• Third Edition •

# Contemporary Literary Criticism

## *Literary and Cultural Studies*

## Robert Con Davis and Ronald Schleifer
*University of Oklahoma*

Longman
New York & London

**Contemporary Literary Criticism:**
**Literary and Cultural Studies,**
**Third Edition**

Longman, 10 Bank Street, White Plains, N.Y. 10606

Associated companies:
Longman Group Ltd., London
Longman Cheshire Pty., Melbourne
Longman Paul Pty., Auckland
Copp Clark Pitman, Toronto

Copyright acknowledgments appear on page 693.

Acquisitions editor: Kathleen M. Schurawich
Development editor: Susan Alkana
Production editor: Ann P. Kearns
Cover design: Silvers Design
Production supervisor: Anne P. Armeny

**Library of Congress Cataloging-in-Publication Data**

Contemporary literary criticism : literary and cultural studies /
    [edited by] Robert Con Davis, Ronald Schleifer. — 3rd ed.
        p.    cm.
    Includes bibliographical references.
    ISBN 0–8013–1113–6
    1. Criticism—History—20th century.   I. Davis, Robert Con.
    II. Schleifer, Ronald.
PN94.C67    1993b
801′.95′0904—dc20                                    93–34856
                                                      CIP


1 2 3 4 5 6 7 8 9 10-MA-9796959493

# Contents

# Preface

This book derives largely from our experience teaching literary criticism in under-graduate and graduate courses at the University of Oklahoma, the University of Tulsa, and Knox College. Additionally, we were enriched and this book has benefited from discussions about contemporary criticism with faculty and students at the University of Washington, Wichita State University, the University of Kansas, Kansas State University, Louisiana State University, the University of New Orleans, Georgia Institute of Technology, Eastern Michigan University, the Southern Illinois University at Edwards-ville, as well as several other institutions. This third edition has also been greatly improved by the help and good advice of a host of people who have used the earlier editions. Many of these people were friends and colleagues, but at least equal in number were the many who simply wrote to discuss their experiences of using the book in class.

Finally, this third edition has a complicated relationship with the second. Robert Con Davis edited the first edition of *Contemporary Literary Criticism,* and the second edition came about as the result of our collaboration on other projects. The second edition of *Contemporary Literary Criticism* then led to an ongoing discussion of issues related to the question of cultural critique, and that discussion became *Criticism and Culture: The Role of Critique in Modern Literary Theory* (Longman 1991). That book—closely related to the second edition of *Contemporary Literary Criticism*—explores the history of cultural critique and outlines the cultural work of literary and cultural criticism in the twentieth century. *Criticism and Culture* has had a strong influence on the shape of this third edition of *Contemporary Literary Criticism,* an influence immediately apparent in "Notes Towards a Definition of Cultural Studies"—the final chapter of *Criticism and Culture* and the last piece in *Contemporary Literary Criticism's* third edition. We believe instructors and students may find *Criticism and Culture* useful as an additional guide to the criticism and theory presented in this book since it discusses at some length most of the issues that we think have been foregrounded in *Contemporary Literary Criticism.*

## READING LITERARY CRITICISM

We noted in the second edition the difficulties that teachers of criticism see some students encounter, even while other students have few difficulties from the beginning, do well in class and on papers, and clearly enjoy studying criticism. In some ways the "difficulties" of criticism—its esoteric vocabularies, its high allusiveness, the intricacies of its argument—are a little less apparent when its scope is widened, as it is in the third edition, to take in forms of culture more familiar to late twentieth-century students. Still, the difficulty of critique remains in this edition: the problem of questioning the self-evident, of trying to imagine (in encounters with literary and other forms of cultural discourse) the world being different from the familiar one. The central problem we noted that makes criticism "difficult"—namely, an approach to it that isolates it from the other activities of interpretation we all habitually pursue—is still evident here. To really "work," criticism must be related to something else, and it can be only when it is conceived as an activity, a doing in the human sciences that opens onto the large questions about the relationships of people to culture. Interpretive criticism—of literature, of social and cultural institutions, of personal relations—is one of the more important things a literate person ever does.

Students who do well with this material not only recognize criticism as essentially an activity to be performed but also understand its importance. Other students tend to regard criticism as simply a body of knowledge to be learned in which failure is always lurking so that each new critical position or school they encounter could be something to confuse and confound them. They imagine that successful completion of the course means getting through it unscathed, "mastering" criticism, but basically remaining untouched by the critical positions they have examined, their own views on literature still intact. In "Psychoanalysis and Education" in "Psychology and Psychoanalysis," Shoshana Felman discusses these two versions of learning. They are related, as she demonstrates, to Jonathan Culler's discussion of "Convention and Meaning" in "Deconstruction and Poststructualism," and tutored by the recent turn in psychology and psychoanalysis discussed by Jacques Lacan, Catherine Belsey, Michael Warner, and others throughout this book. Felman presents a "performative" version of learning that encourages students to view a course in criticism as a tour on which they will explore a number of worlds from the "inside." In this version of education students should be able to learn from literary rhetoric, as Barbara Johnson suggests, to apprehend the function of rhetoric in the most pressing controversies of our society. When they read Louis Marin's structural analysis of Disneyland, in another example, as much as possible they should "become" structuralists and see the world of experience as capable of being subjected to "textual" analysis. When they read poststructuralism, they should come to know a text as decentered by the play of difference and learn to read by undoing the fixation of hierarchical authority. As Marxist critics they should try to understand a text as situated within an ideological superstructure in relation to an historical and "material" base, while as feminist or gender critics, they should self-consciously read with a sense of the overwhelming importance of gender in relation to the understanding of personal and cultural experience.

In other words, "becoming" a critic is making the assumptions particular critics make about literature and culture in their reading and understanding. Learning (and "doing") criticism, like learning to play the piano, is something one practices to do. Students may eventually reject some or all of the critical schools presented in this book. However, while studying each area of concern, they can try to see it as one of its adherents might view it, as in fact a central concern of understanding our world and a central concern of attempting to affect the world we live in. Becoming a "member" of the critical school we are studying constitutes a methodological wager that valuable insight can be gained from a sympathetic entry into a critical system, as opposed to an "objective" scrutiny of a foreign object.

At the beginning of this book in "What Is Criticism?" and "What Is Literary Theory?" we present essays that examine the most fundamental assumptions of literary studies to situate the practice of criticism in larger social contexts presented throughout the book—in the classroom, in the profession, in society at large, and even in the larger world outside Western Anglo-American society. However, even these macrocosmic approaches to criticism—these broad "stances"—are positions to be assumed by students. At the book's end in "Cultural Studies," we try to offer a range of discussions of the ways in which the study of literary (and, in James Clifford's ethnographic study of missionary work, "sacred") discourse can raise questions about culture and society that have been more or less implicit throughout the essays of this book. Cultural studies at its best, we believe, fulfills the most ambitious promises of literary studies. It allows us to see criticism not as a set of monuments but as a set of activities undertaken with others who have made a record of their explorations in literary studies to establish a critical stance, an articulation of value, a call to action. In this way criticism may become something that one tries out, tries on, lives in, and lives through. It is an experience that one actively engages in rather than a difficulty that one avoids, fends off, or even "masters."

## READING *CONTEMPORARY LITERARY CRITICISM*

This book is intended to help readers to explore and interrogate contemporary literary criticism and theory. To that end it provides the immediate background for current criticism with essays that attempt to trace the definitions and history of criticism and theory. The Contents includes the publication dates of all the articles so that readers will be able to gauge the broad chronological development of criticism. We think this inclusion of dates will be useful to students in relating the themes and historical development of contemporary literary studies.

Still, the book is organized thematically and theoretically. The first two sections (the longest in the book) examine the ways that contemporary criticism has taught us to reexamine and critique the practice of literary studies themselves in terms of the nature of "literature," the "ethics" of criticism, the profession of intellectual (or "theoretical") study, the formation of literary canons, and the place and efficacy of literary study in the world. The book then presents criticism in terms of six major areas of concern that present particular critical questions or systems of thought—rhetorical, structuralist, poststructuralist, psychological, historical, and gender-based—and a final section that raises explicitly the relationships between interpretation and cultural life. This is not an inclusive listing of contemporary approaches to reading literature—it presents little that deals with traditional literary analysis (such as explicit examples of "New Critical" literary criticism) or more traditional literary history. It also touches too little on the rich, recent work demonstrating the relationship between reading and writing. However, the nine areas covered are arguably major areas of concern that suggest and connect with many of the others and are likely to lead to other developments in this century and beyond.

## THE STRUCTURE OF THE SECTIONS

A significant feature of this book is the manner in which each section is structured. First of all we have chosen the first essay of each section (in "What Is Criticism?" and "What Is Literary Theory?" the first two essays) to provide a relatively clear and basic description of the school or approach of the whole section. Frye, de Man, Miller, Burke, Culler, Moi, Williams, Spivak, and Hall each provide an introduction to a way of thinking about literature—ways of performing, enacting criticism—that helps to situate the essays that follow in each section. Even when we begin with more "classical" statements—Saussure's technical but illuminating attempt to reorient students to language study, Lacan's attempt to rethink psychoanalysis in terms of discourse, Benjamin's sensitive attempt to relate meaning and historical materialism— the next essay performs this duty of introduction. In the first section the opening essays have a conspicuous function. T. S. Eliot's famous "Tradition and the Individual Talent" begins *Contemporary Literary Criticism,* Third Edition, by reminding us that "criticism is as inevitable as breathing," and our introduction in "What Is Criticism?" aims at situating contemporary criticism in relation to modernism and American New Criticism so that students will get a sense of the historicity of criticism, its existence as a dialogue in relation to the intellectual world in which it finds itself, and its sense of the *stakes* of its activity.

## THE STRUCTURE OF THE BOOK

Within each section the essays are designed to raise questions about one another, and the "framing" sections—the introduction in "What Is Criticism?" and "What Is Literary Theory?" and the gesture toward a conclusion in "Cultural Studies"—are especially designed to present the particular debates about crucial issues of the definition, functioning, and value of literary criticism. "What Is Criticism?" offers the argument over whether literature is "disinterested" or "interested," and "What Is Literary Theory?" offers the argument, clearly seen in the juxtaposition of Christian and Gates, about the *value* of literary theory. In the end we offer the implicit controversies concerning the definition of "culture," the nature of knowledge, and the relationship between understanding and social action.

In other words, the essays of this book are closely interrelated as "contests," as Edward Said says, over "forms and values," and the framing sections attempt to make that interrelationship clear. There are two other ways we have attempted to emphasize this. The introduction to each section provides a list of "further" readings at its end. These alternative readings address the concerns of that section from a different vantage point. (In the introduction to "Feminism and Gender Studies" we even give a close reading of Annette Kuhn's "The Body and Cinema: Some Problems for Feminism" in part to suggest an important text for further reading.) Moreover, each section provides cross-references to essays in other sections. In this way students and instructors can choose to follow a thematic rather than paradigmatic exploration of contemporary literary studies. Furthermore, the introduction to each section also offers an overview of the history and concerns governing the essays contained in it, which aims, as far as possible, to relate that section to the others. Just as earlier in the preface we attempted to relate our discussion of ways of reading criticism to the two definitions of teaching that Felman examines in "Psychology and Psychoanalysis"—and then offered a short list of essays in the book that help to define her approach—so the introduction to each section offers discursive relationships among the sections themselves.

We have substantially redesigned *Contemporary Literary Criticism*—substantially changing the essays from the second edition—so that there are twenty-four new essays, and only fourteen remain from the second edition. We have also substantially redefined and reordered the section headings. The most striking addition, we feel, is the creation of a "general introduction" to contemporary criticism in the two initial sections. With the addition of these essays and introductions, we were able to reduce the size of our own "General Introduction." We have attempted with this change to offer a short overview of contemporary literary and cultural criticism. We imagine, in fact, that one possible way of reading this text is to begin with a sequential reading of the section introductions. We think this might present an integrated discussion and serve as a kind of intellectual history of contemporary thought about literature and discourse in general. To this end we have extensively interrelated the discussions across sections. The "General Introduction" examines the history and definition of "literature" and discusses contemporary criticism and the "humanities" in relation to the concept of the "human sciences." In subsequent introductions we emphasize the role of critique in literary studies and the possibilities of reading literary and other cultural texts in terms of ethics, as well as aesthetics. These possibilities, we hope, will help to expand literary to "cultural" studies. The last introduction in many ways sums up all the other sectional introductions, and the introductions together comprise a history—a coherent narrative and survey—of contemporary critical thought.

Thus *Contemporary Literary Criticism,* Third Edition, suggests alternative tables of contents in the cross-referenced essays in the introductions, and it offers, as well, a text-survey of the field of criticism and theory as a whole. Many who offered suggestions and criticism based on using the earlier editions expressed a need for such guides for students and classes, and we hope that these innovations will prove to be useful.


## ACKNOWLEDGMENTS

As we mentioned, a large number of people assisted us in our work on *Contemporary Literary Criticism,* Third Edition. Chief among them is the late Gordon T. R. Anderson of Longman. In the first two editions his work was instrumental in developing this text, and the strong guidance he gave to higher education throughout the United States in his work at Longman is a lasting legacy of his wisdom and generosity. Kathy Schurawich, Susan Alkana, David Fox, and Ann Kearns of Longman saw this third edition through publication with helpful advice and great patience. Our wives, Julie Davis and Nancy Mergler, were equally helpful and far more patient during the revision of the book. Joshua Michael Davis was born literally days before we sent off the final revisions, and it is to him, along with Cyrus and Benjamin Schleifer, that we dedicate this third edition of this book. (Benjamin was born right before we finished our jointly edited book, *Rhetoric and Form: Deconstruction at Yale,* eight years ago; the seven of us are eagerly awaiting the fourth edition.)

Many colleagues and friends at the University of Oklahoma made suggestions, read material, lent books, and endlessly discussed how the second edition could be improved. They include Richard Barney, Hunter Cadzow, Aparna Dharwadker, Vinay Dharwadker, Yvonne Fonteneau, Susan Green, David S. Gross, Henry McDonald, Catherine Peaden, and Alan R. Velie. Also, several colleagues and graduate students who wrote some of the biographical headnotes for the critics in this book are as follows: Dorie Glickman—*T. S. Eliot;* Justin Everett—*Northrop Frye;* Jeannie Rhodes—*Elaine Showalter;* Steve Wilson—*Gerald Graff;* Richard Barney—*Paul de Man* and *Michael Warner;* Vinay Dharwadker—*Henry Louis Gates, Jr.* and *Edward Said;* James Comas—*Kenneth Burke* and *Michel Foucault;* Kate Myers—*Patrocinio Schweickart* and *Shoshana Felman;* Pamela Liggett—*Ferdinand de Saussure;* Anne Despréaux de Saint Sauveur—*Julia Kristeva;* Scott Kelley—*Louis Marin* and *James Clifford;* Susan Williams—*Jonathan Culler;* Scott LaMascus—*Jacques Derrida;* Stephanie Gross—*Catherine Belsey;* Elizabeth Hinds—*Jacques Lacan;* Suzanne Chelius—*Toril Moi;* Katherine Patterson—*Laura Mulvey;* David S. Gross—*Walter Benjamin, Raymond Williams,* and *Terry Eagleton;* Hunter Cadzow—*Stephen Greenblatt;* Margaret Payne—*Gayatri Chakravorty Spivak;* Susan Green—*Paula Bennett;* Thom Conroy—*Donna Haraway;* Karen Sheriff—*Barbara Johnson* and *Stuart Hall;* Melanie Wright—*Meaghan Morris, Robert Con Davis* and *Ronald Schleifer.* We also thank Christina March, our helpful and cheerful assistant on this project for the last three months.

In addition, we would like to thank the following reviewers, whose insightful comments have strengthened the third edition in many ways:

Chester Anderson, University of Minnesota
Mark Anderson, State University of New York—Brockport
Philip Barnard, University of Kansas
David Blakesley, Southern Illinois University
Mark Brocker, Kent State University
Steven Cole, Temple University
Gloria Cronin, Brigham Young University
Richard Emerson, Western Washington University
Mark Facknitz, James Madison University
William Geiger, Whittier College
John Jordan, University of California—Santa Cruz
Gregory Kelly, Emory University
Robert Miklitsch, Ohio University
Ben Slote, Allegheny College
Fred Stern, University of Illinois—Chicago

# General Introduction: A Preliminary Guide to the Study of Literature, Culture, Criticism, and Critique

Many readers new to this book may already have a strong response to criticism and theory. While some may know next to nothing about criticism and theory and may think they do not like these studies, others will have learned that working with criticism and theory can be highly productive. We suspect that both kinds of readers will be surprised to discover in T. S. Eliot's "Tradition and the Individual Talent," the first essay of this book, the claim that "criticism is as inevitable as breathing, and that we should be none the worse for articulating what passes in our minds when we read a book and feel an emotion about it." Equally surprising will be the further assumption implicit in much contemporary literary and cultural criticism. This assumption suggests that while criticism may be an "inevitable" dimension of the encounter with literary and cultural texts, the self-evident ("traditional") practices of reading literary and cultural texts are not inevitable in the particular forms they take. Rather, the way we understand and interpret texts and even the assessing of our emotions in this process exist in bounded and defining contexts of culture, history, and social relations.

In "Convention and Meaning: Derrida and Austin" (in Part V of this book, "Deconstruction and Poststructuralism"), Jonathan Culler even suggests that such cultural contexts govern the very shape and substance of our emotions. The examples he uses are the expressions of love. In a footnote to his essay distinguishing the plain "use" of language from its "mention" (or "quotation"), he asserts that "no matter how wholeheartedly I may wish to 'use' certain expressions, I find myself [merely] mentioning them: 'I love you' is always something of a quotation, as many lovers have attested." In this way many working today in the study of discourse suggest that the most *self-evident* categories of our experience of literature and the sciences—including the category or "object" called *literature,* the seeming "inevitable" process of reading, and the self-evident categories of the humanities and arts—exist in various contexts in which these *activities* are intelligible in relation to the work they do and the effects they have on those who participate in them.

## THE NATURE OF LITERARY STUDY

As much as possible we need to understand the nature of literary study on its own terms, as a discipline of inquiry, the "disciplinary" practice of literary criticism. The traditional view is that the "humanities" is an area of knowledge that examines unique human events. Every "object" of humanistic study—Chaucer's *Canterbury Tales,* the battle of Waterloo, Locke's *Treatise on Human Nature,* Picasso's *Guernica,* Mozart's *Hunt Quartet,* and even Newton's *Principia* and Darwin's *Origin of Species*—is a unique event that occurred only once and, in a manner of speaking, can only be studied through description and paraphrase. As the linguist Louis Hjelmslev noted, according to this traditional view "humanistic, as opposed to natural phenomena, are non-recurrent and for that very reason cannot, like natural phenomena, be subjected to exact and generalizing treatment." "In the field of the humanities," he goes on, "consequently, there would have to be a different method [from science]—namely, mere description, which would be nearer to poetry than to exact science—or, at any event, a method that restricts itself to a discursive form of presentation in which the phenomena pass by, one by one, without being interpreted through a system."

This "method," Hjelmslev suggests, is "history" in its most chronological manifestation. Since the "objects" of humanistic study are unique, they can be cataloged only in chronological order, and so the humanities have traditionally been "historical" studies; for example, the history of philosophy, the history of art, history itself, the history of science, and literary history. Northrop Frye says the same thing about critical practice in "The Function of Criticism at the Present Time" (in "What Is Criticism?"): "literature being as yet unorganized by criticism, it still appears as a huge aggregate or miscellaneous pile of creative efforts. The only organizing principle so far discovered in it is chronology, and when we see the miscellaneous pile strung out along a chronological line, some coherence is given to it by tradition [chronologically conceived]."

Implicit in Frye's and Hjelmslev's remarks is the possibility that the humanities could "reorient" itself and adopt a more scientific model for its study. Instead of following what Frye calls "naive induction," the humanities could be subject to the attempt, as Hjelmslev says, "to rise above the level of mere primitive description to that of a systematic, exact, and generalizing science, in the theory of which all events (possible combinations of elements) are foreseen and the conditions for their realization established." Such a discipline would attempt to account for the objects of the humanistic study in terms of systematic relationships among them (e.g., Frye's attempt to understand genre—poetry, fiction, drama, etc.—as a system governing "literature") or among the elements that combine to constitute those objects rather than their chronological description. In this case the "humanities" could be conceived as the "human sciences." In such a conception, criticism would take its place among the social sciences rather than the natural sciences. In fact such a division can be seen in the social sciences themselves. In the *Course in General Linguistics,* for instance, Saussure specifically distinguishes between two methods of studying economics— economic history and the "synchronic" study of the economic system at any particular moment. Most of the social sciences, in contemporary practice, are divided in this fashion. Psychology, for instance, encompasses the analysis of unique case histories of "clinical" psychology (such as Freud's *Dora* case, which Toril Moi analyzes in "Psychology and Psychoanalysis") and the analysis of the general functioning of mental activity in "experimental" psychology. Anthropology encompasses both the study of unique cultures and, as in Claude Lévi-Strauss's work, the "general" functioning of aspects of culture. Even an earth science such as geology studies both the historical development and the synchronic composition of geological formations.

Literary study also can be seen to offer two "methods" of study—literary history and more or less systematizing criticism. What allows the systemization of criticism, however, is the common and "recurrent" element of traditional humanistic study, the fact that, as Hjelmslev notes, all the humanities deal in the study of language and discourse. Discourse, moreover, is common to the social sciences in general, and consequently a systematic criticism could be a more general theory of discourse, a more general study of cultural (i.e., discursive) formations. Criticism can transform itself into a "human science" that would study the functioning and creation of a host of "discourses" within society, including, of course, "literary" discourse. Such a human science would attempt to describe what distinguishes literature from other language uses and what literature shares with them. It would attempt, as many have already attempted, to situate literary practice within other cultural practices, including linguistics, teaching, politics, psychology, philosophy, ideology, sociology, and even the "professional" debates within literary studies themselves. All of these areas intersect with the instances of literary and cultural studies that are examined in the various essays of this book.

We are suggesting that the study of criticism can profitably be situated as a part—and a leading part—of the study of culture. A more complete justification for this expansion would necessarily involve a discussion of the definition of the term "culture" beyond what we can offer here (see our book *Criticism and Culture: The Role of Critique in Modern Literary Theory*). "Culture," Raymond Williams notes in *Keywords,* is "one of the two or three most complicated words in the English Language." In another book, *Culture,* Williams says that " 'cultural practice' and 'cultural production' are not simply derived from an otherwise constituted social order but are themselves major elements in its constitution." In this conception culture is not some "informing spirit" within society. Rather, Williams writes, it is "the *signifying system* through which necessarily . . . a social system is communicated, reproduced, experienced and explored."

Williams's definitions are not the only valid description of culture, but it is clear from his ideas that literary studies conceived as a systematized critical activity—a criticism that studies "signifying systems" in a more or less systematic, exact, and generalizing way—is in a position to direct its methods and observations to the widest area of the production of meanings, to cultural activities as specific, signifying practices and as a general area of inquiry. A strong argument can be made, which Williams makes in *The Long Revolution,* and which is also made in this text by critics as different as Barbara Christian, Paul de Man, Edward Said, Catherine Belsey, and Shoshana Felman, that the texts that we customarily call "literature" constitute a privileged site where the most important social, psychological, and cultural forces combine and contend. In this way the attention to discourse, to language in all its manifestations, in its production and in its reception, is a "natural" focus of literary studies and a "natural" outgrowth of criticism. One result of such a possibility has been the recent turn in critical activity to the examination of the institution of literary study in the academy. In books like Robert Scholes's *Textual Power,* Sandra Gilbert and Susan Gubar's *The Madwoman in the Attic,* Gerald Graff's *Professing Literature* and *Beyond the Culture Wars,* Jonathan Culler's *Framing the Sign: Criticism and Its Institutions,* Frank Lentricchia's *Criticism and Social Change,* and Edward Said's *Culture and Imperialism*, as well as a host of feminist and African-American studies, the very nature of the study of literature is being examined in relation to other cultural practices. We are attempting in this book—and especially in the last section on cultural studies—to include as much as possible this wider conception of critical practice as cultural critique as an important informing force within contemporary literary criticism.

## LITERATURE AS AN INSTITUTION

Literary studies has traditionally had a role, most often a privileged one, of transmitting definitions and understandings of culture and knowledge from one age to another. (Gerald Graff and J. Hillis Miller both discuss this role in "What Is Criticism?" and "What Is Literary Theory?") Often that institutional role, as Robert Hodge notes in *Literature as Discourse* (1990), takes the form of defining a "regime of literature" whose initial task is to separate "literature" from "non-literature" and then make the many designations among, for example, poem, novel, play, and short story substantiate and support the initial separation and bolster the institution of literature as a category and practice in culture. Aristotle made this distinction when he placed the study of literature before the study of history because of literature's ability to discover that which is representative and exemplary among history's supposed mere records of what has happened. The especially narrow definition of "literature" as fine and artistic writing, as Raymond Williams notes in *Keywords* (1986), dates only to the nineteenth century. In *The English Novel* (1970) Williams also defines literature as that which exists on the foundation of an essential (though temporally specific) "structure of feeling that is lived and experienced," a realm of actual experience that must be in place before the elaborations of culture and literature. In time, Williams believes, those structures get "arranged as [the] institutions" of culture such as art and literature.

The definition of "literature" as a cultural and social institution is a useful and persistent one. However, this, too, is not the only way to view literature. Even in Williams's comments there are overtones of a different view. Whereas Williams clearly treats literature as a cultural and social institution, his concept of a "structure of feeling" (in the understanding of it that Stuart Hall presents in "Cultural Studies: Two Paradigms" in the last section of this book) posits a natural progression from an essential (noncultural) foundation of "feeling" to culture. To the extent that "literature" is an organized outgrowth of "feeling," "feeling" must function to a degree to stipulate a program for the way culture and society will be. In this sense "literature" is not a constructed institution but an expression of the way the world *is*. "The study of English Literature is accepted by most of its practitioners," as Chris Baldick notes in *The Social Mission of English Criticism: 1848–1932* (1987), "as a 'natural' activity without an identifiable historical genesis." "It is only history," Baldick goes on, "which can challenge any assumption of 'timelessness' about literature as an institution." Williams is responsible for advancing precisely this historical critique of literature as well; that is, another interpretation of Williams's "structures of feeling" emphasizes not the "natural" self-evidence of *feeling* but the very socially and historically determined *structures* that give rise to those feelings.

The definition of literature-as-institution remains confusing in part because of the equally persistent view of literature as a realm in its own right, a view glimpsed fleetingly in Williams's comment in *The English Novel.* If literature as a total body or as a tradition is seen in fact as "presumably coherent in and of itself," as Gerald Graff describes this position in "Introduction: The Humanist Myth" (see "What Is Criticism?"), then one conclusion to draw is that the study of literature by criticism would most likely distort or loosen that coherence, "murdering" to dissect in Wordsworth's famous description of rational analysis. The corollary to the view of "literature itself," literature viewed as a privileged aesthetic or "disinterested" realm largely separate from cultural formation, is that literature will be appreciated best in concert with the recognition that *"literature teaches itself."* As implemented in literary studies in America, this credo has meant that, as Graff explains, "great literary works can be freed from the institutional and professional encumbrances that come between students or laymen and the potency of the work itself."

This view, which Graff is explaining and not propounding, is problematic particularly in light of the fact that, as Baldick notes, "the real content of the school and college subject which goes under the name 'English Literature' is not literature in the primary sense, but criticism." Baldick's point is not a theoretical one but a practical observation that "every student in British education [and American education, as well] is required to compose, not tragic dramas, but essays in criticism." All literary courses are perforce criticism courses in the sense that ordinarily in literature courses (as opposed to creative writing courses) students write essays about the material and do not try to write within the genre they are studying. Literature may be, as Terry Eagleton writes, "non-pragmatic discourse" in the specific sense that it "serves no immediate practical purpose, but is to be taken as referring to a general state of affairs." Even as "non-pragmatic discourse," however, literature is always studied in terms of a more or less "critical" discourse about literature that students enact when they speak to each other and when they write. Practically speaking, there will be no access to the "work itself" or "literature itself," whatever form that could take. As Frye says, "all the arts are dumb." The idea of studying Shakespeare or interpreting the Bible directly begins to sound presumptuous, as misdirected, compared to the activity of participating in the critical discourse about these texts.

A pragmatic and probably defensible definition of literature is the *functional* one that Eagleton offers when he says that literature is the "number of ways in which people *relate themselves* to writing." Such strategies of relating, played out in the conflicts of theme and form among and within literary texts, create the patterned effects of what is commonly called "texture" in literature. If we accept this functional definition, then we must probably forget the "illusion" forever, as Eagleton goes on, "that the category 'literature' is 'objective' " or could ever be made so. Remember that his institutional definition of "literature" is functional, being utterly provisional and specific to the time, place, and occasion for defining it in such a way. It is no wonder, as Robert Scholes argues in *Textual Power,* that the teaching of literary texts now means the teaching of the "cultural text" too.

There is one dimension of the definition of literature that draws assent from most quarters, the idea of literature as the vehicle and transmitter of cultural values. "Literature," Eagleton says bluntly, "in the meaning of the word we have inherited, *is* an ideology." He means that as a form of representation, literature reflects the cultural hierarchies that organize the ways in which the world is understood and even experienced. Those hierarchies are ordered by certain values that constitute a specific social ideology. His claiming this is not so different from countless other claims about values in modern literary studies. Eagleton specifically quotes George Gordon, professor of English Literature at Oxford, as saying in his inaugural lecture that "England is sick, and . . . English literature must save it. The Churches (as I understand) having failed, and social remedies being slow, English literature has now a triple function: still, I suppose, to delight and instruct us, but also, and above all, to save our souls and heal the State." With startling candor, Gordon at once views literature as a communicator of value and as a privileged institution in its potential effect on culture. Matthew Arnold, F. R. Leavis, Lionel Trilling, Gayatri Chakravorty Spivak, and many others make a similar claim, if not so extreme, for literature's ability to articulate and transmit cultural value. In the 1920s and 1930s Leavis claimed that literature was the only medium that could effectively transmit value in the modern, industrialized world in which social institutions are in constant and irreversible transition, and even decay. Trilling, too, believed that only literature and its study would allow us to glimpse anything like the "whole" of human experience, the "whole" person—the rational, emotional, sacred, and profane dimensions of being human.

From a contemporary perspective, we will still find the claim that literature and literary studies have a privileged grasp of the materials and forms of culture. We will often find certain arguments advanced that say the power of literature and literary studies is made possible by a certain sophisticated flexibility, even a kind of lack of focus and commitment, in literature regarding any particular dimension of cultural encounter. Literature's broad engagement with culture and cultures may account both for its power and for the frequent difficulty of organizing the findings and methods of literary studies. ("Literature," in Irving Howe's famous statement, "is difficult to organize.") The paradox here is that a certain *lack* of precision in the cultural positioning of literature as a total enterprise—a lack of fixed grounding in what literature means to culture—may explain both the strength and weakness of literary studies as a cultural agent and force.

For example, in current discussions of cultural studies and multi-culturalism there is often considerable questioning about the aims and methods of inquiry and the apparent loss of consensus about the value of traditional cultural goals. Whenever such cultural discourse breaks down and even basic questions of value remain unsettled, as Samuel Weber writes, the "process of *granting*" cultural validity and recognition becomes the focus of attention. "If such a development can be seen today as a characteristic of much modern thought," Weber goes on, "it is no accident that the field of literary studies" is one of the "privileged arenas" for discussion. Weber argues that it is privileged particularly because of a strategic *lack* of grounding in literature. As Weber writes, "the object that defines this field of study—'literature'—has traditionally been distinguished from other 'objects' of study precisely by a certain *lack* of objectivity. . . . And such a lack of objectivity has, from Plato onward, confronted the study of literature (or of art in general) with the problem of its *legitimation,* and hence, with its status as, and in regard to, *institution(s)*." This is another way of saying, as Eagleton does, that literature "has the most intimate relations to questions of social power." If this is true, one can begin to see why literature and literary studies have played such a large role in the development of cultural critique and cultural studies.

## CRITICISM AND CRITIQUE

A student who stays with these issues long enough will soon see that the process of such exploration has been a part of the Western understanding and interpreting of texts since the time of Greek First Philosophy and the Enlightenment of the eighteenth century. This understanding often takes the form not only of understanding a particular text but of recognizing our own working assumptions as we interpret texts. That is, the issue of *what* literature is always gets tied up with the concomitant issue of *how* to read, "practices" of reading. If "literature" as a concept has a history that plays different roles in different historical settings, the very process of reading also has a history, and that history is closely connected to the value imputed to "literature," the value of literacy. In *The Use of Poetry and the Use of Criticism* (1933) Eliot makes the revealing comment about Dr. Samuel Johnson, the great English critic of the eighteenth century, that "had he lived a generation later, he would have been obliged to look more deeply into the foundations [of his critical practices], and so would have been unable to leave us an example of what criticism ought to be for a civilization which, being settled, has no need, while it lasts, to enquire into the function of its parts." Dr. Johnson, in other words, would have been compelled to interrogate the assumptions he was making in the *practice* of interpretation. In this comment Eliot makes the assumption that some ages have the characteristic of being more "critical" than others. He further advances the important idea that there is the specialized activity in criticism of looking "more deeply into the foundations" of our understanding, of being theoretically self-conscious about the nature of the criticism we practice. This questioning of assumptions at the "foundations" of critical practices—the assumptions we make about the nature of texts and the efficacy of our methods—is the particular activity that we are calling *critique*. The questioning that belongs to critique can be distinguished from the different questioning about what texts mean. This second questioning involves actually discussing and interpreting the work and goes under the name of *criticism*. Criticism studies what texts say and how they say it, while critique studies the often unnoticed assumptions within criticism that govern the practices of reading and the definitions of the "object" of reading. This is true when the "object" of critical reading is "literature," but it is also true when criticism "reads" nonliterary texts such as film; historical narratives; psychological narratives; philosophical ideas; social relationships of gender, race, and class; other, "non-Western" cultures; and even the "theories" of criticism and culture themselves. This list describes most of the essays in this book, and in most of these essays one will find both the readings of criticism and the questionings of critique.

Not long after we published the second edition of *Contemporary Literary Criticism,* we found ourselves continuing to think about the distinction between criticism and critique and began to focus on the need for scholars to be clear about the significance of performing one or the other of these forms of understanding. Focusing especially on the practice of critique since the ancient Greeks, on the great attempts at critique in the eighteenth century, and on the many practices of modern criticism, we decided that it would be generally helpful to mark out for students and scholars of criticism and theory the historical path critique has taken to become, among other things, literary and cultural criticism and cultural studies. We also saw that our mapping out of this path in the history of criticism and theory could help students understand what criticism is and how it has developed. Out of all of this thinking, we ended up writing *Criticism and Culture: The Role of Critique in Modern Literary Theory* (Longman 1991) in hopes of clarifying these questions for students and scholars alike. In that book, arising directly from our work on the second edition of this textbook, we explored the interactions between philosophical critique and cultural theory and the many practical hybrids (schools of criticism) that since then have come from that encounter. Thus, while the second edition of *Contemporary Literary Criticism* led us to the writing of *Criticism and Culture,* that book and the perspectives we developed in it are now having a strong influence on the approach we are taking to the third edition of *Contemporary Literary Criticism.*

In light of these concerns, and in addition to many others, we should like students to see at least two related phenomena: the *institutional* dimension of criticism as we discuss it here and the *transformative* potential of critique. The last selection of this book, "Notes Towards a Definition of Cultural Studies," which is also the last chapter of our book *Criticism and Culture*, explicitly addresses the complex relationship between the analysis of instituted cultural formations and bringing the intelligence of analysis to bear in the transformations of cultural institutions, what we call in that essay "the institutional and transformative concerns of cultural studies." (The "subject" and "object" of cultural studies we examine there correspond to the practices of reading and the definitions of literature we are examining in this General Introduction.)

Plato and Aristotle, for example, thought a good deal in their literary and cultural criticism about the forms poetry can take, and they made important critical distinctions about dramatic genres, including comedy and tragedy and the different kinds of heroes and characters appropriate to each. They also focused on the moral implications of using various forms of dramatic and narrative poetry—how poetry could help or hinder governance of the state and affect the education of impressionable children, for instance. Especially in Plato's criticism there is a strong rejection of the transformative potential of critique and a decision to develop, instead, practices supportive of existing educational and governmental goals—institutional practices. Plato chose, in other words, to practice criticism over critique.

In the eighteenth century Immanuel Kant helped to define the nature of critique as a practice and projected a separate realm for the aesthetic effects of literary and other kinds of art. Kant created the foundation for a purely aesthetic dimension of critical understanding and effectively created programmatic ways of thinking about criticism and critique that laid the foundations for many developments in subsequent criticism and theory. Especially influential was his idea about the free play of the imagination and the realm of aesthetics that can be understood in relation to analytical thinking. In the nineteenth century, for example, the French scholar Hippolyte Taine exploited the distinction between criticism and critique in his definition of an inner human core of personality and character that supposedly exists separate from the "outer" world that is subject to change and transformation. Taine succeeded in constructing a historical model for understanding literary and cultural texts that assumed the existence of pure ethnic traits that can be elaborated and manifested in literature. His assumptions about the existence of "pure" ethnic and national character traits serve the institutional ends of criticism and can, by the way, be shown to have racist implications. His accomplishment, nonetheless, was to define a line of historical criticism that continues through the present.

In the twentieth century, dating from early manifestoes of modernism and formalism (which we discuss in the introductions to "What Is Criticism?" and "Structuralism and Semiotics") through the most recent work in gender and cultural theory, there is a large turn of interest toward exploring the transformative potential of critique—a sustained and massive interrogation of the protocols of formal and textual relations, both in how to define texts and in how to interpret them in relation to culture. The questions continually being asked are: What constitutes a text? What are its boundaries? What constitutes reading? What readerly competence is required to interpret a text? What constitutes a persuasive or "valid" interpretation of a text? In the history of modern criticism questions about literary and cultural form and practice have been underwritten or even specifically guided by attempts to theorize the interactions of various cultural and social formations, including literary, cultural, social, political, and economic institutions. The overriding question circulating through this thinking concerns how we are to understand the connections among criticism, critique, and culture in terms of the relationships among them as practices and the priorities and values that they institute.

## PRACTICES OF READING

These questions of the nature of cultural texts, including the practical and historical definitions of "literature" we have touched on here, and of various practices of reading are precisely the issues we take up in *Criticism and Culture: The Role of Critique in Modern Literary Theory*. These concerns have also helped guide our selections in this third edition of *Contemporary Literary Theory: Literary and Cultural Studies*. We have chosen works, for example, that address these important questions in as coherent a fashion as possible. We assume that our readers—undergraduate or graduate students or simply readers interested in criticism and culture—are not passive onlookers, tourists moving easily and quickly over the terrain of modern critical thought. We assume our readers to be actively interested in the question of what criticism has been as it has served institutional ends and how critique may change and transform those ends—in short, how literary and cultural texts interact and why they are constituted as they seem to be and have the effects they do in the world(s) in which we live.

Even readers inexperienced in the practice of criticism and theory soon will note that the essays in this book tend to fall into two categories and deploy the two modes of understanding we have been discussing. Consider "Interpreting the *Variorum*" by Stanley Fish (in "Rhetoric and Reader Response"). At certain moments Fish finds productive ways of interpreting texts. He reads a poem and determines what words, sentences, and images mean, and then he posits a likely reading of a line in that poem. At the next moment he finds his sense of the poem undercut by the implications of interpretation in later lines of the same poem. This process of gaining and losing ground in interpretation happens several times, and Fish begins to question whether the poem as a whole can ever make sense in precisely the way its individual lines seem to. At a certain point this questioning leads him to seek explanations for the way the poem works differently from what was described by the initial explanations. When Fish begins to question his own procedures and look for new ones—that is, when he begins to look for fundamentally new ways of understanding or even conceiving of the poem (as Eliot claims Dr. Johnson was unable to do)—he has begun doing what we call *critique*. While he does make use of strategies of critique in this essay, however, he generally interprets the poem according to rules and assumptions that he already has in mind, that he learned from someone else, or that he established in other essays. In effect, in this act of reading and interpretation he is performing what we are calling *criticism*.

In other words, the next discovery awaiting the inexperienced reader of criticism and theory is that some of the essays in this book lean more toward criticism and that some are closer to critique. Kenneth Burke's "Literature as Equipment for Living," Fish's "Interpreting the *Variorum*," and Toril Moi's "Representation of Patriarchy," one can argue, have important moments of critique but are on the whole criticism. Each one lucidly explains and applies critical notions that have already been established and are, in some sense, generally known to be useful or "true." Eliot's "Tradition and the Individual Talent," Donna Haraway's "A Cyborg Manifesto," and Meaghan Morris's "Banality in Cultural Studies" lean more toward being exploratory critiques—tending more toward interrogation and the testing of the limits of understanding and the potential for discovering new grounds of explanation. This distinction between institutional criticism and transformative critique parallels J. Hillis Miller's distinction between "canny" and "uncanny" criticism, the first being institutional and the second being transformative. Both sets of concepts can be traced back, further, to Claude Lévi-Strauss's different but related distinction between the rational and institutionally oriented "engineer" and the innovating and experimental *"bricoleur,"* or tinker. (In Lévi-Strauss's work, however, a genuinely transformative potential is not present in either term.) When Kristeva analyzes semiotics to define and allow us to rethink the model-building nature of "science," when Derrida analyzes the principle of reason to allow us to rethink the university as an institution, when Shoshana Felman analyzes psychoanalysis to allow us to rethink teaching as an institution, when Walter Benjamin analyzes the philosophy of history to allow us to rethink the relationship between historical events and violence (what he calls "barbarism"), when Michael Warner analyzes psychoanalytic definitions of homosexuality to demonstrate the contradictions and unspoken assumptions in purportedly "objective" and ahistorical descriptions of psychological development, they are all engaging in practices of reading whose aim is not simply "analysis" but also the examination of the modes of understanding that allow certain institutions to exist. In each case the critics are imagining the possibility of transforming those institutions. These activities of critique, as we shall see in a moment, lend themselves to the particular "difficulties" of contemporary literary criticism by developing practices of reading that are different from those we have been taught.

Such practices do not fully participate in the canons of the self-consistent and self-contained mode of reading that lead to simple and well-formed ideas. Take "Feminism and Critical Theory" by Gayatri Chakravorty Spivak (in "Feminism and Gender Studies"). In the headnote to her article Spivak notes four distinctly different moments at which the four "parts" of her essay were developed. Moreover, the "objects" of her critical analysis of these different parts—theoretical modes in relation to feminism, the concept of race, reflections on a novel by Margaret Drabble in 1980, a factory strike in South Korea in 1982—constantly shift, as do the vocabularies used to discuss them. Sometimes the essay is written in the language of psychoanalysis (e.g., "overdetermination") or Marxism ("surplus value") or deconstruction (e.g., " 'as a deconstructivist' ") or feminism (e.g., footnote 32 that discusses the metonymic use of "clitoris") or, most globally, from the situation of a third-world woman. In other words, the essay is neither narrowly self-consistent in its practice of reading nor self-contained as it is defined by its object of analysis. Instead, it strives, as Spivak says, "moment by moment to practice a taxonomy of different forms of understanding, different forms of change, dependent perhaps upon resemblance and seeming substitutability—figuration—rather than on the self-identical category of truth." The *aim* of this reading, as she says in the "middle" of the essay (a position that is modified somewhat at its "end"), is to change "the common currency of the understanding of society." "The kind of work I have outlined," she says, "would infiltrate the male academy and redo the terms of our understanding of the context and substance of literature as part of the human enterprise." That is, her essay's aim is critique.

By foregrounding the distinction between criticism and critique and by choosing the essays we have for this book, we have intended to provide a set of categories for understanding directions in criticism at an early stage of study. Among these are two "basic" categories: definitions of objects of study ("literature," "ideas," "culture," the "agent" or "subject" of experience, etc.) and practices of reading in the processes of study. These two categories are fully integrated—reading defines objects, and objects call for particular reading—but they correspond to the *provisional* opposition between criticism and critique in the analysis and transformation of cultural institutions just as our discussions of Fish's and Spivak's practices of reading define a *provisional* opposition. We hope our readers will actively make use of the terms "criticism" and "critique"—as well as many of the other useful terms the writers in this book develop—as tools with which to teach themselves about criticism and theory and to discover for themselves the historical situation of contemporary literary and cultural criticism.

## THE DIFFICULTY OF CRITICISM

The questioning of self-evident truths and the development of procedures that examine the particular ends that may be contained in seemingly "dis-interested" and "objective" forms of knowledge—two projects that critique defines in examining objects of knowledge and the methods used to examine them—lead to forms of density and seeming obscurity in much contemporary literary criticism. As Roland Barthes says in *S/Z*, the texts of criticism are often "writerly" in their reliance on the participation of the reader for completion rather than offering the "readerly" contextual explanations that characterize much nineteenth-century literature. (The "readerly" that Barthes sees is a characteristic of the seeming stable subject of experience and knowledge of nineteenth-century middle-class culture.) In other words, it has become a commonplace of contemporary thought that much of contemporary criticism and cultural critique—Paul de Man's literary studies, Kristeva's semiotics, Derrida's "deconstructive" philosophy, the psychoanalysis of Lacan, Spivak's feminist discourse, and even Williams's clear prose when he asks us to question self-evident truths—is difficult to follow. But what does it mean exactly for a critical text to be difficult?

In the essay "On Difficulty," George Steiner asks why the reading of contemporary criticism should be this difficult. In response he has suggested that resistance to reading occasioned by *modernist* literature and contemporary criticism can be understood as belonging to one or more of the following four categories of "difficulty"—all of them providing impediments that, if not properly understood, can block access to reading a particular literary work.

The first is *contingent difficulty*. This is the problem one faces when there are things, words or references, in a poem or text that cannot be identified, that the reader simply does not know. In Saussure's discussion of linguistics, for instance, he mentions the "diachronic" study of language. If the reader does not know that term, it must be looked up in a dictionary. Similarly, if students don't know references to critics or critical positions—the New Criticism Paul de Man mentions, the "airy insouciance of postaxiological criticism" Edward Said mentions, or simply the work of Wayne Booth, whom Patrocinio Schweichkart describes without specifically identifying within the debates in the literary studies—they can easily become lost and feel as if they are overhearing a discussion in another language. Moreover, if these contingent difficulties are not resolved, their accumulation can finally prevent students from grasping the central import of an argument. The point is, however, that "contingent difficulties" are a kind of difficulty that can be completely overcome by briefly consulting a reference book.

The second kind of trouble in reading is a *modal difficulty*. This kind of difficulty is more trouble to overcome than contingent difficulties. Modal difficulty occurs when one is not familiar with or cannot follow the form, or mode, of a work. Some people have a "modal difficulty" with MTV: they simply cannot follow and process the quick visual cuts from scene to scene, which are significantly different from the longer scenes in films and television from the 1950s and 1960s. Such "cuts" are the mode of presentation of music videos. Other modal difficulties are the fragmented language of much modernist poetry, T. S. Eliot's famous lack of transitions, for instance. In contemporary literary criticism this can be seen in the shorthand allusiveness in many of the essays here; for example, the vague suggestion (for those who are new to this work) that Derrida has a particular audience or frame of reference in mind or that Lacan's *purpose* in his prose is as much to overpower the reader with a strange vocabulary as it is to convey information. The *agenda* of many contemporary critics—the *agenda* of critique itself as we have described it—is as much to *reorient* understanding as it is to convey or provoke understanding, and this purpose in feminism, Marxism, psychoanalysis, and other schools of criticism presents a different *mode* of understanding from what we have been taught.

Shoshana Felman, in her psychoanalytic discussion of teaching, discusses this different mode of knowledge. Still, "modal difficulty" (like contingent difficulty) can be remedied through learning and practice. It is similar to learning to use a new language that has a different number or division of tenses from English or similar even to learning that the English concepts of "language" and "speech" are reoriented across three terms in French *(langue, parole, langage)*. By rethinking these concepts in relation to one another, the difficulties with the modalities of understanding can be overcome through practice. Thus people can "learn" to follow music videos or the seemingly strange argumentative forms of contemporary criticism. As James Clifford suggests in "The Translation of Cultures" (in "Cultural Studies"), modal difficulties call for a "deep translation" and an "intercultural translation" that are "part of the creative interpretation of two cultures, a liberation and revivification of meanings latent in each" that are necessary "to grasp a moving language."

The third problem a reader can have with texts is *tactical difficulty*. This kind of difficulty is a formidable resistance to received methods of reading that one brings to literature or criticism. Unlike contingent or modal difficulties, which are occasioned by the fact that writers simply use different facts and modes of discourse from those of their readers, "tactical difficulties" are tactics writers use to produce certain effects in their readers. The effect is to situate their readers in such a way that the "easy" and usual ways they understand language and experience no longer effectively account for that experience and language. In "Art as Technique" (in "Structuralism and Semiotics," Viktor Shklovsky examines this "tactical difficulty" under the name of "defamiliarization." "The technique of art," he writes, "is to make objects 'unfamiliar,' to make forms difficult, to increase the difficulty and length of perception." Insofar as the difference between literature and criticism has become a problem explored in contemporary criticism—and we should add now that this problem of categorization is a "modal difficulty" insofar as it raises the question of whether we are in the "mode" of art or of knowledge—then the tactics of defamiliarization and "making strange" that occur throughout the essays here are part of the *critical* project of contemporary criticism. If critique questions the self-evident, including the self-evident validity of standard argumentation, then a tactic to achieve this end is to make the self-evident strange. Such a difficulty is not "overcome" in the same way contingent or modal difficulties are overcome. Its aim is the reorienting of understanding. Gayatri Chakravorty Spivak's essay we discussed earlier offers a good example of the presentation of tactical difficulties.

The final form of difficulty (a version of the "resistance" to reading de Man describes) is *ontological difficulty*. An "ontological difficulty" is the hardest of all to deal with, and many times readers must simply accept this difficulty as insurmountable. It is not simply confusion over contingent facts or modes of understanding or even the attempt to produce reorientations in readers. Rather, "ontological difficulties" involve trying to see and feel the world from a perspective other than your own, and sometimes the gap between perspectives is quite great and virtually unbridgeable. J. Hillis Miller, in "The Search for Grounds in Literary Study" (in "What Is Literary Theory?"), begins his essay with literary presentations of such "ontological" difficulties—presentations of what seems to be a sort of breach within "reality" in Maurice Blanchot, George Eliot, and Wallace Stevens, all texts that he says seem "irreducibly strange, inexplicable, perhaps even mad." He goes on, in this essay, to describe the ways criticism has attempted to account for and tame such uncanny experiences. The scandal presented by contemporary criticism, which goes to the heart of the ontological difficulty, can be described as a radical division, a *split*—the "devastating experience," Miller describes, "of a transformation of the scene which leaves it nevertheless exactly the same."

The pervasive figure of a "split" or contradiction in contemporary criticism and understanding indicates a sense of a fundamental division within texts, specifically concerning their involvement in time in the abstract sense of "aesthetic" moments but also in the concrete sense that forms of literature, culture, and knowledge occur at, and are in part determined by, particular historical moments. Most current theories of textuality, for example, do not emphasize criticism as attempting a unified "reading," or even see a text as defined by "meaning" or "content." They see instead a process, a "split," twofold relationship between text and the process of producing texts. Contemporary criticism, in this regard, is "difficult" because it so severely questions definitions of "literature" and methods of "reading." Concepts central to interpretation, which the New Critics were accustomed to calling "unity" and "wholeness" in form, have become the problem of "interpretation" to be discussed rather than the goal toward which interpretation moves. This development, one could say, has become the source of an exciting difficulty.

## FURTHER READING

Abrams, M. H., *The Mirror and the Lamp: Romantic Theory and the Critical Tradition* (New York: Oxford University Press, 1953).

————, "Rationality and Imagination in Cultural History: A Reply to Wayne Booth," in *Critical Inquiry,* 2 (1976), 247–64.

Arnold, Matthew, *Arnold: Poetry and Prose,* ed. John Bryson (London: Rupert Hart-Davis, 1954).

Baldick, Chris, *The Social Mission of English Criticism: 1848–1932* (Oxford: Clarendon, 1987).

Culler, Jonathan, *Framing the Sign: Criticism and Its Institutions* (Norman: University of Oklahoma Press, 1988).

Davis, Robert Con, and Ronald Schleifer, *Criticism and Culture: The Role of Critique in Modern Literary Theory* (London: Longman, 1991).

Deleuze, Gilles, and Felix Guattari, *A Thousand Plateaus: Capitalism and Schizophrenia* (Minneapolis: University of Minnesota Press, 1987).

Derrida, Jacques, *Limited Inc.* (Evanston, IL: Northwestern University Press, 1988).

Eagleton, Terry, *Literary Theory* (Minneapolis: University of Minnesota Press, 1983).

Eliot, T. S., *The Use of Poetry and the Use of Criticism: Studies in the Relation of Criticism to Poetry in England* (Cambridge, MA: Harvard University Press, 1933).

Frye, Northrop, *Anatomy of Criticism: Four Essays* (Princeton, NJ: Princeton University Press, 1957).

Gallop, Jane, *The Daughter's Seduction* (Ithaca, NY: Cornell University Press, 1982).

Gilligan, Carol, *In a Different Voice* (Cambridge, MA: Harvard University Press, 1982).

Graff, Gerald, *Literature Against Itself: Literary Ideas in Modern Society* (Chicago: University of Chicago Press, 1979).

———, *Professing Literature* (Chicago: University of Chicago Press, 1987).

———, *Beyond the Culture Wars* (New York: W.W. Norton, 1992).

Hjelmslev, Louis, *Prolegomena to a Theory of Language,* trans. Francis Whitfield (Madison: University of Wisconsin Press, 1961).

Hodge, Robert, *Literature as Discourse* (Baltimore: Johns Hopkins University Press, 1990).

Lentricchia, Frank, *Criticism and Social Change* (Chicago: University of Chicago Press, 1983).

Miller, J. Hillis, "Steven's Rock and Criticism as Cure," in *Georgia Review,* 31 (1976), 44−60.

Ohmann, Richard, *English in America* (New York: Oxford University Press, 1976).

Ryan, Michael, *Marxism and Deconstruction: A Critical Articulation* (Baltimore: Johns Hopkins University Press, 1982).

Said, Edward, *Culture and Imperialism* (New York: A. Knopf, 1993).

Schleifer, Ronald, "The Poison of Ink: Post-War Literary Criticism," in *New Orleans Review,* 8 (1981), 241−49.

Scholes, Robert, *Textual Power* (New Haven, CT: Yale University Press, 1985).

Sontag, Susan, *Against Interpretation* (New York: Dell, 1966).

Steiner, George, *On Difficulty and Other Essays* (New York: Oxford University Press, 1978).

Weber, Samuel, *Institution and Interpretation* (Minneapolis: University of Minnesota Press, 1987)

Williams, Raymond, *Keywords* (London: Fontana, 1986).

———, *Culture* (London: Verso, 1981).

———, *The English Novel: From Dickens to Lawrence* (New York: Oxford University Press, 1970).

———, *The Long Revolution* (New York: Columbia University Press, 1961).

# I

# WHAT IS CRITICISM?

Students of literary and cultural studies find that they are significantly advanced in their work by coming to terms with "criticism" as a concept as early in their studies as possible. There is no surer division between the casual reader of texts and observer of culture and the serious student than the willingness to engage in the task of understanding in its self-consciously critical dimensions. There are many possible definitions of criticism, but the general one central to the study of literature and other forms of discourse and language involves giving self-conscious attention to the methods of understanding. Literary criticism, as opposed to the more general and, as Northrop Frye says, the more "philosophical" study of aesthetics, aspires to develop, as we noted in the general introduction to this book, definitions of "literature" and methods of "reading." "Criticism," T. S. Eliot writes in "Tradition and the Individual Talent," "is as inevitable as breathing," and he goes on to say that "we should be none the worse for articulating what passes in our minds when we read a book and feel an emotion about it, for criticizing our own minds in the work of criticism." Others throughout this book provide different and usually complementary definitions of criticism. Criticism, Frye argues in "The Function of Criticism at the Present Time," speaks *for* literature, which, like the "data" that is the object of scientific discourse, remains "dumb."

He goes on to say that the aim or function of criticism is to discover what literary texts and "literature" itself "actually mean as a whole," and it should pursue this task as systematically as other "sciences"—such as mathematics or history. He argues that criticism "preserves the scientific and systematic element in [literary] research" necessary for literary studies as a whole to make "an immediately significant contribution to culture." Roland Barthes argues that criticism is "essentially an activity" that "must include in its discourse . . . an implicit reflection on itself." Its aim is "not to *discover* the work in question but on the contrary to *cover* it as completely as possible by its own language." Criticism, Elaine Showalter writes in "Feminist Criticism in the Wilderness," is positioned between "ideology and the liberal ideal of disinterestedness"; more specifically in the case of feminist criticism, it is positioned between the concern "with the feminist as *reader"* and the concern with "women as *writers."* Here again, criticism studies both "reading" and "literature," but they come together for Showalter—as they do for many in this book—"to make the leap to a new conceptual vantage point" to focus on "the essential question of difference"—"differences" among texts but also "differences" of value and discrimination within texts.

Northrop Frye joins Eliot, Barthes, and Showalter to say that criticism seeks out a "conceptual vantage point" so that "criticism [can deal] with literature in terms of a specific conceptual framework." Frye describes *one* particular "conceptual framework" based on grand "archetypal" patterns of significance, while Barthes, Showalter, and others in *Contemporary Literary Criticism* describe different ones, such as Marxism, psychoanalysis, and different kinds of feminism. Gerald Graff, in "The Humanist Myth," writes one history of the relations among these vantage points in his description of the "institutional history" of literary studies and criticism. His point is that the "humanist myth" concerning literature—beginning, in important ways, in Matthew Arnold's attempt to define "The Function of Criticism at the Present Time" in 1865—assumed that *"literature teaches itself."* "Practical criticism"—criticism that takes as its task the close scrutiny or explication of particular literary texts—often seems to be versions of literature "teaching itself." However, as the detailed interpretations of texts in this book explicitly show—interpretations such as Louis Marin's "semiotic" reading of Disneyland, Stephen Greenblatt's "new historicist" reading of Shakespeare's *Henry IV,* Paula Bennett's "lesbian" reading of Emily Dickinson's poetry, or Toril Moi's close reading of Freud's *Dora*—approaches to practical criticism always carry "silent" assumptions and presuppositions about the nature of reading, the definition of literature, and the cultural work of literary and discursive analyses.

The assumption that literature teaches itself—thus implying that criticism has a very limited use—is clear in Arnold's description of the aim of criticism "to see the object as in itself it *really* is" (emphasis added). With this task accomplished, the critic can then aspire to present "the best that is known and thought in the world." Graff's point is that the seemingly *self-evident truths* of the liberal humanist tradition, most fully articulated in what Graff calls "Arnoldian humanism," presuppose a particular "conceptual framework," or theory, even when that tradition claims to be simply disinterested, simply an attempted "reading," and simply encompassing and promoting the best that is known and thought. Barthes also describes the "guilty silence" of this tradition, which he says, "is not to be blamed for its prejudices but for the fact that it conceals them, masks them under the moral alibi of rigor and objectivity." Showalter argues that feminist criticism discovers a tradition of literary studies (made up of women writers) different from the Arnoldian tradition, a tradition that "has more to learn from women's studies than from English studies, more to learn from international feminist theory than from another seminar on the masters."

In these definitions of criticism—both of *reading* and *literature* itself—these critics, and many others throughout this book, are attempting to create a broader sense of "culture" and "cultural studies" than even Arnold presents in *Culture and Anarchy.* There he defines culture as the "great help out of our present difficulties; culture being a pursuit of our total perfection by means of getting to know, on all the matters which most concern us, the best which has been thought and said in the world; and, through this knowledge, turning a stream of fresh and free thought upon our stock notions and habits." Similarly, Eliot defines culture in the western tradition as shaped by "the mind of Europe." Frye ends his essay by alluding to both Eliot and Arnold: "I even think," he writes, "that the consolidation of literature by criticism into the verbal universe was one of the things that Matthew Arnold meant by culture." Many critics in this text create a broad sense of "culture" by emphasizing more than Eliot and Frye (and even than Arnold) the *local historical* sense of cultural work (as opposed to Eliot's *universal historical sense*). Edward Said says in "The Politics of Knowledge" (in "What Is Literary Theory?") that such work is both *interested* and *unprovincial.* In his history of the relationship between ideas and institutions, Graff emphasizes this double and seemingly self-contradictory task in his attempt to trace "questions about the nature and cultural functions of literature" that literary criticism more generally pursues.

## THE DOUBLE TASK OF CRITICISM

In Geoffrey Hartman's *Criticism in the Wilderness* (1980), from which Showalter borrows the title of her essay here, Hartman explores "the gulf between philosophic criticism [in Continental Europe] and *practical criticism* [in England and the United States]," repeatedly assuring us that "criticism" must be accorded its status as "a genre, or a primary text" too. In this comment Hartman articulates a kind of anxiety associated with criticism, one occasioned by the possibility that criticism might be more than just commentary, more, in fact, than "just" literary. Hillis Miller in "The Search for Grounds in Literary Study" (in "What Is Literary Theory?") focuses his discussion around Arnold and contemporary understandings of his critical practice to isolate an "imperial" element in literary criticism. Miller argues that, beginning in the eighteenth century at least, literary criticism has attempted to address wider areas of cultural practice beyond literature. The study of literature "has been weighted down in our culture with the burden of carrying from generation to generation the whole freight of the values of that culture, what Matthew Arnold called 'the best that is known and thought in the world.' "

Miller raises the questions of why this should be. What historical events in the eighteenth and nineteenth centuries might have contributed to this practice? What implications does this practice have for the study of literature? Many of the essays throughout *Contemporary Literary Criticism,* but especially those in "What Is Literary Theory?" raise questions about the *interest* of criticism. Who is served by the historical forms criticism has taken? Who is left out? How do silent assumptions about the nature and construction of "reading," "literature," "culture," "self-evidence," and "rigor and objectivity" affect people in particular places—in the classroom, in Australia, in Korea, in Melanesia, in jail, at the national convention for the Modern Language Association, and in the particular self-concepts and social concepts created by gender, race, and class? (These are all "places" described in different essays in this book.) Who is served when criticism is conceived as either simply commentary on literature (a method of reading) or a conceptual framework that allows a text to be considered to be "literary" (the definition of "literature")? One goal of this book is to specify and localize different contexts in which reading and literature are defined, to help describe what Showalter calls "the essential question of difference" in cultural and social terms.

Such questions suggest why critics—at least since the time of Arnold—have been nervous or even willfully unclear about what they do, and why many students, following the critics and critical debates they read, are curious but also anxious about the study of criticism. Despite the wide practice of criticism and formulation of literary theory, the conflict within critical practice that Arnold and Frye describe stimulates great intellectual debate. This activity rises out of the contradiction between roles for criticism. Criticism is the modest activity of creating a situation in which the best that is known and thought can have wide currency (Frye's description of the job of criticism is "to get as many people in contact with the best that has been and is being thought and said"). Criticism also has the imperial "burden" of maintaining cultural values in general (Frye's description of the "verbal universe, in which life and reality are inside literature" and which only the methods of criticism can help us to understand). In fact, as the subtitle of this book *(Literary and Cultural Studies)* suggests, the very *function* of criticism has changed or become more self-reflexive in recent time. Contemporary criticism has expanded its horizon to include a vast array of questions that heretofore seemed outside, or only implicit within, its purview. These include questions of politics, semantics, the philosophy of language, and sexual and social relations, as well as the nature of literary study—its responsibilities and its very objects of study.

Such expansion has occasioned much controversy and debate, exacerbating rather than resolving the contradiction within criticism and the anxiety of its practice. The exploration of wider cultural questions has come in recent times to be called literary "cultural studies," and it has often met tremendous opposition, not only within the academy, which has tended to make explicit the very contradiction in criticism that occasioned Arnold's anxiety, but in the popular press as well. In the academy, however, criticism is positioned, as Barthes says, self-consciously to explore and situate what it is doing. This is precisely the burden of Graff's argument: that literary studies should explore rather than cover up its own contradictions and controversies. Such controversies have a history that extends to the early articulations of modern literary criticism in the beginning of the nineteenth century when Friedrich Schlegel imagined criticism to be a "reconstructive" process whereby a critic enhances the development of art. In so doing, as Schlegel imagined (and Hartman later claims), the critic actually elevates criticism as a *genre* to the level of art. Schlegel's romantic view of criticism as an organic outgrowth of art survives in the poetics of the English Romantics and in the theory of such neoclassicists as T. S. Eliot and Ezra Pound as well as in much current thinking.

The contrary view, however, also present in the early nineteenth century—an early version of the "humanist myth"—says that criticism merely supplements art and, at worst, is a parasite draining away its lifeblood. At best it is a "hermeneutics" whose aim is to recover the intentional meanings of the artist and then, mission accomplished, quietly to disappear. Only on occasion, in this view, does criticism marginally increase our appreciation of artistic form, thereby giving support to art in a limited way. This separation of criticism from art is also implicit in Frank Kermode's idea of genre as a "consensus, a set of foreunderstandings exterior to a text which enable us to follow that text." Kermode thus believes that criticism is totally dependent on literature, and he therefore has little sympathy for the conflicts and convolutions of current theory. Criticism is merely an adjunct to literature, and the two—as Kermode believes—belong in different areas of culture anyway.

Current criticism, lacking Schlegel's belief in unity and Kermode's in separation, has intensified this debate. Contemporary criticism in fact is stranded between these two views—"nervous" about criticism's having a separate identity, and yet constantly undermining distinctions separating fiction and poetry, or prose fiction and expository prose, and even (despite what Kermode says) the basic distinction between criticism and literature. Certainty about the discreteness of critical and literary texts has been vanishing for some time, and we are left with a hybrid critical "thing" best described in Henry James's term for the novel as a genre as a baggy monster; that is, criticism and literature intertwined, intermixed, and mutually implicated. Even the aesthetics of a well-formed essay—with a beginning, middle, and end—is disrupted by contemporary literary criticism, as we noted in our discussion of Gayatri Chakravorty Spivak's essay, "Feminism and Critical Theory" (in "Feminism and Gender Studies"), whose parts were written and presented at different occasions so that they do not "add up" fully or aesthetically. Walter Benjamin's "Theses on the Philosophy of History" (in "Historical Critique") also assumes this "fragmentary" form, and Toril Moi (in "Psychology and Psychoanalysis") focuses her critical analysis on precisely the opposition between wholeness and fragments in the conceiving of knowledge. For these reasons we consistently find it more difficult than Kermode suggests to place the implicit "and" between criticism/literature and cannot say precisely how the two relate, either merging or in forming a relationship.

## ELIOT AND THE TRADITION OF "NEW CRITICISM"

An important point that we are emphasizing repeatedly in this book involves seeing the specific context, in social and cultural terms, that encompasses every attempt at criticism. In a word, there is no universal criticism or transhistorical approach to literary and cultural study. None has been discovered and none will yet be found. We say this with such emphasis because of our belief that social and cultural contexts frame all critical approaches. The essays in this section tend to comment on the social and cultural frames in relation to the study of literary form—the internal patterning of poetry, fiction, and drama—earlier in the twentieth century. This work goes under the general name of "formalism," and a particular school of this movement is called "New Criticism." The New Criticism was influential in America from the late 1930s through the late 1950s and still has an impact in the final years of the twentieth century. Formalism and New Criticism, in turn, were very much governed by the movement in the arts that occurred in the first 30 years of the twentieth century that early in that period came to be called "Modernism." In this introduction to the exploration of criticism in the context of *contemporary* literary studies, it is necessary to describe the related movements of Modernism and New Criticism to indicate the kind of "universal," "impersonal," and "objective" criticism to which much contemporary literary criticism is responding and against which it is reacting. In part, this is the reason why we begin the book with Eliot's essay, which is an important critical statement of literary Modernism.

Here we want to offer examples of Eliot's modernist sense of literature and culture and the formal treatments of literature that follow from that sense. Eliot is a central figure in literary Modernism, a movement in the Anglo-American world that dates from the early twentieth century and the influence of the French Symbolist poetry of Baudelaire, Mallarmé, Valéry, and others. Modernism is a body of literature and criticism, as well as a critical perspective—or, rather, several related perspectives—that produces some of the great writers and critics of our age. Sometimes Modernism is said to have begun at the turn of the century with Conrad and Yeats; others claim that it is most clearly delineated as a post–World War I phenomenon, best represented by the publications of James Joyce's *Ulysses* and T. S. Eliot's *The Waste Land* in 1922. By some accounts the movement ended in the mid-1930s. Others say it went on until World War II, and some note, Fredric Jameson among them, that contemporary postmodernism is simply another version of modernism. In any case the height of modernist fervor was surely Virginia Woolf's assurance in 1924 that "in or about December, 1910, human character changed." Woolf explained that "all human relations have shifted—those between masters and servants, husbands and wives, parents and children. And when human relations change there is at the same time a change in religion, conduct, politics, and literature." However, even a decade earlier D. H. Lawrence had described a similarly radical reconception of human character "as representing some greater, inhuman will." Like Woolf—and like Eliot in the essay included here—Lawrence presents an antiromantic, antiexpression-ist conception of human character in literature—a conception of the subject that, as Eliot says, is "impersonal" and a conception of literature as something other than "expressive." Their conception is a result of the *forms* of literature and experience rather than of the narrowest sense of "personal," "human" significance.

Modernism, that is, responded to huge historical dislocations at the turn of the twentieth century, the second industrial revolution, the growth of democratic institutions in Europe, the great scientific and technological changes in Europe and America, the conquering of much of the world by European imperialism, and the Great War (resulting in large part from all these things) that devastated much of Europe. The rhetoric of "high" Modernism—at least among its mostly male, middle-class spokespersons—is that of loss, apocalypse, and new beginnings; "make it new!" was Ezra Pound's slogan for Modernism, articulated against the background of lost connections between the cultural past and present. For Modernism, there are no ordained or natural lines of order in the world, no cultural backdrop that gives automatic meaning to a text; there is no providential plan according to which history and its outcomes are meaningfully situated. On the contrary, the disinheritance of modern culture is precisely the loss of belief in such traditional schemes as the Great Chain of Being. Pound and Eliot, in particular, do speak of grand cultural orders ("the mind of Europe," "tradition," "the past," and so on), but these are always distinctly human artifacts that must be reimagined for each poet and each culture.

The Modernists, that is, were involved in a serious reevaluation of the limits of literary form and of the possibilities for a new aesthetic in the arts generally—if not exactly new ways of being human, then at least a new paradigm of presentation for the products of twentieth-century culture. This aesthetic reevaluation took its place within the context of a serious questioning of the *subject* of experience and knowledge occasioned by the vast changes in the West in the early twentieth century. Henceforth, as Irving Babbitt said most forcefully, any romantic or sentimental tendencies in literature must be viewed as mere "emotional naturalism," a dissolving of real-world distinctions and a glossing over of important cultural demarcations. In place of nineteenth-century romantic "sloppiness," Babbitt said, is the emergent "modern spirit," "the positive and critical spirit, the spirit that refuses to take things on authority." Babbitt calls for a further movement away from supposedly "soft" and "uncritical" romanticism to "tough," "critical" modernism. It is a shift, as T. E. Hulme argued, into a contemporary version of the neoclassic sensibility and its modes of precise expression and carefully modulated sentiments. In short, Babbitt and Hulme call for the abandonment of romanticism and for the development of an emergent modern, antiromantic, *formal* sensibility.

Eliot elaborates this process in "Tradition and the Individual Talent" when he argues that "past," "present," and "future" are not given facts or simple realities of experience but a *formal* arrangement of areas of disturbance and discontinuity in the midst of which the poet constructs art and culture in a collage. Similarly, in this period the semiotician Ferdinand de Saussure—Eliot's contemporary (see "Structuralism and Semiotics")—proposes that reality itself is a linguistic arrangement of "signified" and potential meanings, a rational and formal arrangement situated within a context of arbitrariness. Thus, cut off from the past, disinherited from it, the poet, artist, or any user of language can choose to accept the imperative and the responsibility "to make it new" or else remain without any operative sense of past or present culture at all. This modernist version of poetry suggests a highly rational (almost Augustan) practice, but it is a poetic logic shown to exist in the irrational wasteland of modern culture, where the poet toils to make (actually *create*) cultural connections that otherwise would not exist. In other words, poetry introduces form into a cultural flux (the modern world) that by definition cannot be well formed, or "finished," because it remains in transition.

The "double task" of Eliot's work in criticism and in poetry, the presentation of rational objectivity alongside great subjective anxiety, is a defining articulation of literary Modernism. In addition, Eliot's work as a critic and as a poet initiated what Leslie Fiedler describes as the "Age of Eliot," the American literary criticism of the forties and fifties that, under the name of "New Criticism," explored linguistic and literary form as a way of creating the so-called "objective" sense that literature presents and examined the subjective "effects" that result from such literary forms. Paul de Man defines the New Criticism in "The Resistance to Theory" (in "What Is Literary Theory?"): "The perfect embodiment of the New Criticism," he writes, "remains, in many respects, the personality and ideology of T. S. Eliot, a combination of original talent, traditional learning, verbal wit and moral earnestness, an Anglo-American blend of intellectual gentility not so repressed as not to afford tantalizing glimpses of darker psychic and political depths." This position, de Man goes on, assumes "the integrity of a social and historical self": it is based on not only the assertion of but also a grave crisis in the "disinterested" subject of experience and knowledge. In the section "Structuralism and Semiotics," we will examine the closely related European phenomenon of Russian Formalism where, as we mentioned in the Introduction, scientific objectivity goes hand in hand with explorations of strangeness.

The principal American version of formalism, the New Criticism, also participates in literary Modernism. A single orthodoxy for the New Criticism as a broad movement does not exist, but we can isolate several of the key tenets articulated by major Anglo-American critics from the late 1920s through the 1950s, the period of the New Criticism's active development. In particular, the New Criticism tried to displace content in literary analysis and to treat a work's form in a manner analogous to empirical research. Also the New Criticism tried to organize the larger, generic forms of literature in accord with the inner ordering of works as revealed in specific analyses or "close readings." In its objectivity, it defined the subject of (poetic) experience and knowledge formally and thus avoided the "modernist" crisis of subjectivity; in its "close readings" it defined literature solely as impersonal, aesthetic experience and thus attempted to avoid the crisis of cultural institutions everywhere apparent in Modernism. It accomplished both of these tasks by conceiving of literature (to some degree or another) as a self-sustaining "artifact," a "spatial form" in Joseph Frank's words, and form as a self-contained "autonomous" entity. Perhaps most important was the New Critical reliance on "imagery" as a concept with which to define form. Drawing heavily on the work of the modernist writers, New Critics like Cleanth Brooks made the literary image the primary material or constituent of form itself. A New Critical "close reading" of John Donne's poem "The Canonization," for instance, involves a preliminary identification of key images in a recurring pattern of opposition, or as Brooks says, "tension." Only once this pattern of imagery is established do the New Critics attend to any interpretive considerations of form. Just as Eliot uses paradox and irony to pursue his argument in "Tradition and the Individual Talent," the New Critics posited paradox and irony as controlling figures, in effect turning them into a kind of content. As Brooks asserts in *The WellWrought Urn,* paradox and irony actually reflect the structure of the imagination itself.

The definition of literary form is the largest difference between the "substantial" formalism of the New Criticism and the "functional" formalism of Russian Formalism (discussed in "Structuralism and Semiotics"). Whereas the Russian Formalists attempted merely to lay bare the operation of local devices, rejecting any authoritative and final interpretation of a work, the New Critics believed that a work can be read objectively and accurately in light of its actual structure or form. A work can thus have a single, or "correct," interpretation. W. K. Wimsatt and Monroe C. Beardsley in "The Intentional Fallacy" stipulate the manner of reading a work the "right" way. They explain the interference and inaccuracies possible when authorial intentions become a consideration in close reading, which is, according to the New Critics, the "wrong" way to read. In "The Affective Fallacy," they also show how at the other extreme a reader's undisciplined "affective" responses to a text—the very *effects* that Shklovsky attempts to account for—may distort the correct apprehension and interpretation of images. In this thinking the New Critics retrieved from romanticism the concept of aesthetic wholeness and unity, as well as a unified or single interpretation of a work. They argued that a work, properly read, will always be unified by a set of reconceived tensions, as expressed in paradox and irony. In short, the New Critics assumed total coherence in a work.

## CONTEMPORARY LITERARY CRITICISM

Criticism after the New Criticism has pursued very different aims from those of Eliot and the New Critics. In fact the very "traditions" that are critiqued in this section, especially the New Criticism, pursued what Graff calls "the atomized empiricism of research and explication, which trusted that the accumulation of facts and interpretations about literature would somehow of itself add up to a coherent picture." Barthes critiques a similar "tradition" that was concerned with "rigor and objectivity" but in the narrow "establishment of facts." Showalter critiques a version of "scientific criticism [that] struggled to purge itself of the subjective" dimension of interpretation. Even Frye, in the *Anatomy of Criticism,* critiqued the New Criticism as a kind of "delicate learning"—appreciative, narrow, and, above all, certain and unselfconscious in the making of its own critical assumptions.

There is a high degree of self-consciousness in, among other areas, the structuralist and poststructuralist work of Barthes, in Showalter's feminism, and in the historical sense and context Graff brings to literary studies. In Frank Lentricchia's *After the New Criticism* he examines the crisis in criticism that the failure (or fulfillment) of the modernist tradition of New Criticism occasioned. The response to that crisis, as the various "schools" of criticism we examine in this book suggest, was to resubmit literature to self-conscious examination within a cultural and social context of functioning. Such a return, as we will see in the next section, requires that the autonomy of "aesthetics"—with its anonymous subject (or perspective on values), its transparent media, and its seeming separation from the world of controversy and culture—be replaced by "theory" and, on occasion, by aesthetics conceived within the context of theory.

**RELATED ESSAYS IN**
***CONTEMPORARY LITERARY CRITICISM***

J. Hillis Miller, "The Search for Grounds in Literary Study"
Kenneth Burke, "Literature as Equipment for Living"
Viktor Shklovsky, "Art as Technique"
Michel Foucault, "What Is an Author?"
Donna Haraway, "A Cyborg Manifesto"

**FURTHER READING**

Arnold, Matthew, *Arnold: Poetry and Prose,* ed. John Bryson (London: Rupert Hart-Davis, 1954).

Babbitt, Irving, *Rousseau and Romanticism* (Boston and New York: Houghton Mifflin, 1919).

Bennett, Tony, *Formalism and Marxism* (London: Methuen, 1979).

Berman, Marshall, *All That Is Solid Melts into Air: The Experience of Modernity* (New York: Simon & Schuster, 1982).

Bradbury, Malcolm, and James McFarlane, *Modernism: 1890–1930* (New York: Penguin Books, 1976).

Brooker, Peter, ed., *Modernism/Postmodernism* (New York: Longman, 1992).

Brooks, Cleanth, "My Credo: Formalist Critics," in *Kenyon Review,* 13 (1951), 72–81.

———, *The Well-Wrought Urn* (New York: Harcourt, 1975).

Brooks, Cleanth, and Robert Penn Warren, eds., *Understanding Poetry* (New York: Holt, 1983).

Conroy, Mark, *Modernism and Authority: Strategies of Legitimation in Flaubert and Conrad* (Baltimore: Johns Hopkins University Press, 1985).

Crane, R.S., et al., eds., *Critics and Criticism: Ancient and Modern* (Chicago: University of Chicago Press, 1957).

Culler, Jonathan, *Framing the Sign: Criticism and its Institutions* (Norman: University of Oklahoma Press, 1988).

Eliot, T. S., *The Sacred Wood* (London: Methuen, 1920).

Ellmann, Richard, and Charles Feidelson, Jr., *The Modern Tradition: Backgrounds of Modern Literature* (New York: Oxford University Press, 1965).

Frank, Joseph, *The Widening Gyre: Crisis and Mastery in Modern Literature* (New Brunswick, NJ: Rutgers University Press, 1963).

Frye, Northrop, *Anatomy of Criticism: Four Essays* (Princeton, NJ: Princeton University Press, 1957).

Graff, Gerald, *Literature Against Itself: Literary Ideas in Modern Society* (Chicago: University of Chicago Press, 1979).

————, *Professing Literature* (Chicago: University of Chicago Press, 1979).

————, *Beyond the Culture Wars* (New York: W.W. Norton, 1992).

Hartman, Geoffrey H., *Criticism in the Wilderness* (New Haven, CT: Yale University Press, 1980).

Howe, Irving, ed., *Literary Modernism* (New York: Fawcett, 1967).

Jameson, Fredric, *Postmodernism* (Durham: Duke University Press, 1992).

Kenner, Hugh, *A Homemade World: The American Modernist Writers* (New York: Morrow, 1975).

————, *The Pound Era* (Berkeley: University of California Press, 1971).

Kermode, Frank, and John Hollander, eds., *Modern British Literature* (New York: Oxford University Press, 1973).

Lentricchia, Frank, *After the New Criticism* (Chicago: University of Chicago Press, 1980).

Lodge, David, ed., *Twentieth-Century Literary Criticism: A Reader* (White Plains, NY: Longman, 1972).

Miller, J. Hillis, *Poets of Reality* (Cambridge, MA: Harvard University Press, 1965).

Ortega y Gasset, Jose, *The Dehumanization of Art and Other Writings of Art and Culture* (1948); reprint (Garden City, NY: Doubleday, 1956).

Pound, Ezra, *The ABC of Reading* (New Haven, CT: Yale University Press, 1934).

Ransom, John Crowe, *The New Criticism* (New York: New Directions, 1941).

Richards, I. A., *Practical Criticism* (New York: Harcourt, Brace, 1929).

————, *Principles of Literary Criticism* (New York: Harcourt, Brace, 1925).

Schleifer, Ronald, "The Poison of Ink: Post-War Literary Criticism," in *New Orleans Review,* 8 (1981), 241−49.

————, *Rhetoric and Death: The Language of Modernism and Postmodern Discourse Theory* (Urbana: University of Illinois Press, 1990).

Scholes, Robert, *Textual Power* (New Haven, CT: Yale University Press, 1985).

Spender, Stephen, *The Struggle of the Modern* (Berkeley: University of California Press, 1963).

Symons, Arthur, *The Symbolist Movement in Literature* (1899); reprint (New York: Dutton, 1958).

Wimsatt, W. K., *The Verbal Icon* (Lexington: University of Kentucky Press, 1954).

Winters, Yvor, *In Defense of Reason* (Denver: Swallow Press, 1947).

# 1

# T. S. Eliot
# 1888–1965

T. S. (Thomas Stearns) Eliot is best known as a poet, but he is arguably a central modern critic writing in English because of his vast influence in several areas: he almost singlehandedly brought about the reappraisal of sixteenth- and seventeenth-century drama and metaphysical poetry; he demonstrated the necessity of reading American and English literature in relation to European and non-European (especially Oriental) traditions; he helped to formulate a modern way of reading and writing that eschewed romantic values and furthered an aesthetic of "hard, dry" images and sentiments. Eliot thus directed modern readers in what and how to read and how to understand literary texts. These achievements, along with the critical revolution signaled by his own poetry, mark Eliot as a modern critic of the first rank. His major works of criticism include *The Sacred Wood* (1920), *The Use of Poetry and the Use of Criticism* (1933), *Christianity and Culture* (1940), *Notes Towards a Definition of Culture* (1949), *Selected Essays* (1953), and *On Poetry and Poets* (1957).

Eliot directed his criticism as much toward professional literary critics as he did toward the general public. In "Tradition and the Individual Talent" (1919), an essay which could easily borrow Pope's title *Essay on Criticism,* Eliot emphasizes the necessity of critical thinking—"criticism is as inevitable as breathing." This essay shows some of the furthest reaches of Eliot's theories and literary philosophy. He asserts the value of poetic creation as the process by which a whole culture locates itself in the present in relation to an acquired sense of the past. The past is an active force in the present, constituting "the presentness of the past," and is a channel of access to a cultural "mind" larger than any single poet's and ultimately decisive in determining the direction and import of all "significant" art in any age. These ideas had a direct influence on modernist criticism and literature, but—to a greater extent than is sometimes recognized—they also underlie some contemporary cultural theories, such as Reader-Response criticism and various approaches to audience-reception theory. Noteworthy for its coherence and cogency, this essay is perhaps Eliot's most important critical statement.

# Tradition and the Individual Talent

**I**

In English writing we seldom speak of tradition, though we occasionally apply its name in deploring its absence. We cannot refer to "the tradition" or to "a tradition"; at most, we employ that adjective in saying that the poetry of So-and-so is "traditional" or even "too traditional." Seldom, perhaps, does the word appear except in a phrase of censure. If otherwise, it is vaguely approbative, with the implication, as to the work approved, of some pleasing archaeological reconstruction. You can hardly make the word agreeable to English ears without this comfortable reference to the reassuring science of archaeology.

Certainly the word is not likely to appear in our appreciations of living or dead writers. Every nation, every race, has not only its own creative, but its own critical turn of mind; and is even more oblivious of the shortcomings and limitations of its critical habits than of those of its creative genius. We know, or think we know, from the enormous mass of critical writing that has appeared in the French language the critical method or habit of the French; we only conclude (we are such unconscious people) that the French are "more critical" than we, and sometimes even plume ourselves a little with the fact, as if the French were the less spontaneous. Perhaps they are; but we might remind ourselves that criticism is as inevitable as breathing, and that we should be none the worse for articulating what passes in our minds when we read a book and feel an emotion about it, for criticizing our own minds in their work of criticism. One of the facts that might come to light in this process is our tendency to insist, when we praise a poet, upon those aspects of his work in which he least resembles anyone else. In these aspects or parts of his work we pretend to find what is individual, what is the peculiar essence of the man. We dwell with satisfaction upon the poet's difference from his predecessors, especially his immediate predecessors; we endeavour to find something that can be isolated in order to be enjoyed. Whereas if we approach a poet without this prejudice we shall often find that not only the best, but the most individual parts of his work may be those in which the dead poets, his ancestors, assert their immortality most vigorously. And I do not mean the impressionable period of adolescence, but the period of full maturity.

Yet if the only form of tradition, of handing down, consisted in following the ways of the immediate generation before us in a blind or timid adherence to its successes, "tradition" should positively be discouraged. We have seen many such simple currents soon lost in the sand; and novelty is better than repetition. Tradition is a matter of much wider significance. It cannot be inherited, and if you want it you must obtain it by great labour. It involves, in the first place, the historical sense, which we may call nearly indispensable to anyone who would continue to be a poet beyond his twenty-fifth year; and the historical sense involves a perception, not only of the pastness of the past, but of its presence; the historical sense compels a man to write not merely with his own generation in his bones, but with a feeling that the whole of the literature of Europe from Homer and within it the whole of the literature of his own country has a simultaneous existence and composes a simultaneous order. This historical sense, which is a sense of the timeless as well as of the temporal and of the timeless and of the temporal together, is what makes a writer traditional. And it is at the same time what makes a writer most acutely conscious of his place in time, of his own contemporaneity.

No poet, no artist of any art, has his complete meaning alone. His significance, his appreciation is the appreciation of his relation to the dead poets and artists. You cannot value him alone; you must set him, for contrast and comparison, among the dead. I mean this as a principle of aesthetic, not merely historical, criticism. The necessity that he shall conform, that he shall cohere, is not onesided; what happens when a new work of art is created is something that happens simultaneously to all the works of art which preceded it. The existing monuments form an ideal order among themselves, which is modified by the introduction of the new (the really new) work of art among them. The existing order is complete before the new work arrives; for order to persist after the supervention of novelty, the whole existing order must be, if ever so slightly altered; and so the relations, proportions, values of each work of art towards the whole are readjusted; and this is conformity between the old and the new. Whoever has approved this idea of order, of the form of European, of English literature will not find it preposterous that the past should be altered by the present as much as the present is directed by the past. And the poet who is aware of this will be aware of great difficulties and responsibilities.

In a peculiar sense he will be aware also that he must inevitably be judged by the standards of the past. I say judged, not amputated, by them; not judged to be as good as, or worse or better than, the dead; and certainly not judged by the canons of dead critics. It is a judgment, a comparison, in which two things are measured by each other. To conform merely would be for the new work not really to conform at all; it would not be new, and would therefore not be a work of art. And we do not quite say that the new is more valuable because it fits in; but its fitting in is a test of its value—a test,

it is true, which can only be slowly and cautiously applied, for we are none of us infallible judges of conformity. We say: it appears to conform, and is perhaps individual, or it appears individual, and may conform; but we are hardly likely to find that it is one and not the other.

To proceed to a more intelligible exposition of the relation of the poet to the past: he can neither take the past as a lump, an indiscriminate bolus, nor can he form himself wholly on one or two private admirations, nor can he form himself wholly upon one preferred period. The first course is inadmissible, the second is an important experience of youth, and the third is a pleasant and highly desirable supplement. The poet must be very conscious of the main current, which does not at all flow invariably through the most distinguished reputations. He must be quite aware of the obvious fact that art never improves, but that the material of art is never quite the same. He must be aware that the mind of Europe—the mind of his own country—a mind which he learns in time to be much more important than his own private mind—is a mind which changes, and that this change is a development which abandons nothing *en route,* which does not superannuate either Shakespeare, or Homer, or the rock drawing of the Magdalenian draughtsmen. That this development, refinement perhaps, complication certainly, is not from the point of view of the artist, any improvement. Perhaps not even an improvement from the point of view of the psychologist or not to the extent which we imagine; perhaps only in the end based upon a complication in economics and machinery. But the difference between the present and the past is that the conscious present is an awareness of the past in a way and to an extent which the past's awareness of itself cannot show.

Someone said: "The dead writers are remote from us because we know so much more than they did." Precisely, and they are that which we know.

I am alive to a usual objection to what is clearly part of my programme for the *métier* of poetry. The objection is that the doctrine requires a ridiculous amount of erudition (pedantry), a claim which can be rejected by appeal to the lives of poets in any pantheon. It will even be affirmed that much learning deadens or perverts poetic sensibility. While, however, we persist in believing that a poet ought to know as much as will not encroach upon his necessary receptivity and necessary laziness, it is not desirable to confine knowledge to whatever can be put into a useful shape for examinations, drawing rooms, or the still more pretentious modes of publicity. Some can absorb knowledge, the more tardy must sweat for it. Shakespeare acquired more essential history from Plutarch than most men could from the whole British Museum. What is to be insisted upon is that the poet must develop or procure the consciousness of the past and that he should continue to develop this consciousness throughout his career.

What happens is a continual surrender of himself as he is at the moment to something which is more valuable. The progress of an artist is a continual self-sacrifice, a continual extinction of personality.

There remains to define this process of depersonalization and its relation to the sense of tradition. It is in this depersonalization that art may be said to approach the condition of science. I therefore invite you to consider, as a suggestive analogy, the action which takes place when a bit of finely filiated platinum is introduced into a chamber containing oxygen and sulphur dioxide.

## II

Honest criticism and sensitive appreciation are directed not upon the poet but upon the poetry. If we attend to the confused cries of the newspaper critics and the susurrus of popular repetition that follows, we shall hear the names of poets in great numbers; if we seek not Blue-book knowledge but the enjoyment of poetry, and ask for a poem, we shall seldom find it. I have tried to point out the importance of the relation of the poem to other poems by other authors, and suggested the conception of poetry as a living whole of all the poetry that has ever been written. The other aspect of this Impersonal theory of poetry is the relation of the poem to its author. And I hinted, by an analogy, that the mind of the mature poet differs from that of the immature one not precisely in any valuation of "personality," not being necessarily more interesting, or having "more to say," but rather by being a more finely perfected medium in which special, or varied, feelings are at liberty to enter into new combinations.

The analogy was that of the catalyst. When the two gases previously mentioned are mixed in the presence of a filament of platinum, they form sulphurous acid. This combination takes place only if the platinum is present; nevertheless the newly formed acid contains no trace of platinum, and the platinum itself is apparently unaffected: has remained inert, neutral, and unchanged. The mind of the poet is the shred of platinum. It may partly or exclusively operate upon the experience of the man himself; but, the more perfect the artist, the more completely separate in him will be the man who suffers and the mind which creates; the more perfectly will the mind digest and transmute the passions which are its material.

The experience, you will notice, the elements which enter the presence of the transforming catalyst, are of two kinds: emotions and feelings. The effect of a work of art upon the person who enjoys it is an experience different in kind from any experience not of art. It may be formed out of one emotion, or may be a combination of several; and various feelings, inhering for the writer in particular words or phrases or images, may be added to compose the final result. Or great poetry may be made without the direct use of any emotion whatever: composed out of feelings solely. Canto XV of the *Inferno* (Brunetto Latini) is a working up of the emotion evident in the situation; but the effect, though single as that of any work of art, is obtained by considerable complexity of detail. The last quatrain[1] gives an image, a feeling attaching to an image, which "came" which did not develop simply out of what precedes, but which was probably in suspension in the poet's mind until the proper combination arrived for it to add itself to. The poet's mind is in fact a receptacle for seizing and storing up numberless feelings, phrases, images, which remain there until all the particles which can unite to form a new compound are present together.

If you compare several representative passages of the greatest poetry you see how great is the variety of types of combination, and also how completely any semi-ethical criterion of "sublimity" misses the mark. For it is not the "greatness," the intensity, of the emotions, the components, but the intensity of the artistic process, the pressure, so to speak, under which the fusion takes place, that counts. The episode of Paolo and Francesca employs a definite emotion, but the intensity of the poetry is something quite different from whatever intensity in the supposed experience it may give the impression of. It is not more intense, furthermore, than Canto XXVI, the voyage of Ulysses, which has not the direct dependence upon an emotion. Great variety is possible in the process of transmutation of emotion: the murder of Agamemnon, or the agony of Othello, gives an artistic effect apparently closer to a possible original than the scenes from Dante. In the *Agamemnon,* the artistic emotion approximates to the emotion of an actual spectator; in *Othello* to the emotion of the protagonist himself. But the difference between art and

the event is always absolute; the combination which is the murder of Agamemnon is probably as complex as that which is the voyage of Ulysses. In either case there has been a fusion of elements. The ode of Keats contains a number of feelings which have nothing particular to do with the nightingale, but which the nightingale, partly perhaps because of its reputation, served to bring together.

The point of view which I am struggling to attack is perhaps related to the metaphysical theory of the substantial unity of the soul: for my meaning is, that the poet has, not a "personality" to express, but a particular medium, which is only a medium and not a personality, in which impressions and experiences combine in peculiar and unexpected ways. Impressions and experiences which are important for the man may take no place in the poetry, and those which become important in the poetry may play quite a negligible part in the man, the personality.

I will quote a passage which is unfamiliar enough to be regarded with fresh attention in the light—or darkness—of these observations:

And now methinks I could e'en chide
    myself
For doating on her beauty, though her
    death
Shall be revenged after no common action.
Does the silkworm expend her yellow
    labours
For thee? For thee does she undo herself?
Are lordships sold to maintain ladyships
For the poor benefit of a bewildering
    minute?
Why does yon fellow falsify highways,
And put his life between the judge's lips,
To refine such a thing—keeps horse and
    men
To beat their valours for her? . . .[2]

In this passage (as is evident if it is taken in its context) there is a combination of positive and negative emotions: an intensely strong attraction towards beauty and an equally intense fascination by the ugliness which is contrasted with it and which destroys it. This balance of contrasted emotion is in the dramatic situation to which the speech is pertinent, but that situation alone is inadequate to it. This is, so to speak, the structural emotion, provided by the drama. But the whole effect, the dominant tone, is due to the fact that a number of floating feelings, having an affinity to this emotion by no means superficially evident, have combined with it to give us a new art emotion.

It is not in his personal emotions, the emotions provoked by particular events in his life, that the poet is in any way remarkable or interesting. His particular emotions may be simple, or crude, or flat. The emotion in his poetry will be a very complex thing, but not with the complexity of the emotions of people who have very complex or unusual emotions in life. One error, in fact, of eccentricity in poetry is to seek for new human emotions to express; and in this search for novelty in the wrong place it discovers the perverse. The business of the poet is not to find new emotions, but the use of ordinary ones and, in working them up into poetry, to express feelings which are not in actual emotions at all. And emotions which he has never experienced will serve his turn as well as those familiar to him. Consequently, we must believe that "emotion recollected in tranquility"[3] is an inexact formula. For it is neither emotion, nor recollection, nor, without distortion of meaning, tranquility. It is a concentration, and a new thing resulting from the concentration, of a very great number of experiences which to the practical and active person would not seem to be experiences at all; it is a concentration which does not happen consciously or of deliberation. These experiences are not "recollected," and they finally unite in an atmosphere which is "tranquil" only in that it is a passive attending upon the event. Of course this is not quite the whole story. There is a great deal, in the writing of poetry, which must be conscious and deliberate. In fact, the bad poet is usually unconscious where he ought to be conscious, and conscious where he ought to be unconscious. Both errors tend to make him "personal." Poetry is not a turning loose of emotion, but an escape from emotion; it is not the expression of personality, but an escape from personality. But, of course, only those who have personality and emotions know what it means to want to escape from these things.

## III

*ὁ δὲ νοῦς ἴνως θειότερόν τι καὶ ἀπαθές ἐστιν.*[4]

This essay proposes to halt at the frontier of metaphysics or mysticism, and confine itself to such practical conclusions as can be applied by the responsible person interested in poetry. To divert interest from the poet to the poetry is a laudable aim: for it would conduce to a juster estimation of actual poetry, good and bad. There are many people who appreciate the expression of sincere emotion in verse, and there is a smaller number of people who can appreciate technical excellence. But very few know when there is an expression of *significant* emotion, emotion which has its life in the poem and not in the history of the poet. The emotion of art is impersonal. And the poet cannot reach this impersonality without surrendering himself wholly to the work to be done. And he is not likely to know what is to be done unless he believes in what is not merely the present, but the present moment of the past, unless he is conscious, not of what is dead, but of what is already living.

## NOTES

1. In the translation of Dorothy L. Sayers:
   Then he turned round.
   And seemed like one of those who over the flat
     And open course in the fields beside Verona
     Run for the green cloth; and he seemed, at
       that,
   Not like a loser, but the winning runner.

2. Cyril Tourneur, *The Revenger's Tragedy* (1607), III, iv.

3. "Poetry is the spontaneous overflow of powerful feelings: it takes its origins from emotion recollected in tranquility." Wordsworth, Preface to *Lyrical Ballads* (1800).

4. "While the intellect is doubtless a thing more divine and is impassive." Aristotle, *De Anima*.

# 2

# Northrop Frye
# 1912–1991

Northrop Frye's most acclaimed work is *Anatomy of Criticism* (1957), in which he introduced his systematic approach to literature. Among his other works are *The Well-Tempered Critic* (1963); *The Critical Path: An Essay on the Social Context of Literary Criticism* (1971); and *The Stubborn Structure: Essays on Criticism and Society* (1970). He also authored two books on Shakespeare: *Fools of Time: Studies in Shakespearean Tragedy* (1967) and *A Natural Perspective* (1965). His two in-depth studies of Romanticism are *Fearful Symmetry: A Study of William Blake* (1947) and *A Study of English Romanticism* (1968).

In his work Frye offers a concise, fully developed, and systematic approach to the study of literature. Unlike the preceding theories of formalism (which concentrate on the individual work) and historicism (emphasizing the author as creator), his method identifies the whole of literature as a culturally structured entity consisting of the entire canon of poems, dramas, and prose. Frye uses a mythological model to illustrate the morphology of literature: it consists of birth (melodrama), zenith (comedy), death (tragedy), and darkness (ironic literature).

In "The Function of Criticism at the Present Time" (1949), Frye considers it the responsibility of the critic to systematize the previously unorganized study of literature. As the shaper of intellectual tradition, the critic must organize the material within a critical framework that follows the natural contours of literature. Before criticism can exist as an organized system, it must thoroughly—even scientifically—classify literature, reconsidering the all-too-frequent use of unsupported value judgments by many writers in discussing literary works. To truly understand literature, says Frye, requires seeing it as a system of word-symbols, not unlike mathematics, which must be considered as part of its greater structure, separate from the world that gave rise to the ideas it depicts.

## The Function of Criticism at the Present Time

The subject-matter of literary criticism is an art, and criticism is presumably an art too. This sounds as though criticism were a parasitic form of literary expression, an art based on pre-existing art, a second-hand imitation of creative power. The conception of the critic as a creator *manqué* is very popular, especially among artists. Yet the critic has specific jobs to do which the experience of literature has proved to be less ignoble. One obvious function of criticism is to mediate between the artist and his public. Art that tries to do without criticism is apt to get involved in either of two fallacies. One is the attempt to reach the public directly through "popular" art, the assumption being that criticism is artificial and public taste natural. Below this is a further assumption about natural taste which goes back to Rousseau. The opposite fallacy is the conception of art as a mystery, an initiation into an esoteric community. Here criticism is restricted to masonic signs of occult understanding, to significant exclamations and gestures and oblique cryptic comments. This fallacy is like the other one in assuming a rough correlation between the merit of art and the degree of public response to it, though the correlation it assumes is inverse. But art of this kind is cut off from society as a whole, not so much because it retreats from life—the usual charge against it—as because it rejects criticism.

On the other hand, a public that attempts to do without criticism, and asserts that it knows what it likes, brutalizes the arts. Rejection of criticism from the point of view of the public, or its guardians, is involved in all forms of censorship. Art is a continuously emancipating factor in society, and the critic, whose job it is to get as many people in contact with the best that has been and is being thought and said, is, at least ideally, the pioneer of education and the shaper of cultural tradition. There is no immediate correlation either way between the merits of art and its general reception. Shakespeare was more popular than Webster, but not because he was a greater dramatist; W. H. Auden is less popular than Edgar Guest, but not because he is a better poet. But after the critic has been at work for a while, some positive correlation may begin to take shape. Most of Shakespeare's current popularity is due to critical publicity.

Why does criticism have to exist? The best and shortest answer is that it can talk, and all the arts are dumb. In painting, sculpture, or music it is easy enough to see that the art

shows forth, and cannot say anything. And, although it sounds like a frantic paradox to say that the poet is inarticulate or speechless, literary works also are, for the critic, mute complexes of facts, like the data of science. Poetry is a *disinterested* use of words: it does not address a reader directly. When it does so, we feel that the poet has a certain distrust in the capacity of readers and critics to interpret his meaning without assistance, and has therefore stopped creating a poem and begun to talk. It is not merely tradition that impels a poet to invoke a Muse and protest that his utterance is involuntary. Nor is it mere paradox that causes Mr. MacLeish, in his famous "Ars Poetica," to apply the words "mute," "dumb," and "wordless" to a poem. The poet, as Mill saw in a wonderful flash of critical insight, is not heard, but overheard. The first assumption of criticism, and the assumption on which the autonomy of criticism rests, is not that the poet does not know what he is talking about, but that he cannot talk about what he knows, any more than the painter or composer can.

The poet may of course have some critical ability of his own, and so interpret his own work; but the Dante who writes a commentary on the first canto of the *Paradiso is merely one more of Dante's* critics. What he says has a peculiar interest, but not a peculiar authority. Poets are too often the most unreliable judges of the value or even the meaning of what they have written. When Ibsen maintains that *Emperor and Galilean* is his greatest play and that certain episodes in *Peer Gynt* are not allegorical, one can only say that Ibsen is an indifferent critic of Ibsen. Wordsworth's Preface to the *Lyrical Ballads* is a remarkable document, but as a piece of Wordsworthian criticism nobody would give it more than about a B plus. Critics of Shakespeare are often supposed to be ridiculed by the assertion that if Shakespeare were to come back from the dead he would not be able to understand their criticism and would accuse them of reading far more meaning into his work than he intended. This, though pure hypothesis, is likely enough: we have very little evidence of Shakespeare's interest in criticism, either of himself or of anyone else. But all that this means is that Shakespeare, though a great dramatist, was not also the greatest Shakespearean critic. Why should he be?

The notion that the poet is necessarily his own best interpreter is indissolubly linked with the conception of the critic as a parasite or jackal of literature. Once we admit that he has a specific field of activity, and that he has autonomy within that field, we are forced to concede that criticism deals with literature in terms of a specific conceptual framework. This framework is not that of literature itself, for this is the parasite theory again, but neither is it something outside literature, for in that case the autonomy of criticism would again disappear, and the whole subject would be assimilated to something else.

Here, however, we have arrived at another conception of criticism which is different from the one we started with. This autonomous organizing of literature may be criticism, but it is not the activity of mediating between the artist and his public which we at first ascribed to criticism. There is one kind of critic, evidently, who faces the public and another who is still as completely involved in literary values as the poet himself. We may call this latter type the critic proper, and the former the critical reader. It may sound like quibbling to imply such a distinction, but actually the whole question of whether the critic has a real function, independent both of the artist at his most explicit and of the public at its most discriminating, is involved in it.

Our present-day critical traditions are rooted in the age of Hazlitt and Arnold and Sainte-Beuve, who were, in terms of our distinction, critical readers. They represented, not another conceptual framework within literature, but the reading public at its most

expert and judicious. They conceived it to be the task of a critic to exemplify how a man of taste uses and evaluates literature, and thus how literature is to be absorbed into society. The nineteenth century has bequeathed to us the conception of the *causerie,* the man of taste's reflections on works of literature, as the normal form of critical expression. I give one example of the difference between a critic and a critical reader which amounts to a head-on collision. In one of his curious, brilliant, scatter-brained footnotes to *Munera Pulveris,* John Ruskin says:

> Of Shakespeare's names I will afterwards speak at more length; they are curiously—often barbarously—mixed out of various traditions and languages. Three of the clearest in meaning have been already noticed. Desdemona—"δυσδαιμονία" *miserable fortune*—is also plain enough. Othello is, I believe, "the careful"; all the calamity of the tragedy arising from the single flaw and error in his magnificently collected strength. Ophelia, "serviceableness," the true, lost wife of Hamlet, is marked as having a Greek name by that of her brother, Laertes; and its signification is once exquisitely alluded to in that brother's last word of her, where her gentle preciousness is opposed to the uselessness of the churlish clergy: *"A ministering* angel shall my sister be, when thou liest howling."

On this passage Matthew Arnold comments as follows:

> Now, really, what a piece of extravagance all that is! I will not say that the meaning of Shakespeare's names (I put aside the question as to the correctness of Mr. Ruskin's etymologies) has no effect at all, may be entirely lost sight of; but to give it that degree of prominence is to throw the reins to one's whim, to forget all moderation and

proportion, to lose the balance of one's mind altogether. It is to show in one's criticism, to the highest excess, the note of provinciality.

Ruskin is a critic, perhaps the only important one that the Victorian age produced, and, whether he is right or wrong, what he is attempting is genuine criticism. He is trying to interpret Shakespeare in terms of a conceptual framework which belongs to the critic alone, and yet relates itself to the plays alone. Arnold is perfectly right in feeling that this is not the sort of material that the public critic can directly use. But he does not suspect the existence of criticism as we have defined it above. Here it is Arnold who is the provincial. Ruskin has learned his trade from the great iconological tradition which comes down through classical and biblical scholarship into Dante and Spenser, both of whom he knew how to read, and which is incorporated in the medieval cathedrals he had pored over in such detail. Arnold is assuming, as a universal law of nature, certain "plain sense" critical assumptions which were hardly heard of before Dryden's time and which can assuredly not survive the age of Freud and Jung and Frazer and Cassirer. What emerges from this is that the critic and critical reader are each better off when they know of one another's existence, and perhaps best off when their work forms different aspects of the same thing.

However, the *causerie* does not, or at least need not, involve any fallacy in the theory of criticism itself. The same cannot be said of the reaction against the *causerie* which has produced the leading twentieth-century substitute for criticism. This is the integrated system of religious, philosophical, and political ideas which takes in, as a matter of course, a critical attitude to literature. Thus Mr. Eliot defines his outlook as classical in literature, royalist in politics, anglo-catholic in religion; and it is clear that the third of these has been the spark-plug, the motivating power that drives the other two. Mr. Allen Tate describes his own critical attitude as "reactionary" in a sense intended to include political and philosophical overtones, and the same is true of Hulme's *Speculations,* which are primarily political speculations. Mr. Yvor Winters collects his criticism under the title "In Defence of Reason." What earthly business, one may inquire, has a literary critic to defend reason? He might as well be defending virtue. And so we could go through the list of Marxist, Thomist, Kierkegaardian, Freudian, Jungian, Spenglerian, or existential critics, all determined to substitute a critical attitude for criticism, all proposing, not to find a conceptual framework for criticism within literature, but to attach criticism to one of a miscellany of frameworks outside it.

The axioms and postulates of criticism have to grow out of the art that the critic is dealing with. The first thing that the literary critic has to do is to read literature, to make an inductive survey of his own field and let his critical principles shape themselves solely out of his knowledge of that field. Critical principles cannot be taken over ready-made from theology, philosophy, politics, science, or any combination of these. Further, an inductive survey of his own field is equally essential for the critic of painting or of music, and so each art has its own criticism. Aesthetics, or the consideration of art as a whole, is not a form of criticism but a branch of philosophy. I state all this as dogma, but I think the experience of literature bears me out. To subordinate criticism to a critical attitude is to stereotype certain values in literature which can be related to the extra-literary source of the value-judgment. Mr. Eliot does not mean to say that Dante is a greater poet than Shakespeare or perhaps even Milton; yet he imposes on literature an extra-literary schematism, a sort of religio-political colour-filter, which makes Dante leap into prominence, shows Milton up as dark and faulty, and largely obliterates the outlines of Shake-speare. All that the genuine critic can do with this colour-filter is to murmur politely that it shows things in a new light and is indeed a most stimulating contribution to criticism.

If it is insisted that we cannot criticize litera-ture until we have acquired a coherent phi-losophy of criticism with its centre of gravity in something else, the existence of criticism as a separate subject is still being denied. But there is one possibility further. If criticism ex-ists, it must be, we have said, an examination of literature in terms of a conceptual frame-work derivable from an inductive survey of the literary field. The word "inductive" sug-gests some sort of scientific procedure. What if criticism is a science as well as an art? The writing of history is an art, but no one doubts that scientific principles are involved in the historian's treatment of evidence, and that the presence of this scientific element is what dis-tinguishes history from legend. Is it also a scientific element in criticism which distin-guishes it from *causerie* on the one hand, and the superimposed critical attitude on the other? For just as the presence of science changes the character of a subject from the casual to the causal, from the random and intuitive to the systematic, so it also safe-guards the integrity of a subject from external invasions. So we may find in science a means of strengthening the fences of criticism against enclosure movements coming not only from religion and philosophy, but from the other sciences as well.

If criticism is a science, it is clearly a social science, which means that it should waste no time in trying to assimilate its methods to those of the natural sciences. Like psychol-ogy, it is directly concerned with the human mind, and will only confuse itself with statisti-cal methodologies. I understand that there is a Ph.D. thesis somewhere that displays a list of Hardy's novels in the order of the percent-ages of gloom that they contain, but one does not feel that that sort of procedure should be encouraged. Yet as the field is narrowed to the social sciences the distinctions must be kept equally sharp. Thus there can be no such thing as a sociological "approach" to litera-ture. There is no reason why a sociologist should not work exclusively on literary mate-rial, but if he does he should pay no attention to literary values. In his field Horatio Alger and the writer of the Elsie books are more important than Hawthorne or Melville, and a single issue of the *Ladies' Home Journal* is worth all of Henry James. The literary critic using sociological data is similarly under no obligation to respect sociological values.

It seems absurd to say that there *may* be a scientific element in criticism when there are dozens of learned journals based on the as-sumption that there is, and thousands of scholars engaged in a scientific procedure re-lated to literary criticism. Either literary criti-cism is a science, or all these highly trained and intelligent people are wasting their time on a pseudoscience, one to be ranked with phrenology and election forecasting. Yet one is forced to wonder whether scholars as a whole are consciously aware that the as-sumptions on which their work is based are scientific ones. In the growing complication of secondary sources which constitutes liter-ary scholarship, one misses, for the most part, that sense of systematic progressive consoli-dation which belongs to a science. Research begins in what is known as "background," and one would expect it, as it goes on, to organize the foreground as well. The digging up of relevant information about a poet should lead to a steady consolidating prog-ress in the criticism of his poetry. One feels a certain failure of nerve in coming out of the background into the foreground, and re-search seems to prefer to become centrifugal, moving away from the works of art into more and more research projects. I have noticed this particularly in two fields in which I am interested, Blake and Spenser. For every critic of Spenser who is interested in knowing what, say, the fourth book of *The Faerie Queene* actually means as a whole, there are dozens who are interested primarily in how Spenser used Chaucer, Malory, and Ariosto in putting it together. So far as I know there is no book devoted to an analysis of *The Faerie Queene* itself, though there are any number on its sources, and, of course, background. As for Blake, I have read a whole shelf of books on his poetry by critics who did not know what any of his major poems meant. The better ones were distinguishable only by the fact that they did not boast of their ignorance.

The reason for this is that research is ancillary to criticism, but the critic to whom the researcher should entrust his materials hardly exists. What passes for criticism is mainly the work of critical readers or spokesmen of various critical attitudes, and these make, in general, a random and haphazard use of scholarship. Such criticism is therefore often regarded by the researcher as a subjective and regressive dilettantism, interesting in its place, but not real work. On the other hand, the critical reader is apt to treat the researcher as Hamlet did the grave-digger, ignoring everything he throws out except an odd skull that he can pick up and moralize about. Yet unless research consolidates into a criticism which preserves the scientific and systematic element in research, the literary scholar will be debarred by his choice of profession from ever making an immediately significant contribution to culture. The absence of direction in research is, naturally, clearest on the very lowest levels of all, where it is only a spasmodic laying of unfertilized eggs in order to avoid an administrative axe. Here the research is characterized by a kind of desperate tentativeness, an implied hope that some synthesizing critical Messiah of the future will find it useful. A philologist can show the relationship of even the most minute study of dialect to his subject as a whole, because philology is a properly organized science. But the researcher who collects all a poet's references to the sea or God or beautiful women does not know who will find this useful or in what ways it could be used, because he has no theory of imagery.

I am not, obviously, saying that literary scholarship at present is doing the wrong thing or should be doing something else: I am saying that it should be possible to get a clearer and more systematic comprehension of what it is doing. Most literary scholarship could be described as prior criticism (the so-called "lower" criticism of biblical scholarship), the editing of texts and the collecting of relevant facts. Of the posterior (or "higher") criticism that is obviously the final cause of this work we have as yet no theory, no tradition, and above all no systematic organization. We have, of course, a good deal of the thing itself. There is even some good posterior criticism of Spenser, though most of it was written in the eighteenth century. And in every age the great scholar will do the right thing by the instinct of genius. But genius is rare, and scholarship is not.

Sciences normally begin in a state of naïve induction: they come immediately in contact with phenomena and take the things to be explained as their immediate data. Thus physics began by taking the immediate sensations of experience, classified as hot, cold, moist, and dry, as fundamental principles. Eventually physics turned inside out, and discovered that its real function was to explain what heat and moisture were. History began as chronicle; but the difference between the old chronicler and the modern historian is that to the chronicler the events he recorded were also the structure of history, whereas the historian sees these events as historical phenomena, to be explained in terms of a conceptual framework different in shape from them. Similarly each modern science has had to take what Bacon calls (though in another context) an inductive leap, occupying a new vantage ground from which it could see its former principles as new things to be explained. As long as astronomers regarded the movements of heavenly bodies as the *structure* of astronomy, they were compelled to regard their own point of view as fixed. Once they thought of movement as itself an explainable phenomenon, a mathematical theory of movement became the conceptual framework, and so the way was cleared for the heliocentric solar system and the law of gravitation. As long as biology thought of animal and vegetable forms of life as constituting its subject, the different branches of biology were largely efforts of cataloguing. As soon as it was the existence of forms of life themselves that had to be explained, the theory of evolution and the conceptions of protoplasm and the cell poured into biology and completely revitalized it.

It occurs to me that literary criticism is now in such a state of naïve induction as we find in a primitive science. Its materials, the masterpieces of literature, are not yet regarded as phenomena to be explained in terms of a conceptual framework which criticism alone possesses. They are still regarded as somehow constituting the framework or form of criticism as well. I suggest that it is time for criticism to leap to a new ground from which it can discover what the organizing or containing forms of its conceptual framework are. And no one can examine the present containing forms of criticism without being depressed by an overwhelming sense of unreality. Let me give one example.

In confronting any work of literature, one obvious containing form is the genre to which it belongs. And criticism, incredible as it may seem, has as yet no coherent conception of genres. The very word sticks out in an English sentence as the unpronounceable and alien thing it is. In poetry, the common-sense Greek division by methods of performance, which distinguishes poetry as lyric, epic, or dramatic according to whether it is

sung, spoken, or shown forth, survives vestigially. On the whole it does not fit the facts of Western poetry, though in Joyce's *Portrait* there is an interesting and suggestive attempt made to re-define the terms. So, apart from a drama which belongs equally to prose, a handful of epics recognizable as such only because they are classical imitations, and a number of long poems also called epics because they are long, we are reduced to the ignoble and slovenly practice of calling almost the whole of poetry "lyric" because the Greeks had no other word for it. The Greeks did not need to develop a classification of prose forms: we do, but have never done so. The circulating-library distinction between fiction and non-fiction, between books which are about things admitted not to be true and books which are about everything else, is apparently satisfactory to us. Asked what the forms of prose fiction are, the literary critic can only say, "well, er—the novel." Asked what form of prose fiction *Gulliver's Travels,* which is clearly not a novel, belongs to, there is not one critic in a hundred who could give a definite answer, and not one in a thousand who would regard the answer (which happens to be "Menippean satire") as essential to the critical treatment of the book. Asked what he is working on, the critic will invariably say that he is working on Donne, or Shelley's thought, or the period from 1640 to 1660, or give some other answer which implies that history, or philosophy, or literature itself, constitutes the structural basis of criticism. It would never occur to any critic to say, for instance, "I am working on the theory of genres." If he actually were interested in this, he would say that he was working on a "general" topic; and the work he would do would probably show the marks of naïve induction: that is, it would be an effort to classify and pigeon-hole instead of clarifying the tradition of the genre.

If we do not know how to handle even the genre, the most obvious of all critical conceptions, it is hardly likely that subtler instruments will be better understood. In any work of literature the characteristics of the language it is written in form an essential critical conception. To the philologist, literature is a function of language, its works linguistic documents, and to the philologist the phrase "English literature" makes sense. It ought not to make any sense at all to a literary critic. For while the philologist sees English literature as illustrating the organic growth of the English language, the literary critic can only see it as the miscellaneous pile of literary works that happened to get written in English. (I say in English, not in England, for the part of "English literature" that was written in Latin or Norman French has a way of dropping unobtrusively into other departments.) Language is an important secondary aspect of literature, but when magnified into a primary basis of classification it becomes absurdly arbitrary.

Critics, of course, maintain that they know this, and that they keep the linguistic categories only for convenience. But theoretical fictions have a way of becoming practical assumptions, and in no time the meaningless convenience of "English literature" expands into the meaningless inconvenience of the "history of English literature." Now, again, the historian must necessarily regard literature as an historical product and its works as historical documents. It is also quite true that the time a work was written in forms an essential critical conception. But again, to the literary critic, as such, the phrase "history of English literature" ought to mean nothing at all. If he doubts this, let him try writing one, and he will find himself confronted by an insoluble problem of form, or rather by an indissoluble amorphousness. The "history" part of his project is an abstract history, a bald chronicle of names and dates and works and influences, deprived of all the real historical interest that a real historian would give it, however much enlivened with discussions of "background." This chronicle is periodically interrupted by conventional judgments of value lugged in from another world, which confuse the history and yet are nothing by themselves. The *form* of literary history has not been discovered, and probably does not exist, and every successful one has been either a textbook or a *tour de force.* Linear time is not an exact enough category to catch literature, and all writers whatever are subtly belittled by a purely historical treatment.

Biography, a branch of history, presents a similar fallacy to the critic, for the biographer turns to a different job and a different kind of book when he turns to criticism. Again, the man who wrote the poem is one of the legitimate containing forms of criticism. But here we have to distinguish the poet *qua* poet, whose work is a single imaginative body, from the poet as man, who is something else altogether. The latter involves us in what is known as the personal heresy, or rather the heroic fallacy. For a biographer, poetry is an emanation of a personality; for the literary critic it is not, and the problem is to detach it from the personality and consider it on impersonal merits. The no man's land between biography and criticism, the process by which a poet's impressions of his environment are transmuted into poetry, has to be viewed by biographer and critic from opposite points of view. The process is too complex ever to be completely unified, Lowes's *Road to Xanadu* being the kind of exception that goes a long way to prove the rule. In Johnson's *Lives of the Poets* a biographical narrative is followed by a critical analysis, and the break between them is so sharp that it is represented in the text by a space.

In all these cases, the same principle recurs. The critic is surrounded by biography, history, philosophy, and language. No one doubts that he has to familiarize himself with these subjects. But is his job only to be the jackal of the historian, the philologist, and the biographer, or can he use these subjects in his own way? If he is not to sell out to all his neighbours in turn, what is distinctive about his approach to the poet's life, the time when he lived, and the language he wrote? To ask this is to raise one of the problems involved in the whole question of what the containing forms of literature are as they take their place in the conceptual framework of criticism. This confronts me with the challenge to make my criticism of criticism constructive. All I have space to do is to outline what I think the first major steps should be.

We have to see what literature is, and try to distinguish the category of literature among all the books there are in the world. I do not know that criticism has made any serious effort to determine what literature is. Next, as discussed above, we should examine the containing forms of criticism, including the poet's life, his historical context, his language, and his thought, to see whether the critic can impose a unified critical form on these things, without giving place to or turning into a biographer, an historian, a philologist, or a philosopher. Next, we should establish the broad distinctions, such as that between prose and poetry, which are preparatory to working out a comprehensive theory of genres. I do not know that critics have clearly explained what the difference between prose and poetry, for instance, really is. Then we should try to see whether the critic, like his neighbours the historian and the philosopher, lives in his own universe. To the historian there is nothing that cannot be considered historically; to the philosopher nothing that cannot be considered philosophically. Does the critic aspire to contain all things in criticism, and so swallow history and philosophy in his own synthesis, or must he be forever the historian's and philosopher's pupil? If I have shown up Arnold in a poor light, I should say that he is the only one I know who suggests that criticism can be, like history and philosophy, a total attitude to experience. And finally, since criticism may obviously deal with anything in a poem from its superficial texture to its ulti-

mate significance, the question arises whether there are different levels of meaning in literature, and, if so, whether they can be defined and classified.

It follows that arriving at value-judgments is not, as it is so often said to be, part of the immediate tactic of criticism. Criticism is not well enough organized as yet to know what the factors of value in a critical judgment are. For instance, as was indicated above in connection with Blake and Spenser, the question of the quality of a poet's thinking as revealed in the integration of his argument is an essential factor in a value-judgment, but many poets are exhaustively discussed in terms of value without this factor being considered. Contemporary judgments of value come mainly from either the critical reader or from the spokesman of a critical attitude. That is, they must be on the whole either unorganized and tentative, or over-organized and irrelevant. For no one can jump directly from research to a value-judgment. I give one melancholy instance. I recently read a study of the sources of mythological allusions in some of the romantic poets, which showed that for the second part of *Faust* Goethe had used a miscellany of cribs, some of dubious authenticity. "I have now, I hope," said the author triumphantly at the end of his investigation, "given sufficient proof that the second part of *Faust* is not a great work of art." I do not deny the ultimate importance of the value-judgment. I would even consider the suggestion that the value-judgment is precisely what distinguishes the social from the natural science. But the more important it is, the more careful we should be about getting it solidly established.

What literature is may perhaps best be understood by an analogy. We shall have to labour the analogy, but that is due mainly to the novelty of the idea here presented. Mathematics appears to begin in the counting and measuring of objects, as a numerical commentary on the world. But the mathematician does not think of his subject as the counting and measuring of physical objects at all. For him it is an autonomous language, and there is a point at which it becomes in a measure independent of that common field of experience which we think of as the physical world, or as existence, or as reality, according to our mood. Many of its terms, such as irrational numbers, have no direct connection with the common field of experience, but depend for their meaning solely on the interrelations of the subject itself. Irrational numbers in mathematics may be compared to prepositions in verbal languages, which, unlike nouns and verbs, have no external symbolic reference. When we distinguish pure from applied mathematics, we are thinking of the former as a disinterested conception of numerical relationships, concerned more and more with its inner integrity, and less and less with its reference to external criteria.

Where, in that case, is pure mathematics going? We may gain a hint from the final chapter of Sir James Jeans' *Mysterious Universe,* which I choose because it shows some of the characteristics of the imaginative leap to a new conceptual framework already mentioned. There, the author speaks of the failure of physical cosmology in the nineteenth century to conceive of the universe as ultimately mechanical, and suggests that a mathematical approach to it may have better luck. The universe cannot be a machine, but it may be an interlocking set of mathematical formulas. What this means is surely that pure mathematics exists in a mathematical universe which is no longer a commentary on an "outside" world, but contains that world within itself. Mathematics is at first a form of understanding an objective world regarded as its content, but in the end it conceives of the content as being itself mathematical in form, so that when the conception of the mathematical universe is reached, form and content become the same thing.

Jeans was a mathematician, and thought of his mathematical universe as *the* universe. Doubtless it is, but it does not follow that the only way of conceiving it is mathematical. For we think also of literature at first as a commentary on an external "life" or "reality." But just as in mathematics we have to go from three apples to three, and from a square field to a square, so in reading Jane Austen we have to go from the faithful reflection of English society to the novel, and pass from literature as symbol to literature as an autonomous language. And just as mathematics exists in a mathematical universe which is at the circumference of the common field of experience, so literature exists in a verbal universe, which is not a commentary on life or reality, but contains life and reality in a system of verbal relationships. This conception of a verbal universe, in which life and reality are inside literature, and not outside it and being described or represented or approached or symbolized by it, seems to me the first postulate of a properly organized criticism.

It is vulgar for the critic to think of literature as a tiny palace of art looking out upon an inconceivably gigantic "life." "Life" should be for the critic only the seed-plot of literature, a vast mass of potential literary forms, only a few of which will grow up into the greater world of the verbal universe. Similar universes exist for all the arts. "We make to ourselves picture of facts," says Wittgenstein, but by pictures he means representative illustrations, which are not pictures. Pictures as pictures are themselves facts, and exist only in a pictorial universe. It is easy enough to say that while the stars in their courses may form the subject of a poem, they will still remain the stars in their courses, forever outside poetry. But this is pure regression to the common field of experience, and nothing more; for the more strenuously we try to conceive the stars in their courses in non-literary ways, the more assuredly we shall fall into the idioms and conventions of some other mental universe. The conception of a constant external reality acts as a kind of censor principle in the arts. Painting has been much bedevilled by it, and much of the freakishness of modern painting is clearly due to the energy of its revolt against the representational fallacy. Music on the other hand has remained fairly free of it: at least no one, so far as I know, insists that it is flying in the face of common sense for music to do anything but reproduce the sounds heard in external nature. In literature the chief function of representationalism is to neutralize its opposing fallacy of an "inner" or subjective reality.

These different universes are presumably different ways of conceiving the same universe. What we call the common field of experience is a provisional means of unifying them on the level of sense-perception, and it is natural to infer a higher unity, a sort of beautification of common sense. But it is not easy to find any human language capable of reaching such exalted heights. If it is true, as is being increasingly asserted, that metaphysics is a system of verbal constructions with no direct reference to external criteria by means of which its truth or falsehood may be tested, it follows that metaphysics forms part of the verbal universe. Theology postulates an ultimate reality in God, but it does not assume that man is capable of describing it in his own terms, nor does it claim to be itself such a description. In any case, if we assert this final unity too quickly we may injure the integrity of the different means of approaching it. It does not help a poet much to tell him that the function of literature is to empty itself into an ocean of superverbal significance, when the nature of that significance is unknown.

Pure mathematics, we have said, does not relate itself directly to the common field of experience, but indirectly, not to avoid it, but with the ultimate design of swallowing it. It thus presents the appearance of a series of hypothetical possibilities. It by-passes the confirmation from without which is the goal of applied mathematics, and seeks it only

from within: its conclusions are related primarily to its own premises. Literature also proceeds by hypothetical possibilities. The poet, said Sidney, never affirmeth. He never says "this is so"; he says "let there be such a situation," and poetic truth, the validity of his conclusion, is to be tested primarily by its coherence with his original postulate. Of course, there is applied literature, just as there is applied mathematics, which we test historically, by its lifelikeness, or philosophically, by the cogency of its propositions. Literature, like mathematics, is constantly useful, a word which means having a continuing relationship to the common field of experience. But pure literature, like pure mathematics, is disinterested, or useless: it contains its own meaning. Any attempt to determine the category of literature must start with a distinction between the verbal form which is primarily itself and the verbal form which is primarily related to something else. The former is a complex verbal fact, the latter a complex of verbal symbols.

We have to use the mathematical analogy once more before we leave it. Literature is, of course, dependent on the haphazard and unpredictable appearance of creative genius. So actually is mathematics, but we hardly notice this because in mathematics a steady consolidating process goes on, and the work of its geniuses is absorbed in the evolving and expanding patern of the mathematical universe. Literature being as yet unorganized by criticism, it still appears as a huge aggregate or miscellaneous pile of creative efforts. The only organizing principle so far discovered in it is chronology, and when we see the miscellaneous pile strung out along a chronological line, some coherence is given to it by the linear factors in tradition. We can trace an epic tradition by virtue of the fact that Virgil succeeded Homer, Dante Virgil, and Milton Dante. But, as already suggested, this is very far from being the best we can do. Criticism has still to develop a theory of literature which will see this aggregate within a verbal universe, as forms integrated within a total form. An epic, besides occurring at a certain point in time, is also something of a definitive statement of the poet's imaginative experience, whereas a lyric is usually a more fragmentary one. This suggests the image of a kind of radiating circle of literary experience in which the lyric is nearer to a periphery and the epic nearer to a centre. It is only an image, but the notion that literature, like any other form of knowledge, possesses a centre and a circumference seems reasonable enough.

If so, then literature is a single body, a vast organically growing form, and, though of course works of art do not improve, yet it may be possible for criticism to see literature as showing a progressive evolution in time, of a kind rather like what Newman postulates for Catholic dogma. One could collect remarks by the dozen from various critics, many of them quite misleading, to show that they are dimly aware, on some level of consciousness, of the possibility of a critical progress toward a total comprehension of literature which no critical history gives any hint of. When Mr. Eliot says that the whole tradition of Western poetry from Homer down ought to exist simultaneously in the poet's mind, the adverb suggests a transcending by criticism of the tyranny of historical categories. I even think that the consolidation of literature by criticism into the verbal universe was one of the things that Matthew Arnold meant by culture. To begin this process seems to me the function of criticism at the present time.

# 3

# Roland Barthes
# 1915–1980

At the time of his death, Roland Barthes was a professor at the College de France, the highest position in the French academic system. Throughout his academic career he held chairs in lexicology, the social and economic sciences, and finally semiology. The variety of his study indicates the breadth of his published writing. No one essay or book is representative of the complete scope of Barthes's interests, intellectual ability, or influence. His work of the early 1960s articulated the concerns of and objectives for structuralism, as *S/Z* did for poststructuralism in the 1970s. His major works include *Writing Degree Zero* (1953, translated into English 1968); *Michelet par lui-même* (1954); *Mythologies* (1957, trans. 1972); *On Racine* (1963, trans. 1964); *Elements of Semiology* (1964, trans. 1967); *Critique et Verité* (1966); *Systeme de la Mode* (1967); *S/Z* (1970, trans. 1975); *Empire of Signs* (1970, trans. 1982); *Sade/ Fourier/Loyola* (1971, trans. 1976); *The Pleasure of the Text* (1973, trans. 1976); *Roland Barthes by Roland Barthes* (1975, trans. 1977); *A Lover's Discourse: Fragments* (1977, trans. 1978); and *The Grain of the Voice: Interviews 1962–1980* (1981, trans. 1985).

"What Is Criticism?" first appeared in *Critical Essays* (1964), a collection that marks the beginning of Barthes's work in structuralism along with a range of other critical interests. As he states in "The Structuralist Activity," another essay in the collection, structuralism is an *activity*—not a school or movement—that reconstructs an "'object' in such a way as to manifest thereby the rules of functioning . . . of this object." The reconstruction of the object, what Barthes calls a "simulacrum," an "imitation," produces its intelligibility because now its functions, invisible in its "natural" state, are realized.

The critical activity that Barthes describes in "What Is Criticism?" follows the structuralist criteria he sets out in "The Structuralist Activity." He answers not only the question in the title of the essay along structuralist lines but the other questions the essay raises as well. What is the object of criticism? What is the critic's responsibility? What is the critic's task? The answers lie in Barthes's definition of "metalanguage," which is a "second language" or "discourse upon discourse." In a sense the object of criticism—the metalanguage—is similar to the reconstruction of the object, for both produce the text's intelligibility. Thus the critic's responsibility and task are to reconstruct not a work's meaning but the "rules and constraints of that meaning's elaboration"; in other words, the critic reconstructs the *system* of a text because literature is a "language . . . a system of signs."

# What Is Criticism?

It is always possible to prescribe major critical principles in accord with one's ideological situation, especially in France, where theoretical models have a great prestige, doubtless because they give the practitioner an assurance that he is participating at once in a combat, a history, and a totality; French criticism has developed in this way for some fifteen years, with various fortunes, within four major "philosophies." First of all, what is commonly—and questionably—called existentialism, which has produced Sartre's critical works, his *Baudelaire,* his *Flaubert,* the shorter articles on Proust, Mauriac, Giraudoux, and Ponge, and above all his splendid *Genet.* Then Marxism: we know (the argument is already an old one) how sterile orthodox Marxism has proved to be in criticism, proposing a purely mechanical explanation of works or promulgating slogans rather than criteria of values; hence it is on the "frontiers" of Marxism (and not at its avowed center) that we find the most fruitful criticism: Lucien Goldmann's work explicitly owes a great deal to Lukacs; it is among the most flexible and the most ingenious criticism which takes social and political history as its point of departure. And then psychoanalysis; in France today, the best representative of Freudian criticism is Charles Mauron, but here too it is the "marginal" psychoanalysis which has been most fruitful; taking its departure from an analysis of substances (and not of works), following the dynamic distortions of the image in a great number of poets, Bachelard has established something of a critical school, so influential that one might call French criticism today, in its most developed form, a criticism of Bachelardian inspiration (Poulet, Starobinski, Richard). Finally structuralism (or to simplify to an extreme and doubtless abusive degree: formalism): we know the importance, even the vogue of this movement in France since Lévi-Strauss has opened to it the methods of the social sciences and a certain philosophical reflection; few critical works have as yet resulted from it, but they are in preparation, and among them we shall doubtless find, in particular, the influence of linguistic models constructed by Saussure and extended by Jakobson (who himself, early in his career, participated in a movement of literary criticism, the Russian formalist school): it appears possible, for example, to develop an entire literary criticism starting from the two rhetorical categories established by Jakobson: metaphor and metonymy.

As we see, this French criticism is at once "national" (it owes little or nothing to Anglo-American criticism, to Spitzer and his followers, to the Croceans) and contemporary (one might even say "faithless"): entirely absorbed in a certain ideological present, it is reluctant to acknowledge any participation in the critical tradition of Sainte-Beuve, Taine, or Lanson. This last model nonetheless raises a special problem for our contemporary criticism. The work, method, and spirit of Lanson, himself a prototype of the French professor, has controlled, through countless epigones, the whole of academic criticism for fifty years. Since the (avowed) principles of this criticism are rigor and objectivity in the establishment of facts, one might suppose that there is no incompatibility between Lansonism and the ideological criticisms, which are all criticisms of interpretation. However, though the majority of French critics today are themselves professors, there is a certain tension between interpretive criticism and positivist (academic) criticism. This is because Lansonism is itself an ideology; not content to demand the application of the objective rules of all scientific investigation, it implies certain general convictions about man, history, literature, and the relations between author and work; for example, the psychology of Lansonism is utterly dated, consisting essentially of a kind of analogical determinism, according to which the details of a work must *resemble* the details of a life, the soul of a character must *resemble* the soul of the author, etc.—a very special ideology, since it is precisely in the years following its formulation that psychoanalysis, for example, has posited contrary relations, relations of denial, between a work and its author. Indeed, philosophical postulates are inevitable; Lansonism is not to be blamed for its prejudices but for the fact that it conceals them, masks them under the moral alibi of rigor and objectivity: ideology is smuggled into the baggage of scientism like contraband merchandise.

If these various ideological principles are possible at the same time (and for my part, in a certain sense I subscribe to each of them at the same time), it is doubtless because an ideological choice does not constitute the Being of criticism and because "truth" is not its sanction. Criticism is more than discourse in the name of "true" principles. It follows that the capital sin in criticism is not ideology but the silence by which it is masked: this guilty silence has a name: *good conscience,* or again, *bad faith.* How could we believe, in fact, that the work is an object exterior to the psyche and history of the man who interrogates it, an object over which the critic would exercise a kind of extraterritorial right? By what miracle would the profound communication which most critics postulate between the work and its author cease in relation to their own enterprise and their own epoch? Are there laws of creation valid for the writer but not for the critic? All criticism must include in its discourse (even if it is in the most indirect and modest manner imaginable) an implicit reflection on itself; every criticism is a criticism of the work *and* a criticism of itself.

In other words, criticism is not at all a table of results or a body of judgments, it is essentially an activity, i.e., a series of intellectual acts profoundly committed to the historical and subjective existence (they are the same thing) of the man who performs them. Can an activity be "true"? It answers quite different requirements.

Every novelist, every poet, whatever the detours literary theory may take, is presumed to speak of objects and phenomena, even if they are imaginary, exterior and anterior to language: the world exists and the writer speaks: that is literature. The object of criticism is very different; the object of criticism is not "the world" but a discourse, the discourse of someone else: criticism is discourse upon a discourse; it is a second language, or a *metalanguage* (as the logicians would say), which operates on a first language (or *language object*). It follows that the critical language must deal with two kinds of relations: the relation of the critical language to the language of the author studied, and the relation of this language object to the world. It is the "friction" of these two languages which defines criticism and perhaps gives it a great resemblance to another mental activity, logic, which is also based on the distinction between language object and metalanguage.

For if criticism is only a metalanguage, this means that its task is not at all to discover "truths," but only "validities." In itself, a language is not true or false, it is or is not valid: valid, i.e., constitutes a coherent system of signs. The rules of literary language do not concern the conformity of this language to reality (whatever the claims of the realistic schools), but only its submission to the system of signs the author has established (and we must, of course, give the word *system* a very strong sense here). Criticism has no responsibility to say whether Proust has spoken "the truth," whether the Baron de Charlus was indeed the Count de Montesquiou, whether Françoise was Céleste, or even, more generally, whether the society Proust described reproduces accurately the historical conditions of the nobility's disappearance at the end of the nineteenth century; its role is solely to elaborate a language whose coherence, logic, in short whose *systematics* can collect or better still can "integrate" (in the mathematical sense of the word) the greatest possible quantity of Proustian language, exactly as a logical equation tests the validity of reasoning without taking sides as to the "truth" of the arguments it mobilizes. One can say that the critical task (and this is the sole guarantee of its universality) is purely formal: not to "discover" in the work or the author something "hidden," "profound," "secret" which hitherto passed unnoticed (by what miracle? Are we more perspicacious than our predecessors?), but only to adjust the language his period affords him (existentialism, Marxism, psychoanalysis) to the language, i.e., the formal system of logical constraints elaborated by the author according to his own period. The "proof" of a criticism is not of an "alethic" order (it does not proceed from truth), for critical discourse—like logical discourse, moreover—is never anything but tautological: it consists in saying ultimately, though placing its whole being within that delay, what thereby is not insignificant: Racine is Racine, Proust is Proust; critical "proof," if it exists, depends on an aptitude not to *discover* the work in question but on the contrary to *cover* it as completely as possible by its own language.

Thus we are concerned, once again, with an essentially formal activity, not in the esthetic but in the logical sense of the term. We might say that for criticism, the only way of avoiding "good conscience" or "bad faith" is to take as a moral goal not the decipherment of the work's meaning but the reconstruction of the rules and constraints of that meaning's elaboration; provided we admit at once that a literary work is a very special semantic system, whose goal is to put "meaning" in the world, but not "a meaning"; the work, at least the work which ordinarily accedes to critical scrutiny—and this is perhaps a definition of "good" literature—the work is never entirely nonsignifying (mysterious or "inspired"), and never entirely clear; it is, one may say, a *suspended* meaning: it offers itself to the reader as an avowed signifying system yet withholds itself from him as a signified object. This disappointment of meaning explains on the one hand why the literary work has so much power to ask the world questions (undermining the assured meanings which ideologies, beliefs, and common sense seem to possess), yet without ever answering them (there is no great work which is "dogmatic"), and on the other hand why it offers itself to endless decipherment, since there is no reason for us ever to stop speaking of Racine or Shakespeare (unless by a disaffection which will itself be a language): simultaneously an insistent proposition of meaning and a stubbornly fugitive meaning, literature is indeed only a *language,* i.e., a system of signs; its being is not in its message but in this "system." And thereby the critic is not responsible for reconstructing the work's message but only its system, just as the linguist is not responsible for deciphering the sentence's meaning but for establishing the formal structure which permits this meaning to be transmitted.

It is by acknowledging itself as no more than a language (or more precisely, a metalanguage) that criticism can be—paradoxically but authentically—both objective and subjective, historical and existential, totalitarian and liberal. For on the one hand, the language each critic chooses to speak does not come down to him from Heaven; it is one of the various languages his age affords him, it is objectively the end product of a certain historical ripening of knowledge, ideas, intellectual passions—it is a *necessity;* and on the other hand, this necessary language is chosen by each critic as a consequence of a certain existential organization, as the exercise of an intellectual function which belongs to him in his own right, an exercise in which he puts all his "profundity," i.e., his choices, his pleasures, his resistances, his obsessions. Thus begins, at the heart of the critical work, the dialogue of two histories and two subjectivities, the author's and the critic's. But this dialogue is egoistically shifted toward the present: criticism is not an "homage" to the truth of the past or to the truth of "others"—it is a construction of the intelligibility of our own time.

*Translated by Richard Howard*

# 4

# Elaine Showalter
# 1941–

Born in Cambridge, Massachusetts, Elaine Showalter received an M.A. from Brandeis University and a Ph.D. from the University of California at Davis. She has taught at Rutgers University and now teaches at Princeton University. She has edited such volumes as *Women's Liberation and Literature; Female Studies IV; Women's Studies; Signs: Journal of Women, Culture, and Society;* and *The New Feminist Criticism.* Her writings include *A Literature of Their Own: British Women Novelists from Brontë to Lessing* (1977); *Alternative Alcott* (1988); *Speaking of Gender* (1989); *Sexual Anarchy: Gender and Culture at the Fin de Siècle* (1990); and most recently *Sister's Choice: Tradition and Change in American Women's Writing* (1991).

In "Feminist Criticism in the Wilderness" (1981) Showalter asks the question: "What is the *difference* in women's writing?" It is a question with exhilarating possibilities, and once posed by herself and other feminist writers, it began the "shift from an androcentric to a gynocentric feminist criticism." Revisionist readings of the male canon can therefore no longer contain the momentum of women's criticism. In this essay she analyzes four theoretical models that explore this difference: biological, linguistic, psychoanalytic, and cultural. These models are sequential, with each being subsumed and enhanced by the one following. Thus the cultural model provides "a more complete and satisfying way to talk about the specificity and difference of women's writing." Showalter, then, begins the work of providing a ground for feminist criticism, a ground that is not "the serenely undifferentiated universality of texts but the tumultuous and intriguing wilderness of difference itself."

# Feminist Criticism in the Wilderness

## 1. PLURALISM AND THE FEMINIST CRITIQUE

*Women have no wilderness in them,*
*They are provident instead*
*Content in the tight hot cell of their hearts*
*To eat dusty bread.*

Louise Bogan, "Women"

In a splendidly witty dialogue of 1975, Caro- lyn Heilbrun and Catharine Stimpson identified two poles of feminist literary criticism. The first of these modes, righteous, angry, and admonitory, they compared to the Old Testament, "looking for the sins and errors of the past." The second mode, disinterested and seeking "the grace of imagination," they compared to the New Testament. Both are necessary, they concluded, for only the Jeremiahs of ideology can lead us out of the

"Egypt of female servitude" to the promised land of humanism.[1] Matthew Arnold also thought that literary critics might perish in the wilderness before they reached the promised land of disinterestedness; Heilbrun and Stimpson were neo-Arnoldian as befitted members of the Columbia and Barnard faculties. But if, in 1981, feminist literary critics are still wandering in the wilderness, we are in good company; for, as Geoffrey Hartman tells us, *all* criticism is in the wilderness.[2] Feminist critics may be startled to find ourselves in this band of theoretical pioneers, since in the American literary tradition the wilderness has been an exclusively masculine domain. Yet between feminist ideology and the liberal ideal of disinterestedness lies the wilderness of theory, which we too must make our home.

Until very recently, feminist criticism has not had a theoretical basis; it has been an empirical orphan in the theoretical storm. In 1975, I was persuaded that no theoretical manifesto could adequately account for the varied methodologies and ideologies which called themselves feminist reading or writing.[3] By the next year, Annette Kolodny had added her observation that feminist literary criticism appeared "more like a set of interchangeable strategies than any coherent school or shared goal orientation."[4] Since then, the expressed goals have not been notably unified. Black critics protest the "massive silence" of feminist criticism about black and Third-World women writers and call for a black feminist aesthetic that would deal with both racial and sexual politics. Marxist feminists wish to focus on class along with gender as a crucial determinant of literary production.[5] Literary historians want to uncover a lost tradition. Critics trained in deconstructionist methodologies wish to "synthesize a literary criticism that is both textual and feminist."[6] Freudian and Lacanian critics want to theorize about women's relationship to language and signification.

An early obstacle to constructing a theoretical framework for feminist criticism was the unwillingness of many women to limit or bound an expressive and dynamic enterprise. The openness of feminist criticism appealed particularly to Americans who perceived the structuralist, post-structuralist, and deconstructionist debates of the 1970s as arid and falsely objective, the epitome of a pernicious masculine discourse from which many feminists wished to escape. Recalling in *A Room of One's Own* how she had been prohibited from entering the university library, the symbolic sanctuary of the male *logos,* Virginia Woolf wisely observed that while it is "unpleasant to be locked out . . . it is worse, perhaps, to be locked in." Advocates of the antitheoretical position traced their descent from Woolf and from other feminist visionaries, such as Mary Daly, Adrienne Rich, and Marguerite Duras, who had satirized the sterile narcissism of male scholarship and celebrated women's fortunate exclusion from its patriarchal methodolatry. Thus for some, feminist criticism was an act of resistance to theory, a confrontation with existing canons and judgments, what Josephine Donovan calls "a mode of negation within a fundamental dialectic." As Judith Fetterley declared in her book, *The Resisting Reader,* feminist criticism has been characterized by "a resistance to codification and a refusal to have its parameters prematurely set." I have discussed elsewhere, with considerable sympathy, the suspicion of monolithic systems and the rejection of scientism in literary study that many feminist critics have voiced. While scientific criticism struggled to purge itself of the subjective, feminist criticism reasserted the authority of experience.[7]

Yet it now appears that what looked like a theoretical impasse was actually an evolutionary phase. The ethics of awakening have been succeeded, at least in the universities, by a second stage characterized by anxiety about the isolation of feminist criticism from a critical community increasingly theoretical in its interests and indifferent to women's writing. The question of how feminist criticism should define itself with relation to the new critical theories and theorists has occasioned sharp debate in Europe and the United States. Nina Auerbach has noted the absence of dialogue and asks whether feminist criticism itself must accept responsibility:

> Feminist critics seem particularly reluctant to define themselves to the uninitiated. There is a sense in which our sisterhood has become too powerful; as a school, our belief in ourself is so potent that we decline communication with the networks of power and respectability we say we want to change.[8]

But rather than declining communication with these networks, feminist criticism has indeed spoken directly to them, in their own media: *PMLA, Diacritics, Glyph, Tel Quel, New Literary History,* and *Critical Inquiry.* For the feminist critic seeking clarification, the proliferation of communiqués may itself prove confusing.

There are two distinct modes of feminist criticism, and to conflate them (as most commentators do) is to remain permanently bemused by their theoretical potentialities. The first mode is ideological; it is concerned with the feminist as *reader,* and it offers feminist readings of texts which consider the images and stereotypes of women in literature, the omissions and misconceptions about women in criticism, and woman-as-sign in semiotic systems. This is not all feminist reading can do; it can be a liberating intellectual act, as Adrienne Rich proposes:

> A radical critique of literature, feminist in its impulse, would take the work first of all as a clue to how we live, how we have been living, how we have been led to imagine ourselves, how our language has trapped as well as liberated us, how the very act of naming has been till now a male prerogative, and how we can begin to see and name—and therefore live—afresh.[9]

This invigorating encounter with literature, which I will call *feminist reading* or the *feminist critique,* is in essence a mode of interpretation, one of many which any complex text will accommodate and permit. It is very difficult to propose theoretical coherence in an activity which by its nature is so eclectic and wide-ranging, although as a critical practice feminist reading has certainly been very influential. But in the free play of the interpretive field, the feminist critique can only compete with alternative readings, all of which have the built-in obsolescence of Buicks, cast away as newer readings take their place. As Kolodny, the most sophisticated theorist of feminist interpretation, has conceded:

> All the feminist is asserting, then, is her own equivalent right to liberate new (and perhaps different) significances from these same texts; and, at the same time, her right to choose which features of a text she takes as relevant because she is, after all, asking new and different questions of it. In the process, she claims neither definitiveness nor structural completeness for her different readings and reading systems, but only their usefulness in recognizing the particular achievements of woman-as-author and their applicability in conscientiously decoding woman-as-sign.

Rather than being discouraged by these limited objectives, Kolodny found them the happy cause of the "playful pluralism" of feminist critical theory, a pluralism which she believes to be "the only critical stance consistent with the current status of the larger women's movement."[10] Her feminist critic dances adroitly through the theoretical minefield.

Keenly aware of the political issues involved and presenting brilliant arguments, Kolodny nonetheless fails to convince me that feminist criticism must altogether abandon its hope "of establishing some basic conceptual model." If we see our critical job as interpretation and reinterpretation, we must be content with pluralism as our critical stance. But if we wish to ask questions about the process and the contexts of writing, if we genuinely wish to define ourselves to the uninitiated, we cannot rule out the prospect of theoretical consensus at this early stage.

All feminist criticism is in some sense revisionist, questioning the adequacy of accepted conceptual structures, and indeed most contemporary American criticism claims to be revisionist too. The most exciting and comprehensive case for this "revisionary imperative" is made by Sandra Gilbert: at its most ambitious, she asserts, feminist criticism "wants to decode and demystify all the disguised questions and answers that have always shadowed the connections between textuality and sexuality, genre and gender, psychosexual identity and cultural authority."[11] But in practice, the revisionary feminist critique is redressing a grievance and is built upon existing models. No one would deny that feminist criticism has affinities to other contemporary critical practices and methodologies and that the best work is also the most fully informed. Nonetheless, the feminist obsession with correcting, modifying, supplementing, revising, humanizing, or even attacking male critical theory keeps us dependent upon it and retards our progress in solving our own theoretical problems. What I mean here by "male critical theory" is a concept of creativity, literary history, or literary interpretation based entirely on male experience and put forward as universal. So long as we look to androcentric models for our most basic principles— even if we revise them by adding the feminist frame of reference—we are learning nothing new. And when the process is so one-sided,

when male critics boast of their ignorance of feminist criticism, it is disheartening to find feminist critics still anxious for approval from the "white fathers" who will not listen or reply. Some feminist critics have taken upon themselves a revisionism which becomes a kind of homage; they have made Lacan the ladies' man of *Diacritics* and have forced Pierre Macherey into those dark alleys of the psyche where Engels feared to tread. According to Christiane Makward, the problem is even more serious in France than in the United States: "If neofeminist thought in France seems to have ground to a halt," she writes, "it is because it has continued to feed on the discourse of the masters."[12]

It is time for feminist criticism to decide whether between religion and revision we can claim any firm theoretical ground of our own. In calling for a feminist criticism that is genuinely women centered, independent, and intellectually coherent, I do not mean to endorse the separatist fantasies of radical feminist visionaries or to exclude from our critical practice a variety of intellectual tools. But we need to ask much more searchingly what we want to know and how we can find answers to the questions that come from *our* experience. I do not think that feminist criticism can find a usable past in the androcentric critical tradition. It has more to learn from women's studies than from English studies, more to learn from international feminist theory than from another seminar on the masters. It must find its own subject, its own system, its own theory, and its own voice. As Rich writes of Emily Dickinson, in her poem "I Am in Danger—Sir—," we must choose to have the argument out at last on our own premises.

## 2. DEFINING THE FEMININE: GYNOCRITICS AND THE WOMAN'S TEXT

*A woman's writing is always feminine; it cannot help being feminine; at its best it is most feminine; the only difficulty lies in defining what we mean by feminine.*

Virginia Woolf

*It is impossible to define a feminine practice of writing, and this is an impossibility that will remain, for this practice will never be theorized, enclosed, encoded—which doesn't mean that it doesn't exist.*

Hélène Cixous, "The Laugh of the Medusa"

In the past decade, I believe, this process of defining the feminine has started to take place. Feminist criticism has gradually shifted its center from revisionary readings to a sustained investigation of literature by women. The second mode of feminist criticism engendered by this process is the study of women *as writers,* and its subjects are the history, styles, themes, genres, and structures of writing by women; the psychodynamics of female creativity; the trajectory of the individual or collective female career; and the evolution and laws of a female literary tradition. No English term exists for such a specialized critical discourse, and so I have invented the term "gynocritics." Unlike the feminist critique, gynocritics offers many theoretical opportunities. To see women's writing as our primary subject forces us to make the leap to a new conceptual vantage point and to redefine the nature of the theoretical problem before us. It is no longer the ideological dilemma of reconciling revisionary pluralisms but the essential question of difference. How can we constitute women as a distinct literary group? What is *the difference* of women's writing?

Patricia Meyer Spacks, I think, was the first academic critic to notice this shift from an androcentric to a gynocentric feminist criticism. In *The Female Imagination* (1975), she pointed out that few feminist theorists had concerned themselves with women's writing. Simone de Beauvoir's treatment of women writers in *The Second Sex* "always suggests an a priori tendency to take them less seri-

ously than their masculine counterparts"; Mary Ellmann, in *Thinking about Women,* characterized women's literary success as escape from the categories of womanhood; and, according to Spacks, Kate Millett, in *Sexual Politics,* "has little interest in woman imaginative writers."[13] Spacks' wide-ranging study inaugurated a new period of feminist literary history and criticism which asked, again and again, how women's writing had been different, how womanhood itself shaped women's creative expression. In such books as Ellen Moers' *Literary Women* (1976), my own *A Literature of Their Own* (1977), Nina Baym's *Woman's Fiction* (1978), Gilbert and Susan Gubar's *The Madwoman in the Attic* (1979), and Margaret Homans' *Women Writers and Poetic Identity* (1980), and in hundreds of essays and papers, women's writing asserted itself as the central project of feminist literary study.

This shift in emphasis has also taken place in European feminist criticism. To date, most commentary on French feminist critical discourse has stressed its fundamental dissimilarity from the empirical American orientation, its unfamiliar intellectual grounding in linguistics, Marxism, neo-Freudian and Lacanian psychoanalysis, and Derridean deconstruction. Despite these differences, however, the new French feminisms have much in common with radical American feminist theories in terms of intellectual affiliations and rhetorical energies. The concept of *écriture féminine,* the inscription of the female body and female difference in language and text, is a significant theoretical formulation in French feminist criticism, although it describes a Utopian possibility rather than a literary practice. Hélène Cixous, one of the leading advocates of *écriture féminine,* has admitted that, with only a few exceptions, "there has not yet been any writing that inscribes femininity," and Nancy Miller explains that *écriture féminine* "privileges a textuality of the avant-garde, a literary production of the late twentieth century, and it is therefore fundamentally a hope, if not a blueprint, for the future."[14] Nonetheless, the concept of *écriture féminine* provides a way of talking about women's writing which reasserts the *value* of the feminine and identifies the theoretical project of feminist criticism as the analysis of difference. In recent years, the translations of important work by Julia Kristeva, Cixous, and Luce Irigaray and the excellent collection *New French Feminisms* have made French criticism much more accessible to American feminist scholars.[15]

English feminist criticism, which incorporates French feminist and Marxist theory but is more traditionally oriented to textual interpretation, is also moving toward a focus on women's writing.[16] The emphasis in each country falls somewhat differently: English feminist criticism, essentially Marxist, stresses oppression; French feminist criticism, essentially psychoanlytic, stresses repression; American feminist criticism, essentially textual, stresses expression. All, however, have become gynocentric. All are struggling to find a terminology that can rescue the feminine from its stereotypical associations with inferiority.

Defining the unique difference of women's writing, as Woolf and Cixous have warned, must present a slippery and demanding task. Is difference a matter of style? Genre? Experience? Or is it produced by the reading process, as some textual critics would maintain? Spacks calls the difference of women's writing a "delicate divergency," testifying to the subtle and elusive nature of the feminine practice of writing. Yet the delicate divergency of the woman's text challenges us to respond with equal delicacy and precision to the small but crucial deviations, the cumulative weightings of experience and exclusion, that have marked the history of women's writing. Before we can chart this history, we must uncover it, patiently and scrupulously; our theories must be firmly grounded in read-

ing and research. But we have the opportunity, through gynocritics, to learn something solid, enduring, and real about the relation of women to literary culture.

Theories of women's writing presently make use of four models of difference: biological, linguistic, psychoanalytic, and cultural. Each is an effort to define and differentiate the qualities of the woman writer and the woman's text; each model also represents a school of gynocentric feminist criticism with its own favorite texts, styles, and methods. They overlap but are roughly sequential in that each incorporates the one before. I shall try now to sort out the various terminologies and assumptions of these four models of difference and evaluate their usefulness.

## 3. WOMEN'S WRITING AND WOMAN'S BODY

*More body, hence more writing.*
        Cixous, "The Laugh of the Medusa"

Organic or biological criticism is the most extreme statement of gender difference, of a text indelibly marked by the body: anatomy is textuality. Biological criticism is also one of the most sibylline and perplexing theoretical formulations of feminist criticism. Simply to invoke anatomy risks a return to the crude essentialism, the phallic and ovarian theories of art, that oppressed women in the past. Victorian physicians believed that women's physiological functions diverted about twenty percent of their creative energy from brain activity. Victorian anthropologists believed that the frontal lobes of the male brain were heavier and more developed than female lobes and thus that women were inferior in intelligence.

While feminist criticism rejects the attribution of literal biological inferiority, some theorists seem to have accepted the *metaphorical* implications of female biological difference in writing. In *The Madwoman in the Attic,* for example, Gilbert and Gubar structure their analysis of women's writing around metaphors of literary paternity. "In patriarchal western culture," they maintain, ". . . the text's author is a father, a progenitor, a procreator, an aesthetic patriarch whose pen is an instrument of generative power like his penis." Lacking phallic authority, they go on to suggest, women's writing is profoundly marked by the anxieties of this difference: "If the pen is a metaphorical penis, from what organ can females generate texts?"[17]

To this rhetorical question Gilbert and Gilbert offer no reply; but it is a serious question of much feminist theoretical discourse. Those critics who, like myself, would protest the fundamental analogy might reply that women generate texts from the brain or that the word-processor of the near future, with its compactly coded microchips, its inputs and outputs, is a metaphorical womb. The metaphor of literary paternity, as Auerbach has pointed out in her review of *The Madwoman,* ignores "an equally timeless and, for me, even more oppressive metaphorical equation between literary creativity and childbirth."[18] Certainly metaphors of literary *maternity* predominated in the eighteenth and nineteenth centuries; the process of literary creation is analogically much more similar to gestation, labor, and delivery than it is to insemination. Describing Thackeray's plan for *Henry Esmond,* for example, Douglas Jerrold jovially remarked, "You have heard, I suppose, that Thackeray is big with twenty parts, and unless he is wrong in his time, expects the first installment at Christmas."[19] (If to write is metaphorically to give birth, from what organ can males generate texts?)

Some radical feminist critics, primarily in France but also in the United States, insist that we must read these metaphors as more than playful; that we must seriously rethink and redefine biological differentiation and its relation to women's unity. They argue that "women's writing proceeds from the body, that our sexual differentiation is also our source."[20] In *Of Woman Born,* Rich explains her belief that

> female biology . . . has far more radical implications than we have yet come to appreciate. Patriarchal thought has limited female biology to its own narrow specifications. The feminist vision has recoiled from female biology for these reasons; it will, I believe, come to view our physicality as a resource rather than a destiny. In order to live a fully human life, we require not only *control* of our bodies . . . we must touch the unity and resonance of our physicality, the corporeal ground of our intelligence.[21]

Feminist criticism written in the biological perspective generally stresses the importance of the body as a source of imagery. Alicia Ostriker, for example, argues that contemporary American women poets use a franker, more pervasive anatomical imagery than their male counterparts and that this insistent body language refuses the spurious transcendence that comes at the price of denying the flesh. In a fascinating essay on Whitman and Dickinson, Terence Diggory shows that physical nakedness, so potent a poetic symbol of authenticity for Whitman and other male poets, had very different connotations for Dickinson and her successors, who associated nakedness with the objectified or sexually exploited female nude and who chose instead protective images of the armored self.[22]

Feminist criticism which itself tries to be biological, to write from the critic's body, has been intimate, confessional, often innovative in style and form. Rachel Blau DuPlessis' "Washing Blood," the introduction to a special issue of *Feminist Studies* on the subject of motherhood, proceeds, in short lyrical paragraphs, to describe her own experience in adopting a child, to recount her dreams and nightmares, and to meditate upon the "healing unification of body and mind based not only on the lived experiences of motherhood as a social institution . . . but also on a biological power speaking through us."[23] Such criticism makes itself defiantly vulnerable, virtually bares its throat to the knife, since our professional taboos against self-revelation are so strong. When it succeeds, however, it achieves the power and the dignity of art. Its existence is an implicit rebuke to women critics who continue to write, according to Rich, "from somewhere outside their female bodies." In comparison to this flowing confessional criticism, the tight-lipped Olympian intelligence of such texts as Elizabeth Hardwick's *Seduction and Betrayal* or Susan Sontag's *Illness as Metaphor* can seem arid and strained.

Yet in its obsessions with the "corporeal ground of our intelligence," feminist biocriticism can also become cruelly prescriptive. There is a sense in which the exhibition of bloody wounds becomes an initiation ritual quite separate and disconnected from critical insight. And as the editors of the journal *Questions féministes* point out, "it is . . . dangerous to place the body at the center of a search for female identity. . . . The themes of otherness and of the Body merge together, because the most visible difference between men and women, and the only one we know for sure to be permanent . . . is indeed the difference in body. This difference has been used as a pretext to 'justify' full power of one sex over the other" (trans. Yvonne Rochette-Ozzello, *NFF,* p. 218). The study of biological imagery in women's writing is useful and important as long as we understand that factors other than anatomy are involved in it. Ideas about the body are fundamental to understanding how women conceptualize their situation in society; but there can be no expression of the body which is unmediated by linguistic, social, and literary structures. The difference of woman's literary practice, there-

fore, must be sought (in Miller's words) in "the body of her writing and not the writing of her body."[24]

## 4. WOMEN'S WRITING AND WOMEN'S LANGUAGE

> *The women say, the language you speak poisons your glottis tongue palate lips. They say, the language you speak is made up of words that are killing you. They say, the language you speak is made up of signs that rightly speaking designate what men have appropriated.*
>
> Monique Wittig, *Les Guérillères*

Linguistic and textual theories of women's writing ask whether men and women use language differently; whether sex differences in language use can be theorized in terms of biology, socialization, or culture; whether women can create new languages of their own; and whether speaking, reading, and writing are all gender marked. American, French, and British feminist critics have all drawn attention to the philosophical, linguistic, and practical problems of women's use of language, and the debate over language is one of the most exciting areas in gynocritics. Poets and writers have led the attack on what Rich calls "the oppressor's language," a language sometimes criticized as sexist, sometimes as abstract. But the problem goes well beyond reformist efforts to purge language of its sexist aspects. As Nelly Furman explains, "It is through the medium of language that we define and categorize areas of difference and similarity, which in turn allow us to comprehend the world around us. Male-centered categorizations predominate in American English and subtly shape our understanding and perception of reality; this is why attention is increasingly directed to the inherently oppressive aspects for women of a male-constructed language system."[25] According to

Carolyn Burke, the language system is at the center of French feminist theory:

> The central issue in much recent women's writing in France is to find and use an appropriate female language. Language is the place to begin: a *prise de conscience* must be followed by a *prise de la parole*. . . . In this view, the very forms of the dominant mode of discourse show the mark of the dominant masculine ideology. Hence, when a woman writes or speaks herself into existence, she is forced to speak in something like a foreign tongue, a language with which she may be personally uncomfortable.[26]

Many French feminists advocate a revolutionary linguism, an oral break from the dictatorship of patriarchal speech. Annie Leclerc, in *Parole de femme,* calls on women "to invent a language that is not oppressive, a language that does not leave speechless but that loosens the tongue" (trans. Courtivron, *NFF,* p. 179). Chantal Chawaf, in an essay on "La chair linguistique," connects biofeminism and linguism in the view that women's language and a genuinely feminine practice of writing will articulate the body:

> In order to reconnect the book with the body and with pleasure, we must disintellectualize writing. . . . And this language, as it develops, will not degenerate and dry up, will not go back to the fleshless academicism, the stereotypical and servile discourses that we reject.
>
> . . . Feminine language must, by its very nature, work on life passionately, scientifically, poetically, politically in order to make it invulnerable. [Trans. Rochette-Ozzello, *NFF,* pp. 177–78]

But scholars who want a women's language that *is* intellectual and theoretical, that works *inside* the academy, are faced with what seems like an impossible paradox, as Xavière Gauthier has lamented: "As long as women remain silent, they will be outside the historical process. But, if they begin to speak and write *as men do,* they will enter history subdued and alienated; it is a history that, logically speaking, their speech should disrupt" (trans. Marilyn A. August, *NFF,* pp. 162–63). What we need, Mary Jacobus has proposed, is a women's writing that works within "male" discourse but works "ceaselessly to deconstruct it: to write what cannot be written," and according to Shoshana Felman, "the challenge facing the woman today is nothing less than to 'reinvent' language, . . . to speak not only against, but outside of the specular phallogocentric structure, to establish a discourse the status of which would no longer be defined by the phallacy of masculine meaning."[27]

Beyond rhetoric, what can linguistic, historical, and anthropological research tell us about the prospects for a women's language? First of all, the concept of a women's language is not original with feminist criticism; it is very ancient and appears frequently in folklore and myth. In such myths, the essence of women's language is its secrecy; what is really being described is the male fantasy of the enigmatic nature of the feminine. Herodotus, for example, reported that the Amazons were able linguists who easily mastered the languages of their male antagonists, although men could never learn the women's tongue. In *The White Goddess,* Robert Graves romantically argues that a women's language existed in a matriarchal stage of prehistory; after a great battle of the sexes, the matriarchy was overthrown and the women's language went underground, to survive in the mysterious cults of Eleusis and Corinth and the witch covens of Western Europe. Travelers and missionaries in the seventeenth and eighteenth centuries brought back accounts of "women's languages" among American Indians, Africans, and Asians (the differences in linguistic structure they reported were usually superficial). There is some ethnographic evidence that in certain cultures women have evolved a private form of communication out of their need to resist the silence imposed upon them in public life. In ecstatic religions, for example, women, more frequently than men, speak in tongues, a phenomenon attributed by anthropologists to their relative inarticulateness in formal religious discourse. But such ritualized and unintelligible female "languages" are scarcely cause for rejoicing; indeed, it was because witches were suspected of esoteric knowledge and possessed speech that they were burned.[28]

From a political perspective, there are interesting parallels between the feminist problem of a women's language and the recurring "language issue" in the general history of decolonization. After a revolution, a new state must decide which language to make official: the language that is "psychologically immediate," that allows "the kind of force that speaking one's mother tongue permits"; or the language that "is an avenue to the wider community of modern culture," a community to whose movements of thought only "foreign" languages can give access.[29] The language issue in feminist criticism has emerged, in a sense, after our revolution, and it reveals the tensions in the women's movement between those who would stay outside the academic establishments and the institutions of criticism and those who would enter and even conquer them.

The advocacy of a women's language is thus a political gesture that also carries tremendous emotional force. But despite its unifying appeal, the concept of a woman's language is riddled with difficulties. Unlike Welsh, Breton, Swahili, or Amharic, that is, languages of minority or colonized groups, there is no mother tongue, no genderlect spoken by the female population in a society, which differs significantly from the dominant language. English and American linguists agree that "there is absolutely no evidence that would suggest the sexes are preprogrammed to develop structurally different linguistic systems." Furthermore, the many specific differences in male and female speech, intonation, and language use that have been identified cannot be explained in terms of "two separate sex-specific languages" but need to be considered instead in terms of styles, strategies, and contexts of linguistic performance.[30] Efforts at quantitative analysis of language in texts by men or women, such as Mary Hiatt's computerized study of contemporary fiction, *The Way Women Write* (1977), can easily be attacked for treating words apart from their meanings and purposes. At a higher level, analyses which look for "feminine style" in the repetition of stylistic devices, image patterns, and syntax in women's writing tend to confuse innate forms with the overdetermined results of literary choice. Language and style are never raw and instinctual but are always the products of innumerable factors, of genre, tradition, memory, and context.

The appropriate task for feminist criticism, I believe, is to concentrate on women's access to language, on the available lexical range from which words can be selected, on the ideological and cultural determinants of expression. The problem is not that language is insufficient to express women's consciousness but that women have been denied the full resources of language and have been forced into silence, euphemism, or circumlocution. In a series of drafts for a lecture on women's writing (drafts which she discarded or suppressed), Woolf protested against the censorship which cut off female access to language. Comparing herself to Joyce, Woolf noted the differences between their verbal territories: "Now men are shocked if a woman says what she feels (as Joyce does). Yet literature which is always pulling down blinds is not literature. All that we have ought to be expressed—

mind and body—a process of incredible difficulty and danger."[31]

"All that we have ought to be expressed—mind and body." Rather than wishing to limit women's linguistic range, we must fight to open and extend it. The holes in discourse, the blanks and gaps and silences, are not the spaces where female consciousness reveals itself but the blinds of a "prison-house of language." Women's literature is still haunted by the ghosts of repressed language, and until we have exorcised those ghosts, it ought not to be in language that we base our theory of difference.

## 5. WOMEN'S WRITING AND WOMAN'S PSYCHE

Psychoanalytically oriented feminist criticism locates the difference of women's writing in the author's psyche and in the relation of gender to the creative process. It incorporates the biological and linguistic models of gender difference in a theory of the female psyche or self, shaped by the body, by the development of language, and by sex-role socialization. Here too there are many difficulties to overcome; the Freudian model requires constant revision to make it gynocentric. In one grotesque early example of Freudian reductivism, Theodor Reik suggested that women have fewer writing blocks than men because their bodies are constructed to facilitate release: "Writing, as Freud told us at the end of his life, is connected with urinating, which physiologically is easier for a woman—they have a wider bladder."[32] Generally, however, psychoanalytic criticism has focused not on the capacious bladder (could this be the organ from which females generate texts?) but on the absent phallus. Penis envy, the castration complex, and the Oedipal phase have become the Freudian coordinates defining women's relationship to language, fantasy, and culture. Currently the French psy-

choanalytic school dominated by Lacan has extended castration into a total metaphor for female literary and linguistic disadvantage. Lacan theorizes that the acquisition of language and the entry into its symbolic order occurs at the Oedipal phase in which the child accepts his or her gender identity. This stage requires an acceptance of the phallus as a privileged signification and a consequent female displacement, as Cora Kaplan has explained:

> The phallus as a signifier has a central, crucial position in language, for if language embodies the patriarchal law of the culture, its basic meanings refer to the recurring process by which sexual difference and subjectivity are acquired. . . . Thus the little girl's access to the Symbolic, i.e., to language and its laws, is always negative and/or mediated by intro-subjective relation to a third term, for it is characterized by an identification with lack.[33]

In psychoanalytic terms, "lack" has traditionally been associated with the feminine, although Lac(k)anian critics can now make their statements linguistically. Many feminists believe that psychoanalysis could become a powerful tool for literary criticism, and recently there has been a renewed interest in Freudian theory. But feminist criticism based in Freudian or post-Freudian psychoanalysis must continually struggle with the problem of feminine disadvantage and lack. In *The Madwoman in the Attic,* Gilbert and Gubar carry out a feminist revision of Harold Bloom's Oedipal model of literary history as a conflict between fathers and sons and accept the essential psychoanalytic definition of the woman artist as displaced, disinherited, and excluded. In their view, the nature and "difference" of women's writing lies in its troubled and even tormented relationship to female identity; the woman writer experiences her own gender as "a painful obstacle or even a debilitating inadequacy." The nineteenth-century woman writer inscribed her own sickness, her madness, her anorexia, her ago-raphobia, and her paralysis in her texts; and although Gilbert and Gubar are dealing spe-cifically with the nineteenth century, the range of their allusion and quotation suggests a more general thesis:

> Thus the loneliness of the female artist, her feelings of alienation from male predeces-sors coupled with her need for sisterly pre-cursors and successors, her urgent sense of her need for a female audience together with her fear of the antagonism of male readers, her culturally conditioned timidity about self-dramatization, her dread of the patriarchal authority of art, her anxiety about the impropriety of female inven-tion—all these phenomena of "inferioriza-tion" mark the woman writer's struggle for artistic self-definition and differentiate her efforts at self-creation from those of her male counterpart. [*Madwoman,* p. 50]

In "Emphasis Added," Miller takes another approach to the problem of negativity in psy-choanalytic criticism. Her strategy is to ex-pand Freud's view of female creativity and to show how criticism of women's texts has fre-quently been unfair because it has been based in Freudian expectations. In his essay "The Relation of the Poet to Daydreaming" (1908), Freud maintained that the unsatisfied dreams and desires of women are chiefly erotic; these are the desires that shape the plots of women's fiction. In contrast, the dominant fantasies behind men's plots are egoistic and ambitious as well as erotic. Miller shows how women's plots have been granted or denied credibility in terms of their con-formity to this phallocentric model and that a gynocentric reading reveals a repressed ego-istic/ambitious fantasy in women's writing as well as in men's. Women's novels which are centrally concerned with fantasies of roman-

tic love belong to the category disdained by George Eliot and other serious women writ-ers as "silly novels"; the smaller number of women's novels which inscribe a fantasy of power imagine a world for women outside of love, a world, however, made impossible by social boundaries.

There has also been some interesting femi-nist literary criticism based on alternatives to Freudian psychoanalytic theory: Annis Pratt's Jungian history of female archetypes, Barbara Rigney's Laingian study of the divided self in women's fiction, and Ann Douglas' Erik-sonian analysis of inner space in nineteenth-century women's writing.[34] And for the past few years, critics have been thinking about the possibilities of a new feminist psycho-analysis that does *not* revise Freud but in-stead emphasizes the development and con-struction of gender identities.

The most dramatic and promising new work in feminist psychoanalysis looks at the pre-Oedipal phase and at the process of psy-chosexual differentiation. Nancy Chodorow's *The Reproduction of Mothering: Psychoanal-ysis and the Sociology of Gender* (1978) has had an enormous influence on women's studies. Chodorow revises traditional psycho-analytic concepts of differentiation, the pro-cess by which the child comes to perceive the self as separate and to develop ego and body boundaries. Since differentiation takes place in relation to the mother (the primary care-taker), attitudes toward the mother "emerge in the earliest differentiation of the self"; "the mother, who is a woman, becomes and re-mains for children of both genders the other, or object."[35] The child develops core gender identity concomitantly with differentiation, but the process is not the same for boys and girls. A boy must learn his gender identity negatively as being not-female, and this dif-ference requires continual reinforcement. In contrast, a girl's core gender identity is posi-tive and built upon sameness, continuity, and identification with the mother. Women's difficulties with feminine identity come after the Oedipal phase, in which male power and cultural hegemony give sex differences a transformed value. Chodorow's work suggests that shared parenting, the involvement of men as primary caretakers of children, will have a profound effect on our sense of sex difference, gender identity, and sexual preference.

But what is the significance of feminist psychoanalysis for literary criticism? One thematic carry-over has been a critical interest in the mother-daughter configuration as a source of female creativity.[36] Elizabeth Abel's bold investigation of female friendship in contemporary women's novels uses Chodorow's theory to show how not only the relationships of women characters but also the relationship of women writers to each other are determined by the psychodynamics of female bonding. Abel too confronts Bloom's paradigm of literary history, but unlike Gilbert and Gubar she sees a "triadic female pattern" in which the Oedipal relation to the male tradition is balanced by the woman writer's pre-Oedipal relation to the female tradition. "As the dynamics of female friendship differ from those of male," Abel concludes, "the dynamics of female literary influence also diverge and deserve a theory of influence attuned to female psychology and to women's dual position in literary history."[37]

Like Gilbert, Gubar, and Miller, Abel brings together women's texts from a variety of national literatures, choosing to emphasize "the constancy of certain emotional dynamics depicted in diverse cultural situations." Yet the privileging of gender implies not only the constancy but also the immutability of these dynamics. Although psychoanalytically based models of feminist criticism can now offer us remarkable and persuasive readings of individual texts and can highlight extraordinary similarities between women writing in a variety of cultural circumstances, they cannot explain historical change, ethnic difference, or the shaping force of generic and economic factors. To consider these issues, we must go beyond psychoanalysis to a more flexible and comprehensive model of women's writing which places it in the maximum context of culture.

## 6. WOMEN'S WRITING AND WOMEN'S CULTURE

> *I consider women's literature as a specific category, not because of biology, but because it is, in a sense, the literature of the colonized.*
>
> —Christiane Rochefort, "The Privilege of Consciousness"

A theory based on a model of women's culture can provide, I believe, a more complete and satisfying way to talk about the specificity and difference of women's writing than theories based in biology, linguistics, or psychoanalysis. Indeed, a theory of culture incorporates ideas about woman's body, language, and psyche but interprets them in relation to the social contexts in which they occur. The ways in which women conceptualize their bodies and their sexual and reproductive functions are intricately linked to their cultural environments. The female psyche can be studied as the product or construction of cultural forces. Language, too, comes back into the picture, as we consider the social dimensions and determinants of language use, the shaping of linguistic behavior by cultural ideals. A cultural theory acknowledges that there are important differences between women as writers: class, race, nationality, and history are literary determinants as significant as gender. Nonetheless, women's culture forms a collective experience within the cultural whole, an experience that binds women writers to each other over time and space. It is in the emphasis on the binding force of women's culture that this approach differs from Marxist theories of cultural hegemony.

Hypotheses of women's culture have been developed over the last decade primarily by anthropologists, sociologists, and social historians in order to get away from masculine systems, hierarchies, and values and to get at the primary and self-defined nature of female cultural experience. In the field of women's history, the concept of women's culture is still controversial, although there is agreement on its significance as a theoretical formulation. Gerda Lerner explains the importance of examining women's experience in its own terms:

> Women have been left out of history not because of the evil conspiracies of men in general or male historians in particular, but because we have considered history only in male-centered terms. We have missed women and their activities, because we have asked questions of history which are inappropriate to women. To rectify this, and to light up areas of historical darkness we must, for a time, focus on a *woman-centered* inquiry, considering the possibility of the existence of a female culture *within* the general culture shared by men and women. History must include an account of the female experience over time and should include the development of feminist consciousness as an essential aspect of women's past. This is the primary task of women's history. The central question it raises is: What would history be like if it were seen through the eyes of women and ordered by values they define?[38]

In defining female culture, historians distinguish between the roles, activities, tastes, and behaviors prescribed and considered appropriate for women and those activities, behaviors, and functions actually generated out of women's lives. In the late-eighteenth

and nineteenth centuries, the term "woman's sphere" expressed the Victorian and Jacksonian vision of separate roles for men and women, with little or no overlap and with women subordinate. If we were to diagram it, the Victorian model would look like this:

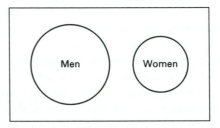

Woman's sphere was defined and maintained by men, but women frequently internalized its precepts in the American "cult of true womanhood" and the English "feminine ideal." Women's culture, however, redefines women's "activities and goals from a woman-centered point of view. . . . The term implies an assertion of equality and an awareness of sisterhood, the communality of women." Women's culture refers to "the broad-based communality of values, institutions, relationships, and methods of communication" unifying nineteenth-century female experience, a culture nonetheless with significant variants by class and ethnic group (*MFP,* pp. 52, 54).

Some feminist historians have accepted the model of separate spheres and have seen the movement from woman's sphere to women's culture to women's-rights activism as the consecutive stages of an evolutionary political process. Others see a more complex and perpetual negotiation taking place between women's culture and the general culture. As Lerner has argued:

> It is important to understand that "woman's culture" is not and should not be seen as a subculture. It is hardly possible

for the majority to live in a subculture. . . . Women live their social existence within the general culture and, whenever they are confined by patriarchal restraint or segregation into separateness (which always has subordination as its purpose), they transform this restraint into complementarity (asserting the importance of woman's function, even its "superiority") and redefine it. Thus, women live a duality—as members of the general culture and as partakers of women's culture. [*MFP*, p. 52]

Lerner's views are similar to those of some cultural anthropologists. A particularly stimulating analysis of female culture has been carried out by two Oxford anthropologists, Shirley and Edwin Ardener. The Ardeners have tried to outline a model of women's culture which is not historically limited and to provide a terminology for its characteristics. Two essays by Edwin Ardener, "Belief and the Problem of Women" (1972) and "The 'Problem' Revisited" (1975), suggest that women constitute a *muted group,* the boundaries of whose culture and reality overlap, but are not wholly contained by, the *dominant (male) group.* A model of the cultural situation of women is crucial to understanding both how they are perceived by the dominant group and how they perceive themselves and others. Both historians and anthropologists emphasize the incompleteness of androcentric models of history and culture and the inadequacy of such models for the analysis of female experience. In the past, female experience which could not be accommodated by androcentric models was treated as deviant or simply ignored. Observation from an exterior point of view could never be the same as comprehension from within. Ardener's model also has many connections to and implications for current feminist literary theory, since the concepts of perception, si-

lence, and silencing are so central to discussions of women's participation in literary culture.[39]

By the term "muted," Ardener suggests problems both of language and of power. Both muted and dominant groups generate beliefs or ordering ideas of social reality at the unconscious level, but dominant groups control the forms or structures in which consciousness can be articulated. Thus muted groups must mediate their beliefs through the allowable forms of dominant structures. Another way of putting this would be to say that all language is the language of the dominant order, and women, if they speak at all, must speak through it. How then, Ardener asks, "does the symbolic weight of that other mass of persons express itself?" In his view, women's beliefs find expression through ritual and art, expressions which can be deciphered by the ethnographer, either female or male, who is willing to make the effort to perceive beyond the screens of the dominant structure.[40]

Let us now look at Ardener's diagram of the relationship of the dominant and the muted group:

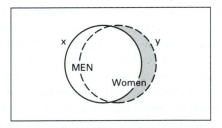

Unlike the Victorian model of complementary spheres, Ardener's groups are represented by intersecting circles. Much of muted circle Y falls within the boundaries of dominant circle X; there is also a crescent of Y which is outside the dominant boundary and therefore (in Ardener's terminology) "wild." We can think of the "wild zone" of women's culture spatially, experientially, or metaphysically. Spatially it stands for an area which is literally no-man's-land, a place forbidden to men, which corresponds to the zone in X which is off limits to women. Experientially it stands for the aspects of the female life-style which are outside of and unlike those of men; again, there is a corresponding zone of male experience alien to women. But if we think of the wild zone metaphysically, or in terms of consciousness, it has no corresponding male space since all of male consciousness is within the circle of the dominant structure and thus accessible to or structured by language. In this sense, the "wild" is always imaginary; from the male point of view, it may simply be the projection of the unconscious. In terms of cultural anthropology, women know what the male crescent is like, even if they have never seen it, because it becomes the subject of legend (like the wilderness). But men do not know what is in the wild.

For some feminist critics, the wild zone, or "female space," must be the address of a genuinely women-centered criticism, theory, and art, whose shared project is to bring into being the symbolic weight of female consciousness, to make the invisible visible, to make the silent speak. French feminist critics would like to make the wild zone the theoretical base of women's difference. In their texts, the wild zone becomes the place for the revolutionary women's language, the language of everything that is repressed, and for the revolutionary women's writing in "white ink." It is the Dark Continent in which Cixous' laughing Medusa and Wittig's *guérillères* reside. Through voluntary entry into the wild zone, other feminist critics tell us, a woman can write her way out of the "cramped confines of patriarchal space."[41] The images of this journey are now familiar in feminist quest fictions and in essays about them. The writer/heroine, often guided by another woman, travels to the "mother country" of liberated

desire and female authenticity; crossing to the other side of the mirror, like Alice in Wonderland, is often a symbol of the passage.

Many forms of American radical feminism also romantically assert that women are closer to nature, to the environment, to a matriarchal principle at once biological and ecological. Mary Daly's *Gyn/Ecology* and Margaret Atwood's novel *Surfacing* are texts which create this feminist mythology. In English and American literature, women writers have often imagined Amazon Utopias, cities or countries situated in the wild zone or on its border: Elizabeth Gaskell's gentle *Cranford* is probably an Amazon Utopia; so is Charlotte Perkins Gilman's *Herland* or, to take a recent example, Joanna Russ' *Whileaway*. A few years ago, the feminist publishing house Daughters, Inc. tried to create a business version of the Amazon Utopia; as Lois Gould reported in the *New York Times Magazine* (2 January 1977), "They believe they are building the working models for the critical next stage of feminism: full independence from the control and influence of "male-dominated" institutions—the news media, the health, education, and legal systems, the art, theater, and literary worlds, the banks."

These fantasies of an idyllic enclave represent a phenomenon which feminist criticism must recognize in the history of women's writing. But we must also understand that there can be no writing or criticism totally outside of the dominant structure; no publication is fully independent from the economic and political pressures of the male-dominated society. The concept of a woman's text in the wild zone is a playful abstraction: in the reality to which we must address ourselves as critics, women's writing is a "double-voiced discourse" that always embodies the social, literary, and cultural heritages of both the muted and the dominant.[42] And insofar as most feminist critics are also women writing, this precarious heritage is one we share; every step that feminist criticism takes toward defining women's writing is a step toward self-understanding as well; every account of a female literary culture and a female literary tradition has parallel significance for our own place in critical history and critical tradition.

Women writing are not, then, *inside* and *outside* of the male tradition; they are inside two traditions simultaneously, "undercurrents," in Ellen Moers' metaphor, of the mainstream. To mix metaphors again, the literary estate of women, as Myra Jehlen says, "suggests . . . a more fluid imagery of interacting juxtapositions, the point of which would be to represent not so much the territory, as its defining borders. Indeed, the female territory might well be envisioned as one long border, and independence for women, not as a separate country, but as open access to the sea." As Jehlen goes on to explain, an aggressive feminist criticism must poise itself on this border and must see women's writing in its changing historical and cultural relation to that other body of texts identified by feminist criticism not simply as literature but as "men's writing."[43]

The difference of women's writing, then, can only be understood in terms of this complex and historically grounded cultural relation. An important aspect of Ardener's model is that there are muted groups other than women; a dominant structure may determine many muted structures. A black American woman poet, for example, would have her literary identity formed by the dominant (white male) tradition, by a muted women's culture, and by a muted black culture. She would be affected by both sexual and racial politics in a combination unique to her case; at the same time, as Barbara Smith points out, she shares an experience specific to her group: "Black women writers constitute an identifiable literary tradition . . . thematically, stylistically, aesthetically, and conceptually. Black women writers manifest common approaches to the act of creating literature as a direct result of the specific political, social, and economic experience they have been obliged to share."[44] Thus the first task of a gynocentric criticism must be to plot the precise cultural locus of female literary identity and to describe the forces that intersect an individual woman writer's cultural field. A gynocentric criticism would also situate women writers with respect to the variables of literary culture, such as modes of production and distribution, relations of author and audience, relations of high to popular art, and hierarchies of genre.

Insofar as our concepts of literary periodization are based on men's writing, women's writing must be forcibly assimilated to an irrelevant grid; we discuss a Renaissance which is not a renaissance for women, a Romantic period in which women played very little part, a modernism with which women conflict. At the same time, the ongoing history of women's writing has been suppressed, leaving large and mysterious gaps in accounts of the development of genre. Gynocentric criticism is already well on the way to providing us with another perspective on literary history. Margaret Anne Doody, for example, suggests that "the period between the death of Richardson and the appearance of the novels of Scott and Austen" which has "been regarded as a dead period, a dull blank" is in fact the period in which late eighteenth-century women writers were developing "the paradigm for women's fiction of the nineteenth century—something hardly less than the paradigm of the nineteenth-century novel itself."[45] There has also been a feminist rehabilitation of the female gothic, a mutation of a popular genre once believed marginal but now seen as part of the great tradition of the novel.[46] In American literature, the pioneering work of Ann Douglas, Nina Baym, and Jane Tompkins, among others, has given us a new view of the power of women's fiction to feminize nineteenth-century American culture.[47] And feminist critics have made us aware that Woolf belonged to a tradition other than modernism and that this tradition surfaces in her work precisely in those places where criticism has hitherto found obscurities, evasions, implausibilities, and imperfections.[48]

Our current theories of literary influence also need to be tested in terms of women's writing. If a man's text, as Bloom and Edward Said have maintained, is fathered, then a woman's text is not only mothered but parented; it confronts both paternal and maternal precursors and must deal with the problems and advantages of both lines of inheritance. Woolf says in *A Room of One's Own* that "a woman writing thinks back through her mothers." But a woman writing unavoidably thinks back through her fathers as well; only male writers can forget or mute half of their parentage. The dominant culture need not consider the muted, except to rail against "the woman's part" in itself. Thus we need more subtle and supple accounts of influence, not just to explain women's writing but also to understand how men's writing has resisted the acknowledgment of female precursors.

We must first go beyond the assumption that women writers either imitate their male predecessors or revise them and that this simple dualism is adequate to describe the influences on the woman's text. I. A. Richards once commented that the influence of G. E. Moore had had an enormous negative impact on his work: "I feel like an obverse of him. Where there's a hole in him, there's a bulge in me."[49] Too often women's place in literary tradition is translated into the crude topography of hole and bulge, with Milton, Byron, or Emerson the bulging bogeys on one side and women's literature from Aphra Behn to Adrienne Rich a pocked moon surface of revisionary lacunae on the other. One of the great advantages of the women's-culture model is that it shows how the female tradition can be a positive source of strength and solidarity as

well as a negative source of powerlessness; it can generate its own experiences and symbols which are not simply the obverse of the male tradition.

How can a cultural model of women's writing help us to read a woman's text? One implication of this model is that women's fiction can be read as a double-voiced discourse, containing a "dominant" and a "muted" story, what Gilbert and Gubar call a "palimpsest." I have described it elsewhere as an object/field problem in which we must keep two alternative oscillating texts simultaneously in view: "In the purest feminist literary criticism we are . . . presented with a radical alteration of our vision, a demand that we see meaning in what has previously been empty space. The orthodox plot recedes, and another plot, hitherto submerged in the anonymity of the background, stands out in bold relief like a thumbprint." Miller too sees "another text" in women's fiction, "more or less muted from novel to novel" but "always there to be read."[50]

Another interpretive strategy for feminist criticism might be the contextual analysis that the cultural anthropologist Clifford Geertz calls "thick description." Geertz calls for descriptions that seek to understand the meaning of cultural phenomena and products by "sorting out the structures of signification . . . and determining their social ground and import."[51] A genuinely "thick" description of women's writing would insist upon gender and upon a female literary tradition among the multiple strata that make up the force of meaning in a text. No description, we must concede, could ever be thick enough to account for all the factors that go into the work of art. But we could work toward completeness, even as an unattainable ideal.

In suggesting that a cultural model of women's writing has considerable usefulness for the enterprise of feminist criticism, I don't mean to replace psychoanalysis with cultural anthropology as the answer to all our theoretical problems or to enthrone Ardener and Geertz as the new white fathers in place of Freud, Lacan, and Bloom. No theory, however suggestive, can be a substitute for the close and extensive knowledge of women's texts which constitutes our essential subject. Cultural anthropology and social history can perhaps offer us a terminology and a diagram of women's cultural situation. But feminist critics must use this concept in relation to what women actually write, not in relation to a theoretical, political, metaphoric, or visionary ideal of what women ought to write.

I began by recalling that a few years ago feminist critics thought we were on a pilgrimage to the promised land in which gender would lose its power, in which all texts would be sexless and equal, like angels. But the more precisely we understand the specificity of women's writing not as a transient by-product of sexism but as a fundamental and continually determining reality, the more clearly we realize that we have misperceived our destination. We may never reach the promised land at all; for when feminist critics see our task as the study of women's writing, we realize that the land promised to us is not the serenely undifferentiated universality of texts but the tumultuous and intriguing wilderness of difference itself.

## NOTES

1. Carolyn G. Heilbrun and Catharine R. Stimpson, "Theories of Feminist Criticism: A Dialogue," in *Feminist Literary Criticism,* ed. Josephine Donovan (Lexington, Ky., 1975), p. 64. I also discuss this distinction in my "Towards a Feminist Poetics," in *Women Writing and Writing about Women,* ed. Mary Jacobus (New York, 1979), pp. 22–41; a number of the ideas in the first part of the present essay are raised more briefly in the earlier piece.

2. No women critics are discussed in Hartman's *Criticism in the Wilderness* (New Haven, Conn., 1980), but he does describe a feminine spirit called "the Muse of Criticism": "more a governess than a Muse, the stern

daughter of books no longer read under trees and in the fields" (p. 175).

3. See my "Literary Criticism," *Signs* 1 (Winter 1975): 435–60.

4. Annette Kolodny, "Literary Criticism," *Signs* 2 (Winter 1976): 420.

5. On black criticism, see Barbara Smith, "Towards a Black Feminist Criticism," *Conditions Two* 1 (1977): 25, and Mary Helen Washington, "New Lives and New Letters: Black Women Writers at the End of the Seventies," *College English* 43 (January 1981): 1–11. On Marxist criticism, see the Marxist-Feminist Literature Collective's "Women's Writing," *Ideology and Consciousness* 3 (Spring 1978): 27, a collectively written analysis of several nineteenth-century women's novels which gives equal weight to gender, class, and literary production as textual determinants.

6. Margaret Homans, *Women Writers and Poetic Identity* (Princeton, N.J., 1980), p. 10.

7. Donovan, "Afterward: Critical Revision," *Feminist Literary Criticism,* p. 74. Judith Fetterley, *The Resisting Reader: A Feminist Approach to American Fiction* (Bloomington, Ind., 1978), p. viii. See my "Towards a Feminist Poetics," pp. 37–39. *The Authority of Experience* is the title of an anthology edited by Lee Edwards and Arlyn Diamond (Amherst, Mass., 1977).

8. Nina Auerbach, "Feminist Criticism Reviewed," in *Gender and Literary Voice,* ed. Janet Todd (New York, 1980), p. 258.

9. Adrienne Rich, "When We Dead Awaken: Writing as Re-Vision," *On Lies, Secrets, and Silence* (New York, 1979), p. 35.

10. Kolodny, "Dancing through the Minefield: Some Observations on the Theory, Practice, and Politics of a Feminist Literary Criticism," *Feminist Studies* 6 (Spring 1980): 19, 20. The complete theoretical case for a feminist hermeneutics is outlined in Kolodny's essays, including "Some Notes on Defining a 'Feminist Literary Criticism,' " *Critical Inquiry* 2 (Autumn 1975): 75–92; "A Map for Rereading; or, Gender and the Interpretation of Literary Texts," *New Literary History* (1980): 451–67; and "The Theory of Feminist Criticism" (paper delivered at the National Center for the Humanities Conference on Feminist Criticism, Research Triangle Park, N.C., March 1981).

11. Sandra M. Gilbert, "What Do Feminist Critics Want?; or, A Postcard from the Volcano," *ADE Bulletin* (Winter 1980): 19.

12. Christiane Makward, "To Be or Not to Be. . . . A Feminist Speaker," in *The Future of Difference,* ed. Hes-

ter Eisenstein and Alice Jardine (Boston, 1980), p. 102. On Lacan, see Jane Gallop, "The Ladies' Man," *Diacritics* 6 (Winter 1976): 28–34; on Macherey, see the Marxist-Feminist Literature Collective's "Women's Writing."

13. Patricia Meyer Spacks, *The Female Imagination* (New York, 1975), pp. 19, 32.

14. Hélène Cixous, "The Laugh of the Medusa," trans. Keith and Paula Cohen, *Signs* 1 (Summer 1976): 878. Nancy K. Miller, "Emphasis Added: Plots and Plausibilities in Women's Fiction," *PMLA* 96 (January 1981): 37.

15. For an overview, see Domna C. Stanton, "Language and Revolution: The Franco-American Dis-Connection," in *Future of Difference,* pp. 73–87, and Elaine Marks and Isabelle de Courtivron, eds., *New French Feminisms* (Amherst, Mass., 1979); all further references to *New French Feminisms,* abbreviated *NFF,* will hereafter be included with translator's name parenthetically in the text.

16. Two major works are the manifesto of the Marxist-Feminist Literature Collective, "Women's Writing," and the papers from the Oxford University lectures on women and literature, *Women Writing and Writing about Women,* ed. Jacobus.

17. Gilbert and Gubar, *The Madwoman in the Attic: The Woman Writer and the Nineteenth-Century Literary Imagination* (New Haven, Conn., 1979), pp. 6, 7; all further references to this work will hereafter be included parenthetically in the text.

18. Auerbach, review of *Madwoman, Victorian Studies* 23 (Summer 1980): 506.

19. Douglas Jerrold, quoted in Kathleen Tillotson, *Novels of the Eighteen-Forties* (London, 1961), p. 39 n. James Joyce imagined the creator as female and literary creation as a process of gestation; see Richard Ellmann, *James Joyce: A Biography* (London, 1959), pp. 306–8.

20. Carolyn Burke, "Report from Paris: Women's Writing and the Women's Movement," *Signs* 3 (Summer 1978): 851.

21. Rich, *Of Woman Born: Motherhood as Experience and Institution* (New York, 1977), p. 62. Biofeminist criticism has been influential in other disciplines as well: e.g., art critics, such as Judy Chicago and Lucy Lippard, have suggested that women artists are compelled to use a uterine or vaginal iconography of centralized focus, curved lines, and tactile or sensuous forms. See Lippard, *From the Center: Feminist Essays on Women's Art* (New York, 1976).

22. See Alicia Ostriker, "Body Language: Imagery of the Body in Women's Poetry," in *The State of the Language,* ed. Leonard Michaels and Christopher Ricks (Berkeley, 1980), pp. 247–63, and Terence Diggory, "Armoured

Women, Naked Men: Dickinson, Whitman, and Their Successors," in *Shakespeare's Sisters: Feminist Essays on Women Poets,* ed. Gilbert and Gubar (Bloomington, Ind., 1979), pp. 135–50.

23. Rachel Blau DuPlessis, "Washing Blood," *Feminist Studies* 4 (June 1978): 10. The entire issue is an important document of feminist criticism.

24. Miller, "Women's Autobiography in France: For a Dialectics of Identification," in *Women and Language in Literature and Society,* ed. Sally McConnell-Ginet, Ruth Borker, and Nelly Furman (New York, 1980), p. 271.

25. Furman, "The Study of Women and Language: Comment on Vol. 3, No. 3," *Signs* 4 (Autumn 1978): 182.

26. Burke, "Report from Paris," p. 844.

27. Jacobus, "The Difference of View," in *Women's Writing and Writing about Women,* pp. 12–13. Shoshana Felman, "Women and Madness: The Critical Phallacy," *Diacritics* 5 (Winter 1975): 10.

28. On women's language, see Sarah B. Pomeroy, *Goddesses, Whores, Wives, and Slaves: Women in Classical Antiquity* (New York, 1976), p. 24; McConnell-Ginet, "Linguistics and the Feminist Challenge," in *Women and Language,* p. 14; and Ioan M. Lewis, *Ecstatic Religion* (1971), cited in Shirley Ardener, ed., *Perceiving Women* (New York, 1977), p. 50.

29. Clifford Geertz, *The Interpretation of Cultures* (New York, 1973), pp. 241–42.

30. McConnell-Ginet, "Linguistics and the Feminist Challenge," pp. 13, 16.

31. Woolf, "Speech, Manuscript Notes," *The Pargiters,* ed. Mitchell A. Leaska (London, 1978), p. 164.

32. Quoted in Erika Freeman, *Insights: Conversations with Theodor Reik* (Englewood Cliffs, N.J., 1971), p. 166. Reik goes on, "But what the hell, writing! The great task of a woman is to bring a child into the world."

33. Cora Kaplan, "Language and Gender" (unpublished paper, University of Sussex, 1977, p. 3).

34. See Annis Pratt, "The New Feminist Criticisms," in *Beyond Intellectual Sexism,* ed. Joan I. Roberts (New York, 1976); Barbara Rigney, *Madness and Sexual Politics* (Athens, Ohio, 1979); and Ann Douglas, "Mrs. Sigourney and the Sensibility of the Inner Space," *New England Quarterly* 45 (June 1972): 163–81.

35. Nancy Chodorow, "Gender, Relation, and Difference in Psychoanalytic Perspective," in *Future of Difference,* p. 11. See also Chodorow et al., "On *The Reproduction of Mothering:* A Methodological Debate," *Signs* 6 (Spring 1981): 482–514.

36. See, e.g., *The Lost Tradition: Mothers and Daughters in Literature,* ed. Cathy M. Davison and E. M. Broner (New York, 1980); this work is more engaged with myths and images of matrilineage than with redefining female identity.

37. Elizabeth Abel, "(E)Merging Identities: The Dynamics of Female Friendship in Contemporary Fiction by Women," *Signs* 6 (Spring 1981): 434.

38. Gerda Lerner, "The Challenge of Women's History," *The Majority Finds Its Past* (New York, 1981); all further references to this book, abbreviated *MFP,* will hereafter be included parenthetically in the text.

39. See, e.g., Tillie Olsen, *Silences* (New York, 1978); Sheila Rowbotham, *Woman's Consciousness, Man's World* (Harmondsworth, 1976), pp. 31–37; and Marcia Landy, "The Silent Woman: Towards a Feminist Critique," in *Authority of Experience* (n. 7 above), pp. 16–27.

40. Edwin Ardener, "Belief and the Problem of Women," in *Perceiving Women* (n. 28 above) p. 3.

41. Mari McCarty, "Possessing Female Space: 'The Tender Shoot,'" *Women's Studies* 8 (1981): 368.

42. Susan Lanser and Evelyn Torton Beck, "[Why] Are There No Great Women Critics? And What Difference Does It Make?" in *The Prism of Sex: Essays in the Sociology of Knowledge,* ed. Beck and Julia A. Sherman (Madison, Wis., 1979), p. 86.

43. Myra Jehlen, "Archimedes and the Paradox of Feminist Criticism," *Signs* 6 (Autumn 1981): 582.

44. Smith, "Black Feminist Criticism," p. 32. See also Gloria T. Hull, "Afro-American Women Poets: A Bio-Critical Survey," in *Shakespeare's Sisters,* pp. 165–82, and Marks, "Lesbian Intertextuality," in *Homosexualities and French Literature,* ed. Marks and George Stambolian (Ithaca, N.Y., 1979).

45. Margaret Anne Doody, "George Eliot and the Eighteenth-Century Novel," *Nineteenth Century Fiction* 35 (December 1980): 267–68.

46. See, e.g., Judith Wilt, *Ghosts of the Gothic: Austen, Eliot, and Lawrence* (Princeton, N.J., 1980).

47. See Douglas, *The Feminization of American Culture* (New York, 1977); Nina Baym, *Woman's Fiction: A Guide to Novels by and about Women in America,* 1820–1870 (Ithaca, N.Y., 1978); and Jane Tompkins, "Sentimental Power: *Uncle Tom's Cabin* and the Politics of Literary History," *Glyph* 8 (1981): 79–102.

48. See, e.g., the analysis of Woolf in Gilbert, "Costumes of the Mind: Transvestism as Metaphor in Modern Literature," *Critical Inquiry* 7 (Winter 1980): 391–417.

49. I. A. Richards, quoted in John Paul Russo, "A Study in Influence: The Moore-Richards Paradigm," *Critical Inquiry* 5 (Summer 1979): 687.

50. Showalter, "Literary Criticism," p. 435; Miller, "Emphasis Added," p. 47. To take one example, whereas *Jane Eyre* had always been read in relation to an implied "dominant" fictional and social mode and had thus been perceived as flawed, feminist readings foreground its muted symbolic strategies and explore its credibility and coherence in its own terms. Feminist critics revise views like those of Richard Chase, who describes Rochester as castrated thus implying that Jane's neurosis is penis envy, and G. Armour Craig, who sees the novel as Jane's struggle for superiority, to see Jane instead as healthy within her own system, that is, a *women's* society. See Chase, "The Brontës; or, Myth Domesticated," *Jane Eyre* (New York, 1971), pp. 462–71; G. Armour Craig, "The Unpoetic Compromise: On the Relation between Private Vision and Social Order in Nineteenth-Century English Fiction," in *Self and Society,* ed. Mark Schorer (New York, 1956), pp. 30–41; Nancy Pell, "Resistance, Rebellion, and Marriage: The Economics of *Jane Eyre,*" *Nineteenth Century Fiction* 31 (March 1977): 397–420; Helene Moglen, *Charlotte Brontë: The Self Conceived* (New York, 1977); Rich, "*Jane Eyre:* The Temptations of a Motherless Woman," *MS,* October 1973; and Maurianne Adams, "*Jane Eyre:* Woman's Estate," in *Authority of Experience,* pp. 137–59.

51. Geertz, *Interpretation of Cultures,* p. 9.

# 5

# Gerald Graff
## 1937–

Gerald Graff was born in Chicago and received his Ph.D. from Stanford University in 1963. He has taught at Northwestern University and currently teaches at the University of Chicago. His major publications approach the conflicts within modern literary studies from a wide range of disciplines dealing with pedagogy, cultural studies, history, criticism, education, and literary theory. His writings include *Poetic Statements and Critical Dogma* (1970), *Criticism in the University* (1985), *Literature Against Itself: Literary Ideas in Modern Society* (1979), and *Beyond the Culture Wars: How Teaching the Conflicts Can Revitalize American Education* (1992). Many of his articles such as "Other Voices, Other Rooms: Organizing and Teaching the Humanities Conflict" (1990) and "Teach the Conflicts" (1990) also deal with the problems inherent in the multifaceted and often fractured humanities.

*Professing Literature: An Institutional History* (1987), possibly Graff's best-known work, illuminates the history of the dissonance in literary instruction that has existed in the instruction of literature in American universities "roughly from the Yale Report in 1828 . . . to the waning of New Criticism in the 1960s." In his "Introduction: The Humanist Myth" Graff traces the origin of the cycle of displacement and the inability of the academy to present a well-functioning (much less a cohesive) policy of literary instruction to "the union of Arnoldian humanism and scientific research which gave birth to academic literary studies." Graff writes of his agreement with Marxist critic Terry Eagleton, who in *Literary Theory* says that literary studies are used for ends other than the study of literature. Graff sees such study as reflective of whichever academic ideal holds sway at a given time. Graff also says, as does Michel Foucault, that the very boundaries and classifications that are articulated by literary studies also define them. Unlike Eagleton and Foucault, however, Graff refuses to brand the attempt at classification as an evil. He "see[s] nothing inherently self-undoing or illegitimate about all idealizations such as deconstructionists do," nor does he think deconstructive criticism can "distinguish between legitimate and illegitimate forms of institutional or rhetorical power." At the same time Graff rejects Allan Bloom's and E. D. Hirsch's recollection of a sentimental golden age of literary study in the American academy. Thus Graff chooses to be a centrist and study the past to point out the divisions that have existed for the purpose of generating discussion and, perhaps, discovering ways of sharing and understanding the differences that do exist.

The remainder of Graff's book addresses specific patterns of conflict that emerge between the "traditional" approach of the time and whichever counter approaches appear. Graff deals with each in a manner that is fascinating and immediate and explores the complaints of Latin students or the confusion in the speeches of many Modern Language Association presidents who were trying to come to grips with a rapidly changing field.

# Introduction: The Humanist Myth

*When a sufficient number of specialists are assembled on a college faculty, the subject of which each knows only a small part is said to be covered, and the academic department to which they all belong is regarded as fully manned. In ancient Ireland, if legend is to be trusted, there was a tower so high that it took two persons to see to the top of it. One would begin at the bottom and look up as far as sight could reach, the other would begin where the first left off, and see the rest of the way.*

John Erskine

*It's hard to organize literature.*

Irving Howe

*Professing Literature* is a history of academic literary studies in the United States, roughly from the Yale Report of 1828, which assured the primacy of the classical over the vernacular languages in American colleges for another half-century, to the waning of the New Criticism in the 1960s and subsequent controversies over literary theory. Strictly speaking, there were no "academic literary studies" in America or anywhere else until the formation of language and literature departments in the last quarter of the nineteenth century. But the use of literature as a vehicle of education goes back to ancient times, and in America since the Colonial era literary texts had been studied in college classes in Greek and Latin, English grammar, and rhetoric and elocution. These early practices assumed a theory of the social function of literature that affected the shape of literature departments when they finally emerged.

But the idea that literature could or should be taught—rather than simply enjoyed or absorbed as part of the normal upbringing of gentlefolk—was a novel one, and no precedents existed for organizing such an enterprise. To "organize literature" is difficult under any circumstances, but particularly when it means reconstituting as a curriculum under more or less democratic conditions something that had previously been part of the socialization of a particular class. My account suggests that this project was never thought through in all its ramifications, but, if anything, early educators were more alert to its difficulties than we are today, since they had the advantage of a historical perspective that was lost once academic literary studies became established and complacent and once it no longer could remember a preacademic literary culture for comparison.

Any single-volume treatment of so vast a subject must omit some matters and reduce others to schematic proportions. Though I refer generically to "academic literary studies" and "the literature department," most of my evidence is drawn from research-oriented departments of English at major universities, and I make only occasional attempts to distinguish patterns in English from those in other modern language departments or departments of comparative literature. Perhaps I ought to have subtitled the book "A History of English Studies," but I decided that essential traits have been similar enough to warrant the broader label.

My account does not do justice to the small-college experience, however. And I suspect that some of the conditions I treat as chronic dilemmas will be seen as grounds for envy in institutions where literature, as distinct from composition, has become a luxury. I deal only in passing with the teaching of composition, though the pioneer work of William Riley Parker, Wallace Douglas, and Richard Ohmann has shown that without that enterprise the teaching of literature could never have achieved its central status, and none of the issues I discuss would matter very much. I have made only occasional mention of British universities, despite the influence they exerted on native developments.

The aim of my concluding chapter is not to examine recent controversies over literary theory in detail—something outside the scope of this kind of book—but to point out how these controversies echo old ones as far back as the beginnings of the profession. My aim here is also to suggest that literary theory can help illuminate old and new conflicts in ways that might infuse some welcome self-consciousness into literary studies. As I use the term, there is a sense in which all teachers of literature are "theorists" and have a stake in theoretical disputes. For that matter, there is a sense in which a literature department (and curriculum) is itself a theory, though it has been largely an incoherent theory, and this incoherence strengthens the impression that the department has no theory.

It is possible to defend the infusion of theory into the curriculum on traditional grounds, namely, that students need theoretical concepts in order to be able to make sense of literature and talk about it intelligently. We shall see that until recently, in fact, the word "theory" was embraced by educational traditionalists, in reaction against the atomized empiricism of research and explication, which trusted that the accumulation of facts and interpretations about literature would somehow of itself add up to a coherent picture. This is not to deny that much current theory amounts to a radical attack on the premises and values of traditional literary humanism. But such attacks on traditional literary humanism raise the kinds of questions about the nature and cultural functions of literature that used to be the concern of traditional humanists, even as they reject the traditional humanistic answers to those questions as no longer sufficient. The real enemy of tradition is the kind of orthodox literary study that neglects theoretical questions about ends, values, and definitions in the hope that they will take care of themselves. It was the breakdown of agreement (or ostensible agreement) on these questions that inspired the current theory explosion and ensures, I think, that it will not be a passing fad.

When I first began this inquiry I vaguely assumed that the founders of academic literary studies must originally have had a shared idea of their rationale that had somehow got lost along the way. I imagined that this shared rationale had something to do with concepts like "humanism" and "cultural tradition," more or less in the sense associated with the name of Matthew Arnold. What I discovered, however, was that although the transmission of humanism and cultural tradition in the Matthew Arnold sense was indeed the official goal of the literature department, there were from the outset fundamental disagreements about how that goal should be pursued. Early educators who identified themselves with the Matthew Arnold view of literature and culture strenuously objected to the philological and historical literary scholarship that had qualified literary studies for departmental status in the new research university.

The union of Arnoldian humanism and scientific research which gave birth to academic literary studies was never free from strain. Traditional humanists argued that the compartmentalization of literature in narrowly specialized and disconnected "fields" and the glorification of quantitative "production" in research tended to undermine Arnold's ideal of broad general culture and his view of literature as a coherent criticism of life. The research fetish seemed only another example of that triumph of practical and technical "machinery" over ethical and cultural ends that Arnold had deplored in so many features of the modern world—and that seemed peculiarly unrestrained in the United States.

It is worth pondering that the kind of scholarship we now think of as traditionally humanistic was regarded as a subversive innovation by the traditionalists of an earlier era, whatever its roots may have been in the classical humanism of the Renaissance. It is also worth pondering that traditional humanists of the same era indicted research scholarship for many of the very same sins for which later traditionalists indicted the New Criticism and present day traditionalists indict literary theory: elevating esoteric, technocratic jargon over humanistic values, coming between literature itself and the student, turning literature into an elitist pastime for specialists. Whatever the sins of recent theory, those who blame the problems of the humanities on them—and on other post-1960 developments—only illustrate their own pet maxim that those who forget the past are condemned to repeat it. The solutions they propose—a return to a great tradition with no investigation of why that tradition has come to be questioned—figures only to send us yet one more time around what we will see has been an oft-repeated cycle.

Of course the research scholars who were the targets of the earliest criticism did not see matters the way their critics did. They too saw themselves as legitimate heirs of Matthew Arnold, and they dismissed their detractors as dilettantes and victims of mere nostalgia, as many of them were. Even so, a surprising number of these early research scholars could not help agreeing with their critics that there was a disturbing disparity between their traditional humanistic ideals and their professional practices. They spent much of their time at the early meetings of the Modern Language Association exhorting one another to do something about the disparity, though few of them went beyond ineffectual assertions, reiterated countless times by now, that teaching should be restored to equal importance with research, that the "general culture" of the undergraduate college should be reasserted against the specialization of the graduate school, and (above all) that literature itself should somehow be restored to primacy over scholarship and methodology. The very nature of this diagnosis led the critics of the profession to lapse into fatalism, blaming their problems on the inherent philistinism of American democracy, the inherent vulgarity of the modern age, or the incurable inferiority of their students.

The complaint that research and publication have displaced teaching has always resembled the parallel complaint that technology or bureaucracy has displaced more human or communal relations. Whatever its justifications, such a complaint leads nowhere, for it envisages no role for the professional interests of the scholar except to extinguish themselves. The diagnosis on which the complaint rests blames the problems of the institution on the process of professionalization itself, not distinguishing between professionalism as such and the specific forms professionalism has taken under the peculiar circumstances of the new university, forms which—it must be stressed—need not be the only forms possible. But however limited their value as present guides, these early critics can at least cure us of the delusion that academic literary studies at some point underwent a falling-away from genuine Arnoldian humanism.

Helping prop up this humanist myth, however, is the habit of thinking of institutions as if they were unmediated projections of the values, methods, and ideologies of major individuals and movements. This procedure is convenient and seems to accord with common sense, but it ignores, for one thing, the substantial changes that even the dominant critical values, methods, and ideologies may undergo when they become institutionalized in the form of scholarly fields, curricula, and pedagogy. "Professionalization" and "academicization" are not neutral principles of organization, but agents that transform the cultural and literary-critical "isms" fed into them, often to the point of subverting their original purpose, or so deflecting them that they become unrecognizable to outsiders. What goes in is not necessarily what comes out, and this is one reason why the things the institution seems self-evidently to stand for to insiders may scarcely register on outsiders.

In calling this book an institutional history, I mean to underscore that its concern is not only with particular scholarly and critical practices, but also with what has happened to those practices once they have become institutionalized in modern universities—in ways that are not the only possible ones. My emphasis, in other words, is not only on what "goes on" in the shape of individual scholarly accomplishments and trends, but on what "comes out" as an operational totality and how that totality is perceived, misperceived, or not perceived at all by outsiders. Most histories of criticism properly ignore such matters and concentrate on major figures and movements, but for this reason their results may not yield a safe basis for an institutional analysis. For even major figures and movements can fail to stamp their values on the institution as a whole. In large degree Arnoldian humanism has been the outlook of singular individuals, individuals who have exerted a powerful and still-present influence on students and followers, but who have repeatedly failed to make their values visibly characteristic of the totality. Without going into the complex history of the term, we can

note that already by the turn of the century, "Humanist"—in its association with Irving Babbitt and his group—was the name of one particular professional faction, one "field" among many, more or less estranged from the established ones. It is no accident that many of the exemplary Arnoldian humanists from Babbitt to Walter Jackson Bate have ended up as bitter critics of the profession.

Their failure does not seem to me a state of affairs to be lamented, since it is after all the inability of their Arnoldian humanism to become an effective umbrella concept that has gradually opened academic literary studies to a variety of competing views of literature, scholarship, and culture. The discouraging thing is not that such institutional conflicts have gone unresolved—unresolved conflict being just the sort of thing a democratic educational system should thrive on—but how little of the potential educational value of such conflicts the professional system has been able to turn into part of what it studies and teaches, instead of a source of paralysis. Not all the conflicts of literary studies have been so esoteric as to lack potential interest to outsiders, and even those that have a large esoteric dimension (like the current cold war between theorists and humanists) have a surprising way of exemplifying cultural conflicts of potentially general interest. But educational-cultural battles tend at present to be fought out only behind the scenes, as it were, in specialized journals, technical vocabularies, and private faculty meetings. They are exemplified rather than foregrounded by the department and the curriculum and thus do not become part of the context of the average student's education or the average professor's professional life.

The pretense that humanism and the cultural tradition preside over the various dispersed activities of literary studies is one of the things which has permitted ideological conflicts to be kept out of public view. But another powerful cause lies in the field-coverage model of departmental organization, which has conceived literature departments as aggregates arranged to cover an array of historical and generic literary fields. The field-coverage principle accompanied the modernization and professionalization of education of the 1870s and 1880s, when schools and colleges organized themselves into departments corresponding to what were deemed to be the major subjects and research fields. For reasons having to do equally with ensuring humanistic breadth and facilitating specialized research, the literature department adopted the assumption that it would consider itself respectably staffed once it had amassed instructors competent to "cover" a more or less balanced spread of literary periods and genres, with a scattering of themes and special topics.

The field-coverage principle seems so innocuous as to be hardly worth looking at, and we have lived with it so long that we hardly even see it, but its consequences have been far reaching. Its great advantage was to make the department and the curriculum virtually self-regulating. By assigning each instructor a commonly understood role—to cover a predefined period or field—the principle created a system in which the job of instruction could proceed as if on automatic pilot, without the need for instructors to debate aims and methods. Assuming individual instructors were competently trained—and the system of graduate work which developed rapidly in America after the 1890's took care of that—instructors could be left on their own to get on with teaching and research, with little need for elaborate supervision and management.

The second advantage of the field-coverage principle was to give the institution enormous flexibility in assimilating new ideas, subjects, and methods. In the model of education that had preceded the modern school or university, where a primary goal was to enforce a Christian religious and social ideology, any innovation that challenged the prevailing way of doing things was disruptive

and had to be excluded or expelled. In the coverage model, by contrast, innovation even of a threatening kind could be welcomed by simply *adding* another unit to the aggregate of fields to be covered. Fierce resistance to innovation arose frequently, of course, but since all instructors were on their own, the absorption of innovation did not oblige pre-established habits to change, so that in the long run—and increasingly it was not a very long run—resistance tended to give way. It is only the field-coverage principle that explains how the literature department has managed to avoid incurring paralyzing clashes of ideology during a period when it has preserved much of its earlier traditional orientation while incorporating disruptive novelties such as contemporary literature, black studies, feminism, Marxism, and deconstruction.

The field-coverage principle made the modern educational machine friction free, for by making individuals functionally independent in the carrying out of their tasks it prevented conflicts from erupting which would otherwise have had to be confronted, debated, and worked through. An invisible hand—fortified by the faith that humanism in the Matthew Arnold sense pervaded all the branches of the department's and the profession's activities—saw to it that the sum of the parts added up to a coherent whole. Yet these very strengths of the field-coverage principle were also liabilities. By making the teaching staff and the curriculum self-regulating, the principle let instructors get on with the job of teaching and research in an efficient and untroubled way, but it also relieved them of the need to discuss the reasons they were doing what they were doing. Organizational structure left the faculty without the need to confer about matters of fundamental concern with colleagues in their own and other departments. Not that there was any lack of controversy, of course—this has always been plentiful enough—but controversy was curiously screened from students and outsiders. The tacit assumption has been that students should be exposed only to the *results* of professional controversies, not to the controversies themselves, which would presumably confuse or demoralize them. The curriculum has been determined by political trade-offs, while the clashing principles that might at least have made the process edifying have been removed from view.

The division of fields according to the least controversial principles made the department easy to administer but masked its most interesting conflicts and connections. To put it another way, the field-coverage principle enabled administrative organization to take the place of principled thought and discussion. The presence of an array of fully staffed fields made it unnecessary for anybody to have a theoretical idea of the department's goals in order for it to get on with its work. The grid of literary periods, genres, and themes in the catalog was a sufficiently clear expression of what the department was about.

Critics objected to the department's compartmentalization as if that in itself was the problem, but division of labor is necessary in any bureaucraticized system. It was not the compartmentalizations which created the problem but their disconnection, which rendered invisible the relations and contrasts that could have forced the meanings of the department's divisions into relief. Since the courses in periods and genres did not address one another, teachers tended not to raise the question of what connections or contrasts the different periods and genres might bear to one another, what was meant by a particular periodization or by "period" in general, or what it might mean to approach literature in a historical or generic (and later a "New Critical") way. It was as if categories existed in order to make it unnecessary to think about them and to recognize that they were the product of theoretical choices.

By organizing itself on a principle of systematic non-relationship in which all parties

tacitly agreed not to ask how they might be connected or opposed, the department prevented potentially edifying conflicts from becoming part of what literary studies was about. Students (and instructors) were thus deprived of a means of situating themselves in relation to the cultural issues of their time. For students learn not just by exposure to individual instructors, but by sensing how the teaching aggregate hangs together or divides, so that to obscure these relations robs students of one of the central means of making sense of education and the cultural world. Latent conflicts of method and ideology that had divided the faculty from the first did not have to be confronted; it was up to each instructor (within increasingly flexible limits) to determine method and ideology without correlation with one another. Thus, even though conflicts over method and ideology were becoming more frequent and intense as the profession developed, the myth of shared humanistic values and purposes could always be maintained. Not only was there no need to ask what theoretical assumptions underlay these values, the illusion could be kept up that nobody had a theory.

This effect operated vertically as well as horizontally, as the methodologies of literary study became detached from the cultural rationales that originally had given point to them. This pattern of detachment, whereby methods become separated from their goals, first arose in the pre-professional era, but professionalization, with its multiplication of technical methodologies, greatly intensified it. Usually the blame falls on the inherent tendency of methodology itself to become a monster grinding out research and criticism without their producers knowing why they are producing it. Again, however, it is arguably not methodology that necessarily invites such routinization, but a system which, by isolating functions, separates methodology from the contexts and theories which would keep its justifications visible.

The field-coverage principle effected at the administrative level what the humanist myth perpetuated at the level of ideology. In combination, the two provided a solution to the problem of how to "organize literature" that removed the need for continued collective discussion. Just as the literature faculty was self-regulating as long as periodization predefined the functions of individuals, literature was self-interpreting as long as it remained an expression of humanism. Hence there arose a curriculum that expressed the faith that exposure to a more or less balanced array of periods, genres, and themes would add up in the mind of the student to an appreciation of humanism and the cultural tradition. More succinctly, the assumption implicit in the humanist myth and the field-coverage principle has been that *literature teaches itself*. Since the literary tradition is presumably coherent in and of itself, it should naturally dictate the way teachers collectively organize themselves. That literature teaches itself is not necessarily the conscious assumption of individual teachers (though many have embraced it, as we will see), but something presupposed by the overall structure.

Unfortunately the assumption has never proved true—but the dream still persists that it might, if the encumbrances of scholarship, criticism, or theory could somehow be prevented from getting in the way. One of the recurrent motifs in the present history is the appeal to "literature itself" against various forms of commentary *about* literature as a cure for institutional dilemmas. The hope is that salvation can be achieved if only the great literary works can be freed from the institutional and professional encumbrances that come between students or laymen and the potency of the work itself. For a long time it was positivistic scholarship that was the target of this view, then it became analytic criticism, and today it has become literary theory and various attempts to historicize literature. But the basic form of the "literature

itself" argument remains the same, bespeaking the perennial wish to believe that if the quality of individual instruction is good and the right works are taught, the effect of the whole will take care of itself.

Literary studies have not yet found a way to institutionalize the lesson of recent criticism that no text is an island, that every work of literature is a rejoinder in a conversation or dialogue that it presupposes but may or may not mention explicitly. It is in this spirit that Robert Scholes argues, in his recent book, *Textual Power,* that to teach the literary text one must teach the "cultural text" as well. Many instructors already do so, but individual pedagogy alone can have only limited effects when it conflicts with institutional structure. The disconnection between the divisions that organize the literature department and the university tends to efface the larger cultural conversation to which works of literature refer. The cultural text tends to fall into the cracks separating periods, genres, and fields, criticism, creative writing, and composition. Nobody is responsible for it since it is nobody's field—or else someone is responsible for it only as one field among others.

One might expect traditionalists to show some sympathy with such a conservatively historical argument as this, yet the idea still remains powerful that students are best introduced to literature by being put in "direct" contact with texts themselves, with a minimum of contextualizing interference. Those who hold this view cling to it tenaciously, believing it has been validated by the historical experience they have lived through for the past thirty or forty years. They recall so vividly the disastrously mechanical kinds of contextualizing they were subjected to under the old positivistic literary history that when they hear words like "contextualize," "historicize," and "theorize," they envision students even more bored and disaffected than they were before the New Criticism put the old historicism out of its misery. But the remedy for a poor contextualizing of literature is not no contextualizing but better contextualizing. That did not arise out of the compromise between New Criticism and background study that resolved disciplinary controversies after World War II. Nobody can doubt that the turn to "close reading" at that time constituted an immense improvement over what came before, but it has proved to be a short-term solution whose costs are now increasingly apparent. By treating the contexts of literature as an extrinsic matter, however important, the compromise between New Critical and historical pedagogy that stabilized literature departments over the past three or four decades has only reinforced the inveterate assumption that these contexts will take care of themselves if a balanced spread of fields is represented, and thus that they do not need to be collectively worked out or organized. By treating the contexts of literature as an extrinsic affair, the New Criticism made it all the more unnecessary to worry about how those contexts might be organized institutionally. But without a context, the student's "direct" experience of literature itself tends to result either in uncertainty or facile acquiescence in an interpretive routine.

Current radical critiques of academic literary studies have effectively exposed the pretensions of "unproblematic" appeals to literature itself, and my analysis often echoes them. I agree with Terry Eagleton's argument, in *Literary Theory,* that literary studies have arbitrarily narrowed the concept of "literature," and that the goal should be to repair the disabling dislocation of literature "from other cultural and social practices." I echo Foucault in looking at the way seemingly neutral, disciplinary classifications and boundaries actually constitute the fields they organize. Like certain deconstructionists, I am concerned with the way idealizations such as "humanism" have functioned rhetorically to mask the conflicts that constituted them.

At the same time, I see nothing inherently self-undoing or illegitimate about all idealizations, as the deconstructionists do, and I doubt that all institutional patterns can be explained as effects of ideology, power, "logocentrism," or subjugation. Valuable as they are, these forms of critique seem to lack a criterion that would enable them to distinguish between legitimate and illegitimate forms of institutional or rhetorical power. Furthermore, they tend to accept the same working model of institutional history as the traditionalists, merely "reinscribing" it in an accusatory vocabulary. Like the Right, the Left mistakes pious wishes and pronouncements for institutional fact. A case in point is Eagleton's account of the rise and development of "English" as a project of "controlling and incorporating the working class" through the consolidation of the national literature.

There is some truth in this "social control" theory of academic literary studies, for many members of the founding generation did conceive these studies explicitly and openly as a means of reinstating cultural uniformity and thus controlling those unruly democratic elements that were entering higher education for the first time after the Civil War. What Eagleton describes in England was true in the United States as well, that "in the work of 'English' pioneers like F. D. Maurice and Charles Kingsley, the emphasis was on solidarity between the social classes, the cultivation of 'larger sympathies,' the instillation of national pride and the transmission of 'moral' values." But the question remains, how successfully was this nationalistic mission for literary studies carried out? Did the ideology of the founders remain "the distinctive hallmark of literary studies" down to the present, as Eagleton claims?

If their testimony can be taken seriously, those who most wanted the mission to succeed thought it had failed right from the start. The hope that the study of English would restore national leadership to the academic custodians of high culture disintegrated very clearly. On the one hand, high literary culture was increasingly marginal to the commercial and corporate interests dominating modern life, making laughable the pretensions of the literary elite to cultural leadership. On the other hand, even within the university the old elite was losing control—at least it complained bitterly that the new academic professionalism tended to place the interests of the research field above the interests of the nation. Underlying the animus of many early Arnoldian humanists against the professional research industry was the view that research sacrificed literature's potential as an instrument of socialization to the narrow interests of a professional clique. Although the turn of the century saw the imposition of a uniform canon of English literature, traditionalists complained that the curriculum had all but dissipated the civic potential of the canon by breaking it up into such disconnected fragments that students could get no clear sense of its unity. Far from being organized on a centralized logocentric model, the American university is itself something of a deconstructionist, proliferating a variety of disciplinary vocabularies that nobody can reduce to the common measure of any metalanguage. This in fact is one of the reasons why such institutions are so hard to change.

My evidence, in any case, suggests that professionalization not only failed to turn academic literary studies into the effective instrument of nationalist ideology some of the founders hoped they would be, but in some ways it subverted that ideology. Again, the American situation may have to be distinguished from that of France and England, where the traditional social elites were more powerful and more able to resist professionalization than were their counterparts in the United States. In the American university, the frustration of cultural nationalism is particularly obvious in the late and grudging academic recognition accorded to America's national literature, which was at first excluded from departments because it did not suit the prevailing research methods and then, when at last incorporated, proceeded to be so assimilated to those methods that its coherence as an expression of the national spirit was rendered all but invisible. Professional literary studies would not have encountered so many problems of identity had they not come into being at the very moment when the principle of nationality, for most of the nineteenth century the major way of conceptualizing literature as a whole, was losing its effectiveness.

The point needs to be kept in mind when considering recent critiques of the canon. Unquestionably, the exclusion of blacks, women, and other heterodox traditions from the canon has had major ideological effects. What is prevented from "going in" to begin with can hardly have an effect on what comes out. But this is not to say that what comes out is ideologically of a piece. When critics like Jane Tompkins argue that the academic remaking of the American literature canon gave "the American people a conception of themselves and their history," they fail to ask whether the canon was ever taught homogeneously or effectively enough to convey a clear conception of the national spirit to students, much less to "the American people" as a whole. In order to specify the ideological effects of the canon, it should be necessary to do more than make inferences from the canonized texts and interpretations. Though recent reader-centered criticism has taught us that readers appropriate texts in heterogeneous ways, this lesson tends to be forgotten when the ideology of the canon is at stake.

Both the accusatory and the honorific view of literary studies—which turn out, curiously, to be the same view—rest on wishful thinking. They credit the institution with a more cohesive impact than it has ever achieved. Like other inventions of the Progressive Era, academic literary studies have combined class, ethnic, and gender prejudices with a genuinely democratic egalitarianism—that is what has made it possible for radical critics to find a home in them. Literary studies have been no beacon of political enlightenment, but they have not been an instrument of dominant ideology and social control either—or, if so, they have been a singularly inefficient one.

As I have told it, then, the story of academic literary studies in America is a tale not of triumphant humanism, nationalism, or any single professional model, but of a series of conflicts that have tended to be masked by their very failure to find visible institutional expression. This emphasis on conflicts is seen in the successive oppositions that organize my narrative: classicists versus modern-language scholars; research investigators versus generalists; historical scholars versus critics; New Humanists versus New Critics; academic critics versus literary journalists and culture critics; critics and scholars versus theorists. These controversies have seemed to me to possess greater richness and vitality than any of the conclusions they led to about the nature of literary studies as a discipline or the nature of literature as an object. Among the matters in dispute have been not just the nature of literature and the discipline, but whether there is—or needs to be—such a thing as a "discipline" of literary studies at all, or such a thing as "literature" in some univocal sense, as opposed to a variety of different literary and critical activities made coherent, if at all, only by their conflicts. If one conflict subsumes the others in my story, however, it is the one which has pitted scholars against critics. We tend to forget that until recently the terms were considered antithetical: scholars did research and dealt with verifiable facts, whereas critics presided over interpretations and values, which supposedly had no objective basis and therefore did not qualify for serious academic study. This state of affairs changed so rapidly that the implications of the change hardly had time to be assessed.

Whereas "academic criticism" had been a contradiction in terms, it suddenly became a redundancy, as criticism, once the province of nonacademic journalists and men of letters, became (with important exceptions) virtually the monopoly of university departments.

Yet the old antagonism of scholar and critic did not disappear as much as it became submerged, after World War II, in an atmosphere where methodological and conceptual progress seemed more desirable than ideological confrontation. Many of the old issues reappeared under a realignment of the parties that has now set scholars and critics on the same side in opposition to theorists. Among these issues are the nature of literature (or whether it has a nature), the nature of literary interpretation and evaluation, the relation between the "intrinsic" domain of literature and the "extrinsic" ones of history, society, philosophy, and psychology, and above all, the issue of whether or in what way literature should be historicized and assimilated to social and political contexts.

Those who argue that the humanities have become disablingly incoherent seem to me right, but many of them fail to see that coherence can no longer be grounded on some restored consensus, whether it be traditional "basics," revolutionary ideological critique, or something else. In the final analysis, what academic literary studies have had to work with is not a coherent cultural tradition, but a series of conflicts that have remained unresolved, unacknowledged, and assumed to be outside the proper sphere of literary education. To bring these conflicts inside that sphere will mean thinking of literary education as part of a larger cultural history that includes the other humanities as well as the sciences even while acknowledging that terms like "humanities," "science," "culture," and "history" are contested.

# II

# WHAT IS LITERARY THEORY?

Over the last two decades "literary theory" has emerged as a cultural event of significant proportions. In his 1986 presidential address to the Modern Language Association, J. Hillis Miller described the "violence and irrationality" surrounding the "attacks on theory" even as theory seemed to "triumph" as a noteworthy cultural event. He discussed the controversy of theory as linked somehow to widespread reconsiderations of the nature of knowledge and of aesthetic experience. The use here and elsewhere of the term "theory" in literary studies is curious and deserves some discussion. In 1949 W. K. Wimsatt argued that the semantic basis of literary art was too broad to be encompassed within the study of aesthetics and required its own study in what he called "literary theory." "Literary theorists of our day," Wimsatt argued, "have been content to say little about 'beauty' or about any overall aesthetic concept. In his most general formulation the literary theorist is likely to be content with something like 'human interest' " even though "disinterestedness, we remember, is something that Kant made a character of art." We will remember from the previous section of this book that 1949 was the same year in which Northrop Frye called for the "scientific" study of literature in his essay "The Function of Criticism at the Present Time" (in "What Is Criticism?").

Wimsatt marks "theory" as an attempt to replace the aesthetic focus on the disinterested effects of art by focusing, to some degree, on the relationship between literary meaning and *interested* writers and readers. Wimsatt's term *theory,* like Miller's use of the term, is tied up with the *problem* of knowledge conceived as the object of disinterested scientific investigation. Jurgen Habermas describes this problem in his account of the term's origin. "The *theoros,* " he notes, "was the representative sent by Greek cities to public celebrations. Through *theoria,* that is through looking on, he abandoned himself to the sacred events. In philosophical language, *theoria* was transferred to contemplation of the cosmos." Similarly, Jacques Derrida, in "The Principle of Reason," notes the relationship between "knowledge" and the sense of sight, leading to modes of objectification ("Deconstruction and Poststructuralism"). Habermas, unlike Derrida, goes on to oppose this "scientific" conception of "theory" to its use in the nonscientific discourses of the "historical-hermeneutic" sciences where theory contemplates meaning and not facts provided by observation. Habermas is repeating the gesture made by Michel Foucault in "What Is an Author?" ("Deconstruction and Poststructuralism") when he distinguishes between scientific theorists who establish particular scientific practices and the initiators of "discursive practice." Derrida calls for the questioning of "scientific normativity"—the assumptions behind scientific, as well as interpretative, understanding—and for analyses of "the rhetoric, the rites, the modes of presentation and demonstration that [the sciences] continue to respect." (See also Donna Haraway's "A Cyborg Manifesto" in "Feminism and Gender Studies.")

The conception of "theory" as the contemplation of meaning is congruent with Wimsatt's "literary theory" and Frye's argument that criticism should take its place among the social sciences. That is, if theory makes understanding and not the world its object, it does so by examining understanding outside of categories of aesthetic subjectivity. For this reason Miller in his presidential address defines "theory" as "the displacement in literary studies from a focus on the meaning of texts to a focus on the ways meaning is conveyed." As Barthes says of criticism (in "What Is Criticism?"), theory is the use of language to talk about language, or as Paul de Man says in this section, theory is a focus on referentiality as a problem rather than as something that reliably and unambiguously relates a reader to the "real world" of history and society. On the other hand, Frank Lentricchia describes "theory" very differently from this: "Theory," he writes, "is primarily a *process* of discovery of the lesson that I am calling historical; any single, formulable theory is a reduced version of the process, a frozen proposition which will tend to cover up the process it grew out of by projecting itself as an uncontingent system of ideas."

Like Lentricchia, in "The Race for Theory" Barbara Christian contests a general definition of theory by describing theory as a short-lived, fixed "constellation of ideas," "with its linguistic jargon, its emphasis on quoting its prophets, its tendency towards 'Biblical' exegesis, its refusal even to mention specific works of creative writers, far less contemporary ones, its preoccupations with mechanical analyses of language, graphs, algebraic equations, its gross generalizations about culture." In this critique Christian defines in "theory" a kind of passive acceptance of the status quo, another version of the political quietism and the esoteric aestheticism of the New Criticism. Others see in "theory" a kind of coterie from which they have been excluded. Still others, as Edward Said suggests in the "academic" narrative at the beginning of "The Politics of Knowledge," see it in solely political terms, between the activism of engagement of a fully politicized "cultural studies" and the old aesthetic traditionalism.

In her critique Christian is careful to distinguish herself from "traditionalist" criticisms of theory made by "the neutral humanists who see literature as pure expression and will not admit to the obvious control of its production, value, and distribution by those who have power." That is, she distinguishes herself from someone like E. D. Hirsch who describes what he calls "the Great Literary Theory Debate" as an "interest conflict" between those who seek to recover "primary interpretations"—namely, the intentional meanings of literary authors—and those who seek "secondary interpretation, or what Foucault calls 'resemanticizing the text.' " The struggle he sees in this debate is between "the needs and interests of undergraduates" who presumably simply want to get to "know" literature and its authors—who simply want to achieve the "humane [and aesthetic] pleasure of particular books"—and "the institutional advantages of secondary interpretation in the sphere of professorial publication."

Throughout the debate over the meaning of theory we can see a striking phenomenon of the past decade in which 'theory," as Martin Kreiswirth and Mark Cheetham have noted, "more and more, appears . . . on its own, without delimiting modifiers, either before or after. No longer is the term wedded to antecedent adjectives, as in *critical theory, literary theory,* or *psychoanalytic theory.* No longer does it routinely drag behind trailing genitives—*of social action, of language,* etc." This is so because "theory" has come to designate critique—as J. Hillis Miller says in this section, "it is 'criticism' in the fundamental sense of 'critique,' discriminating, testing out, in this case a testing out of the medium of which the bridge between theory and practice is made." Even Wimsatt uses the term "theory" in this way. "The mark of 'theory,' " Gerald Graff and Reginald Gibbons argue, "is inevitable at a moment when once-accepted definitions, categories and disciplinary boundaries have become matters of debate and controversy." Critique breaches the self-standing boundaries of knowledge. "While criticism . . . stands outside the object it criticizes, asserting norms against facts, and the dictates of reason against the unreasonableness of the world," Seyla Benhabib has argued, "critique refuses to stand outside its object and instead juxtaposes the immanent, normative self-understanding of its object to the material actuality of this object." Critique, then (as we suggested in the General Introduction), goes beyond the aesthetic wholeness of knowledge, questioning its seeming simplicity, its generalizing wholeness, and even the modalities of its accuracy. This is what Barthes means by the "active role" of theory he describes in *The Grain of the Voice:* its aim "is to reveal as past what we still believe to be present: theory mortifies, and that is what makes it avant-garde."

## THEORY, IDEOLOGY, AND THE AESTHETICS OF TRUTH

Literary theory arose, as Graff and Gibbons note, as an enactment of *critique*—the very questioning of the assumptions of understanding and personal aesthetic experience. It arose as the questioning of the assumptions governing the definition and understanding of "literature" itself (see the General Introduction). The form this critique has taken, to one degree or another, is to question the "disinterested" nature of personal aesthetic experience. Aesthetics claims various kinds of "disinterestedness" for itself. It claims, first of all, that it is a recognizable kind of phenomenon that is *self-consistent* (the possible object of knowledge) and *self-evident* (unmediated by linguistic, psychological, or culturally specific forms). Moreover, it claims that it is *self-contained* and is not affected by the status of the subject of (aesthetic) experience because its experience has no ulterior motives, no purposes beyond itself. It is *disengaged* from both personal and cultural history. The critique of aesthetics questions all of these assumptions. It questions the self-consistent and self-evident "truth" of aesthetics, and it questions the disengaged, disinterested "situation" of aesthetics. This is why the key terms of this section, along with "theory" and "aesthetics," are "ideology," "politics," and, implicitly along with these, "ethics." Paul de Man and J. Hillis Miller examine the "ideology" of aesthetics—what de Man has called "aesthetic ideology." Barbara Christian, Henry Louis Gates, Jr., and Edward Said, by contrast, explore the "politics" of aesthetics and literary studies—what Said calls the "politics of knowledge." (Derrida also uses the phrase, "politics of knowledge," in "The Principle of Reason.") Together they present a complex sense of the work of literary theory.

Such work needs to focus on ideology and ethics. Ideology, as Paul de Man says in "The Resistance to Theory," "is precisely the confusion of linguistic with natural reality, of reference with phenomenalism." Ideology takes the product of human activity as "natural"; it functions as the unconscious "ground" of self-evident truth. Catherine Belsey gives the most thorough discussion of ideology in *Contemporary Literary Criticism* in "Constructing the Subject: Deconstructing the Text" in ("Deconstruction and Poststructuralism"). Ideology, she says, "is not, therefore, to be thought of as a system of ideas in people's heads, nor as the expression at a higher level of real material relationships, but as the necessary condition of action within the social formation." It is the "condition of action" in this definition that links ideology to ethics. In the terms we have been pursuing here, ideology makes seemingly "disinterested" aesthetic experience—the object of the "humanist myth"—the *end* rather than the object of analysis. When such experience becomes the object of analysis, we have "theory." "The advent of theory," de Man says, "the break that is now so often being deplored and that sets it aside from literary history and from literary criticism, occurs with the introduction of linguistic terminology in the metalanguage of literature." Theory, he says, "upsets rooted ideologies by revealing the mechanics of their workings; it goes against a powerful philosophical tradition of which aesthetics is a prominent part; it upsets the established canon of literary works and blurs the borderlines between literary and non-literary discourse."

De Man pursues this thesis—in what is, as we shall note in the introduction to "Deconstruction and Poststructuralism," a classical "deconstructive" argument—by exploding the self-consistent truth of the concepts he employs. "Intuition," he writes, "implies perception, consciousness, experience, and leads at once into the world of logic and of understanding with all its correlatives, among which aesthetics occupies a prominent place." Yet it is the aim of theory precisely to analyze the self-consistency of "perception, consciousness, experience." De Man does this in "Resistance to Theory" by arguing that "a tension develops between methods of understanding and the knowledge which those methods allow one to reach"—that is, a tension between the methods of reading and definitions of literature we discussed in the "General Introduction." He does this, as he does throughout the closely argued essays that have been his contribution to literary scholarship, through a rigorous and ascetic mode of reasoning. In an essay by de Man things are defined precisely to arrive at a situation where those definitions can no longer function. At the beginning of "Resistance to Theory" he defines teaching as a rigorously "cognitive process in which self and other are only tangentially and contiguously involved," only to argue by the end of the essay that "persuasion by *proof*"—the very model of impersonal cognition—becomes an example of and "inseparable from" the "purely affective and intentional realm" of rhetoric. However, rhetoric is always involved with the contiguous involvement of self and other.

Similarly, de Man begins by asserting the "impossibility" of defining "literary theory," even though throughout the essay he offers a number of rigorously self-evident senses of "theory." He asserts, for instance, that theory possesses "impersonal consistency"; that it is both "philosophical," yet beyond the aesthetic categories of philosophy to the extent that "literary theory may now well have become a legitimate concern of philosophy but it cannot be assimilated to it." Its basis in linguistic analysis makes "the resistance to theory . . . a resistance to the rhetoric and tropological dimension of language." "Theory" for de Man is thoroughly *rhetorical*—a mode of "rhetorical reading," but as such it is "theory and not theory at the same time, the universal theory of the impossibility of theory." In this formulation "self-consistency" breaks down, and he concludes that "nothing can overcome the resistance to theory since theory *is* itself this resistance. The loftier the aims and the better the methods of literary theory, the less possible it becomes." In this paradox de Man has followed the path of logic and precision to demonstrate the "impossibility" of their self-consistency. Literature is the *site* of these contradictions, where both "aesthetic categories" and "mimetic" imitation—self-evident personal experience and self-consistent objects in the world—are "voided." That is, "the resistance to theory is a resistance to the rhetorical or tropological dimension of language, a dimension which is perhaps more explicitly in the foreground in literature (broadly conceived) than in other verbal manifestations or—to be somewhat less vague—which can be revealed in any verbal event when it is read textually."

If de Man examines the "truth" of aesthetic self-consistency, then J. Hillis Miller examines the "truth" of aesthetic self-evidence in "The Search for Grounds in Literary Study." Miller begins from a viewpoint directly at odds with the unexamined assumption of the self-evident value of literary education whose history Gerald Graff examines in "Introduction: The Humanist Myth" ("What Is Criticism?"). Miller describes four basic assumptions or "grounds" that govern literary study. These assumptions make understanding possible by "grounding" the "play" of the discourse—what Michel Foucault calls "the cancerous and dangerous proliferation of significations within a world where one is thrifty not only with one's resources and riches, but also with one's discourses and their significations." Foucault, in "What Is an Author?" ("Deconstruction and Poststructuralism"), is describing the ways in which an "author" grounds such proliferation.

The "author" (or "author-function") is an aspect of one of the grounds Miller describes, fitting within psychological taming of discourse, which reduces the play of meanings to the conscious and unconscious intentions of the subject of discourse. This "ground" governs the varieties of contemporary psychoanalytic criticism exampled throughout this book. A second ground Miller describes is social, which reduces the play of meanings to articulations of more or less explicit social forces: the Marxist "base," Foucauldian "power" and social "function," feminist "phallologocentrism," the "discursive organization" of society Michael Warner describes (in "Feminism and Gender Studies"), or most generally Burke's rhetorical definition of language and literature as "equipment for living" with other people. A third ground is language itself—the linguistics and rhetoric de Man describes—which reduces the play of meanings to the linguistic forms and structures analyzed by the linguistic methods of structuralist criticism.

The final ground Miller describes is, as he says, "properly religious, metaphysical, or ontological, though hardly in a traditional or conventional way." This ground, in Miller's argument, is the basis of Derrida's unconventional metaphysics. Like the "anagogic" framework of Frye's vision of literature as a "verbal universe" (as he calls it in *Anatomy of Criticism*), it grounds particular articulations in an overriding vision of the whole of "discourse" or cultural life. In fact, along with Frye's essay in "What Is Criticism?," these grounds also correspond to Barthes's

structural-linguistic definition of criticism, Showalter's feminist-subjective definition
of criticism, and Graff's historical definition of criticism in that section. (In this
schema, Eliot would correspond to the unself-conscious "appreciation" of criticism,
what de Man describes as his and New Criticism's "combination of original talent,
traditional learning, verbal wit and moral earnestness, an Anglo-American blend of
intellectual gentility.")

The point of Miller's discussion, however, is *ethical.* He—like Said, Spirak,
Derrida, and many others writing today—wants to test these assumptions against the
tasks they are set to perform. Most globally, he wants to test "literature" itself against
the "whole freight of the values" of culture that traditional humanistic education
claimed for it. To this end he describes the "imperialism" of each of the grounds he
describes, their tendency to reduce and dismiss all other explanations—that is, to
make each mode of understanding, in turn, a "base" to the superstructure and
epiphenomena of other discursive formations. Along with this tendency he also
describes the blind and almost hysterical resistance that contemporary versions of
these grounds—psychoanalytic, Marxist, structuralist, and deconstructive—have encountered in polemics, which have reduced what Derrida describes as the loss of "all
sense of proportion and control" among those attacking him and his followers
("Deconstruction and Poststructuralism"). (Derrida also presents a thorough discussion of the term "ground" Miller uses.)

The two aspects of "grounds" Miller describes—the "self-evident" ability to
account for everything by their adherents and the equally self-evident dismissal by
those who do not subscribe to them—have ethical implications. They define the
responsibility of criticism according to the larger aspects of human life, what Edward
Said calls "the central factor of human work, the actual participation of peoples in the
making of human life." When the study of literature is reducible to the study of
language, then criticism becomes "scientific" and "objective." It tends not to suggest
the cultural values Miller is describing and turns its attention to the linguistic conditions that allow such values to arise. When it is reducible to the study of psychology,
it becomes either a symtomatics, diagnosing particular authors or even particular eras
in terms of "health," or more usually, "disease," or it becomes a model for understanding based on more or less autonomous subjects. When it is reducible to the study
of society, then criticism becomes a program for social action—what Lentricchia calls
in *Criticism and Social Change* "the production of knowledge to the ends of power."
In this case the study of literature focuses on cultural values, but those values themselves are only defined collectively and socially and, like the other grounding gestures, leave out what it cannot describe as "basic." Finally, if the study of literature is
expandable to one, all-encompassing, "anagogic" vision or another, it leads too
readily to a preexisting vision of the world, to the "indeterminacies" of de Man's
deconstructive readings, or to Frye's Christian quest romance—or even to Eliot's
"mind of Europe," which is "much more important" than the poet's own private mind
and only accessible, as Eliot says, to "those who have personality and emotions [and
consequently] know what it means to want to escape from these things."

Both imperialism and resistance are acts that call for ethical judgment, what
Derrida describes as the questioning of the "values" that govern and authorize particular practices. Based on particular "grounds" of literary study, the theoretical ap-

proaches Miller describes account for only so much, even though each claims, as Raymond Williams says (in "Historical Critique"), "to exhaust the full range of human practice, human energy, human intention (. . . that extraordinary range of variations, both practiced and imagined, of which human beings are and have shown themselves to be capable)." The job for ethics, in John Dewey's traditional terms, is to deal "with conduct in its entirety, with reference . . . to what makes it conduct, its *ends,* its real meaning." Its job, in Julia Kristeva's more contemporary sense, is no longer its "coercive, customary manner of ensuring the cohesiveness of a particular group." Now, she continues, "ethics crops up wherever a code (mores, social contract) must be shattered in order to give way to the free play of negativity, need, desire, pleasure, and *jouissance,* before being put together again." In both cases—of the "old" traditional humanism and the new sense of theoretical uprootings that de Man describes in the contemporary debate—the issue can be and is being understood in terms of ethics rather than aesthetics. This requires a focus on the place of value in human affairs and, more specifically, the relationship that ethics always attempts to understand between *particular* and *local* activities and more *general* principles by which to judge them.

## THE ETHICS OF THEORY

If de Man and Miller pursue the intellectual "grounds" of theory, the other selections in this section examine the historical activity of theory—that is to say, the relationship, in Henry Louis Gates's terms, between "global, imperial theory" and the fact that "our own theoretical reflections must be as provisional, reactive, and local as the texts we reflect upon." In these terms, the debate in this section between Gates and Christian for and against theory is more complicated and less resolvable than it first seems precisely because, in their different ways, *both* are focused on the "politics" of theory and literary studies more generally. In fact Christian, Gates, and Said all see "politics" as the realm of the local and particular. When Christian distinguishes herself from "neutral humanists," she does so by explicitly mentioning their denial that "literature is, of necessity, political." Such a conception of "politics" can also be seen in Gates's catalog of the uses of Frantz Fanon's work in "classifying postcolonial theorists." If, as he argues, Derrida's general term "writing" can be renamed "colonial discourse" (Gates is following Gayatri Chakravorty Spivak here), it is because the *general* theory—de Man's "impersonal consistency"—can be related, provisionally, to the special case. Said makes a similar "move from the realm of interpretation to the realm of world politics," although he sees that this is "risky." The risk is that "the real work, the hard work" of intellectual activity will be lost in "identity politics" (the "politics" of asserting only particular identities and local interests). The work of intellectual activity, Said argues, "is nothing less than the reintegration of all those people and cultures, once confined and reduced to peripheral status, with the rest of the human race."

Such work is an activity of ethics. If aesthetics seems to relate particular experiences to a general system of experiences to achieve some regular relationship between feeling and meaning—some possibility of *disinterested* experience—then ethics seeks to relate particular and *interested* activities to a general—or "human"—system of values. This is always difficult because ethics has traditionally and repeatedly been used as a weapon in warfare between peoples, a way of asserting dominance of one group over another. This surely is Christian's objection to and fear of "theory": that while claiming to serve all, it serves only a few. This is why her question of *interests*—the "central question today," namely, "for whom are we doing what we are doing when we do literary criticism?"—is crucially a question of ethics and the central *theoretical* question when theory is conceived of in terms of ethics. For her, as she says, criticism "is done in order to save my own life. . . . For me literature is a way of knowing that I am not hallucinating." For Gates, in his tracing of uses of Fanon, ethics attempts to understand "the disruptive relation between narratives of subject-formation and narratives of [social] liberation"—the relation, as he says, between Freud and Marx. For this reason his larger discussion of the nature of colonialism and postcolonialism as they are defined in the theory and reading of literary and nonliterary texts enacts an intellectual politics that is not so very different from Christian's critique of theory.

Ethics, unlike aesthetics, does not do away with interests and the "politics" that accompany interests but attempts to situate them, as Said says, within a purview that is "unprovincial." Unlike aesthetics, ethics remains, in Said's term, a form of "worldliness" that judges values in terms of human work, which is always local, interested, and particular, but that also judges that work "by an appreciation not of some tiny, defensively constituted corner of the world, but of the large, many-windowed house of human culture as a whole." The reconsideration of the "ties between the text and the world" that Said describes as the larger work of "theory"—it is also, as we have suggested in the "General Introduction," the larger of work of "cultural studies" in departments of literature and language—remains an interested ethical activity. Said ends his essay with the "central" ethical question of interest. "Who benefits from leveling attacks on the canon?" he asks. "Certainly not the disadvantaged person or class whose history, if you bother to read it at all, is full of evidence that popular resistance to injustice has always derived immense benefits from literature and culture in general. . . ." "The crucial lesson," he goes on, "is that great antiauthoritarian uprisings made their earliest advances, not by denying the humanitarian and universalist claims of the general dominant culture, but by attacking the adherents of that culture for failing to uphold their own declared standards, for failing to extend them to all, as opposed to a small fraction, of humanity." These are, he says, "the great revisionary gestures" of literary theory.

This "theory," as we see, is a site of debate, "the contest for forms and values which any decent cultural work embodies, realizes, and contains." Such a contest is an ethical enterprise. Among other things, that enterprise weighs methods of understanding against objects of knowledge. As literary theory, it makes criticism self-conscious and examines explicitly methods of reading and definitions of literature. Whatever else they do, all the selections in this section do this. De Man defines literature as a mode of rhetoric that confounds the "grammars" of theory. Miller defines literature as the uncanny, dreadful, unmasterable: "the devastating experience of a transfiguration of the scene which leaves it nevertheless exactly the same," which calls for methods of mastery, the "slow reading" he cites from Nietzsche.

Christian defines literature as the site of intelligible feeling, so that both social and personal experience is validated, and, at the same time, reading itself is governed by this experience so that "literature" "compels you to read differently." Gates defines literature in relation to "social action" as he traces specifically in terms of the work of Frantz Fanon the kinds of approaches Miller describes abstractly.

Finally, Said defines literature as a site where "intellectual life" may be granted "the right to exist in a relatively disengaged atmosphere, and allow it a status that isn't disqualified by partisanship" so that "the ties between the text and the world" may be reconsidered "in a serious and uncoercive way." This site—both "partisan" and "global," "unprovincial" and "interested"—allows literary theory to move beyond "the indeterminacy of deconstructive reading, the airy insouciance of postaxiological criticism, [and] the casual reductiveness of some (but by no means all) ideological schools" to explore what is at stake in the contest for forms and values in literary and cultural studies.

## RELATED ESSAYS IN
## *CONTEMPORARY LITERARY CRITICISM*

Kenneth Burke, "Literature as Equipment for Living"
Jacques Derrida, "The Principle of Reason"
Shoshana Felman, "Psychoanalysis and Education"
Raymond Williams, "Base and Superstructure in Marxist Cultural Theory"
Gayatri Chakravorty Spivak, "Feminism and Critical Theory"
Donna Haraway, "A Cyborg Manifesto"
Meaghan Morris, "Banality in Cultural Studies"

## FURTHER READING

Barthes, Roland, *The Grain of the Voice: Interviews 1962–1980,* trans. Linda Coverdale (New York: Hill and Wang, 1985).

Benhabib, Seyla, *Critique, Norm, and Utopia: A Study of the Foundations of Critical Theory* (New York: Columbia University Press, 1986).

Dewey, John, "Outlines of a Critical Theory of Ethics," in *Early Works,* vol. 3, ed. Jo Ann Boydaton (Carbondale: Southern Illinois University Press, 1969).

Graff, Gerald, and Reginald Gibbons, "Preface," in *Criticism in the University,* eds. Gerald Graff and Reginald Gibbons (Evanston, IL: Northwestern University Press, 1985), 7–12.

Habermas, Jurgen, "Knowledge and Human Interests: A General Perspective," in *Knowledge and Human Interests,* trans. Jeremy Shapiro (Boston: Beacon Press, 1971).

Hirsch, E. D., "Back to History," in *Criticism in the University,* eds. Gerald Graff and Reginald Gibbons (Evanston, IL: Northwestern University Press, 1985), 189–97.

Hunter, Ian, "Aesthetics and Cultural Studies," in *Cultural Studies,* eds. Lawrence Grossberg, Cary Nelson and Paula Treicher (New York: Routledge, 1992), 347–367.

Jameson, Fredric, *Postmodernism, or, the Cultural Logic of Late Capitalism* (Durham; NC: Duke University Press, 1991).

Kreiswirth, Martin, and Mark Cheetham, "Introduction: 'Theory-Mad Beyond Redemption' (?)," in *Theory Between the Disciplines,* eds. Martin Kreiswirth and Mark Cheetham (Ann Arbor: University of Michigan Press, 1990), 1–16.

Kristeva, Julia, "The Ethics of Linguistics," in *Desire in Language,* trans. Thomas Gora, Alice Jardine, and Leon Roudiez (New York: Columbia University Press, 1980).

Lentricchia, Frank, *Criticism and Social Change* (Chicago: University of Chicago Press, 1983).

———, "On Behalf of Theory," in *Criticism in the University,* eds. Gerald Graff and Reginald Gibbons (Evanston, IL: Northwestern University Press, 1985), 105–10.

McGee, Patrick. *Telling the Other: The Question of Value in Modern and Postcolonial Writing* (Ithaca, NY: Cornell University Press, 1992).

Merod, Jim, *The Political Responsibility of the Critic* (Ithaca NY: Cornell University Press, 1987).

Miller, J. Hillis, *The Ethics of Reading* (New York: Columbia University Press, 1986).

———, "Presidential Address: The Triumph of Theory, the Resistance to Reading, and the Question of the Material Base," in *PMLA,* 102 (1987), 281–91.

Norris, Christopher, *Paul de Man: Deconstruction and the Critique of Aesthetic Ideology* (New York: Routledge, 1988).

Said, Edward, *The World, the Text, and the Critic* (Cambridge, MA: Harvard University Press, 1983).

Schleifer, Ronald, "The Advent of Theory and the Transformation of Journal Editing," in *Editors' Notes: Bulletin of the Council of Editors of Learned Journals,* 10, No. 1 (1991), 38–45.

Schleifer, Ronald, Robert Con Davis, and Nancy Mergler, *Culture and Cognition: The Boundaries of Literary and Scientific Understanding* (Ithaca NY: Cornell University Press, 1992).

Wimsatt, W. K., "The Domain of Criticism," in *The Verbal Icon* (Lexington: University of Kentucky Press, 1954), 221–32.

# 6

# Paul de Man
# 1919–1983

Paul de Man was born in Antwerp and received a Ph.D. from Harvard University in 1960. At the time of his death he was Sterling Professor of French and comparative literature at Yale University. In the course of his academic career—especially in its last decade—he became a major intellectual force in American literary studies. In large part this was because of his early and articulate understanding of the importance of Continental philosophy to literary studies and the ease with which he moved between philosophy and literature and among English, French, and German texts. His major form was the philosophical-literary essay, written in a severe and difficult, yet rewarding style. All his books are collections of essays, including *Blindness and Insight: Essays in the Rhetoric of Contemporary Criticism* (1971, reprint 1983); *Allegories of Reading: Figural Language in Rousseau, Nietzsche, Rilke, and Proust* (1979); *The Rhetoric of Romanticism* (1984); and *The Resistance to Theory* (1986). Soon after his death, a number of articles he wrote for the collaborationist press of Nazi-occupied Belgium were discovered and reprinted. These articles, and the fact that he never made public references to his youthful activity, have occasioned a great deal of controversy and much rereading of his work.

Still, that work has been immensely important in literary criticism for the last twenty years: it most clearly articulated the literary implications of post–World War II Continental philosophy. In his early work de Man described a kind of Sartrean existential approach to literature, and later he turned to the phenomenological criticism occasioned by Husserl and Heidegger. His major work since 1970, however, is marked by the influence of Nietzsche and poststructuralist thought—especially that of Jacques Derrida—and, with his Yale colleagues J. Hillis Miller and Geoffrey Hartman, he helped to define a distinctively American brand of deconstructive literary criticism.

The following essay, "The Resistance to Theory" (1982), is part of this effort, because ultimately de Man defines the general project of literary theory in terms strongly resonant with Yale School deconstruction. First published near the end of his life, this piece offers a condensed survey of de Man's views concerning philosophy, language, literature, and rhetoric. He argues that during the 1960s, literary theory emerged when approaches to literary texts became based on linguistics rather than history or aesthetics. A focus on the specific dynamics of language, he claims, defines an integral and transhistorical way by which to articulate literature's function—a consequence that can explain more traditional critics' resistance. However, since de Man describes language as a signifying system whose logical and grammatical dimensions are ineluctably undermined and destabilized by the rhetorical dimension of tropes or metaphors, literary theory itself becomes a self-divided project. On the one hand, its refined analytic techniques articulate, sometimes unwittingly, a critical process de Man summarizes as "reading," which documents how the unreliability of rhetorical tropes makes texts' meanings indeterminate. On the other hand, since this very linguistic feature threatens to unravel theory's own aspirations to formulate general literary principles, de Man claims that "resistance may be a built-in constituent of its discourse." Turning this paradoxical screw one notch further, he concludes that "technically correct rhetorical readings . . . are theory and not theory at the same time, the universal theory of the impossibility of theory." This is a dilemma without clear recourse since, as de Man explains in his own devious trope, rejecting theory on this basis "would be like rejecting anatomy because it has failed to cure mortality."

# The Resistance to Theory

This essay was not originally intended to address the question of teaching directly, although it was supposed to have a didactic and an educational function—which it failed to achieve. It was written at the request of the Committee on Research Activities of the Modern Language Association as a contribution to a collective volume entitled *Introduction to Scholarship in Modern Languages and Literatures.* I was asked to write the section on literary theory. Such essays are expected to follow a clearly determined program: they are supposed to provide the reader with a select but comprehensive list of the main trends and publications in the field, to synthesize and classify the main problematic areas and to lay out a critical and programmatic projection of the solutions which can be expected in the foreseeable future. All this with a keen awareness that, ten years later, someone will be asked to repeat the same exercise.

I found it difficult to live up, in minimal good faith, to the requirements of this program and could only try to explain, as concisely as possible, why the main theoretical interest of literary theory consists in the impossibility of its definition. The Committee rightly judged that this was an inauspicious way to achieve the pedagogical objectives of

the volume and commissioned another article. I thought their decision altogether justified, as well as interesting in its implications for the teaching of literature.

I tell this for two reasons. First, to explain the traces in the article of the original assignment which account for the awkwardness of trying to be more retrospective and more general than one can legitimately hope to be. But, second, because the predicament also reveals a question of general interest: that of the relationship between the scholarship (the key word in the title of the MLA volume), the theory, and the teaching of literature.

Overfacile opinion notwithstanding, teaching is not primarily an intersubjective relationship between people but a cognitive process in which self and other are only tangentially and contiguously involved. The only teaching worthy of the name is scholarly, not personal; analogies between teaching and various aspects of show business or guidance counseling are more often than not excuses for having abdicated the task. Scholarship has, in principle, to be eminently teachable. In the case of literature, such scholarship involves at least two complementary areas: historical and philological facts as the preparatory condition for understanding, and methods of reading or interpretation. The latter is admittedly an open discipline, which can, however, hope to evolve by rational means, despite internal crises, controversies and polemics. As a controlled reflection on the formation of method, theory rightly proves to be entirely compatible with teaching, and one can think of numerous important theoreticians who are or were also prominent scholars. A question arises only if a tension develops between methods of understanding and the knowledge which those methods allow one to reach. If there is indeed something about literature, as such, which allows for a discrepancy between truth and method, between *Wahrheit* and *Methode,* then scholarship and theory are no longer necessarily compatible; as a first casualty of this complication, the notion of "literature as such" as well as the clear distinction between history and interpretation can no longer be taken for granted. For a method that cannot be made to suit the "truth" of its object can only teach delusion. Various developments, not only in the contemporary scene but in the long and complicated history of literary and linguistic instruction, reveal symptoms that suggest that such a difficulty is an inherent focus of the discourse about literature. These uncertainties are manifest in the hostility directed at theory in the name of ethical and aesthetic values, as well as in the recuperative attempts of theoreticians to reassert their own subservience to these values. The most effective of these attacks will denounce theory as an obstacle to scholarship and, consequently, to teaching. It is worth examining whether, and why, this is the case. For if this is indeed so, then it is better to fail in teaching what should not be taught than to succeed in teaching what is not true.

A general statement about literary theory should not, in theory, start from pragmatic considerations. It should address such questions as the definition of literature (what is literature?) and discuss the distinction between literary and non-literary uses of language, as well as between literary and non-verbal forms of art. It should then proceed to the descriptive taxonomy of the various aspects and species of the literary genus and to the normative rules that are bound to follow from such a classification. Or, if one rejects a scholastic for a phenomenological model, one should attempt a phenomenology of the literary activity as writing, reading or both, or of the literary work as the product, the correlate of such an activity. Whatever the approach taken (and several other theoretically justifiable starting-points can be imagined) it is certain that considerable difficulties will arise at once, difficulties that cut so deep that even the most elementary task of scholarship, the delimitation of the corpus and the *état présent* of the question, is bound to end in confusion, not necessarily because the bibliography is so large but because it is impossible to fix its borderlines. Such predictable difficulties have not prevented many writers on literature from proceeding along theoretical rather than pragmatic lines, often with considerable success. It can be shown however that, in all cases, this success depends on the power of a system (philosophical, religious or ideological) that may well remain implicit but that determines an *a priori* conception of what is "literary" by starting out from the premises of the system rather than from the literary thing itself—if such a "thing" indeed exists. This last qualification is of course a real question which in fact accounts for the predictability of the difficulties just alluded to: if the condition of existence of an entity is itself particularly critical, then the theory of this entity is bound to fall back into the pragmatic. The difficult and inconclusive history of literary theory indicates that this is indeed the case for literature in an even more manifest manner than for other verbalized occurrences such as jokes, for example, or even dreams. The attempt to treat literature theoretically may as well resign itself to the fact that it has to start out from empirical considerations.

Pragmatically speaking, then, we know that there has been, over the last fifteen to twenty years, a strong interest in something called literary theory and that, in the United States, this interest has at times coincided with the importation and reception of foreign, mostly but not always continental, influences. We also know that this wave of interest now seems to be receding as some satiation or disappointment sets in after the initial enthusiasm. Such an ebb and flow is natural enough, but it remains interesting, in this case, because it makes the depth of the resistance to literary theory so manifest. It is a recurrent strategy of any anxiety to defuse what it considers threatening by magnification or minimization, by attributing to it claims to power of which it is bound to fall short. If a cat is called a tiger it can easily be dismissed as a paper tiger; the question remains however why one was so scared of the cat in the first place. The same tactic works in reverse: calling the cat a mouse and then deriding it for its pretense to be mighty. Rather than being drawn into this polemical whirlpool, it might be better to try to call the cat a cat and to document, however briefly, the contemporary version of the resistance to theory in this country.

The predominant trends in North American literary criticism, before the nineteen sixties, were certainly not averse to theory, if by theory one understands the rooting of literary exegesis and of critical evaluation in a system of some conceptual generality. Even the most intuitive, empirical and theoretically low-key writers on literature made use of a minimal set of concepts (tone, organic form, allusion, tradition, historical situation, etc.) of at least some general import. In several other cases, the interest in theory was publicly asserted and practiced. A broadly shared methodology, more or less overtly proclaimed, links together such influential text books of the era as *Understanding Poetry* (Brooks and Warren), *Theory of Literature* (Wellek and Warren) and *The Fields of Light* (Reuben Brower) or such theoretically oriented works as *The Mirror and the Lamp, Language as Gesture* and *The Verbal Icon*.

Yet, with the possible exception of Kenneth Burke and, in some respects, Northrop Frye, none of these authors would have considered themselves theoreticians in the post-1960 sense of the term, nor did their work provoke as strong reactions, positive or negative, as that of later theoreticians. There were polemics, no doubt, and differences in approach that cover a wide spectrum of divergencies, yet the fundamental curriculum of literary studies as well as the talent and training expected for them were not being seriously challenged. New Critical approaches experienced no difficulty fitting into the academic establishments without their practitioners having to betray their literary sensibilities in any way; several of its representatives pursued successful parallel careers as poets or novelists next to their academic functions. Nor did they experience difficulties with regard to a national tradition which, though certainly less tyrannical than its European counterparts, is nevertheless far from powerless. The perfect embodiment of the New Criticism remains, in many respects, the personality and the ideology of T. S. Eliot, a combination of original talent, traditional learning, verbal wit and moral earnestness, an Anglo-American blend of intellectual gentility not so repressed as not to afford tantalizing glimpses of darker psychic and political depths, but without breaking the surface of an ambivalent decorum that has its own complacencies and seductions. The normative principles of such a literary ambiance are cultural and ideological rather than theoretical, oriented towards the integrity of a social and historical self rather than towards the impersonal consistency that theory requires. Culture allows for, indeed advocates, a degree of cosmopolitanism, and the literary spirit of the American Academy of the fifties was anything but provincial. It had no difficulty appreciating and assimilating outstanding products of a kindred spirit that originated in Europe: Curtius, Auerbach, Croce, Spitzer, Alonso, Valéry and also, with the exception of some of his works, J. P. Sartre. The inclusion of Sartre in this list is important, for it indicates that the dominant cultural code we are trying to evoke cannot simply be assimilated to a political polarity of the left and the right, of the academic and non-academic, of Greenwich Village and Gambier, Ohio. Politically oriented and predominantly non-academic journals, of which the *Partisan Review* of the fifties remains the best example, did not (after due allowance is made for all proper reservations and distinctions) stand in any genuine opposition to the New Critical approaches. The broad, though negative, consensus that brings these extremely diverse trends and individuals together is their shared resistance to theory. This diagnosis is borne out by the arguments and complicities that have since come to light in a more articulate opposition to the common opponent.

The interest of these considerations would be at most anecdotal (the historical impact of twentieth-century literary discussion being so slight) if it were not for the theoretical implications of the resistance to theory. The local manifestations of this resistance are themselves systematic enough to warrant one's interest.

What is it that is being threatened by the approaches to literature that developed during the sixties and that now, under a variety of designations, make up the ill-defined and somewhat chaotic field of literary theory? These approaches cannot be simply equated with any particular method or country. Structuralism was not the only trend to dominate the stage, not even in France, and structuralism as well as semiology are inseparable from

prior tendencies in the Slavic domain. In Germany, the main impulses have come from other directions, from the Frankfurt school and more orthodox Marxists, from post-Husserlian phenomenology and post-Heideggerian hermeneutics, with only minor inroads made by structural analysis. All these trends have had their share of influence in the United States, in more or less productive combinations with nationally rooted concerns. Only a nationally or personally competitive view of history would wish to hierarchize such hard-to-label movements. The possibility of doing literary theory, which is by no means to be taken for granted, has itself become a consciously reflected-upon question and those who have progressed furthest in this question are the most controversial but also the best sources of information. This certainly includes several of the names loosely connected with structuralism, broadly enough defined to include Saussure, Jakobson and Barthes as well as Greimas and Althusser, that is to say, so broadly defined as to be no longer of use as a meaningful historical term.

Literary theory can be said to come into being when the approach to literary texts is no longer based on non-linguistic, that is to say historical and aesthetic, considerations or, to put it somewhat less crudely, when the object of discussion is no longer the meaning or the value but the modalities of production and of reception of meaning and of value prior to their establishment—the implication being that this establishment is problematic enough to require an autonomous discipline of critical investigation to consider its possibility and its status. Literary history, even when considered at the furthest remove from the platitudes of positivistic historicism, is still the history of an understanding of which the possibility is taken for granted. The question of the relationship between aesthetics and meaning is more complex, since aesthetics apparently has to do with the *effect* of meaning rather than with its content *per se*. But aesthetics is in fact, ever since its development just before and with Kant, a phenomenalism of a process of meaning and understanding, and it may be naive in that it postulates (as its name indicates) a phenomenology of art and of literature which may well be what is at issue. Aesthetics is part of a universal system of philosophy rather than a specific theory. In the nineteenth-century philosophical tradition, Nietzsche's challenge of the system erected by Kant, Hegel and their successors is a version of the general question of philosophy. Nietzsche's critique of metaphysics includes, or starts out from, the aesthetic, and the same could be argued for Heidegger. The invocation of prestigious philosophical names does not intimate that the present-day development of literary theory is a by-product of larger philosophical speculations. In some rare cases, a direct link may exist between philosophy and literary theory. More frequently, however, contemporary literary theory is a relatively autonomous version of questions that also surface, in a different context, in philosophy, though not necessarily in a clearer and more rigorous form. Philosophy, in England as well as on the Continent, is less freed from traditional patterns than it sometimes pretends to believe and the prominent, though never dominant, place of aesthetics among the main components of the system is a constitutive part of this system. It is therefore not surprising that contemporary literary theory came into being from outside philosophy and sometimes in conscious rebellion against the weight of its tradition. Literary theory may now well have become a legitimate concern of philosophy but it cannot be assimilated to it, either factually or theoretically. It contains a necessarily pragmatic moment that certainly weakens it as theory but that adds a subversive element of unpredictability and makes it something of a wild card in the serious game of the theoretical disciplines.

The advent of theory, the break that is now so often being deplored and that sets it aside from literary history and from literary criticism, occurs with the introduction of linguistic terminology in the metalanguage about literature. By linguistic terminology is meant a terminology that designates reference prior to designating the referent and takes into account, in the consideration of the world, the referential function of language or, to be somewhat more specific, that considers reference as a function of language and not necessarily as an intuition. Intuition implies perception, consciousness, experience, and leads at once into the world of logic and of understanding with all its correlatives, among which aesthetics occupies a prominent place. The assumption that there can be a science of language which is not necessarily a logic leads to the development of a terminology which is not necessarily aesthetic. Contemporary literary theory comes into its own in such events as the application of Saussurian linguistics to literary texts.

The affinity between structural linguistics and literary texts is not as obvious as, with the hindsight of history, it now may seem. Peirce, Saussure, Sapir and Bloomfield were not originally concerned with literature at all but with the scientific foundations of linguistics. But the interest of philologists such as Roman Jakobson or literary critics such as Roland Barthes in semiology reveals the natural attraction of literature to a theory of linguistic signs. By considering language as a system of signs and of signification rather than as an established pattern of meanings, one displaces or even suspends the traditional barriers between literary and presumably non-literary uses of language and liberates the corpus from the secular weight of textual canonization. The results of the encounter between semiology and literature went considerably further than those of many other theoretical models—philological, psychological or classically epistemological—which writers on literature in quest of such models had tried out before. The responsiveness of literary texts to semiotic analysis is visible in that, whereas other approaches were unable to reach beyond observations that could be paraphrased or translated in terms of common knowledge, these analyses revealed patterns that could only be described in terms of their own, specifically linguistic, aspects. The linguistics of semiology and of literature apparently have something in common that only their shared perspective can detect and that pertains distinctively to them. The definition of this something, often referred to as literariness, has become the object of literary theory.

Literariness, however, is often misunderstood in a way that has provoked much of the confusion which dominates today's polemics. It is frequently assumed, for instance, that literariness is another word for, or another mode of, aesthetic response. The use, in conjunction with literariness, of such terms as style and stylistics, form or even "poetry" (as in "the poetry of grammar"), all of which carry strong aesthetic connotations, helps to foster this confusion, even among those who first put the term in circulation. Roland Barthes, for example, in an essay properly and revealingly dedicated to Roman Jakobson, speaks eloquently of the writer's quest for a perfect coincidence of the phonic properties of a word with its signifying function. "We would also wish to insist on the Cratylism of the name (and of the sign) in Proust. . . . Proust sees the relationship between signifier and signified as motivated, the one copying the other and representing in its material form the signified essence of the thing (and not the thing itself). . . . This realism (in the scholastic sense of the word), which conceives of names as the 'copy' of the ideas, has taken, in Proust, a radical form. But one may well ask whether it is not more or less consciously present in all writing and whether it is possible to be a writer without some sort of belief

in the natural relationship between names and essences. The poetic function, in the widest sense of the word, would thus be defined by a Cratylian awareness of the sign, and the writer would be the conveyor of this secular myth which wants language to imitate the idea and which, contrary to the teachings of linguistic science, thinks of signs as motivated signs."[1] To the extent that Cratylism assumes a convergence of the phenomenal aspects of language, as sound, with its signifying function as referent, it is an aesthetically oriented conception; one could, in fact, without distortion, consider aesthetic theory, including its most systematic formulation in Hegel, as the complete unfolding of the model of which the Cratylian conception of language is a version. Hegel's somewhat cryptic reference to Plato, in the *Aesthetics,* may well be interpreted in this sense. Barthes and Jakobson often seem to invite a purely aesthetic reading, yet there is a part of their statement that moves in the opposite direction. For the convergence of sound and meaning celebrated by Barthes in Proust and, as Gérard Genette has decisively shown,[2] later dismantled by Proust himself as a seductive temptation to mystified minds, is also considered here to be a mere *effect* which language can perfectly well achieve, but which bears no substantial relationship, by analogy or by ontologically grounded imitation, to anything beyond that particular effect. It is a rhetorical rather than an aesthetic function of language, an identifiable trope (paronomasis) that operates on the level of the signifier and contains no responsible pronouncement on the nature of the world—despite its powerful potential to create the opposite illusion. The phenomenality of the signifier, as sound, is unquestionably involved in the correspondence between the name and the thing named, but the link, the relationship between word and thing, is not phenomenal but conventional.

This gives the language considerable freedom from referential restraint, but it makes it epistemologically highly suspect and volatile, since its use can no longer be said to be determined by considerations of truth and falsehood, good and evil, beauty and ugliness, or pleasure and pain. Whenever this autonomous potential of language can be revealed by analysis, we are dealing with literariness and, in fact, with literature as the place where this negative knowledge about the reliability of linguistic utterance is made available. The ensuing foregrounding of material, phenomenal aspects of the signifier creates a strong illusion of aesthetic seduction at the very moment when the actual aesthetic function has been, at the very least, suspended. It is inevitable that semiology or similarly oriented methods be considered formalistic, in the sense of being aesthetically rather than semantically valorized, but the inevitability of such an interpretation does not make it less aberrant. Literature involves the voiding, rather than the affirmation, of aesthetic categories. One of the consequences of this is that, whereas we have traditionally been accustomed to reading literature by analogy with the plastic arts and with music, we now have to recognize the necessity of a non-perceptual, linguistic moment in painting and music, and learn to *read* pictures rather than to *imagine* meaning.

If literariness is not an aesthetic quality, it is also not primarily mimetic. Mimesis becomes one trope among others, language choosing to imitate a non-verbal entity just as paronomasis "imitates" a sound without any claim to identity (or reflection on difference) between the verbal and non-verbal elements. The most misleading representation of literariness, and also the most recurrent objection to contemporary literary theory, considers it as pure verbalism, as a denial of the reality principle in the name of absolute fictions, and for reasons that are said to be ethically and politically shameful. The attack reflects the anxiety of the aggressors rather than the guilt of the accused. By allowing for the necessity of a non-phenomenal linguistics, one frees the discourse on literature from naive oppositions between fiction and reality, which are themselves an offspring of an uncritically mimetic conception of art. In a genuine semiology as well as in other linguistically oriented theories, the referential function of language is not being denied—far from it; what is in question is its authority as a model for natural or phenomenal cognition. Literature is fiction not because it somehow refuses to acknowledge "reality," but because it is not *a priori* certain that language functions according to principles which are those, or which are *like* those, of the phenomenal world. It is therefore not *a priori* certain that literature is a reliable source of information about anything but its own language.

It would be unfortunate, for example, to confuse the materiality of the signifier with the materiality of what it signifies. This may seem obvious enough on the level of light and sound, but it is less so with regard to the more general phenomenality of space, time or especially of the self; no one in his right mind will try to grow grapes by the luminosity of the word "day," but it is very difficult not to conceive the pattern of one's past and future existence as in accordance with temporal and spatial schemes that belong to fictional narratives and not to the world. This does not mean that fictional narratives are not part of the world and of reality; their impact upon the world may well be all too strong for comfort. What we call ideology is precisely the confusion of linguistic with natural reality, of reference with phenomenalism. It follows that, more than any other mode of inquiry, including economics, the linguistics of literariness is a powerful and indispensable tool in the unmasking of ideological aberrations, as well as a determining factor in accounting for their occurrence. Those who reproach literary theory for being oblivious to social and historical (that is to say ideological) reality are merely stating their fear at having their own ideological mystifications exposed by the tool they are trying to discredit. They are, in short, very poor readers of Marx's *German Ideology*.

In these all too summary evocations of arguments that have been much more extensively and convincingly made by others, we begin to perceive some of the answers to the initial question: what is it about literary theory that is so threatening that it provokes such strong resistance and attacks? It upsets rooted ideologies by revealing the mechanics of their workings; it goes against a powerful philosophical tradition of which aesthetics is a prominent part; it upsets the established canon of literary works and blurs the borderlines between literary and non-literary discourse. By implication, it may also reveal the links between ideologies and philosophy. All this is ample enough reason for suspicion, but not a satisfying answer to the question. For it makes the tension between contemporary literary theory and the tradition of literary studies appear as a mere historical conflict between two modes of thought that happen to hold the stage at the same time. If the conflict is merely historical, in the literal sense, it is of limited theoretical interest, a passing squall in the intellectual weather of the world. As a matter of fact, the arguments in favor of the legitimacy of literary theory are so compelling that it seems useless to concern oneself with the conflict at all. Certainly, none of the objections to theory, presented again and again, always misinformed or based on crude misunderstandings of such terms as mimesis, fiction, reality, ideology, reference and, for that matter, relevance, can be said to be of genuine rhetorical interest.

It may well be, however, that the development of literary theory is itself overdetermined by complications inherent in its very project and unsettling with regard to its status as a scientific discipline. Resistance may be a built-in constituent of its discourse, in a manner that would be inconceivable in the natural sciences and unmentionable in the social sciences. It may well be, in other words, that the polemical opposition, the systematic non-understanding and misrepresentation, the unsubstantial but eternally recurrent objections, are the displaced symptoms of a resistance inherent in the theoretical enterprise itself. To claim that this would be sufficient reason not to envisage doing literary theory would be like rejecting anatomy because it has failed to cure mortality. The real debate of literary theory is not with its polemical opponents but rather with its own methodological assumptions and possibilities. Rather than asking why literary theory is threatening, we should perhaps ask why it has such difficulty going about its business and why it lapses so readily either into the language of self-justification and self-defense or else into the overcompensation of a programmatically euphoric utopianism. Such insecurity about its own project calls for self-analysis, if one is to understand the frustrations that attend upon its practitioners, even when they seem to dwell in serene methodological self-assurance. And if these difficulties are indeed an integral part of the problem, then they will have to be, to some extent, a-historical in the temporal sense of the term. The way in which they are encountered on the present local literary scene as a resistance to the introduction of linguistic terminology in aesthetic and historical discourse about literature is only one particular version of a question that cannot be reduced to a specific historical situation and called modern, post-modern, post-classical or romantic (not even in Hegel's sense of the term), although its compulsive way of forcing itself upon us in the guise of a system of historical periodization is certainly part of its problematic nature. Such difficulties can be read in the text of literary theory at all times, at whatever historical moment one wishes to select. One of the main achievements of the present theoretical trends is to have restored some awareness of this fact. Classical, medieval and Renaissance literary theory is now often being read in a way that knows enough about what it is doing not to wish to call itself "modern."

We return, then, to the original question in an attempt to broaden the discussion enough to inscribe the polemics inside the question rather than having them determine it. The resistance to theory is a resistance to the use of language about language. It is therefore a resistance to language itself or to the possibility that language contains factors or functions that cannot be reduced to intuition. But we seem to assume all too readily that, when we refer to something called "language," we know what it is we are talking about, although there is probably no word to be found in the language that is as overdetermined, self-evasive, disfigured and disfiguring as "language." Even if we choose to consider it at a safe remove from any theoretical model, in the pragmatic history of "language," not as a concept, but as a didactic assignment that no human being can bypass, we soon find ourselves confronted by theoretical enigmas. The most familiar and general of all linguistic models, the classical *trivium,* which considers the science of language as consisting of grammar, rhetoric, and logic (or dialectics), is in fact a set of unresolved tensions powerful enough to have generated an infinitely prolonged discourse of endless frustration of which contemporary literary theory, even at its most self-assured, is one more chapter. The difficulties extend to the internal articulations between the constituent parts as well as the articulation of the field of language with the knowledge of the world in general, the link between the *trivium* and the *quadrivium,* which covers the non-verbal sciences of number (arithmetic), of space (geometry), of motion (astronomy), and of time (music). In the history of philosophy, this link is traditionally, as well as substantially, accomplished by way of logic, the area where the

rigor of the linguistic discourse about itself matches up with the rigor of the mathematical discourse about the world. Seventeenth-century epistemology, for instance, at the moment when the relationship between philosophy and mathematics is particularly close, holds up the language of what it calls geometry *(mos geometricus),* and which in fact includes the homogeneous concatenation between space, time and number, as the sole model of coherence and economy. Reasoning *more geometrico* is said to be "almost the only mode of reasoning that is infallible, because it is the only one to adhere to the true method, whereas all other ones are by natural necessity in a degree of confusion of which only geometrical minds can be aware."[3] This is a clear instance of the interconnection between a science of the phenomenal world and a science of language conceived as definitional logic, the pre-condition for a correct axiomatic-deductive, synthetic reasoning. The possibility of thus circulating freely between logic and mathematics has its own complex and problematic history as well as its contemporary equivalences with a different logic and a different mathematics. What matters for our present argument is that this articulation of the sciences of language with the mathematical sciences represents a particularly compelling version of a continuity between a theory of language, as logic, and the knowledge of the phenomenal world to which mathematics gives access. In such a system, the place of aesthetics is preordained and by no means alien, provided the priority of logic, in the model of the *trivium,* is not being questioned. For even if one assumes, for the sake of argument and against a great deal of historical evidence, that the link between logic and the natural sciences is secure, this leaves open the question, within the confines of the *trivium* itself, of the relationship between grammar, rhetoric and logic. And this is the point at which literariness, the use of language that foregrounds the rhetorical over the grammatical and the logical function, intervenes as a decisive but unsettling element which, in a variety of modes and aspects, disrupts the inner balance of the model and, consequently, its outward extension to the nonverbal world as well.

Logic and grammar seem to have a natural enough affinity for each other and, in the tradition of Cartesian linguistics, the grammarians of Port-Royal experienced little difficulty at being logicians as well. The same claim persists today in very different methods and terminologies that nevertheless maintain the same orientation toward the universality that logic shares with science. Replying to those who oppose the singularity of specific texts to the scientific generality of the semiotic project, A. J. Greimas disputes the right to use the dignity of "grammar" to describe a reading that would not be committed to universality. Those who have doubts about the semiotic method, he writes, "postulate the necessity of constructing a grammar for each particular text. But the essence *(le propre)* of a grammar is its ability to account for a large number of texts, and the metaphorical use of the term . . . fails to hide the fact that one has, in fact, given up on the semiotic project."[4] There is no doubt that what is here prudently called "a large number" implies the hope at least of a future model that would in fact be applicable to the generation of all texts. Again, it is not our present purpose to discuss the validity of this methodological optimism, but merely to offer it as an instance of the persistent symbiosis between grammar and logic. It is clear that, for Greimas as for the entire tradition to which he belongs, the grammatical and the logical functions of language are co-extensive. Grammar is an isotope of logic.

It follows that, as long as it remains grounded in grammar, any theory of language, including a literary one, does not threaten what we hold to be the underlying principle of all cognitive and aesthetic linguistic systems. Grammar stands in the service of logic which, in turn, allows for the passage to the knowledge of the world. The study of grammar, the first of the *artes liberales,* is the necessary pre-condition for scientific and humanistic knowledge. As long as it leaves this principle intact, there is nothing threatening about literary theory. The continuity between theory and phenomenalism is asserted and preserved by the system itself. Difficulties occur only when it is no longer possible to ignore the epistemological thrust of the rhetorical dimension of discourse, that is, when it is no longer possible to keep it in its place as a mere adjunct, a mere ornament within the semantic function.

The uncertain relationship between grammar and rhetoric (as opposed to that between grammar and logic) is apparent, in the history of the *trivium,* in the uncertain status of figures of speech or tropes, a component of language that straddles the disputed borderlines between the two areas. Tropes used to be part of the study of grammar but were also considered to be the semantic agent of the specific function (or effect) that rhetoric performs as persuasion as well as meaning. Tropes, unlike grammar, pertain primordially to language. They are text-producing functions that are not necessarily patterned on a non-verbal entity, whereas grammar is by definition capable of extra-linguistic generalization. The latent tension between rhetoric and grammar precipitates out in the problem of reading, the process that necessarily partakes of both. It turns out that the resistance to theory is in fact a resistance to reading, a resistance that is perhaps at its most effective, in contemporary studies, in the methodologies that call themselves theories of reading but nevertheless avoid the function they claim as their object.

What is meant when we assert that the study of literary texts is necessarily dependent on an act of reading, or when we claim that this act is being systematically avoided? Certainly more than the tautology that one has to have read at least some parts, however small, of a text (or read some part, however small, of a text about this text) in order to be able to make a statement about it. Common as it may be, criticism by hearsay is only rarely held up as exemplary. To stress the by no means self-evident necessity of reading implies at least two things. First of all, it implies that literature is not a transparent message in which it can be taken for granted that the distinction between the message and the means of communication is clearly established. Second, and more problematically, it implies that the grammatical decoding of a text leaves a residue of indetermination that has to be, but cannot be, resolved by grammatical means, however extensively conceived. The extension of grammar to include para-figural dimensions is in fact the most remarkable and debatable strategy of contemporary semiology, especially in the study of syntagmatic and narrative structures. The codification of contextual elements well beyond the syntactical limits of the sentence leads to the systematic study of metaphrastic dimensions and has considerably refined and expanded the knowledge of textual codes. It is equally clear, however, that this extension is always strategically directed towards the replacement of rhetorical figures by grammatical codes. This tendency to replace a rhetorical by a grammatical terminology (to speak of hypotaxis, for instance, to designate anamorphic or metonymic tropes) is part of an explicit program, a program that is entirely admirable in its intent since it tends towards the mastering and the clarification of meaning. The replacement of a hermeneutic by a semiotic model, of interpretation by decoding, would represent, in view of the baffling historical instability of textual meanings (including, of course, those of canonical texts), a

considerable progress. Much of the hesitation associated with "reading" could thus be dispelled.

The argument can be made, however, that no grammatical decoding, however refined, could claim to reach the determining figural dimensions of a text. There are elements in all texts that are by no means ungrammatical, but whose semantic function is not grammatically definable, neither in themselves nor in context. Do we have to interpret the genitive in the title of Keats' unfinished epic *The Fall of Hyperion* as meaning "Hyperion's Fall," the case story of the defeat of an older by a newer power, the very recognizable story from which Keats indeed started out but from which he increasingly strayed away, or as "Hyperion Falling," the much less specific but more disquieting evocation of an actual process of falling, regardless of its beginning, its end or the identity of the entity to whom it befalls to be falling? This story is indeed told in the later fragment entitled *The Fall of Hyperion,* but it is told about a character who resembles Apollo rather than Hyperion, the same Apollo who, in the first version (called *Hyperion*), should definitely be triumphantly standing rather than falling if Keats had not been compelled to interrupt, for no apparent reason, the story of Apollo's triumph. Does the title tell us that Hyperion is fallen and that Apollo stands, or does it tell us that Hyperion and Apollo (and Keats, whom it is hard to distinguish, at times, from Apollo) are interchangeable in that all of them are necessarily and constantly falling? Both readings are grammatically correct, but it is impossible to decide from the context (the ensuing narrative) which version is the right one. The narrative context suits neither and both at the same time, and one is tempted to suggest that the fact that Keats was unable to complete either version manifests the impossibility, for him as for us, of reading his own title. One could then read the word "Hyperion" in the title *The Fall of Hyperion* figurally, or, if one wishes, intertextually, as referring not to the historical or mythological character but as referring to the title of Keats' own earlier text *(Hyperion)*. But are we then telling the story of the failure of the first text as the success of the second, the Fall of *Hyperion* as the Triumph of *The Fall of Hyperion?* Manifestly, yes, but not quite, since the second text also fails to be concluded. Or are we telling the story of why all texts, as texts, can always be said to be falling? Manifestly yes, but not quite, either, since the story of the fall of the first version, as told in the second, applies to the first version only and could not legitimately be read as meaning also the fall of *The Fall of Hyperion*. The undecidability involves the figural or literal status of the proper name Hyperion as well as of the verb falling, and is thus a matter of figuration and not of grammar. In "Hyperion's Fall," the word "fall" is plainly figural, the representation of a figural fall, and we, as readers, read this fall standing up. But in "Hyperion Falling," this is not so clearly the case, for if Hyperion can be Apollo and Apollo can be Keats, then he can also be us and his figural (or symbolic) fall becomes his and our literal falling as well. The difference between the two readings is itself structured as a trope. And it matters a great deal how we read the title, as an exercise not only in semantics, but in what the text actually does to us. Faced with the ineluctable necessity to come to a decision, no grammatical or logical analysis can help us out. Just as Keats had to break off his narrative, the reader has to break off his understanding at the very moment when he is most directly engaged and summoned by the text. One could hardly expect to find solace in this "fearful symmetry" between the author's and reader's plight since, at this point, the symmetry is no longer a formal but an actual trap, and the question no longer "merely" theoretical.

This undoing of theory, this disturbance of the stable cognitive field that extends from grammar to logic to a general science of man and of the phenomenal world, can in its turn be made into a theoretical project of rhetorical analysis that will reveal the inadequacy of grammatical models of non-reading. Rhetoric, by its actively negative relationship to grammar and to logic, certainly undoes the claims of the *trivium* (and by extension, of language) to be an epistemologically stable construct. The resistance to theory is a resistance to the rhetorical or tropological dimension of language, a dimension which is perhaps more explicitly in the foreground in literature (broadly conceived) than in other verbal manifestations or—to be somewhat less vague—which can be revealed in any verbal event when it is read textually. Since grammar as well as figuration is an integral part of reading, it follows that reading will be a negative process in which the grammatical cognition is undone, at all times, by its rhetorical displacement. The model of the *trivium* contains within itself the pseudo-dialectic of its own undoing and its history tells the story of this dialectic.

This conclusion allows for a somewhat more systematic description of the contemporary theoretical scene. This scene is dominated by an increased stress on reading as a theoretical problem or, as it is sometimes erroneously phrased, by an increased stress on the reception rather than on the production of texts. It is in this area that the most fruitful exchanges have come about between writers and journals of various countries and that the most interesting dialogue has developed between literary theory and other disciplines, in the arts as well as in linguistics, philosophy and the social sciences. A straightforward *report* on the present state of literary theory in the United States would have to stress the emphasis on reading, a direction which is already present, moreover, in the New Critical tradition of the forties and the fifties. The methods are now more technical, but the contemporary interest in a poetics of literature is clearly linked, traditionally enough, to the problems of reading. And since the models that are being used certainly are no longer *simply* intentional and centered on an identifiable self, nor *simply* hermeneutic in the postulation of a single originary, pre-figural and absolute text, it would appear that this concentration on reading would lead to the rediscovery of the theoretical difficulties associated with rhetoric. This is indeed the case, to some extent; but not quite. Perhaps the most instructive aspect of contemporary theory is the refinement of the techniques by which the threat inherent in rhetorical analysis is being avoided at the very moment when the efficacy of these techniques has progressed so far that the rhetorical obstacles to understanding can no longer be mistranslated in thematic and phenomenal commonplaces. The resistance to theory which, as we saw, is a resistance to reading, appears in its most rigorous and theoretically elaborated form among the theoreticians of reading who dominate the contemporary theoretical scene.

It would be a relatively easy, though lengthy, process to show that this is so for theoreticians of reading who, like Greimas or, on a more refined level, Riffaterre or, in a very different mode, H. R. Jauss or Wolfgang Iser—all of whom have a definite, though sometimes occult, influence on literary theory in this country—are committed to the use of grammatical models or, in the case of *Rezeptionsästhetik,* to traditional hermeneutic models that do not allow for the problematization of the phenomenalism of reading and therefore remain uncritically confined within a theory of literature rooted in aesthetics. Such an argument would be easy to make because, once a reader has become aware of the rhetorical dimensions of a text, he will not be amiss in finding textual instances that are irreducible to grammar or to historically determined meaning, provided only he is willing to acknowledge what he is bound to notice. The problem quickly becomes the more baffling one of having to account for the shared reluctance to acknowledge the obvious. But the argument would be lengthy because it has to involve a textual analysis that cannot avoid being somewhat elaborate; one can succinctly suggest the grammatical indetermination of a title such as *The Fall of Hyperion,* but to confront such an undecidable enigma with the critical reception and reading of Keats' text requires some space.

The demonstration is less easy (though perhaps less ponderous) in the case of the theoreticians of reading whose avoidance of rhetoric takes another turn. We have witnessed, in recent years, a strong interest in certain elements in language whose function is not only not dependent on any form of phenomenalism but on any form of cognition as well, and which thus excludes, or postpones, the consideration of tropes, ideologies, etc., from a reading that would be primarily performative. In some cases, a link is reintroduced between performance, grammar, logic, and stable referential meaning, and the resulting theories (as in the case of Ohmann) are not in essence distinct from those of avowed grammarians or semioticians. But the most astute practitioners of a speech act theory of reading avoid this relapse and rightly insist on the necessity to keep the actual performance of speech acts, which is conventional rather than cognitive, separate from its causes and effects—to keep, in their terminology, the illocutionary force separate from its perlocutionary function. Rhetoric, understood as persuasion, is forcefully banished (like Coriolanus) from the performative moment and exiled in the affective area of perlocution. Stanley Fish, in a masterful essay, convincingly makes this point.[5] What awakens one's suspicion about this conclusion is that it relegates persuasion, which is indeed inseparable from rhetoric, to a purely affective and intentional realm and makes no allowance for modes of persuasion which are no less rhetorical and no less at work in literary texts, but which are of the order of persuasion by *proof* rather than persuasion by seduction. Thus to empty rhetoric of its epistemological impact is possible only because its tropological, figural functions are being bypassed. It is as if, to return for a moment to the model of the *trivium,* rhetoric could be isolated from the generality that grammar and logic have in common and considered as a mere correlative of an illusionary power. The equation of rhetoric with psychology rather than with epistemology opens up dreary prospects of pragmatic banality, all the drearier if compared to the brilliance of the performative analysis. Speech act theories of reading in fact repeat, in a much more effective way, the grammatization of the *trivium* at the expense of rhetoric. For the characterization of the performative as sheer convention reduces it in effect to a grammatical code among others. The relationship between trope and performance is actually closer but more disruptive than what is here being proposed. Nor is this relationship properly captured by reference to a supposedly "creative" aspect of performance, a notion with which Fish rightly takes issue. The performative power of language can be called positional, which differs considerably from conventional as well as from "creatively" (or, in the technical sense, intentionally) constitutive. Speech act oriented theories of reading read only to the extent that they prepare the way for the rhetorical reading they avoid.

But the same is still true even if a "truly" rhetorical reading that would stay clear of any undue phenomenalization or of any undue grammatical or performative codification of the text could be conceived—something which is not necessarily impossible and for which the aims and methods of literary theory should certainly strive. Such a reading would indeed appear as the methodical undoing of the grammatical construct and, in its systematic disarticulation of the *trivium,* will be theoretically sound as well as effective. Technically correct rhetorical readings may be boring, monotonous, predictable and unpleasant, but they are irrefutable. They are also totalizing (and potentially totalitarian) for since the structures and functions they expose do not lead to the knowledge of an entity (such as language) but are an unreliable process of knowledge production that prevents all entities, including linguistic entities, from coming into discourse as such, they are indeed universals, consistently defective models of language's impossibility to be a model language. They are, always in theory, the most elastic theoretical and dialectical model to end all models and they can rightly claim to contain within their own defective selves all the other defective models of reading-avoidance, referential, semiological, grammatical, performative, logical, or whatever. They are theory and not theory at the same time, the universal theory of the impossibility of theory. To the extent however that they are theory, that is to say teachable, generalizable and highly responsive to systematization, rhetorical readings, like the other kinds, still avoid and resist the reading they advocate. Nothing can overcome the resistance to theory since theory *is* itself this resistance. The loftier the aims and the better the methods of literary theory, the less possible it becomes. Yet literary theory is not in danger of going under; it cannot help but flourish, and the more it is resisted, the more it flourishes, since the language it speaks is the language of self-resistance. What remains impossible to decide is whether this flourishing is a triumph or a fall.

## NOTES

1. Roland Barthes, "Proust et les noms," in *To Honor Roman Jakobson* (The Hague: Mouton, 1967), part I, pp. 157–58.

2. "Proust et le language indirect," in *Figures II* (Paris: Seuil, 1969).

3. Blaise Pascal, "De l'esprit géométrique et de l'art de persuader," in *Oeuvres complètes,* L. Lafuma, ed. (Paris: Seuil, 1963), pp. 349ff.

4. A. J. Greimas, *Du Sens* (Paris: Seuil, 1970), p. 13.

5. Stanley Fish, "How to Do Things with Austin and Searle: Speech Act Theory and Literary Criticism," in *MLN* 91 (1976), pp. 983–1025. See especially p. 1008.

# 7

# J. Hillis Miller
# 1928–

J. Hillis Miller, a distinguished critic and scholar, received a Ph.D. from Harvard University in 1951. He taught for more than two decades at Johns Hopkins University and fourteen years at Yale University. He is now Distinguished Professor of English and comparative literature at the University of California, Irvine. At Yale with Geoffrey Hartman and Paul de Man, Miller had been vital in introducing Continental literary studies and philosophy to the Anglo-American academic community, practicing versions of deconstructive and poststructuralist criticism. Miller's work has always been at the forefront of critical discourse in the United States; in fact his career—including a formalist dissertation, books that approach texts from a phenomenological perspective, and his present work in deconstructive criticism—epitomizes postwar American literary studies. His major works include *Charles Dickens: The World of His Novels* (1958); *The Disappearance of God* (1963); *The Poets of Reality: Six Twentieth-Century Writers* (1965); *The Form of Victorian Fiction* (1968); *Thomas Hardy: Distance and Desire* (1970); *Fiction and Repetition* (1982); *The Linguistic Moment* (1985); *The Ethics of Reading* (1987); *Hawthorne and History: Defacing It* (1991); *Theory Now and Then* (1991); *Tropes, Parables, Performatives: Essays on Twentieth-Century Literature* (1991); *Victorian Subjects* (1991); *Ariadne's Thread: Story Lines* (1992); and *Illustration* (1992).

The most striking aspect of Miller's work is his lucid faithfulness to the literary or critical texts he examines in the context of the most profound questions of the experience of those texts. Throughout his career Miller has sought in many ways for such a "metaphysical" reading of literature, but never without maintaining a close sense of the literary texts themselves. As he wrote in *Fiction and Repetition,* "A theory is all too easy to refute or deny, but a reading can be controverted only by going through the difficult task of rereading the work in question and proposing an alternate reading."

In "The Search for Grounds in Literary Study" (1984) Miller specifically returns to Matthew Arnold in the kind of rereading he is suggesting. In this essay he is attempting to do several things simultaneously. First of all, he is trying to account for the *experience* of reading, to make sense of—or at least describe—the strange uncanny experience reading sometimes creates. Second, he is trying to articulate the unconscious assumptions that govern critical writing: he argues that there are four "grounds" on which to base reading—linguistic, social, psychological, and ontological or metaphysical—and that various critics and schools of critics assume one or the other of these. Moreover, these grounds have two striking qualities: first, they are "imperialist," by which Miller means they tend to reduce all understanding to their own base, and second, they each occasion remarkable resistance, almost hysterical denial (in the Freudian sense of the word) way beyond proportion. A third aim of this essay is to question the larger "ground" of literary study, to ask why it is that literature since Arnold's time has been "burdened" with the weight of carrying and maintaining cultural values. For Miller this is not a necessary aspect of literature, and one can indeed question why so many people have seen this as a function of criticism, what he calls the "scrupulously slow reading" of which Nietzsche speaks in his call "back to the texts!"

# The Search for Grounds in Literary Study

*You ask me in what I think or have thought you going wrong: in this: that you would never take your assiette as something determined final and unchangeable for you and proceed to work away on the basis of that: but were always poking and patching and cobbling at the assiette itself—*

(Matthew Arnold, *Letters to Clough*)[1]

*. . . perhaps one is a philologist still, that is to say, a teacher of slow reading [ein Lehrer des langsamen Lesens].*

(Friedrich Nietzsche, "Preface" to *Daybreak*)[2]

An important passage in George Eliot's *Daniel Deronda* (1876) speaks of the liability of the heroine, Gwendolen Harleth, to sudden, inexplicable fits of hysterical terror or of "spiritual dread." She has these fits when faced with open spaces: "Solitude in any wide scene impressed her with an undefined feeling of immeasurable existence aloof from her, in the midst of which she was helplessly incapable of asserting herself."[3]

A strange little paragraph by Maurice Blanchot entitled "Une scène primitive," "A Primitive Scene," and published just a century later, in 1976, describes a "similar" "experience," ascribed this time to a child of seven or eight standing at the window and looking at a wintry urban or suburban scene outside:

Ce qu'il voit, le jardin, les arbres d'hiver, le mur d'une maison; tandis qu'il voit, sans doute à la manière d'un enfant, son espace de jeu, il se lasse et lentement regarde en haut vers le ciel ordinaire, avec les nuages, la lumière grise, le jour terne et sans lointain. Ce qui se passe ensuite: le ciel, le *même* ciel, soudain ouvert, noir absolument et vide absolument, révélant (comme par la vitre brisée) une telle absence que tout s'y est depuis toujours et à jamais perdu, au point que s'y affirme et s'y dissipe le savoir vertigineux que rien est ce qu'il y a, et d'abord rien au-delà.

[What he saw, the garden, the winter trees, the wall of a house; while he looked, no doubt in the way a child does, at his play area, he got bored and slowly looked higher toward the ordinary sky, with the clouds, the grey light, the day flat and without distance. What happened then: the sky, the *same* sky, suddenly opened, black absolutely and empty absolutely, revealing (as if the window had been broken) such an absence that everything is since forever and for forever lost, to the point at which there was affirmed and dispersed there the vertiginous knowledge that nothing is what there is there, and especially nothing beyond.][4]

"Rien est ce qu'il y a, et d'abord rien au-delà": nothing is what there is there, and first of all nothing beyond. As in the case of Wallace Stevens's "The Snow Man," where the listener and watcher in the snow, "nothing himself, beholds/Nothing that is not there and the nothing that is,"[5] the devastating experience of a transfiguration of the scene which leaves it nevertheless exactly the same, the *same* sky, is the confrontation of a nothing which somehow is, has being, and which absorbs into itself any beyond or transcendence. In this primitive scene, original and originating, for Blanchot's child, or possibly even for Blanchot as a child, the sky definitely does not open to reveal heavenly light or choirs of angels singing "Glory, glory, glory." If the effect on Gwendolen Harleth in Eliot's novel of confronting open space in solitude is sometimes hysterical outbursts, the effect on Blanchot's child of an opening of the sky which does not open is seemingly endless tears of a "ravaging joy [joie ravagéant]."

I take these details from *Daniel Deronda* and from Blanchot's little scene, quite arbitrarily, or almost quite arbitrarily, as parables for the terror or dread readers may experience when they confront a text which seems irreducibly strange, inexplicable, perhaps even mad, for example Blanchot's *Death Sentence* [*L'arrêt de mort*]. As long as we have not identified the law by which the text can be made reasonable, explicable, it is as if we have come face to face with an immeasurable existence aloof from us, perhaps malign, perhaps benign, in any case something we have not yet mastered and assimilated into what we already know. It is as if the sky had opened, while still remaining the same sky, for are not those words there on the page familiar and ordinary words, words in our own language or mother tongue, words whose meaning we know? And yet they have suddenly opened and become terrifying, inexplicable. On the one hand, our task as readers is to transfer to reading Henry James's

injunction to the observer of life, the novice writer: "Try to be one of those on whom nothing is lost." A good reader, that is, especially notices oddnesses, gaps, anacoluthons, non sequiturs, apparently irrelevant details, in short, all the marks of the inexplicable, all the marks of the unaccountable, perhaps of the mad, in a text. On the other hand, the reader's task is to reduce the inexplicable to the explicable, to find its reason, its law, its ground, to make the mad sane. The task of the reader, it will be seen, is not too different from the task of the psychoanalyst.

Current criticism tends to propose one or another of the three following grounds on the basis of which the anomalies of literature may be made lawful, the unaccountable accountable: society, the more or less hidden social or ideological pressures which impose themselves on literature and reveal themselves in oddnesses; individual psychology, the more or less hidden psychic pressures which impose themselves on a work of literature and make it odd, unaccountable; language, the more or less hidden rhetorical pressures, or pressures from some torsion within language itself as such, which impose themselves on the writer and make it impossible for his work to maintain itself as an absolutely lucid and reasonable account.

The stories or *récits* of Maurice Blanchot, as well as his criticism, propose a fourth possibility. Though this possibility is, in the case of Blanchot at least, exceedingly difficult to name in so many words, and though the whole task of the reader of Blanchot could be defined as a (perhaps impossible) attempt to make this definition clear to oneself or to others, it can be said that this fourth possibility for the disturber of narrative sanity and coherence, a disruptive energy neither society nor individual psychology nor language itself, is properly religious, metaphysical, or ontological, though hardly in a traditional or conventional way. To borrow a mode of locution familiar to readers of Blanchot it is an ontology without ontology. Nor is it to be defined simply as a species of negative theology. Blanchot gives to this "something" that enters into the words or between the words the names, among others, of it [*il*]; the thing [*la chose*]; dying [*mourir*]; the neutral [*le neutre*]; the non-presence of the eternal return [*le retour éternel*]; writing [*écrire*]; the thought [*la pensée*]; the truth [*la verité*]; the other of the other [*l'autre de l'autre*]; meaning something encountered in our relations to other people, especially relations involving love, betrayal, and that ultimate betrayal by the other of our love for him or her, the death of the other. To list these names in this way cannot possibly convey very much, except possibly, in their multiplicity and incoherence, a glimpse of the inadequacy of any one of them and of the fact that all of them must in one way or another be figurative rather than literal. What sort of "thing" is it which cannot be pinned down and labelled with one single name, so that all names for it are improper, whether proper or generic? All Blanchot's writing is a patient, continual, long-maintained attempt to answer this question, the question posed by the experience recorded in "A Primitive Scene."

Two further features may be identified of my four proposed modes of rationalizing or accounting for or finding grounds for the irrational or unaccountable in any literary account.

The first feature seems obvious enough, though it is evaded often enough to need emphasizing. This is the exclusivity or imperialism of any one of the four. Each has a mode of explanation or of grounding the anomalous in literature which demands to exercise sovereign control over the others, to make the others find their ground in *it*. You cannot have all four at once or even any two of them without ultimately grounding, or rather without having already implicitly grounded, all but one in the single regal ur-explanation. Psychological explanations tend to see lin-

guistic, religious, or social explanations as ultimately finding *their* cause in individual human psychology. Social explanations see human psychology, language, and religion as epiphenomena of underlying and determining social forces, the "real" conditions of class, production, consumption, exchange. Linguistic explanations tend to imply or even openly to assert that society, psychology, and religion are "all language," generated by language in the first place and ultimately to be explained by features of language. Metaphysical explanations see society, psychology, and language as secondary, peripheral. Each of these modes of grounding explanation asserts that it is the true "principle of reason," the true *Satz vom Grund,* the others bogus, an abyss not a ground. Each asserts a jealous will to power over the others.

The second feature of these four modes of explaining oddnesses in literature is the strong resistance each of them seems to generate in those to whom they are proposed. The resistance, for example, to Sigmund Freud's assertion of a universal unconscious sexual etiology for neurosis is notorious, and that resistance has by no means subsided. In Marxist theory, for example that of Louis Althusser in *For Marx,* "ideology" is the name given to the imaginary structures, whereby men and women resist facing directly the real economic and social conditions of their existence. "Ideology, then," says Althusser, "is the expression of the relation between men and their 'world,' that is, the (overdetermined) unity of the real relation and the imaginary relation between them and their real conditions of existence."[6] There is a tremendous resistance to totalizing explanations which say, "It's all language," the resistance encountered, for example, by structuralism, semiotics, and by misunderstandings of so-called "deconstruction" today. Many people, finally, seem able to live on from day to day and year to year, even as readers of literature, without seeing religious or metaphysical questions as having any sort of force or substance. It is not the case that man is everywhere and universally a religious or metaphysical animal. George Eliot, speaking still of Gwendolen, describes eloquently the latter's resistance to two of my sovereign principles of grounding:

> She had no permanent consciousness of other fetters, or of more spiritual restraints, having always disliked whatever was presented to her under the name of religion, in the same way that some people dislike arithmetic and accounts: it had raised no other emotion in her, no alarm, no longing; so that the question whether she believed it had not occurred to her, any more than it had occurred to her to inquire into the conditions of colonial property and banking, on which, as she had had many opportunities of knowing, the family fortune was dependent. (pp. 89–90)

Why this resistance to looking into things, including works of literature, all the way down to the bottom is so strong and so universal I shall not attempt here to explain. Perhaps it is inexplicable. Perhaps it is a general consensus that, as Conrad's Winnie Verloc in *The Secret Agent* puts it, "life doesn't stand much looking into."[7] It might be better not to know.

Is it legitimate to seek in literature a serious concern for such serious topics, to see works of literature as in one way or another interrogations of the ground, taking ground in the sense of a sustaining metaphysical foundation outside language, outside nature, and outside the human mind? The role granted to poetry or to "literature" within our culture and in particular within our colleges and universities today is curiously contradictory. The contradiction is an historical inheritance going back at least to Kant and to eighteenth-century aesthetic theory or "critical philosophy." The tradition comes down from the en-

lightenment through Romantic literary theory and later by way of such figures as Matthew Arnold (crucial to the development of the "humanities" in American higher education) to the New Criticism and the academic humanism of our own day. On the one hand the enjoyment of poetry is supposed to be the "disinterested" aesthetic contemplation of beautiful or sublime organic forms made of words. It is supposed to be "value free," without contamination by use of the poem for any cognitive, practical, ethical, or political purposes. Such appropriations, it is said, are a misuse of poetry. According to this aestheticizing assumption one ought to be able to read Dante and Milton, for example, or Aeschylus and Shelley, without raising either the question of the truth or falsity of their philosophical and religious beliefs, or the question of the practical consequences of acting on those beliefs. Cleanth Brooks, for example, in a recent essay vigorously reaffirming the tenets of the New Criticism, presents *Paradise Lost* as a case in point: "Milton tells us in the opening lines of *Paradise Lost* that his purpose is to 'justify the ways of God to men,' and there is no reason to doubt that this was what he hoped to do. But what we actually have in the poem is a wonderful interconnected story of events in heaven and hell and upon earth, with grand and awesome scenes brilliantly painted and with heroic actions dramatically rendered. In short, generations of readers have found that the grandeur of the poem far exceeds any direct statement of theological views. The point is underscored by the fact that some readers who reject Milton's theology altogether nevertheless regard *Paradise Lost* as a great poem."[8]

On the other hand, literature has been weighted down in our culture with the burden of carrying from generation to generation the whole freight of the values of that culture, what Matthew Arnold called "the best that is known and thought in the world."[9] Cleanth Brooks elsewhere in his essay also reiterates this traditional assumption about literature. Walter Jackson Bate, in a recent polemical essay, sees specialization, including the New Criticism's specialization of close reading, as greatly weakening the humanities generally and departments of English in particular. Bate regrets the good old days (from 1930 to 1950) when departments of English taught everything under the sun but reading as such, in a modern reincarnation of the Renaissance ideal of *litterae humaniores*. The literature components of the humanities in our colleges and universities, and departments of English in particular, have with a good conscience undertaken, after hurrying through a soupçon of rhetoric and poetics, to teach theology, metaphysics, psychology, ethics, politics, social and intellectual history, even the history of science and natural history, in short, "Allerleiwissenschaft," like Carlyle's Professor Diogenes Teufelsdröck.[10]

The implicit reasoning behind this apparently blatant contradiction may not be all that difficult to grasp, though the reasoning will only restate the contradiction. It is just because, and only because, works of literature are stable, self-contained, value-free objects of disinterested aesthetic contemplation that they can be trustworthy vehicles of the immense weight of values they carry from generation to generation uncontaminated by the distortions of gross reality. Just because the values are enshrined in works of literature, uninvested, not collecting interest, not put out to vulgar practical use, they remain pure, not used up, still free to be reappropriated for whatever use we may want to make of them. Has not Kant in the third critique, the *Critique of Judgment,* once and for all set works of art as reliable and indispensable middle member *(Mittelglied),* between cognition (pure reason, theory, the subject of the first critique) and ethics (practical reason, praxis, ethics, the subject of the second critique)? And has not Kant defined beauty, as embodied for example in a poem, as "the symbol of moral-

ity [*Symbol der Sittlichkeit*]"?[11] Both Bate and René Wellek, the latter in another outspoken polemical essay with the nice title of "Destroying Literary Studies," invoke Kant, or rather their understanding of Kant, as having settled these matters once and for all, as if there were no more need to worry about them, and as if our understanding of Kant, or rather theirs, could safely be taken for granted: ". . . Why not," asks Bate, "turn to David Hume, the greatest skeptic in the history of thought . . . and then turn to Kant, by whom so much of this is answered?" (p. 52); "One can doubt the very existence of aesthetic experience," says Wellek, "and refuse to recognize the distinctions, clearly formulated in Immanuel Kant's *Critique of Judgment,* between the good, the true, the useful, and the beautiful."[12] So much is at stake here that it is probably a good idea to go back and read Kant for ourselves, no easy task to be sure, in order to be certain that he says what Bate and Wellek say he says.

When Matthew Arnold, the founding father, so to speak, of the American concept of the humanities, praises the virtues of disinterested contemplation, he is being faithful to the Kantian inheritance, no doubt by way of its somewhat vulgarizing distortions in Schiller. It was, and is, by no means necessary to have read Kant to be a Kantian of sorts. Arnold's full formulaic definition of criticism, in "The Function of Criticism at the Present Time" (1864), is "a disinterested endeavour to learn and propagate the best that is known and thought in the world."[13] He speaks elsewhere in the same essay of the "disinterested love of a free play of the mind on all subjects, for its own sake."[14] When Arnold, in a well-known statement in "The Study of Poetry" (1880) which has echoed down the decades as the implicit credo of many American departments of English, says: "The future of poetry is immense, because in poetry, where it is worthy of its high destinies, our race, as time goes on, will find an ever surer and surer stay," he goes on to make it clear that poetry is a "stay" just because it is detached from the question of its truth or falsity as fact. Poetry can therefore replace religion when the fact fails religion. Poetry is cut off from such questions, sequestered in a realm of disinterested fiction. Just for this reason poetry is a "stay," a firm resting place when all else gives way, like a building without a solid foundation. "There is not a creed which is not shaken," says Arnold in his melancholy litany, "not an accredited dogma which is not shown to be questionable, not a received tradition which does not threaten to dissolve. Our religion has materialized itself in the fact, in the supposed fact; it has attached its emotion to the fact, and now the fact is failing it. But for poetry the idea is everything; the rest is a world of illusion, of divine illusion. Poetry attaches its emotion to the idea; the idea *is* the fact."[15] The image here is that of a self-sustaining linguistic fiction or illusion which holds itself up by a kind of intrinsic magic of levitation over the abyss, like an aerial floating bridge over chaos, as long as one does not poke and patch at the assiette. This bridge or platform may therefore hold up also the ideas the poem contains and the readers who sustain themselves by these ideas.

Arnold had this double or even triple notion of the staying power of poetry already in mind when, in 1848 or 1849, many years before writing "The Study of Poetry," he wrote to Arthur Hugh Clough: "Those who cannot read G[ree]k sh[ou]ld read nothing but Milton and parts of Wordsworth: the state should see to it. . . ."[16] Most Freshman and Sophomore courses in American colleges and universities in "Major English Authors" are still conceived in the spirit of Arnold's categorical dictum. The uplifting moral value of reading Milton and parts of Wordsworth, so important that it should be enforced by the highest civil authority, is initially stylistic. Arnold opposes the solemn, elevated, composing "grand" style of Homer, or, failing that, of Milton and parts of Wordsworth, to the "confused multitudinousness" (ibid.) of Browning, Keats, and Tennyson, the Romantics and Victorians generally, excepting that part of Wordsworth. The occasion of Arnold's letter to Clough is the devastating effect on him of reading Keats's letters: "What a brute you were to tell me to read Keats's Letters. However it is over now: and reflexion resumes her power over agitation" (p. 96). From Keats Arnold turns to the Greeks, to Milton, and to those parts of Wordsworth to subdue his inner agitation as well as to protect himself from the agitation without.

Only secondary to the sustaining effect of the grand style as such are the "ideas" expressed in that style. A writer, says Arnold, "must begin with an Idea of the world in order not to be prevailed over by the world's multitudinousness" (ibid., p. 97). The Idea, so to speak, is the style, or the style is the Idea, since the grand style is nothing but the notion of composure, elevation, coherence, objectivity, that is, just the characteristics of the grand style. This combination of grand elevated style and presupposed, preconceived, or preposited grand comprehensive Idea of the world (never mind whether it is empirically verifiable) not only composes and elevates the mind but also fences it off from the confused multitudinousness outside and the danger therefore of confused multitudinousness within. The latter, Arnold, in the "Preface" of 1853, calls "the dialogue of the mind with itself."[17] He associates it especially with the modern spirit, and fears it more than anything else. It is the dissolution of the mind's objectivity, calm, and unity with itself. This composing, lifting up, and fencing out through literature takes place, to borrow from one of the authors Arnold tells us exclusively to read, as God organizes chaos in the work of creation, or as Milton, at the beginning of *Paradise Lost,* prays that his interior chaos, likened to the unformed Abyss, may be illuminated, elevated, impregnated, and grounded by the Holy Spirit or heavenly muse: "Thou from the first/Was present, and with mighty wings outspread/Dove-like satst brooding on the vast Abyss/And madst it pregnant: What in me is dark/Illumine, what is low raise and support" (*Paradise Lost,* I, 19–23).

It is only a step from Kant's image in paragraph 59 of the *Critique of Judgment* of art or poetry as *hypotyposis* [*Hypotypose*], indirect symbols of intuitions for which there is no direct expression,[18] to Hegel's assertion that sublime poetry, like parable, fable, and apologue, is characterized by the non-adequation and dissimilarity between symbol and symbolized, what he calls the *Sichnichtentsprechen beider,* the noncorrespondence of the two.[19] It is only another step beyond that to I. A. Richards' assertion, in *Principles of Literary Criticism,* with some help from Jeremy Bentham's theory of fictions, that the function of poetry is to produce an equilibrium among painfully conflicting impulses and thereby to provide fictive solutions to real psychological problems. Another step in this sequence (which is not even a progression, radicalizing or deepening, but a movement in place), takes us to Wallace Stevens's resonant formulation in the *Adagia* of what all these writers in somewhat different ways are saying: "The final belief is to believe in a fiction, which you know to be a fiction, there being nothing else. The exquisite truth is to know that it is a fiction and that you believe in it willingly."[20]

Proof that Matthew Arnold still plays an indispensable role within this sequence as the presumed base for a conservative humanism is a forceful recent article by Eugene Goodheart, "Arnold at the Present Time," with accompanying essays and responses by George Levine, Morris Dickstein, and Stuart M. Tave.[21] As is not surprising, the oppositions among these essays come down to a question of how one reads Arnold. If Goodheart grossly misrepresents "deconstruction" and

the sort of "criticism as critique" I advocate (which is not surprising), he is also a bad reader or a non-reader of Arnold. Goodheart takes for granted the traditional misreading of Arnold which has been necessary to make him, as Goodheart puts it, "the inspiration of humanistic study in England and America" (p. 451). Levine, Dickstein, and Tave are, it happens, far better and more searching readers of Arnold. Adjudication of differences here is of course possibly only by a response to that call, "Back to the texts!," which must be performed again and again in literary study. Nothing previous critics have said can be taken for granted, however authoritative it may seem. Each reader must do again for himself the laborious task of a scrupulous slow reading, trying to find out what the texts actually say rather than imposing on them what she or he wants them to say or wishes they said. Advances in literary study are not made by the free invention of new conceptual or historical schemes (which always turn out to be old ones anew in any case), but by that grappling with the texts which always has to be done over once more by each new reader. In the case of Arnold the poetry and prose must be read together, not assumed to be discontinuous units or an early negative stage and a late affirmative stage negating the earlier negation. Far from offering a firm "assiette" to the sort of humanism Goodheart advocates, such a careful reading of Arnold will reveal him to be a nihilist writer through and through, nihilist in the precise sense in which Nietzsche or Heidegger defines the term: as a specifically historical designation of the moment within the development of Western metaphysics when the highest values devalue themselves and come to nothing as their transcendent base dissolves:[22] "There is not a creed which is not shaken, not an accredited dogma which is not shown to be questionable, not a received tradition which does not threaten to dissolve." "I am nothing and very probably never shall be anything," said Arnold in one of the letters to Clough.[23]

A house built on sand, in this case a humanistic tradition built on the shaky foundation of a misreading of Matthew Arnold, cannot stand firmly. To put this another way, the affirmations of Goodheart, Bate, Wellek, and others like them participate inevitably in the historical movement of nihilism ("the history of the next two centuries," Nietzsche called it)[24] which they contest. Most of all they do this in the act itself of contestation. "The question arises," says Heidegger in the section on nihilism in his *Nietzsche,* "whether the innermost essence of nihilism and the power of its dominion do not consist precisely in considering the nothing merely as a nullity [*nur für etwas Nichtiges*], considering nihilism as an apotheosis of the merely vacuous [*der blossen Leere*], as a negation [*eine Verneinung*] that can be set to rights at once by an energetic affirmation."[25]

In a brilliant essay on "The Principle of Reason: The University in the Eyes of its Pupils,"[26] Jacques Derrida identifies the way the modern university and the study of literature within it are based on the domination of the Leibnizian principle of reason, what in German is called "der Satz vom Grund," the notion that everything can and should be accounted for, *Omnis veritatis reddi ratio potest,* that nothing is without reason, *nihil est sine ratione.* Following Nietzsche and Heidegger, Derrida also argues that so-called nihilism is an historical moment which is "completely symmetrical to, thus dependent on, the principle of reason" (p. 15). Nihilism arises naturally and inevitably during a period, the era of technology, when the principle of universal accountability holds sway in the organization of society and of the universities accountable to that society. "For the principle of reason," says Derrida, "may have obscurantist and nihilist effects. They can be seen more or less everywhere, in Europe and America among those who believe they are defending philosophy, literature, and the humanities against these new modes of questioning that are also a new relation to language and tradition, a new affirmation, and new ways of taking responsibility. We can easily see on which side obscurantism and nihilism are lurking when on occasion great professors or representatives of prestigious institutions lose all sense of proportion and control; on such occasions they forget their principles that they claim to defend in their work and suddenly begin to heap insults, to say whatever comes into their heads on the subject of texts that they obviously have never opened or that they have encountered through a mediocre journalism that in other circumstances they would pretend to scorn" (p. 15). Obviously much is at stake here, and we must go carefully, looking before and after, testing the ground carefully, taking nothing for granted.

If such a tremendous burden is being placed on literature throughout all the period from Kant to academic humanists of our own day like Bate and Goodheart, it is of crucial importance to be sure that literature is able to bear the weight, or that it is a suitable instrument to perform its function. The question is too grave for its answer to be left untested. To raise the question of the weight-bearing capacities of the medium of poetry is of course not the only thing criticism can do or ought to do, but I claim it is one all-important task of literary study. The question in question here is not of the thematic content of or the assertions made by works of literature but of the weight-bearing characteristics of the medium of literature, that is, of language. It is a question of what the language of poetry is and does. Is it indeed solid enough and trustworthy enough to serve, according to the metaphor Kant proposes at the end of the introduction to the *Critique of Judgment,* as the fundamentally necessary bridge passing back and forth between pure cognition and moral action, between *theoria* and *praxis?* "The realm of the natural concept under the one legislation," says Kant, "and that of the concept of freedom under the other are entirely removed [*gänzlich abgesondert*] from all mutual influence [*wechselseitigen Einfluss*] which they might have on one another (each according to its fundamental laws) by the great gulf [*die grosse Kluft*] that separates the supersensible from phenomena [*das Übersinnliche von den Erscheinungen*]. The concept of freedom determines nothing in respect of the theoretical cognition of nature, and the internal concept determines nothing in respect of the practical laws of freedom. So far, then, it is not possible to throw a bridge from the one realm to the other [*eine Brücke von einem Gebiete zu dem andern hinüber zu schlagen*]."[27]

Art or the aesthetic experience is the only candidate for a possible bridge. The whole of the *Critique of Judgment* is written to test out the solidity, so to speak, of the planks by which this indispensable bridge from the realm of knowledge to the realm of moral action might be built, across the great gulf that separates them. If the "beauty" of the work of art is the sensible symbol of morality, it is, on the other hand, the sensible embodiment of the pure idea, what Hegel was to call, in a famous formulation, and in echo of Kant's word *Erscheinungen,* "the sensible shining forth of the idea [*das sinnliche 'scheinen' der Idee*]."[28] As Hegel elsewhere puts it, "art occupies the intermediate ground between the purely sensory and pure thought [*steht in der 'Mitte' zwischen der umittelbaren Sinnlichkeit und dem ideellen Gedanken*]" (Ibid., I, 60, my trans.). Whether Kant or Hegel establish satisfactorily the solidity of this ground, its adequacy as a bridge, is another question, one that a full reading of Kant's third *Kritik* and of Hegel's *Ästhetik* would be necessary to answer. That the answer is affirmative does not go without saying, nor of course that it is negative either.

Others are at work on this task of re-reading Kant and Hegel.

The sort of interrogation for which I am calling is neither a work of "pure theory" nor a work of pure praxis, a series of explications. It is something between those two or preparatory to them, a clearing of the ground and an attempt to sink foundations. It is "criticism" in the fundamental sense of "critique," discriminating testing out, in this case a testing out of the medium of which the bridge between theory and practice is made. If criticism as critique is between theory and practice, it is also neither to be identified with hermeneutics, or the search for intentional meaning, on the one side, nor with poetics, or the theory of how texts have meaning, on the other side, though it is closely related to the latter. Critique, however, is a testing of the grounding of language in this or that particular text, not in the abstract or in abstraction from any particular case.

If this sort of investigation of the weight-bearing features of language is often an object of suspicion these days from the point of view of a certain traditional humanism, the humanism of *litterae humaniores,* it is also under attack from the other direction, from the point of view of those who see the central work of literary study as the reinsertion of the work of literature within its social context. The reproaches from the opposite political directions are strangely similar or symmetrical. They often come to the same thing or are couched in the same words. It is as if there were an unconscious alliance of the left and the right to suppress something which is the bad conscience of both a conservative humanism and a "radical" politicizing or sociologizing of the study of literature. A specific problematic is associated with the latter move, which attempts to put literature under the law of economy, under the laws of economic change and social power. I shall examine this problematic in detail elsewhere,[29] but it may be said here that the most resolute attempts to bracket linguistic considerations in the study of literature, to take the language of literature for granted and shift from the study of the relations of word with word to the study of the relations of words with things or with subjectivities, will only lead back in the end to the study of language. Any conceivable encounter with things or with subjectivities in literature or in discourse about literature must already have represented things and subjects in words, numbers, or other signs. Any conceivable representation of the relations of words to things, powers, persons, modes of production and exchange, juridical or political systems (or whatever name the presumably non-linguistic may be given) will turn out to be one or another figure of speech. As such, it will require a rhetorical interpretation, such as that given by Marx in *Capital* and in the *Grundrisse*. Among such figures are that of mimesis, mirroring reflection or representation. This turns out to be a species of metaphor. Another such figure is that of part to whole, work to surrounding and determining milieu, text to context, container to thing contained. This relation is one variety or another of synecdoche or of metonymy. Another figure of the relation of text to social context is that of anamorphosis or of ideology, which is a species of affirmation by denial, abnegation, what Freud called *Verneinung*. Sociologists of literature still all too often do no more than set some social fact side by side with some citation from a literary work and assert that the latter reflects the former, or is accounted for by it, or is determined by it, or is an intrinsic part of it, or is grounded in it. It is just in this place, in the interpretation of this asserted liaison, that the work of rhetorical analysis is indispensable. The necessary dialogue between those practicing poetics or rhetoric and sociologists of literature has scarcely begun. Conservative humanists and "radical" sociologists of literature have this at least in common: both tend to suppress, displace, or replace what I call

the linguistic moment in literature.[30] Here too, however, denegation is affirmation. The covering over always leaves traces behind, tracks which may be followed back to those questions about language I am raising.

Kant, once more, in the "Preface" to the *Critique of Judgment* has admirably formulated the necessity of this work of critique: "For if such a system is one day to be completed [*einmal zu Stande kommen soll*] under the general name of metaphysic . . . , the soil for the edifice [*den Boden zu diesem Gebaude*] must be explored by critique [*die Kritik*] as deep down as the foundation [*die erste Grundlage*] of the faculty of principles independent of experience, in order that it may sink in no part [*damit es nicht an irgend einem Teile sinke*], for this would inevitably bring about the downfall [*Einsturz*] of the whole" (Eng. 4; Ger. 74–75). Elsewhere, in the *Critique of Pure Reason,* the same metaphor has already been posited as the foundation of the edifice of pure thought: "But though the following out of these considerations is what gives to philosophy its peculiar dignity, we must meantime occupy ourselves with a less resplendent [*nicht so glänzenden*], but still meritorious task, namely, to level the ground, and to render it sufficiently secure for moral edifices of these majestic dimensions [*den Boden zu jenen majestätischen sittlichen Gebäuden eben und baufest zu machen*]. For this ground has been honeycombed by subterranean workings [*allerlei Maulwurfsgänge:* all sorts of mole tunnels: Smith's translation effaces the figure] which reason, in its confident but fruitless search for hidden treasures has carried out in all directions, and which threaten the security of the superstructures [*und die jenes Bauwerk unsicher machen*]."[31]

Which is critique? Is it groundbreaking to be distinguished from mole-tunnelling and a repair of it, as the second quotation claims, or is critique, as the first quotation affirms, the work of tunnelling itself, the underground search for bedrock which in that process hollows out the soil? Does this contradiction in Kant's formulations not have something to do with the fact that Kant uses a metaphor from art, or to put this another way, throws out a little artwork of his own in the form of an architectural metaphor, in order to define the work of criticism which is supposed to be a testing out of the very instrument of bridging of which the definition makes use? This is an example of a *mise en abyme* in the technical sense of placing within the larger sign system a miniature image of that larger one, a smaller one potentially within that, and so on, in a filling in and covering over of the abyss, gulf, or *Kluft* which is at the same time an opening of the abyss. Such a simultaneous opening and covering over is the regular law of the *mise en abyme*.

Have I not, finally, by an intrinsic and unavoidable necessity, done the same thing as Kant, with my images of bridges, tunnels, bedrock, pathways, and so on, and with my strategy of borrowing citations from Arnold, Kant, and the rest to describe obliquely my own enterprise? This somersaulting, self-constructing, self-undermining form of language, the throwing out of a bridge where no firm bedrock exists, in place of the bedrock, is a fundamental feature of what I call critique. Groundlevelling, it appears, becomes inevitably tunnelling down in search of bedrock, as, to quote Milton again, beneath the lowest deep a lower deep still opens.

I end by drawing several conclusions from what I have said, and by briefly relating what I have said to the question of genre. The first conclusion is a reiteration of my assertion that the stakes are so large in the present quarrels among students of literature that we must go slowly and circumspectly, testing the ground carefully and taking nothing for granted, returning once more to those founding texts of our modern tradition of literary study and reading them anew with patience and care. To put this another way, the teaching of

philology, of that "slow reading" or *langsamen Lesen* for which Nietzsche calls, is still a fundamental responsibility of the humanities, at no time more needed than today. Second conclusion: Disagreements among students of literature can often be traced to often more covert disagreements about the presupposed ground of literature—whether that ground is assumed to be society, the self, language, or the "thing." One of these four presuppositions may be taken so for granted by a given critic that he is not even aware that it determines all his procedures and strategies of interpretation. Much will be gained by bringing the fundamental causes of these disagreements into the open. Third conclusion: Though the intellectual activity of ground-testing and of testing out the very idea of the ground or of the principle of reason, through slow reading, has a long and venerable tradition under the names of philology and of critical philosophy, nevertheless such testing has a peculiar role in the university. It is likely to seem subversive, threatening, outside the pale of what is a legitimate activity within the university, if research within the university, including research and teaching in the humanities, is all under the sovereign and unquestioned rule of the principle of reason. Nevertheless, moving forward to the necessary new affirmation and the new taking of responsibility for the humanities and within the humanities depends now, as it always has, on allowing that interrogation to take place.

This new taking of responsibility for language and literature, for the language of literature, which I am calling critique, has, finally, important implications for genre theory or for generic criticism. What I have said would imply not that generic classifications or distinctions and the use of these as a guide to interpretation and evaluation are illegitimate, without grounds, but that they are in a certain sense superficial. They do not go all the way to the ground, and the choice of a ground (or being chosen by one) may be more decisive for literary interpretation than generic distinctions and even determine those generic distinctions and their import. It is only on the grounds of a commitment to language, society, the self, or the "it," one or another of these, that generic distinctions make sense and have force. The choice of a ground determines both the definition of each genre and the implicit or explicit hierarchy among them. It is possible, it makes sense, to say "This is a lyric poem," or "This is a novel," and to proceed on the basis of that to follow certain interpretative procedures and ultimately to say, "This is a good lyric poem," or "This is a bad novel." Nevertheless, it is possible and makes sense to do these things only on the grounds of a prior commitment, perhaps one entirely implicit or even unthought, to founding assumptions about the ultimate ground on which all these genres are erected as so many different dwelling places or cultural forms for the human spirit to live in and use.

Beyond that, it might be added that what I am calling critique, in its double emphasis on rhetoric as the study of tropes, on the one hand, in a work of whatever genre, and, on the other hand, on the way any work of literature, of whatever genre, tells a story with beginning, middle, end, and underlying *logos* or *Grund* and at the same time interrupts or deconstructs that story—this double emphasis tends to break down generic distinctions and to recognize, for example, the fundamental role of tropes in novels, the way any lyric poem tells a story and can be interpreted as a narrative, or the way a work of philosophy may be read in terms of its tropological patterns or in terms of the story it tells. Much important criticism today goes against the grain of traditional generic distinctions, while at the same time perpetuating them in new ways in relation to one or another of my four grounds, just as many important works of recent primary literature do not fit easily into any one generic pigeon-hole.

## NOTES

1. *The Letters of Matthew Arnold to Arthur Hugh Clough,* ed. H. F. Lowry (London and New York: Oxford University Press, 1932), 130.

2. Friedrich Nietzsche, *Daybreak: Thoughts on the Prejudices of Morality,* trans. R. J. Hollingdale (Cambridge: Cambridge University Press, 1982), 5, trans. slightly altered; German: Friedrich Nietzsche, *Morgenröte,* "Vorrede," *Werke in Drei Bänden,* ed. Karl Schlecta, I (Munich: Carl Hanser Verlag, 1966), 1016. Further citations will be from these editions.

3. George Eliot, *Daniel Deronda,* I, *Works,* Cabinet Edition (Edinburgh and London: William Blackwood and Sons, n. d.), chap. 6, p. 90. Further references will be to this volume of this edition.

4. In *Première Livraison* (1976), my trans.

5. Wallace Stevens, *The Collected Poems* (New York: Alfred A. Knopf, 1954), 10.

6. Louis Althusser, *For Marx,* trans. Ben Brewster (New York: Vintage Books, 1970), pp. 233–34.

7. Joseph Conrad, *The Secret Agent* (Garden City, N.Y.: Doubleday, Page, 1925), xiii.

8. Cleanth Brooks, "The Primacy of the Author," *The Missouri Review,* 6 (1982), 162.

9. Matthew Arnold, "The Function of Criticism at the Present Time," *Lectures and Essays in Criticism, The Complete Prose Works,* ed. R. H. Super, III (Ann Arbor: The University of Michigan Press, 1962), 270.

10. See Walter Jackson Bate, "The Crisis in English Studies," *Harvard Magazine,* 85, No. 1 (1982), 46–53, esp. pp. 46–47. For a vigorous reply to Bate's essay see Paul de Man, "The Return to Philology," *The Times Literary Supplement,* No. 4, 158 (Friday, December 10, 1982), 1355–56.

11. Immanuel Kant, paragraph 59, "Of Beauty as the Symbol of Morality," *Critique of Judgment,* trans. J. H. Bernard (New York: Hafner Publishing Company, 1951), p. 196; German: *Kritik der Urteilskraft, Werkausgabe,* ed. Wilhelm Weischedel, X (Frankfurt am Main: Suhrkamp Verlag, 1979), 294.

12. René Wellek, "Destroying Literary Studies," *The New Criterion* (December 1983), 2.

13. Matthew Arnold, "The Function of Criticism at the Present Time," p. 282.

14. Ibid., p. 268.

15. Matthew Arnold, "The Study of Poetry," *English Literature and Irish Politics, The Complete Prose Works,* ed.

R. H. Super, IX (Ann Arbor: The University of Michigan Press, 1973), 161.

16. *Letters to Clough,* p. 97.

17. Matthew Arnold, *Poems,* ed. Kenneth Allott (London: Longmans, Green and Co. Ltd., 1965), p. 591.

18. See Kant, *Critique of Judgment,* eds. cit.: Eng., pp. 197–98; Ger., pp. 295–297.

19. G. W. F. von Hegel, *Aesthetics: Lectures on Fine Art,* trans. T. M. Knox, I (New York: Oxford University Press, 1975), 378; *Vorlesungen über die Ästhetik,* I (Frankfurt am Main: Surhkamp, 1970), 486.

20. Wallace Stevens, *Opus Posthumous* (New York: Alfred A. Knopf, 1957), p. 163.

21. "The Function of Matthew Arnold at the Present Time," *Critical Inquiry,* 9 (1983), 451–516. Goodheart's essay, "Arnold at the Present Time," is on pp. 451–68.

22. See Friedrich Nietzsche, "European Nihilism," *The Will to Power,* trans. Walter Kaufmann and R. J. Hollingdale (New York: Vintage Books, 1968), pp. 5–82. These notes are dispersed in chronological order with the other notes traditionally making up *Der Wille zur Macht* in Nietzsche, "Aus dem Nachlass der Achtzigerjahre," *Werke in Drei Bänden,* III, 415–925. See also Martin Heidegger, "Nihilism," *Nietzsche,* trans. Frank A. Capuzzi, IV (San Francisco: Harper & Row, 1982); German: *Nietzsche,* II (Pfullingen: Verlag Günther Neske, 1961), 31–256; 335–98.

23. *Letters to Clough,* p. 135.

24. *The Will to Power,* p. 3.

25. Heidegger, "Nihilism," *Nietzsche,* IV, 21; German: *Nietzsche,* II, 53.

26. Trans. Catherine Porter and Edward P. Morris, *Diacritics,* 13 (1983), 3–20.

27. Kant, *Critique of Judgment,* Eng., p. 32; Ger., p. 106.

28. Hegel, *Ästhetik,* I, 151, my trans.

29. In "Economy," in *Penelope's Web: On the External Relations of Narrative,* forthcoming.

30. A book on nineteenth and twentieth-century poetry with that title is forthcoming from Princeton University Press.

31. Immanuel Kant, *Critique of Pure Reason,* trans. Norman Kemp Smith (New York: St. Martin's Press, 1965), pp. 313–14; German: *Kritik der reinen Vernunft,* A (1781), p. 319; B (1787), pp. 375–76, *Werkausgabe,* ed. cit., III, 325–26. For a discussion of the image of the mole in Kant, Hegel, and Nietzsche see David Farrell Krell, *"Der Maulwurf: Die philosophische Wühlarbeit bei Kant, Hegel und Nietzsche/*The Mole: Philosophic Burrowings in Kant, Hegel, and Nietzsche," *Boundary,* 2, 9 and 10 (Spring/Fall, 1981), 155–79.

# 8

# Barbara T. Christian
# 1943–

Barbara T. Christian received her B.A. from Marquette University in Milwaukee and her M.A. and Ph.D. from Columbia University. She has been extensively involved in developing and implementing programs directed at America's underprivileged and undervalued: these include the SEEK program at City College in New York for disadvantaged black and Puerto Rican students and numerous projects for black and women's communities in and around Berkeley. She was the first black woman to receive tenure at the University of California at Berkeley, where she presently teaches. She has written or edited numerous books, including *Black Women Novelists* (1983), *Teaching Guide to Accompany Black Foremothers: Three Lives* (1980), *Black Feminist Criticism* (1985), and *From the Inside Out: Afro-American Women's Literacy and the State* (1987).

In "The Race for Theory" (1987), Christian questions the need for theoretical approaches to the literary issues of Afro-American theory. She argues for the primacy of literary experience, for a kind of trueness to that experience, without the need for great amplification by theoretical discourse. She believes, further, that the academic preoccupation with theory may be detrimental to third world scholars, who have the great responsibility of creating institutional room for a literature that has been ignored or even suppressed by the dominant culture. In this discussion she enters a contemporary debate with Henry Louis Gates, Jr., Joyce A. Joyce, and Houston Baker concerning the place of theory in the cultural life and struggles of black America. She also joins Horace, Schlegel, Dante, Wordsworth, and many others in the debate over the value of nature versus nurture, in this case preferring the nature of literature to theoretical nurture.

## The Race for Theory

I have seized this occasion to break the silence among those of us, critics, as we are now called, who have been intimidated, devalued by what I call the race for theory. I have become convinced that there has been a takeover in the literary world by Western philosopers from the old literary élite, the neutral humanists. Philosophers have been able to effect such a takeover because so much of the literature of the West has become pallid, laden with despair, self-indulgent, and disconnected. The New Philosophers, eager to understand a world that is today fast escaping their political control, have redefined literature so that the distinctions implied by that term, that is, the distinctions between everything written and those things written to evoke feeling as well as to express thought, have been blurred. They have changed literary critical language to suit their own purposes as philosophers, and they have reinvented the meaning of theory.

My first response to this realization was to ignore it. Perhaps, in spite of the egocentrism of this trend, some good might come of it. I had, I felt, more pressing and interesting things to do, such as reading and studying the history and literature of black women, a history that had been totally ignored, a contemporary literature bursting with originality, passion, insight, and beauty. But unfortunately it is difficult to ignore this new takeover, since theory has become a commodity which helps determine whether we are hired or promoted in academic institutions— worse, whether we are heard at all. Due to this new orientation, works (a word which evokes labor) have become texts. Critics are no longer concerned with literature, but with other critics' texts, for the critic yearning for attention has displaced the writer and has conceived of himself as the center. Interestingly in the first part of this century, at least in England and America, the critic was usually also a writer of poetry, plays, or novels. But today, as a new generation of professionals develops, he or she is increasingly an academic. Activities such as teaching or writing one's response to specific works of literature have, among this group, become subordinated to one primary thrust, that moment when one creates a theory, thus fixing a constellation of ideas for a time at least, a fixing which no doubt will be replaced in another month or so by somebody else's competing theory as the race accelerates. Perhaps because those who have effected the takeover have the power (although they deny it) first of all to be published, and thereby to determine the ideas which are deemed valuable, some of our most daring and potentially radical critics (and by *our* I mean black, women,

third world) have been influenced, even coopted, into speaking a language and defining their discussion in terms alien to and opposed to our needs and orientation. At least so far, the creative writers I study have resisted this language.

For people of color have always theorized—but in forms quite different from the Western form of abstract logic. And I am inclined to say that our theorizing (and I intentionally use the verb rather than the noun) is often in narrative forms, in the stories we create, in riddles and proverbs, in the play with language, since dynamic rather than fixed ideas seem more to our liking. How else have we managed to survive with such spiritedness the assault on our bodies, social institutions, countries, our very humanity? And women, at least the women I grew up around, continuously speculated about the nature of life through pithy language that unmasked the power relations of their world. It is this language, and the grace and pleasure with which they played with it, that I find celebrated, refined, critiqued in the works of writers like Morrison and Walker. My folk, in other words, have always been a race for theory—though more in the form of the hieroglyph, a written figure which is both sensual and abstract, both beautiful and communicative. In my own work I try to illuminate and explain these hieroglyphs, which is, I think, an activity quite different from the creating of the hieroglyphs themselves. As the Buddhists would say, the finger pointing at the moon is not the moon.

In this discussion, however, I am more concerned with the issue raised by my first use of the term, the *race for theory,* in relation to its academic hegemony, and possibly of its inappropriateness to the energetic emerging literatures in the world today. The pervasiveness of this academic hegemony is an issue continually spoken about—but usually in hidden groups, lest we, who are disturbed by it, appear ignorant to the reigning academic élite. Among the folk who speak in muted tones are people of color, feminists, radical critics, creative writers, who have struggled for much longer than a decade to make their voices, their various voices, heard, and for whom literature is not an occasion for discourse among critics but is necessary nourishment for their people and one way by which they come to understand their lives better. Clichéd though this may be, it bears, I think, repeating here.

The race for theory, with its linguistic jargon, its emphasis on quoting its prophets, its tendency towards "Biblical" exegesis, its refusal even to mention specific works of creative writers, far less contemporary ones, its preoccupations with mechanical analyses of language, graphs, algebraic equations, its gross generalizations about culture, has silenced many of us to the extent that some of us feel we can no longer discuss our own literature, while others have developed intense writing blocks and are puzzled by the incomprehensibility of the language set adrift in literary circles. There have been, in the last year, any number of occasions on which I had to convince literary critics who have pioneered entire new areas of critical inquiry that they did have something to say. Some of us are continually harassed to invent wholesale theories regardless of the complexity of the literature we study. I, for one, am tired of being asked to produce a black feminist literary theory as if I were a mechanical man. For I believe such theory is prescriptive—it ought to have some relationship to practice. Since I can count on one hand the number of people attempting to be black feminist literary critics in the world today, I consider it presumptuous of me to invent a theory of how we *ought* to read. Instead, I think we need to read the works of our writers in our various ways and remain open to the intricacies of the intersection of language, class, race, and gender in the literature. And it would help if we share our process, that is,

our practice, as much as possible since, finally, our work *is* a collective endeavor.

The insidious quality of this race for theory is symbolized for me by the very name of this special issue—Minority Discourse—a label which is borrowed from the reigning theory of the day and is untrue to the literatures being produced by our writers, for many of our literatures (certainly Afro-American literature) are central, not minor, and by the titles of many of the articles, which illuminate language as an assault on the other, rather than as possible communication, and play with, or even affirmation of another. I have used the passive voice in my last sentence construction, contrary to the rules of Black English, which like all languages has a particular value system, since I have not placed responsibility on any particular person or group. But that is precisely because this new ideology has become so prevalent among us that it behaves like so many of the other ideologies with which we have had to contend. It appears to have neither head nor center. At the least, though, we can say that the terms "minority" and "discourse" are located firmly in a Western dualistic or "binary" frame which sees the rest of the world as minor, and tries to convince the rest of the world that it *is* major, usually through force and then through language, even as it claims many of the ideas that we, its "historical" other, have known and spoken about for so long. For many of us have never conceived of ourselves only as somebody's *other*.

Let me not give the impression that by objecting to the race for theory I ally myself with or agree with the neutral humanists who see literature as pure expression and will not admit to the obvious control of its production, value, and distribution by those who have power, who deny, in other words, that literature is, of necessity, political. I am studying an entire body of literature that has been denigrated for centuries by such terms as *political*. For an entire century Afro-American writers, from Charles Chesnutt in the nine-teenth century through Richard Wright in the 1930s, Imamu Baraka in the 1960s, Alice Walker in the 1970s, have protested the liter-ary hierarchy of dominance which declares when literature is literature, when literature is great, depending on what it thinks is to its advantage. The Black Arts Movement of the 1960s, out of which Black Studies, the Femi-nist Literary Movement of the 1970s, and Women's Studies grew, articulated precisely those issues, which came *not* from the decla-rations of the New Western philosophers but from these groups' reflections on their own lives. That Western scholars have long be-lieved their ideas to be universal has been strongly opposed by many such groups. Some of my colleagues do not see black criti-cal writers of previous decades as eloquent enough. Clearly they have not read Wright's "Blueprint for Negro Writing," Ellison's *Shadow and Act,* Chesnutt's resignation from being a writer, or Alice Walker's "Search for Zola Neale Hurston." There are two reasons for this general ignorance of what our writer-critics have said. One is that black writing has been generally ignored in this country. Since we, as Toni Morrison has put it, are seen as a discredited people, it is no surprise, then, that our creations are also discredited, but this is also due to the fact that until recently domi-nant critics in the Western World have also been creative writers who have had access to the upper middle class institutions of educa-tion and until recently our writers have decid-edly been excluded from these institutions and in fact have often been opposed to them. Because of the academic world's general ig-norance about the literature of black people and of women, whose work too has been discredited, it is not surprising that so many of our critics think that the position arguing that literature is political begins with these New Philosophers. Unfortunately, many of our young critics do not investigate the rea-sons *why* that statement—literature is politi-

cal—is now acceptable when before it was not; nor do we look to our own antecedents for the sophisticated arguments upon which we can build in order to change the tendency of any established Western idea to become hegemonic.

For I feel that the new emphasis on literary critical theory is as hegemonic as the world which it attacks. I see the language it creates as one which mystifies rather than clarifies our condition, making it possible for a few people who know that particular language to control the critical scene—that language sur-faced, interestingly enough, just when the lit-erature of peoples of color, of black women, of Latin Americans, of Africans began to move to "the center." Such words as *center* and *periphery* are themselves instructive. *Dis-course, canon, texts,* words as latinate as the tradition from which they come, are quite familiar to me. Because I went to a Catholic Mission school in the West Indies I must con-fess that I cannot hear the word "canon" without smelling incense, that the word "text" immediately brings back agonizing memories of Biblical exegesis, that "dis-course" reeks for me of metaphysics forced down my throat in those courses that traced *world* philosophy from Aristotle through Thomas Aquinas to Heidegger. "Periphery" too is a word I heard throughout my child-hood, for if anything was seen as being at the periphery, it was those small Caribbean is-lands which had neither land mass nor mili-tary power. Still I noted how intensely impor-tant this periphery was, for U.S. troups were continually invading one island or another if any change in political control even seemed to be occurring. As I lived among folk for whom language was an absolutely necessary way of validating our existence, I was told that the minds of the world lived only in the small continent of Europe. The metaphysical language of the New Philosophy, then, I must admit, is repulsive to me and is one reason why I raced from philosophy to literature, since the latter seemed to me to have the possibilities of rendering the world as large and as complicated as I experienced it, as sensual as I knew it was. In literature I sensed the possibility of the integration of feeling/ knowledge, rather than the split between the abstract and the emotional in which Western philosophy inevitably indulged.

Now I am being told that philosophers are the ones who write literature, that authors are dead, irrelevant, mere vessels through which their narratives ooze, that they do not work nor have they the faintest idea what they are doing; rather they produce texts as disembodied as the angels. I am frankly astonished that scholars who call themselves Marxists or post-Marxists could seriously use such metaphysical language even as they attempt to deconstruct the philosophical tradition from which their language comes. And as a student of literature, I am appalled by the sheer ugliness of the language, its lack of clarity, its unnecessarily complicated sentence constructions, its lack of pleasurableness, its alienating quality. It is the kind of writing for which composition teachers would give a freshman a resounding F.

Because I am a curious person, however, I postponed readings of black women writers I was working on and read some of the prophets of this new literary orientation. These writers did announce their dissatisfaction with some of the cornerstone ideas of their own tradition, a dissatisfaction with which I was born. But in their attempt to change the orientation of Western scholarship, they, as usual, concentrated on themselves and were not in the slightest interested in the worlds they had ignored or controlled. Again I was supposed to know *them,* while they were not at all interested in knowing *me.* Instead they sought to "deconstruct" the tradition to which they belonged even as they used the same forms, style, language of that tradition, forms which necessarily embody its values. And increasingly as I read them and saw their

substitution of their philosophical writings for literary ones, I began to have the uneasy feeling that their folk were not producing any literature worth mentioning. For they always harkened back to the masterpieces of the past, again reifying the very texts they said they were deconstructing. Increasingly, as *their* way, *their* terms, *their* approaches remained central and became the means by which one defined literary critics, many of my own peers who had previously been concentrating on dealing with the other side of the equation, the reclamation and discussion of past and *present* third world literatures, were diverted into continually discussing the new literary theory.

From my point of view as a critic of contemporary Afro-American women's writing, this orientation is extremely problematic. In attempting to find the deep structures in the literary tradition, a major preoccupation of the new New Criticism, many of us have become obsessed with the nature of reading itself to the extent that we have stopped writing about literature being written today. Since I am slightly paranoid, it has begun to occur to me that the literature being produced *is* precisely one of the reasons why this new philosophical-literary-critical theory of relativity is so prominent. In other words, the literature of blacks, women of South America and Africa, etc., as overtly "political" literature was being preempted by a new Western concept which proclaimed that reality does not exist, that everything is relative, and that every text is silent about something—which indeed it must necessarily be.

There is, of course, much to be learned from exploring how we know what we know, how we read what we read, an exploration which, of necessity, can have no end. But there also has to be a "what," and that "what," when it is even mentioned by the new philosophers, are texts of the past, primarily Western male texts, whose norms are again being transferred onto third world, female texts as theories of reading proliferate. Inevitably a hierarchy has now developed between what is called theoretical criticism and practical criticism, as mind is deemed superior to matter. I have no quarrel with those who wish to philosophize about how we know what we know. But I do resent the fact that this particular orientation is so privileged and has diverted so many of us from doing the first readings of the literature being written today as well as of past works about which nothing has been written. I note, for example, that there is little work done on Gloria Naylor, that most of Alice Walker's works have not been commented on—despite the rage around *The Color Purple*—that there has yet to be an in-depth study of Frances Harper, the nineteenth-century abolitionist poet and novelist. If our emphasis on theoretical criticism continues, critics of the future may have to reclaim the writers we are now ignoring, that is, if they are even aware these artists exist.

I am particularly perturbed by the movements to exalt theory, as well, because of my own adult history. I was an active member of the Black Arts Movement of the sixties and know how dangerous theory can become. Many today may not be aware of this, but the Black Arts Movement tried to create Black Literary Theory and in doing so became prescriptive. My fear is that when Theory is not rooted in practice, it becomes prescriptive, exclusive, élitist.

An example of this prescriptiveness is the approach the Black Arts Movement took towards language. For it, blackness resided in the use of black talk which they defined as hip urban language. So that when Nikki Giovanni reviewed Paule Marshall's *Chosen Place, Timeless People,* she criticized the novel on the grounds that it was not black, for the language was too elegant, too white. Blacks, she said, did not speak that way. Having come from the West Indies where we do, some of the time, speak that way, I was

amazed by the narrowness of her vision. The emphasis on *one way* to be black resulted in the works of Southern writers being seen as non-black since the black talk of Georgia does not sound like the black talk of Philadelphia. Because the ideologues, like Baraka, come from the urban centers they tended to privilege their way of speaking, thinking, writing, and to condemn other kinds of writing as not being black enough. Whole areas of the canon were assessed according to the dictum of the Black Arts Nationalist point of view, as in Addison Gayle's *The Way of the New World,* while other works were ignored because they did not fit the scheme of cultural nationalism. Older writers like Ellison and Baldwin were condemned because they saw that the intersection of Western and African influences resulted in a new Afro-American culture, a position with which many of the Black Nationalist idealogues disagreed. Writers were told that writing love poems was not being black. Further examples abound.

It is true that the Black Arts Movement resulted in a necessary and important critique both of previous Afro-American literature and of the white-established literary world. But in attempting to take over power, it, as Ishmael Reed satirizes so well in *Mumbo Jumbo,* became much like its opponent, monolithic and downright repressive.

It is this tendency towards the monolithic, monotheistic, etc., which worries me about the race for theory. Constructs like the *center* and the *periphery* reveal that tendency to want to make the world less complex by organizing it according to one principle, to fix it through an idea which is really an ideal. Many of us are particularly sensitive to monolithism since one major element of ideologies of dominance, such as sexism and racism, is to dehumanize people by stereotyping them, by denying them their variousness and complexity. Inevitably, monolithism becomes a metasystem, in which there is a controlling ideal, especially in relation to pleasure. Language as one form of pleasure is immediately restricted, and becomes heavy, abstract, prescriptive, monotonous.

Variety, multiplicity, eroticism are difficult to control. And it may very well be that these are the reasons why writers are often seen as *persona non grata* by political states, whatever form they take, since writers/artists have a tendency to refuse to give up their way of seeing the world and of playing with possibilities; in fact, their very expression relies on that insistence. Perhaps that is why creative literature, even when written by politically reactionary people, can be so freeing, for in having to embody ideas and recreate the world, writers cannot merely produce "one way."

The characteristics of the Black Arts Movement are, I am afraid, being repeated again today, certainly in the other area to which I am especially tuned. In the race for theory, feminists, eager to enter the halls of power, have attempted their own prescriptions. So often I have read books on feminist literary theory that restrict the definition of what *feminist* means and overgeneralize about so much of the world that most women as well as men are excluded. Nor seldom do feminist theorists take into account the complexity of life—that women are of many races and ethnic backgrounds with different histories and cultures and that as a rule women belong to different classes that have different concerns. Seldom do they note these distinctions, because if they did they could not articulate a theory. Often as a way of clearing themselves they do acknowledge that women of color, for example, do exist, then go on to do what they were going to do anyway, which is to invent a theory that has little relevance for us.

That tendency towards monolithism is precisely how I see the French feminist theorists. They concentrate on the female body as the means to creating a female language, since language, they say, is male and necessarily conceives of woman as other. Clearly many of them have been irritated by the theories of Lacan for whom language is phallic. But suppose there are peoples in the world whose language was invented primarily in relation to women, who after all are the ones who relate to children and teach language. Some Native American languages, for example, use female pronouns when speaking about non-gender specific activity. Who knows who, according to gender, created languages. Further, by positing the body as the source of everything French feminists return to the old myth that biology determines everything and ignore the fact that gender is a social rather than a biological construct.

I could go on critiquing the positions of French feminists who are themselves more various in their points of view than the label which is used to describe them, but that is not my point. What I am concerned about is the authority this school now has in feminist scholarship—the way it has become *authoritative discourse,* monologic, which occurs precisely because it does have access to the means of promulgating its ideas. The Black Arts Movement was able to do this for a time because of the political movements of the 1960s—so too with the French feminists who could not be inventing "theory" if a space had not been created by the Women's Movement. In both cases, both groups posited a theory that excluded many of the people who made that space possible. Hence one of the reasons for the surge of Afro-American women's writing during the 1970s and its emphasis on sexism in the black community is precisely that when the ideologues of the 1960s said *black,* they meant *black male*.

I and many of my sisters do not see the world as being so simple. And perhaps that is why we have not rushed to create abstract theories. For we know there are countless women of color, both in America and in the rest of the world to whom our singular ideas would be applied. There is, therefore, a caution we feel about pronouncing black feminist theory that might be seen as a decisive statement about Third World women. This is not to say we are not theorizing. Certainly our literature is an indication of the ways in which our theorizing, of necessity, is based on our multiplicity of experiences.

There is at least one other lesson I learned from the Black Arts Movement. One reason for its monolithic approach had to do with its desire to destroy the power which controlled black people, but it was a power which many of its ideologues wished to achieve. The nature of our context today is such that an approach which desires power singlemindedly must of necessity become like that which it wishes to destroy. Rather than wanting to change the whole model, many of us want to be at the center. It is this point of view that writers like June Jordan and Audre Lorde continually critique even as they call for empowerment, as they emphasize the fear of difference among us and our need for leaders rather than a reliance on ourselves.

For one must distinguish the desire for power from the need to become empowered—that is, seeing oneself as capable of and having the right to determine one's life. Such empowerment is partially derived from a knowledge of history. The Black Arts Movement did result in the creation of Afro-American Studies as a concept, thus giving it a place in the university where one might engage in the reclamation of Afro-American history and culture and pass it on to others. I am particularly concerned that institutions such as Black Studies and Women's Studies, fought for with such vigor and at some sacrifice, are not often seen as important by many of our black or women scholars precisely because the old hierarchy of traditional departments is seen as superior to these "marginal" groups. Yet, it is in this context that many others of us are discovering the extent of our complexity, the interrelationships of different areas of knowledge in relation to a distinctly Afro-American

or female experience. Rather than having to view our world as subordinate to others, or rather than having to work as if we were hybrids, we can pursue ourselves as subjects.

My major objection to the race for theory, as some readers have probably guessed by now, really hinges on the question, "for whom are we doing what we are doing when we do literary criticism?" It is, I think, the central question today especially for the few of us who have infiltrated the academy enough to be wooed by it. The answer to that question determines what orientation we take in our work, the language we use, the purposes for which it is intended.

I can only speak for myself. But what I write and how I write is done in order to save my own life. And I mean that literally. For me literature is a way of knowing that I am not hallucinating, that whatever I feel/know *is*. It is an affirmation that sensuality is intelligence, that sensual language is language that makes sense. My response, then, is directed to those who write what I read and to those who read what I read—put concretely—to Toni Morrison and to people who read Toni Morrison (among whom I would count few academics). That number is increasing, as is the readership of Walker and Marshall. But in no way is the literature Morrison, Marshall, or Walker create supported by the academic world. Nor given the political context of our society, do I expect that to change soon. For there is no reason, given who controls these institutions, for them to be anything other than threatened by these writers.

My readings do presuppose a need, a desire among folk who like me also want to save their own lives. My concern, then, is a passionate one, for the literature of people who are not in power has always been in danger of extinction or of cooptation, not because we do not theorize, but because what we can even imagine, far less who we can reach, is constantly limited by societal structures. For me, literary criticism is promotion as well as understanding, a response to the writer to whom there is often no response, to folk who need the writing as much as they need anything. I know, from literary history, that writing disappears unless there is a response to it. Because I write about writers who are now writing, I hope to help ensure that their tradition has continuity and survives.

So my "method," to use a new "lit. crit." word, is not fixed but relates to what I read and to the historical context of the writers I read *and* to the many critical activities in which I am engaged, which may or may not involve writing. It is a learning from the language of creative writers, which is one of surprise, so that I might discover what language I might use. For my language is very much based on what I read and how it affects me, that is, on the surprise that comes from reading something that compels you to read differently, as I believe literature does. I, therefore, have no set method, another prerequisite of the new theory, since for me every work suggests a new approach. As risky as that might seem, it is, I believe, what intelligence means—a tuned sensitivity to that which is alive and therefore cannot be known until it is known. Audre Lorde puts it in a far more succinct and sensual way in her essay "Poetry is not a Luxury":

As they become known to and accepted by us, our feelings and the honest exploration of them become sanctuaries and spawning grounds for the most radical and daring of ideas. They become a safe-house for that difference so necessary to change and the conceptualization of any meaningful action. Right now, I could name at least ten ideas I would have found intolerable or incomprehensible and frightening, except as they came after dreams and poems. This is not idle fantasy, but a disciplined attention to the true meaning of "it feels right to me." We can train ourselves to respect our feelings and to transpose them into a language so they can be shared. And where that language does not yet exist, it is our poetry which helps to fashion it. Poetry is not only dream and vision; it is the skeleton architecture of our lives. It lays the foundations for a future of change, a bridge across our fears of what has never been before.[1]

**NOTE**

1. Audre Lord, *Sister Outsider* (Trumansburg, N.Y.: The Crossing Press, 1984), 37.

# 9

# Henry Louis Gates, Jr.
# 1950–

Henry Louis Gates, Jr., is W. E. B. Du Bois Professor of the Humanities and Chairman of the Afro-American Studies Department at Harvard University. In the course of the 1980s and early 1990s he has emerged as the leading new theorist, historical scholar, and critical interpreter of African-American literature and culture and has begun to play a national and international role as a contemporary cultural commentator. Among his notable books on African-American and African literatures and cultures and on present-day issues of race, history, and politics are *Figures in Black* (1987), *The Signifying Monkey* (1988), and *Loose Canons* (1992). He is an editor of several literary and critical anthologies, the general editor of the multivolume *Schomberg Library of Nineteenth-Century Black Women Writers,* and a coeditor of the journal *Transition.*

In "Critical Fanonism" (1991) Gates identifies and analyzes a network of theoretical positions that have appeared across nationalities and historical contexts since the middle of the twentieth century and have concerned colonial and postcolonial discourse. This web of critical intertextuality, Gates argues, has been spun around the central figure of Frantz Fanon, the Lacanian psychoanalyst who emigrated from the Caribbean French colony of Martinique to French Algeria and in the 1950s and 1960s became an internationally celebrated theorist and activist-critic of "the colonial paradigm." For many contemporary scholars of colonial and postcolonial discourse Fanon's writings in books like *Black Skin, White Masks* and *The Wretched of the Earth* have become a primary historical and theoretical referent for the discussion of subaltern identity, resistance, and revolution. Those who invoke Fanon include Foucauldian and materialist critics such as Edward Said (who writes frequently about Europe and the Middle East), Marxist-feminist deconstructionists such as Gayatri Spivak and Lacanian deconstructionists such as Homi Bhabha (both of whom write mainly about India and Great Britain), South African historians of the British literature of empire such as Benita Parry, cultural theorists of colonial Africa such as Abdul R. JanMohamed, colonial critics of French Algeria such as Albert Memmi, and even "mainstream" humanist and historicist commentators on Anglo-American literature such as Jerome McGann. Gates examines the various ways and contexts in which these scholars invoke and use Fanon's theoretical accounts of colonialism and anticolonial resistance, offering his own illuminating comments on cultural domination, minority discourse, and colonial and postcolonial identity formation in the past and in the future.

# Critical Fanonism

*This book, it is hoped, will be a mirror.*
— Frantz Fanon, *Black Skin, White Masks*

One of the signal developments in contemporary criticism over the past several years has been the ascendancy of the colonial paradigm. In conjunction with this new turn, Frantz Fanon has now been reinstated as a global theorist, and not simply by those engaged in Third World or subaltern studies. In a recent collection centered on British romanticism, Jerome McGann opens a discussion of William Blake and Ezra Pound with an extended invocation of Fanon. Donald Pease has used Fanon to open an attack on Stephen Greenblatt's reading of the Henriad and the interdisciplinary practices of the new historicism. And Fanon, and published interpretations of Fanon, have become regularly cited in the rereadings of the Renaissance that have emerged from places like Sussex, Essex, and Birmingham.[1]

My intent is not to offer a reading of Fanon to supplant these others, but to read, even if summarily, some of these readings of Fanon. By focussing on successive appropriations of this figure, as both totem and text, I think we can chart out an itinerary through contemporary colonial discourse theory. I want to stress, then, that my ambitions here are extremely limited: what follows may be a prelude to a reading of Fanon, but does not even begin that task itself.[2]

Fanon's current fascination for us has something to do with the convergence of the problematic of colonialism with that of subject-formation. As a psychoanalyst of culture, as a champion of the wretched of the earth, he is an almost irresistible figure for a criticism that sees itself as both oppositional and postmodern. And yet there's something Rashomon-like about his contemporary guises. It may be a matter of judgement whether his writings are rife with contradiction or richly dialectical, polyvocal, and multivalent; they are in any event highly porous, that is, wide open to interpretation, and the readings they elicit are, as a result, of unfailing *symptomatic* interest: Frantz Fanon, not to put too fine a point on it, is a Rorschach blot with legs.

We might begin with a recent essay by Edward Said, entitled "Representing the Colonized." To Jean-Francois Lyotard's vision of the decline of grand narrative, Said counterposes the counternarratives of emergent peoples, the counternarratives of liberation that Fanon (as he says) "forces on a Europe playing 'le jeu irresponsable de la belle au bois dormant.'" And Said goes on to argue:

> Despite its bitterness and violence, the whole point of Fanon's work is to force the European metropolis to think its history *together with* the history of colonies awakening from the cruel stupor and abused immobility of imperial dominion. . . .
>
> I do not think that the anti-imperialist challenge represented by Fanon and Césaire or others like them has by any means been met; neither have we taken them seriously as models or representations of human effort in the contemporary world. In fact Fanon and Césaire—of course I speak of them as types—jab directly at the question of identity and of identitarian thought, that secret sharer of present anthropological reflection on "otherness" and "difference." What Fanon and Césaire required of their own partisans, even during the heat of struggle, was to abandon fixed ideas of settled identity and culturally authorized definition.[3]

I've given some space to these remarks because it is, preeminently, in passages such as this one that Fanon as global theorist has been produced.

And yet some have found cause for objection here. Reading the passage above, they say that given the grand narrative in which Fanon is himself inserted, it seems beside the point to ask about the extent to which the historical Fanon really did abandon all fixity of identity; beside the point to raise questions about his perhaps ambivalent relation to counternarratives of identity; beside the point to address his growing political and philosophical estrangement from Aimé Césaire. Fanon's individual specificity seems beside the point because what we have here is explicitly a composite figure, indeed, an ethnographic construct. It's made clear by the formulaic reference to Fanon, Césaire, and "others like them." It's made clear when he writes, "of course I speak of them as types": to which some readers will pose the question, why "of course"? And they will answer: because the ethnographer always speaks of his subjects as types. Or they find the answer in Albert Memmi, who explains that a usual "sign of the colonized's depersonalization is what one might call the mark of the plural. The colonized is never characterized in an individual manner; he is entitled only to drown in an anonymous collectivity."[4]

Thus, while calling for a recognition of the *situatedness* of all discourses, the critic delivers a Fanon as a global theorist *in vacuo;* in the course of an appeal for the specificity of the Other, we discover that his global theorist of alterity is emptied of his own specificity; in the course of a critique of identitarian thought, Fanon is conflated with someone who proved, in important respects, an ideological antagonist. And so on.

These moves are, I think, all too predictable: and, yes, even beside the point. Said has delivered a brief for a usable culture; it is not to be held against him that his interest is in

mobilizing a usable Fanon. Indeed, this is his own counternarrative, in the terrain of postcolonial criticism. But Said's use of Fanon to allegorize the site of counterhegemonic agency must also be read as an implicit rejoinder to those who have charged him with ignoring the self-representations of the colonized. Homi Bhabha's objection that Said's vision of Orientalism suggests that "power and discourse is possessed entirely by the colonizer" is typical in this regard.[5]

Certainly Bhabha's own readings of Fanon are the most elaborated that have been produced in the field of post-structuralism. And his readings are designed to breach the disjunction Said's essay may appear to preserve, that is, between the discourse of the colonized and that of the colonizer. For Bhabha, colonial ambivalence "makes the boundaries of colonial 'positionality'—the division of self/other—and the question of colonial power—the differentiation of colonizer/colonized—different from both the Hegelian master/slave dialectic or the phenomenological projection of Otherness."[6] Accordingly, he has directed attention to (what he sees as) the disruptive articulations of the colonized as inscribed in colonial discourse, that is, the discourse of the colonized. Bhabha's reading requires a model of self-division, of "alienation within identity," and he has enlisted Lacanian psychoanalysis to this end:

> [Minority discourse] is not simply the attempt to invert the balance of power within an unchanged order of discourse, but to redefine the symbolic process through which the social Imaginary—Nation, Culture, or Community—become "subjects" of discourse and "objects" of psychic identification.[7]

From Fanon, he educes the question, "how can a human being live Other-wise?" And he juxtaposes to his reflections on *Black Skin,*

*White Masks* the following remarks of Jacques Lacan's:

"In the case of display . . . the play of combat in the form of intimidation, the being gives of himself, or receives from the other, something that is like a mask, a double, an envelope, a thrown-off skin, thrown off in order to cover the frame of a shield. It is through this separated form of himself that the being comes into play in his effects of life and death."[8]

Bhabha may be Fanon's closest reader, and it is an oddly touching performance of a coaxing devotion: he regrets aloud those moments in Fanon that cannot be reconciled to the post-structuralist critique of identity because he wants Fanon to be even better than he is. Benita Parry has described Bhabha as proffering Fanon as "a premature poststructuralist," and I don't think Bhabha would disagree.[9]

In this same vein, Bhabha redescribes Fanon's "Manichean delirium" as a condition internalized within colonial discourse, as a form of self-misrecognition. "In articulating the problem of colonial cultural alienation in the psychoanalytic language of demand and desire, Fanon radically questions the formation of both individual and social authority as they come to be developed in the discourse of Social Sovereignty" ("RF," p. xiii). Fanon's representation "turns on the idea of Man *as* his alienated image, not Self and Other but the 'Otherness' of the Self inscribed in the perverse palimpsest of colonial identity" ("RF," pp. xiv–xv). It's interesting to note, however, that Bhabha's mobilization of Lacan stands as an explicit correction of Fanon's own citation of Lacan in *Black Skin, White Masks*.

Here, then, is the originary irruption of Lacan into colonial discourse theory. With reference to the mirror stage, Fanon writes:

When one has grasped the mechanism described by Lacan, one can have no further doubt that the real Other for the white man is and will continue to be the black man. And conversely. Only for the white man The Other is perceived on the level of the body image, absolutely as the not-self—that is, the unidentifiable, the unassimilable. For the black man, as we have shown, historical and economic realities come into the picture.[10]

(Hence for the delirious Antillean, Fanon tells us, "the mirror hallucination is always neutral. When Antilleans tell me that they have experienced it, I always ask the same question: 'What color were you?' Invariably they reply: 'I had no color' " [*BS,* p. 162, n. 25].)

Bhabha cautions, however, that

The place of the Other must not be imaged as Fanon sometimes suggests as a fixed phenomenological point, opposed to the self, that represents a culturally alien consciousness. The Other must be seen as the necessary negation of a primordial identity—cultural or psychic—that introduces the system of differentiation which enables the 'cultural' to be signified as a linguistic, symbolic, historic reality. ["RF," p. xviii]

In other words, he wants Fanon to mean Lacan rather than, say, Jean-Paul Sartre, but acknowledges that Fanon does tend to slip:

At times Fanon. . . . turns too hastily from the ambivalences of identification to the antagonistic identities of political alienation and cultural discrimination; he is too quick to name the Other, to personalize its presence in the language of colonial racism. . . . These attempts . . . can, at times, blunt the edge of Fanon's brilliant illustrations of the complexity of psychic projections in the pathological colonial relation. ["RF," pp. xix–xx]

Bhabha is charmingly up front about the pull-ing and pushing involved in turning Fanon into *le Lacan noir;* he regrets the moments when Fanon turns to "an existentialist hu-manism that is as banal as it is beatific" ("RF," p. xx). Indeed, Bhabha's rather passionate essay, entitled "Remembering Fanon," can as easily be read as an index to all that Bhabha wants us to forget.

For some oppositional critics, however, the hazards of Bhabha's approach may go beyond interpretive etiquette. Thus, in a prel-ude to his own Lacanian reading of colonial discourse, Abdul JanMohamed takes Bhabha to task for downplaying the negativity of the colonial encounter; and not surprisingly, his critique pivots on his own positioning of Fanon. JanMohamed writes: "Though he cites Frantz Fanon, Bhabha completely ignores Fanon's definition of the conqueror/native relation as a 'Manichean' struggle—a defini-tion that is not a fanciful metaphoric carica-ture but an accurate representation of a pro-found conflict." "What does it mean, in prac-tice, to imply as Bhabha does that the native, whose entire economy and culture are de-stroyed, is somehow in 'possession' of colo-nial power?" he asks. JanMohamed charges that Bhabha asserts "the unity of the 'colonial subject' " and so "represses the political his-tory of colonialism."[11]

The critical double bind these charges raise is clear enough. You can empower discur-sively the native, and open yourself to charges of downplaying the epistemic (and literal) violence of colonialism; or play up the absolute nature of colonial domination, and be open to charges of negating the subjectiv-ity and agency of the colonized, thus textually replicating the repressive operations of colonialism. In agency, so it seems, begins responsibility.

But of course JanMohamed does not argue that colonialism completely destroyed the na-tive's culture. Conversely, it can't be the case that Bhabha ignores Fanon's discussion of

colonialism's self-representation as a Mani-chean world, since he explicitly reflects on what Fanon calls the "Manichean delirium." But certainly Bhabha's different account of colonialism makes it unlikely that he posits a unity of the colonial subject in the way Jan-Mohamed construes it, for Bhabha's account denies the unity of either subject in the first place. Properly reframed, JanMohamed's ar-gument might be seen as another version of a critique of Lacan advanced by (among oth-ers) Stephen Heath, who argues that "the im-portance of this idea of the Other [as the "locus" of the symbolic, which produces the subject as constitutively divided] and the sym-bolic is crucial to Lacan exactly because it allows him to abstract from problems of so-cial-historical determinations."[12] As against Fredric Jameson's famous injunction, then, Lacan's motto would turn out to be: Never historicize, never explain.

But far from turning against the psychoana-lytic model of colonial discourse, Jan-Mohamed's concern is, of course, to advance an explicitly Lacanian account of these dis-courses. To be sure, the allure of Lacan for both Bhabha and JanMohamed is only tan-gentially related to its appearance in Fanon: as I've suggested, Lacan's discourse exem-plarily maps a problematic of subject-forma-tion onto a Self-Other model that seems to lend itself to the Colonial Encounter. On the other hand, it's unclear whether Jan-Mohamed really wants to make space for all the distinctively Lacanian ramifications spelled out by Bhabha.

For his part, JanMohamed reinstates the notions of alterity that Bhabha rejected. "Faced with an incomprehensible and multi-faceted alterity," he writes, "the European theoretically has the option of responding to the Other in terms of identity or difference" ("EMA," p. 83). Here, the Other exists as such prior to and independent of the encounter; but a little further we find the limits of the Lacanian register in JanMohamed's analysis:

"Genuine and thorough comprehension of Otherness," he writes, requires "the virtually impossible task of negating one's very being" ("EMA," p. 84). This "virtually impossible" encounter is neither a provisional, negotiated difference nor the Lacanian Other in whose field the self must constitute itself. Rather, it is a close encounter of the third kind, involving the disputed notion of radical alterity.[13]

And the duality supports his division of colonialist literature into the two categories of the imaginary and the symbolic. In the imaginary text, the native functions as mirror— though in fact as a negative image. The symbolic text uses the native as mediator of European desires, introducing a realm of "intersubjectivity, heterogeneity, and particularity" ("EMA," p. 85) as opposed to the infantile specularity of Otherness that the imaginary text enacts.

While this use of Lacan to demarcate literary categories has uncertain value as a means of classifying colonial literature (it has been criticized as crudely empiricist), it has appeal in classifying postcolonial theorists. Here one might station JanMohamed's penchant for Manichean allegories in the imaginary register, Bhaba's negotiations in the symbolic. I suppose (to continue the conceit) we might cast Fanon as the Other that mediates between them and the historical Real.

Yet the most problematic feature of Jan-Mohamed's theorizing is what critics describe as an overly mimetic conception of oppositional literature. Here we should turn to a recent overview of colonial discourse theory by the radical South African expatriate, Benita Parry. In the course of her explicitly Fanonian critique of JanMohamed's study, Parry finds him lacking "Fanon's grasp of the paradoxes and pitfalls of 'rediscovering tradition' and representing it within a western system of meanings. What for Fanon is a transitional process of liberating the consciousness of the oppressed into a new reality, JanMohamed treats as the arrival of the definitive opposi-

tional discourse" ("PCT," p. 47). In fact, she is concerned even more with the critique of alteritism as pursued in the work of Bhabha and Gayatri Chakravorty Spivak. Parry asks: "What are the politics of projects which dissolve the binary opposition colonial self/colonized other, encoded in colonialist language as a dichotomy necessary to domination, but also differently inscribed in the discourse of liberation as a dialectic of conflict and a call to arms?" ("PCT," p. 29). Thus Parry says of Bhabha's reading that it "obscures Fanon's paradigm of the colonial condition as one of implacable enmity between native and invader, making armed opposition both a cathartic and a pragmatic necessity" ("PCT," p. 32). (To be sure, Fanon also spoke of the metaphysics of the dualism as "often quite fluid" [*BS,* p. 10].)

Of both Spivak and Bhabha, Parry asserts: "because their theses admit of no point outside of discourse from which opposition can be engendered, their project is concerned to place incendiary devices within the dominant structures of representation and not to confront these with another knowledge" ("PCT," p. 43). Considering the subaltern voice to be irretrievable, they devalue the actual counter-narratives of anticolonialist struggle as mere reverse discourse. But what Fanon shows us, according to Parry, and what "colonial discourse theory has not taken on board," is that "a cartography of imperialist ideology more extensive than its address in the colonialist space, as well as a conception of the native as historical subject and agent of an oppositional discourse is needed" ("PCT," p. 45).

To such positions in contemporary theory, Parry contrasts what she implies is a more properly Fanonian critical mode, one that

also rejects totalizing abstracts of power as falsifying situations of domination and subordination, [and in which] the notion of hegemony is inseparable from that of a counter-hegemony. In this theory of

power and contest, the process of procuring the consent of the oppressed and the marginalized to the existing structure of relationships through ideological inducements, necessarily generates dissent and resistance, since the subject is conceived as being constituted by means of incommensurable solicitations and heterogeneous social practices. The outcome of this agonistic exchange, in which those addressed challenge their interlocutors, is that the hegemonic discourse is ultimately abandoned as scorched earth when a different discourse, forged in the process of disobedience and combat, occupying new, never colonized and 'utopian' territory, and prefiguring other relationships, values, and aspirations, is enunciated. ["PCT," pp. 43–44]

Some people might describe this utopian moment as the externalization of the quest romance. But note the emergence here of the familiar historicist dialectic of subversion and containment: that power produces its own subversion is held to be a fact about the constitution of the subject itself. And some will be skeptical about the notion of a revolutionary literature that is implicit here. If Said made of Fanon an advocative of post-postmodern counternarratives of liberation; if Jan-Mohamed made of Fanon a Manichean theorist of colonialism as absolute negation; and if Bhabha cloned, from Fanon's *theoria,* another Third World post-structuralist, Parry's Fanon (which I generally find persuasive) turns out to confirm her own rather optimistic vision of literature and social action. "This book, it is hoped, will be a mirror," wrote a twenty-six-year-old Fanon, and in rereading these readings, it's hard to avoid a sort of tableau of narcissism, with Fanon himself as the Other that can only reflect and consolidate the critical self.

And perhaps we can hear a warning about the too uncritical appropriations of a Fanon

in Spivak's recent rebuttal to the criticism concerning the recuperation or effacement of the native's voice. The course we've been plotting leads us, then, to what is, in part, Spivak's critique of Parry's critique of Jan-Mohamed's critique of Bhabha's critique of Said's critique of colonial discourse.

Now, in Spivak's view, Parry "is, in effect, bringing back the 'native informant syndrome' and using it differently in a critique of neocolonialism. . . . ' "When Benita Parry takes us—and by this I mean Homi Bhabha, Abdul JanMohamed, Gayatri Spivak—to task for not being able to listen to the natives or to let the native speak, she forgets that we are natives, too. We talk like Defoe's Friday, only much better." ' "[14] Thus, in straining for a voice of indigenous resistance, we can succumb to another quest romance, this time for the

transparent "real" voice of the native. This has so many of the properties of a somewhat displaced model in the 19th-century class-stratified management of the culture of imperialism, that I believe that it is my task now to be vigilant about this desire to hear the native. Also, let me tell you that the native is not a fool and within the fact of this extraordinary search for the "true" native which has been going on for decades, perhaps even a century or more, the native himself or herself is aware of this particular value. ["N," pp. 92–93]

So we need to reject, says Spivak, that insidious image of the native as a parahuman creature "who is there to give us evidence that we must always trust (as we wouldn't trust the speech of people to whom we ascribe the complexity of being human)" ("N," p. 93).

I think this is an elegant reminder and safeguard against the sentimental romance of alterity. On the other hand, it still leaves space for some versions of Parry's critique. I suggest that we try to distinguish more sharply between the notions of cultural resistance, on the one hand, and of cultural alterity, on the other, even as we note the significance of their conflation. There may well be something familiar about Spivak's insistence on the totalizing embrace of colonial discourse, and Parry's unease with the insistence.

My claim is that what Jacques Derrida calls writing, Spivak, in a brilliant reversal, has renamed colonial discourse. So it is no accident that the two terms share precisely the same functionality. The Derridian *mot,* that there is nothing outside the text, is reprised as the argument that there is nothing outside (the discourse of) colonialism. And it leads, as well, to the argument that this very discourse must be read as heterogeneous to itself, as laced with the aporias and disjunctures that any deconstructive reading must elicit and engage. (It's in just these terms that Spivak joins in the critique of alteritism: "I am critical of the binary opposition Coloniser/Colonised. I try to examine the heterogeneity of 'Colonial Power', and to disclose the complicity of the two poles of that opposition as it constitutes the disciplinary enclave of the critique of imperialism.")[15] Indeed, I think Spivak's argument, put in its strongest form, entails the corollary that all discourse is colonial discourse.

But perhaps the psychoanalytic model of culture makes this a foregone conclusion. When Fanon asserted that "only a psychoanalytical interpretation of the black problem" could explain "the structure of the complex" (*BS,* p. 12), he was perhaps only extending a line of Freud's, which Greenblatt has focussed attention to: " 'Civilization behaves toward sexuality as a people or a stratum of its population does which has subjected another one to its exploitation.' "[16] Freud's pessimistic vision of "analysis interminable" would then refer us to a process of decolonization interminable. I spoke of this double session of paradigms, in which the Freudian

mechanisms of psychic repression are set in relation to those of colonial repression; but it's still unclear whether we are to speak of convergence or mere parallelism. Again, the Fanonian text casts the problem in sharpest relief.

Stephan Feuchtwang has recently argued, in an essay entitled "Fanonian Spaces," that

the use of psychoanalytic categories for descriptions of social situations has tremendous analogical virtues. One is their capacity to indicate a directionality of affect in the situations, of forces mobilized and immobilized rather than a mere disposition of intelligible elements and their rationality. Another is their focus on the relational, truly the social facts. Fanon does not analyze the colonial situation as a contact of cultural subjects or as an interaction of interested subjects as if they were logically prior to the situation. Instead, the relations of the situation are analyzed to see how their organization forms cultural subjects.[17]

Feuchtwang speaks of "tremendous analogical virtues": but are they *merely* analogical? Further—accepting the force of the Freudian rereading—do we really want to elide the distance between political repression and individual neurosis: the *positional* distance between Steve Biko and, say, Woody Allen? On the other hand, Feuchtwang does point to the problematic relation between individual case studies and analyses of the collective state in *Black Skin, White Masks.* We've heard Fanon speak of the necessity for the "psychoanalytic interpretation"; yet he subsequently juxtaposes a notion of socioanalysis to Freud's psychoanalysis: "It will be seen that the black man's alienation is not an individual question. Beside [the Freudian contribution of] phylogeny and ontogeny stands sociogeny" (*BS,* p. 13). Or as Memmi simplifies the question, in the preface to his classic *The Colonizer and the Colonized:* "Does psychoanalysis win out over Marxism? Does all depend on the individual or on society?"[18] And, of course, the tension—which we endlessly try to theorize away—persists in all political appropriations of the psychoanalytic.

Indeed, doesn't this tension plague our appropriation of Fanon as a collectivized individual, as alterity in revolt, as the Third World of Theory itself? I speak of course, of *our* Fanon, of whom Sartre wrote in the preface to *The Wretched of the Earth:* "the Third World finds *itself* and speaks to *itself* through his voice."[19] I speak of the black Benjamin who, as McGann writes, presents "the point of view of a Third World, where the dialectic of the first two worlds is completely reimagined," because he writes from "the perspective of an actual citizen of the actual Third World."[20]

So I want to turn, finally, to yet another Fanon, the ironic figure analyzed by the Tunisian novelist and philosopher Albert Memmi. Memmi's Fanon is, emphatically, not the Fanon we have recuperated for global colonial discourse theory. He is, indeed, a far more harried subject, a central fact of whose life is his dislocation from the "actual Third World." Of course, we know from his biographers and from his own account that Fanon, whose mother was of Alsatian descent, grew up in Martinique thinking of himself as white and French: and that his painful reconstitution as a black West Indian occurred only when he arrived at the French capital. Yet at this point—again, in Memmi's narrative—Fanon loses himself as a black Martinican: *"Fanon's private drama is that, though henceforth hating France and the French, he will never return to Negritude and to the West Indies,"* indeed, he "never again set foot in Martinique."[21] Yet his attempts to identify himself as an Algerian proved equally doomed. As Fanon's biographers remind us, most Algerian revolutionaries scant his role and remain irritated by the attention paid to him in the West as a figure in Algerian decolonization: to them—and how ironic this is to his Western admirers—he remained a European interloper.

Though he worked as a psychiatrist in Algeria and Tunisia, in neither country did he even understand the language: his psychiatric consultations were conducted through an interpreter (see M, p. 5). And the image here—of the psychoanalysis of culture being conducted, quite literally, through an *interpreter*—does speak eloquently of the ultimately mediated nature of the most anticolonialist analysis.

Far from championing the particularities and counternarratives of the oppressed, Memmi's Fanon is an interloper without the patience or interest to acquaint himself with the local specificities of culture: "He grew impatient, and failed to hide his scorn of regional particularisms, the tenacity of traditions and customs that distinguish cultural and national aspirations, not to speak of contradictory interests" (M, p. 5). And while Memmi's own insertion in colonial politics is certainly complex, his version is consistent with that of the revolutionary elite of postindependence Algeria.

Memmi's Fanon was devoted to a dream of a third world, a third world where he could look into a mirror and have no color: yet he lived in the Third World, which rebuffed his most ardent desires for identification. What remained for him, Memmi writes, "but to propose a completely novel man?" (M, p. 5).

We've seen inscribed on the Fanonian text (as well as in contemporary colonial discourse theory more widely) the disruptive relation between narratives of subject-formation and narratives of liberation. Here, Memmi is quite blunt: Fanon does, on the one hand, claim an absolute disjunction between colonial representations of the colonized and the subject of representation. But doesn't colonialism inscribe itself on the colonized? "For that matter, is Fanon's own thinking on this point really coherent? I too could cite a great many contradictory passages of his, where he speaks of 'mutilation,' 'inferiorization,' 'criminal impulse,'—results, obviously, of colonization." Actually, Memmi goes on to say, Fanon must have seen that the personality of the colonized was affected in these ways. But

> he found them embarrassing and repulsive. This is because, like many other defenders of the colonized, he harbored a certain amount of revolutionary romanticism. . . . As for most social romantics, so for him the victim remained proud and intact throughout oppression; he suffered but did not let himself be broken. And the day oppression ceases, the new man is supposed to appear before our eyes immediately.

But, says Memmi, "this is not the way it happens."[22]

I believe that the Antillean mirror which reflects no color at all haunts Fanon. Memmi is surely right to locate the utopian moment in Fanon in his depiction of decolonization as engendering a "kind of *tabula rasa,*" as "quite simply the replacing of a certain 'species' of men by another 'species' of men";[23] so that the fear that we will continue to be (as Fanon puts it) "overdetermined from without" was never reconciled with his political vision of emancipation. This may be the clearest way of representing Fanon's own self-divisions, that is, as an agon between psychology and a politics, between ontogeny and sociogeny, between—to recur to Memmi—Marx and Freud.

Fanon's vision of the New Man emerges as a central tableau in identity politics, for us as for him. At the intersection of colonial and psychoanalytic discourse, Fanon wonders how to create a new identity. The problem remains, again for us as for him, that—as Memmi remarked about Fanon's own project of personal transformation—"one doesn't

leave one's own self behind as easily as all that" (M, p. 5).

Rehistoricizing Fanon, we can hear a lament concerning the limits of liberation, concerning the very intelligibility of his dream of decolonization. And while the colonial paradigm proved valuable in foregrounding issues of power and position, it may be time to question its ascendance in literary and cultural studies, especially because the "disciplinary enclave" of anti-imperialist discourse has proved a last bastion for the project, and dream, of global theory. In the context of the colonial binarism, we've seldom admitted fully how disruptive the psychoanalytic model can be, elaborating a productive relation between oppressed and oppressor—productive of each as speaking subjects. And yet we can chart the torsional relation of the discourses in the exceptional instability of Fanon's own rhetoric.

But this requires of us that we no longer allow Fanon to remain a kind of icon or "screen memory," rehearsing dimly remembered dreams of postcolonial emancipation. It means *reading* him, with an acknowledgment of his own historical particularity, as an actor whose own search for self-transcendence scarcely exempts him from the heterogenous and conflictual structures that we have taken to be characteristic of colonial discourse. It means not to elevate him above his localities of discourse as a transcultural, transhistorical Global Theorist, nor simply to cast him into battle, but to recognize him as a battlefield in himself. Fanon wrote, with uncanny and prescient insistence: "In no fashion should I undertake to prepare the world that will come later. I belong irreducibly to my time" (*BS,* p. 15). This is one proviso we ignore at our own risk.

Do we still need global, imperial theory—in this case, a grand unified theory of oppression; or, indeed, even the whole universalizing model of Theory that it presupposes, a model of total theory that quests for finality and an exclusive lien on the last word? It's no longer any scandal that our own theoretical reflections must be as provisional, reactive, and local as the texts we reflect upon. Of course, discarding the imperial agenda of global theory also means not having to choose *between* Spivak and Said, Greenblatt, Pease, or Jameson, Bhabha or JanMohamed or Parry, even Fanon or Memmi; or, rather, it means not representing the choice as simply one of epistemic hygiene. And it requires a recognition that we, too, just as much as Fanon, may be fated to rehearse the agonisms of a culture that may never earn the title of *post*colonial.[24]

## NOTES

1. See Jerome McGann, "The Third World of Criticism," in *Rethinking Historicism: Critical Readings in Romantic History,* ed. Marjorie Levinson et al. (New York, 1989), pp. 85–107, and Donald Pease, "Toward a Sociology of Literary Knowledge: Greenblatt, Colonialism, and the New Historicism," in *Consequences of Theory,* ed. Barbara Johnson and Jonathan Arc (Baltimore, 1991).

2. A properly contextualized reading of Fanon's *Black Skin, White Masks,* the text to which I most frequently recur, should situate it in respect to such germinal works as Jean-Paul Sartre's *Réflexions sur la question Juive* (Paris, 1946), Dominique O. Mannoni's *Psychologie de la colonisation* (Paris, 1950), Germaine Guex's *La Névrose d'abandon* (Paris, 1950), as well as many lesser known works. But this is only to begin to sketch out the challenge of rehistoricizing Fanon.

3. Edward W. Said, "Representing the Colonized: Anthropology's Interlocutors," *Critical Inquiry* 15 (Winter 1989): 223.

4. Albert Memmi, *The Colonizer and the Colonized,* trans. Howard Greenfield (New York, 1965), p. 85.

5. Homi K. Bhabha, "Difference, Discrimination, and the Discourse of Colonialism," in *The Politics of Theory,* ed. Francis Barker (Colchester, 1983), p. 200.

6. Bhabha, "Signs Taken for Wonders: Questions of Ambivalence and Authority under a Tree Outside Delhi, May 1817," in *"Race," Writing, and Difference,* ed. Henry Louis Gates, Jr. (Chicago, 1986), p. 169.

7. Bhabha, "Difference, Discrimination, and the Discourse of Colonialism," p. 200.

8. Bhabha, "Remembering Fanon: Self, Psyche and the Colonial Condition," foreword to Frantz Fanon, *Black Skin, White Masks* (London, 1986), p. xxv; hereafter abbreviated "RF."

9. Benita Parry, "Problems in Current Theories of Colonial Discourse," *Oxford Literary Review* 9 (Winter 1987): 31; hereafter abbreviated "PCT."

10. Fanon, *Black Skin, White Masks,* p. 161 n. 25; hereafter abbreviated *BS.*

11. Abdul R. JanMohamed, "The Economy of Manichean Allegory: The Function of Racial Difference in Colonialist Literature," in *"Race," Writing, and Difference,* pp. 78, 79; hereafter abbreviated "EMA."

12. Stephen Heath, *"Le Père Noël," October,* no. 26 (1983): 77.

13. Gayatri Chakravorty Spivak may keep him company here: "No perspective *critical* of imperialism can turn the Other into a self, because the project of imperialism has always already historically refracted what might have been the absolutely Other into a domesticated Other that consolidates the imperialist self' (Spivak, "Three Women's Texts and a Critique of Imperialism," in *"Race," Writing, and Difference,* p. 272). The "absolutely Other" here seems to be something we find (or fail to find), rather than make. I should stress that it's not the notion of otherness as such but of absolute otherness that I want to question.

14. Maria Koundoura, "Naming Gayatri Spivak," *Stanford Humanities Review* (Spring 1989): 91–92; hereafter abbreviated "N."

15. Angela McRobbie, "Strategies of Vigilance: An Interview with Gayatri Spivak," *Block* 10 (1985): 9.

16. Quoted in Stephen Greenblatt, *Renaissance Self-Fashioning: From More to Shakespeare* (Chicago, 1980), p. 173. See Sigmund Freud, *Civilization and Its Discontents,* trans. James Strachey (New York, 1962); p. 51.

17. Stephan Feuchtwang, "Fanonian Spaces," *New Formations* 1 (Spring 1987):127.

18. Memmi, *The Colonizer and the Colonized,* p. xiii.

19. Jean-Paul Sartre, preface, in Fanon, *The Wretched of the Earth,* trans. Constance Farrington (New York, 1968), p. 10.

20. McGann, "The World of Criticism," pp. 86, 87.

21. Memmi, review of *Fanon,* by Peter Geismar, and *Frantz Fanon,* by David Caute, *New York Times Book Review,* 14 Mar. 1971, p. 5; hereafter abbreviated M.

22. Memmi, "Franz Fanon and the Notion of 'Deficiency,' " trans. Eleanor Levieux, *Dominated Man: Notes towards a Portrait* (New York, 1968), p. 88.

23. Fanon, *The Wretched of the Earth*, p. 35.

24. This paper was originally prepared for and delivered (in abridged form) at the 1989 Modern Language Association panel on "Race and Psychoanalysis," at the invitation of Jane Gallop, which partly explains why my references to Fanon are largely to his first and most overtly psychoanalytic book, *Black Skin, White Masks.* Since Fanon's oeuvre receives scant attention in my paper, I should remind readers unfamiliar with his works that early and late Fanon (say) cannot be simply conflated, and that many oppositional critics regard the later essays to be his most valuable contribution. See, for example, *Toward the African Revolution: Political Essays,* trans. Haakon Chevalier (New York, 1967). Finally, I'm grateful to Hazel Carby, Jonathan Culler, K. A. Appiah, Arnold I. Davidson, Benita Parry, and Henry Finder, who commented on an earlier draft, even though I have failed to respond to their criticisms as I would have wished.

# 10

# Edward W. Said
# 1935–

Edward Said is Parr Professor of English and comparative literature at Columbia University. An Arab-Palestinian intellectual and activist who has lived much of his adult life in "exile" in the United States, Said is one of the principal twentieth-century theorists and scholars of cultural theory and colonial and postcolonial discourse. Since the early 1970s he has also been an influential interpreter in the English-speaking world of European poststructuralism, mediating especially between Michel Foucault's discourse- and institution-centered cultural critique and Jacques Derrida's philosophical deconstruction. In addition, he has contributed significantly to the criticism and interpretation of Anglo-American, Continental, and colonial and post-colonial novelistic fiction and nonfictional prose from the eighteenth century to the present. His diverse scholarly, critical, and political engagements have shaped much of the critique of Eurocentrism and of the Western literary and cultural canon that has affected academic studies in the humanities around the world during the last two decades. Among his most frequently cited books are *Beginnings* (1976), *Orientalism* (1978), *The World, the Text, and the Critic* (1983), and *Culture and Imperialism* (1993).

In "The Politics of Knowledge" (1991) Said argues again for a "worldly criticism" that can accomplish what Raymond Williams's cultural materialism and Foucault's analyses of discursive and cultural practices, disciplinary formations, and institutional histories were intended to accomplish. From Said's viewpoint, both literature and criticism (where the latter brings together engagements with history, politics, interpretation, and theory) are inescapably "worldly," material practices, and constantly need to be understood as such. To analyze their worldliness or materiality adequately, the engaged intellectual and critic needs to focus on concrete historical particulars, as well as on such relatively abstract, global phenomena as culture, imperialism, domination, subjection, racism, native resistance, and nationalism. The critique of such phenomena, however, now runs into several problems arising from, for example, dogmatic contemporary demands for "political correctness," as well as complicitous, postcolonial, non-Western defenses of "the benefits of colonization." Said argues against both types of objections to his work by claiming that "we ought . . . to reconsider the ties between the text and the world in a serious and uncoercive way," and that "it does not finally matter *who* wrote what, but rather *how* a work is written and *how* it is read." In taking this position, Said generates a space for criticism in which "it is not necessary to regard every reading or interpretation of a text as the moral equivalent of a war or a political crisis," even as we remember "to underline the fact that whatever else they are, works of literature are not merely texts."

# The Politics of Knowledge

Last fall I was invited to participate in a seminar at a historical studies center of a historically renowned American university. The subject of the seminar for this and the next academic year is imperialism, and the seminar discussions are chaired by the center's director. Outside participants are asked to send a paper before their arrival; it is then distributed to the members of the seminar, who are graduate students, fellows, and faculty. They will have read the paper in advance, precluding any reading of a lecture to them by the visitor, who is instead asked to summarize its main points for about ten minutes. Then for an hour and a half, there is an open discussion of the paper—a fairly rigorous but stimulating exercise. Since I have been working for some years on a sequel to *Orientalism*—it will be a long book that deals with the relationship between modern culture and imperialism—I sent a substantial extract from the introduction, in which I lay out the main lines of the book's argument. I there begin to describe the emergence of a global consciousness in Western knowledge at the end of the nineteenth century, particularly in such apparently unrelated fields as geography and comparative literature. I then go on to argue that the appearance of such cultural disciplines coincides with a fully global imperial perspective, although such a coincidence can only be made to seem significant from the point of view of later history, when nearly everywhere in the colonized world there emerged resistance to certain oppressive aspects of imperial rule like theories of subject races and peripheral regions, and the notions of backward, primitive or undeveloped cultures. *Because* of that native resistance—for instance, the appearance of many nationalist and independence movements in India, the Caribbean, Africa, the

Middle East—it is now evident that culture and imperialism in the West could be understood as offering support, each to the other. Here I referred to the extraordinary work of a whole range of non-Western writers and activists, including Tagore, Fanon, C. L. R. James, Yeats, and many others, figures who have given integrity to anti-imperialist cultural resistance.

The first question after my brief resumé was from a professor of history, a black woman of some eminence who had recently come to the university, but whose work was unfamiliar to me. She announced in advance that her question was to be hostile, "a very hostile one in fact." She then said something like the following: for the first thirteen pages of your paper you talked only about white European males. Thereafter, on page fourteen, you mention some names of non-Europeans. "How could you do such a thing?" I remonstrated somewhat, and tried to explain my argument in greater detail—after all, I said, I was discussing European imperialism, which would not have been likely to include in its discourse the work of African-American women. I pointed out that in the book I say quite a bit about the response to imperialism all over the world; that point was a place in my argument where it would be pertinent to focus on the work of such writers as—and here I again mentioned the name of a great Caribbean writer and intellectual whose work has a special importance for my own—C. L. R. James. To this my critic replied with a stupefying confidence that my answer was not satisfactory since C. L. R. James was dead! I must admit that I was nonplussed by the severity of this pronouncement. James indeed *was* dead, a fact that needn't, to a historian, have made further discussion impossible. I waited for her to resume, hoping that she might expatiate on what she meant by having suggested that even in discussions of what dead white European males said on a given topic it was inappropriate to confine oneself to what they said while leaving out the work of living African-American, Arab, and Indian writers.

But she did not proceed, and I was left to suppose that she considered her point sufficiently and conclusively made: I was guilty of not mentioning living non-European non-males, even when it was not obvious to me or, I later gathered, to many members of the seminar, what their pertinence might have been. I noted to myself that my antagonist did not think it necessary to enumerate what specifically in the work of living non-Europeans I should have used, or which books and ideas by them she found important and relevant. All I had been given to work with was the asserted necessity to mention some approved names—which names did not really matter—as if the very act of uttering them was enough. I was also left unmistakably with the impression that as a nonwhite—a category incidentally to which as an Arab I myself belong—she was saying that to affirm the existence of non-European "others" took the place of evidence, argument, discussion.

It would be pointless to deny that the exchange was unsettling. Among other things I was chagrined at the distortions of my position and for having responded to the distortions so clumsily. It did not seem to matter that a great deal of my own work has concerned itself with just the kind of omission with which I was being charged. What apparently mattered now was that having contributed to an early trend, in which Western and European intellectuals were arraigned for having their work constructed out of the suffering and deprivations of so many people of color, I was now allegedly doing what such complicit intellectuals had always done. For if in one place you criticize the exclusion of Orientals, as I did in *Orientalism,* the exclu-

sion of "others" from your work in another place becomes, on one level, difficult to justify or explain. I was disheartened not because I was being attacked, but because the general validity of the point made in *Orientalism* still obtained and yet was now being directed at me. It was *still* true that various Others—the word has acquired a sheen of modishness that has become extremely objectionable—were being represented unfairly, their reality distorted, their truth either denied or twisted with malice. Yet instead of joining in their behalf, I felt I was being asked to get involved in an inconsequential academic contest. I had wanted to say, but didn't, "Is all that matters about the issue of exclusion and misrepresentation the fact that *names* were left out? Why are you detaining us with such trivialities?"

To make matters worse, a few minutes later in the discussion I was attacked by a retired professor of Middle Eastern studies, himself an Orientalist. Like me, he was an Arab, but he had consistently identified himself with intellectual tendencies of which I had always been critical. He now intervened to defend imperialism, saying in tones of almost comic reverence, that it had accomplished things that natives couldn't have done for themselves. It had taught them, among other things, he said, how to appreciate the cuneiform and hieroglyphics of their own traditions. As he droned on about the imperial schools, railroads, hospitals, and telegraphs in the Third World that stood for examples of British and French largesse, the irony of the whole thing seemed overpowering. It appeared to me that there had to be something to say that surrendered neither to the caricatural reductiveness of the two positions by then arrayed against me, and against each other, nor to that verbal quality in each that was determined to remain ideologically correct and little else.

I was being reminded by such negative flat-minded examples of thinking, that the one thing that intellectuals *cannot* do without is the full intellectual process itself. Into it goes historically informed research as well as the presentation of a coherent and carefully argued line that has taken account of alternatives. In addition, there must be, it seems to me, a theoretical presumption that in matters having to do with human history and society any rigid theoretical ideal, any simple additive or mechanical notion of what is or is not factual, must yield to the central factor of human work, the actual participation of peoples in the making of human life. If that is so then it must also be true that, given the very nature of human work in the construction of human society and history, it is impossible to say of it that its products are so rarified, so limited, so beyond comprehension as to exclude most other people, experiences, and histories. I mean further, that this kind of human work, which is intellectual work, is worldly, that it is situated in the world, and about that world. It is not about things that are so rigidly constricted and so forbiddingly arcane as to exclude all but an audience of like-minded, already fully convinced persons. While it would be stupid to deny the importance of constituencies and audiences in the construction of an intellectual argument, I think it has to be supposed that many arguments can be made to more than one audience and in different situations. Otherwise we would be dealing not with intellectual argument but either with dogma, or with a technological jargon designed specifically to repel all but a small handful of initiates or coteries.

Lest I fall into the danger myself of being too theoretical and specialized, I shall be more specific now and return to the episode I was discussing just a moment ago. At the heart of the imperial cultural enterprise I analyzed in *Orientalism* and also in my new book, was a politics of identity. That politics has needed to assume, indeed needed firmly to believe, that what was true about Orientals or Africans was *not* however true about or for Europeans. When a French or German scholar tried to identify the main characteristics of, for instance, the Chinese mind, the work was only partly intended to do that; it was also intended to show how different the Chinese mind was from the Western mind.

Such constructed things—they have only an elusive reality—as the Chinese mind or the Greek spirit have always been with us; they are at the source of a great deal that goes into the making of individual cultures, nations, traditions, and peoples. But in the modern world considerably greater attention has generally been given to such identities than was ever given in earlier historical periods, when the world was larger, more amorphous, less globalized. Today a fantastic emphasis is placed upon a politics of national identity, and to a very great degree, this emphasis is the result of the imperial experience. For when the great modern Western imperial expansion took place all across the world, beginning in the late eighteenth century, it accentuated the interaction between the identity of the French or the English and that of the colonized native peoples. And this mostly antagonistic interaction gave rise to a separation between people as members of homogenous races and exclusive nations that was and still is one of the characteristics of what can be called the epistemology of imperialism. At its core is the supremely stubborn thesis that everyone is principally and irreducibly a member of some race or category, and that race or category cannot ever be assimilated to or accepted by others—except as itself. Thus came into being such invented essences as the Oriental or Englishness, as Frenchness, Africanness, or American exceptionalism, as if each of those had a Platonic idea behind it that guaranteed it as pure and unchanging from the beginning to the end of time.

One product of this doctrine is nationalism, a subject so immense that I can treat it only very partially here. What interests me in the politics of identity that informed imperialism in its global phase is that just as natives were considered to belong to a different category—racial or geographical—from that of the Western white man, it also became true that in the great anti-imperialist revolt represented by decolonization this same category was mobilized around, and formed the resisting identity of, the revolutionaries. This was the case everywhere in the Third World. Its most celebrated instance is the concept of *négritude,* as developed intellectually and poetically by Aimé Césaire, Leopold Senghor, and, in English, W. E. B. Du Bois. If blacks had once been stigmatized and given inferior status to whites, then it has since become necessary not to deny blackness, and not to aspire to whiteness, but to accept and celebrate blackness, to give it the dignity of poetic as well as metaphysical status. Thus *négritude* acquired positive Being where before it had been a mark of degradation and inferiority. Much the same revaluation of the native particularity occurred in India, in many parts of the Islamic world, China, Japan, Indonesia, and the Philippines, where the denied or repressed native essence emerged as the focus of, and even the basis for, nationalist recovery.

It is important to note that much of the early cultural resistance to imperialism on which nationalism and independence movements were built was salutary and necessary. I see it essentially as an attempt on the part of oppressed people who had suffered the bondage of slavery, colonialism, and—most important—spiritual dispossession, to reclaim their identity. When that finally occurred in places such as Algeria, the grander nationalist efforts amounted to little short of a reconstructed communal political and cultural program of independence. Where the white man had once only seen lazy natives and exotic customs, the insurrection against imperialism produced, as in Ireland for exam-

ple, a national revolt, along with political parties dedicated to independence, which, like the Congress party in India, was headed by nationalist figures, poets, and military heroes. There were remarkably impressive results from this vast effort at cultural reclamation, most of which are well known and celebrated.

But while the whole movement toward autonomy and independence produced in effect newly independent and separate states constituting the majority of new nations in the postcolonial world today, the nationalist politics of identity has nonetheless quickly proved itself to be insufficient for the ensuing period.

Inattentive or careless readers of Frantz Fanon, generally considered one of the two or three most eloquent apostles of anti-imperialist resistance, tend to forget his marked suspicions of unchecked nationalism. So while it is appropriate to draw attention to the early chapters on violence in *The Wretched of the Earth,* it should be noticed that in subsequent chapters he is sharply critical of what he called the pitfalls of national consciousness. He clearly meant this to be a paradox. And for the reason that while nationalism is a necessary spur to revolt against the colonizer, national consciousness must be immediately transformed into what he calls "social consciousness," just as soon as the withdrawal of the colonizer has been accomplished.

Fanon is scathing on the abuses of the post-independence nationalist party, on, for instance, the cult of the Grand Panjandrum (or maximum leader), or the centralization of the capital city, which Fanon said flatly needed to be deconsecrated, and most importantly, on the hijacking of common sense and popular participation by bureaucrats, technical experts, and jargon-wielding obfuscators. Well before V. S. Naipaul, Fanon was arguing against the politics of mimicry and separatism which produced the Mobutus, Idi Amins, and

Saddams, as well as the grotesqueries and pathologies of power that gave rise to tyrannical states and praetorian guards while obstructing democratic freedoms in so many countries of the Third World. Fanon also prophesied the continuing dependency of numerous postcolonial governments and philosophies, all of which preached the sovereignty of the newly independent people of one or another new Third World state, and, having failed to make the transition from nationalism to true liberation, were in fact condemned to practice the politics, and the economics, of a new oppression as pernicious as the old one.

At bottom, what Fanon offers most compellingly is a critique of the separatism and mock autonomy achieved by a pure politics of identity that has lasted too long and been made to serve in situations where it has become simply inadequate. What invariably happens at the level of knowledge is that signs and symbols of freedom and status are taken for the reality: you want to be named and considered for the sake of being named and considered. In effect this really means that just to be an independent postcolonial Arab, or black, or Indonesian is not a program, nor a process, nor a vision. It is no more than a convenient starting point from which the real work, the hard work, might begin.

As for that work, it is nothing less than the reintegration of all those people and cultures, once confined and reduced to peripheral status, with the rest of the human race. After working through *négritude* in the early sections of *Cahier d'un retour,* Aimé Césaire states this vision of integration in his poem's climatic moment: "no race possesses the monopoly of beauty, of intelligence, of force, and there is a place for all at the rendez-vous of victory."

Without this concept of "place for all at the rendez-vous of victory," one is condemned to an impoverishing politics of knowledge based only upon the assertion and reassertion of identity, an ultimately uninteresting alternation of presence and absence. If you are weak, your affirmation of identity for its own sake amounts to little more than saying that you want a kind of attention easily and superficially granted, like the attention given an individual in a crowded room at a roll call. Once having such recognition, the subject has only to sit there silently as the proceedings unfold as if in his or her absence. And, on the other hand, though the powerful get acknowledged by the sheer force of presence, this commits them to a logic of displacement, as soon as someone else emerges who is as, or more, powerful.

This has proved a disastrous process, whether for postcolonials, forced to exist in a marginal and dependent place totally outside the circuits of world power, or for powerful societies, whose triumphalism and imperious wilfullness have done so much to devastate and destabilize the world. What has been at issue between Iraq and the United States is precisely such a logic of exterminism and displacement, as unedifying as it is unproductive. It is risky, I know, to move from the realm of interpretation to the realm of world politics, but it seems to me true that the relationship between them is a real one, and the light that one realm can shed on the other is quite illuminating. In any case the politics of knowledge that is based principally on the affirmation of identity is very similar, is indeed directly related to, the unreconstructed nationalism that has guided so many postcolonial states today. It asserts a sort of separatism that wishes only to draw attention to itself; consequently it neglects the integration of that earned and achieved consciousness of self within "the rendez-vous of victory." On the national and on the intellectual level the problems are very similar.

Let me return therefore to one of the intellectual debates that has been central to the humanities in the past decade, and which underlies the episode with which I began. The ferment in minority, subaltern, feminist, and postcolonial consciousness has resulted in so many salutary achievements in the curricular and theoretical approach to the study of the humanities as quite literally to have produced a Copernican revolution in all traditional fields of inquiry. Eurocentrism has been challenged definitively; most scholars and students in the contemporary American academy are now aware, as they were never aware before, that society and culture have been the heterogenous product of heterogenous people in an enormous variety of cultures, traditions, and situations. No longer does T. S. Eliot's idea of the great Western masterpieces enduring together in a constantly redefining pattern of monuments have its old authority; nor do the sorts of patterns elucidated with such memorable brilliance in formative works like *Mimesis* or *The Anatomy of Criticism* have the same cogency for today's student or theorist as they did even quite recently.

And yet the great contest about the canon continues. The success of Allan Bloom's *The Closing of the American Mind,* the subsequent publication of such works as Alvin Kernan's *The Death of Literature,* and Roger Kimball's *Tenured Radicals* as well as the rather posthumous energies displayed in journals like *The American Scholar* (now a neo-conservative magazine), *The New Criterion,* and *Commentary*—all this suggests that the work done by those of us who have tried to widen the area of awareness in the study of culture is scarcely finished or secure. But our point, in my opinion, cannot be simply and obdurately to reaffirm the paramount importance of formerly suppressed or silenced forms of knowledge and leave it at that, nor can it be to surround ourselves with the sanctimonious piety of historical or cultural victimhood as a way of making our intellectual presence felt. Such strategies are woefully insufficient. The whole effort to de-

consecrate Eurocentrism cannot be interpreted, least of all by those who participate in the enterprise, as an effort to supplant Eurocentrism with, for instance, Afrocentric or Islamocentric approaches. On its own, ethnic particularity does not provide for intellectual process—quite the contrary. At first, you will recall, it was a question, for some, of adding Jane Austen to the canon of male Western writers in humanities courses; then it became a matter of displacing the entire canon of American writers like Hawthorne and Emerson with best-selling writers of the same period like Harriet Beecher Stowe and Susan Warner. But after that the logic of displacement became even more attenuated, and the mere names of politically validated living writers became more important than anything about them or their works.

I submit that these clamorous dismissals and swooping assertions are in fact caricatural reductions of what the great revisionary gestures of feminism, subaltern or black studies, and anti-imperialist resistance originally intended. For such gestures it was never a matter of replacing one set of authorities and dogmas with another, nor of substituting one center for another. It was always a matter of opening and participating in a central strand of intellectual and cultural effort and of showing what had always been, though indiscernibly, a part of it, like the work of women, or of blacks and servants—but which had been either denied or derogated. The power and interest of—to give two examples particularly dear to me—Tayib Salih's *Season of Migration to the North* is not only how it memorably describes the quandary of a gifted young Sudanese who has lived in London but then returns home to his ancestral village alongside the Nile; the novel is also a rewriting of Conrad's *Heart of Darkness,* seen now as the tale of someone who voyages into the heart of light, which is modern Europe, and discovers there what had been hidden deep within him. To read the Sudanese writer is of course to interpret an Arabic novel written during the late sixties at a time of nationalism and a rejection of the West. The novel is therefore affiliated with other Arabic novels of the postwar period including the works of Mahfouz and Idriss; but given the historical and political meaning of a narrative that quite deliberately recalls and reverses Conrad—something impossible for a black man at the time *Heart of Darkness* was written—Tayib Salih's masterpiece is necessarily to be viewed as, along with other African, Indian, and Caribbean works, enlarging, widening, refining the scope of a narrative form at the center of which had heretofore always been an exclusively European observer or center of consciousness.

There is an equally complex resonance to Ghassan Kanafani's *Men in the Sun,* a compelling novella about the travails of three Palestinian refugees who are trying to get from Basra in Iraq to Kuwait. Their past in Palestine is evoked in order to contrast it with the poverty and dispossession of which they are victims immediately after 1948. When they find a man in Basra whose occupation is in part to smuggle refugees across the border in the belly of his empty watertruck, they strike a deal with him, and he takes them as far as the border post where he is detained in conversation in the hot sun. They die of asphyxiation, unheard and forgotten. Kanafani's novella belongs to the genre of immigrant literature contributed to by an estimable number of postwar writers—Rushdie, Naipaul, Berger, Kundera, and others. But it is also a poignant meditation on the Palestinian fate, and of course eerily prescient about Palestinians in the current Gulf crisis. And yet it would do the subject of the work and its literary merit an extraordinary disservice were we to confine it to the category of national allegory, to see in it only a mirroring of the actual plight of Palestinians in exile. Kanafani's work is literature connected both to its specific historical and cultural situations as well as to a whole world of other literatures

and formal articulations, which the attentive reader summons to mind as the interpretation proceeds.

The point I am trying to make can be summed up in the useful notion of worldliness. By linking works to each other we bring them out of the neglect and secondariness to which for all kinds of political and ideological reasons they had previously been condemned. What I am talking about therefore is the opposite of separatism, and also the reverse of exclusivism. It is only through the scrutiny of these works *as* literature, as style, as pleasure and illumination, that they can be brought in, so to speak, and kept in. Otherwise they will be regarded only as informative ethnographic specimens, suitable for the limited attention of experts and area specialists. *Worldliness* is therefore the restoration to such works and interpretations of their place in the global setting, a restoration that can only be accomplished by an appreciation not of some tiny, defensively constituted corner of the world, but of the large, many-windowed house of human culture as a whole.

It seems to me absolutely essential that we engage with cultural works in this unprovincial, interested manner while maintaining a strong sense of the contest for forms and values which any decent cultural work embodies, realizes, and contains. A great deal of recent theoretical speculation has proposed that works of literature are completely determined as such by their situation, and that readers themselves are totally determined in their responses by their respective cultural situations, to a point where no value, no reading, no interpretation can be anything other than the merest reflection of some immediate interest. All readings and all writing are reduced to an assumed historical emanation. Here the indeterminacy of deconstructive reading, the airy insouciance of postaxiological criticism, the casual reductiveness of some (but by no means all) ideological schools are principally at fault. While it is true to say that because a text is the product of an unrecapturable past, and that contemporary criticism can to some extent afford a neutral disengagement or opposed perspective impossible for the text in its own time, there is no reason to take the further step and exempt the interpreter from *any* moral, political, cultural, or psychological commitments. All of these remain at play. The attempt to read a text in its fullest and most integrative context commits the reader to positions that are educative, humane, and engaged, positions that depend on training and taste and not simply on a technologized professionalism, or on the tiresome playfulness of "postmodern" criticism, with its repeated disclaimers of anything but local games and pastiches. Despite Lyotard and his acolytes, we are still in the era of large narratives, of horrendous cultural clashes, and of appallingly destructive war—as witness the recent conflagration in the Gulf—and to say that we are against theory, or beyond literature, is to be blind and trivial.

I am not arguing that every interpretive act is equivalent to a gesture either for or against life. How could anyone defend or attack so crudely general a position? I am saying that once we grant intellectual work the right to exist in a relatively disengaged atmosphere, and allow it a status that isn't disqualified by partisanship, we ought then to reconsider the ties between the text and the world in a serious and uncoercive way. Far from repudiating the great advances made when Eurocentrism and patriarchy began to be demystified, we should consolidate these advances, using them so as to reach a better understanding of the degree to which literature and artistic genius belong to and are some part of the world where all of us also do other kinds of work.

This wider application of the ideas I've been discussing cannot even be attempted if we simply repeat a few names or refer to a handful of approved texts ritualistically or sanctimoniously. Victimhood, alas, does not guarantee or necessarily enable an enhanced

sense of humanity. To testify to a history of oppression is necessary, but it is not sufficient unless that history is redirected into intellectual process and universalized to include all sufferers. Yet too often testimony to oppression becomes only a justification for further cruelty and inhumanity, or for high sounding cant and merely "correct" attitudes. I have in mind, for instance, not only the antagonists mentioned at the beginning of this essay but also the extraordinary behavior of an Elie Wiesel who has refused to translate the lessons of his own past into consistent criticisms of Israel for doing what it has done and is doing right now to Palestinians.

So while it is not necessary to regard every reading or interpretation of a text as the moral equivalent of a war or a political crisis, it does seem to me to be important to underline the fact that whatever else they are, works of literature are not merely texts. They are in fact differently constituted and have different values, they aim to do different things, exist in different genres, and so on. One of the great pleasures for those who read and study literature is the discovery of longstanding norms in which all cultures known to me concur: such things as style and performance, the existence of good as well as lesser writers, and the exercise of preference. What has been most unacceptable during the many harangues on both sides of the so-called Western canon debate is that so many of the combatants have ears of tin, and are unable to distinguish between good writing and politically correct attitudes, as if a fifth-rate pamphlet and a great novel have more or less the same significance. Who benefits from leveling attacks on the canon? Certainly not the disadvantaged person or class whose history, if you bother to read it at all, is full of evidence that popular resistance to injustice has always derived immense benefits from literature and culture in general, and very few from invidious distinctions made between ruling-class and subservient cultures. After all, the crucial lesson of C. L. R. James's *Black Jacobins,* or of E. P. Thompson's *Making of the English Working Class* (with its reminder of how important Shakespeare was to nineteenth-century radical culture), is that great antiauthoritarian uprisings made their earliest advances, not by denying the humanitarian and universalist claims of the general dominant culture, but by attacking the adherents of that culture for failing to uphold their own declared standards, for failing to extend them to all, as opposed to a small fraction, of humanity. Toussaint L'Ouverture is the perfect example of a downtrodden slave whose struggle to free himself and his people was informed by the ideas of Rousseau and Mirabeau.

Although I risk over-simplification, it is probably correct to say that it does not finally matter *who* wrote what, but rather *how* a work is written and *how* it is read. The idea that because Plato and Aristotle are male and the products of a slave society they should be disqualified from receiving contemporary attention is as limited an idea as suggesting that *only* their work, because it was addressed to and about elites, should be read today. Marginality and homelessness are not, in my opinion, to be gloried in; they are to be brought to an end, so that more, and not fewer, people can enjoy the benefits of what has for centuries been denied the victims of race, class, or gender.

# III

# RHETORIC AND
# READER RESPONSE

"As individual speech acts are to the language in which they are spoken, so are many other individual actions to the codes of the cultures in which they occur." Although speaking as a semiotician, Robert Scholes in these opening words from *Textual Power* underlines the contemporary sense of language as a field of action. He also catches the sense of action as an arrangement and effect within the rhetoric of texts and lived lives. This broad view of rhetoric as applicable to a multiplicity of sites in life and letters, as "equipment for living" (as Kenneth Burke says), is indeed a contemporary but also an ancient idea about rhetoric's utility. Tracing the history of rhetoric as equipment for living entails the recognition of rhetoric as the oldest form of textual criticism in Western culture—the oldest rigorous study of verbal texts. In the ancient world and throughout the Middle Ages, rhetoric, the method of teaching the practical uses and effects of language, was the avenue to reading, speaking, and writing in areas such as politics, law, and even theology. Rhetoric then and now studies the *effects* of language at its various sites of significance in verbal texts, as well as texts of social practice. This includes the effects of certain tropes and strategies, how to be persuasive, how to elicit emotional affect, how to achieve clarity, and attempts to understand how language functions to reach these ends and to have an effect on the world.

Rhetoric, in other words, emphasizes the essential function but also the *social* aspect of language and literature, its intersubjective effects, and its impact in particular situations as potential equipment for living. As such, the aims of rhetoric are as far from the formalist approaches to language and literature as possible, as we describe them in relation to New Criticism and Russian Formalism (in "What Is Criticism?" and "Structuralism and Semiotics"). Yet, in another sense, rhetoric participates in all of the schools of contemporary criticism examined in this book because all criticism at some point must address the effects of language, however those effects are achieved or defined.

There have always been two distinct conceptions of the nature of rhetoric that correspond to the functions of criticism and critique that we discuss in the "General Introduction." On the one hand, rhetoric examines how language persuades and uses so-called "ornaments" to achieve certain ends in the world—to say, in short, what could have been said differently but, instead, was modulated to create a certain effect. A special and instructive case of language as instrument is the way that the philosopher John Searle defines "speech acts." For Searle speech acts are uses of language that clearly accomplish immediate ends, where language directly is an action in the world, as in saying "I do" in a court room or wedding ceremony. This is rhetoric in the utterly pragmatic sense of criticism, as an accounting for the function of and "explaining" certain effects. The debate between Searle and Jacques Derrida over the meaning of speech acts hinges on Searles's pragmatic and common-sensical definition of speech acts. Terry Eagleton, in "Brecht and Rhetoric" (in "Historical Critique") more fully expands on this sense of rhetoric when he adds that " 'rhetoric' here means grasping language and action in the context of the politico-discursive conditions inscribed within them." In another essay, describing the global, dual sense of rhetoric, Eagleton examines "the ways discourses are constructed in order to achieve certain effects." Rhetoric, in this view, looks at the "concrete performance . . . and at people's responses to discourse in terms of linguistic structures and the material situations in which they functioned." He goes on to say that

> Rhetoric, or discourse theory, shares with Formalism, structuralism and semiotics an interest in the formal devices of language, but like reception theory it is also concerned with how these devices are actually effective at the point of "consumption"; its preoccupation with discourse as a form of power and desire can learn much from deconstruction and psychoanalytical theory, and its belief that discourse can be a humanly transformative affair shares a good deal with liberal humanism.

On the other hand, rhetoric can study the discontinuous and nonformal spheres in which language operates, the possibilities of figures and tropes that govern rather than ornament meaning—in effect, that govern power in the verbal and nonverbal dimensions of a social context. This is Derrida's implicit definition of speech acts. In his essay "Semiology and Rhetoric" (in *Allegories of Reading*), Paul de Man emphasizes the latter understanding of rhetoric—rhetoric as "the study of tropes and of figures (. . . not in the derived sense of comment or of eloquence or persuasion)." This would potentially be rhetoric, as Susan Miller writes in *Textual Carnivals: The Politics of Composition,* conceived as a "radical theory of language as constitutive of a greater reality" than the formal sphere of rhetoric can show. To see language in its social context and as defining the limits of meaning is to see it "as a form of power." "Understanding discourse," in this sense of rhetoric, Miller continues, "means understanding its relation to power." It follows that all schools of criticism and theory can be understood in their formal interworkings and patterning *and* in terms of the force of their social impact—their worldly effect. It is in this dual sense that rhetoric can be said to run interference for and encompass all contemporary literary criticism.

## TEXTUAL RHETORIC

The two definitions of rhetoric create a useful distinction beyond the narrow conception of rhetoric as the study of the interpersonal effects of language, a distinction that corresponds to the two modes of formalism we examined in our introduction to "What Is Criticism?" In the current section we see this division in the study of the rhetoric of particular texts, what Burke calls "the attempt to treat literature from the standpoint of situations and strategies." Burke examines such strategies in terms of the sociology of literature—what Susan Miller helpfully redesignates as a "cognitive sociology of the text." This position on the "sociological view of rhetoric" shares much with the Marxist approach of Mikhail Bakhtin throughout his work (see especially his early essay, published under the name V. N. Vološinov, "Discourse in Life and Discourse in Art (Concerning Sociological Poetics)" and *Speech Genres and Other Late Essays*). In both works literature and its rhetorical effects are essentially "functional," not aiming at articulating global or transcendental truths or human nature or a vision of "reality" or anything else "for its own sake." Literature and rhetorical effects, rather, are a form of social activity and a gesture that accomplishes an end, maybe not always the end that was intended but an end with social consequences nonetheless.

In his early and valuable contributions to contemporary rhetorical studies, critic and rhetorician Walter Ong has pursued a similar rhetorical conception of literature. Ong is best known for his work on the relationship between oral and written discourses, an area fully embedded in rhetorical analyses of literature. Working out of Peter Ramus, Eric Havelock, and Marshall McLuhan—though more conservatively than the "sociological" descriptions of Burke and Bakhtin—he attempts to describe literary history in terms of the different "roles" that written literature creates for its readers throughout literary history; oral literature, he notes, always has a *present* audience. Ong examines how the responses of an audience to a text are fully determined by the written text. Such an approach, as Patrocinio Schweickart says, is fully "text dominant." The "fiction" of the audience's role is determined by textual rhetoric in the sense that the language of the text constructs particular roles for the reader, and Ong studies both those roles and the language creating them in work that looks forward to Stanley Fish's rhetoric of style and postulation of "interpretive communities." In his work Ong attempts to mark the place where contemporary literary criticism and practical and theoretical discussions of composition intersect in the examination of rhetorical practices selected to reach an imagined, but absent, audience. The technologies of print in relation to oral cultures, and the dynamics of power between them in both the ancient and modern worlds, provide a context for understanding the relays of power and the intricacies of ideology as one cultural sphere acts on another.

## THE RHETORIC OF READER RESPONSE

The school of criticism called "reader response" is largely a derivative of rhetorical criticism. That is, whereas textual rhetoric examines the relationships of tropes and verbal devices in writing and speech, another accounting for the effects of rhetoric focuses on the reader's response in the relationship between interpretation and the protocols of reading. Criticism that focuses on readers has always been a dimension of classical rhetoric itself at least since Aristotle. In the *Poetics* Aristotle speaks of the cathartic, purging effect of tragedy and in this way Aristotle defines a major component of tragedy as a genre in terms of a reader's reaction to rhetoric. Coleridge, too, emphasizes the importance of a reader's response in his conception—a major part of romantic poetics—of esemplastic power. By esemplastic power he means the reader's sympathetic response to natural forms in nature and in literature, and in important ways romantic sensibility is defined by this human ability to interact with the rhetorical effects of nature. In the 1920s the British critic I. A. Richards proposed to catalog readers' strategies for understanding and interpreting poetry. In a manner quite distinct from the New Critics he influenced so heavily, he discussed the practical steps readers actually go through and the assumptions they make as they read. Kenneth Burke, too, in work that is only recently finding full appreciation, attempted to chart what readers actually do, the strategies by which they adopt "terministic screens" and "dramatistic" poses in reading literature. In sum, these critics, among others, have found the reading activity itself to be a primary channel for understanding textual experience.

Modern Reader-Response theory, from the late 1960s through the present, concentrates intensely on what readers do and how they do it. This movement draws significant inspiration from psychoanalysis, but a major formulation of Reader-Response theory, found in the work of Wolfgang Iser and Hans Robert Jauss, is phenomenology. As defined by Edmund Husserl and Martin Heidegger, phenomenology is a philosophical view that posits a continuous field of experience between the perceiver (subject) and the object of experience and focuses on bringing to light the relations of subject and object. A phenomenologist believes that objects-in-the-world cannot be the valid focus of a rigorous philosophical investigation. Rather, the contents of consciousness itself—"objects" as constituted by the mechanism of consciousness—should be investigated. As elaborated by Maurice Merleau-Ponty, Ludwig Binswanger, Hans-Georg Gadamer, and Gaston Bachelard, this view defines literary experience as a gestalt, holistically, with a minimal sense of separation between text and its interpretation. Phenomenology posits the inseparability of text and its reception.

Georges Poulet's "Phenomenology of Reading," to which Schweickart alludes in her essay included here, is a primary, early document of Reader-Response theory. Poulet sees the dynamics of the reading process as centered on the reader. This focus, because it reveals new and unfamiliar material—always confronting something strange within a familiar context—produces an experience of the unfamiliar, "otherness." The reader begins a text presumably "thinking one's own thought," as Poulet says. This means that readers initially are comfortable with a misrecognition—their early false sense of a familiar encounter as they read an unknown text. Eventually, however, the text offers up unfamiliar encounters and reveals itself as alien to the reader's experience prior to this text and, in its own way, quite odd. These "alien" thoughts then coalesce into a kind of alternative consciousness as a counter perspective separate from and *not* the reader's own. The result of this process is that eventually "my consciousness [as a reader] behaves as though it were the consciousness of another." This other consciousness, as Poulet reasons, must be held as a thought by someone, by a subject. He then posits that "this *thought* which is alien to me and yet in me, must also have [created] in me a *subject* which is alien to me."

This process of discovering "otherness" in reading culminates in a direct confrontation with a kind of transcendental subjectivity, a "being" or other outside of one's own experience. That is, "when reading a literary work," as Poulet goes on, "there is a moment when it seems to me that the subject *present* in this work disengages itself from all that surrounds it, and stands alone." This confrontation with independent "being" is such that "no object can any longer express it, no structure can any longer define it; it is exposed in its ineffability and in its fundamental indeterminancy." The act of reading, in this way, begins with the gradual discovery of "otherness" but eventually opens upon an experience wherein the difference, or gap, separating subjects from objects, and reader from text, is transcended altogether. In reading, subject and object ultimately are shown to be merged—in fact, were never "really" separate—in a continuous field of experience.

On this basis phenomenological literary criticism explores not just the dynamics of individual texts but the boundaries and operations of each author's "world," a particular staging of the process that opens upon the disengaged subject. The philosopher Ludwig Binswanger, along this line, has explored Henrik Ibsen's dramatic "world," and J. Hillis Miller—in the phenomenological phase of his work—investigated the fictional "world" of Charles Dickens just as he explored the "experience" (the "world") of modernity in *Poets of Reality* (1965) and Victorian culture in *The Disappearance of God* (1963). In each case the emphasis is on a "descriptive" approach that gradually, and painstakingly, isolates the text's presentation of subject/object relations. Out of these connections, usually made for several works or for a writer's whole corpus, emerges the consciousness that constitutes the authorial world. The descriptive technique of this phenomenological criticism appears to link it with formalism, but the aim here, by contrast, is precisely to capture "experience," not form, and to disregard and overrun formal limits—particularly a work's chronology, the functions of language, and the like—in characterizing the essential aspects of any text.

Much contemporary reader-oriented criticism is carried out against the background of this earlier work—as well as the background of textual rhetoric—but tends, as Steven Mailloux notes, to divide into three separate strains: phenomenology, subjectivism, and structuralism. The line of phenomenology moves through Poulet, Hans-Georg Gadamer, Hans Robert Jauss, and Wolfgang Iser. Particularly important theoretically is Gadamer's *Truth and Method* (trans. 1975), which attempts to rethink the confluence of phenomenology and literary criticism by returning to Heidegger's discussion of consciousness as always *situated* culturally, what Heidegger called *Dasein*—"being there," or "being-in-the-world." Gadamer's work brought about a minor revival of interest in phenomenological reading, not least because of his influence on Hans Robert Jauss, also a phenomenologist, who examines a work's reception (what Jauss calls "reception esthetic") within a cultural milieu and attempts to establish a "horizon of expectation," or a "paradigm" accounting for that culture's responses to literature at a certain moment. His work, especially in medieval studies, has stimulated a new kind of "historical" criticism and has even been useful to the "New Historicism" examined in the introductory essay to "Historical Critique."

Wolfgang Iser gives another influential version of Reader-Response work, one still in the phenomenological camp but intensely concerned with the pragmatics of reading in actual interpretation. Wolfgang Iser builds a reader-oriented theory around the concept of narrative "gaps." "Gaps" for Iser mean the details or connections—the vaguenesses—within a story that a reader must fill in or make up from his or her own experience. No story, no matter how "realistic," can provide the number of details that would obviate such gaps. The structural need to fill these gaps is the text's way of completing itself through the reader's experience and of ensuring the reader's investment in that work. Ambiguous in this thinking, however, is the question of the reader's apparent control of the reading experience. Is the text in charge of reading, or does the reader virtually write the text by filling its gaps without external constraint? The problem of deciding if the text (author) or the reader is in charge in the act of reading is a recurrent and as yet unanswered question in Reader-Response criticism.

In the related school that Mailloux calls subjectivism, this same problem concerning the authority of interpretation is intensified. Drawing from psychoanalytic theory, David Bleich, for instance, practices a "subjective criticism" that assumes that literary interpretation is never more than an elaboration of a person's most personal motivations and desires, which are projected or "discovered," perhaps even "disavowed," in the literary text. Bleich's method involves establishing the connection between literary interpretation, the aesthetic effect of a text, and the individual search for self-knowledge. By psychologizing the reading process in this way, Bleich resolves the text/reader question in the reader's favor. The reader is in charge, but this strategy, as some believe, leaves the text virtually undefined and without intrinsic meaning— "blank," so to speak.

Initially, Norman N. Holland, also a Freudian and an important literary critic of the mid–twentieth century, seemed to resolve the text/reader question without losing the text, but the result of his criticism (with some differences) is similar to Bleich's. In *5 Readers Reading* (1975) and *Poems in Persons* (1973) Holland attempts "to understand the combination of text and personal association," an approach suggesting evenhandedness in the text-reader dispute. For Holland, as Mailloux points out, "the reader makes sense of the text by creating a meaningful unity out of its elements." There is no unity "in the text [itself] but [only] in the mind of the reader." More pointedly, concerning the text's authority, Holland says in *5 Readers Reading* that "the reader is surely responding to *something*. The literary text may be only so many marks on a page—at most a matrix of psychological possibilities for its readers." This minimalist sense of the literary text as "marks on a page," much like Bleich's subjective criticism, again leaves little sense of the text as anything more than a reflection, a mirroring, of the reader's personal concerns. The text-reader question is resolved completely in the reader's favor, leaving the literary text in the role of mere stimulus (again, a virtually "blank" text) for the reader's response.

Stanley E. Fish and Jonathan Culler try to avoid the ambiguities of Bleich's and Holland's subjectivism through a third approach to reading, one that Mailloux calls structuralism. They begin by imagining, as do Bleich and Holland, that reading and interpretation initially are "free" activities virtually ungoverned by the texts being read. Fish and Culler then move to place constraints on reading to lay the foundation for what may be considered a "valid" interpretation of a particular text. In "Interpreting the *Variorum*," Fish's major document about Reader-Response criticism, Fish explains how the stylistic economy of a text initially elicits multiple and conflicting responses. Any one text, though, will not finally be read in a multiplicity of ways by a single reader. Readers all have personal limitations and tend to interpret texts in fairly narrow and prescribed ways. Particular interpretive choices are based on the reader's belonging to an "interpretive community" of other readers, and this community will allow certain readings as normative and reject others as untenable. From this communal censoring activity, in other words, will emerge "valid," or normative, readings of a text.

In a similar way, drawing on Noam Chomsky's distinction between competence and performance, Culler posits a set of reading conventions, or strategies for understanding written texts, that a qualified reader in a culture will learn and employ. A person's measurable ability to implement these conventions constitutes reading "competence," which for Fish and Culler—under different names—becomes nearly the whole substance of the reading activity. Again, in this focus on competence we are witnessing the virtual obliteration of any sense of an objective "text."

Fish and Culler go on to place "common-sense" restrictions on an activity that most readers would tend to agree is, in some way, bounded or constrained. Readers do not generally report reading from every conceivable perspective simultaneously and experience the extremes of indeterminacy in interpretation only at the initial stage of reading, before external constraints of an interpretive community come into play. Unlike Bleich and Holland, Fish and Culler—most explicitly in Culler's *Structuralist Poetics* (1975)—attempt to articulate a conception of the "facts" in literature in a way that grows out of Saussure's description of the nature of linguistic fact (see Saussure's texts in "Structuralism and Semiotics"). Fish also describes the contextual and conventional nature of literary "facts" when he says that "phonological 'facts' are no more uninterpreted (or less conventional) than the 'facts' of orthography; the distinctive features that make articulation and reception possible are the product of a system of differences that must be *imposed* before it can be recognized." "The patterns the ear hears (like the patterns the eye sees)," Fish goes on, "are the patterns its perceptual habits make available."

Reader-Response criticism, as we can see here, draws on pragmatic notions about the nature of reading and making sense of reading. It does seem reasonable to assume, with Fish and Culler, that constraints on reading do exist and that those constraints are analogous to the constraints on language at its elemental level of functioning. The hypothesis about an interpretive community's implementation of constraints on reading is difficult to verify. One must grant with Bleich and Holland that meaning, or the authority of any single interpretation, is difficult to locate or prove within a text. Few contemporary theorists or critics would maintain that a text is self-defining or authorizing. Texts do not tell readers how to read them or exercise textual or interpretive judgments to support a particular interpretation. Can an inanimate text even be thought to possess an intention? In the practices of contemporary criticism, there are many different answers to this question. However, the simple relocation of interpretive authority from the text to a community that decides about interpreting texts may not be a solution to the problem. Who can know all of the interpretive communities to which any one reader belongs? Who will be sufficiently "competent" to determine the proper communal interpretation of any one text? How is the authority of an interpretive community established?

A moment's reflection on these and other questions reveals that the "interpretive community" cannot be set up as a clear arbitrator of interpretation. Interpretive community is no more of a decidable, unambiguous concept in interpretation than is the idea of "textual" authority. Fish and Culler have apparently "solved" the problem of interpretation once again by deferring it. The "interpretive community" and "competence" are themselves indeterminate and problematic concepts, in effect, new difficulties with which to deal. The text-reader question remains as open for Fish and Culler as for Bleich and Holland.

## THE NEW RHETORIC OF THE TEXT

While current Reader-Response criticism has not actually solved many primary questions about its procedures, it has been and continues to be a creative and vital movement nonetheless. Like many critical schools since World War II, Reader-Response argues against the exclusive use of formalist approaches to literature by emphasizing reading or interpretation as an *activity,* as an ongoing performative rather than static or contained event. At the same time, Reader-Response criticism participates in the generalizing practices of formalism that Burke argues against. Schweickart addresses this issue in the feminist critique of "Reading Ourselves: Toward a Feminist Theory of Reading" and offers a helpful overview of various practices of Reader-Response criticism, exploring the universalizing and "utopian" aim within contemporary criticism. Schweickart notes that much contemporary theory and criticism overlooks the issues of race, class, and sex.

After surveying the various schools of Reader-Response criticism, Schweickart then discusses the gender-based aspects of reading and describes two different *kinds* of reader-response. The first is carried out "under the sign of the 'Resisting Reader,' " wherein the goal is to *resist* the "fiction" intended for a male audience and, in doing so, to expose "the androcentricity of what has customarily passed for the universal." The second kind of reader response is that which creates a new role for the reader, a feminine role for the reader of women's writing, that—eschewing "mainstream reader-response theories [which are] preoccupied with issues of control and partition"—seeks to discover "the dialectic of communication informing the relationship between the feminist reader and the female author/text." In this description Schweickart is attempting to articulate a rhetoric of reading—functioning "equipment"—that is both textual and reader oriented. In her feminist critique, Schweickart is describing ways in which contemporary rhetorical analyses of literature can create new ways of reading and understanding.

Barbara Johnson's "Apostrophe, Animation, and Abortion" exemplifies the operation of a rhetorical dialectic—in this case, the relationship between the feminist reader and the female author/text. In Johnson's conception of rhetoric, there are no encompassing interpretive communities of response to texts but, rather, particular practices and tactics. This conception of rhetoric has the obvious strength of being situated complexly in relation to particular rhetorical strategies in the text and the particular strategies of readers in relation to those texts. This is a conception of rhetoric that highlights the social force of certain rhetorical strategies and the potential of an ideological critique that can focus on the relation among texts in a specific and situated sense. In the manner of Schweickart, Johnson examines the poetic tropes used to address abortion, showing that "there are striking and suggestive parallels between the 'different voices' involved in the abortion debate and the shifting ad-dress-structures of poems like Gwendolyn Brooks's 'The Mother.' " Johnson explores the extent to which abortion and miscarriage as the objects of discourse are "inextri-cably connected to the figure of apostrophe."

Johnson is at once specific in her use of literary and other texts and critical in her rhetorical exploration of those texts. Johnson deploys rhetorical tropes to represent the positions and investments of gender. In this way rhetoric focuses on the relations of value and ideology at different sites of the cultural text. In the manner of cultural studies, following what Gilles Deleuze and Felix Guattari call the "rhizomic" logic of cultural determination, she finds in the course of this inquiry that "rhetorical, psycho-analytical, and political structures are profoundly implicated in one another."

Rhetorical criticism in America is now moving strongly in the direction of the situated understanding—the circumstances of history and the specifics of institu-tional housing—of all denominations of writing and rhetorical practice. Gerald Graff begins his recent *Beyond the Culture Wars: How Teaching the Conflicts Can Revital-ize American Education* by saying, "Writing for a general audience is not an easy thing for the average academic. As writers we academics are spoiled. We are used to writing for other academics, usually those in our particular fields, and this protection from outside perspectives lets us fall into cozy ways of thinking and expressing ourselves." Graff's attempt to contextualize the jargony in-writing typical of most "academic" writers is a way, as Scholes says, of teaching the "cultural text." In light of this contextualization, Graff's plain style of writing his book without the implicit layering of presupposition and guild recognition among specialist academics consti-tutes a rhetorical stance with evident ideological implications. For instance, in these lines just quoted Graff avoids all technical reference and convoluted periodic sen-tence construction. His rhetorical strategy suggests that an academic writer should no longer use as a cover for bad writing the blanket excuse that academic complexity and richness of thought can only be housed in convoluted rhetoric and the most special-ized terminology. In this way Graff's relatively new and accessible prose style is itself a critique of and a challenge to other academic writers. In something as seemingly "ornamental" as style, there is a message and an implicit definition of the nature of efficacious work in a pluralistic democratic culture.

The study of contemporary rhetorical practice, in short, is currently taking the form of a cognitive sociology of the text in its examination of working subjectivities—or working sets of assumptions about value—evident in the perspectives created by actual written and other kinds of texts. This approach potentially takes in, as Susan Miller writes, "the 'actual' [production of texts] and systems of control, theorized horizontal and vertical planes on which social practices and discursive formations meet." The study of rhetoric and writing in this way becomes a kind of study of cultural production, a view of each text as "deployed" by the culture—situated where it is in terms of social class and social relationships to serve a specific and definable end. Even Walter Ong sees and admits, as Miller notes, "that classical rhetoric was itself a combative, disciplined, male pursuit and has accounted for its [own] disap-pearance with curious . . . arguments."

This current, cultural-studies approach to rhetoric not only assumes the connect-edness and cross-indexed relations of different rhetorical texts in the culture, it also chooses sites for rhetorical critique that were once thought to be marginal. This choice in itself becomes, by implication, a focused critique of the customary and accepted sites for rhetorical analysis in canonical literature and well-defined subcultures. By contrast, rhetoricians are now willing and able to look at the previously ignored circumstances of standard (but largely "invisible" in the impact of their circumstances) writing situations. In *Textual Carnivals,* for example, Miller examines the cultural frame that produces the "required subjectivity [which is "infantilized"] of the composition student." She discusses the "characterizations of the composition course as a transition to college life and its reliance on pedagogies often used at much earlier levels, but also from the persistent objectification/subjection of the student that follows from requirements, from placement and 'diagnostic' exams, and from the absence of choice among the emphases or conduct of sections of one course taught by those described in class schedules as anonymous 'staff.'" Working within this cultural text marked as marginalized and insignificant, the composition teacher, in the context of institutional structures, wields the power, in this instance, to initiate "students into the culture's discourse on language, which is always at one with action, emotion, and regulatory establishments."

Significant here in Miller's analysis are the theoretical critique of the subject in a writing situation and also the critique of the choice of a writing situation itself. The rhetorical situation of a college composition course is merely "factual" and without need of comment or critique according to many previous rhetorical analyses. In Miller's analysis, however, the choice of a previously marginalized set of circumstances for writing (unremarkable and seldom remarked on) is a strategic move that defines rhetorical analysis not simply in the explanatory terms of criticism but also in the transformative potential of critique and the instigation of change. This transformative potential of rhetorical analysis is foregrounded in many current practices as an intentionally probing and somewhat disruptive version of the textual analysis that has always been the strength of rhetorical criticism. Current practices in the rhetorical analysis of literary and nonliterary texts appropriate the techniques of classical and contemporary analyses to serve goals that are no longer set exclusively within established institutional models. Evident in current practices is the emergence of a practice as yet unnamed—strong rhetorical critique as a tool of cultural understanding and change.

## RELATED ESSAYS IN
## *CONTEMPORARY LITERARY CRITICISM*

Paul de Man, "The Resistance to Theory"
J. Hillis Miller, "The Search for Grounds in Literary Study"
Jonathan Culler, "Convention and Meaning"
Shoshana Felman, "Psychoanalysis and Education"
Terry Eagleton, "Brecht and Rhetoric"
Paula Bennett, "The Pea That Duty Locks"

## FURTHER READING

Bakhtin, M. M., *Speech Genres and Other Late Essays,* trans. Vern McGee (Austin: University of Texas Press, 1986).

———— [V. N. Volosinov], "Discourse in Life and Discourse in Art (Concerning Sociological Poetics)," in *Marxism and the Philosophy of Language,* trans. Ladislav Matejka and I. R. Titunik (Cambridge, MA: Harvard University Press, 1986).

Bleich, David, *Readings and Feelings: An Introduction to Subjective Criticism* (New York: Harper & Row, 1977).

————, *Subjective Criticism* (Baltimore: Johns Hopkins University Press, 1978).

Booth, Wayne C., *The Rhetoric of Fiction* (Chicago: University of Chicago Press, 1961).

Chabot, Barry C., ". . . Reading Readers Reading Readers Reading . . . ," in *Diacritics,* 5, No. 3 (1975), 24–38.

Chatman, Seymour, *Narrative Structure in Fiction and Film* (Ithaca, NY: Cornell University Press, 1978).

Culler, Jonathan, "Stanley Fish and the Righting of the Reader," in *Diacritics,* 5, No. 1 (1975), 26–31).

————, *Structuralist Poetics* (Ithaca, NY: Cornell University Press, 1975).

de Man, Paul, "Semiology and Rhetoric," in *Allegories of Reading* (New Haven, CT: Yale University Press, 1979).

Fish, Stanley, *Is There a Text in This Class?* (Cambridge, MA: Harvard University Press, 1980).

————, *Self-Consuming Artifacts: The Experience of Seventeenth-Century Literature* (Berkeley: University of California Press, 1972).

————, *Surprised by Sin: The Reader in Paradise Lost* (Berkeley: University of California Press, 1967).

————, "Why No One's Afraid of Wolfgang Iser," in *Diacritics,* 11, No. 1 (1981), 2–13.

Graff, Gerald, *Beyond the Culture Wars: How Teaching the Conflicts Can Revitalize American Education* (New York: W.W. Norton, 1992).

Havelock, Eric, *Preface to Plato* (Cambridge, MA: Harvard University Press, 1963).

Holland, Norman N., *The Dynamics of Literary Response* (New York: Oxford University Press, 1968).

————, *5 Readers Reading* (New Haven, CT: Yale University Press, 1975).

————, *Poems in Persons* (New York: W. W. Norton, 1973).

Ingarden, Roman, *The Cognition of the Literary Work of Art* (Evanston, IL: Northwestern University Press, 1973).

Iser, Wolfgang, *The Act of Reading* (Baltimore: Johns Hopkins University Press, 1978).

————, *The Implied Reader: Patterns of Communication in Prose Fiction from Bunyan to Beckett* (Baltimore: Johns Hopkins University Press, 1974).

Jauss, Hans Robert, "Literary History as a Challenge to Literary Theory," in *New Directions in Literary History,* ed. Ralph Cohen (Baltimore: Johns Hopkins University Press, 1974), 11–41.

————, *Toward an Aesthetic of Reception,* trans. Timothy Bahti (Minneapolis: University of Minnesota Press, 1982).

Mailloux, Steven, *Interpretive Conventions: The Reader in the Study of American Fiction* (Ithaca, NY: Cornell University Press, 1982).

Miller, Susan, *Textual Carnivals: The Politics of Composition* (Carbondale and Edwardsville: Southern Illinois University Press, 1991).

Ong, Walter, S.J., *Fighting for Life: Contest, Sexuality, and Consciousness* (Ithaca NY: Cornell University Press, 1981).

————, *Orality and Literacy* (New York: Methuen, 1982).

————, *Rhetoric, Romance, and Technology.* (Ithaca NY: Cornell University Press, 1971).

Poulet, Georges, "Phenomenology of Reading." Trans. Richard Macksey, *New Literary History*, 1 (1969), 53–68.

Pratt, Mary Louise, *Toward a Speech Act Theory of Literary Discourse* (Bloomington: Indiana University Press, 1977).

Prince, Gerald, "Introduction à l'étude de narrataire," in *Poetique,* 14 (1973), 178–96.

"Reading, Interpretation, Response," Special section of *Genre,* 10 (1977), 363–453.

Roudiez, Leon, "Notes on the Reader as Subject," in *Semiotext(e),* 1, No. 3 (1975), 69–80.

Scoles, Robert, *Textual Power* (New Haven, CT: Yale University Press, 1985).

Starobinski, Jean, *Word Upon Words* (New Haven, CT: Yale University Press, 1979).

Suleiman, Susan, and Inge Corsman, eds., *The Reader in the Text: Essays on Audience and Interpretation* (Princeton, NJ: Princeton University Press, 1980).

Tompkins, Jane, ed., *Reader-Response Criticism* (Baltimore: Johns Hopkins University Press, 1980).

# 11

# Kenneth Burke
# 1897–

In an era of critical thought that understands itself increasingly in terms of movements and schools, Kenneth Burke has produced over sixty years of criticism and theory that distances itself from any single approach to literature. This antinomian attitude is captured in one of Burke's mottoes: "When in Rome, do as the Greeks"; and it is this role of gadfly within the critical establishment that makes Burke a central figure in the development of American criticism. However, to say that Burke continually opposed himself to prevailing critical schools is not to say that he disdained critical method— quite the contrary. In fact one might characterize the trajectory of his thought as a search for a method adequate not only to an understanding of literature but adequate to an understanding of all aspects of human behavior. This broader concern with human behavior begins to develop after the publication of his first book, *Counter-Statement* (1931), when he turns his attention to the question of human motivation, focusing on the nature of perspective, or what he often calls "attitude." The major publications from this early concern are *Permanence and Change* (1935) and *Attitudes Toward History* (1937). It is during this transitional period that "Literature as Equipment for Living" is written. During the following years, Burke writes his best known works: *A Grammar of Motives* (1945), *A Rhetoric of Motives* (1950), and the essays collected in *Language as Symbolic Action* (1966). Interest in these works, as in Burke's thought in general, has increased over the past fifteen years, as American critics influenced by Continental theories of language have rediscovered Burke's concern with the relationship of language, knowledge, and social structures.

"Literature as Equipment for Living" was published initially in 1937, in the first volume of the American leftist journal *Direction,* which Burke later joined as an associate editor. In this essay Burke positions his critical method, more or less explicitly, in relation to three currents in American criticism, all of which, according to Burke, neutralize the vitality of literature. The first is the idea that literature is detached from everyday life and, consequently, more "pure" than the practicalities of living; but in opposition to this idea, Burke asserts that we use literature to deal with recurrent situations in our lives. The second current, which Burke discusses toward the end of the essay, is the drive toward specialization that is encouraged by academic criticism; the tendency of academic criticism, because it excludes other areas of learning, is to reify older literary classifications and thereby to stifle the development of literary criticism. In opposition to these first two currents, Burke calls for a "sociological criticism," but, as he suggests in his opening paragraph, his idea of a sociological criticism has an emphasis different from traditional sociological criticism. Burke appears to be referring to Marxist critics such as Van Wyck Brooks, Granville Hicks, and V. F. Calverton, whose work he had reviewed unfavorably as positing a simplistic economic determinism between literary work and social context. In opposition to this determinism, Burke suggests a broader range of motivations that could affect the production of a literary work and redefines sociological criticism as the codifying of "the various strategies which artists have developed with relation to the naming of situations."

# Literature as Equipment for Living

Here I shall put down, as briefly as possible, a statement in behalf of what might be catalogued, with a fair degree of accuracy, as a *sociological* criticism of literature. Sociological criticism in itself is certainly not new. I shall here try to suggest what partially new elements or emphasis I think should be added to this old approach. And to make the "way in" as easy as possible. I shall begin with a discussion of proverbs.

**1**

Examine random specimens in *The Oxford Dictionary of English Proverbs*. You will note, I think, that there is no "pure" literature here. Everything is "medicine." Proverbs are designed for consolation or vengeance, for admonition or exhortation, for foretelling.

Or they name typical, recurrent situations. That is, people find a certain social relationship recurring so frequently that they must "have a word for it." The Eskimos have special names for many different kinds of snow (fifteen, if I remember rightly) because variations in the quality of snow greatly affect their living. Hence, they must "size up" snow much more accurately than we do. And the same is true of social phenomena. Social structures give rise to "type" situations, subtle subdivisions of the relationships involved in competitive and cooperative acts. Many proverbs seek to chart, in more or less homey and

picturesque ways, these "type" situations. I submit that such naming is done, not for the sheer glory of the thing, but because of its bearing upon human welfare. A different name for snow implies a different kind of hunt. Some names for snow imply that one should not hunt at all. And similarly, the names for typical, recurrent social situations are not developed out of "disinterested curiosity," but because the names imply a command (what to expect, what to look out for).

To illustrate with a few representative examples:

Proverbs designed for consolation: "The sun does not shine on both sides of the hedge at once." "Think of ease, but work on." "Little troubles the eye, but far less the soul." "The worst luck now, the better another time." "The wind in one's face makes one wise." "He that hath lands hath quarrels." "He knows how to carry the dead cock home." "He is not poor that hath little, but he that desireth much."

For vengeance: "At length the fox is brought to the furrier." "Shod in the cradle, barefoot in the stubble." "Sue a beggar and get a louse." "The higher the ape goes, the more he shows his tail." "The moon does not heed the barking of dogs." "He measures another's corn by his own bushel." "He shuns the man who knows him well." "Fools tie knots and wise men loose them."

Proverbs that have to do with foretelling: (The most obvious are those to do with the weather.) "Sow peas and beans in the wane of the moon, Who soweth them sooner, he soweth too soon." "When the wind's in the north, the skilful fisher goes not forth." "When the sloe tree is as white as a sheet, sow your barley whether it be dry or wet." "When the sun sets bright and clear, An easterly wind you need not fear. When the sun sets in a bank, A westerly wind we shall not want."

In short: "Keep your weather eye open": be realistic about sizing up today's weather, because your accuracy has bearing upon tomorrow's weather. And forecast not only the meteorological weather, but also the social weather: "When the moon's in the full, then wit's in the wane." "Straws show which way the wind blows." "When the fish is caught, the net is laid aside." "Remove an old tree, and it will wither to death." "The wolf may lose his teeth, but never his nature." "He that bites on every weed must needs light on poison." "Whether the pitcher strikes the stone, or the stone the pitcher, it is bad for the pitcher." "Eagles catch no flies." "The more laws, the more offenders."

In this foretelling category we might also include the recipes for wise living, sometimes moral, sometimes technical: "First thrive, and then wive." "Think with the wise but talk with the vulgar." "When the fox preacheth, then beware your geese." "Venture a small fish to catch a great one." "Respect a man, he will do the more."

In the class of "typical, recurrent situations" we might put such proverbs and proverbial expressions as: "Sweet appears sour when we pay." "The treason is loved but the traitor is hated." "The wine in the bottle does not quench thirst." "The sun is never the worse for shining on a dunghill." "The lion kicked by an ass." "The lion's share." "To catch one napping." "To smell a rat." "To cool one's heels."

By all means, I do not wish to suggest that this is the only way in which the proverbs could be classified. For instance, I have listed in the "foretelling" group the proverb, "When the fox preacheth, then beware your geese." But it could obviously be "taken over" for vindictive purposes. Or consider a proverb like, "Virtue flies from the heart of a mercenary man." A poor man might obviously use it either to console himself for being poor (the implication being, "Because I am poor in money I am rich in virtue") or to strike at another (the implication being, "When he got money, what else could you expect of him but deterioration?"). In fact, we could even say that such symbolic vengeance would itself be an aspect of solace. And a proverb like "The sun is never the worse for shining on a dunghill" (which I have listed under "typical recurrent situations") might as well be put in the vindictive category.

The point of issue is not to find categories that "place" the proverbs once and for all. What I want is categories that suggest their active nature. Here there is no "realism for its own sake." There is realism for promise, admonition, solace, vengeance, foretelling, instruction, charting, all for the direct bearing that such acts have upon matters of welfare.

## 2

Step two: Why not extend such analysis of proverbs to encompass the whole field of literature? Could the most complex and sophisticated works of art legitimately be considered somewhat as "proverbs writ large"? Such leads, if held admissible, should help us to discover important facts about literary organization (thus satisfying the requirements of technical criticism). And the kind of observation from this perspective should apply beyond literature to life in general (thus helping to take literature out of its separate bin and give it a place in a general "sociological" picture).

The point of view might be phrased in this way: Proverbs are *strategies* for dealing with *situations.* In so far as situations are typical and recurrent in a given social structure, people develop names for them and strategies for handling them. Another name for strategies might be *attitudes.*

People have often commented on the fact that there are contrary *proverbs.* But I believe that the above approach to proverbs suggests a necessary modification of that comment. The apparent contradictions depend upon differences in *attitude,* involving a correspondingly different choice of *strategy.* Consider, for instance, the *apparently* opposite pair: "Repentance comes too late" and "Never too late to mend." The first is admonitory. It says in effect: "You'd better look out, or you'll get yourself too far into this business." The second is consolatory, saying in effect: "Buck up, old man, you can still pull out of this."

Some critics have quarreled with me about my selection of the word "strategy" as the name for this process. I have asked them to suggest an alternative term, so far without profit. The only one I can think of is "method." But if "strategy" errs in suggesting to some people an overly *conscious* procedure, "method" errs in suggesting an overly *"methodical"* one. Anyhow, let's look at the documents:

*Concise Oxford Dictionary:* "Strategy: Movement of an army or armies in a compaign, art of so moving or disposing troops or ships as to impose upon the enemy the place and time and conditions for fighting preferred by oneself' (from a Greek word that refers to the leading of an army).

*New English Dictionary:* "Strategy: The art of projecting and directing the larger military movements and operations of a campaign."

André Cheron, *Traité Complet d'Echecs:* "On entend par stratégie les manoeuvres qui ont pour but la sortie et le bon arrangement des pièces."

Looking at these definitions, I gain cour-

age. For surely, the most highly alembicated and sophisticated work of art, arising in complex civilizations, could be considered as designed to organize and command the army of one's thoughts and images, and to so organize them that one "imposes upon the enemy the time and place and conditions for fighting preferred by oneself." One seeks to "direct the larger movements and operations" in one's campaign of living. One "maneuvers," and the maneuvering is an "art."

Are not the final results one's "strategy"? One tries, as far as possible, to develop a strategy whereby one "can't lose." One tries to change the rules of the game until they fit his own necessities. Does the artist encounter disaster? He will "make capital" of it. If one is a victim of competition, for instance, if one is elbowed out, if one is willy-nilly more jockeyed against than jockeying, one can by the solace and vengeance of art convert this very "liability" into an "asset." One tries to fight on his own terms, developing a strategy for imposing the proper "time, place, and conditions."

But one must also, to develop a full strategy, be *realistic.* One must *size things up* properly. One cannot accurately know how things *will* be, what is promising and what is menacing, unless he accurately knows how things are. So the wise strategist will not be content with strategies of merely a self-gratifying sort. He will "keep his weather eye open." He will not too eagerly "read into" a scene an attitude that is irrelevant to it. He won't sit on the side of an active volcano and "see" it as a dormant plain.

Often, alas, he will. The great allurement in our present popular "inspirational literature," for instance, may be largely of this sort. It is a strategy for easy consolation. It "fills a need," since there is always a need for easy consolation—and in an era of confusion like our own the need is especially keen. So people are only too willing to "meet a man halfway" who will *play down* the realistic naming of our situation and *play up* such strategies as make solace cheap. However, I should propose a reservation here. We usually take it for granted that people who consume our current output of books on "How to Buy Friends and Bamboozle Oneself and Other People" are reading as *students* who will attempt applying the recipes given. Nothing of the sort. *The reading of a book on the attaining of success is in itself the symbolic attaining of that success.* It is *while they read* that these readers are "succeeding." I'll wager that, in by far the great majority of cases, such readers made no serious attempt to apply the book's recipes. The lure of the book resides in the fact that the reader, while reading it, is then living in the aura of success. What he wants is *easy* success; and he gets it in symbolic form by the mere reading itself. To attempt applying such stuff in real life would be very difficult, full of many disillusioning difficulties.

Sometimes a different strategy may arise. The author may remain realistic, avoiding too easy a form of solace—yet he may get as far off the track in his own way. Forgetting that realism is an aspect for foretelling, he may take it as an end in itself. He is tempted to do this by two factors: (1) an *ill-digested* philosophy of science, leading him mistakenly to assume that "relentless" naturalistic "truthfulness" is a proper end in itself, and (2) a merely *competitive* desire to outstrip other writers by being "more realistic" than they. Works thus made "efficient" by tests of competition internal to the book trade are a kind of academicism not so named (the writer usually thinks of it as the *opposite* of academicism). Realism thus stepped up competitively might be distinguished from the proper sort by the name of "naturalism." As a way of "sizing things up," the naturalistic tradition tends to become as inaccurate as the "inspirational" strategy, though at the opposite extreme.

Anyhow, the main point is this: A work like *Madame Bovary* (or its homely American translation, *Babbitt*) is the strategic naming of a situation. It singles out a pattern of experience that is sufficiently often *mutandis mutatis,* for people to "need a word for it" and to adopt an attitude towards it. Each work of art is the addition of a word to an informal dictionary (or, in the case of purely derivative artists, the addition of a subsidiary meaning to a word already given by some originating artist). As for *Madame Bovary,* the French critic Jules de Gaultier proposed to add it to our formal dictionary by coining the word "Bovarysme" and writing a whole book to say what he meant by it.

Mencken's book on *The American Language,* I hate to say, is splendid. I console myself with the reminder that Mencken didn't write it. Many millions of people wrote it, and Mencken was merely the amanuensis who took it down from their dictation. He found a true "vehicle" (that is, a book that could be greater than the author who wrote it). He gets the royalties, but the job was done by a collectivity. As you read that book, you see a people who were up against a new set of typical recurrent situations, situations typical of their business, their politics, their criminal organizations, their sports. Either there were no words for these in standard English, or people didn't know them, or they didn't "sound right." So a new vocabulary arose, to "give us a word for it." I see no reason for believing that Americans are unusually fertile in word-coinage. American slang was not developed out of some exceptional gift. It was developed out of the fact that new typical situations had arisen and people needed names for them. They had to "size things up." They had to console and strike, to promise and admonish. They had to describe for purposes of forecasting. And "slang" was the result. It is, by this analysis, simple *proverbs not so named,* a kind of "folk criticism."

3

With what, then, would "sociological criticism" along these lines be concerned? It would seek to codify the various strategies which artists have developed with relation to the naming of situations. In a sense, much of it would even be "timeless," for many of the "typical, recurrent situations" are not peculiar to our own civilization at all. The situations and strategies framed in Aesop's Fables, for instance, apply to human relations now just as fully as they applied in ancient Greece. They are, like philosophy, sufficiently "generalized" to extend far beyond the particular combination of events named by them in any one instance. They name an "essence." Or, as Korzybski might say, they are on a "high level of abstraction." One doesn't usually think of them as "abstract," since they are usually so concrete in their stylistic expression. But they invariably aim to discern the "general behind the particular" (which would suggest that they are good Goethe).

The attempt to treat literature from the standpoint of situations and strategies suggests a variant of Spengler's notion of the "contemporaneous." By "contemporaneity" he meant corresponding stages of different cultures. For instance, if modern New York is much like decadent Rome, then we are "contemporaneous" with decadent Rome, or with some corresponding decadent city among the Mayas, etc. It is in this sense that situations are "timeless," "nonhistorical," "contemporaneous." A given human relationship may be at one time named in terms of foxes and lions, if there are foxes and lions about; or it may now be named in terms of salesmanship, advertising, the tactics of politicians, etc. But beneath the change in particulars, we may often discern the naming of the one situation.

So sociological criticism, as here understood, would seek to assemble and codify this lore. It might occasionally lead us to outrage good taste, as we sometimes found ex-

emplified in some great sermon or tragedy or abstruse work of philosophy the same strategy as we found exemplified in a dirty joke. At this point, we'd put the sermon and the dirty joke together, thus "grouping by situation" and showing the range of possible particularizations. In his exceptionally discerning essay, "A Critic's Job of Work," R. P. Blackmur says, "I think on the whole his (Burke's) method could be applied with equal fruitfulness to Shakespeare, Dashiell Hammett, or Marie Corelli." When I got through wincing, I had to admit that Blackmur was right. This article is an attempt to say for the method what can be said. As a matter of fact, I'll go a step further and maintain: You can't properly put Marie Corelli and Shakespeare apart until you have first put them together. First genus, then differentia. The strategy in common is the genus. The *range* or *scale of spectrum* of particularizations is the differentia.

Anyhow, that's what I'm driving at. And that's why reviewers sometime find in my work "intuitive" leaps that are dubious as "science." They are not "leaps" at all. They are classifications, groupings, made on the basis of some strategic element common to the items grouped. They are neither more nor less "intuitive" than *any* grouping or classification of social events. Apples can be grouped with bananas as fruits, and they can be grouped with tennis balls as round. I am simply proposing, in the social sphere, a method of classification with reference to *strategies*.

The method of these things to be said in its favor: It gives definite insight into the organization of literary works; and it automatically breaks down the barriers erected about literature as a specialized pursuit. People can classify novels by reference to three kinds, eight kinds, seventeen kinds. It doesn't matter. Students patiently copy down the professor's classification and pass examinations on it, because the range of possible academic classifications is endless. Sociological classification, as herein suggested, would derive its relevance from the fact that it should apply both to works of art and to social situations outside of art.

It would, I admit, violate current pieties, break down current categories, and thereby "outrage good taste." But "good taste" has become *inert*. The classifications I am proposing would be *active*. I think that what we need is active categories.

These categories will lie on the bias across the categories of modern specialization. The new alignment will outrage in particular those persons who take the division of faculties in our universities to be an exact replica of the way in which God himself divided up the universe. We have had the Philosophy of the Being; and we have had the Philosophy of the Becoming. In contemporary specialization, we have been getting the Philosophy of the Bin. Each of these mental localities has had its own peculiar way of life, its own values, even its own special idiom for seeing, thinking, and "proving." Among other things, a sociological approach should attempt to provide a reintegrative point of view, a broader empire of investigation encompassing the lot.

What would such sociological categories be like? They would consider works of art, I think, as strategies for selecting enemies and allies, for socializing losses, for warding off evil eye, for purification, propitiation, and desanctification, consolation and vengeance, admonition and exhortation, implicit commands or instructions of one sort or another. Art forms like "tragedy" or "comedy" or "satire" would be treated as *equipments for living,* that size up situations in various ways and in keeping with correspondingly various attitudes. The typical ingredients of such forms would be sought. Their relation to typical situations would be stressed. Their comparative values would be considered, with the intention of formulating a "strategy of strategies," the "over-all" strategy obtained by inspection of the lot.

# 12

# Stanley Fish
# 1938–

Stanley Fish has taught at the University of California at Berkeley, Johns Hopkins University, and Duke University. His training was in seventeenth-century British literature, but as a critic he has been identified with the development of Reader-Response criticism since the publication of *Surprised by Sin: The Reader in "Paradise Lost"* (1967). His approach to reading is fiercely pragmatic, and he tends to shun philosophical or abstract formulation of his methods. The temperament and tone of his work place it close to that of ordinary-language philosophers (especially John L. Austin). His method consists largely of anticipating the direction of narrative development and then discussing in detail how closely actual development coincides with or frustrates what was expected. He tends to think of interpretive strategies as guided by a reader's "interpretive community." His work, in addition to many essays, includes *John Skelton's Poetry* (1965); *Self-Consuming Artifacts: The Experience of Seventeenth-Century Literature* (1972); *Is There a Text in This Class?* (1980); and *Doing What Comes Naturally: Change, Rhetoric, and the Practice of Theory in Literary and Legal Studies* (1989).

Fish's "Interpreting the *Variorum*" (1980) is a critical document remarkable for its insight into reading and for its candor. Fish looks at volumes of the Milton *Variorum Commentary,* noting that again and again the *Variorum* gives evidence for multiple readings of key passages in Milton's work. Fish then does two things. First, he demonstrates how a reader transforms an interpretive dispute by making it "signify, first by regarding it as evidence of an experience and then by specifying for that experience a meaning." This reader-oriented approach, however, is marked by its "inability to say how it is that one ever begins" to read and interpret. Fish's answer is that readers are guided by "interpretive communities" of readers. Second, Fish asks, "how can any one of us know whether or not he is a member of the same interpretive community as any other of us?" His answer is that we can never be sure, but that our commonsense experience tends to confirm the existence of such reading communities.

# Interpreting the *Variorum*

## I

The first two volumes of the Milton *Variorum Commentary* have now appeared, and I find them endlessly fascinating. My interest, however, is not in the questions they manage to resolve (although these are many) but in the theoretical assumptions which are responsible for their occasional failures. These failures constitute a pattern, one in which a host of commentators—separated by as much as two hundred and seventy years but contemporaries in their shared concerns—are lined up on either side of an interpretive crux. Some of these are famous, even infamous: what is the two-handed engine in *Lycidas?* what is the meaning of Haemony in *Comus?* Others, like the identity of whoever or whatever comes to the window in *L'Allegro,* line 46, are only slightly less notorious. Still others are of interest largely to those who make editions: matters of pronoun referents, lexical ambiguities, punctuation. In each instance, however, the pattern is consistent: every position taken is supported by wholly convincing evidence—in the case of *L'Allegro* and the coming to the window there is a persuasive champion for every proper noun within a radius of ten lines—and the editorial procedure always ends either in the graceful throwing up of hands, or in the recording of a disagreement between the two editors themselves. In short, these are problems that apparently cannot be solved, at least not by the methods traditionally brought to bear on them. What I would like to argue is that they are not *meant* to be solved, but to be experienced (they signify), and that consequently any procedure that attempts to determine which of a number of readings is correct will necessarily fail. What this means is that the commentators and editors have been asking the wrong questions and that a new set of questions based on new assumptions must be formulated. I would like at least to make a beginning in that direction by examining some of the points in dispute in Milton's sonnets. I choose the sonnets because they are brief and because one can move easily from them to the theoretical issues with which this paper is finally concerned.

Milton's twentieth sonnet—"Lawrence of virtuous father virtuous son"—has been the subject of relatively little commentary. In it the poet invites a friend to join him in some distinctly Horatian pleasures—a neat repast intermixed with conversation, wine, and song; a respite from labor all the more enjoyable because outside the earth is frozen and the day sullen. The only controversy the sonnet has inspired concerns its final two lines:

> Lawrence of virtuous father virtuous son,
>> Now that the fields are dank, and ways are mire,
>> Where shall we sometimes meet, and by the fire
>> Help waste a sullen day; what may be won
> 5 From the hard season gaining; time will run
>> On smoother, till Favonius reinspire
>> The frozen earth; and clothe in fresh attire
>> The lily and rose, that neither sowed nor spun.
>> What neat repast shall feast us, light and choice,
> 10　Of Attic taste, with wine, whence we may rise
>> To hear the lute well touched, or artful voice
>> Warble immortal notes and Tuscan air?

He who of those delights can judge,
    and spare
To interpose them oft, is not unwise.[1]

The focus of the controversy is the word "spare," for which two readings have been proposed: leave time for and refrain from. Obviously the point is crucial if one is to resolve the sense of the lines. In one reading "those delights" are being recommended—he who can leave time for them is not unwise; in the other, they are the subject of a warning—he who knows when to refrain from them is not unwise. The proponents of the two interpretations cite as evidence both English and Latin syntax, various sources and analogues, Milton's "known attitudes" as they are found in his other writings, and the unambiguously expressed sentiments of the following sonnet on the same question. Surveying these arguments, A. S. P. Woodhouse roundly declares: "It is plain that all the honours rest with" the meaning "refrain from" or "forbear to." This declaration is followed immediately by a bracketed paragraph initialled D. B. for Douglas Bush, who, writing presumably after Woodhouse has died, begins "In spite of the array of scholarly names the case for 'forbear to' may be thought much weaker, and the case for 'spare time for' much stronger, than Woodhouse found them."[2] Bush then proceeds to review much of the evidence marshaled by Woodhouse and to draw from it exactly the opposite conclusion. If it does nothing else, this curious performance anticipates a point I shall make in a few moments: evidence brought to bear in the course of formalist analyses—that is, analyses generated by the assumption that meaning is embedded in the artifact—will always point in as many directions as there are interpreters; that is, not only will it prove something, it will prove anything.

It would appear then that we are back at square one, with a controversy that cannot be settled because the evidence is inconclusive. But what if that controversy is *itself* regarded as evidence, not of an ambiguity that must be removed, but of an ambiguity that readers have always experienced? What, in other words, if for the question "what does 'spare' mean?" we substitute the question "what does the fact that the meaning of 'spare' has always been an issue mean"? The advantage of this question is that it can be answered. Indeed it has already been answered by the readers who are cited in the *Variorum Commentary*. What these readers debate is the judgment the poem makes on the delights of recreation; what their debate indicates is that the judgment is blurred by a verb that can be made to participate in contradictory readings. (Thus the important thing about the evidence surveyed in the *Variorum* is not how it is marshaled, but that it could be marshaled at all, because it then becomes evidence of the equal availability of both interpretations.) In other words, the lines first generate a pressure for judgment—"he who of those delights can judge"—and then decline to deliver it; the pressure, however, still exists, and it is transferred from the words on the page to the reader (the reader is "he who"), who comes away from the poem not with a statement, but with a responsibility, the responsibility of deciding when and how often—if at all—to indulge in "those delights" (they remain delights in either case). This transferring of responsibility from the text to its readers is what the lines ask us to do—it is the essence of their experience—and in my terms it is therefore what the lines *mean*. It is a meaning the *Variorum* critics attest to even as they resist it, for what they are laboring so mightily to do by fixing the sense of the lines is to give the responsibility back. The text, however, will not accept it and remains determinedly evasive, even in its last two words, "not unwise." In their position these words confirm the impossibility of extracting from the poem a moral formula, for the assertion (certainly too strong a word) they complete is of the form, "He who does such and such, of him it cannot be said that he is unwise"; but of course neither can it be said that he is wise. Thus what Bush correctly terms the "defensive" "not unwise" operates to prevent us from attaching the label "wise" to any action, including *either* of the actions—leaving time for or refraining from—represented by the ambiguity of "spare." Not only is the pressure of judgment taken off the poem, it is taken off the activity the poem at first pretended to judge. The issue is finally not the moral status of "those delights"—they become in seventeenth-century terms "things indifferent"—but on the good or bad uses to which they can be put by readers who are left, as Milton always leaves them, to choose and manage by themselves.

Let us step back for a moment and see how far we've come. We began with an apparently insoluble problem and proceeded, not to solve it, but to make it signify; first by regarding it as evidence of an experience and then by specifying for that experience a meaning. Moreover, the configurations of that experience, when they are made available by a reader-oriented analysis, serve as a check against the endlessly inconclusive adducing of evidence which characterizes formalist analysis. That is to say, any determination of what "spare" means (in a positivist or literal sense) is liable to be upset by the bringing forward of another analogue, or by a more complete computation of statistical frequencies, or by the discovery of new biographical information, or by anything else; but if we first determine that everything in the line before "spare" creates the expectation of an imminent judgment, then the ambiguity of "spare" can be assigned a significance in the context of that expectation. (It disappoints it and transfers the pressure of judgment to us.) That context is experiential, and it is within its contours and constraints that significances are established (both in

the act of reading and in the analysis of that act). In formalist analyses the only constraints are the notoriously open-ended possibilities and combination of possibilities that emerge when one begins to consult dictionaries and grammars and histories; to consult dictionaries, grammars, and histories is to assume that meanings can be specified independently of the activity of reading; what the example of "spare" shows is that it is in and by that activity that meanings— experiential, not positivist—are created.

In other words, it is the structure of the reader's experience rather than any structures available on the page that should be the object of description. In the case of Sonnet XX, that experiential structure was uncovered when an examination of formal structures led to an impasse; and the pressure to remove that impasse led to the substitution of one set of questions for another. It will more often be the case that the pressure of a spectacular failure will be absent. The sins of formalist-positivist analysis are primarily sins of omission, not an inability to explain phenomena, but an inability to see that they are there because its assumptions make it inevitable that they will be overlooked or suppressed. Consider, for example, the concluding lines of another of Milton's sonnets, "Avenge O Lord thy slaughtered saints."

> Avenge O Lord thy slaughtered saints,
>     whose bones
>     Lie scattered on the Alpine mountains
>     cold,
>     Even them who kept thy truth so
>     pure of old
>     When all our fathers worshipped
>     stocks and stones,
> 5 Forget not: in thy book record their
>     groans
>     Who were thy sheep and in their
>     ancient fold
>     Slain by the bloody Piedmontese that
>     rolled

Mother with infant down the rocks.
Their moans
The vales redoubled to the hills, and
they
10    To heaven. Their martyred blood and
ashes sow
O'er all the Italian fields where still
doth sway
The triple Tyrant: that from these may
grow
A hundredfold, who having learnt thy
way
Early may fly the Babylonian woe.

In this sonnet, the poet simultaneously petitions God and wonders aloud about the justice of allowing the faithful—"Even them who kept thy truth"—to be so brutally slaughtered. The note struck is alternately one of plea and complaint, and there is more than a hint that God is being called to account for what has happened to the Waldensians. It is generally agreed, however, that the note of complaint is less and less sounded and that the poem ends with an affirmation of faith in the ultimate operation of God's justice. In this reading, the final lines are taken to be saying something like this: From the blood of these martyred, O God, raise up a new and more numerous people, who, by virtue of an early education in thy law, will escape destruction by fleeing the Babylonian woe. Babylonian woe has been variously glossed[3]; but whatever it is taken to mean it is always read as part of a statement that specifies a set of conditions for the escaping of destruction or punishment; it is a warning to the reader as well as a petition to God. As a warning, however, it is oddly situated since the conditions it seems to specify were in fact met by the Waldensians, who of all men most followed God's laws. In other words, the details of their story would seem to undercut the affirmative moral the speaker proposes to draw from it. It is further undercut by a reading that is fleetingly available, although no one has

acknowledged it because it is a function, not of the words on the page, but of the experience of the reader. In that experience, line 13 will for a moment be accepted as a complete sense unit and the emphasis of the line will fall on "thy way" (a phrase that has received absolutely no attention in the commentaries). At this point "thy way" can refer only to the way in which God has dealt with the Waldensians. That is, "thy way" seems to pick up the note of outrage with which the poem began, and if we continue to so interpret it, the conclusion of the poem will be a grim one indeed: since by this example it appears that God rains down punishment indiscriminately, it would be best perhaps to withdraw from the arena of his service, and thereby hope at least to be safely out of the line of fire. This is not the conclusion we carry away, because as line 14 unfolds, another reading of "thy way" becomes available, a reading in which "early" qualifies "learnt" and refers to something the faithful should do (learn thy way at an early age) rather than to something God has failed to do (save the Waldensians). These two readings are answerable to the pulls exerted by the beginning and ending of the poem: the outrage expressed in the opening lines generates a pressure for an explanation, and the grimmer reading is answerable to that pressure (even if it is also disturbing); the ending of the poem, the forward and upward movement of lines 10–14, creates the expectation of an affirmation, and the second reading fulfills that expectation. The criticism shows that in the end we settle on the more optimistic reading—it feels better—but even so the other has been a part of our experience, and because it has been a part of our experience, it *means*. What it means is that while we may be able to extract from the poem a statement affirming God's justice, we are not allowed to forget the evidence (of things seen) that makes the extraction so difficult (both for the speaker and for us). It is a difficulty we experience in the act of reading, even though a criticism which takes no account of that act has, as we have seen, suppressed it.

## II

In each of the sonnets we have considered, the significant word or phrase occurs at a line break where a reader is invited to place it first in one and then in another structure of syntax and sense. This moment of hesitation, of semantic or syntactic slide, is crucial to the experience the verse provides, but, in a formalist analysis, that moment will disappear, either because it has been flattened out and made into an (insoluble) interpretive crux, or because it has been eliminated in the course of a procedure that is incapable of finding value in temporal phenomena. In the case of "When I consider how my light is spent," these two failures are combined.

> When I consider how my light is spent,
>   Ere half my days, in this dark world
>     and wide,
>   And that one talent which is death to
>     hide,
>   Lodged with me useless, though my
>     soul more bent
> 5 To serve therewith my maker, and
>     present
>   My true account, lest he returning
>     chide,
>   Doth God exact day-labour, light
>     denied,
>   I fondly ask; but Patience to prevent
>   That murmur, soon replies, God doth
>     not need
> 10    Either man's work or his own gifts,
>     who best
>   Bear his mild yoke, they serve him
>     best, his state
>   Is kingly. Thousands at his bidding
>     speed

And post o'er land and ocean without
    rest:
They also serve who only stand and
    wait.

The interpretive crux once again concerns the final line: "They also serve who only stand and wait." For some this is an unqualified acceptance of God's will, while for others the note of affirmation is muted or even forced. The usual kinds of evidence are marshaled by the opposing parties, and the usual inconclusiveness is the result. There are some areas of agreement. "All the interpretations," Woodhouse remarks, "recognize that the sonnet commences from a mood of depression, frustration [and] impatience."[4] The object of impatience is a God who would first demand service and then take away the means of serving, and the oft noted allusion to the parable of the talents lends scriptural support to the accusation the poet is implicitly making: you have cast the wrong servant into unprofitable darkness. It has also been observed that the syntax and rhythm of these early lines, and especially of lines 6–8, are rough and uncertain; the speaker is struggling with his agitated thoughts and he changes directions abruptly, with no regard for the line as a unit of sense. The poem, says one critic, "seems almost out of control."[5]

The question I would ask is "whose control?"; for what these formal descriptions point to (but do not acknowledge) is the extraordinary number of adjustments required of readers who would negotiate these lines. The first adjustment is the result of the expectations created by the second half of line 6—"lest he returning chide." Since there is no full stop after "chide," it is natural to assume that this will be an introduction to reported speech, and to assume further that what will be reported is the poet's anticipation of the voice of God as it calls him, to an unfair accounting. This assumption does not survive line 7—"Doth God exact day-labour, light denied"—which rather than chiding the poet for his inactivity seems to rebuke him for having expected that chiding. The accents are precisely those heard so often in the Old Testament when God answers a reluctant Gideon, or a disputatious Moses, or a self-justifying Job: do you presume to judge my ways or to appoint my motives? Do you think I would exact day labor, light denied? In other words, the poem seems to turn at this point from a questioning of God to a questioning of that questioning; or, rather, the reader turns from the one to the other in the act of revising his projection of what line 7 will say and do. As it turns out, however, that revision must itself be revised because it had been made within the assumption that what we are hearing is the voice of God. This assumption falls before the very next phrase "I fondly ask," which requires not one, but two adjustments. Since the speaker of line 7 is firmly identified as the poet, the line must be reinterpreted as a continuation of his complaint—Is that the way you operate, God, denying light, but exacting labor?—but even as that interpretation emerges, the poet withdraws from it by inserting the adverb "fondly," and once again the line slips out of the reader's control.

In a matter of seconds, then, line 7 has led four experiential lives, one as we anticipate it, another as that anticipation is revised, a third when we retroactively identify its speaker, and a fourth when that speaker disclaims it. What changes in each of these lives is the status of the poet's murmurings—they are alternately expressed, rejected, reinstated, and qualified—and as the sequence ends, the reader is without a firm perspective on the question of record: does God deal justly with his servants?

A firm perspective appears to be provided by Patience, whose entrance into the poem, the critics tell us, gives it both argumentative and metrical stability. But in fact the presence of Patience in the poem finally assures its continuing instability by making it impossible

to specify the degree to which the speaker approves, or even participates in, the affirmation of the final line: "They also serve who only stand and wait." We know that Patience to prevent the poet's murmur soon replies (not soon enough however to prevent the murmur from registering), but we do not know when that reply ends. Does Patience fall silent in line 12, after "kingly"? or at the conclusion of line 13? or not at all? Does the poet appropriate these lines or share them or simply listen to them, as we do? These questions are unanswerable, and it is because they remain unanswerable that the poem ends uncertainly. The uncertainty is not in the statement it makes—in isolation line 14 is unequivocal—but in our inability to assign that statement to either the poet or to Patience. Were the final line marked unambiguously for the poet, then we would receive it as a resolution of his earlier doubts; and were it marked for Patience, it would be a sign that those doubts were still very much in force. It is marked for neither, and therefore we are without the satisfaction that a firmly conclusive ending (in *any* direction) would have provided. In short, we leave the poem unsure, and our unsureness is the realization (in our experience) of the unsureness with which the affirmation of the final line is, or is not, made. (This unsureness also operates to actualize the two possible readings of "wait": wait in the sense of expecting, that is waiting for an opportunity to serve actively; or wait in the sense of waiting *in* service, a waiting that is itself fully satisfying because the impulse to self-glorifying action has been stilled.)

The question debated in the *Variorum Commentary* is, how far from the mood of frustration and impatience does the poem finally move? The answer given by an experiential analysis is that you can't tell, and the fact that you can't tell is responsible for the uneasiness the poem has always inspired. It is that uneasiness which the critics inadvertently acknowledge when they argue about the force of the last line, but they are unable to make analytical use of what they acknowledge because they have no way of dealing with or even recognizing experiential (that is, temporal) structures. In fact, more than one editor has eliminated those structures by punctuating them out of existence: first by putting a full stop at the end of line 6 and thereby making it unlikely that the reader will assign line 7 to God (there will no longer be an expectation of reported speech), and then by supplying quotation marks for the sestet in order to remove any doubts one might have as to who is speaking. There is of course no warrant for these emendations, and in 1791 Thomas Warton had the grace and honesty to admit as much. "I have," he said, "introduced the turned commas both in the question and answer, not from any authority, but because they seem absolutely necessary to the sense."[6]

## III

Editorial practices like these are only the most obvious manifestations of the assumptions to which I stand opposed: the assumption that there *is* a sense, that it is embedded or encoded in the text, and that it can be taken in at a single glance. These assumptions are, in order, positivist, holistic, and spatial, and to have them is to be committed both to a goal and to a procedure. The goal is to settle on a meaning, and the procedure involves first stepping back from the text, and then putting together or otherwise calculating the discrete units of significance it contains. My quarrel with this procedure (and with the assumptions that generate it) is that in the course of following it through the reader's activities are at once ignored and devalued. They are ignored because the text is taken to be self-sufficient—everything is *in* it—and they are devalued because when they are thought of at all, they are thought of as the disposable machinery of extraction. In the procedures I would urge, the reader's activities are at the center of attention, where they are regarded, not as leading to meaning, but as *having* meaning. The meaning they have is a consequence of their not being empty; for they include the making and revising of assumptions, the rendering and regretting of judgments, the coming to and abandoning of conclusions, the giving and withdrawing of approval, the specifying of causes, the asking of questions, the supplying of answers, the solving of puzzles. In a word, these activities are interpretive—rather than being preliminary to questions of value they are at every moment settling and resettling questions of value—and because they are interpretive, a description of them will also be, and without any additional step, an interpretation, not after the fact, but of the fact (of experiencing). It will be a description of a moving field of concerns, at once wholly present (not waiting for meaning, but constituting meaning) and continually in the act of reconstituting itself.

As a project such a description presents enormous difficulties, and there is hardly time to consider them here;[7] but it should be obvious from my brief examples how different it is from the positivist-formalist project. Everything depends on the temporal dimension, and as a consequence the notion of a mistake, at least as something to be avoided, disappears. In a sequence where a reader first structures the field he inhabits and then is asked to restructure it (by changing an assignment of speaker or realigning attitudes and positions) there is no question of priority among his structurings; no one of them, even if it is the last, has privilege; each is equally legitimate, each equally the proper object of analysis, because each is equally an event in his experience.

The firm assertiveness of this paragraph only calls attention to the questions it avoids. Who is this reader? How can I presume to describe his experiences, and what do I say to readers who report that they do not have the experiences I describe? Let me answer these questions or rather make a beginning at answering them in the context of another example, this time from Milton's *Comus*. In line 46 of *Comus* we are introduced to the villain by way of a genealogy:

Bacchus that first from out the purple
    grape,
Crushed the sweet poison of misused wine.

In almost any edition of this poem, a footnote will tell you that Bacchus is the god of wine. Of course most readers already know that, and because they know it, they will be anticipating the appearance of "wine" long before they come upon it in the final position. Moreover, they will also be anticipating a negative judgment on it, in part because of the association of Bacchus with revelry and excess, and especially because the phrase "sweet poison" suggests that the judgment has already been made. At an early point then, we will have both filled in the form of the assertion and made a decision about its moral content. That decision is upset by the word "misused"; for what "misused" asks us to do is transfer the pressure of judgment from wine (where we have already placed it) to the abusers of wine, and therefore when "wine" finally appears, we must declare it innocent of the charges we have ourselves made.

This, then, is the structure of the reader's experience—the transferring of a moral label from a thing to those who appropriate it. It is an experience that depends on a reader for whom the name Bacchus has precise and immediate associations; another reader, a reader for whom those associations are less precise will not have that experience because he will not have rushed to a conclusion in relation to which the word "misused" will stand as a challenge. Obviously I am discriminating between these two readers and

between the two equally real experiences they will have. It is not a discrimination based simply on information, because what is important is not the information itself, but the action of the mind which its possession makes possible for one reader and impossible for the other. One might discriminate further between them by noting that the point at issue—whether value is a function of objects and actions or of intentions—is at the heart of the seventeenth-century debate over "things indifferent." A reader who is aware of that debate will not only *have* the experience I describe; he will recognize at the end of it that he has been asked to take a position on one side of a continuing controversy; and that recognition (also a part of his experience) will be part of the disposition with which he moves into the lines that follow.

It would be possible to continue with this profile of the optimal reader, but I would not get very far before someone would point out that what I am really describing is the intended reader, the reader whose education, opinions, concerns, linguistic competences, etc. make him capable of having the experience the author wished to provide. I would not resist this characterization because it seems obvious that the efforts of readers are always efforts to discern and therefore to realize (in the sense of becoming) an author's intention. I would only object if that realization were conceived narrowly, as the single act of comprehending an author's purpose, rather than (as I would conceive it) as the succession of acts readers perform in the continuing assumption that they are dealing with intentional beings. In this view discerning an intention is no more or less than understanding, and understanding includes (is constituted by) all the activities which make up what I call the structure of the reader's experience. To describe that experience is therefore to describe the reader's efforts at understanding, and to describe the reader's efforts at understanding is to describe his realization (in two senses) of an author's intention. Or to put it another way, what my analyses amount to are descriptions of a succession of decisions made by readers about an author's intention; decisions that are not limited to the specifying of purpose but include the specifying of every aspect of successively intended worlds; decisions that are precisely the shape, because they are the content, of the reader's activities.

Having said this, however, it would appear that I am open to two objections. The first is that the procedure is a circular one. I describe the experience of a reader who in his strategies is answerable to an author's intention, and I specify the author's intention by pointing to the strategies employed by that same reader. But this objection would have force only if it were possible to specify one independently of the other. What is being specified from either perspective are the conditions of utterance, of what could have been understood to have been meant by what was said. That is, intention and understanding are two ends of a conventional act, each of which necessarily stipulates (includes, defines, specifies) the other. To construct the profile of the informed or at-home reader is at the same time to characterize the author's intention and vice versa, because to do either is to specify the *contemporary* conditions of utterance, to identify, by becoming a member of, a community made up of those who share interpretive strategies.

The second objection is another version of the first: if the content of the reader's experience is the succession of acts he performs in search of an author's intentions, and if he performs those acts at the bidding of the text, does not the text then produce or contain everything—intention *and* experience— and have I not compromised my antiformalist position? This objection will have force only if the formal patterns of the text are assumed to exist independently of the reader's experience, for only then can priority be claimed for

them. Indeed, the claims of independence and priority are one and the same; when they are separated it is so that they can give circular and illegitimate support to each other. The question "do formal features exist independently?" is usually answered by pointing to their priority: they are "in" the text before the reader comes to it. The question "are formal features prior?" is usually answered by pointing to their independent status: they are "in" the text before the reader comes to it. What looks like a step in an argument is actually the spectacle of an assertion supporting itself. It follows then that an attack on the independence of formal features will also be an attack on their priority (and vice versa), and I would like to mount such an attack in the context of two short passages from *Lycidas*.

The first passage (actually the second in the poem's sequence) begins at line 42:

The willows and the hazel copses green
Shall now no more be seen,
Fanning their joyous leaves to thy soft lays.
[L1. 42−44]

It is my thesis that the reader is always making sense (I intend "making" to have its literal force), and in the case of these lines the sense he makes will involve the assumption (and therefore the creation) of a completed assertion after the word "seen," to wit, the death of Lycidas has so affected the willows and the hazel copses green that, in sympathy, they will wither and die (will no more be seen by *anyone*). In other words at the end of line 43 the reader will have hazarded an interpretation, or performed an act of perceptual closure, or made a decision as to what is being asserted. I do not mean that he has done four things, but that he has done one thing the description of which might take any one of four forms—making sense, interpreting, performing perceptual closure, deciding about what is intended. (The importance of this point will become clear later.) Whatever he has done (that is, however we characterize it) he will undo it in the act of reading the next line; for here he discovers that his closure, or making of sense, was premature and that he must make a new one in which the relationship between man and nature is exactly the reverse of what was first assumed. The willows and the hazel copses green will in fact be seen, but they will not be seen by Lycidas. It is he who will be no more, while they go on as before, fanning their joyous leaves to someone else's soft lays (the whole of line 44 is now perceived as modifying and removing the absoluteness of "seen"). Nature is not sympathetic, but indifferent, and the notion of her sympathy is one of those "false surmises" that the poem is continually encouraging and then disallowing.

The previous sentence shows how easy it is to surrender to the bias of our critical language and begin to talk as if poems, not readers or interpreters, did things. Words like "encourage" and "disallow" (and others I have used in this paper) imply agents, and it is only "natural" to assign agency first to an author's intentions and then to the forms that assumedly embody them. What really happens, I think, is something quite different: rather than intention and its formal realization producing interpretation (the "normal" picture), interpretation creates intention and its formal realization by creating the conditions in which it becomes possible to pick them out. In other words, in the analysis of these lines from *Lycidas* I did what critics always do: I "saw" what my interpretive principles permitted or directed me to see, and then I turned around and attributed what I had "seen" to a text and an intention. What my principles direct me to "see" are readers performing acts; the points at which I find (or to be more precise, declare) those acts to have been performed become (by a sleight of hand) demarcations *in* the text; those demarcations are then available for the designation "formal features," and as formal features they

can be (illegitimately) assigned the responsibility for producing the interpretation which in fact produced them. In this case, the demarcation my interpretation calls into being is placed at the end of line 42; but of course the end of that (or any other) line is worth noticing or pointing out only because my model *demands* (the word is not too strong) perceptual closures and therefore locations at which they occur; in that model this point will be one of those locations, although (1) it needn't have been (not every line ending occasions a closure) and (2) in another model, one that does not give value to the activities of readers, the possibility of its being one would not have arisen.

What I am suggesting is that formal units are always a function of the interpretative model one brings to bear; they are not "in" the text, and I would make the same argument for intentions. That is, intention is no more embodied "in" the text than are formal units; rather an intention, like a formal unit, is made when perceptual or interpretive closure is hazarded; it is verified by an interpretive act, and I would add, it is not verifiable in any other way. This last assertion is too large to be fully considered here, but I can sketch out the argumentative sequence I would follow were I to consider it: intention is known when and only when it is recognized; it is recognized as soon as you decide about it; you decide about it as soon as you make a sense; and you make a sense (or so my model claims) as soon as you can.

Let me tie up the threads of my argument with a final example from *Lycidas:*

He must not float upon his wat'ry bier
Unwept . . .

[L1. 13–14]

Here the reader's experience has much the same career as it does in lines 42–44: at the end of line 13 perceptual closure is hazarded, and a sense is made in which the line is taken to be a resolution bordering on a promise: that is, there is now an expectation that something will be done about this unfortunate situation, and the reader anticipates a call to action, perhaps even a program for the undertaking of a rescue mission. With "Unwept," however, that expectation and anticipation are disappointed, and the realization of that disappointment will be inseparable from the making of a new (and less comforting) sense: nothing will be done; Lycidas will continue to float upon his wat'ry bier, and the only action taken will be the lamenting of the fact that no action will be efficacious, including the actions of speaking and listening to this lament (which in line 15 will receive the meretricious and self-mocking designation "melodious tear"). Three "structures" come into view at precisely the same moment, the moment when the reader having resolved a sense unresolves it and makes a new one; that moment will also be the moment of picking out a formal pattern or unit, end of line/beginning of line, and it will also be the moment at which the reader having decided about the speaker's intention, about what is meant by what has been said, will make the decision again and in so doing will make another intention.

This, then, is my thesis: that the form of the reader's experience, formal units, and the structure of intention are one, that they come into view simultaneously, and that therefore the questions of priority and independence do not arise. What does arise is another question: what produces *them?* That is, if intention, form, and the shape of the reader's experience are simply different ways of referring to (different perspectives on) the same interpretive act, what is that act an interpretation *of?* I cannot answer that question, but neither, I would claim, can anyone else, although formalists try to answer it by pointing to patterns and claiming that they are available independently of (prior to) interpretation. These patterns vary according to the proce-

dures that yield them: they may be statistical (number of two-syllable words per hundred words), grammatical (ratio of passive to active constructions, or of right-branching to left-branching sentences, or of anything else); but whatever they are I would argue that they do not lie innocently in the world but are themselves constituted by an interpretive act, even if, as is often the case, that act is unacknowledged. Of course, this is as true of my analyses as it is of anyone else's. In the examples offered here I appropriate the notion "line ending" and treat it as a fact of nature; and one might conclude that as a fact it is responsible for the reading experience I describe. The truth I think is exactly the reverse: line endings exist by virtue of perceptual strategies rather than the other way around. Historically, the strategy that we know as "reading (or hearing) poetry" has included paying attention to the line as a unit, but it is precisely that attention which has made the line as a unit (either of print or of aural duration) available. A reader so practiced in paying that attention that he regards the line as a brute fact rather than as a convention will have a great deal of difficulty with concrete poetry; if he overcomes that difficulty, it will not be because he has learned to ignore the line as a unit but because he will have acquired a new set of interpretive strategies (the strategies constitutive of "concrete poetry reading") in the context of which the line as a unit no longer exists. In short, what is noticed is what has been *made* noticeable, not by a clear and undistorting glass, but by an interpretive strategy.

This may be hard to see when the strategy has become so habitual that the forms it yields seem part of the world. We find it easy to assume that alliteration as an effect depends on a "fact" that exists independently of any interpretive "use" one might make of it, the fact that words in proximity begin with the same letter. But it takes only a moment's reflection to realize that the sameness, far from being natural, is enforced by an ortho-graphic convention; that is to say, it is the product of an interpretation. Were we to sub-stitute phonetic conventions for orthographic ones (a "reform" traditionally urged by pur-ists), the supposedly "objective" basis for al-literation would disappear because a pho-netic transcription would require that we dis-tinguish between the initial sounds of those very words that enter into alliterative relation-ships; rather than conforming to those rela-tionships the rules of spelling make them. One might reply that, since alliteration is an aural rather than a visual phenomenon when poetry is heard, we have unmediated access to the physical sounds themselves and hear "real" similarities. But phonological "facts" are no more uninterpreted (or less conven-tional) than the "facts" of orthography; the distinctive features that make articulation and reception possible are the product of a sys-tem of differences that must be *imposed* before it can be recognized; the patterns the ear hears (like the patterns the eye sees) are the patterns its perceptual habits make availa-ble.

One can extend this analysis forever, even to the "facts" of grammar. The history of lin-guistics is the history of competing paradigms each of which offers a different account of the constituents of language. Verbs, nouns, cleft sentences, transformations, deep and surface structures, semes, rhemes, tagmemes—now you see them, now you don't, depending on the descriptive apparatus you employ. The critic who confidently rests his analyses on the bedrock of syntactic descriptions is rest-ing on an interpretation; the facts he points to *are* there, but only as a consequence of the interpretive (man-made) model that has called them into being.

The moral is clear: the choice is never be-tween objectivity and interpretation but be-tween an interpretation that is unacknowl-edged as such and an interpretation that is at least aware of itself. It is this awareness

that I am claiming for myself, although in doing so I must give up the claims implicitly made in the first part of this paper. There I argue that a bad (because spatial) model had suppressed what was really happening, but by my own declared principles the no-tion "really happening" is just one more in-terpretation.

## IV

It seems then that the price one pays for de-nying the priority of either forms or intentions is an inability to say how it is that one ever begins. Yet we do begin, and we continue, and because we do there arises an immediate counter-objection to the preceding pages. If interpretive acts are the source of forms rather than the other way around, why isn't it the case that readers are always performing the same acts or a random succession of forms? How, in short, does one explain these two "facts" of reading?: (1) the same reader will perform differently when reading two "dif-ferent" (the word is in quotation marks be-cause its status is precisely what is at issue) texts; and (2) different readers will perform similarly when reading the "same" (in quotes for the same reason) text. That is to say, both the stability of interpretation among readers and the variety of interpretation in the career of a single reader would seem to argue for the existence of something independent of and prior to interpretive acts, something which produces them. I will answer this challenge by asserting that both the stability and the variety are functions of interpretive strategies rather than of texts.

Let us suppose that I am reading *Lycidas*. What is it that I am doing? First of all, what I am not doing is "simply reading," an activity in which I do not believe because it implies the possibility of pure (that is, disinterested) perception. Rather, I am proceeding on the basis of (at least) two interpretive decisions:

(1) that *Lycidas* is a pastoral and (2) that it was written by Milton. (I should add that the notions "pastoral" and "Milton" are also interpretations; that is they do not stand for a set of indisputable, objective facts; if they did, a great many books would not now be getting written.) Once these decisions have been made (and if I had not made these I would have made others, and they would be consequential in the same way), I am immediately predisposed to perform certain acts, to "find," by looking for, themes (the relationship between natural processes and the careers of men, the efficacy of poetry or of any other action), to confer significances (on flowers, streams, shepherds, pagan deities), to mark out "formal" units (the lament, the consolation, the turn, the affirmation of faith, etc.). My disposition to perform these acts (and others; the list is not meant to be exhaustive) constitutes a set of interpretive strategies, which, when they are put into execution, become the large act of reading. That is to say, interpretive strategies are not put into execution after reading (the pure act of perception in which I do not believe); they are the shape of reading, and because they are the shape of reading, they give texts their shape, making them rather than, as it is usually assumed, arising from them. Several important things follow from this account:

1. I did not have to execute this particular set of interpretive strategies because I did not have to make those particular interpretive (pre-reading) decisions. I could have decided, for example, that *Lycidas* was a text in which a set of fantasies and defenses find expression. These decisions would have entailed the assumption of another set of interpretive strategies (perhaps like that put forward by Norman Holland in *The Dynamics of Literary Response*) and the execution of that set would have made another text.

2. I could execute this same set of strategies when presented with texts that did not bear the title (again a notion which is itself an interpretation) *Lycidas, A Pastoral Monody. . . .* I could decide (it is a decision some have made) that *Adam Bede* is a pastoral written by an author who consciously modeled herself on Milton (still remembering that "pastoral" and "Milton" are interpretations, not facts in the public domain); or I could decide, as Empson did, that a great many things not usually considered pastoral were in fact to be so read; and either decision would give rise to a set of interpretive strategies, which, when put into action, would *write* the text I write when reading *Lycidas.* (Are you with me?)

3. A reader other than myself who, when presented with *Lycidas,* proceeds to put into execution a set of interpretive strategies similar to mine (how he could do so is a question I will take up later), will perform the same (or at least a similar) succession of interpretive acts. He and I then might be tempted to say that we agree about the poem (thereby assuming that the poem exists independently of the acts either of us performs); but what we really would agree about is the way to write it.

4. A reader other than myself who, when presented with *Lycidas* (please keep in mind that the status of *Lycidas* is what is at issue), puts into execution a different set of interpretive strategies will perform a different succession of interpretive acts. (I am assuming, it is the article of my faith, that a reader will always execute some set of interpretive strategies and therefore perform some succession of interpretive acts.) One of us might then be tempted to complain to the other that we could not possibly be reading the same poem (literary criticism is full of such complaints) and he would be right; for each of us would be reading the poem he had made.

The large conclusion that follows from these four smaller ones is that the notions of the "same" or "different" texts are fictions. If I read *Lycidas* and *The Waste Land* differently (in fact I do not), it will not be because the formal structures of the two poems (to term them such is also an interpretive decision) call forth different interpretive strategies but because my predisposition to execute different interpretive strategies will *produce* different formal structures. That is, the two poems are different because I have decided that they will be. The proof of this is the possibility of doing the reverse (that is why point 2 is so important). That is to say, the answer to the question "why do different texts give rise to different sequences of interpretive acts?" is that *they don't have to,* an answer which implies strongly that "they" don't exist. Indeed it has always been possible to put into action interpretive strategies designed to make all texts one, or to put it more accurately, to be forever making the same text. Augustine urges just such a strategy, for example, in *On Christian Doctrine* where he delivers the "rule of faith" which is of course a rule of interpretation. It is dazzlingly simple: everything in the Scriptures, and indeed in the world when it is properly read, points to (bears the meaning of) God's love for us and our answering responsibility to love our fellow creatures for His sake. If only you should come upon something which does not at first seem to bear this meaning, that "does not literally pertain to virtuous behavior or to the truth of faith," you are then to take it "to be figurative" and proceed to scrutinize it "until an interpretation contributing to the reign of charity is produced." This then is both a stipulation of what meaning there is and a set of directions for finding it, which is of course a set of directions—of interpretive strategies—for making it, that is, for the endless reproduction of the same text. Whatever one may think of this interpretive program, its success and ease of execution are attested to by centuries of Christian exegesis. It is my contention that any interpretive program, any set of interpretive strategies, can have a similar success, although few have been as spectacularly successful as this one. (For some time now, for at least three hundred years, the most successful interpretive program has gone under the name "ordinary language.") In our own discipline programs with the same characteristic of always reproducing one text include psychoanalytic criticism, Robertsonianism (always threatening to extend its sway into later and later periods), numerology (a sameness based on the assumption of innumerable fixed differences).

The other challenging question—"why will different readers execute the same interpretive strategy when faced with the 'same' text?"—can be handled in the same way. The answer is again that *they don't have to,* and my evidence is the entire history of literary criticism. And again this answer implies that the notion "same text" is the product of the possession by two or more readers of similar interpretive strategies.

But why should this ever happen? Why should two or more readers ever agree, and why should regular, that is, habitual, differences in the career of a single reader ever occur? What is the explanation on the one hand of the stability of interpretation (at least among certain groups at certain times) and on the other of the orderly variety of interpretation if it is not the stability and variety of texts? The answer to all of these questions is to be found in a notion that has been implicit in my argument, the notion of *interpretive communities.* Interpretive communities are made up of those who share interpretive strategies not for reading (in the conventional sense) but for writing texts, for constituting their properties and assigning their intentions. In other words these strategies exist prior to the act of reading and therefore determine the shape of what is read rather than, as is usually assumed, the other way around. If it is an article of faith in a particular community that there are a variety of texts, its members will boast a repertoire of strategies for making them. And if a community believes in the existence of only one text, then the single strategy its members employ will be forever writing it. The first community will accuse the members of the second of being reductive, and they in turn will call their accusers superficial. The assumption in each community will be that the other is not correctly perceiving the "true text," but the truth will be that each perceives the text (or texts) its interpretive strategies demand and call into being. This, then, is the explanation both for the stability of interpretation among different readers (they belong to the same community) and for the regularity with which a single reader will employ different interpretive strategies and thus make different texts (he belongs to different communities). It also explains why there are disagreements and why they can be debated in a principled way: not because of a stability in texts, but because of a stability in the makeup of interpretive communities and therefore in the opposing positions they make possible. Of course this stability is always temporary (unlike the longed for and timeless stability of the text). Interpretive communities grow larger and decline, and individuals move from one to another; thus while the alignments are not permanent, they are always there, providing just enough stability for the interpretive battles to go on, and just enough shift and slippage to assure that they will never be settled. The notion of interpretive communities thus stands between an impossible ideal and the fear which leads so many to maintain it. The ideal is of perfect agreement and it would require texts to have a status independent of interpretation. The fear is of interpretive anarchy, but it would only be realized if interpretation (text making) were completely random. It is the fragile but real consolidation of interpretive communities that allows us to talk to one another, but with no hope or fear of ever being able to stop.

In other words interpretive communities are no more stable than texts because interpretive strategies are not natural or universal, but *learned*. This does not mean that there is a point at which an individual has not yet learned any. The ability to interpret is not acquired; it is constitutive of being human. What is acquired are the ways of interpreting and those same ways can also be forgotten or supplanted, or complicated or dropped from favor ("no one reads that way anymore"). When any of these things happens, there is a corresponding change in texts, not because they are being read differently, but because they are being written differently.

The only stability, then, inheres in the fact (at least in my model) that interpretive strategies are always being deployed, and this means that communication is a much more chancy affair than we are accustomed to think it. For if there are no fixed texts, but only interpretive strategies making them; and if interpretive strategies are not natural, but learned (and are therefore unavailable to a finite description), what is it that utterers (speakers, authors, critics, me, you) do? In the old model utterers are in the business of handing over ready made or prefabricated meanings. These meanings are said to be encoded, and the code is assumed to be in the world independently of the individuals who are obliged to attach themselves to it (if they do not they run the danger of being declared deviant). In my model, however, meanings are not extracted but made and made not by encoded forms but by interpretive strategies that call forms into being. It follows then that what utterers do is give hearers and readers the opportunity to make meanings (and texts) by inviting them to put into execution a set of strategies. It is presumed that the invitation will be recognized, and that presumption rests on a projection on the part of a speaker or author of the moves *he* would make if confronted by the sounds or marks he is uttering or setting down.

It would seem at first that this account of things simply reintroduces the old objection; for isn't this an admission that there is after all a formal encoding, not perhaps of meanings, but of the directions for making them, for executing interpretive strategies? The answer is that they will only *be* directions to those who already have the interpretive strategies in the first place. Rather than producing interpretive acts, they are the product of one. An author hazards his projection, not because of something "in" the marks, but because of something he assumes to be in his reader. The very existence of the "marks" is a function of an interpretive community, for they will be recognized (that is, made) only by its members. Those outside that community will be deploying a different set of interpretive strategies (interpretation cannot be withheld) and will therefore be making different marks.

So once again I have made the text disappear, but unfortunately the problems do not disappear with it. If everyone is continually executing interpretive strategies and in that act constituting texts, intentions, speakers, and authors, how can any one of us know whether or not he is a member of the same interpretive community as any other of us? The answer is that he can't, since any evidence brought forward to support the claim would itself be an interpretation (especially if the "other" were an author long dead). The only "proof" of membership is fellowship, the nod of recognition from someone in the

same community, someone who says to you what neither of us could ever prove to a third party: "we know." I say it to you now, knowing full well that you will agree with me (that is, understand) only if you already agree with me.

## NOTES

1. All references are to *The Poems of John Milton,* ed. John Carey and Alastair Fowler (London, 1968).

2. *A Variorum Commentary on the Poems of John Milton,* vol. 2, pt. 2. ed. A. S. P. Woodhouse and Douglas Bush (New York, 1972), p. 475.

3. It is first of all a reference to the city of iniquity from which the Hebrews are urged to flee in Isaiah and Jeremiah. In Protestant polemics Babylon is identified with the Roman Church whose destruction is prophesied in the book of Revelation. And in some Puritan tracts, Babylon is the name for Augustine's earthly city, from which the faithful are to flee inwardly in order to escape the fate awaiting the unregenerate. See *Variorum Commentary,* pp. 440–41.

4. *Variorum Commentary,* p. 469.

5. Ibid., p. 457.

6. *Poems Upon Several Occasions, English, Italian, And Latin, With Translations, By John Milton,* ed. Thomas Warton (London, 1791), p. 352.

7. See my *Surprised by Sin: The Reader in* Paradise Lost (London and New York, 1967); *Self-consuming Artifacts: The Experience of Seventeenth-Century Literature* (Berkeley, 1972); "What Is Stylistics and Why are They Saying Such Terrible Things About It?" in *Approaches to Poetics,* ed. Seymour Chatman (New York, 1973), pp. 109–52; "How Ordinary Is Ordinary Language?" in *New Literary History,* 5 (Autumn 1973): 41–54; "Facts and Fictions: A Reply to Ralph Rader," *Critical Inquiry,* 1 (June 1975): 883–91.

# 13

# Patrocinio Schweickart
# 1942–

Patrocinio Schweickart is a leader in the development of new theories of feminist Reader-Response criticism. She has published articles on literary theory and women's literature in *Reader, Modern Fiction Studies, Signs,* and the *Canadian Journal of Social and Political Theory*. With Elizabeth A. Flynn she edited *Gender and Reading* (1986), and her essay "Engendering Critical Discourse" is included in *The Current in Criticism: Essays on the Present and Future of Literary Theory* (1987). Schweickart is associate professor of English at the University of New Hampshire.

Schweickart's "Reading Ourselves: Toward a Feminist Theory of Reading" won the 1984 Florence Howe Award for Outstanding Feminist Scholarship. In this essay Schweickart calls for a change in the "utopian" nature of standard forms of Reader-Response criticism (both the text-oriented and reader-oriented varieties) to include considerations of gender. She asserts that if it is possible to locate the "difference" in women's writing, then it must be possible to locate the "difference" in women's reading. Feminist critics and Reader-Response theorists must develop "reading strategies consonant with the concerns, experiences, and formal devices" that inform women's reading. Women, especially women in the academy, have been "immasculated" by their training; they have been taught to read as men, therefore denying meaning that a text may have for them as women. Rather than accepting a traditional interpretation women must learn to read a text as it was "not meant to be read," to read it "against itself." In doing so, Schweickart hopes, women readers may be able to reverse the process of immasculation. Such a reversal may lead not only to a reevaluation of texts by male writers but to a reevaluation of women writers whose works have been devalued by years of misreading.

## Reading Ourselves: Toward a Feminist Theory of Reading

### THREE STORIES OF READING

A. Wayne Booth begins his Presidential Address to the 1982 MLA Convention by considering and rejecting several plausible myths that might enable us "to dramatize not just our inescapable plurality but the validity of our sense that [as teachers and scholars of literature and composition] we belong together, somehow working on common ground." At last he settles on one story that is "perhaps close enough to our shared experience to justify the telling."[1]

Once upon a time there was a boy who fell in love with books. When he was very young he heard over and over the legend of his great-grandfather, a hard-working weaver who so desired knowledge that he figured out a way of working the loom with one hand, his legs, and his feet, leaving the other hand free to hold a book, and worked so steadily in that crooked position that he became permanently crippled. The boy heard other stories about the importance of reading. Salvation, he came to believe, was to be found in books. When he was six years old, he read *The Wizard of Oz*—his first *real* book—and was rewarded by his Great-Aunt Manda with a dollar.

When the boy grew up, he decided to become a teacher of "litcomp." His initiation into the profession was rigorous, and there were moments when he nearly gave up. But gradually, "there emerged from the trudging a new and surprising love, a love that with all my previous reading I had not dreamed of: the love of skill, of craft, of getting clear in my mind and then in my writing what a great writer had got right in his work" (Booth, p. 315). Eventually, the boy, now grown, got his doctorate, and after teaching for thirteen years in small colleges, he returned to his graduate institution to become one of its eminent professors.

Booth caps his narration by quoting from *The Autobiography of Malcolm X*. It was in prison that Malcolm learned to read:

For the first time I could pick up a book and now begin to understand what the book was saying. Anyone who has read a great deal can imagine the new world that opened. Let me tell you something: from then until I left that prison, in every free moment I had, if I was not reading in the library, I was reading on my bunk. . . . [M]onths passed without my even thinking about being imprisoned. In fact, up to then, I never had been so truly free in my life. (As quoted by Booth, p. 317)

"Perhaps," says Booth, "when you think back now on my family's story about great-grandfather Booth, you will understand why reading about Malcolm X's awakening speaks to the question of where I got my 'insane love' [for books]" (p. 317).

B. When I read the Malcolm X passage quoted in Booth's address, the ellipsis roused my curiosity. What, exactly, I wondered, had been deleted? What in the original exceeded the requirements of a Presidential Address to the MLA? Checking, I found the complete sentence to read: "Between Mr. Muhammad's teachings, my correspondence, my visitors—usually Ella and Reginald—and my reading, months passed without my even thinking about being imprisoned."[2] Clearly, the first phrase is the dissonant one. The reference to the leader of the notorious Black Muslims suggests a story of reading very different from Booth's. Here is how Malcolm X tells it. While serving time in the Norfolk Prison Colony, he hit on the idea of teaching himself to read by copying the dictionary.

In my slow, painstaking, ragged handwriting, I copied into my tablet every thing on that first page, down to the punctuation marks. . . . Then, aloud, to myself, I read back everything I'd written on the table. . . . I woke up the next morning thinking about these words—immensely proud to realize that not only had I written so much at one time, but I'd written words that I never knew were in the world. . . . That was the way I started copying what eventually became the entire dictionary. (P. 172)

After copying the dictionary, Malcolm X began reading the books in the prison library. "No university would ask any student to devour literature as I did when this new world opened to me, of being able to read and *understand*" (p. 173). Reading had changed the course of his life. Years later, he would reflect on how "the ability to read awoke inside me some long dormant craving to be mentally alive" (p. 179).

What did he read? What did he understand? He read Gregor Mendel's *Findings in Genetics* and it helped him to understand "that if you started with a black man, a white man could be produced; but starting with a white man, you never could produce a black man—because the white chromosome is recessive. And since no one disputes that there was but one Original Man, the conclusion is clear" (p. 175). He read histories, books by Will Durant and Arnold Toynbee, by W. E. B. du Bois and Carter G. Woodson, and he saw how "the glorious history of the black man" had been "bleached" out of the history books written by white men.

> [His] eyes opened gradually, then wider and wider, to how the world's white men had indeed acted like devils, pillaging and raping and bleeding and draining the whole world's non-white people. . . . I will never forget how shocked I was when I began reading about slavery's total horror. . . . The world's most monstrous crime, the sin and the blood on the white man's hands, are almost impossible to believe. (P. 175)

He read philosophy—the works of Schopenhauer, Kant, Nietzsche, and Spinoza—and he concluded that the "whole stream of Western Philosophy was now wound up in a cul-de-sac" as a result of the white man's "elaborate, neurotic necessity to hide the black man's true role in history" (p. 180). Malcolm X read voraciously, and book after book confirmed the truth of Elijah Muhammad's teachings. "It's a crime, the lie that has been told to generations of black men and white both. . . . Innocent black children growing up, living out their lives, dying of old age—and all of their lives ashamed of being

black. But the truth is pouring out of the bag now" (p. 181).

Wayne Booth's story leads to the Crystal Ballroom of the Biltmore Hotel in Los Angeles, where we attend the protagonist as he delivers his Presidential Address to the members of the Modern Language Association. Malcolm X's love of books took him in a different direction, to the stage of the Audubon Ballroom in Harlem, where, as he was about to address a mass meeting of the Organization of Afro-American Unity, he was murdered.

C. As we have seen, an ellipsis links Wayne Booth's story of reading to Malcolm X's. Another ellipsis, this time not graphically marked, signals the existence of a third story. Malcolm X's startling reading of Mendel's genetics overlooks the most rudimentary fact of human reproduction: whether you start with a black man or a white man, without a woman, you get *nothing*. An excerpt from Virginia Woolf's *A Room of One's Own* restores this deleted perspective.[3]

The heroine, call her Mary, says Woolf, goes to the British Museum in search of information about women. There she discovers to her chagrin that woman is, "perhaps, the most discussed animal in the universe?"

> Why does Samuel Butler say, "Wise men never say what they think of women"? Wise men never say anything else apparently. . . . Are they capable of education? Napoleon thought them incapable. Dr. Johnson thought the opposite. Have they souls or have they not souls? Some savages say they have none. Others, on the contrary, say women are half divine and worship them on that account. Some sages hold that they are shallower in the brain; others that they are deeper in consciousness. Goethe honoured them; Mussolini despises them. Wherever one looked men

thought about women and thought differently. (Pp. 29–30)

Distressed and confused, Mary notices that she has unconsciously drawn a picture in her notebook, the face and figure of Professor von X. engaged in writing his monumental work, *The Mental, Moral, and Physical Inferiority of the Female Sex*. "His expression suggested that he was labouring under some emotion that made him jab his pen on the paper as if he were killing some noxious insect as he wrote, but even when he had killed it that did not satisfy him; he must go on killing it. . . . A very elementary exercise in psychology . . . showed me . . . that the sketch had been made in anger" (pp. 31–32).

Nothing remarkable in that, she reflects, given the provocation. But "How explain the anger of the professor? . . . For when it came to analysing the impression left by these books, . . . there was [an] element which was often present and could not be immediately identified. Anger, I called it. . . . To judge from its effects, it was anger disguised and complex, not anger simple and open" (p. 32).

Disappointed with essayists and professors, Mary turns to historians. But apparently women played no significant role in history. What little information Mary finds is disturbing: "Wife-beating, I read, was a recognized right of a man, and was practiced without shame by high as well as low" (p. 44). Oddly enough, literature presents a contradictory picture.

If women had not existence save in fiction written by men, we would imagine her to be a person of utmost importance; very various; heroic and mean; splendid and sordid; infinitely beautiful and hideous in the extreme; as great as a man, some think even greater. But this is women in fiction. In fact, as Professor Trevelyan points out, she was locked up, beaten and flung about the room. (P. 45)

At last, Mary can draw but one conclusion from her reading. Male professors, male historians, and male poets can not be relied on for the truth about women. Woman herself must undertake the study of woman. Of course, to do so, she must secure enough money to live on and a room of her own.

Booth's story, we recall, is told within the framework of a professional ritual. It is intended to remind us of "the loves and fears that inform our daily work" and of "what we do when we are at our best," to show, if not a unity, then enough of a "center" "to shame us whenever we violate it." The principal motif of the myth is the hero's insane love for books, and the way this develops with education and maturity into "critical understanding," which Booth defines as that synthesis of thought and passion which should replace, "on the one hand, sentimental and uncritical identifications that leave minds undisturbed, and on the other, hypercritical negations that freeze or alienate" (pp. 317–18). Booth is confident that the experience celebrated by the myth is archetypal. "Whatever our terms for it, whatever our theories about how it happens or why it fails to happen more often, can we reasonably doubt the importance of the moment, at any level of study, when any of us—you, me, Malcolm X, my great-grandfather—succeeds in entering other minds, or 'taking them in,' as nourishment for our own?" (p. 318).

Now, while it is certainly true that something one might call "critical understanding" informs the stories told by Malcolm X and Virginia Woolf, these authors fill this term with thoughts and passions that one would never suspect from Booth's definition. From the standpoint of the second and third stories of reading, Booth's story is utopian. The powers and resources of his hero are equal to the challenges he encounters. At each stage he finds suitable mentors. He is assured by the people around him, by the books he reads, by the entire culture, that he is right for the part. His talents and accomplishments are acknowledged and justly rewarded. In short, from the perspective of Malcolm X's and Woolf's stories, Booth's hero is fantastically privileged.

*Utopian* has a second meaning, one that is by no means pejorative, and Booth's story is utopian in this sense as well. In overlooking the realities highlighted by the stories of Malcolm X and Virginia Woolf, Booth's story anticipates what might be possible, what "critical understanding" might mean for *everyone,* if only we could overcome the pervasive systemic injustices of our time.

## READER-RESPONSE THEORY AND FEMINIST CRITICISM

Reader-response criticism, as currently constituted, is utopian in the same two senses. The different accounts of the reading experience that have been put forth overlook the issues of race, class, and sex, and give no hint of the conflicts, sufferings, and passions that attend these realities. The relative tranquility of the tone of these theories testifies to the privileged position of the theorists. Perhaps, someday, when privileges have withered away or at least become more equitably distributed, some of these theories will ring true. Surely we ought to be able to talk about reading without worrying about injustice. But for now, reader-response criticism must confront the disturbing implications of our historical reality. Paradoxically, utopian theories that elide these realities betray the utopian impulses that inform them.

To put the matter plainly, reader-response criticism needs feminist criticism. The two have yet to engage each other in a sustained and serious way, but if the promise of the former is to be fulfilled, such an encounter must soon occur. Interestingly, the obvious question of the significance of gender has

already been explicitly raised, and—this testifies to the increasing impact of feminist criticism as well as to the direct ideological bearing of the issue of gender on reader-response criticism—not by a feminist critic, but by Jonathan Culler, a leading theorist of reading: "If the experience of literature depends upon the qualities of a reading self, one can ask what difference it would make to the experience of literature and thus to the meaning of literature if this self were, for example, female rather than male. If the meaning of a work is the experience of a reader, what difference does it make if the reader is a woman?"[4]

Until very recently this question has not occurred to reader-response critics. They have been preoccupied with other issues. Culler's survey of the field is instructive here, for it enables us to anticipate the direction reader-response theory might take when it is shaken from its slumber by feminist criticism. According to Culler, the different models (or "stories") of reading that have been proposed are all organized around three problems. The first is the issue of control: Does the text control the reader, or vice versa? For David Bleich, Normal Holland, and Stanley Fish, the reader holds controlling interest. Readers read the poems they have made. Bleich asserts this point most strongly: the constraints imposed by the words on the page are "trivial," since their meaning can always be altered by "subjective action." To claim that the text supports this or that reading is only to "moralistically claim . . . that one's own objectification is more authoritative than someone else's."[5]

At the other pole are Michael Riffaterre, Georges Poulet, and Wolfgang Iser, who acknowledge the creative role of the reader, but ultimately take the text to be the dominant force. To read, from this point of view, is to create the text according to *its* own promptings. As Poulet puts it, a text, when invested with a reader's subjectivity, becomes a "subjectified object," a "second self" that depends on the reader, but is not, strictly speaking, identical with him. Thus, reading "is a way of giving way not only to a host of alien words, images and ideas, but also to the very alien principle which utters and shelters them. . . . I am on loan to another, and this other thinks, feels, suffers and acts within me."[6] Culler argues persuasively that, regardless of their ostensible theoretical commitments, the prevailing stories of reading generally vacillate between these reader-dominant and text-dominant poles. In fact, those who stress the subjectivity of the reader as against the objectivity of the text ultimately portray the text as determining the responses of the reader. "The more active, projective, or creative the reader is, the more she is manipulated by the sentence or by the author" (p. 71).

The second question prominent in theories of reading is closely related to the first. Reading always involves a subject and an object, a reader and a text. But what constitutes the objectivity of the text? What is "in" the text? What is supplied by the reader? Again, the answers have been equivocal. On the face of it, the situation seems to call for a dualistic theory that credits the contributions of both text and reader. However, Culler argues, a dualistic theory eventually gives way to a monistic theory, in which one or the other pole supplies everything. One might say, for instance, that Iser's theory ultimately implies the determinacy of the text and the authority of the author: "The author guarantees the unity of the work, requires the reader's creative participation, and through his text, prestructures the shape of the aesthetic object to be produced by the reader."[7] At the same time, one can also argue that the "gaps" that structure the reader's response are not built into the text, but appear (or not) as a result of the particular interpretive strategy employed by the reader. Thus, "there is no distinction between what the text gives and what the reader supplies; he supplies *everything*."[8] Depending on which aspects of the theory

one takes seriously, Iser's theory collapses either into a monism of the text or a monism of the reader.

The third problem identified by Culler concerns the ending of the story. Most of the time stories of reading end happily. "Readers may be manipulated and misled, but when they finish the book their experience turns into knowledge . . . as though finishing the book took them outside the experience of reading and gave them mastery of it" (p. 79). However, some critics—Harold Bloom, Paul de Man, and Culler himself—find these optimistic endings questionable, and prefer instead stories that stress the impossibility of reading. If, as de Man says, rhetoric puts "an insurmountable obstacle in the way of any reading or understanding," then the reader "may be placed in impossible situations where there is no happy issue, but only the possibility of playing out the roles dramatized in the text" (Culler, p. 81).

Such have been the predominant preoccupations of reader-response criticism during the past decade and a half. Before indicating how feminist critics could affect the conversation, let me consider an objection. A recent and influential essay by Elaine Showalter suggests that we should not enter the conversation at all. She observes that during its early phases, the principal mode of feminist criticism was "feminist critique," which was counter-ideological in intent and concerned with the feminist as *reader*. Happily, we have outgrown this necessary but theoretically unpromising approach. Today, the dominant mode of feminist criticism is "gynocritics," the study of woman as *writer,* of the "history, styles, themes, genres, and structures of writing by women; the psychodynamics of female creativity; the trajectory of the individual or collective female career; and the evolution and laws of a female literary tradition." The shift from "feminist critique" to "gynocritics"—from emphasis on woman as reader to emphasis on woman as writer—has put us in the position of developing a feminist criticism that is "genuinely woman-centered, independent, and intellectually coherent."

> To see women's writing as our primary subject forces us to make the leap to a new conceptual vantage point and to redefine the nature of the theoretical problem before us. It is no longer the ideological dilemma of reconciling revisionary pluralisms but the essential question of difference. How can we constitute women as a distinct literary group? What is the *difference* of women's writing?[9]

But why should the activity of the woman writer be more conducive to theory than the activity of the woman reader is? If it is possible to formulate a basic conceptual framework for disclosing the "difference" of women's writing, surely it is no less possible to do so for women's reading. The same difference, be it linguistic, biological, psychological, or cultural, should apply in either case. In addition, what Showalter calls "gynocritics" is in fact constituted by feminist *criticism*—that is, *readings*—of female texts. Thus, the relevant distinction is not between woman as reader and woman as writer, but between feminist readings of male texts and feminist readings of female texts, and there is no reason why the former could not be as theoretically coherent (or irreducibly pluralistic) as the latter.

On the other hand, there are good reasons for feminist criticism to engage reader-response criticism. Both dispute the fetishized art object, the "Verbal Icon," of New Criticism, and both seek to dispel the objectivist illusion that buttresses the authority of the dominant critical tradition. Feminist criticism can have considerable impact on reader-response criticism, since, as Culler has noticed, it is but a small step from the thesis that the reader is an active producer of meaning to the recognition that there are many different kinds of readers, and that women—because of their numbers if because of nothing else—constitute an essential class. Reader-response critics cannot take refuge in the objectivity of the text, or even in the idea that a gender-neutral criticism is possible. Today they can continue to ignore the implications of feminist criticism only at the cost of incoherence or intellectual dishonesty.

It is equally true that feminist critics need to question their allegiance to text- and author-centered paradigms of criticism. Feminist criticism, we should remember, is a mode of *praxis*. The point is not merely to interpret literature in various ways; the point is to *change the world*. We cannot afford to ignore the activity of reading, for it is here that literature is realized as *praxis*. Literature acts on the world by acting on its readers.

To return to our earlier question: What will happen to reader-response criticism if feminists enter the conversation? It is useful to recall the contrast between Booth's story and those of Malcolm X and Virginia Woolf. Like Booth's story, the "stories of reading" that currently make up reader-response theory are mythically abstract, and appear, from a different vantage point, to be by and about readers who are fantastically privileged. Booth's story had a happy ending; Malcolm's and Mary's did not. For Mary, reading meant encountering a tissue of lies and silences; for Malcolm it meant the verification of Elijah Muhammad's shocking doctrines.

Two factors—gender and politics—which are suppressed in the dominant models of reading gain prominence with the advent of a feminist perspective. The feminist story will have *at least* two chapters: one concerned with feminist readings of male texts, and another with feminist readings of female texts. In addition, in this story, gender will have a prominent role as the locus of political struggle. The story will speak of the difference between men and women, of the way the experience and perspective of women have been systematically and fallaciously assimilated into the generic masculine, and of the need to correct this error. Finally, it will identify literature—the activities of reading and writing—as an important arena of political struggle, a crucial component of the project of interpreting the world in order to change it.

Feminist criticism does not approach reader-response criticism without preconceptions. Actually, feminist criticism has always included substantial reader-centered interests. In the next two sections of this paper, I will review these interests, first with respect to male texts, then with respect to female texts. In the process, I will uncover some of the issues that might be addressed and clarified by a feminist theory of reading.

## THE FEMALE READER AND THE LITERARY CANON

Although reader-response critics propose different and often conflicting models, by and large the emphasis is on features of the process of reading that do not vary with the nature of the reading material. The feminist entry into the conversation brings the nature of the text back into the foreground. For feminists, the question of *how* we read is inextricably linked with the question of *what* we read. More specifically, the feminist inquiry into the activity of reading begins with the realization that the literary canon is androcentric, and that this has a profoundly damaging effect on women readers. The documentation of this realization was one of the earliest tasks undertaken by feminist critics. Elaine Showalter's 1971 critique of the literary curriculum is exemplary of this work.

> [In her freshman year a female student]
> ... might be assigned an anthology of essays, perhaps such as *The Responsible Man,* ... or *Conditions of Man,* or *Man in Crisis,* or again, *Representative Man: Cult*

*Heroes of Our Time,* in which thirty-three men represent such categories of heroism as the writer, the poet, the dramatist, the artist, and the guru, and the only two women included are the actress Elizabeth Taylor, and the existential Heroine Jacqueline Onassis.

Perhaps the student would read a collection of stories like *The Young Man in American Literature: The Initiation Theme,* or sociological literature like *The Black Man and the Promise of America.* In a more orthodox literary program she might study eternally relevant classics, such as *Oedipus;* as a professor remarked in a recent issue of *College English,* all of us want to kill our fathers and marry our mothers. And whatever else she might read, she would inevitably arrive at the favorite book of all Freshman English courses, the classic of adolescent rebellion, *The Portrait of the Artist as a Young Man.*

By the end of her freshman year, a woman student would have learned something about intellectual neutrality; she would be learning, in fact, how to think like a man. And so she would go on, increasingly with male professors to guide her.[10]

The more personal accounts of other critics reinforce Showalter's critique.

> The first result of my reading was a feeling that male characters were at the very least more interesting than women to the authors who invented them. Thus if, reading their books as it seemed their authors intended them, I naively identified with a character, I repeatedly chose men; I would rather have been Hamlet than Ophelia, Tom Jones instead of Sophia Western, and, perhaps, despite Dostoevsky's intention, Raskolnikov not Sonia.
> More peculiar perhaps, but sadly unsurprising, were the assessments I accepted

about fictional women. For example, I quickly learned that power was unfeminine and powerful women were, quite literally, monstrous. . . . Bitches all, they must be eliminated, reformed, or at the very least, condemned. . . . Those rare women who are shown in fiction as both powerful and, in some sense, admirable are such because their power is based, if not on beauty, then at least on sexuality.[11]

For a woman, then, books do not necessarily spell salvation. In fact, a literary education may very well cause her grave psychic damage: schizophrenia "is the bizarre but logical conclusion of our education. Imagining myself male, I attempted to create myself male. Although I knew the case was otherwise, it seemed I could do nothing to make this other critically real."[12]

To put the matter theoretically, androcentric literature structures the reading experience differently depending on the gender of the reader. For the male reader, the text serves as the meeting ground of the personal and the universal. Whether or not the text approximates the particularities of his own experience, he is invited to validate the equation of maleness with humanity. The male reader feels his affinity with the universal, with the paradigmatic human being, precisely because he is male. Consider the famous scene of Stephen's epiphany in *The Portrait of the Artist as a Young Man.*

A girl stood before him in midstream, alone and still, gazing out to sea. She seemed like one whom magic had changed into the likeness of a strange and beautiful seabird. Her long slender bare legs were delicate as a crane's and pure save where an emerald trail of seaweed had fashioned itself as a sign upon the flesh. Her thighs, fuller and softhued as ivory, were bared almost to the hips, where the white fringes of her drawers were like feathering of soft white down.

Her slateblue skirts were kilted boldly about her waist and dovetailed behind her. Her bosom was a bird's, soft and slight, slight and soft, as the breast of some dark plummaged dove. But her long fair hair was girlish: and touched with the wonder of mortal beauty, her face.[13]

A man reading this passage is invited to identify with Stephen, to feel "the riot in his blood," and, thus, to ratify the alleged universality of the experience. Whether or not the sight of a girl on the beach has ever provoked similar emotions in him, the male reader is invited to feel his *difference* (concretely, *from the girl*) and to equate that with the universal. Relevant here is Lévi-Strauss's theory that woman functions as currency exchanged between men. The woman in the text converts the text into a woman, and the circulation of this text/woman becomes the central ritual that establishes the bond between the author and his male readers.[14]

The same text affects a woman reader differently. Judith Fetterley gives the most explicit theory to date about the dynamics of the woman reader's encounter with androcentric literature. According to Fetterley, notwithstanding the prevalence of the castrating bitch stereotype, "the cultural reality is not the emasculation of men by women, but the *immasculation* of women by men. As readers and teachers and scholars, women are taught to think as men, to identify with a male point of view, and to accept as normal and legitimate a male system of values, one of whose central principles is misogyny."[15]

The process of immasculation does not impart virile power to the woman reader. On the contrary, it doubles her oppression. She suffers "not simply the powerlessness which derives from not seeing one's experience articulated, clarified, and legitimized in art, but more significantly, the powerlessness which results from the endless division of self against self, the consequence of the invocation to identify as male while being reminded that to be male—to be universal— . . . is to be *not female.*"[16]

A woman reading Joyce's novel of artistic awakening, and in particular the passage quoted above, will, like her male counterpart, be invited to identify with Stephen and therefore to ratify the equation of maleness with the universal. Androcentric literature is all the more efficient as an instrument of sexual politics because it does not allow the woman reader to seek refuge in her difference. Instead, it draws her into a process that uses her against herself. It solicits her complicity in the elevation of male difference into universality and, accordingly, the denigration of female difference into otherness without reciprocity. To be sure, misogyny is abundant in the literary canon.[17] It is important, however, that Fetterley's argument can stand on a weaker premise. Androcentricity is a sufficient condition for the process of immasculation.

Feminist critics of male texts, from Kate Millett to Judith Fetterley, have worked under the sign of the "Resisting Reader." Their goal is to disrupt the process of immasculation by exposing it to consciousness, by disclosing the androcentricity of what has customarily passed for the universal. However, feminist criticism written under the aegis of the resisting reader leaves certain questions unanswered, questions that are becoming ripe for feminist analysis: Where does the text get its power to draw us into its designs? Why do some (not all) demonstrably sexist texts remain appealing even after they have been subjected to thorough feminist critique? The usual answer—that the power of male texts is the power of the false consciousness into which women as well as men have been socialized—oversimplifies the problem and prevents us from comprehending both the force of literature and the complexity of our responses to it.

Fredric Jameson advances a thesis that seems to me to be a good starting point for the feminist reconsideration of male texts: "The effectively ideological is also at the same time necessarily utopian."[18] This thesis implies that the male text draws its power over the female reader from authentic desires, which it rouses and then harnesses to the process of immasculation.

A concrete example is in order. Consider Lawrence's *Women in Love,* and for the sake of simplicity, concentrate on Birkin and Ursula. Simone de Beauvoir and Kate Millet have convinced me that this novel is sexist. Why does it remain appealing to me? Jameson's thesis prompts me to answer this question by examining how the text plays not only on my false consciousness but also on my authentic liberatory aspirations—that is to say, on the very impulses that drew me to the feminist movement.

The trick of role reversal comes in handy here. If we reverse the roles of Birkin and Ursula, the ideological components (or at least the most egregious of these, e.g., the analogy between women and horses) stand out as absurdities. Now, if we delete these absurd components while keeping the roles reversed, we have left the story of a woman struggling to combine her passionate desire for autonomous conscious being with an equally passionate desire for love and for other human bonds. This residual story is not far from one we would welcome as expressive of a feminist sensibility. Interestingly enough, it also intimates a novel Lawrence might have written, namely, the proper sequel to *The Rainbow.*

My affective response to the novel Lawrence did write is bifurcated. On the one hand, because I am a woman, I am implicated in the representation of Ursula and in the destiny Lawrence has prepared for her: man is the son of god, but woman is the daughter of man. Her vocation is to witness his transcendence in rapt silence. On the other hand, Fetterley is correct that I am also induced to identify with Birkin, and in so doing, I am drawn into complicity with the reduction of Ursula, and therefore of myself, to the role of the other.

However, the process of immasculation is more complicated than Fetterley allows. When I identify with Birkin, I unconsciously perform the two-stage rereading described above. I reverse the roles of Birkin and Ursula and I suppress the obviously ideological components that in the process show up as absurdities. The identification with Birkin is emotionally effective because, stripped of its patriarchal trappings, Birkin's struggle and his utopian vision conform to my own. To the extent that I perform this feminist rereading *unconsciously,* I am captivated by the text. The stronger my desire for autonomous selfhood and for love, the stronger my identification with Birkin, and the more intense the experience of bifurcation characteristic of the process of immasculation.

The full argument is beyond the scope of this essay. My point is that *certain* (not all) male texts merit a dual hermeneutic: a negative hermeneutic that discloses their complicity with patriarchal ideology, and a positive hermeneutic that recuperates the utopian moment—the authentic kernel—from which they draw a significant portion of their emotional power.[19]

## READING WOMEN'S WRITING

Showalter is correct that feminist criticism has shifted emphasis in recent years from "critique" (primarily) of male texts to "gynocritics," or the study of women's writing. Of course, it is worth remembering that the latter has always been on the feminist agenda. *Sexual Politics,* for example, contains not only the critique of Lawrence, Miller, and Mailer that won Millett such notoriety, but also her memorable rereading of *Villette.*[20] It is equally true that interest in women's writing has not entirely supplanted the critical study

of patriarchal texts. In a sense "critique" has provided the bridge from the study of male texts to the study of female texts. As feminist criticism shifted from the first to the second, "feminist critique" turned its attention from androcentric texts per se to the androcentric critical strategies that pushed women's writing to the margins of the literary canon. The earliest examples of this genre (for instance, Showalter's "The Double Critical Standard," and Carol Ohmann's "Emily Brontë in the Hands of Male Critics") were concerned primarily with describing and documenting the prejudice against women writers that clouded the judgment of well-placed readers, that is, reviewers and critics.[21] Today we have more sophisticated and more comprehensive analyses of the androcentric critical tradition.

One of the most cogent of these is Nina Baym's analysis of American literature.[22] Baym observes that, as late as 1977, the American canon of major writers did not include a single woman novelist. And yet, in terms of numbers and commercial success, women novelists have probably dominated American literature since the middle of the nineteenth century. How to explain this anomaly?

One explanation is simple bias of the sort documented by Showalter, Ohmann, and others. A second is that women writers lived and worked under social conditions that were not particularly conducive to the production of "excellent" literature: "There tended to be a sort of immediacy in the ambitions of literary women leading them to professionalism rather than artistry, by choice as well as by social pressure and opportunity."[23] Baym adduces a third, more subtle, and perhaps more important reason. There are, she argues, "gender-related restrictions that do not arise out of the cultural realities contemporary with the writing woman, but out of later critical theories . . . which impose their concerns anachronistically, after the fact, on an earlier period."[24] If one reads the critics most instrumental in forming the current theories about American literature (Matthiessen, Chase, Feidelson, Trilling, etc.), one finds that the theoretical model for the canonical American novel is the "melodrama of beset manhood." To accept this model is also to accept as a consequence the exclusion from the canon of "melodramas of beset womanhood," as well as virtually all fiction centering on the experience of women.[25]

The deep symbiotic relationship between the androcentric canon and androcentric modes of reading is well summarized by Kolodny.

> *Insofar as we are taught to read, what we engage are not texts, but paradigms. . . .* Insofar as literature is itself a social institution, so, too, reading is a highly socialized—or learned—activity. . . . We read well, and with pleasure, what we already know how to read; and what we know how to read is to a large extent dependent on what we have already read [works from which we have developed our expectations and learned our interpretive strategies]. What we then choose to read—and, by extension, teach and thereby "canonize"—usually follows upon our previous reading.[26]

We are caught, in other words, in a rather vicious circle. An androcentric canon generates androcentric interpretive strategies, which in turn favor the canonization of androcentric texts and the marginalization of gynocentric ones. To break this circle, feminist critics must fight on two fronts: for the revision of the canon to include a significant body of works by women, and for the development of the reading strategies consonant with the concerns, experiences, and formal devices that constitute these tests. Of course, to succeed, we also need a community of women readers who are qualified by experience, commitment, and training, and who

will enlist the personal and institutional resources at their disposal in the struggle.[27]

The critique of androcentric reading strategies is essential, for it opens up some ideological space for the recuperation of women's writing. Turning now to this project, we observe, first, that a large volume of work has been done, and, second, that this endeavor is coming to look even more complicated and more diverse than the criticism of male texts. Certainly, it is impossible in the space of a few pages to do justice to the wide range of concerns, strategies, and positions associated with feminist readings of female texts. Nevertheless, certain things can be said. For the remainder of this section, I focus on an exemplary essay: "Vesuvius at Home: The Power of Emily Dickinson," by Adrienne Rich.[28] My commentary anticipates the articulation of a paradigm that illuminates certain features of feminist readings of women's writing.

I am principally interested in the rhetoric of Rich's essay, for it represents an implicit commentary on the process of reading women's writing. Feminist readings of male texts are, as we have seen, primarily resisting. The reader assumes an adversarial or at least a detached attitude toward the material at hand. In the opening pages of her essay, Rich introduces three metaphors that proclaim a very different attitude toward her subject.

> The methods, the exclusions, of Emily Dickinson's existence could not have been my own; yet more and more, as a woman poet finding my own methods, I have come to understand her necessities, could have served as witness in her defense. (P. 158)

> I am traveling at the speed of time, along the Massachusetts Turnpike. . . . "Home is not where the heart is," she wrote in a letter, "but the house and adjacent buildings." . . . I am traveling at the speed of time, in the direction of the house and buildings. . . . For years, I have been not so

much envisioning Emily Dickinson as trying to visit, to enter her mind through her
poems and letters, and through my own
intimations of what it could have meant to
be one of the two mid-nineteenth century
American geniuses, and a woman, living in
Amherst, Massachusetts. (Pp. 158–59)

For months, for most of my life, I have been
hovering like an insect against the screens
of an existence which inhabited Amherst,
Massachusetts between 1830 and 1886. (P.
158) . . . Here [in Dickinson's bedroom] I
become again, an insect, vibrating at the
frames of windows, clinging to the panes
of glass, trying to connect. (P. 161)

A commentary on the process of reading is
carried on silently and unobtrusively through
the use of these metaphors. The first is a judicial metaphor: the feminist reader speaks as a
witness in defense of the woman writer. Here
we see clearly that gender is crucial. The feminist reader takes the part of the woman writer
against patriarchal misreadings that trivialize
or distort her work.[29] The second metaphor
refers to a principal tenet of feminist criticism:
a literary work cannot be understood apart
from the social, historical, and cultural context within which it was written. As if to ac-
quiesce to the condition Dickinson had imposed on her friends, Rich travels through
space and time to visit the poet on her own
*premises*. She goes to Amherst, to the house
where Dickinson lived. She rings the bell, she
goes in, then upstairs, then into the bedroom
that had been "freedom" for the poet. Her
destination, ultimately, is Dickinson's mind.
But it is not enough to read the poet's poems
and letters. To reach her heart and mind, one
must take a detour through "the house and
adjacent buildings."

Why did Dickinson go into seclusion? Why
did she write poems she would not publish?
What mean these poems about queens, vol-
canoes, deserts, eternity, passion, suicide,
wild beasts, rape, power, madness, the dae-
mon, the grave? For Rich, these are related
questions. The revisionary re-reading of Dickinson's work is of a piece with the revisionary re-reading of her life. "I have a notion
genius knows itself; that Dickinson chose her
seclusion, knowing what she needed. . . . She
carefully selected her society and controlled
the disposal of her time. . . . Given her vocation, she was neither eccentric nor quaint; she
was determined to survive, to use her powers, to practice necessary economies" (p.
160).

To write [the poetry that she needed to
write] she had to enter chambers of the self
in which
Ourself, concealed—
Should startle most—
and to relinquish control there, to take
those risks, she had to create a relationship
to the outer world where she could feel in
control. (P. 175)

The metaphor of visiting points to another
feature of feminist readings of women's writing, namely, the tendency to construe the text
not as an object, but as the manifestation of
the subjectivity of the absent author—the
"voice" of another woman. Rich is not content to revel in the textuality of Dickinson's
poems and letters. For her, these are door-
ways to the "mind" of a "woman of genius."
Rich deploys her imagination and her considerable rhetorical skill to evoke "the figure of
powerful will" who lives at the heart of the
text. To read Dickinson, then, is to try to visit
with her, to hear her voice, to make her live
*in* oneself, and to feel her impressive "personal dimensions."[30]

At the same time, Rich is keenly aware that
visiting with Dickinson is *only* a metaphor for
reading her poetry, and an inaccurate one at
that. She signals this awareness with the third
metaphor. It is no longer possible to visit with
Dickinson; one can only enter her mind

through her poems and letters as one can enter her house—through the backdoor out of which her coffin was carried. In reading, one encounters only a text, the trail of an absent author. Upstairs, at last, in the very room where Dickinson exercised her astonishing craft, Rich finds herself again "an insect, vibrating at the frames of windows, clinging to panes of glass, trying to connect." But though "the scent is very powerful," Dickinson herself is absent.

Perhaps the most obvious rhetorical device employed by Rich in this essay, more obvious even than her striking metaphors, is her use of the personal voice. Her approach to Dickinson is self-consciously and unabashedly subjective. She clearly describes her point of view—what she saw as she drove across the Connecticut Valley toward Amherst (ARCO stations, McDonald's, shopping plazas, as well as "light-green spring softening the hills, dogwood and wild fruit trees blossoming in the hollows"), and what she thought about (the history of the valley, "scene of Indian uprisings, religious revivals, spiritual confrontations, the blazing-up of the lunatic fringe of the Puritan coal," and her memories of college weekends in Amherst). Some elements of her perspective—ARCO and McDonald's—would have been alien to Dickinson; others—the sight of dogwood and wild fruit trees in the spring, and most of all, the experience of being a woman poet in a patriarchal culture—would establish their affinity.

Rich's metaphors together with her use of the personal voice indicate some key issues underlying feminist readings of female texts. On the one hand, reading is necessarily subjective. On the other hand, it must not be wholly so. One must respect the autonomy of the text. The reader is a visitor and, as such, must observe the necessary courtesies. She must avoid unwarranted intrusions—she must be careful not to appropriate what belongs to her host, not to impose herself on the other woman. Furthermore, reading is at once an intersubjective encounter and something less than that. In reading Dickinson, Rich seeks to enter her mind, to feel her presence. But the text is a screen, an inanimate object. Its subjectivity is only a projection of the subjectivity of the reader.

Rich suggests the central motivation, the regulative ideal, that shapes the feminist reader's approach to these issues. If feminist readings of male texts are motivated by the need to disrupt the process of immasculation, feminist readings of female texts are motivated by the need "to connect," to recuperate, or to formulate—they come to the same thing—the context, the tradition, that would link women writers to one another, to women readers and critics, and to the larger community of women. Of course, the recuperation of such a context is a necessary basis for the nonrepressive integration of women's point of view and culture into the study of a Humanities that is worthy of its name.[31]

## FEMINIST MODELS OF READING: A SUMMARY

As I noted in the second section, mainstream reader-response theory is preoccupied with two closely related questions: (1) Does the text manipulate the reader, or does the reader manipulate the text to produce the meaning that suits her own interests? and (2) What is "in" the text? How can we distinguish what it supplies from what the reader supplies? Both of these questions refer to the subject-object relation that is established between reader and text during the process of reading. A feminist theory of reading also elaborates this relationship, but for feminists, gender—the gender inscribed in the text as well as the gender of the reader—is crucial. Hence, the feminist story has two chapters, one concerned with male texts and the other with female texts.

The focus of the first chapter is the experience of the woman reader. What do male texts *do* to her? The feminist story takes the subject-object relation of reading through three moments. The phrasing of the basic question signals the first moment. Control is conferred on the text: the woman reader is immasculated by the text. The feminist story fits well at this point in Iser's framework. Feminists insist that the androcentricity of the text and its damaging effects on women readers are not figments of their imagination. These are implicit in the "schematized aspects" of the text. The second moment, which is similarly consonant with the plot of Iser's story, involves the recognition of the crucial role played by the subjectivity of the woman reader. Without her, the text is *nothing*. The process of immasculation is latent in the text, but it finds its actualization only through the reader's activity. In effect, the woman reader is the agent of her own immasculation.[32]

Here we seem to have a corroboration of Culler's contention that dualistic models of reading inevitably disintegrate into one of two monisms. Either the text (and, by implication, the author) or the woman reader is responsible for the process of immasculation. The third moment of the subject-object relation—ushered in by the trasnfiguration of the heroine into a feminist—breaks through this dilemma. The woman reader, now a feminist, embarks on a critical analysis of the reading process, and she realizes that the text has power to structure her experience. Without androcentric texts she will not suffer immasculation. However, her recognition of the power of the text is matched by her awareness of her essential role in the process of reading. Without her, the text is nothing—it is inert and harmless. The advent of feminist consciousness and the accompanying commitment to emancipatory *praxis* reconstitutes the subject-object relationship within a dialectical rather than a dualistic framework, thus averting the impasse described by Culler

between the "dualism of narrative" and the "monism of theory." In the feminist story, the breakdown of Iser's dualism does not indicate a mistake or an irreducible impasse, but the necessity of *choosing* between two modes of reading. The reader can submit to the power of the text, or she can take control of the reading experience. The recognition of the existence of a choice suddenly makes visible the normative dimension of the feminist story: She *should* choose the second alternative.

But what does it mean for a reader to take control of the reading experience? First of all, she must do so without forgetting the androcentricity of the text or its power to structure her experience. In addition, the reader taking control of the text is not, as in Iser's model, simply a matter of selecting among the concretizations allowed by the text. Recall that a crucial feature of the process of immasculation is the woman reader's bifurcated response. She reads the text both as a man and as a woman. But in either case, the result is the same: she confirms her position as other. Taking control of the reading experience means reading the text as it was *not* meant to be read, in fact, reading it against itself. Specifically, one must identify the nature of the choices proffered by the text and, equally important, what the text precludes—namely, the possibility of reading as a woman *without* putting one's self in the position of the other, of reading so as to affirm womanhood as another, equally valid, paradigm of human existence.

All this is easier said than done. It is important to realize that reading a male text, no matter how virulently misogynous, could do little damage if it were an isolated event. The problem is that within patriarchal culture, the experience of immasculation is paradigmatic of women's encounters with the dominant literary and critical traditions. A feminist cannot simply refuse to read patriarchal texts, for they are everywhere, and they condition her participation in the literary and critical enter-prise. In fact, by the time she becomes a femi-nist critic, a woman has already read numer-ous male texts—in particular, the most au-thoritative texts of the literary and critical canons. She has introjected not only andro-centric texts, but also androcentric reading strategies and values. By the time she be-comes a feminist, the bifurcated response characteristic of immasculation has become second nature to her. The feminist story stresses that patriarchal constructs have ob-jective as well as subjective reality; they are inside and outside the text, inside and outside the reader.

The pervasiveness of androcentricity drives feminist theory beyond the individualistic models of Iser and of most reader-response critics. The feminist reader agrees with Stan-ley Fish that the production of the meaning of a text is mediated by the interpretive commu-nity in which the activity of reading is situ-ated: the meaning of the text depends on the interpretive strategy one applies to it, and the choice of strategy is regulated (explicitly or implicitly) by the canons of acceptability that govern the interpretive community.[33] How-ever, unlike Fish, the feminist reader is also aware that the ruling interpretive communi-ties are androcentric, and that this androcen-tricity is deeply etched in the strategies and modes of thought that have been introjected by all readers, women as well as men.

Because patriarchal constructs have psy-chological correlates, taking control of the reading process means taking control of one's reactions and inclinations. Thus, a feminist reading—actually a re-reading—is a kind of therapeutic analysis. The reader recalls and examines how she would "naturally" read a male text in order to understand and there-fore undermine the subjective predisposi-tions that had rendered her vulnerable to its designs. Beyond this, the pervasiveness of immasculation necessitates a collective rem-edy. The feminist reader hopes that other women will recognize themselves in her story, and join her in her struggle to transform the culture.[34]

"Feminism affirms women's point of view by revealing, criticizing and examining its im-possibility."[35] Had we nothing but male texts, this sentence from Catherine MacKinnon's brilliant essay on jurisprudence could serve as the definition of the project of the feminist reader. The significant body of literature writ-ten by women presents feminist critics with another, more heartwarming, task: that of recovering, articulating, and elaborating posi-tive expressions of women's point of view, of celebrating the survival of this point of view in spite of the formidable forces that have been ranged against it.

The shift to women's writing brings with it a shift in emphasis from the negative her-meneutic of ideological unmasking to a posi-tive hermeneutic whose aim is the recovery and cultivation of women's culture. As Show-alter has noted, feminist criticism of women's writing proposes to articulate woman's dif-ference: What does it mean for a woman to express herself in writing? How does a woman write as a woman? It is a central con-tention of this essay that feminist criticism should also inquire into the correlative pro-cess of *reading:* What does it mean for a woman to read without condemning herself to the position of other? What does it mean for a woman, reading as a woman, to read literature written by a woman writing as a woman?[36]

The Adrienne Rich essay discussed in the preceding section illustrates a contrast be-tween feminist readings of male texts and feminist readings of female texts. In the for-mer, the object of the critique, whether it is regarded as an enemy or as symptom of a malignant condition, is the text itself, *not* the reputation or the character of the author.[37] This impersonal approach contrasts sharply with the strong personal interest in Dickinson exhibited by Rich. Furthermore, it is not merely a question of friendliness toward the text. Rich's reading aims beyond "the unfolding of the text as a living event," the goal of aesthetic reading set by Iser. Much of the rhetorical energy of Rich's essay is directed toward evoking the personality of Dickinson, toward making *her* live as the substantial, palpable presence animating her works.

Unlike the first chapter of the feminist story of reading, which is centered around a single heroine—the woman reader battling her way out of a maze of patriarchal constructs—the second chapter features two protagonists—the woman reader and the woman writer—in the context of two settings. The first setting is judicial: one woman is standing witness in defense of the other; the second is dialogic: the two women are engaged in intimate conversation. The judicial setting points to the larger political and cultural dimension of the project of the feminist reader. Feminist critics may well say with Harold Bloom that reading always involves the "art of defensive warfare."[38] What they mean by this, however, would not be Bloom's individualistic, agonistic encounter between "strong poet" and "strong reader," but something more akin to "class struggle." Whether concerned with male or female texts, feminist criticism is situated in the larger struggle against patriarchy.

The importance of this battle cannot be overestimated. However, feminist reading of women's writing opens up space for another, equally important, critical project, namely, the articulation of a model of reading that is centered on a female paradigm. While it is still too early to present a full-blown theory, the dialogic aspect of the relationship between the feminist reader and the woman writer suggests the direction that such a theory might take. As in all stories of reading, the drama revolves around the subject-object relationship between text and reader. The feminist story—exemplified by the Adrienne Rich essay discussed earlier—features an inter-subjective construction of this relationship. The reader encounters not simply a text, but a "subjectified object": the "heart and mind" of another woman. She comes into close contact with an interiority—a power, a creativity, a suffering, a vision—that is *not* identical with her own. The feminist interest in construing reading as an intersubjective encounter suggests an affinity with Poulet's (rather than Iser's) theory, and, as in Poulet's model, the subject of the literary work is its author, *not* the reader: "A book is not only a book; it is a means by which an author actually preserves [her] ideas, [her] feelings, [her] modes of dreaming and living. It is a means of saving [her] identity from death. . . . To understand a literary work, then, is to let the individual who wrote it reveal [herself] to us *in* us."[39]

For all this initial agreement, however, the dialogic relationship the feminist reader establishes with the female subjectivity brought to life in the process of reading is finally at odds with Poulet's model. For the interiorized author is "alien" to Poulet's reader. When he reads, he delivers himself "bound hand and foot, to the omnipotence of fiction." He becomes the "prey" of what he reads. "There is no escaping this takeover." His consciousness is "invaded," "annexed," "usurped." He is "dispossessed" of his rightful place on the "center stage" of his own mind. In the final analysis, the process of reading leaves room for only one subjectivity. The work becomes "a sort of human being" at "the expense of the reader whose life it suspends."[40] It is significant that the metaphors of mastery and submission, of violation and control, so prominent in Poulet's essay, are entirely absent in Rich's essay on Dickinson. In the paradigm of reading implicit in her essay, the dialectic of control (which shapes feminist readings of male texts) gives way to the dialectic of communication. For Rich, reading is a matter of "trying to connect" with the existence behind the text.

This dialectic also has three moments. The

first involves the recognition that genuine intersubjective communication demands the duality of reader and author (the subject of the work). Because reading removes the barrier between subject and object, the division takes place *within* the reader. Reading induces a doubling of the reader's subjectivity, so that one can be placed at the disposal of the text while the other remains with the reader. Now, this doubling presents a problem, for in fact there is only one subject present—the reader. The text—the words on the page—has been written by the writer, but meaning is always a matter of interpretation. The subjectivity roused to life by reading, while it may be attributed to the author, is nevertheless not a separate subjectivity but a projection of the subjectivity of the reader. How can the duality of subjects be maintained in the absence of the author? In an actual conversation, the presence of another person preserves the duality. Because each party must assimilate and interpret the utterances of the other, we still have the introjection of the subject-object division, as well as the possibility of hearing only what one wants to hear. But in a real conversation, the other person can interrupt, object to an erroneous interpretation, provide further explanations, change her mind, change the topic, or cut off conversation altogether. In reading, there are no comparable safeguards against the appropriation of the text by the reader. This is the second moment of the dialectic— the recognition that reading is necessarily subjective. The need to keep it from being *totally* subjective ushers in the third moment of the dialectic.

In the feminist story, the key to the problem is the awareness of the double context of reading and writing. Rich's essay is wonderfully illustrative. To avoid imposing an alien perspective on Dickinson's poetry, Rich informs her reading with the knowledge of the circumstances in which Dickinson lived and worked. She repeatedly reminds herself and her readers that Dickinson must be read in light of her *own* premises, that the "exclusions" and "necessities" she endured, and, therefore, her choices, were conditioned by her own world. At the same time, Rich's sensitivity to the context of writing is matched by her sensitivity to the context of reading. She makes it clear throughout the essay that her reading of Dickinson is necessarily shaped by her experience and interests as a feminist poet living in the twentieth-century United States. The reader also has her own premises. To forget these is to run the risk of imposing them surreptitiously on the author.

To recapitulate, the first moment of the dialectic of reading is marked by the recognition of the necessary duality of subjects; the second, by the realization that this duality is threatened by the author's absence. In the third moment, the duality of subjects is referred to the duality of contexts. Reading becomes a mediation between author and reader, between the context of writings and the context of reading.

Although feminists have always believed that objectivity is an illusion, Rich's essay is the only one, as far as I know, to exhibit through its rhetoric the necessary subjectivity of reading coupled with the equally necessary commitment to reading the text as it was meant to be read.[41] The third moment of the dialectic is apparent in Rich's weaving—not blending—of the context of writing and the context of reading, the perspective of the author and that of the reader. The central rhetorical device effecting this mediation is her use of the personal voice. As in most critical essays, Rich alternates quotes from the texts in question with her own commentary, but her use of the personal voice makes a difference. In her hands, this rhetorical strategy serves two purposes. First, it serves as a reminder that her interpretation is informed by her own perspective. Second, it signifies her tactful approach to Dickinson; the personal voice serves as a gesture warding off any inclination to appropriate the authority of the text as a warrant for the validity of the interpretation. Because the interpretation is presented as an *interpretation,* its claim to validity rests on the cogency of the supporting arguments, *not* on the authorization of the text.

Rich accomplishes even more than this. She reaches out to Dickinson not by identifying with her, but by establishing their affinity. Both are American, both are women poets in a patriarchal culture. By playing this affinity against the differences, she produces a context that incorporates both reader and writer. In turn, this common ground becomes the basis for drawing the connections that, in her view, constitute the proper goal of reading.

One might ask: Is there something distinctively female (rather than "merely feminist") in this dialogic model? While it is difficult to specify what "distinctively female" might mean, there are currently very interesting speculations about differences in the way males and females conceive of themselves and of their relations with others. The works of Jean Baker Miller, Nancy Chodorow, and Carol Gilligan suggest that men define themselves through individuation and separation from others, while women have more flexible ego boundaries and define and experience themselves in terms of their affiliations and relationships with others.[42] Men value autonomy, and they think of their interactions with others principally in terms of procedures for arbitrating conflicts between individual rights. Women, on the other hand, value relationships, and they are most concerned in their dealings with others to negotiate between opposing needs so that the relationship can be maintained. This difference is consistent with the difference between mainstream models of reading and the dialogic model I am proposing for feminist readings of women's writing. Mainstream reader-response theories are preoccupied with issues of control and partition—how to distinguish

the contribution of the author/text from the contribution of the reader. In the dialectic of communication informing the relationship between the feminist reader and the female author/text, the central issue is not of control or partition, but of managing the contradictory implications of the desire for relationship (one must maintain a minimal distance from the other) and the desire for intimacy, up to and including a symbiotic merger with the other. The problematic is defined by the drive "to connect," rather than that which is implicit in the mainstream preoccupation with partition and control—namely, the drive to get it right. It could also be argued that Poulet's model represents reading as an intimate, intersubjective encounter. However, it is significant that in his model, the prospect of close rapport with another provokes both excitement and anxiety. Intimacy, while desired, is also viewed as a threat to one's integrity. For Rich, on the other hand, the prospect of merging with another is problematical, but not threatening.

Let me end with a word about endings. Dialectical stories look forward to optimistic endings. Mine is no exception. In the first chapter the woman reader becomes a feminist, and in the end she succeeds in extricating herself from the androcentric logic of the literary and critical canons. In the second chapter the feminist reader succeeds in effecting a mediation between her perspective and that of the writer. These "victories" are part of the project of producing women's culture and literary tradition, which in turn is part of the project of overcoming patriarchy. It is in the nature of people working for revolutionary change to be optimistic about the prospect of redirecting the future.

Culler observes that optimistic endings have been challenged (successfully, he thinks) by deconstruction, a method radically at odds with the dialectic. It is worth noting that there is a deconstructive moment in Rich's reading of Dickinson. Recall her third metaphor: the reader is an insect "vibrating the frames of windows, clinging to the panes of glass, trying to connect." The suggestion of futility is unmistakable. At best, Rich's interpretation of Dickinson might be considered as a "strong misreading" whose value is in its capacity to provoke other misreadings.

We might say this—but must we? To answer this question, we must ask another: What is at stake in the proposition that reading is impossible? For one thing, if reading is impossible, then there is no way of deciding the validity of an interpretation—the very notion of validity becomes problematical. Certainly it is useful to be reminded that the validity of an interpretation cannot be decided by appealing to what the author "intended," to what is "in" the text, or to what is "in" the experience of the reader. However, there is another approach to the problem of validation, one that is consonant with the dialogic model of reading described above. We can think of validity not as a property inherent in an interpretation, but rather as a *claim* implicit in the *act* of propounding an interpretation. An interpretation, then, is not valid or invalid in itself. Its validity is contingent on the agreement of others. In this view, Rich's interpretation of Dickinson, which is frankly acknowledged as conditioned by her own experience as a twentieth-century feminist poet, is not necessarily a misreading. In advancing her interpretation, Rich implicitly claims its validity. That is to say, to read a text and then to write about it is to seek to connect not only with the author of the original text, but also with a community of readers. To the extent that she succeeds and to the extent that the community is potentially all-embracing, her interpretation has that degree of validity.[43]

Feminist reading and writing alike are grounded in the interest of producing a community of feminist readers and writers, and in the hope that ultimately this community will expand to include everyone. Of course, this project may fail. The feminist story may yet end with the recognition of the impossibility of reading. But this remains to be seen. At this stage I think it behooves us to *choose* the dialectical over the deconstructive plot. It is dangerous for feminists to be overly enamored with the theme of impossibility. Instead, we should strive to redeem the claim that it is possible for a woman, reading as a woman, to read literature written by women, for this is essential if we are to make the literary enterprise into a means for building and maintaining connections among women.

## NOTES

I would like to acknowledge my debt to David Schweickart for the substantial editorial work he did on this chapter.

1. Wayne Booth, Presidential Address, "Arts and Scandals 1982," *PMLA* 98 (1983): 313. Subsequent references to this essay are cited parenthetically in the text.

2. *The Autobiography of Malcolm X,* written with Alex Haley (New York: Grove Press, 1964), p. 173. Subsequent references are cited parenthetically in the text.

3. Virginia Woolf, *A Room of One's Own* (New York: Harcourt Brace Jovanovich, 1981). Subsequent references are cited parenthetically in the text.

4. Jonathan D. Culler, *On Deconstruction: Theory and Criticism after Structuralism* (Ithaca: Cornell University Press, 1982), p. 42. (Subsequent references are cited parenthetically in the text.) Wayne Booth's essay "Freedom of Interpretation: Bakhtin and the Challenge of Feminist Criticism," *Critical Inquiry* 9 (1982): 45–76, is another good omen of the impact of feminist thought on literary criticism.

5. David Bleich, *Subjective Criticism* (Baltimore: Johns Hopkins University Press, 1978), p. 112.

6. George Poulet, "Criticism and the Experience of Interiority," trans. Catherine and Richard Macksey, in *Reader-Response Criticism: From Formalism to Structuralism,* ed. Jane Tompkins (Baltimore: Johns Hopkins University Press, 1980), p. 43. Poulet's theory is not among those discussed by Culler. However, since he will be useful to us later, I mention him here.

7. This argument was advanced by Samuel Weber in

"The Struggle for Control: Wolfgang Iser's Third Dimension," cited by Culler in *On Deconstruction,* p. 75.

8. Stanley E. Fish, "Why No One's Afraid of Wolfgang Iser," *Diacritics* 11 (1981): 7. Quoted by Culler in *On Deconstruction,* p. 75.

9. Elaine Showalter, "Feminist Criticism in the Wilderness," *Critical Inquiry* 8 (1981): 182–85. Showalter argues that if we see feminist critique (focused on the reader) as our primary critical project, we must be content with the "playful pluralism" proposed by Annette Kolodny: first because no single conceptual model can comprehend so eclectic and wide-ranging an enterprise, and second because "in the free play of the interpretive field, feminist critique can only compete with alternative readings, all of which have the built-in obsolescence of Buicks, cast away as newer readings take their place" (p. 182). Although Showalter does not support Wimsatt and Beardsley's proscription of the "affective fallacy," she nevertheless subscribes to the logic of their argument. Kolodny's "playful pluralism" is more benign than Wimsatt and Beardsley's dreaded "relativism," but no less fatal, in Showalter's view, to theoretical coherence.

10. Elaine Showalter, "Women and the Literary Curriculum," *College English* 32 (1971): 855. For an excellent example of recent work following in the spirit of Showalter's critique, see Paul Lauter, *Reconstructing American Literature* (Old Westbury, N.Y.: Feminist Press, 1983).

11. Lee Edwards, "Women, Energy, and *Middlemarch,"* *Massachusetts Review* 13 (1972): 226.

12. Ibid.

13. James Joyce, *The Portrait of the Artist as a Young Man* (London: Jonathan Cape, 1916), p. 195.

14. See also Florence Howe's analysis of the same passage, "Feminism and Literature," in *Images of Women in Fiction: Feminist Perspectives,* ed. Susan Koppelman Cornillon (Bowling Green, Ohio: Bowling Green State University Press, 1972), pp. 262–63.

15. Judith Fetterley, *The Resisting Reader: A Feminist Approach to American Fiction* (Bloomington: Indiana University Press, 1978), p. xx. Although Fetterley's remarks refer specifically to American Literature, they apply generally to the entire traditional canon.

16. Fetterley, *Resisting Reader,* p. xiii.

17. See Katharine M. Rogers, *The Troublesome Helpmate: A History of Misogyny in Literature* (Seattle: University of Washington Press, 1966).

18. Fredric Jameson, *The Political Unconscious: Narrative as a Socially Symbolic Act* (Ithaca: Cornell University Press, 1981), p. 286.

19. In *Woman and the Demon: The Life of a Victorian Myth* (Cambridge: Harvard University Press, 1982), Nina Auerbach employs a similar—though not identical—positive hermeneutic. She reviews the myths and images of women (as angels, demons, victims, whores, etc.) that feminist critics have "gleefully" unmasked as reflections and instruments of sexist ideology, and discovers in them an "unexpectedly empowering" mythos. Auerbach argues that the "most powerful, if least acknowledged creation [of the Victorian cultural imagination] is an explosively mobile, magic woman, who breaks the boundaries of family within which her society restricts her. The triumph of this overweening creature is a celebration of the corporate imagination that believed in her" (p. 1). See also idem, "Magi and Maidens: The Romance of the Victorian Freud," *Critical Inquiry* 8 (1981): 281–300. The tension between the positive and negative feminist hermeneutics is perhaps most apparent when one is dealing with the "classics." See, for example, Carol Thomas Neely, "Feminist Modes of Shakespeare Criticism: Compensatory, Justificatory, Transformational," *Women's Studies* 9 (1981): 3–15.

20. Kate Millett, *Sexual Politics* (New York: Avon Books, 1970).

21. Elaine Showalter, "The Double Critical Standard and the Feminine Novel," chap. 3 in *A Literature of Their Own: British Women Novelists from Brontë to Lessing* (Princeton: Princeton University Press, 1977), pp. 73–99; Carol Ohmann, "Emily Brontë in the Hands of Male Critics," *College English* 32 (1971): 906–13.

22. Nina Baym, "Melodramas of Beset Manhood: How Theories of American Fiction Exclude Women Authors," *American Quarterly* 33 (1981): 123–39.

23. Ibid., p. 125.

24. Ibid., p. 130. One of the founding works of American Literature is "The Legend of Sleepy Hollow," about which Leslie Fiedler writes: "It is fitting that our first successful homegrown legend would memorialize, however playfully, the flight of the dreamer from the shrew" (*Love and Death in the American Novel* [New York: Criterion, 1960], p. xx).

25. Nina Baym's *Women's Fiction: A Guide to Novels by and about Women in America, 1820–1870* (Ithaca: Cornell University Press, 1978) provides a good survey of what has been excluded from the canon.

26. Annette Kolodny, "Dancing through the Minefield: Some Observations on the Theory, Practice, and Politics of a Feminist Literary Criticism," *Feminist Studies* 6 (1980): 10–12. Kolodny elaborates the same theme in "A Map for Rereading: Or, Gender and the Interpretation of Literary Texts," *New Literary History* 11 (1980): 451–67.

27. For an excellent account of the way in which the feminist "interpretive community" has changed literary

and critical conventions, see Jean E. Kennard, "Convention Coverage, or How to Read Your Own Life," *New Literary History* 8 (1981): 69–88. The programs of the MLA Convention during the last twenty-five years offer more concrete evidence of the changes in the literary and critical canons, and of the ideological and political struggles effecting these changes.

28. In Adrienne Rich, *On Lies, Secrets, and Silence: Selected Prose, 1966–1978* (New York: W.W. Norton, 1979). Subsequent references are cited parenthetically in the text.

29. Susan Glaspell's story "A Jury of Her Peers" revolves around a variation of this judicial metaphor. The parable of reading implicit in this story has not been lost on feminist critics. Annette Kolodny, for example, discusses how it "explores the necessary gender marking which *must* constitute any definition of 'peers' in the complex process of unraveling truth or meaning." Although the story does not exclude male readers, it alerts us to the fact that "symbolic representations depend on a fund of shared recognitions and potential references," and in general, "female meaning" is inaccessible to "male interpretation." "However inadvertently, [the male reader] is a *different kind* of reader and, . . . where women are concerned, he is often an inadequate reader" ("Map for Rereading," pp. 460–63).

30. There is a strong counter-tendency, inspired by French poststructuralism, which privileges the appreciation of textuality over the imaginative recovery of the woman writer as subject of the work. See, for example, Mary Jacobus, "Is There a Woman in This Text?" *New Literary History* 14 (1982): 117–41, especially the concluding paragraph. The last sentence of the essay underscores the controversy: "Perhaps the question that feminist critics should be asking is not 'Is there a woman in this text?' but rather: 'Is there a text in this woman?' "

31. I must stress that although Rich's essay presents a significant paradigm of feminist readings of women's writing, it is not the only such paradigm. An alternative is proposed by Caren Greenberg, "Reading Reading: Echo's Abduction of Language," in *Women and Language in Literature and Society,* ed. Sally McConnell-Ginet, Ruth Borker, and Nelly Furman (New York: Praeger, 1980), pp. 304–9.

Furthermore, there are many important issues that have been left out of my discussion. For example:

a. The relationship of her career as reader to the artistic development of the woman writer. In *Madwoman in the Attic* (New Haven: Yale University Press, 1980) Sandra Gilbert and Susan Gubar show that women writers had to struggle to overcome the "anxiety of authorship" which they contracted from the "sentences" of their predecessors, male as well as female. They also argue

that the relationship women writers form with their female predecessors does not fit the model of oedipal combat proposed by Bloom. Rich's attitude toward Dickinson (as someone who "has been there," as a "foremother" to be recovered) corroborates Gilbert and Gubar's claim.

b. The relationship between women writers and their readers. We need actual reception studies as well as studies of the way women writers conceived of their readers and the way they inscribed them in their texts.

c. The relationship between the positive and the negative hermeneutic in feminist readings of women's writing. Rich's reading of Dickinson emphasizes the positive hermeneutic. One might ask, however, if this approach is applicable to *all* women's writing. Specifically, is this appropriate to the popular fiction written by women, e.g., Harlequin Romances? To what extent is women's writing itself a bearer of patriarchal ideology? Janice Radway addresses these issues in "Utopian Impulse in Popular Literature: Gothic Romances and 'Feminist Protest,' " *American Quarterly* 33 (1981): 140–62, and "Women Read the Romance: The Interaction of Text and Context," *Feminist Studies* 9 (1983): 53–78. See also Tania Modleski, *Loving with a Vengeance: Mass-Produced Fantasies for Women* (New York: Methuen, 1982).

32. Iser writes:

> Text and reader no longer confront each other as object and subject, but instead the "division" takes place within the reader [herself]. . . . As we read, there occurs an artificial division of our personality, because we take as a theme for ourselves something we are not. Thus, in reading there are two levels—the alien "me" and the real, virtual "me"—which are never completely cut off from each other. Indeed, we can only make someone else's thoughts into an absorbing theme for ourselves provided the virtual background of our personality can adapt to it. ("The Reading Process: A Phenomenological Approach," in Tompkins, *Reader-Response Criticism,* p. 67)

Add the stipulation that the alien "me" is a male who has appropriated the universal into his maleness, and we have the process of immasculation described in the third section.

33. Stanley E. Fish, *Is There a Text in This Class? The Authority of Interpretive Communities* (Cambridge: Harvard University Press, 1980), especially pt. 2.

34. Although the woman reader is the "star" of the feminist story of reading, this does not mean that men are excluded from the audience. On the contrary, it is hoped that on hearing the feminist story they will be encouraged to revise their own stories to reflect the fact that they, too, are gendered beings, and that, ultimately, they

will take control of their inclination to appropriate the universal at the expense of women.

35. Catherine A. MacKinnon, "Feminism, Marxism, Method, and the State: Toward Feminist Jurisprudence," *Signs* 8 (1981): 637.

36. There is lively debate among feminists about whether it is better to emphasize the essential similarity of women and men, or their difference. There is much to be said intellectually and politically for both sides. However, in one sense, the argument centers on a false issue. It assumes that concern about women's "difference" is incompatible with concern about the essential humanity shared by the sexes. Surely, "difference" may be interpreted to refer to what is distinctive in women's lives and works, *including* what makes them essentially human; unless, of course, we remain captivated by the notion that the standard model for humanity is male.

37. Although opponents of feminist criticism often find it convenient to characterize such works as a personal attack on authors, for feminist critics themselves, the primary consideration is the function of the text as a carrier of patriarchal ideology, and its effect as such especially (but not exclusively) on women readers. The personal culpability of the author is a relatively minor issue.

38. Harold Bloom, *Kabbalah and Criticism* (New York: Seabury, 1975), p. 126.

39. Poulet, "Criticism and the Experience of Interiority," p. 46.

40. Ibid., p. 47. As Culler has pointed out, the theme of control is prominent in mainstream reader-response criticism. Poulet's story is no exception. The issue of control is important in another way. Behind the question of whether the text controls the reader or vice versa is the question of how to regulate literary criticism. If the text is controlling, then there is no problem. The text itself will regulate the process of reading. But if the text is not necessarily controlling, then, how do we constrain the activities of readers and critics? How can we rule out "off-the-wall" interpretations? Fish's answer is of interest to feminist critics. The constraints, he says, are exercised not by the text, but by the institutions within which literary criticism is situated. It is but a small step from this idea to the realization of the necessarily political character of literature and criticism.

41. The use of the personal conversational tone has been regarded as a hallmark of feminist criticism. However, as Jean E. Kennard has pointed out ("Personally Speaking: Feminist Critics and the Community of Readers," *College English* 43 [1981]: 140–45), this theoretical commitment is not apparent in the overwhelming majority of feminist critical essays. Kennard found only five articles in which the critic "overtly locates herself on the page." (To the five she found, I would add three works cited in this essay: "Women, Energy, and *Middlemarch*," by Lee Edwards; "Feminism and Literature," by Florence Howe; and "Vesuvius at Home," by Adrienne Rich.) Kennard observes further that, even in the handful of essays she found, the personal tone is confined to a few introductory paragraphs. She asks: "If feminist criticism has on the whole remained faithful to familiar methods and tone, why have the few articles with an overt personal voice loomed so large in our minds?" Kennard suggests that these personal introductions are invitations "to share a critical response which depends upon unstated, shared beliefs and, to a large extent, experience; that of being a female educated in a male tradition in which she is no longer comfortable." Thus, these introductory paragraphs do not indicate a "transformed critical methodology; they are devices for transforming the reader. I read the later portions of these essays—and by extension other feminist criticism—in a different way because I have been invited to participate in the underground. . . . I am part of a community of feminist readers" (pp. 143–44).

I would offer another explanation, one that is not necessarily inconsistent with Kennard's. I think the use of a personal and conversational tone represents an overt gesture indicating the dialogic mode of discourse as the "regulative ideal" for all feminist discourse. The few essays—indeed, the few introductory paragraphs—that assert this regulative ideal are memorable because they strike a chord in a significant segment of the community of feminist critics. To the extent that we have been touched or transformed by this idea, it will be implicit in the way we read the works of others, in particular, the works of other women. Although the ideal must be overtly affirmed periodically, it is not necessary to do so in all of our essays. It remains potent as long as it is assumed by a significant portion of the community. I would argue with Kennard's distinction between indicators of a transformed critical methodology and devices for transforming the reader. To the extent that critical methodology is a function of the conventions implicitly or explicitly operating in an interpretive community— that is, of the way members of the community conceive of their work and of the way they read each other— devices for transforming readers are also devices for transforming critical methodology.

42. Jean Baker Miller, *Toward a New Psychology of Women* (Boston: Beacon Press, 1976); and Nancy Chodorow, *The Reproduction of Mothering: Psychoanalysis and the Sociology of Gender* (Berkeley and Los Angeles: University of California Press, 1978); and Carol Gilligan, *In a Different Voice: Psychological Theory and Women's Development* (Cambridge: Harvard University Press, 1982).

43. I am using here Jurgen Habermas's definition of truth or validity as a claim (implicit in the act of making assertions) that is redeemable through discourse—specifically, through the domination-free discourse of an "ideal speech situation." For Habermas, consensus at-tained through domination-free discourse is the warrant for truth. See "Wahrheitstheorien," in *Wirklichkeit und Reflexion: Walter Schulz zum 60. Geburtstag* (Pfullingen: Nesge, 1973), pp. 211–65. I am indebted to Alan Soble's unpublished translation of this essay.

# 14

# Barbara Johnson
# 1947–

Barbara Johnson is currently a professor of comparative literature and French at Harvard University. Her work includes "The Frame of Reference" (1977), *Défigurations du langage poetique* (1979), *The Critical Difference* (1980), the translation of Derrida's *Dissemination* (1981), and *A World of Difference* (1987). She also edited *The Psychological Imperative: Teaching as a Literary Genre* (1982). In her work she consistently shows how language subverts a writer's or speaker's intentions and the authorial position of power.

In "Apostrophe, Animation, and Abortion" (1986), Johnson investigates how the politics encoded in the rhetorical figure apostrophe affect the way we deal with issues such as abortion. She asks, "Is there any *inherent* connection between figurative language and questions of life and death, of who will wield and who will receive violence in a given human society?" Johnson focuses on how apostrophe "manipulates the I/Thou structure" so that an "inanimate entity is . . . made present, animate, and anthropomorphic." In her analysis of Baudelaire's poem, "Moesta et Errabunda" (whose Latin title means "sad and vagabond") and Shelley's "Ode to the West Wind" she discusses the use of direct address to give animation and demonstrate the "desire for the *other's* voice." Accordingly, the absence of direct address is assessed as an acting out of "a *loss* of animation." Johnson, along with Baudelaire and Shelley, also considers how effective rhetorical strategies are in bridging the gaps between life and death, times, and locations, and in healing loss.

The relation between abortion and figurative language is addressed more specifically in her treatment of Gwendolyn Brooks's "The Mother," Lucille Clifton's "The Lost Baby," Anne Sexton's "The Abortion," and Adrienne Rich's "To a Poet," among other poems, and Carol Gilligan's study of gender differences in patterns of ethical thinking and male and female logic in her book *In a Different Voice*. Johnson closes the essay by pointing out "the ways in which legal and moral discussions of abortion tend to employ . . . the figure of apostrophe" and discusses how Lacan's analysis of the verbal development of an infant as originating in a demand addressed to the mother may cause us to see lyric poetry as a "fantastically intricate history of endless elaborations and displacements of the single cry, 'Mama!' "

"What happens when the poet is speaking as a mother—a mother whose cry arises out of—and is addressed to—a dead child?" Whether language alone can "bridge the gaps among birth, life, and death" and heal loss is not only a common theme of all the poems Johnson studies but also the over-riding focus of this article. Language "blurs the boundary between life and death" and, consequently, complicates the question of "when life begins." She says, "It is no wonder that the distinction between addressor and addressee should become so problematic in poems about abortion. It is also no wonder that the debate about abortion should refuse to settle into a single voice."

## Apostrophe, Animation, and Abortion

*The abortion issue is as alive and contro-*
*versial in the*
*body politic as it is in the academy and the*
*courtroom.*

—Jay L. Garfield, *Abortion: Moral and Legal*
*Perspectives*

Although rhetoric can be defined as something politicians often accuse each other of, the political dimensions of the scholarly study of rhetoric have gone largely unexplored by literary critics. What, indeed, could seem more dry and apolitical than a rhetorical treatise? What could seem farther away from budgets and guerrilla warfare than a discussion of anaphora, antithesis, prolepsis, and preterition? Yet the notorious CIA manual[1] on psychological operations in guerrilla warfare ends with just such a rhetorical treatise: an appendix on techniques of oratory which lists definitions and examples for these and many other rhetorical figures. The manual is designed to set up a Machiavellian campaign of propaganda, indoctrination, and infiltration in Nicaragua, underwritten by the visible display and selective use of weapons. Shoot softly, it implies, and carry a big schtick. If rhetoric is defined as language that says one thing and means another, then the manual is in effect attempting to maximize the collusion between deviousness in language and accuracy in violence, again and again implying that targets are most effectively hit when most indirectly aimed at. Rhetoric, clearly, has everything to do with covert operations. But are the politics of violence already en-

coded in rhetorical figures as such? In other words, can the very essence of a political issue—an issue like, say, abortion—hinge on the structure of a figure? Is there any *inherent* connection between figurative language and questions of life and death, of who will wield and who will receive violence in a given human society?

As a way of approaching this question, I will begin in a more traditional way by discussing a rhetorical device that has come to seem almost synonymous with the lyric voice: the figure of apostrophe. In an essay in *The Pursuit of Signs,* Jonathan Culler indeed sees apostrophe as an embarrassingly explicit emblem of procedures inherent, but usually better hidden, in lyric poetry as such.[2] Apostrophe in the sense in which I will be using it involves the direct address of an absent, dead, or inanimate being by a first-person speaker: "O wild West Wind, thou breath of Autumn's being . . . ." Apostrophe is thus both direct and indirect: based etymologically on the notion of turning aside, of digressing from straight speech, it manipulates the I/Thou structure of *direct* address in an indirect, fictionalized way. The absent, dead, or inanimate entity addressed is thereby made present, animate, and anthropomorphic. Apostrophe is a form of ventriloquism through which the speaker throws voice, life, and human form into the addressee, turning its silence into mute responsiveness.

Baudelaire's poem "Moesta et Errabunda,"[3] whose Latin title means "sad and vagabond," raises questions of rhetorical animation through several different grades of apostrophe. Inanimate objects like trains and ships or abstract entities like perfumed paradises find themselves called upon to attend to the needs of a plaintive and restless lyric speaker. Even the poem's title poses questions of life and death in linguistic terms: the fact that Baudelaire here temporarily resuscitates a dead language prefigures the poem's attempts to function as a finder of lost loves. But in the opening lines of the poem, the direct-address structure seems straightforwardly *un*figurative: "Tell me, Agatha." This could be called a minimally fictionalized apostrophe, although that is of course its fiction. Nothing at first indicates that Agatha is any more dead, absent, or inanimate than the poet himself.

The poem's opening makes explicit the relation between direct address and the desire for the *other's* voice: "Tell me—*you* talk." But something strange soon happens to the face-to-face humanness of this conversation. What Agatha is supposed to talk about starts a process of dismemberment that might have something to do with a kind of reverse anthropomorphism: "Does your heart sometimes take flight?" Instead of conferring a human shape, this question starts to undo one. Then, too, why the name Agatha? Baudelaire scholars have searched in vain for a biographical referent, never identifying one, but always presuming that one exists. In the Pléiade edition of Baudelaire's complete works, a footnote sends the reader to the only other place in Baudelaire's oeuvre where the name Agathe appears—a page in his *Carnets* where he is listing debts and appointments. This would seem to indicate that Agathe was indeed a real person. What do we know about her? A footnote to the *Carnets* tells us she was probably a prostitute. Why? See the poem "Moesta et Errabunda." This is a particularly stark example of the inevitable circularity of biographical criticism.

If Agathe is finally only a proper name written on two different pages in Baudelaire, then the name itself must have a function as a name. The name is a homonym for the word "agate," a semiprecious stone. Is Agathe really a stone? Does the poem express the Orphic hope of getting a stone to talk?

In a poem about wandering, taking flight, getting away from "here," it is surprising to find that, structurally, each stanza acts out not a departure but a return to its starting point, a repetition of its first line. The poem's structure is at odds with its *apparent* theme. But we soon see that the object of the voyage is precisely to return—to return to a prior state, planted in the first stanza as virginity, in the second as motherhood (through the image of the nurse and the pun on *mer/mère*), and finally as childhood love and furtive pleasure. The voyage outward in space is a figure for the voyage backward in time. The poem's structure of address backs up, too, most explicitly in the third stanza. The cry apostrophizing train and ship to carry the speaker off leads to a seeming reprise of the opening line, but by this point the inanimate has entirely taken over: instead of addressing Agathe directly, the poem asks whether Agathe's heart ever speaks the line the poet himself has spoken four lines earlier. Agathe herself now drops out of the poem, and direct address is temporarily lost, too, in the grammar of the sentence *("Est-il vrai que . . .")*. The poem seems to empty itself of all its human characters and voices, acting out a *loss* of animation—which is in fact its subject: the loss of childhood aliveness brought about by the passage of time. The poem thus enacts in its own temporality the loss of animation it situates in the temporality of the speaker's life.

At this point it launches into a new apostrophe, a new direct address to an abstract, lost state: "How far away you are, sweet paradise." The poem reanimates, addresses an image of fullness and wholeness, and perfect correspondence ("what we love is worthy of our loves"). This height of liveliness, however, culminates strangely in an image of death. The heart that formerly kept trying to fly away now drowns in the moment of reaching its destination ["Où dans la volupté pure le coeur se noie!"]. There may be something to gain, therefore, by deferring arrival, as the poem next seems to do by interrupting itself before grammatically completing the fifth stanza. The poem again ceases to employ direct address and ends by asking two drawn-out, self-interrupting questions. Is that paradise now farther away than India or China? Can one call it back and animate it with a silvery voice? This last question— "Peut-on le rappeler avec des cris plaintifs/Et l'animer encor d'une voix argentine?"—is a perfect description of apostrophe itself: a trope which, by means of the silvery voice of rhetoric, calls up and animates the absent, the lost, and the dead. Apostrophe itself, then, has become not just the poem's mode but also the poem's theme. In other words, what the poem ends up wanting to know is not how far away childhood is, but whether its own rhetorical strategies can be effective. The final question becomes: can this gap be bridged; can this loss be healed, through language alone?

Shelley's "Ode to the West Wind," which is perhaps the ultimate apostrophic poem, makes even more explicit the relation between apostrophe and animation. Shelley spends the first three stanzas demonstrating that the west wind is a figure for the power to animate: it is described as the breath of being, moving everywhere, blowing movement and energy through the world, waking it from its summer dream, parting the waters of the Atlantic, uncontrollable. Yet the wind animates by bringing death, winter, destruction. How do the rhetorical strategies of the poem carry out this program of animation through the giving of death?

The apostrophe structure is immediately foregrounded by the interjections, four times spelled "O" and four times spelled "oh." One of the bridges this poem attempts to build is the bridge between the "O" of the pure vocative, Jakobson's conative function, or the pure presencing of the second person, and the "oh" of pure subjectivity, Jakobson's emotive function, or the pure presencing of the first person.

The first three stanzas are grammatical amplifications of the sentence "Oh thou, hear, oh, hear!" All the vivid imagery, all the picture painting, come in clauses subordinate to this obsessive direct address. But the poet addresses, gives animation, gives the capacity of responsiveness, to the wind, not in order to make it speak but in order to make it listen to him—in order to make it listen to him doing nothing but address *it*. It takes him three long stanzas to break out of this intense near-tautology. As the fourth stanza begins, the "I" starts to inscribe itself grammatically (but not thematically) where the "thou" has been. A power struggle starts up for control over the poem's grammar, a struggle which mirrors the rivalry named in such lines as: "If I were now what I was then, I would ne'er have *striven as thus with thee* in prayer in my sore need." This rivalry is expressed as a comparison: "less free than thou," but then: "One *too like* thee." What does it mean to be "too like"? Time has created a loss of similarity, a loss of animation that has made the sense of similarity even more hyperbolic. In other words, the poet, in becoming less than—less like the wind—somehow becomes more like the wind in his rebellion against the loss of likeness.

In the final stanza the speaker both inscribes and reverses the structure of apostrophe. In saying "be thou me," he is attempting to restore metaphorical exchange and equality. If apostrophe is the giving of voice, the throwing of voice, the giving of animation, then a poet using it is always in a sense saying to the addressee, "Be thou me." But this implies that a poet has animation to give. And *that* is what this poem is saying is not, or is no longer, the case. Shelley's speaker's own sense of animation is precisely what is in doubt, so that he is in effect saying to the wind, "I will animate you so that you will animate, or reanimate, me." "Make me thy lyre . . . ."

Yet the wind, which is to give animation, is also a giver of death. The opposition between life and death has to undergo another reversal, another transvaluation. If death could somehow become a positive force for animation, then the poet would thereby create hope for his own "dead thoughts." The animator that will blow his words around the world will also instate the power of their deadness, their deadness as power, the place of maximum potential for renewal. This is the burden of the final rhetorical question. Does death necessarily entail rebirth? If winter comes, can spring be far behind? The poem is attempting to appropriate the authority of natural logic—in which spring always does follow winter—in order to clinch the authority of cyclic reversibility for its own prophetic powers. Yet because this clincher is expressed in the form of a rhetorical question, it expresses natural certainty by means of a linguistic device that mimics *no* natural structure and has no stable one-to-one correspondence with a meaning. The rhetorical question, in a sense, leaves the poem in a state of suspended animation. But that, according to the poem, is the state of maximum potential.

Both the Baudelaire and the Shelley, then, end with a rhetorical question that both raises and begs the question of rhetoric. It is as though the apostrophe is ultimately directed toward the reader, to whom the poem is addressing Mayor Koch's question: "How'm I doing?" What is at stake in both poems is, as we have seen, the fate of a lost child—the speaker's own former self—and the possibility of a new birth or a reanimation. In the poems that I will discuss next, these structures of apostrophe, animation, and lost life will take on a very different cast through the foregrounding of the question of mother-

hood and the premise that the life that is lost may be someone else's.

In Gwendolyn Brooks's poem "The Mother," the structures of address are shifting and complex. In the first line ("Abortions will not let you forget"), there is a "you" but there is no "I." Instead, the subject of the sentence is the word "abortions," which thus assumes a position of grammatical control over the poem. As entities that disallow forgetting, the abortions are not only controlling but animate and anthropomorphic, capable of treating persons as objects. While Baudelaire and Shelley addressed the anthropomorphized other in order to repossess their lost selves, Brooks is representing the self as eternally addressed and possessed by the lost, anthropomorphized other. Yet the self that is possessed here is itself already a "you," not an "I." The "you" in the opening lines can be seen as an "I" that has become alienated, distanced from itself, and combined with a generalized other, which includes and feminizes the reader of the poem. The grammatical I/Thou starting point of traditional apostrophe has been replaced by a structure in which the speaker is simultaneously eclipsed, alienated, and confused with the addressee. It is already clear that something has happened to the possibility of establishing a clear-cut distinction in this poem between subject and object, agent and victim.

The second section of the poem opens with a change in the structure of address. "I" takes up the positional place of "abortions," and there is temporarily no second person. The first sentence narrates: "I have heard in the voices of the wind the voices of my dim killed children." What is interesting about this line is that the speaker situates the children's voices firmly in a traditional romantic locus of lyric apostrophe—the voices of the wind, Shelley's "West Wind," say, or Wordsworth's "gentle breeze."[4] Gwendolyn Brooks, in other words, is here explicitly rewriting the male lyric tradition, textually placing aborted children in the spot formerly occupied by all the dead, inanimate, or absent entities previously addressed by the lyric. And the question of animation and anthropomorphism is thereby given a new and disturbing twist. For if apostrophe is said to involve language's capacity to give life and human form to something dead or inanimate, what happens when those questions are literalized? What happens when the lyric speaker assumes responsibility for producing the death in the first place, but without being sure of the precise degree of human animation that existed in the entity killed? What is the debate over abortion about, indeed, if not the question of when, precisely, a being assumes a human form?

It is not until line 14 that Brooks's speaker actually addresses the dim killed children. And she does so not directly, but in the form of a self-quotation: "I have said." This embedding of the apostrophe appears to serve two functions here, just as it did in Baudelaire: a self-distancing function, and a foregrounding of the question of the adequacy of language. But whereas in Baudelaire the distance between the speaker and the lost childhood is what is being lamented, and a restoration of vividness and contact is what is desired, in Brooks the vividness of the contact is precisely the source of the pain. While Baudelaire suffers from the dimming of memory, Brooks suffers from an inability to forget. And while Baudelaire's speaker actively seeks a fusion between present self and lost child, Brooks's speaker is attempting to fight her way out of a state of confusion between self and other. This confusion is indicated by the shifts in the poem's structures of address. It is never clear whether the speaker sees herself as an "I" or a "you," an addressor or an addressee. The voices in the wind are not created *by* the lyric apostrophe; they rather initiate the need for one. The initiative of speech seems always to lie in the other. The poem continues to struggle to clarify the relation between "I" and "you," but in the end it only

succeeds in expressing the inability of its language to do so. By not closing the quotation in its final line, the poem, which began by confusing the reader with the aborter, ends by implicitly including the reader among those aborted—and loved. The poem can no more distinguish between "I" and "you" than it can come up with a proper definition of life. For all the Yeatsian tripartite aphorisms about life as what is past or passing or to come, Brooks substitutes the impossible middle ground between "You were born, you had body, you died" and "It is just that you never giggled or planned or cried."

In line 28, the poem explicitly asks, "Oh, what shall I say, how is the truth to be said?" Surrounding this question are attempts to make impossible distinctions: got/did not get, deliberate/not deliberate, dead/never made. The uncertainty of the speaker's control as a subject mirrors the uncertainty of the children's status as an object. It is interesting that the status of the human subject here hinges on the word "deliberate." The association of deliberateness with human agency has a long (and very American) history. It is deliberateness, for instance, that underlies that epic of separation and self-reliant autonomy, Thoreau's *Walden*. "I went to the woods," writes Thoreau, "because I wished to live deliberately, to front only the essential facts of life" [66]. Clearly, for Thoreau, pregnancy was not an essential fact of life. Yet for him as well as for every human being that has yet existed, someone else's pregnancy is the very *first* fact of life. How might the plot of human subjectivity be reconceived (so to speak) if pregnancy rather than autonomy is what raises the question of deliberateness?

Much recent feminist work has been devoted to the task of rethinking the relations between subjectivity, autonomy, interconnectedness, responsibility, and gender. Carol Gilligan's book *In a Different Voice* (and this focus on "voice" is not irrelevant here) studies gender differences in patterns of ethical thinking. The central ethical question analyzed by Gilligan is precisely the decision whether to have, or not to have, an abortion. The first time I read the book, this struck me as strange. Why, I wondered, would an investigation of gender differences focus on one of the questions about which an even-handed comparison of the male and the female points of view is impossible? Yet this, clearly, turns out to be the point: there is difference because it is not always possible to make symmetrical oppositions. As long as there is symmetry, one is not dealing with difference but rather with versions of the same. Gilligan's difference arises out of the impossibility of maintaining a rigorously logical binary model for ethical choices. Female logic, as she defines it, is a way of rethinking the logic of choice in a situation in which none of the choices are good. "Believe that even in my deliberateness I was not deliberate": believe that the agent is not entirely autonomous, believe that I can be subject and object of violence at the same time, believe that I have not chosen the conditions under which I must choose. As Gilligan writes of the abortion decision, "the occurrence of the dilemma itself precludes nonviolent resolution" [94]. The choice is not between violence and non-violence, but between simple violence to a fetus and complex, less determinate violence to an involuntary mother and/or an unwanted child.

Readers of Brooks's poem have often read it as an argument against abortion. And it is certainly clear that the poem is not saying that abortion is a good thing. But to see it as making a simple case for the embryo's right to life is to assume that a woman who has chosen abortion does not have the right to mourn. It is to assume that no case *for* abortion can take the woman's feelings of guilt and loss into consideration, that to take those feelings into account is to deny the right to choose the act that produced them. Yet the poem makes no such claim: it attempts the impossible task

of humanizing both the mother and the aborted children while presenting the inadequacy of language to resolve the dilemma without violence.

What I would like to emphasize is the way in which the poem suggests that the arguments for and against abortion are structured through and through by the rhetorical limits and possibilities of something akin to apostrophe. The fact that apostrophe allows one to animate the inanimate, the dead, or the absent implies that whenever a being is apostrophized, it is thereby automatically animated, anthropomorphized, "person-ified." (By the same token, the rhetoric of calling makes it difficult to tell the difference between the animate and the inanimate, as anyone with a telephone answering machine can attest.) Because of the ineradicable tendency of language to animate whatever it addresses, rhetoric itself can always have already answered "yes" to the question of whether a fetus is a human being. It is no accident that the anti-abortion film most often shown in the United States should be entitled "The Silent Scream." By activating the imagination to believe in the anthropomorphized embryo's mute responsiveness in exactly the same way that apostrophe does, the film (which is of course itself a highly rhetorical entity) is playing on rhetorical possibilities that are inherent in all linguistically-based modes of representation.

Yet the function of apostrophe in the Brooks poem is far from simple. If the fact that the speaker addresses the children at all makes them human, then she must pronounce herself guilty of murder—but only if she discontinues her apostrophe. As long as she addresses the children, she can keep them alive, can keep from finishing with the act of killing them. The speaker's attempt to absolve herself of guilt depends on never forgetting, never breaking the ventriloquism of an apostrophe through which she cannot define her identity otherwise than as the mother eaten alive by the children she has never fed. Who, in the final analysis, exists by addressing whom? The children are a rhetorical extension of the mother, but she, as the poem's title indicates, has no existence apart from her relation to them. It begins to be clear that the speaker has written herself into a poem she cannot get out of without violence. The violence she commits in the end is to her own language: as the poem ends, the vocabulary shrinks away, words are repeated, nothing but "all" rhymes with "all." The speaker has written herself into silence. Yet hers is not the only silence in the poem: earlier she had said, "You will never . . . silence or buy with a sweet." If sweets are for silencing, then by beginning her apostrophe, "Sweets, if I sinned . . ." the speaker is already saying that the poem, which exists to memorialize those whose lack of life makes them eternally alive, is also attempting to silence once and for all the voices of the children in the wind. It becomes impossible to tell whether language is what gives life or what kills.

> *Women have said again and again "This*
>     *body is my body!"*
> *and they have reason to feel angry, reason*
>     *to feel that it has been like*
> *shouting into the wind.*
>     —Judith Jarvis Thomson, "A Defense of
>         Abortion"

It is interesting to note the ways in which legal and moral discussions of abortion tend to employ the same terms as those we have been using to describe the figure of apostrophe. "These disciplines [philosophy, theology, and civil and canon law] variously approached the question in terms of the point at which the embryo or fetus became 'formed' or recognizably human, or in terms of when a 'person' came into being, that is, infused with a 'soul' or 'animated' " [Blackmun, *Roe vs. Wade, Abortion: Moral and Legal Perspectives,* Garfield and Hennessey,

Eds. 15]. The issue of "fetal personhood" [Garfield and Hennessey, 55] is of course a way of bringing to a state of explicit uncertainty the fundamental difficulty of defining personhood in general [cf. Luker 6]. Even if the question of defining the nature of "persons" is restricted to the question of understanding what is meant by the word "person" in the United States Constitution (since the Bill of Rights guarantees the rights only of "persons"), there is not at present, and probably will never be, a stable legal definition. Existing discussions of the legality and morality of abortion almost invariably confront, leave unresolved, and detour around the question of the nature and boundaries of human life. As Justice Blackmun puts it in *Roe vs. Wade:* "We need not resolve the difficult question of when life begins. When those trained in the respective disciplines of medicine, philosophy, and theology are unable to arrive at any consensus, the judiciary, at this point in the development of man's knowledge, is not in a position to speculate as to the answer" [27]. In the case of *Roe vs. Wade,* the legality of abortion is derived from the pregnant couple's right to privacy—an argument which, as Catherine MacKinnon argues in *'Roe vs. Wade:* A Study in Male Ideology" [Garfield and Hennessey 45–54], is itself problematic for women, since by protecting "privacy" the courts also protect the injustices of patriarchal sexual arrangements. When the issue is an unwanted pregnancy, some sort of privacy has already, in a sense, been invaded. In order for the personal to avoid being reduced once again to the non-political, privacy, like deliberateness, needs to be rethought in terms of sexual politics. Yet even the attempt to re-gender the issues surrounding abortion is not simple. As Kristin Luker convincingly demonstrates, the debate turns around the claims not only of woman vs. fetus or of woman vs. patriarchal state, but also of woman vs. woman:

Pro-choice and pro-life activists live in different worlds, and the scope of their lives, as both adults and children, fortifies them in their belief that their views on abortion are the more correct, more moral, and more reasonable. When added to this is the fact that should "the other side" win, one group of women will see the very real devaluation of their lives and life resources, it is not surprising that the abortion debate has generated so much heat and so little light. [Luker 215]

Are pro-life activists, as they claim, actually reaching their cherished goal of "educating the public to the humanity of the unborn child?" As we begin to seek an answer, we should recall that motherhood is a topic about which people have very complicated feelings, and because abortion has become the battleground for different definitions of motherhood, neither the pro-life nor the pro-choice movement has ever been "representative" of how most Americans feel about abortion. More to the point, all our data suggest that neither of these groups will ever be able to be representative. [224, emphasis in original]

It is often said, in literary-theoretical circles, that to focus on undecidability is to be apolitical. Everything I have read about the abortion controversy in its present form in the United States leads me to suspect that, on the contrary, the undecidable *is* the political. There is politics precisely because there is undecidability.

And there is also poetry. There are striking and suggestive parallels between the "different voices" involved in the abortion debate and the shifting address-structures of poems like Gwendolyn Brooks's "The Mother." A glance at several other poems suggests that there tends indeed to be an overdetermined relation between the theme of abortion and the problematization of structures of address.

In Anne Sexton's "The Abortion," six 3-line stanzas narrate, in the first person, a trip to Pennsylvania where the "I" has obtained an abortion. Three times the poem is interrupted by the italicized lines:

> *Somebody who should have been born*
> *is gone.*

Like a voice-over narrator taking superegoistic control of the moral bottom line, this refrain (or "burden," to use the archaic term for both "refrain" and "child in the womb") puts the first-person narrator's authority in question without necessarily constituting the voice of a separate entity. Then, in the seventh and final stanza, the poem extends and intensifies this split:

> *yes, woman, such logic will lead*
> *to loss without death. Or say what you*
> *    meant,*
> *you coward . . . this baby that I bleed.*

Self-accusing, self-interrupting, the narrating "I" turns on herself (or is it someone else?) as "you," as "woman." The poem's speaker becomes as split as the two senses of the word "bleed." Once again, "saying what one means" can only be done by ellipsis, violence, illogic, transgression, silence. The question of who is addressing whom is once again unresolved.

As we have seen, the question of "when life begins" is complicated partly because of the way in which language blurs the boundary between life and death. In "Menstruation at Forty," Sexton sees menstruation itself as the loss of a child ("two days gone in blood")—a child that exists because it can be called:

> *I was thinking of a son. . . .*
> *You! . . .*
> *Will you be the David or the Susan?*

. . .
*David! Susan! David! David!*
. . .
*my carrot, my cabbage,*
*I would have possessed you before all*
    *women,*
*calling your name,*
*calling you mine.*

The political consequences and complexities of addressing—of "calling"—are made even more explicit in a poem by Lucille Clifton entitled "The Lost Baby Poem." By choosing the word "dropped" ("i dropped your almost body down"), Clifton renders it unclear whether the child has been lost through abortion or through miscarriage. What is clear, however, is that that loss is both mourned and rationalized. The rationalization occurs through the description of a life of hardship, flight, and loss: the image of a child born into winter, slipping like ice into the hands of strangers in Canada, conflates the scene of Eliza's escape in *Uncle Tom's Cabin* with the exile of draft resisters during the Vietnam War. The guilt and mourning occur in the form of an imperative in which the notion of "stranger" returns in the following lines:

*if I am ever less than a mountain*
*for your definite brothers and sisters . . . .*
*. . . let black men call me stranger*
*always for your never named sake.*

The act of "calling" here correlates a lack of name with a loss of membership. For the sake of the one that cannot be called, the speaker invites an apostrophe that would expel *her* into otherness. The consequences of the death of a child ramify beyond the mother-child dyad to encompass the fate of an entire community. The world that has created conditions under which the loss of a baby becomes desirable must be resisted, not joined. For a black woman, the loss of a baby can always be perceived as a com-

plicity with genocide. The black mother sees her own choice as one of being either a stranger or a rock. The humanization of the lost baby addressed by the poem is thus carried out at the cost of dehumanizing, even of rendering inanimate, the calling mother.

Yet each of these poems exists, finally, *because* a child does not.[5] In Adrienne Rich's poem "To a Poet," the rivalry between poems and children is made quite explicit. The "you" in the poem is again aborted, but here it is the mother herself who could be called "dim and killed" by the fact not of abortion but of the institution of motherhood. And again, the structures of address are complex and unstable. The deadness of the "you" cannot be named: not suicide, not murder. The question of the life or death of the addressee is raised in an interesting way through Rich's rewriting of Keats's sonnet on his mortality. While Keats writes, "When I have fears that *I* will cease to be" ["When I Have Fears"], Rich writes "and I have fears that *you* will cease to be." If poetry is at stake in both intimations of mortality, what is the significance of this shift from "I" to "you"? On the one hand, the very existence of the Keats poem indicates that the pen has succeeded in gleaning something before the brain has ceased to be. No such grammatical guarantee exists for the "you." Death in the Keats poem is as much a source as it is a threat to writing. Hence, death, for Keats, could be called the mother of poetry while motherhood, for Rich, is precisely the death of poetry. The Western myth of the conjunction of word and flesh implied by the word "incarnate" is undone by images of language floating and vanishing in the toilet bowl of real-flesh needs. The word is not made flesh; rather, flesh unmakes the mother-poet's word. The difficulty of retrieving the "you" as poet is enacted by the structures of address in the following lines:

*I write this . . . not for you*
*who fight to write your own*

*words fighting up the falls*
*but for another woman . . . dumb*

In saying "I write this not for you," it is almost as though Rich is excluding as addressee anyone who could conceivably be reading this poem. The poem is setting aside both the "I" and the "you"—the pronouns Benveniste associates with personhood—and reaches instead toward a "she," which belongs in the category of "non-person." The poem is thus attempting the impossible task of directly addressing not a second person but a third person—a person who, if she is reading the poem, cannot be the reader the poem has in mind. The poem is trying to include what is by its own grammar excluded from it—to animate through language the non-person, the "other woman." Therefore, this poem, too, is bursting the limits of its own language, inscribing a logic that it itself reveals to be impossible—but necessary. Even the divorce between writing and childbearing is less absolute than it appears: in comparing the writing of words to the spawning of fish, Rich's poem reveals itself to be trapped between the inability to combine and the inability to separate the woman's various roles.

In each of these poems, then, a kind of competition is implicitly instated between the bearing of children and the writing of poems. Something unsettling has happened to the analogy often drawn by male poets between artistic creation and procreation. For it is not true that literature contains no examples of male pregnancy. Sir Philip Sidney, in the first sonnet from "Astrophel and Stella," describes himself as "great with child to speak," but the poem is ultimately produced at the expense of no literalized child. Sidney's labor pains are smoothed away by a midwifely apostrophe ("Fool," said my Muse to me, 'look in thy heart, and write!' ") [*The Norton Anthology of Poetry,* 1: 12–14], and by a sort of poetic Caesarian section, out springs the poem we have, in fact, already finished reading. Mallarmé, in "Don du poème," describes himself

as an enemy father seeking nourishment for his monstrous poetic child from the woman within apostrophe-shot who is busy nursing a literalized daughter. But since the woman presumably has two breasts, there seems to be enough to go around. As Shakespeare assures the fair young man, "But were some child of yours alive that time, / You should live twice in it and in my rhyme" [*Sonnets,* 17: 13–14]. Apollinaire, in his play *Les Mamelles de Tirésias,* depicts woman as a de-maternalized neo-Malthusian leaving the task of childbearing to a surrealistically fertile husband. But again, nothing more disturbing than Tiresian cross-dressing seems to occur. Children are alive and well, and far more numerous than ever. Indeed, in one of the dedicatory poems, Apollinaire indicates that his drama represents a return to health from the literary reign of the *poète maudit:*

*La féconde raison a jailli de ma fable,*
*Plus de femme stérile et non plus*
    *d'avortons . . .*

*[Fertile reason springs out of my fable,*
*No more sterile women, no aborted*
    *children]*

This dig at Baudelaire, among others, reminds us that in the opening poem to *Les Fleurs du Mal* ("Bénédiction"), Baudelaire represents the poet himself as an abortion *manqué,* cursed by the poisonous words of a rejecting mother. The question of the unnatural seems more closely allied with the bad mother than with the pregnant father.

Even in the seemingly more obvious parallel provided by poems written to dead children by male poets, it is not really surprising to find that the substitution of poem for child lacks the sinister undertones and disturbed address exhibited by the abortion poems we have been discussing. Ben Jonson, in "On My First Son," calls his dead child "his best piece of poetry," while Mallarmé, in an only semiguilty *Aufhebung,* transfuses the dead Anatole to the level of an idea. More recently, Jon Silkin has written movingly of the death of a handicapped child ("something like a person") as a change of silence, not a splitting of voice. And Michael Harper, in "Nightmare Begins Responsibility," stresses the powerlessness and distrust of a black father leaving his dying son to the care of a "white-doctor-who-breathed-for-him-all-night." But again, whatever the complexity of the voices in that poem, the speaker does not split self-accusingly or infra-symbiotically in the ways we have noted in the abortion/motherhood poems. While one could undoubtedly find counter-examples on both sides, it is not surprising that the substitution of art for children should not be inherently transgressive for the male poet. Men have in a sense always had no choice but to substitute something for the literal process of birth. That, at least, is the belief that has long been encoded into male poetic conventions. It is as though male writing were by nature procreative, while female writing is somehow by nature infanticidal.

It is, of course, as problematic as it is tempting to draw general conclusions about differences between male and female writing on the basis of these somewhat random examples. Yet it is clear that a great many poetic effects may be colored according to *expectations* articulated through the gender of the poetic speaker. Whether or not men and women would "naturally" write differently about dead children, there is something about the connection between motherhood and death that refuses to remain comfortably and conventionally figurative. When a woman speaks about the death of children in any sense other than that of pure loss, a powerful taboo is being violated. The indistinguishability of miscarriage and abortion in the Clifton poem indeed points to the notion that *any* death of a child is perceived as a crime committed by the mother, something a mother ought by definition to be able to prevent. That these questions should be so inex-

tricably connected to the figure of apostrophe, however, deserves further comment. For there may be a deeper link between motherhood and apostrophe than we have hitherto suspected.

The verbal development of the infant, according to Lacan, begins as a demand addressed to the mother, out of which the entire verbal universe is spun. Yet the mother addressed is somehow a personification, not a person—a personification of presence or absence, of Otherness itself.

> Demand in itself bears on something other than the satisfactions it calls for. It is demand of a presence or of an absence—which is what is manifested in the primordial relation to the mother, pregnant with that Other to be situated *within* the needs that it can satisfy. Insofar as [man's] needs are subjected to demand, they return to him alienated. This is not the effect of his real dependence . . . , but rather the turning into signifying form as such, from the fact that it is from the locus of the Other that its message is emitted. [Ecrits 286]

If demand is the originary vocative, which assures life even as it inaugurates alienation, then it is not surprising that questions of animation inhere in the rhetorical figure of apostrophe. The reversal of apostrophe we noted in the Shelley poem ("animate me") would be no reversal at all, but a reinstatement of the primal apostrophe in which, despite Lacan's disclaimer, there is precisely a link between demand and animation, between apostrophe and life-and-death dependency.[6] If apostrophe is structured like demand, and if demand articulates the primal relation to the mother as a relation to the Other, then lyric poetry itself—summed up in the figure of apostrophe—comes to look like the fantastically intricate history of endless elaborations and displacements of the single cry, "Mama!" The question these poems are asking, then, is what happens when the poet is speaking as a mother—a mother whose cry arises out of—and is addressed to—a dead child?

It is no wonder that the distinction between addressor and addressee should become so problematic in poems about abortion. It is also no wonder that the debate about abortion should refuse to settle into a single voice. Whether or not one has ever been a mother, everyone participating in the debate has once been a child. Rhetorical, psychoanalytical, and political structures are profoundly implicated in one another. The difficulty in all three would seem to reside in the attempt to achieve a full elaboration of any discursive position other than that of child.

## WORKS CITED

Allison et al., Eds. *The Norton Anthology of Poetry,* New York: W. W. Norton, 1975.

Apollinaire, Guillaume. "Les Mamelles de Tirésias." *L'Enchanteur pourrissant.* Paris: Gallimard, 1972.

Baudelaire, Charles. *Oeuvres complètes.* Paris: Pleiade, 1976.

Brooks, Gwendolyn. "The Mother." *Selected Poems.* New York: Harper & Row, 1963.

Clifton, Lucille. "The Lost Baby Poem." *Good News About the Earth.* New York: Random House, 1972.

Cohen, Marion Deutsche, Ed. *The Limits of Miracles.* South Hadley, Eng.: Bergin & Garvey, 1985.

Culler, Jonathan. *The Pursuit of Signs.* Ithaca: Cornell UP, 1981.

de Man, Paul. "Lyrical Voice in Contemporary Theory." *Lyric Poetry: Beyond New Criticism.* Ed. Hosek and Parker. Ithaca: Cornell UP, 1985.

Gilligan, Carol. *In a Different Voice.* Cambridge, MA: Harvard UP, 1982.

Harper, Michael. *Nightmare Begins Responsibility.* Urbana: U of Illinois P, 1975.

Jarrell, Randall. "A Sick Child." *The Voice that is Great within Us.* Ed. Hayden Caruth. New York: Bantam, 1970.

Jonson, Ben. "On My First Son." *The Norton Anthology of Poetry.* Ed. Allison et al. New York: W. W. Norton, 1975.

Keats, John. "When I Have Fears." *The Norton Anthology of Poetry.* Ed. Allison et al. New York: W. W. Norton, 1975.

Lacan, Jacques. *Ecrits.* Trans. Sheridan. New York: W. W. Norton, 1977.

Luker, Kristin. *Abortion and the Politics of Motherhood.* Berkeley: U of California P, 1984.

Mallarmé, Stéphane. *Oeuvres complète.* Paris: Pléiade, 1961.

———. *Pour un tombeau d'Anatole.* Ed. Richard. Paris: Seuil, 1961.

Rich, Adrienne. "To a Poet." *The Dream of a Common Language.* New York: W. W. Norton, 1978.

Sexton, Anne. "The Abortion." *The Complete Poems.* Boston: Houghton Mifflin, 1981.

Shakespeare, William. *Sonnets.* Ed. Booth. New Haven: Yale UP, 1977.

Shelley, Percy Bysshe. "Ode to the West Wind." *The Norton Anthology of Poetry.* Ed. Allison et al. New York: W. W. Norton, 1975.

Sidney, Sir Philip. "Astrophel and Stella." *The Norton Anthology of Poetry.* Ed. Allison et al. New York: W. W. Norton, 1975.

Thomson, Judith Jarvis. "A Defense of Abortion." *Rights, Restitution, Risk.* Ed. William Parent. Cambridge, MA: Harvard UP, 1986.

Thoreau, Henry David. *Walden.* New York: Signet, 1960.

Wordsworth, William. *The Prelude.* Ed. de Selincourt. London: Oxford UP, 1959.

## NOTES

1. I would like to thank Tom Keenan of Yale University for bringing this text to my attention. The present essay has in fact benefited greatly from the suggestions of others, among whom I would like particularly to thank Marge Garber, Rachel Jacoff, Carolyn Williams, Helen Vendler, Steven Melville, Ted Morris, Stamos Metzidakis, Steven Ungar, and Richard Yarborough.

2. Cf. also Paul de Man, in "Lyrical Voice in Contemporary Theory": "Now it is certainly beyond question that the figure of address is recurrent in lyric poetry, to the point of constituting the generic definition of, at the very least, the ode (which can, in turn, be seen as paradigmatic for poetry in general)" [61].

3. For complete texts of the poems under discussion, see the appendix to this article.

4. It is interesting to note that the "gentle breeze," apostrophized as "Messenger" and "Friend" in the 1805–6 *Prelude* (Book I, line 5), is, significantly, not directly addressed in the 1850 version. One might ask whether this change stands as a sign of the much-discussed waning of Wordsworth's poetic inspiration, or whether it is, rather, one of a number of strictly rhetorical shifts that give the impression of a wane, just as the shift in Gwendolyn Brooks's poetry from her early impersonal poetic narratives to her more recent direct-address poems gives the impression of a politicization.

5. For additional poems dealing with the loss of babies, see the anthology, *The Limits of Miracles* collected by Marion Deutsche Cohen. Sharon Dunn, editor of the *Agni Review*, told me recently that she has in fact noticed that such poems have begun to form almost a new genre.

6. An interesting example of a poem in which an apostrophe confers upon the total Other the authority to animate the self is Randall Jarrell's "A Sick Child," which ends: "All that I've never thought of—think of me!"

MOESTA ET ERRABUNDA

Dis-moi, ton coeur parfois s'envole-t-il,
    Agathe,
Loin du noir océan de l'immonde cité,
Vers un autre océan où la splendeur éclate,
Bleu, clair, profond, ainsi que la virginité?
Dis-moi, ton coeur parfois s'envole-t-il,
    Agathe?

La mer, la vaste mer, console nos labeurs!
Quel démon a doté le mer, rauque
    chanteuse
Qu'accompagne l'immense orgue des vents
    grondeurs,
De cette fonction sublime de berceuse?
La mer, la vaste mer, console nos labeurs!

Emporte-moi, wagon! elève-moi, frégate!
Loin, loin! ici la boue est faite de nos
    pleurs!
—Est-il vrai que parfois le triste coeur
    d'Agathe
Dise: Loin des remords, des crimes, des
    douleurs,
Emporte-moi, wagon, enlève-moi, frégate?

Comme vous êtes loin, paradis parfumé,
Où sous un clair azur tour n'est qu'amour
    et joie,
Où tout ce que l'on aime est digne d'être
    aimé,
Où dans la volupté pure le coeur se noie!
Comme vous êtes loin, paradis parfumé!

Mais le vert paradis des amours enfantines,
Les courses, les chansons, les baisers, les
    bouquets,
Les violons vibrant derrière les collines,
Avec les brocs de vin, le soir, dans les
    bosquets,
—Mais le vert paradis des amours
    enfantines,

L'innocent paradis, plein de plaisirs furtifs,
Est-il déjà plus loin que l'Inde et que la
    Chine?
Peut-on le rappeler avec des cris plaintifs,
Et l'animer encor d'une voix argentine,
L'innocent paradis plein de plaisirs furtifs?
                        —Charles Baudelaire

MOESTA ET ERRABUNDA

Tell me, Agatha, does your heart take flight
Far from the city's black and filthy sea
Off to another sea of splendid light,
Blue, bright, and deep as virginity?
Tell me, Agatha, does your heart take
    flight?

Seas, unending seas, console our trials!
What demon gave the sea this raucous
    voice
With organ music from the rumbling skies,
And made it play the role of sublime nurse?
Seas, unending seas, console our trials!

Carry me off, engines! lift me, bark!
Far, far away! our tears here turn to mud!
—Can it be true that sometimes Agatha's
    heart
Says: far from the crimes, remorse, distress,
    and dread
Carry me off, engines! lift me, bark!

How far away you are, sweet paradise,
Where what we love is worthy of our loves,
Where all is pleasure under azure skies,
Where hearts are drowned in pure
    voluptuous floods!
How far away you are, sweet paradise!

That verdant paradise of childhood loves,
The songs and games and kisses and
    bouquets,
The trembling violins in wooded groves,
The wine behind the hills as evening greys,
—That verdant paradise of childhood
    loves,

That paradise of blameless, furtive joys—
Does it lie farther off than China lies?
Can it be called back with a silvery voice
And animated again with plaintive cries,
That paradise of blameless, furtive joys?
                              —Trans. B. Johnson

ODE TO THE WEST WIND

1

O wild West Wind, thou breath of
    Autumn's being.
Thou, from whose unseen presence the
    leaves dead
Are driven, like ghosts from an enchanter
    fleeing.

Yellow, and black, and pale, and hectic
    red,
Pestilence-stricken multitudes: O thou,
Who chariotest to their dark wintry bed

The wingéd seeds, where they lie cold and
    low,
Each like a corpse within its grave, until
Thine azure sister of the Spring shall blow

Her clarion o'er the dreaming earth, and fill
(Driving sweet buds like flocks to feed in
    air)
With living hues and odors plain and hill:

Wild Spirit, which art moving everywhere;
Destroyer and preserver; hear, oh, hear!

2

Thou on whose stream, mid the steep sky's
    commotion,
Loose clouds like earth's decaying leaves
    are shed,
Shook from the tangled boughs of Heaven
    and Ocean,

Angels of rain and lightning: there are
    spread
On the blue surface of thine aëry surge,
Like the bright hair uplifted from the head

Of some fierce Maenad, even from the dim
    verge
Of the horizon to the zenith's height,
The locks of the approaching storm. Thou
    dirge

Of the dying year, to which this closing
    night
Will be the dome of a vast sepulcher,
Vaulted with all thy congregated might

Of vapors, from whose solid atmosphere
Black rain, and fire, and hail will burst: oh,
    hear!

3

Thou who didst waken from his summer
    dreams
The blue Mediterranean, where he lay,
Lulled by the coil of his crystálline streams,

Beside a pumice isle in Baiae's bay,
And say in sleep old palaces and towers
Quivering within the wave's intenser day,

All overgrown with azure moss and flowers
So sweet, the sense faints picturing them!
    Thou
For whose path the Atlantic's level powers

Cleave themselves into chasms, while far
    below

The sea-blooms and the oozy woods which
    wear
The sapless foliage of the ocean, know
Thy voice, and suddenly grow gray with
    fear,
And tremble and despoil themselves: oh,
    hear!

4

If I were a dead leaf thou mightest bear;
If I were a swift cloud to fly with thee;
A wave to pant beneath thy power, and
    share

The impulse of thy strength, only less free
Than thou, O uncontrollable! If even
I were as in my boyhood, and could be

The comrade of thy wanderings over
    Heaven,
As then, when to outstrip thy skyey speed
Scarce seem a vision; I would ne'er have
    striven

As thus with thee in prayer in my sore
    need.
Oh, lift me as a wave, a leaf, a cloud!
I fall upon the thorns of life! I bleed!

A heavy weight of hours has chained and
    bowed
One too like thee: tameless, and swift, and
    proud.

5

Make me thy lyre, even as the forest is:
What if my leaves are falling like its own!
The tumult of thy mighty harmonies

Will take from both a deep, autumnal tone,
Sweet though in sadness. Be thou, Spirit
    fierce,
My spirit! Be thou me, impetuous one!

Drive my dead thoughts over the universe
Like withered leaves to quicken a new
    birth!
And, by the incantation of this verse,

Scatter, as from an unextinguished hearth
Ashes and sparks, my words among
    mankind!
Be through my lips to unawakened earth

The trumpet of a prophecy! O Wind,
If Winter comes, can Spring be far behind?
—Percy Bysshe Shelley

THE ABORTION

*Somebody who should have been born
is gone.*

Just as the earth puckered its mouth,
each bud puffing out from its knot,
I changed my shoes, and then drove south.

Up past the Blue Mountains, where
Pennsylvania humps on endlessly,
wearing, like a crayoned cat, its green hair,

its roads sunken in like a gray washboard;
where, in truth, the ground cracks evilly,
a dark socket from which the coal has
    poured,

*Somebody who should have been born
is gone.*

the grass as bristly and stout as chives,
and me wondering when the ground would
    break,
and me wondering how anything fragile
    survives;

up in Pennsylvania, I met a little man,
not Rumpelstiltskin, at all, at all . . .
he took the fullness that love began.

Returning north, even the sky grew thin
like a high window looking nowhere.
The road was as flat as a sheet of tin.

*Somebody who should have been born
is gone.*

Yes, woman, such logic will lead
to loss without death. Or say what you
    meant,
you coward . . . this baby that I bleed.
—Anne Sexton

#### THE LOST BABY POEM

the time i dropped your almost body down
down to meet the waters under the city
and run one with the sewage to the sea
what did i know about waters rushing back
what did i know about drowning
or being drowned

you would have been born into winter
in the year of the disconnected gas
and no car     we would have made the
      thin
walk over Genessee hill into the Canada
      wind
to watch you slip like ice into strangers'
      hands
you would have fallen naked as snow into
      winter
if you were here i could tell you these
and some other things

if i am ever less than a mountain
for your definite brothers and sisters
let the rivers pour over my head
let the sea take me for a spiller
of seas     let black men call me stranger
always     for your never named sake
                              —Lucille Clifton


#### TO A POET

Ice splits   under the metal
shovel   another day
hazed light off fogged panes
cruelty of winter   landlocked   your life
wrapped round you   in your twenties
an old bathrobe   dragged down
with milkstains   tearstains   dust

Scraping eggcrust from the child's
dried dish   skimming the skin
from cooled milk   wringing diapers
Language floats at the vanishing-point
*incarnate*   breathes the fluorescent bulb

*primary*   states the scarred grain of the
      floor
and on the ceiling in torn plaster
      laughs   *imago*

      *and I have fears that you will cease to
      be*
      *before your pen has glean'd your*
      *teeming brain*

for you are not a suicide
but no-one calls this murder
Small mouths, needy, suck you: *This is love*

I write this   not for you
who fight to write your own
words   fighting up the falls
but for another woman   dumb
with loneliness   dust   seeping plastic bags
with children   in a house
where language floats and spins
*abortion*   in
the bowl
                              —Adrienne Rich


### ACKNOWLEDGMENTS

"The Abortion," from *All My Pretty Ones* by Anne Sexton. Copyright © 1962 by Anne Sexton, renewed 1990 by Linda G. Sexton. Reprinted by permission of Houghton Mifflin, Co. All rights reserved.

"The lost baby poem," by Lucille Clifton, copyright © 1987 by Lucille Clifton. Reprinted from *Good Woman: Poems and a Memoir 1969–1980,* by Lucille Clifton, with the permission of BOA Editions, Ltd., 92 Park Avenue, Brockport, NY 14420.

"To a Poet" is reprinted from *The Dream of a Common Language, Poems 1974–1977,* by Adrienne Rich, by permission of the author and W. W. Norton & Company, Inc. Copyright © 1978 by W. W Norton and Company, Inc.

"A Defense of Abortion," by Judith Jarvis Thomson. Reprinted by permission of the publishers from *Rights, Restitution, and Risk: Essays in Moral Theory* by Judith Jarvis Thomson, edited by William Parent, Cambridge, Mass.: Harvard University Press, Copyright © 1986 by the President and Fellows of Harvard College.

# IV

# STRUCTURALISM AND SEMIOTICS

In many ways structuralism and semiotics are the opposite of the rhetorical analysis of literature, the analysis of the usefulness and persuasiveness of language, described in the last section. Instead of examining the effects or results of language—the *communicative* function of language—structural and semiotic analyses attempt to examine the *conditions* that allow language and meaning to arise in the first place; they seek to know, as Roland Barthes notes in "The Structuralist Activity" (1963), "how meaning is possible." Both structuralism and semiotics grow out of the great advances in twentieth-century linguistics initiated by Ferdinand de Saussure. Structuralism and semiotics, especially in the eastern European branches, also grow out of the literary movement of Russian Formalism, represented in this section by Viktor Shklovsky's essay. Above all, these movements attempted to develop a *scientific* method for understanding social meanings in general and literary meaning in particular. Their great ambition, as Louis Marin says in the last essay of this section, was to analyze systematically "the codes by which people make reality significant, by which they interpret reality, that is, the systems of representation of signs, symbols, and values which recreate, as significant for them, the real conditions of their existence." This attempt, as we can see throughout this book, has had an indelible and important effect on literary and cultural studies. (See, for instance, J. Hillis Miller's schematic analysis of the grounds of literary study in "What Is Literary Theory?" or Stuart Hall's analysis of Lévi-Strauss in "Cultural Studies".)

## STRUCTURAL LINGUISTICS, STRUCTURALISM, AND SEMIOTICS

At the beginning of the twentieth century Ferdinand de Saussure reconceived the study of linguistics by reorienting the kinds of questions linguists asked. Instead of asking where particular linguistic formations came from—their history and cause in the etymological and "diachronic" linguistic methods of nineteenth-century linguistics—he asked how the elements of language are *configured* to produce the results or effects they had. In other words, Saussure replaced the "diachronic" study of language through time, the study of the *development* of language, with the "synchronic" study of the particular formation of language *at a particular moment*. In these developments it is clear that Saussure is related to—and, in fact, influenced—the formalism of Russian Formalism and, indirectly, the New Criticism we mentioned in the Introduction to "What Is Criticism?" As Saussure himself notes in the *Course in General Linguistics,* each element of linguistic science—and of language as well—is *"a form, not a substance."*

From this assumption of the formal nature of linguistic elements comes the crucial, reorienting assumptions of Saussure's linguistic work: (1) Saussure's formal or "structural" linguistics suggests that the nature of linguistic elements is *relational* and that the entities of language are a product of relationship. As Saussure says here, "it is the viewpoint that creates the object" of linguistic science. (2) It further assumes the *arbitrary* nature of the linguistic sign. Since the relationships rather than the "elements" of a system of language are crucial, all the elements of language could be different from what they are. Implicit in this assumption is that language takes whatever material is at hand to create its meanings and communication. (3) Its third assumption is that of the *synchronic* method of study that refuses to seek explanations in terms of cause and effect but, rather, seeks understanding in terms of function and activity. Formal relationships are simultaneous rather than sequential; moreover, meaning is more readily apprehended and analyzed through visual models rather than narrative discourse. (Both Kristeva and Marin in this section make this clear.) (4) Finally, Saussurean formalism suggests the *double nature* of language and linguistic elements, including, most significantly here, the double nature of the linguistic sign as the combination of a signified and a signifier; and the double nature of language itself (the French term Saussure uses is *langage*), its particular manifestations both in speech *(parole)* and in the system (the order or *structure* of its code), language as a system *(la langue).* As Saussure says elsewhere, "the absolutely final law of language is, we dare say, that there is nothing which can ever reside in *one* term, as a direct consequence of the fact that linguistic symbols are unrelated to what they should designate."

These assumptions lead Saussure to posit, as he does here, the possibility of a new science for the twentieth century, *"a science that studies the life of signs within society,"* what he calls "semiology." At the same time Saussure was working, in America Charles Sanders Peirce, philosopher and logician, suggested a similar new science that he called "semiotics." As it is practiced today, semiotics examines *meaningful,* cultural phenomena from the viewpoint of the conditions that make such meaningful phenomena possible, including the structures that give rise to that meaning—"the codes by which people make reality significant" that Marin describes in his semiotic analysis of Disneyland. That is, semiotics takes its methods from the structural linguistics Saussure initiated (and, sometimes, from the *pragmatics* Peirce initiated) to understand the conditions governing meaning in society. Shklovsky does this in his attempt to isolate the formal "devices" that create the effects he finds in literature, but even Northrop Frye calls for a kind of systematic and scientific study of literature in "The Function of Criticism at the Present Time" in Part I. Semiotics pursues this kind of analysis more systematically. It does this whether that meaning is through literary texts or more cultural and "ideological" objects such as Kristeva's "science" and Marin's Disneyland. And it can even take general cultural concepts (such as the concept of "author" and "subjectivity" Foucault and Belsey examine in Part V) or gestural communication or media studies (such as those of Mulvey and Morris in "Psychology and Psychoanalysis" and "Cultural Studies"), or even the myths of "primitive" societies in Lévi-Strauss (or Clifford in "Cultural Studies").

The last example—the semiotic or structural study of myth and culture—has been the lifework of the foremost practitioner of structuralism in western Europe, the French anthropologist Claude Lévi-Strauss. Lévi-Strauss has studied a wide range of myths, mostly Amerindian myths, and has attempted to discover the structure—or what might be called the grammar—of mythological narrative. In other words, Lévi-Strauss has attempted to apply the methods of structural linguistics to narrative so that in just the way linguistics analyzes sentences, structural anthropology—as he calls it—can analyze communal narrative discourse. In this endeavor he has articulated the highest *scientific* ambition of structuralism and semiotics. In *The Raw and the Cooked* he says: "I have tried to transcend the contrast between the tangible and the intelligible by operating from the outset at the sign level. The function of signs is, precisely, to express the one by means of the other." This is the aim of semiotics and structuralism: to attempt to isolate and define the conditions of meaning in culture, to articulate the relationship between the tangible entities of nature and the intelligible meanings of culture.

Structuralism, beginning with Lévi-Strauss's analyses of narrative discourse in the early 1950s in France, has had a huge impact on twentieth-century criticism, much more than the structuralism and semiotics of eastern Europe that was effectively ended by Stalinism and World War II. Anticipating the many developments of poststructuralism, French structuralism of the 1960s and early 1970s has proved to be a watershed in modern criticism, causing a major reorientation in literary studies. Prior to structuralism, literary studies often seemed insular and isolated even in the humanities. After structuralism, literary criticism seemed more actively engaged in the discourse of the human sciences, a vital participant and in some areas a guide. In fact by basing its methods on those of linguistics, structuralism helped to transform the traditional "humanities" into what has come to be called the "human sciences."

At first the rise of structuralism was greeted with considerable hostility by critics in the United States and Europe. It was generally acknowledged that this movement was attempting an ambitious, "scientific" examination of literature in all its dimensions. To some, however, the supposed detachment of such an investigation appeared to be offensively antihumanistic and unrelated to the values of a Western liberal education. Anthropologist Alfred Kroeber argued that "structure" is a redundant concept that needs no articulation, and many literary critics judged this new movement to be an ephemeral fad. Not only was structuralism considered antihumanistic. To the Anglo-American world it was further suspect as a French import, merely an exotic dalliance for a few intellectuals who were arrogantly and blindly worshipping a foreignism. In 1975, however, the Modern Language Association awarded Jonathan Culler's *Structuralist Poetics* the annual James Russell Lowell prize for a literary study, and the Anglo-American academy (if not critics and readers generally) began to acknowledge that, for good or ill, structuralism was in place as a functioning critical system.

Equally notable, in retrospect, are the ways in which structuralism was transformed, almost immediately in the United States, into simply a step or stage in a host of critical and cultural programs that can be called "post-structural." As we can see in essays throughout this book—by Paul de Man, J. Hillis Miller, Catherine Belsey,

Toril Moi, Laura Mulvey, Donna Haraway, and Stuart Hall—rigorous structural analyses form parts of arguments whose aims are very different from the presumably "disinterested" and "scientific" methods of structuralism. Julia Kristeva's article in this section spells out some of the reasons why semiotics requires the "and/or" of a science that also creates the possibility of a critique of science. In these more or less unintended results, the rise of structuralism and semiotics in the 1960s—and the rise of various "post" structuralisms in the 1970s—vividly dramatizes the extent to which modern criticism has become an interdisciplinary phenomenon. Rigorous structuralism and semiotics continue to constitute a scholarly "field" in themselves, with intellectual methods and scholarly journals and conferences. Yet by taking meaning and the varying conditions of meaning as their "objects" of study, they cut through, without being confined to, traditional "humanities" and "social sciences" such as literary studies, philosophy, history, linguistics, psychology, and anthropology, all of which have directly influenced literary theory since the late 1960s.

## LITERARY STRUCTURALISM

Literature, as Kristeva argues, has a special relationship to semiotics both as a privileged field in which to examine the semiotic functioning of meaning and as a particular "object" of semiotic study. Literature, she writes, "is a *particular semiotic practice* which has the advantage of making more accessible than others the problematics of the production of meaning." In the first instance the semiotic study of literature offers methods to study other cultural discursive formations—fashion, advertisements, even Disneyland—what both Kristeva and Marin describe as forms of "ideology." In the second instance it offers a particular systematic method for studying literature. Russian Formalism is a good example of the aims and methods of structural linguistics applied to literary studies, while French structuralism offers examples of wider semiotic practices focused on literature.

### Russian Formalism

In its literary criticism, structuralism is closely related to literary formalism, as represented by both American New Criticism (which we discussed in the Introduction to "What Is Criticism?") and Russian Formalism. The principal aim of these movements was to displace "content" in literary analysis and to focus, instead, on literary "form" in a detailed manner analogous to the methods of empirical scientific research. Both movements also sought to organize the generic structures of literature into a system consistent with the inner ordering of works that close reading revealed. In each case literature is viewed as a complex system of "forms" analyzable with considerable objectivity at different levels of generality—from the specific components of a poetic image or line through the poem's genre to that genre's place in the system of literature. Both New Criticism and Russian Formalism promoted the view of literature as a system and a general scientific approach to literary analysis. (Northrop Frye called for an analogous systematization of literary studies in "The Function of Criticism at the Present Time" in "What Is Criticism?") In the same way that structural linguistics attempts to view language not as something "given" that can only be studied by examining its history but as something that can be analyzed in the way chemistry analyzes molecules and particles, Russian Formalism and literary structuralism—and, to a lesser extent, American New Criticism—attempt to view literature not as constituted by its intrinsic ("natural") meaning, as an imitation of reality, but by relational patterns that are meaningful in a particular work and genre. This systematizing and scientistic impulse, especially as formulated in the linguistically oriented theories of Russian Formalism, is a major link between American New Critical formalism and the structuralism of the 1960s.

Russian Formalism was the work of two groups of critics, the Moscow Linguistic Circle, begun in 1915, and OPOYAZ (Society for the Study of Poetic Language), started in 1916. Both groups were disbanded in 1930 in response to official Soviet condemnation of their willingness to depart from the ideological and aesthetic standards of Soviet socialist realism. Their influence continued strongly in the work of the Prague Linguistic Circle (founded in 1926), of which Roman Jakobson is perhaps the best known figure, and in a few key works such as Vladimir Propp's *Morphology of the Folktale* (1928). It is an oddity of the modern history of ideas, however, that after 1930 the Russian Formalists had almost no impact on Western criticism and theory but resurfaced thirty years later with the advent of literary structuralism in France and the United States in the 1960s.

Like Eliot and the Modernists in general, the Russian Formalists sought to move away from nineteenth-century romantic attitudes in criticism and to avoid all romantic notions about poetic inspiration, genius, or aesthetic organicism. Instead, the Formalists adopted a deliberately mechanistic view of poetry and other literary art as the products of *craft*. Considered as *fancy*, poetry-as-craft may be investigated according to immediately analyzable literary functions. Thus, while the Formalists believed that no particular deployment of words, images, or other language effects is intrinsically literary (there being no such thing as literary language), they saw that literature, like other usages of language, could have a particular *function*, could "work" to accomplish particular ends, an assumption shared with Kenneth Burke (see "Rhetoric and Reader Response"). Yet they are more linguistic rather than "sociological" (as Burke calls his work); they want to see language deployed as *language* and to highlight its linguistic functioning as the object of criticism. Linguistic properties then become the primary concern—instead of "inspiration," "poetic genius," or "poetic organicism"—as a poem's meaning and effect are sought. The Formalists attempted to maintain and extend this view at every step of analysis by identifying formal properties as *effective* properties through detailed dissections of poetic (and narrative) technique.

This impulse in theory toward a literary formalism can be seen most clearly in Viktor Shklovsky's definition of literary "device" aimed at effecting some end (a concept analogous to Saussure's "functional" definition of linguistic entities). Central to Russian Formalism, for example, is Shklovsky's argument against the aesthetic notion of "art as thinking in images" and his promotion, instead, of the importance of literary (and nonimagistic) devices. A concentration on images, Shklovsky maintained, leads one to view a poem as having actual "content," and this assumption inhibits any truly formal or relational analysis. What may appear as "content" needs to be considered as "device," or any operation in language that promotes "defamiliarization." That is, since language is a medium of communication before it is used in art, its expressions and conventions inevitably will be overly familiar to the reader and too feeble to have a fresh or significant impact in a poem. To be made new and poetically useful, such language must be "defamiliarized" and "made strange" through linguistic displacement, which means deploying language in an unusual context or presenting it in a novel way. Rhyme schemes (or lack of rhyme), chiasmus (rhetorical balance and reversal), catachresis (the straining of a word or figure beyond its usual meaning), conceits, mixed metaphors, and so on— all these devices for producing particular effects in literature can be used to defamiliarize language and to awaken readers to the intricacy and texture of verbal structure. Such defamiliarization is, therefore, the manner in which poetry functions to rejuvenate and revivify language. All this is quite different from romantic criticism's view of what happens in a poem as the expressive channel for transcendent (or divine) feelings or poetic (or personal) genius.

## French Structuralism

For structuralism the same assumptions hold. Its aim is to "account for" literature and other cultural objects as fully and objectively as possible, without recourse to such "mysterious" and unanalyzable concepts as "genius" or "inexhaustible richness" or "poetic language" unassimilable into general linguistics and semiotics. Thus, as a school of literary criticism, structuralism is dedicated to explaining literature as a system of signs and codes and the conditions that allow that system to function, including relevant cultural frames. Marin follows this discursive and "literary" project here by describing Disneyland "as a text," that "can be viewed as thousands and thousands of narratives uttered by the visitors" and analyzed "according to the codes (vocabulary and syntax) imposed by the makers of Disneyland." In this we can see that with its intense rationalism and sophisticated models, structuralism at its inception seemed without bounds in what it could "understand." As A. J. Greimas wrote in 1966, "It may be—it is a philosophic and not linguistic question—that the phenomenon of language as such is mysterious, but there are no mysteries in language." As the most ambitious movement in recent literary studies, structuralism in the 1960s seemed poised to explain literature in every respect.

Structuralism's strength as an analytical technique, however, was connected to what many conceive to be its major weakness. The power of structuralism derived, as Barthes said in an early essay, from its being "essentially an *activity*" that could "reconstruct an 'object' in such a way as to manifest thereby the rules of functioning." Julia Kristeva articulates this more formally when she describes semiotics as the "development of *models*, that is, of formal systems whose structure is isomorphic or analogous to the structure of another system." For Barthes the system or rules are manifested as the "intelligible" *imitation* of a literary object. By this, Barthes meant that structuralism focused on the *synchronic* dimension of a literary text *(langue* as opposed to *parole)*, the specific ways in which a text is like other texts. As Barthes notes in "What Is Criticism?" (Part I), the goal of literature is conceived as putting " 'meaning' in the world, but not 'a meaning.' " For this reason the structural comparison of texts is based on similarities of function (character development, plot, theme, ideology, and so on), relationships that Lévi-Strauss called *homologies*. The predominately synchronic analysis of homologies "recreates" the text as a "paradigm," a timeless system of structural possibilities.

Thus, in a structural analysis, changes within and among texts or genres can be accounted for as "transformations" in the synchronic system. However, structuralism, in its scientific project, tends to focus on the fixity of relations within synchronic paradigms at the expense of temporality, or the "diachronic" dimension, which involves history. Marin offers no discussion of the development of Disneyland, for example; he simply wants to analyze the meanings implicit in its "map." This tendency to avoid dealing with time and social change concerned many critics of structuralism from its beginning and ultimately became a main target of deconstruction's critique of the prior movement.

While the critique of structuralism is an important development (that will be discussed in more detail later), structuralism's achievement in practical criticism is undeniable and deserves recognition. Roland Barthes's work, for example, charting a course through the early and late stages of structuralism, illuminated semiotic theory, the system of fashion, narrative structure, textuality, and many other topics. These stand as important achievements in modern criticism. The work of Roman Jakobson is very important in this regard. Marin's terms—including "semantic," *"langue,"* "phatic," "mythic," and "lexie"—are derived from the work of Saussure, Lévi-Strauss, Jakobson, and Barthes. Jakobson is perhaps the most rigorous critic to use linguistic analyses—he made significant contributions to linguistics in both Prague and Paris—using the terms and methods of linguistics to analyze poems and narratives. Others, such as Tzvetan Todorov, have pursued these methods to create analyses of the "system" of literature altogether. Frye pursues a similar aim in *Anatomy of Criticism,* yet it is not a structuralist analysis because, as Todorov has argued, it defines its discussions in terms of literary content rather than the structural relationships that allow that content to be articulated and communicated.

Besides the structural analysis of the "system" of literature that, more or less rigorously, genre theory attempts, structuralism has more broadly attempted to analyze the structures (or grammar) of narrative. As already mentioned, Lévi-Strauss's work has been very important in this regard, leading to such diverse approaches as those of Greimas, Genette, and Bremond. A particularly influential example of structuralism's positive achievement is Claude Lévi-Strauss's early essay "The Structural Study of Myth" (1955), an anthropological study that heavily influenced subsequent literary studies. In this essay Lévi-Strauss presents a structural analysis of narrative in which the diachronic dimension (the story line) is eclipsed in favor of a synchronic "reading" of "mythemes" (recurrent narrative structures) in several versions of the Oedipus story. While this structural analysis seemed quite bold at the time, similar structural connections are now routinely made and assumed to be literary common sense. Thus, Lévi-Strauss codified, extended, and even created structuralist possibilities for literary analysis. Objections arose about the "hidden" subjectivity or the bias of Lévi-Strauss's selection of mythemes for analysis, and even about the arbitrariness of what could be called a "mytheme." Nevertheless, "The Structural Study of Myth" and Lévi-Strauss's work as a whole had a tremendously stimulating effect on narrative study and induced Anglo-American criticism to reexamine its own formalistic and strongly descriptive tendencies.

## THE CRITIQUE OF STRUCTURALISM

Structuralism's self-imposed limitations, especially its lack of concern with diachronic change and its focus on general systems rather than on individual cases, have occasioned several critiques. The French philosopher Jacques Derrida offered a particularly decisive critique, a central example of which is "Structure, Sign, and Play in the Discourse of the Human Sciences," which focuses on the structural anthropology of Lévi-Strauss. Derrida connects structuralism with a traditional Western blindness to the "structurality" of structure, or an unwillingness to examine the theoretical and ideological implications of "structure" as a concept. Derrida points out that the attempt to investigate structure implies the ability to stand outside and apart from it—as if one could move outside of cultural understanding to take a detached view of culture. In specific terms Derrida's critique of Lévi-Strauss (not only in "Structure, Sign and Play" but in his *Grammatology* and many other works) is a critique of the privileging of the opposition between "nature" and "culture"—what in *The Raw and the Cooked* Lévi-Strauss calls the tangible and the intelligible. Derrida argues that since one never transcends culture, one can never examine it from the "outside"; there is no standing free of structure, no so-called "natural" state free of the structural interplay that, in the structuralist analysis, constitutes meaning. There is no objective examination of structure. Therefore, Derrida argues, the attempt to "read" and "interpret" cultural structures cannot be adequately translated into exacting scientific models. If "structure" therefore cannot be isolated and examined, then structuralism is seriously undermined as a method. Derrida in fact argues that in place of structuralism we should recognize the interplay of differences among texts, the activity that he and others call *structuration*.

Kristeva pursues a similar critique by underlining the double nature of the structuralist project in the essay in this section. Semiotics, she argues, is not only a "science." It also is a critique of science in the sense of bringing to light and calling into question the silent (and often unconscious) assumptions that govern scientific "rigor." Chief among these, is the assumption that the objects of science and the elements of scientific method can be simple and "pure": Kristeva even adds in a note that "the classical distinction between the natural and the human sciences also considers the former to be more 'pure' than the latter." Similarly, Lévi-Strauss assumes that both "nature" and "culture" are simply and purely themselves and that the difference between them is self-evidently clear. What Kristeva finds, however, is that "semiotic research" always "ultimately uncovers its own ideological gesture." Semiotics, she writes, "begins with a certain knowledge as its goal, and ends up discovering a *theory* which, since it is itself a signifying system, returns semiotic research to its point of departure, to the model of semiotics itself, which it criticizes or overthrows." In part this is because of the *complex* nature of semiotic study, which seeks to demonstrate both how meaning is conditioned and how it is communicated—the double project of the "articulation" and "communication" of meaning. More importantly, however, it is because of the overwhelmingly *cultural* nature of language and discourse, how it always exists within a context of more than one person, more than one meaning. As a structural linguist, Emile Benveniste has argued, "we can never get back to man separate from language and we shall never see him inventing it. We shall never get back to man reduced to himself and exercising his wits to conceive of the existence of another." Human beings, in this conception, *always* exist in societies of human beings, and their language both communicates their thoughts and articulates and structures what can be thought. For this reason, as Kristeva says, semiotics always turns and returns to "ideology" and the cultural formations in which it works.

Yet even Kristeva's account of semiotics falls between her poles of critical science and a critique of science. The whole of her argument is "impure": she brings together Freud and Marx, as well as Saussure, and argues that the same term can "have *another* meaning in the new ideological field which semiotic research *can* construct." At the same time she is pursuing the kind of "rigorous" analysis associated with "science." In other words, Kristeva offers a structural/semiotic analysis that is both informed by structuralism and has a tendency toward poststructuralism, by the scientific method of semiotics and the deconstructive extension of that method. In so doing, her essay offers a semiotics that demonstrates the importance of structuralism to contemporary cultural and literary studies, a semiotic analysis that, even though it demonstrates how theory can be at odds with itself, nevertheless demonstrates the usefulness of structural and semiotic analyses to understanding.

## RELATED ESSAYS IN
## *CONTEMPORARY LITERARY CRITICISM*

Northrop Frye, "The Function of Criticism at the Present Time"
Roland Barthes, "What Is Criticism?"
Barbara Christian, "The Race for Theory"
Jonathan Culler, "Convention and Meaning"
Stuart Hall, "Cultural Studies: Two Paradigms"
Paul de Man, "The Resistance to Theory"
J. Hillis Miller, "The Search for Grounds in Literary Study"
Edward W. Said, "The Politics of Knowledge"
Gayatri Chakravorty Spivak, "Feminism and Critical Theory"

## FURTHER READING

Barthes, Roland, *Critical Essays,* trans. Richard Howard (Evanston, IL: Northwestern University Press, 1972).

————, *Elements of Semiology,* trans. A. Lavers and C. Smith (New York: Hill and Wang, 1977).

Benveniste, Emile, *Problems in General Linguistics,* trans. Mary Elizabeth Meek (Coral Gables, FL: University of Miami Press, 1971).

Bloom, Harold, *The Anxiety of Influence: A Theory of Poetry* (New York: Oxford University Press, 1973).

Culler, Jonathan, *Ferdinand de Saussure* (Baltimore: Penguin Books, 1976).

————, *Structuralist Poetics: Structuralism, Linguistics, and the Study of Literature* (Ithaca, NY: Cornell University Press, 1975).

Derrida, Jacques, *Of Grammatology,* trans. Gayatri Spivak (Baltimore: Johns Hopkins University Press, 1976).

Ehrmann, Jacques, ed., *Structuralism* (Garden City, NY: Doubleday, 1970).

Galan, F. W., *Historical Structures: The Prague School Project, 1928–1946* (Austin: University of Texas Press, 1985).

Genette, Gerard, *Figures of Discourse,* trans. A. Sheridan (New York: Columbia University Press, 1982).

Greimas, A. J., *Structural Semantics: An Attempt at a Method,* trans. Daniele McDowell, Ronald Schleifer, and Alan Velie, Intro. Ronald Schleifer (Lincoln: University of Nebraska Press, 1983).

————. *On Meaning: Selected Writings in Semiotic Theory,* trans. Paul Perron and Frank Collins (Minneapolis: University of Minnesota Press, 1987).

Hawkes, Terence, *Structuralism and Semiotics* (Berkeley: University of California Press, 1977).

Jakobson, Roman, *Language and Literature,* eds. Krystyna Pomorska and Stephen Rudy (Cambridge, MA: Harvard University Press, 1987).

Jameson, Fredric, *The Prison-House of Language: A Critical Account of Structuralism and Russian Formalism* (Princeton, NJ: Princeton University Press, 1972).

Kristeva, Julia, *Revolution in Poetic Language,* trans. Margaret Waller (New York: Columbia University Press, 1984).

Lentricchia, Frank, *After the New Criticism* (Chicago, IL: University of Chicago Press, 1980).

Lévi-Strauss, Claude, *Structural Anthropology,* trans. Claire Jacobson and Brooke Schoepf (New York: Basic Books, 1963).

————, *Structural Anthropology, Vol. 2,* trans. Monique Layton (New York: Basic Books, 1976).

————, *The Raw and the Cooked,* trans. John and Doreen Weighman (New York: Harper Books, 1975).

Macksey, Richard, and Eugenio Donato, eds., *The Structuralist Controversy* (Baltimore: Johns Hopkins University Press, 1970).

Peirce, Charles S., *Collected Papers,* eds., Charles Hartshorne and Paul Weiss (Cambridge, MA: Harvard University Press, 1931, 1958).

Propp, Vladimir, *The Morphology of the Folktale,* trans. Laurence Scott (Austin: University of Texas Press, 1968).

Riffaterre, Michael, *Semiotics of Poetry* (Bloomington: Indiana University Press, 1978).

Saussure, Ferdinand de, *Course in General Linguistics,* trans. Wade Baskin, (New York: McGraw-Hill, 1966).

Schleifer, Ronald, *A. J. Greimas and the Nature of Meaning: Linguistics, Semiotics, and Discourse Theory* (Lincoln: University of Nebraska Press, 1987).

————, "Semiotics and Criticism," in *Literary Criticism and Theory: The Greeks to the Present,* eds. Robert Con Davis and Laurie Finke (New York: Longman, 1989).

Scholes, Robert, *Structuralism in Literature: An Introduction.* (New Haven, CT: Yale University Press, 1974).

Steiner, Peter, *Russian Formalism: A Metapoetics* (Ithaca, NY: Cornell University Press, 1984).

Todorov, Tzvetan, *The Fantastic: A Structural Approach to a Literary Genre,* trans. R. Howard (Ithaca, NY: Cornell University Press, 1975).

————, *Introduction to Poetics,* trans. R. Howard (Minneapolis: University of Minnesota Press, 1981).

# 15

# Ferdinand de Saussure
# 1857–1913

Ferdinand de Saussure, Swiss linguist, is known as the founder of modern linguistics and structuralism. His intensive theories of language established new ways of studying human behavior and revealed strategies of modernist thought. Speaking French, German, English, and Greek by the age of fifteen, Saussure achieved international fame at twenty-one with *Memoire sur le système primitif des voyelles dans les langues indo-européennes* (Memoir on the Primitive System of Vowels in Indo-European Languages). His value to modern literary theory, however, comes from his work in Paris at Ecole Pratique des hautes Etudes and University of Geneva. This work was only available after his death in 1913 when his students and colleagues published *Course in General Linguistics* (1916) from class notes.

The sections from the *Course* excerpted here present the substance of Saussure's thinking that influenced twentieth-century ideas of how language and texts operate. In the first section Saussure distinguishes various levels of words and sounds and determines that what is fundamental to humans is not the ability to speak but the ability to construct a language or sign system. He details the nature of communication in terms of processes: concept and sound production and concept and sound reception. He also addresses the social relationship of mankind and language and asserts that the reality of language is found in an intellectual process (as opposed to a physical one). Most importantly, he predicts the development of semiotics, the study of all sign systems, as a discipline that could shed light on the basic nature of social life. In the second section Saussure explains the arbitrary nature of the linguistic sign and establishes the duality of its nature as signified (concept) and signifier (sound-image). The third section explains Saussure's understanding of the planes on which language operates, especially the synchronic (simultaneous) versus diachronic (chronological). He begins by asserting that language is a system based entirely on the opposition of units. He then states the need to determine the identity of those units that convey conventional meaning yet simultaneously convey new shades of meaning as well. Saussure is especially concerned with the notion of value in a system where the basic unit has meaning only in relation to another unit. Recent theorists see these processes and realms of study as having larger applications. In fact Saussure's notion of relationships as a focus of study is fundamental to twentieth-century literary theory beginning with structuralism and continuing through deconstruction. Essentially, Saussure saw such complexity and chaos in language that he wished to organize and classify universal qualities. The work in discourse is so rich that the basic thoughts of modern theorists such as Derrida, Fish, de Man, Eagleton, and other Poststructuralists are easily traced back to Saussure.

# *from* Course in General Linguistics
## The Object of Linguistics

### 1. DEFINITION OF LANGUAGE

What is both the integral and concrete object of linguistics? The question is especially difficult; later we shall see why; here I wish merely to point up the difficulty.

Other sciences work with objects that are given in advance and that can then be considered from different viewpoints; but not linguistics. Someone pronounces the French word *nu* 'bare': a superficial observer would be tempted to call the word a concrete linguistic object; but a more careful examination would reveal successively three or four quite different things, depending on whether the word is considered as a sound, as the expression of an idea, as the equivalent of Latin *nudum,* etc. Far from it being the object that antedates the viewpoint, it would seem that it is the viewpoint that creates the object; besides, nothing tells us in advance that one way of considering the fact in question takes precedence over the others or is in any way superior to them.

Moreover, regardless of the viewpoint that we adopt, the linguistic phenomenon always has two related sides, each deriving its values from the other. For example:

1. Articulated syllables are acoustical impressions perceived by the ear, but the sounds would not exist without the vocal organs; an *n,* for example, exists only by virtue of the relation between the two sides. We simply cannot reduce language to sound or detach sound from oral articulation; reciprocally, we cannot define the movements of the vocal organs without taking into account the acoustical impression (see pp. 38 ff.).

2. But suppose that sound were a simple thing: would it constitute speech? No, it is only the instrument of thought; by itself, it has no existence. At this point a new and redoubtable relationship arises: a sound, a complex acoustical-vocal unit, combines in turn with an idea to form a complex physiological-psychological unit. But that is still not the complete picture.

3. Speech has both an individual and a social side, and we cannot conceive of one without the other. Besides:

4. Speech always implies both an established system and an evolution; at every moment it is an existing institution and a product of the past. To distinguish between the system and its history, between what it is and what it was, seems very simple at first glance; actually the two things are so closely related that we can scarcely keep them apart. Would we simplify the question by studying the linguistic phenomenon in its earliest stages—if we began, for example, by studying the speech of children? No, for in dealing with speech, it is completely misleading to assume that the problem of early characteristics differs from the problem of permanent characteristics. We are left inside the vicious circle.

From whatever direction we approach the question, nowhere do we find the integral object of linguistics. Everywhere we are confronted with a dilemma: if we fix our attention on only one side of each problem, we run the risk of failing to perceive the dualities pointed out above; on the other hand, if we study speech from several viewpoints simultaneously, the object of linguistics appears to us as a confused mass of heterogeneous and unrelated things. Either procedure opens the door to several sciences—psychology, anthropology, normative grammar, philology, etc.—which are distinct from linguistics, but which might claim speech, in view of the faulty method of linguistics, as one of their objects.

As I see it there is only one solution to all the foregoing difficulties: *from the very outset we must put both feet on the ground of language and use language as the norm of all other manifestations of speech.* Actually, among so many dualities, language alone seems to lend itself to independent definition and provide a fulcrum that satisfies the mind.

But what is language [*langue*]? It is not to be confused with human speech [*langage*], of which it is only a definite part, though certainly an essential one. It is both a social product of the faculty of speech and a collection of necessary conventions that have been adopted by a social body to permit individuals to exercise that faculty. Taken as a whole, speech is many-sided and heterogeneous; straddling several areas simultaneously—physical, physiological, and psychological—it belongs both to the individual and to society; we cannot put it into any category of human facts, for we cannot discover its unity.

Language, on the contrary, is a self-contained whole and a principle of classification. As soon as we give language first place among the facts of speech, we introduce a natural order into a mass that lends itself to no other classification.

One might object to that principle of classification on the ground that since the use of speech is based on a natural faculty whereas language is something acquired and conventional, language should not take first place but should be subordinated to the natural instinct.

That objection is easily refuted.

First, no one has proved that speech, as it manifests itself when we speak, is entirely natural, i.e. that our vocal apparatus was designed for speaking just as our legs were designed for walking. Linguists are far from agreement on this point. For instance Whitney, to whom language is one of several social institutions, thinks that we use the vocal apparatus as the instrument of language purely through luck, for the sake of convenience: men might just as well have chosen gestures and used visual symbols instead of acoustical symbols. Doubtless his thesis is too dogmatic; language is not similar in all respects to other social institutions (see p. 73 f. and p. 75 f.); moreover, Whitney goes too far in saying that our choice happened to fall on the vocal organs; the choice was more or less imposed by nature. But on the essential point the American linguist is right: language is a convention, and the nature of the sign that is agreed upon does not matter. The question of the vocal apparatus obviously takes a secondary place in the problem of speech.

One definition of *articulated speech* might confirm that conclusion. In Latin, *articulus* means a member, part, or subdivision of a sequence; applied to speech, articulation designates either the subdivision of a spoken chain into syllables or the subdivision of the chain of meanings into significant units; *gegliederte Sprache* is used in the second sense in German. Using the second definition, we can say that what is natural to mankind is not oral speech but the faculty of constructing a language, i.e. a system of distinct signs corresponding to distinct ideas.

Broca discovered that the faculty of speech is localized in the third left frontal convolution; his discovery has been used to substantiate the attribution of a natural quality to speech. But we know that the same part of the brain is the center of *everything* that has to do with speech, including writing. The preceding statements, together with observations that have been made in different cases of aphasia resulting from lesion of the centers of localization, seem to indicate: (1) that the various disorders of oral speech are bound up in a hundred ways with those of written speech; and (2) that what is lost in all cases of aphasia or agraphia is less the faculty of producing a given sound or writing a given sign than the ability to evoke by means of an instrument, regardless of what it is, the signs of a regular system of speech. The obvious implication is that beyond the functioning of the various organs there exists a more general faculty which governs signs and which would be the linguistic faculty proper. And this brings us to the same conclusion as above.

To give language first place in the study of speech, we can advance a final argument: the faculty of articulating words—whether it is natural or not—is exercised only with the help of the instrument created by a collectivity and provided for its use; therefore, to say that language gives unity to speech is not fanciful.

## 2. PLACE OF LANGUAGE IN THE FACTS OF SPEECH

In order to separate from the whole of speech the part that belongs to language, we must examine the individual act from which the speaking-circuit can be reconstructed. The act requires the presence of at least two persons; that is the minimum number necessary to complete the circuit. Suppose that two people, A and B, are conversing with each other:

Suppose that the opening of the circuit is in A's brain, where mental facts (concepts) are

associated with representations of the linguistic sounds (sound-images) that are used for their expression. A given concept unlocks a corresponding sound-image in the brain; this purely *psychological* phenomenon is followed in turn by a *physiological* process: the brain transmits an impulse corresponding to the image to the organs used in producing sounds. Then the sound waves travel from the mouth of A to the ear of B: a purely *physical* process. Next, the circuit continues in B, but the order is reversed: from the ear to the brain, the physiological transmission of the sound-image; in the brain, the psychological association of the image with the corresponding concept. If B then speaks, the new act will follow—from his brain to A's—exactly the same course as the first act and pass through the same successive phases, which I shall diagram as follows:

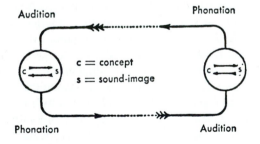

The preceding analysis does not purport to be complete. We might also single out the pure acoustical sensation, the identification of that sensation with the latent sound-image, the muscular image of phonation, etc. I have included only the elements thought to be essential, but the drawing brings out at a glance the distinction between the physical (sound waves), physiological (phonation and audition), and psychological parts (word-images and concepts). Indeed, we should not fail to note that the word-image stands apart from the sound itself and that it is just as psychological as the concept which is associated with it.

The circuit that I have outlined can be further divided into:

**a.** an outer part that includes the vibrations of the sounds which travel from the mouth to the ear, and an inner part that includes everything else;

**b.** a psychological and a nonpsychological part, the second including the physiological productions of the vocal organs as well as the physical facts that are outside the individual;

**c.** an active and a passive part: everything that goes from the associative center of the speaker to the ear of the listener is active, and everything that goes from the ear of the listener to his associative center is passive;

**d.** finally, everything that is active in the psychological part of the circuit is executive ($c \rightarrow s$), and everything that is passive is receptive ($s \rightarrow c$).

We should also add the associative and co-ordinating faculty that we find as soon as we leave isolated signs; this faculty plays the dominant role in the organization of language as a system (see pp. 122 ff.).

But to understand clearly the role of the associative and co-ordinating faculty, we must leave the individual act, which is only the embryo of speech, and approach the social fact.

Among all the individuals that are linked together by speech, some sort of average will be set up: all will reproduce—not exactly of course, but approximately—the same signs united with the same concepts.

How does the social crystallization of language come about? Which parts of the circuit are involved? For all parts probably do not participate equally in it.

The nonpsychological part can be rejected from the outset. When we hear people speaking a language that we do not know, we perceive the sounds but remain outside the social fact because we do not understand them.

Neither is the psychological part of the circuit wholly responsible: the executive side is missing, for execution is never carried out by the collectivity. Execution is always individual, and the individual is always its master: I shall call the executive side *speaking* [*parole*].

Through the functioning of the receptive and co-ordinating faculties, impressions that are perceptibly the same for all are made on the minds of speakers. How can that social product be pictured in such a way that language will stand apart from everything else? If we could embrace the sum of word-images stored in the minds of all individuals, we could identify the social bond that constitutes language. It is a storehouse filled by the members of a given community through their active use of speaking, a grammatical system that has a potential existence in each brain, or, more specifically, in the brains of a group of individuals. For language is not complete in any speaker; it exists perfectly only within a collectivity.

In separating language from speaking we are at the same time separating: (1) what is social from what is individual; and (2) what is essential from what is accessory and more or less accidental.

Language is not a function of the speaker; it is a product that is passively assimilated by the individual. It never requires premeditation, and reflection enters in only for the purpose of classification, which we shall take up later (pp. 122 ff.).

Speaking, on the contrary, is an individual act. It is wilful and intellectual. Within the act, we should distinguish between: (1) the combinations by which the speaker uses the language code for expressing his own thought; and (2) the psychophysical mechanism that allows him to exteriorize those combinations.

Note that I have defined things rather than words; these definitions are not endangered by certain ambiguous words that do not have identical meanings in different languages. For instance, German *Sprache* means both "language" and "speech"; *Rede* almost corresponds to "speaking" but adds the special connotation of "discourse." Latin *sermo* designates both "speech" and "speaking," while *lingua* means "language," etc. No word corresponds exactly to any of the notions specified above; that is why all definitions of words are made in vain; starting from words in defining things is a bad procedure.

To summarize, these are the characteristics of language:

1. Language is a well-defined object in the heterogeneous mass of speech facts. It can be localized in the limited segment of the speaking-circuit where an auditory image becomes associated with a concept. It is the social side of speech, outside the individual who can never create nor modify it by himself; it exists only by virtue of a sort of contract signed by the members of a community. Moreover, the individual must always serve an apprenticeship in order to learn the functioning of language; a child assimilates it only gradually. It is such a distinct thing that a man deprived of the use of speaking retains it provided that he understands the vocal signs that he hears.

2. Language, unlike speaking, is something that we can study separately. Although dead languages are no longer spoken, we can easily assimilate their linguistic organisms. We can dispense with the other elements of speech; indeed, the science of language is possible only if the other elements are excluded.

3. Whereas speech is heterogeneous, language, as defined, is homogeneous. It is a system of signs in which the only essential thing is the union of meanings and sound-images, and in which both parts of the sign are psychological.

4. Language is concrete, no less so than speaking; and this is a help in our study of it. Linguistic signs, though basically psychological, are not abstractions; associations which bear the stamp of collective approval—and which added together constitute language—are realities that have their seat in the brain. Besides, linguistic signs are tangible; it is possible to reduce them to conventional written symbols, whereas it would be impossible to provide detailed photographs of acts of speaking [*actes de parole*]; the pronunciation of even the smallest word represents an infinite number of muscular movements that could be identified and put into graphic form only with great difficulty. In language, on the contrary, there is only the sound-image, and the latter can be translated into a fixed visual image. For if we disregard the vast number of movements necessary for the realization of sound-images in speaking, we see that each sound-image is nothing more than the sum of a limited number of elements or phonemes that can in turn be called up by a corresponding number of written symbols (see pp. 61 ff.). The very possibility of putting the things that relate to language into graphic form allows dictionaries and grammars to represent it accurately, for language is a storehouse of sound-images, and writing is the tangible form of those images.

## 3. PLACE OF LANGUAGE IN HUMAN FACTS: SEMIOLOGY

The foregoing characteristics of language reveal an even more important characteristic. Language, once its boundaries have been marked off within the speech data, can be classified among human phenomena, whereas speech cannot.

We have just seen that language is a social institution; but several features set it a-part from other political, legal, etc. institutions. We must call in a new type of facts in order to illuminate the special nature of language.

Language is a system of signs that express ideas, and is therefore comparable to a system of writing, the alphabet of deaf-mutes, symbolic rites, polite formulas, military signals, etc. But it is the most important of all these systems.

*A science that studies the life of signs within society* is conceivable; it would be a part of social psychology and consequently of general psychology; I shall call it *semiology*[1] (from Greek *semeîon* 'sign'). Semiology would show what constitutes signs, what laws govern them. Since the science does not yet exist, no one can say what it would be; but it has a right to existence, a place staked out in advance. Linguistics is only a part of the general science of semiology; the laws discovered by semiology will be applicable to linguistics, and the latter will circumscribe a well-defined area within the mass of anthropological facts.

To determine the exact place of semiology is the task of the psychologist.[2] The task of the linguist is to find out what makes language a special system within the mass of semiological data. This issue will be taken up again later; here I wish merely to call attention to one thing: if I have succeeded in assigning linguistics a place among the sciences, it is because I have related it to semiology.

Why has semiology not yet been recognized as an independent science with its own object like all the other sciences? Linguists have been going around in circles: language, better than anything else, offers a basis for understanding the semiological problem; but language must, to put it correctly, be studied in itself; heretofore language has almost always been studied in connection with something else, from other viewpoints.

There is first of all the superficial notion of the general public: people see nothing more than a name-giving system in language (see p. 65), thereby prohibiting any research into its true nature.

Then there is the viewpoint of the psychologist, who studies the sign-mechanism in the individual; this is the easiest method, but it does not lead beyond individual execution and does not reach the sign, which is social.

Or even when signs are studied from a social viewpoint, only the traits that attach language to the other social institutions—those that are more or less voluntary—are emphasized; as a result, the goal is by-passed and the specific characteristics of semiological systems in general and of language in particular are completely ignored. For the distinguishing characteristic of the sign—but the one that is least apparent at first sight—is that in some way it always eludes the individual or social will.

In short, the characteristic that distinguishes semiological systems from all other institutions shows up clearly only in language where it manifests itself in the things which are studied least, and the necessity or specific value of a semiological science is therefore not clearly recognized. But to me the language problem is mainly semiological, and all developments derive their significance from that important fact. If we are to discover the true nature of language we must learn what it has in common with all other semiological systems; linguistic forces that seem very important at first glance (e.g., the role of the vocal apparatus) will receive only secondary consideration if they serve only to set language apart from the other systems. This procedure will do more than to clarify the linguistic problem. By studying rites, customs, etc. as signs, I believe that we shall throw new light on the facts and point up the need for including them in a science of semiology and explaining them by its laws.

**NOTES**

1. *Semiology* should not be confused with *semantics,* which studies changes in meaning, and which De

Saussure did not treat methodically; the fundamental principle of semantics is formulated on page 75. [Ed.]

2. Cf. A. Naville, *Classification des Sciences,* (2nd. ed.), p. 104. [Ed.] The scope of semiology (or semiotics) is treated at length in Charles Morris' *Signs, Language and Behavior* (New York: Prentice-Hall, 1946). [Tr.]

## Nature of the Linguistic Sign

### 1. SIGN, SIGNIFIED, SIGNIFIER

Some people regard language, when reduced to its elements, as a naming-process only—a list of words, each corresponding to the thing that it names. For example:

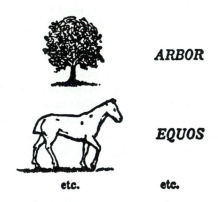

ARBOR

EQUOS

etc.          etc.

This conception is open to criticism at several points. It assumes that ready-made ideas exist before words (on this point, see below); it does not tell us whether a name is vocal or psychological in nature (*arbor,* for instance, can be considered from either viewpoint); finally, it lets us assume that the linking of a name and a thing is a very simple operation—an assumption that is anything but

true. But this rather naive approach can bring us near the truth by showing us that the linguistic unit is a double entity, one formed by the associating of two terms.

We have seen in considering the speaking-circuit that both terms involved in the linguistic sign are psychological and are united in the brain by an associative bond. This point must be emphasized.

The linguistic sign unites, not a thing and a name, but a concept and a sound-image.[1] The latter is not the material sound, a purely physical thing, but the psychological imprint of the sound, the impression that it makes on our senses. The sound-image is sensory, and if I happen to call it "material," it is only in that sense, and by way of opposing it to the other term of the association, the concept, which is generally more abstract.

The psychological character of our sound-images becomes apparent when we observe our own speech. Without moving our lips or tongue, we can talk to ourselves or recite mentally a selection of verse. Because we regard the words of our language as sound-images, we must avoid speaking of the "phonemes" that make up the words. This term, which suggests vocal activity, is applicable to the spoken word only, to the realization of the inner image in discourse. We can avoid that misunderstanding by speaking of the *sounds* and *syllables* of a word provided we remember that the names refer to the sound-image.

The linguistic sign is then a two-sided psychological entity that can be represented by the drawing:

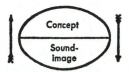

The two elements are intimately united, and each recalls the other. Whether we try to find the meaning of the Latin word *arbor* or the word that Latin uses to designate the concept "tree," it is clear that only the associations sanctioned by that language appear to us to conform to reality, and we disregard whatever others might be imagined.

Our definition of the linguistic sign poses an important question of terminology. I call the combination of a concept and a sound-image a *sign,* but in current usage the term generally designates only a sound-image, a word, for example (*arbor,* etc.). One tends to forget that *arbor* is called a sign only because it carries the concept "tree," with the result that the idea of the sensory part implies the idea of the whole.

Ambiguity would disappear if the three notions involved here were designated by three names, each suggesting and opposing the others. I propose to retain the word *sign* [*signe*] to designate the whole and to replace *concept* and *sound-image* respectively by *signified* [*signifié*] and *signifier* [*signifiant*]; the last two terms have the advantage of indicating the opposition that separates them from each other and from the whole of which they are parts. As regards *sign,* if I am satisfied with it, this is simply because I do not know of any word to replace it, the ordinary language suggesting no other.

The linguistic sign, as defined, has two primordial characteristics. In enunciating them I am also positing the basic principles of any study of this type.

## 2. PRINCIPLE I: THE ARBITRARY NATURE OF THE SIGN

The bond between the signifier and the signified is arbitrary. Since I mean by sign the whole that results from the associating of the signifier with the signified, I can simply say: *the linguistic sign is arbitrary.*

The idea of "sister" is not linked by any inner relationship to the succession of sounds *s-ö-r* which serves as its signifier in French; that it could be represented equally by just any other sequence is proved by differences among languages and by the very existence of different languages: the signified "ox" has as its signifier *b-ö-f* on one side of the border and *o-k-s (Ochs)* on the other.

No one disputes the principle of the arbitrary nature of the sign, but it is often easier to discover a truth than to assign to it its proper place. Principle I dominates all the linguistics of language; its consequences are numberless. It is true that not all of them are equally obvious at first glance; only after many detours does one discover them, and with them the primordial importance of the principle.

One remark in passing: when semiology becomes organized as a science, the question will arise whether or not it properly includes modes of expression based on completely natural signs, such as pantomime. Supposing that the new science welcomes them, its main concern will still be the whole group of systems grounded on the arbitrariness of the sign. In fact, every means of expression used in society is based, in principle, on collective behavior or—what amounts to the same thing—on convention. Polite formulas, for instance, though often imbued with a certain natural expressiveness (as in the case of a Chinese who greets his emperor by bowing down to the ground nine times), are nonetheless fixed by rule; it is this rule and not the intrinsic value of the gestures that obliges one to use them. Signs that are wholly arbitrary realize better than the others the ideal of the semiological process; that is why language, the most complex and universal of all systems of expression, is also the most characteristic; in this sense linguistics can become the master-pattern for all branches of semiology although language is only one particular semiological system.

The word *symbol* has been used to designate the linguistic sign, or more specifically, what is here called the signifier. Principle I in particular weighs against the use of this term. One characteristic of the symbol is that it is never wholly arbitrary; it is not empty, for there is the rudiment of a natural bond between the signifier and the signified. The symbol of justice, a pair of scales, could not be replaced by just any other symbol, such as a chariot.

The word *arbitrary* also calls for comment. The term should not imply that the choice of the signifier is left entirely to the speaker (we shall see below that the individual does not have the power to change a sign in any way once it has become established in the linguistic community); I mean that it is unmotivated, i.e. arbitrary in that it actually has no natural connection with the signified.

In concluding let us consider two objections that might be raised to the establishment of Principle I:

1. *Onomatopoeia* might be used to prove that the choice of the signifier is not always arbitrary. But onomatopoeic formations are never organic elements of a linguistic system. Besides, their number is much smaller than is generally supposed. Words like French *fouet* 'whip' or *glas* 'knell' may strike certain ears with suggestive sonority, but to see that they have not always had this property we need only examine their Latin forms (*fouet* is derived from *fagus* 'beech-tree,' *glas* from *classicum* 'sound of a trumpet'). The quality of their present sounds, or rather the quality that is attributed to them, is a fortuitous result of phonetic evolution.

As for authentic onomatopoeic words (e.g. *glug-glug, tick-tock,* etc.), not only are they limited in number, but also they are chosen somewhat arbitrarily, for they are only approximate and more or less conventional imitations of certain sounds (cf. English *bow-bow* and French *ouaoua*). In addition, once these words have been introduced into the language, they are to a certain extent subjected to the same evolution—phonetic, morphological, etc.—that other words undergo (cf. *pigeon,* ultimately from Vulgar Latin *pīpiō,* derived in turn from an onomatopoeic formation): obvious proof that they lose something of their original character in order to assume that of the linguistic sign in general, which is unmotivated.

2. *Interjections,* closely related to onomatopoeia, can be attacked on the same grounds and come no closer to refuting our thesis. One is tempted to see in them spontaneous expressions of reality dictated, so to speak, by natural forces. But for most interjections we can show that there is no fixed bond between their signified and their signifier. We need only compare two languages on this point to see how much such expressions differ from one language to the next (e.g. the

English equivalent of French *aïe!* is *ouch!*). We know, moreover, that many interjections were once words with specific meanings (cf. French *diable!* 'darn!' *mordieu!* 'golly!' from *mort Dieu* 'God's death,' etc.).²

Onomatopoeic formations and interjections are of secondary importance, and their symbolic origin is in part open to dispute.

## 3. PRINCIPLE II: THE LINEAR NATURE OF THE SIGNIFIER

The signifier, being auditory, is unfolded solely in time from which it gets the following characteristics: (a) it represents a span, and (b) the span is measurable in a single dimension; it is a line.

While Principle II is obvious, apparently linguists have always neglected to state it, doubtless because they found it too simple; nevertheless, it is fundamental, and its consequences are incalculable. Its importance equals that of Principle I; the whole mechanism of language depends upon it (see p. 122 f.). In contrast to visual signifiers (nautical signals, etc.) which can offer simultaneous groupings in several dimensions, auditory signifiers have at their command only the dimension of time. Their elements are presented in succession; they form a chain. This feature becomes readily apparent when they are represented in writing and the spatial line of graphic marks is substituted for succession in time.

Sometimes the linear nature of the signifier is not obvious. When I accent a syllable, for instance, it seems that I am concentrating more than one significant element on the same point. But this is an illusion; the syllable and its accent constitute only one phonational act. There is no duality within the act but only different oppositions to what precedes and what follows (on this subject, see p. 131).

## NOTES

1. The term sound-image may seem to be too restricted inasmuch as beside the representation of the sounds of a word there is also that of its articulation, the muscular image of the phonational act. But for F. de Saussure language is essentially a depository, a thing received from without (see p. 13). The sound-image is par excellence the natural representation of the word as a fact of potential language, outside any actual use of it in speaking. The motor side is thus implied or, in any event, occupies only a subordinate role with respect to the sound-image. [Ed.]

2. Cf. English *goodness!* and *zounds!* (from *God's wounds*). [Tr.]

## The Concrete Entities of Language

### 1. DEFINITION: ENTITY AND UNIT

The signs that make up language are not abstractions but real objects (see p. 15); signs and their relations are what linguistics studies; they are the *concrete entities* of our science.

Let us first recall two principles that dominate the whole issue:

1. The linguistic entity exists only through the associating of the signifier with the signified (see p. 66 ff.). Whenever only one element is retained, the entity

vanishes; instead of a concrete object we are faced with a mere abstraction. We constantly risk grasping only a part of the entity and thinking that we are embracing it in its totality; this would happen, for example, if we divided the spoken chain into syllables, for the syllable has no value except in phonology. A succession of sounds is linguistic only if it supports an idea. Considered independently, it is material for a physiological study, and nothing more than that.

The same is true of the signified as soon as it is separated from its signifier. Considered independently, concepts like "house," "white," "see," etc. belong to psychology. They become linguistic entities only when associated with sound-images; in language, a concept is a quality of its phonic substance just as a particular slice of sound is a quality of the concept.

The two-sided linguistic unit has often been compared with the human person, made up of the body and the soul. The comparison is hardly satisfactory. A better choice would be a chemical compound like water, a combination of hydrogen and oxygen; taken separately, neither element has any of the properties of water.

2. The linguistic entity is not accurately defined until it is *delimited*, i.e. separated from everything that surrounds it on the phonic chain. These delimited entities or units stand in opposition to each other in the mechanism of language.

One is at first tempted to liken linguistic signs to visual signs, which can exist in space without becoming confused, and to assume that separation of the significant elements can be accomplished in the same way, without recourse to any mental process. The word "form," which is often used to indicate them (cf. the expression "verbal form," "noun form")

gives support to the mistake. But we know that the main characteristic of the sound-chain is that it is linear (see p. 70). Considered by itself, it is only a line, a continuous ribbon along which the ear perceives no self-sufficient and clear-cut division; to divide the chain, we must call in meanings. When we hear an unfamiliar language, we are at a loss to say how the succession of sounds should be analyzed, for analysis is impossible if only the phonic side of the linguistic phenomenon is considered. But when we know the meaning and function that must be attributed to each part of the chain, we see the parts detach themselves from each other and the shapeless ribbon break into segments. Yet there is nothing material in the analysis.

To summarize: language does not offer itself as a set of predelimited signs that need only be studied according to their meaning and arrangement; it is a confused mass, and only attentiveness and familiarization will reveal its particular elements. The unit has no special phonic character, and the only definition that we can give it is this: it is *a slice of sound which to the exclusion of everything that precedes and follows it in the spoken chain is the signifier of a certain concept.*

## 2. METHOD OF DELIMITATION

One who knows a language singles out its units by a very simple method—in theory, at any rate. His method consists of using speaking as the source material of language and picturing it as two parallel chains, one of concepts *(A)* and the other of sound-images *(B).*

In an accurate delimitation, the division along the chain of sound-images *(a, b, c)* will correspond to the division along the chain of concepts *(a', b', c'):*

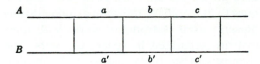

Take French *sižlaprã*. Can we cut the chain after *l* and make *sižl* a unit? No, we need only consider the concepts to see that the division is wrong. Neither is the syllabic division *siž-la-prã* to be taken for granted as having linguistic value. The only possible divisions are these: (1) *si-ž-la-prã (si je la prends* 'if I take it') and (2) *si-ž-l-aprã (si je l'apprends* 'if I learn it'), and they are determined by the meaning that is attached to the words.[1]

To verify the result of the procedure and be assured that we are really dealing with a unit, we must be able in comparing a series of sentences in which the same unit occurs to separate the unit from the rest of the context and find in each instance that meaning justifies the delimitation. Take the two French phrases *laforsdüvã* (la *force* du vent 'the *force* of the wind'), and *abudfors* (a bout de *force* 'exhausted'; *literally:* 'at the end of one's *force'*). In each phrase the same concept coincides with the same phonic slice, *fors;* thus it is certainly a linguistic unit. But in *ilmeforsaparle* (il me *force* a parler 'he *forces* me to talk') *fors* has an entirely different meaning: it is therefore another unit.

## 3. PRACTICAL DIFFICULTIES OF DELIMITATION

The method outlined above is very simple in theory, but is it easy to apply? We are tempted to think so if we start from the notion that the units to be isolated are words. For what is a sentence except a combination of words? And what can be grasped more readily than words? Going back to the example given above, we may say that the analysis of the spoken chain *sižlaprã* resulted in the delimiting of four units, and that the units are words: *si-je-l-apprends*. But we are immediately put on the defensive on noting that there has been much disagreement about the nature of the word, and a little reflection shows that the usual meaning of the term is incompatible with the notion of concrete unit.

To be convinced, we need only think of French *cheval* 'horse' and its plural form *chevaux*. People readily say that they are two forms of the same word; but considered as wholes, they are certainly two distinct things with respect to both meaning and sound. In *mwa (mois,* as in le *mois* de Septembre 'the *month* of September') and *mwaz (mois,* in un *mois* après 'a *month* later') there are also two forms of the same word, and there is no question of a concrete unit. The meaning is the same, but the slices of sound are different. As soon as we try to liken concrete units to words, we face a dilemma: we must either ignore the relation—which is nonetheless evident—that binds *cheval* and *chevaux,* the two sounds of *mwa* and *mwaz,* etc. and say that they are different words, or instead of concrete units be satisfied with the abstraction that links the different forms of the same word. The concrete unit must be sought, not in the word, but elsewhere. Besides, many words are complex units, and we can easily single out their subunits (suffixes, prefixes, radicals). Derivatives like *pain-ful* and *delight-ful* can be divided into distinct parts, each having an obvious meaning and function. Conversely, some units are larger than words: compounds (French *porte-plume* 'penholder'), locutions (*s'il vous plaît* 'please'), inflected forms (*il a été* 'he has been'), etc. But these units resist delimitation as strongly as do words proper, making it extremely difficult to disentangle the interplay of units that are found in a sound-chain and to specify the concrete elements on which a language functions.

Doubtless speakers are unaware of the practical difficulties of delimiting units. Anything that is of even the slightest significance seems like a concrete element to them and they never fail to single it out in discourse. But it is one thing to feel the quick, delicate interplay of units and quite another to account for them through methodical analysis.

A rather widely held theory makes sentences the concrete units of language: we speak only in sentences and subsequently single out the words. But to what extent does the sentence belong to language (see p. 124)? If it belongs to speaking, the sentence cannot pass for the linguistic unit. But let us suppose that this difficulty is set aside. If we picture to ourselves in their totality the sentences that could be uttered, their most striking characteristic is that in no way do they resemble each other. We are at first tempted to liken the immense diversity of sentences to the equal diversity of the individuals that make up a zoological species. But this is an illusion: the characteristics that animals of the same species have in common are much more significant than the differences that separate them. In sentences, on the contrary, diversity is dominant, and when we look for the link that bridges their diversity, again we find, without having looked for it, the word with its grammatical characteristics and thus fall back into the same difficulties as before.

## 4. CONCLUSION

In most sciences the question of units never even arises: the units are delimited from the outset. In zoology, the animal immediately presents itself. Astronomy works with units that are separated in space, the stars. The chemist can study the nature and composition of potassium bichromate without doubting for an instant that this is a well-defined object.

When a science has no concrete units that are immediately recognizable, it is because they are not necessary. In history, for example, is the unit the individual, the era, or the nation? We do not know. But what does it matter? We can study history without knowing the answer.

But just as the game of chess is entirely in the combination of the different chesspieces, language is characterized as a system based entirely on the opposition of its concrete units. We can neither dispense with becoming acquainted with them nor take a single step without coming back to them; and still, delimiting them is such a delicate problem that we may wonder at first whether they really exist.

Language then has the strange, striking characteristic of not having entities that are perceptible at the outset and yet of not permitting us to doubt that they exist and that their functioning constitutes it. Doubtless we have here a trait that distinguishes language from all other semiological institutions.

## NOTE

1. Cf. the sounds [jurmain] in English: "your mine" or "you're mine." [Tr.]

## Identities, Realities, Values

The statement just made brings us squarely up against a problem that is all the more important because any basic notion in static linguistics depends directly on our conception of the unit and even blends with it. This is what I should like successively to demonstrate with respect to the notions of synchronic identity, reality, and value.

A. What is a synchronic *identity?* Here it is not a question of the identity that links the French negation *pas* 'not' to Latin *passum,* a diachronic identity that will be dealt with elsewhere (see p. 181), but rather of the equally interesting identity by virtue of which we state that two sentences like je ne sais *pas* 'I *don't* know' and ne dîtes *pas* cela *'don't* say that' contain the same element. An idle question, one might say; there is identity because the same slice of sound carries the same meaning in the two sentences. But that explanation is unsatisfactory, for if the correspondence of slices of sound and concepts is proof of identity (see above, p. 105, la *force* du vent: a bout de *force*), the reverse is not true. There can be identity without this correspondence. When *Gentlemen!* is repeated several times during a lecture, the listener has the feeling that the same expression is being used each time, and yet variations in utterance and intonation make for appreciable phonic differences in diverse contexts—differences just as appreciable as those that elsewhere separate different words (cf. French *pomme* 'apple' and *paume* 'palm,' *goutte* 'drop' and *je goute* 'I taste,' *fuir* 'flee,' and *fouir* 'stuff,' etc.);[1] besides, the feeling of identity persists even though there is no absolute identity between one *Gentlemen!* and the next from a semantic viewpoint either. In the same vein, a word can express quite different ideas without compromising its identity (cf. French *adopter* une mode 'adopt a fashion' and *adopter* un enfant 'adopt a child,' la *fleur* du pommier 'the *flower* of the apple tree' and la *fleur* de la noblesse 'the *flower* of nobility,' etc.).

The linguistic mechanism is geared to differences and identities, the former being only the counterpart of the latter. Everywhere then, the problem of identities appears; moreover, it blends partially with the problem of entities and units and is only a complication—illuminating at some points—of the larger problem. This characteristic stands out if we draw some comparisons with facts taken from outside speech. For instance, we speak of the identity of two "8:25 p.m. Geneva-to-Paris" trains that leave at twenty-four hour intervals. We feel that it is the same strain each day, yet everything—the locomotive, coaches, personnel—is probably different. Or if a street is demolished, then rebuilt, we say that it is the same street even though in a material sense, perhaps nothing of the old one remains. Why can a street be completely rebuilt and still be the same? Because it does not constitute a purely material entity; it is based on certain conditions that are distinct from the materials that fit the conditions, e.g. its location with respect to other streets. Similarly, what makes the express is its hour of departure, its route, and in general every circumstance that sets it apart from other trains. Whenever the same conditions are fulfilled, the same entities are obtained. Still, the entities are not abstract since we cannot conceive of a street or train outside its material realization.

Let us contrast the preceding examples with the completely different case of a suit which has been stolen from me and which I find in the window of a second-hand store. Here we have a material entity that consists solely of the inert substance—the cloth, its lining, its trimmings, etc. Another suit would not be mine regardless of its similarity to it. But linguistic identity is not that of the garment; it is that of the train and the street. Each time I say the word *Gentlemen!* I renew its substance; each utterance is a new phonic act and a new psychological act. The bond between the two uses of the same word depends neither on material identity nor on sameness in meaning but on elements which must be sought after and which will point up the true nature of linguistic units.

*B.* What is a synchronic *reality?* To what concrete or abstract elements of language can the name be applied?

Take as an example the distinction between the parts of speech. What supports the classing of words as substantives, adjectives, etc.? Is it done in the name of a purely logical, extra-linguistic principle that is applied to grammar from without like the degrees of longitude and latitude on the globe? Or does it correspond to something that has its place in the system of language and is conditioned by it? In a word, is it a synchronic reality? The second supposition seems probable, but the first could also be defended. In the French sentence *ces gants sont bon marché* 'these gloves are cheap,' is *bon marché* an adjective? It is apparently an adjective from a logical viewpoint but not from the viewpoint of grammar, for *bon marché* fails to behave as an adjective (it is invariable, it never precedes its noun, etc.); in addition, it is composed of two words. Now the distinction between parts of speech is exactly what should serve to classify the words of language. How can a group of words be attributed to one of the "parts"? But to say that *bon* 'good' is an adjective and *marché* 'market' a substantive explains nothing. We are then dealing with a

defective or incomplete classification; the division of words into substantives, verbs, adjectives, etc. is not an undeniable linguistic reality.[2]

Linguistics accordingly works continuously with concepts forged by grammarians without knowing whether or not the concepts actually correspond to the constituents of the system of language. But how can we find out? And if they are phantoms, what realities can we place in opposition to them?

To be rid of illusions we must first be convinced that the concrete entities of language are not directly accessible. If we try to grasp them, we come into contact with the true facts. Starting from there, we can set up all the classifications that linguistics needs for arranging all the facts at its disposal. On the other hand, to base the classifications on anything except concrete entities—to say, for example, that the parts of speech are the constituents of language simply because they correspond to categories of logic—is to forget that there are no linguistic facts apart from the phonic substance cut into significant elements.

*C.* Finally, not every idea touched upon in this chapter differs basically from what we have elsewhere called *values*. A new comparison with the set of chessmen will bring out this point (see pp. 88 ff.). Take a knight, for instance. By itself is it an element in the game? Certainly not, for by its material make-up—outside its square and the other conditions of the game—it means nothing to the player; it becomes a real, concrete element only when endowed with value and wedded to it. Suppose that the piece happens to be destroyed or lost during a game. Can it be replaced by an equivalent piece? Certainly. Not only another knight but even a figure shorn of any resemblance to a knight can be declared identical provided the same value is attributed to it. We see then that in semiological systems like language, where elements hold each other in equilibrium in accordance with fixed rules, the notion of identity blends with that of value and *vice versa*.

In a word, that is why the notion of value envelops the notions of unit, concrete entity, and reality. But if there is no fundamental difference between these diverse notions, it follows that the problem can be stated successively in several ways. Whether we try to define the unit, reality, concrete entity, or value, we always come back to the central question that dominates all of static linguistics.

It would be interesting from a practical viewpoint to begin with units, to determine what they are and to account for their diversity by classifying them. It would be necessary to search for the reason for dividing language into words—for in spite of the difficulty of defining it, the word is a unit that strikes the mind, something central in the mechanism of language—but that is a subject which by itself would fill a volume. Next we would have to classify the subunits, then the larger units, etc. By determining in this way the elements that it manipulates, synchronic linguistics would completely fulfill its task, for it would relate all synchronic phenomena to their fundamental principle. It cannot be said that this basic problem has ever been faced squarely or that its scope and difficulty have been understood; in the matter of language, people have always been satisfied with ill-defined units.

Still, in spite of their capital importance, it is better to approach the problem of units through the study of value, for in my opinion value is of prime importance.

*Translated by Wade Baskin*

## NOTES

1. Cf. English *bought: boat, naught: note, far: for: four* (for many speakers). [Tr.]

2. Form, function, and meaning combine to make the classing of the parts of speech even more difficult in English than in French. Cf. *ten-foot: ten feet* in *a ten-foot pole: the pole is ten feet long.* [Tr.]

# 16

# Viktor Shklovsky
# 1893–1984

Viktor Borisovich Shklovsky was one of the leaders of the Russian Formalists, a group of literati (officially called OPOYAZ, Society for the Study of Poetic Languages) that thrived in Moscow from 1916 until 1930. Shklovsky, Boris Eichenbaum, Yary Tynyanov, and other Formalists sought to put literary theory on a par with the natural sciences through rigorous consistency in their systematic elaboration of primary and defensible tenets about literature. At their most expansive they offered a theory of literary function and critical interpretation, as well as a theory of art's purpose. They are most famous for demonstrating and defending the need to emphasize form and structure in literature over content and the fact that social conditions may be said to produce literary works. They tended to view literary works not as monolithic aesthetic wholes with prescribed effects, but as collections of devices that interact in a textual field; the result may or may not produce an overall aesthetic effect. The ultimate purpose of literary art is estrangement, or "making strange," displacing language out of its usual, workaday meaning and freeing it to stimulate and produce fresh linguistic apprehensions—of language itself and of the world. These goals, however, tended to conflict with the governmental aims of socialist realism, and in 1930 the Formalists were officially suppressed.

"Art as Technique" (1917) is Shklovsky's central theoretical statement and one of the primary documents of Russian Formalism. In it Shklovsky attacks then-current aesthetic theories (especially Potebnyaism) about the essence of art being a "thinking in images." The imagist approach to literary art, of course, is highlighted in Anglo-American poetic imagism and in New Criticism. Shklovsky, however, argues against the centrality of "images" and instead defines a field of literary activity in which linguistically based devices (such as metaphor and metonymy) create an experience more complex, and possibly less coherent, than the examination of images can suggest. In *On the Theory of Prose* (1925) and *The Technique of the Writer's Craft* (1928) he elaborated these notions in theoretical and practical criticism. In 1928, though, he began to recant formalist theory—especially in *"War and Peace* of Leo Tolstoy" (1928)—and tried to include sociological material in his interpretations. Both his earlier formalist and later socialist criticism are influential, as we will see later, in structuralism—which in many ways is the extension of work done by the Formalists in their brief but productive fifteen years.

# Art as Technique

"Art is thinking in images." This maxim, which even high school students parrot, is nevertheless the starting point for the erudite philologist who is beginning to put together some kind of systematic literary theory. The idea, originated in part by Potebnya, has spread. "Without imagery there is no art, and in particular no poetry," Potebnya writes.[1] And elsewhere, "Poetry, as well as prose, is first and foremost a special way of thinking and knowing."[2]

Poetry is a special way of thinking; it is, precisely, a way of thinking in images, a way which permits what is generally called "economy of mental effort," a way which makes for "a sensation of the relative ease of the process." Aesthetic feeling is the reaction to this economy. This is how the academician Ovsyaniko-Kulikovsky[3] who undoubtedly read the works of Potebnya attentively, almost certainly understood and faithfully summarized the ideas of his teacher. Potebnya and his numerous disciples consider poetry a special kind of thinking—thinking by means of images; they feel that the purpose of imagery is to help channel various objects and activities into groups and to clarify the unknown by means of the known. Or, as Potebnya wrote:

> The relationship of the image to what is being clarified is that: (a) the image is the fixed predicate of that which undergoes change—the unchanging means of attracting what is perceived as changeable. . . . (b) the image is far clearer and simpler than what it clarifies.[4]

In other words:

> Since the purpose of imagery is to remind us, by approximation, of those meanings for which the image stands, and since, apart from this, imagery is unnecessary for thought, we must be more familiar with the image than with what it clarifies.[5]

It would be instructive to try to apply this principle to Tyutchev's comparison of summer lightning to deaf and dumb demons or to Gogol's comparison of the sky to the garment of God.[6]

"Without imagery there is no art"—"Art is thinking in images." These maxims have led to far-fetched interpretations of individual works of art. Attempts have been made to evaluate even music, architecture, and lyric poetry as imagistic thought. After a quarter of a century of such attempts Ovsyaniko-Kulikovsky finally had to assign lyric poetry, architecture, and music to a special category of imageless art and to define them as lyric arts appealing directly to the emotions. And thus he admitted an enormous area of art which is not a mode of thought. A part of this area, lyric poetry (narrowly considered), is quite like the visual arts: it is also verbal. But, much more important, visual art passes quite imperceptibly into nonvisual art; yet our perceptions of both are similar.

Nevertheless, the definition "Art is thinking in images," which means (I omit the usual middle terms of the argument) that art is the making of symbols, has survived the downfall of the theory which supported it. It survives chiefly in the wake of Symbolism, especially among the theorists of the Symbolist movement.

Many still believe, then, that thinking in images—thinking in specific scenes of "roads and landscape" and "furrows and boundaries"[7]—is the chief characteristic of poetry. Consequently, they should have expected the history of "imagistic art," as they call it, to consist of a history of changes in imagery. But we find that images change little; from century to century, from nation to nation, from poet to poet, they flow on without changing. Images belong to no one: they are "the Lord's." The more you understand an age, the more convinced you become that the images a given poet used and which you thought his own were taken almost unchanged from another poet. The works of poets are classified or grouped according to the new techniques that poets discover and share, and according to their arrangement and development of the resources of language; poets are much more concerned with arranging images than with creating them. Images are given to poets; the ability to remember them is far more important than the ability to create them.

Imagistic thought does not, in any case, include all the aspects of art nor even all the aspects of verbal art. A change in imagery is not essential to the development of poetry. We know that frequently an expression is thought to be poetic, to be created for aesthetic pleasure, although actually it was created without such intent—e.g., Annensky's opinion that the Slavic languages are especially poetic and Andrey Bely's ecstasy over the technique of placing adjectives after nouns, a technique used by eighteenth-century Russian poets. Bely joyfully accepts the technique as something artistic, or more exactly, as intended, if we consider intention as art. Actually, this reversal of the usual adjective-noun order is a peculiarity of the language (which had been influenced by Church Slavonic). Thus a work may be (1) intended as prosaic and accepted as poetic, or (2) intended as poetic and accepted as prosaic. This suggests that the artistry attributed to a given work results from the way we perceive it. By "works of art," in the narrow sense, we mean works created by special techniques designed to make the works as obviously artistic as possible.

Potebnya's conclusion, which can be for-

mulated "poetry equals imagery," gave rise to the whole theory that "imagery equals symbolism," that the image may serve as the invariable predicate of various subjects. (This conclusion, because it expressed ideas similar to the theories of the Symbolists, intrigued some of their leading representatives—Andrey Bely, Merezhkovsky and his "eternal companions"—and, in fact, formed the basis of the theory of Symbolism.) The conclusion stems partly from the fact that Potebnya did not distinguish between the language of poetry and the language of prose. Consequently, he ignored the fact that there are two aspects of imagery: imagery as a practical means of thinking, as a means of placing objects within categories; and imagery as poetic, as a means of reinforcing an impression. I shall clarify with an example. I want to attract the attention of a young child who is eating bread and butter and getting the butter on her fingers. I call, "Hey, butterfingers!" This is a figure of speech, a clearly prosaic trope. Now a different example. The child is playing with my glasses and drops them. I call, "Hey, butterfingers!"[8] This figure of speech is a poetic trope. (In the first example, "butterfingers" is metonymic; in the second, metaphoric—but this is not what I want to stress.)

Poetic imagery is a means of creating the strongest possible impression. As a method it is, depending upon its purpose, neither more nor less effective than other poetic techniques; it is neither more nor less effective than ordinary or negative parallelism, comparison, repetition, balanced structure, hyperbole, the commonly accepted rhetorical figures, and all those methods which emphasize the emotional effect of an expression (including words or even articulated sounds).[9] But poetic imagery only externally resembles either the stock imagery of fables and ballads or thinking in images—e.g., the example in Ovsyaniko-Kulikovsky's *Language and Art* in which a little girl calls a ball a little watermelon. Poetic imagery is but one of the devices of poetic language. Prose imagery is a means of abstraction: a little watermelon instead of a lampshade, or a little watermelon instead of a head, is only the abstraction of one of the object's characteristics, that of roundness. It is no different from saying that the head and the melon are both round. This is what is meant, but it has nothing to do with poetry.

The law of the economy of creative effort is also generally accepted. [Herbert] Spencer wrote:

> On seeking for some clue to the law underlying these current maxims, we may see shadowed forth in many of them, the importance of economizing the reader's or the hearer's attention. To so present ideas that they may be apprehended with the least possible mental effort, is the desideratum towards which most of the rules above quoted point. . . . Hence, carrying out the metaphor that language is the vehicle of thought, there seems reason to think that in all cases the friction and inertia of the vehicle deduct from its efficiency; and that in composition, the chief, if not the sole thing to be done, is to reduce the friction and inertia to the smallest possible amount.[10]

And R[ichard] Avenarius:

> If a soul possess inexhaustible strength, then, of course, it would be indifferent to know how much might be spent from this inexhaustible source; only the necessarily expended time would be important. But since its forces are limited, one is led to expect that the soul hastens to carry out the apperceptive process as expediently as possible—that is, with comparatively the least expenditure of energy, and, hence, with comparatively the best result.

Petrazhitsky, with only one reference to the general law of mental effort, rejects [William]

James's theory of the physical basis of emotion, a theory which contradicts his own. Even Alexander Veselovsky acknowledged the principle of the economy of creative effort, a theory especially appealing in the study of rhythm, and agreed with Spencer: "A satisfactory style is precisely that style which delivers the greatest amount of thought in the fewest words." And Andrey Bely, despite the fact that in his better pages he gave numerous examples of "roughened" rhythm[11] and (particularly in the examples from Baratynsky) showed the difficulties inherent in poetic epithets, also thought it necessary to speak of the law of the economy of creative effort in his book[12]—a heroic effort to create a theory of art based on unverified facts from antiquated sources, on his vast knowledge of the techniques of poetic creativity, and on Krayevich's high school physics text.

These ideas about the economy of energy, as well as about the law and aim of creativity, are perhaps true in their application to "practical" language; they were, however, extended to poetic language. Hence they do not distinguish properly between the laws of practical language and the laws of poetic language. The fact that Japanese poetry has sounds not found in conversational Japanese was hardly the first factual indication of the differences between poetic and everyday language. Leo Jakubinsky has observed that the law of the dissimilation of liquid sounds does not apply to poetic language.[13] This suggested to him that poetic language tolerated the admission of hard-to-pronounce conglomerations of similar sounds. In his article, one of the first examples of scientific criticism, he indicates inductively the contrast (I shall say more about this point later) between the laws of poetic language and the laws of practical language.[14]

We must, then, speak about the laws of expenditure and economy in poetic language not on the basis of an analogy with prose, but on the basis of the laws of poetic language.

If we start to examine the general laws of perception, we see that as perception becomes habitual, it becomes automatic. Thus, for example, all of our habits retreat into the area of the unconsciously automatic; if one remembers the sensations of holding a pen or of speaking in a foreign language for the first time and compares that with his feeling at performing the action for the ten thousandth time, he will agree with us. Such habituation explains the principles by which, in ordinary speech, we leave phrases unfinished and words half expressed. In this process, ideally realized in algebra, things are replaced by symbols. Complete words are not expressed in rapid speech: their initial sounds are barely perceived. Alexander Pogodin offers the example of a boy considering the sentence "The Swiss mountains are beautiful" in the form of a series of letters: *T, S, m, a, b*.[15]

This characteristic of thought not only suggests the method of algebra, but even prompts the choice of symbols (letters, especially initial letters). By this "algebraic" method of thought we apprehend objects only as shapes with imprecise extensions; we do not see them in their entirety but rather recognize them by their main characteristics. We see the object as though it were enveloped in a sack. We know what it is by its configuration, but we see only its silhouette. The object, perceived thus in the manner of prose perception, fades and does not leave even a first impression; ultimately even the essence of what it was is forgotten. Such perception explains why we fail to hear the prose word in its entirety (see Leo Jakubinsky's article[16]) and, hence, why (along with other slips of the tongue) we fail to pronounce it. The process of "algebrization," the overautomatization of an object, permits the greatest economy of perceptive effort. Either objects are assigned only one proper feature—a number, for example—or else they function as though by formula and do not even appear in cognition:

I was cleaning a room and, meandering about, approached the divan and couldn't remember whether or not I had dusted it. Since these movements are habitual and unconscious, I could not remember and felt that it was impossible to remember—so that if I had dusted it and forgot—that is, had acted unconsciously, then it was the same as if I had not. If some conscious person had been watching, then the fact could be established. If, however, no one was looking, or looking on unconsciously, if the whole complex lives of many people go on unconsciously, then such lives are as if they had never been.[17]

And so life is reckoned as nothing. Habitualization devours works, clothes, furniture, one's wife, and the fear of war. "If the whole complex lives of many people go on unconsciously, then such lives are as if they had never been." And art exists that one may recover the sensation of life; it exists to make one feel things, to make the stone stony. The purpose of art is to impart the sensation of things as they are perceived and not as they are known. The technique of art is to make objects "unfamiliar," to make forms difficult, to increase the difficulty and length of perception because the process of perception is an aesthetic end in itself and must be prolonged. *Art is a way of experiencing the artfulness of an object; the object is not important.*

The range of poetic (artistic) work extends from the sensory to the cognitive, from poetry to prose, from the concrete to the abstract: from Cervantes' Don Quixote—scholastic and poor nobleman, half consciously bearing his humiliation in the court of the duke—to the broad but empty Don Quixote of Turgenev; from Charlemagne to the name "king" [in Russian "Charles" and "king" obviously derive from the same root, *korol*]. The meaning of a work broadens to the extent that artfulness and artistry diminish; thus a fable symbolizes more than a poem, and a proverb more than a fable. Consequently, the least self-contradictory part of Potebnya's theory is his treatment of the fable, which, from his point of view, he investigated thoroughly. But since his theory did not provide for "expressive" works of art, he could not finish his book. As we know, *Notes on the Theory of Literature* was published in 1905, thirteen years after Potebnya's death. Potebnya himself completed only the section on the fable.[18]

After we see an object several times, we begin to recognize it. The object is in front of us and we know about it, but we do not see it[19]—hence we cannot say anything significant about it. Art removes objects from the automatism of perception in several ways. Here I want to illustrate a way used repeatedly by Leo Tolstoy, that writer, who, for Merezhkovsky at least, seems to present things as if he himself saw them, saw them in their entirety, and did not alter them.

Tolstoy makes the familiar seem strange by not naming the familiar object. He describes an object as if he were seeing it for the first time, an event as if it were happening for the first time. In describing something he avoids the accepted names of its parts and instead names corresponding parts of other objects. For example, in "Shame" Tolstoy "defamiliarizes" the idea of flogging in this way: "to strip people who have broken the law, to hurl them to the floor, and to rap on their bottoms with switches," and, after a few lines, "to lash about on the naked buttocks." Then he remarks:

Just why precisely this stupid, savage means of causing pain and not any other—why not prick the shoulders or any part of the body with needles, squeeze the hands or the feet in a vise, or anything like that?

I apologize for this harsh example, but it is typical of Tolstoy's way of pricking the con-

science. The familiar act of flogging is made unfamiliar both by the description and by the proposal to change its form without changing its nature. Tolstoy uses this technique of "defamiliarization" constantly. The narrator of "Kholstomer," for example, is a horse, and it is the horse's point of view (rather than a person's) that makes the content of the story seem unfamiliar. Here is how the horse regards the institution of private property:

I understood well what they said about whipping and Christianity. But then I was absolutely in the dark. What's the meaning of "his own," "his colt"? From these phrases I saw that people thought there was some sort of connection between me and the stable. At that time I simply could not understand the connection. Only much later, when they separated me from the other horses, did I begin to understand. But even then I simply could not see what it meant when they called me "man's property." The words "my horse" referred to me, a living horse, and seemed as strange to me as the words "my land," "my air," "my water."

But the words made a strong impression on me. I thought about them constantly, and only after the most diverse experiences with people did I understand, finally, what they meant. They meant this: In life people are guided by words, not by deeds. It's not so much that they love the possibility of doing or not doing something as it is the possibility of speaking with words, agreed on among themselves, about various topics. Such are the words "my" and "mine," which they apply to different things, creatures, objects, and even to land, people, and horses. They agree that only one may say "mine" about this, that, or the other thing. And the one who says "mine" about the greatest number of things is, according to the game which they've agreed to among themselves, the one they consider the most happy. I don't know the point of all this, but it's true. For a long time I tried to explain it to myself in terms of some kind of real gain, but I had to reject that explanation because it was wrong.

Many of those, for instance, who called me their own never rode on me—although others did. And so with those who fed me. Then again, the coachman, the veterinarians, and the outsiders in general treated me kindly, yet those who called me their own did not. In due time, having widened the scope of my observations, I satisfied myself that the notion "my," not only in relation to us horses, has no other basis than a narrow human instinct which is called a sense of or right to private property. A man says "this house is mine" and never lives in it; he only worries about its construction and upkeep. A merchant says "my shop," "my dry goods shop," for instance, and does not even wear clothes made from the better cloth he keeps in his own shop.

There are people who call a tract of land their own, but they never set eyes on it and never take a stroll on it. There are people who call others their own, yet never see them. And the whole relationship between them is that the so-called "owners" treat the others unjustly.

There are people who call women their own, or their "wives," but their women live with other men. And people strive not for the good in life, but for goods they can call their own.

I am now convinced that this is the essential difference between people and ourselves. And therefore, not even considering the other ways in which we are superior, but considering just this one virtue, we can bravely claim to stand higher than men on the ladder of living creatures. The actions of men, at least those with whom I have had dealings, are guided by *words*—ours, by deeds.

The horse is killed before the end of the story, but the manner of the narrative, its technique, does not change:

Much later they put Serpukhovsky's body, which had experienced the world, which had eaten and drunk, into the ground. They could profitably send neither his hide, nor his flesh, nor his bones anywhere.

But since his dead body, which had gone about in the world for twenty years, was a great burden to everyone, its burial was only a superfluous embarrassment for the people. For a long time no one had needed him; for a long time he had been a burden on all. But nevertheless, the dead who buried the dead found it necessary to dress this bloated body, which immediately began to rot, in a good uniform and good boots; to lay it in a good new coffin with new tassels at the four corners, then to place this new coffin in another of lead and ship it to Moscow; there to exhume ancient bones and at just that spot, to hide this putrefying body, swarming with maggots, in its new uniform and clean boots, and to cover it over completely with dirt.

Thus we see that at the end of the story Tolstoy continues to use the technique even though the motivation for it [the reason for its use] is gone.

In *War and Peace* Tolstoy uses the same technique in describing whole battles as if battles were something new. These descriptions are too long to quote; it would be necessary to extract a considerable part of the four-volume novel. But Tolstoy uses the same method in describing the drawing room and the theater:

The middle of the stage consisted of flat boards; by the sides stood painted pictures representing trees, and at the back a linen cloth was stretched down to the floor boards. Maidens in red bodices and white skirts sat on the middle of the stage. One, very fat, in a white silk dress, sat apart on a narrow bench to which a green pasteboard box was glued from behind. They were all singing something. When they had finished, the maiden in white approached the prompter's box. A man in silk with tight-fitting pants on his fat legs approached her with a plume and began to sing and spread his arms in dismay. The man in the tight pants finished his song alone; then the girl sang. After that both remained silent as the music resounded; and the man, obviously waiting to begin singing his part with her again, began to run his fingers over the hand of the girl in the white dress. They finished their song together, and everyone in the theater began to clap and shout. But the men and women on stage, who represented lovers, started to bow, smiling and raising their hands.

In the second act there were pictures representing monuments and openings in the linen cloth representing the moonlight, and they raised lamp shades on a frame. As the musicians started to play the bass horn and counter-bass, a large number of people in black mantles poured onto the stage from right and left. The people, with something like daggers in their hands, started to wave their arms. Then still more people came running out and began to drag away the maiden who had been wearing a white dress but who now wore one of sky blue. They did not drag her off immediately, but sang with her for a long time before dragging her away. Three times they struck on something metallic behind the side scenes, and everyone got down on his knees and began to chant a prayer. Several times all of this activity was interrupted by enthusiastic shouts from the spectators.

The third act is described:

. . . But suddenly a storm blew up. Chromatic scales and chords of diminished sevenths were heard in the orchestra. Everyone ran about and again they dragged one of the bystanders behind the scenes as the curtain fell.

In the fourth act, "There was some sort of devil who sang, waving his hands, until the boards were moved out from under him and he dropped down."[20]

In *Resurrection* Tolstoy describes the city and the court in the same way; he uses a similar technique in "Kreutzer Sonata" when he describes marriage—"Why, if people have an affinity of souls, must they sleep together?" But he did not defamiliarize only those things he sneered at:

Pierre stood up from his new comrades and made his way between the campfires to the other side of the road where, it seemed, the captive soldiers were held. He wanted to talk with them. The French sentry stopped him on the road and ordered him to return. Pierre did so, but not to the campfire, not to his comrades, but to an abandoned, unharnessed carriage. On the ground, near the wheel of the carriage, he sat cross-legged in the Turkish fashion, and lowered his head. He sat motionless for a long time, thinking. More than an hour passed. No one disturbed him. Suddenly he burst out laughing with his robust, good natured laugh—so loudly that the men near him looked around, surprised at his conspicuously strange laughter.

"Ha, ha, ha," laughed Pierre. And he began to talk to himself. "The soldier didn't allow me to pass. They caught me, barred me. Me—me—my immortal soul. Ha, ha, ha," he laughed with tears starting in his eyes.

Pierre glanced at the sky, into the depths of the departing, playing stars. "And all this is mine, all this is in me, and all this is I," thought Pierre. "And all this they caught and put in a planked enclosure." He smiled and went off to his comrades to lie down to sleep.[21]

Anyone who knows Tolstoy can find several hundred such passages in his work. His method of seeing things out of their normal context is also apparent in his last works. Tolstoy described the dogmas and rituals he attacked as if they were unfamiliar, substituting everyday meanings for the customarily religious meanings of the words common in church ritual. Many persons were painfully wounded; they considered it blasphemy to present as strange and monstrous what they accepted as sacred. Their reaction was due chiefly to the technique through which Tolstoy perceived and reported his environment. And after turning to what he had long avoided, Tolstoy found that his perceptions had unsettled his faith.

The technique of defamiliarization is not Tolstoy's alone. I cited Tolstoy because his work is generally known.

Now, having explained the nature of this technique, let us try to determine the approximate limits of its application. I personally feel that defamiliarization is found almost everywhere form is found. In other words, the difference between Potebnya's point of view and ours is this: An image is not a permanent referent for those mutable complexities of life which are revealed through it; its purpose is not to make us perceive meaning, but to create a special perception of the object—*it creates a "vision" of the object instead of serving as a means for knowing it.*

The purpose of imagery in erotic art can be studied even more accurately; an erotic object is usually presented as if it were seen for the first time. Gogol, in "Christmas Eve," provided the following example:

Here he approached her more closely, coughed, smiled at her, touched her

plump, bare arm with his fingers, and expressed himself in a way that showed both his cunning and his conceit.

"And what is this you have, magnificent Solokha?" and having said this, he jumped back a little.

"What? An arm, Osip Nikiforovich!" she answered.

"Hmm, an arm! *He, he, he!*" said the secretary cordially, satisfied with his beginning. He wandered about the room.

"And what is this you have, dearest Solokha?" he said in the same way, having approached her again and grasped her lightly by the neck, and in the very same way he jumped back.

"As if you don't see, Osip Nikoforovich!" answered Solokha, "a neck, and on my neck a necklace."

"Hmm! On the neck a necklace! *He, he, he!*" and the secretary again wandered about the room, rubbing his hands.

"And what is this you have, incomparable Solokha?" . . . It is not known to what the secretary would stretch his long fingers now.

And Knut Hamsum has the following in "Hunger": "Two white prodigies appeared from beneath her blouse."

Erotic subjects may also be presented figuratively with the obvious purpose of leading us away from their "recognition." Hence sexual organs are referred to in terms of lock and key[22] or quilting tools[23] or bow and arrow, or rings and marlinspikes, as in the legend of Stavyor, in which a married man does not recognize his wife, who is disguised as a warrior. She proposes a riddle:

"Remember, Stavyor, do you recall
How we little ones walked to and fro in the
    street?
You and I together sometimes played with
    a marlinspike—
You had a silver marlinspike,

But I had a gilded ring?
I found myself at it just now and then,
But you fell in with it ever and always."
Says Stavyor, son of Godinovich,
"What! I didn't play with you at
    marlinspikes!"
Then Vasilisa Mikulichna: "So he says.
Do you remember, Stavyor, do you recall,
Now must you know, you and I together
    learned to read and write;
Mine was an ink-well of silver,
And yours a pen of gold?
But I just moistened it a little now and
    then,
And I just moistened it ever and always."[24]

In a different version of the legend we find a
key to the riddle:

Here the formidable envoy Vasilyushka
Raised her skirts to the very navel,
And then the young Stavyor, son of
    Godinovich,
Recognized her gilded ring. . . .[25]

But defamiliarization is not only a technique of the erotic riddle—a technique of euphemism—it is also the basis and point of all riddles. Every riddle pretends to show its subject either by words which specify or describe it but which, during the telling, do not seem applicable (the type: "black and white and 'red'—read—all over") or by means of odd but imitative sounds (" 'Twas brillig, and the slithy toves / Did gyre and gimble in the wabe").[26]
Even erotic images not intended as riddles are defamiliarized ("boobies," "tarts," "piece," etc.). In popular imagery there is generally something equivalent to "trampling the grass" and "breaking the guelder-rose." The technique of defamiliarization is absolutely clear in the widespread image—a motif of erotic affectation—in which a bear and other wild beasts (or a devil, with a different reason for nonrecognition) do not recognize a man.[27]

The lack of recognition in the following tale is quite typical:

A peasant was plowing a field with a piebald mare. A bear approached him and asked, "Uncle, what's made this mare piebald for you?"
"I did the piebalding myself."
"But how?"
"Let me, and I'll do the same for you."
The bear agreed. The peasant tied his feet together with a rope, took the ploughshare from the two-wheeled plough, heated it on the fire, and applied it to his flanks. He made the bear piebald by scorching his fur down to the hide with the hot ploughshare. The man untied the bear, which went off and lay down under a tree.
A magpie flew at the peasant to pick at the meat on his shirt. He caught her and broke one of her legs. The magpie flew off to perch in the same tree under which the bear was lying. Then, after the magpie, a horsefly landed on the mare, sat down, and began to bite. The peasant caught the fly, took a stick, shoved it up its rear, and let it go. The fly went to the tree where the bear and the magpie were. There all three sat.
The peasant's wife came to bring his dinner to the field. The man and his wife finished their dinner in the fresh air, and he began to wrestle with her on the ground.
The bear saw this and said to the magpie and the fly, "Holy priests! The peasant wants to piebald someone again."
The magpie said, "No, he wants to break someone's legs."
The fly said, "No, he wants to shove a stick up someone's rump."[28]

The similarity of technique here and in Tolstoy's "Kholstomer," is, I think, obvious.
Quite often in literature the sexual act itself is defamiliarized; for example, the Decameron refers to "scraping out a barrel," "catching nightingales," "gay wool-beating work" (the last is not developed in the plot). Defa-

miliarization is often used in describing the sexual organs.

A whole series of plots is based on such a lack of recognition; for example, in Afanasyev's *Intimate Tales* the entire story of "The Shy Mistress" is based on the fact that an object is not called by its proper name—or, in other words, on a game of nonrecognition. So too in Onchukov's "Spotted Petticoats," tale no. 525, and also in "The Bear and the Hare" from *Intimate Tales,* in which the bear and the hare make a "wound."

Such constructions as "the pestle and the mortar," or "Old Nick and the infernal regions" *(Decameron),* are also examples of the technique of defamiliarization. And in my article on plot construction I write about defamiliarization in psychological parallelism. Here, then, I repeat that the perception of disharmony in a harmonious context is important in parallelism. The purpose of parallelism, like the general purpose of imagery, is to transfer the usual perception of an object into the sphere of a new perception—that is, to make a unique semantic modification.

In studying poetic speech in its phonetic and lexical structure as well as in its characteristic distribution of words and in the characteristic thought structures compounded from the words, we find everywhere the artistic trademark—that is, we find material obviously created to remove the automatism of perception; the author's purpose is to create the vision which results from that deautomatized perception. A work is created "artistically" so that its perception is impeded and the greatest possible effect is produced through the slowness of the perception. As a result of this lingering, the object is perceived not in its extension in space, but, so to speak, in its continuity. Thus "poetic language" gives satisfaction. According to Aristotle, poetic language must appear strange and wonderful; and, in fact, it is often actually foreign: the Sumerian used by the Assyrians, the Latin of Europe during the Middle Ages, the Arabisms of the Persians, the

Old Bulgarian of Russian literature, or the elevated, almost literary language of folk songs. The common archaisms of poetic language, the intricacy of the sweet new style [*dolce stil nuovo*],[29] the obscure style of the language of Arnaut Daniel with the "roughened" [harte] forms *which make pronunciation difficult*—these are used in much the same way. Leo Jakubinsky has demonstrated the principle of phonetic "roughening" of poetic language in the particular case of the repetition of identical sounds. The language of poetry is, then, a difficult, roughened, impeded language. In a few special instances the language of poetry approximates the language of prose, but this does not violate the principle of "roughened" form.

> Her sister was called Tatyana.
> For the first time we shall
> Wilfully brighten the delicate
> Pages of a novel with such a name.

wrote Pushkin. The usual poetic language for Pushkin's contemporaries was the elegant style of Derzhavin; but Pushkin's style, because it seemed trivial then, was unexpectedly difficult for them. We should remember the consternation of Pushkin's contemporaries over the vulgarity of his expressions. He used the popular language as a special device for prolonging attention, just as his contemporaries generally used Russian words in their usually French speech (see Tolstoy's examples in *War and Peace*).

Just now a still more characteristic phenomenon is under way. Russian literary language, which was originally foreign to Russia, has so permeated the language of the people that it has blended with their conversation. On the other hand, literature has now begun to show a tendency towards the use of dialects (Remizov, Klyuyev, Essenin, and others,[30] so unequal in talent and so alike in language, are intentionally provincial) and of barbarisms (which gave rise to the Severyanin group[31]). And currently Maxim Gorky is changing his diction from the old literary language to the new literary colloquialism of Leskov.[32] Ordinary speech and literary language have thereby changed places (see the work of Vyacheslav Ivanov and many others). And finally, a strong tendency, led by Khlebnikov, to create a new and properly poetic language has emerged. In the light of these developments we can define poetry as *attenuated, tortuous* speech. Poetic speech is formed speech. Prose is ordinary speech—economical, easy, proper, the goddess of prose [*dea prosae*] is a goddess of the accurate, facile type, of the "direct" expression of a child. I shall discuss roughened form and retardation as the general law of art at greater length in an article on plot construction.[33]

Nevertheless, the position of those who urge the idea of the economy of artistic energy as something which exists in and even distinguishes poetic language seems, at first glance, tenable for the problem of rhythm. Spencer's description of rhythm would seem to be absolutely incontestable:

> Just as the body in receiving a series of varying concussions, must keep the muscles ready to meet the most violent of them, as not knowing when such may come: so, the mind in receiving unarranged articulations, must keep its perspectives active enough to recognize the least easily caught sounds. And as, if the concussions recur in definite order, the body may husband its forces by adjusting the resistance needful for each concussion; so, if the syllables be rhythmically arranged, the mind may economize its energies by anticipating the attention required for each syllable.[34]

This apparently conclusive observation suffers from the common fallacy, the confusion of the laws of poetic and prosaic language. In *The Philosophy of Style* Spencer failed utterly to distinguish between them. But rhythm of prose, or of a work song like "Dubinushka," permits the members of the work crew to do their necessary "groaning together" and also eases the work by making it automatic. And, in fact, it is easier to march with music than without it, and to march during an animated conversation is even easier, for the walking is done unconsciously. Thus the rhythm of prose is an important automatizing element; the rhythm of poetry is not. There is "order" in art, yet not a single column of a Greek temple stands exactly in its proper order; poetic rhythm is similarly disordered rhythm. Attempts to systematize the irregularities have been made, and such attempts are part of the current problem in the theory of rhythm. It is obvious that the systematization will not work, for in reality the problem is not one of complicating the rhythm but of disordering the rhythm—a disordering which cannot be predicted. Should the disordering of rhythm became a convention, it would be ineffective as a device for the roughening of language. But I will not discuss rhythm in more detail since I intend to write a book about it.[35]

*Translated by Lee T. Lemon and Marion J. Reis*

## NOTES

1. Alexander Potebnya, *Iz zapisok po teorii slovesnosti* [Notes on the Theory of Language] (Kharkov, 1905), 83.

2. Ibid., p. 97.

3. Dmitry Ovsyaniko-Kulikovsky (1835–1920), a leading Russian scholar, was an early contributor to Marxist periodicals and a literary conservative, antagonistic towards the deliberately meaningless poems of the Futurists. *Trans. note.*

4. Potebnya, *Iz zapisok poi teorii slovesnosti*, p. 314.

5. Ibid., p. 291.

6. Fyodor Tyutchev (1803–1873), a poet, and Nicholas Gogol (1809–1852), a master of prose fiction and satire, are mentioned here because their bold use of imagery cannot be accounted for by Potebnya's theory. Shklovsky

is arguing that writers frequently gain their effects by comparing the commonplace to the exceptional rather than vice versa. *Trans. note.*

7. This is an allusion to Vyacheslav Ivanov's *Borozdy i mezhi* [*Furrows and Boundaries*] (Moscow, 1916), a major statement of Symbolist theory. *Trans. note.*

8. The Russian text involves a play on the word for "hat," colloquial for "clod," "duffer," etc. *Trans. note.*

9. Shklovsky is here doing two things of major theoretical importance: (1) he argues that different techniques serve a single function, and that (2) no single technique is all-important. The second permits the Formalists to be concerned with any and all literary devices; the first permits them to discuss the devices from a single consistent theoretical position. *Trans. note.*

10. Herbert Spencer, *The Philosophy of Style* [(Humboldt Library, Vol. XXXIV; New York, 1882), 2–3. Shklovsky's quoted reference, in Russian, preserves the idea of the original but shortens it].

11. The Russian *zatrudyonny* means "made difficult." The suggestion is that poems with "easy" or smooth rhythms slip by unnoticed; poems that are difficult or "roughened" force the reader to attend to them. *Trans. note.*

12. *Simvolizm*, probably. *Trans. note.*

13. Leo Jakubinsky, "O zvukakh poeticheskovo yazyka" ["On the Sounds of Poetic Language"], *Sborniki*, I (1916), 38.

14. Leo Jakubinsky, "Skopleniye odinakovykh plavnykh v prakticheskom i poeticheskom yazykakh" ["The Accumulation of Identical Liquids in Practical and Poetic Language"], *Sborniki*, II (1917), 13–21.

15. Alexander Pogodin, *Yazyk, kak tvorchestvo [Language as Art]* (Kharkov, 1913), 42. [The original sentence was in French, *"Les montaignes de la Suisse sont belles,"* with the appropriate initials.]

16. Jakubinsky, *Sborniki,* I (1916).

17. Leo Tolstoy's *Diary,* entry dated February 29, 1897. [The date is transcribed incorrectly; it should read March 1, 1897.]

18. Alexander Potebnya, *Iz lektsy po teorii slovesnosti* [Lectures on the Theory of Language] (Kharkov, 1914).

19. Victor Shklovsky, *Voskresheniye slova [The Resurrection of the Word]* (Petersburg, 1914).

20. The Tolstoy and Gogol translations are ours. The passage occurs in Vol. II, Part 8, Chap. 9 of the edition of *War and Peace* published in Boston by the Dana Estes Co., in 1904–1912. *Trans. note.*

21. Leo Tolstoy, *War and Peace,* IV, Part 13. Chap. 14. *Trans. note.*

22. [Dimitry] Savodnikov, *Zagadki russkovo naroda [Riddles of the Russian People]* (St. Petersburg, 1901), Nos. 102–107.

23. Ibid., Nos. 588–591.

24. A. E. Gruzinsky, ed., *Pesni, sobrannye P[avel]N. Rybnikovym [Songs Collected by P. N. Rybnikov]* (Moscow, 1909–1910), No. 30.

25. Ibid., No. 171.

26. We have supplied familiar English examples in place of Shklovsky's wordplay. Shklovsky is saying that we create words with no referents or with ambiguous referents in order to force attention to the objects represented by the similar-sounding words. By making the reader go through the extra step of interpreting the nonsense word, the writer prevents an automatic response. A toad is a toad, but "tove" forces one to pause and think about the beast. *Trans. note.*

27. E. R. Romanov, "Besstrashny barin," *Velikoruskiye skazki (Zapiski Imperskovo Russkovo Geograficheskovo Obschestva,* XLII, No. 52). Belorussky sbornik, "Spravyadlivy soldat" ["The Intrepid Gentleman," *Great Russian Tales (Notes of the Imperial Russian Geographical Society,* XLII, No. 52). *White Russian Anthology,* "The Upright Soldier" (1886–1912)].

28. D[mitry] S. Zelenin, *Velikorusskiye skazki Permskoy gubernii [Great Russian Tales of the Permian Province* (St. Petersburg, 1913)], No. 70.

29. Dante, *Purgatorio,* 24:56. Dante refers to the new lyric style of his contemporaries. *Trans. note.*

30. Alexy Remizov (1877–1957) is best known as a novelist and satirist: Nicholas Klyuyev (1885–1937) and Sergey Essenin (1895–1925) were "peasant poets." All three were noted for their faithful reproduction of Russian dialects and coloquial language. *Trans. note.*

31. A group noted for its opulent and sensuous verse style. *Trans. note.*

32. Nicholas Leskov (1831–1895), novelist and short story writer, helped popularize the *skaz,* or yarn, and hence, because of the part dialect peculiarities play in the *skaz,* also altered Russian literary language. *Trans. note.*

33. Shklovsky is probably referring to his *Razvyortyvaniye syuzheta [Plot Development]* (Petrograd, 1921). *Trans. note.*

34. Spencer [p. 169. Again the Russian text is shortened from Spencer's original].

35. We have been unable to discover the book Shklovsky promised. *Trans. note.*

# 17

# Julia Kristeva
# 1941–

Julia Kristeva, a Parisienne born in Bulgaria, since 1966 has carried on a radical critique of what she calls the "signifying practice" of literature and discourse. From linguistics to semiotics, from politics to psychoanalysis and fiction writing, Kristeva appears as a versatile and eminent intellectual. She maintains a common denominator in all works, however: the importance of differences, the constant questioning of theory and practice. Her frequent travels to the United States give her a privileged stance to build bridges between Continental and American thinking. A renowned linguist, semiotician, feminist, psychoanalyst, and novelist, Kristeva is undoubtedly one of the most influential European thinkers of our postmodern era. Her major publications include *Semiotiké: recherches pour une semanalyse* (1969); *Le texte du roman* (1970); *About Chinese Women* (1974, trans. 1977); *The Revolution in Poetic Language* (1974, trans. 1984); *Polylogue* (1977, trans. 1980); *Powers of Horror: An Essay on Abjection* (1980, trans. 1982); *Tales of Love* (1982, trans. 1987); *Black Sun* (1987); *Strangers to Ourselves* (1989, trans. 1991); *The Samurai* (1990, trans. 1992); *Le vieil homme et les loups* (1992); and *Les nouvelles maladies de l'âme* (1993).

Kristeva, who had studied Russian Formalism in Bulgaria and who was a student of Roland Barthes in Paris in the late sixties, has gradually developed a criticism of formalism and structuralism. The center of her theory is the notion of the signifying practice in literature. Kristeva has developed a theory of semiotics that focuses on the nature of poetic language and the structuralist notion of the sign while also including the extralinguistic factors of history and psychology. She thus redefined the text as an ongoing process in which the writer confronts the ideological givens of a different culture and subverts the linguistic signifiers in unanticipated ways. In the seventies, Kristeva, in search of a dialectic that would not exclude the historical subject of its system, turned to psychoanalysis. Since then Kristeva has continued her investigation in the territories of subjectivity and multiplicity and has kept the concept of heterogeneity and multiplicity borrowed from a linguistic and semiotic approach as the cornerstone of her research.

"Semiotics: A Critical Science and/or a Critique of Science" (1968) was written and published in the midst of the student strikes in France. This period, as Kristeva vividly recalls it in *The Samurai,* was a period of intense political reflection, and Marxism was becoming influential in literary criticism. Numerous intellectuals, including the members of the group *Tel Quel,* took an active part in the remodeling of Marxist theory by introducing the concept of subjectivity through the works of Freud and Lacan. In this article, Kristeva argues that semiotics is not constricted to linguistics only but is a theory of processes, a production of models that simultaneously offers a critique of theory itself. By using the concepts of work in both Marx and Freud,

Kristeva discovers in semiotics a new dynamic of production that will encompass the unrepresentable—the unconscious—while maintaining itself as a social practice and a reflection on social constructs and signifying systems. In doing so, Kristeva hopes to avoid a simplifying and positivist position; instead, she favors complexity within each signifying system. She finally argues that literature is the best example of semiotics as the site of a critique of the production of meaning since literature is not reducible to a simple, normative object. Such a semiotic analysis of literature presents itself as a process that cannot be reduced to representation but can only be seen as an ongoing activity of production. In other words, Kristeva wants to maintain the possibility of multiple meanings in discourse.

# Semiotics: A Critical Science and/or a Critique of Science

In a decisive move towards self-analysis, (scientific) discourse today has begun to re-examine languages in order to isolate their (its) models or patterns. In other words, since social practice (the economy, mores, "art," etc.) is envisaged as a signifying system that is "structured like a language," any practice can be scientifically studied as a secondary model in relation to natural language, modelled on this language and in turn becoming a model or pattern for it.[1] It is in this precise area that semiotics today is articulated or rather is searching for its identity.

We shall attempt to isolate a few of the characteristics which give semiotics a precise place in the history of knowledge and ideology, a place which makes this kind of discourse a clear register of the cultural subversion which our civilization is undergoing. These characteristics account for the barely disguised animosity of the bourgeois word (or "conscience") in its various guises (ranging from esoteric aestheticism to scientific positivism, and from "liberal" journalism to a restrictive sense of "commitment") which calls this research "obscure," "gratuitous," "schematic" or "impoverishing," when it doesn't actually recuperate the lesser by-products of this inquiry by

seeing it as a kind of harmless fringe activity.

Faced with the expansion (and the oppositional nature) of semiotics, we must formulate a theory of its evolution that will place it within the history of science and thought about science, and link up with the epistemological research at present being undertaken seriously only in the Marxist work written or inspired by Louis Althusser. The following notes are no more than an indication of this necessity. I shall therefore say less about the nature of semiotics than about its potential.

## I    SEMIOTICS AS THE MAKING OF MODELS

As soon as we try to define this new form of research, the complexity of the problem becomes apparent. For Saussure, who introduced the term (*Course in General Linguistics,* 1916), *semiology* designated an enormous science of signs of which linguistics was only a part. But it soon became clear that whatever semiology's sign-object happens to be (gesture, sound, image, etc.) it can only be known through language.[2] It follows that "linguistics is not part of the general science of signs, not even a privileged part; rather, it is semiology which is part of linguistics, and specifically that part responsible for the large signifying units of speech".[3] It is not possible here to discuss the advantages and disadvantages of this significant reversal which itself is destined to be modified precisely because of the new openings it has made possible.[4] Following the example of Jacques Derrida, we shall indicate the scientific and ideological limitations which the phonological model risks imposing on a science that aims to offer a model for translinguistic practice. But we shall none the less retain the fundamental gesture of semiotics: a formalization or production of models.[5] Thus, when we say semiotics, we mean the (as yet unrealized) development of *models,* that is, of formal systems whose structure is isomorphic or analogous to the structure of another system (the system under study).[6]

In other words, by borrowing its models from the formal sciences (such as mathematics or logic, which in this way are reduced to being a branch of the vast "science" of language-models), semiotics could eventually become the axiomatization of signifying systems, without being hindered by its epistemological dependence on linguistics. The latter could then in turn renew itself by adopting these models.

In this sense, rather than speak of a semiotics, we prefer to talk of a semiotic level, which is that of the axiomatization, or formalization, of signifying systems.[7]

By defining semiotics as the production of models, however, we not only designate its object, but also touch on the characteristic that distinguishes it from the other "sciences."[8] The models elaborated by semiotics, like those of the exact sciences, are representations and, as such, are produced within spatio-temporal coordinates.[9] But this is where semiotics differs from the exact sciences, for the former is also the production of the theory of its own model-making, a the-

ory which in principle can accommodate that which does not belong to the order of representation. Obviously, a theory is always implicit in the models of any science. But semiotics manifests this theory, or rather cannot be separated from the theory constituting it, that is, a theory which constitutes both its object (the semiotic level of the practice under study) and its instruments (the type of model corresponding to a certain semiotic structure designated by the theory). In each particular case of semiotic research, a theoretical reflection isolates the signifying function being axiomatized, which is then represented in a formal manner. (Note that this action is synchronic and dialectic, and is only called diachronic in order to ease representation.)

Semiotics is therefore a mode of thought where science sees itself as (is conscious of itself as) a theory. At every instant of its production, semiotics thinks of its object, its instruments and the relation between them, and in so doing thinks (of) itself: as a result of this reflection, it becomes the theory of the very science it constitutes. This means that semiotics is at once a re-evaluation of its object and/or of its models, a critique both of these models (and therefore of the sciences from which they are borrowed) and of itself (as a system of stable truths). As the meeting-point of the sciences and an endless theoretical process, semiotics cannot harden into *a* science let alone into *the* science, for it is an open form of research, a constant critique that turns back on itself and offers its own auto-critique. As it is its own theory, semiotics is the kind of thought which, without raising itself to the level of a system, is still capable of modelling (thinking) itself.

But this reflexive movement is not a circular one. Semiotic research remains a form of inquiry that ultimately uncovers its own ideological gesture, only in order to record and deny it before starting all over again. "No key to no mystery," as Levi-Strauss said. It begins with a certain knowledge as its goal, and ends up discovering a *theory* which, since it is itself a signifying system, returns semiotic research to its point of departure, to the model of semiotics itself, which it criticizes or overthrows. This tells us that semiotics can only exist as a *critique of semiotics,* a critique which opens on to something other than semiotics, namely *ideology*. Through this method, which Marx was the first to practise, semiotics becomes the moment when the history of knowledge breaks with the tradition for and in which

> science exhibits itself as a *circle* returning upon itself, the end being wound back into the beginning, the simple ground, by the mediation; this circle is moreover a *circle of circles,* for each individual member as ensouled by the method is reflected into itself, so that in returning into the beginning it is at the same time the beginning of a new member. Links of this chain are the individual sciences (of logic, nature and spirit), each of which has an *antecedent* and a *successor*—or, expressed more accurately, *has* only the *antecedent* and *indicates its successor* in its conclusion.[10]

Semiotic practice breaks with this teleological vision of a science that is subordinated to a philosophical *system* and consequently even destined itself to become a system.[11] Without becoming a system, the site of semiotics, where models and theories are developed, is a place of dispute and self-questioning, a "circle" that remains open. Its "end" does not rejoin its "beginning," but, on the contrary, rejects and rocks it, opening up the way to another discourse, that is, another subject and another method; or rather, there is no more end than beginning, the end is a beginning and vice versa.

No form of semiotics, therefore, can exist other than as a critique of semiotics. As the place where the sciences die, semiotics is both the knowledge of this death and the revival, *with* this knowledge, of the "scientific"; less (or more) than a science, it marks instead the aggressivity and disillusionment that takes place within scientific discourse itself. We might argue that semiotics is that "science of ideologies" suggested in revolutionary Russia,[12] but it is also an ideology of sciences.

Such a conception of semiotics does not at all imply a relativism or agnostic scepticism. On the contrary, it unites with the scientific practice of Marx to the extent that it rejects an absolute system (including a scientific one), but retains a scientific approach, that is, a development of models doubled by the theory underlying the very same models. Created as it is by the constant movement between model and theory while at the same time being situated at a distance from them (thus taking up a position in relation to current social practice), this form of thought demonstrates the "epistemological break" introduced by Marx.

The status here given to semiotics has consequences for: (1) the specific relation of semiotics to the other sciences and especially to linguistics, mathematics and logic from whom it borrows its models; and (2) the introduction of a new terminology and the subversion of the existing terminology.

The semiotics concerning us here uses linguistic, mathematical and logical models and *joins* them to the signifying practices it approaches. This junction is as theoretical as it is scientific, and therefore constitutes a profoundly ideological fact which demystifies the exactitude and "purity" of the discourse of the so-called "human" sciences. It subverts the exact premises of the scientific process, such that for semiotics, linguistics, logic and mathematics are "subverted premises" which have little or nothing to do with their status outside semiotics. Far from being simply a stock of models on which semiotics can draw, these annexed sciences are also the object which semiotics *challenges* in order to make itself into an explicit critique. Mathematical terms such as "theorem of existence" or "axiom of choice"; terms from physics like "isotrope"; linguistic ones such as "competence," "performance," "generation" or "anaphora"; terms from logic such as "disjunction," "orthocomplementary structure," etc. can acquire a different meaning when taken out of the conceptual field in which the retrospective terms were conceived and applied to a new ideological subject, such as that of contemporary semiotics. Playing on this "novelty of non-novelty," or on the different meanings a term acquires in different theoretical contexts, semiotics reveals how science is born in ideology: "The new object may well still retain some link with the old ideological object, *elements* may be found in it which belong to the old object, too: but the meaning of these elements changes with the new *structure,* which precisely confers to them their meaning. These apparent similarities in isolated elements may mislead a superficial glance unaware of the function of the structure in the constitution of the meaning of the elements of an object."[13] Marx practised this subversion of the terms of a preceding science: to the mercantilists, "surplus-value" "arises out of the addition to the value of the product." Marx gave the same word a new meaning: in so doing he brought to light "the novelty of the non-novelty of a reality which appears in *two different discourses,* i.e., the question of the theoretical modality of this 'reality' in two theoretical discourses."[14] But if the semiotic approach provokes this displacement of meaning in terms, why use a terminology that already has a strict usage?

We know that any renewal of scientific thought is carried out by and through a renewal of terminology: there is only invention as such when a new term appears, be it oxygen or infinitesimal calculus. "Every new aspect of a science involves a revolution in the technical terms *(Fachausdrucken)* of that science . . . Political economy has generally been content to take, just as they were, the

terms of commercial and industrial life, and to operate with them, entirely failing to see that *by so doing, it confined itself within the narrow circle of ideas expressed by those terms. . . .*"[15] As semiotics today regards the capitalist system and its accompanying discourse as ephemeral phenomena, it uses terms different from those employed by previous discourses in the "human sciences," when it articulates its signifying practices in the source of its critique. Semiotics therefore rejects a humanist and subjectivist terminology, and addresses itself to the vocabulary of the exact sciences. But, as we have indicated above, these terms have *another* meaning in the new ideological field which semiotic research *can* construct; an alterity to which we shall return. The use of terms from the exact sciences does not erase the possibility of introducing a completely new terminology, at the most crucial points of semiotic research.

## II    SEMIOTICS AND PRODUCTION

So far we have defined the subject of semiotics as a semiotic *level,* as a *section* through signifying practices where the signifier is taken as the model of the signified. This definition in itself suffices in order to designate the novelty of the semiotic process in relation to previous "human sciences" and to science in general: a novelty by means of which semiotics allies itself to Marx's strategy when he presents an economy or society (a signified) as a permutation of elements (signifiers). If, sixty years after the appearance of the term, we can speak today of a "classical" semiotics, it is precisely because its strategies fall under this definition. We none the less feel that we can place ourselves in the *opening afforded* by contemporary thought (Marx, Freud, Husserl) if we define the subject of semiotics in the following more subtle way.

It has already been frequently stressed that the great novelty of Marxist economy was to think of the social as being a particular *mode of production*. Work ceases to be a *subjectivity* or *an essence* of man: Marx replaces the concept of "a supernatural creative power" *(Critique of the Gotha Programme)* with that of "production" viewed in its double mode: as a work process, and as the social relations of production whose elements make up a *combinatoire* with its own specific logic. We might say that the possible combinations are the different kinds of semiotic *systems*. Marxist thought is therefore the first to *pose* the problematics of productive work as a major element in the definition of a semiotic system. This occurs, for example, when Marx explodes the concept of "value" and speaks of it only as a crystallization of social work.[16] He even goes so far as to introduce concepts (surplus-value) which owe their existence to work that is unmeasurable and which themselves are measurable only through their effects (the circulation of merchandise, exchange).

But if Marx sees production as a problematics and a specific structure of meaning [*combinatoire*] that determines the social (or value), it is nevertheless studied only from the point of view of the social (value) and therefore only in terms of the distribution and circulation of goods, and not from the inside of production itself. Marx's work is therefore a study of capitalist society, of the laws of exchange and capital. Within this space and to this end, work is "reified" into an object occupying a precise place (which, for Marx, is determining) in the process of exchange, but which is none the less examined from the angle of this exchange. In this way, Marx is led to study work as *value,* to adopt the distinction between use value and exchange value, and while still following the laws of capitalist society, to limit himself to a study of the latter. Marxist analysis rests on *exchange value,* that is, on the circulating *product* of work that enters the capitalist system as value ("a unit of work"), and it is in this way that

Marx analyses its combinatory forces (workforce, workers, masters, object of production, instrument of production).

Therefore, when he tackles work itself and distinguishes between the different "work" concepts, he does it from the point of view of circulation: circulation of a utility (in which case work is *concrete:* "expenditure of human force in such-and-such a productive form, determined by a particular fact, and consequently of a *concrete* and *useful* nature, producing exchange-values or utilities"[17]); or circulation of a value (in which case work is abstract: "expenditure of human form in the psychological sense"). Let us stress in passing that Marx insists on the relativity and historicity of value and above all of exchange value. Therefore, when he tries to approach use value, in order to escape momentarily from this abstract process of (symbolic) circulation of exchange values in a bourgeois economy, Marx is content to indicate (and the terms used here are very significant) that it concerns a *body* and an *expenditure.* "Use values, that is, the *body* of goods, are the result of a combination of two elements, matter and work . . . Work is not, then, the only source of the use values, or material riches it produces. It is the *father* and the earth is the *mother.*"[18] "Quite apart from its usefulness, all productive activity is ultimately an *expenditure* of human force" (my emphasis).[19]

Marx states the problems clearly: from the point of view of distribution and social consumption, or, if you like, of *communication,* work is always a value, be it use value or exchange value. In other words: if, in communication, values are always a crystallized form of work, work *represents* nothing outside the value in which it is crystallized. This work-value can only be measured by its own value, that is, by the amount of social time taken to produce it.

Such a conception of work, taken out of its space of production, that is, a capitalist space, can lead to a valorization of production and provoke a pertinent critique from Heideggerian philosophy.

But Marx clearly outlines another possibility: another space where work can be apprehended without any consideration of value, that is, beyond any question of the circulation of merchandise. There, on a scene where work does not yet *represent* any value or *mean* anything, our concern is with the relation of a *body* to *expenditure.* Marx had neither the wish nor the means to tackle this notion of a productive labour prior to value or meaning. He gives only a *critical* description of political economy: a critique of the system of exchange of signs (values) that hides a work-value. When it is read as a critique, Marx's text on the circulation of money is one of the high-points achieved by a (communicative) discourse that can speak only of *measurable* communication, which exists against a background of production that is merely indicated. In this, Marx's critical reflections on the system of exchange resemble the contemporary critique of the sign and the circulation of meaning: moreover, the critical discourse on the sign acknowledges its similarity to the critical discourse on money. Thus, when Derrida opposes his theory of writing to the theory of the circulation of signs, he writes of Rousseau:

> This movement of analytical abstraction in the circulation of arbitrary signs is quite parallel to that within which money is constituted. Money replaces things by their signs, not only within a society but from one culture to another, or from one economic organization to another. That is why the alphabet is commercial, a trader. It must be understood *within the monetary moment of economic rationality. The critical description of money is the faithful reflection of the discourse on writing* [my emphasis].[20]

It is the long development of the science of discourse, and of the laws of its permutations and annulments, as well as a long meditation on the principles and limits of the Logos as a model for the system of communication of meaning (value), which has enabled us to create this *concept* of a "work" that "means nothing," and of a silent production that marks and transforms while remaining prior to all circular "speech," to communication, exchange or meaning. It is a concept that is formed by reading, for example, texts such as those by Derrida when he writes "trace," "gramma," *"différance"* or "writing before the letter," while criticizing "sign" and "meaning."

In this development, we must note the masterly contribution made by *Husserl and Heidegger, but above all by Freud,* who was the first to think of the work involved in the process of signification as anterior to the meaning produced and/or the representative discourse: in other words, the dream-process. The chapter-heading from *The Interpretation of Dreams:* "The Dream-Work," shows how Freud revealed production itself to be a *process* not of exchange (or use) or meaning (value), but of playful permutation which provides the very model for production. Freud therefore opens up the problematics of *work as a particular semiotic system,* as distinct from that of exchange: this work exists within the communicative word but differs essentially from it. On the level of manifestation it is a *hieroglyph,* while on a latent level it is a *dream-thought.* "Dream-work" becomes a theoretical concept that triggers off a new research, one that touches on *pre-representative production,* and the development of "thinking" before *thought.* In this new inquiry a radical break separates the *dream-work* from the work of conscious thought and is "for that reason not immediately comparable with it." The dream-work "does not think, calculate or judge in any way at all; it restricts itself to giving things a new form."[21]

This seems to encapsulate the whole problem of contemporary semiotics: either it continues to formalize the semiotic systems from the point of view of communication (in the same way, to risk a brutal comparison, that Ricardo regarded surplus-value from the point of view of distribution and consumption), or else it opens up to the internal problematics of communication (inevitably offered by all social problematics) the "other scene" of the production of meaning prior to meaning.

If we opt for this second route, two possibilities are offered: either we isolate a measurable and consequently representable aspect of the signifying system under study against the background of an unmeasurable concept (work, production, gramma, trace, *différance*); or else we try to construct a new scientific problematics (in the sense given above of a science that is also a theory) to which this new concept necessarily must give rise. In other words, the second case involves the construction of a new "science" once a definition has been reached of a new subject: *work* as a different semiotic practice of exchange.

Several events in the current social and scientific environment justify, if not demand, such an endeavour. Irrupting on to the historical scene, the world of work claims its rights and protests against the system of exchange, demanding that "knowledge" change its perspective so as to transform "exchange based on production" into "production regulated by exchange."

Exact science itself is already tackling the problems of the unpresentable and the unmeasurable, as it tries to think of them not as "deviations" from the observable world, but as a structure with special laws. We are no longer in the age of Laplace where one believed in a superior intelligence that was capable of embracing "in the same formula the movements of the largest bodies and the lightest atoms in the universe: nothing would remain unknown to it, and both future and past would be present in its eyes."[22] Quantum mechanics is aware that our discourse ("intelligence") needs to be "fractured," and must change objects and structures in order to be able to tackle a problematics that can no longer be contained within the framework of classical reason. Consequently, one talks of the *unobserved object*[23] and searches for new logical and mathematical models of formalization. The semiotics of production has inherited this infiltration of the unpresentable by scientific thought and will no doubt use these models elaborated by the exact sciences (polyvalent logic, topology). But since the semiotics of production is a science-theory of discourse and so of itself, and since it tends to emphasize the dynamics of production over the actual product, it consequently rebels against representation even as it uses representative models, and overthrows the very formalization that gives it substance with an unstable theory of the unrepresentable and the unmeasurable. This semiotics of production will therefore accentuate the *alterity* of its object in its relation with the representable and representative object of exchange examined by the exact sciences. At the same time it will accentuate the upheaval of (exact) scientific terminology by shifting it towards that other scene of work that exists prior to value and which can only be glimpsed today.

It is here that semiotic's difficulties lie, both for itself and for those who wish to come to understand it. It is virtually impossible to comprehend such a semiotics when it poses the problem of a production that is not that of communication but which at the same time is constituted through communication, unless one accepts the radical break which separates the problematics of exchange and work. Let us indicate just one of the many consequences entailed by such a semiotics: it replaces the concept of *linear historicity* with the necessity of establishing a typology of signifying practices from the particular models of the production of meaning which actually found them. This approach therefore differs from that of traditional historicism, which it replaced by a plurality of productions that cannot be reduced to one another and even less so to the thought of exchange. Let me stress that I do not wish to establish a list of the *modes* of production: Marx suggested this by limiting himself to the point of view of the circulation of goods. I rather wish to look at the difference between the *types* of signifying production prior to the product (value): oriental philosophies have attempted to tackle this from the point of view of work prior to communication.[24] These kinds of production will perhaps constitute what has been called a "monumental history" to the extent that it literally becomes the foundation or background in relation to a "cursive," figurative (teleological) history.[25]

## III        SEMIOTICS AND "LITERATURE"

In the field thus defined of semiotics, does "literary" practice occupy a privileged place?

Literature does not exist for semiotics. It does not exist as an utterance [*parole*] like others and even less as an aesthetic object. It is a *particular semiotic practice* which has the advantage of making more accessible than others the problematic of the production of meaning posed by a new semiotics, and consequently it is of interest only to the extent that it ("literature") is envisaged as irreducible to the level of an object for normative linguistics (which deals with the codified and denotative word [*parole*]). In this way we can adopt the term of *writing* when it concerns a text seen as a production, in order to distinguish it from the concepts of "literature" and "speech." It then becomes apparent that it is

thoughtless if not dishonest to write "speech [*parole*] (or writing)," "spoken (or written) language."

Seen as a practice, the literary text

is not assimilable to the historically determined concept of "literature." (It) implies the overthrow and complete revision of the place and effects of this concept . . . In other words, the specific problematics of writing isolates itself completely from myth and representation in order to think (of) itself in its own literality and space. The practice must be defined on the level of the "text" to the extent that from now on this word refers to a function that writing does not "express," but rather which it has at its *disposal*. A dramatic economy whose "geometric place" cannot be represented (it is in play).[26]

Any "literary" text may be envisaged as productivity. Literary history since the end of the nineteenth century has given us modern texts which, even structurally, perceive themselves as a production that cannot be reduced to representation (Joyce, Mallarmé, Lautréamont, Roussel). Therefore, a semiotics of production must tackle these texts precisely in order to join a scriptural practice concerned with its own production to a scientific thought in search of production. And it must do so in order to bring out all the consequences of such a confrontation, that is, the reciprocal upheavals which the two practices inflict on one another.

Developed from and in relation to these modern texts the new semiotic models then turn to the *social text,* to those social practices of which "literature" is only one unvalorized variant, in order to conceive of them as so many ongoing transformations and/or productions.

*Translated by Seán Hand*

## NOTES

1. See "Troudy po znadowym sisteman" (Work on signifying systems), vols I, II, III (Estonia: University of Tartu, 1965).

2. "Semiology, sooner or later, is bound to come up against ('true') language, not just as a model, but also as a component, relay or signified." R. Barthes, "Eléments de semiologie," *Communications* 4.

3. Loc. cit.

4. On this point, see the critique of J. Derrida, *De la grammatologie* (Paris: Minuit, 1967), p. 75 (*Of Grammatology,* tr. G. Spivak, Baltimore, Md.: Johns Hopkins University Press, 1974, p. 57).

5. See A. Rosenbluth and W. Wiener, "The role of models in science," *Philosophy of Sciences,* 12, no. 4 (1945), p. 314. Let us note, in passing, the etymology of the word "model" in order to clarify the concept: lat. *modus* = measure, melody, mode, cadence, suitable limit, moderation, way, manner.

6. The notion of analogy, which seems to shock the purists, must be taken here in the serious sense which Mallarmé defined "poetically" as follows: "Herein lies the whole mystery: to pair things off and establish secret identities that gnaw at objects and wear them away in the name of a central purity."

7. "We can say that the semiological is a sort of signifier which, under the control of some anagogical level, articulates the symbolic signified and constitutes it within a network of different significations." A. J. Greimas, *Sémantique structurale* (Paris: Larousse, 1966), p. 60 (*Structural Semantics: an attempt at method,* Lincoln: Neb.: University of Nebraska Press, 1984).

8. The classical distinction between the natural and human sciences also considers the former to be more "pure" than the latter.

9. "The model is always a representation. The problem is to know what is represented and how the function of representation appears." G. Frey, "Symbolische und ikonische Modelle," *Synthèse,* 12, no. 2–3 (1960), p. 213.

10. G. W. F. Hegel, *Science of Logic,* tr. A. V. Miller (London: Allen & Unwin, 1969), p. 842.

11. "It is here that the *content* of cognition as such first enters into the circle of consideration, since, as deduced, it now belongs to the method. The method itself by means of this moment expands itself into a *system.*" Ibid., p. 838.

12. "The Marxist science of ideologies raises two fundamental problems: 1) the problem of the characteristics and forms of the ideological material which is organized like a signifying material; 2) the problem of the characteristics and forms of the social communication that produces this signification." P. N. Medvedev, *Formalnyi metod v literaturovedenci, Kriticheskoïe wedenie v sotsiologicheskuïu poetiku* (Leningrad, 1928) (*The Formal Method in Literary Scholarship,* tr. A. J. Wehrle, Baltimore, Md.: Johns Hopkins University Press, 1978). We shall return to the importance of this distinction.

13. L. Althusser, *Lire le Capital,* vol. II (Paris: Maspéro, 1966), p. 125 (*Reading Capital,* tr. B. Brewster, London: New Left Books, 1979, p. 157).

14. *Lire le Capital,* vol. II, pp. 114–15 (*Reading Capital,* pp. 149–50).

15. F. Engels, preface to the English edition of *Capital,* 1886, vol. I, pp. 4–6 (quoted by L. Althusser, *Lire le Capital,* vol. II, p. 112 (*Reading Capital,* p. 147)).

16. K. Marx, *A Contribution to the Critique of Political Economy* (London: Lawrence & Wishart, 1971), p. 38.

17. *Capital.*

18. Ibid.

19. Ibid.

20. J. Derrida, *De la grammatologie* (Paris: Minuit, 1967), p. 424 (*Of Grammatology,* tr. G. Spivak, Baltimore, Md.: Johns Hopkins University Press, 1974, p. 300).

21. S. Freud, *The Interpretation of Dreams, Standard Edition,* vol. V (London: Hogarth Press, 1953), p. 507.

22. Laplace, *Essai philosophique sur les probabilités* (Paris: Gauthier-Villard, 1921), p. 3.

23. H. Reichenbach, *Philosophic Foundations of Quantum Mechanics* (Berkeley, Calif., and Los Angeles: University of California Press, 1944).

24. For a trial typology of signifying practices, see "For a semiology of paragrams," in *Séméiotiké: recherches pour une sémanalyse* (Paris: Seuil, 1969), pp. 174–207, as well as "Distance and antipresentation," *Tel Quel,* 32, pp. 49–53.

25. Ph. Sollers, "Programme," *Tel Quel,* 31, reprinted in *Logiques* (Paris: Seuil, 1968).

26. Ibid.

# 18

# Louis Marin
# 1931–1992

Louis Marin, author of a wide range of studies on Christianity, Pascal, autobiography, Poussin, and Renaissance painting, the semiotics of the Bible and of seventeenth century absolutism, and the representation of the body in art and literature, posed questions throughout his career about the critical activity of reading and the ways we make meaning of human experience, be it an afternoon at an amusement park or our understanding of a particular work of art or literature. Marin taught at the Ecole des Hautes Etudes en Sciences Sociales in Paris. Currently, four of his books have been translated into English: *Semiotics of the Passion Narrative* (1971; trans. 1980); *Utopics: Spatial Play* (1973; trans. 1984); *Portrait of the King* (1981; trans. 1988); and *Food for Thought* (1986; trans. 1989).

"Disneyland: A Degenerate Utopia" (1977) is based on the study of utopias that he conducted in *Utopics: Spatial Play*. In his book Marin looked at utopia from the meaning suggested by its etymology: Greek *ou,* "no," + Greek *topos,* "place." In contemporary usage utopia is something in which we find (or construct) an unlikely state of perfection. However, this involves a contradiction between utopia as a place and its self-proclaimed "no-place" neutrality, a contradiction that Marin seizes by asking: "Is it possible to dispel the contradiction in utopia without destroying utopia as well?" In the essay here Marin focuses his attention on popular culture and examines a utopian prototype of American cultural life: the amusement park. Taking Disneyland as his model, Marin shows that such modern-day theme parks have a function that runs much deeper than mere amusement: such utopian playgrounds negate historical and social reality through the representation of opposites. In this case the opposite of contemporary history is transcendental fantasy, or Disneyland.

The first objective of the essay is to illustrate the function and the permanence of utopian spaces through the "critical power" that they possess—the ability to represent *"differences* between social reality" and the ideal. In other words, what Disneyland does for us, says Marin, is reverse the content of a perception, show us how *unlike* utopia our world really is. This function, the ability to call attention to something by representing its opposite, is what Marin calls "metadiscourse," a form of critique that substitutes a practical activity (reading a map of Disneyland) for an ideological one (indulging the Disney fantasy). The second objective of the essay is to show how utopias undermine historical awareness, how they relegate meaning to the sphere of "entertainment," myth or fantasy. The dominant culture, says Marin, prevents our experience of Disneyland from having any meaningful relation to the culture on which it is based, and instead dissolves knowledge into "fantasmic projections." These "fantasmic projections" are meant to amuse us; they are not to be taken seriously. To see beyond the fantasyland shrouded in the euphoria of the fantastic, we must become "liberated from [utopia's] fascinating grasp." To fail to do this is to be alienated from one's own history, transported to a "no-place" where we become the actors of a mythic drama on the stage of Fantasyland.

# Disneyland: A Degenerate Utopia

MY REFLECTION on utopia was provoked by fascination with the signifier Ou-topia in which "something" was inscribed by Thomas More on a geographical chart: a name given by him at the beginning of the sixteenth century to a blessed island *between* England and America, *between* the Old and the New World.

The name Utopia is obviously written, through its Greek etymology, as a geographical referent; simultaneously in this writing, in this name, a play on words is also evident: Ou-topia is also Eu-topia, a play on words written by More in the margins of his book entitled *Utopia*. Sometimes, if not always, edges and borders have the precise and concealed function of indicating the center. Outopia can be written Eutopia by substitution of the first letters of the two words. I shall analyze such a play on words, through the play on spaces, as the core of the matrix of utopia. This play on words is also a play on letters which may be read as an indication of the utopian question: Nowhere, or the place of happiness.

Let me say, and this is my first step in another path toward utopia—a path leading my reading astray, a perverted path—that the topographical, political, social spaces articulated by the utopian text *play,* they shrink and swell, they warp, they do not fit exactly together: there are empty places between these spaces. The discourse held on utopia attempts, through the constructed reading of the text, to make the spaces signified by the utopian text coherent and consistent by filling them up with its own signifying substance. When the discourse on utopia dismantles the parts of the utopian totality in order to explain how utopia is functioning, it prohibits the utopian text to play. The quasi-system of the utopian construction becomes, by this metadiscourse, a real system, a structured whole where space no longer plays. This is the essential critique I make of my former study of utopia.[1] It did not leave the text playing and the only way to restore the utopian text is to displace its inconsistencies, its deficiencies, and its excesses, its quasi-system toward mere fantasy, mere ludicity, to take our pleasure without speculative or practical interest in order to inquire ultimately into the nature of the instantaneous manifestation of this pleasure.

I might say that, in my first attempts on utopia, I tried to formalize what its name indicates—*ou-topia,* no-where—with the notion of "neutrality" which was also approached by Blanchot and Derrida. Such a notion does not concern origin and *telos;* the question is not that of the neutrality of the institutionalized power, be this power that of the dominant truth. What is in question is not this imaginary representation where utopia unfolds its architectural perfection by fulfilling its wish of escaping the historical determinations. Neutral is the name given to limits, to contradiction itself. It seems that the fate of all theoretical knowledge and of the practice which derives from it is to dissolve contradiction, to solve it in a change that neutralizes it by overtaking it, a change by which the whole reconstitutes itself, in its identity, on every synthetic level it reaches. So the traces of contradiction, of differentiation are nothing else than the determinations of the totality which capitalizes them as its properties. All forms of dialectical thinking and knowledge are apparent in this description.

Is it possible to think of and to formulate the contradiction signified by that notion of neutral? And to keep it working? I try to discern in the utopian texts the traces of contradiction as its *fiction,* opposed to concept or image. Being such a fiction, utopia transforms contradiction into a representation and, in its turn, my own discourse about utopia transformed it into theory. A reading authority, an interpretive power settled down in the nowhere of the limits, occupied this noplace, possessed it in the name of truth, repeating the gesture already accomplished by utopia itself which endlessly recuperates the unbearable neutral with a logic joining together the contradictory terms. To take a paradigmatic example in More's *Utopia* at the very moment when wealth and poverty are negated—utopia is neither rich nor poor—More creates the harmonious image or representation of a society which is at the same time rich and poor, rich to corrupt and dominate its imaginary outside, poor to maintain virtue and to build with its citizens the ethicoreligious monument of the State.

Moreover, a discourse on utopia can formulate the critical analysis of More's *Utopia* and discern, in the synoptic and totalizing image derived from the esthetic *affabulation,* the power of a scheme of pure imagination, to use Kantian language, and in the matrix of that scheme, the communication between concept and history. Without any doubt, a discourse on utopia can attempt to display the "vertical" relationships, formulated in terms of misreading and recognition, which allow the levels of the utopian text to generate each other and to sketch what Lyotard has called a figure in the discourse.[2] A figurative

mode of discourse, utopia as the textual product of utopian practice or fiction is produced, in its turn, by the critical discourse as a possible synthesis of an historical contradiction. The critical-theoretical discourse will show, but always *post festum,* how a representation can have been produced from the negation of contemporary history; history that is the absent referent of the utopian representation. The utopian representation denotes a reality which is not signified by the utopian figure, but whose true signified is the critical discourse given at the end of the representation's own historical time.

To be effective, such a critical discourse on utopia has to lean back against the wall, (the thesis) of a final truth of history, a place from which it is formulated. But what would happen to its authority if the wall cracks and splits?

In other words and to conclude this introduction, I might say that in describing the utopian space in a critical way, my theoretical discourse was formulated in terms of a topic and its fabricated utopian figure consisted in making coherent the spatial inconsistencies which the utopian image structured as a whole. I would not emphasize the topic of the utopian fantasy, which is also a fantasmatic topic since the theoretical discourse about utopia operates (like in dreams, the screen memory) by filling up the gaps and the blanks of the utopian text, of the utopian space, by producing the systematic elements which are necessary to make the text intelligible. This production was possible only *après coup,* in a site supposed to be the true knowledge of the end of history that is the end of utopia as well. The topic of utopian fantasy as well as the fantasmatic topic of the critical-theoretical discourse on utopia rest on that basis.

In trying to analyse Disneyland as a utopian space, I aim at two targets. [A more detailed version of this analysis originally appeared in *Utopiques, jeux d'espaces.*—Eds.] First, I mean to show the permanence of some patterns of spatial organization which the history of ideas and myths allows us to call utopian. We find these patterns in the architectural schemes and the texts which can roughly be viewed as utopian, but which also fill a specific function with regard to reality, history, and social relationships. This function is a critical one: it shows, through the picture drawn by the utopian writer or designer, the *différences* between social reality and a projected model of social existence. But the utopian representation possesses this critical power without being aware of it; that is, unconsciously. In a sense, I apply to utopian texts (or spaces) what has been suggested by Lévi-Strauss' methodology of distinguishing models—the conscious representation built by societies to explain and legitimate their specific existences—and structures—the "unconscious" set of transformations that the anthropologist's analysis displays in the models themselves. The critical impact of utopia is not the fact of the model itself, but the differences between the model and reality; these differences being exhibited by the utopian picture. But this critical discourse, which is a latent characteristic of all utopias, is not separated from dominant systems of ideas and values: it expresses itself through the structures, the vocabulary of those systems by which individuals, a social class, decision-making groups represent the real conditions of their existence. It is this latent critique which is unfolded, *post-festum,* by a theory of society, a metadiscourse which, generally speaking, substitutes a rational understanding of the social reality for what it considers to be an ideological system of representation. Utopia is a social theory, the discourse of which has not yet attained theoretical status. In other words, utopia expresses a "possible" intervention of reason in the social field, but a "possible" which remains possible. Utopia is the real, iconic, or textual picture of this

"possible." Therefore, utopia has a two-sided nature. On the one hand, it expresses what is absolutely new, the "possible as such," what is unthinkable in the common categories of thought used by the peoples of a given time in its history. So it employs fiction, fable to say what it has to say. On the other hand, utopia cannot transcend the common and ordinary language of a period and of a place. It cannot transgress completely the codes by which people make reality significant, by which they interpret reality, that is, the systems of representation of signs, symbols, and values which recreate, as significant for them, the real conditions of their existence. So Disneyland shows us the structure and the functions of utopia in its real topography and through its use by the visitor. From this vantage point, the possible tour which the visitor commences when he comes to Disneyland can be viewed as the narrative which characterizes utopia. The map of Disneyland he buys in order to know how to go from one place to another can play the role of the description; it performs the part of the representational picture which also characterizes utopia.

But Disneyland is more interesting from another point of view which is the second aim of our analysis: to show how a utopian structure and utopian functions degenerate, how the utopian representation can be entirely caught in a dominant system of ideas and values and, thus, be changed into a myth or a collective fantasy. Disneyland is the representation realized in a geographical space of the imaginary relationship which the dominant groups of American society maintain with their real conditions of existence or, more precisely, with the real history of the United States and with the space outside of its borders. Disneyland is a fantasmatic projection of the history of the American nation, of the way in which this history was conceived with regard to other peoples and to the natural world. Disneyland is an immense and displaced metaphor of the system of representations and values unique to American society.[3]

This projection has the precise function of alienating the visitor by a distorted and fantasmatic representation of daily life, by a fascinating picture of the past and the future, of what is estranged and what is familiar: comfort, welfare, consumption, scientific and technological progress, superpower, and morality. But this projection no longer has its critical impact: yes, to be sure, all the forms of alienation are represented in Disneyland, and we could believe Disneyland is the stage of these representations thanks to which they are known as such and called into critical question. But, in fact, this critical process is not possible in Disneyland in so far as the visitor to Disneyland is not a spectator estranged from the show, distanced from the myth, and liberated from its fascinating grasp. The visitor is on the stage; he performs the play; he is alienated by his part without being aware of performing a part. In "performing" Disney's utopia, the visitor realizes the models and the paradigms of his society in the mythical story by which he imagines his social community has been constructed.

## THE LIMIT

One of the most notable features of the utopian picture is its limit: the utopian discourse inscribes the utopian representation in the imaginary space of a map, but at the same time, it makes this inscription in a geographical map impossible. We can make the survey of the blessed island described by Thomas More, but we cannot draw the geographical map in which this survey could take place. The utopian land belongs to "our world," but there is an insuperable gap between our world and utopia. More has given the paradigmatic example of this distance; he explains that when someone asked Raphael: "Where is the island of Utopia?" Raphael gave

the precise information, but his words were hidden by a servant's cough. This mark in the discourse ironically designates the figurative process by signifying one of the conditions of the possibility of representation: it is a semiotic transposition of the frame of a painting.

This gap is a neutral space, the place of the limit between reality and utopia: by this distance which is a zero-point, utopia appears to be not a world beyond, but the reverse side of this world.

In Disneyland, the neutral space of the limit is displayed by three places, each of these having a precise function. (1) The outer limit is the parking area, an open, unlimited space, weakly structured by the geometrical net of the parking lot. The parking area, where the visitor leaves his car, is the limit of the space of his daily life of which the car is one of the most powerful markers. The fact of leaving his car is an over determined sign of a codical change; for pragmatic utility, for his adjustment to a certain system of signs and behavior, the visitor substitutes another system of signs and behaviors, the system of playful symbols, the free field of consumption for nothing, the *passeist* and aleatory tour in the show. (2) The intermediary limit is lineal and discontinuous: the row of booths where a monetary substitution takes place. With his money, the visitor buys the Disneyland money, the tickets which allow him to participate in the Disneyland life. Thus, the Disneyland money is less a money than a language; with his real money the visitor buys the signs of the Disneyland vocabulary thanks to which he can perform his part, utter his "speech" or his individual narrative, take his tour in Disneyland. The amount of the exchange of real money for utopian signs determines the importance of his visit, the semantic volume of his tour, the number and the nature of its entertainments, in other words, it indirectly determines the number of syntactic rules which can be set working to coordinate the different signifying units. For example, with six dollars (four years ago), I received ten utopian signs—one A, one B, two C, three D, three E—and I was able to give utterance to a series of alternative narratives. (3) The inner limit is circular, linear, continuous, and articulated. It is the embankment of the Sante Fe and Disneyland Railway with its stations. This last limit is not a border line for the visitor or the "performer," since he does not necessarily use the train to go into Disneyland, but it is a limit for the utopian space which is encircled and closed by it. This limit belongs to the picture, to the representation, or to the map more than it appears as a limit to the traveller and to the tour he takes in the land. When he passes beyond the embankment, he is definitely in Disneyland. What I mean is that this element, the Railway, is a limit *in the map* for a dominant, all seeing eye; it is not a limit for the visitor, the consumer, or performer of Disneyland; it is the first of the entertainments which he can consume. But, in fact, without being aware of it, the visitor is forced to spell the vocabulary in the right order. In other words, this structure which belongs to the map is a concealed *rule* of behavior for the visitor.

## THE ACCESS TO THE CENTER

Disneyland is a centered space. Main Street USA leads the visitor to the center. But this route toward the central plaza is also the way toward Fantasyland, one of the four districts of Disneyland. So the most obvious axis of Disney's utopia leads the visitor not only from the circular limit or perimeter to the core of the closed space, but also from reality to fantasy. This fantasy is the trademark, the sign, the symbolic image of Disney's utopia. Fantasyland is made up of images, characters, animals of the tales illustrated by Disney in his animated films, magazines, books, and so on. This district is constituted by images; of particular significance is the fact that these im-

ages are realized, are made living by their transformation into real materials, wood, stone, plaster . . . and through their animation by men and women disguised as movie or storybook characters. Image is duplicated by reality in two opposite senses: on the one hand, it becomes real, but on the other, reality is changed into image, is grasped by the "imaginary." Thus, the visitor who has left reality outside finds it again, but as a real *"imaginaire";* a fixed, stereotyped, powerful fantasy. The utopian place to which Main Street USA leads is the fantasmatic return of reality, its hallucinatory presence. This coming back of reality as a fantasy, as an hallucinatory wish-fulfillment, is in fact mediated by a complete system of representations elaborated by Walt Disney which constitutes a rhetorical and iconic code and vocabulary that have been perfectly mastered by the visitor-performer. So this coming back appears to be brought about through a secondary process which is not only the stuff of images and representations molded by wish, but which constitutes the very actuality of the fantasy where wish is caught in its snare. That snare is the collective, totalitarian form taken by the *"imaginaire"* of a society, blocked by its specular self-image. One of the essential functions of the utopian image is to make apparent a wish in a *free* image of itself, in an image which can play in opposition to the fantasy which is an inert, blocked, and recurrent image. Disneyland is on the side of the fantasy and not on that of a free or utopian representation.

Main Street USA is the way of access to the center, to begin the visitor's tour, to narrate his story, to perform his speech. From the center, he can articulate the successive sequences of his narrative by means of the signs he has received in exchange for his money at the entrance. If we consider Disneyland as a text, Main Street USA is the channel of transmission of the story narrated by the visitor in making his tour. It allows him to communicate. Its function is phatic: it is the most primitive function of the communication since it only permits communication to take place without communicating anything. Thus, Disneyland can be viewed as thousands and thousands of narratives uttered by the visitors. Its text is constituted by this plurality of "lexies," to speak like Barthes, which are exchanged endlessly by the visitors according to the codes (vocabulary and syntax) imposed by the makers of Disneyland.

Now this semiotic function, the condition of possibility of all the messages, all the tours, all the stories told by the visitors, is taken into account structurally in a "lexie" belonging to a superior level, in the diagrammatic scheme of all the possible tours, an open and yet finite totality, the Disneyland map. When we look at this map (figure 18.1), we acknowledge a feature which we do not perceive when we recite the story in passing from the entrance to the center: the fact that Main Street USA is not only a street, but a "district,"

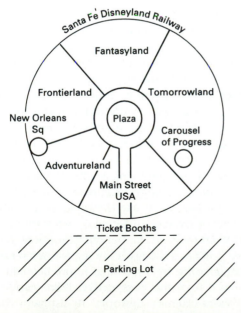

**FIGURE 18.1** Disneyland Diagram

a land which separates and links Frontierland and Adventureland on the one hand, and Tomorrowland on the other. For the visitor-performer, Main Street USA is an axis which allows him to begin to tell his story. For the spectator, it is a place in the map which articulates two worlds; this place makes him look at the relations and at the differences between these worlds. But as a route to Fantasyland, it is the axis of the founding principle of Disneyland.

We can sum up this analysis in the following terms: Main Street USA is a universal operator which articulates and builds up the text of Disneyland on all of its levels. We have discovered three functions of this operator, (1) *phatic:* it allows all the possible stories to be narrated; (2) *referential:* through it, reality becomes a fantasy and an image, a reality; (3) *integrative:* it is the space which divides Disneyland into two parts, left and right, and which relates these two parts to each other. It is at the same time a condition by which the space takes on meaning for the viewer and a condition by which the space can be narrated by the visitor (the actor). These three functions are filled up by a semantic content. Main Street USA is the place where the visitor can buy, in a nineteenth-century American decor, actual and real commodities with his real, actual money. Locus of exchange of meanings and symbols in the imaginary land of Disney, Main Street USA is also the real place of exchange of money and commodity. It is the locus of the societal truth—consumption—which is the truth for all of Disneyland. With Main Street USA, we have a part of the whole which is as good as the whole, which is equivalent to the whole. The fact that this place is also an evocation of the past is an attempt to reconcile or to exchange, in the space occupied by Main Street USA, the past and the present, that is, an ideal past and a real present. *USA Today* appears to be the *term referred to and represented;* it is the term through which all the contrary poles of the structure are exchanged, in the semantic and economic meanings of the term, or, in other words, through which they are fictively reconciled. And by his narrative, the visitor performs, enacts reconciliation. This is the mythical aspect of Disneyland.

## DISNEYLAND'S WORLDS: FROM THE NARRATIVE TO THE SYSTEM OF READINGS

Let us now leave the narrator-visitor and his *énonciation* to the hazards of his possible tours. As we have seen, the syntax of his "discourse-tour" is defined first by his passing through the limits and by his journey to the center. The visitor has learned the codes of the language of Disneyland and has thus been given the possibilities to tell his individual story. Yet, his freedom, the freedom of his *parole* (his tour) is constrained not only by these codes but also by the representation of an imaginary history. This imaginary history is contained in a stereotyped system of representations. In order to utter his own story, the visitor is forced to borrow these representations. He is manipulated by the system, even when he seems to freely choose his tour. Now these remarks allow us to substitute the analysis of the map for a possible narrative and for its performative narration; the analysis of the map or the description not of a *parcours* in time (which is always a narrative) but of a picture, the parts of which coexist in the space of the analogue-model. Methodologically, we assume that the narrative tours constitute a total system and that the map is the structure of this total system. But we have had to justify this substitution by ascertaining that the possible tours in Disneyland are absolutely constrained by the codes which the visitors are given. The interplay of the codes is reduced to nothing. In a real town, in an actual house, there are some codes constraining the freedom or the randomness of the

individual routes or passageways, but these codes do not inform the totality of the messages emitted by the inhabitants of the town or the house. By *realizing* a pure model, that is, by making an "abstract" model a reality, the makers of Disneyland have excluded any possibility of code interference, of code interplay. Not only are the different possible tours strictly determined, but the map of Disneyland can be substituted for a visit. In other words, Disneyland is an example of a *langue* reduced to a univocal code, without *parole*, even though its visitors have the feeling of living a personal and unique adventure on their tour. And since this *langue* is a stereotyped fantasy, the visitor is caught in it, without any opportunity to escape. This can be a definition of an ideological conditioning, or of a collective neurosis. But Disneyland provides us with a valuable lesson. If the substitution of the map for the narrative is somehow a necessary condition of the analysis of a town, a house, etc., we must remember not to jumble together the narrative processes by which people live, thus consuming their town or their house and the textual system which gives them the signs, the symbols, and the syntactic rules through which they display and perform these narrative processes. An architectural set is at the same time a set of places, routes, and pathways and a visible, "spectacular" totality. From this point of view, a progressive architecture seems to me to be defined as an attempt to build up a totality in which different codes are competing, are in conflict, are not coherent, in order to give to people living in this totality, and consuming it, an opportunity to perform their specific *parole,* to use the town as a multi-coded or overcoded totality, codes subverting each other to the benefit of a poetic *parole.* I mean a totality allowing for behaviors characterized by a factor of unpredictability. Viewed from this perspective, Disneyland is an extra-ordinary dystopia. It displaces the spatial habitability, what we have called its

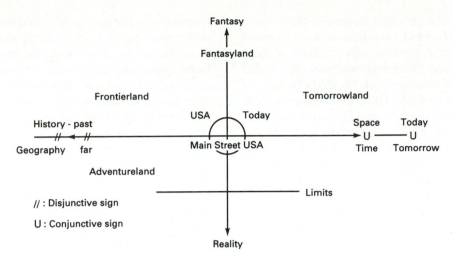

**FIGURE 18.2**   Semantic Structure of the Map

narrativity, into its spectacular representation; it reduces the dynamic organization of the places, the aleatory unity of a possible tour to a univocal scheme allowing only the same redundant behavior. So we are justified in viewing the map of Disneyland as an analogue-model which assimilates the possible narratives of its space.

On the left of the map, two districts: Adventureland and Frontierland. The first is the representation of scenes of wildlife in exotic countries which are viewed during a boat trip on a tropical river. The second is the representation of scenes of the final conquest of the West. The latter district signifies the temporal distance of the past history of the American nation, the former, the spatial distance of the outside geographical world, the world of natural savagery. The two left districts represent the two distances of history and geography, and distance represented inside America in the first, and the distance represented outside in the second.

The right of the map is occupied by a single district: Tomorrowland, which consists principally of representations of the Future-as-Space, Einsteinian Time-Space which realizes the harmonious synthesis of the two-dimensional world represented on the left part as time and space, time as historical, national past and space as strange, exotic primitivism. Tomorrowland is space as time, the universe captured by science and technology. In each of the two parts of Disneyland, we find an eccentric center, New Orleans Square on the left and the Carrousel of Progress, a gift of the General Electric Corporation, on the right. We can construct two models which are secondary representations of the map. The first is a purely analogous diagram, the second, a semantic structure (see figures 18.1 and 18.2).

Consideration of the center of these two models elicits the following remarks: (1) The center in the map is not the center in the semantic structure; in other words, the structure is not a simplified map. In the structure, the center is the sign of the numerous semiotic functions of Main Street USA as a route to the mapped center, an axis converting reality into fantasy, and vice versa, and an axis exchanging a scientific and technological conjunction of space and time for the historico-geographical distance.

(2) In the semantic structure, Main Street USA appears to be on different levels, formal and material, semiotic and semantic, a place of *exchange:* exchange of commodities and objects of consumption, but also of significations and symbols. The center of the structure functions at once inside and outside the structure. Inside, it is determined rigorously by the two main correlations of which it is made up—reality and fantasy: historic-geographical distance and space-time. But it is not only an intersecting point of these two semantic axes; somehow it produces them as well. Through it, the contrary poles of the correlations exchange their meaning: reality becomes fantasmatic and fantasy, actual. The remoteness of exotic places and of the American national past becomes the universal space-time of science and technology and this universality becomes American. In the semiotic theory of the narrative, the center is the representation of the dialectical mediation from which springs the narrative solution: it is the image of the inventions determined by the story on its different levels.

(3) It is not without significance that in this case, this image, this representation is named USA and is declined in the present tense. The ultimate meaning of the center is the conversion of history into representation, a conversion by which the utopian space itself is caught in the representation. This representational mediation makes it clear that in the utopian place, commodities are significations and significations are commodities. By the selling of up-to-date consumer goods in the setting of a nineteenth-century street, between the adult reality and the childish fantasy, Walt Disney's utopia converts the commodities into significations. Reciprocally, what is bought there are signs, but these signs are *commodities.*

(4) *The Eccentric Centers:* I shall just describe the Pirates of the Caribbean attraction at the New Orleans Square center, in the left part of the map. This place reveals all of its semantic content only in its narration. So the visitor must begin to speak again in order to recite the underground tour, for the syntagmatic organization of his ride displays a primary and essential level of meaning. The first sequence of the narrative discourse is a place where skulls and skeletons are lying on heaps of gold and silver, diamonds and pearls. Next, the visitor goes through a naval battle in his little boat; then he sees off shore the attack of a town launched by the pirates. In the last sequence, the spoils are piled up in the pirate ships, the visitor is cheered by pirates feasting and revelling; and his tour is concluded. The narrative unfolds its moments in a reverse chronological order; the first scene in the tour-narrative is the last scene in the "real" story. And this inversion has an ethical meaning: crime does not pay. The morality of the fable is presented before the reading of the story in order to constrain the comprehension of the fable by a preexisting moral code. The potential force of the narrative, its unpredictability, is neutralized by the moral code which makes up all of the representation. But if we introduce the story into the structural scheme of the map and especially if we do so by relating it to the structural center, another meaning appears beneath the moral signification. The center, you remember, is a place of exchange of actual products and commodities of *today:* it is a marketplace and a place of consumption. Correlated to the eccentric center of the left part, Main Street USA signifies to the visitor that life is an endless exchange and a constant consumption and, reciprocally, that the feudal accumulation of riches, the Spanish hoarding of treasure, the Old World conception of gold and money are not only morally criminal, but they are, economically, signs and symptoms of death. The treasure buried in the ground is a dead thing, a corpse. The commodity produced and sold is a living good because it can be consumed.

I do not want to overemphasize this point;

but in Tomorrowland, on the right side of the map, the same meaning is made obvious by another eccentric center, the Carrousel of Progress. Here, the visitor becomes a spectator, immobilized and passive, seated in front of a circular and moving stage which shows him successive scenes taken from family life in the nineteenth century, the beginning of the twentieth century, today, and tomorrow. It is the *same* family that is presented in these different historical periods; the story of this "permanent" family is told to visitors who no longer narrate their own story. History is neutralized; the scenes only change in relation to the increasing quantity of electric implements, the increasing sophistication of the utensil-dominated human environment. The individual is shown to be progressively mastered, dominated by utensility. The scenic symbols of wealth are constructed by the number and variety of the means and tools of consumption, that is, by the quantity and variation of the technical and scientific mediations of consumption. The circular motion of the stage expresses this endless technological progress, as well as its necessity, its fate. And the specific organization of the space of representation symbolizes the passive satisfaction of endlessly increasing needs.

So the eccentric centers have powerful meaning-effects on Disneyland as a totality and on its districts.

We shall conclude our analysis with the following brief remarks. The left side of the map illustrates both the culture supplied by Americans to nineteenth-century America, and the one produced, at the same time, by adult, civilized, male, white people in exotic and remote countries. The living beings of Adventureland and Frontierland are only reproductions of reality. All that is living is an artifact; Nature is a simulacrum. Nature is a wild, primitive, savage world, but this world is only the appearance taken on by the machine in the utopian play. In other words, what is signified by the left part of the map is

this assumption that the Machine is the truth, the actuality of the living. Mechanism and a mechanistic conception of the world, which are basic tenets of the utopian mode of thinking from the sixteenth century until today, are at work in Disneyland, no longer as a form of knowledge but as a disguised apparatus which can be taken for its contrary, the natural life.

On the right side of the map, the underlying truth of the left side becomes obvious. In Tomorrowland, machines are everywhere: from the atomic submarine to the moon rocket. The concealed meaning of the left side is now revealed thanks to the mediating center, Main Street USA. But these machines are neither true nor false; they are not, as in the left part, false reproductions. Instead, they are scaled-down models of the actual machines. We have false duplicates of living beings and concealed mechanistic springs on the left, obvious machines and true models on the right. Real nature is an appearance and the reduced model of the machine is reality. The ideology of representation and machine is all-pervading, and man is twice removed from Nature and science. Nature, which he sees, is a representation, the reverse side of which is a machine. Machines that he uses and with which he sometimes plays are the reduced models of a machinery which seizes him and which plays with him.

We find the same function of the reduced models, but on a different plane, in Fantasyland. This district is constituted by the real-realized images of the tales animated by Walt Disney. Fantasyland is the return of reality in a regressive and hallucinatory form. This imaginary *real* is a reproduction of the scenes the visitor has seen in the pirates' cave; but it is a regressive reproduction on a tiny and childish scale. We find the same fantasies of death, superpower, violence, destruction, and annihilation, but as reduced models of the attractions of the left side. Reduced models like those of Tomorrowland, but reduced

**FIGURE 18.3** Semantic Structure of the Ideological Representation in Disneyland Utopia

models of death, strangeness, exoticism in the imaginary; they are the opposite of the reduced models of the right side, which show life, consumption, and techniques in their images. The realm of the Living in life-size is the realm of natural appearance in its historical past or geographical, anthropological remoteness. The realm of the Machine as a reduced model is the cultural truth of the American way of life, here and now, looking at itself as a universal way of living.

The function of Disney's utopia is to represent the exchange of the first and second realms of Natural Life and Scientific Technique and to express the ideology of this exchange on the stage and in the decor of utopia. Disneyland's ideological exchange can be illustrated by an elaboration of the semantic structure of the map (see figure 18.3).

Five years ago, I concluded my first visit to Disneyland by making the following statements:

*Axioms:* 1. An ideology is a system of representations of the imaginary relationships which individuals have with their real living conditions.

2. Utopia is an ideological locus: it belongs to the ideological discourse.

3. Utopia is an ideological locus where ideology is put into play and called into question. Utopia is the stage where an ideology is performed or represented.

4. A myth is a narration which fantastically "resolves" a fundamental contradiction in a given society.

*Theorem:* A degenerate utopia is a fragment of the ideological discourse realized in the form of a myth or a collective fantasy.

It seems to me, today, that these statements articulate only one side of the utopian problem, a side that relies on some questionable philosophical presuppositions, as I attempted to show at the beginning of this essay. Perhaps I was not aware five years ago that my own discourse in the past and, in a sense, the paper I publish today are also degenerate utopias, critical myths, theoretical fantasies.

Perhaps I was not fully aware that science, theory have to get out of their Disneylands to discover their utopias.

## NOTES

1. *Utopiques, jeux d'espaces* (Paris: Editions de Minuit, Collection Critique, 1973).

2. See Jean-François Lyotard, *Discours, Figure* (Paris: Klincksieck, 1971).

3. However, today I would be more careful: these statements are perhaps like the statements of an anthropologist visiting his research field for the first time. They may be characteristic of a foreigner reading the "Other" by superimposing upon it his own set of values and notions.

# V

# DECONSTRUCTION AND POSTSTRUCTURALISM

The introduction to "Structuralism and Semiotics" ended with a discussion of Jacques Derrida's "deconstructive" critique of structuralism and a brief look at the Derrida essay, "Structure, Sign, and Play in the Discourse of the Human Sciences." We also discussed how Julia Kristeva examined the critique implicit in the semiotic project. Structuralism and semiotics, as Kristeva and Derrida both suggest, are firmly embedded in the tradition of Western thought and science. Their aim, typical of most Western thought, is to find ways of "understanding" phenomena through models of explanation that offer *coherent* pictures of the order of things, a picture that embodies what Michel Foucault calls a "principle of unity," the *self-consistency* we mentioned in the introduction to "What Is Literary Theory?" As Jonathan Culler says in his discussion of the relation between Derrida and the English philosopher J. L. Austin, the aim of understanding is to find a way to present and master the context of whatever is to be understood. "Meaning," Culler writes, "is context-bound." In Part VIII, "Feminism and Gender Studies," Gayatri Chakravorty Spivak treads closely to the limits of self-consistency and coherence in the repeated changes on the context of discourse in "Feminism and Critical Theory," and much of the criticism that John Searle directs at Derrida in the controversy that Culler recounts can be understood as a criticism of Derrida's questioning of the assumptions of "common-sense" limits and *definitions* (i.e., "delimitations") that allow understanding.

The overall aim of *post*-structuralism and deconstructive "critique" is different from the rigorous and "scientific" analyses of structuralism. Instead of attempting to account for how things are, their order, deconstruction and poststructualism aim at describing the limits of understanding in terms of such various factors as the intellectual assumptions that allow limits and definitions to be assumed, the social relationships of power that are served by these definitions, individual and "subjective" ends that are served, and other such matters. As J. Hillis Miller says in "The Search for Grounds in Literary Study" (in "What Is Literary Theory?"), "the fundamental sense of [deconstructive] 'critique' [is] discriminating [and] testing out." That is, deconstructive critique examines and tests the assumptions supporting intellectual insight to interrogate the "self-evident" truths on which they are based. It tests the legitimacy of the contextual "bounds" (or "definitions") that understanding both presents and requires. Rather than seeking a way of "understanding"—that is, a way of incorporating new phenomena into coherent (i.e., "bounded") existing or modified models—a deconstructive critique seeks to undercover the unexamined axioms that give rise to those models and their boundaries.

## DECONSTRUCTION

"Deconstruction" is an important mode of the kind of "critique" we described in the introduction to "What Is Literary Theory?" It was named in the sixties by Jacques Derrida, who in 1967 began to describe certain events he saw taking place in the history of philosophy, that is, events in Western modes of conceiving and articulating knowledge. In sweeping analyses Derrida noted that traditional embodiments of legitimate authority have traditionally been taken to be self-evident in their absolute "rightness," as is the case with concepts such as "goodness," "naturalness," "reason," and "truth." The same is true of more abstract versions of authority such as (in Derrida's examples) *"aletheia,* transcendentality, consciousness, or conscience, God, man, and so forth"—all assumed in the West to be self-evident givens of understanding and, therefore, "correct." He also noted that such concepts are necessarily defined in relation to their opposites. Further, Derrida explained in "Sign, Structure, and Play," authority in the West is generally conceived as existing in a structure and thought to be the precise *center* "at which the substitution of contents, elements, or terms is no longer possible." "It has always been thought," Derrida wrote, "that [this] center, which is by definition unique, constituted that very thing within a structure which governs the structure, while escaping structurality." Certain aspects of understanding, in other words, are themselves taken to be self-evidently "true." Thus the concept of "center," or foundation of knowledge, is an epistemologically immovable mover, on which structures and hierarchies of belief or understanding have been thought to be based or securely "centered."

One version of this "center," Derrida argues in "The Principle of Reason," is the Enlightenment conception of reason as the *ground* of understanding. However, Derrida has focused on many other "central" concepts as well: the self-evidence of speech, the simple humanity of "man" (as opposed to gendered individuals), the solidity of "seriousness" (as opposed to playfulness), the profundity of "philosophy" (as opposed to literature), and the basic category of "nature" (as opposed to culture). Throughout his career Derrida has attempted to "deconstruct" the self-evidence of such concepts, to subject the very basic assumptions governing the apprehension of knowledge to critical analysis. That attempt involves demonstrating the local and historical nature of seemingly universal concepts. The word "deconstruction" itself is Derrida's coinage in response to the philosopher Martin Heidegger's idea of "destructive" analysis, the attempt to introduce time as a decisive element of the way we understand the world. In the same way that time inevitably upsets and reshapes any human scheme of understanding, so too are—as Derrida shows—meanings and values, by their very nature, so mutually interdependent in *local* systems of thought that they continually destabilize each other and even themselves. This is why Derrida is at such pains to demonstrate that even "reason" itself has a history, and that history also involves its seeming opposite, irrationality: "the theme of extravagance as an irrationalism," he writes, ". . . dates from the period when the principle of reason was being formulated," the Enlightenment period of Leibniz and Kant.

Deconstruction is a "concept"—though Derrida would say, as he does of his neologism *différance,* it is "neither a word nor a concept"—that focuses on this instability of meaning. However, by "instability" it does not suggest that there are *no* meanings (as many of its critics argue), but rather that meaning is historical, local, and subject to change. The principle of reason, for instance, is a powerful local concept defined, as it was by Kant, as the opposite of "applied" reason (or technology) that, as Derrida says, "we can no longer dissociate . . . from the very idea of technology." Deconstruction rises out of Derrida's recognition that in modern conceptions of knowledge there is a temporal "decentering" or a "rupture" in the conventional order—the secular, liberal-humanist Enlightenment order that began in the West in the seventeenth and eighteenth centuries (which Michel Foucault mentions as decisive moments in the history of the concept of "author"). That order is based (or "grounded") on reason, which is why "The Principle of Reason," as Christopher Norris suggests, is so important. Derrida records or enacts a dramatic and decisive shift in this traditional, "rational," humane relation to authority, what might be termed a radical challenge to all authority. That is, the Western mind has learned to accept authority only by positing its underlying basis—what both Derrida and Miller ("What Is Literary Theory?") describe as its "ground"—around or on which that "authority" is founded and beyond which one cannot go.

The opposite of reason, as it is found in René Descartes at the beginning of the Enlightenment, Ernest Gellner has recently argued, is "culture." For Descartes, he argues, "liberation from error requires liberation from culture, from 'example and custom' as he calls it." Enlightenment reason—and the "liberal humanism" Catherine Belsey describes and to which reason gives rise—aims at *universalizing* understanding by detaching it from the particular and local historical contexts in which it arises, the very "custom" and "tradition" to which Descartes opposes reason. Similarly, Enlightenment understanding is *individualized*. As Gellner says, Enlightenment rationalism is "profoundly individualist." Whatever is "collective," as well as whatever is "customary," "is non-rational, and the overcoming of unreason and of collective custom are one and the same process." Enlightenment rationalism posits a unitary *subject* of reason who participates in *universal* and *transhistorical* truths. Such a rational subject is, in fact, universal. As Samuel Johnson says, reason itself is always the same so that even the Creator is subject to its power: "it is no limitation on omnipotence," he wrote in *Rasselas* in 1759, "to suppose that one thing is not consistent with another, that the same proposition cannot be at once true and false, that the same number cannot be even and odd, that cogitation cannot be conferred on that which is created incapable of cogitation." Moreover, even feeling comes within the compass of Enlightenment reason. As Terry Eagleton has argued, the same forces in the Enlightenment that gave rise to rationality and liberal humanism also gave rise to philosophical aesthetics in the eighteenth century. (See the discussion of aesthetics in the introduction to "What Is Literary Theory?") In fact, when Paul de Man suggests that persuasion by proof—that is, by *rational* argument—is a form of rhetoric in "The Resistance to Theory"—he is "deconstructing" the opposition between reason and feeling, showing them to "rise" out of the same local conditions.

The opposite to the Enlightenment "order" of reason is the order of culture, which is historical and collective. Another "opposite" to this order is the irrationalism Derrida mentions that arose with rationalism in the seventeenth and eighteenth centuries or the philosophy of feeling Eagleton traces in aesthetics. This is why the deconstructive critique of Enlightenment reason—and Derrida, among others, has important discussions of Leibniz, Kant, Rousseau, and other figures of the eighteenth century—focuses so often on the local nature of seemingly universal ideas. In this way the investigation or "interrogation" of deconstructive critique reveals an underlying "authority" (or "center" or "ground") beneath or temporally prior to the present authority, and so on.

In Derrida's critique of Kant, it is the valorization of the "objectivity" of reason and the self-evidence of its "representations" beneath Kant's attempt to demonstrate the priority of "pure" over "applied" science. In this regress of certainty and absolute reference points, modern thought—especially in the nineteenth and twentieth centuries—brings about a depreciation, or displacement, of conventional cultural references, of notions such as "truth," "objectivity," and so on. This "decentering," in other words, deeply undercuts or destroys notions of self-evident and absolute grounds in knowledge. In short, as Nietzsche said, God, or any absolute reference point, really does "die" (does become "decentered") for the modern world. Accordingly, there is the recognition in modern thought of what Derrida calls the "structurality of structure" in "Structure, Sign, and Play" and of what he describes in "The Principle of Reason" as the special status of sight, the fact that "theory" is closely linked to visual contemplation. Such contemplation presents as self-evident the equation of knowledge and *spatial structures,* knowledge conceived as ideal "form" beginning with Plato and Aristotle. Among other things Derrida wants to suggest that this is ultimately problematic and "undecidable," that we can also think about knowledge, as Heidegger does, in terms of apostrophe and hearing.

## DECONSTRUCTIVE CRITICISM

As it bears on literary criticism, as our allusion to de Man suggests, deconstruction is a *strategy* of reading. Derrida describes deconstructive reading as starting from a philosophical hierarchy in which two opposed terms are presented as the "superior" general case and the "inferior" special case. These oppositions are Western culture's most important categories of thought such as truth/error, health/disease, male/female, nature/culture, philosophy/literature, speech/writing, seriousness/play, and reason/practice. De Man adds the certainties of grammar/the uncertainties of rhetoric to this list; and Jonathan Culler gives the example of language conceived as "constative" (i.e., as essentially a system of true or false meanings) versus language conceived as "performative" (i.e., the actual *activity* of using language). Another example, as much of the feminist criticism in this book suggests, is the generally accepted use of "man" to mean "human" and "woman" to mean only the special case of a female human being. Also, as Belsey argues, we can see yet another example in the opposition between the project of "total explicitness, total verisimilitude in the interests of a plea for scientificity" embodied not only in the methods of Sherlock Holmes but in literary "realism" more generally, as opposed to the "shadowy, mysterious and often silent women" that "haunt" the Holmes detective stories.

Deconstruction isolates such oppositions and points out that they are indeed *hierarchically* opposed, general to special case. It then reverses such crucial hierarchies to elevate the "inferior" over the "superior"—making, as Culler says, "the constative a special case of the performative," or reason a "case" of technology. The purpose of these reversals, however, is not merely to invert value systems. Doing so, Derrida says elsewhere, would only "confirm" the old system of opposition that is the object of analysis. Rather, deconstruction attempts to "explode" (in Derrida's metaphor) the original relationship of "superior" and "inferior" that gives rise to the semantic horizon—the possibility of any particular meaning, the possibility of particular "definitions"—in a discourse. Deconstruction attempts, as Derrida says in "Structure, Sign, and Play," to confront one interpretation "of interpretation, of structure, of sign, of freeplay"—one that seeks "a truth or an origin which is free from freeplay and from the order of the sign"—with another interpretation of interpretation "which is no longer turned toward the origin, [but] affirms freeplay and tries to pass beyond man and humanism." In de Man's terms this second interpretation refuses the specific meanings of grammar for the "suspended" logic and meanings of rhetoric, the "tropological dimension" of language that de Man chooses to call "literature." It refuses the propositional logic of language conceived as constative, information or knowledge as exclusively "true or false," for the open-ended "promises" of performative language. Such a confrontation, though, should not constitute itself into a new hierarchy. Rather, it presents an "undecidability," an inability to choose, an "aporia" in rhetorical terms—the inability to decide how to proceed.

While in de Man such a confrontation remains more or less "rhetorical," it can also create the basis of critique that goes beyond the "institutional" critique of linguistic analysis to "transformative" forms of critique. As Belsey says, "The object of deconstructing the text is to examine the *process of production*—not the private experience of individual authors, but the mode of production, the materials and their arrangement in the work. The aim is to locate the point of contradiction within the text, the point at which it transgresses the limits within which it is constructed, breaks free of the constraints imposed by its own realist form. Composed of contradictions," she concludes, "the text is no longer restricted to a single, harmonious and authoritative reading." Neither, as she argues, is the psychological "subject," the social "experience" (of ideology), or even the canons of positive "science." Each of these things can be shown to be inhabited by "the contrary meanings which are the inevitable condition of its existence as a signifying practice" so that they "are unable to explain an area which none the less they cannot ignore." Such moments of contradiction allow for the possibilities of transformation, as well as of analysis, that inhabit critique.

Before we turn to these possibilities—the "possibilities" of poststructuralism—we can take three issues from Derrida's general theories and specific commentaries that have a direct bearing on literary theory and criticism: textuality, undecidability, and strategy. By textuality, Derrida means largely what the structuralists mean by that term: anything that can be known will be articulated *as a text* within a system of differences—in Saussure's description, *without positive terms*. Consequently, because it is a system without positive terms (i.e., without a "center"), textuality is subject to a certain instability, or undecidability. That is, texts of any sort (social or literary phenomena, for example) will produce meanings, but since the production of meaning cannot be arrested through a relationship with absolute referents (positive terms) or absolutely closed contexts (centers or grounds), textuality will always be in progress and unfinished—thus undecidable. The notion of deconstructive textuality, as de Man, J. Hillis Miller, Barbara Johnson, Shoshana Felman, Gayatri Chakravorty Spivak, and others have shown, is easily applicable in practical criticism. Indeed, in practical criticism the dimension of undecidability separates the structuralist from the deconstructionist version of the text.

Most decisive for deconstructive literary criticism, though, is the issue of deconstructive strategy we have described above, its two strategic "moves." A deconstructive analysis of literature involves reversing and reinscribing the terms of a hierarchy. Such reversal and reinscription are of course playful, but it is a playfulness intended to be radically disruptive—in a way, to institute a kind of nonsense. But however innocuous such a strategy of "non-sense" may seem, Derrida is playful with the "seriousness" of the "new responsibilities" he mentions in "The Principle of Reason": responsibilities toward a "future" created by "new modes of questioning that are also a new relation to language and tradition, a new *affirmation,* and new ways of taking responsibility." This new mode of responsibility includes "play" that is intended to subvert the most fundamental strictures of seriousness and, thus, to displace and "contaminate" the very basis of (Western) authority. (The issue of seriousness is central to Culler's discussion in this section.) It is play, in other words, aimed at producing revolutionary changes in thought. In fact deconstructive play offers a virtual model of the continual revolution (political and intellectual) of critique in its drive to overturn the status quo and then to institute a new order. In this way, as Derrida and other deconstructionists have become more playful, rhetorically and conceptually, they have also become more intent about instituting new practices in writing and thinking.

Such readings of literature can be seen in Belsey's reading of Doyle or Barbara Johnson's reading of poetry. Similarly, Stanley Fish presents a deconstructive reading of "reading" in "Interpreting the *Variorum,"* which is even more playful than de Man's discussion, and both Toril Moi and Shoshana Felman offer "deconstructive" readings of Freud and Lacan. What these readings all do, to different extents, is confront the performances of authors/narrators/texts with their "constative" meanings to exam what is going on in literature. These critics make us confront the two senses of rhetoric discussed in the introduction to "Rhetoric and Reader Response."

Along with this confrontation, deconstruction, as Derrida himself suggests, involves a reversal and reinscription of the usual patterns of interpretation—that is, it examines criticism, as well as literature. In fact one hierarchical opposition that deconstruction has brought into question is the opposition between literature and criticism, "primary" and "secondary" texts, and in this, perhaps more than anywhere else, deconstructive criticism has encountered resistance. Among others, critics who taught and wrote at Yale University during the 1970s (J. Hillis Miller and Geoffrey Hartman along with de Man) attempted to challenge the "superiority" of literature over criticism. De Man, in particular, claims a "literary" status for critique itself—"the key to this critique of metaphysics," he writes in *Allegories of Reading,* ". . . is the rhetorical model of the trope or, if one prefers to call it that, literature"—and claims the essentially "critical" nature of literature.

By conceiving of literature or rhetoric as the site of critique, more or less "deconstructive" strategies, following from Derrida's work, can be seen in many areas of literary criticism. Current psychoanalytic criticism, influenced by Lacan, decenters the traditional Freudian version of the "subject" and is distinctly deconstructive in its practice. Feminism, too, especially in the work of Hélène Cixous, Luce Irigaray, Sarah Kofman, Gayatri Chakravorty Spivak, and Barbara Johnson, uses deconstructive strategies for displacing maleness and "male" readings of literary texts (and Gayatri Spivak even uses deconstructive critique to displace the universalized "female" in feminist criticism). Marxist critics, especially Louis Althusser, Fredric Jameson, John Ellis, Rosalind Coward, and Michael Ryan have found deep affinities between the Marxist and deconstructive critiques of cultural production. All these critics have adopted a deconstructive approach to literary texts and have attempted from different angles to understand the forces that shape and "rupture" those texts. In one sense deconstructive poststructuralism can be said to cover all post-Derridean developments in criticism, including the contemporary rhetoric examined earlier in this book (though it could be plausibly argued—Newton Garver and Richard Rorty have made this argument—that Derrida is the latest example of a long tradition in philosophy that is quintessentially *rhetorical*). It is, in any event, difficult to find the limits of deconstruction's influence. More conservatively, these approaches to literary texts arise from definitions of literature and criticism that have followed from Derrida's ideas about textuality, undecidability, and strategy.

## POSTSTRUCTURALISM

Still, the deconstructive critique of reading can be extended, as "The Principle of Reason" suggests, to Western epistemology as a whole, and this has led to the deconstruction of many institutions of Western culture—that is, it has led to the extension of linguistic and epistemological analyses into areas of actual practice and, thus, to first-hand investigations of the cultural changes originally described in general terms. As we see in Belsey, this has been done extensively with psychoanalysis and literary criticism (especially theories of representation, or mimesis). These studies have proceeded to offer another sense of "poststructuralism" that is equally important; namely, the articulation of a *critique* of deconstruction itself. For, as we have already suggested, the constant danger of deconstruction is that it falls prey to the same hierarchies it attempts to expose. Derrida himself is quite aware of this danger, and his response—really a *rhetorical* response—is recurrently to present "deconstruction" in relation to particular textual practices, those of Lévi-Strauss or Saussure or Austin, and recurrently to articulate that practice in terminology specific to those contexts ("writing" in discussing Saussure, "structure" in relation to Lévi-Strauss, "iteration" in relation to Austin, "render" in relation to reason, etc.). Nevertheless, if deconstruction aims, as does rhetoric, at situating the concepts that are assumed in any particular discourse, then deconstruction can have its own focus on discourse also subject to examination.

In "What Is an Author," Michel Foucault performs this very "post-structuralist" critique. In that essay Foucault examines the *function* of the author-role as a social function, a "position" (like the positions that structural analysis describes). It is not enough "to repeat the empty affirmation that the author has disappeared," Foucault writes. "Instead, we must locate the space left empty by the author's disappearance, follow the distribution of gaps and breaches, and watch for the openings that this disappearance uncovers." In this way Foucault attempts to describe the social and political "role" of the author, the ends it serves as a principle of unity, its links with juridical and institutional systems, its function within different classes, and, finally, its changing nature.

Foucault's essay can be profitably contrasted with Roland Barthes's essay "The Death of the Author" (1968), which is more conventionally a "deconstructive," post-structuralist work. There Barthes argues that in discourse "it is language which speaks, not the author; to write is, through a prerequisite impersonality . . . to reach that point where only language acts, 'performs,' and not 'me.'" In this discussion Barthes hypothesizes "language" rather than situating it; instead of examining the "death" of the author in situated terms related to what Foucault calls the "author-function," he reverses the opposition between author and reader and claims, in a deconstructive gesture of reversal, that it is in "the place of the reader, not . . . the author" that writing exists: "a text's unity lies not in its origin but in its destination." In the second move of deconstruction Barthes explodes this opposition altogether by making the reader and the author equally unrecoverable; "this destination," he adds, "cannot any longer be personal: the reader is without history, biography, or psychology. He is simply that *someone* who holds together in a single field all the traces by which the written text is constituted." However, what Barthes fails to do is precisely what constitutes Foucault's implicit critique: he fails to show what situated function the role of author—or even Barthes's role of reader—serves, how it *works* within the confines of particular discursive practices that are, also, practices of power.

In this essay Foucault is offering an implicit critique of deconstruction that is analogous to the critique of scientific structuralism Kristeva offers or the critique of reader-response criticism Schweickart presents. Like deconstruction itself, Foucault's critique uses the categories of the object of critique to demonstrate its shortcomings. Yet Foucault—unlike Kristeva or Derrida—never makes that critique explicit. Instead, he offers a reading of a cultural and socially defined category, the "author," which Barthes "deconstructs" and both modernist formalism and structuralism erase in their different ways (Eliot in his talk of the "impersonality" of poetry and Lévi-Strauss in his description of structuralism as "Kantianism without a transcendental subject") to show the relationship between discursive social "categories" and practices and strategies of power within culture itself. Such an analysis, as we shall see, offers the possibility, articulated by Stephen Greenblatt in the section on "Historical Critique," of a "new historicism" in literary criticism.

**RELATED ESSAYS IN**
*CONTEMPORARY LITERARY CRITICISM*

Paul de Man, "The Resistance to Theory"
J. Hillis Miller, "The Search for Grounds in Literary Study"

Stanley Fish, "Interpreting the *Variorum*"
Barbara Johnson, "Apostrophe, Animation, and Abortion"
Ferdinand de Saussure, Selections from *Course in General Linguistics*
Toril Moi, "Representation of Patriarchy"
Gayatri Chakravorty Spivak, "Feminism and Critical Theory"

**FURTHER READING**

Arac, Jonathan, et al., *The Yale Critics: Deconstruction in America* (Minneapolis: University of Minnesota Press, 1983).

Barthes, Roland, *S/Z,* trans. Richard Miller (New York: Hill and Wang, 1974).

———, "The Death of the Author," in *Image-Music-Text,* trans. Stephen Heath (New York: Hill and Wang, 1977).

Bloom, Harold, et al., *Deconstruction and Criticism* (New York: Continuum, 1979).

Culler, Jonathan, *On Deconstruction: Theory and Criticism After Structuralism* (Ithaca, NY: Cornell University Press, 1982).

———, *The Pursuit of Signs: Semiotics, Literature, Deconstruction* (Ithaca, NY: Cornell University Press, 1981).

Davis, Robert Con, and Ronald Schleifer, eds., *Rhetoric and Form: Deconstruction at Yale* (Norman: University of Oklahoma Press, 1985).

de Man, Paul, *Allegories of Reading: Figural Language in Rousseau, Nietzsche, Rilke, and Proust* (New Haven: Yale University Press, 1979).

———, *Blindness and Insight: Essays in the Rhetoric of Contemporary Criticism* (Minneapolis: University of Minnesota Press, 1983).

Derrida, Jacques, "Differance," in *Speech and Phenomena, and Other Essays on Husserl's Theory of Signs,* trans. David B. Allison (Evanston, IL: Northwestern University Press, 1973).

———, *Dissemination,* trans. Barbara Johnson (Chicago: University of Chicago Press, 1981).

———, *Of Grammatology,* trans. Gayatri Spivak (Baltimore: Johns Hopkins University Press, 1976).

———, "Structure, Sign, and Play in the Discourse of the Human Sciences," in *The Structuralist Controversy,* eds. Richard Macksey and Eugenio Donato (Baltimore: Johns Hopkins University Press, 1972), 247–272.

———, *Writing and Difference,* trans. Alan Bass (Chicago: University of Chicago Press, 1978).

Eagleton, Terry, *The Ideology of the Aesthetic* (Cambridge, MA: B. Blackwell, 1990).

Eco, Umberto, *A Theory of Semiotics* (Bloomington: Indiana University Press, 1976).

Felman, Shoshana, *The Literary Speech Act: Don Juan with J.L. Austin, or Seduction in Two Languages,* trans. Catherine Porter (Ithaca, NY: Cornell University Press, 1983).

Garver, Newton, "Preface," in Jacques Derrida, *Speech and Phenomena, and Other Essays on Husserl's Theory of Signs,* trans. David B. Allison (Evanston, IL: Northwestern University Press, 1973).

Gasché, Rodolphe, "Deconstruction as Criticism," in *Glyph,* 6 (1979), 177–215.

Harari, Josué, ed., *Textual Strategies: Perspectives in Post-Structuralist Criticism* (Ithaca, NY: Cornell University Press, 1979).

Hartman, Geoffrey H., *Criticism in the Wilderness* (New Haven: Yale University Press, 1980).

Irwin, John T., *American Hieroglyphics* (New Haven: Yale University Press, 1980).

Johnson, Barbara, *The Critical Difference: Essays in the Contemporary Rhetoric of Reading* (Baltimore: Johns Hopkins University Press, 1980).

Leitch, Vincent B., *Deconstructive Criticism: An Advanced Introduction and Survey* (New York: Columbia University Press, 1982).

Norris, Christopher, *Derrida* (Cambridge, MA: Harvard University Press, 1987).

Rorty, Richard, *Consequences of Pragmaticism* (Minneapolis: University of Minnesota Press, 1982).

Ryan, Michael, *Marxism and Deconstruction* (Baltimore: Johns Hopkins University Press, 1982).

Schleifer, Ronald, "Deconstruction and Linguistic Analysis," in *College English,* 49 (1987), 381–95.

# 19

# Jonathan Culler
# 1944–

Born in Ohio in 1944, Jonathan Culler completed his undergraduate degree at Harvard in 1966 and was a Rhodes scholar from 1966 until 1969. He completed his D.Phil. (the British equivalent of the Ph.D.) at Oxford in 1972, and until 1977, when he became professor of English and comparative literature at Cornell University, was a lecturer at Cambridge and Oxford. In 1975, while a visiting professor in French and comparative literature at Yale, Culler received the prestigious James Russell Lowell Prize for his second book, *Structuralist Poetics* (1975). This book is a revised and expanded version of his doctoral dissertation, which was an investigation of contemporary French criticism's theoretical foundations and a discussion of the usefulness of the model of structural linguistics for literary criticism. Culler has also written *Flaubert: The Uses of Uncertainty* (1974); *Saussure* (1976); *Roland Barthes* (1983); *On Deconstruction* (1982); and *Framing the Sign: Criticism and Its Institutions* (1988). He also served as translator for Derrida's *Memoires for Paul de Man* (1986, 1989).

The following article, "Convention and Meaning: Derrida and Austin" (1981) is an excerpt from *On Deconstruction,* where it appears in expanded form as the chapter "Meaning and Iterability." The article provides an account of the debate between the American philosopher and speech-act theorist John Searle and the French philosopher Jacques Derrida concerning their different readings of J. L. Austin's *How to Do Things with Words,* a seminal British work in ordinary-language philosophy. Culler takes Derrida's part in the debate, discussing to what extent Searle's responses to Derrida miss the thrust of Derrida's approach. The article is a significant contribution to literary criticism because it summarizes and clarifies a debate of much importance to both literary critics and philosophers studying the philosophy of language. Moreover, Culler's article makes an understanding of Derrida's deconstruction of texts accessible to a wide audience that might sometimes be overwhelmed by the rhetoric of Derrida's work in deconstruction.

Very briefly, Culler begins with Austin's attempt to address the meaning of utterances in terms of a system of speech acts, a system to provide conventional rules of meaning involving the contextual features of utterances. Austin's attempt purportedly provides an account of utterance and meaning that is independent of a speaker's intention—what the speaker has in mind to say when speaking. However, in providing his account in *How to Do Things with Words,* Austin introduces a distinction between serious and nonserious speech acts. Derrida contends that this introduction provides the wedge by which the speaker's intention is reintroduced into the account of meaning, thus defeating Austin's project—a project with which Derrida is somewhat sympathetic. Searle's counter contention, in defense of Austin, is that Derrida misunderstands Austin's methodological use of "serious" and makes more of this use than is warranted. In the article, Culler discusses Searle's failure to address the issues Derrida raises in his criticism of Austin, as well as Searle's possible oversight on the scope of Austin's project: "The project of clarifying all possible ways and varieties of *not exactly doing things,"* Culler quotes Austin, ". . . has to be carried through if we are to understand properly what doing this is."

In reading Culler one should pay particular attention to the account of supplementarity and iterability, key concepts to understanding the fundamentals of the Searle/Derrida debate. Supplementarity is a Derridean term that (in French) means both a supplement—an addition—to something and a substitution—a supplanting—of something. Iterability, the possibility of repeating discourse, is the notion of an infinite number of contexts for an utterance that make for the undecidability of meaning without reference to a code for the conventions of context. However, it is Derrida's point, ultimately, that the possibility of an infinite number of conventions defeats the project of providing a systematic code for them.

# Convention and Meaning: Derrida and Austin[1]

In the Saussurian perspective, meaning is the product of linguistic conventions, the effect of a system of differences. To account for meaning is to set forth the relations of contrast and the possibilities of combination that constitute a language. However, as many have observed, a theory that derives meaning from linguistic conventions does not account for it completely. If one conceives of meaning as the effect of linguistic relations manifested in an utterance, then one must contend with the fact that, as we say, a speaker can mean different things by the same linguistic sequence on different occasions. "Could you move that box?" may be a request, or a question about one's interlocutor's strength, or even, as rhetorical question, the resigned indication of an impossibility.

Such examples seem to reinstate a model in which the subject—the consciousness of the speaker—is made the source of meaning: despite the contribution of linguistic structure, the meaning of the utterance varies from case to case; its meaning is what the speaker means by it. Confronted with such a model, the partisan of structural explanation will ask what makes it possible for the speaker to mean these several things by the one utterance. Just as we account for the meaning of sentences by analyzing the linguistic system, so we should account for the meaning of utterances (or as Austin calls it, their illocutionary force) by analyzing another system; the system of speech acts. As the founder of speech act theory, Austin is, in fact, repeating at another level (though less explicitly) the crucial move made by Saussure: to account for signifying events *(parole)* one attempts to describe the system that makes them possible.

Thus Austin argues, for example, that to mean something by an utterance is not to perform an inner act of meaning that accompanies the utterance. The notion that I may mean different things by "Can you move this box?" seems to urge that we explain meaning by inquiring what the speaker has in mind, as though this were the determining factor, but this is what Austin denies. What makes an utterance a command or a promise or a request is not the speaker's state of mind at the moment of utterance but conventional rules involving features of the context. If in appropriate circumstances I say "I promise to return this to you," I have made a promise, whatever was running through my mind at the time; and conversely, when earlier in this sentence I wrote the words "I promise to return this to you," I did not succeed in making a promise, even if the thoughts in my mind were similar to those that occurred on an occasion when I did make a promise. Promising is an act governed by certain conventions which the theorist of speech acts attempts to make explicit.

Austin's project is thus an attempt at structural explanation which offers a pertinent critique of logocentric premises, but in his discussion he reintroduces precisely those assumptions that his project puts in question. Derrida outlines this self-deconstructive movement in a section of "Signature événement contexte" in *Marges de la philosophie,* but John Searle's egregious misunderstanding in his "Reiterating the Differences: A Reply to Derrida" indicates that it may be important to proceed more slowly than Derrida does, with fuller discussion of Austin's project and Derrida's observations.

Austin begins *How to Do Things with Words* with the observation that "it was for too long the assumption of philosophers that the business of a 'statement' can only be to 'describe' some state of affairs, or to 'state some fact,' which it must do either truly or falsely.'[2] The normal sentence was conceived as a true or false representation of a state of affairs, and numerous sentences which failed to correspond to this model were treated either as unimportant exceptions or as deviant "pseudo-statements." "Yet we, that is, even philosophers, set some limits to the amount of nonsense that we are prepared to admit we talk; so that it was natural to go on to ask, as a second stage, whether many apparent

pseudo-statements really set out to be 'statements' at all."

Austin thus proposes to attend to cases previously ignored as marginal and problematic and to treat them not as failed statements but as an independent type. He proposes a distinction between statements, or *constative* utterances, which describe a state of affairs and are true or false, and another class of utterances which are not true or false and which actually perform the action to which they refer (e.g., "I promise to pay you tomorrow" accomplishes the act of promising). These he calls *performatives.*

This distinction between *performative* and *constative* has proved very fruitful in the analysis of language, but as Austin presses further in his description of the distinctive features of the performative and the various forms it can take, he reaches a surprising conclusion. An utterance such as "I hereby affirm that the cat is on the mat" seems also to possess the crucial feature of accomplishing the act (of affirming) to which it refers. *I affirm X,* like *I promise X,* is neither true nor false but performs the act it denotes. It would thus seem to count as a performative. But another important feature of the performative, Austin has shown, is the possibility of deleting the explicit performative verb. Instead of saying "I promise to pay you tomorrow," one can in appropriate circumstances perform the act of promising by saying "I will pay you tomorrow"—a statement whose illocutionary force remains performative. Similarly, one can perform the act of affirming or stating while omitting "I hereby affirm that." "The cat is on the mat" may be seen as a shortened version of "I hereby state that the cat is on the mat" and thus a performative. But, of course, "The cat is on the mat" is the classic example of a constative utterance.

Austin's analysis provides a splendid instance of the logic of supplementarity at work. Starting from the philosophical hierarchy that makes true or false statements the norm of language and treats other utterances as flawed statements or as extra—supplementary—forms, Austin's investigation of the qualities of the marginal case leads to a deconstruction and inversion of the hierarchy: the performative is not a flawed constative; rather, the constative is a special case of the performative. The conclusion that a constative is a performative from which one of various performative verbs has been deleted has since been adopted by numerous linguists. John Lyons notes, "It is natural to consider the possibility of deriving all sentences from underlying structures with an optionally deletable main clause containing a first-person subject, a performative verb of saying and optionally an indirect-object expression referring to the addressee."[3]

This would be a way of extending grammar to account for part of the force of utterances. Instead of saying that speakers can mean different things by the sentence "This chair is broken," linguists can extend the linguistic system to account for certain variations in meaning. "This chair is broken" can have different meanings because it can be derived from any of several underlying strings— strings which could be expressed as "I warn you that this chair is broken," "I inform you that this chair is broken," "I concede to you that this chair is broken," "I proclaim to you that this chair is broken," "I complain to you that this chair is broken."

Austin does not cast his theory in this form and would be skeptical of such attempts to extend grammar. He cites relationships between such pairs as "I warn you that this chair is broken" and "This chair is broken" to show that illocutionary force does not necessarily follow from grammatical structure. Indeed, he proposes a distinction between locutionary and illocutionary acts. When I say "This chair is broken," I perform the locutionary act of uttering a particular English sentence and the illocutionary act of stating, warning, proclaiming, or complaining. (There is also what

Austin calls a perlocutionary act, the act I may accomplish by my performance of the locutionary and illocutionary acts: by arguing I may persuade you, by proclaiming something I may bring you to know it.) The rules of the linguistic system account for the meaning of the locutionary act; the goal of speech act theory is to account for the meaning of the illocutionary act or, as Austin calls it, the illocutionary force of an utterance.

To explain illocutionary force is to set forth the conventions that make it possible to perform various illocutionary acts: what one has to do in order to promise, to warn, to complain, to command. "Besides the uttering of the words of the so-called performative," Austin writes, "a good many other things have as a general rule to be right and to go right if we are to be said to have happily brought off our action. What these are we may hope to discover by looking at and classifying types of case in which something goes wrong and the act—marrying, betting, bequeathing, christening, or what not—is therefore at least to some extent a failure" (*How to . . .*, p. 14). Austin thus does not treat failure as an external accident that befalls performatives and has no bearing on their nature. The possibility of failure is internal to the performative and a point of departure for investigating it. Something cannot be a performative unless it can go wrong.

This approach may seem unusual, but in fact it accords with the basic axioms of semiotics. "A sign," writes Umberto Eco in *A Theory of Semiotics,* "is everything which can be taken as significantly substituting for something else. . . . *Semiotics is in principle the discipline studying everything which can be used in order to lie.* If something cannot be used to tell a lie, conversely it cannot be used to tell the truth."[4] "The bat is on my hat" would not be a signifying sequence if it were not possible to utter it falsely. Similarly, "I now pronounce you man and wife" is not a performative unless it is possible for it to misfire, to be used in inappropriate circumstances and without the effect of performing a marriage.

For the smooth functioning of a performative, Austin says, "(A.1) There must exist an accepted conventional procedure having a certain conventional effect, that procedure to include the uttering of certain words by certain persons in certain circumstances, and further, (A.2) the particular persons and circumstances in a given case must be appropriate for the invocation of the particular procedure invoked. (B.1) The procedure must be executed by all participants both correctly and (B.2) completely" (*How to . . .*, pp. 14–15). As these formulations suggest, to promise is to utter one of the conventional formulae in appropriate circumstances. It would be wrong, Austin argues, to think of the utterance "as (merely) the outward and visible sign, for convenience or other record or for information, of an inward and spiritual act" (*How to . . .*, p. 9). For example, "the act of marrying, like, say, the act of betting, is at least *preferably . . .* to be described as *saying certain words,* rather than as performing a different, inward and spiritual, action of which these words are merely the outward and audible sign. That this is so can perhaps hardly be proved, but it is, I should claim, a fact" (*How to . . .*, p. 13).

Austin refuses to explain meaning in terms of a state of mind and proposes, rather, an analysis of the conventions of discourse. Can such an account be developed? Can Austin proceed without reinstating the notion of meaning as a signifying intention present to consciousness at the moment of utterance and thus treating the meaning of a speech act as ultimately determined by or grounded in a consciousness whose intention is fully present to itself? Derrida's reading focuses on the way in which this reintroduction occurs. An especially interesting moment in which the argument can be shown to involve such an appeal occurs in the opening pages of *How to Do Things with Words,* as Austin is staking out the ground for his enterprise. After chastizing philosophers for treating as marginal any utterances that are not true or false statements and thus leading us to suppose that he himself will be concerned with such things as fictional utterances which are neither true nor false, Austin proposes an objection to the notion of performative utterance: "Surely the words must be spoken 'seriously' and so as to be taken 'seriously'? This is, though vague, true enough in general—it is an important commonplace in discussing the purport of any utterance whatsoever. I must not be joking, for example, nor writing a poem" (*How to . . .*, p. 9).

The rhetorical structure of this passage is itself quite revealing. Although he proposes to exclude the nonserious, Austin offers no characterization of it, presumably because he is particularly anxious at this point to avoid the reference to an inner intention that such description would doubtless involve. Instead his text posits an anonymous objection which introduces "seriously" in quotation marks, as if it were itself not altogether serious. Doubling itself to produce this objection whose key term remains unanchored, the text can then grant the objection as something to be taken for granted.

Once, Austin has already told us, it was customary for philosophers to exclude—unjustifiably—utterances that were not true or false statements. Now his own text makes it appear customary to exclude utterances that are not serious. We have here, as the remark about the vagueness of the "serious" indicates, not a rigorous move within philosophy but a customary exclusion on which philosophy relies.

This exclusion is repeated in a longer passage which helps to indicate what is at stake. After listing various failures that may prevent the accomplishment of a performative, Austin notes that performatives are subject to certain other kinds of ill which infect all utterances. And these likewise, though again they might be brought into a more general account, we are deliberately at present excluding. I mean, for example, the following: a performative utterance will, for example, be in a peculiar way hollow or void if said by an actor on the stage, or if introduced in a poem, or spoken in soliloquy. This applies in a similar manner to any and every utterance—a sea-change in special circumstances. Language in such circumstances is in special ways—intelligibly—used not seriously, but in ways parasitic upon its normal use—ways which fall under the doctrine of the etiolations of language. All this we are excluding from consideration. Our performative utterances, felicitous or not, are to be understood as issued in ordinary circumstances. [How to . . . , pp. 21–22]

As the image of the parasite suggests, we have here a familiar relationship of supplementarity: the nonserious use of language is something extra, added to ordinary language and wholly dependent upon it. It need not be taken into consideration in discussing ordinary language use since it is only a parasite.

John Searle argues in his reply to Derrida that this exclusion is of no importance but purely provisional.

Austin's idea is simply this: if we want to know what it is to make a promise or make a statement we had better not start our investigation with promises made by actors on stage in the course of a play or statements made in a novel by novelists about characters in the novel, because in a fairly obvious way such utterances are not standard cases of promises and statements. . . . Austin correctly saw that it was necessary to hold in abeyance one set of questions, about parasitic discourse, until one

has answered a logically prior set of questions about "serious" discourse.[5]

This may well have been "Austin's idea," but the appropriateness of such an idea is precisely what is in question. "What is at stake," Derrida writes, "is above all the structural impossibility and illegitimacy of such an 'idealization,' even one which is methodological and provisional."[6] Indeed, Austin himself, who begins his investigation of performatives by looking at ways in which they can go wrong, contests Searle's notion of simple logical priority: "The project of clarifying all possible ways and varieties of *not exactly doing things* . . . has to be carried through if we are to understand properly what doing things is" (Austin's italics).[7] To set aside as parasitic certain uses of language in order to base one's theory on other, "ordinary" uses of language is to beg precisely those questions about the essential nature of language that a theory of language ought to answer. Austin objected to such an exclusion by his predecessors: in assuming that the ordinary use of language was to make true or false statements, they excluded precisely those cases that enable him to conclude that statements are a particular case of performative. When Austin then performs a similar exclusion, his own example prompts us to ask whether it is not equally illicit, especially since both he and Searle, by putting "serious" in quotation marks, suggest the dubiousness of the hierarchical opposition serious/nonserious. The fact that Austin's own writing is often highly playful and seductive, or that he does not hesitate to undermine distinctions that he proposes, only emphasizes the inappropriateness of excluding nonserious discourse from consideration.[8]

Searle uses his "Reply to Derrida" not to explore this problem but dogmatically to reaffirm the structure in question. "The existence of the pretended form of the speech act is logically dependent on the possibility of the nonpretended speech act in the same way that any pretended form of behavior is dependent on nonpretended forms of behavior, and in that sense the pretended forms are *parasitical* on the nonpretended forms."9

In what sense is the pretended dependent upon the nonpretended? Searle gives an example: "There could not, for example, be promises made by actors in a play if there were not the possibility of promises made in real life." We are certainly accustomed to thinking in this way: a promise I make is real; a promise in a play is a fictional imitation of a real promise, an empty iteration of a formula used to make real promises. But in fact one can argue that the relation of dependency works the other way. If it were not possible for a character in a play to make a promise, there could be no promises in real life, for what makes it possible to promise, as Austin tells us, is the existence of a conventional procedure, of formulae one can repeat. For me to be able to make a promise in "real life," there must be iterable procedures or formulae, such as are used on stage.

"Could a performative utterance succeed," Derrida asks or pretends to ask, "if its formulation did not repeat a 'coded' or iterable utterance, or in other words, if the formula I pronounce in order to open a meeting, to launch a ship or a marriage were not identifiable as *conforming* with an iterable model, if it were not thus identifiable in some way as 'citation'?"10 For the "standard case" of promising to occur, it must be recognizable as the repetition of conventional procedure, and the actor's performance on the stage is an excellent model of such repetition. The possibility of "serious" performatives depends upon the possibility of performances, because performatives depend upon the iterability that is most explicitly manifested in performances.11 Just as Austin reversed his predecessors' hierarchical opposition by showing that constatives were a special case of performatives, so we can reverse Austin's opposition between the serious and the parasitic by showing that his so-called serious performatives are only a special case of performances.

Indeed, this is a principle of considerable breadth. Something can be a signifying sequence only if it is iterable, only if it can be repeated in various serious and nonserious contexts, cited, and parodied. Imitation is not an accident that befalls an original but its condition of possibility. There is such a thing as an original Hemingway style only if it can be cited, imitated, and parodied. For there to be such a style, there must be recognizable features that characterize it and produce its distinctive effects; for features to be recognizable, one must be able to isolate them as elements that could be repeated, and thus the iterability manifested in the inauthentic, the derivative, the imitative, the parodic is what makes possible the authentic or original.

A deconstructive reading of Austin focuses on the way he repeats the move that he identifies and criticizes in others and on the way in which the distinction between the serious and the parasitic, which makes it possible for him to undertake an analysis of speech acts, is undone by the implications of that analysis. Since any serious performative can be reproduced in various ways and is itself a repetition of a conventional procedure, the possibility of repetition is not something external that may afflict the serious performative. On the contrary, Derrida insists, the performative is from the outset structured by this possibility. "This *possibility* is part of the so-called 'standard case.' It is an essential, internal, and permanent part, and to exclude what Austin himself admits is a constant possibility from one's description is to describe something other than the so-called standard case."12

Nevertheless, Austin's exclusion of the parasitic is not simply an error, an error he might have avoided. It is a strategic part of his enterprise. As we saw above, for Austin an utterance can function as a performative and thus have a certain meaning or illocutionary force when there exists a conventional procedure involving "the utterance of certain words by certain persons in certain circumstances" and when these specified conditions are actually fulfilled. Illocutionary force is thus held to depend upon context, and the theorist must, in order to account for meaning, specify the necessary features of the context—the nature of the words, persons, and circumstances required. What happens when one attempts such specification? Marriage is an example Austin cites. When the minister says "I now pronounce you man and wife," his utterance successfully performs the act of uniting a couple in marriage if the context meets certain conditions. The speaker must be one authorized to perform weddings; the persons he addresses must be a man and a woman who are not married, who have obtained a license to marry, and who have uttered the required phrases in the preceding ceremony. But when one formulates such conditions regarding the words, persons, and circumstances that are necessary for an utterance to have a particular meaning or force, a listener or critic can usually without great difficulty imagine circumstances that fit these conditions but in which the utterance would not have the illocutionary force that is supposed to follow from them. Suppose that the requirements for a marriage ceremony were met but that one of the parties were under hypnosis, or again that the ceremony were impeccable in all respects but had been called a "rehearsal," or finally, that while the speaker was a minister licensed to perform weddings and the couple had obtained a license, the three of them were on this occasion acting in a play that, coincidentally, included a wedding ceremony.

When anyone proposes an example of a meaningless sentence, listeners can usually imagine a context in which it would in fact have meaning; by placing a frame around it, they can make it signify. This aspect of the functioning of language, the possibility of

grafting a sequence onto a context that alters its functioning, is also at work in the case of performatives. For any specification of the circumstances under which an utterance counts as a promise, we can either imagine further details that would make a difference or else place a further frame around the circumstances. (We imagine that the conditions are fulfilled on a stage or in an example.)

In order to arrest or control this process, which threatens the possibility of a successful theory of speech acts, Austin is led to reintroduce the notion, previously rejected, that the meaning of an utterance depends on the presence of a signifying intention in the consciousness of the speaker. First, he sets aside the nonserious—a notion not explicitly defined but which clearly would involve reference to intention: a "serious" speech act is one in which the speaker consciously assents to the act he appears to be performing. Second, he introduces intention as one feature of the circumstances by setting aside speech acts performed unintentionally—"done under duress, or by accident, or owing to this or that variety of mistake, say, or otherwise unintentionally" (*How to* . . . , p. 21).

However, this reintroduction does not solve the problem; intention cannot serve as the decisive determinant or the ultimate foundation of a theory of speech acts. To see this, one need only consider what would happen if, after apparently completing a marriage ceremony, one of the parties said that he had been joking when he uttered his lines—only pretending, just rehearsing, or acting under duress. Assuming that the others believe his report of his intention, it will not in itself be decisive. What he had in mind at the moment of utterance does not determine what speech act his utterance performed. On the contrary, the question of whether a marriage did indeed take place will depend upon further discussion of the circumstances. If the minister had said that there would be a full dress rehearsal immediately before the real ceremony, or if the groom can sustain his claim that throughout the ceremony the bride's father was threatening him with a pistol, then one might reach a different conclusion about the illocutionary force of their utterances. What counts is the plausibility of the description of the circumstances: whether the features of the context adduced create a frame that alters the illocutionary force of the utterances.

Thus the possibility of grafting an utterance upon a new context, of repeating a formula in different circumstances, does not discredit the principle that illocutionary force is determined by context rather than by intention. On the contrary, it confirms this principle: in citation, iteration, or framing, it is new contextual features that alter illocutionary force. We are here approaching a general principle of considerable importance. What the indissociability of performative and performance puts in question is not the determination of illocutionary force by context but the possibility of mastering the domain of speech acts by exhaustively specifying the contextual determinants of illocutionary force. A theory of speech acts must in principle be able to specify every feature of context that might affect the success or failure of a given speech act or that might affect what particular speech act an utterance effectively performed. This would require, as Austin recognizes, a mastery of the total context: "The total speech act in the total speech situation is the only actual phenomenon which, in the last resort, we are engaged in elucidating" (*How to . . .* , p. 148). But total context is unmasterable, both in principle and in practice. Meaning is context-bound, but context is boundless.[13]

This is true in two senses. First, any given context is always open to further description. There is no limit in principle to what might be included in a given context, to what might be shown relevant to the interpretation of a particular speech act. This structural openness of context is essential to all disciplines: the sci-

entist discovers that factors previously disregarded are relevant to the behavior of particular objects; the historian brings new or reinterpreted data to bear on a particular event; the critic relates a particular passage or text to contexts that make it appear in a new light. A striking instance of the possibilities of further specification of context, Derrida notes, is the question of the unconscious. In his *Speech Acts* Searle proposes, as one of the conditions of promising, that "if a purported promise is to be non-defective, the thing promised must be something the hearer wants done, or considers to be in his interest."[14] An utterance that promised to do what the listener apparently wants but unconsciously dreads might thus cease to be a promise and become instead a threat; conversely, an utterance that seemed a defective promise—a threat to do what the listener claims not to want—may become a well-formed promise, should unconscious desire be specified as part of the total context.[15] This example illustrates very well how meaning is determined by context and for that very reason open to further possibilities.

Context is also unmasterable in a second sense: any attempt to codify context can always be grafted onto the context it sought to describe, yielding a new context which escapes the previous formulation. Attempts to describe limits always make possible a displacement of those limits, so that Wittgenstein's suggestion that one cannot say "bububu" and mean "if it does not rain I shall go out for a walk" has, paradoxically, made it possible to do just that. Its denial establishes a connection that can be exploited. Adepts of speech act theory, interested in excluding nonserious utterances from the corpus they are attempting to master, might admire the principle at work in a sign displayed in certain American airports at the spot where passengers and hand luggage are searched: "All remarks concerning bombs and weapons will be taken seriously." Designed to master signification by specifying the illocutionary force of certain statements in this context, it attempts to preclude the possibility of saying in jest "I have a bomb in my shoe" by identifying such utterances as serious statements. But this codification fails to arrest the play of meaning, nor is its failure an accident. The structure of language grafts this codification onto the context it attempts to master, and the new context creates new opportunities for obnoxious behavior. "If I were to remark that I had a bomb in my shoe, you would have to take it seriously, wouldn't you?" is only one of numerous remarks whose force is a function of context but which escape the prior attempt to codify contextual force. A metasign, "All remarks about bombs and weapons, including remarks about remarks about bombs and weapons, will be taken seriously," would escalate the struggle without arresting it, engendering the possibility of obnoxious remarks about this sign about remarks.

But if this seems a nonserious example, let us consider a more serious instance. What speech act is more serious than the act of signing a document, a performance whose legal, financial, and political implications may be enormous? Austin cites the act of signature as the equivalent in writing of explicit performative utterances with the form "I hereby . . . ," and indeed it is in appending a signature that one can in our culture most authoritatively take responsibility for an utterance. By signing a document, one intends its meaning and seriously performs the signifying act it accomplishes.

Derrida concludes "Signature évènement contexte" with what he calls an "improbable signature," the "reproduction" of a "J. Derrida" in script above a printed "J. Derrida," accompanied by the following "Remark": "(Remark: the—written—text of this—oral—communication should have been sent to the Association des sociétés de philosophie de langue française before the meeting.

That dispatch should thus have been signed. Which I do, and counterfeit, here. Where? There. J.D.)."[16] Is the cursive "J. Derrida" a signature even if it is a citation of the signature appended to the copy of this text sent through the mails? Is it still a signature when the supposed signatory calls it counterfeit? Can one counterfeit one's own signature? What, in sum, is a signature?

Traditionally, as Austin's remarks suggest, a signature is supposed to attest to the presence to consciousness of a signifying intention at a particular moment. Whatever my thoughts before or after, there was a moment when I fully intended a particular meaning. The notion of signature thus seems to imply a moment of presence to consciousness which is the origin of subsequent obligations or other effects. But if we ask what enables a signature to function in this way, we find that effects of signature depend on iterability. As Derrida writes, "The condition of possibility of those effects is simultaneously, once again, the condition of their impossibility, of the impossibility of their rigorous purity. In order to function, that is, to be readable, a signature must have a repeatable, iterable, imitable form; it must be able to be detached from the present and singular intention of its production. It is its sameness which, by corrupting its identity and its singularity, divides its seal."[17]

A proper signature, one that will validate a check or some other document, is one that conforms to a model and can be recognized as a repetition. This iterability, an essential feature of the structure of the signature, introduces as part of its structure an independence from any signifying intention. If the signature on a check corresponds to the model, the check can be cashed whatever my intentions at the moment of signature. So true is this that the empirical presence of the signatory is not even an essential feature of the signature. It is part of the structure of the signature that it can be produced by a stamp or by a machine. We can, fortunately, cash checks signed by a machine and receive a salary even though the signatory never saw the check nor entertained a specific intention to pay us the sum in question.

It is tempting to think of checks signed by a machine as a perverse exception irrelevant to the fundamental nature of signatures. Logocentric idealization sets aside such cases as accidents, "supplements," or "parasites" in its attempt to preserve a model predicated upon the presence of a full intention to consciousness at the moment of signature. But such cases could not occur if they did not belong to the structure of the phenomenon in question, and far from being a perverse exception, the check signed by machine is a logical and explicit example of the fundamental iterability of signatures. The requirement that a signature be recognizable as a repetition introduces the possibility of a machine as part of the structure of the signature at the same time as it eliminates the need for any particular intention at the point of signature.

Signatures thus ought to be included in what Derrida calls "a typology of forms of iteration":

In such a typology the category of intention will not disappear: it will have its place, but from that place it will no longer be able to govern the entire scene and system of utterance. Above all, we will then be dealing with different kinds of marks or chains of iterable marks and not with an opposition between citational utterances on the one hand and singular and original event-utterances on the other. The first consequence of this will be the following: given that structure of iteration, the intention animating the utterance will never be through and through present to itself and to its content. The iteration structuring it introduces into it a priori an essential dehiscence and cleft [*brisure*].[18]

It is not a matter of denying that signatories have intentions but of situating those intentions. One way of doing this would be to take the unconscious, as Vincent Descombes has argued, "not as a phenomenon of the will but as a phenomenon of enunciation."[19] The thesis of the unconscious "makes sense only in relation to the subject of enunciation: he does not know what he says."[20] The unconscious is the excess of what one says over what one knows, or of what one says over what one wants to say. Either the speaker's intention is whatever content is present to consciousness at the moment of utterance, in which case it is variable and incomplete, unable to account for the illocutionary force of utterances, or else it is comprehensive and divided—conscious and unconscious—a structural intentionality which is never anywhere present and which includes implications that never, as we say, entered my mind. This latter notion of intention, marked by what Derrida calls an essential cleft or division, is indeed quite common. When questioned about the implications of an utterance, I may quite routinely include in my intention implications that had never occurred to me before I was questioned.

Either way, intention is perhaps best thought of as a product. To the extent one can ever "fully intend" what one's signature accomplishes, it is because one has read the document and one's signature as an iterable act, an act with certain consequences on any occasion when it is performed, and thus anticipates further explanations one might give if questioned on any point. Intentions are not a delimited content but open sets of discursive possibilities—what one will say in response to questions about an act.

The example of the signature thus presents us with the same structure we encountered in the case of other speech acts: (1) the dependence of meaning on conventional and contextual factors, but (2) the impossibility of exhausting contextual possibilities so as to specify the limits of illocutionary force, and thus (3) the impossibility of controlling effects of signification or the force of discourse by a theory, whether it appeal to intentions of subjects or to codes and contexts.

The view of meaning to which this leads is not simple: it entails, on the one hand, the contextual, conventional determination of meaning and, on the other hand, the impossibility of ever saturating or limiting context so as to control or rigorously determine the "true" meaning. It is thus possible, and even appropriate, to proclaim the indeterminacy of meaning—though the smug iconoclasm apparent in many such proclamations is irritating. On the other hand, it is necessary and appropriate to continue to interpret texts, classify speech acts, and generally elucidate as far as possible the conditions of signification. Though Austin demonstrates the collapse of his distinction between performative and constative, he does not for that reason abandon his attempt to discriminate various classes of performative. Even though one may have reason to believe, as Derrida says, that "the language of theory always leaves a residue that is neither formalizable nor idealizable in terms of that theory of language," this is no reason to stop work on theory.[21] In mathematics, for example, Gödel's demonstration of the incompleteness of metamathematics (the impossibility of constructing a theoretical system within which all true statements of number theory are theorems) does not lead mathematicians to abandon their work. The humanities, however, often seem touched with the belief that a theory which asserts the ultimate indeterminacy of meaning renders all effort pointless. The fact that such assertions emerge from essays that propose numerous particular determinations of meaning, specific interpretations of passages and texts, should indicate that we are dealing with a double, not a simple, view of meaning: if language always evades its conventions, it also depends on them.

## NOTES

1. This is an excerpt from my book *On Deconstruction: Literary Theory in the 1970s,* published in 1982 by the Cornell University Press.

2. J. L. Austin, *How to Do Things with Words* (Cambridge, Mass., 1975), p. 1; hereafter cited in text as "How to. . . ."

3. John Lyons, *Semantics* II (Cambridge, 1977), p. 778.

4. Umberto Eco, *A Theory of Semiotics* (Bloomington, 1976), p. 7.

5. John Searle, "Reiterating the Differences: A Reply to Derrida," *Glyph* 1 (1977), pp. 204–5.

6. Jacques Derrida, *Limited Inc* (Baltimore, 1977) [supplement to *Glyph* 2], 39. English translation: "Limited Inc a b c . . . ," *Glyph* 2 (1977), p. 206.

7. Austin, *Philosophical Papers* (London, 1970), p. 27.

8. Shoshana Felman, in a fascinating discussion, casts Austin in the role of a Don Juan who seduces readers and disrupts all norms. She attempts to set aside Austin's exclusion of nonserious discourse by arguing that when Austin writes "I must not be joking, for example, or writing a poem" (in the example cited above), "cette phrase ne pourrait-elle pas être considérée elle-même comme une dénégation—comme une plaisanterie?" ["Could not this sentence itself be considered as a denial—as a joke?"], *Le Scandale du corps parlant: Don Juan avec Austin, ou la séduction en deux langues* (Paris, 1980), p. 188. This is a clever suggestion, part of a sustained attempt to attribute to Austin everything she has learned from Derrida—in order then to accuse Derrida of misreading Austin. But to treat the exclusion of jokes as a joke prevents one from explaining the logical economy of Austin's project, which can admit infelicities and exploit them so profitably only by excluding the fictional and the nonserious. This logic is what is at stake, not Austin's attitude or his liking for what Felman calls "le fun." Felman does argue convincingly, however, that by comparison with his successors, who see misfires and infelicities as events to be eliminated by a more rigorous idealization, Austin is a powerful defender of the irreducibility of the negative.

9. Searle, "Reiterating the Differences," p. 205.

10. Jacques Derrida, "Signature événement contexte," *Marges de la philosophie* (Paris, 1972), 389. English translation: "Signature Event Context," *Glyph* 1 (1977), pp. 191–92.

11. Searle accuses Derrida of confusing "no less than three separate and distinct phenomena: iterability, citationality, and parasitism." "There is a basic difference in

that in parasitic discourse the expressions are being *used* and not *mentioned*"—a difference Derrida is said not to understand ("Reiterating the Differences," p. 206). But the distinction between use and mention is precisely one of the hierarchizations that Derrida's argument contests. The distinction seems clear and important in the classic examples: "Boston is populous" uses the word or expression *Boston,* while *"Boston* is disyllabic" does not use the expression but mentions it—mentions the word *Boston* by using an expression which is a metaname. Here the distinction seems important because it points to the difference between using a word to talk about a city and talking about a word. But when we turn to other examples of citation the problem becomes more complicated. If I write of a scholar, "Some of my colleagues think his work 'boring and incompetent' or 'pointless,' " what have I done? Have I used the expressions *boring* and *incompetent* and *pointless* as well as mentioned them? If we wish to preserve the distinction between use and mention here, we shall fall back on those notions of seriousness and of intention which Derrida claims are involved. I use the expressions insofar as I seriously intend the meanings of the sign sequences I utter; I mention them when I reiterate some of these signs (within quotation marks, for example) without committing myself to the meaning they convey. Mentioning, for Searle, would thus be parasitic upon use, and the distinction would separate the proper use of language, where I seriously intend the meaning of the signs I use, from a derivative reiteration that only mentions. We thus have a distinction—am I "seriously" applying the expressions boring, incompetent, and pointless or only mentioning them?—between two sorts of iteration, apparently based on intention, and Derrida is quite right to claim that use/mention is ultimately a hierarchy of the same sort as serious/nonserious and speech/writing. Each attempts to control language by characterizing distinctive aspects of its iterability as parasitic, derivative. A deconstructive reading would demonstrate that the hierarchy should be inverted and that use is but a special case of mentioning.

The distinction is still useful: among other things it helps us to describe how language subverts it. However much I may wish only to mention to a friend what others say about him, I effectively use these expressions, giving them meaning and force in my discourse. And no matter how wholeheartedly I may wish to "use" certain expres-

sions, I find myself mentioning them: "I love you" is always something of a quotation, as many lovers have attested.

12. Derrida, *Limited Inc,* p. 61; "Limited Inc a b c . . . ," p. 231.

13. For discussion of this perspective, see Stanley Fish, *Is There a Text in This Class?* (Cambridge, 1980), 268–92 and 305–21; and esp. Susan Horton, *Interpreting Interpreting: Interpreting Dickens' "Dombey"* (Baltimore, 1979). In an excellent analysis of how interpretations are produced and justified, Horton argues that "each situation permits of innumerable acts of contextualizing" (p. 128) and that "what is responsible for those apparently infinite and infinitely variable interpretations of our texts, including Dombey and Son, is that everything else in that hermeneutical circle and not just the reader is in motion at the same time" (p. 17). Horton helped me to see that "interpretive conventions," on which Fish and I had tended to focus, should be seen as part of this boundless context. For another argument that breaks down the distinction between convention and context—but then draws the wrong conclusions—see Jay Schleusener, "Convention and the Context of Reading," *Critical Inquiry*, 6, No. 4 (Summer 1980), 669–80.

14. Searle, *Speech Acts: An Essay on the Philosophy of Language* (Cambridge, 1969), 59.

15. Derrida, *Limited Inc*, p. 47; "Limited Inc a b c . . . ," p. 215.

16. Derrida, "Signature événement contexte," p. 393; "Signature Event Context," p. 196.

17. "Signature événement contexte," pp. 391–92; "Signature Event context," p. 194.

18. "Signature événement contexte," p. 389; "Signature Event Context," p. 192.

19. Vincent Descombes, *L'Inconscient malgré lui* (Paris, 1977), p. 85.

20. Descombes, p. 15.

21. Derrida, *Limited Inc*, p. 41; "Limited Inc a b c . . . ," p. 209. The first part of this sentence is missing from the French text of *Limited Inc*. A line of typescript has apparently been omitted from line 35 of p. 41 following "toujours."

# 20

# Jacques Derrida
# 1930–

Born in Algiers and educated in France, Jacques Derrida has become one of the most prominent thinkers of the poststructuralist movement. He teaches the history of philosophy at the Ecole Normale Superieur in Paris and teaches regularly at universities in the United States. Although he is not primarily a literary critic, Derrida's work, particularly his articulation and development of "deconstruction," has had great influence on literary studies. Since the 1960s, the force of his ideas has affected other areas, including theology, sociology, and the interdisciplinary practice of discourse theory. Although some might call his ideas "subversive" and others might argue they are visionary, few doubt their impact on literary criticism and classroom practice. He is a prolific writer in many areas of study (including literature, art, psychology, linguistics, theater, theology, and philosophy). His books include *Speech and Phenomena* (1967; trans. 1973); *Writing and Difference* (1967; trans. 1978); *Of Grammatology* (1967; trans. 1976); *Margins of Philosophy* (1972; trans. 1983); *Dissemination* (1972; trans. 1981); *Glas* (1974; trans. 1987); *The Postcard* (1980; trans. 1987); and *The Other Heading: Reflections on Today's Europe* (1991; trans. 1992). (For a useful bibliography see Peggy Kamuf's *A Derrida Reader: Between the Blinds* New York: Columbia University Press, 1991).

Originally given as an inaugural address by Derrida as Cornell University's Andrew Dickson White Professor-at-Large, "The Principle of Reason: The University in the Eyes of Its Pupils" (1983) is an important articulation of the relationship between academic understanding, philosophy, and discourse. Significant in part because Derrida moves his critique of Western metaphysics to the university and its modes of inquiry, but perhaps also because of its on-going connections to the literature of crisis surrounding the humanities in the academy, Derrida's comments here remain crisp and relevant. His "deconstruction" of the binary opposition between reason and unreason in the cultural context of institutions of learning is a notable refocusing of his philosophical work.

This essay probes the nature of the university by considering its point of view and how it responds to sight. Derrida is trying to "view viewing," as he calls it. He begins with the question "What can the University's body see or not see of its own destination, of that in view of which it stands its ground? Is the University the master of its own diaphragm?" This question frames his inquiry as an issue of opening the eyes or closing them to privilege other senses and other ways of knowing—a trope Derrida juxtaposes with the idea of the university's role in Enlightenment. By contrasting the relationships of the university to that which surrounds it and by considering its *raison d'être*—both the functions of reason and the nature of being—Derrida probes Leibniz's concept of the moral imperative behind rendering reason. This sense of obligation, Derrida argues, leads to the important issue of the university's "responsibility." He asks: "But is answering *to* the principle of reason the same act as answering *for* the principle of reason?" The question leads to the dilemmas related to grounding the university in reason—what Derrida calls grounding it in the principle of grounding.

The implications of these issues for the modern university, and indeed for inquiry itself (including the reasoned discourse of literary criticism), are sharply focused in the last half of the essay, where Derrida brings the abstractions of Aristotle, Kant, Heidegger, and Nietzsche into the realm of the modern university in the larger questions concerning the nature of "normative" knowledge—of "objectivity"—and concerning who or what is served by the disciplinary "knowledge" of the university, what he calls the "politics of knowledge." Even those, he writes, who work "on structures of the simulacrum or of literary fiction, on a poetic rather than an informative value of language, on the effects of undecidability, and so on, by that very token . . . are interested in possibilities that arise at the outer limits of the authority and the power of the principle of reason."

# The Principle of Reason: The University in the Eyes of Its Pupils

Today, how can we not speak of the university?

I put my question in the negative, for two reasons. On the one hand, as we all know, it is impossible, now more than ever, to dissociate the work we do, within one discipline or several, from a reflection on the political and institutional conditions of that work. Such a reflection is unavoidable. It is no longer an external complement to teaching and research; it must make its way through the very objects we work with, shaping them as it goes, along with our norms, procedures, and aims. We cannot not speak of such things. On the other hand, the question "how can we not" gives notice of the *negative,* or perhaps we should say *preventive,* complexion of the preliminary reflections I should like to put to you. Indeed, since I am seeking to initiate discussion, I shall content myself with saying how one should not speak of the university. Some of the typical risks to be avoided, it

seems to me, take the form of a bottomless pit, while others take the form of a protectionist barrier.

Does the university, today, have what is called a *raison d'être?* I have chosen to put my question in a phrase—*raison d'être,* literally, "reason to be"—which is quite idiomatically French. In two or three words, that phrase names everything I shall be talking about: reason and being, of course, and the essence of the University in its connections to reason and being; but also the cause, purpose, direction, necessity, justification, meaning and mission of the University; in a word, its destination. To have a *raison d'être,* a reason for being, is to have a justification for existence, to have a meaning, an intended purpose, a destination; but also, to have a cause, to be explainable according to the "principle of reason" or the "law of sufficient reason," as it is sometimes called—in terms of a reason which is also a cause (a ground, *ein Grund*), that is to say also a footing and a foundation, ground to stand on. In the phrase *raison d'être,* that idea of causality takes on above all the sense of final cause, in the wake of Leibniz, the author of the formulation—and it was much more than a formulation—"the Principle of Reason." To ask whether the University has a reason for being is to wonder why there is a University, but the question "why" verges on "with a view to what?" The University with a view to what? What is the University's view? What are its views? Or again: what do we see from the University, whether for instance, we are simply in it, on board; or whether, puzzling over destinations, we look out from it while in port or, as French has it, *"au large,"* on the open sea, "at large"? As you may have noticed, in asking "what is the view from the University?" I was echoing the title of the impeccable parable James Siegel published in *Diacritics* two years ago: "Academic Work: The View from Cornell" [Spring, 1981]. Today, indeed, I shall do no more than decipher that parable in my own way. More precisely, I shall be transcribing in a different code what I read in that article—the dramatic, exemplary nature of the topology and politics of this university, in terms of its views and its site: the topolitics of the Cornellian point of view.

Starting with its first words, Metaphysics associates sight with knowledge, and knowledge with knowing how to learn and knowing how to teach. I am referring of course to Aristotle's *Metaphysics*. I shall return presently to the political import of its opening lines; for the moment, let us look at the very first sentence: "All men, by nature, have the desire to know." Aristotle thinks he sees a sign of this in the fact that sensations give pleasure, "even apart from their usefulness." The pleasure of useless sensations explains the desire to know for the sake of knowing, the desire for knowledge with no practical purpose. And this is more true of sight than of the other senses. We give preference to sensing "through the eyes" not only for taking action, but even when we have no praxis in view. This one sense, naturally theoretical and contemplative, goes beyond practical usefulness and provides us with more to know than any other; indeed, it unveils countless differences. We give preference to sight just as we give preference to the uncovering of difference.

But is sight enough? For learning and teaching, does it suffice to know how to unveil differences? In certain animals, sensation engenders memory, and that makes them more intelligent and more capable of learning. But for knowing how to learn, and learning how to know, sight, intelligence and memory are not enough. We must also know how to hear, and to listen. I might suggest somewhat playfully that we have to know how to shut our eyes in order to be better listeners. Bees know many things, since they can see; but they cannot learn, since they are among the animals that lack the faculty of hearing. Thus, despite appearances to the contrary, the University, the place where people know how to learn and learn how to know, can never be a kind of hive. Aristotle, let us note in passing, has ushered in a long tradition of frivolous remarks on the philosophical commonplace of the bee, the sense and senses of the bee, and the bee's reason for being. Marx was doubtless not the last to have overworked that topos, when he insisted on distinguishing human industry from animal industry, as exemplified in bee society. Seeking such nectar as may be gathered from the vast anthology of philosophical bees, I find a remark of Schelling's, in his *Lessons on the Method of Academic Studies,* [1] more to my taste. An allusion to the sex of bees often comes to the aid of the rhetoric of naturalism, organicism, or vitalism as it plays upon the theme of the complete and interdisciplinary unity of knowledge, the theme of the university as an organic social system. This is in the most classic tradition of interdisciplinary studies. I quote Schelling:

> The aptitude for doing thoughtful work in the specialized sciences, the capacity to work in conformity with that higher inspiration which is called scientific genius, depends upon the ability to see each thing, including specialized knowledge, in its cohesion with what is originary and unified. Any thought which has not been formed in this spirit of unity and totality [*der Ein- und Allheit*] is empty in itself, and must be challenged; whatever is incapable of fitting harmoniously within that budding, living totality is a dead shoot which sooner or later will be eliminated by organic laws; doubtless there also exist, within the realm of science, numerous sexless bees [*geschlechtlose Bienen*] who, since they have not been granted the capacity to create, multiply in inorganic shoots the outward signs of their own witlessness [*ihre eigne Geistlosigkeit*]. [*Philosophies de l'université*, p. 49]

(I don't know what bees, not only deaf but sexless, Schelling had in mind at the time. But I am sure that even today such rhetorical weapons would find many an eager buyer. One professor has recently written that a certain theoretical movement was mostly supported, within the university, by homosexuals and feminists—a fact which seemed very significant to him, and doubtless a sign of asexuality.)

Opening the eyes to know, closing them—or at least listening—in order to know how to learn and to learn how to know: here we have a first sketch of the rational animal. If the University is an institution for science and teaching, does it have to go beyond memory and sight? In what rhythm? To hear better and learn better, must it close

its eyes or narrow its outlook? In cadence? What cadence? Shutting off sight in order to learn is of course only a figurative manner of speaking. No one will take it literally, and I am not proposing to cultivate an art of blinking. And I am resolutely in favor of a new university Enlightenment [*Aufklärung*]. Still, I shall run the risk of extending my figuration a little farther, in Aristotle's company. In his *De anima* (421b) he distinguishes between man and those animals that have hard, dry eyes [*tôn sklerophtalmôn*], the animals lacking eyelids, that sort of sheath or tegumental membrane [*phragma*] which serves to protect the eye and permits it, at regular intervals, to close itself off in the darkness of inward thought or sleep. What is terrifying about an animal with hard eyes and a dry glance is that it always sees. Man can lower the sheath, adjust the diaphragm, narrow his sight, the better to listen, remember, and learn. What might the University's diaphragm be? The University must not be a sclerophthalmic animal, a hard-eyed animal; when I asked, a moment ago, how it should set its sights and adjust its views, that was another way of asking about its reasons for being and its essence. What American English calls "the faculty," those who teach, is in French *le corps enseignant,* the teaching corps (just as we say "the diplomatic corps") or teaching body. What can the University's body see or not see of its own destination, of that in view of which it stands its ground? Is the University the master of its own diaphragm?

Now that I have opened up this perspective, allow me to close it off quick as a wink and, in the twinkling of an eye, let me confide in you, to make what in French I could call a *confidence* but in English must call a confession.

Before preparing the text of a lecture, I find I must prepare myself for the scene I shall encounter as I speak. That is always a painful experience, an occasion for silent, paralytic deliberation. I feel like a hunted animal, looking in darkness for a way out where none is to be found. Every exit is blocked. In the present case, the task seemed triply impossible.

In the first place, this was not to be just a lecture like any other; rather, it had to be something like an inaugural address. Of course, Cornell University has welcomed me generously many times since I first came to speak here in 1975. I have many friends here, and Cornell is in fact the first American university I ever taught for. That was in Paris, in 1967–68, as David Grossvogel will undoubtedly remember: he was in charge of a program that had also been directed by Paul de Man. But today, for the first time, I am taking the floor to speak as an Andrew Dickson White Professor-at-Large. In French, "Au large" is the expression a great ship uses to hail a small craft about to cross her course: "Wear off. Give way." In this case, the title with which your university has honored me at once brings me closer to you and adds to the anguish of the cornered animal. Was this inaugural lecture a well-chosen moment to ask whether the University has a reason for being? Wasn't I about to act with all the unseemliness of a stranger who in return for noble hospitality plays prophet of doom with his hosts, or at best eschatological harbinger, like Elijah denouncing the power of kings or announcing the end of the realm?

A second cause for worry is that I find myself involved already, quite imprudently, that is, blindly and without foresight, in an act of dramaturgy, writing out the play of that view in which Cornell, from its beginnings, has felt so much to be at stake. The question of the view has informed the writing-out of the institutional scene, the landscape of your university, the alternatives of expansion and enclosure, life and death. From the first it was considered vital not to close off the view. This was recognized by Andrew Dickson White, Cornell's first president: may I pay him this

homage? At a moment when the trustees wanted to locate the university closer to town, Ezra Cornell took them to the top of East Hill to show them the sights, and the site, he had in mind. "We viewed the landscape," writes Andrew Dickson White. "It was a beautiful day and the panorama was magnificent. Mr. Cornell urged reasons on behalf of the upper site, the main one being that there was so much more room for expansion."[2] Ezra Cornell gave good reasons, and since the Board of Trustees, reasonably enough, concurred with them, reason won out. But in this case was reason quite simply on the side of life? Drawing on K. C. Parsons' account of the planning of the Cornell campus, James Siegel observes (and I quote) that

> for Ezra Cornell the association of the view with the university had something to do with death. Indeed Cornell's plan seems to have been shaped by the thematics of the Romantic sublime, which practically guaranteed that a cultivated man in the presence of certain landscapes would find his thoughts drifting metonymically through a series of topics—solitude, ambition, melancholy, death, spirituality, "classical inspiration"—which could lead, by an easy extension, to questions of culture and pedagogy. [p. 69]

A matter of life and death. The question arose once again in 1977, when the university administration proposed to erect protective railings on the Collegetown bridge and the Fall Creek suspension bridge to check thoughts of suicide inspired by the view of the gorge. "Barriers" was the term used; we could say "diaphragm," borrowing a word which in Greek literally means "partitioning fence." Beneath the bridges linking the university to its surroundings, connecting its inside to its outside, lies the abyss. In testimony before the Campus Council, one member of the faculty did not hesitate to express his opposition to the barriers, those diaphragmatic eyelids, on the grounds that blocking the view would mean, to use his words, "destroying the essence of the university." What did he mean? What is the essence of the university?

Perhaps now you can better imagine with what shudders of awe I prepared myself to speak to you on the subject—quite properly sublime—of the essence of the University. Sublime in the Kantian sense of the term: in the *Conflict of the Faculties,* Kant averred that the University should be governed by "an idea of reason," the idea of the whole field of what is presently teachable [*das ganze gegenwärtige Feld der Gelehrsamkeit*]. As it happens, no experience in the present allows for an adequate grasp of that present, presentable totality of doctrine, of teachable theory. But the crushing sense of that inadequacy is the exalting, desperate sense of the sublime, suspended between life and death.

Kant says, too, that the approach of the sublime is first heralded by an inhibition. There was a third reason for the inhibition I myself felt as I thought about speaking to you today. I was resolved of course to limit myself to preliminary, preventive remarks—propedeutical remarks, to use the word German took over from Greek to designate the teaching that comes before teaching. I would speak only of the risks to be avoided, the abyss, and bridges, and boundaries as one struggles with such fearful questions. But that would still be too much, because I wouldn't know how to pick and choose. In my teaching in Paris I have devoted a year-long seminar to the question of the University. Furthermore, I was recently asked by the French government to write a proposal for the establishment of an International College of Philosophy, a proposal which for literally hundreds of pages considers all of the difficulties involved. To speak of such things in an hour would be more than just a challenge. As I sought to encourage myself, daydreaming a

bit, it occurred to me that I didn't know how many meanings were conveyed by the phrase "at large," as in "professor at large." I wondered whether a professor at large, not belonging to any department, nor even to the university, wasn't rather like the person who in the old days was called *un ubiquiste*, a "ubiquitist," if you will, in the University of Paris. A ubiquitist was a doctor of theology not attached to any particular college. Outside that context, in French, an *ubiquiste* is someone who travels a lot and travels fast, giving the illusion of being everywhere at once. Perhaps a professor at large, while not exactly a ubiquitist, is also someone who, having spent a long time on the high seas, "*au large*," occasionally comes ashore, after an absence which has cut him off from everything. He is unaware of the context, the proper rituals, and the changed environment. He is given leave to consider matters loftily, from afar. People indulgently close their eyes to the schematic, drastically selective views he has to express in the rhetoric proper to an academic lecture about the academy. But they may be sorry that he spends so much time in a prolonged and awkward attempt to capture the benevolence of his listeners.

As far as I know, nobody has ever founded a university against reason. So we may reasonably suppose that the University's reason for being has always been reason itself, and some essential connection of reason to being. But what is called the principle of reason is not simply reason. We cannot for now plunge into the history of reason, its words and concepts, into the puzzling scene of translation which has shifted *logos* to *ratio* to *raison, reason, Grund,* ground, *Vernunft,* and so on. What for three centuries now has been called the principle of reason was thought out and formulated, several times, by Leibniz. His most often quoted statement holds that "Nothing is without reason, no effect is without cause." According to Heidegger, though, the only formulation Leibniz himself considered authentic, authoritative, and rigorous is found in a late essay, *Specimen inventorum*: "There are two first principles in all reasoning, the principle of non-contradiction, of course . . . and the principle of rendering reason." The second principle says that for any truth—for any true proposition, that is—a reasoned account is possible. *"Omnis veritatis reddi ratio potest."* Or, to translate more literally, for any true proposition, reason can be rendered.[3]

Beyond all those big philosophical words—reason, truth, principle—that generally command attention, the principle of reason also holds that reason must be rendered. (In French the expression corresponding to Leibniz's *reddere rationem* is *rendre raison de quelque chose;* it means to explain or account for something.) But what does "render" mean with respect to reason? Could reason be something that gives rise to exchange, circulation, borrowing, debt, donation, restitution? But in that case, who would be responsible for that debt or duty, and to whom? In the phrase *reddere rationem, "ratio"* is not the name of a faculty or power (*Logos, Ratio, Reason, Vernunft*) that is generally attributed by metaphysics to man, *zoon logon ekon*, the rational animal. If we had more time, we could follow out Leibniz's interpretation of the semantic shift which leads from the *ratio* of the *principium reddendae rationis*, the principle of rendering reason, to reason as the rational faculty—and in the end, to Kant's definition of reason as the faculty of principles. In any case, if "reason" in the principle of reason is not the rational faculty or power, that does not mean it is a thing, encountered somewhere among the beings and the objects in the world, which must be rendered up, given back. The question of this reason cannot be separated from a question about the modal verb "must" and the phrase "must be rendered." The "must" seems to cover the essence of our relationship to prin-

ciple, it seems to mark out for us requirement, debt, duty, request, command, obligation, law, the imperative. Whenever reason can be rendered (*reddi potest*), it must. Can we, without further precautions, call this a moral imperative, in the Kantian sense of pure practical reason? It is not clear that the sense of "practical," as it is determined by a critique of pure practical reason, gets to the bottom of the "must," or reveals its origin, although such a critique has to presuppose such a "must." It could be shown, I think, that the critique of practical reason continually calls on the principle of reason, on its "must" which, although it is certainly not of a theoretical order, is nonetheless not simply "practical" or "ethical" in the Kantian sense.

A responsibility is involved here, however. We have to respond to the call of the principle of reason. In *Der Satz vom Grund* [*The Principle of Reason*], Heidegger names that call *Anspruch:* requirement, claim, request, demand, command, convocation; it always entails a certain addressing of speech. The word is not seen, it has to be heard and listened to, this apostrophe that enjoins us to respond to the principle of reason.

A question of responsibility, to be sure. But is answering *to* the principle of reason the same act as answering *for* the principle of reason? Is the scene the same? Is the landscape the same? And where is the university located within this space?

To respond to the call of the principle of reason is to "render reason," to explain effects through their causes, rationally; it is also to ground, to justify, to account for on the basis of principles or roots. Keeping in mind that Leibnizian moment whose originality should not be underestimated, the response to the call of the principle of reason is thus a response to the Aristotelian requirements, those of metaphysics, of primary philosophy, of the search for "roots," "principles," and "causes." At this point, scientific and techno-scientific requirements lead back to a common origin. And one of the most insistent questions in Heidegger's meditation is indeed that of the long "incubation" time that separated this origin from the emergence of the principle of reason in the seventeenth century. Not only does that principle constitute the verbal formulation of a requirement present since the dawn of Western science and philosophy, it provides the impetus for a new era of purportedly "modern" reason, metaphysics and technoscience. And one cannot *think* the possibility of the modern university, the one that is re-structured in the nineteenth century in all the Western countries, without inquiring into that event, that institution of the principle of reason.

But to answer for the principle of reason (and thus for the university), to answer for this call, to raise questions about the origin or ground of this principle of foundation (*Der Satz vom Grund*), is not simply to obey it or to respond in the face of this principle. We do not listen in the same way when we are responding to a summons as when we are questioning its meaning, its origin, its possibility, its goal, its limits. Are we obeying the principle of reason when we ask what grounds this principle which is itself a principle of grounding? We are not—which does not mean that we are disobeying it, either. Are we dealing here with a circle or with an abyss? The circle would consist in seeking to account for reason by reason, to render reason to the principle of reason, in appealing to the principle in order to make it speak of itself at the very point where, according to Heidegger, the principle of reason says nothing about reason itself. The abyss, the hole, the *Abgrund,* the empty "gorge" would be the impossibility for a principle of grounding to ground itself. This very grounding, then, like the university, would have to hold itself suspended above a most peculiar void. Are we to use reason to account for the principle of reason? Is the reason for reason rational? Is it rational to worry about reason and its princi-

ple? Not *simply;* but it would be over-hasty to seek to disqualify this concern and to refer those who experience it back to their own irrationalism, their obscurantism, their nihilism. Who is more faithful to reason's call, who hears it with a keener ear, who better sees the difference, the one who offers questions in return and tries to think through the possibility of that summons, or the one who does not want to hear any question about the reason of reason? This is all played out, along the path of the Heideggerian question, in a subtle difference of tone or stress, according to the particular words emphasized in the formula *nihil est sine ratione*. This statement has two different implications according to whether *"nihil"* and *"sine"* are stressed, or *"est"* and *"ratione."* I shall not attempt here, given the limits of this talk, to pursue all of the reckonings involved in this shift of emphasis. Nor shall I attempt—among other things, and for the same reasons—to reconstitute a dialogue between Heidegger and for example Charles Sanders Peirce. A strange and necessary dialogue on the compound theme, indeed, of the university and the principle of reason. In a remarkable essay on "The limits of Professionalism," Samuel Weber quotes Peirce who, in 1900, "in the context of a discussion on the role of higher education" in the United States, concludes as follows:

Only recently have we seen an American man of science and of weight discuss the purpose of education, without once alluding to the only motive that animates the genuine scientific investigator. I am not guiltless in this matter myself, for in my youth I wrote some articles to uphold a doctrine called pragmatism, namely, that the meaning and essence of every conception lies in the application that is to be made of it. That is all very well, when properly understood. I do not intend to recant it. But the question arises, *what* is the ultimate application; and at that time I seem to have been inclined to subordinate the *conception* to the *act*, knowing to doing. Subsequent experience of life has taught me that the only thing that is really *desirable* without a reason for being so, is to render ideas and things reasonable. *One cannot well demand a reason for reasonableness itself.*[4]

To bring about such a dialogue between Peirce and Heidegger, we would have to go beyond the conceptual opposition between "conception" and "act," between "conception" and "application," theoretical view and praxis, theory and technique. This passage *beyond* is sketched out briefly by Peirce in the very movement of his dissatisfaction: what might the ultimate application be? What Peirce only outlines is the path where Heidegger feels the most to be at stake, especially in *Der Satz vom Grund*. Being unable to follow this path myself here in the way I have attempted to follow it elsewhere, I shall merely draw from it two assertions, at the risk of oversimplifying.

1. The modern dominance of the principle of reason had to go hand in hand with the interpretation of the essence of beings as objects, an object present as representation [*Vortsellung*], an object placed and positioned *before* a subject. This latter, a man who says "I," an ego certain of itself, thus ensures his own technical mastery over the totality of what is. The "re-" of *repraesentatio* also expresses the movement that accounts for—"renders reason to"—a thing whose presence is encountered by rendering it present, by bringing it to the subject of representation, to the knowing self. This would be the place, if we only had the time, to consider the way Heidegger makes the language do its work (the interaction between *begegnen, entgegen, Gegenstand, Gegenwart* on the one hand. *Stellen, Vorstellen, Zustellen* on the other hand.)[5] This relation of representation—which in its whole extension is not merely a relation of knowing—has to be grounded, ensured, protected: that is what we are told by the principle of reason, the *Satz vom Grund*. A dominance is thus assured for representation, for *Vorstellen,* for the relation to the object, that is, to the being that is located *before* a subject that says "I" and assures itself of its own present existence. But this dominance of the "being-before" does not reduce to that of sight or of *theoria*, nor even to that of a metaphor of the optical (or indeed sklerophthalmic) dimension. It is in *Der Satz vom Grund* that Heidegger states all his reservations on the very presuppositions of such rhetoricizing interpretations. It is not a matter of distinguishing here between sight and nonsight, but rather between two ways of thinking of sight and of light, as well as between two conceptions of listening and voice. But it is true that a caricature of representational man, in the Heideggerian sense, would readily endow him with hard eyes permanently open to a nature that he is to dominate, to rape if necessary, by fixing it in front of himself, or by swooping down on it like a bird of prey. The principle of reason installs its empire only to the extent that the abyssal question of the being that is hiding within it remains hidden, and with it the question of the grounding of the ground itself, of grounding as gruden (to ground, to give or take ground: *Boden-nehmen*), as *begrunden* (to motivate, justify, authorize) or especially as *stitten* (to erect or institute, a meaning to which Heidegger accords a certain pre-eminence).[6]

2. Now that institution of modern technoscience that is the university *Stiftung* is built both on the principle of reason and

on what remains hidden in that principle. As if in passing, but in two passages that are important to us, Heidegger asserts that the modern university is "grounded" [*gegrundet*], "built" [*gebaut*] on the principle of reason, it "rests" [*ruht*] on this principle.[7] But if today's university, locus of modern science, "is grounded on the principle of grounding," that is, on reason [*grundet auf dem Satz vom Grund*], nowhere do we encounter within it the principle of reason itself, nowhere is this principle thought through, scrutinized, interrogated as to its origin. Nowhere, within the university as such, is anyone wondering from where that call [*Anspruch*] of reason is voiced, nowhere is anyone inquiring into the origin of that demand for grounds, for reason that is to be provided, rendered, delivered: *"Woher spricht dieser Anspruch des Grundes aus seine Zustellung?"* And this dissimulation of its origin within what remains unthought is not harmful, quite the contrary, to the development of the modern university; indeed, Heidegger in passing makes certain laudatory remarks about that university: progress in the sciences, its militant interdisciplinarity, its discursive zeal, and so on. But all this is elaborated above an abyss, suspended over a "gorge"—by which we mean on grounds whose own grounding remains invisible and unthought.

Having reached this point in my reading, instead of involving you in a micrological study of Heidegger's *Der Satz vom Grund* or of his earlier texts on the University (in particular his inaugural lesson of 1929, *Was ist Metaphysik,* or the Rector's Speech of 1933, *Die Selbstbehauptung der deutschen Universitat*)—a study which I am attempting elsewhere, in Paris, and to which we shall doubtless refer in the discussions that come after this talk—instead of meditating

at the edge of the abyss—even if on a bridge protected by "barriers"—I prefer to return to a certain concrete actuality in the problems that assail us in the university.

The framework of grounding, or foundation, and the dimension of the fundamental impose themselves on several counts in the space of the university, whether we are considering the question of its reason for being in general, or its specific missions, or the politics of teaching and research. Each time, what is at stake is the principle of reason as principle of grounding, foundation or institution. A major debate is under way today on the subject of the politics of research and teaching, and on the role that the university may play in this arena: whether this role is central or marginal, progressive or decadent, collaborative with or independent of that of other research institutions sometimes considered better suited to certain ends. The terms of this debate tend to be analogous—I am not saying they are identical—in all the highly industrialized countries, whatever their political regime, whatever role the State traditionally plays in this arena (and, as we all know, even the Western democracies vary considerably in this respect). In the so-called "developing countries," the problem takes shape according to models that are certainly different but in all events inseparable from the preceding ones.

Such a problematics cannot always—cannot any longer—be reduced to a problematics centered on the nation-state; it is now centered instead on multinational military-industrial complexes or techno-economic networks, or rather international technomilitary networks that are apparently multi- or trans-national in form. In France, for some time, this debate has been organized around what is called the "orientation" [*finalisation*] of research. "Oriented" research is research that is programmed, focused, organized in an authoritarian fashion *in view* of its utilization (in view of *"ta khreia,"* Aristotle would say), whether we are talking about technology, economy, medicine, psychosociology, or military power—and in fact we are talking about all of these at once. There is doubtless greater sensitivity to this problem in countries where the politics of research depend closely upon state-managed or "nationalized" structures, but I believe that conditions are becoming more and more homogeneous among all the technologically advanced industrialized societies. We speak of "oriented" research where, not so long ago, we spoke—as Peirce did—of "application." For it is growing more and more obvious that, without being immediately applied or applicable, research may "pay off," be usable, "end-oriented," in more or less deferred ways. And what is at stake is not merely what sometimes used to be called the techno-economic, medical, or military "by-products" of pure research. The detours, delays and relays of "orientation," its random aspects as well, are more disconcerting than ever. Hence the attempt, by every possible means, to take them into account, to integrate them to the rational calculus of programmed research. A term like "orient" is preferred to "apply," in addition, because the word is less "utilitarian," it leaves open the possibility that noble aims may be written into the program.

You may wonder what is being advocated, in France, in opposition to this concept of oriented research. The answer is basic, "fundamental" research, disinterested research with aims that would not be pledged in advance to some utilitarian purpose. Once upon a time it was possible to believe that pure mathematics, theoretical physics, philosophy (and, within philosophy, especially metaphysics and ontology) were basic disciplines shielded from power, inaccessible to programming by the pressures of the State or, under cover of the State, by civil society or capital interests. The sole concern of such basic research would be knowledge, truth, the disinterested exercise of reason, under the sole authority of the principle of reason.

And yet we know better than ever before what must have been true for all time, that this opposition between the basic and the end-oriented is of real but limited relevance. It is difficult to maintain this opposition with thoroughgoing conceptual as well as practical rigor, especially in the modern fields of the formal sciences, theoretical physics, astrophysics (consider the remarkable example of the science of astronomy, which is becoming useful after having been for so long the paradigm of disinterested contemplation), chemistry, molecular biology, and so forth. Within each of these fields—and they are more interrelated than ever—the so-called basic philosophical questions no longer simply take the form of abstract, sometimes epistemological questions raised after the fact; they arise at the very heart of scientific research in the widest variety of ways. One can no longer distinguish between technology on the one hand and theory, science and rationality on the other. The term techno-science has to be accepted, and its acceptance confirms the fact that an essential affinity ties together objective knowledge, the principle of reason, and a certain metaphysical determination of the relation to truth. We can no longer—and this is finally what Heidegger recalls and calls on us to think through—we can no longer dissociate the principle of reason from the very idea of technology in the realm of their modernity. One can no longer maintain the boundary that Kant, for example, sought to establish between the schema that he called "technical" and the one he called "architectonic" in the systematic organization of knowledge—which was also to ground a systematic organization of the university. The architectonic is the art of systems. "Under the government of reason, our knowledge in general," Kant says, "should not form a rhapsody, but it must form a system in which alone it can support and favor the essential aims of reason." To that pure rational unity of the architectonic, Kant opposes the scheme of the merely technical unity that is empirically oriented, according to views and ends that are incidental, not essential. It is thus a limit between two aims that Kant seeks to define, the essential and noble ends of reason that give rise to a fundamental science versus the incidental and empirical ends which can be systematized only in terms of technical schemas and necessities.

Today, in the orientation or "finalization" of research—forgive me for presuming to recall such obvious points—it is impossible to distinguish between these two sets of aims. It is impossible, for example, to distinguish programs that one would like to consider "worthy," or even technically profitable for humanity, from other programs that would be destructive. This is not new; but never before has so-called basic scientific research been so deeply committed to aims that are at the same time military aims. The very essence of the military, the limits of military technology and even the limits of its accountability are no longer definable. When we hear that two million dollars a minute are being spent in the world today for armaments, we may assume that this figure represents simply the cost of weapons manufacture. But military investments do not stop at that. For military power, even police power, and more generally speaking the entire defensive and offensive security establishment benefits from more than just the "byproducts" of basic research. In the advanced technological societies, this establishment programs, orients, orders, and finances, directly or indirectly, through the State or otherwise, the front-line research that is apparently the least "end-oriented" of all. This is all too obvious in such areas as physics, biology, medicine, biotechnology, bioprogramming, data processing and telecommunications. We have only to mention telecommunications and data processing to assess the extent of the phenomenon: the "orientation" of research is limitless, everything in these areas proceeds "in view" of

technical and instrumental security. At the service of war, of national and international security, research programs have to encompass the entire field of information, the stockpiling of knowledge, the workings and thus also the essence of language and of all semiotic systems, translation, coding and decoding, the play of presence and absence, hermeneutics, semantics, structural and generative linguistics, pragmatics, rhetoric. I am accumulating all these disciplines in a haphazard way, on purpose, but I shall end with literature, poetry, the arts and fiction in general: the theory that has these disciplines as its object may be just as useful in ideological warfare as it is in experimentation with variables in all-too-familiar perversions of the referential function. Such a theory may always be put to work in communications strategy, the theory of commands, the most refined military pragmatics of jussive utterances (by what token, for example, will it be clear that an utterance is to be taken as a command in the new technology of telecommunications? How are the new resources of simulation and simulacrum to be controlled? And so on . . .). One can just as easily seek to use the theoretical formulations of sociology, psychology, even psychoanalysis in order to refine what was called in France during the Indochinese or Algerian wars the powers of "psychological action"—alternating with torture. From now on, so long as it has the means, a military budget can invest in anything at all, in view of deferred profits: "basic" scientific theory, the humanities, literary theory and philosophy. The compartment of philosophy which covered all this, and which Kant thought ought to be kept unavailable to any utilitarian purpose and to the orders of any power whatsoever in its search for truth, can no longer lay claim to such autonomy. What is produced in this field can always be used. And even if it should remain useless in its results, in its productions, it can always serve to keep the masters of discourse busy: the experts, professionals of rhetoric, logic or philosophy who might otherwise be applying their energy elsewhere. Or again, it may in certain situations secure an ideological bonus of luxury and gratuitousness for a society that can afford it, within certain limits. Furthermore, when certain random consequences of research are taken into account, it is always possible to have in view some eventual benefit that may ensue from an apparently useless research project (in philosophy or the humanities, for example). The history of the sciences encourages researchers to integrate that margin of randomness into their centralized calculation. They then proceed to adjust the means at their disposal, the available financial support, and the distribution of credits. A State power or the forces that it represents no longer need to prohibit research or to censor discourse, especially in the West. It is enough that they can limit the means, can regulate support for production, transmission, and diffusion. The machinery for this new "censorship" in the broad sense is much more complex and omnipresent than in Kant's day, for example, when the entire problematics and the entire topology of the university were organized around the exercise of royal censorship. Today, in the Western democracies, that form of censorship has almost entirely disappeared. The prohibiting limitations function through multiple channels that are decentralized, difficult to bring together into a system. The unacceptability of a discourse, the noncertification of a research project, the illegitimacy of a course offering are declared by evaluative actions: studying such evaluations is, it seems to me, one of the tasks most indispensable to the exercise of academic responsibility, most urgent for the maintenance of its dignity. Within the university itself, forces that are apparently external to it (presses, foundations, the mass media) are intervening in an ever more decisive way. University presses play a mediating role that entails the most serious responsibilities, since

scientific criteria, in principle represented by the members of the university corporation, have to come to terms with many other aims. When the margin of randomness has to be narrowed, restrictions on support affect the disciplines that are the least profitable in the short run. And that provokes, within the professions, all kinds of effects, certain ones of which seem to have lost any direct relation to that causality—which is itself still largely overdetermined. The shifting determination of the margin of randomness always depends upon the techno-economic situation of a society in its relation to the entire world arena. In the United States, for example (and it is not just one example among others), without even mentioning the economic regulation that allows certain surplus values—through the channel of private foundations among others—to sustain research or creative projects that are not immediately or apparently profitable, we also know that military programs, especially those of the Navy, can very rationally subsidize linguistic, semiotic or anthropological investigations. These in turn are related to history, literature, hermeneutics, law, political science, psychoanalysis, and so forth.

The concept of information or informatization is the most general operator here. It integrates the basic to the oriented, the purely rational to the technical, thus bearing witness to that original intermingling of the metaphysical and the technical. The value of "form" is not foreign to it; but let us drop this difficult point for now. In *Der Satz vom Grund*, Heidegger locates this concept of "information" (understood and pronounced as in English, he says at the time when he is putting America and Russia side by side like two symmetrical and homogeneous continents of metaphysics as technique) in a dependence upon the principle of reason, as a principle of integral calculability. Even the principle of uncertainty (and he would have said the same thing of a certain interpretation of undecidability) continues to operate within the problematics of representation and of the subject-object relation. Thus he calls this the atomic era and quotes a book of popularization entitled "We shall live thanks to atoms" with prefaces both by Otto Hahn, Nobel prize-winner and "fundamentalist" physicist, and Franz Joseph Strauss, then minister of national defense. Information ensures the insurance of calculation and the calculation of insurance. In this we recognize the period of the principle of reason. Leibniz, as Heidegger recalls, is considered to have been the inventor of life insurance. In the form of information [in *der Gestalt der Information*], Heidegger says, the principle of reason dominates our entire representation [*Vorstellen*] and delineates a period for which everything depends upon the delivery of atomic energy. Delivery in German is *Zustellung,* a word that also applies, as Heidegger points out, to the delivery of mail. It belongs to the chain of *Gestell*, from the *Stellen* group [*Vorstellen*, *Nachstellen*, *Zustellen*, *Sicherstellen*] that characterizes technological modernity. "Information" in this sense is the most economic, the most rapid and the clearest (univocal, *eindeutig*) stockpiling, recording and communication of news. It must instruct men about the safeguarding [*Sicherstellung*] of what will meet their needs, *ta khreia*. Computer technology, data banks, artificial intelligences, translating machines, and so forth, all these are constructed on the basis of that instrumental determination of a calculable language. Information does not inform merely by delivering an information content, it gives form, "*in-formiert*," "*formiert zugleich*." It installs man in a form that permits him to ensure his mastery on earth and beyond. All this has to be pondered as the effect of the principle of reason, or, put more rigorously, has to be analyzed as the effect of a dominant interpretation of that principle, of a certain emphasis in the way we heed its summons. But I have said that I cannot deal with the question of such stress here; it lies outside the scope of my topic.

What, then, is my topic? What do I have in view that has led me to present things as I have done so far? I have been thinking especially of the necessity to awaken or to resituate a responsibility, in the university or in face of the university, whether one belongs to it or not.

Those analysts who study the informative and instrumental value of language today are necessarily led to the very confines of the principle of reason thus interpreted. This can happen in any number of disciplines. But if the analysts end up for example working on the structures of the simulacrum or of literary fiction, on a poetic rather than an informative value of language, on the effects of undecidability, and so on, by that very token they are interested in possibilities that arise at the outer limits of the authority and the power of the principle of reason. On that basis, they may attempt to define new responsibilities in the face of the university's total subjection to the technologies of informatization. Not so as to refuse them; not so as to counter with some obscurantist irrationalism (and irrationalism, like nihilism, is a posture that is completely symmetrical to, thus dependent upon, the principle of reason). The theme of extravagance as an irrationalism—there is very clear evidence for this—dates from the period when the principle of reason was being formulated. Leibniz denounced it in his *New Essays on Human Understanding*. To raise these new questions may sometimes protect an aspect of philosophy and the humanities that has always resisted the influx of knowledge; it may also preserve the memory of what is much more deeply buried and ancient than the principle of reason. But the approach I am advocating here is often felt by certain guardians of the "humanities" or of the positive sciences as a threat. It is interpreted as such by those who most often have never sought to understand the history and the system of norms specific to their own institution, the deontology of their own profession. They do not wish to know how their discipline has been constituted, particularly in its modern professional form, since the beginning of the nineteenth century and under the watchful vigilance of the principle of reason. For the principle of reason may have obscurantist and nihilist effects. They can be seen more or less everywhere, in Europe and in America among those who believe they are defending philosophy, literature and the humanities against these new modes of questioning that are also a new relation to language and tradition, a new *affirmation*, and new ways of taking responsibility. We can easily see on which side obscurantism and nihilism are lurking when on occasion great professors or representatives of prestigious institutions lose all sense of proportion and control; on such occasions they forget the principles that they claim to defend in their work and suddenly begin to heap insults, to say whatever comes into their heads on the subject of texts that they obviously have never opened or that they have encountered through a mediocre journalism that in other circumstances they would pretend to scorn.[8]

It is possible to speak of this new responsibility that I have invoked only by sounding a call to practice it. It would be the responsibility of a community of thought for which the frontier between basic and oriented research would no longer be secured, or in any event not under the same conditions as before. I call it a community of thought in the broad sense—"at large"—rather than a community of research, of science or philosophy, since these values are most often subjected to the unquestioned authority of a principle of reason. Now reason is only one species of thought—which does not mean that thought is "irrational." Such a community would interrogate the essence of reason and of the principle of reason, the values of the basic, of

the principial, of radicality, of the *arkhe* in general, and it would attempt to draw out all the possible consequences of this questioning. It is not certain that such thinking can bring together a community or found an institution in the traditional sense of these words. What is meant by community and institution must be rethought. This thinking must also unmask—an infinite task—all the ruses of end-orienting reason, the paths by which apparently disinterested research can find itself indirectly reappropriated, reinvested by programs of all sorts. That does not mean that "orientation" is bad in itself and that it must be combatted, far from it. Rather, I am defining the necessity for a new way of educating students that will prepare them to undertake new analyses in order to evaluate these ends and to choose, when possible, among them all.

As I mentioned earlier, along with some colleagues I was asked last year by the French government to prepare a report in view of the creation of an International College of Philosophy. I insisted, in that report, on stressing the dimension that in this context I am calling "thought"—a dimension that is not reducible to technique, nor to science, nor to philosophy. This International College would not only be a College of Philosophy but also a place where philosophy itself would be questioned. It would be open to types of research that are not perceived as legitimate today, or that are insufficiently developed in French or foreign institutions, including some research that could be called "basic"; but it would not stop there. We would go one step further, providing a place to work on the *value and meaning* of the basic, the fundamental, on its opposition to goal-orientation, on the ruses of orientation in all its domains. As in the seminar that I mentioned earlier, the report confronts the political, ethical, and juridical consequences of such an undertaking. I cannot go into more detail here without keeping you much too long.

These new responsibilities cannot be purely academic. If they remain extremely difficult to assume, extremely precarious and threatened, it is because they must at once keep alive the memory of a tradition and make an opening beyond any program, that is, toward what is called the future. And the discourse, the works, or the position-taking that these responsibilities inspire, as to the institution of science and research, no longer stem solely from the sociology of knowledge, from sociology or politology. These disciplines are doubtless more necessary than ever; I would be the last to want to disqualify them. But whatever conceptual apparatus they may have, whatever axiomatics, whatever methodology (Marxist or neo-Marxist, Weberian or neo-Weberian, Mannheimian, some combination of these or something else entirely), they never touch upon that which, in themselves, continues to be based on the principle of reason and thus on the essential foundation of the modern university. They never question scientific normativity, beginning with the value of objectivity or of objectivation, which governs and authorizes their discourse. Whatever may be their scientific value—and it may be considerable—these sociologies of the institution remain in this sense internal to the university, intra-institutional, controlled by the deepseated standards, even the programs, of the space that they claim to analyze. This can be observed, among other things, in the rhetoric, the rites, the modes of presentation and demonstration that they continue to respect. Thus I shall go so far as to say that the discourse of Marxism and psychoanalysis, including those of Marx and Freud, inasmuch as they are standardized by a project of scientific practice and by the principle of reason, are intra-institutional, in any event homogeneous with the discourse that dominates the university in the last analysis. And the fact that this discourse is occasionally proffered by people who are not professional academics changes nothing essen-

tial. It simply explains, to a certain extent, the fact that even when it claims to be revolutionary, this discourse does not always trouble the most conservative forces of the university. Whether it is understood or not, it is enough that it does not threaten the fundamental axiomatics and deontology of the institution, its rhetoric, its rites and procedures. The academic landscape easily accommodates such types of discourse more easily within its economy and its ecology; however, when it does not simply exclude those who raise questions at the level of the foundation or non-foundation of the foundation of the university, it reacts much more fearfully to those that address sometimes the same questions to Marxism, to psychoanalysis, to the sciences, to philosophy and the humanities. It is not a matter simply of questions that one formulates while submitting oneself, as I am doing here, to the principle of reason, but also of preparing oneself thereby to transform the modes of writing, approaches to pedagogy, the procedures of academic exchange, the relation to languages, to other disciplines, to the institution in general, to its inside and its outside. Those who venture forth along this path, it seems to me, need not set themselves up in opposition to the principle of reason, nor need they give way to "irrationalism." They may continue to assume within the university, along with its memory and tradition, the imperative of professional rigor and competence. There is a double gesture here, a double postulation: to ensure professional competence and the most serious tradition of the university even while going as far as possible, theoretically and practically, in the most directly underground thinking about the abyss beneath the university, to think at one and the same time the entire "Cornellian" landscape—the campus on the heights, the bridges, and if necessary the barriers above the abyss—and the abyss itself. It is this double gesture that appears unsituatable and thus unbearable to certain university professionals in every country who join ranks to foreclose or to censure it by all available means, simultaneously denouncing the "professionalism" and the "antiprofessionalism" of those who are calling others to these new responsibilities.

I shall not venture here to deal with the debate on "professionalism" that is developing in your country. Its features are, to a certain extent at least, specific to the history of the American university. But I shall conclude on this general theme of "professions." At the risk of contradicting what I have been urging here, I should like to caution against another kind of precipitous reaction. For the responsibility that I am trying to situate cannot be simple. It implies multiple sites, a stratified terrain, postulations that are undergoing continual displacement, a sort of strategic rhythm. I said earlier that I would be speaking only of a certain rhythm, for example that of the blinking of an eye, and that I would only be playing one risk off against another, the barrier against the abyss, the abyss against the barrier, the one with the other and the one under the other.

Beyond technical goal-orientation, even beyond the opposition between technical goal-orientation and the principle of sufficient reason, beyond the affinity between technology and metaphysics, what I have here called "thought" risks in its turn (but I believe this risk is unavoidable—it is the risk of the future itself) being reappropriated by socio-political forces that could find it in their own interest in certain situations. Such a "thought" indeed cannot be produced outside of certain historical, techno-economic, politico-institutional and linguistic conditions. A strategic analysis that is to be as vigilant as possible must thus with its eyes wide open attempt to ward off such reappropriations. (I should have liked to situate at this point certain questions about the "politics" of Heideggerian thought, especially as elaborated prior to *Der Satz vom Grund*, for exam-

ple in the two inaugural discourses of 1929 and 1933.)

I shall limit myself, however, to the double question of "professions." First: does the university have as its essential mission that of producing professional competencies, which may sometimes be external to the university? Second: is the task of the university to ensure within itself—and under what conditions—the reproduction of professional competence by preparing professors for pedagogy and for research who have respect for a certain code? One may answer the second question in the affirmative without having done so for the first, and seek to keep professional forms and values internal to the university outside the market place while keeping the goal-orientation of social work outside of the university. The new responsibility of the "thought" of which we are speaking cannot fail to be accompanied at least by a movement of suspicion, even of rejection with respect to the professionalization of the university in these two senses, and especially in the first, which regulates university life according to the supply and demand of the marketplace and according to a purely technical ideal of competence. To this extent at least, such "thought" may, at a minimum, result in reproducing a highly traditional politics of knowledge. And the effects may be those that belong to a social hierarchy in the exercise of technopolitical power. I am not saying that this "thought" is identical with that politics, and that it is therefore necessary to abstain from it; I am saying that under certain conditions it can serve that politics, and that everything thus comes down to the analysis of those conditions. In modern times, Kant, Nietzsche, Heidegger and numerous others have all said as much, quite unmistakably: the essential feature of academic responsibility must not be professional education (and the pure core of academic autonomy, the essence of the university, is located in the philosophy department, according to Kant). Does this affirmation not repeat the profound and hierarchizing political evaluation of Metaphysics, I mean of Aristotle's *Metaphysics*? Shortly after the passage that I read at the beginning (981b and following), one sees a theoretico-political hierarchy being put into place. At the top, there is theoretical knowledge. It is not sought after in view of its utility; and the holder of this knowledge, which is always a knowledge of causes and of principles, is the leader or *arkhitekton* of a society at work, is positioned above the manual laborer [*kheiroteknes*] who acts without knowing, just as a fire burns. Now this theoretician leader, this knower of causes who has no need of "practical" skill, is in essence a *teacher*. Beyond the fact of knowing causes and of possessing reason [*to logon ekhein*], he bears another mark [*semeion*] of recognition: the "capacity to teach" [*to dunasthai didaskein*]. To teach, then, and at the same time to direct, steer, organize the empirical work of the laborers. The theoretician-teacher or "architect" is a leader because he is on the side of the *arkhe*, of beginning and commanding. He commands—he is the premier or the prince—because he knows causes and principles, the "whys" and thus also the "wherefores" of things. Before the fact, and before anyone else, he answers to the principle of reason which is the first principle, the principle of principles. And that is why he takes orders from no one; it is he, on the contrary, who orders, prescribes, lays down the law (982a 18). And it is normal that this superior science, with the power that it confers by virtue of its very lack of utility, is developed in places [*topoi*], in regions where leisure is possible. Thus Aristotle points out that the mathematical arts were developed in Egypt owing to the leisure time enjoyed by the priestly caste [*to ton iereon ethnos*], the priestly folk.

Kant, Nietzsche and Heidegger, speaking of the university, premodern or modern, do not say exactly what Aristotle said, nor do all three of them say exactly the same thing. But they also do say the same thing. Even though he admits the industrial model of the division of labor into the university, Kant places the so-called "lower" faculty, the faculty of philosophy—a place of pure rational knowledge, a place where truth has to be spoken without controls and without concern for "utility," a place where the very meaning and the autonomy of the university meet—Kant places this faculty above and outside professional education: the architectonic schema of pure reason is above and outside the technical schema. In his *Lectures on the Future of our Educational Establishments*, Nietzsche condemns the division of labor in the sciences, condemns utilitarian and journalistic culture in the service of the State, condemns the professional ends of the University. The more one does [*tut*] in the area of training, the more one has to think [*denken*]. And, still in the first Lecture: "*Man muss nicht nur Standpunkte, sondern auch Gedanken haben!*"; one must not have viewpoints alone, but also thoughts! As for Heidegger, in 1929, in his inaugural lesson entitled "What is Metaphysics," he deplores the henceforth technical organization of the university and its compartmentalizing specialization. And even in his Rector's Speech, at the very point where he makes an appeal on behalf of the three services (*Arbeitsdienst*, *Wehrdienst*, *Wissensdienst*, the service of work, the military, and knowledge), at the very point where he is recalling that these services are of equal rank and equally original (he had recalled earlier that for the Greeks *theoria* was only the highest form of *praxis* and the mode, par excellence, of *energeia*), Heidegger nevertheless violently condemns disciplinary compartmentalization and "exterior training in view of a profession," as "an idle and inauthentic thing" [*Das Mussige und Unechte ausserlicher Berufsabrichtung* . . .].

Desiring to remove the university from "useful" programs and from professional ends, one may always, willingly or not, find oneself serving unrecognized ends, reconstituting powers of caste, class, or corporation. We are in an implacable political topography: one step further in view of greater profundity or radicalization, even going beyond the "profound" and the "radical," the principal, the *arkhe*, one step further toward a sort of original an-archy risks producing or reproducing the hierarchy. "Thought" requires *both* the principle of reason *and* what is beyond the principle of reason, the *arkhe* and an-archy. Between the two, the difference of a breath or an accent, only the *enactment* of this "thought" can decide. That decision is always risky, it always risks the worst. To claim to eliminate that risk by an institutional program is quite simply to erect a barricade against a future. The decision of thought cannot be an intra-institutional event, an academic moment.

All this does not define a politics, nor even a responsibility. Only, at best, some negative conditions, a "negative wisdom," as the Kant of *The Conflict of the Faculties* would say: preliminary cautions, protocols of vigilance for a new *Aufklärung*, what must be seen and kept in sight in a modern re-elaboration of that old problematics. Beware of the abysses and the gorges, but also of the bridges and the barriers. Beware of what opens the university to the outside and the bottomless, but also of what, closing it in on itself, would create only an illusion of closure, would make the university available to any sort of interest, or else render it perfectly useless. Beware of ends; but what would a university be without ends?

Neither in its medieval nor in its modern form has the university disposed freely of its own absolute autonomy and of the rigorous conditions of its own unity. During more than eight centuries, "university" has been the name given by a society to a sort of supplementary body that at one and the same time it wanted to project outside itself and to keep jealously to itself, to emancipate and to control. On this double basis, the university was supposed to *represent* society. And in a certain way it has done so: it has reproduced society's scenography, its views, conflicts, contradictions, its play and its differences, and also its desire for organic union in a total body. Organicist language is always associated with "techno-industrial" language in "modern" discourse on the university. But with the relative autonomy of a technical apparatus, indeed that of a machine and of a prosthetic body, this artifact that is the university has *reflected society* only in giving it the chance for reflection, that is, also, for *dissociation*. The time for reflection, here, signifies not only that the internal rhythm of the university apparatus is relatively independent of social time and relaxes the urgency of command, ensures for it a great and precious freedom of play. An empty place for chance: the invagination of an inside pocket. The time for reflection is also the chance for turning back on the very conditions of reflection, in all the senses of that word, as if with the help of a new optical device one could finally see sight, could not only view the natural landscape, the city, the bridge and the abyss, but could view viewing. As if through an acoustical device one could hear hearing, in other words, seize the inaudible in a sort of poetic telephony. Then the time of reflection is also an other time, it is heterogeneous with what it reflects and perhaps gives time for what calls for and is called thought. It is the chance for an event about which one does not know whether or not, presenting itself *within* the university, it belongs to the history of the university. It may also be brief and paradoxical, it may tear up time, like the instant invoked by Kierkegaard, one of those thinkers who are foreign, even hostile to the university, who give us more to think about, with respect to the essence of the university, than academic reflections themselves. The chance for this event is the chance of an instant, an *Augenblick*, a "wink" or a "blink," it takes place "in the twinkling of an eye." I would say, rather, "in the twilight of an eye," for it is in the most crepuscular, the most westerly situations of the Western university that the chances of this "twinkling" of thought are multiplied. In a period of "crisis," as we say, a period of decadence and renewal, when the institution is "on the blink," provocation to think brings together in the *same* instant the desire for memory and exposure to the future, the fidelity of a guardian faithful enough to want to keep even the chance of a future, in other words the singular responsibility of what he does not have and of what is not yet. Neither in his keeping nor in his purview. Keep the memory and keep the chance—is this possible? And chance—can it be kept? Is it not, as its name indicates, the risk or the advent of the fall, even of decadence, the falling-due that befalls you at the bottom of the "gorge"? I don't know. I don't know if it is possible to keep both memory and chance. I am tempted to think, rather, that the one cannot be kept without the other, without keeping the other and being kept from the other. Differently. That double guard will be assigned, as its responsibility, to the strange destiny of the university. To its law, to its reason for being and to its truth. Let us risk one more etymological wink: truth is what keeps, that is, both preserves and is preserved. I am thinking here of *Wahrheit*, of the *Wahren* of *Wahrheit* and of *veritas*—whose name figures on the coat of arms of so many American universities. It institutes guardians and calls upon them to watch faithfully—truthfully—over itself.

Let me recall my *incipit* and the single question that I raised at the outset: how can we not speak, today, of the university? Have I said it, or done it? Have I said how one must not speak, today, of the university? Or have I rather spoken as one should not do today, within the University? Only others can answer. Beginning with you.

*Translated by Catherine Porter and*
*Edward P. Morris*

## NOTES

1. In regard to this "naturalism" (a frequent, but not general phenomenon that Kant, for example, eludes at the beginning of the *Conflict of the Faculties*), and also to the classic motif of interdiscipinarity as an effect of the architectonic totality; see, for example, Schleiermacher's 1808 essay "Geregenther Gedanken über Universitaten in deutschem Sinn, nepst einem Annang über ein neu zu errontence." French translation of this text appears in a noteworthy collection, *Philosophies de l'université l'idéalism allemand et la question de l'Université,* ed. Ferry, Pesron, Renault [Paris: Pavon, 1979].

2. James Siegel, "Academic Work: The View from Cornell," *Diacritics* 11:1 [Spring 1981], 68–83; the quotation, on page 69, is taken from Kermit Parsons, *The Cornell Campus: A History of Its Planning and Development* [Ithaca: Cornell University Press, 1968].

3. Translator's Note. About national idioms and idioms which, like Latin, aspire to greater catholicity: Leibniz's *rationem reddere*—a phrase by no means his exclusive property, but common to philosophy at large—is easily carried over into ordinary French as *rendre raison, rendre raison de quelque chose;* but in English, today, "render reason" sounds outlandish. The Oxford dictionary shows that English had the idiom at one time; setting aside a willfully archaic and dialectical sentence from Walter Scott, the most recent example adduced is from *An Exposition of the Creed,* by John Pearson, bishop of Chester, published in London in 1659, and it is an example not without interest for our purposes. "Thus," says Pearson as he expounds Article IX, "the Church of Christ in it's [sic] primary institution was made to be of a diffusive nature, to spread and extend itself from the City of *Jerusalem,* where it first began, to all the parts and corners of the earth. This reason did the ancient fathers render why the Church was called Catholick." [*An Exposition . . .,* (Ann Arbor, Michigan: University Microfilms, 1968), p. 697.] He then goes on to say that for a second reason the church is called catholic because it teaches everything, or at least everything necessary to Christian faith. Apparently, there was a whole teaching of diffusion and dissemination well before our own time. To judge from the quotations given by OED, *to render reason* (to give it back, as it were) worked in exchange and concert with *to yield reason* and *to give reason:* any one of the three could mean to give grounds for one's thoughts and assertions, but also, to give an account of one's acts or conduct, when summoned to do so: to be held accountable and to speak accordingly. In 1690, writing not of reason but only of understanding, Locke argued that we rank things under distinct names "according to complex ideas in us," as he says, "and not according to precise, distinct, real essences in them." We cannot denominate things by their real essences, as Locke puts the matter, for

the good reason that "we know them not." Even the familiar objects of our everyday world are composed we know not how; they must have their reason, but we cannot give it back to them. Thus, for all his practical bent, Locke is drawn to say, and I quote him once again, "When we come to examine the stones we tread on, or the iron we daily handle, we presently find that we know not their make, and can give no reason of the different qualities we find in them" [*An Essay concerning Human Understanding,* III, vi, 8–9]. In English, as in French or Latin, at one time people could give reason, or render it, or not be able to render it.—E.P.M.

4. In this quotation from Peirce's *Values in a Universe of Chance* [(Stanford, Ca.: Stanford University Press, 1958), p. 332], in addition to the last sentence, I have italicized the allusion to *desire* in order to echo the opening words of Aristotle's *Metaphysics.* Weber's article appeared in a double issue of *The Oxford Literary Review* 5: 1–2 (1982), pp. 59–79.

5. Here is but one example: "Rationem reddere heisst: den Grund zurückgeben. Weshal zurück und wohin zurück? Weil es sich in den Bewisgängen, allgemein gesprochen im Erkennen um das *Vor*-stellen der Gegenstände handelt, kommt dieses zurück ins Spiel. Die lateinische Sprache der Philosophie sagt es deutlicher: das Vorstellen is re-praesentatio. Das Begegnende wird auf das vorstellende Ich zu, auf es zurück und ihm entgegen praesentiert, in eine Gegenwart gestellt. Gemäss dem principium reddendae rationis muss das Vorstellen, wenn es ein erkennendes sein soll, den Grund des Gegegnenden auf das Vorstellen zu un d.h. ihm zurückgeben (reddere). Im erkennenden Vorstellen wird dem erkennenden Ich der Grund zu-gestellt. Dies Verlangt das principium rationis. Des Satz vom Grund is darum für Leibniz der Grundsatz des zuzustellenden Grundes" [*Der Satz vom Grund* (Pfullingen: G. Neske, 1957), p. 45].

6. In "Vom Wesen des Grundes," *Wegmarken* [Frankfurt am Main: Klostermann, 1976], pp. 60–61.

7. "And yet, without this all powerful principle there would be no modern science, and without such a science there would be no university today. The latter rests upon the princple of reason [*Diese gründet auf dem Satz vom Grund*]. How should we represent that to ourselves [*Wie sollen wir uns dies vorstellen*], the university founded *gegründet* on a sentence (a primary proposition: *auf einen Satz*)? Can we risk such an assertion [*Dürfen wir eine solche Behauptung wagen*]" [*Der Satz vom Grund. Dritte Stunde,* p. 49].

8. Among many possible examples, I shall mention only two recent articles. They have at least one trait in common: their authors are highly placed representatives of two institutions whose power and influence hardly need to be recalled. I refer to "The Crisis in English Studies" by Walter Jackson Bate, Kingsley Porter University Professor at Harvard [*Harvard Magazine,* Sept./Oct. 1982], and to "The Shattered Humanities" by Willis J. Bennett, Chairman of the National Endowment for the Humanities [*Wall Street Journal,* Dec. 31, 1982]. The latter of these articles carries ignorance and irrationality so far as to write the following: "A popular movement in literary criticism called "Deconstruction" denies that there are any texts at all. If there are no texts, there are no great texts, and no argument for reading." The former makes remarks about deconstruction—and this is not by chance—that are, we might say, just as unnerved. As Paul de Man notes in an admirable short essay ["The Return to Philogy," *Times Literary Supplement,* December 10, 1982], Professor Bate "has this time confined his sources of information to *Newsweek* magazine. . . . What is left is a matter of law-enforcement rather than a critical debate. One must be feeling very threatened indeed to become so aggressively defensive."

# 21

# Michel Foucault
# 1926–1984

Along with Jacques Derrida, Michel Foucault has become one of the most prominent European influences directing the pursuit of theory in recent American literary studies. Foucault's thought, however, has not been as readily integrated into literary criticism as have the ideas of Derrida and the "poststructuralist" work of Roland Barthes, Jacques Lacan, and Julia Kristeva (even though he has written on Gustave Flaubert, Maurice Blanchot, and Raymond Roussel). This difficulty of integration results from the specific concerns of his work. Unlike most "Poststructuralists," Foucault is less concerned with language at the level of the sign and much more concerned with the relationship of language and social institutions, a relationship that he calls "discourse." To examine language at the level of discourse is to identify the institutional rules that make possible particular significations and, consequently, make possible particular forms of knowledge.

This concern with underlying rules that govern the production of knowledge is found in Foucault's early major work, in which he identifies the conditions that made possible the emergence and development of modern areas of knowledge and their corresponding institutions: the diagnosis of madness and the emergence of asylums (*Madness and Civilization*, 1961; trans. 1965), scientific medicine and the emergence of clinics (*Birth of the Clinic*, 1963; trans. 1973), and the emergence of the human sciences in eighteenth-century Europe (*The Order of Things*, 1966; trans. 1970). Though Foucault, in his later work, remained interested in the social conditions of knowledge, his focus shifted following the failed leftist uprising in Paris during May 1968. The failure of this uprising led Foucault to an analysis of the exercise of power through social practices, including uses of language, or "discursive practices." This shift of interest coincided with a prestigious appointment to the College de France in 1970. His inaugural lecture in this position, *The Discourse on Language* (1971; trans. 1972), set the agenda for future work by outlining the ways in which "in every society the production of discourse is at once controlled, selected, organized and redistributed according to a certain number of procedures. . . ." In *Discipline and Punish* (1975; trans. 1977) Foucault combined his interest in the emergence of social institutions (in this case, the rise of prisons in the early nineteenth-century) and the exercise of power through discipline, especially discipline of the body. This interest in the application of discipline through discursive and other practices continues in the last of Foucault's major work, the three volumes of *History of Sexuality* (1976, 1984; trans. 1978, 1986). Foucault's thought therefore does not lend itself to commentaries on individual literary works as much as it directs us to view literature as a socially determined discursive practice. Also Foucault's work has influenced several American critics to examine literary criticism (and its history) as a discursive practice.

"What Is an Author?" was first published in 1969, and, while it continues to probe the institutional forces that affect writing and knowledge (a project that he theorized in *The Archeology of Knowledge*, 1969; trans. 1972), it was the first work to reflect his new concern with the exercise of power. Foucault frames the essay by observing a contradiction in modern culture: in many ways our culture regards the author as unimportant (for example, formalist literary criticism and the structuralist approach to the human sciences), yet in our criticism we do not hesitate to use the names of authors. On the basis of this contradiction, Foucault sets the direction of his inquiry: "I am not certain that consequences derived from the disappearance or death of the author have been fully explored or that the importance of this event has been appreciated." Foucault therefore, in posing the question, What is an author? is asking, In what ways do we use the notion of author? Foucault observes that we use the name of an author to do more than to refer to a person; instead, the notion of author, unlike the notion of writer, is used to authorize certain writings, to privilege those writings. Thus by focusing on the notion of author, Foucault is able to raise the more general questions of what conditions and interests allow one writer to be regarded an "author" and another writer not. Also Foucault uses this insight into the social/political nature of the notion of author to problematize the subjectivity of the writer, that is, to assert that a text is never the product of a unified consciousness (the author) but consists in several, socially determined roles, or "author-functions."

# What Is an Author?

The coming into being of the notion of "author" constitutes the privileged moment of *individualization* in the history of ideas, knowledge, literature, philosophy, and the sciences. Even today, when we reconstruct the history of a concept, literary genre, or school of philosophy, such categories seem relatively weak, secondary, and superimposed scansions in comparison with the solid and fundamental unit of the author and the work.

I shall not offer here a sociohistorical analysis of the author's persona. Certainly it would be worth examining how the author became individualized in a culture like ours, what status he has been given, at what moment studies of authenticity and attribution began, in what kind of system of valorization the author was involved, at what point we began to recount the lives of authors rather than of heroes, and how this fundamental category of "the-man-and-his-work criticism" began. For the moment, however, I want to deal solely with the relationship between text and author and with the manner in which the text points to this "figure" that, at least in appearance, is outside it and antecedes it.

Beckett nicely formulates the theme with which I would like to begin: " 'What does it matter who is speaking,' someone said, 'what does it matter who is speaking.' " In this indifference appears one of the fundamental ethical principles of contemporary writing *(écriture)*. I say "ethical" because this indifference is not really a trait characterizing the manner in which one speaks and writes, but rather a kind of immanent rule, taken up over and over again, never fully applied, not designating writing as something completed, but dominating it as a practice. Since it is too familiar to require a lengthy analysis, this immanent rule can be adequately illustrated here by tracing two of its major themes.

First of all, we can say that today's writing has freed itself from the dimension of expression. Referring only to itself, but without being restricted to the confines of its interiority, writing is identified with its own unfolded exteriority. This means that it is an interplay of signs arranged less according to its signified content than according to the very nature of the signifier. Writing unfolds like a game *(jeu)* that invariably goes beyond its own rules and transgresses its limits. In writing, the point is not to manifest or exalt the act of writing, nor is it to pin a subject within language; it is rather a question of creating a space into which the writing subject constantly disappears.

The second theme, writing's relationship with death, is even more familiar. This link subverts an old tradition exemplified by the Greek epic, which was intended to perpetuate the immortality of the hero: if he was willing to die young, it was so that his life, consecrated and magnified by death, might pass into immortality; the narrative then redeemed this accepted death. In another way, the motivation, as well as the theme and the pretext of Arabian narratives—such as *The Thousand and One Nights*—was also the eluding of death: one spoke, telling stories into the early morning, in order to forestall death, to postpone the day of reckoning that would silence the narrator. Scheherazade's narrative is an effort, renewed each night, to keep death outside the circle of life.

Our culture has metamorphosed this idea of narrative, or writing, as something designed to ward off death. Writing has become linked to sacrifice, even to the sacrifice of life: it is now a voluntary effacement which does not need to be represented in books, since it is brought about in the writer's very exis-

tence. The work, which once had the duty of providing immortality, now possesses the right to kill, to be its author's murderer, as in the cases of Flaubert, Proust, and Kafka. That is not all, however: this relationship between writing and death is also manifested in the effacement of the writing subject's individual characteristics. Using all the contrivances that he sets up between himself and what he writes, the writing subject cancels out the signs of his particular individuality. As a result, the mark of the writer is reduced to nothing more than the singularity of his absence; he must assume the role of the dead man in the game of writing.

None of this is recent; criticism and philosophy took note of the disappearance—or death—of the author some time ago. But the consequences of their discovery of it have not been sufficiently examined, nor has its import been accurately measured. A certain number of notions that are intended to replace the privileged position of the author actually seem to preserve that privilege and suppress the real meaning of his disappearance. I shall examine two of these notions, both of great importance today.

The first is the idea of the work. It is a very familiar thesis that the task of criticism is not to bring out the work's relationships with the author, nor to reconstruct through the text a thought or experience, but rather, to analyze the work through its structure, its architecture, its intrinsic form, and the play of its internal relationships. At this point, however, a problem arises: "What is a work? What is this curious unity which we designate as a work? Of what elements is it composed? Is it not what an author has written?" Difficulties appear immediately. If an individual were not an author, could we say that what he wrote, said, left behind in his papers, or what has been collected of his remarks, could be called a "work"? When Sade was not considered an author, what was the status of his papers? Were they simply rolls of paper onto which he ceaselessly uncoiled his fantasies during his imprisonment?

Even when an individual has been accepted as an author, we must still ask whether everything that he wrote, said, or left behind is part of his work. The problem is both theoretical and technical. When undertaking the publication of Nietzsche's works, for example, where should one stop? Surely everything must be published, but what is "everything"? Everything that Nietzsche himself published, certainly. And what about the rough drafts for his works? Obviously. The plans for his aphorisms? Yes. The deleted passages and the notes at the bottom of the page? Yes. What if, within a workbook filled with aphorisms, one finds a reference, the notation of a meeting or of an address, or a laundry list: is it a work, or not? Why not? And so on, ad infinitum. How can one define a work amid the millions of traces left by someone after his death? A theory of the work does not exist, and the empirical task of those who naively undertake the editing of works often suffers in the absence of such a theory.

We could go even further: does *The Thousand and One Nights* constitute a work? What about Clement of Alexandria's *Miscellanies* or Diogenes Laertius' *Lives?* A multitude of questions arises with regard to this notion of the work. Consequently, it is not enough to declare that we should do without the writer (the author) and study the work in itself. The word "work" and the unity that it designates are probably as problematic as the status of the author's individuality.

Another notion which has hindered us from taking full measure of the author's disappearance, blurring and concealing the moment of this effacement and subtly preserving the author's existence, is the notion of writing [*écriture*]. When rigorously applied, this notion should allow us not only to circumvent references to the author, but also to situate his recent absence. The notion of writing, as currently employed, is concerned with neither the act of writing nor the indication—be it symptom or sign—of a meaning which someone might have wanted to express. We try, with great effort, to imagine the general condition of each text, the condition of both the space in which it is dispersed and the time in which it unfolds.

In current usage, however, the notion of writing seems to transpose the empirical characteristics of the author into a transcendental anonymity. We are content to efface the more visible marks of the author's empiricity by playing off, one against the other, two ways of characterizing writing, namely, the critical and the religious approaches. Giving writing a primal status seems to be a way of retranslating, in transcendental terms, both the theological affirmation of its sacred character and the critical affirmation of its creative character. To admit that writing is, because of the very history that it made possible, subject to the test of oblivion and repression, seems to represent, in transcendental terms, the religious principle of the hidden meaning (which requires interpretation) and the critical principle of implicit significations, silent determinations, and obscured contents (which gives rise to commentary). To imagine writing as absence seems to be a simple repetition, in transcendental terms, of both the religious principle of inalterable and yet never fulfilled tradition, and the aesthetic principle of the work's survival, its perpetuation beyond the author's death, and its enigmatic *excess* in relation to him.

This usage of the notion of writing runs the risk of maintaining the author's privileges under the protection of writing's a priori status: it keeps alive, in the grey light of neutralization, the interplay of those representations that formed a particular image of the author. The author's disappearance, which, since Mallarmé, has been a constantly recurring event, is subject to a series of transcendental barriers. There seems to be an important dividing line between those who believe that they can still locate today's discontinuities *(ruptures)* in the historicotranscendental tradition of the nineteenth century, and those who try to free themselves once and for all from that tradition.[1]

It is not enough, however, to repeat the empty affirmation that the author has disappeared. For the same reason, it is not enough to keep repeating (after Nietzsche) that God and man have died a common death. Instead, we must locate the space left empty by the author's disappearance, follow the distribution of gaps and breaches, and watch for the openings that this disappearance uncovers.

First, we need to clarify briefly the problems arising from the use of the author's name. What is an author's name? How does it function? Far from offering a solution, I shall only indicate some of the difficulties that it presents.

The author's name is a proper name, and therefore it raises the problems common to all proper names. (Here I refer to Searle's analyses, among others.[2] Obviously, one cannot turn a proper name into a pure and simple reference. It has other than indicative functions: more than an indication, a gesture, a finger pointed at someone, it is the equivalent of a description. When one says "Aristotle," one employs a word that is the equivalent of one, or a series of, definite descriptions, such as "the author of the *Analytics*," "the founder of ontology," and so forth. One cannot stop there, however, because a proper name does not have just one signification. When we discover that Rimbaud did not write *La Chasse spirituelle,* we cannot pretend that the meaning of this proper name, or that of the author, has been altered. The proper name and the author's name are situated between the two poles of description and designation: they must have a certain link with what they name, but one that is neither entirely in the mode of designation nor in that of description; it must be a *specific* link. How-

ever—and it is here that the particular difficulties of the author's name arise—the links between the proper name and the individual named and between the author's name and what it names are not isomorphic and do not function in the same way. There are several differences.

If, for example, Pierre Dupont does not have blue eyes, or was not born in Paris, or is not a doctor, the name Pierre Dupont will still always refer to the same person; such things do not modify the link of designation. The problems raised by the author's name are much more complex, however. If I discover that Shakespeare was not born in the house that we visit today, this is a modification which, obviously, will not alter the functioning of the author's name. But if we proved that Shakespeare did not write those sonnets which pass for his, that would constitute a significant change and affect the manner in which the author's name functions. If we proved that Shakespeare wrote Bacon's *Organon* by showing that the same author wrote both the works of Bacon and those of Shakespeare, that would be a third type of change which would entirely modify the functioning of the author's name. The author's name is not, therefore, just a proper name like the rest.

Many other facts point out the paradoxical singularity of the author's name. To say that Pierre Dupont does not exist is not at all the same as saying that Homer or Hermes Trismegistus did not exist. In the first case, it means that no one has the name Pierre Dupont; in the second, it means that several people were mixed together under one name, or that the true author had none of the traits traditionally ascribed to the personae of Homer or Hermes. To say that X's real name is actually Jacques Durand instead of Pierre Dupont is not the same as saying that Stendhal's name was Henri Beyle. One could also question the meaning and functioning of propositions like "Bourbaki is so-and-so, so-

and-so, etc." and "Victor Eremita, Climacus, Anticlimacus, Frater Taciturnus, Constantine Constantius, all of these are Kierkegaard."

These differences may result from the fact that an author's name is not simply an element in a discourse (capable of being either subject or object, of being replaced by a pronoun, and the like); it performs a certain role with regard to narrative discourse, assuring a classificatory function. Such a name permits one to group together a certain number of texts, define them, differentiate them from and contrast them to others. In addition, it establishes a relationship among the texts. Hermes Trismegistus did not exist, nor did Hippocrates—in the sense that Balzac existed—but the fact that several texts have been placed under the same name indicates that there has been established among them a relationship of homogeneity, filiation, authentification of some texts by the use of others, reciprocal explication, or concomitant utilization. The author's name serves to characterize a certain mode of being of discourse: the fact that the discourse has an author's name, that one can say "this was written by so-and-so" or "so-and-so is its author," shows that this discourse is not ordinary everyday speech that merely comes and goes, not something that is immediately consumable. On the contrary, it is a speech that must be received in a certain mode and that, in a given culture, must receive a certain status.

It would seem that the author's name, unlike other proper names, does not pass from the interior of a discourse to the real and exterior individual who produced it; instead, the name seems always to be present, marking off the edges of the text, revealing, or at least characterizing, its mode of being. The author's name manifests the appearance of a certain discursive set and indicates the status of this discourse within a society and a culture. It has no legal status, nor is it located in the fiction of the work; rather, it is located in the break that founds a certain discursive

construct and its very particular mode of being. As a result, we could say that in a civilization like our own there are a certain number of discourses that are endowed with the "author-function," while others are deprived of it. A private letter may well have a signer—it does not have an author; a contract may well have a guarantor—it does not have an author. An anonymous text posted on a wall probably has a writer—but not an author. The author-function is therefore characteristic of the mode of existence, circulation, and functioning of certain discourses within a society.

Let us analyze this "author-function" as we have just described it. In our culture, how does one characterize a discourse containing the author-function? In what way is this discourse different from other discourses? If we limit our remarks to the author of a book or a text, we can isolate four different characteristics.

First of all, discourses are objects of appropriation. The form of ownership from which they spring is of a rather particular type, one that has been codified for many years. We should note that, historically, this type of ownership has always been subsequent to what one might call penal appropriation. Texts, books, and discourses really began to have authors (other than mythical, "sacralized" and "sacralizing" figures) to the extent that authors became subject to punishment, that is, to the extent that discourses could be transgressive. In our culture (and doubtless in many others), discourse was not originally a product, a thing, a kind of goods; it was essentially an act—an act placed in the bipolar field of the sacred and the profane, the licit and the illicit, the religious and the blasphemous. Historically, it was a gesture fraught with risks before becoming goods caught up in a circuit of ownership. Once a system of ownership for texts came into being, once strict rules concerning author's rights, author-publisher relations, rights of reproduction, and related matters were enacted—at the end of the eighteenth and the beginning of the nineteenth century—the possibility of transgression attached to the act of writing took on, more and more, the form of an imperative peculiar to literature. It is as if the author, beginning with the moment at which he was placed in the system of property that characterizes our society, compensated for the status that he thus acquired by rediscovering the old bipolar field of discourse, systematically practicing transgression and thereby restoring danger to a writing which was now guaranteed the benefits of ownership.

The author-function does not affect all discourses in a universal and constant way, however. This is its second characteristic. In our civilization, it has not always been the same types of texts which have required attribution to an author. There was a time when the texts that we today call "literary" (narratives, stories, epics, tragedies, comedies) were accepted, put into circulation, and valorized without any question about the identity of their author; their anonymity caused no difficulties since their ancientness, whether real or imagined, was regarded as a sufficient guarantee of their status. On the other hand, those texts that we now would call scientific—those dealing with cosmology and the heavens, medicine and illnesses, natural sciences and geography—were accepted in the Middle Ages, and accepted as "true," only when marked with the name of their author. "Hippocrates said," "Pliny recounts," were not really formulas of an argument based on authority; they were the markers inserted in discourses that were supposed to be received as statements of demonstrated truth.

A reversal occurred in the seventeenth or eighteenth century. Scientific discourses began to be received for themselves, in the anonymity of an established or always redemonstrable truth; their membership in a sys-

tematic ensemble, and not the reference to the individual who produced them, stood as their guarantee. The author-function faded away, and the inventor's name served only to christen a theorem, proposition, particular effect, property, body, group of elements, or pathological syndrome. By the same token, literary discourses came to be accepted only when endowed with the author-function. We now ask of each poetic or fictional text: from where does it come, who wrote it, when, under what circumstances, or beginning with what design? The meaning ascribed to it and the status or value accorded it depend upon the manner in which we answer these questions. And if a text should be discovered in a state of anonymity—whether as a consequence of an accident or the author's explicit wish—the game becomes one of rediscovering the author. Since literary anonymity is not tolerable, we can accept it only in the guise of an enigma. As a result, the author-function today plays an important role in our view of literary works. (These are obviously generalizations that would have to be refined insofar as recent critical practice is concerned.)

The third characteristic of this author-function is that it does not develop spontaneously as the attribution of a discourse to an individual. It is, rather, the result of a complex operation which constructs a certain rational being that we call "author." Critics doubtless try to give this intelligible being a realistic status, by discerning, in the individual, a "deep" motive, a "creative" power, or a "design," the milieu in which writing originates. Nevertheless, these aspects of an individual which we designate as making him an author are only a projection, in more or less psychologizing terms, of the operations that we force texts to undergo, the connections that we make, the traits that we establish as pertinent, the continuities that we recognize, or the exclusions that we practice. All these operations vary according to periods and types of discourse. We do not construct a "philosophical author" as we do a "poet," just as, in the eighteenth century, one did not construct a novelist as we do today. Still, we can find through the ages certain constants in the rules of author-construction.

It seems, for example, that the manner in which literary criticism once defined the au-thor—or rather constructed the figure of the author beginning with existing texts and dis-courses—is directly derived from the manner in which Christian tradition authenticated (or rejected) the texts at its disposal. In order to "rediscover" an author in a work, modern criticism uses methods similar to those that Christian exegesis employed when trying to prove the value of a text by its author's saintli-ness. In *De viris illustribus,* Saint Jerome ex-plains that homonymy is not sufficient to identify legitimately authors of more than one work: different individuals could have had the same name, or one man could have, il-legitimately, borrowed another's patronymic. The name as an individual trademark is not enough when one works within a textual tra-dition.

How then can one attribute several dis-courses to one and the same author? How can one use the author-function to determine if one is dealing with one or several individuals? Saint Jerome proposes four criteria: (1) if among several books attributed to an author one is inferior to the others, it must be with-drawn from the list of the author's works (the author is therefore defined as a constant level of value); (2) the same should be done if certain texts contradict the doctrine ex-pounded in the author's other works (the au-thor is thus defined as a field of conceptual or theoretical coherence); (3) one must also ex-clude works that are written in a different style, containing words and expressions not ordinarily found in the writer's production (the author is here conceived as a stylistic unity); (4) finally, passages quoting state-ments that were made, or mentioning events that occurred after the author's death must be

regarded as interpolated texts (the author is here seen as a historical figure at the cross-roads of a certain number of events).

Modern literary criticism, even when—as is now customary—it is not concerned with questions of authentication, still defines the author the same way: the author provides the basis for explaining not only the presence of certain events in a work, but also their trans-formations, distortions, and diverse modifi-cations (through his biography, the determi-nation of his individual perspective, the anal-ysis of his social position, and the revelation of his basic design). The author is also the principle of a certain unity of writing—all differences having to be resolved, at least in part, by the principles of evolution, matura-tion, or influence. The author also serves to neutralize the contradictions that may emerge in a series of texts: there must be—at a cer-tain level of his thought or desire, of his con-sciousness or unconscious—a point where contradictions are resolved, where incompat-ible elements are at last tied together or orga-nized around a fundamental or originating contradiction. Finally, the author is a particu-lar source of expression that, in more or less completed forms, is manifested equally well, and with similar validity, in works, sketches, letters, fragments, and so on. Clearly, Saint Jerome's four criteria of authenticity (criteria which seem totally insufficient for today's ex-egetes) do define the four modalities accord-ing to which modern criticism brings the au-thor-function into play.

But the author-function is not a pure and simple reconstruction made secondhand from a text given as passive material. The text always contains a certain number of signs re-ferring to the author. These signs, well known to grammarians, are personal pro-nouns, adverbs of time and place, and verb conjugation. Such elements do not play the same role in discourses provided with the author-function as in those lacking it. In the latter, such "shifters" refer to the real speaker and to the spatio-temporal coordinates of his discourse (although certain modifications can occur, as in the operation of relating discourses in the first person). In the former, however, their role is more complex and variable. Everyone knows that, in a novel narrated in the first person, neither the first person pronoun, nor the present indicative refer exactly either to the writer or to the moment in which he writes, but rather to an alter ego whose distance from the author varies, often changing in the course of the work. It would be just as wrong to equate the author with the real writer as to equate him with the fictitious speaker; the author-function is carried out and operates in the scission itself, in this division and this distance.

One might object that this is a characteristic peculiar to novelistic or poetic discourse, a "game" in which only "quasi-discourses" participate. In fact, however, all discourses endowed with the author-function do possess this plurality of self. The self that speaks in the preface to a treatise on mathematics—and that indicates the circumstances of the treatise's composition—is identical neither in its position nor in its functioning to the self that speaks in the course of a demonstration, and that appears in the form of "I conclude" or "I suppose." In the first case, the "I" refers to an individual without an equivalent who, in a determined place and time, completed a certain task; in the second, the "I" indicates an instance and a level of demonstration which any individual could perform provided that he accept the same system of symbols, play of axioms, and set of previous demonstrations. We could also, in the same treatise, locate a third self, one that speaks to tell the work's meaning, the obstacles encountered, the results obtained, and the remaining problems; this self is situated in the field of already existing or yet-to-appear mathematical discourses. The author-function is not assumed by the first of these selves at the expense of the other two, which would then be nothing more than

a fictitious splitting in two of the first one. On the contrary, in these discourses the author-function operates so as to effect the dispersion of these three simultaneous selves.

No doubt analysis could discover still more characteristic traits of the author-function. I will limit myself to these four, however, because they seem both the most visible and the most important. They can be summarized as follows: (1) the author-function is linked to the juridical and institutional system that encompasses, determines, and articulates the universe of discourses; (2) it does not affect all discourses in the same way at all times and in all types of civilization; (3) it is not defined by the spontaneous attribution of a discourse to its producer, but rather by a series of specific and complex operations; (4) it does not refer purely and simply to a real individual, since it can give rise simultaneously to several selves, to several subjects—positions that can be occupied by different classes of individuals.

Up to this point I have unjustifiably limited my subject. Certainly the author-function in painting, music, and other arts should have been discussed, but even supposing that we remain within the world of discourse, as I want to do, I seem to have given the term "author" much too narrow a meaning. I have discussed the author only in the limited sense of a person to whom the production of a text, a book, or a work can be legitimately attributed. It is easy to see that in the sphere of discourse one can be the author of much more than a book—one can be the author of a theory, tradition, or discipline in which other books and authors will in their turn find a place. These authors are in a position which we shall call "transdiscursive." This is a recurring phenomenon—certainly as old as our civilization. Homer, Aristotle, and the Church Fathers, as well as the first mathematicians and the originators of the Hippocratic tradition, all played this role.

Furthermore, in the course of the nineteenth century, there appeared in Europe another, more uncommon, kind of author, whom one should confuse with neither the "great" literary authors, nor the authors of religious texts, nor the founders of science. In a somewhat arbitrary way we shall call those who belong in this last group "founders of discursivity." They are unique in that they are not just the authors of their own works. They have produced something else: the possibilities and the rules for the formation of other texts. In this sense, they are very different, for example, from a novelist, who is, in fact, nothing more than the author of his own text. Freud is not just the author of *The Interpretation of Dreams* or *Jokes and their Relation to the Unconscious;* Marx is not just the author of the *Communist Manifesto* or *Capital:* they both have established an endless possibility of discourse.

Obviously, it is easy to object. One might say that it is not true that the author of a novel is only the author of his own text; in a sense, he also, provided that he acquires some "importance," governs and commands more than that. To take a very simple example, one could say that Ann Radcliffe not only wrote *The Castles of Athlin and Dunbayne* and several other novels, but also made possible the appearance of the Gothic horror novel at the beginning of the nineteenth century; in that respect, her author-function exceeds her own work. But I think there is an answer to this objection. These founders of discursivity (I use Marx and Freud as examples, because I believe them to be both the first and the most important cases) make possible something altogether different from what a novelist makes possible. Ann Radcliffe's texts opened the way for a certain number of resemblances and analogies which have their model or principle in her work. The latter contains characteristic signs, figures, relationships, and structures which could be reused by others. In other words, to say that Ann Radcliffe founded the Gothic horror novel means that

in the nineteenth-century Gothic novel one will find, as in Ann Radcliffe's works, the theme of the heroine caught in the trap of her own innocence, the hidden castle, the character of the black, cursed hero devoted to making the world expiate the evil done to him, and all the rest of it.

On the other hand, when I speak of Marx or Freud as founders of discursivity, I mean that they made possible not only a certain number of analogies, but also (and equally important) a certain number of differences. They have created a possibility for something other than their discourse, yet something belonging to what they founded. To say that Freud founded psychoanalysis does not (simply) mean that we find the concept of the libido or the technique of dream analysis in the works of Karl Abraham or Melanie Klein; it means that Freud made possible a certain number of divergences—with respect to his own texts, concepts, and hypotheses—that all arise from the psychoanalytical discourse itself.

This would seem to present a new difficulty, however: is the above not true, after all, of any founder of a science, or of any author who has introduced some important transformation into a science? After all, Galileo made possible not only those discourses that repeated the laws that he had formulated, but also statements very different from what he himself had said. If Cuvier is the founder of biology or Saussure the founder of linguistics, it is not because they were imitated, nor because people have since taken up again the concept of organism or sign; it is because Cuvier made possible, to a certain extent, a theory of evolution diametrically opposed to his own fixism; it is because Saussure made possible a generative grammar radically different from his structural analyses. Superficially, then, the initiation of discursive practices appears similar to the founding of any scientific endeavor.

Still, there is a difference, and a notable one. In the case of a science, the act that founds it is on an equal footing with its future transformations; this act becomes in some respects part of the set of modifications that it makes possible. Of course, this belonging can take several forms. In the future development of a science, the founding act may appear as little more than a particular instance of a more general phenomenon which unveils itself in the process. It can also turn out to be marred by intuition and empirical bias; one must then reformulate it, making it the object of a certain number of supplementary theoretical operations which establish it more rigorously, etc. Finally, it can seem to be a hasty generalization which must be limited, and whose restricted domain of validity must be retraced. In other words, the founding act of a science can always be reintroduced within the machinery of those transformations that derive from it.

In contrast, the initiation of a discursive practice is heterogeneous to its subsequent transformations. To expand a type of discursivity, such as psychoanalysis as founded by Freud, is not to give it a formal generality that it would not have permitted at the outset, but rather to open it up to a certain number of possible applications. To limit psychoanalysis as a type of discursivity is, in reality, to try to isolate in the founding act an eventually restricted number of propositions or statements to which, alone, one grants a founding value, and in relation to which certain concepts or theories accepted by Freud might be considered as derived, secondary, and accessory. In addition, one does not declare certain propositions in the work of these founders to be false: instead, when trying to seize the act of founding, one sets aside those statements that are not pertinent, either because they are deemed inessential, or because they are considered "prehistoric" and derived from another type of discursivity. In other words, unlike the founding of a science, the initiation of a discursive practice does not participate in its later transformations.

As a result, one defines a proposition's theo-

retical validity in relation to the work of the founders—while, in the case of Galileo and Newton, it is in relation to what physics or cosmology *is* (in its intrinsic structure and "normativity") that one affirms the validity of any proposition that those men may have put forth. To phrase it very schematically: the work of initiators of discursivity is not situated in the space that science defines; rather, it is the science or the discursivity which refers back to their work as primary coordinates.

In this way we can understand the inevitable necessity, within these fields of discursivity, for a "return to the origin." This return, which is part of the discursive field itself, never stops modifying it. The return is not a historical supplement which would be added to the discursivity, or merely an ornament; on the contrary, it constitutes an effective and necessary task of transforming the discursive practice itself. Re-examination of Galileo's text may well change our knowledge of the history of mechanics, but it will never be able to change mechanics itself. On the other hand, re-examining Freud's texts modifies psychoanalysis itself just as a re-examination of Marx's would modify Marxism.[3]

What I have just outlined regarding the initiation of discursive practices is, of course, very schematic; this is true, in particular, of the opposition that I have tried to draw between discursive initiation and scientific founding. It is not always easy to distinguish between the two; moreover, nothing proves that they are two mutually exclusive procedures. I have attempted the distinction for only one reason: to show that the author-function, which is complex enough when one tries to situate it at the level of a book or a series of texts that carry a given signature, involves still more determining factors when one tries to analyze it in larger units, such as groups of works or entire disciplines.

To conclude, I would like to review the reasons why I attach a certain importance to what I have said.

First, there are theoretical reasons. On the one hand, an analysis in the direction that I have outlined might provide for an approach to a typology of discourse. It seems to me, at least at first glance, that such a typology cannot be constructed solely from the grammatical features, formal structures, and objects of discourse: more likely there exist properties or relationships peculiar to discourse (not reducible to the rules of grammar and logic), and one must use these to distinguish the major categories of discourse. The relationship (or nonrelationship) with an author, and the different forms this relationship takes, constitute—in a quite visible manner—one of these discursive properties.

On the other hand, I believe that one could find here an introduction to the historical analysis of discourse. Perhaps it is time to study discourses not only in terms of their expressive value or formal transformations, but according to their modes of existence. The modes of circulation, valorization, attribution, and appropriation of discourses vary with each culture and are modified within each. The manner in which they are articulated according to social relationships can be more readily understood, I believe, in the activity of the author-function and in its modifications, than in the themes or concepts that discourses set in motion.

It would seem that one could also, beginning with analyses of this type, re-examine the privileges of the subject. I realize that in undertaking the internal and architectonic analysis of a work (be it a literary text, philosophical system, or scientific work), in setting aside biographical and psychological references, one has already called back into question the absolute character and founding role of the subject. Still, perhaps one must return to this question, not in order to re-establish the theme of an originating subject, but to grasp the subject's points of insertion, modes of functioning, and system of dependencies. Doing so means overturning the traditional problem, no longer raising the questions "How can a free subject penetrate the substance of things and give it meaning? How can it activate the rules of a language from within and thus give rise to the designs which are properly its own?" Instead, these questions will be raised: "How, under what conditions and in what forms can something like a subject appear in the order of discourse? What place can it occupy in each type of discourse, what functions can it assume, and by obeying what rules?" In short, it is a matter of depriving the subject (or its substitute) of its role as originator, and of analyzing the subject as a variable and complex function of discourse.

Second, there are reasons dealing with the "ideological" status of the author. The question then becomes: How can one reduce the great peril, the great danger with which fiction threatens our world? The answer is: One can reduce it with the author. The author allows a limitation of the cancerous and dangerous proliferation of significations within a world where one is thrifty not only with one's resources and riches, but also with one's discourses and their significations. The author is the principle of thrift in the proliferation of meaning. As a result, we must entirely reverse the traditional idea of the author. We are accustomed, as we have seen earlier, to saying that the author is the genial creator of a work in which he deposits, with infinite wealth and generosity, an inexhaustible world of significations. We are used to thinking that the author is so different from all other men, and so transcendent with regard to all languages that, as soon as he speaks, meaning begins to proliferate, to proliferate indefinitely.

The truth is quite the contrary: the author is not an indefinite source of significations which fill a work; the author does not precede the works, he is a certain functional principle by which, in our culture, one limits, excludes, and chooses; in short, by which one impedes the free circulation, the free manipulation, the free composition, decomposition, and recomposition of fiction. In fact, if we are accustomed to presenting the author as a genius, as a perpetual surging of invention, it is because, in reality, we make him function in exactly the opposite fashion. One can say that the author is an ideological product, since we represent him as the opposite of his historically real function. (When a historically given function is represented in a figure that inverts it, one has an ideological production.) The author is therefore the ideological figure by which one marks the manner in which we fear the proliferation of meaning.

In saying this, I seem to call for a form of culture in which fiction would not be limited by the figure of the author. It would be pure romanticism, however, to imagine a culture in which the fictive would operate in an absolutely free state, in which fiction would be put at the disposal of everyone and would develop without passing through something like a necessary or constraining figure. Although, since the eighteenth century, the author has played the role of the regulator of the fictive, a role quite characteristic of our era of industrial and bourgeois society, of individualism and private property, still, given the historical modifications that are taking place, it does not seem necessary that the author-function remain constant in form, complexity, and even in existence. I think that, as our society changes, at the very moment when it is in the process of changing, the author-function will disappear, and in such a manner that fiction and its polysemic texts will once again function according to another mode, but still with a system of constraint—one which will no longer be the author, but which will have to be determined or, perhaps, experienced.

All discourses, whatever their status, form, value, and whatever the treatment to which they will be subjected, would then develop in the anonymity of a murmur. We would no longer hear the questions that have been rehashed for so long: "Who really spoke? Is it really he and not someone else? With what authenticity or originality? And what part of his deepest self did he express in his discourse?" Instead, there would be other questions, like these: "What are the modes of existence of this discourse? Where has it been used, how can it circulate, and who can appropriate it for himself? What are the places in it where there is room for possible subjects? Who can assume these various subject-functions?" And behind all these questions, we would hear hardly anything but the stirring of an indifference: "What difference does it make who is speaking?"

*Translated by Josué V. Harari*

## NOTES

1. For a discussion of the notions of discontinuity and historical tradition see Foucault's *Les Mots et les choses* (Paris: Gallimard, 1966), translated as *The Order of Things* (New York: Pantheon, 1971).—Trans.

2. John Searle, *Speech Acts: An Essay in the Philosophy of Language* (Cambridge: Cambridge University Press, 1969), pp. 162–174.—Trans.

3. To define these returns more clearly, one must also emphasize that they tend to reinforce the enigmatic link between an author and his works. A text has an inaugurative value precisely because it is the work of a particular author, and our returns are conditioned by this knowledge. As in the case of Galileo, there is no possibility that the rediscovery of an unknown text by Newton or Cantor will modify classical cosmology or set theory as we know them (at best, such an exhumation might modify our historical knowledge of their genesis). On the other hand, the discovery of a text like Freud's "Project for a Scientific Psychology"—insofar as it is a text by Freud—always threatens to modify not the historical knowledge of psychoanalysis, but its theoretical field, even if only by shifting the accentuation or the center of gravity. Through such returns, which are part of their make-up, these discursive practices maintain a relationship with regard to their "fundamental" and indirect author unlike that which an ordinary text entertains with its immediate author.—Trans.

# 22

# Catherine Belsey
# 1940–

Catherine Belsey lectures in English at the University of Wales, College of Cardiff. She is the author of *Critical Practice* (1980), *The Subject of Tragedy: Identity and Difference in Renaissance Drama* (1985), and *John Milton: Language, Gender, Power* (1988). She is also editor, with Jane Moore, of *The Feminist Reader: Essays in Gender and the Politics of Literary Criticism* (1989). Belsey's *Critical Practice* was one of the most influential books introducing contemporary French Marxist, feminist, psychoanalytical, and poststructuralist theory to the English-speaking world. Along with Terry Eagleton, she argued for the materialist and historical view of literature and culture championed in France by Louis Althusser and Pierre Machery and in the early work of Roland Barthes. Her work has drawn the ire of defenders of traditional liberal humanism, who see her ideas on the cultural constitution of the subject or self and the systemic shaping effects of discourse as threats to the ethical basis of Western civilization. Belsey, however, uses theory to support a broad cultural and intellectual critique of endemic class and gender-based oppression under the surface of parliamentary democracy and humanist "freedoms."

At the heart of Belsey's account of critical practice is the critique of the "normal," "self-evident" view of the human self or subject and its relation to language and to power relations in society. In "Constructing the Subject: Deconstructing the Text" (1985), she again concentrates on the constitution of the self in and through discourse, and on the particular functions of literature, "as one of the more persuasive uses of language," in affecting the ways in which people understand themselves and their relations with each other and the world. Belsey reiterates here, as in *Critical Practice,* the implications of Saussure's theory of language: "there is no unmediated experience," and "[t]he subject is constructed in language and in discourse and, since the symbolic order in its discursive use is closely related to ideology, in ideology." Ideology "suppresses the role of language in the construction of the subject" and as a result people "misrecognize" themselves according to the ways in which society "interpellates" them. In this way the role of constituted "subjects" is twofold, Belsey argues. Within bourgeois ideology, which relies on the idea of individual fixed identities, lies the "subjected being" who believes she is choosing freely to accept what is, in fact, a constructed identity.

These basic assumptions, of course, have implications for the authors of literature, as well as for the texts themselves. Relying on Lacan and Macherey, Belsey looks carefully in this article at classic realism and the gap "between the ideological project and the specifically literary form," noting that "[t]he text is no more a transcendent unity than the human subject." Belsey suggests a way of reading for the critic that is "precisely contrary to traditional Anglo-American critical practice, where the quest is for the unity of the work" and for a closure that ultimately colludes with and gives allegiance to dominant ideology. Belsey's critical objective is to expose the multiplicity of meaning within the text, including and most especially its contradictions, within which may be found the "process of its production." As Belsey has stated in many different places and ways, no form of interpretation is a politically neutral act.

# Constructing the Subject: Deconstructing the Text

## THE SUBJECT IN IDEOLOGY

One of the central issues for feminism is the cultural construction of subjectivity. It seems imperative to many feminists to find ways of explaining why women have not simply united to overthrow patriarchy. Why, since all women experience the effects of patriarchal practices, are not all women feminists? And why do those of us who think of ourselves as feminists find ourselves inadvertently colluding, at least from time to time, with the patriarchal values and assumptions prevalent in our society? Since the late seventeenth century feminists have seen subjectivity as itself subject to convention, education, culture in its broadest sense. Now feminist criticism has allowed that fiction too plays a part in the process of constructing subjectivity. But how?

In his influential essay, "Ideology and ideological state apparatuses," Louis Althusser includes literature among the ideological apparatuses which contribute to the process of *reproducing* the *relations of production,* the social relationships which are the necessary condition for the existence and perpetuation of the capitalist mode of production. He does not here develop the argument concerning literature, but in the context both of his concept of ideology and also of the work of Roland Barthes on literature and Jacques Lacan on psychoanalysis it is possible to

construct an account of some of the implications for feminist critical theory and practice of Althusser's position. The argument is not only that literature represents the myths and imaginary versions of real social relationships which constitute ideology, but also that classic realist fiction, the dominant literary form of the nineteenth century and arguably of the twentieth, "interpellates" the reader, addresses itself to him or her directly, offering the reader as the position from which the text is most "obviously" intelligible, the position of the *subject in (and of) ideology*.

According to Althusser's reading (re-reading) of Marx, ideology is not simply a set of illusions, as *The German Ideology* seems to argue, but a system of representations (discourses, images, myths) concerning the real relations in which people live. But what is represented in ideology is "not the system of the real relations which govern the existence of individuals, but the imaginary relation of those individuals to the real relations in which they live' (Althusser 1971, p. 155). In other words, ideology is both a real and an imaginary relation to the world—real in that it is the way in which people really live their relationship to the social relations which govern their conditions of existence, but imaginary in that it discourages a full understanding of these conditions of existence and the ways in which people are socially constituted within them. It is not, therefore, to be thought of as a system of ideas in people's heads, nor as the expression at a higher level of real material relationships, but as the necessary condition of action within the social formation. Althusser talks of ideology as a "material practice" in this sense: it exists in the behaviour of people acting according to their beliefs (ibid., pp. 155–9).

As the necessary condition of action, ideology exists in commonplaces and truisms as well as in philosophical and religious systems. It is apparent in all that is "obvious" to us, in "obviousnesses which we cannot *fail to recognise* and before which we have the inevitable and natural reaction of crying out (aloud or in the 'still, small voice of conscience'): 'That's obvious! That's right! That's true!'" (ibid., p. 161). If it is true, however, it is not the whole truth. Ideology obscures the real conditions of existence by presenting partial truths. It is a set of omissions, gaps rather than lies, smoothing over contradictions, appearing to provide answers to questions which in reality it evades, and masquerading as coherence in the interests of the social relations generated by and necessary to the reproduction of the existing mode of production.

It is important to stress, of course, that ideology is in no sense a set of deliberate distortions foisted upon a helpless working class by a corrupt and cynical bourgeoisie (or upon victimized women by violent and power hungry men). If there are groups of sinister men in shirt-sleeves purveying illusions to the public these are not the real makers of ideology. Ideology has no creators in that sense, since it exists necessarily. But according to Althusser ideological practices are supported and reproduced in the institutions of our society which he calls Ideological State Apparatuses (ISAs). The phrase distinguishes from the Repressive State Apparatus which works by force (the police, the penal system, the army) those institutions whose existence

helps to guarantee consent to the existing mode of production. The central ISA in contemporary capitalism is the educational system, which prepares children to act consistently with the values of society by inculcating in them the dominant versions of appropriate behaviour as well as history, social studies and, of course, literature. Among the allies of the educational ISA are the family, the law, the media and the arts, all helping to represent and reproduce the myths and beliefs necessary to enable people to work within the existing social formation.

The destination of all ideology is the subject (the individual in society) and it is the role of ideology to *construct people as subjects:*

> I say: the category of the subject is constitutive of all ideology, but at the same time and immediately I add that *the category of the subject is only constitutive of all ideology in so far as all ideology has the function (which defines it) of "constituting" concrete individuals as subjects.* (ibid., p. 160)

Within the existing ideology it appears "obvious" that people are autonomous individuals, possessed of subjectivity or consciousness which is the source of their beliefs and actions. That people are unique, distinguishable, irreplaceable identities is "the elementary ideological effect" (ibid., p. 161).

The obviousness of subjectivity has been challenged by the linguistic theory which has developed on the basis of the work of Saussure. As Emile Benveniste argues, it is language which provides the possibility of subjectivity because it is language which enables the speaker to posit himself or herself as "I," as the subject of a sentence. It is in language that people constitute themselves as subjects. Consciousness of self is possible only through contrast, differentiation: "I" cannot be conceived without the conception "non-I," "you," and dialogue, the fundamental condition of language, implies a reversible polarity between "I" and "you." "Language is possible only because each speaker sets himself up as a *subject* by referring to himself as *I* in his discourse" (Benveniste 1971, p. 225). But if language is a system of differences with no positive terms, "I" designates only the subject of a specific utterance. "And so it is literally true that the basis of subjectivity is in the exercise of language. If one really thinks about it, one will see that there is no other objective testimony to the identity of the subject except that which he himself thus gives about himself" (ibid., p. 226).

Within ideology, of course, it seems "obvious" that the individual speaker is the origin of the meaning of his or her utterance. Post-Saussurean linguistics, however, implies a more complex relationship between the individual and meaning, since it is language itself which, by differentiating between concepts, offers the possibility of meaning. In reality, it is only by adopting the position of the subject within language that the individual is able to produce meaning. As Derrida puts it,

> what was it that Saussure in particular reminded us of? That "language [which consists only of differences] is not a function of the speaking subject." This implies that the subject (self-identical or even conscious of self-identity, self-conscious) is inscribed in the language, that he is a "function" of the language. He becomes a *speaking* subject only by conforming his speech . . . to the system of linguistic prescriptions taken as the system of differences. (Derrida 1973, pp. 145–6)

Derrida goes on to raise the question whether, even if we accept that it is only the signifying system which makes possible the speaking subject, the signifying subject, we cannot none the less conceive of a non-speaking, non-signifying subjectivity, "a silent and intuitive consciousness" (ibid., p.

146). The problem here, he concludes, is to define consciousness-in-itself as distinct from consciousness of something, and ultimately as distinct from consciousness of self. If consciousness is finally consciousness of self, this in turn implies that consciousness depends on differentiation, and specifically on Benveniste's differentiation between "I" and "you," a process made possible by language.

The implications of this concept of the primacy of language over subjectivity have been developed by Jacques Lacan's reading of Freud. Lacan's theory of the subject as constructed in language confirms the *decentring* of the individual consciousness so that it can no longer be seen as the origin of meaning, knowledge and action. Instead, Lacan proposes that the infant is initially an "hommelette"—"a little man and also like a broken egg spreading without hindrance in all directions" (Coward and Ellis 1977, p. 101). The child has no sense of identity, no way of conceiving of itself as a unity, distinct from what is "other," exterior to it. During the "mirror-phase" of its development, however, it "recognizes" itself in the mirror as a unit distinct from the outside world. This "recognition" is an identification with an "imaginary" (because imaged) unitary and autonomous self. But it is only with its entry into language that the child becomes a full subject. If it is to participate in the society into which it is born, to be able to act deliberately within the social formation, the child must enter into the symbolic order, the set of signifying systems of culture of which the supreme example is language. The child who refuses to learn the language is "sick," unable to become a full member of the family and of society.

In order to speak the child is compelled to differentiate; to speak of itself it has to distinguish "I" from "you." In order to formulate its needs the child learns to identify with the first person singular pronoun, and this identification constitutes the basis of subjectivity.

Subsequently it learns to recognize itself in a series of subject-positions ("he" or "she," "boy" or "girl," and so on) which are the positions from which discourse is intelligible to itself and others. "Identity," subjectivity, is thus a matrix of subject-positions, which may be inconsistent or even in contradiction with one another.

Subjectivity, then, is linguistically and discursively constructed and displaced across the range of discourses in which the concrete individual participates. It follows from Saussure's theory of language as a system of differences that the world is intelligible only in discourse: there is no unmediated experience, no access to the raw reality of self and others. Thus:

> As well as being a system of signs related among themselves, language incarnates meaning in the form of the series of positions it offers for the subject from which to grasp itself and its relations with the real. (Nowell-Smith 1976, p. 26)

The subject is constructed in language and in discourse and, since the symbolic order in its discursive use is closely related to ideology, in ideology. It is in this sense that ideology has the effect, as Althusser argues, of constituting individuals as subjects, and it is also in this sense that their subjectivity appears "obvious." Ideology suppresses the role of language in the construction of the subject. As a result, people "recognize" (misrecognize) themselves in the ways in which ideology "interpellates" them, or in other words, addresses them as subjects, calls them by their names and in turn "recognizes" their autonomy. As a result, they "work by themselves" (Althusser 1971, p. 169), they "willingly" adopt the subject-positions necessary to their participation in the social formation. In capitalism they "freely" exchange their labour-power for wages, and they "voluntarily" purchase the commodities produced. In pa-

triarchal society women "choose" to do the housework, to make sacrifices for their children, not to become engineers. And it is here that we see the full force of Althusser's use of the term "subject," originally borrowed, as he says, from law. The subject is not only a grammatical subject, "a centre of initiatives, author of and responsible for its actions," but also a *subjected being* who submits to the authority of the social formation represented in ideology as the Absolute Subject (God, the king, the boss, Man, conscience): "the individual *is interpellated as a (free) subject in order that he shall submit freely to the commandments of the Subject, i.e. in order that he shall (freely) accept his subjection*" (ibid., p. 169).

Ideology interpellates concrete individuals as subjects, and bourgeois ideology in particular emphasizes the fixed identity of the individual. "I'm just *like* that"—cowardly, perhaps, or aggressive, generous or impulsive. Astrology is only an extreme form of the determinism which attributes to us given essences which cannot change. Popular psychology and popular sociology make individual behaviour a product of these essences. And underlying them all, ultimately unalterable, is "human nature." In these circumstances, how is it possible to suppose that, even if we could break in theoretical terms with the concepts of the ruling ideology, we are ourselves capable of change, and therefore capable both of acting to change the social formation and of transforming ourselves to constitute a new kind of society? A possible answer can be found in Lacan's theory of the precariousness of conscious subjectivity, which in turn depends on the Lacanian conception of the unconscious.

In Lacan's theory the individual is not in reality the harmonious and coherent totality of ideological misrecognition. The mirror-phase, in which the infant perceives itself as other, an image, exterior to is own perceiving self, necessitates a splitting between the *I* which is perceived and the *I* which does the perceiving. The entry into language necessitates a secondary division which reinforces the first, a split between the *I* of discourse, the subject of the utterance, and the *I* who speaks, the subject of the enunciation. There is thus a contradiction between the conscious self, the self which appears in its own discourse, and the self which is only partly represented there, the self which speaks. The unconscious comes into being in the gap which is formed by this division. The unconscious is constructed in the moment of entry into the symbolic order, simultaneously with the construction of the subject. The repository of repressed and pre-linguistic signifiers, the unconscious is a constant source of potential disruption of the symbolic order. To summarize very briefly what in Lacan is a complex and elusive theory, entry into the symbolic order liberates the child into the possibility of social relationship; it also reduces its helplessness to the extent that it is now able to articulate its needs in the form of demands. But at the same time a division within the self is constructed. In offering the child the possibility of formulating its desires the symbolic order also betrays them, since it cannot by definition formulate those elements of desire which remain unconscious. Demand is always only a metonymy of desire (Lemaire 1977, p. 64). The subject is thus the site of contradiction, and is consequently perpetually in the process of construction, thrown into crisis by alterations in language and in the social formation, capable of change. And in the fact that the subject is a *process* lies the possibility of transformation.

In addition, the displacement of subjectivity across a range of discourses implies a range of positions from which the subject grasps itself and its relations with the real, and these positions may be incompatible or contradictory. It is these incompatibilities and contradictions within what is taken for granted which exert a pressure on concrete individuals to seek new, non-contradictory subject-positions. Women as a group in our society are both produced and inhibited by contradictory discourses. Very broadly, we participate both in the liberal-humanist discourse of freedom, self-determination and rationality and at the same time in the specifically feminine discourse offered by society of submission, relative inadequacy and irrational intuition. The attempt to locate a single and coherent subject-position within these contradictory discourses, and in consequence to find a non-contradictory pattern of behaviour, can create intolerable pressures. One way of responding to this situation is to retreat from the contradictions and from discourse itself, to become "sick"—more women than men are treated for mental illness. Another is to seek a resolution of the contradictions in the discourses of feminism. That the position of women in society has changed so slowly, in spite of such a radical instability in it, may be partly explained in terms of the relative exclusion of women from the discourse of liberal humanism. This relative exclusion, supported in the predominantly masculine institutions of our society, is implicit, for example, in the use of masculine terms as generic ("rational man," etc.).

Women are not an isolated case. The class structure also produces contradictory subject-positions which precipitate changes in social relations not only between whole classes but between concrete individuals within those classes. Even at the conscious level, although this fact may itself be unconscious, the individual subject is not a unity, and in this lies the possibility of deliberate change.

This does not imply the reinstatement of individual subjects as the agents of change and changing knowledge. On the contrary, it insists on the concept of a dialectical relationship between concrete individuals and the language in which their subjectivity is constructed. In consequence, it also supports the concept of subjectivity as in process.

It is because subjectivity is perpetually in

process that literary texts can have an important function. No one, I think, would suggest that literature alone could precipitate a crisis in the social formation. None the less, if we accept Lacan's analysis of the importance of language in the construction of the subject it becomes apparent that literature as one of the most persuasive uses of language may have an important influence on the ways in which people grasp themselves and their relation to the real relations in which they live. The interpellation of the reader in the literary text could be argued to have a role in reinforcing the concepts of the world and of subjectivity which ensure that people "work by themselves" in the social formation. On the other hand, certain critical modes could be seen to challenge these concepts, and to call in question the particular complex of imaginary relations between individuals and the real conditions of their existence which helps to reproduce the present relations of class, race and gender.

## THE SUBJECT AND THE TEXT

Althusser analyses the interpellation of the subject in the context of ideology in general; Benveniste in discussing the relationship between language and subjectivity is concerned with language in general. None the less, it readily becomes apparent that capitalism in particular needs subjects who work by themselves, who freely exchange their labour-power for wages. It is in the epoch of capitalism that ideology emphasizes the value of individual freedom, freedom of conscience and, of course, consumer choice in all the multiplicity of its forms. The ideology of liberal humanism assumes a world of non-contradictory (and therefore fundamentally unalterable) individuals whose unfettered consciousness is the origin of meaning, knowledge and action. It is in the interest of this ideology above all to suppress the role of

language in the construction of the subject, and its own role in the interpellation of the subject, and to present the individual as a free, unified, autonomous subjectivity. Classic realism, still the dominant popular mode in literature, film and television drama, roughly coincides chronologically with the epoch of industrial capitalism. It performs, I wish to suggest, the work of ideology, not only in its representation of a world of consistent subjects who are the origin of meaning, knowledge and action, but also in offering the reader, as the position from which the text is most readily intelligible, the position of subject as the origin both of understanding and of action in accordance with that understanding.

It is readily apparent that Romantic and post-Romantic poetry, from Wordsworth through the Victorian period at least to Eliot and Yeats, takes subjectivity as its central theme. The developing self of the poet, his consciousness of himself as poet, his struggle against the constraints of an outer reality, constitute the preoccupations of *The Prelude, In Memoriam* or *Meditations in Time of Civil War*. The "I" of these poems is a kind of super-subject, experiencing life at a higher level of intensity than ordinary people and absorbed in a world of selfhood which the phenomenal world, perceived as external and antithetical, either nourishes or constrains. This transcendence of the subject in poetry is not presented as unproblematic, but it is entirely overt in the poetry of this period. The "I" of the poem directly addresses an individual reader who is invited to respond equally directly to this interpellation.

Fiction, however, in this same period, frequently appears to deal rather in social relationships, the interaction between the individual and society, to the increasing exclusion of the subjectivity of the author. Direct intrusion by the author comes to seem an impropriety; impersonal narration, "showing" (the truth) rather than "telling" it, is a requirement of prose fiction by the end of the nineteenth century. In drama too the author is apparently absent from the self-contained fictional world on the stage. Even the text effaces its own existence as text: unlike poetry, which clearly announces itself as formal, if only in terms of the shape of the text on the page, the novel seems merely to transcribe a series of events, to report on a palpable world, however fictional. Classic realist drama displays transparently and from the outside how people speak and behave.

Nevertheless, as we know while we read or watch, the author is present as a shadowy authority and as source of the fiction, and the author's presence is substantiated by the name on the cover of the programme: "a novel by Thomas Hardy," "a new play by Ibsen." And at the same time, as I shall suggest in this section, the *form* of the classic realist text acts in conjunction with the expressive theory and with ideology by interpellating the reader as subject. The reader is invited to perceive and judge the "truth" of the text, the coherent, non-contradictory interpretation of the world as it is perceived by an author whose autonomy is the source and evidence of the truth of the interpretation. This model of intersubjective communication, of shared understanding of a text which re-presents the world, is the guarantee not only of the truth of the text but of the reader's existence as an autonomous and knowing subject in a world of knowing subjects. In this way classic realism constitutes an ideological practice in addressing itself to readers as subjects, interpellating them in order that they freely accept their subjectivity and their subjection.

It is important to reiterate, of course, that this process is not inevitable, in the sense that texts do not determine like fate the ways in which they *must* be read. I am concerned at this stage primarily with ways in which they are conventionally read: conventionally, since language is conventional, and since

modes of writing as well as ways of reading are conventional, but conventionally also in that new conventions of reading are available. In this sense meaning is never a fixed essence inherent in the text but is always constructed by the reader, the result of a "circulation" between social formation, reader and text (Heath 1977–8, p. 74). In the same way, "inscribed subject positions are never hermetically sealed into a text, but are always positions in ideologies" (Willemen 1978, p. 63). To argue that classic realism interpellates subjects in certain ways is not to propose that this process is ineluctable; on the contrary it is a matter of choice. But the choice is ideological: certain ranges of meaning (there is always room for debate) are "obvious" within the currently dominant ideology, and certain subject-positions are equally "obviously" the positions from which these meanings are apparent.

Classic realism is characterized by "illusionism," narrative which leads to "closure," and a "hierarchy of discourses" which establishes the "truth" of the story. "Illusionism" is, I hope, self-explanatory. The other two defining characteristics of classic realism need some discussion. Narrative tends to follow certain recurrent patterns. Classic realist narrative, as Barthes demonstrates in *S/Z,* turns on the creation of enigma through the precipitation of disorder which throws into disarray the conventional cultural and signifying systems. Among the commonest sources of disorder at the level of plot in classic realism are murder, war, a journey or love. But the story moves inevitably towards closure which is also disclosure, the dissolution of enigma through the re-establishment of order, recognizable as a reinstatement or a development of the order which is understood to have preceded the events of the story itself.

The moment of closure is the point at which the events of the story become fully intelligible to the reader. The most obvious instance is the detective story where, in the final pages, the murderer is revealed and the motive made plain. But a high degree of intelligibility is sustained throughout the narrative as a result of the hierarchy of discourses in the text. The hierarchy works above all by means of a privileged discourse which places as subordinate all the discourses that are literally or figuratively between inverted commas.

By these means classic realism offers the reader a position of knowingness which is also a position of identification with the narrative voice. To the extent that the story first constructs, and then depends for its intelligibility, on a set of assumptions shared between narrator and reader, it confirms both the transcendent knowingness of the reader-as-subject and the "obviousness" of the shared truths in question.

## DECONSTRUCTING THE TEXT

Ideology, masquerading as coherence and plenitude, is in reality inconsistent, limited, contradictory, and the realist text as a crystallization of ideology participates in this incompleteness even while it diverts attention from the fact in the apparent plenitude of narrative closure. The object of deconstructing the text is to examine the *process of its production*— not the private experience of the individual author, but the mode of production, the materials and their arrangement in the work. The aim is to locate the point of contradiction within the text, the point at which it transgresses the limits within which it is constructed, breaks free of the constraints imposed by its own realist form. Composed of contradictions, the text is no longer restricted to a single, harmonious and authoritative reading. Instead it becomes *plural*, open to rereading, no longer an object for passive consumption but an object of work by the reader to produce meaning.

It is the work of Derrida which has been most influential in promoting deconstruction

as a critical strategy. Refusing to identify meaning with authorial intention or with the theme of the work, deconstruction tends to locate meaning in areas which traditional criticism has seen as marginal—in the metaphors, the set of oppositions or the hierarchies of terms which provide the framework of the text. The procedure, very broadly, is to identify in the text the contrary meanings which are the inevitable condition of its existence as a signifying practice, locating the trace of otherness which undermines the overt project.

Derrida, however, says little specifically about literary criticism or about the question of meaning in fiction. Nor is his work directly political. In order to produce a politics of reading we need to draw in addition on the work of Roland Barthes and Pierre Macherey. In *S/Z*, first published in 1970 (English translation 1975), Barthes deconstructs (without using the word) a short story by Balzac. *Sarrasine* is a classic realist text concerning a castrato singer and a fortune. The narrative turns on a series of enigmas (What is the source of the fortune? Who is the little old man? Who is La Zambinella? What is the connection between all three?). Even in summarizing the story in this way it is necessary to "lie": there are not "three" but two, since the little old "man" is "La" Zambinella. Barthes breaks the text into fragments of varying lengths for analysis, and adds a number of "divagations," pieces of more generalized commentary and exploration, to show *Sarrasine* as a "limit-text," a text which uses the modes of classic realism in ways which constitute a series of "transgressions" of classic realism itself. The sense of plenitude, of a full understanding of a coherent text which is the normal result of reading the realist narrative, cannot here be achieved. It is not only that castration cannot be named in a text of this period. The text is compelled to transgress the conventional antithesis between the genders whenever it uses a pronoun to speak of the castrato. The story concerns the scandal of castration and the death of desire which follows its revelation; it concerns the scandalous origin of wealth; and it demonstrates the collapse of language, of antithesis (difference) as a source of meaning, which is involved in the disclosure of these scandals.

Each of these elements of the text provides a point of entry into it, none privileged, and these approaches constitute the degree of polyphony, the "parsimonious plural" of the readable *(lisible)* text. The classic realist text moves inevitably and irreversibly to an end, to the conclusion of an ordered series of events, to the disclosure of what has been concealed. But even in the realist text certain modes of signification within the discourse—the symbolic, the codes of reference and the *semes*—evade the constraints of the narrative sequence. To the extent that these are "reversible," free-floating and of indeterminate authority, the text is plural. In the writable *(scriptible),* wholly plural text all statements are of indeterminate origin, no single discourse is privileged, and no consistent and coherent plot constrains the free play of the discourses. The totally writable, plural text does not exist. At the opposite extreme, the readable text is barely plural. The readable text is merchandise to be consumed, while the plural text requires the production of meanings through the identification of its polyphony. Deconstruction in order to reconstruct the text as a newly intelligible, plural object is the work of criticism.

Barthes's own mode of writing demonstrates his contempt for the readable: *S/Z* is itself a polyphonic critical text. It is impossible to summarize adequately, to reduce to systematic accessibility, and it is noticeable that the book contains no summarizing conclusion. Like *Sarrasine, S/Z* offers a number of points of entry, critical discourses which generate trains of thought in the reader, but it would be contrary to Barthes's own (anarchist) argument to order all these into a sin-

gle, coherent methodology, to constitute a new unitary way of reading, however comprehensive, and so to become the (authoritative) author of a new critical orthodoxy. As a result, the experience of reading *S/Z* is at once frustrating and exhilarating. Though it offers a model in one sense—it implies a new kind of critical practice—it would almost certainly not be possible (or useful) to attempt a wholesale imitation of its critical method(s).

It seems clear that one of the most influential precursors of *S/Z,* though Barthes does not allude to it, was Pierre Macherey's (Marxist) *A Theory of Literary Production,* first published in 1966 (English translation 1978). Despite real and important differences between them, there are similarities worth noting. For instance, Macherey anticipates Barthes in demonstrating that contradiction is a condition of narrative. The classic realist text is constructed on the basis of enigma. Information is initially withheld on condition of a "promise" to the reader that it will finally be revealed. The disclosure of this "truth" brings the story to an end. The movement of narrative is thus both towards disclosure—the end of the story—and towards concealment—prolonging itself by delaying the end of the story through a series of "reticences," as Barthes calls them, snares for the reader, partial answers to the questions raised, equivocations (Macherey 1978, pp. 28−9; Barthes 1975, pp. 75−6). Further, narrative involves the reader in an experience of the inevitable in the form of the unforeseen (Macherey 1978, p. 43). The hero encounters an obstacle: will he attempt to overcome it or abandon the quest? The answer is already determined, though the reader, who has only to turn the page to discover it, experiences the moment as one of choice for the hero. In fact, of course, if the narrative is to continue the hero must go on (Barthes 1975, p. 135). Thus the author's autonomy is to some degree illusory. In one sense the author determines the nature of the story: he or she decides what happens. In another sense, however, this decision is itself determined by the constraints of the narrative (Macherey 1978, p. 48), or by what Barthes calls the "interest" (in both the psychological and the economic senses) of the story (Barthes 1975, p. 135).

The formal constraints imposed by literary form on the project of the work in the process of literary production constitute the structural principle of Macherey's analysis. It is a mistake to reduce the text to the product of a single cause, authorial determination *or* the mechanics of the narrative. On the contrary, the literary work "is composed from a real diversity of elements which give it substance" (Macherey 1978, p. 49). There may be a direct contradiction between the project and the formal constraints, and in the transgression thus created it is possible to locate an important object of the critical quest.

Fiction for Macherey (he deals mainly with classic realist narrative) is intimately related to ideology, but the two are not identical. Literature is a specific and irreducible form of discourse, but the language which constitutes the raw material of the text is the language of ideology. It is thus an inadequate language, incomplete, partial, incapable of concealing the real contradictions it is its purpose to efface. This language, normally in flux, is arrested, "congealed" by the literary text.

The realist text is a determinate representation, an intelligible structure which claims to convey intelligible relationships between its elements. In its attempt to create a coherent and internally consistent fictive world the text, in spite of itself, exposes incoherences, omissions, absences and transgressions which in turn reveal the inability of the language of ideology to create coherence. This becomes apparent because the contradiction between the diverse elements drawn from different discourses, the ideological project and the literary form, creates an absence at the centre of the work. The text is divided,

split as the Lacanian subject is split, and Macherey compares the "lack" in the consciousness of the work, its silence, what it cannot say, with the unconscious which Freud explored (ibid., p. 85).

The unconscious of the work (*not,* it must be insisted, of the author) is constructed in the moment of its entry into literary form, in the gap between the ideological project and the specifically literary form. Thus the text is no more a transcendent unity than the human subject. The texts of Jules Verne, for instance, whose work Macherey analyses in some detail, indicate that "if Jules Verne chose to be the spokesman of a certain ideological condition, he could not choose to be what he in fact became" (ibid., p. 94). What Macherey reveals in Verne's *The Secret of the Island* is an unpredicted and contradictory element, disrupting the colonialist ideology which informs the conscious project of the work. Within the narrative, which concerns the willing surrender of nature to improvement by a team of civilized and civilizing colonizers, there *insists* an older and contrary myth which the consciousness of the text rejects. Unexplained events imply another mysterious presence on what is apparently a desert island. Captain Nemo's secret presence, and his influence on the fate of the castaways from a subterranean cave, is the source of the series of enigmas and the final disclosure which constitute the narrative. But his existence in the text has no part in the overt ideological project. On the contrary, it represents the return of the repressed in the form of a re-enacting of the myth of Robinson Crusoe. This myth evokes both a literary ancestor— Defoe's story—on which all subsequent castaway stories are to some degree conditional, and an ancestral relationship to nature—the creation of an economy by Crusoe's solitary struggle to appropriate and transform the island—on which subsequent bourgeois society is also conditional. The Robinson Crusoe story, the antithesis of the conscious project of the narrative, is also the condition of its existence. It returns, as the repressed experience returns to the consciousness of the patient in dreams and slips of the tongue and in doing so it unconsciously draws attention to an origin and a history from which both desert island stories and triumphant bourgeois ideology are unable to cut themselves off, and with which they must settle their account. *The Secret of the Island* thus reveals, through the discord within it between the conscious project and the insistence of the disruptive unconscious, the *limits* of the coherence of nineteenth-century ideology.

The object of the critic, then, is to seek not the unity of the work, but the multiplicity and diversity of its possible meanings, its incompleteness, the omissions which it displays but cannot describe, and above all its contradictions. In its absences, and in the collisions between its divergent meanings, the text implicitly criticizes its own ideology; it contains within itself the critique of its own values, in the sense that it is available for a new process of production of meaning by the reader, and in this process it can provide a knowledge of the limits of ideological representation.

Macherey's way of reading is precisely contrary to traditional Anglo-American critical practice, where the quest is for the unity of the work, its coherence, a way of repairing any deficiencies in consistency by reference to the author's philosophy or the contemporary world picture. In thus smoothing out contradiction, closing the text, criticism becomes the accomplice of ideology. Having created a canon of acceptable texts, criticism then provides them with acceptable interpretations, thus effectively censoring any elements in them which come into collusion with the dominant ideology. To deconstruct the text, on the other hand, is to open it, to release the possible positions of its intelligibility, including those which reveal the partiality (in both senses) of the ideology inscribed in the text.

## THE CASE OF SHERLOCK HOLMES

In locating the transitions and uncertainties of the text it is important to remember, Macherey insists, sustaining the parallel with psychoanalysis, that the problem of the work is not the same as its *consciousness* of a problem (Macherey 1978, p. 93). In "Charles Augustus Milverton," one of the short stories from *The Return of Sherlock Holmes,* Conan Doyle presents the reader with an ethical problem. Milverton is a blackmailer; blackmail is a crime not easily brought to justice since the victims are inevitably unwilling to make the matter public; the text therefore proposes for the reader's consideration that in such a case illegal action may be ethical. Holmes plans to burgle Milverton's house to recover the letters which are at stake, and both Watson and the text appear to conclude, after due consideration, that the action is morally justifiable. The structure of the narrative is symmetrical: one victim initiates the plot, another concludes it. While Holmes and Watson hide in Milverton's study a woman shoots him, protesting that he has ruined her life. Inspector Lestrade asks Holmes to help catch the murderer. Holmes replies that certain crimes justify private revenge, that his sympathies are with the criminal and that he will not handle the case. The reader is left to ponder the ethical implications of his position.

Meanwhile, on the fringes of the text, another narrative is sketched. It too contains problems but these are not foregrounded. Holmes's client is the Lady Eva Blackwell, a beautiful debutante who is to be married to the Earl of Dovercourt. Milverton has secured letters she has written "to an impecunious young squire in the country." Lady Eva does not appear in the narrative in person. The content of the letters is not specified, but they are "imprudent, Watson, nothing worse." Milverton describes them as "sprightly." Holmes's sympathies, and ours, are with the

Lady Eva. None the less we, and Holmes, accept without question on the one hand that the marriage with the Earl of Dovercourt is a desirable one and on the other that were he to see the letters he would certainly break off the match. The text's elusiveness on the content of the letters, and the absence of the Lady Eva herself, deflects the reader's attention from the potentially contradictory ideology of marriage which the narrative takes for granted.

This second narrative is also symmetrical. The murderer too is a woman with a past. She is not identified. Milverton has sent her letters to her husband who in consequence "broke his gallant heart and died." Again the text is unable to be precise about the content of the letters since to do so would be to risk losing the sympathy of the reader for either the woman or her husband.

In the mean time Holmes has become engaged. By offering to marry Milverton's housemaid he has secured information about the layout of the house he is to burgle. Watson remonstrates about the subsequent fate of the girl, but Holmes replies:

"You can't help it, my dear Watson. You must play your cards as best you can when such a stake is on the table. However, I rejoice to say that I have a hated rival who will certainly cut me out the instant that my back is turned. What a splendid night it is."

The housemaid is not further discussed in the story.

The sexuality of these three shadowy women motivates the narrative and yet is barely present in it. The disclosure which ends the story is thus scarcely a disclosure at all. Symbolically Holmes has burnt the letters, records of women's sexuality. Watson's opening paragraph constitutes an apology for the "reticence" of the narrative: "with *due suppression* the story may be told"; "The

reader will excuse me if I conceal the date *or any other fact*" (my italics).

The project of the Sherlock Holmes stories is to dispel magic and mystery, to make everything explicit, accountable, subject to scientific analysis. The phrase most familiar to all readers—"Elementary, my dear Watson"—is in fact a misquotation, but its familiarity is no accident since it precisely captures the central concern of the stories. Holmes and Watson are both men of science. Holmes, the "genius," is a scientific conjuror who insists on disclosing how the trick is done. The stories begin in enigma, mystery, the impossible, and conclude with an explanation which makes it clear that logical deduction and scientific method render all mysteries accountable to reason:

I am afraid that my explanation may disillusionize you, but it has always been my habit to hide none of my methods, either from my friend Watson or from anyone who might take an intelligent interest in them. ("The Reigate Squires," *The Memoirs of Sherlock Holmes*)

The stories are a plea for science not only in the spheres conventionally associated with detection (footprints, traces of hair or cloth, cigarette ends), where they have been deservedly influential on forensic practice, but in all areas. They reflect the widespread optimism characteristic of their period concerning the comprehensive power of positivist science. Holmes's ability to deduce Watson's train of thought, for instance, is repeatedly displayed, and it owes nothing to the supernatural. Once explained, the reasoning process always appears "absurdly simple," open to the commonest of common sense.

The project of the stories themselves, enigma followed by disclosure, echoes precisely the structure of the classic realist text. The narrator himself draws attention to the parallel between them:

"Excellent!" I cried.

"Elementary," said he. "It is one of those instances where the reasoner can produce an effect which seems remarkable to his neighbour because the latter has missed the one little point which is the basis of the deduction. The same may be said, my dear fellow, for the effect of some of these little sketches of yours, which is entirely meretricious, depending as it does upon your retaining in your own hands some factors in the problem which are never imparted to the reader. Now, at present I am in the position of these same readers, for I hold in this hand several threads of one of the strangest cases which ever perplexed a man's brain, and yet I lack the one or two which are needful to complete my theory. But I'll have them, Watson, I'll have them!" ("The crooked man," *Memoirs*)

(The passage is quoted by Macherey (1978, p. 35) in his discussion of the characteristic structure of narrative.)

The project also requires the maximum degree of "realism"—verisimilitude, plausibility. In the interest of science no hint of the fantastic or the implausible is permitted to remain once the disclosure is complete. This is why even their own existence as writing is so frequently discussed within the texts. The stories are alluded to as Watson's "little sketches," his "memoirs." They resemble fictions because of Watson's unscientific weakness for story-telling:

"I must admit, Watson, that you have some power of selection which atones for much which I deplore in your narratives. Your fatal habit of looking at everything from the point of view of a story instead of as a scientific exercise has ruined what might have been an instructive and even classical series of demonstrations." ("The Abbey Grange," *The Return of Sherlock Holmes*)

In other words, the fiction itself accounts even for its own fictionality, and the text thus appears wholly transparent. The success with which the Sherlock Holmes stories achieve an illusion of reality is repeatedly demonstrated. In their Foreword to *The Sherlock Holmes Companion* (1962) Michael and Mollie Hardwick comment on their own recurrent illusion "that we were dealing with a figure of real life rather than of fiction. How vital Holmes appears, compared with many people of one's own acquaintance."

De Waal's bibliography of Sherlock Holmes lists twenty-five "Sherlockian" periodicals apparently largely devoted to conjectures, based on the "evidence" of the stories, concerning matters only hinted at in the texts—Holmes's education, his income and his romantic and sexual adventures. According to *The Times* in December 1967, letters to Sherlock Holmes were then still commonly addressed to 221B Baker Street, many of them asking for the detective's help.

None the less these stories, whose overt project is total explicitness, total verisimilitude in the interests of a plea for scientificity, are haunted by shadowy, mysterious and often silent women. Their silence repeatedly conceals their sexuality, investing it with a dark and magical quality which is beyond the reach of scientific knowledge. In "The Greek interpreter" *(Memoirs)* Sophie Kratides has run away with a man. Though she is the pivot of the plot she appears only briefly: "I could not see her clearly enough to know more than that she was tall and graceful, with black hair, and clad in some sort of loose white gown." Connotatively the white gown marks her as still virginal and her flight as the result of romance rather than desire. At the same time the dim light surrounds her with shadow, the unknown. "The crooked man" concerns Mrs Barclay, whose husband is found dead on the day of her meeting with her lover of many years before. Mrs Barclay is now insensible, "temporarily insane" since the night of the murder and therefore unable to speak. In "The dancing men" *(Return)* Mrs Elsie Cubitt, once engaged to a criminal, longs to speak but cannot bring herself to break her silence. By the time Holmes arrives she is unconscious, and she remains so for the rest of the story. Ironically the narrative concerns the breaking of the code which enables her former lover to communicate with her. Elsie's only contribution to the correspondence is the word, "Never." The precise nature of their relationship is left mysterious, constructed of contrary suggestions. Holmes says she feared and hated him; the lover claims, "She had been engaged to me, and she would have married me, I believe, if I had taken over another profession." When her husband moves to shoot the man whose coded messages are the source of a "terror" which is "wearing her away," Elsie restrains him with compulsive strength. On the question of her motives the text is characteristically elusive. Her husband recounts the story:

> "I was angry with my wife that night for having held me back when I might have caught the skulking rascal. She said that she feared that I might come to harm. For an instant it had crossed my mind that what she really feared was that *he* might come to harm, for I could not doubt that she knew who this man was and what he meant by those strange signals. But there is a tone in my wife's voice, Mr Holmes, and a look in her eyes which forbid doubt, and I am sure that it was indeed my own safety that was in her mind."

After her husband's death Elsie remains a widow, faithful to his memory and devoting her life to the care of the poor, apparently expiating something unspecified, perhaps an act or a state of feeling, remote or recent.

"The dancing men" is "about" Holmes's method of breaking the cipher. Its project is to dispel any magic from the deciphering process. Elsie's silence is in the interest of the

story since she knows the code. But she also "knows" her feelings towards her former lover. Contained in the completed and fully disclosed story of the decipherment is another uncompleted and undisclosed narrative which is more than merely peripheral to the text as a whole. Elsie's past is central and causal. As a result, the text with its project of dispelling mystery is haunted by the mysterious state of mind of a woman who is unable to speak.

The classic realist text had not yet developed a way of signifying women's sexuality except in a metaphoric or symbolic mode whose presence disrupts the realist surface. Joyce and Lawrence were beginning to experiment at this time with modes of sexual signification but in order to do so they largely abandoned the codes of realism. So much is readily apparent. What is more significant, however, is that the presentation of so many women in the Sherlock Holmes stories as shadowy, mysterious and magical figures precisely contradicts the project of explicitness, transgresses the values of the texts, and in doing so throws into relief the poverty of the contemporary concept of science. These stories, pleas for a total explicitness about the world, are unable to explain an area which none the less they cannot ignore. The version of science which the texts present would constitute a clear challenge to ideology: the interpretation of all areas of life, physical, social and psychological, is to be subject to rational scrutiny and the requirements of coherent theorization. Confronted, however, by an area in which ideology itself is uncertain, the Sherlock Holmes stories display the limits of their own project and are compelled to manifest the inadequacy of a bourgeois scientificity which, working within the constraints of ideology, is thus unable to challenge it.

Perhaps the most interesting case, since it introduces an additional area of shadow, is "The second stain" *(Return),* which concerns two letters. Lady Hilda Trelawney Hope does speak. She has written before her marriage "an indiscreet letter . . . a foolish letter, a letter of an impulsive, loving girl." Had her husband read the letter his confidence in her would have been for ever destroyed. Her husband is none the less presented as entirely sympathetic, and here again we encounter the familiar contradiction between a husband's supposed reaction, accepted as just, and the reaction offered to the reader by the text. In return for her original letter Lady Hilda gives her blackmailer a letter from "a certain foreign potentate" stolen from the dispatch box of her husband, the European Secretary of State. This political letter is symbolically parallel to the first sexual one. Its contents are equally elusive but it too is "indiscreet," "hot-headed"; certain phrases in it are "provocative." Its publication would produce "a most dangerous state of feeling" in the nation. Lady Hilda's innocent folly is the cause of the theft: she knows nothing of politics and was not in a position to understand the consequences of her action. Holmes ensures the restoration of the political letter and both secrets are preserved.

Here the text is symmetrically elusive concerning both sexuality and politics. Watson, as is so often the case where these areas are concerned, begins the story by apologizing for his own reticence and vagueness. In the political instance what becomes clear as a result of the uncertainty of the text is the contradictory nature of the requirements of verisimilitude in fiction. The potentate's identity and the nature of his indiscretion cannot be named without involving on the part of the reader either disbelief (the introduction of a patently fictional country would be dangerous to the project of verisimilitude) or belief (dangerous to the text's status as fiction, entertainment; also quite possibly politically dangerous). The scientific project of the texts require that they deal in "facts," but their nature as fiction forbids the introduction of facts.

The classic realist text instills itself in the space between fact and illusion through the presentation of a simulated reality which is plausible but *not real.* In this lies its power as myth. It is because fiction does not normally deal with "politics" directly, except in the form of history or satire, that it is ostensibly innocent and therefore ideologically effective. But in its evasion of the real also lies its weakness as "realism." Through their transgression of their own values of explicitness and verisimilitude, the Sherlock Holmes stories contain within themselves an implicit critique of their limited nature as characteristic examples of classic realism. They thus offer the reader through the process of deconstruction a form of knowledge, not about "life" or "the world," but about the nature of fiction itself.

Thus, in adopting the form of classic realism, the only appropriate literary mode, positivism is compelled to display its own limitations. Offered as science, it reveals itself to a deconstructive reading as ideology at the very moment that classic realism, offered as verisimilitude, reveals itself as fiction. In claiming to make explicit and *understandable* what appears mysterious, these texts offer evidence of the tendency of positivism to push to the margins of experience whatever it cannot explain or understand. In the Sherlock Holmes stories classic realism ironically tells a truth, though not the truth about the world which is the project of classic realism. The truth the stories tell is the truth about ideology, the truth which ideology represses, its own existence as ideology itself.

## REFERENCES

Althusser, Louis (1971) *Lenin and Philosophy and Other Essays,* tr. Ben Brewster (London: New Left Books).

Barthes, Roland (1975), *S/Z,* tr. Richard Miller (London: Cape).

Benveniste, Emile (1971), *Problems in General Linguistics* (Miami: University of Miami Press).

Conan Doyle, Arthur (1950) *The Memoirs of Sherlock Holmes* (Harmondsworth: Penguin).

Conan Doyle, Arthur (1976) *The Return of Sherlock Holmes* (London: Pan).

Coward, Rosalind and John Ellis (1977) *Language and Materialism* (London: Routledge & Kegan Paul).

Derrida, Jacques (1973) *Speech and Phenomena*, tr. David B. Allison (Evanston: Northwestern University Press).

De Waal, Ronald (1972) *The World Bibliography of Sherlock Holmes* (Greenwich, Conn.: New York Graphic Society).

Hardwick, Michael and Mollie (1962) *The Sherlock Holmes Companion* (London: John Murray).

Heath, Stephen (1977–8) "Notes on Suture" *Screen* 18:4, pp. 48–76.

Lemaire, Anika (1977) *Jacques Lacan*, tr. David Macey (London: Routledge & Kegan Paul).

Macherey, Pierre (1978) *A Theory of Literary Production*, tr. Geoffrey Wall (London: Routledge & Kegan Paul).

Nowell-Smith, Geoffrey (1976) "A note on history discourse," *Edinburgh 76 Magazine*, 1, pp. 26–32.

Saussure, Ferdinand de (1974) *Course in General Linguistics*, tr. Wade Baskin (London: Fontana).

Willemen, Paul (1978) "Notes on subjectivity—on reading 'Subjectivity Under Siege' " *Screen* 19:1, pp. 41–69.

# VI

# PSYCHOLOGY AND PSYCHOANALYSIS

Psychoanalysis has inspired much of the literary and cultural criticism in the twentieth century. This influence ranges from early attempts at criticism by Ernest Jones, Marie Bonaparte, and Freud himself to more recent work by Jacques Lacan and a whole generation of feminists to reimagine Freudian thought in relation to literary texts, language, female sexuality, and political power. The use of psychoanalysis has taken many forms in literary and cultural studies and continues to undergo radical and frequent revision. The incorporation of depth psychology—whether Jungian or Freudian—in literary studies was characteristic of modernist culture in the twentieth century for at least two reasons. The more important reason is the possibility of interpreting disconnected or fragmented aspects of modern culture within the revealing schemes of psychoanalysis. The second, closely connected reason is that psychoanalysis can show a literary or cultural text to have multiple meanings of various kinds on several levels simultaneously. There could be elements of an Oedipal complex in *Hamlet*'s overall dramatic structure, and this argument would depend little on a discussion of character makeup. The attention given to the interpretation of fragments and to coordinating a multiplicity of meanings strongly connected psychoanalysis and modernism generally.

As a basis for much cultural theory, psychoanalysis provides the frame for relating many aspects of culture, the events and texts of everyday life, the history of religion, art, sexuality, and so on. This potential to connect various sectors of culture and society, to underwrite interpretive change in productive ways, does much to explain the strong continuing interest in the psychoanalytic understanding of literature and culture throughout this century. At the end of the century, in the work of Jacques Lacan and others on the Continent and in the United States, the extension of psychoanalysis into the discourse on language, cultural critique, female sexuality, and forms of power has made Freudian thought vital in contemporary criticism.

## ARCHETYPAL CRITICISM

Before moving to the contemporary scene, however, let us think first about the once influential but now much-diminished offshoot of Freudian criticism called archetypal criticism. At mid-century there were two dominant formalist movements in American and European criticism: the New Criticism and *explication du texte*. Each approach prescribed a method of close reading and attempted to account for a variety of textual information, including imagery and image patterns, rhythm, sound, tone, and overall structure. Each method presented itself as potentially exhaustive, able to discover and catalog *all* pertinent textual details in a manner approximating empirical observation in thoroughness and supposed objectivity. In the Anglo-American academy, however, the active development of the New Criticism came to an end in the late 1950s with the rise of archetypal criticism associated with the psychologist Carl Jung, which rapidly supplanted the New Criticism in practical influence and prestige. Archetypal criticism exploited certain aspects of the New Criticism (mainly, the deployment of paradox and irony) and then moved directly into areas that the New Criticism refused or failed to develop, particularly the relationship between literature and objects of study that exist "outside" the narrow formalist conception of literature. This included areas such as "mind," or personal psychology, history, and culture. It also included attempts to systemize the understanding of literature and culture in what Northrop Frye specifically called the "conceptual framework" of literature conceived as a "properly organized" intellectual discipline; that is, the system of literature taken as more than "a huge aggregate or miscellaneous pile of creative efforts." (See "The Function of Criticism at the Present Time" in "What Is Criticism?") On this issue Frye thought that the New Critics such as Cleanth Brooks, W. K. Wimsatt and Monroe Beardsley, John Crowe Ransom, Mark Schorer, and Joseph Frank had taken literary criticism outside of history and could no longer account for the changes that take place in culture.

Approaches to archetypal criticism are varied, but the central paradigm for interpretation comes from the work of Carl Jung. Jung was Freud's close friend and protegé through the 1920s. Freud had already described a psychoanalytic theory of archetypes in his book *Totem and Taboo* (1918). Jung went on to develop an explicit theory, through which he separated himself from Freud, of the "collective unconscious," a realm of transpersonal imagery preserved and repeated throughout human experience. Belonging to the human race and also to individual people (at levels "below" consciousness), the collective unconscious contains "archetypes," or fundamental patterns and forms of human experience, such as "mother," "rebirth," "spirit," and "trickster." Apprehendable only as fragments, or incomplete representations, the archetypes are like the light flickering on the walls of Plato's cave. Archetypal images, that is—never the totality of an archetype—are cast on the screen of conscious thought, constituting informative patterns that are never quite unambiguous or completely unified.

In literary interpretation, archetypes show up in character, plot, and setting. Apparently unrelated textual elements, as well as realistic, representational details, form patterns suggestive of one or more of the archetypes. These patterns establish an archetypal orientation in the work and reflect what lies "beneath" the work's narrative and imagistic surface. Archetypal interpretation organizes each literary text into a narrative surface composed of images and a textual "depth" where the connection with archetypes takes place. A full archetypal interpretation seeks to make explicit what is only implicit in the text's fragmented evocation of archetypes. An archetypal understanding of a text, in short, necessitates seeing how the appearance of merely suggestive details in a minimal sequence is, in reality, a disguised archetypal pattern.

The possibility of narrative progression in archetypal criticism is crucial for understanding archetypalism's ascendancy over the New Criticism. After all, the New Critical emphasis on imagery as the object of analysis depends on evidence drawn from poetry, particularly modernism's highly figurative, nonnarrative poetry (such as that of Eliot). Also, as is often noted, the New Critics foundered on the difficulty of applying imagery and paradox/irony (essentially static and even pictorial in their avoidance of history) to fiction and its profoundly temporal dimension. Only late in the movement's development, during the late 1940s and 1950s, did Joseph Frank and Mark Schorer seek to recast the poetic image as "spatial form" and suggest "technique as [a form of] discovery" in prose fiction. By contrast, archetypalism from its start attempted to define itself precisely in relation to a temporal order, that of the "monomyth" or "quest." As Erich Neumann and others have shown, the coherence of the archetypes rests precisely on their placement within a narrative development that moves from total narcissism toward the hero's individuation and relative autonomy, each stage in the quest being a further step toward independence from the Great Mother. This pattern is *monomythic* because it encompasses all possible human change and growth within a single story. The quest-narrative unites the repeatable form of each archetype with the principle of change dictated by the ongoing temporal development of a story itself. The potential circularity of merely locating self-defining archetypes in literature—wherein discoveries are dictated by foreknown patterns—is avoided through the necessity of accounting for the dynamic operation of narrative ("mythic") progression in particular cases.

The definitive archetypal approach to literature is presented in Frye's *Anatomy of Criticism* (1957) (for which "The Function of Criticism at the Present Time," included in "What Is Criticism?," became the "Polemical Introduction"). Frye was the most formidable archetypal critic to announce a decisive break, as he said, with the "ironic provincialism" and "delicate learning" of the New Criticism. Uncharacteristically disdainful in his appraisal of this literary school, Frye rejected what he considered the New Criticism's limited range and lack of sophistication. Also the implicit religious—and "typological"—perspective of Frye's criticism conflicted with the implicit skepticism of the New Criticism. His harshest slap at the New Criticism was his choice of a title for the *Anatomy*'s first essay, "Historical Criticism: Theory of Modes," where with polemical bravado Frye is attempting to situate the archetypal project on the very historical terrain abandoned by the New Criticism. Frye proclaimed, in effect, that archetypal criticism's success would be precisely where the prior movement had failed. He then went on in "four essays" to erect the monomyth's structure over the whole of culture in a "proto-structuralist" reading of Western literature's archetypal development—from prehistoric and sacred "myth" to present-day "irony." In a remarkable elaboration of literary archetypes, Frye presented a comprehensive catalog of literary forms (genre, sound, rhythm, tone, and so on) as part of his complex presentation of the archetypal paradigm. Implicit in his discussion is, in fact, a sense of the "development" of Western literature—his "Historical Criticism"—as Frye simultaneously suggested both an archetypal "conceptual framework" for criticism and an examination of the "history" of literature.

Throughout the 1960s Frye's version of archetypalism influenced much theory and practical criticism, especially in Medieval and Renaissance studies. Gradually, however, Frye's approach came under attack from three directions: historical critics, structuralists, and feminists. Historicists like A. S. P. Woodhouse, Roy Harvey Pearce, and Lionel Trilling began to point out the failure of both the New Criticism and archetypalism in dealing with history except within narrow bounds. They argued that archetypalism developed a "historical" theory of modes (myth, romance, high mimetic, low mimetic, and irony) merely to turn Western literature itself into a huge, static structure—an all-inclusive closed system. Whereas historical criticism should be able to analyze change, account for the as yet unmet and unthought, archetypalism apparently did nothing more than impose a static grid over literature and culture as a substitute for historical understanding.

The structuralists of the 1960s and 1970s argued with Frye's complicated but, in their view, often naive and overly rigid schema. In the first chapter of *The Fantastic,* for example, Tzvetan Todorov criticized Frye's tendency to analyze literature for "content," actual images (like a "tree" and "shore") in literature, when his professed aim was to examine literary structure as positioned beyond concrete examples. Todorov also noted the formal rigidity of Frye's schema and simultaneous logical lapses in it—for example, the seasonal four-part structure of the "mythoi" as opposed to the five-part structure of his historical "modes." Most devastating, though, was the feminist critique of Frye, focused on the Jungian paradigm and the notion of the monomyth standing behind Frye's work. As Catherine Belsey charged in *Critical Practice,* "underlying Frye's formalism, therefore, [was] a concept of human nature and of culture which sees literature as imitating not the world but rather 'the total dream of *man'* " (emphasis added). Many feminists pointed out that the archetypal hero is at base a male figure attempting to bring reconciliation with an "original" female (the Great Mother) and with a potential "anima" figure who is both the hero's ideal mate and his reward for success on the quest. This exclusively male paradigm assumes a male subject, and nowhere in Jung's thought, or Frye's, is there a serious attempt to reconceive a woman's experience outside of support for a man. While some teachers and practical critics have continued to employ archetypalism for specific ends, especially to create contexts for genre distinctions, the influence of archetypalism has declined markedly. Nevertheless, it should be remembered that archetypalism had a particular historical and critical value as a major critique of the New Criticism and contributed to the revaluation of formalism that is still very much in evidence today.


## FREUDIAN CRITICISM

Psychoanalysis is the intellectual parent of archetypalism, but, as it happens, psychoanalytic criticism both precedes archtypalism in the first-generation Freudians beginning in the twenties and thirties and succeeds it in the more recent movement, the semiotic "return to Freud." Archetypal criticism, for all its virtues and power, and in spite of its criticism of the New Criticism, finally participates in a version of the positivist assumptions that govern New Critical formalism and the earlier criticism of Freudian ego psychologists (even if the positive "objects" of study are not independent texts but rather particular, transcendental archetypes). This can be seen, in fact, in Frye's attempt to develop a discipline of criticism as a social science in "The

Function of Criticism at the Present Time." By contrast, the great strength of contemporary psychoanalytic criticism—contemporary Freudian criticism—is that it goes beyond some of the positivist assumptions of its master to use Freud's work to critique those assumptions and develop discursive modes of interpretations not only of individuals but of larger social formations.

Critical movements tend to develop through a life cycle and then eventually fade away even as they stimulate and then make way for new movements to follow. With psychoanalysis the pattern has been a persistent cycle of rebirths. A first generation of Freudian criticism continued until the 1940s and included such names as Ernest Jones, Marie Bonaparte, and Edmund Wilson. After World War II a group of university critics came into prominence, such as Lionel Trilling, Frederick Crews, Frederick Hoffman, and Norman Holland. Then a new literary Freudianism, based initially on the suggestions made in Jacques Lacan's seminars, was reborn in France in the 1960s. Since the mid-1970s the "French Freud" approach to understanding literature and culture has been extremely influential in the United States, Europe, and around the world.

This new Freudian criticism came out of the intellectual joining of Ferdinand de Saussure (see "Structuralism and Semiotics") with Sigmund Freud: semiotics and psychoanalysis. This combining of intellectual paradigms took place in Jacques Lacan's work first, but it is Lacan's claim that Freud developed semiotic insights and semiotic methods of analysis all through the development of psychoanalysis. In the late nineteenth- and early twentieth-century work of Charles Sanders Peirce and Ferdinand de Saussure emerged the idea of *signifiers* as the smallest constituent units of meaning. In turn, those units (such as words) are elaborated according to the invariant mechanisms of meaning production—how texts work—that govern the operation of signifiers in all cultures. (This "scientific" approach to semiotics was prevalent early in the twentieth century, though now it is much challenged by poststructuralism.) Signifiers are combined by particular cultures as meaningful ("significant") units according to the signifying practices already established as that society's system of culture. It was Lacan's insight to see that Freud had made the same basic claim about the workings of signification in his formulation of psychoanalysis. Freud's theories were simply a formulation of the workings of the locally invariant cultural scheme for understanding the semiotic practices of neurotic and psychotic patients—as well as whole cultures.

Lacan argues, in effect, that both semiotics and psychoanalysis have the potential to dislodge and reorient traditional ways of understanding human experience. Lacan advances this notion in his critique of the Western, generally Cartesian, notion of human understanding as grounded in a substantial self who does *all* of the understanding. That is, the Cartesian view Lacan critiques argues that a generally independent observer exists within each one of us. We then have the potential, if disciplined and trained, to collect data and information through disinterested observation. This nonparticipant observer can examine a world that stays forever separate from the activity of observing that world. In this model knowledge as the product of inquiry matches the conscious formulation of intentions and aims, both in the generation and understanding of texts. For example, according to this model, a literary text would tend to "make sense" when the author's "actual" aims can be retrieved and accurately understood, that is, as a message intended by the author and actually received by the reader. The textual "form" conveying this message takes shape around the manifest representational figures (characters, settings, images deployed in both, etc.) that appear more or less empirically in and form the substance of the text. (Jacques Derrida critiques another aspect of the Cartesian framework of understanding in "The Principle of Reason" in "Deconstruction and Poststructuralism.")

Compared to this view of the text, Lacan's idea of reading and interpretation (of a person's experience or of an event in culture) may at first seem counterintuitive and indeed odd. The Lacanian idea of the text (much like Saussure's definition) opposes—as Lacan says in "The Mirror Stage"—"any philosophy directly issuing from the *Cogito* [substantial ego]." For Lacan, rather, interpretation begins with the idea of a text as an unending interplay of signifiers—not a substantial, fixed message, an absolute given to be investigated empirically in the process of reading—but differential and semiotic. The text is not a continuous, fixed form at all, or a "substance," but a network of signifiers. Thus constituted semiotically as a network of signs, texts are also composed of gaps and inconsistencies. There can be no inherently meaningful sign or entity, not part of a semiotic network, for the letter, as Lacan says in one of his seminars, is "a pure signifier" determined by its position within discourse. Barbara Johnson makes the same point in her essay on the relationship between Derrida and Lacan, "The Frame of Reference," when she says that "the letter, then, acts as a signifier not because its contents are lacking, but because its function is not dependent on the knowledge or nonknowledge of those contents. . . . It is not something with 'an identity to itself inaccessible to dismemberment' as Derrida interprets it; it is a difference."

In this sense, as Lacan explains in *Ecrits,* the signifier has "priority in relation to the signified" and is an activity of making meaning more than a fixable meaning in and of itself. Signifying (semiosis)—in short—precedes and creates the matrix of meaning, and not vice versa. In fact, Lacan says, "we teach that the unconscious means that man is inhabited by [constituted by] the signifier." To be thus inhabited by the signifier, in Johnson's words, is to be "knotted up, entangled in semiotic relations." Signifiers create "texts," and "knot" captures the etymological sense of the figural weaving that constitutes them. This weaving can be seen in the complex strands that constitute Freud's *Dora* text. In "Representation of Patriarchy" Toril Moi locates a series of misplaced signifiers of desire that comprises a whole narrative of misrecognition and displacement—a daughter's misrecognition of her own desire for her mother, her father's misrecognition of his own desire for his mistress, and Freud's misrecognizing of his desire for (and counter-transference in relation to) Dora. The interweaving of these signifiers, the "knot" that is the *Dora* text, can be read and interpreted by untying and sorting out the various signifying strands. Moi's reading of Freud's text, including her reading of Freud into the text, proceeds in precisely this semiotic/psychoanalytic manner of identifying and relating the situating of certain codes within a psychoanalytic framework. That is, she shows this text to be comprised of signifiers of desire linked together and deployed according to the analytic codes that Freud identified in the workings of the unconscious. Moi's interpretation of Freud's *Dora* text, moreover, plays out against the background of Lacan's idea that "the unconscious . . . is structured like a language." That is, in both the case of the unconscious and of language meaning and significance are always textual effects produced by semiotic processes.

The language of contemporary psychoanalysis may be the most difficult of all the contemporary discourses in the sense that it consistently attempts, as Johnson describes, to create effects of "power" in itself—effects "on" and "within" the reader—as much as descriptions of meaning. Shoshana Felman highlights this dimension of psychoanalysis in "Psychoanalysis and Education: Teaching Terminable and Interminable" when she discusses the nature and role of teaching. "Teaching," she says, "like analysis, does not deal so much with lack of knowledge as with resistances to knowledge." Felman analyzes the relationships of knowledge and ignorance—between teacher and student—in a way suggestive of structuralism's reconsideration of the actual phenomenal occurrences of language—what it calls "language-effects" —as opposed to the unconscious (nonphenomenal) structures that allow language to function. In this way Felman attempts to *situate* the practice of pedagogy, that is, to "reorient" it in relation to the interpersonal relationships of power that discourse conveys along with its "knowledge."

Teaching, Felman argues, must learn to learn from ignorance, as ignorance is not simply the absence of knowledge, but a kind of resistance to knowledge itself. Teaching "is not the transmission of ready-made knowledge; it is rather the creation of a new condition of knowledge." The analyst's "competence, insists Lacan, lies in 'what I would call textual knowledge,' " which is, Felman says, "the very stuff the literature teacher is supposed to deal in— . . . knowledge of the functioning of language, of symbolic structures, of the signifier, knowledge at once derived from— and directed towards—interpretation."

According to this idea of what the teacher does, knowledge "cannot be exchanged[;] it has to be used." Teaching uncovers the conditions of knowledge, and it functions as much by performative "utterances" as it does by constative statements. (For a discussion of these terms, see Jonathan Culler, "Convention and Meaning" in "Deconstruction and Poststructuralism.") "Misinterpretations of the psychoanalytical critique of pedagogy," Felman argues, "refer exclusively to Lacan's or Freud's explicit statements about pedagogy, and thus fail to see the illocutionary force, the didactic function, of the utterance as opposed to the mere content of the statement."

One of the most influential understandings of this performative dimension of culture in psychoanalytic terms is Laura Mulvey's "Visual Pleasure and Narrative Cinema." In this often-cited article, Mulvey isolates the scenario of viewing the "classic Hollywood" film and reads it as a performance text. Key here, and this is a dimension to note carefully in her work, is the situating of a semiotic text (the genre of the Hollywood film) within a broad historical and social situation. In this case a genre is understood as a cultural institution intended for a mass audience. In other words, in what has been a groundbreaking study for film and cultural criticism, Mulvey relates the material conditions of film viewing to the ideological implications of the gender relations that dominate in Hollywood film. She then situates these generic concerns to the capitalistic production mode of the American film industry. In working this way across signifying codes, Mulvey brings to realization a certain potential of psychoanalysis to function synthetically and quite effectively as cultural critique on several levels.

This manner of positing a semiotic "subject" within a cultural institution, of projecting meaning *and* interpretation as semiotic operations, has made Freud (via Lacan) newly useful for feminists, Marxists, and others working in cultural theory. Feminist critics such as Luce Irigaray, Hélène Cixous, Laura Mulvey, Julia Kristeva, and Shoshana Felman have found in the "French Freud" a potential for interpreting literary texts from other than a male (or "phallogocentric") perspective. Starting with Lacan's work, but often revising his critique of the subject of interpretation, feminists have profitably read literary and other cultural texts psychoanalytically. Likewise, Marxist critics such as Fredric Jameson and Louis Althusser have worked from Lacan's figure of the split subject to integrate the political and the psychological critiques of literary texts. An important result of this project is the idea of a "political unconscious," an approach to power relations that uses Freud's model to analyze manifest and unconscious discourses. For both feminists and Marxists, Lacanian thought can be deployed in a strategy for overturning the traditional Western subject and reinscribing (reimagining) the workings of subjectivity in a largely unconscious discourse.

The importance of psychoanalysis is everywhere evident in contemporary literary criticism. In "Constructing the Subject: Deconstructing the Text" (in "Deconstruction and Poststructuralism") Catherine Belsey uses a Lacanian mode of analysis to bring together the work of feminism and of Marxist and ideological analyses of culture. Similarly, Gayatri Spivak expands Lacanian psychoanalysis to a wider, cultural use in "Feminism and Critical Theory" (in "Feminism and Gender Studies"). Finally, in "Notes Towards a Definition of Cultural Studies" (in "Cultural Studies"), we try to show the central place of the critique of the subject initiated by psychoanalysis in contemporary literary and cultural studies. Lacan's is a difficult view of the text, but it is precisely the radicality—the semiotic and deconstructive dimension—in the "new" psychoanalysis that has once more given Freud urgent importance in contemporary literary and cultural criticism.

## RELATED ESSAYS IN
## *CONTEMPORARY LITERARY CRITICISM*

Henry Louis Gates, Jr., "Critical Fanonism"
Barbara Johnson, "Apostrophe, Animation, and Abortion"
Ferdinand de Saussure, Selections from the *Course in General Linguistics*
Catherine Belsey, "Constructing the Subject: Deconstructing the Text"
Michael Warner, "Homo-Narcissism; or, Heterosexuality"
Stuart Hall, "Cultural Studies: Two Paradigms"

## FURTHER READING

Abraham, Nicolas, and Maria Torok, *Cryptonymie: Le Verbier de l'homme aux loups* (Paris: Aubier-Flammarion, 1976).
Bellemin-Noel, Jean, *Vers l'inconscient du texts* (Paris: Presses Universitaires de France, 1979).
Belsey, Catherine, *Critical Practice* (New York: Methuen, 1980).

Bodkin, Maud, *Archetypal Patterns in Poetry* (New York: Vintage, 1958).

Brooks, Peter, "Fictions of the Wolfman: Freud and Narrative Understanding," *Diacritics,* 9, No. 1 (1979), 72–83.

Campbell, Joseph, *The Hero with a Thousand Faces* (New York: Pantheon, 1949).

Caroll, David, "Freud and the Myth of Origins," *New Literary History,* 6 (1975), 511–28.

Crews, Frederick C., *Out of My System* (New York: Oxford University Press, 1975).

———, ed., *Psychoanalysis and Literary Process* (Cambridge, MA: Winthrop, 1970).

———, *The Sins of the Fathers* (New York: Oxford University Press, 1966).

Davis, Robert Con, ed., *The Fictional Father: Lacanian Readings of the Text* (Amherst: University of Massachusetts Press, 1981).

———, "Freud, Lacan, and the Subject of Cultural Studies," in *College Literature* 18, 2 (June 1991): 22–37.

———, ed., *Lacan and Narration: The Psychoanalytic Difference in Narrative Theory* (Baltimore: Johns Hopkins University Press, 1984).

Derrida, Jacques, *The Post Card: From Socrates to Freud and Beyond,* trans. Alan Bass (Chicago: University of Chicago Press, 1987).

———, "Freud and the Scene of Writing," in his *Writing and Difference,* trans. Alan Bass (Chicago: University of Chicago Press, 1978), 196–231.

Felman, Shoshana, *The Literary Speech Act: Don Juan with J. L. Austin, or Seduction in Two Languages,* trans. Catherine Porter (Ithaca, NY: Cornell University Press, 1983).

———, ed., *Literature and Psychoanalysis: The Question of Reading—Otherwise* (Baltimore: Johns Hopkins University Press, 1982).

Frank, Joseph, *The Widening Gyre* (New Brunswick, NJ: Rutgers University Press, 1963).

Freud, Sigmund, *Totem and Taboo,* trans. A. A. Brill (New York: Moffat, Yard, 1918).

Frye, Northrop, *Anatomy of Criticism: Four Essays* (Princeton, NJ: Princeton University Press, 1957).

Gallop, Jane, *The Daughter's Seduction: Feminism and Psychoanalysis* (Ithaca, NY: Cornell University Press, 1982).

Goux, Jean-Joseph, *Freud, Marx: economie et symbolique* (Paris: Editions du Seuil, 1973).

Grosz, Elizabeth, *Sexual Subversions: Three French Feminists* (Sydney: Allen and Unwin, 1989).

Hartman, Geoffrey H., "Psychoanalysis: The French Connection," in *Psychoanalysis and the Question of the Text,* ed. Geoffrey H. Hartman (Baltimore: Johns Hopkins University Press, 1978), 86–113.

Hertz, Neil, "Freud and the Sandman," in *Textual Strategies,* ed. Josué Harari (Ithaca, NY: Cornell University Press, 1979), 296–321.

Hoffman, Frederick J., *Freudianism and the Literary Mind,* 2nd ed. (Baton Rouge: Louisiana State University Press, 1957).

Holland, Norman N., *The Dynamics of Literary Response* (New York: Oxford University Press, 1968).

———, *5 Readers Reading* (New Haven: Yale University Press, 1975).

———, *Poems in Persons* (New York: Norton, 1973).

Johnson, Barbara, "The Frame of Reference," in *Yale French Studies, 55/56* (1977), 457–505.

Lacan, Jacques, *Ecrits: A Selection,* Trans. Alan Sheridan (New York: Norton, 1977).

————, *Speech and Language in Psychoanalysis,* trans., notes, and commentary by Anthony G. Wilden (Baltimore: Johns Hopkins University Press, 1982).

———— and the Ecole Freudienne, *Feminine Sexuality,* ed. Juliet Mitchell and Jacqueline Rose, trans. J. Rose (New York: Norton, 1982).

Lesser, Simon O., *Fiction and the Unconscious* (Boston: Beacon Press, 1957).

MacCabe, Colin, ed., *The Talking Cure: Essays in Psychoanalysis and Language* (London: Macmillan, 1981).

Mulvey, Laura, *Visual and Other Pleasures* (London: Macmillan, 1989).

Penley, Constance, ed., *Feminism and Film Theory* (New York: Routledge and Bfl Publishing, 1989).

————, *The Future of an Illusion: Film, Feminism and Psychoanalysis* (Minneapolis: University of Minnesota Press, 1989).

Rose, Jacqueline, *Sexuality in the Field of Vision* (London: Verso, 1985).

Schorer, Mark, *The World We Imagine: Selected Essays* (New York: Farrar, Straus, and Giroux, 1968).

Spivack, Gayatri Chakravorty, "The Letter as Cutting Edge," in *Yale French Studies, 55/56* (1977), 208–26.

Todorov, Tzvetan, *The Fantastic* (Cleveland, OH: Press of Case Western Reserve University, 1973).

Trilling, Lionel, *Freud and the Crisis of Our Culture* (Boston: Beacon Press, 1955).

————, *The Liberal Imagination* (New York: Viking, 1951).

Wilson, Edmund, *The Triple Thinkers* (New York: Harcourt, Brace, 1938).

————, *The Wound and the Bow* (Boston: Houghton Mifflin, 1941).

Wright, Elizabeth, *Psychoanalytic Criticism: Theory in Practice* (London: Methuen, 1984).

# 23

# Jacques Lacan
# 1901–1981

From his earliest writings, including his doctoral thesis (1932), Jacques Lacan expressed discontent with the limits of traditional psychoanalysis as practiced by rigid Freudians. After parting ways first with the French and then the international psychoanalytic establishment, in 1953 Lacan began weekly seminars attended by students, philosophers, and linguists. Along with his essays, most of which appear in his *Ecrits* (1966; trans. 1977), these seminars provided Lacan with a field for his most important work. Lacan's intent was to reinterpret Freud, with special attention to Freud's treatment of the unconscious, which communicates its formal structure through a specialized language. For Lacan, the true subject—of psychoanalysis and discourse—is the unconscious rather than the ego; at the same time, Lacan refused to reify the unconscious, given that a unified subject, he argued, is illusory.

Like Lévi-Strauss, Foucault, Barthes, and Derrida, Lacan's work was deeply affected by structural linguistics, and in it he particularly concentrates on the functions of signs. From this study Lacan determined that the unconscious is "structured like language" and reveals meaning only in the connections among signifiers. This linguistic model surfaced in Lacan's *Rome Discourse* (1953; trans. 1968) entitled "The function and field of speech and language in psychoanalysis." Lacan's seminar on Poe's "The Purloined Letter" (1956; trans. 1972) best illustrates his nexus of discourse and the psychoanalytic process; in tracing the path of the displaced signifier, Poe's story became, for Lacan, a parable of the linguistic sign in its creation of the speaking subject. His 1957 essay in *Ecrits,* "The instance of the letter, or reason since Freud," a Saussurian reading of the unconscious, took this attention to the signifier one step further by making the signifier the primary component of the signifier/signified schema, thereby reversing the traditional Western notion of the primacy of the concept.

Lacan's essay reprinted here, "The mirror stage as formative of the function of the I as revealed in psychoanalytic experience" (1949), identifies the point at which the *I* (that is, the ego) begins to formulate itself as a socially constructed agent, or a subject fabricated by virtue of the preexisting social order of language. In the infant's recognition of his mirror image as his own, Lacan identifies the first stage of development toward an eventual sense of both "permanence of the *I*"—its fundamentally spatial reality—and alienation of the *I* from a unified sense of self. The mirror image's reduplication begins the process of mediating the *I* through the desire of and identification with others, a stage entailing the profit of recognizing the self as an agent among others in history and the loss of perceived unified sufficiency. In one move, therefore, Lacan joins the phenomena of doubling and narcissism to tease out a source, psychoanalytically speaking, for what literary critics will see as two ubiquitous literary tropes, metaphor and metonymy.

# The Mirror Stage as Formative of the Function of the I as Revealed in Psychoanalytic Experience

*Delivered at the 16th International Congress of Psychoanalysis, Zürich, July 17, 1949*

The conception of the mirror stage that I introduced at our last congress, thirteen years ago, has since become more or less established in the practice of the French group. However, I think it worthwhile to bring it again to your attention, especially today, for the light it sheds on the formation of the *I* as we experience it in psychoanalysis. It is an experience that leads us to oppose any philosophy directly issuing from the *Cogito.*

Some of you may recall that this conception originated in a feature of human behaviour illuminated by a fact of comparative psychology. The child, at an age when he is for a time, however short, outdone by the chimpanzee in instrumental intelligence, can nevertheless already recognize as such his own image in a mirror. This recognition is indicated in the illuminative mimicry of the *Aha-Erlebnis,* which Köhler sees as the expression of situational apperception, an essential stage of the act of intelligence.

This act, far from exhausting itself, as in the case of the monkey, once the image has been mastered and found empty, immediately rebounds in the case of the child in a series of gestures in which he experiences in play the relation between the movements assumed in the image and the reflected environment, and between this virtual complex and the reality it reduplicates—the child's own body, and the persons and things, around him.

This event can take place, as we have known since Baldwin, from the age of six months, and its repetition has often made me reflect upon the startling spectacle of the infant in front of the mirror. Unable as yet to walk, or even to stand up, and held tightly as he is by some support, human or artificial (what, in France, we call a "trotte-bébé"), he nevertheless overcomes, in a flutter of jubilant activity, the obstructions of his support and, fixing his attitude in a slightly leaning-forward position, in order to hold it in his gaze, brings back an instantaneous aspect of the image.

For me, this activity retains the meaning I have given it up to the age of eighteen months. This meaning discloses a libidinal dynamism, which has hitherto remained problematic, as well as an ontological structure of the human world that accords with my reflections on paranoiac knowledge.

We have only to understand the mirror stage *as an identification,* in the full sense that analysis gives to the term: namely, the transformation that takes place in the subject when he assumes an image—whose predestination to this phase-effect is sufficiently indicated by the use, in analytic theory, of the ancient term *imago.*

This jubilant assumption of his specular image by the child at the *infans* stage, still sunk in his motor incapacity and nursling dependence, would seem to exhibit in an exemplary situation the symbolic matrix in which the *I* is precipitated in a primordial form, before it is objectified in the dialectic of identification with the other, and before language restores to it, in the universal, its function as subject.

This form would have to be called the

Ideal-I,[1] if we wished to incorporate it into our usual register, in the sense that it will also be the source of secondary identifications, under which term I would place the functions of libidinal normalization. But the important point is that this form situates the agency of the ego, before its social determination, in a fictional direction, which will always remain irreducible for the individual alone, or rather, which will only rejoin the coming-into-being *(le devenir)* of the subject asymptotically, whatever the success of the dialectical syntheses by which he must resolve as *I* his discordance with his own reality.

The fact is that the total form of the body by which the subject anticipates in a mirage the maturation of his power is given to him only as *Gestalt,* that is to say, in an exteriority in which this form is certainly more constituent than constituted, but in which it appears to him above all in a contrasting size *(un relief de stature)* that fixes it and in a symmetry that inverts it, in contrast with the turbulent movements that the subject feels are animating him. Thus, this *Gestalt*—whose pregnancy should be regarded as bound up with the species, though its motor style remains scarcely recognizable—by these two aspects of its appearance, symbolizes the mental permanence of the *I,* at the same time as it prefigures its alienating destination; it is still pregnant with the correspondences that unite the *I* with the statue in which man projects himself, with the phantoms that dominate him, or with the automation in which, in an ambiguous relation, the world of his own making tends to find completion.

Indeed, for the *imagos*—whose veiled faces it is our privilege to see in outline in our daily experience and in the penumbra of symbolic efficacity[2]—the mirror-image would seem to be the threshold of the visible world, if we go by the mirror disposition that the *imago of one's own body* presents in hallucinations or dreams, whether it concerns its individual features, or even its infirmities, or

its object-projections; or if we observe the role of the mirror apparatus in the appearances of the *double,* in which psychical realities, however heterogeneous, are manifested.

That a *Gestalt* should be capable of formative effects in the organism is attested by a piece of biological experimentation that is itself so alien to the idea of psychical causality that it cannot bring itself to formulate its results in these terms. It nevertheless recognizes that it is a necessary condition for the maturation of the gonad of the female pigeon that it should see another member of its species, of either sex; so sufficient in itself is this condition that the desired effect may be obtained merely by placing the individual within reach of the field of reflection of a mirror. Similarly, in the case of the migratory locust, the transition within a generation from the solitary to the gregarious form can be obtained by exposing the individual, at a certain stage, to the exclusively visual action of a similar image, provided it is animated by movements of a style sufficiently close to that characteristic of the species. Such facts are inscribed in an order of homeomorphic identification that would itself fall within the larger question of the meaning of beauty as both formative and erogenic.

But the facts of mimicry are no less instructive when conceived as cases of heteromorphic identification, in as much as they raise the problem of the signification of space for the living organism—psychological concepts hardly seem less appropriate for shedding light on these matters than ridiculous attempts to reduce them to the supposedly supreme law of adaptation. We have only to recall how Roger Caillois (who was then very young, and still fresh from his breach with the sociological school in which he was trained) illuminated the subject by using the term *"legendary psychasthenia"* to classify morphological mimicry as an obsession with space in its derealizing effect.

I have myself shown in the social dialectic

that structures human knowledge as para-noiac[3] why human knowledge has greater autonomy than animal knowledge in relation to the field of force of desire, but also why human knowledge is determined in that "little reality" *(ce peu de réalité),* which the Surrealists, in their restless way, saw as its limitation. These reflections lead me to recognize in the spatial captation manifested in the mirror-stage, even before the social dialectic, the effect in man of an organic insufficiency in his natural reality—in so far as any meaning can be given to the word "nature."

I am led, therefore, to regard the function of the mirror-stage as a particular case of the function of the *imago,* which is to establish a relation between the organism and its reality—or, as they say, between the *Innenwelt* and the *Umwelt.*

In man, however, this relation to nature is altered by a certain dehiscence at the heart of the organism, a primordial Discord betrayed by the signs of uneasiness and motor unco-ordination of the neo-natal months. The objective notion of the anatomical incompleteness of the pyramidal system and likewise the presence of certain humoral residues of the maternal organism confirm the view I have formulated as the fact of a real *specific prematurity of birth* in man.

It is worth noting, incidentally, that this is a fact recognized as such by embryologists, by the term *foetalization,* which determines the prevalence of the so-called superior apparatus of the neurax, and especially of the cortex, which psycho-surgical operations lead us to regard as the intra-organic mirror.

This development is experienced as a temporal dialectic that decisively projects the formation of the individual into history. The *mirror stage* is a drama whose internal thrust is precipitated from insufficiency to anticipation—and which manufactures for the subject, caught up in the lure of spatial identification, the succession of phantasies that extends from a fragmented body-image to a form of its totality that I shall call orthopae-dic—and, lastly, to the assumption of the armour of an alienating identity, which will mark with its rigid structure the subject's entire mental development. Thus, to break out of the circle of the *Innenwelt* into the *Umwelt* generates the inexhaustible quadrature of the ego's verifications.

This fragmented body—which term I have also introduced into our system of theoretical references—usually manifests itself in dreams when the movement of the analysis encounters a certain level of aggressive disintegration in the individual. It then appears in the form of disjointed limbs, or of those organs represented in exoscopy, growing wings and taking up arms for intestinal persecutions—the very same that the visionary Hieronymus Bosch has fixed, for all time, in painting, in their ascent from the fifteenth century to the imaginary zenith of modern man. But this form is even tangibly revealed at the organic level, in the lines of "fragilization" that define the anatomy of phantasy, as exhibited in the schizoid and spasmodic symptoms of hysteria.

Correlatively, the formation of the *I* is symbolized in dreams by a fortress, or a stadium—its inner arena and enclosure, surrounded by marshes and rubbish-tips, dividing it into two opposed fields of contest where the subject flounders in quest of the lofty, remote inner castle whose form (sometimes juxtaposed in the same scenario) symbolizes the id in a quite startling way. Similarly, on the mental plane, we find realized the structures of fortified works, the metaphor of which arises spontaneously, as if issuing from the symptoms themselves, to designate the mechanisms of obsessional neurosis—inversion, isolation, reduplication, cancellation and displacement.

But if we were to build on these subjective givens alone—however little we free them from the condition of experience that makes us see them as partaking of the nature of a linguistic technique—our theoretical attempts would remain exposed to the charge of projecting themselves into the unthinkable of an absolute subject. This is why I have sought in the present hypothesis, grounded in a conjunction of objective data, the guiding grid for a *method of symbolic reduction*.

It establishes in the *defences of the ego* a genetic order, in accordance with the wish formulated by Miss Anna Freud, in the first part of her great work, and situates (as against a frequently expressed prejudice) hysterical repression and its returns at a more archaic stage than obsessional inversion and its isolating processes, and the latter in turn as preliminary to paranoic alienation, which dates from the deflection of the specular *I* into the social *I*.

This moment in which the mirror-stage comes to an end inaugurates, by the identification with the *imago* of the counterpart and the drama of primordial jealousy (so well brought out by the school of Charlotte Bühler in the phenomenon of infantile *transitivism*), the dialectic that will henceforth link the *I* to socially elaborated situations.

It is this moment that decisively tips the whole of human knowledge into mediatization through the desire of the other, constitutes its objects in an abstract equivalence by the co-operation of others, and turns the I into that apparatus for which every instinctual thrust constitutes a danger, even though it should correspond to a natural maturation—the very normalization of this maturation being henceforth dependent, in man, on a cultural mediation as exemplified, in the case of the sexual object, by the Oedipus complex.

In the light of this conception, the term primary narcissism, by which analytic doctrine designates the libidinal investment characteristic of that moment, reveals in those who invented it the most profound awareness of semantic latencies. But it also throws light on the dynamic opposition between this libido and the sexual libido, which the first analysts tried to define when they invoked destructive and, indeed, death instincts, in order to explain the evident connection between the narcissistic libido and the alienating function of the *I*, the aggressivity it releases in any relation to the other, even in a relation involving the most Samaritan of aid.

In fact, they were encountering that existential negativity whose reality is so vigorously proclaimed by the contemporary philosophy of being and nothingness.

But unfortunately that philosophy grasps negativity only within the limits of a self-sufficiency of consciousness, which, as one of its premises, links to the *méconnaissances* that constitute the ego, the illusion of autonomy to which it entrusts itself. This flight of fancy, for all that it draws, to an unusual extent, on borrowings from psychoanalytic experience, culminates in the pretention of providing an existential psychoanalysis.

At the culmination of the historical effort of a society to refuse to recognize that it has any function other than the utilitarian one, and in the anxiety of the individual confronting the "concentrational"[4] form of the social bond that seems to arise to crown this effort, existentialism must be judged by the explanations it gives of the subjective impasses that have indeed resulted from it; a freedom that is never more authentic than when it is within the walls of a prison; a demand for commitment, expressing the impotence of a pure consciousness to master any situation; a voyeuristic-sadistic idealization of the sexual relation; a personality that realizes itself only in suicide; a consciousness of the other that can be satisfied only by Hegelian murder.

These propositions are opposed by all our experience, in so far as it teaches us not to regard the ego as centered on the *perception-consciousness system*, or as organized by the "reality principle"—a principle that is the expression of a scientific prejudice most hostile to the dialectic of knowledge. Our experience shows that we should start instead from the *function of méconnaissance* that characterizes the ego in all its structures, so markedly articulated by Miss Anna Freud. For, if the *Verneinung* represents the patent form of that function, its effects will, for the most part, remain latent, so long as they are not illuminated by some light reflected on to the level of fatality, which is where the id manifests itself.

We can thus understand the inertia characteristic of the formations of the *I,* and find there the most extensive definition of neurosis—just as the captation of the subject by the situation gives us the most general formula for madness, not only the madness that lies behind the walls of asylums, but also the madness that deafens the world with its sound and fury.

The sufferings of neurosis and psychosis are for us a schooling in the passions of the soul, just as the beam of the psychoanalytic scales, when we calculate the tilt of its threat to entire communities, provides us with an indication of the deadening of the passions in society.

At this junction of nature and culture, so persistently examined by modern anthropology, psychoanalysis alone recognizes this knot of imaginary servitude that love must always undo again, or sever.

For such a task, we place no trust in altruistic feeling, we who lay bare the aggressivity that underlies the activity of the philanthropist, the idealist, the pedagogue, and even the reformer.

In the recourse of subject to subject that we preserve, psychoanalysis may accompany the patient to the ecstatic limit of the *"Thou art that,"* in which is revealed to him the cipher of his mortal destiny, but it is not in our mere power as practitioners to bring him to that point where the real journey begins.

*Translated by Alan Sheridan*

## NOTES

1. Throughout this article I leave in its peculiarity the translation I have adopted for Freud's *Ideal-Ich* [i.e., "je-idéal"], without further comment, other than to say that I have not maintained it since.

2. Cf. Claude Lévi-Strauss, *Structural Anthropology,* Chapter X.

3. Cf. "Aggressivity in Psychoanalysis," p. 8 and *Écrits,* p. 180.

4. *"Concentrationnaire,"* an adjective coined after World War II (this article was written in 1949) to describe the life of the concentration-camp. In the hands of certain writers it became, by extension, applicable to many aspects of "modern" life [Tr.].

# 24

# Toril Moi
## 1953–

Toril Moi, a Norwegian living in Britain, since 1981 has published work that is vital to feminism in its critique of feminist theory and its proposals for change. While her criticism has been primarily written for an American audience, it has been largely based on the writings of French feminists. In her work she strives to combine feminism, psychoanalysis, deconstruction, and Marxism. Moi's work includes *Jealousy and Sexual Difference* (1982); *Psychoanalytic Approaches to Sartre's* "Les Mots" (1982); *Sexual/Textual Politics: Feminist Literary Theory* (1985); *Power, Sex and Subjectivity: Feminist Reflections on Foucault* (1985); *Existentialism and Feminism: The Rhetoric of Biology in* "The Second Sex" (1986); *Feminist Literary Criticism* (1986); *Feminism, Postmodernism and Style: Recent Feminist Criticism in the U.S.* (1988); *Patriarchal Thought and the Drive for Knowledge* (1989); and *Feminist Theory and Simone de Beauvoir* (1990).

Moi's "Representation of Patriarchy: Sexuality and Epistemology in Freud's Dora" (1981) reflects her interest in refining feminist theory to make it a powerful tool capable of achieving its political ends. Moi incorporates Cixous and Clément's *La jeune née,* as well as other feminist interpretations, into her own analysis of Freud's first full-length case history, *Dora,* the study of a young, hysterical woman. Focusing primarily on the conflicting epistemological ideologies of fragmentation and wholeness that plagued Freud in his composition of Dora's case, Moi's criticism links Freud's obsession with proving the completeness of his work to his fear of castration. In his longing to possess a knowledge of Dora's case that is self-contained and whole, Freud is continually frustrated by the piecemeal nature of Dora's secrets. Moi understands that Freud's analysis of Dora's case privileges the epistemology of patriarchal mastery. His limited epistemology necessarily denies the validity of the fragmentary nature of Dora's own presentation of her case. Moi identifies Freud's misinterpretation of Dora's transference, as well as Freud's failure to identify his own countertransference, to be the crucial oversights that further complicate the nature of the case. Moi does not grant Freud the position of "neutral, scientific observer" that he claims in *Dora.* Instead, she interprets Dora's eventual dismissal of Freud to be the event that "rescues" Freud from "further epistemological insecurity." Dora's dismissal allows Freud to publish the case as his own *complete* work. Using the tools of psychoanalysis and deconstruction, Moi is able to expose the "lack of 'natural' foundation" in Freud's attempt to restore his own sense of mutilation in the form of a complete, published work. In this analysis Moi uses the the methods of psychoanalytic narrative and discourse analysis—"its own weapons"—to subvert Freud's epistemological phallocentrism from within.

# Representation of Patriarchy: Sexuality and Epistemology in Freud's Dora

Over the past few years Freud's account of his treatment of the eighteen-year-old Dora has provoked many feminists to take up their pen, in anger or fascination. Dora had for some time suffered from various hysterical symptoms (nervous cough, loss of voice, migraine, depression, and what Freud calls "hysterical unsociability" and *'taedium vitae'*), but it was not until the autumn of 1900, when her parents found a suicide note from her, that Dora's father sent her to Freud for treatment. Freud's case history reveals much about the situation of a young woman from the Viennese bourgeoisie at the turn of the century. Dora's psychological problems can easily be linked to her social background. She has very little, if any, scope for independent activity, is strictly guarded by her family, and feels under considerable pressure from her father. She believes (and Freud agrees) that she is being used as a pawn in a game between her father and Herr K., the husband of her father's mistress. The father wants to exchange Dora for Frau K. ("If I get your wife, you get my daughter"), so as to be able to carry on his affair with Frau K. undisturbed. Dora claims that her father only sent her to psychiatric treatment because he hoped that she would be "cured" into giving up her opposition to her father's affair with Frau K., accept her role as a victim of the male power game, and take Herr K. as her lover.

Freud, then, becomes the person who is to help Dora handle this difficult situation. But Freud himself is the first to admit that his treatment of Dora was a failure. Freud has his own explanations of this failure, but these are not wholly convincing. Feminists have been quick to point out that the reasons for Freud's failure are clearly sexist: Freud is authoritarian, a willing participant in the male power game conducted between Dora's father and Herr K., and at no time turns to consider Dora's own experience of the events. That Freud's analysis fails because of its inherent sexism is the common feminist conclusion.

But *Dora* is a complex text, and feminists have stressed quite different points in their reading of it. Hélène Cixous and Catherine Clément discuss the political potential of hysteria in their book *La jeune née* and agree that Dora's hysteria developed as a form of protest, a silent revolt against male power.[1] They differ, however, as I shall show later, in their evaluation of the importance of hysteria as a political weapon. Cixous and Clément do not discuss in any detail the interaction between Freud and Dora, but Hélène Cixous returned to this theme in 1976, when she published her play *Portrait de Dora*.[2] Here Dora's story is represented in dreamlike sequences from Dora's own viewpoint. Cixous plays skillfully with Freud's text: she quotes, distorts, and displaces the "father text" with great formal mastery. This technique enables her to create new interpretations of Dora's symptoms in a playful exposure of Freud's limitations.

Jacqueline Rose's article, "Dora: Fragment of an Analysis," differs considerably from these two French texts. Rose sees *Dora* as a text that focuses with particular acuteness on the problem of the representation of femininity and discusses several modern French psychoanalytical theories of femininity (particularly Michèle Montrelay and Luce Irigaray in relation to Lacan). She concludes by rejecting that simplistic reading of *Dora* which would

see Dora the woman opposed to and oppressed by Freud the man. According to Rose,
*Dora* reveals how Freud's concept of the feminine was incomplete and contradictory, thus
delineating a major problem in psychoanalytical theory: its inability to account for the feminine. A valuable contribution to a feminist
reading of psychoanalysis, Rose's essay is nevertheless silent on its political consequences.

The same is true of Suzanne Gearhart's
"The Scene of Psychoanalysis: The Unanswered Questions of Dora." Gearhart reads
*Dora* principally through Lacan's and Irigaray's discussions of Dora's case, arguing that
the central problem in the text is "the symbolic status of the father." According to Gearhart, *Dora* must be seen as Freud's "interrogation of the principle of paternity"; it is in
the correct understanding of the text's handling of this problem that we will find the key
to the ultimate explanation of Dora's illness
and also the basis of the identity of Freud and
his work. Gearhart's highly sophisticated
reading of *Dora* shows that the status of the
father in *Dora* is problematical, and the father
himself made marginal, because Freud wants
to avoid the central insight that the (Lacanian)
Imaginary and Symbolic realms are fundamentally complicit. Theoretically valuable
though this essay is, it fails to indicate the
consequences of its reading of *Dora* for a
feminist approach to psychoanalysis.

Maria Ramas' long study of Dora, "Freud's
Dora, Dora's Hysteria," is the most accessible
article on Dora to date. Whereas Rose and
Gearhart use a sophisticated theoretical vocabulary, Ramas writes in a lucid, low-key
style. But her "theoretical" inquiry advances
little beyond a scrupulous, somewhat tedious
resumé of Freud's text. Ramas argues that
"Ida's problem [Ramas uses Dora's real name,
Ida Bauer, throughout her text] was her unconscious belief that "femininity, bondage,
and debasement were synonymous." Since
Freud unconsciously shared this belief, she

claims, he could only reinforce Dora's problems rather than free her from them.

This, at least, is a traditional feminist reading: it implies that Dora could escape her
hysteria only through feminist consciousness-
raising—that if she could stop equating femininity with bondage she would be liberated.
But it is also a sadly partial and superficial
account, failing to encompass many controversial areas of Freud's text. Despite one brief
reference to Jacqueline Rose's article, Ramas
seems to find the status of the term *femininity* in the text quite unproblematical; she
unquestioningly accepts Freud's automatic
reduction of oral sex to fellatio (a point I shall
return to later) and does not even notice
many of Freud's more eccentric concerns in
the case study. Qualifying her own essay as
pure "feminist polemics," Ramas suggests
that further study of *Dora* would lead beyond
feminism: "If this were Freud's story, we
would have to go beyond feminist polemics
and search for the sources of the negative
countertransference—the unanalyzed part of
Freud—that brought the analysis to an
abrupt end."[3]

I believe that it is precisely through an exploration of the "unanalyzed part of Freud"
that we may uncover the relations between
sexual politics and psychoanalytical theory in
*Dora,* and therefore also in Freud's works in
general. In my reading of *Dora* I want to
show that neither Rose's and Gearhart's
depoliticized theorizing nor Ramas' rather
simplistic "feminist polemics" will really do.
Feminists must neither reject theoretical discussion as "beyond feminist polemics" nor
forget the ideological context of theory.

## FRAGMENT OR WHOLE?

The first version of *Dora* was written in 1901.
Freud entitled it "Dreams and Hysteria" and
had the greatest ambitions for the text: this

was his first great case history, and it was to continue and develop the work presented in *The Interpretation of Dreams,* published in the previous year. But Freud recalled *Dora* from his publisher and curiously enough delayed publication until 1905, the year of the *Three Essays on Sexuality*. Why would Freud hesitate for more than four years before deciding to publish *Dora?* According to Jacqueline Rose, this hesitation may have been because *Dora* was written in the period between the theory of the unconscious, developed in *The Interpretation of Dreams,* and the theory of sexuality, first expressed in the *Three Essays. Dora* would then mark the transition between these two theories, and Freud's hesitation in publishing the text suggests the theoretical hesitation within it. Jacqueline Rose may well be right in this supposition. It is at any rate evident that among Freud's texts *Dora* marks an unusual degree of uncertainty, doubt, and ambiguity.

This uncertainty is already revealed in the title of the work: the true title is not "Dora," but "Fragment of an Analysis of a Case of Hysteria." Freud lists three reasons for calling his text a fragment. First, the analytic results are fragmentary both because Dora interrupted the treatment before it was completed and because Freud did not write up the case history until after the treatment was over. The only exceptions to this are Dora's two dreams, which Freud took down immediately. The text we are reading, in other words, is constructed from fragmentary notes and Freud's fragmentary memory. Second, Freud insists on the fact that he has given an account only of the (incomplete) analytic *results* and not at all of the *process* of interpretation—that is to say, Freud willfully withholds the *technique of the analytic work*. To describe the analytic technique, Freud argues, would have led to "nothing but hopeless confusion" (*SE* 7:13; *P* 41; *C* 27). Finally, Freud stresses that no *one* case history can provide the answer to *all* the problems presented by

hysteria: all case histories are in this sense incomplete answers to the problem they set out to solve.

It is of course perfectly normal to state, as Freud does here, the limitations of one's project in the preface to the finished work, but Freud does more than that. In his Prefatory Remarks to *Dora,* Freud seems positively obsessed with the incomplete status of his text. He returns to the subject again and again, either to excuse the fact that he is presenting a fragment or to express his longings for a *complete* text after all. His Prefatory Remarks oscillate constantly between the theme of fragmentation and the notion of totality. These two themes, however, are not presented as straight opposites. Having expressed his regrets that the case history is incomplete, he writes: "But its shortcomings are connected with the very circumstances which have made its publication possible. . . . I should not have known how to deal with the material involved in the history of a treatment which had lasted, perhaps, for a whole year" (*SE* 7:11; *P* 40; *C* 26). Freud here totally undermines any notion of a fundamental opposition between fragment and whole: it would have been impossible to write down a *complete* case history. The fragment can be presented as a complete book; the complete case history could not. Nevertheless, Freud insists on the fact that the fragment *lacks* something:

> In the face of the incompleteness of my analytic results, I had no choice but to follow the example of those discoverers whose good fortune it is to bring to the light of day after their long burial the priceless though mutilated relics of antiquity. I have restored what is missing, taking the best models known to me from other analyses; but like a conscientious archaeologist, I have not omitted to mention in each case where the authentic parts end and my construction begins. (*SE* 7:21; *P* 41: *C* 27)

Once again, Freud candidly admits that his results are incomplete—only to claim in the same breath that he has "restored what is missing"; Freud's metaphors in this context are significant. Dora's story is compared to the "priceless though mutilated relics of antiquity," and Freud himself figures as an archeologist, digging relics out from the earth. His claim here is that when he adds something to the "mutilated relics," completeness is established *malgré tout*. But this new completeness is after all not quite complete. On the same page as the above quotation, Freud writes that the psychoanalytic technique (which he jealously retains for himself) does not by its nature lend itself to the creation of complete sequences: "Everything that has to do with the clearing-up of a particular symptom emerges piecemeal, woven into various contexts, and distributed over widely separated periods of time" (*SE* 7:12, *P* 41; *C* 27). The "completeness" achieved by Freud's supplementary conjectures is doubly incomplete: it consists of Dora's story (the "mutilated relics of antiquity"), to which Freud's own assumptions have been added. But Dora's story is not only a fragment: it is a fragment composed of information that has emerged "piecemeal, woven into various contexts, and distributed over widely separated periods of time." We must assume that it is Freud himself who has imposed a fictional coherence on Dora's story, in order to render the narrative readable. But Dora's story is in turn only one part of the finished work entitled "Fragment of an Analysis of a Case of Hysteria." The other part is supplemented by Freud. In itself Dora's story is too fragmentary; it is readable only when Freud supplies the necessary supplement. But that supplement is based on Freud's experience from other cases of hysteria, cases that must have been constructed in the same way as Dora's: by information provided "piecemeal, over widely separated periods of time." The fragment depends on the supplement, which depends on

other fragments depending on other supplements, and so on ad infinitum.

We are, in other words, surprisingly close to Jacques Derrida's theories of the production of meaning as *"différance."*[4] According to Derrida, meaning can never be seized as presence: it is always deferred, constantly displaced onto the next element in the series, in a chain of signification that has no end, no transcendental signified that might provide the final anchor point for the production of sense. This, need one say, is not Freud's own *conscious* theory: he clings to his dream of "complete elucidation" (*SE* 7:24; *P* 54; *C* 39), refusing to acknowledge that according to his own account of the status of the *Dora* text, completeness is an unattainable illusion. Even when he insists strongly on the fragmentary status of his text, he always implies that completeness is within reach. He can, for instance, write, "If the work had been continued, we should no doubt have obtained the fullest possible enlightenment upon every particular of the case" (*SE* 7:12; *P* 40; *C* 26). Freud's text oscillates endlessly between his desire for complete insight or knowledge and an unconscious realization (or fear) of the fragmentary, deferring status of knowledge itself.

## TRANSFERENCE AND COUNTERTRANSFERENCE

We have seen that in his Prefatory Remarks Freud discloses that "Dora's story" *is* largely "Freud's story": he is the author, the one who has conjured a complete work from these analytic fragments. This in itself should alert the reader eager to discover Dora's own view of her case to the dangers of taking Freud's words too much at face value. His account of the analysis of Dora must instead be scanned with the utmost suspicion.

The better part of the Postscript is devoted to a discussion of the reasons why the analysis of Dora was at least in part a failure. Freud's main explanation is that he failed to discover the importance of the *transference* for the analysis; he did not discover in time that Dora was transferring the emotions she felt for Herr K. onto Freud himself. Psychoanalytic theory holds that transference is normal in the course of analysis, that it consists in the patient's transferring emotions for some other person onto the analyst, and that if the analyst, unaware of the transference, cannot counteract it, the analysis will in consequence go awry.

Freud adds this information in this Postscript. But if we are to grasp what is being acted out between Freud and Dora, it is important to keep in mind from the outset this transference on Dora's part from Herr K. to Freud. Transference, however, is something the patient does to the analyst. Freud does not mention at all the opposite phenomenon, *countertransference,* which consists in the analyst's transferring his or her own unconscious emotions onto the patient. Jacques Lacan has discussed precisely this problem in *Dora* in an article entitled "Intervention sur le transfert."[5] According to Lacan, Freud unconsciously identifies with Herr K. in his relationship to Dora, which makes him (Freud) far too interested in Dora's alleged love for Herr K. and effectively blind to any other explanation of her problems. Thus the countertransference contributes decisively to the failure of Dora's analysis.

The fact of transference and countertransference between Freud and Dora considerably complicates the task of the *Dora* reader. *Freud's attempts to posit himself as the neutral, scientific observer who is merely noting down his observations and reflections can no longer be accepted.* The archeologist must be suspected of having mutilated the relics he finds. We must remember that Freud's version of the case is colored not only by his own unconscious countertransference but also by the fact that he signally fails to notice the

transference in Dora, and therefore systematically misinterprets her transference symptoms throughout the text. This, oddly, is something the reader is not told until the "Postscript."

Freud's interpretation of Dora's case can be summarized as follows. Dora develops hysterical symptoms because she represses sexual desire. But her case has an added, oedipal dimension: one must suppose that Dora originally desired her father, but since her father disappointed her by starting an affair with Frau K., Dora now pretends to hate him. Herr K. represents the father for Dora, particularly because he is also Frau K.'s husband. Dora's repression of her sexual desire for Herr K. is therefore at once a hysterical reaction (repression of sexual desire) *and* an oedipal reaction (rejection of the father through rejection of Herr K.). Based on this interpretation, Freud's treatment of Dora consists in repeated attempts to get her to admit her repressed desire for Herr K., a "confession" Dora resists as best she can.

We have already seen that, according to Lacan, the analysis failed because of Freud's unconscious identification with Herr K. Since Dora is at the same time identifying Freud with Herr K., the result is inevitably that she must experience Freud's insistence on the necessity of acknowledging her desire for Herr K. as a repetition of Herr K.'s attempt to elicit sexual favors from her. In the end she rejects Freud in the same way she rejected Herr K.—by giving him two weeks' notice. Herr K. had earlier had an affair with the governess of his children, and Dora felt greatly insulted at being courted like a servant by the same man. Her revenge is to treat both Freud and Herr K. as servants in return.

But Freud's incessant identification with Herr K., the rejected lover, leads to other interesting aspects of the text. One of the most important episodes in the study is Freud's interpretation of Herr K.'s attempt to kiss Dora, then fourteen, after having tricked her into being alone with him in his office. Freud writes that Herr K.

> suddenly clasped the girl to him and pressed a kiss upon her lips. This was surely just the situation to call up a distinct feeling of sexual excitement in a girl of fourteen who had never before been approached. But Dora had at that moment a violent feeling of disgust, tore herself free from the man, and hurried past him to the staircase and from there to the street door. (*SE* 7:28; *P* 59; *C* 43)

At this moment in the text Freud is completely in the grip of his countertransference: he must at all costs emphasize that Dora's reaction was abnormal and writes that "the behaviour of this child of fourteen was already entirely and completely hysterical" (*SE* 7:28; *P* 59; *C* 44). Her reaction was hysterical because she was already repressing sexual desire: "Instead of the genital sensation which would certainly have been felt by a healthy girl in such circumstances, Dora was overcome by . . . disgust" (*SE* 7:29; *P* 60; *C* 44). It is, of course, resplendently clear to any scientific observer that any normal girl of fourteen would be overwhelmed by desire when a middle-aged man "suddenly clasps her to him" in a lonely spot.

Freud then links Dora's feeling of disgust to *oral* impulses and goes on to interpret as a "displacement" Dora's statement that she clearly felt the pressure from the upper part of Herr K.'s body against her own. What she really felt, according to Freud, and what aroused such strong oral disgust, was the pressure of Herr K.'s erect penis. The thought of this unmentionable organ was then repressed, and the feeling of pressure displaced from the lower to the upper part of the body. The oral disgust is then related to Dora's habit of thumb-sucking as a child, and Freud connects the oral satisfaction resulting from this habit to Dora's nervous cough. He interprets

the cough (irritation of oral cavity and throat) as a revealing symptom of Dora's sexual fantasies: she must be fantasizing a scene where sexual satisfaction is obtained by using the mouth (*per os,* as Freud puts it) (*SE* 7:48; *P* 81; *C* 65), and this scene is one that takes place between Frau K. and Dora's father.

Having said as much, Freud spends the next few pages defending himself against accusations of using too foul a language with his patients. These passages could be read as betraying a certain degree of unconscious tension in Freud himself, but it is enough to point out here that he argues his way from exhortations to tolerance to the high social status of "the perversion which is the most repellent to us, the sensual love of a man for a man" (*SE* 7:50; *P* 93; *C* 67) in ancient Greece, before returning to Dora's oral fantasy and making it plain that what he had in mind was fellatio, or "sucking at the male organ" (*SE* 7:51; *P* 85; *C* 68). It would not be difficult to detect in Freud a defensive reaction-formation in this context, since on the next page he feels compelled to allude to "this excessively repulsive and perverted phantasy of sucking at a penis" (*SE* 7:52; *P* 86; *C* 69). It is little wonder that he feels the need to defend himself against the idea of fellatio, since it is more than probable that the fantasy exists, not in Dora's mind, but in his alone. Freud has informed us that Dora's father was impotent, and assumes this to be the basis of Dora's "repulsive and perverted phantasy." According to Freud, the father cannot manage penetration, so Frau K. must perform fellatio instead. But as Lacan has pointed out, this argument reveals an astonishing lack of logic on Freud's part. In the case of male impotence, the man is obviously much more likely, *faute de mieux,* to perform cunnilingus. As Lacan writes: "Everyone knows that cunnilingus is the artifice most commonly adopted by 'men of means' whose powers begin to abandon them." It is in this logical flaw that Freud's countertransference is seen at its strongest. The illogicality reveals his own unconscious wish for gratification, a gratification Freud's unconscious alter ego, Herr K., might obtain if only Dora would admit her desire for him.

Freud's countertransference blinds him to the possibility that Dora's hysteria may be due to the repression of desire, not for Herr K., but for his wife, Frau K. A fatal lack of insight into the transferential process prevents Freud from discovering Dora's homosexuality early enough. Dora's condition as a victim of male dominance here becomes starkly visible. She is not only a pawn in the game between Herr K. and her father; her doctor joins the male team and untiringly tries to ascribe to her desires she does not have and to ignore the ones she does have.

## PATRIARCHAL PREJUDICES

Freud's oppressive influence on Dora does not, however, stem only from the countertransference. There are also more general ideological tendencies to sexism at work in his text. Freud, for instance, systematically refuses to consider female sexuality as an active, independent drive. Again and again he exhorts Dora to accept herself as an object for Herr K. Every time Dora reveals active sexual desires, Freud interprets them away, either by assuming that Dora is expressing masculine identification (when she fantasizes about female genitals, Freud instantly assumes that she wants to penetrate them) or by supposing that she desires to be penetrated by the male (Dora's desire for Frau K. is interpreted as her desire to be in Frau K.'s place in order to gain access to Herr K.). His position is self-contradictory: he is one of the first to acknowledge the existence of sexual desire in women, and at the same time he renders himself incapable of seeing it as more than the impulse to become passive recipients for male desire. Lacan assumes precisely the same attitude

when he states that the problem for Dora (and all women) is that she "must accept herself as the object of male desire" (Lacan) and that this is the reason for Dora's adoration of Frau K.

Feminists cannot help feeling relieved when Dora finally dismisses Freud like another servant. It is tempting to read Dora's hysterical symptoms, as do Cixous and Clément, as a silent revolt against male power over women's bodies and women's language. But at the same time it is disconcerting to see how inefficient Dora's revolt turned out to be. Felix Deutsch describes Dora's tragic destiny in an article written in 1957. She continued to develop various hysterical symptoms, made life unbearable for her family, and grew to resemble her mother (whom Freud dismissed as a typical case of "housewife psychosis"). According to Deutsch, Dora tortured her husband throughout their marriage; he concluded that "her marriage had served only to cover up her distaste of men" (see essay 1). Dora suffers continuously from psychosomatic constipation and dies from cancer of the colon. Deutsch concludes, "Her death . . . seemed a blessing to those who were close to her. She had been, as my informant phrased it, one of the most repulsive hysterics he had ever met."

It may be gratifying to see the young, proud Dora as a radiant example of feminine revolt (as does Cixous); but we should not forget the image of the old, nagging, whining, and complaining Dora she later becomes, achieving nothing. Hysteria is not, *pace* Hélène Cixous, the incarnation of the revolt of women forced to silence but rather a declaration of defeat, the realization that there is no other way out. Hysteria is, as Catherine Clément perceives, a cry for help when defeat becomes real, when the woman sees that she is efficiently gagged and chained to her feminine role.

Now if the hysterical woman is gagged and chained, Freud posits himself as her liberator.

And if the emancipatory project of psycho-analysis fails in the case of Dora, it is because Freud the liberator happens also to be, *objectively,* on the side of oppression. He is a male in patriarchal society, and moreover not just any male but an educated bourgeois male, incarnating *malgré lui* patriarchal values. His own emancipatory project profoundly conflicts with his political and social role as an oppressor of women.

The most telling instance of this deeply unconscious patriarchal ideology in *Dora* is to be found in Freud's obsession with the sources of his patient's sexual information. After stressing the impossibility of tracing the sources of Dora's sexual information (*SE* 7:31; *P* 62; *C* 46), Freud nevertheless continually returns to the subject, suggesting alternately that the source may have been books belonging to a former governess (*SE* 7:36; *P* 68; *C* 52), Mantegazza's *Physiology of Love* (*SE* 7:62; *P* 97; *C* 80), or an encyclopedia (*SE* 7:99; *P* 140; *C* 120). He finally realizes that there must have been an *oral* source of information, in addition to the avid reading of forbidden books, then sees, extremely belatedly, that the oral source must have been none other than the beloved Frau K.

The one hypothesis that Freud does not entertain is that the source of oral information may have been Dora's mother—the mother who is traditionally charged with the sexual education of the daughters. This omission is wholly symptomatic of Freud's treatment of Dora's mother. Although he indicates Dora's identification with her mother (*SE* 7:75; *P* 111; *C* 93), he nevertheless strongly insists that Dora had withdrawn completely from her mother's influence (*SE* 7:23; *C* 38). Dora's apparent hatred of her mother is mobilized as evidence for this view.

But Freud ought to know better than to accept a daughter's hatred of her mother as an inevitable consequence of the mother's objective unlikableness ("housewife's psychosis"). Even his own oedipal explanation of Dora's rejection of Herr K. should contribute to a clearer understanding of the mother's importance for Dora. Oedipally speaking, Dora would be seen as the mother's rival in that competition for the father's love, but this rivalry also implies the necessity of identifying with the mother: the daughter must become like the mother in order to be loved by the father. Freud notes that Dora is behaving like a jealous wife and that this behavior shows that "she was clearly putting herself in her mother's place" (*SE* 7:56; *P* 90; *C* 73), but he draws no further conclusions from these observations. He also points out that Dora identifies with Frau K., her father's mistress, but is still quite content to situate her mainly in relation to her father and Herr K. He fails to see that Dora is caught up in an ambivalent relationship to her mother and an idealizing and identifying relationship to Frau K., the other mother-figure in this text. Freud's patriarchal prejudices force him to ignore relationships between women and instead center all his attention on relationships with men. This grievous underestimation of the importance of other women for Dora's psychic development contributes decisively to the failure of the analysis and the cure—not least in that it makes Freud unaware of the *preoedipal* causes for Dora's hysteria. Maria Ramas writes: "By Freud's own admission, the deepest level of meaning of hysterical symptoms is not a thwarted desire for the father, but a breakthrough of the prohibited desire for the mother."

## SEXUALITY AND EPISTEMOLOGY

Freud's particular interest in the sources of Dora's sexual information does not, however, merely reveal that for as long as possible he avoids considering oral relations between women as such a source; it also indicates that Freud overestimates the importance of this question. There is nothing in Dora's story to indicate that a successful analysis depends on the elucidation of this peripheral problem. Why then would Freud be so obsessed by these sources of knowledge?

First, because he himself desires total knowledge: his aim is nothing less than the *complete elucidation* of Dora, despite his insistence on the fragmentary nature of his material. The absence of information on this one subject is thus tormenting, since it so obviously ruins the dream of completeness. But such a desire for total, absolute knowledge exposes a fundamental assumption in Freud's epistemology. *Knowledge for Freud is a finished, closed whole.* Possession of knowledge means possession of power. Freud, the doctor, is curiously proud of his hermeneutical capacities. After having interpreted Dora's fingering of her little purse as an admission of infantile masturbation, he writes with evident satisfaction:

> When I set myself the task of bringing to light what human beings keep hidden within them, not by the compelling power of hypothesis, but by observing what they say and what they show, I thought the task was a harder one than it really is. He that has eyes to see and ears to hear may convince himself that no mortal can keep a secret. If his lips are silent, he chatters with his finger tips; betrayal oozes out of him at every pore. And thus the task of making conscious the most hidden recesses of the mind is one which it is quite possible to accomplish. (*SE* 7:77–8; *P* 114; *C* 96)

Freud in other words possesses powers more compelling than those of hypnosis. He is the one who discloses and unlocks secrets; he is Oedipus solving the Sphinx's riddle. But like Oedipus he is ravaged by a terrible anxiety: the fear of castration. If Freud cannot solve Dora's riddle, the unconscious punishment for this failure will be castration. In this struggle for the possession of knowledge, a

knowledge that is power, Dora reveals herself both as Freud's alter ego and as his rival. She possesses the secret Freud is trying to discover. At this point we must suspect Freud of countertransference to Dora: he identifies with the hysterical Dora in the search for information about sexual matters. Freud has his own secret, as Dora has hers: the analytic technique, which, as we have seen, cannot be exposed without causing "total confusion." Freud jealously keeps his secret, as Dora keeps hers: her homosexual desire for Frau K.

But since Dora is a woman, and a rather formidable one at that, a young lady who hitherto has had only scorn for the incompetent (and, surely, impotent) doctors who have treated her so far, she becomes a threatening rival for Freud. If he does not win the fight for knowledge, he will also be revealed as incompetent/impotent, his compelling powers will be reduced to nothing, he will be castrated. If Dora wins the knowledge game, her model for knowledge will emerge victorious, and Freud's own model will be destroyed. Freud here finds himself between Scylla and Charybdis: if he identifies with Dora in the search for knowledge, he becomes a woman, that is to say, castrated; but if he chooses to cast her as his rival, he *must* win out, or the punishment will be castration.

The last point (that the punishment in case of defeat will be castration) requires further explanation. We have seen that Dora's sources of knowledge have been characterized as female, oral, and scattered. Freud, on the contrary, presents his knowledge as something that creates a unitary whole. In both cases we are discussing sexual knowledge. But Freud's own paradigmatic example of the desire for sexual knowledge is the sexual curiosity in children, and Freud's most important text on this topic is *Little Hans*. Moving from *Dora* to *Little Hans,* the reader is struck by this remarkable difference in tone between the two texts. The five-year-old little Hans, straining to understand the mysteries of sexuality, is strongly encouraged in his epistemophilia (Freud's own word, from *Three Essays on Sexuality*). Freud never ceases to express his admiration for the intelligence of the little boy, in such laudatory statements as, "Here the little boy was displaying a really unusual degree of clarity" (*SE* 10:44; *P* 206), or "Little Hans has by a bold stroke taken the conduct of the analysis into his own hands. By means of a brilliant symptomatic act . . ." (*SE* 10:86; *P* 246). This tone is far removed from Freud's stern admonitions of Dora, his continuous *et tu quoque* ripostes to her interpretation of her own situation.

Why this differential treatment? It is arguable that in *Little Hans* Freud equates the desire for knowledge and the construction of theories with the desire to discover the role of the penis in procreation. The penis, in other words, becomes the epistemological object par excellence for Freud. But if this is so, knowledge and theory must be conceptualized as whole, rounded, finished—just like the penis. Little Hans becomes in this sense a penis for Freud. He is both a pleasurable object to be studied, a source of excitation and enthusiasm, *and* Freud's double: a budding sexual theoretician emerging to confirm Freud's own epistemological activities. But where Little Hans confirms, Dora threatens. Her knowledge cannot be conceptualized as a whole; it is dispersed and has been assembled piecemeal from feminine sources. Dora's epistemological model becomes the female genitals, which in Freud's vision emerge as unfinished, diffuse, and fragmentary; they cannot add up to a complete whole and must therefore be perceived as castrated genitals. If Freud were to accept Dora's epistemological model, it would be tantamout to rejecting the penis as the principal symbol for human desire for knowledge, which again would mean accepting castration.

Freud's masculine psyche therefore perceives Dora as more fundamentally threatening than he can consciously express. Instead, his fear of epistemological castration manifests itself in various disguises: in his obsessive desire to discover the sources of Dora's knowledge, and in his oddly intense discussion of the fragmentary status of the *Dora* text. To admit that there are holes in one's knowledge is tantamount to transforming the penis to a hole, that is to say, to transforming the man into a woman. Holes, empty spaces, open areas are at all cost to be avoided; and with this in mind we can discern further layers of meaning in the passage quoted earlier:

> In the face of the incompleteness of my analytic results, I had no choice but to follow the example of those discoverers whose good fortune it is to bring to the light of day after their long burial the priceless though mutilated relics of antiquity. I have restored what is missing. (*SE* 7:12; *P* 41; *C* 27)

"The priceless though mutilated relics of antiquity" are not only Dora's story: they are Dora herself, her genitals and the feminine epistemological model. Freud makes sure that the message here is clear: "mutilated" is his usual way of describing the effect of castration, and "priceless" also means just what it says: price-less, without value. For how can there be value when the valuable piece has been cut off?[6] The relics are mutilated, the penis has been cut. Freud's task is therefore momentous: he must "restore what is missing"; his penis must fill the epistemological hole represented by Dora.

But such a task can only be performed by one who possesses what is missing. And this is precisely what Freud occasionally doubts in his text: the fear of castration is also the fear of discovering that one has already been castrated. Freud's hesitation in *Dora* between insisting on completeness and admitting fragmentary status indicates that in his text the penis is playing a kind of *fort-da* game with its author (now you have it, now you don't).[7]

Freud's book about Dora is the narrative of an intense power struggle between two protagonists—a struggle in which the male character's virility is at stake and in which he by no means always has the upper hand.

When Dora dismisses Freud like a servant, she paradoxically rescues him from further epistemological insecurity. He is left, then, the master of the *writing* of Dora. And even though his text bears the scars of the struggle between him and his victim, it is a victorious Freud who publishes it. Dora dismissed him, but Freud got his revenge: Dora was the name Freud's own sister, Rosa, had foisted on her maid in place of her real one, which also was Rosa (*The Psychopathology of Everyday Life, SE* 6:241). So Ida Bauer, in a bitter historical irony, was made famous under the name of a servant after all.

Freud's epistemology is clearly phallocentric. The male is the bearer of knowledge; he alone has the power to penetrate woman and text; woman's role is to let herself be penetrated by such truth. Such epistemological phallocentrism is by no means specifically Freudian; on the contrary, it has so far enjoyed universal sway in our patriarchal civilization, and one could hardly expect Freud to emerge untouched by it. It is politically important, however, to point out that this pathological division of knowledge into masculine totality and feminine fragment is completely mystifying and mythological. There is absolutely no evidence for the actual existence of two such gender-determined sorts of knowledge, to be conceptualized as parallel to the shapes of human genitals. Dora can be perceived as the bearer of feminine epistemology in the study only because Freud selected her as his opponent in a war over cognition, creating her as his symbolic antagonist. To champion Dora's "feminine values" means meekly accepting Freud's own definitions of masculine and feminine. Power always creates its own definitions, and this is particularly true of the distinctions between

masculine and feminine constructed by patriarchal society. Nowhere is patriarchal ideology to be seen more clearly than in the definition of the feminine as the negative of the masculine—and this is precisely how Freud defines Dora and the "feminine" epistemology she is supposed to represent.

To undermine this phallocentric epistemology means to expose its lack of "natural" foundation. In the case of *Dora,* however, we have been able to do this only because of Freud's own theories of femininity and sexuality. The attack upon phallocentrism must come from within, since there can be no "outside," no space where true femininity, untainted by patriarchy, can be kept intact for us to discover. We can only destroy the mythical and mystifying constructions of patriarchy by using its own weapons. We have no others.

## NOTES

This essay was first published in *Feminist Review* (1981), 9:60–73. The main sources were oral: it would never have been written were it not for the invaluable insight I gained both from Neil Hertz's seminars on "Freud and Literature" at Cornell University in the fall semester of 1980, and from the exciting and extremely inspiring discussions in the Women's Group on Psychoanalysis at Cornell that same autumn.

1. Hélène Cixous and Catherine Clément, *La jeune née* (Paris: Editions 10/18, 1975).

2. Hélène Cixous, *Portrait de Dora* (Paris: Editions des femmes, 1976). This play has been translated by Sarah Burd in *Diacritics* (Spring 1983), pp. 2–32. Another translation, by Anita Barrows, has been published in *Benmussa Directs* (London: Calder, 1979; Dallas: Riverrun Press, 1979).

3. Maria Ramas cut this passage from the shortened version of her essay published in this book. The full version is in *Feminist Studies,* (Fall 1980), 6(3):500—Editors' note.

4. Jacques Derrida, *Marges de la philosophie* (Paris: Minuit, 1972).

5. Jacques Lacan, *Écrits* (Paris: Seuil, 1966), p. 224. See

Jacqueline Rose's translation of "Intervention sur le trans-fert," essay 4 of this book.

6. Freud always assumes that castration means the cutting off of the penis. This is quite odd; not so much because real castration consists in the cutting off of the testicles, but because he nowhere refers to this discrepancy between his own definition of castration and the real practice.

7. The *fort-da* game is the game in which the child, by rejecting and retrieving a toy, enacts the absence and presence of the mother. *Fort-da* means roughly *"here-gone."*

# 25

---

# Shoshana Felman
# 1942–

---

Shoshana Felman is the Thomas E. Donnelley Professor of French and comparative literature at Yale University. She is a leading exponent of psychoanalytic literary criticism. Her lucid explications of the theories of Jacques Lacan and, through Lacan, of Freud, and her practical applications of those theories to the study of literature have helped make the practice of psychoanalytic literary criticism accessible to a wide audience. Felman's work includes *La "Folie" dans l'oeuvre romanesques de Stendhal* (1971); *The Literary Speech Act: Don Juan with Austin* (1980; trans. 1983); *Madness and Writing* (1978; trans. 1985); *Jacques Lacan and the Adventure of Insight* (1987); and *Testimony: Crises of Witnessing in Literature, Psychoanalysis and History* (1991). She also edited *Literature and Psychoanalysis* (1982).

In "Psychoanalysis and Education: Teaching Terminable and Interminable" (1982), Felman discusses what she calls the "radical impossibility of teaching." With close attention to the writings of Freud and Lacan, she demonstrates the similarities between the relationships of teacher and student and analyst and analysand, indicating the ways in which psychoanalytic methodology may be used as a tool to facilitate the learning process. That is, she argues that there is a parallel between the analysand's "repression" or "resistance" in psychotherapy and students' "ignorance." Teaching, like psychoanalysis, must "deal not so much with *lack* of knowledge as with *resistances* to knowledge"; the teacher, like the analyst, must learn not to *"exchange"* knowledge with students but to *"use"* his or her knowledge to help students discover (or rediscover) their own. Psychoanalytic methods are, in Felman's view, especially applicable to the teaching of literature; literature, like the recovering analysand and the brighter student, *"knows it knows, but does not know the meaning of its knowledge*—it does not know *what* it knows."

---

## Psychoanalysis and Education: Teaching Terminable and Interminable

*In memory of Jacques Lacan*

---

*Meno: Can you tell me, Socrates, if virtue can be taught? Or is it not teachable but the result of practice, or is it neither of these, but men possess it by nature?*

*Socrates: . . . You must think me happy indeed if you think I know whether virtue can be taught . . . I am so far from knowing whether virtue can be taught or not that I do not even have any knowledge of what virtue itself is.*

*. . .*

*Meno: Yes, Socrates, but how do you mean that we do not learn, but that what we call learning is recollection? Can you teach me how this is so?*

*Socrates: . . . Meno, you are a rascal. Here you are asking me to give you my "teaching," I who claim that there is no such thing as teaching, only recollection.*

—Plato, *Meno*[1]

## THE MEASURE OF A TASK

Socrates, that extraordinary teacher who taught humanity what pedagogy is, and whose name personifies the birth of pedagogics as a science, inaugurates his teaching practice, paradoxically enough, by asserting not just his own ignorance, but the radical impossibility of teaching.

Another extraordinarily effective pedagogue, another one of humanity's great teachers, Freud, repeats, in his own way, the same conviction that teaching is a fundamentally impossible profession. "None of the applications of psychoanalysis," he writes, "has excited so much interest and aroused so many hopes . . . as its use in the theory and practice of education . . .":

My personal share in this application of psychoanalysis has been very slight. At an early stage I had accepted the *bon mot* which lays it down that there are three impossible professions—educating, healing, governing—and I was already fully occupied with the second of them.[2]

In a later text—indeed the very last one that he wrote—Freud recapitulates this paradoxical conviction which time and experience seem to have only reinforced, confirmed:

It almost looks as if analysis were the third of those 'impossible' professions in which one can be sure beforehand of achieving unsatisfying results. The other two, which have been known much longer, are education and government. [Standard, XXIII, 248]

If teaching is impossible—as Freud and Socrates both point out—what are we teachers doing? How should we understand—and carry out—our task? And why is it precisely two of the most effective teachers ever to appear in the intellectual history of mankind, who regard the task of teaching as impossible? Indeed, is not their radical enunciation of the impossibility of teaching itself actively engaged in teaching, itself part of the lesson they bequeath us? And if so, what can be learnt from the fact that it is impossible to teach? What can the impossibility of teaching teach us?

As much as Socrates, Freud has instituted, among other things, a revolutionary pedagogy. It is my contention—which I will here attempt to elucidate and demonstrate—that it is precisely in giving us unprecedented insight into the impossibility of teaching, that psychoanalysis has opened up unprecedented teaching possibilities, renewing both the questions and the practice of education.

This pedagogical renewal was not, however, systematically thought out by Freud himself, or systematically articulated by any of his followers; nor have its thrust and scope been to date fully assimilated or fully grasped, let alone utilized, exploited in the classroom. The only truly different pedagogy to have practically emerged from what might be called the psychoanalytic lesson is the thoroughly original teaching-style of Jacques Lacan, Freud's French disciple and interpreter. If Lacan is, as I would argue, Freud's best student—that is, the most radical effect of the insights of Freud's teaching—perhaps his teaching practice might give us a clue to the newness of the psychoanalytic lesson about lessons, and help us thus define both the actual and, more importantly, the potential contribution of psychoanalysis to pedagogy.

## WHAT IS A CRITIQUE OF PEDAGOGY?

Lacan's relationship with pedagogy has, however, been itself—like that of Freud—mostly oversimplified, misunderstood, reduced. The reason for the usual misinterpretations of both Lacan's and Freud's pedagogical contribution lies in a misunderstanding of the critical position taken by psychoanalysis with respect to traditional methods and assumptions of education. Lacan's well-known critique of what he has pejoratively termed "academic discourse" *(le discours universitaire)* situates "the radical vice" in "the transmission of knowledge." "A Master of Arts," writes Lacan ironically, "as well as other titles, protect the secret of a substantialized knowledge,"[3] Lacan thus blames "the narrow-minded horizon of pedagogues" for having "reduced" the "strong notion" of "teaching"[4] to a "functional apprenticeship" (E 445).

Whereas Lacan's pedagogical critique is focused on grown-up training—on academic education and the ways it handles and structures knowledge, Freud's pedagogical critique is mainly concerned with children's education and the ways it handles and structures repression. "Let us make ourselves clear," writes Freud, "as to what the first task of education is":

The child must learn to control his instincts. It is impossible to give him liberty to carry out all his impulses without restriction . . . Accordingly, *education must inhibit, forbid and suppress*[5] and this is abundantly seen in all periods of history. But we have learnt from analysis that precisely this suppression of instincts involves

the risk of neurotic illness. . . . Thus education has to find its way between the Scylla of non-interference and the Charybdis of frustration. . . . An optimum must be discovered which will enable education to achieve the most and damage the least. . . . A moment's reflection tells us that hitherto education has fulfilled its task very badly and has done children great damage. [Standard, XXII, 149]

Thus, in its most massive statements and in its polemical pronouncements, psychoanalysis, in Freud as well as in Lacan—although with different emphases—is first and foremost *a critique of pedagogy*. The legacy of this critique has been, however, misconstrued and greatly oversimplified, in that the critical stance has been understood—in both Lacan's and Freud's case—as a desire to escape the pedagogical imperative: a desire—whether possible or impossible—to do away with pedagogy altogether. "Psychoanalysis," writes Anna Freud, "whenever it has come into contact with pedagogy, has always expressed the wish to *limit education*. Psychoanalysis has brought before us the quite definite danger arising from education."[6]

The illocutionary force of the psychoanalytical (pedagogical) critique of pedagogy has thus been reduced, either to a simple negativity, or to a simple positivity, of that critique. Those who, in an oversimplification of the Freudian lesson, equate the psychoanalytic critical stance with a simple positivity, give consequently positive advice to educators, in an attempt to conceive of more liberal methods for raising children—methods allowing "to each stage in the child's life the right proportion of instinct-gratification and instinct-restriction."[7] Those who, on the other hand, in an oversimplification of the Lacanian lesson, equate the psychoanalytical critical stance with a simple negativity, see in psychoanalysis "literally an inverse pedagogy": "the analytic process is in effect a kind of reverse pedagogy, which aims at undoing what has been established by education."[8] In the title of a recent book on the relationship of Freud to pedagogy, Freud is thus defined as "The Anti-Pedagogue."[9] This one-sidedly negative interpretation of the relation of psychoanalysis to pedagogy fails to see that every true pedagogue is in effect an anti-pedagogue, not just because every pedagogy has historically emerged as a critique of pedagogy (Socrates: "There's a chance, Meno, that we, you as well as me . . . have been inadequately educated, you by Gorgias, I by Prodicus"[10]), but because, in one way or another, every pedagogy stems from its confrontation with the impossibility of teaching (Socrates: "You see, Meno, that I am not teaching . . . anything, but all I do is question . . ."[11]). The reductive conception of "Freud: The Anti-Pedagogue" thus fails to see that there is no such thing as an anti-pedagogue: an anti-pedagogue is *the* pedagogue par excellence. Such a conception overlooks, indeed, and fails to reckon with, Freud's own stupendous pedagogical performance, and its relevance to his declarations about pedagogy.

The trouble, both with the positivistic and with the negativistic misinterpretations of the psychoanalytical critique of pedagogy, is that they refer exclusively to Lacan's or Freud's explicit *statements* about pedagogy, and thus fail to see the illocutionary force, the didactic function of the *utterance* as opposed to the mere content of the statement. They fail to see, in other words, the pedagogical situation—the pedagogical dynamic in which statements function not as simple truths but as performative speech-*acts*. Invariably, all existing psychoanalytically-inspired theories of pedagogy fail to address the question of the pedagogical speech-act of Freud himself, or of Lacan himself: what can be learnt about pedagogy not just from their theories (which only fragmentarily and indirectly deal with the issue of education) but from their way of

*teaching* it, from their own practice as teachers, from their own pedagogical performance.

Lacan refers explicitly to what he calls the psychoanalyst's "mission of teaching" (E 241, N 34 TM),[12] and speaks of his own teaching—the bi-monthly seminar he gave for forty years—as a vocation, "a function . . . to which I have truly devoted my entire life" (S-XI, 7, N 1).[13] Unlike Lacan, Freud addresses the issue of teaching more indirectly, rather by refusing to associate his person with it:

> But there is one topic which I cannot pass over so easily—*not, however, because I understand particularly much about it* or have contributed very much to it. Quite the contrary: *I have scarcely concerned myself with it at all*. I must mention it because it is so exceedingly important, so rich in hopes for the future, perhaps the most important of all the activities of analysis. What I am thinking of is the application of psychoanalysis to education. [Standard, XXII, 146]

This statement thus promotes pedagogy to the rank of "perhaps the most important of all the activities of analysis" only on the basis of Freud's denial of his own personal involvement with it. However, this very statement, this very denial is itself engaged in a dramatic pedagogical performance; it itself is part of an imaginary "lecture," significantly written in the form of an academic public address and of a dialogue with students—a pedagogic dialogue imaginarily conducted by a Freud who, in reality terminally ill and having undergone an operation for mouth-cancer, is no longer capable of speech:

> My *Introductory Lectures on Psychoanalysis* were delivered . . . in a lecture room of the Vienna Psychiatric Clinic before an audience gathered from all the Faculties of the University. . . .

These new lectures, unlike the former ones, have never been delivered. My age had in the meantime absolved me from the obligation of giving expression to my membership in the University (which was in any case a peripheral one) by delivering lectures; and a surgical operation had made speaking in public impossible for me. If, therefore, I once more take my place in the lecture room during the remarks that follow, it is only by an artifice of the imagination; it may help me not to forget to bear the reader in mind as I enter more deeply into my subject. . . . Like their predecessors, [these lectures] are addressed to the multitude of educated people to whom we may perhaps attribute a benevolent, even though cautious, interest in the characteristics and discoveries of the young science. This time once again it has been my chief aim to make no sacrifice to an appearance of being simple, complete or rounded-off, not to disguise problems and not to deny the existence of gaps and uncertainties. [Standard, XXII, 5–6]

No other such coincidence of fiction and reality, biography and theory, could better dramatize Freud's absolutely fundamental pedagogic gesture. What better image could there be for the pedagogue in spite of himself, the pedagogue in spite of everything— the dying teacher whose imminent death, like that of Socrates, only confirms that he is a born teacher—than this pathetic figure, this living allegory of the speechless speaker, of the teacher's teaching out of— through—the very radical impossibility of teaching?

Pedagogy in psychoanalysis is thus not just a theme: it is a rhetoric. It is not just a statement: it is an utterance. It is not just a meaning: it is action; an action which itself may very well, at times, belie the stated meaning, the didactic *thesis,* the theoretical assertion. It

is essential to become aware of this complexity of the relationship of pedagogy and psychoanalysis, in order to begin to think out what the psychoanalytic teaching about teaching might well be.

Discussing "The Teaching of Psychoanalysis in Universities," Freud writes: "it will be enough if [the student] learns something *about* psychoanalysis and something *from* it" (Standard, XVII, 173). To learn "something *from* psychoanalysis" is a very different thing than to learn "something *about* it: "it means that psychoanalysis is not a simple *object* of the teaching, but its *subject.* In his essay, "Psychoanalysis and its Teaching," Lacan underlines the same ambiguity, the same dynamic complexity, indicating that the true object of psychoanalysis, the object of his teaching, can only be that mode of learning which institutes psychoanalysis itself as subject—as the purveyor of the act of teaching. "How can what psychoanalysis teaches us be taught?," he asks (E 439).

As myself both a student of psychoanalysis and a teacher, I would here like to suggest that the lesson to be learnt about pedagogy from psychoanalysis is less that of "the *application* of psychoanalysis to pedagogy" than that of the *implication* of psychoanalysis in pedagogy and of pedagogy in psychoanalysis. Attentive, thus, both to the pedagogical speech act of Freud and to the teaching-practice of Lacan, I would like to address the question of teaching as itself a psychoanalytic question. Reckoning not just with the pedagogical thematics *in* psychoanalysis, but with the pedagogical rhetoric *of* psychoanalysis, not just with what psychoanalysis says *about* teachers but with psychoanalysis *itself as teacher,* I will attempt to analyze the ways in which—modifying the conception of what *learning* is and of what *teaching* is—psychoanalysis has shifted pedagogy by radically displacing our very modes of intelligibility.

## ANALYTICAL APPRENTICESHIP

Freud conceives of the process of a psychoanalytic therapy as a learning process—an apprenticeship whose epistemological validity far exceeds the contingent singularity of the therapeutic situation:

> Psychoanalysis sets out to explain . . . uncanny disorders; it engages in careful and laborious investigations . . . until at length it can speak thus to the ego:
> ". . . A part of the activity of your own mind has been withdrawn from your knowledge and from the command of your will . . . you are using one part of your force to fight the other part. . . . A great deal more must constantly be going on in your mind than can be known to your consciousness. Come, *let yourself be taught . . . !* What is in your mind does not coincide with what you are conscious of; whether something is going on in your mind and whether you hear of it, are two different things. In the ordinary way, I will admit, the intelligence which reaches your consciousness is enough for your needs; and *you may cherish the illusion that you learn of all the more important things.* But in some cases, as in that of an instinctual conflict . . . your intelligence service breaks down. . . . In every case, the news that reaches your consciousness is incomplete and often not to be relied on. . . . Turn your eyes inward . . . *learn first to know yourself!* . . .
> It is thus that *psychoanalysis has sought to educate the ego.* [Standard, XVII, 142–143]

Psychoanalysis is thus a pedagogical experience: as a process which gives access to new knowledge hitherto denied to consciousness, it affords what might be called a lesson in cognition (and in miscognition), an epistemological instruction.

Psychoanalysis institutes, in this way, a unique and radically original mode of learning: original not just in its procedures, but in the fact that it gives access to information unavailable through any other mode of learning—unprecedented information, hitherto *unlearnable*. "We learnt," writes Freud, "a quantity of things which could not have been learnt except through analysis" (Standard, XXII, 147).

This new mode of investigation and of learning has, however, a very different temporality than the conventional linear—cumulative and progressive—temporality of learning, as it has traditionally been conceived by pedagogical theory and practice. Proceeding not through linear progression, but through breakthroughs, leaps, discontinuities, regressions, and deferred action, the analytic learning-process puts indeed in question the traditional pedagogical belief in intellectual perfectibility, the progressistic view of learning as a simple one-way road from ignorance to knowledge.

It is in effect the very concept of both ignorance and knowledge—the understanding of what "to know" and "not to know" may really mean—that psychoanalysis has modified, renewed. And it is precisely the originality of this renewal which is central to Lacan's thought, to Lacan's specific way of understanding the cultural, pedagogical and epistemological revolution implied by the discovery of the unconscious.

## KNOWLEDGE

Western pedagogy can be said to culminate in Hegel's philosophical didacticism: the Hegelian concept of "absolute knowledge"—which for Hegel defines at once the potential aim and the actual end of dialectics, of philosophy—is in effect what pedagogy has always aimed at as its ideal: the exhaustion—through methodical investigation—of all there is to know; the absolute completion—

termination—of apprenticeship. Complete and totally appropriated knowledge will become—in all senses of the word—a *mastery.* "In the Hegelian perspective," writes Lacan, "the complete discourse" is "an instrument of power, the scepter and the property of those who know" (S-II, 91). "What is at stake in absolute knowledge is the fact that discourse closes back upon itself, that it is entirely in agreement with itself" (S-II, 91).

But the unconscious, in Lacan's conception, is precisely the discovery that human discourse can by definition never be entirely in agreement with itself, entirely identical to its knowledge of itself, since, as the vehicle of unconscious knowledge, it is constitutively the material locus of a signifying difference from itself.

What, indeed, is the unconscious, if not a kind of *unmeant knowledge* which escapes intentionality and meaning, a knowledge which is spoken by the language of the subject (spoken, for instance, by his "slips" or by his dreams), but which the subject cannot recognize, assume as *his,* appropriate; a speaking knowledge which is nonetheless denied to the speaker's knowledge. In Lacan's own terms, the unconscious is "knowledge which can't tolerate one's knowing that one knows" (Seminar, Feb. 19, 1974; unpublished). "Analysis appears on the scene to announce that there is *knowledge which does not know itself,* knowledge which is supported by the signifier as such" (S-XX, 88). "It is from a place which differs from any capture by a subject that a knowledge is surrendered, since that knowledge offers itself only to the subject's slips—to his misprision" (*Scilicet* I, 38).[14] "The discovery of the unconscious . . . is that the implications of meaning infinitely exceed the signs manipulated by the individual" (S-II, 150). "As far as signs are concerned, man is always mobilizing many more of them than he knows" (S-II, 150).

If this is so, there can constitutively be no such thing as absolute knowledge: absolute knowledge is knowledge that has exhausted its own articulation; but articulated knowledge is by definition what cannot exhaust its own self-knowledge. For knowledge to be spoken, linguistically articulated, it would constitutively have to be supported by the ignorance carried by language, the ignorance of the *excess of signs* that of necessity its language—its articulation—"mobilizes." Thus, human knowledge is, by definition, that which is *untotalizable,* that which rules out any possibility of totalizing what it knows or of eradicating its own ignorance.

The epistemological principle of the irreducibility of ignorance which stems from the unconscious, receives an unexpected confirmation from modern science, to which Lacan is equally attentive in his attempt to give the theory of the unconscious its contemporary scientific measure. The scientific a-totality of knowledge is acknowledged by modern mathematics, in set theory (Cantor: "the set of all sets in a universe does not constitute a set"); in contemporary physics, it is the crux of what is known as "the uncertainty principle" of Heisenberg:

> This is what the Heisenberg principle amounts to. When it is possible to locate, to define precisely one of the points of the system, it is impossible to formulate the others. When the place of electrons is discussed . . . it is no longer possible to know anything about . . . their speed. And inversely . . . [S-II, 281]

From the striking and instructive coincidence between the revolutionary findings of psychoanalysis and the new theoretical orientation of modern physics, Lacan derives the following epistemological insight—the following pathbreaking pedagogical principle:

> Until further notice, we can say that *the elements do not answer in the place where*

*they are interrogated.* Or more exactly, as soon as they are interrogated somewhere, it is impossible to grasp them in their totality. [S-II, 281]


## IGNORANCE

Ignorance is thus no longer simply *opposed* to knowledge: it is itself a radical condition, an integral part of the very *structure* of knowledge. But what does ignorance consist of, in this new epistemological and pedagogical conception?

If ignorance is to be equated with the a-totality of the unconscious, it can be said to be a kind of forgetting—of forgetfulness: while learning is obviously, among other things, remembering and memorizing ("all learning is recollection," says Socrates), ignorance is linked to what is *not remembered,* what will not be memorized. But what will not be memorized is tied up with repression, with the imperative to forget—the imperative to exclude from consciousness, to not admit to knowledge. Ignorance, in other words, is not a passive state of absence—a simple lack of information: it is an active dynamic of negation, an active refusal of information. Freud writes:

It is a long superseded idea . . . that the patient suffers from a sort of ignorance, and that if one removes this ignorance by giving him information (about the causal connection of his illness with his life, about his experiences in childhood, and so on) he is bound to recover. The pathological factor is not his ignorance in itself, but the root of this ignorance in his *inner resistances;* it was they who first called this ignorance into being, and they still maintain it now. The task of the treatment lies in combating these resistances. [Standard, XI, 225]

Teaching, like analysis, has to deal not so much with *lack* of knowledge as with *resistances* to knowledge. Ignorance, suggests Lacan, is a "passion." Inasmuch as traditional pedagogy postulated a desire for knowledge, an analytically informed pedagogy has to reckon with "the passion for ignorance" (S-XX, 110). Ignorance, in other words is nothing other than a *desire to ignore:* its nature is less cognitive than performative; as in the case of Sophocles' nuanced representation of the ignorance of Oedipus, it is not a simple lack of information but the incapacity—or the refusal—to acknowledge *one's own implication* in the information.

The new pedagogical lesson of psychoanalysis is not subsumed, however, by the revelation of the dynamic nature—and of the irreducibility—of ignorance. The truly revolutionary insight—the truly revolutionary *pedagogy* discovered by Freud—consists in showing the ways in which, however irreducible, *ignorance itself can teach us something*—become itself *instructive.* This is, indeed, the crucial lesson that Lacan has learnt from Freud:

It is necessary, says Freud, to interpret the phenomenon of doubt as an integral part of the message. [S-II, 155]

The forgetting of the dream is . . . itself part of the dream. [S-II, 154]

The message is not forgotten in any manner. . . . A censorship is an intention. Freud's argumentation properly reverses the burden of the proof—"In these elements that you cite in objection to me, the memory lapses and the various degradations of the dream, I continue to see a meaning, and even an additional meaning. When the phenomenon of forgetting intervenes, it interests me all the more . . . *These negative phenomena. I add them to the interpretation of the meaning. I recognize that they too have the function of a message.* Freud discovers this dimension. . . . What interests Freud . . . [is] *the message as an interrupted discourse,* and which insists. [S-II, 153]

The pedagogical question crucial to Lacan's own teaching will thus be: *Where does it resist?* Where does a text (or a signifier in a patient's conduct) precisely make no sense, that is, *resist interpretation?* Where does what I see—and what I read—resist my understanding? Where is the *ignorance*—the resistance to knowledge—located? And what can I thus *learn* from the locus of that ignorance? How can I interpret *out of* the dynamic ignorance I analytically encounter, both in others and in myself? How can I turn ignorance into an instrument of teaching?

> . . . Teaching—says Lacan—is something rather problematic. . . . As an American poet has pointed out, no one has ever seen a professor who has fallen short of the task because of ignorance . . .
>
> One always knows enough in order to occupy the minutes during which one exposes oneself in the position of the one who knows. . . .
>
> This makes me think that there is no true teaching other than the teaching which succeeds in provoking in those who listen an insistence—this desire to know which can only emerge when they themselves have *taken the measure of ignorance as such*—of ignorance inasmuch as it is, as such, fertile—in the one who teaches as well. [S-II, 242]

## THE USE OF THAT WHICH CANNOT BE EXCHANGED

Teaching, thus, is not the transmission of ready-made knowledge, it is rather the creation of a new *condition* of knowledge—the creation of an original learning-disposition. "What I teach you," says Lacan, "does nothing other than express the *condition* thanks to which what Freud says is possible" (S-II, 368). The lesson, then, does not "teach" Freud: it teaches the "condition" which makes it *possible to learn* Freud—the condition which makes possible Freud's teaching. What is this condition?

In analysis, what sets in motion the psychoanalytical apprenticeship is the peculiar pedagogical structure of the analytic situation. The analysand speaks to the analyst, whom he endows with the authority of the one who possesses knowledge—knowledge of what is precisely lacking in the analysand's own knowledge. The analyst, however, knows nothing of the sort. His only competence, insists Lacan, lies in "what I would call *textual knowledge,* so as to oppose it to the referential notion which only masks it" (*Scilicet* 1, 21). Textual knowledge—the very stuff the literature teacher is supposed to deal in—is knowledge of the functioning of language, of symbolic structures, of the signifier, knowledge at once derived from—and directed towards—interpretation.

But such knowledge cannot be acquired (or possessed) once and for all: each case, each text, has its own specific, singular symbolic functioning, and requires thus a different—an original—interpretation. The analysts, says Lacan, are "those who share this knowledge only at the price, on the condition of their *not being able to exchange it*" (*Scilicet* I, 59). Analytic (textual) knowledge cannot be *exchanged,* it has to be *used*—and used in each case differently, according to the singularity of the case, according to the specificity of the text. Textual (or analytic) knowledge is, in other words, that peculiarly specific knowledge which, unlike any commodity, is subsumed by its *use* value, having no exchange value whatsoever.[15] Analysis has thus no use for ready-made interpretations, for knowledge given in advance. Lacan insists on "the insistence with which Freud recommends to us to approach each new case as if we had never learnt anything from his first interpretations" (*Scilicet,* I, 20). "What the analyst must know," concludes Lacan, "is how to ignore what he knows."

## DIALOGIC LEARNING, OR THE ANALYTICAL STRUCTURE OF INSIGHT

Each case is thus, for the analyst as well as for the patient, a new apprenticeship. "If it's true that our knowledge comes to the rescue of the patient's ignorance, it is not less true that, for our part, we, too, are plunged in ignorance" (S-I, 78). While the analysand is obviously ignorant of his own unconscious, the analyst is doubly ignorant: pedagogically ignorant of his suspended (given) knowledge; actually ignorant of the very knowledge the analysand presumes him to possess of his own (the analysand's) unconscious: knowledge of the very knowledge he—the patient—lacks. In what way does knowledge, then, emerge in and from the analytic situation?

Through the analytic dialogue the analyst, indeed, has first to learn where to situate the ignorance: where his own textual knowledge is *resisted*. It is, however, out of this resistance, out of the patient's active ignorance, out of the patient's speech which says much more than it itself knows, that the analyst will come to *learn* the *patient's own* unconscious *knowledge,* that knowledge which is inaccessible to itself because it cannot tolerate knowing that it knows; and it is the signifiers of this constitutively a-reflexive knowledge coming from the patient that the analyst *returns* to the patient from his different vantage point, from his non-reflexive, asymmetrical position as an Other. Contrary to the traditional pedagogical dynamic, in which the teacher's question is addressed to an answer from the other—from the student—which is totally reflexive, and expected, "the true Other" says Lacan, "is the Other who gives the answer one does not expect" (S-II, 288). Coming from the Other, knowledge is, by definition, that which comes as a surprise, that which is constitutively the return of a difference:

TEIRESIAS:  . . . You are the land's pollution.
OEDIPUS:  How shamelessly you started up this taunt! How do you think you will escape?
TEIRESIAS:  . . . I have escaped; the truth is what I cherish and that's my strength.
OEDIPUS:  And *who has taught you* truth? Not your profession surely!
TEIRESIAS:  *You have taught me,* for you have made me speak against my will.
OEDIPUS:  Speak what? Tell me again that I may *learn* it better.
TEIRESIAS:  Did you not understand before or would you provoke me into speaking?
OEDIPUS:  *I did not grasp it, not so to call it known.* Say it again.
TEIRESIAS:  I say you are the murderer of the king whose murderer you seek.[16]

As Teiresias—so as to be able to articulate the truth—must have been *"taught"* not by "his profession" but *by Oedipus,* so the analyst precisely must be *taught* by the analysand's unconscious. It is by structurally occupying the position of the analysand's unconscious, and by thus making himself a *student of the patient's knowledge,* that the analyst becomes the patient's teacher—makes the patient learn what would otherwise remain forever inaccessible to him.

For teaching to be realized, for knowledge to be learnt, the position of alterity is therefore indispensable: knowledge is what is already there, but always in the Other. Knowledge, in other words, is not a *substance* but a structural dynamic: it is not *contained* by any individual but comes about out of the mutual apprenticeship between two partially unconscious speeches which both say more than they know. Dialogue is thus the radical condition of learning and of knowledge, the analytically constitutive condition through which ignorance becomes structurally informative; knowledge is essentially, irreducibly dialogic. "No knowledge," writes Lacan, "can be supported or transported by one alone" [*Scilicet* I, 59].

Like the analyst, the teacher, in Lacan's eyes, cannot in turn be, alone, a *master* of the knowledge which he teaches. Lacan transposes the radicality of analytic dialogue—as a newly understood structure of insight—into the pedagogical situation. This is not simply to say that he encourages "exchange" and calls for students' interventions—as many other teachers do. Much more profoundly and radically, he attempts to *learn from the students his own knowledge.* It is the following original pedagogical appeal that he can thus address to the audience of his seminar:

It seems to me I should quite naturally be the point of convergence of the questions that may occur to you.

Let everybody tell me, in his own way, *his idea of what I am driving at.* How, for him, is opened up—or closed—or how already he resists, the question as I pose it. [S-II, 242]

## THE SUBJECT PRESUMED TO KNOW

This pedagogical approach, which makes no claim to total knowledge, which does not even claim to be in possession of its own knowledge, is, of course, quite different from the usual pedagogical pose of mastery, different from the image of the self-sufficient, self-possessed proprietor of knowledge, in

which pedagogy has traditionally featured the authoritative figure of the teacher. This figure of infallible human authority implicitly likened to a God, that is, both modeled on and guaranteed by divine *omniscience,* is based on an illusion: the illusion of a consciousness transparent to itself. "It is the case of the unconscious," writes Lacan, "that it abolishes the postulate of the subject presumed to know" (*Scilicet* I, 46).

Abolishing a postulate, however, doesn't mean abolishing an illusion: while psychoanalysis uncovers the mirage inherent in the function of the subject presumed to know, it also shows the prestige and the affective charge of that mirage to be constitutively irreducible, to be indeed most crucial to, determinant of, the emotional dynamic of all discursive human interactions, of all human relationships founded on sustained interlocution. The psychoanalytical account of the functioning of this dynamic is the most directly palpable, the most explicit lesson psychoanalysis has taught us about teaching.

In a brief and peculiarly introspective essay called "Some Reflections on Schoolboy Psychology," the already aging Freud nostalgically probes into his own "schoolboy psychology," the affect of which even time and intellectual achievements have not entirely extinguished. "As little as ten years ago," writes Freud, "you may have had moments at which you suddenly felt quite young again":

As you walked through the streets of Vienna—already a grey-beard and weighed down by all the cares of family life—you might come unexpectedly on some well-preserved, elderly gentleman, and would greet him humbly almost, because you had recognized him as one of your former schoolmasters. But afterwards, you would stop and reflect: "Was that really he? or only someone deceptively like him? How youthful he looks! And how old you yourself have grown! . . . *Can it be possible that the men who used to stand for us as types of adulthood were so little older than we were?"* [Standard, XIII, 241]

Commenting on "my emotion at meeting my old schoolmaster," Freud goes on to give an analytical account of the emotional dynamic of the pedagogical situation:

> It is hard to decide whether what affected us more . . . was our concern with the sciences that we were taught or with . . . our teachers . . . In many of us *the path to the sciences led only through our teachers.* . . .
>
> We courted them and turned our backs on them, we imagined sympathies and antipathies which probably had no existence . . .
>
> . . . *psychoanalysis has taught us* that the individual's emotional attitudes to other people . . . are . . . established at an unexpectedly early age. . . . The people to whom [the child] is in this way fixed are his parents . . . His later acquaintances are . . . obliged to *take over a kind of emotional heritage,* they encounter sympathies and antipathies to the production of which they themselves have contributed little . . .
>
> These men [the teachers] became our *substitute fathers.* That was why, even though they were still quite young, *they struck us as so mature and so unattainably adult.* We *transferred* to them *the respect and expectations attaching to the omniscient father of our childhood,* and then we began to treat them as we treated our own fathers at home. We confronted them with the *ambivalence* that we had acquired in our own families and with its help we struggled with them as we had been in the habit of struggling with our fathers . . . [Standard, XI, 242–44]

This phenomenon of the compulsive unconscious reproduction of an archaic emotional pattern, which Freud called "transfer-

ence" and which he saw both as the energetic spring and as the interpretive key to the psychoanalytic situation, further thought out by Lacan as what accounts for the functioning of authority in general: as essential, thus, not just to any pedagogic situation but to the problematics of knowledge as such. "As soon as there is somewhere a subject presumed to know, there is transference," writes Lacan (S-XI, 210).

Since "transference is the acting out of the reality of the unconscious" (S-XI, 150, 240, N 174, 267), teaching is not a purely cognitive, informative experience, it is also an emotional, erotical experience. "I deemed it necessary," insists Lacan, "to support the idea of transference, as indistinguishable from love, with the formula of the subject presumed to know. I cannot fail to underline the new resonance with which this notion of knowledge is endowed. The person in whom I presume knowledge to exist, thereby acquires my love" (S-XX, 64). "The question of love is thus linked to the question of knowledge" (S-XX, 84). "Transference *is* love . . . I insist: it is love directed toward, addressed to, knowledge" (*Scilicet* V, 16).

"Of this subject presumed to know, who," asks Lacan, "can believe himself to be entirely invested?—That is not the question. The question, first and foremost, for each subject, is how to situate *the place from which he himself addresses* the subject presumed to know?" (S-XX, 211). Insofar as knowledge is itself *a structure of address,* cognition is always both motivated and obscured by love; theory, both guided and misguided by an implicit transferential structure.

## ANALYTIC PEDAGOGY, OR DIDACTIC PSYCHOANALYSIS: THE INTERMINABLE TASK

In human relationships, sympathies and antipathies usually provoke—and call for—a similar emotional response in the person they are addressed to. Transference on "the sub-ject presumed to know"—the analyst or the teacher—may provoke a counter-transfer-ence on the latter's part. The analytic or the pedagogical situation may thus degenerate into an imaginary mirror-game of love and hate, where each of the participants would unconsciously enact past conflicts and emo-tions, unwarranted by the current situation and disruptive with respect to the real issues, unsettling the topical stakes of analysis or ed-ucation.

In order to avoid this typical degeneration, Freud conceived of the necessity of a prelimi-nary psychoanalytic training of "the subjects presumed to know," a practical didactic train-ing through their own analysis which, giving them insight into their own transferential structure, would later help them understand the students' or the patients' transferential mechanisms and, more importantly, keep under control their own—avoid being en-trapped in counter-transference. "The only appropriate preparation for the profession of educator," suggests Freud, "is a thorough psycho-analytic training . . . The analysis of teachers and educators seems to be a more efficacious prophylactic measure than the analysis of children themselves" (Standard, XXII, 150).

While this preliminary training (which has come to be known as "didactic psychoanaly-sis") is, however, only a recommendation on Freud's part as far as teachers are concerned, it is an absolute requirement and precondi-tion for the habilitation—and qualifica-tion—of the psychoanalyst. In his last and therefore, in a sense, testamentary essay, "Analysis Terminable and Interminable," Freud writes:

Among the factors which influence the prospects of analytic treatment and add to its difficulties in the same manner as the resistances, must be reckoned not only the nature of the patient's ego but the individu-ality of the analyst.

It cannot be disputed that *analysts . . . have not invariably come up to the stan-dard* of psychical normality *to which they wish to educate their patients*. Opponents of analysis often point to this fact with scorn and use it as an argument to show the uselessness of analytic exertions. We might reject this criticism as making unjus-tifiable demands. *Analysts are people who have learnt to practice a particular art;* alongside of this, they may be allowed to be *human beings like anyone else*. After all, nobody maintains that a physician is incapable of treating internal diseases if his own internal organs are not sound; on the contrary, it may be argued that there are certain advantages in a man who is himself threatened with tuberculosis specializing in the treatment of persons suffering from that disease. . . .

It is reasonable, [however,] . . . to expect of an analyst, as part of his qualifications, a considerable degree of mental normality and correctness. In addition, he must pos-sess some kind of superiority, so that in certain analytic situations he can *act as a model for his patient* and in others *as a teacher*. And finally, we must not forget that the analytic relationship is based on a love of truth—that is, on a recognition of reality—and that it precludes any kind of sham or deceit. . . .

It almost looks as if analysis were the third of those 'impossible' professions . . . *Where is the poor wretch to acquire the ideal qualifications* which he will need in his profession? *The answer is, in an analy-sis of himself,* with which his preparation for his future activity begins. For practical reasons this analysis can only be short and incomplete. . . . It has accomplished its purpose if it gives *the learner* a firm con-viction of the existence of the unconscious, if it enables him . . . to perceive in himself things which would otherwise be incred-ible to him, and if it shows him a first ex-ample of the technique . . . in analytic work. *This alone would not suffice for his instruction; but we reckon on the stimuli he has received in his own analysis not ceasing when it ends* and *on the process of remodelling the ego continuing* spontaneously in the analysed subject and making use of all subsequent experiences in this newly-acquired sense. This does in fact happen, and *in so far as it happens, it makes the analysed subject qualified to be an analyst.* [Standard, XXIII, 247–49]

Nowhere else does Freud describe as keenly *the revolutionary radicality of the very nature of the teaching* to be (practically and theoretically) derived from the originality of the psychoanalytical experience. The analysand is qualified to be an analyst as of the point at which he understands his own analysis to be inherently unfinished, incomplete, as of the point, that is, at which he settles into his own didactic analysis—or his own analytical apprenticeship—as fundamentally interminable. It is, in other words, as of the moment the student recognizes that *learning has no term,* that he can himself become a teacher, assume the position of the teacher. But the position of the teacher is itself the position of *the one who learns,* of the one who *teaches* nothing other than *the way he learns.* The subject of teaching is interminably—a student; the subject of teaching is interminably—a learning. This is the most radical, perhaps the most far-reaching insight psychoanalysis can give us into pedagogy.

Freud pushes this original understanding of what pedagogy is to its logical limit. Speaking of the "defensive" tendency of psychoanalysts "to divert the implications and demands of analysis from themselves (probably by directing them on to other people)"—of the analysts' tendency, that is, "to *withdraw from the critical and corrective influence of analysis,"* as well as of the temptation of power threatening them in

the very exercise of their profession, Freud enjoins:

> Every analyst should periodically—at intervals of five years or so—submit himself to analysis once more, without feeling ashamed of taking this step. This would mean, then, that not only the therapeutic analysis of patients[17] but *his own analysis would change from a terminable into an interminable task.* [Standard, XXIII, 249]

Of all Freud's followers, Lacan alone has picked up on the radicality of Freud's pedagogical concern with didactic psychoanalysis, not just as a subsidiary technical, pragmatic question (how should analysts be trained?), but as a major theoretical concern, as a major pedagogical investigation crucial to the very innovation, to the very revolutionary core of psychoanalytic insight. The highly peculiar and surprising style of Lacan's own teaching-practice is, indeed, an answer to, a follow-up on, Freud's ultimate suggestion—in Lacan's words—"to make psychoanalysis and education (training) collapse into each other" (E 459).

This is the thrust of Lacan's original endeavor both as psychoanalyst and as teacher: "in the field of psychoanalysis," he writes, "what is necessary is the restoration of the identical status of didactic psychoanalysis and of the teaching of psychoanalysis, in their common scientific opening" (E 236).

As a result of this conception, Lacan considers not just the practical analyses which he—as analyst—directs, but his own public teaching, his own seminar—primarily directed towards the (psychoanalytical) training of analysts—as partaking of didactic psychoanalysis, as itself, thus, analytically didactic and didactically analytical, in a new and radical way.

"How can what psychoanalysis teaches us be taught?" (E 439)—Only by continuing, in one's own teaching, one's own interminable didactic analysis. Lacan has willingly trans-formed himself into the *analysand* of his Seminar[18] so as to teach, precisely, psycho-analysis *as* teaching, and teaching *as* psycho-analysis.

Psychoanalysis as teaching, and teaching as psychoanalysis, radically subvert the de-marcation-line, the clear-cut opposition be-tween the analyst and the analysand, be-tween the teacher and the student (or the learner)—showing that what counts, in both cases, is precisely the transition, the struggle-filled *passage* from one position to the other. But the passage is itself interminable; it can never be crossed once and for all: "The psy-choanalytic act has but to falter slightly, and it is the analyst who becomes the analysand" (*Scilicet* I, 47). Lacan denounces, thus, "the reactionary principle" of the professional be-lief in "the duality of the one who suffers and the one who cures," in "the opposition be-tween the one who knows and the one who does not know. . . . The most corrupting of comforts is intellectual comfort, just as one's *worst* corruption is the belief that one is *bet-ter*" (E 403).

Lacan's well-known polemical and con-troversial stance—his *critique of psycho-analysis*—itself partakes, then, of his under-standing of the pedagogical imperative of didactic psychoanalysis. Lacan's original en-deavor is to submit *the whole discipline of psychoanalysis* to what Freud called "the critical and corrective influence of analysis" (Standard, XXIII, 249). Lacan, in other words, is the first to understand that the psychoanalytic discipline is an unprece-dented one in that its *teaching* does not just reflect upon itself, but turns back upon itself so as to *subvert itself,* and truly *teaches* only insofar as it subverts itself. Psychoanalytic teaching is pedagogically unique in that it is inherently, interminably, self-critical. Lacan's amazing pedagogical performance thus sets forth the unparalleled example of a teach-ing whose fecundity is tied up, paradoxi-cally enough, with the inexhaustibility—the interminability—of its *self-critical po-tential.*

From didactic analysis, Lacan derives, in-deed, a whole new theoretical (didactic) mode of *self-subversive self-reflection*.

A question suddenly arises . . .: in the case of the knowledge yielded solely to the sub-ject's mistake, what kind of subject could ever be in a position to know it in advance? [*Scilicet* I, 38]

Retain at least what this text, which I have tossed out in your direction, bears witness to: my enterprise does not go beyond the act in which it is caught, and, therefore, its only chance lies in its being mistaken. [*Scilicet* I, 41]

This lesson seems to be one that should not have been forgotten, had not psycho-analysis precisely taught us that it is, as such, forgettable. [E 232]

Always submitting analysis itself to the in-struction of an unexpected analytic turn of the screw, to the surprise of an additional reflexive turn, of an additional self-subversive ironic twist, didactic analysis becomes for Lacan what might be called a *style:* a teaching style which has become at once a life-style and a writing style: "the ironic style of calling into question the very foundations of the dis-cipline" (E 238).

Any return to Freud founding a teaching worthy of the name will occur only on that pathway where truth . . . becomes manifest in the revolutions of culture. That pathway is the only training we can claim to transmit to those who follow us. It is called—a style. [E 458]

Didactic analysis is thus invested by Lacan not simply with the practical, pragmatic value, but with the theoretical significance—the allegorical instruction—of a paradigm: a paradigm, precisely, of the interminability, not just of teaching (learning) and of analyzing (being analyzed), but of the very act of thinking, theorizing: of teaching, analyzing, thinking, theorizing, in such a way as to make of psychoanalysis "what it has never ceased to be: an act that is yet to come" (*Scilicet* I, 9).

## TEACHING AS A LITERARY GENRE

Among so many other things, Lacan and Freud thus teach us teaching, teach us—in a radically new way—what it might mean to teach. Their lesson, and their pedagogical performance, profoundly renew at once the meaning and the status of the very act of teaching.

If they are both such extraordinary teachers, it is—I would suggest—because they both are, above all, quite extraordinary learners. In Freud's case, I would argue, the extraordinary teaching stems from Freud's original—unique—position as a student; in Lacan's case, the extraordinary teaching stems from Lacan's original—unique—position as disciple.

"One might feel tempted," writes Freud, "to agree with the philosophers and the psychiatrists and like them, rule out the problem of dream-interpretation as a purely fanciful task. *But I have been taught better"* (Standard, IV, 100).

*By whom* has Freud been taught—taught better than by "the judgement of the prevalent science of today," better than by the established scholarly authorities of philosophy and psychiatry? Freud has been taught *by dreams* themselves: his own, and those of others; Freud has been taught by his own patients: *"My patients . . . told me their dreams and so taught me . . . ————"* (Standard, VI, 100–101).

Having thus been taught by dreams, as well as by his patients, that—contrary to the established scholarly opinion—dreams do have meaning, Freud is further taught by a literary text:

This discovery is confirmed by a legend that has come down to us from antiquity. . . .

While the poet . . . brings to light the guilt of Oedipus, he is at the same time compelling us to recognize our own inner minds . . .

Like Oedipus, we live in ignorance of these wishes . . . and after their revelation, we may all of us well seek to close our eyes to the scenes of our childhood. [Standard, VI, 261–263]

"But I have been taught better." What is unique about Freud's position as a student—as a learner—is that he learns from, or puts in the position of his teacher, the least authoritative sources of information that can be imagined: that he knows how to derive a teaching, or a lesson, from the very unreliability—the very *non-authority*—of literature, of dreams, of patients. For the first time in the history of learning, Freud, in other words, has recourse—scientific recourse—to a knowledge which is not authoritative, which is not that of a master, a knowledge which does not know what it knows, and is thus *not in possession of itself.*

Such, precisely, is the very essence of literary knowledge. "I went to the poets," says Socrates; ". . . I took them some of the most elaborate passages in their own writings, and asked them what was the meaning of them—thinking that they would teach me something. Will you believe me? I am almost ashamed to confess the truth, but I must say that there is hardly a person present who would not have talked better about their poetry than they did themselves. Then I knew that *not by wisdom do poets write poetry, but by a sort of genius or inspiration;* they are like diviners or soothsayers who also *say many fine things, but do not understand the meaning of them.* The poets appeared to me to be much in the same case."[19] From a philosophical perspective, knowledge is mastery—that which is in mastery of its own meaning. Unlike Hegelian philosophy, which *believes it knows all that there is to know;* unlike Socratic (or contemporary post-Nietzschean) philosophy, which *believes it knows it does not know*—literature, for its part, *knows it knows, but does not know the meaning of its knowledge*—does not know *what* it knows.

For the first time then, Freud gives authority to the instruction—to the teaching—of a knowledge which does not know its own meaning, to a knowledge (that of dreams, of patients, of Greek tragedy) which we might define as literary: knowledge that is not in mastery of itself.

Of all Freud's students and disciples, Lacan alone has understood and emphasized the *radical* significance of Freud's indebtedness to literature: the role played by *literary knowledge* not just in the historical constitution of psychoanalysis, but in the very actuality of the psychoanalytic act, of the psychoanalytic (ongoing) *work* of learning and of teaching. Lacan alone has understood and pointed out the ways in which Freud's teaching—in all senses of the word—is not accidentally, but radically and fundamentally, a *literary* teaching. Speaking of "the training of the analysts of the future," Lacan thus writes:

One has only to turn the pages of his works for it to become abundantly clear that Freud regarded a study . . . of the resonances . . . of literature and of the significations involved in works of art as necessary to an understanding of the text of our experience. Indeed, Freud himself is a striking instance of his own belief: he derived his

inspiration, his ways of thinking and his technical weapons, from just such a study. But he also regarded it as a necessary condition in any teaching of psychoanalysis. [E 435, N 144]

This [new] technique [of interpretation] would require for its teaching as well as for its learning a profound assimilation of the resources of a language, and especially of those that are concretely realized in its poetic texts. It is well known that Freud was in this position in relation to German literature, which, by virtue of an incomparable translation, can be said to include Shakespeare's plays. Every one of his works bears witness to this, and to the continual recourse he had to it, no less in his technique than in his discovery. [E 295, N 83]

The psychoanalytic experience has rediscovered in man the imperative of the Word as the law that has formed him in its image. It manipulates the poetic function of language to give to his desire its symbolic mediation. [E 322, N 106]

Freud had, eminently, this feel for meaning, which accounts for the fact that any of his works, *The Three Caskets,* for instance, gives the reader the impression that it is written by a soothsayer, that it is guided by that kind of meaning which is of the order of poetic inspiration. [S-II, 353]

It is in this sense, among others, that Lacan can be regarded as Freud's best student: Lacan is the sole Freudian who has sought to learn from Freud how to learn Freud: Lacan is "taught" by Freud in much the same way Freud is "taught" by dreams; Lacan reads Freud in much the same way Freud reads *Oedipus the King,* specifically seeking in the text its *literary knowledge.* From Freud as teacher, suggests Lacan, we should learn to derive that kind of *literary teaching* he himself derived in an unprecedented way from literary texts. Freud's text should thus itself be read as a poetic text:

> ... the notion of the death instinct involves a basic irony, since its meaning has to be sought in the conjunction of two contrary terms: instinct ... being the law that governs ... a cycle of behavior whose goal is the accomplishment of a vital function; and death appearing first of all as the destruction of life. ...

> This notion must be approached through its resonances in what I shall call *the poetics of the Freudian corpus,* the first way of access to the penetration of its meaning, and the essential dimension, from the origins of the work to the apogee marked in it by this notion, for an understanding of its dialectical repercussions. [E 316–17, N 101–02]

It is here, in conjunction with Lacan's way of relating to Freud's literary teaching and of learning from Freud's literary knowledge, that we touch upon the historical uniqueness of Lacan's position as disciple, and can thus attempt to understand the way in which this pedagogically unique discipleship accounts for Lacan's astounding originality as a teacher.

"As Plato pointed out long ago," says Lacan, "it is not at all necessary that the poet know what he is doing, in fact, it is preferable that he not know. That is what gives a primordial value to what he does. We can only bow our heads before it" (Seminar, April 9, 1974, unpublished). Although apparently Lacan seems to espouse Plato's position, his real pedagogical stance is, in more than one way, at the antipodes of that of Plato; and not just because he bows his head to poets, whereas Plato casts them out of the Republic. If Freud himself, indeed, bears witness, in his text, to some poetic—literary—knowledge, it is to

the extent that, like the poets, he, too, cannot exhaust the meaning of his text—he too partakes of the poetic ignorance of his own knowledge. Unlike Plato who, from his position as an admiring disciple, reports Socrates' assertion of his ignorance without—it might be assumed—really believing in the *non-ironic truth* of that assertion ("For the hearers," says Socrates, "always imagine that I myself possess the wisdom I find wanting in others"[20]), Lacan can be said to be the first disciple in the whole history of pedagogy and of culture who *does indeed believe in the ignorance of his teacher—of his master.* Paradoxically enough, this is why he can be said to be, precisely, Freud's best student: a student of Freud's own revolutionary way of learning, of Freud's own unique position as the unprecedented student of unauthorized, unmastered knowledge. "The truth of the subject," says Lacan, "even when he is the position of a master, is not in himself" (S-XI, 10).

> [Freud's] texts, to which for the past ... years I have devoted a two-hour seminar every Wednesday ... without having covered a quarter of the total, ... , have given me, and those who have attended my seminars, the surprise of genuine discoveries. These discoveries, which range from concepts that have remained unused to clinical details uncovered by our exploration, demonstrate *how far the field investigated by Freud extended beyond the avenues that he left us to tend,* and how little his observation, which sometimes gives an impression of exhaustiveness, was the slave of what he had to demonstrate. Who ... has not been moved by this research in action, whether in 'The Interpretation of Dreams,' 'The Wolf Man,' or 'Beyond the Pleasure Principle?' [E 404, N 117, TM]

Commenting on *The Interpretation of Dreams,* Lacan situates in Freud's text the discoverer's own transferential structure—Freud's own unconscious structure of address:

> What polarizes at the moment Freud's discourse; what organizes the whole of Freud's existence, is the conversation with Fliess. . . . It is in this dialogue that Freud's self-analysis is realized. . . . This vast speech addressed to Fliess will later become the whole written work of Freud.
>
> The conversation of Freud with Fliess, this fundamental discourse, which at that moment is unconscious, is the essential dynamic element [of *The Interpretation of Dreams*]. Why is it unconscious at that moment? Because its significance goes far beyond what both of them, as individuals, can consciously apprehend or understand of it at the moment. As individuals, they are nothing other, after all, than two little erudites who are in the process of exchanging rather weird ideas.
>
> The discovery of the unconscious, in the full dimension with which it is revealed at the very moment of its historical emergence, is that the scope, the implications of meaning go far beyond the signs manipulated by the individual. As far as signs are concerned, man is always mobilizing many more of them than he knows. [S-II, 150]

It is to the extent that Lacan precisely teaches us to read in Freud's text (in its textual excess) the signifiers of Freud's ignorance—his ignorance of his own knowledge—that Lacan can be considered Freud's best reader, as well as the most compelling teacher of the Freudian pedagogical imperative: the imperative to learn from and through the insight which does not know its own meaning, from and through the knowledge which is not entirely in mastery—in possession—of itself.

This unprecedented *literary* lesson, which

Lacan derives from Freud's revolutionary way of learning and in the light of which he learns Freud, is transformed, in Lacan's own work, into a deliberately literary style of teaching. While—as a subject of praise or controversy—the originality of Lacan's eminently literary, eminently "poetic" style has become a stylistic *cause célèbre* often commented upon, what has not been understood is the extent to which this style—this poetic theory or theoretical poetry—is *pedagogically* poetic: poetic in such a way as to raise, through every answer that it gives, the literary question of its non-mastery of itself. In pushing its own thought beyond the limit of its self-possession, beyond the limitations of its own capacity for mastery, in passing on understanding which does not fully understand what it understands; in *teaching,* thus, *with blindness*—with and through the very blindness of its literary knowledge, of insights not entirely transparent to themselves—Lacan's unprecedented theoretically *poetic pedagogy* always implicitly opens up onto the infinitely literary, infinitely *teaching* question: What is the "navel"[21] of my own theoretical dream of understanding? What is the specificity of my incomprehension? What is the riddle which I in effect here pose under the guise of knowledge?

> "But what was it that Zarathustra once said to you? That poets lie too much? But Zarathustra too is a poet. Do you believe that in saying this he spoke the truth? Why do you believe that?"
>
> The disciple answered, "I believe in Zarathustra.[22] But Zarathustra shook his head and smiled."
>
> Any return to Freud founding a teaching worthy of the name will occur only on that pathway where truth . . . becomes manifest in the revolutions of culture. That pathway is the only training we can claim to transmit to those who follow us. It is called—a style. [E 458][23]

## NOTES

1. Plato, *Meno,* 70a, 71a, 82a. Translated by G.M.A. Grube (Indianapolis: Hackett Publishing Company, 1980), pp. 3, 14 (translation modified).

2. *The Complete Psychological Works of Sigmund Freud,* translated from the German under the general editorship of James Strachey (London: The Hogarth Press and the Institute of Psychoanalysis), volume XIX, p. 273. Hereafter, this edition will be referred to as "Standard," followed by volume number (in roman numerals) and page number (in arabic numerals).

3. Jacques Lacan, *Ecrits* (Paris: Seuil, 1966), p. 233, my translation. Henceforth I will be using the abbreviations: "E" (followed by page number)—for this original French edition of the *Ecrits,* and "N" (followed by page number) for the corresponding Norton edition of the English translation (*Ecrits: A Selection,* translated by Alan Sheridan, New York: Norton, 1977). When the reference to the French edition of the *Ecrits* (E) is not followed by a reference to the Norton English edition (N), the passage quoted (as in this case) is in my translation and has not been included in the "Selection" of the Norton edition.

4. Which for Lacan involves "the relationship of the individual to language": E445.

5. Italics mine. As a rule, in the quoted passages, italics are mine unless otherwise indicated.

6. Anna Freud, *Psychoanalysis for Teachers and Parents,* translated by Barbara Low (Boston: Beacon Press, 1960), pp. 95–6.

7. Ibid., p. 105.

8. Catherine Millot, interview in *l'Ane, le magasine freudien*. No. 1, April–May 1981, p. 19.

9. Catherine Millot, *Freud Anti-Pedagogue* (Paris: Bibliothèque d'Ornicar, 1979).

10. Plato, *Meno,* 96 d, op. cit., p. 28 (translation modified).

11. Ibid., 82 e, p. 15.

12. The abbreviation "TM"—"translation modified"—will signal my alterations of the official English translation of the work in question.

13. The abbreviation S-XI (followed by page number) refers to Jacques Lacan, *Le Séminaire, livre XI, Les Quatre concepts fondamentaux de la psychoanalyse* (Paris: Seuil, 1973). The following abbreviation "N" (followed by page number) refers to the corresponding English edition: *The Four Fundamental Concepts of Psychoanalysis,* edited by Jacques-Alain Miller, translated by Alan Sheridan (New York: Norton, 1978).

As for the rest of Lacan's Seminars which have appeared in book form, the following abbreviations will be used:

*S-I* (followed by page number), for: J. Lacan, *Le Séminaire, livre I: Les Ecrits techniques de Freud* (Paris: Seuil, 1975);

*S-II* (followed by page number), for: J. Lacan, *Le Séminaire, livre II: le Moi dans la théorie de Freud et dans la techniquè de la psychoanalyse* (Paris: Seuil, 1978);

*S-XX* (followed by page number), for: J. Lacan, *Le Séminaire, livre XX: Encore* (Paris: Seuil, 1975).

All quoted passages from these (as yet untranslated) Seminars are here in my translation.

14. Abbreviated for Lacan's texts published in *Scilicet: Tu peux savoir ce qu'en pense l'école freudienne de Paris* (Paris: Seuil). The roman numeral stands for the issue number (followed by page number). Number 1 appeared in 1968.

15. As soon as analytic knowledge *is* exchanged, it ceases to be knowledge and becomes opinion, prejudice, presumption: "the sum of prejudices that every knowledge contains, and that each of us transports. . . . Knowledge is always, somewhere, only one's belief that one knows" (S-II, 56).

16. Sophocles, *Oedipus the King,* translated by David Grene, in *Sophocles I,* (Chicago & London: The University of Chicago Press, 1954), pp. 25–6.

17. The therapeutic analysis of patients is "interminable" to the extent that repression can never be totally lifted, only displaced. Cf. Freud's letter to Fliess, dated April 16, 1900. "E's career as a patient has at last come to an end . . . His riddle is *almost* completely solved, his condition is excellent . . . At that moment a residue of his symptoms remains. I am beginning to understand that the apparently interminable nature of the treatment is something determined by law and is dependent on the transference." Hence, Freud speaks of "the asymptotic termination of treatment" (Standard, XXIII, 215) Freud's italics.

18. The occasional master's pose—however mystifying to the audience—invariably exhibits itself as a parodic symptom of the analysand.

19. Plato, *Apology,* 22 a–c, in *Dialogues of Plato.* Jowett translation, edited by J. D. Kaplan, (New York: Washington Square Press, Pocket Books, 1973), p. 12.

20. Plato, *Apology,* 22 a–c, op. cit., p. 12.

21. "There is," writes Freud, "at least one spot in every dream at which it is unplumbable—a navel, as it were, that is its point of contact with the unknown" (Standard IV, III).

22. Nietzsche, *Thus Spoke Zarathustra,* translated by

Walter Kaufmann, (T.M.) in *The Portable Nietzsche* (New York: The Viking Press, 1971), p. 239, "On Poets."

23. The present essay is a chapter from my forthcoming book, *Psychoanalysis in Contemporary Culture: Jacques Lacan and the Adventure of Insight.*

The news of Lacan's death (on September 9, 1981) reached me as I was writing the section here entitled "The Interminable Task." The sadness caused by the cessation of a life as rich in insight and as generous in instruction, was thus accompanied by an ironic twist which itself felt like a typical Lacanian turn, one of the ironies of his teaching, teaching terminable and interminable . . . Few deaths, indeed, have been as deeply inscribed as a lesson in a teaching, as Lacan's, who always taught the implications of the Master's death. "Were I to go away," he said some time ago, "tell yourselves that it is in order to at last be truly Other."

I have deliberately chosen not to change, and to pursue, the grammatical present tense which I was using to describe Lacan's teaching; since his life has ceased to be, his teaching is, indeed, all the more present, all the more alive, all the more interminably "what it has never ceased to be: an act that is yet to come."

# 26

# Laura Mulvey
## 1941–

Laura Mulvey is a British film theorist and filmmaker, currently teaching film at the University of East Anglia. Her semiological analyses of film seek to deconstruct the classical tropes of traditional narrative cinema with a discourse employing Feminist, Marxist, and Freudian concepts. Mulvey's text, "Visual Pleasure and Narrative Cinema" (1975), was first published in *Screen*. Since its publication in the mid-seventies, this article has helped initiate a new vocabulary through which visual analysis may simultaneously articulate a feminist critique. Mulvey has published on the broad spectrum of issues of spectatorship involving not only film, but also photography, art, and myth. In addition to the films entitled *Penthesilea* (1974), *Riddles of the Sphinx* (1978), *Amyl* (1980), *Crystal Gazing* (1981), and *The Bad Sister* (1983), Mulvey has published two books, *Visual and Other Pleasures* in 1989 and *Citizen Kane* in 1992. As Mulvey states in *Visual and Other Pleasures,* her 1975 article "has seemed, over the last decade, to take on a life of its own." Noting the response its publication generated, Mulvey wrote "Afterthoughts on Visual Pleasure and Narrative Cinema" inspired by King Vidor's *Duel in the Sun,* which appeared in *Framework* in 1981.

Mulvey's article "Visual Pleasure and Narrative Cinema" seeks to shatter the patriarchal "pleasure" of classical narrative cinema in which, as Mulvey states, "the meaning of woman is sexual difference." Unacknowledged systems of film convention construct male identity in association with activity, subjectivity, and voyeurism while female identity is rendered as a passive (disempowered) icon of sexuality, utterly fetishized as "other," and as an object of the male gaze. Mulvey describes this male gaze as projecting its "phantasy" onto the female body "which is styled accordingly." "In their traditional exhibitionist role," she argues, "women are simultaneously looked at and displayed, with their appearance coded for strong visual and erotic impact so that they can be said to connote to-be-looked-at-ness" in what Mulvey terms "a heterosexual division of labor" that controls narrative structure. In her argument Mulvey describes an indissoluble link between heterosexism and patriarchal capitalism. In the language of psychoanalysis, she also identifies the male desire in film as a drive to fetishize and contain—to "demystify"—woman as a drive to destroy what it cannot understand in its quest for self-reflection. Mulvey asserts that for Freud the tension between voyeurism and narcissism was crucial in ego construction, and that this binary tension applies fundamentally to the ways in which cinema coerces the audience's looking as voyeurism and scopophilia (just as the characters in classical narrative cinema are conditioned by the same processes of looking and of "being looked at"). Through a textual analysis of film form, and by defining the three looks of cinema, Mulvey provides a new discourse to the analysis of media and of gender representation.

# Visual Pleasure and Narrative Cinema[1]

## I  INTRODUCTION

### (a) A Political Use of Psychoanalysis

This paper intends to use psychoanalysis to
discover where and how the fascination of
film is reinforced by pre-existing patterns of
fascination already at work within the individual subject and the social formations that
have moulded him. It takes as its starting-
point the way film reflects, reveals and even
plays on the straight, socially established interpretation of sexual difference which controls images, erotic ways of looking and spectacle. It is helpful to understand what the cinema has been, how its magic has worked in
the past, while attempting a theory and a
practice which will challenge this cinema of
the past. Psychoanalytic theory is thus appropriated here as a political weapon, demonstrating the way the unconscious of patriarchal society has structured film form.

The paradox of phallocentrism in all its
manifestations is that it depends on the image
of the castrated woman to give order and
meaning to its world. An idea of woman
stands as linchpin to the system: it is her lack
that produces the phallus as a symbolic presence, it is her desire to make good the lack
that the phallus signifies. Recent writing in
*Screen* about psychoanalysis and the cinema
has not sufficiently brought out the importance of the representation of the female form
in a symbolic order in which, in the last resort, it speaks castration and nothing else. To
summarise briefly: the function of woman in
forming the patriarchal unconscious is two-
fold: she firstly symbolises the castration
threat by her real lack of a penis and secondly
thereby raises her child into the symbolic.

Once this has been achieved, her meaning in
the process is at an end. It does not last into
the world of law and language except as a
memory, which oscillates between memory
of maternal plenitude and memory of lack.
Both are posited on nature (or on anatomy in
Freud's famous phrase). Woman's desire is
subjugated to her image as bearer of the
bleeding wound; she can exist only in relation to castration and cannot transcend it. She
turns her child into the signifier of her own
desire to possess a penis (the condition, she
imagines, of entry into the symbolic). Either
she must gracefully give way to the word, the
name of the father and the law, or else struggle to keep her child down with her in the
half-light of the imaginary. Woman then
stands in patriarchal culture as a signifier for
the male other, bound by a symbolic order in
which man can live out his fantasies and
obsessions through linguistic command by
imposing them on the silent image of woman
still tied to her place as bearer, not maker, of
meaning.

There is an obvious interest in this analysis for feminists, a beauty in its exact rendering of the frustration experienced under the
phallocentric order. It gets us nearer to the
roots of our oppression, it brings closer an
articulation of the problem, it faces us with
the ultimate challenge: how to fight the unconscious structured like a language
(formed critically at the moment of arrival of
language) while still caught within the language of the patriarchy? There is no way in
which we can produce an alternative out of
the blue, but we can begin to make a break
by examining patriarchy with the tools it
provides, of which psychoanalysis is not the
only but an important one. We are still sepa-

rated by a great gap from important issues for the female unconscious which are scarcely relevant to phallocentric theory: the sexing of the female infant and her relationship to the symbolic, the sexually mature woman as non-mother, maternity outside the signification of the phallus, the vagina. But, at this point, psychoanalytic theory as it now stands can at least advance our understanding of the *status quo,* of the patriarchal order in which we are caught.

### (b) Destruction of Pleasure as a Radical Weapon

As an advanced representation system, the cinema poses questions about the ways the unconscious (formed by the dominant order) structures ways of seeing and pleasure in looking. Cinema has changed over the last few decades. It is no longer the monolithic system based on large capital investment exemplified at its best by Hollywood in the 1930s, 1940s and 1950s. Technological advances (16mm and so on) have changed the economic conditions of cinematic production, which can now be artisanal as well as capitalist. Thus it has been possible for an alternative cinema to develop. However self-conscious and ironic Hollywood managed to be, it always restricted itself to a formal *mise en scène* reflecting the dominant ideological concept of the cinema. The alternative cinema provides a space for the birth of a cinema which is radical in both a political and an aesthetic sense and challenges the basic assumptions of the mainstream film. This is not to reject the latter moralistically, but to highlight the ways in which its formal preoccupations reflect the psychical obsessions of the society which produced it and, further, to stress that the alternative cinema must start specifically by reacting against these obsessions and assumptions. A politically and aesthetically avant-garde cinema is now possi-

ble, but it can still only exist as a counterpoint.

The magic of the Hollywood style at its best (and of all the cinema which fell within its sphere of influence) arose, not exclusively, but in one important aspect, from its skilled and satisfying manipulation of visual pleasure. Unchallenged, mainstream film coded the erotic into the language of the dominant patriarchal order. In the highly developed Hollywood cinema it was only through these codes that the alienated subject, torn in his imaginary memory by a sense of loss, by the terror of potential lack in fantasy, came near to finding a glimpse of satisfaction: through its formal beauty and its play on his own formative obsessions. This article will discuss the interweaving of that erotic pleasure in film, its meaning and, in particular, the central place of the image of woman. It is said that analysing pleasure, or beauty, destroys it. That is the intention of this article. The satisfaction and reinforcement of the ego that represent the high point of film history hitherto must be attacked. Not in favour of a reconstructed new pleasure, which cannot exist in the abstract, nor of intellectualised unpleasure, but to make way for a total negation of the ease and plenitude of the narrative fiction film. The alternative is the thrill that comes from leaving the past behind without simply rejecting it, transcending outworn or oppressive forms, and daring to break with normal pleasurable expectations in order to conceive a new language of desire.

### II PLEASURE IN LOOKING/ FASCINATION WITH THE HUMAN FORM

**A.** The cinema offers a number of possible pleasures. One is scopophilia (pleasure in looking). There are circumstances in which looking itself is a source of pleasure, just as, in the reverse formation, there is pleasure in being looked at. Originally, in his *Three Es-*

*says on Sexuality,* Freud isolated scopophilia as one of the component instincts of sexuality which exist as drives quite independently of the erotogenic zones. At this point he associated scopophilia with taking other people as objects, subjecting them to a controlling and curious gaze. His particular examples centre on the voyeuristic activities of children, their desire to see and make sure of the private and forbidden (curiosity about other people's genital and bodily functions, about the presence or absence of the penis and, retrospectively, about the primal scene). In this analysis scopophilia is essentially active. (Later, in "Instincts and Their Vicissitudes," Freud developed his theory of scopophilia further, attaching it initially to pre-genital auto-eroticism, after which, by analogy, the pleasure of the look is transferred to others. There is a close working here of the relationship between the active instinct and its further development in a narcissistic form.) Although the instinct is modified by other factors, in particular the constitution of the ego, it continues to exist as the erotic basis for pleasure in looking at another person as object. At the extreme, it can become fixated into a perversion, producing obsessive voyeurs and Peeping Toms whose only sexual satisfaction can come from watching, in an active controlling sense, an objectified other.

At first glance, the cinema would seem to be remote from the undercover world of the surreptitious observation of an unknowing and unwilling victim. What is seen on the screen is so manifestly shown. But the mass of mainstream film, and the conventions within which it has consciously evolved, portray a hermetically sealed world which unwinds magically, indifferent to the presence of the audience, producing for them a sense of separation and playing on their voyeuristic fantasy. Moreover the extreme contrast between the darkness in the auditorium (which also isolates the spectators from one another)

and the brilliance of the shifting patterns of light and shade on the screen helps to promote the illusion of voyeuristic separation. Although the film is really being shown, is there to be seen, conditions of screening and narrative conventions give the spectator an illusion of looking in on a private world. Among other things, the position of the spectators in the cinema is blatantly one of repression of their exhibitionism and projection of the repressed desire onto the performer.

**B.** The cinema satisfies a primordial wish for pleasurable looking, but it also goes further, developing scopophilia in its narcissistic aspect. The conventions of mainstream film focus attention on the human form. Scale, space, stories are all anthropomorphic. Here, curiosity and the wish to look intermingle with a fascination with likeness and recognition: the human face, the human body, the relationship between the human form and its surroundings, the visible presence of the person in the world. Jacques Lacan has described how the moment when a child recognises its own image in the mirror is crucial for the constitution of the ego. Several aspects of this analysis are relevant here. The mirror phase occurs at a time when children's physical ambitions outstrip their motor capacity, with the result that their recognition of themselves is joyous in that they imagine their mirror image to be more complete, more perfect than they experience in their own body. Recognition is thus overlaid with misrecognition: the image recognised is conceived as the reflected body of the self, but its misrecognition as superior projects this body outside itself as an ideal ego, the alienated subject which, reintrojected as an ego ideal, prepares the way for identification with others in the future. This mirror moment predates language for the child.

Important for this article is the fact that it is an image that constitutes the matrix of the imaginary, of recognition/misrecognition and identification, and hence of the first articulation of the I, of subjectivity. This is a moment when an older fascination with looking (at the mother's face, for an obvious example) collides with the initial inklings of self-awareness. Hence it is the birth of the long love affair/despair between image and self-image which has found such intensity of expression in film and such joyous recognition in the cinema audience. Quite apart from the extraneous similarities between screen and mirror (the framing of the human form in its surroundings, for instance), the cinema has structures of fascination strong enough to allow temporary loss of ego while simultaneously reinforcing it. The sense of forgetting the world as the ego has come to perceive it (I forgot who I am and where I was) is nostalgically reminiscent of that pre-subjective moment of image recognition. While at the same time, the cinema has distinguished itself in the production of ego ideals, through the star system for instance. Stars provide a focus or centre both to screen space and screen story where they act out a complex process of likeness and difference (the glamorous impersonates the ordinary).

**C.** Sections A and B have set out two contradictory aspects of the pleasurable structures of looking in the conventional cinematic situation. The first, scopophilic, arises from pleasure in using another person as an object of sexual stimulation through sight. The second, developed through narcissism and the constitution of the ego, comes from identification with the image seen. Thus, in film terms, one implies a separation of the erotic identity of the subject from the object on the screen (active scopophilia), the other demands identification of the ego with the object on the screen through the spectator's fascination with and recognition of his like. The first is a function of the sexual instincts, the second of ego libido. This dichotomy was crucial for Freud. Although he saw the two as interact-

ing and overlaying each other, the tension between instinctual drives and self-preservation polarises in terms of pleasure. But both are formative structures, mechanisms without intrinsic meaning. In themselves they have no signification, unless attached to an idealisation. Both pursue aims in indifference to perceptual reality, and motivate eroticised phantasmagoria that affect the subject's perception of the world to make a mockery of empirical objectivity.

During its history, the cinema seems to have evolved a particular illusion of reality in which this contradiction between libido and ego has found a beautifully complementary fantasy world. In *reality* the fantasy world of the screen is subject to the law which produces it. Sexual instincts and identification processes have a meaning within the symbolic order which articulates desire. Desire, born with language, allows the possibility of transcending the instinctual and the imaginary, but its point of reference continually returns to the traumatic moment of its birth: the castration complex. Hence the look, pleasurable in form, can be threatening in content, and it is woman as representation/image that crystallises this paradox.

## III   WOMAN AS IMAGE, MAN AS BEARER OF THE LOOK

**A.** In a world ordered by sexual imbalance, pleasure in looking has been split between active/male and passive/female. The determining male gaze projects its fantasy onto the female figure, which is styled accordingly. In their traditional exhibitionist role women are simultaneously looked at and displayed, with their appearance coded for strong visual and erotic impact so that they can be said to connote *to-be-looked-at-ness*. Woman displayed as sexual object is the *leitmotif* of erotic spectacle: from pin-ups to strip-tease, from Ziegfeld to Busby Berkeley, she holds the look, and plays to and signifies male desire. Mainstream film neatly combines spectacle and narrative. (Note, however, how in the musical song-and-dance numbers interrupt the flow of the diegesis.) The presence of woman is an indispensable element of spectacle in normal narrative film, yet her visual presence tends to work against the development of a story-line, to freeze the flow of action in moments of erotic contemplation. This alien presence then has to be integrated into cohesion with the narrative. As Budd Boetticher has put it:

> What counts is what the heroine provokes, or rather what she represents. She is the one, or rather the love or fear she inspires in the hero, or else the concern he feels for her, who makes him act the way he does. In herself the woman has not the slightest importance.

(A recent tendency in narrative film has been to dispense with this problem altogether; hence the development of what Molly Haskell has called the "buddy movie," in which the active homosexual eroticism of the central male figures can carry the story without distraction.) Traditionally, the woman displayed has functioned on two levels: as erotic object for the characters within the screen story, and as erotic object for the spectator within the auditorium, with a shifting tension between the looks on either side of the screen. For instance, the device of the showgirl allows the two looks to be unified technically without any apparent break in the diegesis. A woman performs within the narrative; the gaze of the spectator and that of the male characters in the film are neatly combined without breaking narrative verisimilitude. For a moment the sexual impact of the performing woman takes the film into a no man's land outside its own time and space. Thus Marilyn Monroe's first appearance in *The River of No Return* and Lauren Bacall's

songs in *To Have and Have Not*. Similarly, conventional close-ups of legs (Dietrich, for instance) or a face (Garbo) integrate into the narrative a different mode of eroticism. One part of a fragmented body destroys the Renaissance space, the illusion of depth demanded by the narrative; it gives flatness, the quality of a cut-out or icon, rather than verisimilitude, to the screen.

**B.** An active/passive heterosexual division of labour has similarly controlled narrative structure. According to the principles of the ruling ideology and the psychical structures that back it up, the male figure cannot bear the burden of sexual objectification. Man is reluctant to gaze at his exhibitionist like. Hence the split between spectacle and narrative supports the man's role as the active one of advancing the story, making things happen. The man controls the film fantasy and also emerges as the representative of power in a further sense: as the bearer of the look of the spectator, transferring it behind the screen to neutralise the extra-diegetic tendencies represented by woman as spectacle. This is made possible through the processes set in motion by structuring the film around a main controlling figure with whom the spectator can identify. As the spectator identifies with the main male protagonist, he projects his look onto that of his like, his screen surrogate, so that the power of the male protagonist as he controls events coincides with the active power of the erotic look, both giving a satisfying sense of omnipotence. A male movie star's glamorous characteristics are thus not those of the erotic object of the gaze, but those of the more perfect, more complete, more powerful ideal ego conceived in the original moment of recognition in front of the mirror. The character in the story can make things happen and control events better than the subject/spectator, just as the image in the mirror was more in control of motor co-ordination.

In contrast to woman as icon, the active male figure (the ego ideal of the identification process) demands a three-dimensional space corresponding to that of the mirror recognition, in which the alienated subject internalised his own representation of his imaginary existence. He is a figure in a landscape. Here the function of film is to reproduce as accurately as possible the so-called natural conditions of human perception. Camera technology (as exemplified by deep focus in particular) and camera movements (determined by the action of the protagonist), combined with invisible editing (demanded by realism), all tend to blur the limits of screen space. The male protagonist is free to command the stage, a stage of spatial illusion in which he articulates the look and creates the action. (There are films with a woman as main protagonist, of course. To analyse this phenomenon seriously here would take me too far afield. Pam Cook and Claire Johnston's study of *The Revolt of Mamie Stover* in Phil Hardy (ed.), *Raoul Walsh* (Edinburgh, 1974), shows in a striking case how the strength of this female protagonist is more apparent than real.)

**C1.** Sections III A and B have set out a tension between a mode of representation of woman in film and conventions surrounding the diegesis. Each is associated with a look: that of the spectator in direct scopophilic contact with the female form displayed for his enjoyment (connoting male fantasy) and that of the spectator fascinated with the image of his like set in an illusion of natural space, and through him gaining control and possession of the woman within the diegesis. (This tension and the shift from one pole to the other can structure a single text. Thus both in *Only Angels Have Wings* and in *To Have and Have Not,* the film opens with the woman as object of the combined gaze of spectator and all the male protagonists in the film. She is isolated, glamorous, on display, sexualized. But as the

narrative progresses she falls in love with the main male protagonist and becomes his property, losing her outward glamorous characteristics, her generalised sexuality, her show-girl connotations; her eroticism is subjected to the male star alone. By means of identification with him, through participation in his power, the spectator can indirectly possess her too.)

But in psychoanalytic terms, the female figure poses a deeper problem. She also connotes something that the look continually circles around but disavows: her lack of a penis, implying a threat of castration and hence unpleasure. Ultimately, the meaning of woman is sexual difference, the visually ascertainable absence of the penis, the material evidence on which is based the castration complex essential for the organisation of entrance to the symbolic order and the law of the father. Thus the woman as icon, displayed for the gaze and enjoyment of men, the active controllers of the look, always threatens to evoke the anxiety it originally signified. The male unconscious has two avenues of escape from this castration anxiety: preoccupation with the re-enactment of the original trauma (investigating the woman, demystifying her mystery), counterbalanced by the devaluation, punishment or saving of the guilty object (an avenue typified by the concerns of the *film noir*); or else complete disavowal of castration by the substitution of a fetish object or turning the represented figure itself into a fetish so that it becomes reassuring rather than dangerous (hence overvaluation, the cult of the female star).

This second avenue, fetishistic scopophilia, builds up the physical beauty of the object, transforming it into something satisfying in itself. The first avenue, voyeurism, on the contrary, has associations with sadism: pleasure lies in ascertaining guilt (immediately associated with castration), asserting control and subjugating the guilty person through punishment or forgiveness. This sadistic side fits in well with narrative. Sadism demands a story, depends on making something happen, forcing a change in another person, a battle of will and strength, victory/defeat, all occurring in a linear time with a beginning and an end. Fetishistic scopophilia, on the other hand, can exist outside linear time as the erotic instinct is focused on the look alone. These contradictions and ambiguities can be illustrated more simply by using works by Hitchcock and Sternberg, both of whom take the look almost as the content or subject matter of many of their films. Hitchcock is the more complex, as he uses both mechanisms. Sternberg's work, on the other hand, provides many pure examples of fetishistic scopophilia.

**C2.** Sternberg once said he would welcome his films being projected upside-down so that story and character involvement would not interfere with the spectator's undiluted appreciation of the screen image. This statement is revealing but ingenuous: ingenuous in that his films do demand that the figure of the woman (Dietrich, in the cycle of films with her, as the ultimate example) should be identifiable; but revealing in that it emphasises the fact that for him the pictorial space enclosed by the frame is paramount, rather than narrative or identification processes. While Hitchcock goes into the investigative side of voyeurism, Sternberg produces the ultimate fetish, taking it to the point where the powerful look of the male protagonist (characteristic of traditional narrative film) is broken in favour of the image in direct erotic rapport with the spectator. The beauty of the woman as object and the screen space coalesce; she is no longer the bearer of guilt but a perfect product, whose body, stylised and fragmented by close-ups, is the content of the film and the direct recipient of the spectator's look.

Sternberg plays down the illusion of screen depth; his screen tends to be one-dimensional, as light and shade, lace, steam, foliage,

net, streamers and so on reduce the visual field. There is little or no mediation of the look through the eyes of the main male protagonist. On the contrary, shadowy presences like La Bessière in *Morocco* act as surrogates for the director, detached as they are from audience identification. Despite Sternberg's insistence that his stories are irrelevant, it is significant that they are concerned with situation, not suspense, and cyclical rather than linear time, while plot complications revolve around misunderstanding rather than conflict. The most important absence is that of the controlling male gaze within the screen scene. The high point of emotional drama in the most typical Dietrich films, her supreme moments of erotic meaning, take place in the absence of the man she loves in the fiction. There are other witnesses, other spectators watching her on the screen, their gaze is one with, not standing in for, that of the audience. At the end of *Morocco,* Tom Brown has already disappeared into the desert when Amy Jolly kicks off her gold sandals and walks after him. At the end of *Dishonoured,* Kranau is indifferent to the fate of Magda. In both cases, the erotic impact, sanctified by death, is displayed as a spectacle for the audience. The male hero misunderstands and, above all, does not see.

In Hitchcock, by contrast, the male hero does see precisely what the audience sees. However, although fascination with an image through scopophilic eroticism can be the subject of the film, it is the role of the hero to portray the contradictions and tensions experienced by the spectator. In *Vertigo* in particular, but also in *Marnie* and *Rear Window,* the look is central to the plot, oscillating between voyeurism and fetishistic fascination. Hitchcock has never concealed his interest in voyeurism, cinematic and non-cinematic. His heroes are exemplary of the symbolic order and the law—a policeman *(Vertigo),* a dominant male possessing money and power *(Marnie)*—but their erotic drives lead them into compromised situations. The power to subject another person to the will sadistically or to the gaze voyeuristically is turned onto the woman as the object of both. Power is backed by a certainty of legal right and the established guilt of the woman (evoking castration, psychoanalytically speaking). True perversion is barely concealed under a shallow mask of ideological correctness—the man is on the right side of the law, the woman on the wrong. Hitchcock's skilful use of identification processes and liberal use of subjective camera from the point of view of the male protagonist draw the spectators deeply into his position, making them share his uneasy gaze. The spectator is absorbed into a voyeuristic situation within the screen scene and diegesis, which parodies his own in the cinema.

In an analysis of *Rear Window,* Douchet takes the film as a metaphor for the cinema. Jeffries is the audience, the events in the apartment block opposite correspond to the screen. As he watches, an erotic dimension is added to his look, a central image to the drama. His girlfriend Lisa had been of little sexual interest to him, more or less a drag, so long as she remained on the spectator side. When she crosses the barrier between his room and the block opposite, their relationship is reborn erotically. He does not merely watch her through his lens, as a distant meaningful image, he also sees her as a guilty intruder exposed by a dangerous man threatening her with punishment, and thus finally giving him the opportunity to save her. Lisa's exhibitionism has already been established by her obsessive interest in dress and style, in being a passive image of visual perfection; Jeffries's voyeurism and activity have also been established through his work as a photo-journalist, a maker of stories and captor of images. However, his enforced inactivity, binding him to his seat as a spectator, puts him squarely in the fantasy position of the cinema audience.

In *Vertigo,* subjective camera predominates. Apart from one flashback from Judy's point of view, the narrative is woven around what Scottie sees or fails to see. The audience follows the growth of his erotic obsession and subsequent despair precisely from his point of view. Scottie's voyeurism is blatant: he falls in love with a woman he follows and spies on without speaking to. Its sadistic side is equally blatant: he has chosen (and freely chosen, for he had been a successful lawyer) to be a policeman, with all the attendant possibilities of pursuit and investigation. As a result, he follows, watches and falls in love with a perfect image of female beauty and mystery. Once he actually confronts her, his erotic drive is to break her down and force her *to tell* by persistent cross-questioning.

In the second part of the film, he re-enacts his obsessive involvement with the image he loved to watch secretly. He reconstructs Judy as Madeleine, forces her to conform in every detail to the actual physical appearance of his fetish. Her exhibitionism, her masochism, make her an ideal passive counterpart to Scottie's active sadistic voyeurism. She knows her part is to perform, and only by playing it through and then replaying it can she keep Scottie's erotic interest. But in the repetition he does break her down and succeeds in exposing her guilt. His curiosity wins through; she is punished.

Thus, in *Vertigo,* erotic involvement with the look boomerangs: the spectator's own fascination is revealed as illicit voyeurism as the narrative content enacts the processes and pleasures that he is himself exercising and enjoying. The Hitchcock hero here is firmly placed within the symbolic order, in narrative terms. He has all the attributes of the patriarchal superego. Hence the spectator, lulled into a false sense of security by the apparent legality of his surrogate, sees through his look and finds himself exposed as complicit, caught in the moral ambiguity of looking. Far from being simply an aside on the perversion of the police, *Vertigo* focuses on the implications of the active/looking, passive/looked-at split in terms of sexual difference and the power of the male symbolic encapsulated in the hero. Marnie, too, performs for Mark Rutland's gaze and masquerades as the perfect to-be-looked-at image. He, too, is on the side of the law until, drawn in by obsession with her guilt, her secret, he longs to see her in the act of committing a crime, make her confess and thus save her. So he, too, becomes complicit as he acts out the implications of his power. He controls money and words; he can have his cake and eat it.

## IV   SUMMARY

The psychoanalytic background that has been discussed in this article is relevant to the pleasure and unpleasure offered by traditional narrative film. The scopophilic instinct (pleasure in looking at another person as an erotic object) and, in contradistinction, ego libido (forming identification processes) act as formations, mechanisms, which mould this cinema's formal attributes. The actual image of woman as (passive) raw material for the (active) gaze of man takes the argument a step further into the content and structure of representation, adding a further layer of ideological significance demanded by the patriarchal order in its favourite cinematic form—illusionistic narrative film. The argument must return again to the psychoanalytic background: women in representation can signify castration, and activate voyeuristic or fetishistic mechanisms to circumvent this threat. Although none of these interacting layers is intrinsic to film, it is only in the film form that they can reach a perfect and beautiful contradiction, thanks to the possibility in the cinema of shifting the emphasis of the look. The place of the look defines cinema, the possibility of varying it and exposing it. This is

what makes cinema quite different in its voyeuristic potential from, say, strip-tease, theatre, shows and so on. Going far beyond highlighting a woman's to-be-looked-at-ness, cinema builds the way she is to be looked at into the spectacle itself. Playing on the tension between film as controlling the dimension of time (editing, narrative) and film as controlling the dimension of space (changes in distance, editing), cinematic codes create a gaze, a world and an object, thereby producing an illusion cut to the measure of desire. It is these cinematic codes and their relationship to formative external structures that must be broken down before mainstream film and the pleasure it provides can be challenged.

To begin with (as an ending), the voyeuristic-scopophilic look that is a crucial point of traditional filmic pleasure can itself be broken down. There are three different looks associated with cinema: that of the camera as it records the pro-filmic event, that of the audience as it watches the final product, and that of the characters at each other within the screen illusion. The conventions of narrative film deny the first two and subordinate them to the third, the conscious aim being always to eliminate intrusive camera presence and prevent a distancing awareness in the audience. Without these two absences (the material existence of the recording process, the critical reading of the spectator), fictional drama cannot achieve reality, obviousness and truth. Nevertheless, as this article has argued, the structure of looking in narrative fiction film contains a contradiction in its own premises: the female image as a castration threat constantly endangers the unity of the diegesis and bursts through the world of illusion as an intrusive, static, one-dimensional fetish. Thus the two looks materially present in time and space are obsessively subordinated to the neurotic needs of the male ego. The camera becomes the mechanism for producing an illusion of Renaissance space, flowing movements compatible with the human eye, an ideology of representation that revolves around the perception of the subject; the camera's look is disavowed in order to create a convincing world in which the spectator's surrogate can perform with verisimilitude. Simultaneously, the look of the audience is denied an intrinsic force: as soon as fetishistic representation of the female image threatens to break the spell of illusion, and the erotic image on the screen appears directly (without mediation) to the spectator, the fact of fetishisation, concealing as it does castration fear, freezes the look, fixates the spectator and prevents him from achieving any distance from the image in front of him.

This complex interaction of looks is specific to film. The first blow against the monolithic accumulation of traditional film conventions (already undertaken by radical film-makers) is to free the look of the camera into its materiality in time and space and the look of the audience into dialectics and passionate detachment. There is no doubt that this destroys the satisfaction, pleasure and privilege of the "invisible guest," and highlights the way film has depended on voyeuristic active/passive mechanisms. Women, whose image has continually been stolen and used for this end, cannot view the decline of the traditional film form with anything much more than sentimental regret.

## NOTE

1. Written in 1973 and published in 1975 in *Screen*.

# VII

# HISTORICAL CRITIQUE

Since the 1980s literary critics have focused with renewed intensity on the possibilities of historical understanding in literary and cultural studies. This interest has prompted much productive debate about what constitutes effective historical criticism and how historical criticism can be articulated along with other critical approaches. This movement has been in reaction to more traditional historical criticism that tends to confine itself to inquiry moving strictly along three lines of historical understanding. The first is to shed light on and clarify the text as a document or a kind of material, cultural artifact. This may mean fixing the date of composition and also establishing the authoritative version of a text—addressing such questions as the following: Does it correspond with known manuscripts? Are there spurious editions of this text? The text can also be clarified by identifying actual references to history—allusions to actual people, political events, civic upheavals, economic trends, and so on. This effort locates the text as a historical phenomenon—and it includes the "source study" that Stephen Greenblatt describes in "Shakespeare and the Exorcists" as "the elephants' graveyard of literary history."

The second goal is to describe the author/artist as having a past made up of certain significant events and, in light of that past, a predisposition to write in a certain manner and style. The goal of most literary biography, this approach tends to cover a broad area of intellectual, cultural, and aesthetic concerns, including the "symptomatic" (highly person-oriented) reading of literature that dominated the work of Freudian ego-psychology, which analyzes literature in the same way the psychoanalyst analyzes the discourse of the patient in the "talking cure" of therapy. This last is "history" in the sense of being a single author's "life" or "life and work." Just as Freud analyzes Dora's language to discover the coherent narrative—the case *history*—that Toril Moi examines and critiques in "Representation of Patriarchy" (in "Psychology and Psychoanalysis"), so the literary critic analyzes the author's language to discover the coherent underlying psychoanalytic narrative.

The third goal is to grasp a literary work as it reflects the historical forces that shaped it initially. This approach assumes that a historical moment—enormously complex in its diverse representations—produces the factors that shape a particular work of literary art. This approach projects the historical process itself as the instigator and actual shaper of all dimensions of culture, a kind of ultimate author, both the origin and real composer of specific works, too. Kenneth Burke, in "Literature as Equipment for Living" (in "Rhetoric and Reader Response"), offers an abstract version of this approach in what he calls "sociological categories" that derive their "relevance from the fact that [they] should apply both to works of art and to social situations outside of art." Burke can be contrasted with the psychoanalytic technique Moi presents precisely in the fact that while Freudian psychology analyzes discourse attached to an explicitly named author, Burke is interested in the anonymous social discourse of proverbs.

Successful historical criticism in this traditional mold—criticism that accomplishes all three goals—endeavors, as Hippolyte Taine advanced in the nineteenth century, to recover "from the monuments of literature, a knowledge of the manner in which men thought and felt centuries ago." Taine's approach to historical criticism, known today as the "traditional" approach, thus defines literary interpretation on a *genetic* model, as an explanation of how a work's genesis in a historical situation (where specific causes are manifested) brings the work into being as a distinct aesthetic object. From this standpoint, the literary critic necessarily studies history as an end in itself, since the literary text is an object produced by history's operation. Indeed, since history produces or determines the shape and content of literature, the study of literature must first be a study of history, the virtual master text. From this perspective at least, contrary to Aristotle's opinion, history is superior to literature since it shapes literature and determines its nature.

Such traditional historical study, in Walter Benjamin's penetrating analysis in "Theses on the Philosophy of History," is the opposite of the politically oriented sense of history in Marxist historical materialism. More recently, Stephen Greenblatt defined traditional historical study as "old" historicism as against a "new historicism," the "old" being "the dominant historical scholarship of the past." In the "Introduction" to *The Forms of Power and the Power of Forms in the Renaissance,* he says that the "old" kind "tends to be monological; that is, it is concerned with discovering a single political vision, usually identical to that said to be held by the entire literate class or indeed the entire population." As such, he argues, "this vision can serve as a stable point of reference, beyond contingency, to which literary interpretation can securely refer. Literature is conceived to mirror the period's beliefs, but to mirror them, as it were, from a safe distance." Greenblatt refers specifically to traditional literary scholarship, but he is also voicing the traditional Marxist distinction between the "historical" economic base of social relationships—the modes of production at a given historical moment—and the superstructure of ideology, beliefs, and assumptions embodied in art, intellectual worldviews, and other consciously or unconsciously held ideas.

## MARXIST CRITICISM

Much modern historical criticism has tended to veer away from the "old" historicism and has disrupted the hierarchy of history as superior to literature and has closed the distance between the two domains. Instead of viewing history as the determining context for literature, many critics throughout the twentieth century —Georg Lukács and Raymond Williams, for example—have reconceived history as a field of discourse in which literature and criticism make their own impact as political forces and, in effect, participate in an historical dialectic. In the Marxist view of literary criticism, the critic is a member of a intellectual class that promotes cultural revolution through a political commitment expressed in literary studies. Lukács fulfilled this social commitment by attempting to "lay bare" the "devices" of literature that can show the ideological orientation of a work.

In the case of modernist literature, particularly James Joyce's *Ulysses,* Lukács demonstrated the dehumanizing and fragmenting effect of capitalist culture and, further, showed how a modernist novel can silently promote the acceptance of underlying social principles and values. As Lukács says of Franz Kafka, the "mood of total impotence, of paralysis in the face of the unintelligible power of circumstances, informs" the modernists' worldview and espouses bourgeois ideology. Fredric Jameson, in *The Political Unconscious,* attempts to modify this extreme view of modernism by isolating the "utopian vocation" in modernist discourse, its "mission . . . to restore at least a symbolic experience of libidinal gratification." Patrocinio Schweichkart uses Jameson's concept and offers a helpful example of the dialectical relationship between the negative and positive elements of modernism in "Reading Ourselves" (in "Rhetoric and Reader Response").

Raymond Williams, who has influenced many with his historical and cultural criticism, investigates crucial areas of modern culture in the attempt to understand subtle coercion in the promotion of capitalist ideology. At the same time, he broke with an older Marxism by positing the potential productive effect of cultural developments on dimensions of the economic "base" that was previously thought to dictate all aspects of culture. Typical of Williams is his ground-breaking analysis of "country and city" in English literature. He shows the ways in which certain values have been projected in the ideal pastoral setting of "country" communities. Other values are depicted as primarily urban and even antipastoral. Such an "opposition" is governed, above all, by the contradictions (dialectical contradictions) that drive social life and reveal the "real" relations of the "base" (economic) and "superstructure" (social and cultural) relationship. As Williams notes in "Base and Superstructure in Marxist Cultural Theory" in this section, "it is indeed one of the central propositions of Marx's sense of history that there are deep contradictions in the relationships of production and in the consequent social relationships." The economic "base" of a society, as manifested in the "relations of production," he goes on, determines that society's "superstructure"—its arts and ideology—as a "consequence" of the underlying "mode" of production such as feudalism or capitalism.

On this point Williams articulates a somewhat modified version of the central tenet of Marxist literary criticism (modified in that he recognizes the effect of the superstructure on the base): that literature, art, and culture are social practices inseparable "from other kinds of social practice, in such a way as to make them subject to quite special and distinct laws. They may have quite specific features as practices, but they cannot be separated from the general social process." In the words of Étienne Balibar and Pierre Macherey, literature "does not 'fall from the heavens,' the product of a mysterious 'creation,' but is the product of social practice (rather a particular social practice); neither is it an 'imaginary' activity, albeit it produces imaginary effects, but inescapably part of a material process." The term "imaginary" they use is taken from Lacanian psychoanalysis and applied to social contexts. Catherine Belsey, in "Constructing the Subject: Deconstructing the Text" (in "Deconstruction and Poststructuralism") explicates this "transference" of psychoanalytic categories to social situations in explaining "ideology." She, like Balibar and Macherey, is following the French Marxist theoretician Louis Althuser.

Other Marxist critics also assume that literature and discourse are best analyzed as the product of particular social practices. For instance, the large corpus of work associated with the Russian scholar M. M. Bakhtin aims at exploring the interpersonal and social contexts of art and discourse. Under the term "dialogism"—the study of language in the processes of the social interactions of dialogue and contest—Bakhtin has, in recent years, been greatly influential. (The work associated with him that sometimes was published under the name of friends and associates during Stalin's repressive regime in the Soviet Union demonstrates in the very ambiguity surrounding its "authorship" the very "dialogism" that it propounds.) In his studies of particular authors and genres, Bakhtin attempts to analyze the play of different voices, articulating differing ideological positions, within the discourse of the novel and other literary forms. An early essay, "Discourse in Life and Discourse in Art" (published in 1926 under the name of his friend V. N. Vološinov), maintains that there is not a "social essence of art." "Verbal discourse," this essay asserts, "is a social event; it is not self-contained in the sense of some abstract linguistic quantity, nor can it be derived psychologically from the speaker's subjective consciousness taken in isolation." Rather, the extraverbal—the "historical"—situation enters into verbal discourse, including literary discourse "as an essential constitutive part of the structure of its import." Thus, the audience—the "listener"—is not, as rhetoricians like Walter Ong suggest, simply a function of a text, but rather the listener "has his own independent place in the event of artistic creation." In this way, a Marxist rhetoric is quite different from that of Ong or Peter Ramus. Rather than stabilizing the position of the reader, creating a normative or fictional reader, as Ong advances that literature does in "The Writer's Audience Is Always a Fiction," Terry Eagleton argues in "Brecht and Rhetoric" that the rhetorical function of literature is precisely to *destabilize* the reader, to create an "alienation effect"—not unrelated to the "defamiliarization" of Russian Formalism—that allows the reader or audience to reconceive his or her position as one situated within a particular social structure. Alienation, Eagleton argues, "hollows out the imaginary plenitude of everyday actions, deconstructing them into their social determinants and inscribing within them the conditions of their making." Art, at least as Brecht conceived it, can reveal the artificial in the seemingly "natural" by asking the "crude" question of what ends particular discursive practices serve rather than "refined" questions that assume the stability and permanence of those practices. This, Eagleton argues, is the significance of Brecht's slogan, *"plumpes Denken"*—think crudely.

In this way, contemporary Marxist work situates criticism as it does literature. In *Literary Theory* Terry Eagleton argues "that the history of modern literary theory is part of the political and ideological history of our epoch," and many contemporary critics—including Jameson, Williams, Eagleton, Gayatri Spivak, Edward Said, Catherine Belsey, and most of the feminist critics represented in this book—share a strong sense of criticism as a historically situated activity that deeply involves the critic, so that the critic cannot stand apart from the text being read and interpreted but can only choose to recognize his or her own effect on the text. Any literary theory in use, as Eagleton says, is "indissociably bound up with political beliefs and ideological values"—that is, has taken some stand in relation to such beliefs. In denoting performance and power rather than meaning and knowledge, Brecht's "crude" thinking reminds the reader that the "superstructure" of knowledge and meaning has a material base that has not been produced by the refinements of a superstructure developing from that base. Also it reminds the critic that even the most "disinterested" contemplation of meaning and art—even the most esoteric criticism—is situated in a social and political world and, for that reason, is a more or less "crude" activity with social and political consequences that can never achieve the purity of "disinterestedness."

A good example of this is Walter Benjamin's meditations on history in "Theses on the Philosophy of History." These numbered observations on history, written shortly before Benjamin's suicide in 1940 when he thought he would be arrested by the Nazis for the "crimes" of being both a Marxist and a Jew, offer profound meditations on the very idea of "history" in the modern world. Traditional historians (such as Taine, whom we mentioned earlier), according to Benjamin, aim at "disinterestedness" in their attempt to "blot out everything they know about the later course of history"; they conceive of history as taking place in "homogeneous, empty time" and culminating in "universal history," in which it is possible to distinguish "between major and minor" events. Such distinctions are always made from the point of view of history's "victors," the ruling class that defines the "cultural treasures" of history. From Benjamin's Marxist point of view, history must be read in relation to the activities of the present to allow a dialectic mode of apprehension. Such a mode allows history itself—and its cultural treasures, including literature—to be seen to be inhabited by more than one historical narrative, more than one historical significance: cultural treasures, Benjamin writes, "owe their existence not only to the efforts of great minds and talents who have created them, but also to the anonymous toil of their contemporaries. There is no document of civilization which is not at the same time a document of barbarism." Moreover, such a dialectic allows the past and the present to interpenetrate one another, not only so that the activities of the past inform the present, but more profoundly so that our activities now, in the present, can change or "redeem" the past. In a language that is at once religious and political, Benjamin argues that the historical materialist can recognize "a sign of a Messianic cessation of happening, or, put differently, a revolutionary chance in the fight for the oppressed past." Earlier he writes that "there is a secret agreement between past generations and the present one. Our coming was expected on earth," and the "agreement" of which he speaks would allow the past itself to be changed and revalued by making what it *resulted in*—namely the present—different.

In Benjamin we can see a second way in which contemporary criticism "situates" itself in history. Not only do Marxist critics want criticism to be constantly aware of history—both present and past history. In reading literature, they also demand that criticism become more overtly political, that it attempt, as Marx said, not simply to interpret but to change the world. This sense of the need for commitment and the political responsibility of the literary critic pervades the work of these critics and much of contemporary literary criticism carried out from an historical viewpoint. (Such commitment can be heard in Gates's, Christian's, and Said's essays in "What Is Literary Theory?" as well as in Spivak's and Haraway's essays in "Feminism and Gender Studies.") This stance is clear in Williams's (implicitly "utopian") assertion that human practices are "inexhaustible" and, consequently, one can always imagine and work for a world better than the present world. "No mode of production," he writes, "and therefore no dominant society or order of society, and therefore no dominant culture, in reality exhausts the full range of human practice, human energy, human intention." This stance is evident, too, in Eagleton's description of the function of rhetoric and in Frank Lentricchia's definition of criticism in *Criticism and Social Change* as "the production of knowledge to the ends of power and, maybe, of social change." "The activity that a Marxist literary intellectual preeminently engages in—should engage in—" Lentricchia goes on, "is the activity of interpretation . . . which does not passively 'see,' as Burke put it, but constructs a point of view in its engagement with textual events, and in so constructing produces an image of history as social struggle, of, say, class struggle." "This sort of interpretation," he concludes, "will above all else attempt to displace traditional interpretations which cover up the political work of culture."

Fredric Jameson, who is probably the most prominent Marxist critic in America today, has consistently pursued such politically oriented, cultural work in his literary criticism—what he calls in *Postmodernism, or, The Cultural Logic of Late Capitalism* the disengagment of the "seeds of the future" from the present "both through analysis and through political praxis." This extensive range of vision distinguishes Jameson's work, as it does Williams's. Jameson has consistently attempted to discover the usefulness in a Marxist sense of contemporary literary theory. *The Political Unconscious,* for instance, uses Freudian, structuralist, and poststructuralist concepts in its "political work of culture." In *Postmodernism* Jameson brings the same range of methods and interest to bear in a Marxist analysis. He attempts to present a sophisticated analysis of the relationship between the base and superstructure regarding the specific cultural phenomenon of "postmodernism." Rather than seeing it as an isolated cultural phenomenon, or a mere symptom of the so-called postindustrial society, Jameson tries to show how postmodernism is related to and serves the economic order, how what is most often conducted as an aesthetic debate about the nature of "postmodernism" actually defines "political positions."

The seemingly disinterested aesthetic discussions of such artistic or cultural phenomena as postmodernism, he argues, "can always be shown to articulate visions of history" and can, in fact, be related to "moments of the capitalism from which it emerged." Jameson analyzes the cultural artifacts of contemporary culture ranging from architecture to pop art, from literature to television, in relation to the ideology of late capitalism not simply to interpret culture, but to situate it in relation to its historical "base." His aim is to present an analysis of the social forces that govern consciousness and, consequently, govern action. The aim here, as it was for Marx, is to create a situation from which to imagine the world different from the existing social and political institutions—to change the world.

**THE NEW HISTORICISM**

The New Historicism in America, as a movement since the early 1980s, brings the tools of contemporary critical discourse to the understanding of history and historical texts. Its two most important precursors are Raymond Williams and Michel Foucault. For Williams, especially, with his wide-ranging interest in culture and critical methodology, we can see midcentury historical criticism moving away from the traditional hierarchy of history over literature. Contemporary historical criticism also made this move, at least in part, as Eagleton suggests in his use of the term "deconstruction" in "Brecht and Rhetoric," under the sway of Continental philosopher-critics—particularly the French—who have redrawn the boundaries of history as a discipline. Foucault, in particular, has influenced cultural critics with his view of history as "discursive practice," what it is possible to say in one era as opposed to another.

In "What Is an Author?" (in "Deconstruction and Poststructuralism"), Foucault says that "the author's name manifests the appearance of a certain discursive set and indicates the status of this discourse within a society and a culture." Such discursive practices are, as Williams says, "hegemonic" in their effect, both creating and created by "a whole body of practices and expectations." Hans Robert Jauss, Hans-Georg Gadamer, and Eugene Vance, likewise, have suggested new ways of understanding *history as a language* but also as a horizon for both narration and social activity in relation to which textual effects are constructed.

Stephen Greenblatt, who coined the term "new historicism," asserts that "history cannot be divorced from textuality." The union of history and textuality has led to a rebirth of historical studies in contemporary criticism. It has led to a host of questions about the relationship Hunter Cadzow describes "between texts and the cultural system in which they were produced," between textual practice and historical events. In "Invisible Bullets" Greenblatt examines the construction of a version of social authority and the way a textual economy works within that construction. In this essay his aim is to recover the *power* of ideas in cultural artifacts not "to expose [them] as mere illusion or anachronism," but to trace their functioning within the social world in which they appeared. Here he traces the power and struggle attendant to the use of the idea of "atheism" in seventeenth-century England to show, among other things, that the relationship between political and "cultural" events—between Thomas Harriot's *A Brief and True Report on the New Found Land of Virginia* and Shakespeare's *I Henry IV*—is not a simple hierarchy (of base and superstructure, say) but a complicated interweaving of modes of apprehension. Even the critical term "subversion," Greenblatt argues—a term that he uses throughout his essay—is "historicized": "we locate as 'subversive' in the past precisely those things that are *not* subversion to ourselves, that pose no threat to the order by which we live and allocate resources." More generally, the mode of critical/historical analysis Greenblatt (among others) pursues abandons any notion of history as direct mimesis, any belief in history as a mere imitation of events in the world—history as a reflection of an activity happening "out there." Hayden White, especially, tends to view history as fundamentally a narrative, a narrated sequence always positioned within a genre of historical inquiry.

The sequence of history itself elaborates relationships that belong to an "episteme" (to use Foucault's term), not a mode of thought that characterizes an age (as in the "old" historicism), but the discursive limits in culture on what can be thought (i.e., "discursivized") at any particular moment, so that history as a discipline necessarily traces ruptures rather than continuities, empty spaces of thought within and between epistemes. This is an intentionally problematic view of history, nearly a contradiction in historical terms, in which historicity, as Foucault says in *The Order of Things,* "in its very fabric, makes possible the necessity of an origin which must be both internal and foreign to it." Rather than proposing an integrated story about the world, this model suggests that history is fundamentally comprehensible as a way, or ways, of knowing the world, as successive forms of discourse or, in Greenblatt's term, "textuality." Therefore, insofar as history comes out of an "origin" that is "foreign to it," history is a way of "thinking the Other," a sequential elaboration of the lacunae in experience. Foucault is quick to caution that these gaps in history are not lacunae "that must be filled." They are "nothing more," he explains, "and nothing less, than the unfolding of a space in which it is once more possible to think."

Fundamentally, the writing of history in this new view is a continual renewal of the cultural grids for thinking and constitutes an epistemological posture (a way of knowing—an "episteme") in and "about" the world. It would be misleading to think of this definition of history as solely a contemporary phenomenon. Walter Benjamin's "Theses on the Philosophy of History" from earlier in the century, for example, gives a historical-materialist version of this interactive sense of history, historical writing, and the common perception of everyday life (and Benjamin, too, is influential among New Historicists). This sense of history holds true for the histories we write, as well as for the immediate sense we have of history as "reality," even its personal impact. The new "textual" sense of history—what Stanley Fish calls "wall-to-wall textuality"—difficult and sometimes forbidding in its terminology, has done much to encourage literary critics both to view history as a species of language and to look beyond formalist aesthetics to read literature in the context of power relations and ever wider and deeper contexts of culture.

The current view of history as a "discourse" indeed reverses the hierarchy of history over literature. Now history, similar to literature, is projected as a product of language, and both represent themselves as formed in a sequence of gaps, as a narrative discourse. If fundamentally a breached narrative, history in its constitution is virtually indistinguishable from literature. This comparison should not suggest that history is "made up"—"fictitious" or "mythical" in the derogatory sense—and trivial as a cultural and social pattern of interpretation. On the contrary, the reality of history in this new view (as what "hurts") is as "real" and intractable and even as potentially "hurtful" as it ever was. The new awareness is that history, like a fictional narrative, exists in a dialogue with something "foreign" or "other" to it that can never be contained or controlled by the historian. In this view, instead of being a more-or-less accurate story about what already exists, history is a knowing that is also a making, although a making that never quite makes what was intended.

Alternatively—looking back at traditional views of history—we can try to make of history a process of repetition, as T. S. Eliot imagined, so that what was valuable in the past is continually regained in cultural terms ("made new") through poetry in a kind of cultural retrieval mechanism. Alternatively, we can make of history an apocalyptic promise to be fulfilled in time, as Northrop Frye in *Anatomy of Criticism*—and, indeed, the Bible—envisioned it. And we can project history as a series of irrational ruptures, as Friedrich Nietzsche and Foucault imagined it. Whether as repetition, apocalypse, or rupture, however, history for the New Historicists is not an order in the world that simply is copied but an order of encounter with the world similar to that which Heidegger called Dasein—"being-in-the-world," a conception of making and participating with the world.

As one result of this reconception of history and the historicity of literature, New Historicism attempts to situate literary works, as Marxist criticism does, within an historical matrix. Following Williams, New Historicism does not define that matrix as a one-way relationship between base and superstructure. Rather, following Foucault, as well as Williams, it describes both history and literature in terms that eschew universalizing and transcendental descriptions and draws on the "discursive" presuppositions we have been describing. As Greenblatt says in "Shakespeare and the Exorcists," "for me the study of literature is the study of contingent, particular, intended, and historically embedded works." This is a conception of literature as not being "autonomous, separable from its cultural context and hence divorced from the social, ideological, and material matrix in which all art is produced and consumed."

Joined by the work of Jonathan Goldberg, Louis Marin, Louis Montrose, Leonard Tennenhouse, and others, Greenblatt has produced a significant rereading of Renaissance literature in terms of a sense that, in Tennenhouse's words, "the history of a culture is a history of all its products, literature being just one such product, social organization another, the legal apparatus yet another, and so on." Tennenhouse argues, further, that "one is forced to make an artificial distinction among cultural texts between those which are literary and those which are political in the effort to demonstrate how, in sharing common themes and a common teleology, they actually comprised a seamless discourse." This project of articulating what Greenblatt calls "cultural poetics" has not been limited to Renaissance studies. Nancy Armstrong has "historicized" (in the sense we are discussing) feminist readings of nineteenth-century culture and Walter Ben Michaels has reread American naturalism. Similar work for other periods in literary history is going on, and what they all attempt to do (as does Marxist criticism) is to read in literature what Greenblatt calls "a deeper and unexpressed institutional exchange."

In this project, then, the New Historicism shares a good deal with Marxist literary criticism—in fact, some critics have argued that it is a part of Marxist criticism. Whether this is so—and certainly self-consciously Marxist readers such as Jameson have offered strong critiques of the New Historicism—nevertheless, both Marxism and New Historicism recognize in literary texts, as Catherine Belsey says, "not 'knowledge' but ideology itself in all its inconsistency and partiality." In doing so, they situate literary criticism in a larger framework of cultural criticism, what Eagleton calls "rhetoric" and "discourse theory." Such theory above all attempts to understand literature as historically situated practices that encompass power as much as knowledge.

## RELATED ESSAYS IN
## *CONTEMPORARY LITERARY CRITICISM*

Henry Louis Gates, Jr., "Critical Fanonism"
Edward Said, "The Politics of Knowledge"

Patrocinio Schweickart, "Reading Ourselves: Toward a Feminist Theory of Reading"
Michel Foucault, "What Is an Author?"
Gayatri Chakravorty Spivak, "Feminism and Critical Theory"
Meaghan Morris, "The Banality of Cultural Studies"

## FURTHER READING

Adorno, Theodor W., *Prisms,* trans. Samuel Weber and Shierry Weber (Cambridge, MA: MIT Press, 1983).

Althuser, Louis. *For Marx* (New York: Pantheon Books, 1969).

————, *Lenin and Philosophy and Other Essays,* trans. B. Brewster (New York: Monthly Review, 1971).

Armstrong, Nancy, *Desire and Domestic Fiction* (New York: Oxford University Press, 1987).

Auerbach, Erich. *Mimesis: The Representation of Reality in Western Literature,* trans. Willard Trask (Princeton, NJ: Princeton University Press, 1953).

Bakhtin, M. M., *The Dialogic Imagination: Four Essays* (Austin: University of Texas Press, 1981).

————, "Discourse in Life and Discourse in Art (Concerning Sociological Politics)," in *Freudianism: A Critical Sketch*, trans. I. R. Titunik (Bloomington: Indiana University Press, 1987), 93–116.

Balibar, Étienne, and Pierre Macherey, "On Literature As an Ideological Form," trans. Ian McLeod, John Whitehead, and Ann Wordsworth, in *Untying the Text*, ed. Robert Young (London: Routledge and Kegan Paul, 1981).

Belsey, Catherine, *Critical Practice* (London: Methuen, 1980).

Benjamin, Walter, *Illuminations* (New York: Schocken, 1970).

Bowers, Fredson, *Textual and Literary Criticism* (New York: Cambridge University Press, 1959).

Cadzow, Hunter, "The New Historicism," in *The Johns Hopkins Guide to Literary Theory,* ed. Martin Kreisworth and Michael Gordon (Baltimore: Johns Hopkins University Press, 1993).

Coward, Rosalind, and John Ellis, *Language and Materialism: Developments in Semiology and the Theory of the Subject* (London: Routledge and Kegan Paul, 1977).

Eagleton, Terry, *Criticism and Ideology* (New York: Schocken, 1978).

————, *Literary Theory: An Introduction* (Minneapolis: University of Minnesota Press, 1983).

————, *Marxism and Literary Criticism* (Berkeley: University of California Press, 1976).

Foucault, Michel, *Language, Counter-Memory, Practice,* trans. Donald F. Bouchard (Ithaca, NY: Cornell University Press, 1977).

————, *Madness and Civilization,* trans. Richard Howard (New York: Pantheon, 1965).

————, *The Order of Things* (New York: Pantheon, 1972).

Goldmann, Lucien, *The Hidden God,* trans. Philip Thody (New York: Humanities Press, 1976).

Greenblatt, Stephen, "Shakespeare and the Exorcists," in *Shakespeare and the Question of Theory,* eds. Patricia Parker and Geoffrey Hartman (New York: Methuen, 1985).

Holquist, Michel, *Dialogism: Bakhtin and His World* (New York: Routledge, 1990).

Hicks, Granville, *The Great Tradition* (New York: Macmillan, 1933; rev. 1935).

James, C. Vaughan, *Soviet Socialist Realism: Origins and Theory* (New York: Macmillan, 1973).

Jameson, Fredric, *Marxism and Form: Twentieth-Century Dialectical Theories of Literature* (Princeton, NJ: Princeton University Press, 1971).

————, *The Political Unconscious: Narrative as a Socially Symbolic Act* (Ithaca, NY: Cornell University Press, 1981).

————, *Postmodernism, or, The Cultural Logic of Late Capitalism* (Durham: Duke University Press, 1991).

————, *The Prison-House of Language: A Critical Account of Structuralism and Russian Formalism* (Princeton, NJ: Princeton University Press, 1972).

Jay, Martin, *The Dialectical Imagination: A History of the Frankfurt School* (Boston: Little, Brown 1973).

Lentricchia, Frank, *Criticism and Social Change* (Chicago: University of Chicago Press, 1983).

Lukács, Georg, *The Historical Novel* (London: Merlin Press, 1962).

————, *Realism in Our Time* (New York: Harper Torchbooks, 1971).

Macherey, Pierre, *A Theory of Literary Production,* trans. G. Wall (London: Routledge and Kegan Paul, 1978).

Robertson, D. W., Jr., "Historical Criticism," in *English Institute Essays: 1950,* ed. Alan S. Downer (New York: Columbia University Press, 1951), 3–31.

Sartre, Jean Paul, *What Is Literature?* (New York: Philosophical Library, 1949).

Schleifer, Ronald, "Walter Benjamin and the Crisis of Representation: Multiplicity, Meaning, and Athematic Death," in *Death and Representation,* ed. Sara Goodwin and Elisabeth Bronfen (Baltimore: Johns Hopkins University Press, 1993).

Taine, Hippolyte Adolphe, *History of English Literature,* trans. Henry Van Loun (New York: P. F. Collier, 1900).

Tennenhouse, Leonard, "Representing Power: *Measure for Measure* in Its Time," in *The Power of Forms and the Forms of Power in* the *Renaissance, Genre* 15: 139–56.

Vesser, H. Aram, ed., *The New Historicism* (New York: Routledge, 1990).

Wellek, René, "Literary Theory, Criticism, and History," in *Sewanee Review,* 68 (1960), 1–19.

White, Hayden, *Metahistory: The Historical Imagination in Nineteenth-Century Europe* (Baltimore: Johns Hopkins University Press, 1973).

————, *Tropics of Discourse: Essays in Cultural Criticism* (Baltimore: Johns Hopkins University Press, 1978).

Willett, John, ed., *Brecht on Theatre* (London: Methuen, 1964).

Williams, Raymond, *Marxism and Literature* (New York: Oxford University Press, 1977).

————, *Problems in Materialism and Culture* (New York: Schocken, 1981).

Wimsatt, W. K., Jr., "History and Criticism: A Problematic Relationship," in *PMLA,* 66 (1951), 21–31.

# 27

# Walter Benjamin
# 1882–1940

Walter Benjamin was born in Berlin, into a well-to-do, merchant-class family. He received his doctorate at the University of Frankfurt in 1918 and seemed about to establish himself as an academic with a postdoctoral thesis on what became *On the Origin of German Tragic Drama,* when he abandoned that project and started on the path he was to maintain for the rest of his life as an independent scholar, supporting himself with difficulty as a free-lance writer. He was associated with Theodor Adorno, Herbert Marcuse, and others of "the Frankfurt school," also known as "the New School for Social Research," an important early manifestation of what we now call "cultural studies." Benjamin committed suicide at the French/Spanish border in the Pyrenees in 1940 after an unsuccessful attempt to cross the border and escape Nazism.

Walter Benjamin is probably the most unusual of major theoretical thinkers of this century. Along with Bakhtin, Benjamin is the most important non-Stalinist Marxist thinker of this century in the area of literary and cultural criticism more generally. To classify Benjamin as "Marxist," though, is to do an injustice to the amazing blend of perspectives, commitments, and other passionate attachments that characterize his writing. However, he was always committed to the radical social transformation at the heart of Marxism and its goals. His writings are amazingly varied. He wrote on a wide variety of topics, and although his most important and ambitious work remained unfinished, his published writings now constitute a large body of work. His essays discuss canonical writers of European modernity, obscure German and Jewish writers, modern and contemporary architecture and city planning, and memorabilia and the passion for collecting, all the detritus of commercial and popular culture in Europe from 1850 to 1940. He was one of the first theoreticians of culture to examine the cultural impact of technological innovation on the way art functions in society, as in the famous "The Work of Art in the Age of Mechanical Reproduction." It only compounds his reputation as an almost Gnostic mystic that much of his most exciting work is transcribed from aphoristic notebook fragments.

"Theses on the Philosophy of History" (1940) is the last piece of writing in *Illuminations,* the eclectic collection of essays by which Benjamin is best known in English. (In German, the pieces collected in *Charles Baudelaire: A Lyric Poet in the Age of High Capitalism,* especially the brief, wonderfully titled "Paris, Capital of the Nineteenth Century," are probably better known.) The fame of the piece and its place in *Illuminations* have probably doomed it to being known that way, though many other translations of the title have been suggested—"Theses on the Conception of History" is probably much closer. This is one of Benjamin's most important, strangest, most difficult, and most rewarding works. Each sentence demands a meditative pause to follow it, a little thinking time. Their condensed, aphoristic style is typical of Benjamin's best work, and their cryptic openness resonates perfectly with his Marxist theologian friend Ernst Bloch's great aphorism, "Seek and ye shall wonder." Since his death many different schools of thought have sought to claim Benjamin, and there are those who would read the "Theses" from a uniquely theological, religious perspective that would privilege Benjamin's lifelong fascination with the Cabalistic tradition and other instances of mystical Judaism. However, one should not attempt to choose between that and a historical materialist perspective that was at least as important to Benjamin. Thus, when he speaks of a conception of "the time of the now, shot through with chips of Messianic time," those chips resonate with mystical religion but they also denote a militant revolutionary praxis aimed at radical social transformation. His statement in Thesis VII that "there is no document of civilization which is not also a document of barbarism" has been very influential, anticipating as it does the critique of the canon, a skeptical view of what he here terms "cultural treasures." Much work remains to be done in developing the implications of the writings of this major voice in the area of cultural theory and critique.

# Theses on the Philosophy of History

## I

The story is told of an automaton constructed in such a way that it could play a winning game of chess, answering each move of an opponent with a countermove. A puppet in Turkish attire and with a hookah in its mouth sat before a chessboard placed on a large table. A system of mirrors created the illusion that this table was transparent from all sides. Actually, a little hunchback who was an expert chess player sat inside and guided the puppet's hand by means of strings. One can imagine a philosophical counterpart to this device. The puppet called "historical materialism" is to win all the time. It can easily be a match for anyone if it enlists the services of theology, which today, as we know, is wizened and has to keep out of sight.

## II

"One of the most remarkable characteristics of human nature," writes Lotze, "is, alongside so much selfishness in specific instances, the freedom from envy which the present displays toward the future." Reflection shows us that our image of happiness is thoroughly colored by the time to which the course of our own existence has assigned us. The kind of happiness that could arouse envy in us exists only in the air we have breathed, among people we could have talked to, women who could have given themselves to us. In other words, our image of happiness is indissolubly bound up with the image of redemption. The same applies to our view of the past, which is the concern of history. The past carries with it a temporal index by which it is referred to redemption.

There is a secret agreement between past generations and the present one. Our coming was expected on earth. Like every generation that preceded us, we have been endowed with a *weak* Messianic power, a power to which the past has a claim. That claim cannot be settled cheaply. Historical materialists are aware of that.

## III

A chronicler who recites events without distinguishing between major and minor ones acts in accordance with the following truth: nothing that has ever happened should be regarded as lost for history. To be sure, only a redeemed mankind receives the fullness of its past—which is to say, only for a redeemed mankind has its past become citable in all its moments. Each moment it has lived becomes a *citation à l'ordre du jour*—and that day is Judgment Day.

## IV

*Seek for food and clothing first, then the Kingdom of God shall be added unto you.*
—Hegel, 1807

The class struggle, which is always present to a historian influenced by Marx, is a fight for the crude and material things without which no refined and spiritual things could exist. Nevertheless, it is not in the form of the spoils which fall to the victor that the latter make their presence felt in the class struggle. They manifest themselves in this struggle as courage, humor, cunning, and fortitude. They have retroactive force and will constantly call in question every victory, past and present, of the rulers. As flowers turn toward the sun, by dint of a secret heliotropism the past strives to turn toward that sun which is rising in the sky of history. A historical materialist must be aware of this most inconspicuous of all transformations.

## V

The true picture of the past flits by. The past can be seized only as an image which flashes up at the instant when it can be recognized and is never seen again. "The truth will not run away from us": in the historical outlook of historicism these words of Gottfried Keller mark the exact point where historical materialism cuts through historicism. For every image of the past that is not recognized by the present as one of its own concerns threatens to disappear irretrievably. (The good tidings which the historian of the past brings with throbbing heart may be lost in a void the very moment he opens his mouth.)

## VI

To articulate the past historically does not mean to recognize it "the way it really was" (Ranke). It means to seize hold of a memory as it flashes up at a moment of danger. Historical materialism wishes to retain that image of the past which unexpectedly appears to man singled out by history at a moment of danger. The danger affects both the content of the tradition and its receivers. The same threat hangs over both: that of becoming a tool of the ruling classes. In every era the attempt must be made anew to wrest tradition away from a conformism that is about to overpower it. The Messiah comes not only as the redeemer, he comes as the subduer of Antichrist. Only that historian will have the gift of fanning the spark of hope in the past who is firmly convinced that *even the dead* will not be safe from the enemy if he wins. And this enemy has not ceased to be victorious.

**VII**

*Consider the darkness and the great cold*
*In this vale which resounds with mysery.*
— Brecht, THE THREEPENNY OPERA

To historians who wish to relive an era, Fustel de Coulanges recommends that they blot out everything they know about the later course of history. There is no better way of characterizing the method with which historical materialism has broken. It is a process of empathy whose origin is the indolence of the heart, *acedia,* which despairs of grasping and holding the genuine historical image as it flares up briefly. Among medieval theologians it was regarded as the root cause of sadness. Flaubert, who was familiar with it, wrote: *"Peu de gens devineront combien il a fallu être triste pour ressusciter Carthage."*[1] The nature of this sadness stands out more clearly if one asks with whom the adherents of historicism actually empathize. The answer is inevitable: with the victor. And all rulers are the heirs of those who conquered before them. Hence, empathy with the victor invariably benefits the rulers. Historical materialists know what that means. Whoever has emerged victorious participates to this day in the triumphal procession in which the present rulers step over those who are lying prostrate. According to traditional practice, the spoils are carried along in the procession. They are called cultural treasures, and a historical materialist views them with cautious detachment. For without exception the cultural treasures he surveys have an origin which he cannot contemplate without horror. They owe their existence not only to the efforts of the great minds and talents who have created them, but also to the anonymous toil of their contemporaries. There is no document of civilization which is not at the same time a document of barbarism. And just as such a document is not free of barbarism, barbarism taints also the manner in which it was transmitted from one owner to another. A historical materialist therefore dissociates himself from it as far as possible. He regards it as his task to brush history against the grain.

**VIII**

The tradition of the oppressed teaches us that the "state of emergency" in which we live is not the exception but the rule. We must attain to a conception of history that is in keeping with this insight. Then we shall clearly realize that it is our task to bring about a real state of emergency, and this will improve our position in the struggle against Fascism. One reason why Fascism has a chance is that in the name of progress its opponents treat it as a historical norm. The current amazement that the things we are experiencing are "still" possible in the twentieth century is *not* philosophical. This amazement is not the beginning of knowledge—unless it is the knowledge that the view of history which gives rise to it is untenable.

**IX**

*Mein Flügel ist zum Schwung bereit,*
*ich kehrte gern zurück,*
*denn blieb ich auch lebendige Zeit,*
*ich hätte wenig Glück.*
— Gerhard Scholem, "Gruss vom Angelus"[2]

A Klee painting named "Angelus Novus" shows an angel looking as though he is about to move away from something he is fixedly contemplating. His eyes are staring, his mouth is open, his wings are spread. This is how one pictures the angel of history. His face is turned toward the past. Where we perceive a chain of events, he sees one single catastrophe which keeps piling wreckage upon wreckage and hurls it in front of his feet. The angel would like to stay, awaken the dead, and make whole what has been smashed. But a storm is blowing from Paradise; it has got caught in his wings with such violence that the angel can no longer close them. This storm irresistibly propels him into the future to which his back is turned, while the pile of debris before him grows skyward. This storm is what we call progress.

X

The themes which monastic discipline assigned to friars for meditation were designed to turn them away from the world and its affairs. The thoughts which we are developing here originate from similar considerations. At a moment when the politicians in whom the opponents of Fascism had placed their hopes are prostrate and confirm their defeat by betraying their own cause, these observations are intended to disentangle the political worldlings from the snares in which the traitors have entrapped them. Our consideration proceeds from the insight that the politicians' stubborn faith in progress, their confidence in their "mass basis," and, finally, their servile integration in an uncontrollable apparatus have been three aspects of the same thing. It seeks to convey an idea of the high price our accustomed thinking will have to pay for a conception of history that avoids any complicity with the thinking to which these politicians continue to adhere.

XI

The conformism which has been part and parcel of Social Democracy from the beginning attaches not only to its political tactics but to its economic views as well. It is one reason for its later breakdown. Nothing has corrupted the German working class so much as the notion that it was moving with the current. It regarded technological devel-

opments as the fall of the stream with which it thought it was moving. From there it was but a step to the illusion that the factory work which was supposed to tend toward technological progress constituted a political achievement. The old Protestant ethics of work was resurrected among German workers in secularized form. The Gotha Program[3] already bears traces of this confusion, defining labor as "the source of all wealth and all culture." Smelling a rat, Marx countered that ". . . the man who possesses no other property than his labor power" must of necessity become "the slave of other men who have made themselves the owners. . . ." However, the confusion spread, and soon thereafter Josef Dietzgen proclaimed: "The savior of modern times is called work. The . . . improvement . . . of labor constitutes the wealth which is now able to accomplish what no redeemer has ever been able to do." This vulgar-Marxist conception of the nature of labor bypasses the question of how its products might benefit the workers while still not being at their disposal. It recognizes only the progress in the mastery of nature, not the retrogression of society; it already displays the technocratic features later encountered in Fascism. Among these is a conception of nature which differs ominously from the one in the Socialist utopias before the 1848 revolution. The new conception of labor amounts to the exploitation of nature, which with naïve complacency is contrasted with the exploitation of the proletariat. Compared with this positivistic conception, Fourier's fantasies, which have so often been ridiculed, prove to be surprisingly sound. According to Fourier, as a result of efficient cooperative labor, four moons would illuminate the earthly night, the ice would recede from the poles, sea water would no longer taste salty, and beasts of prey would do man's bidding. All this illustrates a kind of labor which, far from exploiting nature, is capable of delivering her of the creations which lie dormant in her womb as potentials. Nature, which, as Dietzgen puts it, "exists gratis," is a complement to the corrupted conception of labor.

## XII

*We need history, but not the way a spoiled loafer in the garden of knowledge needs it.*
—Nietzsche, OF THE USE AND ABUSE OF HISTORY

Not man or men but the struggling, oppressed class itself is the depository of historical knowledge. In Marx it appears as the last enslaved class, as the avenger that completes the task of liberation in the name of generations of the downtrodden. This conviction, which had a brief resurgence in the Spartacist group,[4] has always been objectionable to Social Democrats. Within three decades they managed virtually to erase the name of Blanqui, though it had been the rallying sound that had reverberated through the preceding century. Social Democracy thought fit to assign to the working class the role of the redeemer of future generations, in this way cutting the sinews of its greatest strength. This training made the working class forget both its hatred and its spirit of sacrifice, for both are nourished by the image of enslaved ancestors rather than that of liberated grandchildren.

## XIII

*Every day our cause becomes clearer and people get smarter.*
—Wilhelm Dietzgen, DIE RELIGION DER SOZIALDEMOKRATIE

Social Democratic theory, and even more its practice, have been formed by a conception of progress which did not adhere to reality but made dogmatic claims. Progress as pictured in the minds of Social Democrats was, first of all, the progress of mankind itself (and not just advances in men's ability and knowledge). Secondly, it was something boundless, in keeping with the infinite perfectibility of mankind. Thirdly, progress was regarded as irresistible, something that automatically pursued a straight or spiral course. Each of these predicates is controversial and open to criticism. However, when the chips are down, criticism must penetrate beyond these predicates and focus on something that they have in common. The concept of the historical progress of mankind cannot be sundered from the concept of its progression through a homogeneous, empty time. A critique of the concept of such a progression must be the basis of any criticism of the concept of progress itself.

## XIV

*Origin is the goal.*
—Karl Kraus, WORTE IN VERSEN, Vol. I

History is the subject of a structure whose site is not homogeneous, empty time, but time filled by the presence of the now [*Jetztzeit*].[5] Thus, to Robespierre ancient Rome was a past charged with the time of the now which he blasted out of the continuum of history. The French Revolution viewed itself as Rome reincarnate. It evoked ancient Rome the way fashion evokes costumes of the past. Fashion has a flair for the topical, no matter where it stirs in the thickets of long ago; it is a tiger's leap into the past. This jump, however, takes place in an arena where the ruling class gives the commands. The same leap in the open air of history is the dialectical one, which is how Marx understood the revolution.

## XV

The awareness that they are about to make the continuum of history explode is characteristic of the revolutionary classes at the moment of their action. The great revolution introduced a new calendar. The initial day of a calendar serves as a historical time-lapse camera. And, basically, it is the same day that keeps recurring in the guise of holidays, which are days of remembrance. Thus the calendars do not measure time as clocks do; they are monuments of a historical consciousness of which not the slightest trace has been apparent in Europe in the past hundred years. In the July revolution an incident occurred which showed this consciousness still alive. On the first evening of fighting it turned out that the clocks in towers were being fired on simultaneously and independently from several places in Paris. An eye-witness, who may have owed his insight to the rhyme, wrote as follows:

Qui le croirait! on dit, qu'irrités contre
    l'heure
De nouveaux Josués au pied de chaque
    tour,
Tiraient sur les cadrans pour arrêter le jour.[6]

## XVI

A historical materialist cannot do without the notion of a present which is not a transition, but in which time stands still and has come to a stop. For this notion defines the present in which he himself is writing history. Historicism gives the "eternal" image of the past; historical materialism supplies a unique experience with the past. The historical materialist leaves it to others to be drained by the whore called "Once upon a time" in historicism's bordello. He remains in control of his powers, man enough to blast open the continuum of history.

## XVII

Historicism rightly culminates in universal history. Materialistic historiography differs from it as to method more clearly than from any other kind. Universal history has no theoretical armature. Its method is additive; it musters a mass of data to fill the homogeneous, empty time. Materialistic historiography, on the other hand, is based on a constructive principle. Thinking involves not only the flow of thoughts, but their arrest as well. Where thinking suddenly stops in a configuration pregnant with tensions, it gives that configuration a shock, by which it crystalizes into a monad. A historical materialist approaches a historical subject only where he encounters it as a monad. In this structure he recognizes the sign of a Messianic cessation of happening, or, put differently, a revolutionary chance in the fight for the oppressed past. He takes cognizance of it in order to blast a specific era out of the homogeneous course of history—blasting a specific life out of the era or a specific work out of the lifework. As a result of this method the lifework is preserved in this work and at the same time canceled[7] in the lifework, the era; and in the era, the entire course of history. The nourishing fruit of the historically understood contains time as a precious but tasteless seed.

## XVIII

"In relation to the history of organic life on earth," writes a modern biologist, "the paltry fifty millennia of *homo sapiens* constitute something like two seconds at the close of a twenty-four-hour day. On this scale, the history of civilized mankind would fill one-fifth of the last second of the last hour." The present, which, as a model of Messianic time, comprises the entire history of mankind in an enormous abridgment, coincides exactly with the stature which the history of mankind has in the universe.

## A

Historicism contents itself with establishing a causal connection between various moments in history. But no fact that is a cause is for that very reason historical. It became historical posthumously, as it were, through events that may be separated from it by thousands of years. A historian who takes this as his point of departure stops telling the sequence of events like the beads of a rosary. Instead, he grasps the *constellation* which his own era has formed with a definite earlier one. Thus he establishes a conception of the present as the "time of the now" which is shot through with chips of Messianic time.

## B

The soothsayers who found out from time what it had in store certainly did not experience time as either homogeneous or empty. Anyone who keeps this in mind will perhaps get an idea of how past times were experienced in remembrance—namely, in just the same way. We know that the Jews were prohibited from investigating the future. The Torah and the prayers instruct them in remembrance, however. This stripped the future of its magic, to which all those succumb

who turn to the soothsayers for enlightenment. This does not imply, however, that for the Jews the future turned into homogeneous, empty time. For every second of time was the strait gate through which the Messiah might enter.

*Translated by Harry Zohn*

## NOTES

1. "Few will be able to guess how sad one had to be in order to resuscitate Carthage."

2. *My wing is ready for flight,*
*I would like to turn back.*
*If I stayed timeless time,*
*I would have little luck.*

3. The Gotha Congress of 1875 united the two German Socialist parties, one led by Ferdinand Lassalle, the other by Karl Marx and Wilhelm Liebknecht. The program, drafted by Liebknecht and Lassalle, was severely attacked by Karl Marx in London. See his "Critique of the Gotha Program."

4. Leftist group, founded by Karl Liebknecht and Rosa Luxemburg at the beginning of World War I in opposition to the pro-war policies of the German Socialist party, later absorbed by the Communist party.

5. Benjamin says *"Jetztzeit"* and indicates by the quotation marks that he does not simply mean an equivalent to *Gegenwart*, that is, present. He clearly is thinking of the mystical *nunc stans*.

6. Who would have believed it! we are told that new Joshuas
at the foot of every tower, as though irritated with time itself, fired at the dials in order to stop the day.

7. The Hegelian term *aufheben* in its threefold meaning: to preserve, to elevate, to cancel.

# 28

# Raymond Williams 1921–1988

Raymond Williams was a professor of drama at Jesus College, Cambridge. Among his nearly twenty published books are *Culture and Society, 1780–1950* (1958); *The Long Revolution* (1961); *Drama from Ibsen to Brecht* (1969); *The English Novel from Dickens to Lawrence* (1970); *The Country and the City* (1973); *Keywords* (1976); *Marxism and Literature* (1977); *Politics and Letters* (interviews, 1979); *Problems in Materialism and Culture* (1981); *Culture* (1981); *The Sociology of Culture* (1982); *Writing in Society* (1983); and four novels, published between 1960 and 1979.

Williams may be the most important British Marxist literary critic and theoretician of culture since World War II. With the publication of *Culture and Society* in 1958 Williams single-handedly changed the image of Marxist literary criticism in the English-speaking world from simplistic notions of culture as economically determined and rigid demands for political orthodoxy to a subtle and complex understanding of all writers and all writing as embedded in specific, concrete relations, all writing as responses to real situations. His impressive body of work spanning the next three decades has continued to demonstrate his keen awareness and understanding of the deep sociology of culture. From close readings of both canonical and mass cultural works to more general, theoretical essays on culture, he seeks always to convince us of the shaping power of social and economic practices and institutions, and of the significant function and effects of cultural practice within the larger social context.

"Base and Superstructure in Marxist Cultural Theory" is drawn from his selected essays, *Problems in Materialism and Culture*. It appeared originally in *New Left Review* in 1973. Much of the essay appeared as well in *Marxism and Literature* in 1977. In this essay Williams is grappling with the central issue for Marxist theory of the determination of culture (and consciousness) by human social existence. He is at pains here to refute the "straw man" of vulgar Marxist economic determinism in which culture is seen as some simple, direct "reflection" of economic forces. At the same time he uses Antonio Gramsci's notion of "hegemony" to argue for the validity of a subtle and carefully argued Marxist position with regard to the real power of dominant political and economic forces in cultural as in other aspects of life. Another key aspect of this influential essay is Williams's formulation—which he develops further in *Marxism and Literature*—with regard to dominant, residual, and emergent strains, which always exist in varying strengths and different configurations, and in differing relations to one another, at any given moment in any culture, with an equally universal struggle, within emergent cultural practices and formations, between the alternative and the oppositional. This schema has been widely taken up by other Marxist critics (see, for example, Fredric Jameson's various essays on postmodernism), and provides an extremely useful analytical tool. Williams's work in the sociology of culture has laid the groundwork for much of the most important contemporary work in the area of cultural studies.

# Base and Superstructure in Marxist Cultural Theory

Any modern approach to a Marxist theory of culture must begin by considering the proposition of a determining base and a determined superstructure. From a strictly theoretical point of view this is not, in fact, where we might choose to begin. It would be in many ways preferable if we could begin from a proposition which originally was equally central, equally authentic: namely the proposition that social being determines consciousness. It is not that the two propositions necessarily deny each other or are in contradiction. But the proposition of base and superstructure, with its figurative element, with its suggestion of a fixed and definite spatial relationship, constitutes, at least in certain hands, a very specialized and at times unacceptable version of the other proposition. Yet in the transition from Marx to Marxism, and in the development of mainstream Marxism itself, the proposition of the determining base and the determined superstructure has been commonly held to be the key to Marxist cultural analysis.

It is important, as we try to analyse this proposition, to be aware that the term of relationship which is involved, that is to say "determines," is of great linguistic and theoretical complexity. The language of determination and even more of determinism was inherited from idealist and especially theological accounts of the world and man. It is significant that it is in one of his familiar inversions, his contradictions of received propositions, that Marx uses the word which becomes, in English translation, "determines" (the usual but not invariable German word is *bestimmen*). He is opposing an ideology that had been insistent on the power of certain forces outside man, or, in its secular version, on an abstract determining consciousness. Marx's own proposition explicitly denies this, and puts the origin of determination in men's own activities. Nevertheless, the particular history and continuity of the term serves to remind us that there are, within ordinary use—and this is true of most of the major European languages—quite different possible meanings and implications of the word "determine." There is, on the one hand, from its theological inheritance, the notion of an external cause which totally predicts or prefigures, indeed totally controls a subsequent activity. But there is also, from the experience of social practice, a notion of determination as setting limits, exerting pressures.[1]

Now there is clearly a difference between a process of setting limits and exerting pressures, whether by some external force or by the internal laws of a particular development, and that other process in which a subsequent content is essentially prefigured, predicted and controlled by a preexisting external force. Yet it is fair to say, looking at many applications of Marxist cultural analysis, that it is the second sense, the notion of prefiguration, prediction or control, which has often explicitly or implicitly been used.

## SUPERSTRUCTURE: QUALIFICATIONS AND AMENDMENTS

The term of relationship is then the first thing that we have to examine in this proposition, but we have to do this by going on to look at the related terms themselves. "Super-structure" *(Überbau)* has had most attention. In common usage, after Marx, it acquired a main sense of a unitary "area" within which all cultural and ideological activities could be placed. But already in Marx himself, in the later correspondence of Engels, and at many points in the subsequent Marxist tradition, qualifications were made about the determined character of certain superstructural activities. The first kind of qualification had to do with delays in time, with complications, and with certain indirect or relatively distant relationships. The simplest notion of a superstructure, which is still by no means entirely abandoned, had been the reflection, the imitation or the reproduction of the reality of the base in the superstructure in a more or less direct way. Positivist notions of reflection and reproduction of course directly supported this. But since in many real cultural activities this relationship cannot be found, or cannot be found without effort or even violence to the material or practice being studied, the notion was introduced of delays in time, the famous lags; of various technical complications; and of indirectness, in which certain kinds of activity in the cultural sphere—philosophy, for example—were situated at a greater distance from the primary economic activities. That was the first stage of qualification of the notion of superstructure: in effect, an operational qualification. The second stage was related but more fundamental, in that the process of the relationship itself was more substantially looked at. This was the kind of reconsideration which gave rise to the modern notion of "mediation," in which something more than simple reflection or reproduction—indeed something radically different from either reflection or reproduction—actively occurs. In the later twentieth century there is the notion of "homologous structures," where there may be no direct or easily apparent similarity, and certainly nothing like reflection or reproduc-

tion, between the superstructural process and the reality of the base, but in which there is an essential homology or correspondence of structures, which can be discovered by analysis. This is not the same notion as "mediation," but it is the same kind of amendment in that the relationship between the base and the superstructure is not supposed to be direct, nor simply operationally subject to lags and complications and indirectnesses, but that of its nature it is not direct reproduction.

These qualifications and amendments are important. But it seems to me that what has not been looked at with equal care is the received notion of the "base" (*Basis, Grundlage*). And indeed I would argue that the base is the more important concept to look at if we are to understand the realities of cultural process. In many uses of the proposition of base and superstructure, as a matter of verbal habit, "the base" has come to be considered virtually as an object, or in less crude cases, it has been considered in essentially uniform and usually static ways. "The base" is the real social existence of man. "The base" is the real relations of production corresponding to a stage of development of the material productive forces. "The base" is a mode of production at a particular stage of its development. We make and repeat propositions of this kind, but the usage is then very different from Marx's emphasis on productive activities, in particular structural relations, constituting the foundation of all other activities. For while a particular stage of the development of production can be discovered and made precise by analysis, it is never in practice either uniform or static. It is indeed one of the central propositions of Marx's sense of history that there are deep contradictions in the relationships of production and in the consequent social relationships. There is therefore the continual possibility of the dynamic variation of these forces. Moreover, when these forces are considered, as Marx always considers them, as the specific activities and relationships of real men, they mean something very much more active, more complicated and more contradictory than the developed metaphorical notion of "the base" could possibly allow us to realize.

## THE BASE AND THE PRODUCTIVE FORCES

So we have to say that when we talk of "the base," we are talking of a process and not a state. And we cannot ascribe to that process certain fixed properties for subsequent translation to the variable processes of the superstructure. Most people who have wanted to make the ordinary proposition more reasonable have concentrated on refining the notion of superstructure. But I would say that each term of the proposition has to be revalued in a particular direction. We have to revalue "determination" towards the setting of limits and the exertion of pressure, and away from a predicted, prefigured and controlled content. We have to revalue "superstructure" towards a related range of cultural practices, and away from a reflected, reproduced or specifically dependent content. And, crucially, we have to revalue "the base" away from the notion of a fixed economic or technological abstraction, and towards the specific activities of men in real social and economic relationships, containing fundamental contradictions and variations and therefore always in a state of dynamic process.

It is worth observing one further implication behind the customary definitions. "The base" has come to include, especially in certain twentieth-century developments, a strong and limiting sense of basic industry. The emphasis on heavy industry, even, has played a certain cultural role. And this raises a more general problem, for we find ourselves forced to look again at the ordinary notion of "productive forces." Clearly what

we are examining in the base is primary productive forces. Yet some very crucial distinctions have to be made here. It is true that in his analysis of capitalist production Marx considered "productive work" in a very particular and specialized sense corresponding to that mode of production. There is a difficult passage in the *Grundrisse* in which he argues that while the man who makes a piano is a productive worker, there is a real question whether the man who distributes the piano is also a productive worker; but he probably is, since he contributes to the realization of surplus value. Yet when it comes to the man who plays the piano, whether to himself or to others, there is no question: he is not a productive worker at all. So piano-maker is base, but pianist superstructure. As a way of considering cultural activity, and incidentally the economics of modern cultural activity, this is very clearly a dead-end. But for any theoretical clarification it is crucial to recognize that Marx was there engaged in an analysis of a particular kind of production, that is capitalist commodity production. Within his analysis of this mode, he had to give to the notion of "productive labour" and "productive forces" a specialized sense of primary work on materials in a form which produced commodities. But this has narrowed remarkably, and in a cultural context very damagingly, from his more central notion of *productive forces,* in which, to give just brief reminders, the most important thing a worker ever produces is himself, himself in the fact of that kind of labour, or the broader historical emphasis of men producing themselves, themselves and their history. Now when we talk of the base, and of primary productive forces, it matters very much whether we are referring, as in one degenerate form of this proposition became habitual, to primary production within the terms of capitalist economic relationships, or to the primary production of society itself, and of men themselves, the material production and reproduction of real life. If we have the broad sense of productive forces, we look at the whole question of the base differently, and we are then less tempted to dismiss as superstructural, and in that sense as merely secondary, certain vital productive social forces, which are in the broad sense, from the beginning, basic.

## USES OF TOTALITY

Yet, because of the difficulties of the ordinary proposition of base and superstructure, there was an alternative and very important development, an emphasis primarily associated with Lukács, on a social "totality." The totality of social practices was opposed to this layered notion of base and a consequent superstructure. This concept of a totality of practices is compatible with the notion of social being determining consciousness, but it does not necessarily interpret this process in terms of a base and a superstructure. Now the language of totality has become common, and it is indeed in many ways more acceptable than the notion of base and superstructure. But with one very important reservation. It is very easy for the notion of totality to empty of its essential content the original Marxist proposition. For if we come to say that society is composed of a large number of social practices which form a concrete social whole, and if we give to each practice a certain specific recognition, adding only that they interact, relate and combine in very complicated ways, we are at one level much more obviously talking about reality, but we are at another level withdrawing from the claim that there is any process of determination. And this I, for one, would be very unwilling to do. Indeed, the key question to ask about any notion of totality in cultural theory is this: whether the notion of totality includes the notion of intention.

If totality is simply concrete, if it is simply

the recognition of a large variety of miscellaneous and contemporaneous practices, then it is essentially empty of any content that could be called Marxist. Intention, the notion of intention, restores the key question, or rather the key emphasis. For while it is true that any society is a complex whole of such practices, it is also true that any society has a specific organization, a specific structure, and that the principles of this organization and structure can be seen as directly related to certain social intentions, intentions by which we define the society, intentions which in all our experience have been the rule of a particular class. One of the unexpected consequences of the crudeness of the base/superstructure model has been the too easy acceptance of models which appear less crude—models of totality or of a complex whole—but which exclude the facts of social intention, the class character of a particular society and so on. And this reminds us of how much we lose if we abandon the superstructural emphasis altogether. Thus I have great difficulty in seeing processes of art and thought as superstructural in the sense of the formula as it is commonly used. But in many areas of social and political thought—certain kinds of ratifying theory, certain kinds of law, certain kinds of institution, which after all in Marx's original formulations were very much part of the superstructure—in all that kind of social apparatus, and in a decisive area of political and ideological activity and construction, if we fail to see a superstructural element we fail to recognize reality at all. These laws, constitutions, theories, ideologies, which are so often claimed as natural, or as having universal validity or significance, simply have to be seen as expressing and ratifying the domination of a particular class. Indeed the difficulty of revising the formula of base and superstructure has had much to do with the perception of many militants—who have to fight such institutions and notions as well as fighting economic battles—

that if these institutions and their ideologies are not perceived as having that kind of dependent and ratifying relationship, if their claims to universal validity or legitimacy are not denied and fought, then the class character of the society can no longer be seen. And this has been the effect of some versions of totality as the description of cultural process. Indeed I think we can properly use the notion of totality only when we combine it with that other crucial Marxist concept of "hegemony."

## THE COMPLEXITY OF HEGEMONY

It is Gramsci's great contribution to have emphasized hegemony, and also to have understood it at a depth which is, I think, rare. For hegemony supposes the existence of something which is truly total, which is not merely secondary or superstructural, like the weak sense of ideology, but which is lived at such a depth, which saturates the society to such an extent, and which, as Gramsci put it, even constitutes the substance and limit of common sense for most people under its sway, that it corresponds to the reality of social experience very much more clearly than any notions derived from the formula of base and superstructure. For if ideology were merely some abstract, imposed set of notions, if our social and political and cultural ideas and assumptions and habits were merely the result of specific manipulation, of a kind of overt training which might be simply ended or withdrawn, then the society would be very much easier to move and to change than in practice it has ever been or is. This notion of hegemony as deeply saturating the consciousness of a society seems to me to be fundamental. And hegemony has the advantage over general notions of totality, that it at the same time emphasizes the facts of domination.

Yet there are times when I hear discussions of hegemony and feel that it too, as a concept,

is being dragged back to the relatively simple, uniform and static notion which "superstructure" in ordinary use had become. Indeed I think that we have to give a very complex account of hegemony if we are talking about any real social formation. Above all we have to give an account which allows for its elements of real and constant change. We have to emphasize that hegemony is not singular; indeed that its own internal structures are highly complex, and have continually to be renewed, recreated and defended; and by the same token, that they can be continually challenged and in certain respects modified. That is why instead of speaking simply of "the hegemony," "a hegemony," I would propose a model which allows for this kind of variation and contradiction, its sets of alternatives and its processes of change.

For one thing that is evident in some of the best Marxist cultural analysis is that it is very much more at home in what one might call *epochal* questions than in what one has to call *historical* questions. That is to say, it is usually very much better at distinguishing the large features of different epochs of society, as commonly between feudal and bourgeois, than at distinguishing between different phases of bourgeois society, and different moments within these phases: that true historical process which demands a much greater precision and delicacy of analysis than the always striking epochal analysis which is concerned with main lineaments and features.

The theoretical model which I have been trying to work with is this. I would say first that in any society, in any particular period, there is a central system of practices, meanings and values, which we can properly call dominant and effective. This implies no presumption about its value. All I am saying is that it is central. Indeed I would call it a corporate system, but this might be confusing, since Gramsci uses "corporate" to mean the subordinate as opposed to the general and dominant elements of hegemony. In any case what I have in mind is the central, effective and dominant system of meanings and values, which are not merely abstract but which are organized and lived. That is why hegemony is not to be understood at the level of mere opinion or mere manipulation. It is a whole body of practices and expectations; our assignments of energy, our ordinary understanding of the nature of man and of his world. It is a set of meanings and values which as they are experienced as practices appear as reciprocally confirming. It thus constitutes a sense of reality for most people in the society, a sense of absolute because experienced reality beyond which it is very difficult for most members of the society to move, in most areas of their lives. But this is not, except in the operation of a moment of abstract analysis, in any sense a static system. On the contrary we can only understand an effective and dominant culture if we understand the real social process on which it depends: I mean the process of incorporation. The modes of incorporation are of great social significance. The educational institutions are usually the main agencies of the transmission of an effective dominant culture, and this is now a major economic as well as a cultural activity; indeed it is both in the same moment. Moreover, at a philosophical level, at the true level of theory and at the level of the history of various practices, there is a process which I call the *selective tradition:* that which, within the terms of an effective dominant culture, is always passed off as "*the* tradition," "*the* significant past." But always the selectivity is the point; the way in which from a whole possible area of past and present, certain meanings and practices are chosen for emphasis, certain other meanings and practices are neglected and excluded. Even more crucially, some of these meanings and practices are reinterpreted, diluted, or put into forms which support or at least do not contradict other elements within the effective dominant culture. The processes of education; the processes of a much wider social training within institutions like the family; the practical definitions and organization of work; the selective tradition at an intellectual and theoretical level: all these forces are involved in a continual making and remaking of an effective dominant culture, and on them, as experienced, as built into our living, its reality depends. If what we learn there were merely an imposed ideology, or if it were only the isolable meanings and practices of the ruling class, or of a section of the ruling class, which gets imposed on others, occupying merely the top of our minds, it would be—and one would be glad—a very much easier thing to overthrow.

It is not only the depths to which this process reaches, selecting and organizing and interpreting our experience. It is also that it is continually active and adjusting; it isn't just the past, the dry husks of ideology which we can more easily discard. And this can only be so, in a complex society, if it is something more substantial and more flexible than any abstract imposed ideology. Thus we have to recognize the alternative meanings and values, the alternative opinions and attitudes, even some alternative senses of the world, which can be accommodated and tolerated within a particular effective and dominant culture. This has been much under-emphasized in our notions of a superstructure, and even in some notions of hegemony. And the under-emphasis opens the way for retreat to an indifferent complexity. In the practice of politics, for example, there are certain truly incorporated modes of what are nevertheless, within those terms, real oppositions, that are felt and fought out. Their existence within the incorporation is recognizable by the fact that, whatever the degree of internal conflict or internal variation, they do not in practice go beyond the limits of the central effective and dominant definitions. This is true, for example, of the practice of parliamentary politics, though its internal oppositions are real. It is true about a whole range of practices and arguments, in any real society, which can by no means be reduced to an ideological cover, but which can nevertheless be properly analysed as in my sense corporate, if we find that, whatever the degree of internal controversy and variation, they do not in the end exceed the limits of the central corporate definitions.

But if we are to say this, we have to think again about the sources of that which is not corporate; of those practices, experiences, meanings, values which are not part of the effective dominant culture. We can express this in two ways. There is clearly something that we can call alternative to the effective dominant culture, and there is something else that we can call oppositional, in a true sense. The degree of existence of these alternative and oppositional forms is itself a matter of constant historical variation in real circumstances. In certain societies it is possible to find areas of social life in which quite real alternatives are at least left alone. (If they are made available, of course, they are part of the corporate organization.) The existence of the possibility of opposition, and of its articulation, its degree of openness, and so on, again depends on very precise social and political forces. The facts of alternative and oppositional forms of social life and culture, in relation to the effective and dominant culture, have then to be recognized as subject to historical variation, and as having sources which are very significant as a fact about the dominant culture itself.

## RESIDUAL AND EMERGENT CULTURES

I have next to introduce a further distinction, between *residual* and *emergent* forms, both of alternative and of oppositional culture. By "residual" I mean that some experiences, meanings and values, which cannot be veri-

fied or cannot be expressed in terms of the dominant culture, are nevertheless lived and practised on the basis of the residue—cultural as well as social—of some previous social formation. There is a real case of this in certain religious values, by contrast with the very evident incorporation of most religious meanings and values into the dominant system. The same is true, in a culture like Britain, of certain notions derived from a rural past, which have a very significant popularity. A residual culture is usually at some distance from the effective dominant culture, but one has to recognize that, in real cultural activities, it may get incorporated into it. This is because some part of it, some version of it—and especially if the residue is from some major area of the past—will in many cases have had to be incorporated if the effective dominant culture is to make sense in those areas. It is also because at certain points a dominant culture cannot allow too much of this kind of practice and experience outside itself, at least without risk. Thus the pressures are real, but certain genuinely residual meanings and practices in some important cases survive.

By "emergent" I mean, first, that new meanings and values, new practices, new significances and experiences, are continually being created. But there is then a much earlier attempt to incorporate them, just because they are part—and yet not a defined part—of effective contemporary practice. Indeed it is significant in our own period how very early this attempt is, how alert the dominant culture now is to anything that can be seen as emergent. We have then to see, first, as it were a temporal relation between a dominant culture and on the one hand a residual and on the other hand an emergent culture. But we can only understand this if we can make distinctions, that usually require very precise analysis, between residual-incorporated and residual not incorporated, and between emergent-incorporated and emergent not incorporated. It is an important fact about any particular society, how far it reaches into the whole range of human practices and experiences in an attempt at incorporation. It may be true of some earlier phases of bourgeois society, for example, that there were some areas of experience which it was willing to dispense with, which it was prepared to assign as the sphere of private or artistic life, and as being no particular business of society or the state. This went along with certain kinds of political tolerance, even if the reality of that tolerance was malign neglect. But I am sure it is true of the society that has come into existence since the last war, that progressively, because of developments in the social character of labour, in the social character of communications, and in the social character of decision, it extends much further than ever before in capitalist society into certain hitherto resigned areas of experience and practice and meaning. Thus the effective decision, as to whether a practice is alternative or oppositional, is often now made within a very much narrower scope. There is a simple theoretical distinction between alternative and oppositional, that is to say between someone who simply finds a different way to live and wishes to be left alone with it, and someone who finds a different way to live and wants to change the society in its light. This is usually the difference between individual and small-group solutions to social crisis and those solutions which properly belong to political and ultimately revolutionary practice. But it is often a very narrow line, in reality, between alternative and oppositional. A meaning or a practice may be tolerated as a deviation, and yet still be seen only as another particular way to live. But as the necessary area of effective dominance extends, the same meanings and practices can be seen by the dominant culture, not merely as disregarding or despising it, but as challenging it.

Now it is crucial to any Marxist theory of culture that it can give an adequate explana-

tion of the sources of these practices and meanings. We can understand, from an ordinary historical approach, at least some of the sources of residual meanings and practices. These are the results of earlier social formations, in which certain real meanings and values were generated. In the subsequent default of a particular phase of a dominant culture, there is then a reaching back to those meanings and values which were created in real societies in the past, and which still seem to have some significance because they represent areas of human experience, aspiration and achievement, which the dominant culture under-values or opposes, or even cannot recognize. But our hardest task, theoretically, is to find a non-metaphysical and non-subjectivist explanation of emergent cultural practice. Moreover, part of our answer to this question bears on the process of persistence of residual practices.

## CLASS AND HUMAN PRACTICE

We have indeed one source to hand from the central body of Marxist theory. We have the formation of a new class, the coming to consciousness of a new class. This remains, without doubt, quite centrally important. Of course, in itself, this process of formation complicates any simple model of base and superstructure. It also complicates some of the ordinary versions of hegemony, although it was Gramsci's whole purpose to see and to create by organization that hegemony of a proletarian kind which would be capable of challenging the bourgeois hegemony. We have then one central source of new practice, in the emergence of a new class. But we have also to recognize certain other kinds of source, and in cultural practice some of these are very important. I would say that we can recognize them on the basis of this proposition: that no mode of production, and therefore no dominant society or order of society, and therefore no dominant culture, in reality exhausts the full range of human practice, human energy, human intention (this range is not the inventory of some original "human nature" but, on the contrary, is that extraordinary range of variations, both practised and imagined, of which human beings are and have shown themselves to be capable). Indeed it seems to me that this emphasis is not merely a negative proposition, allowing us to account for certain things which happen outside the dominant mode. On the contrary, it is a fact about the modes of domination that they select from and consequently exclude the full range of actual and possible human practice. The difficulties of human practice outside or against the dominant mode are, of course, real. It depends very much whether it is in an area in which the dominant class and the dominant culture have an interest and a stake. If the interest and the stake are explicit, many new practices will be reached for, and if possible incorporated, or else extirpated with extraordinary vigour. But in certain areas, there will be in certain periods practices and meanings which are not reached for. There will be areas of practice and meaning which, almost by definition from its own limited character, or in its profound deformation, the dominant culture is unable in any real terms to recognize. This gives us a bearing on the observable difference between, for example, the practices of a capitalist state and a state like the contemporary Soviet Union in relation to writers. Since from the whole Marxist tradition literature was seen as an important activity, indeed a crucial activity, the Soviet state is very much sharper in investigating areas where different versions of practice, different meanings and values, are being attempted and expressed. In capitalist practice, if the thing is not making a profit, or if it is not being widely circulated, then it can for some time be overlooked, at least while

it remains alternative. When it becomes oppositional in an explicit way, it does, of course, get approached or attacked.

I am saying then that in relation to the full range of human practice at any one time, the dominant mode is a conscious selection and organization. At least in its fully formed state it is conscious. But there are always sources of actual human practice which it neglects or excludes. And these can be different in quality from the developing and articulate interests of a rising class. They can include, for example, alternative perceptions of others, in immediate personal relationships, or new perceptions of material and media, in art and science, and within certain limits these new perceptions can be practised. The relations between the two kinds of source—the emerging class and either the dominatively excluded or the more generally new practices—are by no means necessarily contradictory. At times they can be very close, and on the relations between them much in political practice depends. But culturally and as a matter of theory the areas can be seen as distinct.

Now if we go back to the cultural question in its most usual form—what are the relations between art and society, or literature and society?—in the light of the preceding discussion, we have to say first that there are no relations between literature and society in that abstracted way. The literature is there from the beginning as a practice in the society. Indeed until it and all other practices are present, the society cannot be seen as fully formed. A society is not fully available for analysis until each of its practices is included. But if we make that emphasis we must make a corresponding emphasis: that we cannot separate literature and art from other kinds of social practice, in such a way as to make them subject to quite special and distinct laws. They may have quite specific features as practices, but they cannot be separated from the general social process. Indeed one way of emphasizing this is to say, to insist, that literature is not restricted to operating in any one of the sectors I have been seeking to describe in this model. It would be easy to say, it is a familiar rhetoric, that literature operates in the emergent cultural sector, that it represents the new feelings, the new meanings, the new values. We might persuade ourselves of this theoretically, by abstract argument, but when we read much literature, over the whole range, without the sleight-of-hand of calling literature only that which we have already selected as embodying certain meanings and values at a certain scale of intensity, we are bound to recognize that the act of writing, the practices of discourse in writing and speech, the making of novels and poems and plays and theories, all this activity takes place in all areas of the culture.

Literature appears by no means only in the emergent sector, which is always, in fact, quite rare. A great deal of writing is of a residual kind, and this has been deeply true of much English literature in the last half-century. Some of its fundamental meanings and values have belonged to the cultural achievements of long-past stages of society. So widespread is this fact, and the habits of mind it supports, that in many minds "literature" and "the past" acquire a certain identity, and it is then said that there is now no literature: all that glory is over. Yet most writing, in any period, including our own, is a form of contribution to the effective dominant culture. Indeed many of the specific qualities of literature—its capacity to embody and enact and perform certain meanings and values, or to create in single particular ways what would be otherwise merely general truths—enable it to fulfill this effective function with great power. To literature, of course, we must add the visual arts and music, and in our own society the powerful arts of film and of broadcasting. But the general theoretical point should be clear. If we are looking for the relations between literature and society, we cannot either separate out this one practice from a formed body of other practices, nor when we have identified a particular practice can we give it a uniform, static and ahistorical relation to some abstract social formation. The arts of writing and the arts of creation and performance, over their whole range, are parts of the cultural process in all the different ways, the different sectors, that I have been seeking to describe. They contribute to the effective dominant culture and are a central articulation of it. They embody residual meanings and values, not all of which are incorporated, though many are. They express also and significantly some emergent practices and meanings, yet some of these may eventually be incorporated, as they reach people and begin to move them. Thus it was very evident in the sixties, in some of the emergent arts of performance, that the dominant culture reached out to transform, or seek to transform, them. In this process, of course, the dominant culture itself changes, not in its central formation, but in many of its articulated features. But then in a modern society it must always change in this way, if it is to remain dominant, if it is still to be felt as in real ways central in all our many activities and interests.

## CRITICAL THEORY AS CONSUMPTION

What then are the implications of this general analysis for the analysis of particular works of art? This is the question towards which most discussion of cultural theory seems to be directed: the discovery of a method, perhaps even a methodology, through which particular works of art can be understood and described. I would not myself agree that this is the central use of cultural theory, but let us for a moment consider it. What seems to me very striking is that nearly all forms of contemporary critical theory are theories of *consumption*. That is to say, they are concerned with understanding an object in such a way that it can profitably or correctly be consumed. The earliest stage of consumption theory was the theory of "taste," where the link between the practice and the theory was direct in the metaphor. From taste there came the more elevated notion of "sensibility," in which it was the consumption by sensibility of elevated or insightful works that was held to be the essential practice of reading, and critical activity was then a function of this sensibility. There were then more developed theories, in the 1920s with I. A. Richards, and later in New Criticism, in which the effects of consumption were studied directly. The language of the work of art as object then became more overt. "What effect does this work ('the poem' as it was ordinarily described) have on me?" Or, "what impact does it have on me?" as it was later to be put in a much wider area of communication studies. Naturally enough, the notion of the work of art as *object,* as *text,* as an isolated artifact, became central in all these later consumption theories. It was not only that the practices of *production* were then overlooked, though this fused with the notion that most important literature anyway was from the past. The real social conditions of production were in any case neglected because they were believed to be at best secondary. The true relationship was seen always as between the taste, the sensibility or the training of the reader and this isolated work, this object "as in itself it really is," as most people came to put it. But the notion of the work of art as object had a further large theoretical effect. If you ask questions about the work of art seen as object, they may include questions about the components of its production. Now, as it happened, there was a use of the formula of base and superstructure which was precisely in line with this. The components of a work of art were the real activities of the base, and you could study the object to discover these components. Sometimes you even studied the components and

then projected the object. But in any case the relationship that was looked for was one between an object and its components. But this was not only true of Marxist suppositions of a base and a superstructure. It was true also of various kinds of psychological theory, whether in the form of archetypes, or the images of the collective unconscious, or the myths and symbols which were seen as the *components* of particular works of art. Or again there was biography, or psychobiography and its like, where the components were in the man's life and the work of art was an object in which components of this kind were discovered. Even in some of the more rigorous forms of New Criticism and of structuralist criticism, this essential procedure of regarding the work as an object which has to be reduced to its components, even if later it may be reconstituted, came to persist.

## OBJECTS AND PRACTICES

Now I think the true crisis in cultural theory, in our own time, is between this view of the work of art as object and the alternative view of art as a practice. Of course it is at once argued that the work of art *is* an object: that various works have survived from the past, particular sculptures, particular paintings, particular buildings, and these are objects. This is of course true, but the same way of thinking is applied to works which have no such singular existence. There is no *Hamlet,* no *Brothers Karamazov,* no *Wuthering Heights,* in the sense that there is a particular great painting. There is no *Fifth Symphony,* there is no work in the whole area of music and dance and performance, which is an object in any way comparable to those works in the visual arts which have survived. And yet the habit of treating all such works as objects has persisted because this is a basic theoretical and practical presupposition. But in literature (especially in drama), in music and in a very wide area of the performing arts, what we permanently have are not objects but *notations*. These notations have then to be interpreted in an active way, according to the particular conventions. But indeed this is true over an even wider field. The relationship between the making of a work of art and its reception is always active, and subject to conventions, which in themselves are forms of (changing) social organization and relationship, and this is radically different from the production and consumption of an object. It is indeed an activity and a practice, and in its accessible forms, although it may in some arts have the character of a singular object, it is still only accessible through active perception and interpretation. This makes the case of notation, in arts like drama and literature and music, only a special case of a much wider truth. What this can show us here about the practice of analysis is that we have to break from the common procedure of isolating the object and then discovering its components. On the contrary we have to discover the nature of a practice and then its conditions.

Often these two procedures may in part resemble each other, but in many other cases they are of radically different kinds, and I would conclude with an observation on the way this distinction bears on the Marxist tradition of the relation between primary economic and social practices, and cultural practices. If we suppose that what is produced in cultural practice is a series of objects, we shall, as in most current forms of sociological-critical procedure, set about discovering their components. Within a Marxist emphasis these components will be from what we have been in the habit of calling the base. We then isolate certain features which we can so to say recognize in component form, or we ask what processes of transformation or mediation these components have gone through before they arrived in this accessible state.

But I am saying that we should look not for the components of a product but for the con-

ditions of a practice. When we find ourselves looking at a particular work, or group of works, often realizing, as we do so, their essential community as well as their irreducible individuality, we should find ourselves attending first to the reality of their practice and the conditions of the practice as it was then executed. And from this I think we ask essentially different questions. Take for example the way in which an object—"a text"—is related to a genre, in orthodox criticism. We identify it by certain leading features, we then assign it to a larger category, the genre, and then we may find the components of the genre in a particular social history (although in some variants of criticism not even that is done, and the genre is supposed to be some permanent category of the mind).

It is not that way of proceeding that is now required. The recognition of the relation of a collective mode and an individual project—and these are the only categories that we can initially presume—is a recognition of related practices. That is to say, the irreducibly individual projects that particular works are, may come in experience and in analysis to show resemblances which allow us to group them into collective modes. These are by no means always genres. They may exist as resemblances within and across genres. They may be the practice of a group in a period, rather than the practice of a phase in a genre. But as we discover the nature of a particular practice, and the nature of the relation between an individual project and a collective mode, we find that we are analysing, as two forms of the same process, both its active composition and its conditions of composition, and in either direction this is a complex of extending active relationships. This means, of course, that we have no built-in procedures of the kind which is indicated by the fixed character of an object. We have the principles of the relations of practices, within a discoverably intentional organization, and we have the available hypotheses of dominant, residual and emergent. But what we are actively seeking is the true practice which has been alienated to an object, and the true conditions of practice—whether as literary conventions or as social relationships—which have been alienated to components or to mere background.

As a general proposition this is only an emphasis, but it seems to me to suggest at once the point of break and the point of departure, in practical and theoretical work, within an active and self-renewing Marxist cultural tradition.

**NOTE**

1. For a further discussion of the range of meanings in "determine" see *Keywords,* London 1976, pp. 87–91.

# 29

# Terry Eagleton
# 1943–

Terry Eagleton was educated at Cambridge University (where he studied under Raymond Williams) and since 1969 has been a fellow and tutor at Wadham College, Oxford University. His books include *Shakespeare and Society* (1967); *The Body As Language: Outlines of a "New Left" Theology* (1970); *Myths of Power: A Marxist Study of the Brontes* (1976); *Criticism and Ideology* (1978); *Walter Benjamin, or Towards a Revolutionary Criticism* (1981); *The Rape of Clarissa: Writing, Sexuality and Class Struggle in Samuel Richardson* (1982); *Literary Theory: An Introduction* (1983); *The Function of Criticism, From the Spectator to Post-Structuralism* (1984); *Against the Grain* (1986); *Raymond Williams: Critical Perspectives* (1989); *Ideology of the Aesthetic* (1990); *Saint Oscar* (1990); *Saints and Scholars* (1990) *The Significance of Theory* (1990); and *Ideology: An Introduction* (1991).

Eagleton may be the most prominent among the younger generation of Marxist literary critics in the English-speaking world. His work is subtle and sophisticated but also highly partisan and polemical in tone. Like Fredric Jameson, Eagleton shows the influence of French poststructuralist thinkers, especially Lacan and Derrida, and the Marxists Althusser and Machery. As one of his titles suggests, his work also draws on Walter Benjamin. Eagleton's work in cultural theory brings together Frankfurt school Marxism of the 1930s, recent and contemporary theories of discourse that have their root in Saussure and the Formalists, and the tradition of philosophical linguistics, especially Wittgenstein.

"Brecht and Rhetoric" (1982) is one of Eagleton's "selected essays" collected in *Against the Grain*. It originally appeared in *New Literary History*. In this highly condensed essay Eagleton establishes convincingly the kinship between the modernist Marxism of Brecht (and Benjamin) and "left" deconstruction. Eagleton argues that in Brecht we have a prototype for the deconstruction through theory of the illusions of individualism and selfhood. Thus Eagleton joins his Marxist project to the post-structuralist critique of the subject. The self-reflexive, critical position Eagleton advocates—the position toward the self and the subject that is the result or effect of Brechtian theatre—links his work to that of Jameson, Said, and other contemporary oppositional critics.

Two explanatory notes may prove helpful: First, when Eagleton speaks early on of "alienated acting" and the "A-effect," he is referring to a notion at the heart of Brechtian dramaturgy. The word in German is *Verfremdung,* or the "V-effect." The referent is Brecht's idea that there should be a deliberate separation of space between the actor and the role or the words he says. This is part of a larger goal of destroying the illusion of reality in the theater. (Brecht's notion is akin to the "making strange" of the Russian Formalists.) Second, when Eagleton refers to "a piece of *plumpes*

*Denken,"* he refers to Brecht's famous injunction to "think crudely!"—not to get so involved with the complexities of theoretical argument that we lose sight of class conflict, exploitation, and oppression.

# Brecht and Rhetoric

In a notorious comment, J. L. Austin once wrote that "a performative utterance will, for example, be *in a peculiar way* hollow or void if said by an actor on a stage."[1] Perhaps Austin only ever attended amateur theatricals. Bertolt Brecht approved of amateur acting, since the occasional flatness and hollowness of its utterances seemed to him an unwitting form of alienation effect. For Brecht, the whole point of acting was that it should be in a peculiar sense hollow or void. Alienated acting hollows out the imaginary plenitude of everyday actions, deconstructing them into their social determinants and inscribing within them the conditions of their making. The "void" of alienated acting is a kind of Derridean "spacing," rendering a piece of stage business exterior to itself, sliding a hiatus between actor and action and thus, it is hoped, dismantling the ideological self-identity of our routine social behaviour. The actor, Walter Benjamin remarked in "What Is Epic Theatre?," "must be able to space his gestures as the compositor produces spaced type."[2] The dramatic gesture, by miming routine behaviour in contrivedly hollow ways, represents it in all its lack, in its suppression of material conditions and historical possibilities, and thus represents an absence which it at the same time produces. What the stage action represents is the routine action as differenced through the former's non-self-identity, which nevertheless remains self-identical—recognizable—enough to do all this representing rather than merely to "reflect" a "given" non-identity in the world. A certain

structure of presence must, in other words, be preserved: "verisimilitude" between stage and society can be disrupted only if it is posited. Brecht was particularly keen on encouraging his actors to observe and reproduce actions precisely, for without such an element of presence and recognition the absencing of the A-effect would be non-productively rather than productively empty. The internal structure of the effect is one of presence and absence together, or rather a problematic contention of the two in which the distinction between "representation" and "non-representation" is itself thrown into question. The stage action must be self-identical enough to represent as non-self-identical an apparently self-identical world, but in that very act puts its own self-identity into question. This self-cancelling or self-transcending of the theatrical signifier becomes a political metaphor: if political society were to know itself in its difference, there would be no need for this kind of representational theatre. It is because political society does not recognize itself as a *production* that it must be *represented* as such, which (since the concept of production itself overturns classical notions of representation) is bound to result in a self-contradictory aesthetic. It is not surprising that Brecht never seems able to make up his mind about the political value of representation. The A-effect, however, turns this contradiction to fruitful use, positing and subverting simultaneously; as a "supplement" to social reality it posits its solid anterior existence *and* unmasks it as crippledly incomplete.

Another way of putting this is to claim that Brechtian theatre deconstructs social processes into rhetoric, which is to say reveals them as social *practices*. "Rhetoric" here means grasping language and action in the context of the politico-discursive conditions inscribed within them, and Brecht's term for this is *Gest*. To view things gestically is to catch the gist in terms of the gesture, or rather to position oneself at the point where the one German word hovers indeterminately between the two English ones. *Gest* denotes the curve of intentionality, the class of socially typical performative utterances, to which in a piece of *plumpes Denken* the complexities of action or discourse may be reduced. An unpublished fragment by Brecht headed "representation of sentences in a new encyclopaedia" would suggest that he thought all sentences, not just obviously performative ones like theatrical speech, could and should be treated in this way:

1. Who is the sentence of use to?
2. Who does it claim to be of use to?
3. What does it call for?
4. What practical action corresponds to it?
5. What sort of sentences result from it? What sort of sentences support it?
6. In what situation is it spoken? By whom?[3]

All discourse is gestic or rhetorical, but some—dramatic discourse—is more rhetorical than the rest. It *needs* to be, since its task is to reveal the repressed rhetoricity of nontheatrical utterances, a revelation which is for Brecht ineluctably materialist because it involves contextualizing what is said or done in terms of its institutional conditions. The function of theatre is to show that all the world's a stage.

But if all language is performative, what becomes of representation? Brecht's answer to this, briefly, is that what representations represent are performatives. The theatre simply lays bare the process by which we come to grasp "constative" utterances in the first place only by an act of "theatrical" miming. In a piece significantly entitled "Two Essays on Unprofessional Acting," Brecht writes:

One easily forgets that human education proceeds along highly theatrical lines. In a quite theatrical manner the child is taught how to behave; logical arguments only come later. When such-and-such occurs, it is told (or sees), one must laugh. It joins in when there is laughter, without knowing why; if asked why it is laughing it is wholly confused. In the same way it joins in shedding tears, not only weeping because the grown-ups do so but also feeling genuine sorrow. This can be seen at funerals, whose meaning escapes children entirely. These are theatrical events which form the character. The human being copies gestures, miming, tones of voice. And weeping arises from sorrow, but sorrow also arises from weeping.[4]

Rhetoric, in other words, precedes logic: grasping propositions is only possible by participating in specific forms of social life. As children we get the gist by miming the gesture, grow into "appropriate" feelings by performing the behaviours criterial of them. Only later will logic bury rhetoric, the gesture be surreptitiously slid beneath the gist. What utterances "represent" is not referents but practices, including other utterances: "gestures, miming, tones of voice." As with the A-effect, then, Brecht's focus is at once representational and anti-representational, mimetic and performative together. The child grows towards representational meaning by redoubling rhetoric, miming a miming, performing a performative; indeed when Brecht writes (perhaps by a slide of the signifier) of the child *copying miming,* he suggests the possibility of performing the performing of a performance.

The child, one might say, begins as an amateur or Brechtian actor, performing what he does not yet truly feel, and by dint of doing so ends up as a professional or Aristotelian one, fully at one with his forms of life. The aim of Brechtian theory, then, must be to reverse this unhappy process and regress us to a childlike condition once more, make us all amateurs again. The child and the Marxist move in opposite directions but meet in the middle: the child's understanding is at first purely practical, the effect of a spontaneous involvement with forms of life, and only later crystallizes out into a logical or representational system.[5] The Marxist is confronted by that (ideo)logical system and has to work his or her way back to the practical conditions it now suppresses, rewriting it as a piece of rhetoric or mode of social performance. We forget that we have to learn our emotions through sharing in forms of social behaviour, that feelings are social institutions; in the theatre we can re-enact our childhood at a conscious level, observe new forms of behaviour and so develop the forms of subjectivity appropriate to them. In both theatre and childhood, meaning is not "representational" but the effect of representation, the consequence of a certain practical miming. Mimesis is what precedes and encircles meaning, the material conditions for the emergence of logical thought. In the end, child and materialist will come out at the same point: "I now see thinking just as a way of behaving," says the Actor in the *Messingkauf Dialogues,* "and behaving socially at that. It's something that the whole body takes part in, with all its senses."

To "act" is to go through the motions of behaviour without really feeling it, lacking the appropriate experiences. Acting is a kind of fraud; and flagrantly "fraudulent" acting, of an amateur or alienated kind, returns us self-consciously to the fictive formation of the self, re-opens that gap or lag between our action and its appropriate inwardness which was there in the first place as a consequence

of our desiring the desire of the Other. Children are allegorists, confusedly hunting the elusive meaning of behaviour; adults are symbolists, unable to dissociate action and significance. Amateur actors, like political revolutionaries, are those who find the conventions hard to grasp and perform them badly, having never recovered from their childhood puzzlement.

Such puzzlement is perhaps what we call "theory." The child is an incorrigible theoretician, forever urging the most impossibly fundamental questions. The form of a philosophical question, Wittgenstein remarks, is "I don't know my way around"; and since this is literally true of the child, it is driven to pose questions which are not answerable simply in rhetorical terms ("The meaning of this action is this") but which press perversely on to interrogate the whole form of social life which might generate such particular meanings in the first place. Theory is in this sense the logical refuge of those puzzled or naive enough not to find simply rhetorical answers adequate, or who want to widen the boundaries of what mature minds take to be adequate rhetorical explanations. The revolutionary questioner sees the world with the astonishment of a child ("Where does capitalism come from, Mummy?"), and refuses to be fobbed off by the adults' customary Wittgensteinian justifications of their practices: "This is just what we *do,* dear." He or she accepts that all justification is in this sense rhetorical, an appeal to existing practices and conventions, but does not see why one should not do something else for a change. The theoretical question is as utterly estranged as the metaphysician's traditional wonderment about why there is anything at all, rather than just nothing. Why do we have all *these* practices, utterances and institutions, rather than some others?

Since such a question is not of course simply requesting historical information, it is rhetorical in its turn—both in the sense that it implies its own answer (we *shouldn't* rest happy with such practices), and in the sense that like the discourses it addresses it is therefore animated by malice, scorn, insecurity, hostility, the will to reject. If the child's questions are naive, the revolutionary's are *faux naif.* "I don't know my way around" implies, "What the hell is all this?" The theoretical question, then, is as much a performative as the languages it challenges; it is just that it tries to view those other languages in a new way, as Brecht reported that it was only by reading Marx that he was able to understand his own plays. Theory begins to take hold once one realizes that the adults don't know their way around either, even if they *act* as though they do. They act as well as they do precisely because they can no longer see, and so question, the conventions by which they behave. The task of theory is to breed bad actors, of which Brecht's remarks about the A-effect is one small model.

Just as Marxism can be seen as a morality in the properly classical rather than narrowly fashionable sense, concerned with as many as possible of the factors (and not just interpersonal ones) which condition the quality of human behaviour, so "theory" can be seen as rhetorical study in its broadest and richest sense, reckoning in modes of production as well as conventions of promising. Where theory is most importantly performative, however, is in the practical difference it makes to our routine rhetorics. "Lamenting by means of sounds, or better still words," says the Philosopher in the *Messingkauf Dialogues,* "is a vast liberation, because it means that the sufferer isbeginningtoproducesomething.He'sal-

ready mixing his sorrow with an account of the blows he has received; he's already making something out of the utterly devastating. Observation has set in." If the child's trek from rhetoric to logic is part of the problem, the sufferer's transition from screaming to explaining is part of the solution. When lamenting becomes propositional it is transformed: it becomes, like theory, a way of encompassing a situation rather than being its victim. To give an account of one's sorrow even as one grieves; to act and, in alienated style, to observe oneself acting: this is the dialectical feat which, for quite different reasons, neither child nor logician can achieve, and which is central at once to Brecht's dramaturgy and to his politics.

## NOTES

1. J. L. Austin, *How to Do Things with Words,* Cambridge, Mass. 1975, p. 21.

2. Walter Benjamin, *Understanding Brecht,* London 1973, p. 19.

3. *Brecht on Theatre: The Development of an Aesthetic,* translated by John Willett, London 1964, p. 106.

4. Ibid., p. 152.

5. Walter Benjamin admired the way in which, in children, cognition was tied to action, and found in their behaviour a "language of gestures" more basic than conceptual discourse. For Benjamin as for Brecht, children's behaviour was essentially mimetic, a matter of forging bizarre correspondences of the kind that the revolutionary theorist must also generate. See, for this neglected aspect of Benjamin's thought, Susan Buck-Morss, "Walter Benjamin: Revolutionary Writer (11)," *New Left Review* 129, September–October 1981.

# 30

# Stephen J. Greenblatt
# 1943–

For more than a decade now Stephen Greenblatt, the class of 1932 professor of English literature at the University of California, Berkeley, has been a leading contributor to the critical movement called the New Historicism. Greenblatt himself invented this title in the early 1980s to distinguish the reading practices that he and a number of like-minded colleagues, including Louis Montrose and Richard Helgerson, had developed from two interpretive approaches that had shaped much of the research that had been conducted by a previous generation of Renaissance scholars. Rejecting both the New Critical assumption that Renaissance works belong to an autonomous aesthetic realm and the older historicist premise that Renaissance literature mirrored, from a distant point of observation, a coherent worldview, Greenblatt argued that critics who wish to understand Tudor and Stuart writing must situate specific texts within the irreducibly complex network of authorities that constituted Renaissance culture in its entirety.

To spell out the implications of Greenblatt's position, we can briefly summarize the thesis of his highly influential *Renaissance Self-Fashioning* (1980). In this work Greenblatt demonstrates that sixteenth- and seventeenth-century English society was regulated by an array of institutions—for instance, the court, the church, and the colonial administration—that sponsored a varied, occasionally contradictory, assortment of beliefs, customs, and activities. These codes and practices were actually cultural conventions, social constructions of reality, but the authorities that disseminated these systems of comportment invested their positions with the aura of naturalness and thus sought to stigmatize those who sponsored alternative paradigms for understanding behavior—including members of other nations and proponents of other faiths—by describing these rivals as aliens. Since Renaissance writers were endowed with subjectivity or selfhood at the point when they allied themselves with or rose in opposition to one of these formidable institutions, their views were shaped by the cultural authority they identified with or resisted, and they used their texts either to depict the strategies that their allies might deploy to overcome figures of otherness, or to denounce the tactics that a power mobilized to expand its sphere of influence. Given that Renaissance authors were fully engaged with the social problems of their time, the critic's job is to reconstruct the political terrain in which their writers performed their ideological labors, and to chart, in dialectical fashion, the ways that texts both represented a community's behavior patterns and endorsed, perpetuated, or critiqued that culture's dominant codes.

To produce the sophisticated interpretations that his polemical statements invite, Greenblatt forges a powerful interdisciplinary approach to the study of Renaissance writing. Following cultural anthropologists, especially Clifford Geertz, he speaks of public actions as elements in a discursive or signifying system, and this assumption allows him to disclose the ways that apparently minor events such as casual encounters between colonists and native Americans encoded the beliefs, tactics, and values that gave an entire community its coherence. In addition, Greenblatt is indebted to Michel Foucault, for the prominent French theorist provides him with models of coercive and corrective power relations that shape his analysis of Renaissance institutions. Marx and his followers also provide Greenblatt with paradigms that he invokes to discuss the political function of literature; indeed, Althusser's notion that art makes us perceive, by a process of internal distancing, the ideology in which it is held informs many of Greenblatt's comments on the question of whether Renaissance texts could subvert the social order that was dominant at the time when they were written. Having developed this complicated theoretical orientation while authoring *Renaissance Self-Fashioning,* Greenblatt applied it with some modification in his subsequent book-length studies of culture, and as a result he has offered his readers telling analyses of strategies of social reproduction and tactics of colonial domination in *Shakespearian Negotiations* (1988) and *Marvelous Possessions* (1991), respectively.

In the essay that follows, a 1988 revision of an earlier essay, "Invisible Bullets: Renaissance Authority and Its Subversion" (1981), Greenblatt explores an issue that has become one of the leading concerns of the New Historicists, namely how orthodox and defiant impulses are related within the specific cultural formations they study. Contrary to scholars who have posited the existence of radical Renaissance intellectual traditions and scientific communities, Greenblatt argues that the texts of authors who ostensibly seek to celebrate political authority actually register some of Elizabethan society's most subtly subversive insights about power. To prove his point, he examines the practices of testing, recording, and explaining as they appear in *A Brief and True Report of the New Found Land of Virginia,* and he demonstrates that Thomas Harriot can provide a skeptical representation of religion—one that confirms the Machiavellian view that theology is a collection of tricks that allows the civilized to control the savage—precisely because this author is a vigilant defender of a colonial administration that defines itself in opposition to Indian voices it projects as other. In pursuing such an analysis, Greenblatt does not mean to imply that Harriot was fully conscious of the subversive potential implicit in his depiction of power; in fact he takes the unintentionally radical character of the *Report* as a sign that this text replicates mechanisms that shape the apprehensions of an entire community. This maneuver allows Greenblatt to trace in some of Shakespeare's plays the same tactics of testing and recording that he found in Harriot's work, and in doing so he fulfills the New Historicist's obligation to delineate the ways that texts were linked to the network of institutions, practices, and beliefs that constituted a particular culture.

# Invisible Bullets

I

In his notorious police report of 1593 on Christopher Marlowe, the Elizabethan spy Richard Baines informed his superiors that Marlowe had declared, among other monstrous opinions, that "Moses was but a Juggler, and that one Heriots being Sir W Raleighs man Can do more than he."[1] The "Heriots" cast for a moment in this lurid light is Thomas Harriot, the most profound Elizabethan mathematician, an expert in cartography, optics, and navigational science, an adherent of atomism, the first Englishman to make a telescope and turn it on the heavens, the author of the first original book about the first English colony in America, and the possessor throughout his career of a dangerous reputation for atheism.[2] In all of his extant writings, private correspondence as well as public discourse, Harriot professes the most reassuringly orthodox religious faith, but the suspicion persisted. When he died of cancer in 1621, one of his contemporaries, persuaded that Harriot had challenged the doctrinal account of creation *ex nihilo,* remarked gleefully that "a *nihilum* killed him at last: for in the top of his nose came a little red speck (exceeding small), which grew bigger and bigger, and at last killed him."[3]

Charges of atheism leveled at Harriot or anyone else in this period are difficult to assess, for such accusations were smear tactics, used with reckless abandon against anyone whom the accuser happened to dislike. At a dinner party one summer evening in 1593, Sir Walter Ralegh teased an irascible country parson named Ralph Ironside and found himself the subject of a state investigation; at the other end of the social scale, in the same Dorsetshire parish, a drunken servant named Oliver complained that in the Sunday sermon

the preacher had praised Moses excessively but had neglected to mention his fifty-two concubines, and Oliver too found himself under official scrutiny.[4] Few, if any, of these investigations turned up what we would call atheists, even muddled or shallow ones; the stance that seemed to come naturally to me as a green college freshman in mid–twentieth-century America seems to have been almost unthinkable to the most daring philosophical minds of late sixteenth-century England.

The historical evidence is unreliable; even in the absence of social pressure, people lie readily about their most intimate beliefs. How much more must they have lied in an atmosphere of unembarrassed repression. Still, there is probably more than politic concealment involved here. After all, treason was punished as harshly as atheism, yet while the period abounds in documented instances of treason in word and deed, there are virtually no professed atheists.[5] If ever there were a place to confirm that in a given social construction of reality certain interpretations of experience are sanctioned and others excluded, it is here, in the boundaries that contained sixteenth-century skepticism. Like Machiavelli and Montaigne, Thomas Harriot professed belief in God, and there is no justification in any of these cases for dismissing the profession of faith as mere hypocrisy.

I am arguing not that atheism was literally unthinkable in the late sixteenth century but rather that it was almost always thinkable only as the thought of another. This is one of its attractions as a smear; atheism is a characteristic mark of otherness—hence the ease with which Catholics can call Protestant martyrs atheists and Protestants routinely make similar charges against the pope.[6] The pervasiveness and frequency of these charges, then, does not signal the existence of a secret society of freethinkers, a School of Night, but rather registers the operation of a religious authority, whether Catholic or Protestant, that confirms its power by disclosing the threat of atheism. The authority is secular as well as religious, since atheism is frequently adduced as a motive for heinous crimes, as if all men and women would inevitably conclude that if God does not exist, everything is permitted. At Ralegh's 1603 treason trial, for example, Justice Popham solemnly warned the accused not to let "Harriot, nor any such Doctor, persuade you there is no eternity in Heaven, lest you find an eternity of hell-torments."[7] Nothing in Harriot's writings suggests that he held the position attributed to him here, but the charge does not depend upon evidence: Harriot is invoked as the archetypal corrupter, Achitophel seducing the glittering Absalom. If the atheist did not exist, he would have to be invented.

Yet atheism is not the only mode of subversive religious doubt, and we cannot discount the persistent rumors of Harriot's heterodoxy by pointing to either his conventional professions of faith or the conventionality of the attacks upon him. Indeed I want to suggest that if we look closely at *A Brief and True Report of the New Found Land of Virginia* (1588), the only work Harriot published in his lifetime and hence the work in which he was presumably the most cautious, we can find traces of material that could lead to the remark attributed to Marlowe, that "Moses was but a Juggler, and that one Heriots being Sir W Raleighs man Can do more than he." And I want to suggest further that understanding the relation between orthodoxy and subversion in Harriot's text will enable us to construct an interpretive model that may be used to understand the far more complex problem posed by Shakespeare's history plays.

Those plays have been described with impeccable intelligence as deeply conservative and with equally impeccable intelligence as deeply radical. Shakespeare, in Northrop Frye's words, is "a born courtier," the dramatist who organizes his representation of English history around the hegemonic mysticism of the Tudor myth; Shakespeare is also a relentless demystifier, an interrogator of ideology, "the only dramatist," as Franco Moretti puts it, "who rises to the level of Machiavelli in elaborating all the consequences of the separation of political praxis from moral evaluation."[8] The conflict glimpsed here could be investigated, on a performance-by-performance basis, in a history of reception, but that history is shaped, I would argue, by circumstances of production as well as consumption. The ideological strategies that fashion Shakespeare's history plays help in turn to fashion the conflicting readings of the plays' politics. And these strategies are no more Shakespeare's invention than the historical narratives on which he based his plots. As we shall see from Harriot's *Brief and True Report,* in the discourse of authority a powerful logic governs the relation between orthodoxy and subversion.

I should first explain that the apparently feeble wisecrack about Moses and Harriot finds its way into a police file on Marlowe because it seems to bear out one of the Machiavellian arguments about religion that most excited the wrath of sixteenth-century authorities: Old Testament religion, the argument goes, and by extension the whole Judeo-Christian tradition, originated in a series of clever tricks, fraudulent illusions perpetrated by Moses, who had been trained in Egyptian magic, upon the "rude and gross" (and hence credulous) Hebrews.[9] This argument is not actually to be found in Machiavelli, nor does it originate in the sixteenth century; it is already fully formulated in early pagan polemics against Christianity. But it seems to acquire a special force and currency in the Renaissance as an aspect of a heightened consciousness, fueled by the period's prolonged crises of doctrine and church governance, of the social function of religious belief.

Here Machiavelli's writings are important. *The Prince* observes in its bland way that if Moses' particular actions and methods are examined closely, they appear to differ little from those employed by the great pagan princes; the *Discourses* treats religion as if its primary function were not salvation but the achievement of civic discipline, as if its primary justification were not truth but expediency.[10] Thus Romulus's successor Numa Pompilius, "finding a very savage people, and wishing to reduce them to civil obedience by the arts of peace, had recourse to religion as the most necessary and assured support of any civil society" (*Discourses,* 146). For although "Romulus could organize the Senate and establish other civil and military institutions without the aid of divine authority, yet it was very necessary for Numa, who feigned that he held converse with a nymph, who dictated to him all that he wished to persuade the people to." In truth, continues Machiavelli, "there never was any remarkable lawgiver amongst any people who did not resort to divine authority, as otherwise his laws would not have been accepted by the people" (147).

From here it was only a short step, in the minds of Renaissance authorities, to the monstrous opinions attributed to the likes of Marlowe and Harriot. Kyd, under torture, testified that Marlowe had affirmed that "things esteemed to be done by divine power might have as well been done by observation of men," and the Jesuit Robert Parsons claimed that in Ralegh's "school of Atheism," "both Moses and our Savior, the old and the New Testament, are jested at."[11] On the eve of Ralegh's treason trial, some "hellish verses" were lifted from an anonymous tragedy written ten years earlier and circulated as Ralegh's own confession of atheism. At first the earth was held in common, the verses declare, but

this golden age gave way to war, kingship, and property:

> Then some sage man, above the vulgar
> wise,
> Knowing that laws could not in quiet
> dwell,
> Unless they were observed, did first devise
> The names of Gods, religion, heaven, and
> hell
> . . . Only bug-bears to keep the world in
> fear.[12]

The attribution of these lines to Ralegh is instructive: the fictional text returns to circulation as the missing confessional language of real life. That fiction is unlikely to represent an observable attitude in the "real" world, though we can never altogether exclude that possibility; rather it stages a cultural conceit, the recurrent fantasy of the archcriminal as atheist. Ralegh already had a reputation as both a poet and a freethinker; perhaps one of his numerous enemies actually plotted to heighten the violent popular hostility toward him by floating under his name a forgotten piece of stage villainy.[13] But quite apart from a possible conspiracy, the circulation fulfills a strong cultural expectation. When a hated favorite like Ralegh was accused of treason, what was looked for was not evidence but a performance, a theatrical revelation of motive and an enactment of despair. If the motives for treason revealed in this performance could be various—ambition, jealousy, greed, spite, and so forth—what permitted the release of these motives into action would always be the same: atheism. No one who actually loved and feared God would allow himself to rebel against an anointed ruler, and atheism, conversely, would lead inevitably to treason. Since atheism was virtually always, as I have argued, the thought of the other, it would be difficult to find a first-person confession—except, of course, in fiction and above all in the theater. The soliloquy is lifted from its theatrical context and transformed into "verses" that the three surviving manuscripts declare were "devised by that Atheist and Traitor Ralegh as it is said." The last phrase may signal skepticism about the attribution, but such reservations do not count for much: the "hellish verses" are what men like Marlowe, Harriot, or Ralegh would have to think in their hearts.

Harriot does not voice any speculations remotely resembling the hypotheses that a punitive religion was invented to keep men in awe and that belief originated in a fraudulent imposition by cunning "jugglers" on the ignorant, but his recurrent association with the forbidden thoughts of the demonized other may be linked to something beyond malicious slander. If we look attentively at his account of the first Virginia colony, we find a mind that seems interested in the same set of problems, a mind, indeed, that seems to be virtually testing the Machiavellian hypotheses. Sent by Ralegh to keep a record of the colony and to compile a description of the resources and inhabitants of the area, Harriot took care to learn the North Carolina Algonquian dialect and to achieve what he calls a "special familiarity with some of the priests."[14] The Virginian Indians believe, Harriot writes, in the immortality of the soul and in otherworldly punishments and rewards for behavior in this world: "What subtlety soever be in the *Wiroances* and Priests, this opinion worketh so much in many of the common and simple sort of people that it maketh them have great respect to the Governors, and also great care what they do, to avoid torment after death and to enjoy bliss" (374).[15] The split between the priests and people implied here is glimpsed as well in the description of the votive images: "They think that all the gods are of human shape, and therefore they represent them by images in the forms of men, which they call Kewasowak. . . . The common sort think them to be also gods" (373). And the social function of popular belief is underscored in Harriot's note to an illustration showing the priests carefully tending the embalmed bodies of the former chiefs: "These poor souls are thus instructed by nature to reverence their princes even after their death" (De Bry, p. 72).

We have then, as in Machiavelli, a sense of religion as a set of beliefs manipulated by the subtlety of priests to help instill obedience and respect for authority. The terms of Harriot's analysis—"the common and simple sort of people," "the Governors," and so forth—are obviously drawn from the language of comparable social analyses of England; as Karen Kupperman has most recently demonstrated, sixteenth- and seventeenth-century Englishmen characteristically describe the Indians in terms that closely replicate their own self-conception, above all in matters of *status*.[16] The great mass of Indians are seen as a version of "the common sort" at home, just as Harriot translates the Algonquian *weroan* as "great Lord" and speaks of "the chief Ladies," "virgins of good parentage," "a young gentlewoman," and so forth. There is an easy, indeed almost irresistible, analogy in the period between accounts of Indian and European social structure, so that Harriot's description of the inward mechanisms of Algonquian society implies a description of comparable mechanisms in his own culture.[17]

To this we may add a still more telling observation not of the internal function of native religion but of the impact of European culture on the Indians: "Most things they saw with us," Harriot writes, "as mathematical instruments, sea compasses, the virtue of the loadstone in drawing iron, a perspective glass whereby was showed many strange sights, burning glasses, wildlife works, guns, books, writing and reading, spring clocks that seem to go of. themselves, and many other things that we had, were so strange unto them, and so far exceeded their capacities to comprehend the reason and means how they should be made and done, that they thought they were rather the works of gods than of men, or at the leastwisc they had been given and taught us of the gods" (375–76). This delusion, born of what Harriot supposes to be the vast technological superiority of the European, caused the savages to doubt that they possessed the truth of God and religion and to suspect that such truth "was rather to be had from us, whom God so specially loved than from a people that were so simple, as they found themselves to be in comparison of us" (376).

Here, I suggest, is the very core of the Machiavellian anthropology that posited the origin of religion in an imposition of socially coercive doctrines by an educated and sophisticated lawgiver on a simple people. And in Harriot's list of the marvels—from wildfire to reading—with which he undermined the Indians' confidence in their native understanding of the universe, we have the core of the claim attributed to Marlowe: that Moses was but a juggler and that Ralegh's man Harriot could do more than he. The testing of this hypothesis in the encounter of the Old World and the New was appropriate, we may add, for though vulgar Machiavellianism implied that all religion was a sophisticated confidence trick, Machiavelli himself saw that trick as possible only at a radical point of origin: "If any one wanted to establish a republic at the present time," he writes, "he would find it much easier with the simple mountaineers, who are almost without any civilization, than with such as are accustomed to live in cities, where civilization is already corrupt; as a sculptor finds it easier to make a fine statue out of a crude block of marble than out of a statue badly begun by another."[18] It was only with a people, as Harriot says, "so simple, as they found themselves to be in comparison of us," that the imposition of a coercive set of religious beliefs could be attempted.

In Harriot, then, we have one of the earliest instances of a significant phenomenon: the testing upon the bodies and minds of non-Europeans or, more generally, the noncivilized, of a hypothesis about the origin and nature of European culture and belief. In encountering the Algonquian Indians, Harriot not only thought he was encountering a simplified version of his own culture but also evidently believed that he was encountering his own civilization's past.[19] This past could best be investigated in the privileged anthropological moment of the initial encounter, for the comparable situations in Europe itself tended to be already contaminated by prior contact. Only in the forest, with a people ignorant of Christianity and startled by its bearers' technological potency, could one hope to reproduce accurately, with live subjects, the relation imagined between Numa and the primitive Romans, Moses and the Hebrews. The actual testing could happen only once, for it entails not detached observation but radical change, the change Harriot begins to observe in the priests who "were not so sure grounded, nor gave such credit to their traditions and stories, but through conversing with us they were brought into great doubts of their own" (375).[20] I should emphasize that I am speaking here of events as reported by Harriot. The history of subsequent English-Algonquian relations casts doubt on the depth, extent, and irreversibility of the supposed Indian crisis of belief. In the *Brief and True Report,* however, the tribe's stories begin to *collapse* in the minds of their traditional guardians, and the coercive power of the European beliefs begins to show itself almost at once in the Indians' behavior: "On a time also when their corn began to wither by reason of a drought which happened extraordinarily, fearing that it had come to pass by reason that in some thing they had displeased us, many would come to us and desire us to pray to our God of England, that he would preserve their corn, promising that when it was ripe we also should be partakers of their fruit" (377). If we remember that the English, like virtually all sixteenth-century Europeans in the New World, resisted or were incapable of provisioning themselves and in consequence depended upon the Indians for food, we may grasp the central importance for the colonists of this dawning Indian fear of the Christian God.

As early as 1504, during Columbus's fourth voyage, the natives, distressed that the Spanish seemed inclined to settle in for a long visit, refused to continue to supply food. Knowing from his almanac that a total eclipse of the moon was imminent, Columbus warned the Indians that God would show them a sign of his displeasure; after the eclipse, the terrified Indians resumed the supply. But an eclipse would not always be so conveniently at hand. John Sparke, who sailed with Sir John Hawkins in 1564–65, noted that the French colonists in Florida "would not take the pains so much as to fish in the river before their doors, but would have all things put in their mouths."[21] When the Indians wearied of this arrangement, the French turned to extortion and robbery, and before long there were bloody wars. A similar situation seems to have arisen in the Virginia colony: despite land rich in game and ample fishing grounds, the English nearly starved to death when the exasperated Algonquians refused to build fishing weirs and plant corn.[22]

It is difficult to understand why men so aggressive and energetic in other regards should have been so passive in the crucial matter of feeding themselves. No doubt there were serious logistic problems in transporting food and equally serious difficulties adapting European farming methods and materials to the different climate and soil of the New World, yet these explanations seem insufficient, as they did even to the early explorers themselves. John Sparke wrote that "notwithstanding the great want that the Frenchmen had, the ground doth yield victuals sufficient, if they would have taken pains to get the same; but they were being soldiers, desired to live by the sweat of other mens brows" (Hakluyt 10:56). This remark bears close attention: it points not to laziness or negligence but to an occupational identity, a determination to be nourished by the labor of others weaker, more vulnerable, than oneself. This self-conception was not, we might add, exclusively military: the hallmark of power and wealth in the sixteenth century was to be waited on by others. "To live by the sweat of other men's brows" was the enviable lot of the gentleman; indeed in England it virtually defined a gentleman. The New World held out the prospect of such status for all but the poorest cabin boy.[23]

But the prospect could not be realized through violence alone, even if the Europeans had possessed a monopoly of it, because the relentless exercise of violence could actually reduce the food supply. As Machiavelli understood, physical compulsion is essential but never sufficient; the survival of the rulers depends upon a supplement of coercive belief. The Indians must be persuaded that the Christian God is all-powerful and committed to the survival of his chosen people, that he will wither the corn and destroy the lives of savages who displease him by disobeying or plotting against the English. Here is a strange paradox: Harriot tests and seems to confirm the most radically subversive hypothesis in his culture about the origin and function of religion by imposing his religion—with its intense claims to transcendence, unique truth, inescapable coercive force—on others. Not only the official purpose but the survival of the English colony depends upon this imposition. This crucial circumstance licensed the testing in the first place; only as an agent of the English colony, dependent upon its purposes and committed to its survival, is Harriot in a position to disclose the power of human achievements—reading, writing, perspective glasses, gunpowder, and the like—to appear to the ignorant as divine and hence to promote belief and compel obedience.

Thus the subversiveness that is genuine and radical—sufficiently disturbing so that to be suspected of it could lead to imprisonment and torture—is at the same time contained by the power it would appear to threaten. Indeed the subversiveness is the very product of that power and furthers its ends. One may go still further and suggest that the power Harriot both serves and embodies not only produces its own subversion but is actively built upon it: the project of evangelical colonialism is not set over against the skeptical critique of religious coercion but battens on the very confirmation of that critique. In the Virginia colony, the radical undermining of Christian order is not the negative limit but the positive condition for the establishment of that order. And this paradox extends to the production of Harriot's text: *A Brief and True Report,* with its latent heterodoxy, is not a reflection upon the Virginia colony or even a simple record of it—it is not, in other words, a privileged withdrawal into a critical zone set apart from power—but a continuation of the colonial enterprise.

By October 1586, rumors were spreading in England that Virginia offered little prospect of profit, that the colony had been close to starvation, and that the Indians had turned hostile. Harriot accordingly begins his report with a descriptive catalog in which the natural goods of the land are turned into social goods, that is, into "merchantable commodities": "Cedar, a very sweet wood and fine timber; whereof if nests of chests be there made, or timber thereof fitted for sweet and fine bedsteads, tables, desks, lutes, virginals, and many things else, . . . [it] will yield profit" (329–30).[24] The inventory of these commodities is followed by an inventory of edible plants and animals, to prove to readers that the colony need not starve, and then by the account of the Indians, to prove that the colony could impose its will on them. The key to this imposition, as we

have seen, is the coercive power of religious belief, and the source of the power is the impression made by advanced technology upon a "backward" people.

Hence Harriot's text is committed to record what I have called his confirmation of the Machiavellian hypothesis, and hence too the potential subversiveness of this confirmation is invisible not only to those on whom the religion is supposedly imposed but also to most readers and quite possibly to Harriot himself. It may be that Harriot was demonically conscious of what he was doing—that he found himself situated exactly where he could test one of his culture's darkest fears about its own origins, that he used the Algonquians to do so, and that he wrote a report on his own findings, a coded report, since as he wrote to Kepler years later, "our situation is such that I still may not philosophize freely."[25] But this is not the only Harriot we can conjure up. A scientist of the late sixteenth century, we might suppose, would have regarded the natives' opinion that English technology was god-given—indeed divine—with something like corroboratory complacency. It would, as a colleague from whom I borrow this conjecture remarked, "be just like an establishment intellectual, or simply a well-placed Elizabethan bourgeois, to accept that his superior 'powers'—moral, technological, cultural—were indeed signs of divine favor and that therefore the superstitious natives were quite right in their perception of the need to submit to their benevolent conquerors."[26]

Now Harriot does not in fact express such a view of the ultimate origin of his trunk of marvels—and I doubt that he held the view in this form—but it is significant that in the next generation Bacon, perhaps recalling Harriot's text or others like it, claims in *The New Organon* that scientific discoveries "are as it were new creations, and imitations of God's works" that may be justly regarded *as if* they were manifestations not of human skill but of divine power: "Let a man only consider what a difference there is between the life of men in the most civilized province of Europe, and in the wildest and most barbarous districts of New India; he will feel it to be great enough to justify the saying that 'man is a god to man,' not only in regard to aid and benefit, but also by a comparison of condition. And this difference comes not from soil, not from climate, not from race, but from the arts."[27] From this perspective the Algonquian misconception of the origin and nature of English technology would be evidence not of the power of Christianity to impose itself fraudulently on a backward people but of the dazzling power of science and of the naive literalism of the ignorant, who can conceive of this power only as the achievement of actual gods.[28]

Thus, for all his subtlety and his sensitivity to heterodoxy, Harriot might not have grasped fully the disturbing implications of his own text. The plausibility of a picture of Harriot culturally insulated from the subversive energies of his own activity would seem to be enhanced elsewhere in *A Brief and True Report* by his account of his missionary efforts:

Many times and in every town where I came, according as I was able, I made declaration of the contents of the Bible; that therein was set forth the true and only God, and his mighty works, that therein was contained the true doctrine of salvation through Christ, with many particularities of Miracles and chief points of religion, as I was able then to utter, and thought fit for the time. And although I told them the book materially and of itself was not of any such virtue, as I thought they did conceive, but only the doctrine therein contained; yet would many be glad to touch it, to embrace it, to kiss it, to hold it to their breasts and heads, and stroke over all their body with it; to show their hungry desire of that

knowledge which was spoken of. (376–77)

Here the heathens' confusion of material object and religious doctrine does not seem to cast doubts upon the truth of the Holy Book; rather it signals precisely the naive literalism of the Algonquians and hence their susceptibility to idolatry. They are viewed with a touch of amusement, as Spenser in the *Faerie Queene* views the "salvage nation" who seek to worship Una herself rather than the truth for which she stands:

During which time her gentle wit she plyes,
To teach them truth, which worshipt her in
     vaine,
And made her th'Image of Idolatryes;
But when their bootlesse zeale she did
     restraine
From her own worship, they her Asse
     would worship fayn.
                                        (1.6.19)[29]

Harriot, for his part, is willing to temper the view of the savage as idolater by reading the Algonquian fetishism of the book as a promising sign, an allegory of "their hungry desire of that knowledge which was spoken of." Such a reading, we might add, conveniently supports the claim that the English would easily dominate and civilize the Indians and hence advances the general purpose of *A Brief and True Report*.

The apparent religious certainty, cultural confidence, and national self-interest here by no means rule out the possibility of what I have called demonic consciousness—we can always postulate that Harriot found ever more subtle ways of simultaneously recording and disguising his dangerous speculations—but the essential point is that we need no such biographical romance to account for the apparent testing and confirmation of the Machiavellian hypothesis: the colonial power produced the subversiveness in its own interest, as I have argued, and *A Brief and True Report,* appropriately, was published by the great Elizabethan exponent of missionary colonialism, the Reverend Richard Hakluyt.

The thought that Christianity served to shore up the authority of the colonists would not have struck Hakluyt or the great majority of his readers as subversive. On the contrary, the role of religion in preserving the social order was a commonplace that all parties vied with each other in proclaiming. The suggestion that religions should be ranked according to their demonstrated ability to control their adherents would have been unacceptable, however, and the suggestion that reinforcing civil discipline must be the real origin and ultimate purpose of Christianity would have been still worse. These were possible explanations of the religion of another—skeptical arguments about ideological causality always work against beliefs one does not hold—but as we might expect from the earlier discussion of atheism, the application of this explanation to Christianity itself could be aired, and sternly refuted, only as the thought of another. Indeed a strictly functionalist explanation even of false religions was rejected by Christian theologians of the period. "It is utterly vain," writes Calvin, "for some men to say that religion was invented by the subtlety and craft of a few to hold the simple folk in thrall by this device and that those very persons who originated the worship of God for others did not in the least believe that any God existed." He goes on to concede "that in order to hold men's minds in greater subjection, clever men have devised very many things in religion by which to inspire the common folk with reverence and strike them with terror. But they would never have achieved this if men's minds had not already been imbued with a firm conviction about God, from which the inclination toward religion springs as from a seed."[30] Similarly, Hooker argues, "lest any man should here conceive, that it greatly skilleth not of

what sort our religion be, inasmuch as heathens, Turks, and infidels, impute to religion a great part of the same effects which ourselves ascribe thereunto," that the good moral effects of false religions result from their having religious—that is, Christian—truths "entwined" in them.[31]

This argument, which derives from the early chapters of the Epistle to the Romans, is so integral to what John Coolidge has called the Pauline Renaissance in England that Harriot's account of the Algonquians would have seemed, even for readers who sensed something odd about it, closer to confirmation than to subversion of religious orthodoxy. Yet it is misleading, I think, to conclude without qualification that the radical doubt implicit in Harriot's account is *entirely* contained. After all, Harriot was hounded through his whole life by charges of atheism, and, more tellingly, the remark attributed to Marlowe suggests that a contemporary could draw the most dangerous conclusions from the Virginia report. Both of these signs of slippage are compromised by their links to the society's well-developed repressive apparatus: rumors, accusations, police reports. But if we should be wary of naively accepting a version of reality proffered by the secret police, we cannot at the same time dismiss that version altogether. There is a perversely attractive, if bleak, clarity in such a dismissal—in deciding that subversive doubt was totally produced and totally contained by the ruling elite—but the actual evidence is tenebrous. We simply do not know what was thought in silence, what was written and then carefully burned, what was whispered by Harriot to Ralegh. Moreover, the "Atlantic Republican tradition," as Pocock has argued, does grow out of the "Machiavellian moment" of the sixteenth century, and that tradition, with its transformation of subjects into citizens, its subordination of transcendent values to capital values, does ultimately undermine, in the interests of a new power, the religious and secular authorities that had licensed the American enterprise in the first place.[32] In Harriot's text the relation between orthodoxy and subversion seems, at the same interpretive moment, to be both perfectly stable and dangerously volatile.

We can deepen our understanding of this apparent paradox if we consider a second mode of subversion and its containment in Harriot's account. Alongside the *testing* of a subversive interpretation of the dominant culture, we find the *recording* of alien voices or, more precisely, of alien interpretations. The occasion for this recording is another consequence of the English presence in the New World, not in this case the threatened extinction of the tribal religion but the threatened extinction of the tribe: "There was no town where we had any subtle device practiced against us," Harriot writes, "but that within a few days after our departure from every such town, the people began to die very fast, and many in short space; in some towns about twenty, in some forty, in some sixty and in one six score, which in truth was very many in respect of their numbers. The disease was so strange, that they neither knew what it was, nor how to cure it; the like by report of the oldest man in the country never happened before, time out of mind" (378).[33] Harriot is writing, of course, about the effects of measles, smallpox, or perhaps simply influenza on people with no resistance to them, but a conception of the biological basis of epidemic disease lies far, far in the future. For the English the deaths must be a moral phenomenon—this notion for them is as irresistible as the notion of germs for ourselves—and hence the "facts" as they are observed are already moralized: the deaths occurred only "where they used some practice against us," that is, where the Indians conspired secretly against the English. And with the wonderful self-validating circularity that characterizes virtually all powerful constructions of reality, the evidence for these secret conspiracies is precisely the deaths of the Indians.[34]

It is not surprising that Harriot seems to endorse the idea that God protects his chosen people by killing off untrustworthy Indians; what is surprising is to find him interested in the Indians' own anxious speculations about the unintended biological warfare that was destroying them. Drawing upon his special familiarity with the priests, he records a remarkable series of conjectures, almost all of which assume—correctly, as we now know—a link between the Indians' misfortune and the presence of the strangers. "Some people," observing that the English remained healthy while the Indians died, "could not tell," Harriot writes, "whether to think us gods or men"; others, seeing that the members of the first colony were all male, concluded that they were not born of women and therefore must be spirits of the dead returned to mortal form. Some medicine men learned in astrology blamed the disease on a recent eclipse of the sun and on a comet—a theory Harriot considers seriously and rejects—while others shared the prevailing English view and said "that it was the special work of God" on behalf of the colonists. And some who seem in historical hindsight eerily prescient prophesied "that there were more of [the English] generation yet to come, to kill theirs and take their places." The supporters of this theory even worked out a conception of the disease that in some features resembles our own: "Those that were immediately to come after us [the first English colonists], they imagined to be in the air, yet invisible and without bodies, and that they by our entreaty and for the love of us did make the people to die . . . by shooting invisible bullets into them" (380).

For a moment, as Harriot records these competing theories, it may seem to us as if there were no absolute assurance of God's national interest, as if the drive to displace and absorb the other had given way to conversation among equals, as if all meanings were provisional, as if the signification of events stood apart from power. Our impression is intensified because we know that the theory that would ultimately triumph over the moral conception of epidemic disease was already present, at least metaphorically, in the conversation.[35] In the very moment that the moral conception is busily authorizing itself, it registers the possibility (indeed from our vantage point, the inevitability) of its own destruction.

But why, we must ask ourselves, should power record other voices, permit subversive inquiries, register at its very center the transgressions that will ultimately violate it? The answer may be in part that power, even in a colonial situation, is not monolithic and hence may encounter and record in one of its functions materials that can threaten another of its functions; in part that power thrives on vigilance, and human beings are vigilant if they sense a threat; in part that power defines itself in relation to such threats or simply to that which is not identical with it. Harriot's text suggests an intensification of these observations: English power in the first Virginia colony *depends* upon the registering and even the production of potentially unsettling perspectives. "These their opinions I have set down the more at large," Harriot tells the "Adventurers, Favorers, and Wellwishers" of the colony to whom his report is addressed, "that it may appear unto you that there is good hope that they may be brought through discreet dealing and government to the embracing of the truth, and consequently to honor, obey, fear, and love us" (381). The recording of alien voices, their preservation in Harriot's text, is part of the process whereby Indian culture is constituted as a culture and thus brought into the light for study, discipline, correction, transformation. The momentary sense of instability or plenitude— the existence of other voices—is produced by the monological power that ultimately de-

nies the possibility of plenitude, just as the subversive hypothesis about European religion is tested and confirmed only by the imposition of that religion.

We may add that the power of which we are speaking is in effect an allocation method—a way of distributing to some and denying to others critical resources (here primarily corn and game) that prolong life. In a remarkable study of the "tragic choices" societies make in allocating scarce resources (for example, kidney machines) or in determining high risks (for example, the military draft), Guido Calabresi and Philip Bobbitt observe that by complex mixtures of approaches, societies attempt to avert "tragic results, that is, results which imply the rejection of values which are proclaimed to be fundamental." Although these approaches may succeed for a time, it will eventually become apparent that some sacrifice of fundamental values has taken place, whereupon "fresh mixtures of methods will be tried, structured . . . by the shortcomings of the approaches they replace." These too will in time give way to others in a "strategy of successive moves," an "intricate game" that reflects the simultaneous perception of an inherent flaw and the determination to "forget" that perception in an illusory resolution.[36] Hence the simple operation of any systematic order, any allocation method, inevitably risks exposing its own limitations, even (or perhaps especially) as it asserts its underlying moral principle.

This exposure is most intense at moments when a comfortably established ideology confronts unusual circumstances, when the moral value of a particular form of power is not merely assumed but explained. We may glimpse such a moment in Harriot's account of a visit from the colonists' principal Indian ally, the chief Wingina. Wingina, persuaded that the disease ravaging his people was indeed the work of the Christian God, had come to request that the English ask their God to direct his lethal magic against an enemy tribe. The colonists tried to explain that such a prayer would be "ungodly," that their God was indeed responsible for the disease but that in this as in all things, he would act only "according to his good pleasure as he had ordained" (379). Indeed, if men asked God to make an epidemic, he probably would not do it; the English could expect such providential help only if they made sincere "petition for the contrary," that is, for harmony and good fellowship in the service of truth and righteousness.

The problem with these assertions is not that they are self-consciously wicked (in the manner of Richard III or Iago) but that they are dismayingly moral and logically coherent; or rather, what is unsettling is one's experience of them, the nasty sense that they are at once irrefutable ethical propositions and pious humbug with which the English conceal from themselves the rapacity and aggression, or simply the horrible responsibility, implicit in their very presence. The explanatory moment manifests the self-validating, totalizing character of Renaissance political theology—its ability to account for almost every occurrence, even (or above all) apparently perverse or contrary occurrences—and at the same time confirms for us the drastic disillusionment that extends from Machiavelli to its definitive expression in Hume and Voltaire. In his own way, Wingina himself clearly thought his lesson in Christian ethics was polite nonsense. When the disease spread to his enemies, as it did shortly thereafter, he returned to the English to thank them—I presume with the Algonquian equivalent of a sly wink—for their friendly help, for "although we satisfied them not in promise, yet in deeds and effect we had fulfilled their desires" (379). For Harriot, this "marvellous accident," as he calls it, is another sign of the colony's great expectations.

Once again a disturbing vista—a skeptical critique of the function of Christian morality in the New World—is glimpsed only to be immediately closed off. Indeed we may feel at this point that subversion scarcely exists and may legitimately ask ourselves how our perception of the subversive and orthodox is generated. The answer, I think, is that the term *subversive* for us designates those elements in Renaissance culture that contemporary audiences tried to contain or, when containment seemed impossible, to destroy and that now conform to our own sense of truth and reality. That is, we find "subversive" in the past precisely those things that are *not* subversive to ourselves, that pose no threat to the order by which we live and allocate resources: in Harriot's *Brief and True Report,* the function of illusion in the establishment of religion, the displacement of a providential conception of disease by one focused on "invisible bullets," the exposure of the psychological and material interests served by a certain conception of divine power. Conversely, we identify as principles of order and authority in Renaissance texts what we would, if we took them seriously, find subversive for ourselves: religious and political absolutism, aristocracy of birth, demonology, humoral psychology, and the like. That we do not find such notions subversive, that we complacently identify them as principles of aesthetic or political order, replicates the process of containment that licensed the elements we call subversive in Renaissance texts: that is, our own values are sufficiently strong for us to contain alien forces almost effortlessly. What we find in Harriot's *Brief and True Report* can best be described by adapting a remark about the possibility of hope that Kafka once made to Max Brod: There is subversion, no end of subversion, only not for us.

## II

Shakespeare's plays are centrally, repeatedly concerned with the production and containment of subversion and disorder, and the three practices that I have identified in Harriot's text—testing, recording, and explaining—all have their recurrent theatrical equivalents, above all in the plays that meditate on the consolidation of state power.

These equivalents are not unique to Shakespeare; they are the signs of a broad institutional appropriation that is one of the root sources of the theater's vitality. Elizabethan playing companies contrived to absorb, refashion, and exploit some of the fundamental energies of a political authority that was itself already committed to histrionic display and hence was ripe for appropriation. But if he was not alone, Shakespeare nonetheless contrived to absorb more of these energies into his plays than any of his fellow playwrights. He succeeded in doing so because he seems to have understood very early in his career that power consisted not only in dazzling display—the pageants, processions, entries, and progresses of Elizabethan statecraft—but also in a systematic structure of relations, those linked strategies I have tried to isolate and identify in colonial discourse at the margins of Tudor society. Shakespeare evidently grasped such strategies not by brooding on the impact of English culture on far-off Virginia but by looking intently at the world immediately around him, by contemplating the queen and her powerful friends and enemies, and by reading imaginatively the great English chroniclers. And the crucial point is less that he *represented* the paradoxical practices of an authority deeply complicit in undermining its own legitimacy than that he *appropriated* for the theater the compelling energies at once released and organized by these practices.

The representation of a self-undermining authority is the principal concern of *Richard II,* which marks a brilliant advance over the comparable representation in the *Henry VI* trilogy, but the full appropriation for the stage of that authority and its power is not achieved until *1 Henry IV.* We may argue, of course,

that in this play there is little or no "self-undermining" at all: emergent authority in *1 Henry IV*—that is, the authority that begins to solidify around the figure of Hal—is strikingly different from the enfeebled command of Henry VI or the fatally self-wounded royal name of Richard II. "Who does not all along see," wrote Upton in the mid–eighteenth century, "that when prince Henry comes to be king he will assume a character suitable to his dignity?" My point is not to dispute this interpretation of the prince as, in Maynard Mack's words, "an ideal image of the potentialities of the English character,"[37] but to observe that such an ideal image involves as its positive condition the constant production of its own radical subversion and the powerful containment of that subversion.

We are continually reminded that Hal is a "juggler," a conniving hypocrite, and that the power he both serves and comes to embody is glorified usurpation and theft.[38] Moreover, the disenchantment makes itself felt in the very moments when Hal's moral authority is affirmed. Thus, for example, the scheme of Hal's redemption is carefully laid out in his soliloquy at the close of the first tavern scene, but as in the act of *explaining* that we have examined in Harriot, Hal's justification of himself threatens to fall away at every moment into its antithesis. "By how much better than my word I am," Hal declares, "By so much shall I falsify men's hopes" (1.2.210–11). To falsify men's hopes is to exceed their expectations, and it is also to disappoint their expectations, to deceive men, to turn hopes into fictions, to betray.

At issue are not only the contradictory desires and expectations centered on Hal in the play—the competing hopes of his royal father and his tavern friends—but our own hopes, the fantasies continually aroused by the play of innate grace, limitless playfulness, absolute friendship, generosity, and trust. Those fantasies are symbolized by certain echoing, talismanic phrases ("when thou art king," "shall we be merry?" "a thousand pound"), and they are bound up with the overall vividness, intensity, and richness of the theatrical practice itself. Yeats's phrase for the quintessential Shakespearean effect, "the emotion of multitude," seems particularly applicable to *1 Henry IV* with its multiplicity of brilliant characters, its intensely differentiated settings, its dazzling verbal wit, its mingling of high comedy, farce, epic heroism, and tragedy. The play awakens a dream of superabundance, which is given its irresistible embodiment in Falstaff.

But that dream is precisely what Hal betrays or rather, to use his own more accurate term, "falsifies." He does so in this play not by a decisive act of rejection, as at the close of *2 Henry IV,* but by a more subtle and continuous draining of the plentitude. "This chair shall be my state," proclaims Falstaff, improvising the king's part, "this dagger my sceptre, and this cushion my crown." Hal's cool rejoinder cuts deftly at both his real and his surrogate father: "Thy state is taken for a join'd-stool, thy golden sceptre for a leaden dagger, and thy precious rich crown for a pitiful bald crown" (2.4.378–82). Hal is the prince and principle of falsification—he is himself a counterfeit companion, and he reveals the emptiness in the world around him. "Dost thou hear, Hal?" Falstaff implores, with the sheriff at the door. "Never call a true piece of gold a counterfeit. Thou art essentially made, without seeming so" (2.4.491–93). The words, so oddly the reverse of the ordinary advice to beware of accepting the counterfeit for reality, attach themselves to both Falstaff and Hal: do not denounce me to the law for I, Falstaff, am genuinely your adoring friend and not merely a parasite; and also, do not think of yourself, Hal, as a mere pretender, do not imagine that your value depends upon falsification.

The "true piece of gold" is alluring because of the widespread faith that it has an intrinsic value, that it does not depend upon the stamp of authority and hence cannot be arbitrarily duplicated or devalued, that it is indifferent to its circumstances, that it cannot be robbed of its worth. This is the fantasy of identity that Falstaff holds out to Hal and that Hal empties out, as he empties out Falstaff's pockets. "What hast thou found?" "Nothing but papers, my lord" (2.4.532–33).[39] Hal is an anti-Midas: everything he touches turns to dross. And this devaluation is the source of his own sense of value, a value not intrinsic but contingent, dependent upon the circulation of counterfeit coin and the subtle manipulation of appearances:

And like bright metal on a sullen ground,
My reformation, glitt'ring o'er my fault,
Shall show more goodly and attract more
        eyes
Than that which hath no foil to set it off.
I'll so offend, to make offense a skill,
Redeeming time when men think least I
        will.

                                        (1.2.212–17)

Such lines, as Empson remarks, "cannot have been written without bitterness against the prince," yet the bitterness is not incompatible with an "ironical acceptance" of his authority.[40] The dreams of plenitude are not abandoned altogether—Falstaff in particular has an imaginative life that overflows the confines of the play itself—but the daylight world of *1 Henry IV* comes to seem increasingly one of counterfeit, and hence one governed by Bolingbroke's cunning (he sends "counterfeits" of himself out onto the battlefield) and by Hal's calculations. A "starveling"—fat Falstaff's word for Hal—triumphs in a world of scarcity. Though we can perceive at every point, through our own constantly shifting allegiances, the potential instability of the structure of power that has Henry IV and his son at the pinnacle and Robin Ostler, who "never joy'd since the price of oats rose" (2.1.12–13), near the bottom,

Hal's "redemption" is as inescapable and in-evitable as the outcome of those practical jokes the madcap prince is so fond of playing. Indeed, the play insists, this redemption is not something toward which the action moves but something that is happening at every moment of the theatrical representa-tion.

The same yoking of the unstable and the inevitable may be seen in the play's acts of *recording,* that is, the moments in which we hear voices that seem to dwell outside the realms ruled by the potentates of the land. These voices exist and have their apotheosis in Falstaff, but their existence proves to be utterly bound up with Hal, contained politi-cally by his purposes as they are justified aes-thetically by his involvement. The perfect emblem of this containment is Falstaff's company, marching off to Shrewsbury: "dis-carded unjust servingmen, younger sons to younger brothers, revolted tapsters, and os-tlers trade-fall'n, the cankers of a calm world and a long peace" (4.2.27–30). As many a homily would tell us, these are the very types of Elizabethan subversion—the masterless men who rose up periodically in desperate protests against their social superiors. A half century later they would swell the ranks of the New Model Army and be disciplined into a revolutionary force. But here they are pressed into service as defenders of the estab-lished order, "good enough to toss," as Fal-staff tells Hal, "food for powder, food for powder" (4.2.65–66). For power as well as powder, and we may add that this food is produced as well as consumed by the great.

Shakespeare gives us a glimpse of this pro-duction in the odd little scene in which Hal, with the connivance of Poins, reduces the puny tapster Francis to the mechanical repeti-tion of the word "Anon":

PRINCE:  Nay, but hark you, Francis: for the
                sugar thou gavest me, 'twas a penny-
                worth, was't not?

FRANCIS:  O Lord, I would it had been two!
PRINCE:  I will give thee for it a thousand
                pound. Ask me when thou wilt, and
                thou shalt have it.
POINS:  *(Within)* Francis!
FRANCIS:  Anon, anon.
PRINCE:  Anon, Francis? No, Francis; but to-
                morrow, Francis; or, Francis, a' Thurs-
                day; or indeed, Francis, when thou
                wilt.

(2.4.58–67)

The Bergsonian comedy in such a moment resides in Hal's exposing a drastic reduction of human possibility: "That ever this fellow should have fewer words than a parrot," he says at the scene's end, "and yet the son of a woman!" (2.4.98–99). But the chief interest for us resides in Hal's producing the very re-duction he exposes. The fact of this produc-tion, its theatrical demonstration, implicates Hal not only in the linguistic poverty upon which he plays but in the poverty of the five years of apprenticeship Francis has yet to serve: "Five year!" Hal exclaims, "by'r lady, a long lease for the clinking of pewter" (2.4.45–46). And as the prince is implicated in the production of this oppressive order, so is he implicated in the impulse to abrogate it: "But, Francis, dearest thou be so valiant as to play the coward with thy indenture, and show it a fair pair of heels and run from it?" (2.4.46–48).

It is tempting to think of this particular mo-ment—the prince awakening the appren-tice's discontent—as linked darkly with some supposed uneasiness in Hal about his own apprenticeship.[41] The momentary glimpse of a revolt against authority is closed off at once, however, with a few obscure words calculated to return Francis to his trade without enabling him to understand why he must return to it:

PRINCE:  Why then your brown bastard is
                your only drink! for look you, Francis,
                your white canvas doublet will sully.

> In Barbary, sir, it cannot come to so
> much.
> FRANCIS: What, sir?
> POINS: *(Within)* Francis!
> PRINCE: Away, you rogue, dost thou not
> hear them call?
>
> (2.4.73–79)

If Francis takes the earlier suggestion, robs his master and runs away, he will find a place for himself, the play implies, only as one of the "revolted tapsters" in Falstaff's company, men as good as dead long before they march to their deaths as upholders of the crown. Better that he should follow the drift of Hal's deliberately mystifying words and continue to clink pewter. As for the prince, his interest in the brief exchange, beyond what we have already sketched, is suggested by his boast to Poins moments before Francis enters: "I have sounded the very base-string of humility. Sirrah, I am sworn brother to a leash of drawers, and can call them all by their christen names, as Tom, Dick, and Francis" (2.4.5–8). The prince must sound the base-string of humility if he is to play all of the chords and hence be the master of the instrument, and his ability to conceal his motives and render opaque his language offers assurance that he himself will not be played on by another.

I have spoken of such scenes in *1 Henry IV* as resembling what in Harriot's text I have called *recording,* a mode that culminates for Harriot in a glossary, the beginnings of an Algonquian-English dictionary, designed to facilitate further acts of recording and hence to consolidate English power in Virginia. The resemblance may be seen most clearly perhaps in Hal's own glossary of tavern slang: "They call drinking deep, dyeing scarlet, and when you breathe in your watering, they cry 'hem!' and bid you play it off. To conclude, I am so good a proficient in one quarter of an hour, that I can drink with any tinker in his own language during my life" (2.4.15–20). The potential value of these lessons, the func-

tional interest to power of recording the speech of an "under-skinker" and his mates, may be glimpsed in the expressions of loyalty that Hal laughingly recalls: "They take it already upon their salvation, that . . . when I am King of England I shall command all the good lads in Eastcheap" (2.4.9–15).

It may be objected that there is something slightly absurd in likening such moments to aspects of Harriot's text; *1 Henry IV* is a play, not a tract for potential investors in a colonial scheme, and the only values we may be sure Shakespeare had in mind, the argument would go, are theatrical values. But theatrical values do not exist in a realm of privileged literariness, of textual or even institutional self-referentiality. Shakespeare's theater was not isolated by its wooden walls, nor did it merely reflect social and ideological logical forces that lay entirely outside it: rather the Elizabethan and Jacobean theater was itself a *social event* in reciprocal contact with other social events.

One might add that *1 Henry IV* itself insists upon the impossibility of sealing off the interests of the theater from the interests of power. Hal's characteristic activity is playing or, more precisely, theatrical improvisation—his parts include his father, Hotspur, Hotspur's wife, a thief in buckram, himself as prodigal, and himself as penitent—and he fully understands his own behavior through most of the play as a role that he is performing. We might expect that this role playing gives way at the end of his true identity: "I shall hereafter," Hal has promised his father, "Be more myself" (3.2.92–93). With the killing of Hotspur, however, Hal clearly does not reject all theatrical masks but rather replaces one with another. "The time will come," Hal declares midway through the play, "That I shall make this northern youth exchange/His glorious deeds for my indignities" (3.2.144–46); when that time *has* come, at the play's close, Hal hides with his "favors" (that is, a scarf or other emblem, but the word *favor* also has in the sixteenth century the sense of "face") the dead Hotspur's "mangled face" (5.4.96), as if to mark the completion of the exchange.

Theatricality, then, is not set over against power but is one of power's essential modes. In lines that anticipate Hal's promise, the angry Henry IV tells Worcester, "I will from henceforth rather be myself,/Mighty and to be fear'd, than my condition" (1.3.5–6). "To be oneself" here means to perform one's part in the scheme of power rather than to manifest one's natural disposition, or what we would normally designate as the very core of the self. Indeed it is by no means clear that such a thing as a natural disposition exists in the play except as a theatrical fiction: we recall that in Falstaff's hands the word *instinct* becomes histrionic rhetoric, an improvised excuse for his flight from the masked prince. "Beware instinct—the lion will not touch the true prince. Instinct is a great matter; I was now a coward on instinct. I shall think the better of myself, and thee, during my life; I for a valiant lion, and thou for a true prince" (2.4.271–75). Both claims—Falstaff's to natural valor, Hal's to legitimate royalty—are, the lines darkly imply, of equal merit.

Again and again in *1 Henry IV* we are tantalized by the possibility of an escape from theatricality and hence from the constant pressure of improvisational power, but we are, after all, in the theater, and our pleasure depends upon there being no escape, and our applause ratifies the triumph of our confinement. The play operates in the manner of its central character, charming us with its visions of breadth and solidarity, "redeeming" itself in the end by betraying our hopes, and earning with this betrayal our slightly anxious admiration. Hence the odd balance in this play of spaciousness—the constant multiplication of separate, vividly realized realms—and militant claustrophobia: the absorption of all of these realms by a power at once vital and impoverished. The balance is almost perfect, as if Shakespeare had some-

how reached through in *1 Henry IV* to the very center of the system of opposed and interlocking forces that held Tudor society together.

### III

When we turn, however, to the plays that continue the chronicle of Hal's career, *2 Henry IV* and *Henry V,* we find not only that the forces balanced in the earlier play have pulled apart—the claustrophobia triumphant in *2 Henry IV,* the spaciousness triumphant in *Henry V*[42]—but that from this new perspective the familiar view of *1 Henry IV* as a perfectly poised play must be revised. What appeared as "balance" may on closer inspection seem like radical instability tricked out as moral or aesthetic order; what appeared as clarity may seem now like a conjurer's trick concealing confusion in order to buy time and stave off the collapse of an illusion.[43] Not waving but drowning.

In *2 Henry IV* the characteristic operations of power are less equivocal than they had been in the preceding play: there is no longer even the lingering illusion of distinct realms, each with its own system of values, its soaring visions of plenitude, and its bad dreams. There is manifestly a single system now, one based on predation and betrayal. Hotspur's intoxicating dreams of honor are dead, replaced by the cold rebellion of cunning but impotent schemers. The warm, roistering noise overheard in the tavern—noise that seemed to signal a subversive alternative to rebellion—turns out to be the sound of a whore and a bully beating a customer to death. And Falstaff, whose earlier larcenies were gilded by fantasies of innate grace, now talks of turning diseases to commodity (1.2.-248).

Only Prince Hal seems in this play less meanly calculating, subject now to fits of weariness and confusion, though this change serves less to humanize him (as Auerbach argued in a famous essay) than to make it clear that the betrayals are systematic. They happen to him and for him. He need no longer soliloquize his intention to "falsify men's hopes" by selling his wastrel friends: the sale will be brought about by the structure of things, a structure grasped in this play under the twinned names of time and necessity. So too there is no longer any need for heroic combat with a dangerous, glittering enemy like Hotspur (the only reminder of whose voice in this play is Pistol's parody of Marlovian swaggering); the rebels are deftly, if ingloriously, dispatched by the false promises of Hal's younger brother, the primly virtuous John of Lancaster. To seal his lies, Lancaster swears fittingly "by the honor of my blood" (4.2.55)—the cold blood, as Falstaff observes of Hal, that he inherited from his father.

The recording of alien voices—the voices of those who have no power to leave literate traces of their existence—continues in this play, but without even the theatrical illusion of princely complicity. The king is still convinced that his son is a prodigal and that the kingdom will fall to ruin after his death—perhaps he finds a peculiar consolation in the thought—but it is no longer Hal alone who declares (against all appearances) his secret commitment to disciplinary authority. Warwick assures the king that the prince's interests in the good lads of Eastcheap are entirely what they should be:

The Prince but studies his companions
Like a strange tongue, wherein, to gain the
    language,
'Tis needful that the most immodest word
Be look'd upon and learnt, which once
    attain'd,
Your Highness knows, comes to no further
    use
But to be known and hated. So, like gross
    terms,

The Prince will in the perfectness of time
Cast off his followers, and their memory
Shall as a pattern or a measure live,
By which his Grace must mete the lives of
    other,
Turning past evils to advantages.

(4.4.68–78)

At first the language analogy likens the prince's low-life excursions to the search for proficiency: perfect linguistic competence, the "mastery" of a language, requires the fullest possible vocabulary. But the darkness of Warwick's words—"to be known and hated"—immediately pushes the goal of Hal's linguistic researches beyond proficiency. When in *1 Henry IV* Hal boasts of his mastery of tavern slang, we are allowed for a moment at least to imagine that we are witnessing a social bond, the human fellowship of the extremest top and bottom of society in a homely ritual act of drinking together. The play may make it clear, as I have argued, that well-defined political interests are involved, but these interests may be bracketed, if only briefly, for the pleasure of imagining what Victor Turner calls "communitas"—a union based on the momentary breaking of the hierarchical order that normally governs a community.[44] And even when we pull back from this spacious sense of union, we are permitted for much of the play to take pleasure at least in Hal's surprising skill, the proficiency he rightly celebrates in himself.

To learn another language is to acknowledge the existence of another people and to acquire the ability to function, however crudely, in another social world. Hal's remark about drinking with any tinker in his own language suggests, if only jocularly, that for him the lower classes are virtually another people, an alien tribe—immensely more populous than his own—within the kingdom. That this perception extended beyond the confines of Shakespeare's play is suggested by the evidence that middle- and upper-class English settlers in the New World regarded the American Indians less as another race than as a version of their own lower classes; one man's tinker is another man's Indian.[45]

If Hal's glossary initially seems to resemble Harriot's practical word list in the *Brief and True Report,* with its Algonquian equivalents for *fire, food, shelter,* Warwick's account of Hal's intentions suggests a deeper resemblance to a different kind of glossary, one more specifically linked to the attempt to understand and control the lower classes. I refer to the sinister glossaries appended to sixteenth-century accounts of criminals and vagabonds. "Here I set before the good reader the lewd, lousy language of these loitering lusks and lazy lorels," announces Thomas Harman as he introduces (with a comical flourish designed to display his own rhetorical gifts) what he claims is an authentic list, compiled at great personal cost.[46] His pamphlet, *A Caveat for Common Cursitors,* is the fruit, he declares, of personal research, difficult because his informants are "marvellous subtle and crafty." But "with fair flattering words, money, and good cheer," he has learned much about their ways, "not without faithful promise made unto them never to discover their names or anything they showed me" (82). Harman cheerfully goes on to publish what they showed him, and he ends his work not only with a glossary of "peddler's French" but with an alphabetical list of names, so that the laws made for "the extreme punishment" of these wicked idlers may be enforced.

It is not clear that Harman's subjects—upright men, doxies, Abraham men, and the like—bear any more relation to social reality than either Doll Tearsheet or Mistress Quickly.[47] Much of the *Caveat,* like the other cony-catching pamphlets of the period, has the air of a jest book: time-honored tales of tricksters and rogues, dished out as realistic observation. (It is not encouraging that the

rogues' term for the stocks in which they were punished, according to Harman, is "the harmans.") But Harman is concerned to convey at least the impression of accurate observation and recording—clearly, this was among the book's selling points—and one of the principal rhetorical devices he uses to do so is the spice of betrayal: he repeatedly calls attention to his solemn promises never to reveal anything he has been told, for his breaking of his word assures the accuracy and importance of what he reveals.

A middle-class Prince Hal, Harman claims that through dissembling he has gained access to a world normally hidden from his kind, and he will turn that access to the advantage of the kingdom by helping his readers to identify and eradicate the dissemblers in their midst. Harman's own personal interventions—the acts of detection and apprehension he proudly reports (or invents)—are not enough; only his book can fully expose the cunning sleights of the rogues and thereby induce the justices and shrieves to be more vigilant and punitive. Just as theatricality is thematized in the *Henry IV* plays as one of the crucial agents of royal power, so in *A Caveat for Common Cursitors* (and in much of the cony-catching literature of the period in England and France) printing is represented in the text itself as a force for social order and the detection of criminal fraud. The printed book can be widely disseminated and easily revised, so that the vagabonds' names and tricks may be known before they themselves arrive at an honest citizen's door; as if this mobility were not tangible enough, Harman claims that when his pamphlet was only halfway printed, his printer helped him apprehend a particularly sly "counterfeit crank"—a pretended epileptic. In Harman's account the printer turns detective, first running down the street to apprehend the dissembler, then on a subsequent occasion luring him "with fair allusions" (116) and a show of charity into the hands of the constable. With such lurid tales Harman literalizes the power of the book to hunt down vagabonds and bring them to justice.

The danger of such accounts is that the ethical charge will reverse itself, with the forces of order—the people, as it were, of the book—revealed as themselves dependent on dissembling and betrayal and the vagabonds revealed either as less fortunate and well-protected imitators of their betters or, alternatively, as primitive rebels against the hypocrisy of a cruel society. Exactly such a reversal seems to occur again and again in the rogue literature of the period, from the doxies and morts who answer Harman's rebukes with unfailing, if spare, dignity to the more articulate defenders of vice elsewhere who insist that their lives are at worst imitations of the lives of the great:

> Though your experience in the world be not so great as mine [says a cheater at dice], yet am I sure ye see that no man is able to live an honest man unless he have some privy way to help himself withal, more than the world is witness of. Think you the noblemen could do as they do, if in this hard world they should maintain so great a port only upon their rent? Think you the lawyers could be such purchasers if their pleas were short, and all their judgments, justice and conscience? Suppose ye that offices would be so dearly bought, and the buyers so soon enriched, if they counted not pillage an honest point of purchase? Could merchants, without lies, false making their wares, and selling them by a crooked light, to deceive the chapman in the thread or colour, grow so soon rich and to a baron's possessions, and make all their posterity gentlemen?[48]

Though these reversals are at the very heart of the rogue literature, it would be as much of a mistake to regard their intended effect as subversive as to regard in a similar light the

comparable passages—most often articulated by Falstaff—in Shakespeare's histories. The subversive voices are produced by and within the affirmations of order; they are powerfully registered, but they do not undermine that order. Indeed, as the example of Harman—so much cruder than Shakespeare—suggests, the order is neither possible nor fully convincing without both the presence and perception of betrayal.

This dependence on betrayal does not prevent Harman from leveling charges of hypocrisy and deep dissembling at the rogues and from urging his readers to despise and prosecute them. On the contrary, Harman's moral indignation seems paradoxically heightened by his own implication in the deceitfulness that he condemns, as if the rhetorical violence of the condemnation cleansed him of any guilt. His broken promises are acts of civility, necessary strategies for securing social well-being. The "rowsy, ragged rabblement of rakeshells" has put itself outside the bounds of civil conversation; justice consists precisely in taking whatever measures are necessary to eradicate them. Harman's false oaths are the means of identifying and ridding the community of the purveyors of false oaths. The pestilent few will "fret, fume, swear, and stare at this my book," in which their practices, disclosed after they had received fair promises of confidentiality, are laid open, but the majority will band together in righteous reproach: "The honourable will abhor them, the worshipful will reject them, the yeomen will sharply taunt them, the husbandmen utterly defy them, the labouring men bluntly chide them, the women with clapping hands cry out at them" (84). To like reading about vagabonds is to hate them and to approve of their ruthless betrayal.

"The right people of the play," a gifted critic of *2 Henry IV* observes, "merge into a larger order; the wrong people resist or misuse that larger order."[49] True enough, but like Harman's community of vagabond-haters, the "larger order" of the Lancastrian state in this play seems to batten on the breaking of oaths. Shakespeare does not shrink from any of the felt nastiness implicit in this sorting out of the right people and the wrong people; he takes the discursive mode that he could have found in Harman and a hundred other texts and intensifies it, so that the founding of the modern state, like the self-fashioning of the modern prince, is shown to be based upon acts of calculation, intimidation, and deceit. And these acts are performed in an entertainment for which audiences, the subjects of this very state, pay money and applaud.

There is, throughout *2 Henry IV,* a sense of constriction that is only intensified by the obsessive enumeration of details: "Thou didst swear to me upon a parcel-gilt goblet, sitting in my Dolphin chamber, at the round table by a sea-coal fire, upon Wednesday in Wheeson week . . ." (2.1.86–89). We may find, in Justice Shallow's garden, a few twilight moments of release from this oppressive circumstantial and strategic constriction, but Falstaff mercilessly deflates them—and the puncturing is so wonderfully adroit, so amusing, that we welcome it: "I do remember him at Clement's Inn, like a man made after supper of a cheeseparing. When 'a was naked, he was for all the world like a fork'd redish, with a head fantastically carv'd upon it with a knife" (3.2.308–12).

What remains is the law of nature: the strong eat the weak. Yet this is not quite what Shakespeare invites the audience to affirm through its applause. Like Harman, Shakespeare refuses to endorse so badly cynical a conception of the social order; instead actions that should have the effect of radically undermining authority turn out to be the props of that authority. In this play, even more cruelly than in *1 Henry IV,* moral values—justice, order, civility—are secured through the apparent generation of their subversive contraries. Out of the squalid betrayals that preserve the state emerges the "for-

mal majesty" into which Hal at the close, through a final, definitive betrayal—the rejection of Falstaff—merges himself.

There are moments in *Richard II* when the collapse of kingship seems to be confirmed in the discovery of the physical body of the ruler, the pathos of his creatural existence:

> throw away respect,
> Tradition, form, and ceremonious duty,
> For you have but mistook me all this while.
> I live with bread like you, feel want,
> Taste grief, need friends: subjected thus,
> How can you say to me I am a king?
> (3.2.172–77)

By the close of *2 Henry IV* such physical limitations have been absorbed into the ideological structure, and hence justification, of kingship. It is precisely because Prince Hal lives with bread that we can understand the sacrifice that he and, for that matter, his father have made. Unlike Richard II, Henry IV articulates this sacrifice not as a piece of histrionic rhetoric but as a private meditation, the innermost thoughts of a troubled, weary man:

> Why rather, sleep, liest thou in smoky cribs,
> Upon uneasy pallets stretching thee,
> And hush'd with buzzing night-flies to thy
>     slumber,
> Than in the perfum'd chambers of the
>     great,
> Under the canopies of costly state,
> And lull'd with sound of sweetest melody?
> (3.1.9–14)

Who knows? Perhaps it is even true; perhaps in a society in which the overwhelming majority of men and women had next to nothing, the few who were rich and powerful did lie awake at night. But we should understand that this sleeplessness was not a well-kept secret: the sufferings of the great are one of the familiar themes in the literature of the governing classes in the sixteenth century.[50] Henry IV speaks in soliloquy, but as is so often the case in Shakespeare, his isolation only intensifies the sense that he is addressing a large audience: the audience of the theater. We are invited to take measure of his suffering, to understand—here and elsewhere in the play—the costs of power. And we are invited to understand these costs in order to ratify the power, to accept the grotesque and cruelly unequal distribution of possessions: everything to the few, nothing to the many. The rulers earn, or at least pay for, their exalted position through suffering, and this suffering ennobles, if it does not exactly cleanse, the lies and betrayals upon which this position depends.

As so often, Falstaff parodies this ideology, or rather—and more significantly—presents it as humbug *before* it makes its appearance as official truth. Called away from the tavern to the court, Falstaff turns to Doll and Mistress Quickly and proclaims sententiously: "You see, my good wenches, how men of merit are sought after. The undeserver may sleep when the man of action is call'd on" (2.4.374–77). Seconds later this rhetoric—marked out as something with which to impress whores and innkeepers to whom one owes money one does not intend to pay—recurs in the speech and, by convention of the soliloquy, the innermost thoughts of the king.

This staging of what we may term anticipatory, or proleptic, parody is a major structural principle of Shakespeare's play. Its effect is not (as with straightforward parodies) to ridicule the claims of high seriousness but rather to mark them as slightly suspect and to encourage guarded skepticism. Thus in the wake of Falstaff's burlesque of the weariness of the virtuous, the king's insomniac pathos reverberates hollowness as well as poignancy. At such moments *2 Henry IV* seems to be testing and confirming a dark and disturbing hypothesis about the nature of monarchical power in England: that its moral

authority rests upon a hypocrisy so deep that the hypocrites themselves believe it. "Then (happy) low, lie down!/Uneasy lies the head that wears a crown" (3.1.30–31): so the old pike tells the young dace. But the old pike actually seems to believe in his own speeches, just as he may believe that he never really sought the crown, "But that necessity so bow'd the state/That I and greatness were compell'd to kiss" (3.1.73–74). Our privileged knowledge of the network of state betrayals and privileged access to Falstaff's cynical wisdom can make this opaque hypocrisy transparent. Yet even with *2 Henry IV,* where the lies and the self-serving sentiments are utterly inescapable, where the illegitimacy of legitimate authority is repeatedly demonstrated, where the whole state seems—to adapt More's phrase—a conspiracy of the great to enrich and protect their interests under the name of commonwealth, even here the state, watchful for signs of sedition on the stage, was not prodded to intervene. We may choose to attribute this apparent somnolence to incompetence or corruption, but the linkages I have sketched between the history plays and the discursive practices represented by Harriot and Harman suggest another explanation. Once again, though in a still more iron-age spirit than at the close of *1 Henry IV,* the play appears to ratify the established order, with the new-crowned Henry V merging his body into "the great body of our state," with Falstaff despised and rejected, and with Lancaster—the coldhearted betrayer of the rebels—left to admire his still more coldhearted brother: "I like this fair proceeding of the King's" (5.5.97).[51]

The mood at the close remains, to be sure, an unpleasant one—the rejection of Falstaff has been one of the nagging "problems" of Shakespeare criticism—but the discomfort only serves to verify Hal's claim that he has turned away his former self. If there is frustration at the harshness of the play's end, the frustration confirms a carefully plotted official strategy whereby subversive perceptions are at once produced and contained:

> My father is gone wild into his grave;
> For in his tomb lie my affections,
> And with his spirits sadly I survive,
> To mock the expectation of the world,
> To frustrate prophecies, and to rase out
> Rotten opinion. . . .
>
> (5.2.123−28)

## IV

The first part of *Henry IV* enables us to feel at moments that we are like Harriot, surveying a complex new world, testing upon it dark thoughts without damaging the order that those thoughts would seem to threaten. The second part of *Henry IV* suggests that we are still more like the Indians, compelled to pay homage to a system of beliefs whose fraudulence only confirms their power, authenticity, and truth. The concluding play in the series, *Henry V,* insists that we have all along been both colonizer and colonized, king and subject. The play deftly registers every nuance of royal hypocrisy, ruthlessness, and bad faith—testing, in effect, the proposition that successful rule depends not upon sacredness but upon demonic violence—but it does so in the context of a celebration, a collective panegyric to "This star of England," the charismatic leader who purges the commonwealth of its incorrigibles and forges the martial national state.

By yoking together diverse peoples—represented in the play by the Welshman Fluellen, the Irishman Macmorris, and the Scotsman Jamy, who fight at Agincourt alongside the loyal Englishmen—Hal symbolically tames the last wild areas in the British Isles, areas that in the sixteenth century represented, far more powerfully than any New World people, the doomed outposts of a vanishing tribalism.[52] We might expect then that

in *Henry V* the mode that I have called recording would reach its fullest flowering, and in a sense it does. The English allies are each given a distinct accentual notation—" 'a utt'red as prave words at the pridge as you shall see in a summer's day"; "By Chrish law, 'tish ill done! The work ish give over"; "It sall be vary gud, gud feith, gud captens bath, and I sall quit you with gud leve"—a notation that helped determine literary representations of the stock Welshman, Irishman, and Scotsman for centuries to come. But their distinctness is curiously formal, a collection of mechanistic attributes recalling the heightened but static individuality of Jonson's humorous grotesques.

The verbal tics of such characters interest us because they represent not what is alien but what is predictable and automatic. They give pleasure because they persuade an audience of its own mobility and complexity; even a spectator gaping passively at the play's sights and manipulated by its rhetoric is freer than these puppets jerked on the strings of their own absurd accents. Only Fluellen (much of the time an exuberant, bullying prince-pleaser) seems at one moment to articulate perceptions that lie outside the official line, and he arrives at these perceptions not through his foreignness but through his relentless pursuit of classical analogies. Teasing out a Plutarch-like parallel between Hal and "Alexander the Pig"—"There is a river in Macedon, and there is also moreover a river at Monmouth," and so forth—Fluellen reaches the observation that Alexander "did, in his ales and his angers, look you, kill his best friend, Clytus." Gower quickly intervenes: "Our King is not like him in that; he never kill'd any of his friends." But Fluellen persists: "as Alexander kill'd his friend Clytus, being in his ales and his cups; so also Harry Monmouth, being in his right wits and his good judgments, turn'd away the fat knight with the great belly doubled. He was full of jests, and gipes, and knaveries, and mocks—I have forgot his name." Gower provides it: "Sir John Falstaff" (4.7.-26–51).

The moment is potentially devastating. The comparison with drunken Alexander focuses all our perceptions of Hal's sober cold-bloodedness, from his rejection of Falstaff—"The King has kill'd his heart" (2.1.88)—to his responsibility for the execution of his erstwhile boon companion Bardolph. The low-life characters in the earlier plays had been the focus of Hal's language lessons, but as Warwick had predicted, the prince studied them as "gross terms," no sooner learned than discarded.

The discarding in *Henry V* is not an attractive sight but is perfectly consistent with the practice we have analyzed in Harman's *Caveat*. Indeed in a direct recollection of the cony-catching literature, Fluellen learns that Pistol, whom he had thought "as valiant a man as Mark Antony" (3.6.13–14), is "a rogue, that now and then goes to the wars, to grace himself at his return into London under the form of a soldier" (3.6.67–69). "You must learn to know such slanders of the age," remarks Gower in a line that could serve as Harman's epigraph, "or else you may be marvellously mistook" (3.6.79–81). And how does Fluellen learn that Pistol is one of the slanders of the age? What does Pistol do to give himself away? He passionately pleads that Fluellen intervene to save Bardolph, who has been sentenced to die for stealing a "pax of little price." "Let gallows gape for dog, let man go free," rages Pistol, "and let not hemp his windpipe suffocate" (3.6.42–43). Fluellen refuses; Bardolph hangs; and this attempt to save his friend's life marks Pistol as a "rascally, scald, beggarly, lousy, pragging knave" (5.1.5–6). By contrast, Hal's symbolic killing of Falstaff—which might have been recorded as a bitter charge against him—is advanced by Fluellen as the climactic manifestation of his virtues. No sooner is it mentioned than the king himself enters in triumph, lead-

ing his French prisoners. This entrance, with its military "Alarum" followed by a royal "Flourish," is the perfect emblematic instance of a potential dissonance being absorbed into a charismatic celebration. The betrayal of friends does not subvert but rather sustains the moral authority and the compelling glamour of power. That authority, as the play defines it, is precisely the ability to betray one's friends without stain.

If neither the English allies nor the low-life characters seem to fulfill adequately the role of aliens whose voices are "recorded," *Henry V* apparently gives us a sustained, even extreme, version of this practice in the dialogue of the French characters, dialogue that is in part presented untranslated in the performance. This dialogue includes even a language lesson, the very emblem of "recording" in the earlier plays. Yet like the English allies, the French enemies say remarkably little that is alien or disturbing in relation to the central voice of authority in the play. To be sure, several of the French nobles contemptuously dismiss Hal as "a vain, giddy, shallow, humorous youth" (2.4.28), but these terms of abuse are outmoded; it is as if news of the end of *1 Henry IV* or of its sequel had not yet crossed the Channel. Likewise, the easy French assumption of cultural and social superiority to the English—"The emptying of our fathers' luxury,/Our scions, put in wild and savage stock" (3.5.6–7)—is voiced only to be deflated by the almost miraculous English victory. The glamour of French aristocratic culture is not denied (see, for example, the litany of noble names beginning at 3.5.40), but it issues in overweening self-confidence and a military impotence that is explicitly thematized as sexual impotence. The French warriors "hang like roping icicles/Upon our houses' thatch," while the English "Sweat drops of gallant youth in our rich fields!" (3.5.23–25). In consequence, complains the Dauphin,

Our madams mock at us, and plainly say
Our mettle is bred out, and they will give
Their bodies to the lust of English youth.
                                          (3.5.28–30)

Thus the affirmation of French superiority is immediately reprocessed as an enhancement of English potency. By the play's close, with a self-conscious gesture toward the conventional ending of a comedy, the sexualized violence of the invasion is transfigured and tamed in Hal's wooing of Princess Katherine: "I love France so well that I will not part with a village of it; I will have it all mine. And, Kate, when France is mine and I am yours, then yours is France and you are mine" (5.2.-173–76). Acknowledgment of the other has now issued in the complete absorption of the other.

As for the language lesson, it is no longer Hal but the French princess who is the student. There is always a slight amusement in hearing one's own language spoken badly, a gratifying sense of possessing effortlessly what for others is a painful achievement. This sense is mingled at times with a condescending encouragement of the childish efforts of the inept learner, at times with delight at the inadvertent absurdities or indecencies into which the learner stumbles. (I spent several minutes in Bergamo once convulsing passersby with requests for directions to the Colleone Chapel. It was not until much later that I realized that I was pronouncing it the "Coglioni"—"Balls"—Chapel.) In *Henry V* the pleasure is intensified because the French princess is by implication learning English as a consequence of the successful English invasion, an invasion graphically figured as a rape. And the pleasing sense of national and specifically male superiority is crowned by the comic spectacle of the obscenities into which the princess is inadvertently led.[53]

If the subversive force of "recording" is substantially reduced in *Henry V,* the mode I have called explaining is by contrast intensi-

fied in its power to disturb. The war of conquest that Henry V launches against the French is depicted as carefully founded on acts of "explaining." The play opens with a notoriously elaborate account of the king's genealogical claim to the French throne, and, as in the comparable instances in Harriot, this ideological justification of English policy is an unsettling mixture of "impeccable" reasoning (once its initial premises are accepted) and gross self-interest.[54] In the ideological apologies for absolutism, the self-interest of the monarch and the interest of the nation are identical, and both in turn are secured by God's overarching design. Hence Hal's personal triumph at Agincourt is represented as the nation's triumph, which in turn is represented as God's triumph. When the deliciously favorable kill ratio—ten thousand French dead compared to twenty-nine English[55]—is reported to the king, he immediately gives "full trophy, signal, and ostent," as the Chorus later puts it, to God: "Take it, God,/For it is none but thine!" (4.8.11–12).

Hal evidently thinks this explanation of the English victory—this translation of its cause and significance from human to divine agency—needs some reinforcement:

And be it death proclaimed through our
    host
To boast of this, or take that praise from
    God
Which is his only.

                                          (4.8.114–116)

By such an edict God's responsibility for the slaughter of the French is enforced, and with it is assured at least the glow of divine approval over the entire enterprise, from the complex genealogical claims to the execution of traitors, the invasion of France, the threats leveled against civilians, the massacre of the prisoners. Yet there is something disconcerting as well as reinforcing about this draconian mode of ensuring that God receive credit: with a strategic circularity at once compelling and suspect, God's credit for the killing can be guaranteed only by the threat of more killing. The element of compulsion would no doubt predominate if the audience's own survival were at stake—the few Elizabethans who openly challenged the theological pretensions of the great found themselves in deep trouble—but were the stakes this high in the theater? Was it not possible inside the playhouse walls to question certain claims elsewhere unquestionable?

A few years earlier, at the close of *The Jew of Malta,* Marlowe had cast a witheringly ironic glance, worthy of Machiavelli, at the piety of the triumphant: Ferneze's gift to God of the "trophy, signal, and ostent" of the successful betrayal of Barabas is the final bitter joke of a bitter play. Shakespeare does not go so far. But he does take pains to call attention to the problem of invoking a God of battles, let alone enforcing the invocation by means of the death penalty. On the eve of Agincourt, the soldier Williams had responded unenthusiastically to the disguised king's claim that his cause was good:

> But if the cause be not good, the King himself hath a heavy reckoning to make, when all those legs, and arms, and heads, chopp'd off in a battle, shall join together at the latter day and cry all, "We died at such a place"—some swearing, some crying for a surgeon, some upon their wives left poor behind them, some upon the debts they owe, some upon their children rawly left. I am afeard there are few die well that die in a battle; for how can they charitably dispose of any thing, when blood is their argument? (4.1.134–43)

To this the king replies with a string of awkward "explanations" designed to show that "the King is not bound to answer the particular endings of his soldiers" (4.1.155–56)—as if death in battle were a completely unforeseen accident or, alternatively, as if each soldier killed were being punished by God for a hidden crime or, again, as if war were a religious blessing, an "advantage" to a soldier able to "wash every mote out of his conscience" (4.1.179–80). Not only are these explanations mutually contradictory, but they cast long shadows on the king himself. For in the wake of this scene, as the dawn is breaking, Hal pleads nervously with God not to think—at least "not to-day"—upon the crime from which he has benefited: his father's deposition and killing of Richard II. The king calls attention to all the expensive and ingratiating ritual acts that he has instituted to compensate for the murder of the divinely anointed ruler—reinterment of the corpse, five hundred poor "in yearly pay" to plead twice daily for pardon, two chantries where priests say mass for Richard's soul—and he promises to do more. Yet in a moment that anticipates Claudius's inadequate repentance of old Hamlet's murder, inadequate since he is "still possess'd/Of those effects" for which the crime was committed (*Hamlet* 3.3.53–54), Hal acknowledges that these expiatory rituals and even "contrite tears" are worthless:

> Though all that I can do is nothing worth,
> Since that my penitence comes after all,
> Imploring pardon.
>
> (4.1.303–5)[56]

If by nightfall Hal is threatening to execute anyone who denies God full credit for the astonishing English victory, the preceding scenes would seem to have fully exposed the ideological and psychological mechanisms behind such compulsion, its roots in violence, magical propitiation and bad conscience. The pattern disclosed here is one we have glimpsed in *2 Henry IV:* we witness an anticipatory subversion of each of the play's central claims. The archbishop of Canterbury spins out an endless public justification for an invasion he has privately confessed would relieve financial pressure on the church; Hal repeatedly warns his victims that they are bringing pillage and rape upon themselves, but he speaks as the head of the invading army that is about to pillage and rape them; Gower claims that the king has ordered the killing of the prisoners in retaliation for the attack on the baggage train, but we have just been shown that the king's order preceded that attack.[57] Similarly, Hal's meditation on the sufferings of the great—"What infinite heart's ease/Must kings neglect, that private men enjoy!" (4.1.236–37)—suffers from his being almost single-handedly responsible for a war that by his own earlier account and that of the enemy is causing immense civilian misery. And after watching a scene in which anxious, frightened troops sleeplessly await the dawn, it is difficult to be fully persuaded by Hal's climactic vision of the "slave" and "peasant" sleeping comfortably, little knowing "What watch the King keeps to maintain the peace" (4.1.283).

This apparent subversion of the monarch's glorification has led some critics since Hazlitt to view the panegyric as bitterly ironic or to argue, more plausibly, that Shakespeare's depiction of Henry V is radically ambiguous.[58] But in the light of Harriot's *Brief and True Report,* we may suggest that the subversive doubts the play continually awakens originate paradoxically in an effort to intensify the power of the king and his war. The effect is bound up with the reversal that we have noted several times—the great events and speeches all occur twice: the first time as fraud, the second as truth. The intimations of bad faith are real enough, but they are deferred—deferred until after Essex's campaign in Ireland, after Elizabeth's reign, after the monarchy itself as a significant political institution. Deferred indeed even today, for in the wake of full-scale ironic readings and at a time when it no longer seems to matter very much, it is

not at all clear that *Henry V* can be successfully performed as subversive.

The problem with any attempt to do so is that the play's central figure seems to feed on the doubts he provokes. For the enhancement of royal power is not only a matter of the deferral of doubt: the very doubts that Shakespeare raises serve not to rob the king of his charisma but to heighten it, precisely as they heighten the theatrical interest of the play; the unequivocal, unambiguous celebrations of royal power with which the period abounds have no theatrical force and have long since fallen into oblivion. The charismatic authority of the king, like that of the stage, depends upon falsification.

The audience's tension, then, enhances its attention; prodded by constant reminders of a gap between real and ideal, the spectators are induced to make up the difference, to invest in the illusion of magnificence, to be dazzled by their own imaginary identification with the conqueror. The ideal king must be in large part the invention of the audience, the product of a will to conquer that is revealed to be identical to a need to submit. *Henry V* is remarkably self-conscious about this dependence upon the audience's powers of invention. The prologue's opening lines invoke a form of theater radically unlike the one that is about to unfold: "A kingdom for a stage, princes to act,/And monarchs to behold the swelling scene!" (3–4). In such a theater-state there would be no social distinction between the king and the spectator, the performer and the audience; all would be royal, and the role of the performance would be to transform not an actor into a king but a king into a god: "Then should the warlike Harry, like himself,/Assume the port of Mars" (5–6). This is in effect the fantasy acted out in royal masques, but Shakespeare is intensely aware that his play is not a courtly entertainment, that his actors are "flat unraised spirits," and that his spectators are hardly monarchs—"gentles all," he calls them, with fine flattery.[59] "Let us," the prologue begs the audience, "On your imaginary forces work. . . . For 'tis your thoughts that now must deck our kings" (17–18, 28). This "must" is cast in the form of an appeal and an apology—the consequence of the miserable limitations of "this unworthy scaffold"—but the necessity extends, I suggest, beyond the stage: all kings are "decked" out by the imaginary forces of the spectators, and a sense of the limitations of king or theater only excites a more compelling exercise of those forces.

Power belongs to whoever can command and profit from this exercise of the imagination, hence the celebration of the charismatic ruler whose imperfections we are invited at once to register and to "piece out" (Prologue, 23). Hence too the underlying complicity throughout these plays between the prince and the playwright, a complicity complicated but never effaced by a strong counter-current of identification with Falstaff. In Hal, Shakespeare fashions a compelling emblem of the playwright as sovereign "juggler," the minter of counterfeit coins, the genial master of illusory subversion and redemptive betrayal. To understand Shakespeare's conception of Hal, from rakehell to monarch, we need in effect a poetics of Elizabethan power, and this in turn will prove inseparable, in crucial respects, from a poetics of the theater. Testing, recording, and explaining are elements in this poetics, which is inseparably bound up with the figure of Queen Elizabeth, a ruler without a standing army, without a highly developed bureaucracy, without an extensive police force, a ruler whose power is constituted in theatrical celebrations of royal glory and theatrical violence visited upon the enemies of that glory. Power that relies on a massive police apparatus, a strong middle-class nuclear family, an elaborate school system, power that dreams of a panopticon in which the most intimate secrets are open to the view of an invisible authority—such power will have as its appropriate aesthetic form the the realist novel;[60] Elizabethan power, by contrast, depends upon its privileged visibility. As in a theater, the audience must be powerfully engaged by this visible presence and at the same time held at a respectful distance from it. "We princes," Elizabeth told a deputation of Lords and Commons in 1586, "are set on stages in the sight and view of all the world."[61]

Royal power is manifested to its subjects as in a theater, and the subjects are at once absorbed by the instructive, delightful, or terrible spectacles and forbidden intervention or deep intimacy. The play of authority depends upon spectators—"For 'tis your thoughts that now must deck our kings"—but the performance is made to seem entirely beyond the control of those whose "imaginary forces" actually confer upon it its significance and force. These matters, Thomas More imagines the common people saying of one such spectacle, "be king's games, as it were stage plays, and for the more part played upon scaffolds. In which poor men be but the lookers-on. And they that wise be will meddle no farther."[62] Within this theatrical setting, there is a notable insistence upon the paradoxes, ambiguities, and tensions of authority, but this apparent production of subversion is, as we have already seen, the very condition of power. I should add that this condition is not a theoretical necessity of theatrical power in general but a historical phenomenon, the particular mode of this particular culture. "In sixteenth century England," writes Clifford Geertz, comparing Elizabethan and Majapahit royal progresses, "the political center of society was the point at which the tension between the passions that power excited and the ideals it was supposed to serve was screwed to its highest pitch. . . . In fourteenth century Java, the center was the point at which such tension disappeared in a blaze of cosmic symmetry."[63]

It is precisely because of the English form of absolutist theatricality that Shakespeare's drama, written for a theater subject to state censorship, can be so relentlessly subversive: the form itself, as a primary expression of Renaissance power, helps to contain the radical doubts it continually provokes. Of course, what is for the state a mode of subversion contained can be for the theater a mode of containment subverted: there are moments in Shakespeare's career—*King Lear* is the greatest example[64]—when the process of containment is strained to the breaking point. But the histories consistently pull back from such extreme pressure. Like Harriot in the New World, the Henry plays confirm the Machiavellian hypothesis that princely power originates in force and fraud even as they draw their audience toward an acceptance of that power. And we are free to locate and pay homage to the plays' doubts only because they no longer threaten us.[65] There is subversion, no end of subversion, only not for us.

## NOTES

1. John Bakeless, *The Tragicall History of Christopher Marlowe,* 2 vols. (Cambridge, Mass.: Harvard University Press, 1942), 1:111. *Juggler* is a richly complex word, including in its range of associations con man, cheap entertainer, magician, trickster, storyteller, conjurer, actor, and dramatist.

2. On Harriot, see especially *Thomas Harriot, Renaissance Scientist,* ed. John W. Shirley (Oxford: Clarendon Press, 1974); Muriel Rukeyser, *The Traces of Thomas Harriot* (New York: Random House, 1970); and Jean Jacquot, "Thomas Harriot's Reputation for Impiety," *Notes and Records of the Royal Society* 9 (1952): 164–87. Harriot himself appears to have paid close attention to his reputation; see David B. Quinn and John W. Shirley, "A Contemporary List of Hariot References," *Renaissance Quarterly* 22 (1969): 9–26.

3. John Aubrey, *Brief Lives,* 2 vols., ed. Andrew Clark (Oxford: Clarendon Press, 1898), 1:286.

4. For the investigation of Ralegh, see *Willobie His Avisa* (1594), ed. G. B. Harrison (London: John Lane, 1926), app. 3, pp. 255–71; for Oliver's story, see Ernest A. Strathmann, *Sir Walter Ralegh: A Study in Elizabethan Skepticism* (New York: Columbia University Press, 1951), p. 50.

5. There are, to be sure, some evangelical professions of

having been *saved* from atheism. On treason see Lacey Baldwin Smith, "English Treason Trials and Confessions in the Sixteenth Century," *Journal of the History of Ideas* 15 (1954): 471–98.

6. See, for example, the story William Strachey borrows from Henri Estienne's commentary on Herodotus: "Pope Leo the 10. answered Cardinall Bembo that alleadged some parte of the Ghospell into him: 'Lord Cardinall, what a wealth this fable of Jesus Christ hath gotten vs?' " (William Strachey, *The Historie of Travell into Virginia Britania* [1612], ed. Louis B. Wright and Virginia Freund, Hakluyt Society 2d ser., no. 103 [London, 1953], p. 101).

7. Jacquot, "Thomas Harriot's Reputation for Impiety," p. 167. In another official record, Popham is reported to have said ominously, "You know what men say of He-reiat" (John W. Shirley, "Sir Walter Ralegh and Thomas Harriot," in *Thomas Harriot, Renaissance Scientist,* p. 27). The logic (if that is the word for it) would seem to be this: since God clearly supports the established order of things and punishes offenders with eternal torments, a criminal must be someone who has been foolishly persuaded that God does not exist. The alternative theory posits wickedness, a corruption of the will so severe as to lead people against their own better knowledge into the ways of crime. The two arguments are often conflated, since atheism is the heart of the greatest wickedness, as well as the greatest folly.

8. Northrop Frye, *On Shakespeare* (New Haven: Yale University Press, 1986), p. 10 (see also p. 60: "Shakespeare's social vision is a deeply conservative one"); Franco Moretti, " 'A Huge Eclipse': Tragic Form and the Deconsecration of Sovereignty," in *The Power of Forms in the English Renaissance,* ed. Stephen Greenblatt (Norman, Okla.: Pilgrim Books, 1982), p. 31. On the histories as occasioning an interrogation of ideology, see Jonathan Dollimore and Alan Sinfield, "History and Ideology: The Instance of *Henry V,*" in John Drakakis, *Alternative Shakespeares* (London: Methuen, 1985), pp. 205–27.

9. Here is how Richard Baines construes Marlowe's version of this argument: "He affirmeth . . . That the first beginning of Religion was only to keep men in awe. That it was an easy matter for Moyses being brought vp in all the artes of the Egiptians to abuse the Jewes being a rude & grosse people" (C. F. Tucker Brooke, *The Life of Marlowe* [London: Methuen, 1930], app. 9, p. 98). For other versions, see Strathmann, *Sir Walter Ralegh,* pp. 70–72, 87.

10. "To come to those who have become princes through their own merits and not by fortune, I regard as the greatest, Moses, Cyrus, Romulus, Theseus, and their like. And although one should not speak of Moses, he having merely carried out what was ordered him by God, still he deserves admiration, if only for that grace which

made him worthy to speak with God. But regarding Cyrus and others who have acquired or founded kingdoms, they will all be found worthy of admiration; and if their particular actions and methods are examined they will not appear very different from those of Moses, although he had so great a Master [che ebbe si gran precettore]" (Niccolò Machiavelli, *The Prince,* trans. Luigi Ricci, revised E. R. P. Vincent [New York: Random House, 1950], p. 20). Christian Detmold translated the *Discourses,* in the same volume.

The delicate ironies here are intensified in the remarks on ecclesiastical principalities:

> They are acquired either by ability or by fortune; but are maintained without either, for they are sustained by ancient religious customs, which are so powerful and of such quality, that they keep their princes in power in whatever manner they proceed and live. These princes alone have states without defending them, have subjects without governing them, and their states, not being defended are not taken from them; their subjects not being governed do not resent it, and neither think nor are capable of alienating themselves from them. Only those principalities, therefore, are secure and happy. But as they are upheld by higher causes, which the human mind cannot attain to, I will abstain from speaking of them; for being exalted and maintained by God, it would be the work of a presumptuous and foolish man to discuss them. (*The Prince,* 41–42)

The sly wit of this passage depends not only on the subtle mockery but also on the possibility that the "ancient religious customs" are in fact politically efficacious.

11. Kyd, in Brooke, *Life of Marlowe,* app. 12, p. 107; Parsons, in Strathmann, *Sir Walter Ralegh,* p. 25.

12. Quoted in Jean Jacquot, "Ralegh's 'Hellish Verses' and the 'Tragicall Raigne of Selimus,' " *Modern Language Review* 48 (1953): 1.

13. This is the suggestion of Pierre Lefranc, *Sir Walter Ralegh, Ecrivain* (Quebec: Armand Colin, 1968), pp. 673–74; Lefranc gives a slightly different version of the verses (app. N, p. 673).

For a popular instance of Ralegh's reputation as a freethinker, see the poem circulated against him, with the refrain "Damnable friend of hell,/Mischievous Matchivell" (in Lefranc, p. 667). I should add that Ralegh was famous for a theatrical manner, so that it may have seemed all the more plausible to attach to his name verses from a play.

14. Thomas Harriot, *A briefe and true report of the new found land of Virginia: of the commodities there found and to be raysed, as well marchantable, as others for victuall, building and other necessarie uses for those that are and shall be the planters there; and of the nature and manners of the natural inhabitants* (London,

1588), in *The Roanoke Voyages, 1584–1590,* 2 vols., ed. David Beers Quinn, Hakluyt Society 2d ser. no. 104 (London, 1955), p. 375.

The illustrated edition of this account includes John White drawings of these priests and of the ceremonies over which they presided, along with a striking drawing of a dancing figure called "the conjurer." "They have commonly conjurers or jugglers," Harriot's annotation explains, "which use strange gestures, and often contrary to nature in their enchantments: For they be very familiar with devils, of whom they enquire what their enemies do, or other such things. . . . The Inhabitants give great credit unto their speech, which oftentimes they find to be true" (Thomas Harriot, *A Briefe and True Report,* facsimile of the 1590 Theodor De Bry edition [New York: Dover, 1972], p. 54). I will refer to this edition in my text as De Bry.

In the next generation, William Strachey would urge that when the colonists have the power, they should "performe the same acceptable service to god, that Iehu king of Israell did when he assembled all the priests of Baal, and slue them to the last man in their owne Temple" (*Historie of Travell,* p. 94).

The best introduction to the current scholarship on the Algonquians of southern New England is Bruce G. Trigger, ed., *Handbook of North American Indians,* vol. 15, *Northeast* (Washington, D.C.: Smithsonian, 1978).

15. Harriot goes on to note that the disciplinary force of religious fear is supplemented by secular punishment: "although notwithstanding there is punishment ordained for malefactours, as stealers, whoremoonger, and other sortes of wicked doers; some punished with death, some with forfeitures, some with beating, according to the greatness of the factes" (De Bry, p. 26).

16. See Karen Ordahl Kupperman, *Settling with the Indians: The Meeting of English and Indian Cultures in America, 1580–1640* (Totowa, N.J.: Rowman and Littlefield, 1975).

17. I should add that it quickly became a rhetorical trope to describe the mass of Europeans as little better than or indistinguishable from American savages.

18. *Discourses,* p. 148. The context of this observation is the continuing discussion of Numa's wisdom in feigning divine authority: "It is true that those were very religious times, and the people with whom Numa had to deal were very untutored and superstitious, which made it easy for him to carry out his designs, being able to impress upon them any new form. . . . I conclude that the religion introduced by Numa into Rome was one of the chief causes of the prosperity of that city" (147–48).

19. When in 1590 the Flemish publisher Theodor De Bry reprinted Harriot's *Briefe and True Report,* he made this belief explicit: along with engravings of John White's brilliant Virginia drawings, De Bry's edition includes five

engravings of the ancient Picts, "to showe how that the Inhabitants of the great Bretannie haue bin in times past as sauuage as those of Virginia" (De Bry, p. 75).

20. In his notes to the John White engravings, Harriot also records his hopes for a widespread Algonquian conversion to Christianity: "Thes poore soules haue none other knowledge of god although I thinke them verye Desirous to know the truthe. For when as wee kneeled downe on our knees to make our prayers vnto god, they went abowt to imitate vs, and when they saw we moued our lipps, they also dyd the like. Wherfore that is verye like that they might easelye be brought to the knowledge of the gospel. God of his mercie grant them this grace" (De Bry, p. 71).

21. In Richard Hakluyt, *The Principal Navigations, Voyages, Traffiques, and Discoveries of the English Nation,* 12 vols. (Glasgow: James Maclehose and Sons, 1903–5), 10:54.

22. The situation is parodied in Shakespeare's *Tempest* when the drunken Caliban, rebelling against Prospero, sings:

No more dams I'll make for fish,
Nor fetch in firing
At requiring,
Nor scrape trenchering, nor wash dish.
*(2.2.180–83)*

23. For an alternative explanation of the principal sources of the Europeans' apparent apathy, see Karen Ordahl Kupperman, "Apathy and Death in Early Jamestown," *Journal of American History* 66 (1979): 24–40. Kupperman argues that there are significant parallels between the deaths of early colonists and the deaths of American prisoners in Korean prison camps.

24. On these catalogs, see Wayne Franklin, *Discoverers, Explorers, Settlers: The Diligent Writers of Early America* (Chicago: University of Chicago Press, 1979), pp. 69–122.

25. Quoted in Edward Rosen, "Harriot's Science: The Intellectual Background," in Shirley, *Thomas Harriot, Renaissance Scientist,* p. 4.

26. Donald Friedman, private correspondence. Friedman continues: "A point that follows is that Harriot's awareness of 'subversion' might, by this token, be cast in the mode of 'what else can you expect of heathen?' "

27. Francis Bacon, *The New Organon,* bk. 1, aphorism 129, in *Francis Bacon: A Selection of His Works,* ed. Sidney Warhaft (New York: Odyssey, 1965), p. 373. I am indebted for this reference to James Carson.

28. For a further instance of the term *juggler* used of English technology in the New World, see William Wood, *New Englands Prospect* (London, 1634), p. 78; quoted in Karen Ordahl Kupperman, "English Percep-

tions of Treachery, 1583–1640: The Case of the American 'Savages,' " *Historical Journal* 20 (1977): 263–87.

29. In Spenser, this primitive propensity toward idolatrous worship plays into the wicked hands of the Catholic church, and there may be some echoes of this preoccupation in Harriot's text where it would provide further insulation against awareness of a radical self-indictment. The fetishism of religious objects, the confusion of the spiritual and the material, is a frequent Protestant accusation against Catholicism, as is the charge that subtle priests cynically foster idolatry to control the people. In his notes to the White illustrations, Harriot remarks that the Algonquians sometimes have two or three "idols in their churches . . . which they place in a dark corner where they show terrible"; he notes that the priest who guards the bones of the dead chieftains "mumbleth his prayers night and day"; and he describes the posts around which the Indians dance as "carved with heads like to the faces of Nuns covered with their veils" (De Bry, pp. 71–72). This is the familiar language of Protestant polemics, and it may imply that the English will be saving the Algonquians not only from their own false worship but from the oddly cognate false worship spread by the Catholic Spanish and French. But it should be noted that Harriot does not push the resemblance between Indian and Catholic priests very hard.

30. John Calvin, *Institutes of the Christian Religion,* 2 vols., ed. John T. McNeill, trans. Ford Lewis Battles, Library of Christian Classics, vols. 20–21 (Philadelphia: Westminster Press, 1960), 1:1.3.2, pp. 44–45. I am indebted for this and the following reference to John Coolidge.

31. Richard Hooker, *Works,* 3 vols., ed. John Keble (Oxford: Oxford University Press, 1836), 2:5.1.3, p. 21.

32. J. G. A. Pocock, *The Machiavellian Moment: Florentine Political Thought and the Atlantic Republican Tradition* (Princeton: Princeton University Press, 1975).

33. Cf. Walter Bigges's narrative of Drake's visit to Florida in 1586: "The wilde people at first comminge of our men died verie fast and saide amongest themselues, It was the Inglisshe God that made them die so faste" (in Quinn, *The Roanoke Voyages* 1:306).

34. The search for atheists offers a parallel: atheism is the cause of treason, and the occurrence of treason is itself evidence for the existence of atheism.

35. We should note, however, that the conception of "invisible bullets" implies intention and hence morality.

36. Guido Calabresi and Philip Bobbitt, *Tragic Choices* (New York: W. W. Norton, 1978), p. 195. The term *tragic* is misleading, I think, since the same strategies may be perceived in situations that do not invoke the generic expectations or constraints of tragedy.

37. John Upton, *Critical Observations on Shakespeare* (1748), in *Shakespeare: The Critical Heritage,* ed. Brian Vickers, vol. 3, 1733–1752 (London: Routledge and Kegan Paul, 1975), p. 297; Maynard Mack, introduction to the Signet Classic edition of *1 Henry IV* (New York: New American Library, 1965), p. xxxv.

38. Who is the "we" in these sentences? I refer both to the stage tradition of the play and to the critical tradition. This does not mean that the play cannot be staged as a bitter assault upon Hal, but such a staging will struggle against the current that has held sway since the play's inception and indeed since the formation of the whole ideological myth of Prince Hal.

39. In the battle of Shrewsbury, when Falstaff is pretending he is dead, Hal, seeing the body of his friend, thinks with an eerie symbolic appropriateness of having the corpse literally emptied. As Hal exits, Falstaff rises up and protests. If Falstaff is an enormous mountain of flesh, Hal is the quintessential thin man: "you starveling," Falstaff calls him (2.4.244). From Hal's point of view, Falstaff's fat prevents him from having any value at all: "there's no room for faith, truth, nor honesty in this bosom of thine; it is all fill'd up with guts and midriff" (3.3.153–55).

Here and throughout the discussion of *1 Henry IV,* I am indebted to Edward Snow.

40. William Empson, *Some Versions of Pastoral* (London: Chatto and Windus, 1968), p. 103.

41. See S. P. Zitner, "Anon, Anon; or, a Mirror for a Magistrate," *Shakespeare Quarterly* 19 (1968): 63–70.

42. More accurately, the ratios are redistributed. For example, *Henry V* insists that the world represented in the play is extraordinarily spacious, varied, and mobile, while the stage itself is cramped and confining:

> Can this cockpit hold
> The vasty fields of France? Or may we cram
> Within this wooden O the very casques
> That did affright the air at Agincourt?
> *(Prologue, 11–14)*

The Chorus calls attention to this contradiction to exhort the audience to transcend it "In the quick forge and working-house of thought" (5.0.23). We have to do not with a balance of forces but with an imbalance that must be rectified by the labor of the imagination:

> Piece out our imperfections with your
> thoughts;
> Into a thousand parts divide one man,
> And make imaginary puissance.
> *(Prologue, 23–25)*

43. What we took to be the "center" may be part of the remotest periphery. More unsettling still, topographic ac-

counts of both theater and power may be illusions: there may be no way to locate oneself securely in relation to either.

44. See, for example, Victor Turner, *Drama, Fields, and Metaphors: Symbolic Action in Human Society* (Ithaca: Cornell University Press, 1974).

45. The evidence is amply documented by Karen Kupperman, *Settling with the Indians.*

46. Thomas Harman, *A Caueat or Warening, for Commen Cursetors Vulgarely Called Vagabones* (1566), in *Cony-Catchers and Bawdy Baskets,* ed. Gamini Salgado (Middlesex: Penguin, 1972), p. 146.

47. On the problems of Elizabethan representations of the underworld, see A. L. Beier, *Masterless Men: The Vagrancy Problem in England, 1560–1640* (London: Methuen, 1985).

48. [Gilbert Walker?] *A manifest detection of the moste vyle and detestable use of Diceplay* (c. 1552), in Salgado, *Cony-Catchers and Bawdy Baskets,* pp. 42–43.

49. Norman N. Holland, in the Signet Classic edition of *2 Henry IV* (New York: New American Library, 1965), p. xxxvi.

50. See Frank Whigham, *Ambition and Privilege: The Social Tropes of Elizabethan Courtesy Theory* (Berkeley: University of California Press, 1984).

51. The public response to betrayal is extremely difficult to measure. Lawrence Stone suggests that there is a transition in the early years of the seventeenth century: "Up to the end of the sixteenth century men saw nothing dishonorable in attacking by surprise with superior forces, and nothing in hitting a man when he was down. By the second decade of the seventeenth century, however, such behaviour was becoming discreditable and is much less frequently met with" (Lawrence Stone, *The Crisis of the Aristocracy, 1558–1641,* abridged edition [New York: Oxford University Press, 1967], p. 109).

52. The presence of the Irishman among the English forces is especially significant since as the Chorus points out, an English expeditionary army was attempting at the moment of the play to subjugate the Irish. It is not the least of the play's bitter historical ironies that in four hundred years this attempt has not become an anachronism.

53. It would not have escaped at least some members of an Elizabethan audience that an English gentleman or woman would have been far more likely to learn French than a Frenchman English. The language lesson, Steven Mullaney suggests, is Shakespeare's "rearward glance at the improprieties that occupied the ambivalent center of Hal's prodigality." Whereas in the first and second parts of *Henry IV,* the recording of the language of the other has an element of tragedy, its equivalent in *Henry V* has

only the spirit of French farce (Steven Mullaney, "Strange Things, Gross Terms, Curious Customs: The Rehearsal of Cultures in the Late Renaissance," *Representations* 3 [1983]: 63–64).

54. "This does not sound like hypocrisy or cynicism. The Archbishop discharges his duty faithfully, as it stands his reasoning is impeccable. . . . Henry is not initiating aggression" (J. H. Walter, in the Arden edition of *King Henry V* [London: Methuen, 1954], p. xxv).

55. The kill ratio is highly in the English favor in all accounts, but Shakespeare adopts from Holinshed the most extreme figure. Holinshed himself adds that "other writers of greater credit affirm that there were slain above five or six hundred" Englishmen (Holinshed, in the Oxford Shakespeare edition of *Henry V,* ed. Gary Taylor [Oxford: Oxford University Press, 1984], p. 308). Similarly, Shakespeare makes no mention of the tactical means by which the English army achieved its victory. The victory is presented as virtually miraculous.

56. In a long appendix to his edition of *Henry V,* Gary Taylor attempts to defend his emendation of "all" to "ill" in these lines, on the grounds that an interpretation along the lines of Claudius's failed repentance would be difficult for an actor to communicate and, if communicated, would make "the victory of Agincourt morally and dramatically incomprehensible" (Taylor, p. 298). The interpretive framework that I am sketching in this chapter should make the Folio's reading fully comprehensible; the effect of the victory is, by my account, intensified by the play's moral problems.

57. Taylor makes a subtle and, I think, implausible attempt to reduce the unintended irony of Gower's line, "wherefore the King, most worthily, hath caus'd every soldier to cut his prisoner's throat" (4.7.8–10): "Gower is not saying (as all editors and critics seem to have understood him) 'the king *caused* the prisoners to be executed because of the attack on the baggage train' but 'given the barbarity of the subsequent French conduct, the king *has* quite justifiably *caused* the death of his prisoners' " (Taylor, p. 243). Even were we to understand the line in Taylor's sense, it would open a moral problem still worse than the political problem that has been resolved.

58. See the illuminating discussion in Norman Rabkin, *Shakespeare and the Problem of Meaning* (Chicago: University of Chicago Press, 1981), pp. 33–62.

59. This is flattery carefully echoed in Hal's promise to his troops on the eve of Agincourt that "be he ne'er so

vile,/This day shall gentle his condition" (4.3.62–63). The promise is silently forgotten after the battle.

60. For a brilliant exploration of this hypothesis, see D. A. Miller, "The Novel and the Police," in *Glyph* 8 (1981): 127–47.

61. Quoted in J. E. Neale, *Elizabeth I and Her Parliaments, 1584–1601,* 2 vols. (London: Cape, 1965), 2:119. For the complex relation between theater and absolutism, see Stephen Orgel, *The Illusion of Power: Political Theater in the English Renaissance* (Berkeley: University of California Press, 1975); Jonathan Goldberg, *James I and the Politics of Literature: Jonson, Shakespeare, Donne, and Their Contemporaries* (Baltimore: Johns Hopkins University Press, 1983); Jonathan Dollimore, *Radical Tragedy: Religion, Ideology, and Power in the Drama of Shakespeare and His Contemporaries* (Brighton: Harvester, 1983); Greenblatt, *The Power of Forms in the English Renaissance;* Steven Mullaney, "Lying like Truth: Riddle, Representation, and Treason in Renaissance England," *ELH* 47 (1980): 32–47; Paola Colaiacomo, "Il teatro del principe," *Calibano* 4 (1979): 53–98; Christopher Pye, "The Sovereign, the Theater, and the Kingdome of Darknesse: Hobbes and the Spectacle of Power," *Representations* 8 (1984): 85–106.

62. *The History of King Richard III,* ed. R. S. Sylvester, in *The Complete Works of St. Thomas More,* vol. 3 (New Haven: Yale University Press, 1963), p. 80.

63. Clifford Geertz, "Centers, Kings, and Charisma: Reflections on the Symbolics of Power," in *Culture and Its Creators: Essays in Honor of Edward Shils,* ed. Joseph Ben David and Terry Nichols Clark (Chicago: University of Chicago Press, 1977), p. 160.

64. The nameless servant in *Lear* who can no longer endure what he is witnessing and who heroically stabs his master Cornwall, the legitimate ruler of half of England, inhabits a different political world from the one sketched here, a world marked out by Shakespeare as tragic.

65. Perhaps we should imagine Shakespeare writing at a moment when none of the alternatives for a resounding political commitment seemed satisfactory; when the pressure to declare himself unequivocally an adherent of one or another faction seemed narrow, ethically coarse, politically stupid; when the most attractive political solution seemed to be to keep options open and the situation fluid.

# VIII

# FEMINISM AND GENDER STUDIES

Many instances of work being done in contemporary feminist criticism, Susan Sheridan writes in *Grafts: Feminist Cultural Criticism*, "advocate and enact heterogeneity, not as a politically naive pluralism but as an insistence on the complexity of cultural discourses and practices and on the diversity of positions from which feminists engage with them." Her comment can be expanded slightly to say that the current scene, encompassing feminism and gender studies, is so broad that an actual survey of directions and interests would be quickly outdated and impractical. Vastly complicating the picture are the many strong alliances of thought and practice that feminism and gender studies have with cultural studies, Marxist criticism, science studies, and psychoanalysis. It would not even be possible to draw the boundaries with any accuracy among these alliances and hybrids ("cyborgs," in Donna Haraway's word). Evident in this activity and cultural reorientation is the urgency to understand literature and culture from a variety of viewpoints—some of which are traditionally defined as "feminine" and homosocial but only recently have been liberated into active cultural expression. In "The Story So Far" (in *The Feminist Reader*) Catherine Belsey and Jane Moore give a sense of how great the effect of feminist studies has been in recent years. In 1970 they write, "three revolutionary books appeared within a few months of each other . . . Germaine Greer's *The Female Eunuch,* Kate Millett's *Sexual Politics* and *Patriarchal Attitudes* by Eva Figes." "It comes as something of a shock," they continue, "to encounter 'he' as the generalized pronoun in these books published in 1970."

At the time of the publication of these books, there was little engagement with the areas of psychoanalytic and philosophical discourse that since have become a part of the feminist and gender critique of culture. This limited engagement was apparent in Millett's dismissal of psychoanalysis as focused exclusively on a theory of "penis-envy" in *Sexual Politics.* The subsequent, quite different tendency actually to appropriate "theory" (especially psychoanalysis) of all kinds in feminist and gender criticism has empowered feminist and gender critics not only to "identify representations of sexuality and female desire," but to "demonstrate how meanings work and how they can be challenged." "This is done," Belsey and Moore go on, "by seeking out uncertainties—the problems, ambiguities and, above all, contradictions, which the representations reveal." That search for ambiguities has opened gender studies beyond merely traditional representations of women, whether heterosocial or homosocial, and has enabled feminists and gender critics to explore the social construction of gender, even those not explicitly configured as, for example, male/female or straight/gay.

The idea of cultural reorientation, of course, has always been a part of feminist and gender studies. In "Notes Towards a Definition of Cultural Studies" (in "Cultural Studics") we survey a version of this reorientation, citing Elaine Showalter's description of a new mode of reading occasioned by feminism in "Toward a Feminist Poetics" and the kind of "androcentric" reading Patrocinio Schweickart cites in "Reading Ourselves: Toward a Feminist Theory of Reading" (in "Rhetoric and Reader Response") that had obscured this mode of reading. However, the reorientations occasioned by feminism and gender studies have gone further than the kinds of distinctions based on the opposition between male and female that governs feminist literary and cultural criticism of the early seventies to encompass viewpoints never known before (or were never recognized), including those in gay/lesbian culture. Such viewpoints are emerging in the texts of current technoculture as subjectivities "in a post-gender world" that, as Donna Haraway says, has "no truck with bisexuality, pre-oedipal symbiosis, unalienated labour, or other seductions to organic wholeness through a final appropriation of all the power of the parts into a higher unity." In the recent avant-garde developments of feminist and gender studies is the assumption of a diversity of genders and even gender possibilities, according to Haraway and Kathy Acker, that can be conceived only in relation to cybernetic culture, computer interface, and virtual space.

This complex situation is somewhat clarified in terms of the survey of feminist literary criticism Showalter presents in "Feminist Criticism in the Wilderness" (in "What Is Criticism?"). Showalter isolates four approaches to criticism (which we discuss in "Notes Towards a Definition of Cultural Studies"): "biological, linguistic, psychoanalytic, and cultural," all of which "ground" (in J. Hillis Miller's term in "What Is Literary Theory?") particular ways of reading. Feminist approaches also draw from at least four areas of contemporary critical thought, and we have included examples of all of them in this collection. Donna Haraway's "A Cyborg Manifesto" draws on science studies and psychoanalysis in her exploration of the figure of the cyborg (and its artificial "biology") in contemporary technoculture. In the same way, Schweickart's essay in "Rhetoric and Reader Response" examines the linguistic strategies of literature from a feminist viewpoint, and again that orientation encompasses biological, psychological, and cultural concerns within its rhetorical approach. Toril Moi's examination of Freud and Dora in "Psychology and Psychoanalysis"—while offering a feminist reading of contemporary psychoanalytic criticism—highlights the questions of sexual difference, linguistic strategies, and cultural understanding within that framework. A good example of the cultural interweaving of approaches is the essay by Catherine Belsey in "Deconstruction and Poststructuralism." Belsey weaves together the discourses of psychoanalysis, deconstruction, and Marxism to articulate the multifaceted analysis of the representations of women in "realistic" fiction—in Sherlock Holmes stories—to situate those representations within the cultural formations of subjectivity, literature, and ideology.

The essays of this section on feminism and gender studies similarly focus on such larger cultural questions of politics, literary history, the psychoanalytics of (gendered) subjectivity, and even the relationship of science and "knowledge" in relation to gender. Gender studies as a broad category, in short, comprises the set of issues in various disciplines pertinent to cultural experience as always in some relation to gender categories. Just as we suggested in the introduction to "What Is Literary Theory?" that ethics is not a simple "object" of study but rather a set of questions and concerns that can be brought to all our studies, so gender is not simply an "object" of study but a way of critiquing and understanding an array of received ideas. In this way feminism and gender studies challenge literary and cultural theory to confront the difficult task of assimilating the findings of an expanding sphere of inquiry, including—as we see here—forms of *interdisciplinary* inquiry.

## FEMINIST LITERARY AND CULTURAL CRITICISM

As Catherine Belsey and Jane Moore point out, modern feminist criticism continues to be deeply indebted to the work of two writers, Virginia Woolf and Simone de Beauvoir. Their criticism exemplifies the strength, as well as the challenge, of literary feminism as social critique and as an aesthetic of women's texts or an explanation of how writing by women manifests a *distinctively* female discourse. Woolf displays this dual awareness in *A Room of One's Own* (1924) when she describes female writing as shaped primarily by its subject and less by the "shadow across the page" (the imposition of ego) characteristic of male discourse. Woolf suggests a model of textual alinearity and plasticity (female) versus hegemony and rigidity (male) that guides her critique of the social displacement of women in relation to the "shadow" that the ego of the privileged male casts starkly across Western culture. Woolf's "room of one's own," a domain that allows women both privacy and (economic) freedom, simultaneously incorporates the interiority of female discourse and the social sanctuary within which a woman may develop strength.

Simone de Beauvoir in *The Second Sex* (1949) most pointedly criticizes patriarchal culture and analyzes the marginal position of women in society and the arts. She describes a male-dominated social discourse within which particular misogynist practices occur. Tending toward a Marxist analysis—and anticipating Shulamith Firestone—de Beauvoir identifies a capitalist base of political and economic oppression with a kind of "superstructure" of sexist literature and art. De Beauvoir found reflections of socioeconomic injustices in what she saw as fundamentally imitative modes of literature (literature conceived as "reflecting" a social reality). While her work illustrates the double focus also evident in Woolf's criticism, it tends to dismiss literary production per se as a strict reflection (mimesis) of social and ideological schemes.

De Beauvoir and Woolf mark out the terrain of feminist literary criticism from social critique to feminist aesthetic and discourse. Elaine Showalter follows suit with her idea (most fully articulated in "Toward a Feminist Poetics," but also discussed in "Feminist Criticism in the Wilderness") of two "distinct varieties" of feminist criticism as directed toward either the *woman as reader* or *the woman as writer*. The first focuses on the significance of sexual codes ("woman-as-sign") in a historical and political context. This is socially oriented criticism with strong reflections of de Beauvoir's critique. The second focuses on the four categories of gender difference we have already discussed. This second focus is close to Woolf's concern and is the area of feminism that Showalter christens *gynocritics* (in "Toward a Feminist Poetics")—"a female framework for the analysis of women's literature" beginning "at the point when we free ourselves from the linear absolutes of male literary history"—the "malestream," as Sheridan says. From the work of gynocriticism, as Showalter writes, "the lost continent of the female tradition has risen like Atlantis from the sea of English literature."

Extraordinarily influential and still having an impact in America is Hélène Cixous. Through her fiction and criticism she has attempted to free readers, female and male, from patriarchal linear absolutes. In essays such as "Castration or Decapitation?" and "Laugh of the Medusa" she enacts a performative critique of patriarchal textual practices. Cixous combines the categories of woman as reader and as writer in a wide-ranging literary practice that, as Annette Kuhn has noted, is what Cixous herself calls a "woman-text," "a return of the repressed feminine that with its energetic, joyful, and transgressive 'flying in language and making it fly' dislocates the repressive structures of phallologocentrism." "Cixous's own work," Kuhn continues, offers a practice of writing "that aims to do this by posing plurality against unity; multitudes of meanings against single, fixed meanings; diffuseness against instrumentality; openness against closure." Such a discourse is what Rachel Blau DuPlessis calls "situational," "a both/and vision born of shifts, contraries, negations, contradictions; linked to personal vulnerability and need." In *The Newly-Born Woman,* Cixous and Catherine Clement construct a manifesto of such "shifts" away from "single, fixed meanings." They identify strategies of understanding—"exits," "escapes," and "opportunities" *(sorties)*—outside of the traditional understandings of the "malestream."

The difficulty of generating and sustaining such discourse is formidable. Gayatri Chakravorty Spivak in "Feminism and Critical Theory," for example, discusses the "discourse of the clitoris." In this discourse she describes a feminine dimension, a "short-hand," for "women's excess in all areas of production and practice, an excess which must be brought under control to keep business going as usual." In the discourse of excess, writing is not unified but scattered and "lost" along discontinuous and irregular channels. This version of writing under female authority, distinct from the "phallic" continuity and linearity of male writing, is unavoidably difficult precisely because as we attempt to reconceive writing in such different economies, we are inevitably trying to reconceive humans in relation to the world, which, in turn, is being reconceived as well. (Moi addresses this issue in her essay in "Psychology and Psychoanalysis.") Such difficulty is not merely what George Steiner calls a "tactical" problem, or language deployed strategically to jar us from old perceptual patterns. Rather, the difficulty of such feminist discourse goes deeper, to what Steiner calls the "ontological" level (some feminists would say "biological")—the raising of "questions," as Steiner says, "about the nature of human speech [and] about the status of significance." Such discourse forces us to reconceive the very concepts and relations of "self" and "world." The conclusion of these developments in feminist criticism would be a grand enterprise, indeed—a "field" theory, an explanation of the whole range of gender's impact on literature, virtually an ultimate correction of all the world's errors and mysteries, what Nietzsche calls in a very different context a "healing" of the "eternal wound of existence." Like other great inquiries of the twentieth century, to the extent that feminist literary and cultural theory attempts to encompass the entire gender dialectic, the dimensions of Woolf's "room of one's own" and all that lies within its walls, feminism presses on the very questions about private and public life, culture and power, female and male that demand attention in the modern and postmodern world.

"Feminism and Critical Theory," as does the essay by Spivak that we included in this book's second edition ("Imperialism and Sexual Difference"), attempts to situate the very practice of feminist criticism within the context of middle-class academic life and within the international division of labor in the world. To do so Spivak articulates feminist practice within the context of contemporary discourse and deconstructive theory. In a move indicative of her strategy in discursive practices, she defines "woman" in a way that initially appears traditional and conservative and allows that "defining the word 'woman' as resting on the word 'man' " could appear to be "a reactionary position." However, for deconstruction "no rigorous definition of anything is ultimately possible, so that if one wants to, one could go on deconstructing the opposition between man and woman, and finally show that it is a binary opposition that displaces itself."

At the same time, as she writes in "Imperialism and Sexual Difference," "even as we feminist critics discover the troping error of the masculist truth-claim to universality or academic objectivity, we perform the lie of constituting a truth of global sisterhood where the model remains . . . European." She notes, in particular, the "post-romantic concept of irony" articulated by one of her students, which springs "from the imposition of her own historical and voluntarist" position within "U.S. academic feminism as a 'universal' model of the 'natural' reactions of the female psyche." Such a practice, Spivak says, carries with it a *"structural* effect" of colonialism and imperialism as marked as that of colonialist enterprises such as the East India Company in the nineteenth century. In such theoretically oriented criticism, Spivak articulates a critique of imperialism in the West informed by the advances that structuralism, poststructuralism, Marxism, and feminism have brought to the examination of literature and discourse in general. (See Gates's reference to Spivak in "Critical Fanonism" and Said's "The Politics of Knowledge" in "What Is Literary Theory?")

The dimension of change that Spivak theatricalizes in the very structure(s) of "Feminism and Critical Theory," the manner in which she advertises the emergence of new directions in thinking and the continual revision of rethinking, foregrounds a persistent and profound strength in feminist discourse. Feminist critics and theorists such as Spivak, Nancy Hartsock, Hélène Cixous, Luce Irigaray, Monique Wittig, bell hooks, Donna Haraway, Laura Mulvey, Barbara Christian, Laurie Finke, Annette Kuhn, Trinh T. Ha Min, and Meaghan Morris consistently demonstrate both the diversity and strength of contemporary feminisms in that they tend to construct critical discourse according to a model that incorporates and builds on the potential of conflict, of change. By this we mean that they have a strong tendency to view discourse as open and dynamic, always trying to respond to their own cultural situatedness and new developments in the culture itself.

In an article that we take to be an important statement of gender criticism and cultural studies, and which we wish there was room to include here, Annette Kuhn demonstrates the productivity of such open discourse. In "The Body and Cinema: Some Problems for Feminism" in *Grafts,* she demonstrates the strategic coexistence of analytical rigor and discursive openness to emergent insights and formations. Kuhn uses the film *Pumping Iron II—The Women* as a staging for an analysis of contemporary attempts to construct (or reconstruct) the category of the feminine. In the manner of a structuralist, at least initially, she brings forward from the film about female bodybuilders a spectrum of possibility for conceiving of femininity in relation to the absence or presence of muscle and body fat. In this spectrum she opposes Beverly Francis, the extraordinarily muscled newcomer, against Rachel McLish, the traditional female bodybuilder with strong muscles but also a body of soft, fluid lines suggestive of muscles literally smoothed over with body fat. In this structuralist analysis of gender construction, the unmarked signifier of a strong but feminine woman is Rachel McLish. In the muscle competition depicted in this film, however, the extraordinary possibility of marking the female body as feminine but simultaneously a challenge in musculature to a male body, emerges in the person of Beverly Francis. The subordinate (or "subaltern") status of the female to the master (unmarked) text of the male body is then potentially lost in Beverly Francis's establishment of something like symmetry in relation to a strong male body.

The semiotic/structuralist dimension of Kuhn's analysis, however, is only a limited portion of her cultural critique. In addition to analyzing these women bodybuilders as cultural signifiers for current developments in the rethinking of gender categories, Kuhn also constructs a particular subjectivity for undertaking this analysis. She relates the details of her viewing of *Pumping Iron II—The Women* with an "all-female audience" in a "packed auditorium." She describes how this female audience talked back to "characters on the screen, cheering on the 'goodies,' booing the 'baddies.' " "All the viewers," she goes on, "were having a wonderful time, enjoying both the film and the circumstances in which they were watching it." She then narrates the "apparently inconsistent responses of this audience" to the film. They enjoyed the film while watching it, indulging in ironic responses to "good" and "bad" characters, and then advancing a more sustained critique in group discussions after the film. In this narration Kuhn is fully cognizant of the feminist critique (owing greatly to the work of Laura Mulvey, Stephen Heath, Christian Metz, and a number of critics connected with *Screen* magazine) of "male/masculine and female/feminine" positions as established "within the cinematic apparatus" of Hollywood films. "Spectators in cinema," Kuhn writes, "are basically either to take up a masculine subject position . . . or to submit to a masochism of over-identification . . . or to adopt the narcissistic position of taking the screen as mirror and becoming one's own object of desire."

Kuhn never tries to resolve the cultural contradictions that her analysis of *Pumping Iron II—The Women* pushes forward. "The instability of femininity as a subject position [one "potentially monstrous"], and the discomfort involved in identification with it," she writes, "are liable to become evident in looking at this film in ways they are not when such relations are more embedded, more submerged in the text." This assessment of a certain set of relations between gender construction and the medium of film leads Kuhn to explore briefly "representation . . . as a form of regulation" in culture. For all of Kuhn's incisive analysis, however, she never tries to explain away or somehow dismiss the contradictory responses of the "all-female audience" with which she watched the film. She also never tries to distance herself analytically from the particular pleasures associated with the Hollywood cinematic apparatus. In fact it is a strong feature of Kuhn's discourse that she attempts to highlight these "contradictions" of response as markers of the cultural frame from which her critique emanates. In this way, and in the many loose ends that Kuhn narrates but does not attempt to "explain," she is situating herself discursively and ideologically in relation to the discourse that is the object of her analysis.

In short, Kuhn—but also all of these theorists we have mentioned, and many others as well—actively work against formalist clarification and final precision (and thus a closing down) of cultural discourses. In gestures that virtually constitute a signature of feminist discourse and inquiry, so much that is productive and influential about contemporary feminisms is self-consciously open-ended and dialectical in its operation. In the parlance of our General Introduction, we see a strong tendency toward critique in the diversity of practices in such contemporary feminist discourse.

## GENDER STUDIES

The emergence of gender studies in the last decade overlaps with feminism to a great extent but also extends well outside of it. In the broadest interpretation (one employed by the theorist Laurie Finke), gender studies can be taken as an umbrella term encompassing all manner of studying gender—women's studies, feminist theory, and gay/lesbian studies. For those working in all of these areas, the term is especially useful to signal the thread of gender running through a number of questions and issues. In a narrower designation, gender studies sometimes is used to mean a more pluralized focus on the construction of female and male gender roles, including "male" studies as evidenced by the work of Andrew Ross and Michael Warner, but also including specifically gay/lesbian studies. However, those working in gay/lesbian studies—Michael Warner, Michael Moon, Paula Bennett, Adrienne Rich, Monique Wittig, for example—tend to want more specialized designations for their projects. In any case the inquiry into questions of gender is newly emergent in the academy, an extremely important new area of literary and cultural theory that doubtless will be highly productive in the years to come.

A strong example of the relations of lesbian studies to women's studies is Paula Bennett's "The Pea That Duty Locks: Lesbian and Feminist-Heterosexual Readings of Emily Dickinson's Poetry." Assessing recent critical response to Dickinson's poetry, Bennett situates her own work against "feminist retelling of traditional mainstream narratives," such as Dickinson criticism by eleven, well-known "feminist" critics. "Although all of these critics are deeply committed to understanding Dicksinson as a woman poet," Bennett cautions, "the framework for their discussion is the poet's relationship to the male tradition"—to " 'woman's place in man's world.' " Bennett then gives a listing of lesbian critics who read Dickinson's work with the assumption that "Dickinson's relationships with women are of greater significance than her struggles with men or with the male tradition." "While lesbian critics do not necessarily deny the prominence of certain male figures in Dickinson's life," Bennett goes on, "they have dug beneath the more mythic aspects of the poet's heterosexuality . . . to uncover the ways in which Dickinson used her relationships to the female and to individual women . . . to empower herself as a woman and poet." Much of Bennett's reading of Dickinson turns on her interpretation of the trope, interpreted as vaginal lips, of the "lips that never lie" in "A still—Volcano—Life" (#461). (Such a focus on figurative language is similar to that of Sandra Gilbert and Susan Gubar in *The Madwoman in the Attic* in their quite different description of the struggle of women writers with the male tradition.)

In "Homo-Narcissism; or, Heterosexuality," Michael Warner makes a similar argument for seeing gayness not as a category subordinate to the hegemony of heterosexuality but as its own discourse in both personal and cultural dimensions. "This utopian self-relation," he writes, "far from being the pathology of the homosexual, could instead be seen as a historical condition and, in the perverse and un-recuperated mode of homosexual subjectivity, the source of a critical potential." Warner works to this conclusion by beginning, as do so many discussions of gender theory, with Freud's economy of the inevitable "poles of hetero- and homosexuality." Warner critiques the Freudian version of the process of sexual maturation and especially Freud's idea that the "interest in 'an object' " of sexual investment is "normally" a woman. Warner explains that

> Nothing guarantees such an outcome other than the boy's discovery that women are defined as objects to him in a way that other men are not. And since the girl discovers at the same time that her destiny is to be an object of desire, her encounter with alterity is very different from the boy's. She is not offered the same simple distinction between her own subjectivity and the other's objectivity. The discovery of otherness in the other gender, therefore, is neither neutral nor symmetrical. In de Beauvoir's argument, as in the work of other feminists who continue her Hegelian tradition, this construction of gendered otherness is seen as the structure of domination.

Warner's critique focuses on what he calls "the phenomenology of difference"—the reduction of one sort of distinction between people to a defining difference. Yet his ultimate critique focuses on changes under way in contemporary technoculture. Like Haraway, he sees transformations of the lines of power that structure markets and communities as restructuring gendered identity constructions in contemporary culture as well. The changing "forms of exchange in capitalism, the role-detachment that comes with a system-differentiated society, the mass imaginary of video capitalism, rituals and markets of adolescence," and the like open up new choices for postmodern subjectivity to express "the utopian erotics of modern subjectivity." "The work of analyzing the subjectivity of these interarticulated contexts," Warner concludes, "has only begun."

In quite different styles of gender criticism, Warner and Haraway both project a horizon of technoculture and electronic erotics, an amalgam of gender studies, cultural studies, and future shock. Both focus on the revisions of gender categories in contemporary culture and refuse to endorse, in Haraway's words, "anti-science metaphysics, a demonology of technology," and embrace instead the "task of reconstructing the boundaries of daily life." The resulting critique and interpretation may well be, as Haraway says, "an infidel heteroglossia," and that strange designation, in fact, may be fitting for the "cyborg" constructions of subjectivity and gender that she describes as emerging in contemporary technoculture.

In such alliances with cultural studies, gender and gay/lesbian studies often wager their critique on the revelatory developments of the contemporary scene—on developments in popular culture and technology. As the essays here show, this commitment to the "truth" of the hypernew and the post-postmodern often has less to do with faith in the future and the outcome of current developments in culture and technology than with a strategy for the practice of critique. In much gender criticism (Haraway's article here is a good example) is the construction and placement of a vantage point "located" in the future or in the hyperpresent of cultural change. Such a viewpoint functions primarily to enfranchise a certain kind of critique. From that vantage, "in" the culture but by definition a view from "outside" of it, it is possible to direct a massive oppositional critique of dominant Western practices in cultural relations and in the arts, particularly in relation to gender construction and social class. This critique is often of the repressions and constraints of those erotic, technological, and economic practices now being threatened and possibly eroded in Western culture.

We have been trying to show that feminist theory and gender studies are, on a number of fronts, principal theoretical sites and venues of critique in current critical studies. This is so, in part, because feminism and gender studies—like rhetorical studies—have the potential to articulate relations among all of the other schools of criticism we are discussing in this book. Whereas other sites of critical work have made important contributions in the past, feminism and gender studies are currently engaged in helping to shape the future of literary and cultural studies—both in teaching and in research.

**RELATED ESSAYS IN**
***CONTEMPORARY LITERARY CRITICISM***

Elaine Showalter, "Feminist Criticism in the Wilderness"
Barbara Christian, "The Race for Theory"
Patrocinio Schweickart, "Reading Ourselves: Toward a Feminist Theory of Reading"
Barbara Johnson, "Apostrophe, Animation, and Abortion"
Catherine Belsey, "Constructing the Subject: Deconstructing the Text"
Toril Moi, "Representation of Patriarchy"
Laura Mulvey, "Visual Pleasure and Narrative Cinema"
Meaghan Morris, "Banality in Cultural Studies"

**FURTHER READING**

Bauer, Dale M., *Feminist Dialogics* (New York: State University of New York Press, 1988).

Belsey, Catherine, and Jane Moore, eds., "Introduction: The Story So Far," in *The Feminist Reader: Essays in Gender and the Politics of Literary Criticism* (New York: Basil Blackwell, 1989).

Boone, Joseph Allen, ed., *Engendering Men: The Question of Male Feminist Criticism* (New York: Routledge, 1990).

Cixous, Hélène, and Catherine Clement, *The Newly-Born Woman* (Minneapolis: University of Minnesota, 1986).

Daly, Mary, *Beyond God the Father: Towards a Philosophy of Women's Liberation* (Boston: Beacon Press, 1973).

————, *Gyn/Ecology* (Boston: Beacon Press, 1978).

————, "The Transformation of Silence into Language and Action," in *Sinister Wisdom,* 6 (1978).

Davis, Robert Con, and Thaïs Morgan, "A Conversation about Men Doing Feminism," in *Men Writing the Feminine,* ed. Thaïs Morgan (Albany: SUNY Press, 1993).

de Beauvoir, Simone, *The Second Sex,* trans. H. M. Parshley (New York: Knopf, 1953).

Dinnerstein, Dorothy, *The Mermaid and the Minotaur: Sexual Arrangements and Human Malaise* (New York: Harper & Row, 1976).

Donaldson, Laura E., *Decolonizing Feminisms: Race, Gender, and Empire-Building* (Chapel Hill: University of North Carolina Press, 1992).

Donovan, Josephine, ed., *Feminist Literary Criticism* (Lexington: University of Kentucky Press, 1975).

Edwards, Lee, and Arlyn Diamond, eds., *The Authority of Experience: Essays in Feminist Criticism* (Amherst: University of Massachusetts Press, 1977).

Eisenstein, Hester, and Alice Jardine, eds., *The Future of Difference* (Boston: G.K. Hall, 1980).

Ellmann, Mary, *Thinking About Women* (New York: Harcourt, Brace, 1968).

Felman, Shoshana, "Rereading Feminity," in *Yale French Studies,* 62 (1981), 19–44.

————, *"Women and Madness:* The Critical Phallacy," in *Diacritics,* 5, No. 4 (1975), 2–10.

Finke, Laurie, *Feminist Theory, Women's Writing* (Ithaca, NY: Cornell University Press, 1992).

Fuss, Diana, *Essentially Speaking: Feminism, Nature, and Difference* (New York: Routledge, 1989).

Gilbert, Sandra M., and Susan Gubar, *The Madwoman in the Attic* (New Haven: Yale University Press, 1979).

Irigaray, Luce, *This Sex Which Is Not One*, trans. Caroline Porter (Ithaca, NY: Cornell University Press, 1985).

————, *Speculum of the Other Woman*, trans. Gillian C. Gill (Ithaca, NY: Cornell University Press, 1985).

Jacobus, Mary, ed., *Women Writing and Writing About Women* (London: Croom Helm, 1979).

Jardine, Alice, *Gynesis: Configurations of Woman and Modernity* (Ithaca, NY: Cornell University Press, 1985).

Kamuf, Peggy, "Writing Like a Woman," in *Woman and Language in Literature and Society,* ed. Sally McConnell-Ginet et al. (New York: Praeger, 1980), 284–99.

Kofman, Sarah, "Freud's Suspension of the Mother," in *Enclitic,* 4, No. 2 (1980), 17–28.

————, "The Narcissistic Woman: Freud and Girard," in *Diacritics,* 10, No. 3 (1980), 36–45.

Kolodny, Annette, "Some Notes on Defining a 'Feminist Literary Criticism,' " in *Critical Inquiry,* 2 (1975), 75–92.

Kroker, Arthur, and Marilouise Kroker, eds., *The Hysterical Male: New Feminist Theory* (New York: St. Martin's Press, 1991).

Kuhn, Annette, "The Body and Cinema: Some Problems for Feminism," in *Grafts: Feminist Cultural Criticism*, ed. Susan Sheridan (London and New York: Verso, 1988), 11–23.

———, "Introduction to Hélène Cixous's 'Castration or Decapitation?' " in *Signs* 7 (1981): 36–40.

Laqueur, Thomas, *Making Sex: Body and Gender from the Greeks to Freud* (Cambridge, MA: Harvard University Press, 1990).

McConnell-Ginet, Sally, et al., eds., *Women and Language in Literature and Society* (New York: Praeger, 1980).

Marks, Elaine, "Women and Literature in France," in *Signs,* 3 (1978), 832–42.

———, and Isabelle Courtivron, eds., *New French Feminisms: An Anthology* (Amherst: University of Massachusetts Press, 1980).

Millett, Kate, *Sexual Politics* (Garden City, NY: Doubleday, 1970).

Montrelay, Michele, "Inquiry into Feminity," trans. Parveen Adams in *m/f,* 1 (1978), 83–101.

Newton, Judith, and Deborah Rosenfelt, eds., *Feminist Criticism and Social Change* (New York: Methuen, 1985).

Pratt, Annis, *Archetypal Patterns in Women's Fiction* (Bloomington: Indiana University Press, 1981).

Sheridan, Susan, ed., *Grafts: Feminist Cultural Criticism* (London: Verso, 1988).

Showalter, Elaine, *A Literature of Their Own: British Women Novelists from Bronte to Lessing* (Princeton, NJ: Princeton University Press, 1977).

———, "Notes Toward a Feminist Poetics," in *Feminist Criticism*, ed. Elaine Showalter (New York: Pantheon, 1981), 243–70.

Spivak, Gayatri Chakravorty, *In Other Worlds: Essays in Cultural Politics* (New York: Methuen, 1987).

———, "Imperialism and Sexual Difference," in *Oxford Literary Review* 8 (1986): 225–240.

Wittig, Monique, "One is Not Born a Woman," in *Feminist Issues* 1, 2 (Winter 1981): 47–54.

———, "The Category of Sex," in *Feminist Issues* 2, 1 (Fall 1982): 63–68.

———, "On the Social Contract," in *Feminist Issues* 9, 1 (Spring 1989): 3–12.

———, "Homo Sum," in *Feminist Issues* 10, 1 (Spring 1990): 3–11.

Woolf, Virginia, *Collected Essays* (London: Hogarth, 1966).

———, *A Room of One's Own* (New York: Harcourt Brace Jovanovich, 1981).

# 31

# Gayatri Chakravorty Spivak
# 1942–

Born in Calcutta, Gayatri Chakravorty Spivak taught at the universities of Iowa, Texas, and Pittsburgh before assuming her current position at Columbia University. Known for her feminist and Marxist perspectives, she has been instrumental in extracting the issues contained under the rubric "marginality" and bringing them to the forefront of critical discussion. Spivak translated Jacques Derrida's *Of Grammatology* (1976) with a masterful introduction that introduced Derrida's work to the English-speaking world. She has also published a collection of critical essays entitled *In Other Worlds: Essays in Cultural Politics* (1987) and *The Post-Colonial Critic* (1990).

In "Feminism and Critical Theory" (1986) Spivak pursues an analysis of the relationship between deconstruction, Marxism, and feminism in the past few years to establish the boundaries between feminist reading of texts and its activities within real-life treatment of women internationally. Spivak's opening section involves a discussion of the Marxist and Freudian determinations of the placement of women, and especially of the work that they perform within society. This discussion proposes a more practical reading of texts through psychoanalysis and Marxism to determine answerable truths (or at least a closer proximity to them) than past theoretical readings have produced. The placement of "women's work" within the Marxist context is incomplete because the use, exchange, and surplus values of the products of that work—the bearing and raising of children—have been invisible and seemingly intangible within that intellectual framework. Its placement within the Freudian context is problematic as well because of Freud's evident inability to understand female sexuality and expression. To this concern Spivak adds in her final section an ironic description between first world and third world feminism to illustrate the gulf that remains between the two conditioned by class and race. Ultimately, she integrates her ideas into a practical, as well as a critical, examination of the "bourgeois feminism" of the first world in which she asks for new readings—both historical and textual—that are sensitive to class, gender, and race.

## Feminism and Critical Theory

What has been the itinerary of my thinking during the past few years about the relationships among feminism, Marxism, psychoanalysis, and deconstruction? The issues have been of interest to many people, and the configurations of these fields continue to change. I will not engage here with the various lines of thought that have constituted this change, but will try instead to mark and reflect upon the way these developments have been inscribed in my own work. The first section of the essay is a version of a talk I gave several years ago. The second section represents a reflection on that earlier work. The third section is an intermediate moment. The fourth section inhabits something like the present.

## 1.

I cannot speak of feminism in general. I speak of what I do as a woman within literary criticism. My own definition of a woman is very simple: it rests on the word "man" as used in the texts that provide the foundation for the corner of the literary criticism establishment that I inhabit. You might say at this point, defining the word "woman" as resting on the word "man" is a reactionary position. Should I not carve out an independent definition for myself as a woman? Here I must repeat some deconstructive lessons learned over the past decade that I often repeat. One, no rigorous definition of anything is ultimately possible, so that if one wants to, one could go on deconstructing the opposition between man and woman, and finally show that it is a binary opposition that displaces itself.[1] Therefore, "as a deconstructivist," I cannot recommend that kind of dichotomy at all, yet, I feel that definitions are necessary in order to keep us going, to allow us to take a stand. The only way that I can see myself making definitions is in a provisional and polemical one: I construct my definition as a woman not in terms of a woman's putative essence but in terms of words currently in use. "Man" is such a word in common usage. Not *a* word, but *the* word. I therefore fix my glance upon this word even as I question the enterprise of redefining the premises of any theory.

In the broadest possible sense, most critical theory in my part of the academic establishment (Lacan, Derrida, Foucault, the last Bar-

thes) sees the text as that area of the discourse of the human sciences—in the United States called the humanities—in which the *problem* of the discourse of the human sciences is made available. Whereas in other kinds of discourses there is a move toward the final truth of a situation, literature, even within this argument, displays that the truth of a human situation *is* the itinerary of not being able to find it. In the general discourse of the humanities, there is a sort of search for solutions, whereas in literary discourse there is a playing out of the problem as the solution, if you like.

The problem of human discourse is generally seen as articulating itself in the play of, in terms of, three shifting "concepts": language, world, and consciousness. We know no world that is not organized as a language, we operate with no other consciousness but one structured as a language—languages that we cannot possess, for we are operated by those languages as well. The category of language, then, embraces the categories of world and consciousness even as it is determined by them. Strictly speaking, since we are questioning the human being's control over the production of language, the figure that will serve us better is writing, for there the absence of the producer and receiver is taken for granted. A safe figure, seemingly outside of the language-(speech)-writing opposition, is the text—a weave of knowing and not-knowing which is what knowing is. (This organizing principle—language, writing, or text—might itself be a way of holding at bay a randomness incongruent with consciousness.)

The theoreticians of textuality read Marx as a theorist of the world (history and society), as a text of the forces of labor and production-circulation-distribution, and Freud as a theorist of the self, as a text of consciousness and the unconscious. This human textuality can be seen not only *as* world and self, *as* the representation of a world in terms of a self at play with other selves and generating this representation, but also *in* the world and self, all implicated in an "intertextuality." It should be clear from this that such a concept of textuality does not mean a reduction of the world to linguistic texts, books, or a tradition composed of books, criticism in the narrow sense, and teaching.

I am not, then, speaking about Marxist or psychoanalytic criticism as a reductive enterprise which diagnoses the scenario in every book in terms of where it would fit into a Marxist or a psychoanalytical canon. To my way of thinking, the discourse of the literary text is part of a general configuration of textuality, a placing forth of the solution as the unavailability of a unified solution to a unified or homogeneous, generating or receiving, consciousness. This unavailability is often not confronted. It is dodged and the problem apparently solved, in terms perhaps of unifying concepts like "man," the universal contours of a sex-, race-, class-transcendent consciousness as the generating, generated, and receiving consciousness of the text.

I could have broached Marx and Freud more easily. I wanted to say all of the above because, in general, in the literary critical establishment here, those two are seen as reductive models. Now, although nonreductive methods are implicit in both of them, Marx and Freud do also seem to argue in terms of a mode of evidence and demonstration. They seem to bring forth evidence from the world of man or man's self, and thus prove certain kinds of truths about world and self. I would risk saying that their descriptions of world and self are based on inadequate evidence. In terms of this conviction, I would like to fix upon the idea of alienation in Marx, and the idea of normality and health in Freud.

One way of moving into Marx is in terms of use-value, exchange-value, and surplus-value. Marx's notion of use-value is that which pertains to a thing as it is directly consumed by an agent. Its exchange-value (after the emergence of the money form) does not relate to its direct fulfillment of a specific need, but is rather assessed in terms of what it can be exchanged for in either labor-power or money. In this process of abstracting through exchange, by making the worker work longer than necessary for subsistence wages or by means of labor-saving machinery, the buyer of the laborer's work gets more (in exchange) than the worker needs for his subsistence while he makes the thing.[2] This "more-worth" (in German, literally, *Mehrwert*) is surplus-value.

One could indefinitely allegorize the relationship of woman within this particular triad—use, exchange, and surplus—by suggesting that woman in the traditional social situation produces more than she is getting in terms of her subsistence, and therefore is a continual source of the production of surpluses, *for* the man who owns her, or *by* the man for the capitalist who owns *his* labor-power. Apart from the fact that the mode of production of housework is not, strictly speaking, capitalist, such an analysis is paradoxical. The contemporary woman, when she seeks financial compensation for housework, seeks the abstraction of use-value into exchange-value. The situation of the domestic workplace is not one of "pure exchange." The Marxian exigency would make us ask at least two questions: What is the use-value of unremunerated woman's work for husband or family? Is the willing insertion into the wage structure a curse or a blessing? How should we fight the idea, universally accepted by men, that wages are the only mark of value-producing work? (Not, I think, through the slogan "Housework is beautiful.") What would be the implications of denying women entry into the capitalist economy? Radical feminism can here learn a cautionary lesson from Lenin's capitulation to capitalism.

These are important questions, but they do not necessarily broaden Marxist theory from a feminist point of view. For our purpose, the idea of externalization *(Ent-äuBerung/VeräuBerung)* or alienation *(Ent-fremdung)* is of greater interest. Within the capitalist system, the labor process externalizes itself and the worker as commodities. Upon this idea of the fracturing of the human being's relationship to himself and his work as commodities rests the ethical charge of Marx's argument.[3]

I would argue that, in terms of the physical, emotional, legal, custodial, and sentimental situation of the woman's product, the child, this picture of the human relationship to production, labor, and property is incomplete. The possession of a tangible place of production in the womb situates the woman as an agent in any theory of production. Marx's dialectics of externalization-alienation followed by fetish formation is inadequate because one fundamental human relationship to a product and labor is not taken into account.[4]

This does not mean that, if the Marxian account of externalization-alienation were rewritten from a feminist perspective, the special interest of childbirth, childbearing, and childrearing would be inserted. It seems that the entire problematic of sexuality, rather than remaining caught within arguments about overt sociosexual politics, would be fully broached.

Having said this, I would reemphasize the need to interpret reproduction within a Marxian problematic.[5]

In both so-called matrilineal and patrilineal societies the legal possession of the child is an inalienable fact of the property right of the man who "produces" the child.[6] In terms of this legal possession, the common custodial definition, that women are much more nurturing of children, might be seen as a dissimulated reactionary gesture. The man retains legal property rights over the product of a woman's body. On each separate occasion, the custodial decision is a sentimental questioning of man's right. The current struggle over abortion rights has foregrounded this unacknowledged agenda.

In order not simply to make an exception to man's legal right, or to add a footnote from a feminist perspective to the Marxist text, we must engage and correct the theory of production and alienation upon which the Marxist text is based and with which it functions. As I suggested above, much Marxist feminism works on an analogy with use-value, exchange-value, and surplus-value relationships. Marx's own writings on women and children seek to alleviate their condition in terms of a desexualized labor force.[7] If there were the kind of rewriting that I am proposing, it would be harder to sketch out the rules of economy and social ethics; in fact, to an extent, deconstruction as the questioning of essential definitions would operate if one were to see that in Marx there is a moment of major transgression where rules for humanity and criticism of societies are based on inadequate evidence. Marx's texts, including *Capital,* presuppose an ethical theory: alienation of labor must be undone because it undermines the agency of the subject in his work and his property. I would like to suggest that if the nature and history of alienation, labor, and the production of property are reexamined in terms of women's work and childbirth, it can lead us to a reading of Marx beyond Marx.

One way of moving into Freud is in terms of his notion of the nature of pain as the deferment of pleasure, especially the later Freud who wrote *Beyond the Pleasure Principle.*[8] Freud's spectacular mechanics of imagined, anticipated, and avoided pain write the subject's history and theory, and constantly broach the never-quite-defined concept of normality: anxiety, inhibition, paranoia, schizophrenia, melancholy, mourning. I would like to suggest that in the womb, a tangible place of production, there is the possibility that pain exists *within* the concepts of normality and productivity. (This is not to sentimentalize the pain of childbirth.) The problematizing of the phenomenal identity of pleasure and unpleasure should not be operated only through the logic of repression. The opposition pleasure-pain is questioned in the physiological "normality" of woman.

If one were to look at the never-quite-defined concepts of normality and health that run through and are submerged in Freud's texts, one would have to redefine the nature of pain. Pain does not operate in the same way in men and in women. Once again, this deconstructive move will make it much harder to devise the rules.

Freud's best-known determinant of femininity is penis-envy. The most crucial text of this argument is the essay on femininity in the *New Introductory Lectures*.[9] There, Freud begins to argue that the little girl is a little boy before she discovers sex. As Luce Irigaray and others have shown, Freud does not take the womb into account.[10] Our mood, since we carry the womb as well as being carried by it, should be corrective.[11] We might chart the itinerary of womb-envy in the production of a theory of consciousness: the idea of the womb as a place of production is avoided both in Marx and in Freud. (There are exceptions to such a generalization, especially among American neo-Freudians such as Erich Fromm. I am speaking here about invariable presuppositions, even among such exceptions.) In Freud, the genital stage is preeminently phallic, not clitoral or vaginal. This particular gap in Freud is significant. The hysteron remains the place which constitutes only the text of hysteria. Everywhere there is a nonconfrontation of the idea of the womb as a workshop, except to produce a surrogate penis. Our task in rewriting the text of Freud is not so much to declare the idea of penis-envy rejectable, but to make available the idea of a womb-envy as something that interacts with the idea of penis-envy to determine human sexuality and the production of society.[12]

These are some questions that may be asked of the Freudian and Marxist "grounds" or theoretical "bases" that operate our ideas of world and self. We might want to ignore them altogether and say that the business of literary criticism is neither your gender (such a suggestion seems hopelessly dated) nor the theories of revolution or psychoanalysis. Criticism must remain resolutely neuter and practical. One should not mistake the grounds out of which the ideas of world and self are produced with the business of the appreciation of the literary text. If one looks closely, one will see that, whether one diagnoses the names or not, certain kinds of thoughts are presupposed by the notions of world and consciousness of the most "practical" critic. Part of the feminist enterprise might well be to provide "evidence" so that these great male texts do not become great adversaries, or models from whom we take our ideas and then revise or reassess them. These texts must be rewritten so that there is new material for the grasping of the production and determination of literature within the general production and determination of consciousness and society. After all, the people who produce literature, male and female, are also moved by general ideas of world and consciousness to which they cannot give a name.

If we continue to work in this way, the common currency of the understanding of society will change. I think that kind of change, the coining of new money, is necessary. I certainly believe that such work is supplemented by research into women's writing and research into the conditions of women in the past. The kind of work I have outlined would infiltrate the male academy and redo the terms of our understanding of the context and substance of literature as part of the human enterprise.

**2.**

What seems missing in these earlier remarks is the dimension of race. Today I would see my work as the developing of a reading method that is sensitive to gender, race, and class. The earlier remarks would apply indirectly to the development of class-sensitive and directly to the development of gender-sensitive readings.

In the matter of race-sensitive analyses, the chief problem of American feminist criticism is its identification of racism as such with the constitution of racism in America. Thus, today I see the object of investigation to be not only the history of "Third World Women" or their testimony but also the production, through the great European theories, often by way of literature, of the colonial object. As long as American feminists understand "history" as a positivistic empiricism that scorns "theory" and therefore remains ignorant of its own, the "Third World" as its object of study will remain constituted by those hegemonic First World intellectual practices.[13]

My attitude toward Freud today involves a broader critique of his entire project. It is a critique not only of Freud's masculism but of nuclear-familial psychoanalytical theories of the constitution of the sexed subject. Such a critique extends to alternative scenarios to Freud that keep to the nuclear parent-child model, as it does to the offer of Greek mythical alternatives to Oedipus as the regulative type-case of the model itself, as it does to the romantic notion that an extended family, especially a community of women, would necessarily cure the ills of the nuclear family. My concern with the production of colonial discourse thus touches my critique of Freud as well as most Western feminist challenges to Freud. The extended or corporate family is a socioeconomic (indeed, on occasion political) organization which makes sexual constitution irreducibly complicit with historical and political economy.[14] To learn to read that

way is to understand that the literature of the world, itself accessible only to a few, is not tied by the concrete universals of a network of archetypes—a theory that was entailed by the consolidation of a political excuse—but by a textuality of material-ideological-psycho-sexual production. This articulation sharpens a general presupposition of my earlier remarks.

Pursuing these considerations, I proposed recently an analysis of "the discourse of the clitoris."[15] The reactions to that proposal have been interesting in the context I discuss above. A certain response from American lesbian feminists can be represented by the following quotation: "In this open-ended definition of phallus/semination as organically *omnipotent* the only recourse is to name the clitoris as orgasmically phallic and to call the uterus the reproductive extension of the phallus. . . . You must stop thinking of yourself privileged as a heterosexual woman."[16] Because of its physiologistic orientation, the first part of this objection sees my naming of the clitoris as a repetition of Freud's situating of it as a "little penis." To the second part of the objection I customarily respond: "You're right, and one cannot know how far one succeeds. Yet, the effort to put First World lesbianism in its place is not necessarily reducible to pride in female heterosexuality." Other uses of my suggestion, both supportive and adverse, have also reduced the discourse of the clitoris to a physiological fantasy. In the interest of the broadening scope of my critique, I should like to reemphasize that the clitoris, even as I acknowledge and honor its irreducible physiological effect, is, in this reading, also a short-hand for women's excess in all areas of production and practice, an excess which must be brought under control to keep business going as usual.[17]

My attitude toward Marxism now recognizes the historical antagonism between Marxism and feminism, *on both sides*. Hard-core Marxism at best dismisses and at worst patronizes the importance of women's struggle. On the other hand, not only the history of European feminism in its opposition to Bolshevik and Social Democrat women, but the conflict between the suffrage movement and the union movement in this country must be taken into account. This historical problem will not be solved by saying that we need more than an analysis of capitalism to understand male dominance, or that the sexual division of labor as the primary determinant is already given in the texts of Marx. I prefer the work that sees that the "essential truth" of Marxism or feminism cannot be separated from its history. My present work relates this to the ideological development of the theory of the imagination in the eighteenth, nineteenth, and twentieth centuries. I am interested in class analysis of families as it is being practiced by, among others, Elizabeth Fox-Genovese, Heidi Hartman, Nancy Hartsock, and Annette Kuhn. I am myself bent upon reading the text of international feminism as operated by the production and realization of surplus-value. My own earlier concern with the specific theme of reproductive (non) alienation seems to me today to be heavily enough touched by a nuclear-familial hysterocentrism to be open to the critique of psychoanalytic feminism that I suggest above.

On the other hand, if sexual reproduction is seen as the production of a product by an irreducibly determinate means (conjunction of semination-ovulation), in an irreducibly determinate mode (heterogeneous combination of domestic and politico-civil economy), entailing a minimal variation of social relations, then two original Marxist categories would be put into question: use-value as the measure of communist production and absolute surplus-value as the motor of primitive (capitalist) accumulation. For the first: the child, although not a commodity, is also not produced for immediate and adequate consumption or direct exchange. For

the second: the premise that the difference between subsistence-wage and labor-power's potential of production is the origin of original accumulation can only be advanced if reproduction is seen as identical with subsistence; in fact, the reproduction and maintenance of children would make heterogeneous the original calculation in terms of something like the slow displacement of value from fixed capital to commodity.[18] These insights take the critique of wage-labor in unexpected directions.

When I earlier touched upon the relationship between wage-theory and "women's work," I had not yet read the autonomist arguments about wage and work as best developed in the work of Antonio Negri.[19] Exigencies of work and limitations of scholarship and experience permitting, I would like next to study the relationship between domestic and political economies in order to establish the subversive power of "women's work" in models in the construction of a "revolutionary subject." Negri sees this possibility in the inevitable consumerism that socialized capitalism must nurture. Commodity consumption, even as it realizes surplus-value as profit, does not itself produce the value and therefore persistently exacerbates crisis.[20] It is through reversing and displacing this tendency within consumerism, Negri suggests, that the "revolutionary subject" can be released. Mainstream English Marxists sometimes think that such an upheaval can be brought about by political interventionist teaching of literature. Some French intellectuals think this tendency is inherent in the "pagan tradition," which pluralizes the now-defunct narratives of social justice still endorsed by traditional Marxists in a post-industrial world. In contrast, I now argue as follows:

It is women's work that has continuously survived within not only the varieties of capitalism but other historical and geographical modes of production. The economic, political, ideological, and legal heterogeneity of thc relationship between the definitive mode of production and race- and class-differentiated women's and wives' work is abundantly recorded. . . . Rather than the refusal to work of the freed Jamaican slaves in 1834, which is cited by Marx as the only example of zero-work, quickly recuperated by imperialist maneuvers, it is the long history of women's work which is a sustained example of zero-work: work not only outside of wage-work, but, *in one way or another,* "outside" of the definitive modes of production. The displacement required here is a transvaluation, an uncatastrophic *im*plosion of the search for validation via the circuit of productivity. Rather than a miniaturized and thus controlled metaphor for civil society and the state, the power of the *oikos,* domestic economy, can be used as the model of the foreign body unwittingly nurtured by the *polis.*[21]

With psychoanalytic feminism, then, an invocation of history and politics leads us back to the place of psychoanalysis in colonialism. With Marxist feminism, an invocation of the economic text foregrounds the operations of the New Imperialism. The discourse of race has come to claim its importance in this way in my work.

I am still moved by the reversal-displacement morphology of deconstruction, crediting the asymmetry of the "interest" of the historical moment. Investigating the hidden ethico-political agenda of differentiations constitutive of knowledge and judgment interests me even more. It is also the deconstructive view that keeps me resisting an essentialist freezing of the concepts of gender, race, and class. I look rather at the repeated agenda of the situational production of those concepts and our complicity in such a production. This aspect of deconstruction

will not allow the establishment of a hegemonic "global theory" of feminism.

Over the last few years, however, I have also begun to see that, rather than deconstruction simply opening a way for feminists, the figure and discourse of women opened the way for Derrida as well. His incipient discourse of woman surfaced in *Spurs* (first published as "La Question du Style" in 1975), which also articulates the thematics of "interest" crucial to political deconstruction.[22] This study marks his move from the critical deconstruction of phallocentrism to "affirmative" deconstruction (Derrida's phrase). It is at this point that Derrida's work seems to become less interesting for Marxism.[23] The early Derrida can certainly be shown to be useful for feminist practice, but why is it that, when he writes under the sign of woman, as it were, that his work becomes solipsistic and marginal? What is it in the history of that sign that allows this to happen? I will hold this question until the end of this essay.

## 3.

In 1979–80, concerns of race and class were beginning to invade my mind. What follows is in some sense a check list of quotations from Margaret Drabble's *The Waterfall* that shows the uneasy presence of those concerns.[24] Reading literature "well" is in itself a questionable good and can indeed be sometimes productive of harm and "aesthetic" apathy within its ideological framing. My suggestion is to use literature, with a feminist perspective, as a "nonexpository" theory of practice.

Drabble has a version of "the best education" in the Western world: a First Class in English from Oxbridge. The tradition of academic radicalism in England is strong. Drabble was at Oxford when the prestigious journal *New Left Review* was being organized. I am not averse to a bit of simple biographical detail: I began to re-read *The Waterfall* with these things in mind as well as the worrying thoughts about sex, race, and class.

Like many woman writers, Drabble creates an extreme situation, to answer, presumably, the question "Why does love happen?" In place of the mainstream objectification and idolization of the loved person, she situates her protagonist, Jane, in the most inaccessible privacy—at the moment of birthing, alone by choice. Lucy, her cousin, and James, Lucy's husband, take turns watching over her in the empty house as she regains her strength. *The Waterfall* is the story of Jane's love affair with James. In place of a legalized or merely possessive ardor toward the product of his own body, Drabble gives to James the problem of relating to the birthing woman through the birth of "another man's child." Jane looks and smells dreadful. There is blood and sweat on the crumpled sheets. And yet "love" happens. Drabble slows language down excruciatingly as Jane records how, wonders why. It is possible that Drabble is taking up the challenge of feminine "passivity" and making it the tool of analytic strength. Many answers emerge. I will quote two, to show how provisional and self-suspending Jane can be:

I loved him inevitably, of necessity. Anyone could have foreseen it, given those facts: a lonely woman, in an empty world. Surely I would have loved anyone who might have shown me kindness. . . . But of course it's not true, it could not have been anyone else. . . . I know that it was not inevitable: it was a miracle. . . . What I deserved was what I had made: solitude, or a repetition of pain. What I received was grace. Grace and miracles. I don't much care for my terminology. Though at least it lacks that most disastrous concept, the concept of free will. Perhaps I could make a religion that denied free will, that placed God in his true place, arbitrary, carelessly kind, idly malicious, intermittently atten-

tive, and himself subject, as Zeus was, to necessity. Necessity is my God. Necessity lay with me when James did [pp. 49–50].

And, in another place, the "opposite" answer—random contingencies:

I loved James because he was what I had never had: because he belonged to my cousin: because he was kind to his own child: because he looked unkind: because I saw his naked wrists against a striped tea towel once, seven years ago. Because he addressed me an intimate question upon a beach on Christmas day. Because he helped himself to a drink when I did not dare to accept the offer of one. Because he was not serious, because his parents lived in South Kensington and were mysteriously depraved. Ah, perfect love. For these reasons, was it, that I lay there, drowned was it, drowned or stranded, waiting for him, waiting to die and drown there, in the oceans of our flowing bodies, in the white sea of that strange familiar bed [p. 67].

If the argument for necessity is arrived at by slippery happenstance from thought to thought, each item on this list of contingencies has a plausibility far from random.

She considers the problem of making women rivals in terms of the man who possesses them. There is a peculiar agreement between Lucy and herself before the affair begins:

I wonder why people marry? Lucy continued, in a tone of such academic flatness that the topic seemed robbed of any danger. I don't know, said Jane, with equal calm. . . . So arbitrary, really, said Lucy, spreading butter on the toast. It would be nice, said Jane, to think there were reasons. . . . Do you think so? said Lucy. Sometimes I prefer to think we are victims. . . . If there were a reason, said Jane, one would be all the more a victim. She paused, thought, ate a mouthful of the toast. I am wounded, therefore I bleed. I am human, therefore I suffer. Those aren't reasons you're describing, said Lucy. . . . And from upstairs the baby's cry reached them—thin, wailing, desperate. Hearing it, the two women looked at each other, and for some reason smiled [pp. 26–27].

This, of course, is no overt agreement, but simply a hint that the "reason" for female bonding has something to do with a baby's cry. For example, Jane records her own deliberate part in deceiving Lucy this way: "I forgot Lucy. I did not think of her—or only occasionally, lying awake at night *as the baby cried,* I would think of her, with pangs of irrelevant inquiry, pangs endured not by me and in me, but at a distance, pangs as sorrowful and irrelevant as another person's pain" [p. 48; italics mine].

Jane records inconclusively her gut reaction to the supposed natural connection between parent and child: "Blood is blood, and it is not good enough to say that children are for the motherly, as Brecht said, for there are many ways of unmothering a woman, or unfathering a man. . . . And yet, how can I deny that it gave me pleasure to see James hold her in his arms for me? The man I loved and the child to whom I had given birth" [p. 48].

The loose ending of the book also makes Jane's story an extreme case. Is this love going to last, prove itself to be "true," and bring Jane security and Jane and James happiness? Or is it resolutely "liberated," overprotesting its own impermanence, and thus falling in with the times? Neither. The melodramatic and satisfactory ending, the accident which might have killed James, does not in fact do so. It merely reveals all to Lucy, does not end the book, and reduces all to a humdrum kind of double life.

These are not bad answers: necessity if all fails, or perhaps random contingency; an attempt not to rivalize women; blood bonds between mothers and daughters; love free of social security. The problem for a reader like me is that the entire questioning is carried on in what I can only see as a privileged atmosphere. I am not saying, of course, that Jane is Drabble (although that, too, is true in a complicated way). I am saying that Drabble considers the story of so privileged a woman the most worth telling. Not the well-bred lady of pulp fiction, but an impossible princess who mentions in one passing sentence toward the beginning of the book that her poems are read on the BBC.

It is not that Drabble does not want to rest her probing and sensitive fingers on the problem of class, if not race. The account of Jane's family's class prejudice is incisively told. Her father is headmaster of a public school.

> There was one child I shall always remember, a small thin child . . . whose father, he proudly told us, was standing as Labour Candidate for a hopeless seat in an imminent General Election. My father teased him unmercifully, asking questions that the poor child could not begin to answer, making elaborate and hideous semantic jokes about the fruits of labour, throwing in familiar references to prominent Tories that were quite wasted on such . . . tender ears; and the poor child sat there, staring at his roast beef . . . turning redder and redder, and trying, pathetically, sycophantically, to smile. I hated my father at that instant [pp. 56–57].

Yet Drabble's Jane is made to share the lightest touch of her parents' prejudice. The part I have elided is a mocking reference to the child's large red ears. For her the most important issue remains sexual deprivation, sexual choice. *The Waterfall,* the name of a card trick, is also the name of Jane's orgasms, James's gift to her.

But perhaps Drabble is ironic when she creates so class-bound and yet so analytic a Jane? It is a possibility, of course, but Jane's identification with the author of the narrative makes this doubtful. If there is irony to be generated here, it must come, as they say, from "outside the book."

Rather than imposing my irony, I attempt to find the figure of Jane as narrator helpful. Drabble manipulates her to examine the conditions of production and determination of microstructural heterosexual attitudes within her chosen enclosure. This enclosure is important because it is from here that rules come. Jane is made to realize that there are no fixed new rules in the book, not as yet. First World feminists are up against that fact, every day. This should not become an excuse but should remain a delicate responsibility: "If I need a morality, I will create one: a new ladder, a new virtue. If I need to understand what I am doing, if I cannot act without my own approbation—and I must act, I have changed, I am no longer capable of inaction—then I will invent a morality that condones me. Though by doing so, I risk condemning all that I have been" [pp. 52–53].

If the cautions of deconstruction are heeded—the contingency that the desire to "understand" and "change" are as much symptomatic as they are revolutionary—merely to fill in the void with rules will spoil the case again, for women as for human beings. We must strive moment by moment to practice a taxonomy of different forms of understanding, different forms of change, dependent perhaps upon resemblance and seeming substitutability—figuration—rather than on the self-identical category of truth:

Because it's obvious that I haven't told the truth, about myself and James. How could I? Why, more significantly, should I? . . . Of the truth, I haven't told enough. I flinched at the conclusion and can even see in my

hesitance a virtue: it is dishonest, it is inartistic, but it is a virtue, such discretion, in the moral world of love. . . . The names of qualities are interchangeable: vice, virtue: redemption, corruption: courage, weakness: and hence the confusion of abstraction, the proliferation of aphorism and paradox. In the human world, perhaps there are merely likenesses. . . . The qualities, they depended on the supposed true end of life. . . . Salvation, damnation. . . . I do not know which of these two James represented. Hysterical terms, maybe: religious terms, yet again. But then life is a serious matter, and it is not merely hysteria that acknowledges this fact: for men as well as women have been known to acknowledge it. I must make an effort to comprehend it. I will take it all to pieces. I will resolve it to parts, and then I will put it together again, I will reconstitute it in a form that I can accept, a fictitious form [pp. 46, 51, 52].

The categories by which one understands, the qualities of plus and minus, are revealing themselves as arbitrary, situational. Drabble's Jane's way out—to resolve and reconstitute life into an acceptable fictional *form* that need not, perhaps, worry too much about the categorical problems—seems, by itself, a classical privileging of the aesthetic, for Drabble hints at the limits of self-interpretation through a gesture that is accessible to the humanist academic. Within a fictional form, she confides that the exigencies of a narrative's unity had not allowed her to report the whole truth. She then changes from the third person to first.

What can a literary critic do with this? Notice that the move is absurdity twice compounded, since the discourse reflecting the constraints of fiction-making goes on then to fabricate another fictive text. Notice further that the narrator who tells us about the impossibility of truth-in-fiction—the classic privilege of metaphor—is a metaphor as well.[25]

I should choose a simpler course. I should acknowledge this global dismissal of any narrative speculation about the nature of truth and then dismiss it in turn, since it might unwittingly suggest that there is somewhere a way of speaking about truth in "truthful" language, that a speaker can somewhere get rid of the structural unconscious and speak without role playing. Having taken note of the frame, I will thus explain the point Jane is making here and relate it to what, I suppose, the critical view above would call "the anthropomorphic world": when one takes a rational or aesthetic distance from oneself one gives oneself up to the conveniently classifying macrostructures, a move dramatized by Drabble's third-person narrator. By contrast, when one involves oneself in the microstructural moments of practice that make possible and undermine every macrostructural theory, one falls, as it were, into the deep waters of a first person who recognizes the limits of understanding and change, indeed the precarious necessity of the micro-macro opposition, yet is bound not to give up.

The risks of first-person narrative prove too much for Drabble's fictive Jane. She wants to plot her narrative in terms of the paradoxical category—"pure corrupted love"—that allows her to *make* a fiction rather than try, *in* fiction, to report on the unreliability of categories: "I want to get back to that schizoid third-person dialogue. I've one or two more sordid conditions to describe, and then I can get back there to that isolated world of pure corrupted love" [p. 130]. To return us to the detached and macrostructural third person narrative after exposing its limits could be an aesthetic allegory of deconstructive practice.

Thus Drabble fills the void of the female consciousness with meticulous and helpful articulation, though she seems thwarted in any serious presentation of the problems of race and class, and of the marginality of sex. She engages in that microstructural dystopia, the sexual situation in extremis, that begins to

seem more and more a part of women's fiction. Even within those limitations, our motto cannot be Jane's "I prefer to suffer, I think"— the privatist cry of heroic liberal women; it might rather be the lesson of the scene of writing of *The Waterfall:* to return to the third person with its grounds mined under.

## 4.

It is no doubt useful to decipher women's fiction in this way for feminist students and colleagues in American academia. I am less patient with literary texts today, even those produced by women. We must of course remind ourselves, our positivist feminist colleagues in charge of creating the discipline of women's studies, and our anxious students, that essentialism is a trap. It seems more important to learn to understand that the world's women do not all relate to the privileging of essence, especially through "fiction," or "literature," in quite the same way.

In Seoul, South Korea, in March 1982, 237 woman workers in a factory owned by Control Data, a Minnesota-based multinational corporation, struck over a demand for a wage raise. Six union leaders were dismissed and imprisoned. In July, the women took hostage two visiting U.S. vice-presidents, demanding reinstatement of the union leaders. Control Data's main office was willing to release the women; the Korean government was reluctant. On July 16, the Korean male workers at the factory beat up the female workers and ended the dispute. Many of the women were injured and two suffered miscarriages.

To grasp this narrative's overdeterminations (the many telescoped lines—sometimes noncoherent, often contradictory, perhaps discontinuous—that allow us to determine the reference point of a single "event" or cluster of "events") would require a complicated analysis.[26] Here, too, I will give no more than a checklist of the overdeterminants. In the earlier stages of industrial capitalism, the colonies provided the raw materials so that the colonizing countries could develop their manufacturing industrial base. Indigenous production was thus crippled or destroyed. To minimize circulation time, industrial capitalism needed to establish due process, and such civilizing instruments as railways, postal services, and a uniformly graded system of education. This, together with the labor movements in the First World and the mechanisms of the welfare state, slowly made it imperative that manufacturing itself be carried out on the soil of the Third World, where labor can make many fewer demands, and the governments are mortgaged. In the case of the telecommunications industry, making old machinery obsolete at a more rapid pace than it takes to absorb its value in the commodity, this is particularly practical.

The incident that I recounted above, not at all uncommon in the multinational arena, complicates our assumptions about women's entry into the age of computers and the modernization of "women in development," especially in terms of our daily theorizing and practice. It should make us confront the discontinuities and contradictions in our assumptions about women's freedom to work outside the house, and the sustaining virtues of the working-class family. The fact that these workers were women was not merely because, like those Belgian lacemakers, oriental women have small and supple fingers. It is also because they are the true army of surplus labor. No one, including their men, will agitate for an adequate wage. In a two-job family, the man saves face if the woman makes less, even for a comparable job.

Does this make Third World men more sexist than David Rockefeller? The nativist argument that says "do not question Third World mores" is of course unexamined imperialism. There *is* something like an answer, which makes problematic the grounds upon which we base our own intellectual and political activities. No one can deny the dynamism and civilizing power of socialized capital. The irreducible search for greater production of surplus-value (dissimulated as, simply, "productivity") through technological advancement; the corresponding necessity to train a consumer who will need what is produced and thus help realize surplus-value as profit; the tax breaks associated with supporting humanist ideology through "corporate philanthropy"; all conspire to "civilize." These motives do not exist on a large scale in a comprador economy like that of South Korea, which is neither the necessary recipient nor the agent of socialized capital. The surplus-value is realized elsewhere. The nuclear family does not have a transcendent ennobling power. The fact that ideology and the ideology of marriage have developed in the West since the English revolution of the seventeenth century has something like a relationship to the rise of meritocratic individualism.[27]

These possibilities overdetermine any generalization about universal parenting based on American, Western European, or laundered anthropological speculation.

Socialized capital kills by remote control. In this case, too, the American managers watched while the South Korean men decimated their women. The managers denied charges. One remark made by a member of Control Data management, as reported in *Multinational Monitor,* seemed symptomatic in its self-protective cruelty: "Although 'it's true' Chae lost her baby, 'This is not the first miscarriage she's had. She's had two before this' "[28] However active in the production of civilization as a by-product, socialized capital has not moved far from the presuppositions of a slave mode of production. "In Roman theory, the agricultural slave was designated an *instrumentum vocale,* the speaking tool, one grade away from the livestock that constituted an *instrumentum semi-vocale,* and two from the implement which was an *instrumentum mutum.*"[29]

One of Control Data's radio commercials speaks of how its computers open the door to knowledge, at home or in the workplace, for men and women alike. The acronym of this computer system is PLATO. One might speculate that this noble name helps to dissimulate a quantitative and formula-permutational vision of knowledge as an instrument of efficiency and exploitation with an aura of the unique and subject-expressive wisdom at the very root of "democracy." The undoubted historical-symbolic value of the acronym PLATO shares in the effacement of class-history that is the project of "civilization" as such: "The slave mode of production which underlay Athenian civilization necessarily found its most pristine ideological expression in the privileged social stratum of the city, whose intellectual heights its surplus labour in the silent depths below the *polis* made possible."[30]

"Why is it," I asked above, "that when Derrida writes under the sign of woman his work becomes solipsistic and marginal?"

His discovery of the figure of woman is in terms of a critique of propriation—propering, as in the proper name (patronymic) or property.[31] Suffice it to say here that, by thus differentiating himself from the phallocentric tradition under the aegis of a(n idealized) woman who is the "sign" of the indeterminate, of that which has im-propriety as its property, Derrida cannot think that the sign "woman" is indeterminate by virtue of its access to the tyranny of the text of the proper. It is this tyranny of the "proper"—in the sense of that which produces both property and the proper name of the patronymic—that I have called the suppression of the clitoris, and that the news item about Control Data illustrates.[32]

Derrida has written a magically orchestrated book—*La carte postale*—on philosophy as telecommunication (Control Data's

business) using an absent, unnamed, and sexually indeterminate woman (Control Data's victim) as a vehicle, to reinterpret the relationship between Socrates and Plato (Control Data's acronym) taking it through Freud and beyond. The determination of that book is a parable of my argument. Here deconstruction becomes complicit with an essentialist bourgeois feminism. The following paragraph appeared recently in *Ms:* "Control Data is among those enlightened corporations that offer social-service leaves. . . . Kit Ketchum, former treasurer of Minnesota NOW, applied for and got a full year with pay to work at NOW's national office in Washington, D.C. She writes: 'I commend Control Data for their commitment to employing and promoting women. . . .' Why not suggest this to your employer?"[33] Bourgeois feminism, because of a blindness to the *multi*national theater, dissimulated by "clean" national practice and fostered by the dominant ideology, can participate in the tyranny of the proper and see in Control Data an extender of the Platonic mandate to women in general.

The dissimulation of political economy is in and by ideology. What is at work and can be used in that operation is at least the ideology of nation-states, nationalism, national liberation, ethnicity, and religion. Feminism lives in the master-text as well as in the pores. It is not the determinant of the last instance. I think less easily of "changing the world" than in the past. I teach a small number of the holders of the can(n)on, male or female, feminist or masculist, how to read their own texts, as best I can.

## NOTES

1. For an explanation of this aspect of deconstruction, see Gayatri Chakravorty Spivak, "Translator's Preface" to Jacques Derrida, *Of Grammatology* (Baltimore: Johns Hopkins University Press, 1976).

2. It seems appropriate to note, by using a masculine pronoun, that Marx's standard worker is male.

3. I am not suggesting this by way of what Harry Braverman describes as "that favorite hobby horse of recent years which has been taken from Marx without the least understanding of its significance" in *Labor and Monopoly Capital: the Degradation of Work in the Twentieth Century* (New York and London: Monthly Review Press, 1974, pp. 27, 28). Simply put, alienation in Hegel is that structural emergence of negation which allows a thing to sublate itself. The worker's alienation from the product of his labor under capitalism is a particular case of alienation. Marx does not question its specifically *philosophical* justice. The revolutionary upheaval of this philosophical or morphological justice is, strictly speaking, also a harnessing of the principle of alienation, the negation of a negation. It is a mark of the individualistic ideology of liberalism that it understands alienation as *only* the pathetic predicament of the oppressed worker.

4. In this connection, we should note the metaphors of sexuality in *Capital.*

5. I remember with pleasure my encounter, at the initial presentation of this paper, with Mary O'Brien, who said she was working on precisely this issue, and who later produced the excellent book *The Politics of Reproduction* (London: Routledge and Kegan Paul, 1981). I should mention here that the suggestion that mother and daughter have "the same body" and therefore the female child experiences what amounts to an unalienated pre-Oedipality argues from an individualist-pathetic view of alienation and locates as *discovery* the essentialist *presuppositions* about the sexed body's identity. This reversal of Freud remains also a legitimation.

6. See Jack Goody, *Production and Reproduction: A Comparative Study of the Domestic Domain* (Cambridge: Cambridge University Press, 1976), and Maurice Godelier, "The Origins of Male Domination," *New Left Review* 127 (May/June 1981): pp. 3–17.

7. Collected in *Karl Marx on Education, Women, and Children* (New York: Viking Press, 1977).

8. No feminist reading of this text is now complete without Jacques Derrida's "Spéculer—sur Freud," *La Carte postale: de Socrate à Freud et au-delà* (Paris: Aubier-Flammarion, 1980).

9. *The Standard Edition of the Complete Psychological Works of Sigmund Freud,* trans. James Strachey et al. (London: Hogarth Press, 1964), vol. 22.

10. Luce Irigaray, "La tâche aveugle d'un vieux rêve de symétrie," in *Speculum de l'autre femme* (Paris: Minuit, 1974).

11. I have moved, as I explain later, from womb-envy, still bound to the closed circle of coupling, to the suppression of the clitoris. The mediating moment would be the appropriation of the vagina, as in Derrida (see Gaya-tri Chakravorty Spivak, "Displacement and the Discourse of Women," in Mark Krupnick, ed., *Displacement: Derrida and After* (Bloomington: Indiana University Press, 1983).

12. One way to develop notions of womb-envy would be in speculation about a female fetish. If, by way of rather obvious historico-sexual determinations, the typical male fetish can be said to be the phallus, given to and taken away from the mother (Freud, "Fetishism," *Standard Edition,* trans. James Strachey, et al., vol. 21), then, the female imagination in search of a name from a revered sector of masculist culture might well fabricate a fetish that would operate the giving and taking away of a womb to a father. I have read Mary Shelley's *Frankenstein* in this way. The play between such a gesture and the Kantian socio-ethical framework of the novel makes it exemplary of the ideology of moral and practical imagination in the Western European literature of the nineteenth century. See Gayatri Chakravorty Spivak, "Three Women's Texts and a Critique of Imperialism," *Critical Inquiry* 12, no. 1 (Autumn 1985).

13. As I have repeatedly insisted, the limits of hegemonic ideology are larger than so-called individual consciousness and personal goodwill. See "The Politics of Interpretations," pp. 118–33 above; and "A Response to Annette Kolodny," widely publicized but not yet published.

14. This critique should be distinguished from that of Gilles Deleuze and Félix Guattari, *Anti-Oedipus: Capitalism and Schizophrenia,* trans. Robert Hurley, et al. (New York: Viking Press, 1977), with which I am in general agreement. Its authors insist that the family-romance should be seen as inscribed within politico-economic domination and exploitation. My argument is that the family romance-effect should be situated within a larger familial formation.

15. "French Feminism in an International Frame," pp. 134–53 above.

16. Pat Rezabek, unpublished letter.

17. What in man exceeds the closed circle of coupling in sexual reproduction is the entire "public domain."

18. I understand Lise Vogel is currently developing this analysis. One could analogize directly, for example, with a passage such as Karl Marx, *Grundrisse: Foundations of the Critique of Political Economy,* trans. Martin Nicolaus (New York: Vintage Books, 1973), p. 710.

19. Antonio Negri, *Marx Beyond Marx,* trans. Harry Cleaver, et al. (New York: J. F. Bergen, 1984). For another perspective on a similar argument, see Jacques Donzelot, "Pleasure in Work," *I & C* 9 (Winter 1981–82).

20. An excellent elucidation of this mechanism is to be

found in James O'Connor, "The Meaning of Crisis," *International Journal of Urban and Regional Research* 5, no. 3 (1981): pp. 317–29.

21. Jean-François Lyotard, *Instructions païens* (Paris: Union générale d'éditions, 1978). Tony Bennett, *Formalism and Marxism* (London: Methuen, 1979), pp. 145 and passim. Marx, *Grundrisse,* p. 326. The self-citation is from "Woman in Derrida," unpublished lecture, School of Criticism and Theory, Northwestern University, July 6, 1982.

22. See Gayatri Chakravorty Spivak, "Love Me, Love My Ombre, Elle," *Diacritics* (Winter 1984), pp. 19–36.

23. Michael Ryan, *Marxism and Deconstruction: A Critical Articulation* (Baltimore: Johns Hopkins University Press, 1982), p. xiv.

24. Margaret Drabble, *The Waterfall* (Harmondsworth: Penguin, 1971). Subsequent references are included in the text. Part of this reading has appeared in a slightly different form in *Union Seminary Quarterly Review* 35 (Fall–Winter 1979–80): 15–34.

25. As in Paul de Man's analysis of Proust in *Allegories of Reading: Figural Language in Rousseau, Nietzsche, Rilke, and Proust* (New Haven: Yale University Press, 1979), p. 18.

26. For definitions of "overdetermination," see Freud, *Standard Edition,* trans. James Strachey, et al., vol. 4, pp. 279–304; Louis Althusser, *For Marx,* trans. Ben Brewster (New York: Vintage Books, 1970), pp. 89–128.

27. See Gayatri Chakravorty Spivak, response, "Independent India: Women's India," forthcoming in a collection edited by Dilip Basu.

28. "Was Headquarters Responsible? Women Beat Up at Control Data, Korea," *Multinational Monitor* 3, no. 10 (September 1982): 16.

29. Perry Anderson, *Passages from Antiquity to Feudalism* (London: Verso Editions, 1978), pp. 24–25.

30. Ibid., pp. 39–40.

31. Spivak, "Love Me, Love My Ombre, Elle."

32. I have already made the point that "clitoris" here is not meant in a physiological sense alone. I had initially proposed it as the reinscription of a certain physiological emphasis on the clitoris in some varieties of French feminism. I use it as a name (close to a metonym) for women in excess of coupling-mothering. When this excess is in competition in the public domain, it is suppressed in one way or another. I can do no better than refer to the very end of my earlier essay, where I devise a list that makes the scope of the metonym explicit. "French Feminism," p. 184.

33. *Ms.* 10, no. II (May 1982):30. In this connection, it is interesting to note how so gifted an educator as Jane Addams misjudged nascent socialized capital. She was wrong, of course, about the impartiality of commerce: "In a certain sense commercialism itself, at least in its larger aspect, tends to educate the working man better than organized education does. Its interests are certainly world-wide and democratic, while it is absolutely undiscriminating as to country and creed, coming into contact with all climes and races. If this aspect of commercialism were utilized, it would in a measure counterbalance the tendency which results from the subdivision of labor" (*Democracy and Social Ethics,* Cambridge, Mass.: Harvard University Press, 1964), p. 216.

# 32

---

# Paula Bennett
# 1936–

---

One of a generation of women whose return to graduate studies accompanied the broader social and cultural movements of the 1960s, Paula Bennett brings her lesbian critical/theoretical perspective to the study of nineteenth-century American literature. As she describes it, her scholarship took shape hesitatingly as she began to assess the imagery of homoerotic love in Emily Dickinson's poetry in 1976 when she first wrote the essay included here. Between that first exploration and the publication of her two revisionary books on American women poets, *My Life a Loaded Gun: Female Creativity and Feminist Poetics* (orig. pub. Beacon Press, 1986, rpt. Urbana: University of Illinois Press, 1990) and *Emily Dickinson: Woman Poet* (orig. pub. Harvester Press, 1990, rpt. Iowa City: University of Iowa Press, 1991), Bennett weighed the implications of what at first she "believed" to be true and on the other hand "seemed too bizarre, too impossible to be true." Returning to the question of Dickinson's sexual imagery in her book-length studies nearly ten years after her first diffident, though compelling, interpretation, Bennett was ready to assess the cultural significance of images of women's sexuality, first by allowing herself to see the pervasiveness of this imagery, then by exploring the implications of the astounding critical silence regarding clitoral and other images of women's sexuality, not only in nineteenth-century American literary texts but also in psychoanalytic studies beginning with Freud and continuing with his late twentieth-century interpreters. In her two books and in a recent *Signs* article, "Critical Clitoridectomy," she offers an encompassing theoretical analysis of the implications of her reading not only of Dickinson's poetry but in much wider cultural contexts, including contemporary feminist, especially heterosexual, discussions of women's writing.

Bennett currently teaches English at Southern Illinois University, Carbondale.

---

## The Pea That Duty Locks: Lesbian and Feminist-Heterosexual Readings of Emily Dickinson's Poetry

---

*[The clitoris] is endowed with the most intense erotic sensibility, and is probably the prime seat of that peculiar life power, although not the sole one.*

—Charles D. Meigs, *Woman: Her Diseases and Remedies*, 1851

*One would have to dig down very deep indeed to discover . . . some clue to woman's sexuality. That extremely ancient civilization would undoubtedly have a different alphabet, a different language. . . . Woman's desire would not be expected to speak the same language as man's.*

—Luce Irigaray, *This Sex Which Is Not One*, 1985

In a 1985 essay in *Feminist Studies*, Margaret Homans brilliantly analyzes Emily Dickinson's use of vaginal imagery ("lips") as a multivalent figure for female sexual and poetic power (" 'Syllables' " 583–86, 591). Homans quite rightly identifies Dickinson's concept of the volcanic "lips that never lie" in "A still—Volcano—Life" (*The Poems* 461)[1] with the genital/lingual lips from which the hummingbird sucks in "All the letters I can write":

> All the letters I can write
> Are not fair as this—
> Syllables of Velvet—
> Sentences of Plush,
> Depths of Ruby, undrained,
> Hid, Lip, for Thee—
> Play it were a Humming Bird—
> And just sipped—me—
>
> (#334)

Less happily, Homans treats Dickinson's use of genital imagery entirely within the context of the (male) tradition of the romantic love lyric (that is, as a "subversion" of the "scopic" economy, or visual orientation, of masculinist love poetry). Not only does she fail to discuss the poem's homoerotic or lesbian possibilities, she barely notes them—this despite the fact that the poem's only known variant was originally sent—with a flower—to a woman, Dickinson's cousin, Eudocia (Converse) Flynt, of Monson, Massachusetts. For Homans, text—not sex—is the issue.

As in "A still—Volcano—Life," the imagery in "All the letters I can write" is undoubtedly (if not necessarily, consciously) sexual. The reader-lover-bird is told to sip from the well-hidden "depths" of the poet-vagina-

flower: "lip" to lips. But the form of sexual congress which the poet fantasizes in this poem is—as Homans fails to specify—oral; and the sex of the beloved-reader-bird is left deliberately (though, for Dickinson, not atypically), vague. He/she/you is referred to as "it." If this poem overturns the scopic conventions of the male-dominated romantic love lyric, it does so not to critique male "gaze," but to celebrate a kind of sexuality the poet refuses, or is unable, to name.

Because of her ambiguity, which makes variant readings such as the above not only possible but inevitable, Dickinson has become a preeminent example of the splitting of feminist criticism along sexual orientation lines. To those critics who read the poet heterosexually, the central narrative of Dickinson's career is her struggle with the male tradition—whether this tradition is seen as embodied in her lover, father, God, muse, or merely her precursor poets. Critics writing from this perspective (which represents, in effect, a feminist retelling of traditional mainstream narratives of the poet's career) include, in chronological order, Gilbert and Gubar, Margaret Homans, Joanne Feit Diehl, Barbara Antonina Clarke Mossberg, Suzanne Juhasz, Vivian Pollak, Jane Donahue Eberwein, Helen McNeil, Alicia Ostriker, and, most recently, Cynthia Griffin Wolff. Although all of these critics are deeply committed to understanding Dickinson as a woman poet, the framework for their discussion is the poet's relationship to the male tradition. Their concern is with "woman's place in man's world," even when, as in Homans's case, they acknowledge the presence of homoerotic strands in the poet's life and work.

In contrast to these critics are those like Rebecca Patterson, Lillian Faderman, Adalaide Morris, Judy Grahn, Martha Nell Smith, Toni McNaron and myself, who believe that Dickinson's relationships with women are of greater significance than her struggles with men or with the male tradition. While lesbian critics do not necessarily deny the prominence of certain male figures in Dickinson's life, they have dug beneath the more mythic aspects of the poet's heterosexuality (in particular, her supposed "love affair" with a "Master") to uncover the ways in which Dickinson used her relationships to the female and to individual women such as her sister-in-law Susan Gilbert Dickinson to empower herself as a woman and poet. To these critics, the central struggle in Dickinson's career is not, as Joanne Feit Diehl puts it, "to wrest an independent vision" *from* the male ("Reply" 196),[2] but to find a way to identify and utilize specifically female power in her work.

While both heterosexual and lesbian/feminist readings of Dickinson exemplify what Elaine Showalter calls "gynocriticism" (128), that is, both focus on the woman as writer, the difference between these two approaches to the poet—one privileging the male, the other the female—results in remarkably different presentations of Dickinson's biography and art. In this essay, I will discuss what happens to our reading of Dickinson's poetry when we give priority to her homoeroticism—and what happens when we do not. In particular, I will focus on the ways in which the privileging of homoeroticism affects our interpretation of Dickinson's erotic poetry as this poetry projects Dickinson's sense of self as a woman and as a woman poet (the two issues raised by Homans's essay).

For "straight" readers of Dickinson's texts, the poet's struggle with the tradition is mediated through her relationship with a man whom history has come to call the "Master," since his biographical identity (if any) has yet to be confirmed. Whoever or whatever this man was to the poet—whether lover, father, God, or muse—Dickinson's relationship to him is, according to this view of her texts,

fundamental to her poetic development—the means by which she came to define herself. In response to critiques by Lillian Faderman and Louise Bernikow of her theory of a male muse in Dickinson's poetry, Joanne Feit Diehl articulates the underlying assumptions governing the feminist-heterosexual approach to the Master Phenomenon in Dickinson's work:

> Bernikow's and Faderman's remarks offer nothing that would cause me to change my assertion that Dickinson found herself by confronting a male-dominated tradition. My essay acknowledges that she sought inspiration and courage from women poets engaged in similar struggles toward self-definition; however, hundreds of poems attest that her primary confrontations are with the male self. Furthermore, it is Dickinson who enables later women poets to trace a more exclusively female lineage. Refusing to ignore the tradition Bernikow and Faderman would deny her, Dickinson confronts her masculine precursors to wrest an independent vision. No woman poet need ever feel so alone again. ("Reply" 196)

The key word here is "alone." Like a latter-day feminist confronting a totally male-dominated environment (whether home, office, or academic department), Dickinson struggles in isolation to "wrest" vision from a male figure (or "tradition") infinitely more powerful than herself, a figure whom she wishes both to seduce and to defy. Because her Master is superior to her—and, perhaps, because she *does* love him—the form her struggle takes is (as Alicia Ostriker puts it), "subversive" not rebellious (39). Dickinson's tools are traditional female weapons, the "weapons" of those who are subordinate and isolated: play, parody, duplicity, evasion, illogic, silence, role-playing, and renunciation. As Ostriker says of the first five, they are strategies "still practiced by women poets today" (43).

For this particular interpretation of the poet and her plight, "The Daisy follows soft the Sun" has, not surprisingly, become the signature poem, mentioned or analyzed in a striking number of feminist-heterosexual readings:[3]

The Daisy follows soft the Sun—
And when his golden walk is done—
Sits shily at his feet—
He—waking—finds the flower there—
Wherefore—Maurauder—art thou here?
Because, Sir, love is sweet!

We are the Flower—Thou the Sun!
Forgive us, if as days decline—
We nearer steal to Thee!
Enamored of the parting West—
The peace—the flight—the Amethyst—
Night's possibility!

(#106)

In light of the above discussion, the reason for this poem's appeal to feminist-heterosexual readers should be obvious. Duplicity and subversion are the Daisy's essence. Cloaking herself in a veil of modesty (sitting "shily" at her Master's "feet"), the speaker claims to "follow" the Sun all simplicity and adoration, when in fact her real aim is to "steal" from him at night what he will not allow her to have by day: call it love, poetry, or power. The Daisy's reverence for her Master may be sincere, but it is also a cloak for highly disobedient ("Marauder"-like) ambitions, ambitions which only "Night's possibility"— and the Sun's "decline"—can fulfill.

I have no quarrel with this reading of the poem or those like it on which it is based. As Diehl's "hundreds of poems" testify, Dickinson was both attracted to and jealous of male power (from her brother's to God's), and she sought a variety of ways, including duplicity and subversion, seduction and evasion, and

maybe even fantasies of madness and necrophilia, to compensate for—or to change the conditions of—her unwanted subordination. Indeed, the poet's need to claim power equal to the male's is the primary theme of most of her heterosexual love poetry. His is the "Shaggier Vest" against which she asserts her smaller "Acorn" size ("One Year ago—jots what?" #296). His is the "crown" or "name" she wants to bear ("The face I carry with me—last," #336), even if she—and he— must die in order for her to have it:

Think of it Lover! I and Thee
Permitted—face to face to be—
After a Life—a Death—We'll say—
For Death was That—
And This—is Thee—

. . .

Forgive me, if the Grave come slow—
For Coveting to look at Thee—
Forgive me, if to stroke thy frost
Outvisions Paradise!

(from #577)

When writing heterosexually, Dickinson apparently could not imagine achieving equality in any other way. Men had the power. For her to have power equal to her male lover's, she had to take, steal, or seduce it from him—or they both had to be dead. Given nineteenth-century gender arrangements (including the arrangements within the Dickinson household), it is not surprising that the poet thought of heterosexual relationships in this way. But this is not the only kind of "love" poem that Dickinson wrote, nor is this the only kind of love story (or story about power) her poems tell.

As research by feminist historians Carroll Smith-Rosenberg and Lillian Faderman suggests, the rigid separation of the sexes produced by nineteenth-century American gender arrangements did not totally disadvan-

tage women (Smith-Rosenberg 53–76, Faderman, *Surpassing,* 147–230). True,
women spoke of themselves typically as
"low" or "inferior" in respect to men. These
are terms Dickinson herself uses in variants
to a poem on Elizabeth Barrett Browning
(#593). But nineteenth-century women
were not solely reliant on their relationships
with men for their sense of personal or sexual power (as heterosexual woman in our
society tend to be today). On the contrary,
one of the ironies of the doctrine of separate spheres was that it encouraged women
to form close affectional bonds with each
other. Within these bonds, women were
able to affirm themselves and their female
power despite their presumably inferior
state.

Dickinson's letters and poems indicate
that she participated in such relationships
with women throughout her life and, as I
have discussed elsewhere (*My Life a Loaded
Gun* 27–37, 55–63), she drew an enormous
amount of comfort, both emotional and sexual, from them. Indeed, a study of Dickinson's erotic poetry suggests that it was precisely the safety and protection offered by
her relationships with women—that is, by
relationships in which sameness not difference was the dominant factor (Morris in
Juhasz 103 and *passim*)—that allowed her
full access to her sexual feelings. Unlike
unambiguously heterosexual poets such as
Plath, Wakoski, and Olds, Dickinson did not
find male difference exciting. She was awed,
frightened, and, finally, repelled by it. In her
often-quoted "man of noon" letter, sent to
Susan Gilbert prior to the latter's engagement to Austin, the poet's brother, Dickinson compares male love to a sun that "scor-
ches" and "scathes" women (*The Letters*
210). And in her poetry, she exhibits similar
anxieties. Thus, for example, in "In Winter
in my Room," she depicts male sexuality as
a snake "ringed with Power" from whom
her speaker flees in terror:

> I shrank—"How fair you are"!
> Propitiation's claw—
> "Afraid he hissed
> Of me"?
>
> . . .
>
> That time I flew
> Both eyes his way
> Lest he pursue
>                         (from #1670)

And this same response of mingled awe and
repulsion is repeated more subtly in other
poems as well: "I started Early—Took my
Dog," (#520) for instance, and "I had been
hungry, all the Years" (#579). In each of
these poems, the poet's fear of male sexuality—not the arousal of her desire—is the
operative emotion. If she cannot find some
way to reduce male power, to bring it under
control, then she either loses her appetite
for it (as in "I had been hungry, all the
Years") or else she pulls back before she is
engulfed (as in "I started Early—Took my
Dog"). As she says in the latter poem, she
feared male desire "would eat me up"
(#520).

When relating to women, on the other
hand, or when describing female sexuality
(her own included), Dickinson's poetry could
not be more open, eager, and lush. Permeated with images of beauty, nurturance,
and protectiveness, and typically oral in emphasis, this poetry bespeaks the poet's overwhelming physical attraction to her own sex,
and her faith in the power of her own sexuality even when, as in the following poem, Dickinson is presumably writing from a heterosexual point of view:

> I tend my flowers for thee—
> Bright Absentee!
> My Fuschzia's Coral Seams
> Rip—while the Sower—dreams—
> Geraniums—tint—and spot—
> Low Daisies—dot—

My Cactus—splits her Beard
To show her throat—

Carnations—tip their spice—
And Bees—pick up—
A Hyacinth—I hid—
Puts out a Ruffled head—
And odors fall
From flasks—so small—
You marvel how they held—

Globe Roses—break their satin flake—
Upon my Garden floor—

                              (from #339)

At the conclusion of this poem, the speaker vows to "dwell in Calyx—Gray," modestly draping herself while "Her Lord" is away, but the damage, so-to-speak, has already been done. The entire emphasis in the poem lies in the speaker's riotous delight in the sensual joys that female sexuality has to offer. Like a painting by Georgia O'Keeffe or Judy Chicago, "I tend my flowers" takes us into the very heart of the flower: its sight, smell, taste, and feel. It is all coral and satin, spice and rose. In its image of the budding hyacinth coming into bloom, it could well be orgasmic.

As in "The Daisy follows soft the Sun," Dickinson employs a heterosexual context in "I tend my flowers" in order to assert female sexuality subversively, but her focus is obviously on female sexuality itself. It is this (not the charms of her absent male lover) that evokes the poet's intensely colored verse, her sensual reveries. When writing outside a specifically heterosexual context, as in the following poems, Dickinson is able to revel in female sexuality's Edenic pleasures without apology or restraint:

        Come slowly—Eden!
        Lips unused to Thee—
        Bashful—sip thy Jessamines—
        As the fainting Bee—

Reaching late his flower,
Round her chamber hums—
Counts his nectars—
Enters—and is lost in Balms.

                              (#211)

Wild Nights—Wild Nights!
Were I with thee
Wild Nights should be
Our luxury!

. . .

Rowing in Eden—
Ah, the Sea!
Might I but moor—Tonight—
In Thee!

                              (from #249)

        Within that little Hive
        Such Hints of Honey lay
        As made Reality a Dream
        And Dreams, Reality—
                              (#1607)

As Lillian Faderman first observed of "Wild Nights" ("Homoerotic Poetry" 20), these poems are all written from what we would normally think of as a male perspective. That is, they are written from the perspective of one who enters, not one who is entered. Because of this ambiguity, they effectively exclude the male. ("He" is at most a male bee, and hence, being small and round, equivocally, as we shall see, a female symbol.) The poems focus on female sexuality instead. "At sea" with this sexuality, Dickinson's speaker bathes in bliss and moors herself in wonder, eats hidden honey, adds up her nectars and is "lost in balms." The undisguised lushness of the imagery, especially when compared to Dickinson's poems on male sexuality, speaks for itself. For Dickinson, the dangerous aspects of sexual power lay with the male—the power to devour, scorch, and awe. The sweetness and balm (the healing) of sexuality, as well as its abundant pleasures, lay in women. And it was within this basically homoerotic context (a context created and sustained by nineteenth-century female bonding) that Dickinson defines her own desire.

As I discuss in *Emily Dickinson: Woman Poet,* in the poetry in which Dickinson privileges the clitoris even more than in the poetry in which she extols the delights of vaginal entry, she puts into words her subjective awareness of this desire and its paradoxical "little-big" nature. In this poetry, a poetry characterized by images drawn from the "neighboring life"—dews, crumbs, berries, and peas—Dickinson (in Irigaray's words) digs beneath the layers of male civilization to recover the ancient language of female sexuality itself (25). As Dickinson says in a poem sent to Susan Gilbert Dickinson in 1858, it is a language that sings a "different tune":

> She did not sing as we did—
> It was a different tune—
> Herself to her a music
> As Bumble bee of June
>
> . . .
>
> I split the dew—
> But took the morn—
> I chose this single star
> From out the wide night's numbers—
> Sue—forevermore!
>
> (from #14)

In *Literary Women* Ellen Moers observes that women writers—including Dickinson—have a predilection for metaphors of smallness which Moers relates to their small physical size. "Littleness," she writes, "is inescapably associated with the female body, and as long as writers describe women they will all make use of the diminutive in language and the miniature in imagery" (244). Even though Moers summarizes these metaphors suggestively as "the little hard nut, the living stone, something precious . . . to be fondled with the hand or cast away in wrath" (244),

she does not identify such images as clitoral. However, I believe that we should. Indeed, I believe that we must if we are to understand how a great many women—not just Dickinson—have traditionally (if, perhaps, unconsciously) chosen to represent their difference to themselves.

As nineteenth-century gynecologists such as Charles D. Meigs recognized over a hundred and forty years ago (a recognition "lost" later in the century), the clitoris is the "prime seat" of erotic sensibility in woman just as its homologue, the penis, is the prime seat in man (130).[4] It is reasonable to assume, therefore, that the clitoris's size, shape, and function contribute as much to a woman's sense of self—her inner perception of her power—as does her vagina or womb—the sexual organs on which psychoanalytic critics since Freud have chosen to concentrate.[5] Images of smallness in women's writing unquestionably relate to woman's body size and to her social position. But like phallic images (which also serve these other purposes), such images have a sexual base, and so does the power women so paradoxically attribute to them. In identifying their "little hard nut[s]" with "something precious," women are expressing through their symbolism their body's subjective consciousness of itself. That is, they are expressing their conscious or unconscious awareness of the organic foundation of their (oxymoronic) sexual power.

The existence of a pattern of imagery involving small, round objects in Dickinson's writing cannot be disputed. Whether identified as male or female, bees alone appear 125 times in her poetry. Dews, crumbs, pearls, and berries occur 111 times, and with peas, pebbles, pellets, beads, and nuts, the total number of such images comes to 261. In the context of the poems in which they appear, many of these images are neutral, that is, they seem to have no sexual significance. But their repetitiveness is another matter. So is the way in which they are given primacy in many poems. Analysis of the latter suggests that on the deepest psychological level, these images represented to the poet her subjective awareness of her female sexual self, both its "littleness" (when compared to male sex) and the tremendous force nevertheless contained within it. In privileging this imagery, consciously or unconsciously, Dickinson was replacing the hierarchies of male-dominated heterosexual discourse—hierarchies that disempowered her as woman and poet—with a (paradoxical) clitorocentrism of her own, affirming her specifically female power.

Over and over clitoral images appear in Dickinson's poetry as symbols of an indeterminate good in which she delights, yet which she views as contradictory in one way or another. It is small yet great, modest yet vain, not enough yet all she needs. The following poem brings together many of these motifs:

God gave a Loaf to every Bird—
But just a Crumb—to Me—
I dare not eat it—tho' I starve—
My poignant luxury—

To own it—touch it—
Prove the feat—that made the Pellet
        mine—
Too happy—for my Sparrow's chance—
For Ampler Coveting—

It might be Famine—all around—
I could not miss an Ear—
Such Plenty smiles upon my Board—
My Garner shows so fair—

I wonder how the Rich—may feel—
An Indiaman—An Earl—
I deem that I—with but a Crumb—
Am Sovereign of them all—

                                        (#791)

There are a number of things to note here. First, the poet is undecided whether the crumb in her possession satisfies her physical or her material appetite. In the first three stan-zas it takes care of her hunger (albeit, by touching). In the fourth stanza it makes her wealthy, an "Indiaman" or "Earl." She also cannot decide whether she is starving or not. For while she can touch and feel the crumb, she cannot eat it. Owning it is, therefore, a paradoxical business. It is a "poignant luxury," that is, a deeply affecting, possibly hurtful, sumptuousness that has archaic overtones of lust. Finally, poor though she is, the crumb makes this sparrow a "Sovereign," that is, it gives her power. She prefers it to "an Ear," presumably an ear of corn, and hence, given the poem's erotic suggestiveness, a phallus.

From one point of view, this poem is, obviously, a stunning example of Dickinson's ambiguity. Despite the many terms whose status as erotic signifiers can be established by reference to passages elsewhere in her work (loaf, bird, eat, luxury, sparrow, famine, plenty, Indiaman, earl, sovereign), there is no way to "know" what the poem is about. Not only do masturbation and cunnilingus fit but so do having a male or female lover, having some other unnamed good instead, sharing communion with God, and being content with her small/great lot as poet.

But whatever reading one adopts, what matters is that Dickinson has used imagery based upon her body as the primary vehicle through which to make her point. Whether or not she intended this poem to be about the clitoris, the clitoris is the one physical item in a woman's possession that pulls together the poem's disparate and conflicting parts. What other *single* crumb satisfies a woman's appetite even though she cannot eat it, and gives her the power of a "Sovereign" (potent male) whoever she is? In trying to represent her sense of self and the paradoxes of her female situation, consciously or unconsciously, Dickinson was drawn to what she loved most: the body she inhabited, the body she shared with other women. And it is the specific and extraordinary power of this body, its sovereign littleness, that she celebrates in this poem. As she says in another poem, this was the "crumb" for which she sang. As figure and fact, it was the source, motivation, and substance of her song:

> The Robin for the Crumb
> Returns no syllable
> But long records the Lady's name
> In Silver Chronicle.
>
> (#864)

By giving primacy to a clitoral image in this poem, Dickinson is asserting a form of female textuality and female sexuality that falls explicitly *outside* the male tradition. The song this "Robin" sings is "Silver," not golden like the sun/son. It is a "chronicle" that records "the Lady's," not her Master's, "name." And because it is female, it is written in different "syllables" from those of male verse, syllables drawn from the backyard life to which Dickinson's "lot" as a woman had consigned her—the life of robins, bees, and, above all, *crumbs*. From this life comes the "alphabet" in which female desire is reco(r)ded, an alphabet suited to the very different "Pleasure" loving women (as opposed to loving men) gives rise:

> There is an arid Pleasure—
> As different from Joy—
> As Frost is different from Dew—
> Like element—are they—
>
> Yet one—rejoices Flowers—
> And one—the Flowers abhor—
> The finest Honey—curdled—
> Is worthless—to the Bee—
>
> (#782)[6]

For Dickinson, devoting oneself to this homoerotic pleasure inevitably meant writing a different kind of verse:

> As the Starved Maelstrom laps the Navies
> As the Vulture teazed
> Forces the Broods in lonely Valleys
> As the Tiger eased
>
> By but a Crumb of Blood, fasts Scarlet
> Till he meet a Man
> Dainty adorned with Veins and Tissues
> And partakes—his Tongue
>
> Cooled by the Morsel for a moment
> Grows a fiercer thing
> Till he esteem his Dates and Cocoa
> A Nutrition mean
>
> I, of a finer Famine
> Deem my Supper dry
> For but a Berry of Domingo
> And a Torrid Eye.
>
> (#872)

In the first three stanzas of this poem, Dickinson compares the "male-storm"[7] created by male appetite sequentially—and hyperbolically—to a whirlpool, a vulture, and a man-eating tiger. In the final stanza, she celebrates her own "finer Famine," satisfied with "a Berry of Domingo / And a Torrid Eye." The theater of blood and lust which Dickinson depicts in the first three stanzas of this poem is so blatantly exaggerated it seems meant to be humorous. Male appetite is so voracious, the speaker claims, it will consume anything, including, finally, itself. (I read both "Crumb of Blood" and "Dates and Cocoa" as references to women.) In the final stanza, the speaker proudly asserts her own "limited" appetite by way of comparison. It is this appetite which defines her, making her the woman and poet she is: "I, of a finer Famine."

For Dickinson this "finer Famine" was a "sumptuous Destitution" (#1382), a paradoxical source of power and poetry, that nourished her throughout her life. In 1864, the same year in which she wrote "As the Starved Maelstrom laps the Navies," she sent Susan the following poem.

The luxury to apprehend
The luxury 'twould be
To look at Thee a single time
An Epicure of Me
In whatsoever Presence makes
Till for a further food
I scarcely recollect to starve
So first am I supplied—
The luxury to meditate
The luxury it was
To banquet on thy Countenance
A Sumptuousness bestows
On plainer Days,
Whose Table, far
As Certainty—can see—
Is laden with a single Crumb—
The Consciousness of Thee.
                    (#815 Version to Sue)

And in a letter written to Susan in 1883, she declared: "To be Susan is Imagination, / To have been Susan, a Dream— / What depths of Domingo in that torrid Spirit!" (*The Letters* 791). Over the twenty years that intervened between these poems and this letter, Dickinson's patterns of female sexual imagery and the homoerotic values these patterns encoded did not substantially change. Taken together, they were the "berries," "crumbs," and "dews" that—in imagination and in reality—nourished and sustained her as male love (and the male literary tradition) never could.

The importance of Dickinson's commitment to a woman-centered sexuality and textuality seems hard to dispute. But why then have so many feminist critics found it difficult to acknowledge the centrality of Dickinson's homoeroticism to her writing? Put another way, why have so many of them insisted on depicting her, in Diehl's terms, as "alone," even when (given her bonds to other women), she was not? What follows is not meant as a personal attack on these critics, but rather as an exploration of what I believe

to be one of the most difficult issues confronting feminist-heterosexual women today—an issue whose political and sexual nature Dickinson was not only aware of but which she addressed in her poetry.

In *This Sex Which Is Not One,* Luce Irigaray makes the following comments on the (heterosexual) woman's place in the "dominant phallic economy," that is, in male-dominated culture:

> Woman, in this sexual imaginary, is only a more or less obliging prop for the enactment of man's fantasies. That she may find pleasure there in that role, by proxy, is possible, even certain. But such pleasure is above all a masochistic prostitution of her body to a desire that is not her own, and it leaves her in a familiar state of dependency upon man. Not knowing what she wants, ready for anything, even asking for more, so long as he will "take" her as his "object" when he seeks his own pleasure. (25).

Women, Irigaray argues, have been "enveloped in the needs/desires/fantasies of . . . men" (134). As such, they have been cut off from their own sexuality. In Irigaray's terms, they have learned to "masquerade" (133–34), assuming the sexual roles men have imposed upon them, while devaluing their own capacity for autonomous sexual response. As "conceptualized" within the phallic economy, Irigaray writes, "woman's erogenous zones never amount to anything but a clitoris-sex that is not comparable to the noble phallic organ, or a hole-envelope that serves to sheathe and massage the penis in intercourse: a non-sex . . ." (23). That women can be sexually equal to men (agents, as it were, of their own desire) is an idea both men and (many) women resist.

The historical appropriation and devaluation of female sexuality by men is hardly news; women in the nineteenth century were also aware of it. But in "The Malay—took the

Pearl," Dickinson gives this perception a twist by addressing it from a homoerotic perspective, that is, from a perspective shaped by the poet's (homoerotic) awareness of the role the clitoris plays in autonomous woman-centered sex:

> The Malay—took the Pearl—
> Not—I—the Earl—
> I—feared the Sea—too much
> Unsanctified—to touch—
>
> Praying that I might be
> Worthy—the Destiny—
> The Swarthy fellow swam—
> And bore my Jewel—Home—
>
> Home to the Hut! What lot
> Had I—the Jewel—got—
> Borne on a Dusky Breast—
> I had not a deemed Vest
> Of Amber—fit—
>
> The Negro never knew
> I—wooed it—too
> To gain, or be undone—
> Alike to Him—One—
>
> (#452)

Whether the "Pearl" in this poem stands synecdochically for the woman Dickinson loved or metonymically for the sexual and poetic powers which the poet believed were hers,[8] or, as is probable, for both, the poem's main point is clear. The "Jewel" that the Malay takes and then devalues (brings "Home" to his "hut") is an object of desire not just for the man but the speaker also. Indeed, the speaker (presumably a woman even though she cross-dresses as an "Earl") has far more title to the pearl than the Malay since she appreciates its true worth whereas he does not. (He wears it on a "Dusky," sundarkened, "Breast" where she would not deem a "Vest / Of Amber—fit" to bear it.) Nevertheless, she feels she has no right to this prize. She "fears" to touch the sea.

In cross-dressing her speaker in this poem, Dickinson may be expressing some of the awkwardness or perhaps even "unnaturalness" she felt in attributing (active) sexual desire to herself as a woman. As a young woman, Dickinson's problem—as she states in "The Malay—took the Pearl"—had been to gather the courage to appropriate female power for herself, to see herself as equally "sanctified"—and sanctioned—to "dive" (or "climb") into forbidden territories, whether erotic or poetic. In maturity, she lashes out again and again at the damage done women psychologically by such self-serving (masculine) prohibitions, prohibitions that not only prevent women from maturing fully, but turn them into the passive objects of male desire (and male art). Not permitted to act on their own needs or in their own stead, women inevitably become the victims of the men who "envelop" them (or eat them up):

> Over the fence—
> Strawberries—grow—
> Over the fence—
> I could climb—if I tried, I know—
> Berries are nice!
>
> But—if I stained my Apron
> God would certainly scold!
> Oh, dear,—I guess if He were a Boy—
> He'd—climb—if He could!
>
> (#251)

The little girl voice Dickinson adopts in this poem is deliberate and calculated. Boys have a right to "forbidden" fruits, but women (those whose sexual maturation is tied to—and "tied down" by—apron strings) do not. Yet, as this poem's symbolism makes clear, it is precisely women who are the "Berries" that boys so eagerly pick. Hence men's desire to guard their access to this fruit by divine interdiction. The God men worship (or create) protects male right.

What Dickinson is alluding to in this poem

is—and has historically been—the paradox (and tragedy) of female sexuality: that its power is something women themselves have been forbidden to enjoy. It is a paradox Dickinson gives brilliant expression to in one of her most teasing yet trenchant epigrams:

> Forbidden Fruit a flavor has
> That lawful Orchards mocks—
> How luscious lies within the Pod
> The Pea that Duty locks—
>
> (#1377)

Whether this poem is about cunnilingus, masturbation, or something else altogether, the sexual implications of its final line are hard to evade. "Duty," that is, women's sense of obligation to a male-dominated culture's self-serving prohibitions, has made women's sexuality inaccessible to them. Women's loss of their sexuality occurred literally during the nineteenth century as they were propagandized to believe that they did not have orgasms. As we now know, in the space of less than fifty years, the physiological importance of the clitoris was expunged from the record and apparently from many women's conscious awareness as well (Laqueur 1–41).

Symbolically, this silencing of female sexual power continues to occur today in the writing of those critics, including those feminist critics, who ignore the significance of the homoerotic (and autoerotic) elements in poetry like Dickinson's. Indeed, feminist-heterosexual interpretations of Dickinson's poetry testify all too vividly to the degree to which, as Irigaray says, female sexuality remains "enveloped" in the needs and desires of men, despite the woman-centeredness of feminist vision. Committed to a heterosexual perspective (a perspective that makes women sexually as well as emotionally and intellectually dependent on men, no matter how much they may compete with them for power), these critics cannot see the centrality of Dickinson's homoeroticism even

when—as in her clitoral poetry—it is obviously there. They cannot decode the "alphabet" in which these poems are written. Dickinson's relationship to the Master (a paradigm, perhaps, for these critics' own relationship to what Diehl calls "the male self") overwhelms ("envelopes") their eyes.

No one understood the magnitude of the task involved in women's reappropriation of their sexual power better than Dickinson and there were times when she questioned whether her "Pebble" was adequate to the task. It was a struggle of epic proportion in which she was David (indeed, less than David) to her culture's Goliath:

> I took my Power in my Hand—
> And went against the World—
> 'Twas not so much as David—had—
> But I—was twice as bold—
>
> I aimed my Pebble—but Myself
> Was all the one that fell—
> Was it Goliath—was too large—
> Or was myself—too small?
>
> (from #540)

But there were other times when she was able to assert without reservation her absolute right to the "Crown" she knew was hers:

> I'm ceded—I've stopped being Their's—
> The name They dropped upon my face
> With water, in the country church
> Is finished using, now . . .
>
> My second Rank—too small the first—
> Crowned—Crowing—on my Father's
>     breast—
> A half unconscious Queen—
> But this time—Adequate—Erect,
> With Will to choose, or to reject,
> And I choose, just a Crown
>
> (from #508)

The full impact of these lines can only be appreciated when they are read against those poems in which the speaker yearns pathetically for her Master's "Crown." In this poem, she stands masculinely "Erect" and crowns herself. Doing so, she takes back the symbol of her womanhood that men have usurped. In baptizing their daughters (as in wedding their wives), men give their names to women, making them "half unconscious Queens"— Queens who are not in full possession of their power (their "Crown"). In "I'm ceded," these rights (and rites) of male possession come to an end. The woman's vagina-ring-crown is hers. So presumably is the personal (creative) power—the "crumb"—that goes with it.

As I have asserted in *Emily Dickinson: Woman Poet,* Dickinson's ability to pose female sexuality and textuality as valid, autonomous *alternatives* to male sexuality and textuality derives from her romantic commitment to women and from her willingness to see in women sources of love, power, and pleasure independent of what Mary Lyon calls "the other sex" (Quoted by Hitchcock, 301). Her use of female sexual imagery suggests, therefore, not the "subversion" of an existing male tradition—but rather the assertion of a concept of female sexuality and female textuality that renders male sexuality and the poetic discourse around male sexuality irrelevant. In privileging the clitoris over the vagina, Dickinson privileged the female sexual organ whose pleasure was clearly independent of the male. She also privileged the sole organ in either sex whose *only* function is pleasure. For Dickinson, her "crumb" was "small" but it was also "plenty." It was "enough."

## NOTES

This essay deals with issues which troubled me during the writing of *Emily Dickinson: Woman Poet.* In the book, I argue the case for Dickinson's homoeroticism (and autoeroticism) much more fully. Here I wish to look at what feminist-heterosexual critics have—or, rather, have not—made of this material—and why.

1. All subsequent citations to Dickinson's poems will appear parenthetically in the text as the # symbol, followed by the Johnson number of the poem. In quoting from Dickinson's poetry and letters, I have retained her idiosyncratic spelling and punctuation.

2. Diehl's original essay has been republished in her *Dickinson and the Romantic Imagination* (13–33).

3. Analyses of "The Daisy follows soft the Sun" may be found in Gilbert and Gubar (600–601), Homans (203–4), and the essays by Gilbert, Keller, Mossberg, Morris, Homans, and Miller published in *Feminist Critics Read Emily Dickinson,* edited by Suzanne Juhasz.

4. The knowledge which Meigs states so definitively was "lost" in the course of the nineteenth century as part of a general (politically motivated) redefining of female sexuality. See Laqueur (1–41).

5. Naomi Schor is the only critic with whom I am familiar who has treated the subject of clitoral imagery and she discusses it only in relation to the use of synecdoche (detail) in male writing ("Female Paranoia" 204–19). In her full-length study of detail in male writing *(Reading in Detail: Aesthetics and the Feminine),* she drops the idea altogether.

The *locus classicus* for a discussion of uterine imagery in women's "art" is Erik Erikson's influential essay "Womanhood and the Inner Space" (Erikson 261–94). In *Through the Flower,* Judy Chicago discusses her development of vaginal imagery and the empowering effect working with this imagery had on her (especially 51–58).

6. Dickinson identifies two kinds of sexual pleasure in this poem: one that gives the flowers joy and one that dries up *or* freezes them ("arid," "Frost"). If my reading is correct, this latter "pleasure" is the product of male sexuality which Dickinson depicts in some poems as a "sun," and in others as "frost." See for example, "A Visitor in Marl" (#391), and "The Frost of Death was on the Pane" (#1136). In either case, of course, male sexuality's ultimate effect on the women-flowers is the same: death.

7. I am indebted to Ms. Deborah Pfeiffer for calling my attention to this anagram.

8. I have discussed the biographical elements of this poem in *My Life a Loaded Gun* (52–53).

## WORKS CITED

Bennett, Paula, *Emily Dickinson* (London: Harvester, 1990).

———, *My Life a Loaded Gun: Female Creativity and Feminist Poetics* (Boston: Beacon Press, 1986).

Chicago, Judy, *Through the Flower: My Struggle as a Woman Artist.* 1975 (Garden City, N.Y.: Anchor-Doubleday, 1982).

Dickinson, Emily, *The Letters of Emily Dickinson,* ed. Thomas H. Johnson and Theodora Ward, 3 vols. (Cambridge, Mass.: Belknap Press of Harvard University Press, 1958).

———, *The Poems of Emily Dickinson,* ed. Thomas H. Johnson, 3 vols. (Cambridge, Mass.: Belknap Press of Harvard University Press, 1958).

Diehl, Joanne Feit, *Dickinson and the Romantic Imagination* (Princeton, N.J.: Princeton University Press, 1981).

———, "Reply to Faderman and Bernikow," in *Signs,* 4 (1978), 196.

Erikson, Erik, *Identity: Youth and Crisis* (New York: Norton, 1968).

Faderman, Lillian, "Emily Dickinson's Homoerotic Poetry," in *Higginson Journal,* 18 (1978), 19–27.

———, *Surpassing the Love of Men: Romantic Friendship and Love between Women from the Renaissance to the Present* (New York: Morrow, 1981).

Gilbert, Sandra M., and Susan Gubar, *The Madwoman in the Attic: The Woman Writer and the Nineteenth-Century Literary Imagination.* (New Haven, Conn.: Yale University Press, 1979).

Hitchcock, Edward, ed., *The Power of Christian Benevolence Illustrated in the Life and Labors of Mary Lyon* (Northampton, Mass.: Hopkins, Bridgman, 1852).

Homans, Margaret, "'Syllables of Velvet': Dickinson, Rossetti, and the Rhetoric of Sexuality," in *Feminist Studies,* 11 (1985), 569–93.

———, *Women Writers and Poetic Identity: Dorothy Wordsworth, Emily Brontë, and Emily Dickinson* (Princeton, N.J.: Princeton University Press, 1980).

Irigaray, Luce, *This Sex Which Is Not One,* trans. Catherine Porter (Ithaca, N.Y.: Cornell University Press, 1985).

Juhasz, Suzanne, ed., *Feminist Critics Read Emily Dickinson* (Bloomington: Indiana University Press, 1983).

Laqueur, Thomas, "Orgasm, Generation, and the Politics of Reproductive Biology," in *The Making of the Modern Body: Sexuality and Society in the Nineteenth Century,* ed. Catherine Gallagher and Thomas Laqueur (Berkeley: University of California Press, 1988), 1–41.

Meigs, Charles D., *Woman: Her Diseases and Remedies* (Philadelphia: Lea and Blanchard, 1851).

Moers, Ellen, *Literary Women: The Great Writers,* rpt. 1976 (New York: Oxford University Press, 1985).

Ostriker, Alicia Suskind, *Stealing the Language: The Emergence of Women's Poetry in America* (Boston: Beacon Press, 1986).

Schor, Naomi, "Female Paranoia: The Case for Psychoanalytical Criticism," in *Yale French Studies,* 62 (1981): 204–19.

———, *Reading in Detail: Aesthetics and the Feminine* (New York: Methuen, 1987).

Showalter, Elaine, "Toward a Feminist Poetics," in *The New Feminist Criticism: Essays on Women, Literature, and Theory,* ed. Elaine Showalter (New York: Pantheon 1985), 125–43.

Smith-Rosenberg, Carroll, *Disorderly Conduct: Visions of Gender in Victorian America* (New York: Knopf, 1985).

# 33

# Michael Warner
# 1958–

Michael Warner is associate professor of English at Rutgers University, New Brunswick. A Ph.D. graduate from the Johns Hopkins University, Warner's earliest work has been in early modern American literature and culture, an interest that produced his first book, *The Letters of the Republic: Publication and the Public Sphere in Eighteenth-Century America* (1990). From that base in American studies, he has pursued a broad range of critical and theoretical interests, including the history of the profession, American pragmatism, cultural studies, and, perhaps most prominently, the field now called "queer theory." Warner has been not only one of the leading voices in the United States advocating gay and lesbian studies but also one of the most lucid writers tackling theoretical problems in the field. He has coedited, with Gerald Graff, *The Origins of Literary Studies in America: A Documentary Anthology* (1988). His essays have appeared in places such as *Representations, Boundary 2, Criticism, Nineteenth-Century Literature,* and *The Village Voice Literary Supplement*.

"Homo-Narcissism: Or, Heterosexuality" first appeared in a landmark anthology entitled *Engendering Men: The Question of Male Feminist Criticism* (1990), and it represents Warner's attempt to cut through the Gordian knot that in the West has traditionally linked gender and sexuality in the twentieth century. Studying Freud's work on narcissism in detail, Warner explains that psychoanalysis has characterized homoeroticism as a pathological abnormality in which an individual, especially a man, desires "himself in the guise of another," thereby collapsing the distinction between self and Other in hermetically sealed narcissism. However, Freud also recognizes, argues Warner, that erotic relationships of *all* kinds involve such a psychological—and clearly narcissistic—transaction of projecting one's own ego ideals onto a love object. Why have Freud, Lacan, and other intellectuals nonetheless persisted in portraying homosexuality as a pathology producing unitary sameness? Warner answers that these writers have proceeded on a fundamental Western assumption that the difference between self and Other is founded on the difference between gender—that "gender is the phenomenology of difference itself." That assumption, he says, undergirds a general cultural system in which heterosexual ego-identity, despite its own narcissistic dynamic, can be naturalized and therefore can attempt to transcend the basic "role of the imaginary in the formation of the erotic."

Warner moves then to urge a large-scale historical investigation of how and why "modern" heterosexuality has relied on and simultaneously displaced its narcissistic component onto a pathologized homosexuality. Drawing on Jürgen Habermas's claim that modern human identity is based on the tentative formation of the ego rather than on more definable identity roles, Warner suggests the outline of such a history by proposing that homosexuality takes the "multiple sites of ego-reflection in modern liberal capitalism as multiple sites of erotic play and interaction." It therefore has provided an articulation of modern subjectivity's fluid construction while also serving as denial of the dynamic dimension in "normal" human development.

# Homo-Narcissism; or, Heterosexuality

The modern system of sex and gender would not be possible without a disposition to interpret the difference between genders as the difference between self and Other. This elementary structure has been a subject for feminist theory at least since 1949, when Simone de Beauvoir posed it as the central problem of *The Second Sex:* how does it happen that man is constituted as the subject, and woman is constituted as the Other? For de Beauvoir, this is not just what men would like to believe, but the psychic structure of gender. Femininity is learned as a way of constructing oneself as object, a way of attributing full subjectivity only to the masculine. This identification of the male as subject and the female as Other, she argues, underwrites all the asymmetries of gender throughout history.

But the same insidious identification also has a more specially modern variant.[1] In the modern West, having a sexual object of the opposite gender is taken to be the normal and paradigmatic form of an interest either in the Other or, more generally, in others. That is why in our own century it has acquired the name *heterosexuality*—a sexuality of otherness. In this organization of sexuality, heteroerotics can be understood as the opposite *either* of homoerotics *or,* in the more general extension, of autoerotics. Indeed, according to this logic homoerotics is an unrecognized version of autoerotics, or more precisely of narcissism; both are seen as essentially an interest in self rather than in the other. The perverse options are therefore the exceptions that prove the rule, since both are

overcome in the otherness of heterosexuality. The very categories of hetero-, homo-, and auto-erotics are jointly defined by the same understanding of gender as simple alterity.

In *The Second Sex,* for instance, de Beauvoir herself writes a sentence that is both bland and startling: "When the boy reaches the genital phase, his evolution is completed, though he must pass from the autoerotic inclination, in which pleasure is subjective, to the heteroerotic inclination, in which pleasure is bound up with an object, normally woman."[2] As a summary of Freud, this is quite bland. But in the context of de Beauvoir's argument, this way of opposing interest in others simultaneously to autoerotics and to homoerotics is startling. As she shows so eloquently, there is nothing innocent about the slippage from interest in "an object" to the assumption that such an interest is "normally" in woman. Nothing guarantees such an outcome other than the boy's discovery that women are defined as objects to him in a way that other men are not. And since the girl discovers at the same time that her destiny is to be an object of desire, her encounter with alterity is very different from the boy's. She is not offered the same simple distinction between her own subjectivity and the other's objectivity. The discovery of otherness in the other gender, therefore, is neither neutral nor symmetrical. In de Beauvoir's argument, as in the work of other feminists who continue her Hegelian tradition, this construction of gendered otherness is seen as the structure of domination.[3]

If the scenario of gender difference is difficult to imagine without the asymmetries of domination, it is also true that all of our accounts of this scenario bear the stamp of the modern organization of sexuality. Every description of the subject's access to gender and alterity, beginning with Freud's account of the Oedipus complex, seems already to be oriented by the poles of hetero- and homosexuality. Could the modern system of hetero- and homosexualities be imagined without this ideological core, or vice versa? By shifting the question in this way, I mean to indicate how difficult it is to analyze a discourse of sexuality, when our own tools of analysis already *are* that discourse. But I also mean to indicate ways in which gender domination presents problems besides the obvious one that it poses for women.

Where women are "normally" defined by otherness, the transition from autoerotics to heteroerotics entails a peculiar problem for men. To cite de Beauvoir once more, a key feature of male subjectivity comes about as a corollary of the subjugation of women: "For the male it is always another male who is the fellow being, the other who is also the same, with whom reciprocal relations are established."[4] The point of this for feminism is clear: insofar as woman is Other, she stands outside of reciprocity. But an important question for the male subject is less clear. Since sexual desire is directed toward an object, male desire will be directed only toward women, rather than toward the men who are fellow beings, subjects, the same. But what if this does not take place? And well it might not: for the man values other men as fellow beings and will accordingly seek their recognition and desire. At the same time, no matter how much he wants to think of the Other as woman, it remains true that men are others to him as well, just as women are fellow beings. When another man, this "other who is also the same," becomes the object of desire, has the

male subject failed to distinguish self and other?

It may sound absurd, but that is just what psychoanalysis classically concludes. Psychoanalytic theory has from the beginning described homosexuality—especially among men—as a version of narcissism. Freud, for example, declares that the homosexual chooses "not another of the same sex, but himself in the guise of another."[5] This is not a simple judgment. And it would certainly not hold much intuitive force outside of the modern West, where erotic relations either among men or among women are imagined by most cultures as something other than relations of mere sameness.[6] But there has never been a sustained critique of the premises behind Freud's judgment, on this issue so widely taken as common sense. The gay movement has either ignored it or tried to reject it out of hand, no doubt because its invidious consequences are so easy to apprehend. Yet we need not wave away this powerful tradition, nor even deny that one kind of homoerotics in the modern West has the logic of a relation to self. It is imperative, though immensely difficult, for us to retheorize that relation.

The first difficulty lies in appropriating psychoanalysis. Although it is uniquely equipped to analyze the slippage in our culture between understandings of gender and understandings of self and other, traditionally psychoanalysis has been the principal site of that slippage. "Psychoanalysis," de Beauvoir concludes, "fails to explain why woman is the *Other.*"[7] Of course, different directions have been taken by psychoanalytic theory since 1949, and one would not offer so simple a conclusion today. But the related problems of heterosexuality remain as unclear—indeed, ideologically clouded—as they were then. What guarantees that a transition from autoerotics will or should lead to heteroerotics? How does it come to be taken as self-evident that homoerotics is really an arrested form of interest in oneself? Why do we find it so difficult to think about sex and gender without these ideological categories and their teleological narratives? And why do these questions seem linked to the structure of modern liberal society? Only modern liberal society, after all, understands sexuality as a choice between hetero- and homosexualities, conceiving them as sexualities of difference and sameness. The only way to pose such large questions is by examining the theory of narcissism, where the issue of gender and alterity arises with peculiar insistence.

Freud postulated a connection between homosexuality and narcissism before the notion of narcissism was even fully developed. He went so far as to argue that the existence of the link between the two is "the strongest of the reasons which have led us to adopt the hypothesis of narcissism."[8] In the same essay, "On Narcissism," Freud argues that homosexuals express something different from what he calls primary narcissism. In primary narcissism, a child cathects itself in a unity with its parent, without differentiation, without a developed ego. This narcissistic love of the parent-child dyad is what the later love of the parent as a separate person will be propped on. Homosexuality, by contrast, is described by Freud as coming about in the later stage, when the subject's original narcissism encounters "the admonitions of others" and the awakening of his [sic] own critical judgement."[9] The subject's primary attachment to itself, suddenly broken and troubled by criticism, is recuperated in the development of the ego ideals. It then happens, says Freud, that the individual seeks in another some ideal excellence missing from his own ego. And this is the type of narcissistic choice made by the homosexual, by which Freud generally means the male homosexual: the choice of what he himself would like to be.

Without reconstructing any more of the difficulties raised by Freud's problematic essay, I would like to make two observations about his argument. The first is that the two

kinds of narcissism are very different. One is residual, an effect of infancy that lingers into later life. The other is proleptic and utopian. The homosexual (male), according to Freud, develops his narcissism not simply because of the residual attachment to the parent-child dyad, but because of a developmentally advanced ego ideal that is difficult to realize. I will return to this point later; it is important because Freud's thinking here leads him close to breaking his usual frame of reference. Indeed, by foregrounding the development of critical judgment and the admonitions of others, Freud places the subject in a context much larger than that of the restricted family. And by indicating the relation between narcissism and ideals, Freud works no longer in the realm of simple pathology. What is puzzling, then, is that Freud continues to treat homosexuality as regressive. Although one important criticism of Freud's account is that his narrative is rather arbitrarily committed to a hypotactic logic of linear development, an equally important one is that his own analysis, in this essay, does not necessarily show the homosexual's narcissism as a developmental regression.

A second observation then follows: Freud cannot account for the normative implications of his analysis. It is not a neutral analysis. He speaks with an unmistakable tone of condescension toward the homosexuals who are really seeking themselves. He does not imagine that one might speak of narcissism other than pejoratively in this context, though he does in others.[10] Nor does he acknowledge that to describe homosexuality as *merely* a version of narcissism is counterintuitive. The homosexual, after all, is by definition interested in others in a way that is not true of the narcissist in general. Ovid tells us that Narcissus rejects not just the girls who love him, but also the boys. Those boys, then, have an interest in other persons, if not in the other gender, and the myth of Narcissus does not collapse the two. What warrants the forgetting of this difference, which becomes a nondifference, sameness? Why should gender amount to alterity *tout court?*

Freud's secondary narcissism does not preclude a recognition of alterity. Everyone undergoes—and indeed requires—the kind of narcissism Freud describes. Everyone makes identifications with others on the basis of ego ideals. But we call them ideals only insofar as identification is accompanied by alienation and longing. The act of taking up ego ideals therefore does not foreclose a sense of the other's otherness, no matter how much we might like to eliminate that otherness. Indeed, in the last section of "On Narcissism" Freud suggests that this double movement of identification and desire is what makes the subject truly social. In the very action of taking an ideal, the subject apprehends a difference between the ideal and the actual ego. And that difference is just what produces our sense of longing and our search for the recognition of others. Because the ideals remain alien, insofar as they are ideals at all, they drive the subject to the pursuit of the other.

Identification in this sense is not a satisfactory unity; Freud shows that the ideals of identification have a critical relation to the self that the ego will continue to feel as dissonance, especially in the form of guilt.[11] It follows—though this does not always remain clear in Freud—that they are both identifications and objects of longing. And that can be true even of the ideals that are most critical and guilt-inducing. As Kaja Silverman points out, the most normally Oedipal boy in the world is placed in a relation of longing with the image of the father; insofar as the father's image is taken as an ideal, or superego, it remains "susceptible to sexualization."[12] Identification, in short, does not result in a relation of identity, and this is especially the case where another subject is involved. The difference that is therefore inevitably involved in taking the other as a sexual object, an other, cannot entirely be elided—even

where the desire is founded on an identification. But that is what Freud does when he claims that homosexuals "are plainly seeking *themselves* as a love object."

Freud here imagines, in effect, that the dialectic of desire could not continue beyond the first moment of alienated identification. The figure of Narcissus represents that blockage: in Jacqueline Rose's phrase, Narcissus shows how "an apparent reciprocity reveals itself as *no more than* the return of an image to itself."[13] But it is not so easy to explain any erotic attachment as merely the reflexive attachment of a self to itself. Even the apparent return of an image reveals also some forms of reciprocity. When the subject chooses another on the basis of a desired ego ideal, he or she is already engaged in dialogue with others and in multiple perspectives on self. In Freud's account, the individual is encountering the admonitions of others and the development of his or her own critical judgment. As a result, the subject adopts the position of the other toward him- or herself. This kind of narcissism, therefore, already involves the subject in the negativity of speech.[14] If desire arises in these alienated identifications, it by the same token must always reactivate the potential for mutual recognition. Freud does not imagine this possibility long enough to argue against it. He concludes that homosexual desire *reduces* to narcissism without significant remainder and hence is a developmental misdirection.

Freud's conclusion here has hardly proven to be idiosyncratic. It remains the most powerful way of treating homoerotics as a symptomology, and some version of it still dominates every major branch of psychoanalytic theory.[15] Though the DSM III no longer lists homosexuality as a disease, the theoretical tradition continues to reveal it in the light of pathology. Professional psychology and psychoanalysis continue to understand themselves as explaining homosexuality, as giving its causes. But the entire discourse is possible at all only if the pathological status of the homosexual is assumed from the outset. If homosexuality is taken to be a symptom, then etiology provides a logic for saying that it reduces to narcissism. But if the symptomatic character of homosexuality is not simply taken for granted, then it would be necessary to theorize its dialectical and interactive character—precisely that which would prevent a reductive etiology. It is not surprising to find such ideological effects in the medical and scientific institutions that have, after all, generated the modern discourse of hetero- and homosexualities. It is more surprising to find the normalizing conclusion in Freud, since his own account demonstrates the dialectical and interactive movement that leads from the ego to homoerotics. (And back: one more reason Freud might have avoided his normalizing conclusion is that he was intermittently conscious of his own investment in homoerotics, particularly with Josef Breuer and Wilhelm Fliess. After his break with Fliess, Freud wrote to Sandor Ferenczi about his "overcoming" the trauma of the break: "A part of homosexual cathexis has been withdrawn and made use of to enlarge my own ego.")[16]

My point, however, is not simply that we should depathologize the homosexual. There is also a further, equally unremarked problem in the argument. If normal development leads from autoerotics to narcissism to heterosexuality, how would heterosexuality transcend its sources in narcissism more than homosexuality does? Freud assumes, as does psychoanalytic discourse generally, that the heterosexual (male) is a better realist than the homosexual (male). The heterosexual male chooses the Other—woman—but the homosexual male only *thinks* he chooses another. Yet it is not difficult to read Freud's essay as showing that all erotic life—not just the pathology of homosexuals—takes its form from the search for the ego ideal in the position of the other. (This of course is the

direction in which Jacques Lacan will push the inquiry.) When Freud initially describes how the investment of the ego ideal can be transferred into a sexual desire for another, he is describing the pathology of homosexuals. By the end of the essay, he is using the same language to interpret a form of heterosexual romance. The lover, says Freud, overvalues the other in whose eyes he sees *himself* ideally desired. Yet Freud does not draw the obvious inference that it might not be so easy as first appeared to construct a normative hierarchy of hetero- and homosexuality by showing the function of the ego ideal in generating desire.

What, then, is developmental in the development from narcissism to heterosexuality? Or at least, what is developmental here that is not equally characteristic of homosexuality? Freud's various solutions to this problem come to grief because they are in the last analysis based on an *a priori* opposition of the genders as subject and Other. Nowhere are the difficulties of the project more clear than in *The Ego and the Id,* a text in which Freud returns to the unstable problems of the narcissism essay. In the earlier essay, identification and the ego ideals stemmed from the admonitions of others and the development of the subject's critical judgment. Now, in the later work, Freud writes that the "origin of the ego-ideal" lies in "an individual's first and most important identification, his [sic] identification with the father in his own personal prehistory."[17] The difference is that Freud has now introduced the Oedipus complex in an attempt to explain the developmental path that leads to heterosexuality. But why have the male subject and the male parent been singled out as the primary axis of identification?

In an astonishing footnote to this sentence, Freud acknowledges that there is no good reason at all: "Perhaps it would be safer to say 'with the parents'; for before a child has arrived at definite knowledge of the difference between the sexes, the lack of a penis, it does not distinguish in value between its father and its mother. . . . In order to simplify my presentation I shall discuss only identification with the father." According to the footnote, identification with the father has been emphasized only arbitrarily, for convenience. But the text that it glosses shows that the father must not be just any identification, but "the first and most important" one. That is what guarantees the Oedipalized heterosexual outcome. If nothing naturally makes this axis of identification the primary one, then the heterosexual resolution will be no more of a development than a homosexual one. Without this ideological support, Freud's derivation of heterosexual norms is subject to narrative incoherence.

The footnote admits, in effect, that the father has primacy only in his symbolic cultural value, which is learned later; he has no primacy in the simple development of the child's identification. Both parents are subjects of identification, and both are objects of attachment. This leads Freud to postulate both "positive" and "negative" forms of the Oedipal situation. Again, however, he presupposes the chiastic axes of heterosexuality that the model is designed to derive. Freud assumes that an identification with the mother will retain an attachment to the father and vice versa. He does not imagine that one might identify with the mother and yet have an attachment to other women or identify with the father and yet have an attachment to other men. Nor can he justify the primacy of one axis over another. In an especially striking moment of circularity, Freud writes that only the child's "sexual disposition"—i.e., its "masculine" or "feminine" bent—will determine the relative weight of these identification axes.[18] At this point, nothing establishes which axis—if indeed we can assume their constitution as axes—will be primary, or "positive" rather than "negative."

Freud maintains the normative character of

Oedipal resolution only by ignoring these qualifications in a rather blunt declaration that the male child identifies with the father and takes the mother as object. In *Group Psychology and the Analysis of the Ego,* published two years before *The Ego and the Id,* Freud presents this declaration in its most normalized form:

> A little boy will exhibit a special interest in his father; he would like to grow like him and be like him, and take his place everywhere. We may say simply that he takes his father as his ideal. This behaviour has nothing to do with a passive or feminine attitude toward his father (and towards males in general); it is on the contrary typically masculine. It fits very well with the Oedipus complex, for which it helps to prepare the way.
>
> At the same time as this identification with his father, or a little later, the boy has begun to develop a true object cathexis towards his mother according to the attachment [anaclitic] type.[19]

As we know from Freud's qualifications in *The Ego and the Id,* nothing in this narrative can be assumed. The child takes both parents as ideals and has object attachments to both parents. Why does Freud so insist, despite his own observations, on the primacy of this "positive" form of what has already been assumed as a chiastic structure? Both the supremacy of the father and the goal of heterosexuality seem to derive from the Oedipal scene as it is summarized here. If this is the moment when de Beauvoir's mastery relation has been established, it is also the moment when the available object choices have been resolved into hetero- and homosexualities. The father's supremacy is assured since, for children of both sexes, he will be identified with as subject, while the mother's nurturing role will result in an object attachment to her. But what is easier to miss is that Freud has presupposed that the child's identification and its object attachment will be assigned to different genders. Hence Freud's anxious haste to deny that identification with the father results in a "passive or feminine" attitude toward him. Freud consistently supposes that identification desexualizes the parental image, that the positive Oedipus complex cancels out the object choice of the negative complex and vice versa.[20] This is partly because he presupposes that the parents' heterosexual choices will be internalized along with their images, so that identification with the father will simply transfer the father's gendered desire to the boy. (To explain himself in this way, however, would amount to an admission that heterosexual desire is only a status quo.) But it is also partly because Freud's entire account is based on the exclusiveness of identification and attachment.

Identification and attachment are the structuring moments in psychoanalysis that correspond to subject and object. Identification constructs a feature of the world as a feature of the subject; attachment constructs its features as objects. But the opposition is unstable. As Mikkel Borch-Jacobsen shows, the two operations can be read as mutual forms of denial. If identification denies the radical alterity of the other, attachment-desire "is organized as a vehement rejection of all resemblance, all mimesis."[21] Freud's deepest commitment, throughout the changes in his position on the subject, is that these two operations will be exclusive, and one will be reserved for each gender. An admission that it would be possible both to identify with *and* to desire a gendered image would be the most troubling of all. If Freud implies in "On Narcissism" that the homosexual narcissist does just that, he has a very different account in the later works.

Here it is striking that Freud has two entirely different pathologies for homosexuality, and they accompany entirely different accounts of the ego ideal. Both *Group Psychol-*

*ogy* and *The Ego and the Id* attempt to explain the homosexual by means of the chiasmus of gender identification and desire. The ego ideal with which the child identifies is a gendered parental image, and the child's sexual object will accordingly be the parental image of the opposite sex. In both of these later texts, the homosexual is said simply to choose the "negative" axis—for the male child, identifying with the mother and taking on her desire for the father. But in the earliest essay, the sources of the ego ideals had been much more general. They had not necessarily entailed the gendered parental images, with the chiastic Oedipal teleology of those images.

What if it is possible, as Freud implied in the earlier essay, that the boy might both identify with the father and yet desire his image? This possibility is implied insofar as the boy's identification would still not close the gap between himself and the gendered ideal. Indeed, identification could result in a longing because of that gap between actual and ideal. But subject and object would not be distributed to different genders. Freud is therefore obliged in this essay to regard the relation as one of mere sameness. Freud explains homosexuality alternately as sameness (in the earlier essay) or as inverted difference (in the later works). No matter which route of explanation Freud takes, he does not infer from his own insights that difference and sameness might coexist, in both desire and identification, without being reducible to the difference or sameness of gender.

It is only the more striking that Lacan never makes this inference either, since it is he who radicalizes the function of the ego ideal in a way only suggested by Freud. Lacan's analysis of the *imago* of the ego shows it to be *both* the site of identification *and* the source of desire. "We call libidinal investment," he says, "that which makes an object desirable, that is to say, the way it becomes confused with the image we carry within us."[22] Where

Freud initially argued that an intricate confusion of the desired object with the image of what one would like to be is just the pathological derivation of homosexuality, Lacan shows that such an investment always structures the erotic. Lacan cites Goethe's Werther as an example of the way heterosexual investment is based not only on anaclitic parental cathexis but also on the reflective function of the ego ideal. When Werther first sees Lotte, he writes,

> No, I do not deceive myself! In her dark eyes I have read a genuine sympathy for me and my destiny. Yes, I feel . . . that she loves me! Loves me!—And how precious I become in my own eyes, how I—to you as an understanding person I may say it— how I admire myself since she loves me.

With this passage in mind, Lacan says, "That's what love is. It's one's own ego that one loves in love, one's own ego made real on the imaginary level."[23] Of course, there are other things that one could say about Werther; his is not the only form of "what love is." My point is simply that Lacan made it one of the central projects of his career to critique our elementary assumptions about the difference between identification and desire, subject and object. In so doing, he definitively removed any possibility of making narcissism a basis for a normative hierarchy between hetero- and homosexuality. Homosexuality may indeed be a way of loving one's own ego, but so is heterosexual romance.

Yet however radical and subtle Lacan's analysis of the imaginary might be, it seems never to have occurred to him that it might now be unnecessary to pathologize the homosexual's relation to narcissism. Quite the contrary. In a passage from the seminars of the very same year (1954), Lacan takes it on himself to describe homosexuality as a perversion, not because of the contingency of morals, nor because of the supposed needs of biology, but because of the narcissistic structure of homosexual desire. "It is himself," Lacan says of the homosexual," "whom he pursues." What I find especially incomprehensible about this classical assertion is that it appears as a gloss on one of Lacan's most Hegelian formulations: "the [homosexual] subject exhausts himself in pursuing the desire of the other, which he will never be able to grasp as his own desire, because his own desire is the desire of the other."[24] This, as Lacan notes, is the form of "the imaginary intersubjective relation." Nothing about it is peculiar to homosexuality. Moreover, when he is pursuing the Hegelian logic of his analysis, Lacan is capable of treating this same imaginary intersubjectivity as opening onto a dialectic of recognition.[25] In this case, he does not do so.

Compare the tone of his account with the tone of the equally Hegelian description that de Beauvoir had given five years earlier of the logic of lesbianism:

> To be willing to be changed into a passive object is not to renounce all claim to subjectivity: woman hopes in this way to find self-realization under the aspect of herself as a thing; but then she will be trying to find herself in her otherness, her alterity. When alone she does not succeed in really creating her double; if she caresses her own bosom, she still does not know how her breasts seem to a strange hand, nor how they are felt to react under a strange hand; a man can reveal to her the existence of her flesh *for herself*—that is to say, as she herself perceives it, but not what it is *to others*. It is only when her fingers trace the body of a woman whose fingers in turn trace her body that the miracle of the mirror is accomplished.

But de Beauvoir does not mean, by "the miracle of the mirror," an entrapment in a circuit of sameness. Far from it. Because she understands the problem of alterity sketched here as one taking place in a setting of domination, the dialectic of lesbianism is a model of how the imaginary transcends its limitations: "in exact reciprocity each is at once subject and object, sovereign and slave; duality becomes mutuality."[26] This is exactly what Lacan denies. Though he offers no reason for this belief, he asserts that the homosexual is perverse because the recognition of the other's desire remains closed to him. Lacan goes so far as to say that it is "not without reason" that homosexuality is called "a desire which dare not speak its name." (Of course, however, Lacan like Freud assumes that only male homosexuality is in question. If the lesbian dialectic allows women access to their subjectivity in addition to their normal objectivity, we might say the reverse for male homosexuals: they seek access to their objectivity in addition to their normal subjectivity. And because that means that would imply a compromise of privilege, a feminization, it is more unthinkable.)

Lacan's position in this respect is not as different as one would like to think from that of the reactionary Christopher Lasch. Lasch's writings on the subject have infinitely less subtlety and intelligence than Lacan's. But partly for that reason they lay bare the politics of the analytic tradition from which Lacan, less understandably, could not free himself. In a complimentary preface to a book by Chasseguet-Smirgel, Lasch claims that by eradicating differences of gender, the homosexual pervert "erases the more fundamental distinction between the self and the not-self, the source of every other distinction."[27] One hardly knows where to begin with this kind of comment. In the first place, it would simply be absurd to think that homosexuals eradicate gender; the very logic of homosexuality as a category is impossible without gender and its utopian identifications. Equally foolish is the rather crude form of heterosexist ideology in which it is supposed that peo-

ple who have homosexual relations do not also have other kinds.

More deceptive, however, is the assumption that gender is the phenomenology of difference itself. This is the core of the psychoanalytic tradition I am trying to map. It is a staggeringly primitive confusion. Can it actually be imagined that people in homosexual relations have no other way of distinguishing between self and not-self? That no other marker of difference, such as race, could intervene; or that the pragmatics of dialogue would not render alterity meaningful, even in the minimal imaginary intersubjectivity of cruising? Why is gender assumed to be our only access to alterity? It is not even the only line of sameness and difference that structures erotic images. Race, age, and class are capable of doing that as well. Sexuality has any number of forms of the dialectic between identification and desire. But we do not say of people whose erotic objects are chosen partly on the basis of racial identity or of generation or of class that they have eradicated the distinction between self and not-self. We say that only of gender. The difference between hetero- and homosexualities is not, in fact, a difference between sexualities of otherness and sameness. It is an allegory about gender.

We have only to consider the breathtaking simplicity of the premises for the whole argument to dissolve. But let me emphasize that I am not making a point about Lasch's blindness. He merely reproduces an ideological confusion that is axiomatic for the modern sex/gender system. Even Lacan ascribes to what he calls "the cosmic polarity of male and female"[28] nothing less than the transition from ego-identification to dialogue:

For it is a truth of experience for analysis that the subject is presented with the question of his [*sic*] existence, not in terms of the anxiety that it arouses at the level of the ego, and which is only one element in the series, but as an articulated question: 'What am I there?', concerning his sex and his contingency in being, namely, that, on the one hand, he is a man or a woman, and, on the other, that he might not be, the two conjugating their mystery, and binding it in the symbols of procreation and death.[29]

This passage appears exactly as an explanation of how alterity can be grasped within the narcissistic structure of subjectivity. Lacan is explaining the so-called "schema L," which describes the mediations between the subject and the Other, by which Lacan means "the locus from which the question of his existence may be presented to him." He here proposes that it is the otherness of gender that allows the subject to apprehend his or her own ego as an other. If we are to read Lacan generously here, we will emphasize the qualifier "it is a truth *of experience for analysis*" as meaning that the situation he depicts is only a nonnormative description of how gender operates in the present culture. We could then make these assumptions the subject of critique, as does de Beauvoir. But Lacan does not take that step, and it is just as possible to read the emphasis differently: "it is a *truth* of experience for analysis."

The passage is not without a sentimental and mystifying element. Lacan implies that the realization "I am this individual and not that one" not only does but *should* come in the form "I am this gender and not that one." He further assumes that a recognition of gender implicitly contains the particular form of mortality-transcendence found in the myths and rituals of heterosexual conjugality. But the dialectic of identification does not lead without mediation to procreative, genital sexuality. Indeed, Lacan often paints a very different picture himself:

What is my desire? What is my position in the imaginary structuration? This position is only conceivable in so far as one finds a guide beyond the imaginary, on the level of the symbolic plane, of the legal exchange which can only be embodied in the verbal exchange between human beings. This guide governing the subject is the ego-ideal.[30]

Here, as elsewhere, Lacan argues that the narcissism of desire is transcended only by the rule-governed multiple perspectives of symbolic interaction. Language in general brings about forms of difference and norms of reciprocity and thus allows the subject the negativity with which to consider his or her identity in the role of another. Yet no absolute break with narcissistic identification has occurred, since the subject's ability to do this continues to be regulated by the ego ideals. As a picture of the development of subjectivity, Lacan's scene here resembles the "admonitions" and "critical judgment" referred to by Freud as the origin of the ego ideals in "On Narcissism." The subject has encountered the Other, "the locus from which the question of his existence may be presented to him." But significantly, that locus and its questioning do not imply the gender of an object choice.

Lacan moves between this account, in which the decisive factor is symbolic interaction, and another account, closer to the so-called second topography of Freud's later work, in which the ego ideal is specifically the paternal image. Again, the generous reading is that Lacan's analysis is descriptive of the way the father's authority stands for the subjective function he describes in our culture. But again, Lacan is not critical of that cultural equation, and he does not analyze the ways in which it is possible for subjects to interact without the prescribed relation to the paternal image. Instead, as we have seen, he adheres to models of pathology that incorporate and presuppose the normative role of gender defined as the simple apprehension of alterity. Because of this elision, the fundamental phenomenology of gender in Lacan's account often has an ideological character, though his most radical (and most Hegelian) arguments work in another direction. Indeed, if the equation between homosexuality and narcissism in psychoanalysis tells us anything, it is that the central premises and vocabulary of psychoanalysis have been designed for a heterosexist self-understanding. They have totalized gender as an allegory of difference, leaving little analytic space between the development of subjectivity and the production of heterosexual norms.

How does this mystification get sustained? When Lasch declares homosexuality perverse because it eradicates the distinction between self and not-self, does he not realize that many of his readers will come to the passage with the experience that must inevitably disclose its falseness? In fact, I think he does not. The entire psychoanalytic heritage on this subject does not imagine itself in dialogue with those it describes.[31] If I have taken some pains to show this, it is because I consider it a *tactical* necessity to have a better understanding of what the sources of this discourse's power are. If the tradition I have described simply reflects the illiberal intolerance of a few homophobic theorists, then we need not sweat it any more. If it is structural to the premises of psychoanalysis, then we need more of an attack on modern psychoanalysis. If it lies in the heart of modern social organization, then we should consider how, and in what institutions, and where a more organized resistance should begin.

That is not to say that we need a theory of homosexuality in the usual sense. There may be any number of logics lumped together under this heading, from the "lesbian continuum" theorized by Adrienne Rich to the more recent phenomenon of gay communities organized through a discourse of rights. Both for women and for men in our culture there are probably as many ways of cathecting other women or men as there are ways in other cultures, where the discourse of homo-

sexuality remains so foreign. Indeed, part of the oppressiveness of the modern formation is that all forms of erotics among men or among women get classified by the same logic. We might begin to clarify the question by saying that the theorization of homosexuality as narcissism is itself a form of narcissism peculiar to modern heterosexuality. The central imperative of heterosexist ideology is that the homosexual be supposed to be out of dialogue on the subject of his being. Imagining that the homosexual is narcissistically contained in an unbreakable fixation on himself serves two functions at once: it allows a self-confirming pathology by declaring homosexuals' speech, their interrelations, to be an illusion; *and more fundamentally it allows the constitution of heterosexuality as such.*

If that sounds like a strong claim, let me repeat that by heterosexuality I mean the modern discursive organization of sex that treats gender difference as difference in general. It is a sexuality organized by its self-understanding as *hetero*sexuality and therefore also includes the categories of homo- and autoerotics against which it defines itself. What I would like to suggest is that it is possible to read this historically recent discourse as, in part, a reaction formation. The allegory of gender protects against a recognition of the role of the imaginary in the formation of the erotic. It provides reassurance that imaginary intersubjectivity has been transcended. To the extent that our culture relies on the allegorization of gender to disguise from itself its own ego erotics, it will recognize those ego erotics only in the person of the homosexual, apparently bereft of the master trope of difference. If it were possible to admit that any relevant forms of otherness operate in homosexuality, then the main feature of heterosexual self-understanding would be lost. The heterosexual would be no longer be able to interpret the gendered, binary form of his or her own captation in desire as already being the transcendence of that captation.

But there is a broader issue at stake here, and one that could be raised as an objection. What if we are to return to the more generous reading of Lacan, seeing the psychoanalytic account not only as an ideological rationalization, but as an essentially accurate description of the *cultural* mechanisms whereby gender and alterity are equated? For surely Lacan is correct to point out that the equation takes place not just in psychoanalytic theory, but on very elementary levels of subjective experience. It *is* a truth of experience for analysis, in our society, that the subject is presented with the question of his or her existence through the problematic alterity of gender. That is why the *psychoanalytic* tradition of linking narcissism and homosexuality has been so easy to confirm. And although the categories and norms of that tradition can be shown to be ideological and incoherent, they are the categories and norms of subjective experience in our culture, rather than simply the prejudices of a few theorists. The argument that I have made here therefore raises a whole new problem: what is the social and historical character of this organization of sexuality and gender?

This issue challenges us to separate the two problematics that I have brought together in this essay: on the one hand the problem of women's construction as the Other, with its prehistoric sources in phallocentrism; on the other hand, a sex/gender system in which object choice is posed as an apprehension of alterity *tout court*. These two structures of power are currently coarticulated as a unity of experience, but they have different histories. The system of hetero- and homosexualities is a much more recent phenomenon, codified in discourse only for the past century. Through most of Western history erotics among men in particular have been understood precisely along axes of difference: the active/passive difference in the discourse of

sodomy, for instance, or the pedagogic difference of generations in the classical discourse of pederasty. If suddenly it has become necessary and common-sensical to imagine erotics among men or among women as homosexuality, a sexuality of sameness, we might ask how that has come about. We might also ask what relation there might be between this recent organization of sexuality and the longer history of phallocentrism that constructs woman as Other. Indeed, one reason it is so hard for us to imagine hetero- and homosexualities as recent developments is that they have been articulated so closely with that phallocentric construction of Otherness.

Unfortunately, if the organization of sexuality around the axis of the hetero and the homo is the result of historical change, we have virtually no social theory of why its organization in this form should have been so recent or what kind of historical narrative it would call for. The account typically given in the wake of Michel Foucault has been to attribute the system of heterosexuality to its discourse, beginning roughly with the naming of *homosexuality* in the late nineteenth century.[32] The Foucauldian account has an undeniable force in showing that the discourse of sexuality is a form of biotechnical power, not a superstructural effect. Nevertheless, I think my argument suggests, in effect, a different strategy of historicizing the whole organization of sexuality. If I am correct that the ideology of gender as alterity is a special way of not recognizing the imaginary sources of desire, then why should Western society have developed that need for misrecognition so recently? Why should there have been an imperative for such a massive displacement of ego erotics?

To pose the question in this way is to link the problem of heterosexuality not simply to modern society in the sense of recent society, but to the force of modernity. A full critique of heterosexism would involve questions about the role of the ego in post-Enlightenment capitalist society. That debate is a complex one, but I can at least indicate its relevance here. On one side Christopher Lasch, in *The Culture of Narcissism,* laments the ego orientation of consumer society as producing debased forms of individualism and symptomatic perversions such as the gay rights movement.[33] On the other side, Jürgen Habermas can argue that the self-reflection of the autonomous ego is the source of a still progressive modernity. And he can show in a fairly nuanced way that ego-identity becomes both necessary and problematic in a whole new range of social contexts.[34] Both sides agree that a tension between the ego and its ideals has become newly important in post-Enlightenment Western capitalism. In response to that debate, could we speculate that the ego erotics coded in homosexuality is a special feature of this social history?

Obviously, that subject is too large to be treated here. But I should note that the possibility of such an account is already implicit in the way Freud imagines an erotics of the ego ideal. In the essay on narcissism, Freud takes a broad social view. Having once stated that secondary narcissism is possible only after the development of critical judgment and the encountering of the admonitions of others, he returns with an even more general description:

> For what prompted the subject to form an ego ideal, on whose behalf his conscience acts as watchman, arose from the critical influence of his parents (conveyed to him by the medium of the voice), to whom were added, as time went on, those who trained and taught him and the innumerable and indefinable host of all the other people in his environment—his fellow men—and public opinion.

> In this way large amounts of libido of an essentially homosexual kind are drawn into the formation of the narcissistic ego

ideal and find outlet and satisfaction in maintaining it.

Here Freud advances a notion to which he returned often, especially in the *Group Psychology*—the notion that sociality itself is in some essential way a desexualized homosexuality. But when Freud describes the environment to which the subject must relate in such a homosexual way, he depicts an essentially modern society. It is defined by the critical force of training and teaching. It is made up of an "innumerable and indefinable host" of people. And at its limits it finds expression in a highly generalized perspective of criticism: public opinion. This set of social pressures on the ego may also be what Freud has in mind when he links his developmental narrative with the historical transition from traditional to modern. He claims, for instance, that "primitive peoples," like children, orient themselves to the world through primary narcissism rather than secondary.[35] One doesn't have to be uncritical of Freud's ethnocentrism here to imagine that a special role for critical judgment in modern Western societies might also mean that the subject of those societies might be structured by a correspondingly special ego erotics.

Lacan's account also suggests as much, and Lacan in fact often asserts that social modernity has brought about a general pathology of ego erotics.[36] His example of Werther's narcissistic love, we might note, is already articulated within the normative subjectivity of modernity. We can see how that articulated relation works by taking a strikingly similar example from an American admirer and contemporary of Goethe, Charles Brockden Brown, also writing in the context of the late Enlightenment:

> Good God! You say she loves; loves *me!* me, a boy in age; bred in clownish ignorance; scarcely ushered into the world;

more than childishly unlearned and raw; a barn-door simpleton; a plow-tail, kitchen-hearth, turnip-hoeing novice![37]

Arthur Mervyn here encounters his heterosexual love as a relation between his ego ideals and his actual ego. Several things follow. First, it is a moment of narcissistic ego erotics ("loves *me!* me . . ."), but the affective charge is attached to what seems like an unbridgable gulf of difference ("Good God!"). The extravagant otherness of his beloved— she is, in fact, older, foreign, and Jewish— allows her to be the fulcrum of Mervyn's desire-laden self-relation. The passage therefore marks the mutual involvement of a conspicuous *hetero*sexuality with a potentially homoerotic fixation on a reflexive ego erotics. And in fact, its usual charge, both in this novel and in Brown's work generally, is decisively, even sensationally homoerotic. Mervyn's awakening here might be constructed as the origin of heterosexuality, but that only shows how closely linked heterosexuality and homosexuality are in the erotics of the ego.

Mervyn's desirous self-relation, however, is also a moment of critical self-consciousness. In the very act of focusing on himself as a possible object of desire, he confronts the difference between his ideals and his actual ego. He occupies the vantage of a critical public opinion, defining an image of himself there: "a boy in age; bred in clownish ignorance; scarcely ushered into the world; more than childishly unlearned and raw; a barn-door simpleton; a plow-tail, kitchen-hearth, turnip-hoeing novice!" This is exactly the sort of role-detached, posttraditional self-consciousness that Habermas identifies with the normative content of modernity. If this sort of ego erotics seems to bear the stamp of the special social contexts of modernity, with its norm of critical self-consciousness in an environment of equals, then both hetero- and homosexuality share its essential structure.

But I do not wish to emphasize only the normative, critical content of modernity. It should also be possible to specify a whole range of social and historical institutions in which the subject is called on to take an evaluative/desirous posture toward his or her ego ideal. The imaginary register will be important, albeit in different ways, for the discourse of rights, the forms of exchange in capitalism, the role-detachment that comes with a system-differentiated society, the mass imaginary of video capitalism, rituals and markets of adolescence, and the like. The work of analyzing the subjectivity of these interarticulated contexts has only begun.

The possibility I'm trying to indicate is that homosexuality, encoded as such, takes these multiple sites of ego-reflection in modern liberal capitalism as multiple sites of erotic play and interaction. Heterosexuality deploys an understanding of gender as alterity in order to mobilize, but also to obscure, a self-reflexive erotics of the actual ego measured against its ideals. In a modernity constituted by multiple sites of ego erotics, sex ceases to be complacently patriarchal and becomes heterosexual, mystifying its own imaginary register with its liberal logic of difference. Homosexuality, however, engages the same self-reflexive erotics, without the mechanism of obscuring it. The homosexual who makes the choice of "what he himself would like to be" expresses the utopian erotics of modern subjectivity. This utopian self-relation, far from being the pathology of the homosexual, could instead be seen as a historical condition and, in the perverse and unrecuperated mode of homosexual subjectivity, the source of a critical potential. This is why modern heterosexuality needs a discourse about homosexuality as a displacement of its own narcissistic sources. The psychoanalytic tradition enacts and justifies that displacement.

## NOTES

1. The question of what is "modern" can here get a bit tricky. At this point, I mean only the broadest extension of the term: heterosexuality as a cultural system does not date from prehistory, nor is it universally the same. Later on, however, I shall be speaking of links between the sex/gender system of heterosexuality and "modern society." The task then will be to describe the relation of that sex/gender system not simply to a recent period of history, but to the set of social forms and normative principles that are programmatically linked together as "modernity." Included under this heading are the imperatives of universal law and morality, rationalized social life, autonomous disciplines of art, and objective science. And although this development in social organization has sources in the Renaissance, its full and classic expression comes with the height of the Enlightenment and its liberal aftermath. The key descriptions of this term and its history are by Jürgen Habermas; although his defense of modernity is highly controversial, his exposition of its meaning remains unmatched. See, for a brief version, "Modernity—An Incomplete Project," in Hal Foster, ed., *The Anti-Aesthetic* (Seattle: The Bay Press, 1983), 3–15. The much more developed version is in Jürgen Habermas, *The Philosophical Discourse of Modernity,* trans. Frederick Lawrence (Cambridge: MIT Press, 1987), esp. chapters 1 and 2. For the debate about the ongoing value of modernity and Habermas' use of the notion, see the essays in Richard Bernstein, ed., *Habermas and Modernity* (Cambridge: MIT Press, 1985).

2. Simone de Beauvoir, *The Second Sex,* trans. H. M. Parshley (1952; rpt. New York: Vintage, 1974), 44.

3. The best recent example of this tradition is Jessica Benjamin's *The Bonds of Love: Psychoanalysis, Feminism, and the Problem of Domination* (New York: Pantheon, 1988).

4. De Beauvoir, *The Second Sex,* 79.

5. Juliet Mitchell, *Psychoanalysis and Feminism* (New York: Random House, 1974), 34 (summarizing Freud).

6. This appears in a voluminous literature on sexuality in other cultures. For a general survey of the problem of "homo" and "hetero" sexualities, along with the projection of these categories onto cultures that order sexuality differently, see David Greenberg, *The Construction of Homosexuality* (Chicago: University of Chicago Press, 1988).

7. De Beauvoir, *The Second Sex,* 55 (italics in original). In *Psychoanalysis and Feminism,* Juliet Mitchell offers a critical but, in my reading, not entirely fair account of de Beauvoir's rejection of Freud. See pp. 305–18.

8. Sigmund Freud, "On Narcissism," in James Strachey, ed., *The Standard Edition of the Complete Psychological Works of Sigmund Freud,* 24 vols. (London: Hogarth, 1953–1974), 14:88.

9. "As always where the libido is concerned, man has here again shown himself incapable of giving up a satisfaction he had once enjoyed. He is not willing to forgo the narcissistic perfection of his childhood; and when, as he grows up, he is disturbed by the admonitions of others and by the awakening of his own critical judgement, so that he can no longer retain that perfection, he seeks to recover it in the new form of an ego ideal" ("On Narcissism," 94).

10. Several commentators have noted the evaluative instability of the term, usefully surveyed by Arnold Cooper, "Narcissism," in an excellent collection edited by Andrew Morrison: *Essential Papers on Narcissism* (New York: New York University Press, 1986), 112–43.

11. In *The Ego and the Id,* trans. Joan Riviere (New York: Norton, 1962), by which time Freud has begun to treat the ego ideals as the superego, he writes that "the superego manifests itself essentially as a sense of guilt (or rather, as criticism—for the sense of guilt is the perception in the ego answering to this criticism)" (43). This narrowing of the dissonance of the ego ideals is, in my view, too simple and indicates a symbolic valence that has since eroded. For describing the dissonance between ego and its ideals in modernity, "criticism" is probably more accurate.

12. Kaja Silverman, "Masochism and Male Subjectivity," *Camera Obscura* 17 (1988):41.

13. Jacqueline Rose, *Sexuality in the Field of Vision* (London: Verso, 1986), 170 (emphasis added).

14. For a much fuller version of this argument, see John Brenkman, *Culture and Domination* (Ithaca: Cornell University Press, 1987), especially chapter 5, "The Social Constitution of Subjectivity." Explicating the *fort-da* game, Brenkman writes: "It is essential not to collapse the distinctive moments of the dialectic of desire and interaction; the child's mirror play is already marked with the liberating negativity of speech" (165).

15. There are a number of general surveys on this subject. None, as far as I know, is really satisfactory. The most recent is Kenneth Lewes, *The Psychoanalytic Theory of Male Homosexuality* (New York: Simon and Schuster, 1988).

16. Freud to Sandor Ferenczi, 6 October 1910, quoted in Ernest Jones, *The Life and Work of Sigmund Freud,* 3 vols. (New York: Basic Books, 1953), 2:83. On the erotics of Freud's collaborative friendships, see Wayne Koestenbaum, *Double Talk: The Erotics of Male Literary Collaboration* (New York: Routledge, 1989), 17–42.

17. Freud, *The Ego and the Id,* 21.

18. Ibid., 23–24.

19. Sigmund Freud, *Group Psychology and the Analysis of the Ego,* trans. James Strachey (New York: Norton, 1959), 37.

20. See Silverman, "Masochism and Male Subjectivity," 39ff., for a discussion of the implications of this scenario.

21. Mikkel Borch-Jacobsen, *The Freudian Subject,* trans. Catherine Porter (Stanford: Stanford University Press, 1988), 93. The passage continues: "To recognize that I resemble the other, that I resemble myself in him even in my own desire, would be tantamount to admitting the inadmissible: that I am not myself and that my most proper being is over there, in that double who enrages me."

22. Jacques Lacan, *Seminaire* 1 (Paris: Seuil, 1975), 162. Translation modified from the English version: *The Seminar of Jacques Lacan: Book I,* trans. John Forrester (New York: Norton, 1988), 141.

23. Lacan, *Seminar,* 1:142.

24. Ibid., 1:221.

25. There is an excellent article by Wilfried Ver Eecke on this subject: "Hegel as Lacan's Source for Necessity in Psychoanalytic Theory," in Joseph Smith and William Kerrigan, eds., *Interpreting Lacan* (New Haven: Yale University Press, 1983), 113–38.

26. De Beauvoir, *Second Sex,* 464–65.

27. Christopher Lasch, Introduction to Janine Chasseguet-Smirgel, *The Ego Ideal,* trans. Paul Barrows (New York: Norton, 1984), xiii–xiv.

28. Jacques Lacan, "Aggressivity in Psychoanalysis," *Écrits,* trans. Alan Sheridan (New York: Norton, 1977), 27.

29. Jacques Lacan, "On a Question Preliminary to Any Possible Treatment of Psychosis," *Écrits,* 194.

30. Lacan, *Seminar,* 1:141.

31. In this way the discourse on narcissism and homosexuality bears an important resemblance to the psychoanalytic discourse on femininity. See Shoshana Felman, "Rereading Femininity," *Yale French Studies* 62 (1981):19–44.

32. Michel Foucault, *The History of Sexuality, Vol. 1: An Introduction* (New York: Pantheon, 1978). I have no interest in minimizing the value of work that has followed in the same general direction, especially in its value as a critique of the liberal-essentialist discourse of sexuality. For versions that specifically treat the question of homosexuality, see especially Jeffrey Weeks, *Sexuality and Its Discontents: Meanings, Myths, and Modern Sexualities* (London: Routledge, Kegan Paul, 1985); or the work of Eve Sedgwick, most recently exemplified in "Across Gender, Across Sexuality: Willa Cather and Others," *South Atlantic Quarterly* 88 (Winter 1989):53–72; or David M. Halperin, *One Hundred Years of Homosexuality and Other Essays on Greek Love* (New York: Routledge, 1990).

33. Christopher Lasch, *The Culture of Narcissism* (New York: Norton, 1979).

34. See especially Jürgen Habermas, "Moral Development and Ego Identity," in *Communication and the Evolution of Society,* trans. Thomas McCarthy (Boston: Beacon Press, 1979), 69–94. Habermas argues, for instance, that the subject of modernity "takes into account that traditionally settled forms of life can prove to be mere conventions, to be irrational. Thus he has to retract his ego behind the line of all particular roles and norms and stabilize it only through the abstract ability to present himself credibly in any situation as someone who can satisfy the requirements of consistency even in the face of incompatible role expectations and in the passage through a sequence of contradictory periods of life. Role identity is replaced by ego identity; actors meet as individuals across, so to speak, the objective contexts of their lives" (85–86).

35. Freud, "On Narcissism," 75.

36. See, for instance, Lacan, "Aggressivity," 27.

37. Charles Brockden Brown, *Arthur Mervyn* (1799–1800), ed. Sydney Krause et al. (Kent, Ohio: Kent State University Press, 1980), p. 434.

# 34

# Donna Haraway
# 1944–

Born in Denver, Colorado, Donna Haraway received her M.Phil. and Ph.D. from Yale University. Haraway's training as a scientist enables her to fuse the specialized knowledge of science and the history of science with a sociological and feminist discourse. "Biological and bisocial disciplines," she explains, "have been important parts of belief and value systems which may function as expressive control or may be reclaimed for other ends." It has been the effort of Haraway to process and reclaim scientific discourse for the ends of feminism. Her major works include *Crystals, Fabrics, and Fields: Metaphors of Organicism in Twentieth-Century Developmental Biology* (1976); *Primate Visions: Gender, Race and Nature in the World of Modern Science* (1989); and *Simians, Cyborgs, and Women: the Reinvention of Nature* (1991), in which "A Cyborg Manifesto: Science, Technology, and Socialist Feminism in the 1980s" is also reprinted.

Haraway's "A Cyborg Manifesto: Science, Technology, and Socialist Feminism in the 1980s" (1985) is an effort to appropriate the resources of contemporary sciences and technologies in the construction of "an ironic political myth faithful to feminism, socialism, and materialism." The icon of Haraway's new feminist mythology is the Cyborg, a half-organic, half-mechanical offspring of modern science. The Cyborg, situated on the boundary of organism and machine, does not participate in Western mythologies. The Cyborg, Haraway argues, is a post-gender, post-Marxist, post-Western, non-Oedipal creation whose exclusion from traditional epistemologies makes it a viable image of new subjectivity for feminists. Not bound by patriarchal, imperialist, and teleological polarities, it defies "original unity" in the Western humanist sense of the word. "The Cyborg," writes Haraway, "would not recognize the Garden of Eden."

The consciousnesses of gender, race, and class, Haraway explains, are the products of the "terrible historical experience" of the Western tradition. In her critique of formations of identity in traditional Marxism and feminism, Haraway discusses how the unifying emphasis of each has caused it to develop a unified subjectivity based on the exclusion or marginalization of biological reproduction, sex, and race (in traditional Marxism) and labor, social reproduction, and race (in some forms of feminism). A new feminist subjectivity, Haraway contends, must be composed on new principles. Feminist subjectivity in a postmodern world must identify itself with simulation instead of representation, surface instead of depth, stress management instead of hygiene, AIDS instead of tuberculosis, replication instead of reproduction, Lacan instead of Freud, robotics instead of labor, artificial intelligence instead of the mind, Star Wars instead of World War II, and Informatics of Domination instead of white capitalist patriarchy.

In "A Cyborg Manifesto," Haraway claims that a possible feminist entry into the postmodern circuit of Informatics of Domination may be found in the new sciences of communications and biotechnologies. The intense emphasis on the flow of information in these sciences depends on the language of microelectronic coding. This coding, Haraway explains, operates on a new linguistic system of "copies without originals," of signifieds without signifiers, a linguistic system grounded in what Jean Baudrillard has called "pure simulcra." It is through this new language, with its possibilities for almost infinite interfacing, that feminists may construct new social relations, new sexualities, and new ethnicities. Haraway concludes with a construction of a "Cyborg Myth" that integrates women and machines into a new fiction. Haraway offers two possible fictions in the world of "Cyborg Identity": the fiction of the women of color and the fiction of science fiction. For outsider women such as Audre Lorde, author of *Sister Other,* Haraway explains that the ideas of writing and language, so crucial to the technology of the Cyborg, have always been a matter of survival. Science fiction, in which actual Cyborgs abound, challenges many of Western culture's most traditional images of gender, race, class, and human identity. These fictions are two of the first "Cyborg Myths" with which, Haraway argues, feminists must replace the reductionist dualisms, the totalizing polarities, and the god/goddess mythologies of the Western tradition.

# A Cyborg Manifesto: Science, Technology, and Socialist-Feminism in the Late Twentieth Century[1]

## AN IRONIC DREAM OF A COMMON LANGUAGE FOR WOMEN IN THE INTEGRATED CIRCUIT

This chapter is an effort to build an ironic political myth faithful to feminism, socialism, and materialism. Perhaps more faithful as blasphemy is faithful, than as reverent worship and identification. Blasphemy has always seemed to require taking things very seriously. I know no better stance to adopt from within the secular-religious, evangelical traditions of United States politics, including the politics of socialist feminism. Blasphemy protects one from the moral majority within, while still insisting on the need for community. Blasphemy is not apostasy. Irony is about contradictions that do not resolve into larger wholes, even dialectically, about the tension of holding incompatible things together because both or all are necessary and true. Irony is about humour and serious play. It is also a rhetorical strategy and a political method, one I would like to see more honoured within socialist-feminism. At the centre of my ironic faith, my blasphemy, is the image of the cyborg.

A cyborg is a cybernetic organism, a hybrid of machine and organism, a creature of social reality as well as a creature of fiction. Social reality is lived social relations, our most important political construction, a world-changing fiction. The international women's movements have constructed "women's experience," as well as uncovered or discovered this crucial collective object. This experience is a fiction and fact of the most crucial, political kind. Liberation rests on the construction of the consciousness, the imaginative apprehension, of oppression, and so of possibility. The cyborg is a matter of fiction and lived experience that changes what counts as women's experience in the late twentieth century. This is a struggle over life and death, but the boundary between science fiction and social reality is an optical illusion.

Contemporary science fiction is full of cyborgs—creatures simultaneously animal and machine, who populate worlds ambiguously natural and crafted. Modern medicine is also full of cyborgs, of couplings between organism and machine, each conceived as coded devices, in an intimacy and with a power that was not generated in the history of sexuality. Cyborg "sex" restores some of the lovely replicative baroque of ferns and invertebrates (such nice organic prophylactics against heterosexism). Cyborg replication is uncoupled from organic reproduction. Modern production seems like a dream of cyborg colonization work, a dream that makes the nightmare of Taylorism seem idyllic. And modern war is a cyborg orgy, coded by $C^3I$, command-control-communication-intelligence, an \$84 billion item in 1984's US defence budget. I am making an argument for the cyborg as a fiction mapping our social and bodily reality and as an imaginative resource suggesting some very fruitful couplings. Michel Foucault's biopolitics is a flaccid premonition of cyborg politics, a very open field.

By the late twentieth century, our time, a mythic time, we are all chimeras, theorized and fabricated hybrids of machine and organism; in short, we are cyborgs. The cyborg is our ontology; it gives us our politics. The cyborg is a condensed image of both imagination and material reality, the two joined centres structuring any possibility of historical transformation. In the traditions of "Western" science and politics—the tradition of racist, male-dominant capitalism; the tradition of progress; the tradition of the appropriation of nature as resource for the productions of culture; the tradition of reproduction of the self from the reflections of the other—the relation between organism and machine has been a border war. The stakes in the border war have been the territories of production, reproduction, and imagination. This chapter is an argument for *pleasure* in the confusion of boundaries and for *responsibility* in their construction. It is also an effort to contribute to socialist-feminist culture and theory in a postmodernist, non-naturalist mode and in the utopian tradition of imagining a world without gender, which is perhaps a world without genesis, but maybe also a world without end. The cyborg incarnation is outside salvation history. Nor does it mark time on an oedipal calendar, attempting to heal the terrible cleavages of gender in an oral symbiotic utopia or post-oedipal apocalypse. As Zoe Sofoulis argues in her unpublished manuscript on Jacques Lacan, Melanie Klein, and nuclear culture, *Lacklein,* the most terrible and perhaps the most promising monsters in cyborg worlds are embodied in non-oedipal narratives with a different logic of repression, which we need to understand for our survival.

The cyborg is a creature in a post-gender world; it has no truck with bisexuality, pre-oedipal symbiosis, unalienated labour, or other seductions to organic wholeness through a final appropriation of all the powers of the parts into a higher unity. In a sense, the cyborg has no origin story in the Western sense—a "final" irony since the cyborg is also the awful apocalyptic *telos* of the "West's" escalating dominations of abstract individuation, an ultimate self untied at last from all dependency, a man in space. An origin story in the "Western," humanist sense depends on the myth of original unity, fullness, bliss and terror, represented by the phallic mother from whom all humans must separate, the task of individual development and of history, the twin potent myths inscribed most powerfully for us in psychoanalysis and Marxism. Hillary Klein has argued that both Marxism and psychoanalysis, in their concepts of labour and of individuation and gender formation, depend on the plot of original unity out of which difference must be produced and enlisted in a drama of escalating domination of woman/nature. The cyborg skips the step of original unity, of identification with nature in the Western sense. This is its illegitimate promise that might lead to subversion of its teleology as star wars.

The cyborg is resolutely committed to partiality, irony, intimacy, and perversity. It is oppositional, utopian, and completely without innocence. No longer structured by the polarity of public and private, the cyborg defines a technological polis based partly on a revolution of social relations in the *oikos,* the household. Nature and culture are reworked; the one can no longer be the resource for appropriation or incorporation by the other. The relationships for forming wholes from parts, including those of polarity and hierarchical domination, are at issue in the cyborg world. Unlike the hopes of Frankenstein's monster, the cyborg does not expect its father to save it through a restoration of the garden; that is, through the fabrication of a heterosexual mate, through its completion in a finished whole, a city and cosmos. The cyborg does not dream of community on the model of the organic family, this time without the oedipal project. The cyborg would not recognize the Garden of Eden; it is not made of mud and cannot dream of returning to dust. Perhaps that is why I want to see if cyborgs can subvert the apocalypse of returning to nuclear dust in the manic compulsion to name the Enemy. Cyborgs are not reverent; they do not remember the cosmos. They are wary of holism, but needy for connection—they seem to have a natural feel for united front politics, but without the vanguard party. The main trouble with cyborgs, of course, is that they

are the illegitimate offspring of militarism and patriarchal capitalism, not to mention state socialism. But illegitimate offspring are often exceedingly unfaithful to their origins. Their fathers, after all, are inessential.

I will return to the science fiction of cyborgs at the end of this chapter, but now I want to signal three crucial boundary breakdowns that make the following political-fictional (political-scientific) analysis possible. By the late twentieth century in United States scientific culture, the boundary between human and animal is thoroughly breached. The last beachheads of uniqueness have been polluted if not turned into amusement parks—language, tool use, social behaviour, mental events, nothing really convincingly settles the separation of human and animal. And many people no longer feel the need for such a separation; indeed, many branches of feminist culture affirm the pleasure of connection of human and other living creatures. Movements for animal rights are not irrational denials of human uniqueness; they are a clear-sighted recognition of connection across the discredited breach of nature and culture. Biology and evolutionary theory over the last two centuries have simultaneously produced modern organisms as objects of knowledge and reduced the line between humans and animals to a faint trace re-etched in ideological struggle or professional disputes between life and social science. Within this framework, teaching modern Christian creationism should be fought as a form of child abuse.

Biological-determinist ideology is only one position opened up in scientific culture for arguing the meanings of human animality. There is much room for radical political people to contest the meanings of the breached boundary.[2] The cyborg appears in myth precisely where the boundary between human and animal is transgressed. Far from signalling a walling off of people from other living beings, cyborgs signal disturbingly and pleasurably tight coupling. Bestiality has a new status in this cycle of marriage exchange.

The second leaky distinction is between animal-human (organism) and machine. Pre-cybernetic machines could be haunted; there was always the spectre of the ghost in the machine. This dualism structured the dialogue between materialism and idealism that was settled by a dialectical progeny, called spirit or history, according to taste. But basically machines were not self-moving, self-designing, autonomous. They could not achieve man's dream, only mock it. They were not man, an author to himself, but only a caricature of that masculinist reproductive dream. To think they were otherwise was paranoid. Now we are not so sure. Late twentieth-century machines have made thoroughly ambiguous the difference between natural and artificial, mind and body, self-developing and externally designed, and many other distinctions that used to apply to organisms and machines. Our machines are disturbingly lively, and we ourselves frighteningly inert.

Technological determination is only one ideological space opened up by the reconceptions of machine and organism as coded texts through which we engage in the play of writing and reading the world.[3] "Textualization" of everything in poststructuralist, postmodernist theory has been damned by Marxists and socialist feminists for its utopian disregard for the lived relations of domination that ground the "play" of arbitrary reading.[4] It is certainly true that postmodernist strategies, like my cyborg myth, subvert myriad organic wholes (for example, the poem, the primitive culture, the biological organism). In short, the certainty of what counts as nature—a source of insight and promise of innocence—is undermined, probably fatally. The transcendent authorization of interpretation is lost, and with it the ontology grounding "Western" epistemology. But the alternative is not cynicism or faithlessness, that is, some version of abstract existence, like the accounts of tech-

nological determinism destroying "man" by the "machine" or "meaningful political action" by the "text." Who cyborgs will be is a radical question; the answers are a matter of survival. Both chimpanzees and artefacts have politics, so why shouldn't we (de Waal, 1982; Winner, 1980)?

The third distinction is a subset of the second: the boundary between physical and non-physical is very imprecise for us. Pop physics books on the consequences of quantum theory and the indeterminacy principle are a kind of popular scientific equivalent to Harlequin romances [The US equivalent of Mills & Boon] as a marker of radical change in American white heterosexuality: they get it wrong, but they are on the right subject. Modern machines are quintessentially microelectronic devices: they are everywhere and they are invisible. Modern machinery is an irreverent upstart god, mocking the Father's ubiquity and spirituality. The silicon chip is a surface for writing; it is etched in molecular scales disturbed only by atomic noise, the ultimate interference for nuclear scores. Writing, power, and technology are old partners in Western stories of the origin of civilization, but miniaturization has changed our experience of mechanism. Miniaturization has turned out to be about power; small is not so much beautiful as pre-eminently dangerous, as in cruise missiles. Contrast the TV sets of the 1950s or the news cameras of the 1970s with the TV wrist bands or hand-sized video cameras now advertised. Our best machines are made of sunshine; they are all light and clean because they are nothing but signals, electromagnetic waves, a section of a spectrum, and these machines are eminently portable, mobile—a matter of immense human pain in Detroit and Singapore. People are nowhere near so fluid, being both material and opaque. Cyborgs are ether, quintessence.

The ubiquity and invisibility of cyborgs is precisely why these sunshine-belt machines are so deadly. They are as hard to see politically as materially. They are about consciousness—or its simulation.[5] They are floating signifiers moving in pickup trucks across Europe, blocked more effectively by the witch-weavings of the displaced and so unnatural Greenham women, who read the cyborg webs of power so very well, than by the militant labour of older masculinist politics, whose natural constituency needs defence jobs. Ultimately the "hardest" science is about the realm of greatest boundary confusion, the realm of pure number, pure spirit, $C^3I$, cryptography, and the preservation of potent secrets. The new machines are so clean and light. Their engineers are sun-worshippers mediating a new scientific revolution associated with the night dream of post-industrial society. The diseases evoked by these clean machines are "no more" than the minuscule coding changes of an antigen in the immune system, "no more" than the experience of stress. The nimble fingers of "Oriental" women, the old fascination of little Anglo-Saxon Victorian girls with doll's houses, women's enforced attention to the small take on quite new dimensions in this world. There might be a cyborg Alice taking account of these new dimensions. Ironically, it might be the unnatural cyborg women making chips in Asia and spiral dancing in Santa Rita jail [a practice at once both spiritual and political that linked guards and arrested anti-nuclear demonstrators in the Alameda County jail in California in the early 1980s] whose constructed unities will guide effective oppositional strategies.

So my cyborg myth is about transgressed boundaries, potent fusions, and dangerous possibilities which progressive people might explore as one part of needed political work. One of my premises is that most American socialists and feminists see deepened dualisms of mind and body, animal and machine, idealism and materialism in the social practices, symbolic formulations, and physical artefacts associated with "high technology" and scientific culture. From *One-Dimensional Man* (Marcuse, 1964) to *The Death of Nature* (Merchant, 1980), the analytic resources developed by progressives have insisted on the necessary domination of technics and recalled us to an imagined organic body to integrate our resistance. Another of my premises is that the need for unity of people trying to resist world-wide intensification of domination has never been more acute. But a slightly perverse shift of perspective might better enable us to contest for meanings, as well as for other forms of power and pleasure in technologically mediated societies.

From one perspective, a cyborg world is about the final imposition of a grid of control on the planet, about the final abstraction embodied in a Star Wars apocalypse waged in the name of defence, about the final appropriation of women's bodies in a masculinist orgy of war (Sofia, 1984). From another perspective, a cyborg world might be about lived social and bodily realities in which people are not afraid of their joint kinship with animals and machines, not afraid of permanently partial identities and contradictory standpoints. The political struggle is to see from both perspectives at once because each reveals both dominations and possibilities unimaginable from the other vantage point. Single vision produces worse illusions than double vision or many-headed monsters. Cyborg unities are monstrous and illegitimate; in our present political circumstances, we could hardly hope for more potent myths for resistance and recoupling. I like to imagine LAG, the Livermore Action Group, as a kind of cyborg society, dedicated to realistically converting the laboratories that most fiercely embody and spew out the tools of technological apocalypse, and committed to building a political form that actually manages to hold together witches, engineers, elders, perverts, Christians, mothers, and Leninists long enough to disarm the state. Fission Impossible is the name of the affinity group in my town. (Affinity: related not by blood but by choice, the appeal of one chemical nuclear group for another, avidity.)[6]

## FRACTURED IDENTITIES

It has become difficult to name one's feminism by a single adjective—or even to insist in every circumstance upon the noun. Consciousness of exclusion through naming is acute. Identities seem contradictory, partial, and strategic. With the hard-won recognition of their social and historical constitution, gender, race, and class cannot provide the basis for belief in "essential" unity. There is nothing about being "female" that naturally binds women. There is not even such a state as "being" female, itself a highly complex category constructed in contested sexual scientific discourses and other social practices. Gender, race, or class consciousness is an achievement forced on us by the terrible historical experience of the contradictory social realities of patriarchy, colonialism, and capitalism. And who counts as "us" in my own rhetoric? Which identities are available to ground such a potent political myth called "us," and what could motivate enlistment in this collectivity? Painful fragmentation among feminists (not to mention among women) along every possible fault line has made the concept of *woman* elusive, an excuse for the matrix of women's dominations of each other. For me—and for many who share a similar historical location in white, professional middle-class, female, radical, North American, mid-adult bodies—the sources of a crisis in political identity are legion. The recent history for much of the US left and US feminism has been a response to this kind of crisis by endless splitting and searches for a new essential unity. But there has also been a growing recognition of another response through coalition—affinity, not identity.[7]

Chela Sandoval (n.d., 1984), from a consid-eration of specific historical moments in the formation of the new political voice called women of colour, has theorized a hopeful model of political identity called "oppositional consciousness," born of the skills for reading webs of power by those refused stable membership in the social categories of race, sex, or class. "Women of color," a name contested at its origins by those whom it would incorporate, as well as a historical consciousness marking systematic breakdown of all the signs of Man in "Western" traditions, constructs a kind of postmodernist identity out of otherness, difference, and specificity. This postmodernist identity is fully political, whatever might be said about other possible postmodernisms. Sandoval's oppositional consciousness is about contradictory locations and heterochronic calendars, not about relativisms and pluralisms.

Sandoval emphasizes the lack of any essential criterion for identifying who is a woman of colour. She notes that the definition of the group has been by conscious appropriation of negation. For example, a Chicana or US black woman has not been able to speak as a woman or as a black person or as a Chicano. Thus, she was at the bottom of a cascade of negative identities, left out of even the privileged oppressed authorial categories called "women and blacks," who claimed to make the important revolutions. The category "woman" negated all non-white women; "black" negated all non-black people, as well as all black women. But there was also no "she," no singularity, but a sea of differences among US women who have affirmed their historical identity as US women of colour. This identity marks out a self-consciously constructed space that cannot affirm the capacity to act on the basis of natural identification, but only on the basis of conscious coalition, of affinity, of political kinship.[8] Unlike the "woman" of some streams of the white women's movement in the United States, there is no naturalization of the matrix, or at least this is what Sandoval argues is uniquely available through the power of oppositional consciousness.

Sandoval's argument has to be seen as one potent formulation for feminists out of the world-wide development of anti-colonialist discourse; that is to say, discourse dissolving the "West" and its highest product—the one who is not animal, barbarian, or woman; man, that is, the author of a cosmos called history. As orientalism is deconstructed politically and semiotically, the identities of the occident destabilize, including those of feminists.[9] Sandoval argues that "women of colour" have a chance to build an effective unity that does not replicate the imperializing, totalizing revolutionary subjects of previous Marxisms and feminisms which had not faced the consequences of the disorderly polyphony emerging from decolonization.

Katie King has emphasized the limits of identification and the political/poetic mechanics of identification built into reading "the poem," that generative core of cultural feminism. King criticizes the persistent tendency among contemporary feminists from different "moments" or "conversations" in feminist practice to taxonomize the women's movement to make one's own political tendencies appear to be the *telos* of the whole. These taxonomies tend to remake feminist history so that it appears to be an ideological struggle among coherent types persisting over time, especially those typical units called radical, liberal, and socialist-feminism. Literally, all other feminisms are either incorporated or marginalized, usually by building an explicit ontology and epistemology.[10] Taxonomies of feminism produce epistemologies to police deviation from official women's experience. And of course, "women's culture," like women of colour, is consciously created by mechanisms inducing affinity. The rituals of poetry, music, and certain forms of academic practice have been pre-eminent.

The politics of race and culture in the US women's movements are intimately interwoven. The common achievement of King and Sandoval is learning how to craft a poetic/political unity without relying on a logic of appropriation, incorporation, and taxonomic identification.

The theoretical and practical struggle against unity-through-domination or unity-through-incorporation ironically not only undermines the justifications for patriarchy, colonialism, humanism, positivism, essentialism, scientism, and other unlamented -isms, but *all* claims for an organic or natural standpoint. I think that radical and socialist/Marxist-feminisms have also undermined their/our own epistemological strategies and that this is a crucially valuable step in imagining possible unities. It remains to be seen whether all "epistemologies" as Western political people have known them fail us in the task to build effective affinities.

It is important to note that the effort to construct revolutionary standpoints, epistemologies as achievements of people committed to changing the world, has been part of the process showing the limits of identification. The acid tools of postmodernist theory and the constructive tools of ontological discourse about revolutionary subjects might be seen as ironic allies in dissolving Western selves in the interests of survival. We are excruciatingly conscious of what it means to have a historically constituted body. But with the loss of innocence in our origin, there is no expulsion from the Garden either. Our politics lose the indulgence of guilt with the *naïveté* of innocence. But what would another political myth for socialist-feminism look like? What kind of politics could embrace partial, contradictory, permanently unclosed constructions of personal and collective selves and still be faithful, effective—and, ironically, socialist-feminist?

I do not know of any other time in history when there was greater need for political unity to confront effectively the dominations of "race," "gender," "sexuality," and "class." I also do not know of any other time when the kind of unity we might help build could have been possible. None of "us" have any longer the symbolic or material capability of dictating the shape of reality to any of "them." Or at least "we" cannot claim innocence from practising such dominations. White women, including socialist feminists, discovered (that is, were forced kicking and screaming to notice) the non-innocence of the category "woman." That consciousness changes the geography of all previous categories; it denatures them as heat denatures a fragile protein. Cyborg feminists have to argue that "we" do not want any more natural matrix of unity and that no construction is whole. Innocence, and the corollary insistence on victimhood as the only ground for insight, has done enough damage. But the constructed revolutionary subject must give late-twentieth-century people pause as well. In the fraying of identities and in the reflexive strategies for constructing them, the possibility opens up for weaving something other than a shroud for the day after the apocalypse that so prophetically ends salvation history.

Both Marxist/socialist-feminisms and radical feminisms have simultaneously naturalized and denatured the category "woman" and consciousness of the social lives of "women." Perhaps a schematic caricature can highlight both kinds of moves. Marxian socialism is rooted in an analysis of wage labour which reveals class structure. The consequence of the wage relationship is systematic alienation, as the worker is dissociated from his (sic) product. Abstraction and illusion rule in knowledge, domination rules in practice. Labour is the pre-eminently privileged category enabling the Marxist to overcome illusion and find that point of view which is necessary for changing the world. Labour is the humanizing activity that makes man; labour is an ontological category permitting the knowledge of a subject, and so the knowledge of subjugation and alienation.

In faithful filiation, socialist-feminism advanced by allying itself with the basic analytic strategies of Marxism. The main achievement of both Marxist feminists and socialist feminists was to expand the category of labour to accommodate what (some) women did, even when the wage relation was subordinated to a more comprehensive view of labour under capitalist patriarchy. In particular, women's labour in the household and women's activity as mothers generally (that is, reproduction in the socialist-feminist sense), entered theory on the authority of analogy to the Marxian concept of labour. The unity of women here rests on an epistemology based on the ontological structure of "labour." Marxist/socialist-feminism does not "naturalize" unity; it is a possible achievement based on a possible standpoint rooted in social relations. The essentializing move is in the ontological structure of labour or of its analogue, women's activity.[11] The inheritance of Marxian humanism, with its pre-eminently Western self, is the difficulty for me. The contribution from these formulations has been the emphasis on the daily responsibility of real women to build unities, rather than to naturalize them.

Catherine MacKinnon's (1982, 1987) version of radical feminism is itself a caricature of the appropriating, incorporating, totalizing tendencies of Western theories of identity grounding action.[12] It is factually and politically wrong to assimilate all of the diverse "moments" or "conversations" in recent women's politics named radical feminism to MacKinnon's version. But the teleological logic of her theory shows how an epistemology and ontology—including their negations—erase or police difference. Only one of the effects of MacKinnon's theory is the rewriting of the history of the polymorphous field called radical feminism. The major effect is the production of a theory of experience, of women's identity, that is a kind of apocalypse for all revolutionary standpoints. That is, the totalization built into this tale of radical feminism achieves its end—the unity of women—by enforcing the experience of and testimony to radical non-being. As for the Marxist/socialist feminist, consciousness is an achievement, not a natural fact. And MacKinnon's theory eliminates some of the difficulties built into humanist revolutionary subjects, but at the cost of radical reductionism.

MacKinnon argues that feminism necessarily adopted a different analytical strategy from Marxism, looking first not at the structure of class, but at the structure of sex/gender and its generative relationship, men's constitution and appropriation of women sexually. Ironically, MacKinnon's "ontology" constructs a non-subject, a non-being. Another's desire, not the self's labour, is the origin of "woman." She therefore develops a theory of consciousness that enforces what can count as "women's" experience—anything that names sexual violation, indeed, sex itself as far as "women" can be concerned. Feminist practice is the construction of this form of consciousness; that is, the self-knowledge of a self-who-is-not.

Perversely, sexual appropriation in this feminism still has the epistemological status of labour; that is to say, the point from which an analysis able to contribute to changing the world must flow. But sexual objectification, not alienation, is the consequence of the structure of sex/gender. In the realm of knowledge, the result of sexual objectification is illusion and abstraction. However, a woman is not simply alienated from her product, but in a deep sense does not exist as a subject, or even potential subject, since she owes her existence as a woman to sexual appropriation. To be constituted by another's desire is not the same thing as to be alienated in the violent separation of the labourer from his product.

MacKinnon's radical theory of experience is totalizing in the extreme; it does not so much marginalize as obliterate the authority of any other women's political speech and action. It is a totalization producing what Western patriarchy itself never succeeded in doing—feminists' consciousness of the nonexistence of women, except as products of men's desire. I think MacKinnon correctly argues that no Marxian version of identity can firmly ground women's unity. But in solving the problem of the contradictions of any Western revolutionary subject for feminist purposes, she develops an even more authoritarian doctrine of experience. If my complaint about socialist/Marxian standpoints is their unintended erasure of polyvocal, unassimilable, radical difference made visible in anti-colonial discourse and practice, MacKinnon's intentional erasure of all difference through the device of the "essential" nonexistence of women is not reassuring.

In my taxonomy, which like any other taxonomy is a re-inscription of history, radical feminism can accommodate all the activities of women named by socialist feminists as forms of labour only if the activity can somehow be sexualized. Reproduction had different tones of meanings for the two tendencies, one rooted in labour, one in sex, both calling the consequences of domination and ignorance of social and personal reality "false consciousness."

Beyond either the difficulties or the contributions in the argument of any one author, neither Marxist nor radical feminist points of view have tended to embrace the status of a partial explanation; both were regularly constituted as totalities. Western explanation has demanded as much; how else could the "Western" author incorporate its others? Each tried to annex other forms of domination by expanding its basic categories through analogy, simple listing, or addition. Embarrassed silence about race among white radical and socialist feminists was one major, devastating political consequence. History and polyvocality disappear into political taxonomies that try to establish genealogies. There was no structural room for race (or for much else) in theory claiming to reveal the construction of the category woman and social group women as a unified or totalizable whole. The structure of my caricature looks like this:

socialist feminism—structure of
   class//wage labour//alienation
labour, by analogy reproduction, by
   extension sex, by addition race
radical feminism—structure of
   gender//sexual
   appropriation//objectification
sex, by analogy labour, by extension
   reproduction, by addition race

In another context, the French theorist, Julia Kristeva, claimed women appeared as a historical group after the Second World War, along with groups like youth. Her dates are doubtful; but we are now accustomed to remembering that as objects of knowledge and as historical actors, "race" did not always exist, "class" has a historical genesis, and "homosexuals" are quite junior. It is no accident that the symbolic system of the family of man—and so the essence of woman—breaks up at the same moment that networks of connection among people on the planet are unprecedentedly multiple, pregnant, and complex. "Advanced capitalism" is inadequate to convey the structure of this historical moment. In the "Western" sense, the end of man is at stake. It is no accident that woman disintegrates into women in our time. Perhaps socialist feminists were not substantially guilty of producing essentialist theory that suppressed women's particularity and contradictory interests. I think we have been, at least through unreflective participation in the logics, languages, and practices of white humanism and through searching for a single

ground of domination to secure our revolutionary voice. Now we have less excuse. But in the consciousness of our failures, we risk lapsing into boundless difference and giving up on the confusing task of making partial, real connection. Some differences are playful; some are poles of world historical systems of domination. "Epistemology" is about knowing the difference.

## THE INFORMATICS OF DOMINATION

In this attempt at an epistemological and political position, I would like to sketch a picture of possible unity, a picture indebted to socialist and feminist principles of design. The frame for my sketch is set by the extent and importance of rearrangements in worldwide social relations tied to science and technology. I argue for a politics rooted in claims about fundamental changes in the nature of class, race, and gender in an emerging system of world order analogous in its novelty and scope to that created by industrial capitalism; we are living through a movement from an organic, industrial society to a polymorphous, information system—from all work to all play, a deadly game. Simultaneously material and ideological, the dichotomies may be expressed in the following chart of transitions from the comfortable old hierarchical dominations to the scary new networks I have called the informatics of domination:

| | |
|---|---|
| Representation | Simulation |
| Bourgeois novel, realism | Science fiction, postmodernism |
| Organism | Biotic component |
| Depth, integrity | Surface, boundary |
| Heat | Noise |
| Biology as clinical practice | Biology as inscription |

| | |
|---|---|
| Physiology | Communications engineering |
| Small group | Subsystem |
| Perfection | Optimization |
| Eugenics | Population Control |
| Decadence, *Magic Mountain* | Obsolescence, *Future Shock* |
| Hygiene | Stress Management |
| Microbiology, tuberculosis | Immunology, AIDS |
| Organic division of labour | Ergonomics/cybernetics of labour |
| Functional specialization | Modular construction |
| Reproduction | Replication |
| Organic sex role specialization | Optimal genetic strategies |
| Biological determinism | Evolutionary inertia, constraints |
| Community ecology | Ecosystem |
| Racial chain of being | Neo-imperialism, United Nations humanism |
| Scientific management in home/factory | Global factory/Electronic cottage |
| Family/Market/Factory | Women in the Integrated Circuit |
| Family wage | Comparable worth |
| Public/Private | Cyborg citizenship |
| Nature/Culture | Fields of difference |
| Co-operation | Communications enhancement |
| Freud | Lacan |
| Sex | Genetic engineering |
| Labour | Robotics |
| Mind | Artificial Intelligence |
| Second World War | Star Wars |
| White Capitalist Patriarchy | Informatics of Domination |

This list suggests several interesting things.[13] First, the objects on the right-hand side cannot be coded as "natural," a realization that subverts naturalistic coding for the left-hand side as well. We cannot go back ideologically or materially. It's not just that "god" is dead; so is the "goddess." Or both are revivified in the worlds charged with microelectronic and biotechnological politics. In relation to objects like biotic components, one must think not in terms of essential properties, but in terms of design, boundary constraints, rates of flows, systems logics, costs of lowering constraints. Sexual reproduction is one kind of reproductive strategy among many, with costs and benefits as a function of the system environment. Ideologies of sexual reproduction can no longer reasonably call on notions of sex and sex role as organic aspects in natural objects like organisms and families. Such reasoning will be unmasked as irrational, and ironically corporate executives reading *Playboy* and anti-porn radical feminists will make strange bedfellows in jointly unmasking the irrationalism.

Likewise for race, ideologies about human diversity have to be formulated in terms of frequencies of parameters, like blood groups or intelligence scores. It is "irrational" to invoke concepts like primitive and civilized. For liberals and radicals, the search for integrated social systems gives way to a new practice called "experimental ethnography" in which an organic object dissipates in attention to the play of writing. At the level of ideology, we see translations of racism and colonialism into languages of development and under-development, rates and constraints of modernization. Any objects or persons can be reasonably thought of in terms of disassembly and reassembly; no "natural" architectures constrain system design. The financial districts in all the world's cities, as well as the export-processing and free-trade zones, proclaim this elementary fact of "late capitalism." The entire universe of objects that can be known scientifically must be formulated as problems in communications engineering (for the managers) or theories of the text (for those who would resist). Both are cyborg semiologies.

One should expect control strategies to concentrate on boundary conditions and interfaces, on rates of flow across boundaries—and not on the integrity of natural objects. "Integrity" or "sincerity" of the Western self gives way to decision procedures and expert systems. For example, control strategies applied to women's capacities to give birth to new human beings will be developed in the languages of population control and maximization of goal achievement for individual decision-makers. Control strategies will be formulated in terms of rates, costs of constraints, degrees of freedom. Human beings, like any other component or subsystem, must be localized in a system architecture whose basic modes of operation are probabilistic, statistical. No objects, spaces, or bodies are sacred in themselves; any component can be interfaced with any other if the proper standard, the proper code, can be constructed for processing signals in a common language. Exchange in this world transcends the universal translation effected by capitalist markets that Marx analysed so well. The privileged pathology affecting all kinds of components in this universe is stress—communications breakdown (Hogness, 1983). The cyborg is not subject to Foucault's biopolitics; the cyborg simulates politics, a much more potent field of operations.

This kind of analysis of scientific and cultural objects of knowledge which have appeared historically since the Second World War prepares us to notice some important inadequacies in feminist analysis which has proceeded as if the organic, hierarchical dualisms ordering discourse in "the West" since Aristotle still ruled. They have been cannibalized, or as Zoe Sofia (Sofoulis) might put it, they have been "techno-digested." The dichotomies between mind and body, animal and human, organism and machine, public and private, nature and culture, men and women, primitive and civilized are all in question ideologically. The actual situation of women is their integration/exploitation into a world system of production/reproduction and communication called the informatics of domination. The home, workplace, market, public arena, the body itself—all can be dispersed and interfaced in nearly infinite, polymorphous ways, with large consequences for women and others—consequences that themselves are very different for different people and which make potent oppositional international movements difficult to imagine and essential for survival. One important route for reconstructing socialist-feminist politics is through theory and practice addressed to the social relations of science and technology, including crucially the systems of myth and meanings structuring our imaginations. The cyborg is a kind of disassembled and reassembled, postmodern collective and personal self. This is the self feminists must code.

Communications technologies and biotechnologies are the crucial tools recrafting our bodies. These tools embody and enforce new social relations for women world-wide. Technologies and scientific discourses can be partially understood as formalizations, i.e., as frozen moments, of the fluid social interactions constituting them, but they should also be viewed as instruments for enforcing meanings. The boundary is permeable between tool and myth, instrument and concept, historical systems of social relations and historical anatomies of possible bodies, including objects of knowledge. Indeed, myth and tool mutually constitute each other.

Furthermore, communications sciences and modern biologies are constructed by a common move—*the translation of the world into a problem of coding,* a search for a common language in which all resistance to instrumental control disappears and all heterogeneity can be submitted to disassembly, reassembly, investment, and exchange.

In communications sciences, the translation of the world into a problem in coding can be illustrated by looking at cybernetic (feedback-controlled) systems theories applied to telephone technology, computer design, weapons deployment, or data base construction and maintenance. In each case, solution to the key questions rests on a theory of language and control; the key operation is determining the rates, directions, and probabilities of flow of a quantity called information. The world is subdivided by boundaries differentially permeable to information. Information is just that kind of quantifiable element (unit, basis of unity) which allows universal translation, and so unhindered instrumental power (called effective communication). The biggest threat to such power is interruption of communication. Any system breakdown is a function of stress. The fundamentals of this technology can be condensed into the metaphor C³I, command-control-communication-intelligence, the military's symbol for its operations theory.

In modern biologies, the translation of the world into a problem in coding can be illustrated by molecular genetics, ecology, sociobiological evolutionary theory, and immunobiology. The organism has been translated into problems of genetic coding and read-out. Biotechnology, a writing technology, informs research broadly.[14] In a sense, organisms have ceased to exist as objects of knowledge, giving way to biotic components, i.e., special kinds of information-processing devices. The analogous moves in ecology could be examined by probing the history and utility of the concept of the ecosystem. Immunobiology and associated medical practices are rich exemplars of the privilege of coding and recognition systems as objects of knowledge, as constructions of bodily reality for us. Biology here is a kind of cryptography. Research is necessarily a kind of intelligence activity. Ironies abound. A

stressed system goes awry; its communication processes break down; it fails to recognize the difference between self and other. Human babies with baboon hearts evoke national ethical perplexity—for animal rights activists at least as much as for the guardians of human purity. In the US gay men and intravenous drug users are the "privileged" victims of an awful immune system disease that marks (inscribes on the body) confusion of boundaries and moral pollution (Treichler, 1987).

But these excursions into communications sciences and biology have been at a rarefied level; there is a mundane, largely economic reality to support my claim that these sciences and technologies indicate fundamental transformations in the structure of the world for us. Communications technologies depend on electronics. Modern states, multinational corporations, military power, welfare state apparatuses, satellite systems, political processes, fabrication of our imaginations, labour-control systems, medical constructions of our bodies, commercial pornography, the international division of labour, and religious evangelism depend intimately upon electronics. Microelectronics is the technical basis of simulacra; that is, of copies without originals.

Microelectronics mediates the translations of labour into robotics and word processing, sex into genetic engineering and reproductive technologies, and mind into artificial intelligence and decision procedures. The new biotechnologies concern more than human reproduction. Biology as a powerful engineering science for redesigning materials and processes has revolutionary implications for industry, perhaps most obvious today in areas of fermentation, agriculture, and energy. Communications sciences and biology are constructions of natural-technical objects of knowledge in which the difference between machine and organism is thoroughly blurred; mind, body, and tool are on very intimate terms. The "multinational" material organization of the production and reproduction of daily life and the symbolic organization of the production and reproduction of culture and imagination seem equally implicated. The boundary-maintaining images of base and superstructure, public and private, or material and ideal never seemed more feeble.

I have used Rachel Grossman's (1980) image of women in the integrated circuit to name the situation of women in a world so intimately restructured through the social relations of science and technology.[15] I used the odd circumlocution, "the social relations of science and technology," to indicate that we are not dealing with a technological determinism, but with a historical system depending upon structured relations among people. But the phrase should also indicate that science and technology provide fresh sources of power, that we need fresh sources of analysis and political action (Latour, 1984). Some of the rearrangements of race, sex, and class rooted in high-tech-facilitated social relations can make socialist-feminism more relevant to effective progressive politics.

## THE "HOMEWORK ECONOMY" OUTSIDE "THE HOME"

The "New Industrial Revolution" is producing a new world-wide working class, as well as new sexualities and ethnicities. The extreme mobility of capital and the emerging international division of labour are intertwined with the emergence of new collectivities, and the weakening of familiar groupings. These developments are neither gender- nor race-neutral. White men in advanced industrial societies have become newly vulnerable to permanent job loss, and women are not disappearing from the job rolls at the same rates as men. It is not simply that women in Third World countries are the preferred labour force for the science-based multinationals in the export-processing sectors, particularly in electronics. The picture is more systematic and involves reproduction, sexuality, culture, consumption, and production. In the prototypical Silicon Valley, many women's lives have been structured around employment in electronics-dependent jobs, and their intimate realities include serial heterosexual monogamy, negotiating childcare, distance from extended kin or most other forms of traditional community, a high likelihood of loneliness and extreme economic vulnerability as they age. The ethnic and racial diversity of women in Silicon Valley structures a microcosm of conflicting differences in culture, family, religion, education, and language.

Richard Gordon has called this new situation the "homework economy."[16] Although he includes the phenomenon of literal homework emerging in connection with electronics assembly, Gordon intends "homework economy" to name a restructuring of work that broadly has the characteristics formerly ascribed to female jobs, jobs literally done only by women. Work is being redefined as both literally female and feminized, whether performed by men or women. To be feminized means to be made extremely vulnerable; able to be disassembled, reassembled, exploited as a reserve labour force; seen less as workers than as servers; subjected to time arrangements on and off the paid job that make a mockery of a limited work day; leading an existence that always borders on being obscene, out of place, and reducible to sex. Deskilling is an old strategy newly applicable to formerly privileged workers. However, the homework economy does not refer only to large-scale deskilling, nor does it deny that new areas of high skill are emerging, even for women and men previously excluded from skilled employment. Rather, the concept indicates that factory, home, and market are integrated on a new scale and that the places of women are crucial—and need to be analysed for differences among women and for meanings for relations between men and women in various situations.

The homework economy as a world capitalist organizational structure is made possible by (not caused by) the new technologies. The success of the attack on relatively privileged, mostly white, men's unionized jobs is tied to the power of the new communications technologies to integrate and control labour despite extensive dispersion and decentralization. The consequences of the new technologies are felt by women both in the loss of the family (male) wage (if they ever had access to this white privilege) and in the character of their own jobs, which are becoming capital-intensive; for example, office work and nursing.

The new economic and technological arrangements are also related to the collapsing welfare state and the ensuing intensification of demands on women to sustain daily life for themselves as well as for men, children, and old people. The feminization of poverty— generated by dismantling the welfare state, by the homework economy where stable jobs become the exception, and sustained by the expectation that women's wages will not be matched by a male income for the support of children—has become an urgent focus. The causes of various women-headed households are a function of race, class, or sexuality; but their increasing generality is a ground for coalitions of women on many issues. That women regularly sustain daily life partly as a function of their enforced status as mothers is hardly new; the kind of integration with the overall capitalist and progressively war-based economy is new. The particular pressure, for example, on US black women, who have achieved an escape from (barely) paid domestic service and who now hold clerical and similar jobs in large numbers, has large implications for continued enforced black poverty *with* employment. Teenage women in industrializing areas of the Third World increas-

ingly find themselves the sole or major source of a cash wage for their families, while access to land is ever more problematic. These developments must have major consequences in the psychodynamics and politics of gender and race.

Within the framework of three major stages of capitalism (commercial/early industrial, monopoly, multinational)—tied to nationalism, imperialism, and multinationalism, and related to Jameson's three dominant aesthetic periods of realism, modernism, and postmodernism—I would argue that specific forms of families dialectically relate to forms of capital and to its political and cultural concomitants. Although lived problematically and unequally, ideal forms of these families might be schematized as (1) the patriarchal nuclear family, structured by the dichotomy between public and private and accompanied by the white bourgeois ideology of separate spheres and nineteenth-century Anglo-American bourgeois feminism; (2) the modern family mediated (or enforced) by the welfare state and institutions like the family wage, with a flowering of a-feminist heterosexual ideologies, including their radical versions represented in Greenwich Village around the First World War; and (3) the "family" of the homework economy with its oxymoronic structure of women-headed households and its explosion of feminisms and the paradoxical intensification and erosion of gender itself. This is the context in which the projections for world-wide structural unemployment stemming from the new technologies are part of the picture of the homework economy. As robotics and related technologies put men out of work in "developed" countries and exacerbate failure to generate male jobs in Third World "development," and as the automated office becomes the rule even in labour-surplus countries, the feminization of work intensifies. Black women in the United States have long known what it looks like to face the structural underemployment ("feminization") of black men, as well as their own highly vulnerable position in the wage economy. It is no longer a secret that sexuality, reproduction, family, and community life are interwoven with this economic structure in myriad ways which have also differentiated the situations of white and black women. Many more women and men will contend with similar situations, which will make cross-gender and race alliances on issues of basic life support (with or without jobs) necessary, not just nice.

The new technologies also have a profound effect on hunger and on food production for subsistence world-wide. Rae Lessor Blumberg (1983) estimates that women produce about 50 per cent of the world's subsistence food.[17] Women are excluded generally from benefiting from the increased high-tech commodification of food and energy crops, their days are made more arduous because their responsibilities to provide food do not diminish, and their reproductive situations are made more complex. Green Revolution technologies interact with other high-tech industrial production to alter gender divisions of labour and differential gender migration patterns.

The new technologies seem deeply involved in the forms of "privitization" that Ros Petchesky (1981) has analysed, in which militarization, right-wing family ideologies and policies, and intensified definitions of corporate (and state) property as private synergistically interact.[18] The new communications technologies are fundamental to the eradication of "public life" for everyone. This facilitates the mushrooming of a permanent high-tech military establishment at the cultural and economic expense of most people, but especially of women. Technologies like video games and highly miniaturized televisions seem crucial to production of modern forms of "private life." The culture of video games is heavily orientated to individual competition and extraterrestrial warfare. High-tech, gen-

dered imaginations are produced here, imaginations that can contemplate destruction of the planet and a sci-fi escape from its consequences. More than our imaginations is militarized; and the other realities of electronic and nuclear warfare are inescapable. These are the technologies that promise ultimate mobility and perfect exchange—and incidentally enable tourism, that perfect practice of mobility and exchange, to emerge as one of the world's largest single industries.

The new technologies affect the social relations of both sexuality and of reproduction, and not always in the same ways. The close ties of sexuality and instrumentality, of views of the body as a kind of private satisfaction- and utility-maximizing machine, are described nicely in sociobiological origin stories that stress a genetic calculus and explain the inevitable dialectic of domination of male and female gender roles.[19] These sociobiological stories depend on a high-tech view of the body as a biotic component or cybernetic communications system. Among the many transformations of reproductive situations is the medical one, where women's bodies have boundaries newly permeable to both "visualization" and "intervention." Of course, who controls the interpretation of bodily boundaries in medical hermeneutics is a major feminist issue. The speculum served as an icon of women's claiming their bodies in the 1970s; that handcraft tool is inadequate to express our needed body politics in the negotiation of reality in the practices of cyborg reproduction. Self-help is not enough. The technologies of visualization recall the important cultural practice of hunting with the camera and the deeply predatory nature of a photographic consciousness.[20] Sex, sexuality, and reproduction are central actors in high-tech myth systems structuring our imaginations of personal and social possibility.

Another critical aspect of the social relations of the new technologies is the reformulation of expectations, culture, work, and reproduction for the large scientific and technical work-force. A major social and political danger is the formation of a strongly bimodal social structure, with the masses of women and men of all ethnic groups, but especially people of colour, confined to a homework economy, illiteracy of several varieties, and general redundancy and impotence, controlled by high-tech repressive apparatuses ranging from entertainment to surveillance and disappearance. An adequate socialist-feminist politics should address women in the privileged occupational categories, and particularly in the production of science and technology that constructs scientific-technical discourses, processes, and objects.[21]

This issue is only one aspect of enquiry into the possibility of a feminist science, but it is important. What kind of constitutive role in the production of knowledge, imagination, and practice can new groups doing science have? How can these groups be allied with progressive social and political movements? What kind of political accountability can be constructed to tie women together across the scientific-technical hierarchies separating us? Might there be ways of developing feminist science/technology politics in alliance with anti-military science facility conversion action groups? Many scientific and technical workers in Silicon Valley, the high-tech cowboys included, do not want to work on military science.[22] Can these personal preferences and cultural tendencies be welded into progressive politics among this professional middle class in which women, including women of colour, are coming to be fairly numerous?

## WOMEN IN THE INTEGRATED CIRCUIT

Let me summarize the picture of women's historical locations in advanced industrial societies, as these positions have been restructured partly through the social relations of science and technology. If it was ever possible ideologically to characterize women's lives by the distinction of public and private domains—suggested by images of the division of working-class life into factory and home, of bourgeois life into market and home, and of gender existence into personal and political realms—it is now a totally misleading ideology, even to show how both terms of these dichotomies construct each other in practice and in theory. I prefer a network ideological image, suggesting the profusion of spaces and identities and the permeability of boundaries in the personal body and in the body politic. "Networking" is both a feminist practice and a multinational corporate strategy—weaving is for oppositional cyborgs.

So let me return to the earlier image of the informatics of domination and trace one vision of women's "place" in the integrated circuit, touching only a few idealized social locations seen primarily from the point of view of advanced capitalist societies: Home, Market, Paid Work Place, State, School, Clinic-Hospital, and Church. Each of these idealized spaces is logically and practically implied in every other locus, perhaps analogous to a holographic photograph. I want to suggest the impact of the social relations mediated and enforced by the new technologies in order to help formulate needed analysis and practical work. However, there is no "place" for women in these networks, only geometrics of difference and contradiction crucial to women's cyborg identities. If we learn how to read these webs of power and social life, we might learn new couplings, new coalitions. There is no way to read the following list from a standpoint of "identification," of a unitary self. The issue is dispersion. The task is to survive in the diaspora.

*Home:* Women-headed households, serial monogamy, flight of men, old women alone, technology of domestic work, paid homework, reemergence of home sweat-shops, home-based businesses and telecommuting, electronic cottage, urban homelessness, migration, module architecture, reinforced (simulated) nuclear family, intense domestic violence.

*Market:* Women's continuing consumption work, newly targeted to buy the profusion of new production from the new technologies (especially as the competitive race among industrialized and industrializing nations to avoid dangerous mass unemployment necessitates finding ever bigger new markets for ever less clearly needed commodities); bimodal buying power, coupled with advertising targeting of the numerous affluent groups and neglect of the previous mass markets; growing importance of informal markets in labour and commodities parallel to high-tech, affluent market structures; surveillance systems through electronic funds transfer; intensified market abstraction (commodification) of experience, resulting in ineffective utopian or equivalent cynical theories of community; extreme mobility (abstraction) of marketing/financing systems; interpenetration of sexual and labour markets; intensified sexualization of abstracted and alienated consumption.

*Paid Work Place:* Continued intense sexual and racial division of labour, but considerable growth of membership in privileged occupational categories for many white women and people of colour; impact of new technologies on women's work in clerical, service, manufacturing (especially textiles), agriculture, electronics; international restructuring of the working classes; development of new time arrangements to facilitate the homework economy (flex time, part time, over time, no time); homework and out work; increased pressures for two-tiered wage structures;

significant numbers of people in cash-dependent populations world-wide with no experience or no further hope of stable employment; most labour "marginal" or "feminized."

*State:* Continued erosion of the welfare state; decentralizations with increased surveillance and control; citizenship by telematics; imperialism and political power broadly in the form of information rich/information poor differentiation; increased high-tech militarization increasingly opposed by many social groups; reduction of civil service jobs as a result of the growing capital intensification of office work, with implications for occupational mobility for women of colour; growing privatization of material and ideological life and culture; close integration of privatization and militarization, the high-tech forms of bourgeois capitalist personal and public life; invisibility of different social groups to each other, linked to psychological mechanisms of belief in abstract enemies.

*School:* Deepening coupling of high-tech capital needs and public education at all levels, differentiated by race, class, and gender; managerial classes involved in educational reform and refunding at the cost of remaining progressive educational democratic structures for children and teachers; education for mass ignorance and repression in technocratic and militarized culture; growing anti-science mystery cults in dissenting and radical political movements; continued relative scientific illiteracy among white women and people of colour; growing industrial direction of education (especially higher education) by science-based multinationals (particularly in electronics- and biotechnology-dependent companies); highly educated, numerous élites in a progressively bimodal society.

*Clinic-hospital:* Intensified machine-body

relations; renegotiations of public metaphors which channel personal experience of the body, particularly in relation to reproduction, immune system functions, and "stress" phenomena; intensification of reproductive politics in response to world historical implications of women's unrealized, potential control of their relation to reproduction; emergence of new, historically specific diseases; struggles over meanings and means of health in environments pervaded by high technology products and processes; continuing feminization of health work; intensified struggle over state responsibility for health; continued ideological role of popular health movements as a major form of American politics.

*Church:* Electronic fundamentalist "super-saver" preachers solemnizing the union of electronic capital and automated fetish gods; intensified importance of churches in resisting the militarized state; central struggle over women's meanings and authority in religion; continued relevance of spirituality, intertwined with sex and health, in political struggle.

The only way to characterize the informatics of domination is as a massive intensification of insecurity and cultural impoverishment, with common failure of subsistence networks for the most vulnerable. Since much of this picture interweaves with the social relations of science and technology, the urgency of a socialist-feminist politics addressed to science and technology is plain. There is much now being done, and the grounds for political work are rich. For example, the efforts to develop forms of collective struggle for women in paid work, like SEIU's District 925, [Service Employees International Union's office workers' organization in the US] should be a high priority for all of us. These efforts are profoundly tied to technical restructuring of la-

bour processes and reformations of working classes. These efforts also are providing understanding of a more comprehensive kind of labour organization, involving community, sexuality, and family issues never privileged in the largely white male industrial unions.

The structural rearrangements related to the social relations of science and technology evoke strong ambivalence. But it is not necessary to be ultimately depressed by the implications of late twentieth-century women's relation to all aspects of work, culture, production of knowledge, sexuality, and reproduction. For excellent reasons, most Marxisms see domination best and have trouble understanding what can only look like false consciousness and people's complicity in their own domination in late capitalism. It is crucial to remember that what is lost, perhaps especially from women's points of view, is often virulent forms of oppression, nostalgically naturalized in the face of current violation. Ambivalence towards the disrupted unities mediated by high-tech culture requires not sorting consciousness into categories of "clear-sighted critique grounding a solid political epistemology" versus "manipulated false consciousness," but subtle understanding of emerging pleasures, experiences, and powers with serious potential for changing the rules of the game.

There are grounds for hope in the emerging bases for new kinds of unity across race, gender, and class, as these elementary units of socialist-feminist analysis themselves suffer protean transformations. Intensifications of hardship experienced world-wide in connection with the social relations of science and technology are severe. But what people are experiencing is not transparently clear, and we lack sufficiently subtle connections for collectively building effective theories of experience. Present efforts—Marxist, psychoanalytic, feminist, anthropological—to clarify even "our" experience are rudimentary.

I am conscious of the odd perspective provided by my historical position—a PhD in biology for an Irish Catholic girl was made possible by Sputnik's impact on US national science-education policy. I have a body and mind as much constructed by the post-Second World War arms race and cold war as by the women's movements. There are more grounds for hope in focusing on the contradictory effects of politics designed to produce loyal American technocrats, which also produced large numbers of dissidents, than in focusing on the present defeats.

The permanent partiality of feminist points of view has consequences for our expectations of forms of political organization and participation. We do not need a totality in order to work well. The feminist dream of a common language, like all dreams for a perfectly true language, of perfectly faithful naming of experience, is a totalizing and imperialist one. In that sense, dialectics too is a dream language, longing to resolve contradiction. Perhaps, ironically, we can learn from our fusions with animals and machines how not to be Man, the embodiment of Western logos. From the point of view of pleasure in these potent and taboo fusions, made inevitable by the social relations of science and technology, there might indeed be a feminist science.

## CYBORGS: A MYTH OF POLITICAL IDENTITY

I want to conclude with a myth about identity and boundaries which might inform late twentieth-century political imaginations. I am indebted in this story to writers like Joanna Russ, Samuel R. Delany, John Varley, James Tiptree, Jr., Octavia Butler, Monique Wittig, and Vonda McIntyre.[23] These are our storytellers exploring what it means to be embodied in high-tech worlds. They are theorists for cyborgs. Exploring conceptions of bodily boundaries and social order, the anthropologist Mary Douglas (1966, 1970) should be

credited with helping us to consciousness about how fundamental body imagery is to world view, and so to political language. French feminists like Luce Irigaray and Monique Wittig, for all their differences, know how to write the body; how to weave eroticism, cosmology, and politics from imagery of embodiment, and especially for Wittig, from imagery of fragmentation and reconstitution of bodies.[24]

American radical feminists like Susan Griffin, Audre Lorde, and Adrienne Rich have profoundly affected our political imaginations—and perhaps restricted too much what we allow as a friendly body and political language.[25] They insist on the organic, opposing it to the technological. But their symbolic systems and the related positions of ecofeminism and feminist paganism, replete with organicisms, can only be understood in Sandoval's terms as oppositional ideologies fitting the late twentieth century. They would simply bewilder anyone not preoccupied with the machines and consciousness of late capitalism. In that sense they are part of the cyborg world. But there are also great riches for feminists in explicitly embracing the possibilities inherent in the breakdown of clean distinctions between organism and machine and similar distinctions structuring the Western self. It is the simultaneity of breakdowns that cracks the matrices of domination and opens geometric possibilities. What might be learned from personal and political "technological" pollution? I look briefly at two overlapping groups of texts for their insight into the construction of a potentially helpful cyborg myth: constructions of women of colour and monstrous selves in feminist science fiction.

Earlier I suggested that "women of colour" might be understood as a cyborg identity, a potent subjectivity synthesized from fusions of outsider identities and in the complex political-historical layerings of her "biomythography," *Zami* (Lorde, 1982; King, 1987a,

1987b). There are material and cultural grids mapping this potential, Audre Lorde (1984) captures the tone in the title of her *Sister Outsider*. In my political myth, Sister Outsider is the offshore woman, whom US workers, female and feminized, are supposed to regard as the enemy preventing their solidarity, threatening their security. Onshore, inside the boundary of the United States, Sister Outsider is a potential amidst the races and ethnic identities of women manipulated for division, competition, and exploitation in the same industries. "Women of colour" are the preferred labour force for the science-based industries, the real women for whom the world-wide sexual market, labour market, and politics of reproduction kaleidoscope into daily life. Young Korean women hired in the sex industry and in electronics assembly are recruited from high schools, educated for the integrated circuit. Literacy, especially in English, distinguishes the "cheap" female labour so attractive to the multinationals.

Contrary to orientalist stereotypes of the "oral primitive," literacy is a special mark of women of colour, acquired by US black women as well as men through a history of risking death to learn and to teach reading and writing. Writing has a special significance for all colonized groups. Writing has been crucial to the Western myth of the distinction between oral and written cultures, primitive and civilized mentalities, and more recently to the erosion of that distinction in "postmodernist" theories attacking the phallogocentrism of the West, with its worship of the monotheistic, phallic, authoritative, and singular work, the unique and perfect name.[26] Contests for the meanings of writing are a major form of contemporary political struggle. Releasing the play of writing is deadly serious. The poetry and stories of US women of colour are repeatedly about writing, about access to the power to signify; but this time that power must be neither phallic nor innocent. Cyborg writing must not be about the

Fall, the imagination of a once-upon-a-time wholeness before language, before writing, before Man. Cyborg writing is about the power to survive, not on the basis of original innocence, but on the basis of seizing the tools to mark the world that marked them as other.

The tools are often stories, retold stories, versions that reverse and displace the hierarchical dualisms of naturalized identities. In retelling origin stories, cyborg authors subvert the central myths of origin of Western culture. We have all been colonized by those origin myths, with their longing for fulfilment in apocalypse. The phallogocentric origin stories most crucial for feminist cyborgs are built into the literal technologies—technologies that write the world, biotechnology and microelectronics—that have recently textualized our bodies as code problems on the grid of $C^3I$. Feminist cyborg stories have the task of recording communication and intelligence to subvert command and control.

Figuratively and literally, language politics pervade the struggles of women of colour; and stories about language have a special power in the rich contemporary writing by US women of colour. For example, retellings of the story of the indigenous woman Malinche, mother of the mestizo "bastard" race of the new world, master of languages, and mistress of Cortés, carry special meaning for Chicana constructions of identity. Cherríe Moraga (1983) in *Loving in the War Years* explores the themes of identity when one never possessed the original language, never told the original story, never resided in the harmony of legitimate heterosexuality in the garden of culture, and so cannot base identity on a myth or a fall from innocence and right to natural names, mother's or father's.[27] Moraga's writing, her superb literacy, is presented in her poetry as the same kind of violation as Malinche's mastery of the conqueror's language—a violation, an illegitimate production, that allows survival. Moraga's language is not "whole"; it is self-consciously spliced, a chimera of English and Spanish, both conqueror's languages. But it is this chimeric monster, without claim to an original language before violation, that crafts the erotic, competent, potent identities of women of colour. Sister Outsider hints at the possibility of world survival not because of her innocence, but because of her ability to live on the boundaries, to write without the founding myth of original wholeness, with its inescapable apocalypse of final return to a deathly oneness that Man has imagined to be the innocent and all-powerful Mother, freed at the End from another spiral of appropriation by her son. Writing marks Moraga's body, affirms it as the body of a woman of colour, against the possibility of passing into the unmarked category of the Anglo father or into the orientalist myth of "original illiteracy" of a mother that never was. Malinche was mother here, not Eve before eating the forbidden fruit. Writing affirms Sister Outsider, not the Woman-before-the-Fall-into-Writing needed by the phallogocentric Family of Man.

Writing is pre-eminently the technology of cyborgs, etched surfaces of the late twentieth century. Cyborg politics is the struggle for language and the struggle against perfect communication, against the one code that translates all meaning perfectly, the central dogma of phallogocentrism. That is why cyborg politics insist on noise and advocate pollution, rejoicing in the illegitimate fusions of animal and machine. These are the couplings which make Man and Woman so problematic, subverting the structure of desire, the force imagined to generate language and gender, and so subverting the structure and modes of reproduction of "Western" identity, of nature and culture, of mirror and eye, slave and master, body and mind. "We" did not originally choose to be cyborgs, but choice grounds a liberal politics

and epistemology that imagines the reproduction of individuals before the wider replications of "texts."

From the perspective of cyborgs, freed of the need to ground politics in "our" privileged position of the oppression that incorporates all other dominations, the innocence of the merely violated, the ground of those closer to nature, we can see powerful possibilities. Feminisms and Marxisms have run aground on Western epistemological imperatives to construct a revolutionary subject from the perspective of a hierarchy of oppressions and/or a latent position of moral superiority, innocence, and greater closeness to nature. With no available original dream of a common language or original symbiosis promising protection from hostile "masculine" separation, but written into the play of a text that has no finally privileged reading or salvation history, to recognize "oneself" as fully implicated in the world, frees us of the need to root politics in identification, vanguard parties, purity, and mothering. Stripped of identity, the bastard race teaches about the power of the margins and the importance of a mother like Malinche. Women of colour have transformed her from the evil mother of masculinist fear into the originally literate mother who teaches survival.

This is not just literary deconstruction, but liminal transformation. Every story that begins with original innocence and privileges the return to wholeness imagines the drama of life to be individuation, separation, the birth of the self, the tragedy of autonomy, the fall into writing, alienation; that is, war, tempered by imaginary respite in the bosom of the Other. These plots are ruled by a reproductive politics—rebirth without flaw, perfection, abstraction. In this plot women are imagined either better or worse off, but all agree they have less selfhood, weaker individuation, more fusion to the oral, to Mother, less at stake in masculine autonomy. But there is another route to having less at stake in masculine autonomy, a route that does not pass through Woman, Primitive, Zero, the Mirror Stage and its imaginary. It passes through women and other present-tense, illegitimate cyborgs, not of Woman born, who refuse the ideological resources of victimization so as to have a real life. These cyborgs are the people who refuse to disappear on cue, no matter how many times a "Western" commentator remarks on the sad passing of another primitive, another organic group done in by "Western" technology, by writing.[28] These real-life cyborgs (for example, the Southeast Asian village women workers in Japanese and US electronics firms described by Aihwa Ong) are actively rewriting the texts of their bodies and societies. Survival is the stakes in this play of readings.

To recapitulate, certain dualisms have been persistent in Western traditions; they have all been systemic to the logics and practices of domination of women, people of colour, nature, workers, animals—in short, domination of all constituted as others, whose task is to mirror the self. Chief among these troubling dualisms are self/other, mind/body, culture/nature, male/female, civilized/primitive, reality/appearance, whole/part, agent/resource, maker/made, active/passive, right/wrong, truth/illusion, total/partial, God/man. The self is the One who is not dominated, who knows that by the service of the other, the other is the one who holds the future, who knows that by the experience of domination, which gives the lie to the autonomy of the self. To be One is to be autonomous, to be powerful, to be God; but to be One is to be an illusion, and so to be involved in a dialectic of apocalypse with the other. Yet to be other is to be multiple, without clear boundary, frayed, insubstantial. One is too few, but two are too many.

High-tech culture challenges these dualisms in intriguing ways. It is not clear who makes and who is made in the relation between human and machine. It is not clear what is mind and what body in machines that resolve into coding practices. In so far as we know ourselves in both formal discourse (for example, biology) and in daily practice (for example, the homework economy in the integrated circuit), we find ourselves to be cyborgs, hybrids, mosaics, chimeras. Biological organisms have become biotic systems, communications devices like others. There is no fundamental, ontological separation in our formal knowledge of machine and organism, of technical and organic. The replicant Rachel in the Ridley Scott film *Blade Runner* stands as the image of a cyborg culture's fear, love, and confusion.

One consequence is that our sense of connection to our tools is heightened. The trance state experienced by many computer users has become a staple of science-fiction film and cultural jokes. Perhaps paraplegics and other severely handicapped people can (and sometimes do) have the most intense experiences of complex hybridization with other communication devices.[29] Anne McCaffrey's pre-feminist *The Ship Who Sang* (1969) explored the consciousness of a cyborg, hybrid of girl's brain and complex machinery, formed after the birth of a severely handicapped child. Gender, sexuality, embodiment, skill: all were reconstituted in the story. Why should our bodies end at the skin, or include at best other beings encapsulated by skin? From the seventeenth century till now, machines could be animated—given ghostly souls to make them speak or move or to account for their orderly development and mental capacities. Or organisms could be mechanized—reduced to body understood as resource of mind. These machine/organism relationships are obsolete, unnecessary. For us, in imagination and in other practice, machines can be prosthetic devices, intimate components, friendly selves. We don't need organic holism to give impermeable wholeness, the total woman and her feminist variants (mutants?). Let me conclude this point by a very partial reading of the logic of the cyborg monsters of my second group of texts, feminist science fiction.

The cyborgs populating feminist science fiction make very problematic the statuses of man or woman, human, artefact, member of a race, individual entity, or body. Katie King clarifies how pleasure in reading these fictions is not largely based on identification. Students facing Joanna Russ for the first time, students who have learned to take modernist writers like James Joyce or Virginia Woolf without flinching, do not know what to make of *The Adventures of Alyx* or *The Female Man,* where characters refuse the reader's search for innocent wholeness while granting the wish for heroic quests, exuberant eroticism, and serious politics. *The Female Man* is the story of four versions of one genotype, all of whom meet, but even taken together do not make a whole, resolve the dilemmas of violent moral action, or remove the growing scandal of gender. The feminist science fiction of Samuel R. Delany, especially *Tales of Nevèrÿon,* mocks stories of origin by redoing the neolithic revolution, replaying the founding moves of Western civilization to subvert their plausibility. James Tiptree, Jr, an author whose fiction was regarded as particularly manly until her "true" gender was revealed, tells tales of reproduction based on non-mammalian technologies like alternation of generations of male brood pouches and male nurturing. John Varley constructs a supreme cyborg in his arch-feminist exploration of Gaea, a mad goddess-planet-trickster-old woman-technological device on whose surface an extraordinary array of post-cyborg symbioses are spawned. Octavia Butler writes of an African sorceress pitting her powers of transformation against the genetic manipulations of her rival *(Wild Seed),* of time warps that bring a modern US black woman into slavery where her actions in relation to her white master-ancestor determine the possibility of her own birth *(Kindred),*

and of the illegitimate insights into identity and community of an adopted cross-species child who came to know the enemy as self *(Survivor).* In *Dawn* (1987), the first instalment of a series called *Xenogenesis,* Butler tells the story of Lilith Iyapo, whose personal name recalls Adam's first and repudiated wife and whose family name marks her status as the widow of the son of Nigerian immigrants to the US. A black woman and a mother whose child is dead, Lilith mediates the transformation of humanity through genetic exchange with extra-terrestrial lovers/rescuers/destroyers/genetic engineers, who reform earth's habitats after the nuclear holocaust and coerce surviving humans into intimate fusion with them. It is a novel that interrogates reproductive, linguistic, and nuclear politics in a mythic field structured by late twentieth-century race and gender.

Because it is particularly rich in boundary transgressions, Vonda McIntyre's *Superluminal* can close this truncated catalogue of promising and dangerous monsters who help redefine the pleasures and politics of embodiment and feminist writing. In a fiction where no character is "simply" human, human status is highly problematic. Orca, a genetically altered diver, can speak with killer whales and survive deep ocean conditions, but she longs to explore space as a pilot, necessitating bionic implants jeopardizing her kinship with the divers and cetaceans. Transformations are effected by virus vectors carrying a new developmental code, by transplant surgery, by implants of microelectronic devices, by analogue doubles, and other means. Laenea becomes a pilot by accepting a heart implant and a host of other alterations allowing survival in transit at speeds exceeding that of light. Radu Dracul survives a virus-caused plague in his outerworld planet to find himself with a time sense that changes the boundaries of spatial perception for the whole species. All the characters explore the limits of language; the dream of communicating experience; and the necessity of limitation, partiality, and intimacy even in this world of protean transformation and connection. *Superluminal* stands also for the defining contradictions of a cyborg world in another sense; it embodies textually the intersection of feminist theory and colonial discourse in the science fiction I have alluded to in this chapter. This is a conjunction with a long history that many "First World" feminists have tried to repress, including myself in my readings of *Superluminal* before being called to account by Zoe Sofoulis, whose different location in the world system's informatics of domination made her acutely alert to the imperialist moment of all science fiction cultures, including women's science fiction. From an Australian feminist sensitivity, Sofoulis remembered more readily McIntyre's role as writer of the adventures of Captain Kirk and Spock in TV's *Star Trek* series than her rewriting the romance in *Superluminal*.

Monsters have always defined the limits of community in Western imaginations. The Centaurs and Amazons of ancient Greece established the limits of the centred polis of the Greek male human by their disruption of marriage and boundary pollutions of the warrior with animality and woman. Unseparated twins and hermaphrodites were the confused human material in early modern France who grounded discourse on the natural and supernatural, medical and legal, portents and diseases—all crucial to establishing modern identity.[30] The evolutionary and behavioural sciences of monkeys and apes have marked the multiple boundaries of late twentieth-century industrial identities. Cyborg monsters in feminist science fiction define quite different political possibilities and limits from those proposed by the mundane fiction of Man and Woman.

There are several consequences to taking seriously the imagery of cyborgs as other than our enemies. Our bodies, ourselves; bodies are maps of power and identity. Cyborgs are no exception. A cyborg body is not innocent; it was not born in a garden; it does not seek unitary identity and so generate antagonistic dualisms without end (or until the world ends); it takes irony for granted. One is too few, and two is only one possibility. Intense pleasure in skill, machine skill, ceases to be a sin, but an aspect of embodiment. The machine is not an *it* to be animated, worshipped, and dominated. The machine is us, our processes, an aspect of our embodiment. We can be responsible for machines; *they* do not dominate or threaten us. We are responsible for boundaries; we are they. Up till now (once upon a time), female embodiment seemed to be given, organic, necessary; and female embodiment seemed to mean skill in mothering and its metaphoric extensions. Only by being out of place could we take intense pleasure in machines, and then with excuses that this was organic activity after all, appropriate to females. Cyborgs might consider more seriously the partial, fluid, sometimes aspect of sex and sexual embodiment. Gender might not be global identity after all, even if it has profound historical breadth and depth.

The ideologically charged question of what counts as daily activity, as experience, can be approached by exploiting the cyborg image. Feminists have recently claimed that women are given to dailiness, that women more than men somehow sustain daily life, and so have a privileged epistemological position potentially. There is a compelling aspect to this claim, one that makes visible unvalued female activity and names it as the ground of life. But *the* ground of life? What about all the ignorance of women, all the exclusions and failures of knowledge and skill? What about men's access to daily competence, to knowing how to build things, to take them apart, to play? What about other embodiments? Cyborg gender is a local possibility taking a global vengeance. Race, gender, and capital require a cyborg theory of wholes and parts.

There is no drive in cyborgs to produce total theory, but there is an intimate experience of boundaries, their construction and deconstruction. There is a myth system waiting to become a political language to ground one way of looking at science and technology and challenging the informatics of domination—in order to act potently.

One last image: organisms and organismic, holistic politics depend on metaphors of rebirth and invariably call on the resources of reproductive sex. I would suggest that cyborgs have more to do with regeneration and are suspicious of the reproductive matrix and of most birthing. For salamanders, regeneration after injury, such as the loss of a limb, involves regrowth of structure and restoration of function with the constant possibility of twinning or other odd topographical productions at the site of former injury. The regrown limb can be monstrous, duplicated, potent. We have all been injured, profoundly. We require regeneration, not rebirth, and the possibilities for our reconstitution include the utopian dream of the hope for a monstrous world without gender.

Cyborg imagery can help express two crucial arguments in this essay: first, the production of universal, totalizing theory is a major mistake that misses most of reality, probably always, but certainly now; and second, taking responsibility for the social relations of science and technology means refusing an antiscience metaphysics, a demonology of technology, and so means embracing the skilful task of reconstructing the boundaries of daily life, in partial connection with others, in communication with all of our parts. It is not just that science and technology are possible means of great human satisfaction, as well as a matrix of complex dominations. Cyborg imagery can suggest a way out of the maze of dualisms in which we have explained our bodies and our tools to ourselves. This is a dream not of a common language, but of a powerful infidel heteroglossia. It is an imagination of a feminist speaking in tongues to strike fear into the circuits of the supersavers of the new right. It means both building and destroying machines, identities, categories, relationships, space stories. Though both are bound in the spiral dance, I would rather be a cyborg than a goddess.

## NOTES

1. Research was funded by an Academic Senate Faculty Research Grant from the University of California, Santa Cruz. An earlier version of the paper on genetic engineering appeared as "Lieber Kyborg als Göttin: für eine sozialistisch-feministische Unterwanderung der Gentechnologie," in Bernd-Peter Lange and Anna Marie Stuby, eds.", Berlin: Argument-Sonderband 105, 1984, pp 66–84. The cyborg manifesto grew from my "New machines, new bodies, new communities: political dilemmas of a cyborg feminist," "The Scholar and the Feminist X: The Question of Technology," Conference, Barnard College, April 1983.

The people associated with the History of Consciousness Board of UCSC have had an enormous influence on this paper, so that it feels collectively authored more than most, although those I cite may not recognize their ideas. In particular, members of graduate and undergraduate feminist theory, science, and politics, and theory and methods courses contributed to the cyborg manifesto. Particular debts here are due Hilary Klein (1989), Paul Edwards (1985), Lisa Lowe (1986), and James Clifford (1985).

Parts of the paper were my contribution to a collectively developed session, "Poetic Tools and Political Bodies: Feminist Approaches to High Technology Culture," 1984 California American Studies Association, with History of Consciousness graduate students Zoe Sofoulis, "Jupiter space"; Katie King, "The pleasures of repetition and the limits of identification in feminist science fiction: reimaginations of the body after the cyborg"; and Chela Sandoval, "The construction of subjectivity and oppositional consciousness in feminist film and video." Sandoval's (n.d.) theory of oppositional consciousness was published as "Women respond to racism: A Report on the National Women's Studies Association Conference." For Sofoulis's semiotic-psychoanalytic readings of nuclear culture, see Sofia (1984). King's unpublished papers ("Questioning tradition: canon formation and the veiling of power"; "Gender and genre: reading the science fiction of Joanna Russ"; "Varley's *Titan* and *Wizard:* feminist parodies of nature, culture, and hardware") deeply informed the cyborg manifesto.

Barbara Epstein, Jeff Escoffier, Rusten Hogness, and Jaye Miler gave extensive discussion and editorial help.

Members of the Silicon Valley Research Project of UCSC and participants in SVRP conferences and workshops were very important, especially Rick Gordon, Linda Kimball, Nancy Snyder, Langdon Winner, Judith Stacey, Linda Lim, Patricia Fernandez-Kelly, and Judith Gregory. Finally, I want to thank Nancy Hartsock for years of friendship and discussion on feminist theory and feminist science fiction. I also thank Elizabeth Bird for my favourite political button: "Cyborgs for Earthly Survival."

2. Useful references to left and/or feminist radical science movements and theory and to biological/biotechnical issues include: Bleier (1984, 1986), Harding (1986), Fausto-Sterling (1985), Gould (1981), Hubbard *et al.* (1982), Keller (1985), Lewontin *et al.* (1984), *Radical Science Journal* (became *Science as Culture* in 1987), 26 Freegrove Road, London N7 9RQ; *Science for the People,* 897 Main St, Cambridge, MA 02139.

3. Starting points for left and/or feminist approaches to technology and politics include: Cowan (1983), Rothschild (1983), Traweek (1988), Young and Levidow (1981, 1985), Weizenbaum (1976), Winner (1977, 1986), Zimmerman (1983), Athanasiou (1987), Cohn (1987a, 1987b), Winograd and Flores (1986), Edwards (1985). *Global Electronics Newsletter,* 867 West Dana St, #204, Mountain View, CA 94041; *Processed World,* 55 Sutter St, San Francisco, CA 94104; ISIS, Women's International Information and Communication Service, PO Box 50 (Cornavin), 1211 Geneva 2, Switzerland, and Via Santa Maria Dell'Anima 30, 00186 Rome, Italy. Fundamental approaches to modern social studies of science that do not continue the liberal mystification that it all started with Thomas Kuhn, include: Knorr-Cetina (1981), Knorr-Cetina and Mulkay (1983), Latour and Woolgar (1979), Young (1979). The 1984 Directory of the Network for the Ethnographic Study of Science, Technology, and Organizations lists a wide range of people and projects crucial to better radical analysis; available from NESSTO, PO Box 11442, Stanford, CA 94305.

4. A provocative, comprehensive argument about the politics and theories of "postmodernism" is made by Fredric Jameson (1984), who argues that postmodernism is not an option, a style among others, but a cultural dominant requiring radical reinvention of left politics from within; there is no longer any place from without that gives meaning to the comforting fiction of critical distance. Jameson also makes clear why one cannot be for or against postmodernism, an essentially moralist move. My position is that feminists (and others) need continuous cultural reinvention, postmodernist critique, and historical materialism; only a cyborg would have a chance. The old dominations of white capitalist patriarchy seem nostalgically innocent now: they normalized heterogeneity, into man and woman, white and black, for example. "Advanced capitalism" and postmodernism release heterogeneity without a norm, and

we are flattened, without subjectivity, which requires depth, even unfriendly and drowning depths. It is time to write *The Death of the Clinic.* The clinic's methods required bodies and works; we have texts and surfaces. Our dominations don't work by medicalization and normalization any more; they work by networking, communications redesign, stress management. Normalization gives way to automation, utter redundancy. Michel Foucault's *Birth of the Clinic* (1963), *History of Sexuality* (1976), and *Discipline and Punish* (1975) name a form of power at its moment of implosion. The discourse of biopolitics gives way to technobabble, the language of the spliced substantive; no noun is left whole by the multinationals. These are their names, listed from one issue of *Science:* Tech-Knowledge, Genentech, Allergen, Hybritech, Compupro, Genen-cor, Syntex, Allelix, Agrigenetics Corp., Syntro, Codon, Repligen, MicroAngelo from Scion Corp., Percom Data, Inter Systems, Cyborg Corp., Statcom Corp., Intertec. If we are imprisoned by language, then escape from that prison-house requires language poets, a kind of cultural restriction enzyme to cut the code; cyborg heteroglossia is one form of radical cultural politics. For cyborg poetry, see Perloff (1984); Fraser (1984). For feminist modernist/postmodernist "cyborg" writing, see HOW(ever), 871 Corbet Ave, San Francisco, CA 94131.

5. Baudrillard (1983). Jameson (1984, p. 66) points out that Plato's definition of the simulacrum is the copy for which there is no original, i.e., the world of advanced capitalism, of pure exchange. See *Discourse* 9 (Spring/Summer 1987) for a special issue on technology (cybernetics, ecology, and the postmodern imagination).

6. For ethnographic accounts and political evaluations, see Epstein (forthcoming), Sturgeon (1986). Without explicit irony, adopting the spaceship earth/whole earth logo of the planet photographed from space, set off by the slogan "Love Your Mother," the May 1987 Mothers and Others Day action at the nuclear weapons testing facility in Nevada none the less took account of the tragic contradictions of views of the earth. Demonstrators applied for official permits to be on the land from officers of the Western Shoshone tribe, whose territory was invaded by the US government when it built the nuclear weapons test ground in the 1950s. Arrested for trespassing, the demonstrators argued that the police and weapons facility personnel, without authorization from the proper officials, were the trespassers. One affinity group at the women's action called themselves the Surrogate Others; and in solidarity with the creatures forced to tunnel in the same ground with the bomb, they enacted a cyborgian emergence from the constructed body of a large, non-heterosexual desert worm.

7. Powerful developments of coalition politics emerge from "Third World" speakers, speaking from nowhere, the displaced centre of the universe, earth: "We live on

the third planet from the sun"—*Sun Poem* by Jamaican writer, Edward Kamau Braithwaite, review by Mackey (1984). Contributors to Smith (1983) ironically subvert naturalized identities precisely while constructing a place from which to speak called home. See especially Reagon (in Smith, 1983, pp. 356–68). Trinh T. Minh-ha (1986–87).

8. Hooks (1981, 1984); Hull *et al.* (1982). Bambara (1981) wrote an extraordinary novel in which the women of colour theatre group, The Seven Sisters, explores a form of unity. See analysis by Butler-Evans (1987).

9. On orientalism in feminist works and elsewhere, see Lowe (1986); Said (1978); Mohanty (1984); *Many Voices, One Chant: Black Feminist Perspectives* (1984).

10. Katie King (1986, 1987a) has developed a theoretically sensitive treatment of the workings of feminist taxonomies as genealogies of power in feminist ideology and polemic. King examines Jaggar's (1983) problematic example of taxonomizing feminisms to make a little machine producing the desired final position. My caricature here of socialist and radical feminism is also an example.

11. The central role of object relations versions of psychoanalysis and related strong universalizing moves in discussing reproduction, caring work, and mothering in many approaches to epistemology underline their authors' resistance to what I am calling postmodernism. For me, both the universalizing moves and these versions of psychoanalysis make analysis of "women's place in the integrated circuit" difficult and lead to systematic difficulties in accounting for or even seeing major aspects of the construction of gender and gendered social life. The feminist standpoint argument has been developed by: Flax (1983), Harding (1986), Harding and Hintikka (1983), Hartsock (1983a, b), O'Brien (1981), Rose (1983), Smith (1974, 1979). For rethinking theories of feminist materialism and feminist standpoints in response to criticism, see Harding (1986, pp. 163–96), Hartsock (1987), and H. Rose (1986).

12. I make an argumentative category error in "modifying" MacKinnon's positions with the qualifier "radical," thereby generating my own reductive critique of extremely heterogeneous writing, which does explicitly use that label, by my taxonomically interested argument about writing which does not use the modifier and which brooks no limits and thereby adds to the various dreams of a common, in the sense of univocal, language for feminism. My category error was occasioned by an assignment to write from a particular taxonomic position which itself has a heterogeneous history, socialist-feminism, for *Socialist Review*. A critique indebted to MacKinnon, but without the reductionism and with an elegant feminist account of Foucault's paradoxical conservatism

on sexual violence (rape), is de Lauretis (1985; see also 1986, pp. 1–19). A theoretically elegant feminist social-historical examination of family violence, that insists on women's, men's, and children's complex agency without losing sight of the material structures of male domination, race, and class, is Gordon (1988).

13. This chart was published in 1985. My previous efforts to understand biology as a cybernetic command-control discourse and organisms as "natural-technical objects of knowledge" were Haraway (1979, 1983, 1984). The 1979 version of this dichotomous chart appears in this vol., ch. 3; for a 1989 version, see ch. 10. The differences indicate shifts in argument.

14. For progressive analyses and action on the biotechnology debates: *GeneWatch, a Bulletin of the Committee for Responsible Genetics,* 5 Doane St, 4th Floor, Boston, MA 02109; Genetic Screening Study Group (formerly the Sociobiology Study Group of Science for the People), Cambridge, MA; Wright (1982, 1986); Yoxen (1983).

15. Starting references for "women in the integrated circuit": D'Onofrio-Flores and Pfafflin (1982), Fernandez-Kelly (1983), Fuentes and Ehrenreich (1983), Grossman (1980), Nash and Fernandez-Kelly (1983), Ong (1987), Science Policy Research Unit (1982).

16. For the "homework economy outside the home" and related arguments: Gordon (1983); Gordon and Kimball (1985); Stacey (1987); Reskin and Hartmann (1986); *Women and Poverty* (1984); S. Rose (1986); Collins (1982); Burr (1982); Gregory and Nussbaum (1982); Piven and Coward (1982); Microelectronics Group (1980); Stallard *et al.* (1983) which includes a useful organization and resource list.

17. The conjunction of the Green Revolution's social relations with biotechnologies like plant genetic engineering makes the pressures on land in the Third World increasingly intense. AID's estimates (*New York Times,* 14 October 1984) used at the 1984 World Food Day are that in Africa, women produce about 90 per cent of rural food supplies, about 60–80 per cent in Asia, and provide 40 per cent of agricultural labour in the Near East and Latin America. Blumberg charges that world organizations' agricultural politics, as well as those of multinationals and national governments in the Third World, generally ignore fundamental issues in the sexual division of labour. The present tragedy of famine in Africa might owe as much to male supremacy as to capitalism, colonialism, and rain patterns. More accurately, capitalism and racism are usually structurally male dominant. See also Blumberg (1981); Hacker (1984); Hacker and Bovit (1981); Busch and Lacy (1983); Wilfred (1982); Sachs (1983); International Fund for Agricultural Development (1985); Bird (1984).

18. See also Enloe (1983a, b).

19. For a feminist version of this logic, see Hrdy (1981). For an analysis of scientific women's story-telling practices, especially in relation to sociobiology in evolutionary debates around child abuse and infanticide, see this vol., ch. 5.

20. For the moment of transition of hunting with guns to hunting with cameras in the construction of popular meanings of nature for an American urban immigrant public, see Haraway (1984–5, 1989b), Nash (1979), Sontag (1977), Preston (1984).

21. For guidance for thinking about the political/cultural/racial implications of the history of women doing science in the United States see: Haas and Perucci (1984); Hacker (1981); Keller (1983); National Science Foundation (1988); Rossiter (1982); Schiebinger (1987); Haraway (1989b).

22. Markoff and Siegel (1983). High Technology Professionals for Peace and Computer Professionals for Social Responsibility are promising organizations.

23. King (1984). An abbreviated list of feminist science fiction underlying themes of this essay: Octavia Butler, *Wild Seed, Mind of My Mind, Kindred, Survivor,* Suzy McKee Charnas, *Motherliness;* Samuel R. Delany, the Nevèrÿon series; Anne McCaffery, *The Ship Who Sang, Dinosaur Planet;* Vonda McIntyre, *Superluminal, Dreamsnake;* Joanna Russ, *Adventures of Alyx, The Female Man;* James Tiptree, Jr., *Star Songs of an Old Primate, Up the Walls of the World;* John Varley, *Titan, Wizard, Demon.*

24. French feminisms contribute to cyborg heteroglossia. Burke (1981); Irigaray (1977, 1979); Marks and de Courtivron (1980); *Signs* (Autumn 1981); Wittig (1973); Duchen (1986). For English translation of some currents of francophone feminism see *Feminist Issues: A Journal of Feminist Social and Political Theory,* 1980.

25. But all these poets are very complex, not least in their treatment of themes of lying and erotic, decentred collective and personal identities. Griffin (1978), Lorde (1984), Rich (1978).

26. Derrida (1976, especially part II); Lévi-Strauss (1961, especially "The Writing Lesson"); Gates (1985); Kahn and Neumaier (1985); Ong (1982); Kramarae and Treichler (1985).

27. The sharp relation of women of colour to writing as theme and politics can be approached through: Program for "The Black Woman and the Diaspora: Hidden Connections and Extended Acknowledgments," an International Literary Conference, Michigan State University, October 1985; Evans (1984); Christian (1985); Carby (1987); Fisher (1980); *Frontiers* (1980, 1983); Kingston (1977); Lerner (1973); Giddings (1985); Moraga and Anzaldúa (1981); Morgan (1984). Anglophone European and Euro-American women have also crafted special relations to their writing as a potent sign: Gilbert and Gubar (1979), Russ (1983).

28. The convention of ideologically taming militarized high technology by publicizing its applications to speech and motion problems of the disabled/differently abled takes on a special irony in monotheistic, patriarchal, and frequently anti-semitic culture when computer-generated speech allows a boy with no voice to chant the Haftorah at his bar mitzvah. See Sussman (1986). Making the always context-relative social definitions of "ableness" particularly clear, military high-tech has a way of making human beings disabled by definition, a perverse aspect of much automated battlefield and Star Wars R&D. See Welford (1 July 1986).

29. James Clifford (1985, 1988) argues persuasively for recognition of continuous cultural reinvention, the stubborn non-disappearance of those "marked" by Western imperializing practices.

30. DuBois (1982), Daston and Park (n.d.), Park and Daston (1981). The noun *monster* shares its root with the verb *to demonstrate.*

# IX

# CULTURAL STUDIES

Someone new to cultural studies, an advanced undergraduate or graduate student reading this book for the first time, could well describe cultural studies as an interdisciplinary movement with a lot of theory in it, a theory-oriented version of American or Victorian studies but with much broader interests. The many readings in cultural studies in this book—not only the synthesis pieces in this section called "Cultural Studies" but many others by Gates, Said, Johnson, Mulvey, Spivak, Haraway, for example—will show that cultural studies, indeed both interdisciplinary and theoretical, remains an active area of inquiry that has scarcely solidified into a program of well-defined interests and methods. Cultural studies is shaped by postcolonial inquiries into colonial strategies of cultural oppression and also by tactics (to use Michel de Certeau's term) for resisting those practices. It is shaped by gender study, feminist and gay-lesbian, as well as by psychoanalysis and Marxist social theory. It is shaped in relation to, and often as a critique of, traditional practices of anthropology, which use the term "culture" as a central concept. But it is also shaped in relation to, and as a critique of, traditional practices of literary studies and aesthetics, for which "culture" is also central. Comprised variously by what Henry Louis Gates, Jr., calls "that uneasy, shifting set of alliances formed by feminist critics, critics of so-called minority culture and Marxist and post-structuralist critics generally—in short, the rainbow coalition of contemporary critical theory," cultural studies consistently, since the early 1960s, has asked what it means to know about and be in culture(s) and also what can be done to change and improve culture(s). These are the twin tasks of analyzing existing institutions and transforming those institutions we describe as "the institutional and transformative concerns of cultural study" in "Notes Towards a Definition of Cultural Studies" in this section. Challenging the adequacy of previous, formal "academic" critiques of culture and social practices, this work has shifted cultural and political priorities in what is taught and *how* teaching happens, as well as in the kind of inquiries and critiques that get published. In many manifestations, cultural studies is a form of academic rebellion against status quo assumptions about academic work so that it sometimes seems to be a kind of academic "protest" movement seeking to change the nature of what is studied in the academy and even the relations between scholarship and the society that bounds it.

## "CULTURE" AS A CONCEPT

The term *cultural studies* is often associated with the work of Raymond Williams. In 1958 Williams published a very influential book, *Culture and Society: 1780–1950,* which pursued the thesis that "the idea of culture, and the word itself in its general modern uses, came into English thinking in the period which we commonly describe as that of the Industrial Revolution." Following the different uses of the term "culture" in different historical settings, Williams examines the social need for this "idea" in English writers and intellectuals. Later, in his book *Keywords* Williams examines "the issues and problems" that could be traced in particular words, whose "uses bound together certain ways of seeing culture and society." This procedure, as we mention in *Criticism and Culture* and note in passing in "Notes Towards a Definition of Cultural Studies," is remarkably parallel to Michel Foucault's description (and pursuit) of Nietzsche's procedure of "genealogy." The parallel between Williams and Foucault, like the comparison between Williams and Claude Lévi-Strauss that Stuart Hall offers in "Cultural Studies: Two Paradigms" in this section, shows the convergence on a set of issues by the two very different intellectual traditions of Anglo-American pragmatism and Continental rationalism.

In *Marxism and Literature* Williams specifically describes the "complexity of the concept of 'culture.'" The term "culture," he writes, "became a noun of 'inner' process, specialized to its presumed agencies in 'intellectual life' and 'the arts.' It became also a noun of general process, specialized to its presumed configurations in 'whole ways of life.' It played a crucial role in definitions of 'the arts' and 'the humanities,' from the first sense. It played an equally crucial role in definitions of the 'human sciences' and the 'social sciences,' in the second sense. Each tendency is ready to deny any proper use of the concept to the other, in spite of many attempts at reconciliation." In this analysis, as we note in this section, "culture" encompasses the world of art, "imagination," and ideas, and it also encompasses the social grouping of people where, in some sense, the whole is greater than the sum of its parts. It describes the ways in which societies make sense of the common experience of its members, situating "culture" within the domain of "ideas," and, in Williams' repeated phrase, it describes "a whole way of living of a people."

These two "tendencies" indicate two different intellectual disciplines for which the term "culture" has been crucial, literary/intellectual studies and anthropology. In other words, just as we argued in the General Introduction that the concept of "literature" has a history that has been affected by the institutions that define and preserve it, so "culture" has a history of the ways it has been put to use. An early use of the term was that of Matthew Arnold in *Culture and Anarchy* (1869), where he attempts to find a system of values in a world where traditional religious and social values were crumbling, a world where the aristocracy no longer commanded the coherence of society, and the middle-class ideology of laissez-faire capitalism did not address the needs of social and "cultural" coherence. Another early use was that of E. B. Tylor in *Primitive Culture* (1871), a book that is often described as a founding document in the establishment of anthropology as an intellectual discipline. Unlike Arnold's description of the culture as an agency of intellectual life and the arts, Tylor describes culture as whole ways of life. (Following Williams's sense of culture as the particular "ways" people live their lives together, Meaghan Morris describes the ordinariness and "banality" of this sense of culture.) Instead of Arnold's normative and singular term, Taylor offers the possibility of many different "cultures." That is, the opposition between Arnold and Tylor, as George Stocking has argued, is (paradoxically) the opposition between Arnold's view of culture as a transindividual tradition and Tylor's view of cultures as a plurality of unrelated instances.

Still, it is necessary, we think, for cultural studies to acknowledge its relation to the social sciences, as well as the humanities: in many ways, the translation of "humanities" into the "human sciences" we mentioned in the General Introduction gestures in this direction. The inclusion here of James Clifford's essay, "The Translation of Cultures," aims to suggest these links. Clifford brings together Arnold's "traditional" view of culture in the religious culture of Maurice Leenhardt, the evangelical missionary at New Caledonia at the turn of the twentieth century, and, at the same time, the scientific anthropological study of different cultures in the examination of the confrontation of different languages. The crucial problem for both views of culture—the problem of what Clifford calls "deep translation"—is that of "otherness" or "difference." These terms (or implications of them) have reappeared throughout this book—in Showalter, Gates, Said, Schweickart, Kristeva, Derrida, Moi, Greenblatt, Spivak, Bennett, and Morris—and they are always implicated in any discussion of culture. (Even Arnold, in defining the cultural work of criticism in "The Function of Criticism at the Present Time" in 1865, felt it necessary to discuss the differences of class.) That is, the *problem* of cultural studies is the difficult task of *both* acknowledging cultural and human differences and discovering means of creating culture and community where whatever people share with one another is not lost in acknowledged difference. In relation to literary criticism, the problem of cultural studies, as Said says, is the difficulty of linking literary and cultural works to each other to bring particular works "out of the neglect and secondariness to which for all kinds of political and ideological reasons they had previously been condemned." Williams describes such "otherness" in historical and temporal terms (as opposed to the spatial terms of Clifford's anthropology) when he notes in *The Long Revolution* that different generations "never quite talk 'the same language,' " and Clifford describes it in his narration of Leenhardt's "intercultural translation."

## THE COMPLEXITY OF CULTURAL STUDIES

The large body of writing and thought that comprises "cultural studies" within literary studies at present blends vocabularies drawn from classical Marxist and current political theory, psychoanalysis, feminism, philosophy, and semiotics. In view of this complex blending, cultural studies discourse at times may be formidable in its technical terminology and diversity. The reading of a few formative essays, however, can assist immensely to open up for inspection the significant debates about "culture" centered on cultural studies. Stuart Hall's "Cultural Studies: Two Paradigms" is one such article (see also the more recent "Cultural Studies and Its Theoretical Legacies" 1992). Hall divides the expanse of work in cultural studies into the "culturalist" and the "structuralist" initiatives. Culturalism he defines as moving in a line from Matthew Arnold, F. R. Leavis, and down through Raymond Williams. Those who speak of culture in this setting generally assume, in Williams's words, the existence of a "common culture" through which occurs "the sharing of common meanings." Here "culture" means "a whole way of life" that springs from a ground of shared natural experience. This version of "culture," relying on the priority of "experience" conceived as a substance giving form to culture, is essentialist in orientation.

The other principal mode for understanding cultural studies in Hall's discussion is the "structuralist" view of culture. Largely semiotic in orientation, "experience" in this view is culturally—and socially—constructed, never "natural" or universal in its range but always specific to a particular culture. In "The Translation of Cultures," Clifford discusses the "translation" of one culture to another as the "nuanced understanding" of what he calls "reciprocal translation," the attempt of cultures to recognize each other's otherness. All through Clifford's discussion is the constant reminder that "reciprocal translation," whatever its relative success, also means untranslatability, the suggestion that in a fundamental way cultures may speak to but not *for* each other. In this structuralist line, drawing on modern linguistics and semiotics, are Claude Lévi-Strauss, Michel Foucault, Julia Kristeva, Jacques Lacan, and Jacques Derrida. In their thinking, the languages and codes of culture produce the experiential effects that, as part of their power as instituted practices, give the appearance of being inevitable and unalterable, "natural." Many of the critics working currently in cultural studies are aligned on this structuralist side. Hall, however, wisely resists the theoretical closure of choosing one paradigm over the other. He writes in "Cultural Studies: Two Paradigms" that by themselves "neither structuralism nor culturalism will do[;] as self-sufficient paradigms of study, they [together] have a centrality to the field which all the other contenders lack. . . ." The "essential" move of taking a particular position to speak from and the representational function of language that one uses when speaking from that position are not two different assumptions that we can choose between. They are themselves constituent dimensions of what culture can be. As the abstract markers for other possibilities, he goes on, together "they address what must be the *core problem* of cultural studies," the relations of essentialism and representation, saying and doing, as represented in the coupling "culture/ideology."

A number of disciplines have been influenced by cultural studies since the 1960s, including pedagogy, communication, literary criticism, women's studies, and legal studies. In each case is a recasting of traditional conceptions of inquiry in light of the social use of knowledge. Much influenced by Raymond Williams's idea of the "politics of intellectual work," these diverse practices all move in the direction of framing "knowing" within the social context of inquiry at a particular historical moment. Knowledge, from this view, can never be disinterested in the manner Arnold took it to be; as an actual *act* in the world, not something simply that *is,* knowledge is simultaneously an enablement to some who can perform it in a particular way and an impediment to others. Always taking the form of an actual *act,* knowledge is and can always be conceived as part of a discourse, as having a sender and receiver—in other words, as having agency. Cultural studies and this definition of knowledge as an act are currently shaping English and literary studies as a discipline. English and rhetoric, in their *performative* dimension as activities of analysis and interpretation, also help to establish in cultural studies this sense of knowledge as a kind of action taken. (For related discussions, see the examinations of rhetoric in "Rhetoric and Reader Response"; Culler's discussion of the opposition between performative and constative aspects of language in "Deconstruction and Poststructuralism"; and Felman's and Moi's discussions of knowledge in "Psychology and Psychoanalysis.")

The "performative" conception of knowledge in cultural studies implies a general rejection of knowledge taken as an abstract reference separate from the realm of human activity. Rather, knowledge is something that happens within a scenario of material conditions, within and in relation to the *local* conditions from which it arose. As we noted in the introduction to "Deconstruction and Poststructuralism," the aim of Enlightenment "reason" was to *universalize* and *individualize* understanding by detaching it from the particular and local historical contexts in which it arises, the very "custom" and "tradition" to which Descartes objected. Custom and tradition are the sources and loci of "culture," and cultural studies—whatever discipline or disciplines from which it is working—attempts to make knowledge more complex by returning it to the customs and traditions from which it arises. That is, cultural studies attempts to understand and locate knowledge as a phenomenon that is conditioned not by an individual subject but by a social world. It is against this background of knowledge seen in its performative dimension that the performing of cultural work, the "struggle" over "whole ways of life," to use Williams's words, can be seen as actually creating the dimensions of culture that, when fully instituted, will appear to be inevitable and "natural."

## THE POLITICS OF CULTURAL STUDIES

Cultural studies, in its complexity, its interdisciplinarity—even as informed by semiotics—aims, however, at creating new practices, new "cultural" life, as well as new objects and forms of knowledge. In other words, its "complex" definition of knowledge as never fully achieving detachment and disinterestedness means that even in the academy it is measured by performance, as well as understanding. Other interdisciplinary inquiries in American studies, comparative literature, and African-American studies have not in every instance been highly effective, in actual practice. Henry Giroux, David Shumway, Paul Smith, and James Sosnoski in "The Need for Cultural Studies: Resisting Intellectual and Oppositional Public Spheres," advance a withering discussion of the prior era of interdisciplinary studies in the 1960s. They argue that interdisciplinary programs such as American studies, Victorian studies, and Black studies joined and harmonized too well with the institutions of which they were a part. (Patrick Brantlinger also offers a good history of these programs in relation to cultural studies.) In effect, these programs ceased to be *critical* practices in the sense of "transformative critique" common to and useful in cultural studies. We can argue that more consistently successful in the performing of cultural critique have been individual figures active in cultural studies both in and outside of the academy, such as Gayatri Spivak, Edward Said, and Cornel West—in addition to the project at the Birmingham Centre for the Study of Popular Culture in England. The impetus of such movements, as Spivak argues in *Other Worlds: Essays in Cultural Politics* (1987) and *The Post-Colonial Critic* (1990), is the result of the work of those positioned on the periphery of culture, paradoxically, those who represent discourses that have been denied access to cultural and intellectual power. Such figures speak in a voice closely linked to their status as cultural agents for particular ideological positions, voices "marked" by the signifiers (skin tone, accent, place of origin, gender, etc.) for social marginalization.

However, insofar as such critics work in accord with certain principles or interests, the possibility of "interested" critics and scholars, at least in America, has to be a peculiarity. American academics, with few exceptions historically, traditionally go about their work estranged from other sites of social struggle and commitment and, in the process, often fulfill a "merely" intellectual role in society: they seem, at best, "merely" to analyze the phenomena of the human sciences, the *institutions* of social life. In this situation, an intellectual becomes liable to the charge of being "in some undismissible sense," as Jim Merod says in *The Political Responsibility of the Critic,* simply "an agent of that power" that supposedly was being analyzed and critiqued. Those working in cultural studies, many of whom work in state-supported colleges and universities around the country, are faced with the dilemma concerning how to maintain the effectiveness of a critique that seeks to *transform* institutions of knowledge and power when working within such institutions. One solution to this dilemma would be "to find an institutional practice in cultural studies that might produce an organic intellectual," that is, one who is aligned, as Hall says in "Cultural Studies and Its Theoretical Legacies, "with an emerging historic movement." If such practices could be found, such an intellectual would be "organic" in the sense of finding his or her own genesis *as* an intellectual within specific communal needs at a specific moment. The question of whether such a figure as an organic intellectual (Antonio Gramsci's term) can exist in any form is a key question of cultural studies. (In a different register, Henry Louis Gates pursues an analysis of this problem in "What Is Literary Theory?")

## THE SUBJECTS OF CULTURE: KNOWLEDGE AND POWER

The concept and definition of "organic" intellectual emphasizes the *local* nature of cultural studies: cultural studies addresses situations that occur at a particular place and a particular time, so that the "interests" of cultural studies and knowledge can be self-consciously formed in relation to local conditions—in the classroom, in discussions of curricula, in the creation of possibilities of intellectual and other activities. This definition may help to formulate the "problem" of cultural studies in contemporary culture. For insofar as the academic intellectual (both student and teacher) has a stake in the status quo, what can move critical inquiry in the direction of interested inquiry without losing the "critical" and "ethical" dimensions? In other words, to what extent can approaches to cultural studies, potentially or at present, produce practices with salutary effects socially and culturally? And how are such "effects" to be identified and measured—by what standard? Dinesh D'Souza's idea in *Illiberal Education*—in some ways the only idea of his book—is that contemporary cultural inquiry is defined and practiced subjectively. In this, in a certain sense, he is correct. A primary tenet of the cultural-studies agenda, as advanced by the Birmingham Centre and in much actual practice in Australia and the United States, is that cultural studies is fundamentally "subjective" in nature—this is a form of the *local* nature of knowledge—what D'Souza mistakenly parodies in *Illiberal Education* as a practice malleable and frivolous, what he identifies as a set of largely Lilliputian abstractions about texts and theoretical approaches to multiculturalism. He advances that a few bleeding hearts with left-leaning politics are attempting to fix education and the world by projecting their own values into education. However, in a sense that D'Souza misses, cultural studies traditionally is, in fact, subjective. This is not to say that it is non-"objective" or nonrigorous but, rather, "subjective" in the sense of paying attention to the situation and the context within which we find any inquiring subject.

Hall argues that it became necessary to theorize the "subject" after the rise of structuralism in the 1950s and 1960s. Given the constructionist view in many of the social sciences and cultural studies that says "experience," even when taken to be natural or naturally occurring, is the effect of a certain subjectivity and cultural practice, a critical examination of culture must also define and understand the cultural viewpoint, or "subject," the set of assumptions on which a particular cultural construction is built. Here the "subject" means, as Hall writes in this section, "a set of positions in language and knowledge, from which culture can appear to be enunciated." So even what we might call observable experience would have to be investigated within the context of the subjectivity that produced it. For these reasons cultural studies is indeed "subjective" in the sense that insofar as it is "critical," it can never escape examining the perspective and the assumptions that make a critical investigation possible.

Given the working assumption that we cannot investigate anything without examining who is doing the investigating, cultural studies necessarily will be an activity defined by specific cultural subjects with specific *interests*. In the absence of a universal or neutral way of studying culture, in the absence of a ground outside of the positions of discourse and interests, there is also no such thing as an innocent observer of culture. As Williams notes, no one can possibly be unaligned and unpositioned culturally. In the "The Principle of Reason: The University in the Eyes of Its Pupils" (in "Deconstruction and Poststructuralism") Derrida makes the same argument about the structure and alignment of institutional knowledge. As we discuss in "Notes Toward a Definition of Cultural Studies," the Western university as a site for producing knowledge is a product of the eighteenth-century separation of pure knowledge from ethics, disinterested inquiry from the world of practicality. Aesthetics and art occupy a kind of middle ground between disinterestedness and practicality. They are not categorizable purely as knowledge or practical activity (ethics and/or power). They function, though, as the mediators between and, in this way, provide an important bridge between, knowledge and power. The object of cultural studies as a form of knowledge and the activity of knowing—the difficulty of precisely formulating this conjunction and its uneasy elements is the double task of cultural studies—are the "texts" of social and cultural experience. These texts are located in precisely that material and historical situation between knowledge and power. Linking knowledge and power engenders a new organization of academic "disciplines" and can create a definite sense of what it means for an inquiry to be *interested*. "Knowing" anything, in this engaged sense that characterizes cultural studies, necessarily involves the specific relation of ethical responsibility in relation to the discourse of inquiry itself.

To speak of "interests" in this way—as Hall notes in "Cultural Studies and Its

Theoretical Legacies"—is to admit that inquiry has "some stake in the choices it makes." To have a stake in choices, in the sense of preferring one social outcome over another in a particular set of conditions, is, as Hall says, "the 'political' aspect of cultural studies," the way in which it is situated in power relations. This connection with the issue of power does not hold just for the large, institutional dimensions of inquiry but includes "the question of the personal as political." This is a "radical expansion of the notion of power" in that it does include the personal and private realms of cultural manifestation. By "personal" is meant particularly the areas of "gender and sexuality [as part of] the understanding of power itself." So if cultural studies is professedly "subjective" and "interested" in this manner, then it can be said to be ideologically oriented. Part of knowing itself as a subject necessarily involves cultural studies' acknowledgment of its interests in the contest of competing interests, "the contest for forms and values" Said describes. Cultural studies of course has an agenda and an aim, "some will to connect," as Hall says. Whereas rational and traditional scientific inquiry stipulates empirical and detached observation as instrumental to the testing of an hypothesis, in cultural studies there must instead be an acknowledgment of the participants' interests within a historical frame—as well as cultural studies' own interests as a project.

In this formulation of the cultural-studies agenda there is the acknowledgment of the constructed subject within a cultural and historical context—cultural studies as always "subjective." That acknowledgment of subjectivity then facilitates an awareness of the social and economic ties that define an interested participant. Cultural critique is then maintained as an actual possibility through a continual resituating of the inquiring subject as a particular organization of power within discourse—cultural studies inquiry, in other words, as an interested and purposeful activity, always ideologically oriented. Indeed the power to speak about oppression comes from the recognition of economic and ideological interests within history, one's commitment, finally, to the choice of how we want our lives to be and the responsibility defined by that commitment.

## CULTURE AS LOCAL

Thus far we have outlined an abstract and rather broad critical agenda for cultural studies. The actual work in this field is often controversial and can present formidable difficulties. Meaghan Morris, in "Banality in Cultural Studies," investigates the manner in which "theory" can function as "an objectified and objectifying . . . force strategically engaged in an ever more intense process of commodification." She discusses the influential work of Jean Baudrillard and finds that the "banality" of contemporary culture "is associated, quite clearly and conventionally, with negative aspects of media . . . a gross platitudinousness of the all-pervasive present." The banality of culture is judged negatively according to the " 'aristocratic' ideal of maintaining an elite, arbitrary, and avowedly artificial order." "Baudrillard's theory calls for," she writes, "an aesthetic order (fatality) to deal with mass cultural anarchy (banality)." Her concern is that cultural studies could succeed as a coherent practice but fail as actual cultural critique. This could happen because the elitism of its theory could have the effect "of discrediting" the "voices of grumpy feminists and cranky leftists." "To discredit such voices is, as I understand it," she goes on, "one of the immediate political functions of the current boom in cultural studies (as distinct from the intentionality of projects invested by it)."

At present most people are cautious about making claims for the achievements of cultural studies. Cultural studies is not a "school" in any formal sense, and it can be called a "movement" in the loosest configuration only dating back to the late 1950s and early 1960s. Along with the critiques of gender studies and the "New Historicism," though, cultural-studies critics have succeeded in foregrounding pressing issues arising out of the articulation of culture and politics. They have elaborated strategies for viewing culture ideologically and dynamically without the reductionism of an old-fashioned and oversimplified base/superstructure relationship. They have helped us, in fact, to rethink the very nature of culture and its institutions, to understand cultural and political choices and how we make them, and generally, to render problematic prior assumptions about the separation of culture and politics. In the new cultural-studies criticism there is the prospect (and not necessarily the full "realization") of a profoundly historical and critical understanding of the relationships of power and culture, and it is for this reason, above all, that cultural studies has attracted such interest.

Still, the reasons for this interest are not always the "same." In this book the local arguments and critiques of received ideas (which are often encountered under the form of disinterested, "aesthetic" ideas) by Showalter, Christian, Said, Gates, Johnson, Moi, Morris, Clifford, Derrida, Warner, and many others often have greatly varied goals and agendas. These differences, we think, have allowed cultural studies to revitalize the reading and writing of literary criticism in remarkable ways. Most importantly, cultural studies underlines the various *stakes* in reading and interpreting texts: how these activities, like the "knowledge" they discover and define, make a difference in the world. These stakes are not always congruent or compatible: J. Hillis Miller's attempt to acknowledge the uncanny in reading can (and has) seemed to some as a form of quietism in a world of great social injustice; Showalter's attempt to delineate a feminist criticism can (and has) seemed to some as an activity for privileged, middle-class women; Derrida's critique of reason can (and has) seemed to some as simple, irresponsible wordplay; Christian's attempt to define "theory" as always tending toward the monolithic can (and has) seemed to some as participating in mystification; and even our raising so many of these issues associated with cultural studies in this book and in "Notes Towards a Definition of Cultural Studies" can (and has) seemed to some as participating in the ways "the current boom in cultural studies" blunts, as Morris says, other kinds of political action. For others, new contexts create new ways of understanding: for Paul de Man, for instance, the revelation of both his youthful sympathetic newspaper writings for the collaborationist press during the Nazi occupation of Belgium and his longtime silence about this matter has seemed to make an enormous difference in understanding the rigorous irony of his work. In some important way, these facts cannot be ignored.

Not ignoring local circumstances is a part of what the anthropologist Clifford Geertz means by describing the work of cultural studies as "thick description." However, as we have said, "description" itself—especially if it presents itself as objective and disinterested—is one of the things that cultural studies has asked us to reexamine in light of the question of the social and cultural function it serves. Such a reexamination is what we have called ethics, and ethics calls for procedures—this is part of our point about cultural studies more generally—that do not necessarily have to participate in the simple "wholeness" of what we have described as Enlightenment aesthetics. The parts of cultural studies don't have to hold together "for all time." Rather, like any genuine *ethical* activity, these studies cannot avoid the *local* and the judgment between local considerations and larger "cultural" concerns. As a local activity, its different activities have to be judged individually, in terms of the contest for forms and values in which each one participates. That is, rather than compatibility and congruence, cultural studies seeks local activity that can *always* be subject to critique because some particular form or value is always at stake, and as we said before, the stake of "knowledge" as an actual *act* in the world—*its* reexamination—is simultaneously an enablement to some who can perform it in a particular way and an impediment to others.

In this, we think, we can see one reason that cultural studies has been attractive to literary criticism: criticism, too, like cultural studies and like ethical considerations, is always *local*. As George Steiner asks in his "Introduction" to Walter Benjamin's *Origin of German Tragic Drama*, "how can there be a general and generalizing treatment of artistic-literary objects which are, by definition, unique?" The answer, as Said and others suggest in this book—we saw it also, in a very different way, in the definition of the humanities by the linguist, Louis Hjelmslev, in the General Introduction—is that for the "humanities," as for "culture," we do not have to choose, once and for all, between disinterested knowledge and interested action, between "thick" local description and generalizing "human" relevance. This is not to mystify or idealize "literature." Rather, literature is one place—there are many others—where the forms and values of human life lend themselves to analyses that make clear that knowledge and action, different levels of interest, various modes of interhuman relationships, and different grounds for association and activity are *alternative* responses to our experience. We can return to the site of that experience—in this case, "literature"—repeatedly as our interests change, our sympathy for others grows, our understanding of such terms as "knowledge" and "reading" alters, and as we sense that there is work in the world, locally and on larger scenes, that demands our responsibility. That these things and others are at stake in literary criticism marks the importance, we believe, of cultural studies, and we hope they can be found everywhere in this book.

**RELATED ESSAYS IN**
***CONTEMPORARY LITERARY CRITICISM***

Elaine Showalter, "Feminist Criticism in the Wilderness"
Barbara Christian, "The Race for Theory"
Henry Louis Gates, Jr., "Critical Fanonism"
Edward Said, "The Politics of Knowledge"

Barbara Johnson, "Apostrophe, Animation, and Abortion"
Jacques Derrida, "The Principle of Reason"
Toril Moi, "Representation of Patriarchy"
Walter Benjamin, "Theses on the Philosophy of History"
Michael Warner, "Homo-Narcissism; or, Heterosexuality"

## FURTHER READING

Brantlinger, Patrick, *Crusoe's Footprint: Cultural Studies in Britain and America* (New York: Routledge, 1990).

Davis, Robert Con, "Cixous, Spivak, and Oppositional Theory," in *Lit* 4/1 (1992): 29–42.

———, "Freud, Lacan, and the Subject of Cultural Studies," in *College Literature* 18, 2 (1991): 22–37.

———, *The Paternal Romance: Reading God-the-Father in Early Western Culture* (Urbana: University of Illinois Press, 1993).

D'Souza, Dinesh, *Illiberal Education: The Politics of Race and Sex on Campus* (New York: The Free Press, 1991).

Fish, Stanley, "Being Interdisciplinary Is So Very Hard to Do," in *Profession,* 89 (1989), 15–22.

Gates, Henry Louis, Jr., "Whose Canon Is It, Anyway?" in *New York Times,* 26 February 1989, 7, 1:1.

Giroux, Henry, David Shumway, Paul Smith, and James Sosnoski, "The Need for Cultural Studies: Resisting Intellectual and Oppositional Public Spheres," in *Dalhousie Review,* 64, 2 (Summer 1984), 472–486.

Grossberg, Lawrence, Cary Nelson and Paula Treichler, eds. *Cultural Studies* (New York: Routledge, 1992).

Hall, Stuart, "Cultural Studies and Its Theoretical Legacies," in *Cultural Studies,* eds. Lawrence Grossberg, Cary Nelson, and Paula A. Treichler (New York: Routledge, 1992), 277–294.

Heath, Stephen, *The Sexual Fix* (London: Macmillan, 1982).

Hebdige, Dick, *Subculture: The Meaning of Style* (New York: Routledge, 1979).

"Instituting Cultural Studies: A Dialogue with Gerald Graff, Janice Radway, Gita Rajan, and Robert Con Davis," in *Instituting Cultural Studies,* ed. Isaiah Smithson and Nancy Ruff (Champaign: University of Illinois Press, 1993).

Kamuf, Peggy, and Nancy K. Miller, "Parisian Letters: Between Feminism and Deconstruction," in *Conflicts in Feminism,* eds. Marianne Hirsch and Evelyn Fox Keller (New York: Routledge, 1990), 121–133.

Merod, Jim, *The Political Responsibility of the Critic* (Ithaca, NY: Cornell University Press, 1987).

Modleski, Tania, ed., *Studies in Entertainment: Critical Approaches to Mass Culture* (Bloomington: Indiana University Press, 1986).

Rodway, Janice, *Reading the Romance: Women, Patriarchy, and Popular Literature* (Chapel Hill: University of North Carolina Press, 1984).

Schleifer, Ronald, "The Institutions of Cultural Studies," in *Surfaces,* 2, 14 (1992), 3–22.

Schleifer, Ronald, Robert Con Davis, and Nancy Mergler, *Culture and Cognition* (Ithaca, NY: Cornell University Press, 1992).

Sheridan, Susan, *Grafts: Feminist Cultural Criticism* (New York: Verso, 1988).

Spivak, Gayatri Chakravorty, *In Other Worlds: Essays in Cultural Politics* (New York: Methuen, 1987).

————, *The Post-Colonial Critic: Interviews, Strategies, Dialogues,* ed. Sarah Harasym (New York: Routledge, 1990).

Steiner, George, "Introduction" to Walter Benjamin, *The Origin of German Tragic Drama* (London: Verso, 1977).

Stocking, George, *Race, Culture, and Evolution* (New York: Free Press, 1968).

Williams, Raymond, *Culture and Society*: 1780–1950 (New York: Columbia University Press, 1958).

————, *The Long Revolution* (New York: Columbia University Press, 1961).

————, *Marxism and Literature* (New York: Oxford University Press, 1977).

————, *Keywords,* revised edition (New York: Oxford University Press, 1983).

# 35

# Stuart Hall
# 1932–

Stuart Hall, who is currently a professor of sociology at the Open University, was for a decade the director of the Centre for Contemporary Cultural Studies in Birmingham. Much of Hall's work is done in the style of an interventionist who continually maneuvers himself into conflicts with cultural practices to manipulate understandings of "culture" as a phenomenon and as a field of study. He recently published *The Hard Road to Renewal: Thatcherism and the Crisis of the Left* and coauthored *Policing the Crisis. Culture, Media, Language, Resistance Through Rituals* and *New Times* are two of the numerous volumes he has coedited.

In "Cultural Studies: Two Paradigms" (1980), Hall identifies the "refounding" of cultural studies as "a distinct problematic" and emphasizes "significant *breaks*" of thought worth noting because of the "complex articulation between thinking and historical reality, reflected in the social categories of thought, and the continuous dialectic between 'knowledge' and 'power.' " He begins and ends this essay with the idea that there is "no single, unproblematic definition of 'culture' " and that "the concept remains a complex one—a site of convergent interest, rather than a logically or conceptually clarified idea." By analyzing the perspectives of Raymond Williams, E. P. Thompson, Lucien Goldmann, and Claude Lévi-Strauss, he overlaps and counterposes the precepts of culturalism and structuralism. Whether "experience" is seen as the ground or the effect of consciousness and social conditions, how to "think [about] *both* the specificity of different practices and the forms of the articulated unity they constitute," and how to deal with the "terrain marked out by those strongly coupled but not mutually exclusive concepts culture/ideology" are three primary questions Hall addresses here. In the course of this questioning, Hall calls on Lacanian psychoanalytic vocabularies and figures from Marxism (such as the "political economy" of culture and the metaphor of "base" and "superstructure") and pursues the "concrete analysis of particular ideological and discursive formations" that is often associated with Gramsci and Foucault. Hall doesn't describe either culturalism or structuralism as self-sufficient paradigms for the study of culture but instead believes that between them they begin to define the "space . . . and limits within which such a synthesis might be constituted." As "mutually reinforcing antagonisms," they ensure "no promise of an easy synthesis" but instead a recognition that questions and differing views of dialectics are fundamental in constructing the domain of cultural studies.

# Cultural Studies: Two Paradigms

In serious, critical intellectual work, there are no "absolute beginnings" and few unbroken continuities. Neither the endless unwinding of "tradition," so beloved on the History of Ideas, nor the absolutism of the "epistemological rupture," punctuating Thought into its "false" and "correct" parts, once favoured by the Althussereans, will do. What we find, instead, is an untidy but characteristic unevenness of development. What is important are the significant *breaks*—where old lines of thought are disrupted, older constellations displaced, and elements, old and new, are regrouped around a different set of premises and themes. Changes in a problematic do significantly transform the nature of the questions asked, the forms in which they are proposed, and the manner in which they can be adequately answered. Such shifts in perspective reflect, not only the results of an internal intellectual labour, but the manner in which real historical developments and transformations are appropriated in thought, and provide Thought, not with its guarantee of "correctness" but with its fundamental orientations, its conditions of existence. It is because of this complex articulation between thinking and historical reality, reflected in the social categories of thought, and the continuous dialectic between "knowledge" and "power," that the breaks are worth recording.

Cultural Studies, as a distinctive problematic, emerges from one such moment, in the mid-1950s. It was certainly not the first time that its characteristic questions had been put on the table. Quite the contrary. The two books which helped to stake out the new terrain—Hoggart's *Uses of Literacy* and Williams's *Culture and Society*—were both, in different ways, works (in part) of recovery. Hoggart's book took its reference from the "cultural debate," long sustained in the argu-

ments around "mass society" and in the tradition of work identified with Leavis and *Scrutiny*. *Culture and Society* reconstructed a long tradition which Williams defined as consisting, in sum, of "a record of a number of important and continuing reactions to . . . changes in our social, economic and political life" and offering "a special kind of map by means of which the nature of the changes can be explored" (p. 16). The books looked, at first, simply like updating of these earlier concerns, with reference to the post-war world. Retrospectively, their "breaks" with the traditions of thinking in which they were situated seem as important, if not more so, than their continuity with them. The *Uses of Literacy* did set out—much in the spirit of "practical criticism"—to "read" working class culture for the values and meanings embodied in its patterns and arrangements: as if they were certain kinds of "texts." But the application of this method to a living culture, and the rejection of the terms of the "cultural debate" (polarized around the high/low culture distinction) was a thorough-going departure. *Culture and Society*—in one and the same movement—constituted a tradition (*the* "culture-and-society" tradition), defined its "unity" (not in terms of common positions but in its characteristic concerns and the idiom of its inquiry), itself made a distinctive modern contribution to it—*and* wrote its epitaph. The Williams book which succeeded it—*The Long Revolution*—clearly indicated that the "culture-and-society" mode of reflection could only be completed and developed by moving somewhere else—to a significantly different kind of analysis. The very difficulty of some of the writing in *The Long Revolution*—with its attempt to "theorize" on the back of a tradition resolutely empirical and particularist in its idiom of thought, the experiential "thickness" of its concepts, and the generalizing movement of argument in it—stems, in part, from this determination to *move on* (Williams's work, right through to the most recent *Politics And Letters,* is exemplary precisely in its sustained developmentalism). The "good" and the "bad" parts of *The Long Revolution* both arise from its status as a work "of the break." The same could be said of E. P. Thompson's *Making of the English Working Class,* which belongs decisively to this "moment," even though, chronologically it appeared somewhat later. It, too, had been "thought" within certain distinctive historical traditions: English marxist historiography, Economic and "Labour" History. But in its foregrounding of the questions of culture, consciousness and experience, and its accent on agency, it also made a decisive break: with a certain kind of technological evolutionism, with a reductive economism and an organizational determinism. Between them, these three books constituted the *caesura* out of which—among other things—"Cultural Studies" emerged.

They were, of course, seminal and formative texts. They were not, in any sense, "textbooks" for the founding of a new academic sub-discipline: nothing could have been farther from their intrinsic impulse. Whether historical or contemporary in focus, they were, themselves, focused *by,* organized through and constituted responses to, the immediate pressures of the time and society in which they were written. They not only took "culture" seriously—as a dimension without which historical transformations, past and present, simply could not adequately be thought. They were, themselves, "cultural" in the *Culture and Society* sense. They forced on their readers' attention the proposition that "concentrated in the word *culture* are questions directly raised by the great historical changes which the changes in industry, democracy and class, in their own way, represent, and to which the changes in art are a

closely related response" (p. 16). This was a question for the 1960s and 70s, as well as the 1860s and 70s. And this is perhaps the point to note that this line of thinking was roughly coterminous with what has been called the "agenda" of the early New Left, to which these writers, in one sense or another, belonged, and whose texts these were. This connection placed the "politics of intellectual work" squarely at the centre of Cultural Studies from the beginning—a concern from which, fortunately, it has never been, and can never be, freed. In a deep sense, the "settling of accounts" in *Culture and Society,* the first part of *The Long Revolution,* Hoggart's densely particular, concrete study of some aspects of working-class culture and Thompson's historical reconstruction of the formation of a class culture and popular traditions in the 1790—1830 period formed, between them, the break, and defined the space from which a new area of study and practice opened. In terms of intellectual bearings and emphases, this was—if ever such a thing can be found—Cultural Studies moment of "refounding." The institutionalization of Cultural Studies—first, in the Centre at Birmingham, and then in courses and publications from a variety of sources and places—with its characteristic gains and losses, belongs to the 1960s and later.

"Culture" was the site of the convergence. But what definitions of this core concept emerged from this body of work? And, since this line of thinking has decisively shaped Cultural Studies, and represents the most formative *indigenous* or "native" tradition, around what space was its concerns and concepts unified? The fact is that no single, unproblematic definition of "culture" is to be found here. The concept remains a complex one—a site of convergent interests, rather than a logically or conceptually clarified idea. This "richness" is an area of continuing tension and difficulty in the field. It might be useful, therefore, briefly to resume the characteristic stresses and emphases through which the concept has arrived at its present state of (in)-determinacy. (The characterizations which follow are necessarily crude and over-simplified, synthesizing rather than carefully analytic.) Two main problematics only are discussed.

Two rather different ways of conceptualizing "culture" can be drawn out of the many suggestive formulations in Raymond Williams's *Long Revolution*. The first relates "culture" to the sum of the available descriptions through which societies make sense of and reflect their common experiences. This definition takes up the earlier stress on "ideas", but subjects it to a thorough reworking. The conception of "culture" is itself democratized and socialized. It no longer consists of the sum of the "best that has been thought and said," regarded as the summits of an achieved civilization—that ideal of perfection to which, in earlier usage, all aspired. Even "art"—assigned in the earlier framework a privileged position, as touchstone of the highest values of civilization—is now redefined as only one, special, form of a general social process: the giving and taking of meanings, and the slow development of "common" meanings—a common culture: "culture," in this special sense, "is ordinary" (to borrow the title of one of Williams's earliest attempts to make his general position more widely accessible). If even the highest, most refined of descriptions offered in works of literature are also "part of the general process which creates conventions and institutions, through which the meanings that are valued by the community are shared and made active" (p. 55), then there is no way in which this process can be hived off or distinguished or set apart from the other practices of the historical process: "Since our way of seeing things is literally our way of living, the process of communication is in fact the process of community: the sharing of common meanings, and thence common activities and pur-

poses; the offering, reception and comparison of new meanings, leading to tensions and achievements of growth and change" (p. 55). Accordingly, there is no way in which the communication of descriptions, understood in this way, can be set aside and compared externally with other things. "If the art is part of society, there is no solid whole, outside it, to which, by the form of our question, we concede priority. The art is there, as an activity, with the production, the trading, the politics, the raising of families. To study the relations adequately we must study them actively, seeing all activities as particular and contemporary forms of human energy."

If this first emphasis takes up and re-works the connotation of the term "culture" with the domain of "ideas," the second emphasis is more deliberately anthropological, and emphasizes that aspect of "culture" which refers to social *practices*. It is from this second emphasis that the somewhat simplified definition—"culture is a whole way of life"—has been rather too neatly abstracted. Williams did relate this aspect of the concept to the more "documentary"—that is, descriptive, even ethnographic—usage of the term. But the earlier definition seems to me the more central one, into which "way of life" is integrated. The important point in the argument rests on the active and indissoluble relationships between elements or social practices normally separated out. It is in *this* context that the "theory of culture" is defined as "the study of relationships between elements in a whole way of life." "Culture" is not *a* practice; nor is it simply the descriptive sum of the "mores and folkways" of societies—as it tended to become in certain kinds of anthropology. It is threaded through *all* social practices, and is the sum of their inter-relationship. The question of what, then, is studied, and how, resolves itself. The "culture" is those patterns of organization, those characteristic forms of human energy which can be discovered as revealing themselves—in "unexpected identities and correspondences" as well as in "discontinuities of an unexpected kind" (p. 63)—within or underlying *all* social practices. The analysis of culture is, then, "the attempt to discover the nature of the organization which is the complex of these relationships." It begins with "the discovery of patterns of a characteristic kind." One will discover them, not in the art, production, trading, politics, the raising of families, treated as separate activities, but through "studying a general organization in a particular example" (p. 61). Analytically, one must study "the relationships between these patterns." The purpose of the analysis is to grasp how the interactions between all these practices and patterns are lived and experienced as a whole, in any particular period. This is its "structure of feeling."

It is easier to see what Williams was getting at, and why he was pushed along this path, if we understand what were the problems he addressed, and what pitfalls he was trying to avoid. This is particularly necessary because *The Long Revolution* (like many of Williams's work[s]) carries on a submerged, almost "silent" dialogue with alternative positions, which are not always as clearly identified as one would wish. There is a clear engagement with the "idealist" and "civilizing" definitions of culture—both the equation of "culture" with *ideas,* in the idealist tradition; and the assimilation of culture to an *ideal,* prevalent in the elitist terms of the "cultural debate." But there is also a more extended engagement with certain kinds of Marxism, against which Williams's definitions are consciously pitched. He is arguing against the literal operations of the base/superstructure metaphor, which in classical Marxism ascribed the domain of ideas and of meanings to the "superstructures," themselves conceived as merely reflective of and determined in some simple fashion by "the base"; without a social effectivity of their own. That is to say, his argument is constructed against a vulgar material-

ism and an economic determinism. He offers, instead, a radical interactionism: in effect, the interaction of all practices in and with one another, skirting the problem of determinacy. The distinctions between practices is overcome by seeing them all as variant forms of *praxis*—of a general human activity and energy. The underlying patterns which distinguish the complex of practices in any specific society at any specific time are the characteristic "forms of its organization" which underlie them all, and which can therefore be traced in each.

There have been several, radical revisions of this early position: and each has contributed much to the redefinition of what Cultural Studies is and should be. We have acknowledged already the exemplary nature of Williams's project, in constantly rethinking and revising older arguments—in going on thinking. Nevertheless, one is struck by a marked line of continuity through these seminal revisions. One such moment is the occasion of his recognition of Lucien Goldmann's work, and through him, of the array of marxist thinkers who had given particular attention to superstructural forms and whose work began, for the first time, to appear in English translation in the mid-1960s. The contrast between the alternative marxist traditions which sustained writers like Goldman and Lukacs, as compared with Williams's isolated position and the impoverished Marxist tradition he had to draw on, is sharply delineated. But the points of convergence—both what they are against, and what they are about—are identified in ways which are not altogether out of line with his earlier arguments. Here is the negative, which he sees as linking his work to Goldmann's: "I came to believe that I had to give up, or at least to leave aside, what I knew as the Marxist tradition: to attempt to develop a theory of social totality; to see the study of culture as the study of relations between elements in a whole way of life; to find ways of studying structure . . . which could stay in touch with and illuminate particular art works and forms, but also forms and relations of more general social life; to replace the formula of base and superstructure with the more active idea of a field of mutually if also unevenly determining forces" (*NLR* 67, May–June 1971). And here is the positive—the point where the convergence is marked between Williams's "structure of feeling" and Goldmann's "genetic structuralism": "I found in my own work that I had to develop the idea of a structure of feeling . . . But then I found Goldmann beginning . . . from a concept of structure which contained, in itself, a relation between social and literary facts. This relation, he insisted, was not a matter of content, but of mental structures: "categories which simultaneously organize the empirical consciousness of a particular social group, and the imaginative world created by the writer." By definition, these structures are not individually but collectively created. The stress there on the interactivity of practices and on the underlying totalities, and the homologies between them, is characteristic and significant. "A correspondence of content between a writer and his world is less significant than this correspondence of organization, of structure."

A second such "moment" is the point where Williams really takes on board E. P. Thompson's critique of *The Long Revolution* (cf. the review in *NLR* 9 and 10)—that no "whole way of life" is without its dimension of struggle and confrontation between opposed *ways* of life—and attempts to rethink the key issues of determination and domination via Gramsci's concept of "hegemony." This essay ("Base and Superstructure," *NLR* 82, 1973) is a seminal one, especially in its elaboration of dominant, residual and emergent cultural practices, and its return to the problematic of determinacy as "limits and pressures." None the less, the earlier emphases recur, with force: "we cannot separate literature and art from other kinds of social practice, in such a way as to make them subject to quite special and distinct laws." And, "no mode of production, and therefore no dominant society or order of society, and therefore no dominant culture, in reality exhausts human practice, human energy, human intention." And this note is carried forward—indeed, it is radically accented—in Williams's most sustained and succinct recent statement of his position: the masterly condensations of *Marxism and Literature*. Against the structuralist emphasis on the specificity and "autonomy" of practices, and their analytic separation of societies into their discrete instances, Williams's stress is on "constitutive activity" in general, on "sensuous human activity, as practice," from Marx's first "thesis" on Feuerbach; on different practices conceived as a "whole indissoluble practice"; on "totality". "Thus, contrary to one development in Marxism, it is not 'the base' and 'the superstructure' that need to be studied, but specific and indissoluble real processes, within which the decisive relationship, from a Marxist point of view, is that expressed by the complex idea of 'determination' " (*M & L,* pp. 30–31, 82).

At one level, Williams's and Thompson's work can only be said to converge around the terms of the same problematic through the operation of a violent and schematically dichotomous theorization. The organizing terrain of Thompson's work—classes as relations, popular struggle, and historical forms of consciousness, class cultures in their historical particularity—is foreign to the more reflective and "generalizing" mode in which Williams typically works. And the dialogue between them begins with a very sharp encounter. The review of *The Long Revolution,* which Thompson undertook, took Williams sharply to task for the evolutionary way in which culture as a "whole way of life" had been conceptualized; for his tendency to absorb conflicts between class cultures into the terms of an extended "conversation"; for his impersonal tone—above the contending classes, as it were; and for the imperializing sweep of his concept of "culture" (which, heterogeneously, swept everything into its orbit because it was the study of the interrelationships between the forms of energy and organization underlying *all* practices. But wasn't this—Thompson asked—where History came in?) Progressively, we can see how Williams has persistently rethought the terms of his original paradigm to take these criticisms into account—though this is accomplished (as it so frequently is in Williams) obliquely: via a particular appropriation of Gramsci, rather than in a more direct modification.

Thompson also operates with a more "classical" distinction than Williams, between "social being" and "social consciousness" (the terms he infinitely prefers, from Marx, to the more fashionable "base and superstructure"). Thus, where Williams insists on the absorption of all practices into the totality of "real, indissoluble practice," Thompson does deploy an older distinction between what is "culture" and what is "not culture." "Any theory of culture must include the concept of the dialectical interaction between culture and something that is *not* culture." Yet the definition of culture is not, after all, so far removed from Williams's: "We must suppose the raw material of life experience to be at one pole, and all the infinitely complex human disciplines and systems, articulate and inarticulate, formalised in institutions or dispersed in the least formal ways, which 'handle,' transmit or distort this raw material to be at the other." Similarly, with respect to the commonality of "practice" which underlies all the distinct practices: "It is the active process—which is at the same time the process through which men make their history—that I am insisting upon" (*NLR* 9, p. 33, 1961). And the two positions come closer together around—again—certain distinctive negatives and positives. Negatively, against the

"base/superstructure" metaphor, and a reductionist or "economistic" definition of determinacy. On the first: "The dialectical intercourse between social being and social consciousness—or between 'culture' and '*not* culture'—is at the heart of any comprehension of the historical process within the Marxist tradition. . . . The tradition inherits a dialectic that is right, but the particular mechanical metaphor through which it is expressed is wrong. This metaphor from constructional engineering . . . must in any case be inadequate to describe the flux of conflict, the dialectic of a changing social process. . . . All the metaphors which are commonly offered have a tendency to lead the mind into schematic modes and away from the interaction of being-consciousness." And on "reductionism": "Reductionism is a lapse in historical logic by which political or cultural events are 'explained' in terms of the class affiliations of the actors. . . . But the mediation between 'interest' and 'belief' was not through Nairn's 'complex of superstructures' but through the people themselves" ("Peculiarities of the English," *Socialist Register,* 1965, pp. 351–352). And, more positively—a simple statement which may be taken as defining virtually the whole of Thompson's historical work, from *The Making* to *Whigs and Hunters, The Poverty of Theory* and beyond—"capitalist society was founded upon forms of exploitation which are simultaneously economic, moral and cultural. Take up the essential defining productive relationship . . . and turn it round, and it reveals itself now in one aspect (wage-labour), now in another (an acquisitive ethos), and now in another (the alienation of such intellectual faculties as are not required by the worker in his productive role)" (ibid., p. 356).

Here, then, despite the many significant differences, is the outline of one significant line of thinking in Cultural Studies—some would say, *the* dominant paradigm. It stands opposed to the residual and merely-reflective rôle assigned to "the cultural." In its different ways, it conceptualizes culture as interwoven with all social practices; and those practices, in turn, as a common form of human activity: sensuous human praxis, the activity through which men and women make history. It is opposed to the base-superstructure way of formulating the relationship between ideal and material forces, especially where the "base" is defined as the determination by "the economic" in any simple sense. It prefers the wider formulation—the dialectic between social being and social consciousness: neither separable into its distinct poles (in some alternative formulations, the dialectic between "culture" and "non-culture"). It defines "culture" as *both* the meanings and values which arise amongst distinctive social groups and classes, on the basis of their given historical conditions and relationships, through which they "handle" and respond to the conditions of existence; *and* as the lived traditions and practices through which those "understandings" are expressed and in which they are embodied. Williams brings together these two aspects—definitions and ways of life—around the concept of "culture" itself. Thompson brings the two elements—consciousness and conditions—around the concept of "experience." Both positions entail certain difficult fluctuations around these key terms. Williams so totally absorbs "definitions of experience" into our "ways of living," and both into an indissoluble real material practice-in-general, as to obviate any distinction between "culture" and "not-culture." Thompson sometimes uses "experience" in the more usual sense of consciousness, as the collective ways in which men "handle, transmit or distort" their given conditions, the raw materials of life; sometimes as the domain of the "lived," the mid-term *between* "conditions" and "culture"; and sometimes as the objective conditions themselves—against which particular modes of consciousness are counterposed. But, whatever the terms, both

positions tend to read structures of relations in terms of how they are "lived" and "experienced." Williams's "structure of feeling"—with its deliberate condensation of apparently incompatible elements—is characteristic. But the same is true of Thompson, despite his far fuller historical grasp of the "givenness" or structuredness of the relations and conditions into which men and women necessarily and involuntarily enter, and his clearer attention to the determinacy of productive and exploitative relations under capitalism. This is a consequence of giving culture-consciousness and experience so pivotal a place in the analysis. The *experiential pull* in this paradigm, and the emphasis on the creative and on historical agency, constitutes the two key elements in the *humanism* of the position outlined. Each, consequently accords "experience" an authenticating position in any cultural analysis. It is, ultimately, where and how people experience their conditions of life, define them and respond to them, which, for Thompson defines why every mode of production is also a culture, and every struggle between classes is always also a struggle between cultural modalities; and which, for Williams, is what a "cultural analysis," in the final instance, should deliver. In "experience," all the different practices intersect; within "culture" the different practices interact—even if on an uneven and mutually determining basis. This sense of cultural totality—of *the whole* historical process—over-rides any effort to keep the instances and elements distinct. Their real interconnection, under given historical conditions, must be matched by a totalizing movement "in thought," in the analysis. It establishes for both the strongest protocols against any form of analytic abstraction which distinguishes practices, or which sets out to test the "actual historical movement" in all its intertwined complexity and particularity by any more sustained logical or analytical operation. These positions, especially in their more concrete historical rendering (*The Making, The Country and the City*) are the very opposite of a Hegelian search for underlying Essences. Yet, in their tendency to reduce practices to *praxis* and to find common and homologous "forms" underlying the most apparently differentiated areas, their movement is "essentialising." They have a particular way of understanding the totality—though it is with a small "t," concrete and historically determinate, uneven in its correspondences. They understand it "expressively." And since they constantly inflect the more traditional analysis towards the experiential level, or read the other structures and relations downwards from the vantage point of how they are "lived," they are properly (even if not adequately or fully) characterized as "culturalist" in their emphasis: even when all the caveats and qualifications against a too rapid "dichotomous theorizing" have been entered. (Cf. for "culturalism," Richard Johnson's two seminal articles on the operation of the paradigm: in "Histories of Culture/Theories of Ideology," *Ideology and Cultural Production,* eds. M. Barrett, P. Corrigan *et al.,* Croom Helm, 1979; and "Three Problematics" in *Working Class Culture:* Clarke, Critcher and Johnson, Hutchinsons and CCCS, 1979. For the dangers in "dichotomous theorizing," cf. the Introduction, "Representation and Cultural Production," to Barrett, Corrigan *et al.*)

The "culturalist" strand in Cultural Studies was interrupted by the arrival on the intellectual scene of the "structuralisms." These, possibly more varied than the "culturalisms," nevertheless shared certain positions and orientations in common which makes their designation under a single title not altogether misleading. It has been remarked that whereas the "culturalist" paradigm can be defined without requiring a conceptual reference to the term "ideology" (the *word,* of course, does appear: but it is not a key concept), the "structuralist" interventions have been largely articulated around the concept of "ideology": in keeping with its more impeccably Marxist lineage, "culture" does not figure so prominently. Whilst this may be true of the Marxist structuralists, it is at best less than half the truth about the structuralist enterprise as such. But it is now a common error to condense the latter exclusively around the impact of Althusser and all that has followed in the wake of his interventions—where "ideology" has played a seminal, but modulated rôle: and to omit the significance of Lévi-Strauss. Yet, in strict historical terms, it was Lévi-Strauss, and the early semiotics, which made the first break. And though the Marxist structuralisms have superseded the latter, they owed, and continue to owe, an immense theoretical debt (often fended off or down-graded into footnotes, in the search for a retrospective orthodoxy) to his work. It was Lévi-Strauss's structuralism which, in its appropriation of the linguistic paradigm, after Saussure, offered the promise to the "human sciences of culture" of a paradigm capable of rendering them scientific and rigorous in a thoroughly new way. And when, in Althusser's work, the more classical Marxist themes were recovered, it remained the case that Marx was "read"—and reconstituted—through the terms of the linguistic paradigm. In *Reading Capital,* for example, the case is made that the mode of production—to coin a phrase—could best be understood as if "structured like a language" (through the selective combination of invariant elements). The a-historical and synchronic stress, against the historical emphases of "culturalism," derived from a similar source. So did a preoccupation with "the social, *sui generis*"—used not adjectivally but substantively: a usage Lévi-Strauss derived, not from Marx, but from Durkheim (the Durkheim who analysed the social categories of thought—e.g. in *Primitive Classification*—rather than the Durkheim of *The Division of Labour,* who became the founding father of American structural-functionalism).

Lévi-Strauss did, on occasion, toy with certain Marxist formulations. Thus, "Marxism, if not Marx himself, has too commonly reasoned as though practices followed directly from praxis. Without questioning the undoubted primacy of infrastructures, I believe that there is always a mediator between praxis and practices, namely, the conceptual scheme by the operation of which matter and form, neither with any independent existence, are realized as structures, that is as entities which are both empirical and intelligible." But this—to coin another phrase—was largely "gestural." This structuralism shared with culturalism a radical break with the terms of the base/superstructure metaphor, as derived from the simpler parts of the *German Ideology*. And, though "It is to this theory of the superstructures, scarcely touched on by Marx" to which Lévi-Strauss aspired to contribute, his contribution was such as to break in a radical way with its whole terms of reference, as finally and irrevocably as the "culturalists" did. Here—and we must include Althusser in this characterization—culturalists and structuralists alike ascribed to the domains hitherto defined as "superstructural" a specificity and effectivity, a constitutive primacy, which pushed them beyond the terms of reference of "base" and "superstructure." Lévi-Strauss and Althusser, too, were anti-reductionist and anti-economist in their very cast of thought, and critically attacked that transitive causality which, for so long, had passed itself off as "classical Marxism."

Lévi-Strauss worked consistently with the term "culture." He regarded "ideologies" as of much lesser importance: mere "secondary rationalizations." Like Williams and Goldmann, he worked, not at the level of correspondences between the *content* of a practice, but at the level of their forms and structures. But the manner in which these were conceptualized were altogether at variance with either the "culturalism" of Williams or Goldmann's "genetic structuralism." This di-vergence can be identified in three distinct ways. First, he conceptualized "culture" as the categories and frameworks in thought and language through which different societies classified out their conditions of existence—above all (since Levi-Strauss was an anthropologist), the relations between the human and the natural worlds. Second, he thought of the manner and practice through which these categories and mental frameworks were produced and transformed, largely on an analogy with the ways in which language itself—the principal medium of "culture"—operated. He identified what was specific to them and their operation as the "production of meaning": they were, above all, *signifying* practices. Third, after some early flirtations with Durkheim and Mauss's social categories of thought, he largely gave up the question of the relation *between* signifying and non-signifying practices—between "culture" and "not-culture," to use other terms—for the sake of concentrating on the *internal* relations within signifying practices by means of which the categories of meaning were produced. This left the question of determinacy, of totality, largely in abeyance. The causal logic of determinacy was abandoned in favour of a structuralist causality—a logic of *arrangement,* of internal relations, of articulation of parts within a structure. Each of these aspects is also positively present in Althusser's work and that of the Marxist structuralists, even when the terms of reference had been regrounded in Marx's "immense theoretical revolution." In one of Althusser's seminal formulations about ideology—defined as the themes, concepts and representations through which men and women "live," in an imaginary relation, their relation to their real conditions of existence—we can see the skeleton outline of Levi-Strauss's "conceptual schemes between praxis and practices." "Ideologies" are here being conceptualized, not as the contents and surface forms of ideas, but as the unconscious categories through which conditions are represented and lived. We have already commented on the active presence in Althusser's thinking of the linguistic paradigm—the second element identified above. And though, in the concept of "over-determination"—one of his most seminal and fruitful contributions—Althusser did return to the problems of the relations *between* practices and the question of determinacy (proposing, incidentally, a thoroughly novel and highly suggestive reformulation, which has received far too little subsequent attention), he did tend to reinforce the "relative autonomy" of different practices, and their internal specificities, conditions and effects at the expense of an "expressive" conception of the totality, with its typical homologies and correspondences.

Aside from the wholly distinct intellectual and conceptual universes within which these alternative paradigms developed, there were certain points where, despite their apparent overlaps, culturalism and structuralism were starkly counterposed. We can identify this counterposition at one of its sharpest points precisely around the concept of "experience," and the rôle the term played in each perspective. Whereas, in "culturalism," experience was the ground—the terrain of "the lived"—where consciousness and conditions intersected, structuralism insisted that "experience" could not, by definition, be the ground of anything, since one could only "live" and experience one's conditions *in and through* the categories, classifications and frameworks of the culture. These categories, however, did not arise from or in experience: rather, experience was their "effect." The culturalists had defined the forms of consciousness and culture as collective. But they had stopped far short of the radical proposition that, in culture and in language, the subject was "spoken by" the categories of culture in which he/she thought, rather than "speaking them." These categories were, however, not merely collective rather than individual

productions: they were *unconscious* structures. That is why, though Lévi-Strauss spoke only of "Culture," his concept provided the basis for an easy translation, by Althusser, into the conceptual framework of ideology: "Ideology is indeed a system of 'representations,' but in the majority of cases these representations have nothing to do with 'consciousness': . . . it is above all as structures that they impose on the vast majority of men, not via their 'consciousness' . . . it is within this ideological unconsciousness that men succeed in altering the 'lived' relation between them and the world and acquiring that new form of specific unconsciousness called 'consciousness' " (*For Marx,* p. 233). It was, in this sense, that "experience" was conceived, not as an authenticating source but as an effect: not as a reflection of the real but as an "imaginary relation." It was only a short step—the one which separates *For Marx* from the "Ideological State Apparatuses" essay—to the development of an account of how this "imaginary relation" served, not simply the dominance of a ruling class over a dominated one, but (through the reproduction of the relations of production, and the constitution of labour-power in a form fit for capitalist exploitation) the expanded reproduction of the mode of production itself. Many of the other lines of divergence between the two paradigms flow from this point: the conception of "men" as bearers of the structures that speak and place them, rather than as active agents in the making of their own history; the emphasis on a structural rather than a historical "logic"; the preoccupation with the constitution—in "theory"—of a non-ideological, scientific discourse; and hence the privileging of conceptual work and of Theory as guaranteed; the recasting of history as a march of the structures (cf. passim, *The Poverty of Theory*): the structuralist "machine". . . .

There is no space in which to follow through the many ramifications which have followed from the development of one or other of these "master paradigms" in Cultural Studies. Though they by no means account for all, or even nearly all, of the many strategies adopted, it is fair to say that, between them, they have defined the principal lines of development in the field. The seminal debates have been polarized around their thematics; some of the best concrete work has flowed from the efforts to set one or other of these paradigms to work on particular problems and materials. Characteristically—the sectarian and self-righteous climate of critical intellectual work in England being what it is, and its dependency being so marked—the arguments and debates have most frequently been over-polarized into their extremes. At these extremities, they frequently appear only as mirror-reflections or inversions of one another. Here, the broad typologies we have been working with—for the sake of convenient exposition—become the prison-house of thought.

Without suggesting that there can be any easy synthesis between them, it might usefully be said at this point that neither "culturalism" nor "structuralism" is, in its present manifestation, adequate to the task of constructing the study of culture as a conceptually clarified and theoretically informed domain of study. Nevertheless, something fundamental to it emerges from a rough comparison of their respective strengths and limitations.

The great strength of the structuralisms is their stress on "determinate conditions." They remind us that unless the dialectic really can be held, in any particular analysis, between both halves of the proposition—that "men make history . . . on the basis of conditions which are not of their making"—the result will inevitably be a naïve humanism, with its necessary consequence: a voluntarist and populist political practice. The fact that "men" can become conscious of their conditions, organize to struggle against them and in fact transform them—without which no active politics can even be conceived, let alone practised—must not be allowed to override the awareness of the fact that, in capitalist relations, men and women are placed and positioned in relations which constitute them as agents. "Pessimism of the intellect, optimism of the will" is a better starting point than a simple heroic affirmation. Structuralism does enable us to begin to think—as Marx insisted—of the *relations* of a structure on the basis of something other than their reduction to relationships between "people." This was Marx's privileged level of abstraction: that which enabled him to break with the obvious but incorrect starting point of "political economy"—bare individuals.

But this connects with a second strength: the recognition by structuralism not only of the necessity of abstraction as the instrument of thought through which "real relations" are appropriated, but also of the presence, in Marx's work, of a continuous and complex movement *between different levels of abstraction*. It is, of course, the case—as "culturalism" argues—that, in historical reality, practices do not appear neatly distinguished out into their respective instances. However, to think about or to analyse the complexity of the real, the act of practice of thinking is required; and this necessitates the use of the power of abstraction and analysis, the formation of concepts with which to cut into the complexity of the real, in order precisely to reveal and bring to light relationships and structures which cannot be visible to the naïve naked eye, and which can neither present nor authenticate themselves: "In the analysis of economic forms, neither microscopes nor chemical reagents are of assistance. The power of abstraction must replace both." Of course, structuralism has frequently taken this proposition to its extreme. Because thought is impossible without "the power of abstraction," it has confused this with giving an absolute primacy to the level of the formation of concepts—and at the highest, most abstract level of abstraction only: Theory with a capital "T" then becomes judge and jury. But this is precisely to lose the insight just won from Marx's own practice. For it is clear in, for example, *Capital,* that the *method*—whilst, of course, taking place "in thought" (as Marx asked in the 1857 Introduction, where else?)—rests, not on the simple exercise of abstraction but on the movement and relations which the argument is constantly establishing between *different levels* of abstraction: at each, the premises in play must be distinguished from those which—for the sake of the argument—have to be held constant. The movement to another level of magnification (to deploy the microscope metaphor) requires the specifying of further conditions of existence not supplied at a previous, more abstract level: in this way, by successive abstractions of different magnitudes, to *move towards* the constitution, the *reproduction,* of "the concrete in thought" as an effect of a certain kind of thinking. This method is adequately represented in *neither* the absolutism of Theoretical Practice, in structuralism, nor in the anti-abstraction "Poverty of Theory" position into which, in reaction, culturalism appears to have been driven or driven itself. Nevertheless it is intrinsically *theoretical,* and must be. Here, structuralism's insistence that thought does not reflect reality, but is articulated on and appropriates it, is a necessary starting point. An adequate *working through* of the consequences of this argument might begin to produce a method which takes us outside the permanent oscillations between abstraction/anti-abstraction and the false dichotomies of Theoreticism *vs.* Empiricism which have both marked and disfigured the structuralism/culturalism encounter to date.

Structuralism has another strength in its conception of "the whole." There is a sense in which, though culturalism constantly insists on the radical particularity of its practices, its mode of conceptualizing the "totality" has something of the complex simplicity of an expressive totality behind it. Its complexity is constituted by the fluidity with which practices move into and out of one another: but this complexity is reducible, conceptually, to the "simplicity" of praxis—human activity, as such—in which the same contradictions constantly appear, homologously reflected in each. Structuralism goes too far in erecting the machine of a "Structure," with its self-generating propensities (a "Spinozean eternity," whose function is only the sum of its effects: a truly structural*ist* deviation), equipped with its distinctive instances. Yet it represents an advance over culturalism in the conception it has of the necessary *complexity* of the unity of a structure (over-determination being a more successful way of thinking this complexity than the combinatory invariance of structuralist causality). Moreover, it has the conceptual ability to think of a unity which is constructed through the *differences* between, rather than the homology of, practices. Here, again, it has won a critical insight about Marx's method: one thinks of the complex passages of the 1857 Introduction to the *Grundrisse* where Marx demonstrates how it is possible to think of the "unity" of a social formation as constructed, not out of identity but out of *difference.* Of course, the stress on difference can—and has—led the structuralisms into a fundamental conceptual heterogeneity, in which all sense of structure and totality is lost. Foucault and other post-Althussereans have taken this devious path into the absolute, not the relative, autonomy of practices, via their necessary heterogeneity and "necessary non-correspondence." But the emphasis on unity-in-difference, on complex unity—Marx's concrete as the "unity of many determinations"—can be worked in another, and ultimately more fruitful direction: towards the problematic of relative autonomy and "over-determination," and the study of *articulation*. Again, articulation contains the danger of a high formalism. But it also has the considerable advantage of enabling us to think of how specific practices (articulated around contradictions which do not all arise in the same way, at the same point, in the same moment), can nevertheless be thought *together*. The structuralist paradigm thus does—if properly developed— enable us to begin really to *conceptualize* the specificity of different practices (analytically distinguished, abstracted out), without losing its grip on the ensemble which they constitute. Culturalism constantly affirms the specificity of different practices—"culture" must not be absorbed into "the economic": but it lacks an adequate way of establishing this specificity theoretically.

The third strength which structuralism exhibits lies in its decentering of "experience" and its seminal work in elaborating the neglected category of "ideology." It is difficult to conceive of a Cultural Studies thought within a Marxist paradigm which is innocent of the category of "ideology." Of course, culturalism constantly make[s] reference to this concept: but it does not in fact lie at the centre of its conceptual universe. The authenticating power and reference of "experience" imposes a barrier between culturalism and a proper conception of "ideology." Yet, without it, the effectivity of "culture" for the reproduction of a particular mode of production cannot be grasped. It is true that there is a marked tendency in the more recent structuralist conceptualisations of "ideology" to give it a functionalist reading—as the necessary cement of the social formation. From this position, it is indeed impossible—as culturalism would correctly argue—to conceive either of ideologies which are not, by definition, "dominant": or of the concept of struggle (the latter's appearance in Althusser's famous ISA's article being—to coin yet another phrase—largely "gestural"). Nevertheless, work is already being done which sug-

gests ways in which the field of ideology may be adequately conceptualized as a terrain of struggle (through the work of Gramsci, and more recently, of Laclau), and these have structuralist rather than culturalist bearings.

Culturalism's strengths can almost be derived from the weaknesses of the structuralist position already noted, and from the latter's strategic absences and silences. It has insisted, correctly, on the affirmative moment of the development of conscious struggle and organization as a necessary element in the analysis of history, ideology and consciousness: against its persistent down-grading in the structuralist paradigm. Here, again, it is largely Gramsci who has provided us with a set of more refined terms through which to link the largely "unconscious" and given cultural categories of "common sense" with the formation of more active and organic ideologies, which have the capacity to intervene in the ground of common sense and popular traditions and, through such interventions, to organize masses of men and women. In this sense, culturalism *properly* restores the dialectic between the unconsciousness of cultural categories and the moment of conscious organization: even if, in its characteristic movement, it has tended to match structuralism's over-emphasis on "conditions" with an altogether too-inclusive emphasis on "consciousness." It therefore not only recovers— as the necessary moment of any analysis— the process by means of which classes-in-themselves, defined primarily by the way in which economic relations position "men" as agents—become active historical and political forces—for-themselves: it also—against its own anti-theoretical good sense—*requires* that, when properly developed, each moment must be understood in terms of the level of abstraction at which the analysis is operating. Again, Gramsci has begun to point a way through this false polarization in his discussion of "the passage between the structure and the sphere of the complex superstructures," and its distinct forms and moments.

We have concentrated in this argument largely on a characterization of what seem to us to be the two seminal paradigms at work in Cultural Studies. Of course, they are by no means the only active ones. New developments and lines of thinking are by no means adequately netted with reference to them. Nevertheless, these paradigms can, in a sense, be deployed to measure what appear to us to be the radical weaknesses or inadequacies of those which offer themselves as alternative rallying-points. Here, briefly, we identify three.

The first is that which follows on from Levi-Strauss, early semiotics and the terms of the linguistic paradigm, and the centering on "signifying practices," moving by way of psychoanalytic concepts and Lacan to a radical recentering of virtually the whole terrain of Cultural Studies around the terms "discourse" and "the subject." One way of understanding this line of thinking is to see it as an attempt to fill that empty space in early structuralism (of both the Marxist and non-Marxist varieties) where, in earlier discourses, "the subject" and subjectivity might have been expected to appear but did not. This is, of course, precisely one of the key points where culturalism brings its pointed criticisms to bear on structuralism's "process without a subject." The difference is that, whereas culturalism would correct for the hyper-structuralism of earlier models by restoring the unified subject (collective or individual) of consciousness at the centre of "the Structure," discourse theory, by way of the Freudian concepts of the unconscious and the Lacanian concepts of how subjects are constituted in language (through the entry into the Symbolic and the Law of Culture), restores the *decentered* subject, the contradictory subject, as a set of positions in language and knowledge, from which culture can appear to be enunciated. This approach clearly identifies a

gap, not only in structuralism but in Marxism itself. The problem is that the manner in which this "subject" of culture is conceptualized is of a trans-historical and "universal" character: it addresses the subject-in-general, not historically-determinate social subjects, or socially determinate particular languages. Thus it is incapable, so far, of moving its in-general propositions to the level of concrete historical analysis. The second difficulty is that the processes of contradiction and struggle—lodged by early structuralism wholly at the level of "the structure"—are now, by one of those persistent mirror-inversions, lodged exclusively at the level of the unconscious processes of the subject. It may be, as culturalism often argues, that the "subjective" is a necessary moment of any such analysis. But this is a very different proposition from dismantling the whole of the social processes of particular modes of production and social formations, and reconstituting them exclusively at the level of unconscious psychoanalytic processes. Though important work has been done, both within this paradigm and to define and develop it, its claims to have replaced *all* the terms of the earlier paradigms with a more adequate set of concepts seem wildly over-ambitious. Its claims to have integrated Marxism into a more adequate materialism are, largely, a semantic rather than a conceptual claim.

A second development is the attempt to return to the terms of a more classical "political economy" of culture. This position argues that the concentration on the cultural and ideological aspects has been wildly over-done. It would restore the older terms of "base/superstructure," finding, in the last-instance determination of the cultural-ideological by the economic, that hierarchy of determinations which both alternatives appear to lack. This position insists that the economic processes and structures of cultural production are more significant than their cultural-ideological aspect: and that these are quite adequately caught in the more classical terminology of profit, exploitation, surplus-value and the analysis of culture as commodity. It retains a notion of ideology as "false consciousness."

There is, of course, some strength to the claim that both structuralism and culturalism, in their different ways, have neglected the economic analysis of cultural and ideological production. All the same, with the return to this more "classical" terrain, many of the problems which originally beset it also reappear. The specificity of the effect of the cultural and ideological dimension once more tends to disappear. It tends to conceive the economic level as not only a "necessary" but a "sufficient" explanation of cultural and ideological effects. Its focus on the analysis of the commodity form, similarly, blurs all the carefully established distinctions between different practices, since it is the most *generic* aspects of the commodity-form which attract attention. Its deductions are therefore, largely, confined to an epochal level of abstraction: the generalizations about the commodity-form hold true throughout the capitalist epoch as a whole. Very little by way of concrete and conjunctural analysis can be derived at this high-level "logic of capital" form of abstraction. It also tends to its own kind of functionalism—a functionalism of "logic" rather than of "structure" or history. This approach, too, has insights which are well worth following through. But it sacrifices too much of what has been painfully secured, without a compensating gain in explanatory power.

The third position is closely related to the structuralist enterprise, but has followed the path of "difference" through into a radical heterogeneity. Foucault's work currently enjoying another of those uncritical periods of discipleship through which British intellectuals reproduce today their dependency on yesterday's French ideas—has had an exceedingly positive effect: above all because—in suspending the nearly-insoluble problems of

determination Foucault has made possible a welcome return to the concrete analysis of particular ideological and discursive formations, and the sites of their elaboration. Foucault and Gramsci between them account for much of the most productive work on *concrete analysis* now being undertaken in the field: thereby reinforcing and—paradoxically—supporting the sense of the concrete historical instance which has always been one of culturalism's principal strengths. But, again, Foucault's example is positive only if his general epistemological position is not swallowed whole. For in fact Foucault so resolutely suspends judgment, and adopts so thoroughgoing a scepticism about any determinacy or relationship between practices, other than the largely contingent, that we are entitled to see him, not as an agnostic on these questions, but as deeply committed to the necessary non-correspondence of all practices to one another. From such a position neither a social formation, nor the State, can be adequately thought. And indeed Foucault is constantly falling into the pit which he has dug for himself. For when—against his well-defended epistemological positions—he stumbles across certain "correspondences" (for example, the simple fact that all the major moments of transition he has traced in each of his studies—on the prison, sexuality, medicine, the asylum, language and political economy—all appear to converge around exactly that point where industrial capitalism and the bourgeoisie make their fateful, historical rendezvous), he lapses into a vulgar reductionism, which thoroughly belies the sophisticated positions he has elsewhere advanced.[1]

I have said enough to indicate that, in my view, the line in Cultural Studies which has attempted to *think forwards* from the best elements in the structuralist and culturalist enterprises, by way of some of the concepts elaborated in Gramsci's work, comes closest to meeting the requirements of the field of study. And the reason for that should by now also be obvious. Though neither structuralism nor culturalism will do, as self-sufficient paradigms of study, they have a centrality to the field which all the other contenders lack because, between them (in their divergences as well as their convergences) they address what must be the *core problem* of Cultural Studies. They constantly return us to the terrain marked out by those strongly coupled but not mutually exclusive concepts culture/ideology. They pose, together, the problems consequent on trying to think *both* the specificity of different practices and the forms of the articulated unity they constitute. They make a constant, if flawed, return to the base/superstructure metaphor. They are correct in insisting that this question—which resumes all the problems of a non-reductive determinacy—is the heart of the matter: and that, on the solution of this problem will turn the capacity of Cultural Studies to supercede the endless oscillations between idealism and reductionism. They confront—even if in radically opposed ways—the dialectic between conditions and consciousness. At another level, they pose the question of the relation between the logic of thinking and the "logic" of historical process. They continue to hold out the promise of a properly materialist theory of culture. In their sustained and mutually reinforcing antagonisms they hold out no promise of an easy synthesis. But, between them, they define where, if at all, is the space, and what are the limits, within which such a synthesis might be constituted. In Cultural Studies, theirs are the "names of the game".

**NOTE**

1. He is quite capable of wheeling in through the back door the classes he recently expelled from the front.

# 36

# James Clifford
# 1945–

James Clifford has written extensively on anthropology and ethnography in such books as *The Predicament of Culture: Twentieth-Century Ethnography, Literature, and Art* (1988), *Writing Culture: The Poetics and Politics of Ethnography* (1986), and most recently, *Person and Myth: Maurice Leenhardt in the Melanesian World* (1988). His work is of increasing importance to the field of cultural studies in its focus on the aesthetic, social, and political issues central to an understanding of non-Western cultures.

"The Translation of Cultures" (1980) describes a twenty-five-year fragment in the life of the early twentieth-century Protestant missionary, Maurice Leenhardt. Through Leenhardt, Clifford explores the boundaries of person and culture, focusing on the question of how cultures are mediated by traditional structures of power. Leenhardt is an interesting subject for Clifford for several reasons. First, Leenhardt's letters to his family reveal that conventional theory on the religious "conversion" process had virtually no application value in the field. Second, Leenhardt discloses a strong *personal* involvement in his missionary work (as opposed to strictly professional involvement), which was often at odds with the doctrine of the Société des Missions, his sponsoring church in Paris. Third, Leenhardt confessed to his father that parts of the Christian message itself had to be modified for the native culture to be understood. This led, Clifford shows, to the reconfiguration of Leenhardt's political beliefs regarding missionary work. Translation took on new meaning for Leenhardt.

The application of Clifford's sense of translation reaches well beyond religion. He points out not only the problems Leenhardt encountered in finding synonyms for Christian terminology in a pagan dialect but also of the more slippery problem of interpretation. Clifford shows us the extraordinary flexibility that must accompany any attempt to mediate between foreign cultures. For example, Leenhardt found that in Houailou (the Melanesian language), the word for "God" translated as "*Bao,*" which had multiple meanings as spiritual deity, human corpse, old person, and a dead ancestor. Such latitude in meaning is unthinkable for the translator, but Leenhardt turned the situation to his advantage by letting these multiple connotations in meaning stand. However, in doing so he faced one of the most important decisions in his work at Caledonia: torn between the necessity to ensure that the Christian sense of *Bao* became fully integrated into the Melanesian belief system, he struggled to preserve Christianity's taboo of immanent and graven images of God. This crisis of accommodation led to a revolution in cultural translation. What Leenhardt called "inverse acculturation" was the result of his reconciliation of two apparent opposites: pagan heterodoxy and Christian theology. The possibility—even the task—of a reconciliation of this order challenged both the frontiers of language and the core of *both* Christian and Melanesian belief systems. For conversion, as Leenhardt learned, is not merely a matter of transferring one belief system intact into another language but rather involves reciprocity between cultures—a two-way street of sorts—in which the ethnographer's cultural norms, practices, and dogmas are challenged to the limits of their ability to accommodate difference.

# The Translation of Cultures
*Maurice Leenhardt's Evangelism, New Caledonia 1902–1926*

It is becoming increasingly difficult to speak without second thoughts of "the missionary type" or of a "missionary attitude." The range of "missionary occasions," to appropriate the title of Burridge's thoughtful essay,[1] is broad, so broad that it is no easy matter to decide what essential set of orientations to culture change and to the religious life may be said to unite the intentions and experiences of a list like the following: fire and brimstone fundamentalists, contributors to *Missiology,* intrepid young Mormons, medical technicians, aiders and abettors of national liberation movements, back-country hermits, Billy Graham-style revivalists, and so on. In a postcolonial world the all too familiar sharp silhouette of the evangelist has blurred. But was it in fact ever sharp? Alongside the "man of God"—unbending extirpator of the devil in the bush, in Colin Turnbull's unforgettable and venomous portrait—has always stood the romantic "Father Lobo," also painted by Turnbull, whose church in the jungle is built by Christians, Moslems, and Pagans, and whose joyous service of dedication is attended by dancing pygmies trailing vines.[2]

Between these poles, historians investigating "typical" missionary discourse may, in fact, discover in common words like "god," "adultery," "holy spirit," "devil," "the Word," "conversion," and so on, a spectrum of local renderings, inventions, and heterodox interpretations. The historian of missions must be prepared to discover intransigence coexisting in unexpected ways with what Burridge calls "mutual metanoia," an unpublicized other conversion process that Maurice Leenhardt some time ago termed "acculturation in two directions" and recommended to all participants in colonial situations.[3] The present case is a contribution to a more nuanced understanding of these processes and to a more adequate portrait of the liberal evangelist. It is an example of how a missionary can, perhaps must, be personally involved, and changed, in the complex productive work of reciprocal translation inadequately glossed by the term "conversion."

Maurice Leenhardt's exemplary career is becoming somewhat better known thanks to the recent English edition of his best known work, *Do Kamo: Person and Myth in the Melanesian World,* and thanks to a special issue of the *Journal de la Société des Océanistes.*[4] The present essay is a portion of a longer study[5] and is devoted solely to Leenhardt's translation work, seen as the core of his evangelical practice and as a personal quest for religious authenticity—a work that would become, also, the primary basis of his ethnological production. It is unfortunately not possible here to discuss Leenhardt's extensive ethnographic *oeuvre* and his second career during the 1930s and 40s as a Paris-based ethnologist. He was founder and first president of the Société des Océanistes and the

Institute Français d'Océanie, Professor at the École Pratique des Hautes Études and the Musée de l'Homme, and an enthusiastic ethnographer on renewed field trips in French Melanesia. Here I can only present a part of Leenhardt's total missionary effort in New Caledonia, from 1902 until 1926, ignoring, along with his scientific work, his important "pro-native" political activities on the island.[6] I am not primarily concerned with the history of New Caledonian Protestantism and I do not discuss the actual outcome of Leenhardt's religious work, its dilution by his missionary successors in the 1930s and 1940s, and the history of schism and internal conflict which followed his departure.[7] I am offering merely a description of his interrelated evangelical and personal quests, an account based largely on unpublished family papers (journals and an extensive correspondence with his pastor-naturalist father in France) as well as on materials in the Archives of the Société des Missions Évangeliques in Paris, the missionary society to which Leenhardt belonged.[8]

Maurice Leenhardt was born in 1878 at Montauban where his father, an eminent geologist, taught natural science to pastoral students of France's principal Protestant theological seminary. As a secondary student in the 1890s Leenhardt was won for missions by the vogue for African exploration and evangelism, particularly by the French examples of Casalis in Lessoto and the Livingstone-like Coillard in the upper Zambeze. An independent-minded student of an idealistic and aesthetic temperament, he was unhappy within the lock-step of the French Classical Baccalaureate. He saw in missions an *ouverture,* a constructive escape from a cultural and religious life that had become rigid, hierarchical and abstract. As Bachelor of Theology he wrote a sympathetic study of South African Ethiopianism which openly attacked colonial abuses and evangelical hypocrisy.[9] At his consecration service, just prior to leaving for New Caledonia with his wife Jeanne, he revealed his hopes for mission work in a discourse from which the rhetoric of conquest was notably absent:

> The Christian church seems nowhere so pure as in missions, where it finds itself liberated from the dogmatic political debris with which history has burdened it. Those who have just laid on me their hands will understand what I mean when I speak of the privilege of sowing in a virgin land rather than incessantly pruning sprouts from sick roots. And perhaps, God only knows, it is the young churches in pagan lands who will provide us with the fresh blood needed for the vitalization of our tired milieux.[10]

This, very briefly, was the 24-year-old who in 1902 established himself at Houailou on the east coast of the Grande Terre, or New Caledonian mainland. He remained, to all intents and purposes, the sole European Protestant evangelist on the large island until the early 20s. Communications were slow with colleagues on the Loyalty Islands; the missionary society in Paris was distant; thus Leenhardt enjoyed considerable leeway in deciding mission policy. He was seconded, and in important respects instructed, by about 40 Melanesian pastors called *natas,* "messengers," originating from the Loyalty Islands—and increasingly, as his pastoral school took hold, from New Caledonia. After two decades of sometimes bitter conflict—with the Noumea administration, with farmers and cattlemen, with Catholic evangelical competitors—the Protestant mission radiating from Leenhardt's station, Do Neva, finally established itself securely on the island and was able to claim the stable allegiance of about a third of the Melanesian population. This was accomplished against far superior Marxist resources. The "Melanesian" evangelical style of the Protestant pastoral corps, accepted and systematized by Leenhardt, seems to have been a significant advantage.[11]

The first years at Do Neva were difficult. Beyond the practical and political struggles (Protestantism, "the English religion," was perceived as subversive in the colony), Leenhardt was confronted with the intellectual problem of understanding his pastors, men of experience and, to the young evangelist, often inscrutable—"pagano-protestants," he called them, inelegantly but accurately. Leenhardt was being forced to accept the fact that the land on which he had hoped to sow his faith was anything but virgin. At the end of his first three years, after a series of misunderstandings with the *natas,* resistances, rules imposed by authority, etc., the wiser and considerably bruised evangelist wrote to his father that his work urgently required him to study what he called the "complete psychology" of his Melanesian Christians. "I'm astounded at all the pathways different from ours that I've discovered in their hearts. But it's not enough to discover a country, you've got to know how to map it." Melanesian resistances had to be grasped sympathetically and with considerable relativism: "We don't know how to judge others without comparing them to ourselves; and surely divine wisdom consists in weighing each according to its own measure."[12]

Leenhardt's growing relativism caused him to question seriously the notion of religious "conversion." He criticized (privately) the naiveté of Loyalty Islands colleagues like Philadelphe Delord. Delord, a veteran evangelist and innovator in the treatment of leprosy, was one of those missionaries who knew how to sway an audience with tales of dramatic transformations. He believed in the existence of simple peoples, desirous of the faith. Their "paganism" was for him merely a sort of natural state, not a living culture rooted in a complex reality. Leenhardt was increasingly critical of this approach. Rather than imagine a people yearning for the gos-

pels, it is better, he said, simply to see "various tribes, looking for a support."[13] As a veteran, Leenhardt went further. In the native people's adherence to a religion, he wrote to his wife, prestige plays a key role: they become Protestant in English colonies and Catholic in French. Conversion is for them a means of becoming involved in the white world. Adoption of a new religion can be a method of observation of the white. And finally, it can spring from a "need to react against the deadly breath of civilization." Religious adherence in this case involves a "judgement" of one culture by another. Moreover, the *natas'* message had been essentially this-worldly, a promise of better explanation, prediction, and control of a changing environment. Christianity's other-worldly significance, concentrated in personal communion with a transcendent God, was not so easily accepted.[14] Adherence to the practical religion of the *natas* did not necessarily entail even an elementary acquaintance with Christ.

As a consequence of such views, Leenhardt had difficulty in adopting the modes of discourse proper to his profession. His mother prodded him repeatedly to include more "touching stories" and "edifying conversations" in his reports. Anyone who has leafed through mission journals will know the sort of thing she wanted. But Leenhardt could not bring himself to adopt a language he felt to be fundamentally meaningless. Only with difficulty could he write using "the little touch which creates sympathy." In early 1905, he expressed the radical opinion that, since his arrival, he had seen no real conversions at all, only mass and individual "adherences."[15] He could be mordant in his deflation of colleagues:

> how dangerous it is to always portray the march of the Kingdom of God as if it advanced overstriding all contingencies. It makes me think of Delord moving an audience with a Caledonian woman's story

about how the prayer of a *nata* had swayed a pagan chief. But at the same time, the *nata* had sent 2 [other] chiefs as delegates with 25F of persuasion. The prayer stands, but so does the contingency—and the chief is still pagan.[16]

Leenhardt's mother, in pressing him to recount stories like Delord's, wrote not simply as an orthodox believer but also as a fund raiser. Sentimental stories brought in donations; her son's infrequent, long, and rather dryly descriptive reports did not. At one point Leenhardt promised his parents he would write more "sentimentalism." But he added in exasperation: "I gave myself dispassionately to this work. Why can't Christians learn to give—dispassionately?"[17] Leenhardt was chided, too, by Alfred Boegner, president of the Paris mission society, for not writing the right kind of reports for the Mission Journal, not including enough of his personal experience. The missionary replied: "It must therefore be the case that to interest people in a mission you've got to be able to interest them in yourself. But I feel myself incapable of doing for us what Delord does so well." And he added, once more, his plea for dispassion.[18] Important issues of evangelical method were at stake. The Delord, Coillard style of mission, centring on the romantic figure of the evangelist, seemed dangerous to Leenhardt. It diverted attention from the real work, which was the encouragement of indigenous churches. His own reports tended to leave himself out of the picture and to describe political and cultural circumstances in the Grande Terre, including frequent portraits of individual Melanesian Christians.

Leenhardt, like many a missionary, was torn between the real needs of his work and the demands of his publicity. He had somehow to avoid sacrificing the former to the latter. And this choice involved struggle, for missionary practice was deeply enmeshed in the fantasy systems of European religious sentimentality. Many evangelists never really

chose between their audience in the metropole and their audience in the bush. Leenhardt felt the attraction of "pure" primitivism. Small-scale, anti-clerical Christianity had always been his ideal, and in the back hills he rediscovered "the true *canaque* of before, . . . who has not rubbed against the White. He is more savage, a hundred times better, and in him one sees the lost soul to be brought home so much more clearly than among the poor natives who have been made corrupt and cynical [*désabusés*]."[19] But Leenhardt had to resist this taste for the primitive. He did not question the need for education and change, and traditional socio-religious structures were, he thought, collapsing. Thus his greatest energies were devoted to students and *natas*. These, he thought, were minds in transition, searching for a new conception of themselves which could be guaranteed only through a personal relation with divinity. The conversion process, as Leenhardt analyzes it in a number of subsequent works, consists of an interrelated series of movements: from concrete toward abstract modes of thought and expression, from a diffuse, participatory consciousness toward self-consciousness, from the affective domain of myth toward detached observation and analysis. The process must not, however, be accomplished in simple imitation of whites. It must develop as "some kind of appropriate civilization, affirming itself gradually."[20] In religious terms conversion was the emergence of an internalized moral conscience based on an intimate communion with Christ. True conversion was never collective.

To encourage the necessary individual experience, Leenhardt urged his students to write down as best they could their life stories—to testify to themselves. The missionary and ethnologist learned a great deal from these documents. For example, in a notebook written by Eleisha Nebay at Guilgal in November 1911 we learn that the Christian God appeared to the young convert as a new father *and* mother. Eleisha testifies also to a new feeling, something he had not experienced before becoming a *nata*-in-training. Previously, "there seemed to be only one man in my heart . . ."

> At that time my eyes saw well what they saw and my heart was direct [*droit*]. After a few years in God's work, I've found there to be two men within me, disputing in eloquence every day till the present. I used to wonder whether the first state was God's will. I prayed to him ceaselessly to take the other away. I'm opening myself, telling you what isn't clear to me; but that's how it seemed in my heart.[21]

The conception of conversion as struggle within a divided heart has its origin in the literature of the early Church. To Leenhardt in colonial Melanesia it was a hopeful sign, indicating that his students were growing in self consciousness. People like Eleisha, he thought, would henceforth be able to separate themselves out from the flux of events, making clear choices. This would make resistance to colonial temptations possible, an active selection of alternative moral values within the new, ambiguous context. Other readers of Eleisha Nebay's notebook may be less content with what appears as the birth of modern self-alienation. And indeed, Leenhardt was aware of the danger that the newly individualized Christian person might develop into an experience of separations, without healing communions. The person, he believed, must not abandon myth for rationality, becoming severed from passionate involvements with land and kin. If conversion involved a process of separation and self-discrimination, it had also to be based on translation, a knowing search for equivalents and mediations uniting the old and new, pagan and Christian, mythic and rational.

Leenhardt believed at first that the Melanesian experience of divinity could be brought directly over into Christianity. In 1905 he began experimenting with using the *bao* (a spirit, ancestor, or corpse) to clarify in the native language the "visions" spoken of in the gospels. The development of his translation researches will be treated more fully below. It is worth noting here that for Leenhardt this kind of activity represented a form of questioning which sometimes verged on rebellion. For example, after describing in a letter his use of the *bao* in teaching, he added: "Mama shouldn't think I'm playing the rebel. The thing is too serious here, and why rebel when there's no one to scandalize?"[22] But of course there was someone to scandalize, for Leenhardt, at the antipodes, remained a member of the French Protestant extended family. His father had told him to devise a "simplistic theology" for his students.[23] Leenhardt's problem was to do more—to purify as well as to simplify the Christianity he was teaching. His faith had to be conceived as concretely as possible: this was a prerequisite of communication. The immediate aim was subtle and effective evangelization; but more than just that was at stake. The idea of a cross-culturally translatable Christianity coincided with the sort of lived religion and morality which the young missionary was seeking for himself. From the start he was worried about the need for absolute sincerity in his classes. He was free to follow his feelings, but at the same time he felt uneasy about the great leeway he enjoyed and the resultant dangers of teaching a heterodoxy. "My entire difficulty," he wrote, "is to teach them nothing that I don't believe myself."[24]

In 1913 he sent a report to his Society in Paris for publication in its Journal.[25] In it he hinted at the supple method of evangelization he had for some time been practising. The article was composed in Leenhardt's best "missionary style"; "From Shadows into the Light" was its title. It described halting and apparently rather quaint attempts by *natas* and Do Neva students to grasp the true message of Christ. Various strange native prayers and mistaken concepts are portrayed and explained. Then the concept of "God" is discussed. God had to have a vernacular name, Leenhardt argued, or rather He had to co-opt the generic term for the traditional gods and spirits. Otherwise, as a new and foreign term, the Christian God might be simply added to the roster of deities as *primus inter pares*. Other missionaries, for example Patteson, and Codrington of the English Melanesian Mission, had opted for the European term "God." They feared the inevitable misunderstandings involved in the adaptation of a pagan name. But Leenhardt believed that a certain confusion was part of any process of change and education; and unless native terms could be brought to new significances there would be no real conversion.

Thus the Christian God had to appropriate the essence of Melanesian spirits by taking possession of their generic name, *Bao*. In the process of co-optation, Leenhardt suggested, Christianity was in fact recovering a religious essence which pre-existed the magical gods and spirits, an affective, communal essence that he later identified with totemism and worship of the landscape. This approach to conversion, amounting in some ways to a reversion, was dangerously close to heterodoxy. Where did the Christian missionary draw the line in making use of archaic concepts and terms?

It is interesting to see, from the private letters, that Leenhardt had already censored his article. Writing to his father he revealed that he had begun with an account which would have been much more specific and controversial than the one he finally sent. In the original version he had discussed openly

> the heart of the question . . . which is to determine: is God the revelation man has of Spirit with which we are in relation, and which man then personifies according to his mentality in various spirits etc . . . , until he even succeeds in systematizing and hierarchizing these spirits; or is God much

more transcendant, not discoverable by man?

God is either "immanent or transcendant"; and if he is the former . . .

> If Jehovah is really that which is visible since the creation . . . then the pagans must have an obscure revelation of God at the heart of their beliefs. This is a minimum of experiences upon which the preaching of the Gospel can be based. And thus we shouldn't reject the entire jumble of their gods in order to give them a new god with a foreign name; rather we should search for the word in their language, even the strangest word, into which can be translated the visible experience of God.[26]

The *natas,* he adds, had already been doing this, "openly adopting the pagan name." Leenhardt sympathized, but he felt himself to be walking a fine line.

We cannot know exactly what Leenhardt felt he should exclude from his article, or just how he recast its style. But we can compare a passage he allowed to remain with a later analysis of the same passage. He quotes a prayer overheard on the lips of a Melanesian Protestant: "Oh God who is wholly long, you came to our Néporo and Asana families; then you stretched yourself out again and arrived in Monéo, and again stretching yourself you came to Paci." In the article as printed Leenhardt cited this curious prayer merely as a poetic image for the gospel's progress throughout the land. But the "long god" meant something much more profound to a Melanesian. It evoked the elemental flux, or life force, emanating from the totem and passing into the present generations through the blood of the maternal lineage. If the Christian God was called "wholly long" it meant that it had appropriated this potent myth. In a lecture given much later at the Paris Ecole des Missions Leenhardt describes the relation of the "long god" to the totemic flow of "life" and adds that "this god who stretches out may make us smile when we don't understand paganism. But when we are familiar with the "long god," the image is a moving one, touching the Missionary's heart."[27] This was the sort of comment Leenhardt could not permit himself in his original article, where the *"dieu long"* remained a picturesque image. In 1913 Leenhardt was still unsure of his missionary-ethnology. He asked his father whether it was permissible to affix pagan names and properties to the Christian God. And the question posed once more the basic theological problem for Leenhardt: that of mediating an apparent choice between immanence and transcendence.

> . . . so that according to whether God is transcendent or immanent (I mean glimpsed as such, for I think he is both) we translate using the foreign name or the pagan name; and who knows whether we're being orthodox or heterodox?

Was God in effect already present in Melanesian language and experience? Or did He have to be imported? Leenhardt's instincts were all on the side of immanence, but he needed encouragement:

> I wish father would tell me what he thinks of all this; because I wrote that article as a search, and seeing that I was heading straight for heterodoxy, I began again and turned it into edification. But if Father tells me I'm on the right track, I'll feel a lot more courage in searching for God among the pagans.[28]

In the ambiguous freedom of his mission work, Leenhardt had to develop enough self-confidence to see God for himself in strange contexts. This was a problem of personal identity, or "sincerity" in the language of Leenhardt which was that of Rousseau. However the romantic route of introspection and confession made no claim on the activist. He looked for his "god among the pagans," among the others—and in this he opened himself personally to the conversion process.

"Inverse acculturation" was Leenhardt's way of describing, later, in an ethnological context, a desirable colonial reciprocity in which the European would learn from the Melanesian.[29] Before an audience of young evangelists he put it rather differently. The missionary, he insists, keeps his mind open—but not in order to be influenced by primitivism so much as to be, simply, a purer Christian and man.

> The missionary is called to bring the Gospel of Jesus Christ and not the Gospel of whites. His purpose is not the founding of a white church. In remaining perfectly loyal to the mandate given him by God, not men, he must become a man, and not the representative of a civilization. Otherwise . . . his message will not be that of pure Gospel; it will contain a mixture of voices . . . [30]

The purity required of the missionary was not a form of dogma or divine inspiration. It was an attitude of openness—a poetic negative capability. "The Gospel of Jesus," the veteran said in his lecture, "adapts itself to all peoples." As an evangelist Leenhardt had to learn to recognize true translation when it was already at work in an unfamiliar idiom.

The *nata* Joané Nigoth had already produced a Houailou version of the Gospel of Matthew. The translation of the remaining New Testament was a collective enterprise spanning more than 15 years which became, for Leenhardt, an intense focus for ethnolinguistic research. A letter sets out his procedure:

Just a word while waiting for Boesoou, my old teacher with whom I can't manage to find a few quiet hours to work on translations. By now he's used to the work and gives the correct word fairly quickly. For two hours a week I read completed chapters to the students, and it's very interesting to see them satisfied by a good word which makes clear in their minds something they hadn't understood; or protesting sometimes against a word which doesn't satisfy them. After their verdict I give the rough draft to Apou to copy . . .[31]

It was often almost impossible to find meaningful equivalents for Christian religious concepts, and Leenhardt went to great lengths to avoid imposing a foreign expression. It was important not to be in a hurry. He would try to hold an open mind and keep discussing a troublesome idea whenever he could, in classes and sermons, until some Houailou-speaker arrived spontaneously at a meaningful rendition.

An example of how the process sometimes worked is given in Leenhardt's article of 1922 on translating the New Testament. He was having difficulty with the rendering of a key concept in the Epistle to the Romans.

While I was seeking for the meaning of the term "propitiatory," I heard a native Christian explain the text of Romans 3:25 with these words, which I translate literally, "God has made Jesus an object *of sacrifice, and the healing and propitiatory leaf* is his blood for those who have faith." This confusing and awkward expression is translated in Caledonian by a very short word, "Demo." Its original significance is "leaf cicatrization, or living leaf, the ideas of healing and of life being connected. But this should not lead us to think that it is the leaf which cicatrizes; in that case the phrase would be "cicatrizing leaf," *"De Pemo."* The leaf is only the vehicle for a virtue

transmitted through the benevolence of a divinity in the course of a sacrifice. Without this sacrifice or an offering, the leaf does not act. This virtue, originally given to a leaf, must have been extended later to other objects, for the word designating it has a generic sense and is applied to all objects provoking or soliciting divine influence. In this very primitive idea, the medicinal value of the leaf has not been grasped; the leaf is effective only by virtue of its propitiatory value. When *Canaques* applied this word to Jesus Christ, they perceived that the death of Christ modified the relations between man and God, and took away their sin, as these leaves in sacrifices formerly altered their condition and took away their sufferings. This is perceived from a wholly simple and concrete standpoint.[32]

Leenhardt goes on to suggest that the Melanesian—who propitiates a god or totem using the *demo* leaf as part of his everyday activities of fishing or gardening, etc.—probably grasps the expiatory role of Christ in a manner that is more alive than that of many Christians, tied to a juridical mode of comprehension.

In the same context, Leenhardt tells how he finally arrived at a term which would express the idea of redemption. Previous missionaries had interpreted it in terms of exchange—an exchange of life, that of Jesus for ours. But in Melanesian thinking more strict equivalents were demanded in the exchanges structuring social life. It remained unclear to them how Jesus's sacrifice could possibly redeem mankind. So unclear was it that even the *natas* gave up trying to explain a concept they didn't understand very well themselves and simply employed the term "release." So the matter stood, with the missionary driven to the use of cumbersome circumlocutions, until one day during a conversation on I Corinthians 1:30 Boesoou Erijisi used a surprising expression. The term *nawi* which he employed referred to the custom of planting a small tree on land cursed either by the blood of battle or some calamity. "Jesus was thus the one who has accomplished the sacrifice and has planted himself like a tree, as though to absorb all the misfortunes of men and to free the world from its taboos." Here at last was a concept which seemed to render that of redemption, while reaching deeply enough into living modes of thought. "The idea was a rich one, but how could I be sure I understood it right?" The key test was in the reaction of students and *natas* to his provisional version. They were, he reports, overjoyed with the deep translation.

Often enough, Melanesian terms seemed to express the elemental meaning of the Bible more truly than the French or the Greek, both of which were less concrete tongues than the original language of the gospels. Thus Leenhardt's intercultural translation was more than a simple scriptural exegesis. His "primitivizing" of the gospel restored to it a rich, immediate context and concrete significance. An example of the kinship between the Biblical and the Melanesian, which Leenhardt would elaborate again and again throughout his ethnological career, was the term for "word" or "speech" (French, *parole,* Houailou, *no*). "In the beginning was the Word . . ." was first translated by the Loyalty missionaries using the Greek, and pronouncing it in native fashion. "In the beginning the logos."

*Canaques* are intelligent people: I've never heard them using words which have no meaning. But when a *Canaque* speaks French, he translates his thoughts as best he can. He has no trouble at all expressing himself concerning the man who has conceived good things, has said them, done them, or even accomplished the three acts at once: "The word [*parole*] of this man is good." Thought, speech, and action are all

included in the Caledonian term *No*. Thus in speaking of an adulterous man, one may say: "He has done an evil word." One may speak of a chief whose character is uncertain, who does not think, organize, or act correctly, as—"His word is not good." The expression "the Word of God," which we limit to divine discourse or literature, here includes the thoughts and acts of God. "God spoke and it was done." We need search no farther; we translate using *No* this term of such richness—the *Logos* of the first verses of John that the native attempts to transpose into French using *"parole."* The term for Word takes on a broad, living meaning, worthy of the God whose creative will it must make intelligible. Things become clearer. The native has no trouble seeing the word becoming action, the word made flesh, the word as phenomenon.[33]

The opening of the Book of John was particularly effective in Melanesian vernacular. Another "improved" passage was Matthew 19:6, *New English Bible:*

"Have you never read that the Creator made them from the beginning male and female?"; and he added, "For this reason a man shall leave his father and mother, and be made one with his wife; and the two shall become one flesh. It follows that they are no longer two individuals: they are one flesh. What God has joined together, man must not separate."

These words were "more expressive in Houailou."[34] Leenhardt was discovering that the vernacular abounded in locutions of duality and plurality. These were substantives, and they did not imply the additive combination of separate parts. Rather, they were one flesh, as with husband and wife. It was also true for other couplings, grandfather and grandson, nephew and maternal uncle, the relation of homonyms. What in Western languages would be seen as composites would in Houailou be expressed as ensembles, substantial entities or "images."[35]

For Leenhardt, translation was part of the creative interpenetration of two cultures, a liberation and revivification of meanings latent in each. In the process it was essential not simply to find accurate expressions, but to locate and use *meaningful* expressions. In this concern he anticipated modern, ethnolinguistic approaches to Bible translation, the search for "dynamic equivalences."[36] Imposed terminology had no place in real translation. Spontaneously borrowed and adapted foreign words were accepted, after scrutiny. Archaic expressions, words which once had sense but had been abandoned, were left to their fate. On the other hand, "those expressions which spring from the native mind in an attempt to formulate new concepts revealed by the knowledge of the gospel or by contact with [Western] civilization, exhibit a great variety. And their value is far greater; for these are not artificial words, but truly living words."[37]

Leenhardt is attempting here to grasp a moving language. He values those usages which, although they might appear corrupt when judged against an imagined, static, primitive standard, are in reality the most vital elements of a parlance. He works within a dynamic conception of culture. Rather than simply transferring meanings from one cultural code to another, a situation of dialogue is created in which the language of all parties is enriched. As opposed to the ethnographer, who typically concentrates on making an alien expressive system understandable, Leenhardt works at making himself and his belief system understood—to others and, in the process, to himself. A context of exchange is initiated. By contrast, scientific ethnology runs the risk of overemphasizing the univocal translation of exotic cultures and languages, as if they were inert texts

*(langues)* rather than evolving expressivities *(paroles)*. Perhaps in order to translate "them" into "us," one must be prepared to translate "us" into "them." The missionary's summary of the translator's role is relevant—in some degree—to all ethnographic encounters:

> The work of the translator is not to interrogate his native helpers, as if compiling human dictionaries, but rather he must solicit their interest, awaken their thinking [ . . . ] He does not create a language; this is composed by the native himself; it is the product and translation of his thoughts. And the translator, he who has initiated this thinking, merely transcribes the words he has aroused, overheard, seized upon— fixing them in writing.[38]

The translator seizes a moment of intercultural "thinking." He is participant and midwife in language's perpetual process of rebirth in the encounter with other languages.

The importance of this process for Leenhardt was two-fold. First, in cooperation with Melanesians, he hoped to preserve an endangered expressivity, not as a static ethnological document, but in words which would be "acts of life inspired by experience." Living New Caledonian culture required living languages. Secondly, for himself and his own culture, Leenhardt uncovered in the translation process a purified and concretized Christianity.

> The missionary has once more experienced the power of the Gospel, and now the natives have helped him in better understanding this power. He perceives that if psychological and theological terms are abstract and indefinite, words as they spring from the experience of the believer are concrete and precise. He realizes that the religious fact expressed in abstract terms is without active value and consti-

tutes merely a dead formula whose spirit has departed. [ . . . ] Christianity will appear to [the missionary] stripped of the various historical garments which conceal it from the eyes of so many in Europe. And [he] will glimpse the entire beauty of the Gospel, light and life-force for those who seek it with simplicity.[39]

Thus the translator's credo. As Leenhardt conceived the process involved, there could be no simple importation of a Western divinity into a Melanesian religious landscape. For the European, "God" would take on unexpected forms. He watched and listened: *"Para bao we kei pai ae para rhe we ke mi roi powè."* (Tous les dieux à cause les hommes, d'autre part tous les totems à cause venir selon femmes.) A phrase "overheard in the mouth of a *Canaque*" provided Leenhardt with a key to the complex structure of New Caledonian religion.[40] "Gods come from men, totems proceed from women."

The *natas,* as we have seen, had translated the Christian "God" as *"Bao."* Perhaps it was disconcerting for their young missionary when he discovered that *Bao* could be a term for cadaver. (He was probably not as confused, however, as his missionary predecessors on Lifou who for a time had translated "Bible" as "container of the Word," until they discovered that the islanders also called their penis sheath "container of the word.")[41] Leenhardt considered all translations to be provisional; he let *Bao* stand, and began looking into the term's wide variety of connotations. *Bao,* he found, could be a magical spirit of recent origin used in magic and sorcery, like the "red god," *doki.*[42] *Bao* could be a human corpse, or even a very old person, still alive; it could also be an ancestor deceased in recent memory; it could be a more distant ancestor, founder of an island or region; it could be an almost forgotten deity, remembered by a single exaggerated trait or identified with an element of nature or geog-

raphy. Finally, *bao* could refer to a totem which had become confused with an ancestor and was thus also a "god." *Bao,* Leenhardt discovered, was generally identified with the male ancestral lineage, heritage of the clan and the chief. Its properties were masculine, its virtue was "power." Leenhardt observed that the *bao* most actively worshipped were magical manifestations—spirits of fairly recent origin, linked to present occasions. As he understood better the common usages of *bao,* he worried that the Christian deity's status might be that of one more magical "god." It might—like the *doki,* recently imported from Lifou—fail to express really ancient mythic attachments. How could the missionary-translator be sure that *Bao,* the Christian god, would penetrate to the deepest strata of Melanesian feeling and belief?

Leenhardt was at first much impressed with the power in New Caledonian life of the *bao* ancestor-gods. This was most manifest in the authority of chiefs, representatives of the masculine clan lineage, and mediators with the *bao.* But as he became more sensitive to local custom, he discovered that in practice the chiefs often deferred to uterine kin, members of clans from which the paternal clan received its wives. The maternal uncle, or *kanya,* had to be given gifts at births, deaths, *pilou* festivals, marriages, to ensure the counter gift of female life.[43] But the *kanya* did not hold power in himself any more than the chief did. The latter was spokesman, *parole,* of the clan accestors; the former was representative of the maternal line. The *chef* incarnated the heritage of masculine "power," the *kanya* of feminine "life." An elemental living force flowed as blood from mother to child; its original source was the totem, or *rhë.* The totem was an animal, plant, or mineral, peculiar to a clan and recognized by a system of ritual gestures and sacrifices.[44] Prior to Leenhardt's identification of *rhë* as "totem," New Caledonian culture had been classified as nontotemic. The missionary now had to explain the coexistence of two parallel sources of authority, *bao*-chief, and totem-*kanya*. At first he hypothesized a society in transition from matriarchy to patriarchy. But after further research he dropped these terms, and with them abandoned a theoretical stance tending to explain incongruous elements in a culture as survivals, or evidences of past historical stages. Nineteenth-century evolutionism frequently posited that culture in its early periods had passed from matriarchy to patriarchy. However Leenhardt rejected the notion of opposed, successive states. He found that in New Caledonia duality was structural, with opposition best understood as complementarity. He came to see the lineages of "power" and "life," male and female, in reciprocal union. The missionary, in looking hard at Melanesian religion, had done more than derive a simple equivalent for "God." He had identified a coherent socio-religious system.[45]

Although Leenhardt admired the aesthetic balance of the Melanesian sociomythic order, he nonetheless judged it to be no longer viable. New modes of thought were required, to deal with new conditions. The mythic landscape in which the deeper forms of ancestor worship and totemic identification had found expression was shattered. A new person, less externalized, more centred in an individually defined ego would have to develop. (This Western person, Lévi-Strauss has remarked, seems to have as "totem" his own personality.)[46] Leenhardt's concern was with the spiritual health of this new individual, the quality of "life" available to it. He did not wish to encourage the development of a belief system reduced to merely technical, magical, or rational manipulation of an objective environment. Deeper attachments were needed. Leenhardt identified these affective attitudes primarily with totemic myth as well as with older forms of ancestor-nature worship. It seemed to Leenhardt that acculturation was likely to result in a shift away from myth in the direction of magic, the latter involving a

more instrumental attitude toward the world. But he did not wish the Christian *Bao* to be simply a powerful new tool for the understanding and control of immediate events. This would be to encourage shallowness of belief and to promote the development of sorcery and messianism, unstable means of socio-religious problem solving.

Beneath the changing repertoire of *bao*-gods lay the more authentic attachments of myth, geographic and totemic. Something of these forces would need to be co-opted into the new, personal "God" if modes of mythic participation were to co-exist with, not simply be replaced by, techniques of rational manipulation. Thus, the missionary could be delighted, even moved, to hear an old man participating in a Christian festival address a temperance commitment to "his mountains."[47] Much of this religious essence might be excluded in naming "God" *Bao*. The Supreme Being might be thought of as just another lesser god, magical, this worldly, and merely useful for dealing with the white world. There was a risk of excluding the entire female-totemic "side" of the traditional socio-religious structure. The first Loyalty Islands *natas* had tried to use the name "Jehovah," but their New Caledonian converts preferred *"Bao,"* and Leenhardt respected their instinct, though he knew the translation to be imperfect.[48] The *bao* concept would have to be reunderstood, not as a generic term but capitalized, as a personal name. And mythic depth might be added to it through the annexation of as much totemic language as was possible. Leenhardt was encouraged by his discovery that *bao* was, traditionally, a highly adaptable concept. It could apply not merely to a corpse, recent ancestor, or magical divinity, but its masculine "power" could sometimes fuse spontaneously with the feminine-totemic principle of "life." It sometimes happened that a mythic founding father might in collective memory become identified with a totem. Leenhardt had also discovered an encouraging composite usage of *bao,* the "long god" which we have already mentioned. Here was a masculine "god" being associated with the curving flow of the female lineage. If such "totem-god" associations could naturally occur, there was hope for a similar mediation in the person of the Christian *Bao.* "God" could be a "long god," a source of both "power" and "life."

The religious language of Leenhardt's Houailou *New Testament (Peci Arii)* is drawn from a broad range of sources. Totemic expressions abound.[49] The new *Bao* is characterized in language drawn from the expressive systems of myth, of social morality, of magic. The Christian God had to embrace the totality of Melanesian life. It had to co-opt the all-encompassing "peaceful abode" *("séjour paisible,"* Houailou *maciri)* so effectively incarnated in the traditional village, with its symbolic male and female alleyways inserted in a living, mythic landscape.[50] Leenhardt tried to preach in a concrete local language, expressive of wholeness and quality. He wrote to his father that he was teaching the Melanesians that "the god to whom they give boiled yams and from whom they ask an abundant harvest (*maciri,* the kingdom, same word as kingdom of heaven, *maciri, re néko*) is the same whose hand they now ask for, to help them walk in righteousness."[51] But to appeal to the traditional "peaceful abode" was to invoke immanent spatial attachments, relationships mythical, ecological and social, not habitually thought of as "a" god. This quotation is from an early letter; Leenhardt would become more sophisticated in his translations. But the general aim revealed to his father remained: somehow a localized, immediate mythic experience had to be encompassed by the "person" of a transcendent deity.

In adopting the language of totemic myth in order to evoke the Christian Bao, and in identifying Him with *maciri,* the "peaceful abode" and traditional village, Leenhardt in effect broadened the God of European orthodoxy in two crucial ways. In translating his deity the missionary made "Him" more androgynous, a totem-*bao* of feminine "life" as well as masculine "power." He also rendered God less transcendent, expressing Him through myths of immediate social and religious experience—this worldly and participative.[52]

The Houailou translation of the *New Testament* fairly successfully incarnates Leenhardt's religious ideal. But it was quite another thing to achieve as precise and nuanced a translation in the actual beliefs of Melanesian Protestants. When Leenhardt and his wife returned to New Caledonia in 1938, they found evidence that many *natas* were preaching the Christian *Bao* as if it were "added" onto traditional religion.[53] The missionary's successors had de-emphasized the use of Houailou in religious instruction and ritual and were not as sophisticated as he had been in detecting when Christianity was in danger of slipping either into a syncretist or merely magical-instrumental status. It is difficult today to know precisely how much of the mythic depth Leenhardt strove to preserve in the language of New Caledonian Christianity in fact survives. French is the island's *lingua franca,* and the young have largely forgotten the old religious words.

On the other hand, there are solid indications that an immanent attachment, at once social, mythic, and ecological, to land and habitat has in fact survived to a significant degree in Christian New Caledonia. And a passing firsthand acquaintance with Protestantism on the Grande Terre has persuaded the present author at least (in the absence of any detailed study) that there is more to "modernization" here than meets the eye. There are still, for example, Protestants who, during their regional church festivals, "pass along the young girl," in the form of a symbolic gift, back and forth between clans united by ancient exchanges of uterine blood (life). Moreover, the desire for a return of expropriated ancestral habitats is the most constant and profound current of political agitation among the island's Melanesians. If Leenhardt's specific Houailou translations have been superseded by events beyond his control, there has been no rejection of the spirit in which they were collectively made. For the missionary, in any event, there were no final versions. Authenticity was a process—the translation of cultures, creative and humanly indeterminate.

## NOTES

1. K. O. L. Burridge, "Missionary Occasions," in J. Boutilier, D. Hughes, and S. Tiffany (eds.), *Mission, Church and Sect in Oceania* (Ann Arbor 1978), 1–30.

2. Colin Turnbull, *The Lonely African* (New York 1962), 105–20, 123–4.

3. Maurice Leenhardt, *Gens de la Grande Terre* (Paris, revised ed., 1952), "Deuxième avant-propos," 8.

4. Maurice Leenhardt, *Do Kamo, Person and Myth in the Melanesian World* (Chicago 1979), Intro. by Vincent Crapanzano; "Centenaire de Maurice Leenhardt," special number, *Journal de la Société des Océanistes,* XXXIV: 58–59 (1978); see also Leenhardt issue of *Objets et Mondes, la revue du Musée de l'Homme,* XVII: 2 (1977); Roselène Dousset-Leenhardt, "Maurice Leenhardt," *L'Homme,* XVII (1977), 105–15.

5. James Clifford, "Maurice Leenhardt: Ethnologist and Missionary," PhD dissertation, Harvard University (Cambridge 1977).

6. On Leenhardt's political work see: Clifford, op. cit., ch. 4; Jean Guiart, "Maurice Leenhardt, missionaire et sociologue," *Le Monde Non Chrétien,* XXXIII (1955), 52–71; and "Maurice Leenhardt inconnu: l'homme d'action," *Objets et Mondes,* XVII: 2 (1977), 75–85; *Journal de la Société des Océanistes,* XXXIV: 58–59, (1978), 9–42.

7. See J. Guiart, *Destin d'une église et d'un peuple: étude monographique d'une oeuvre protestante missionaire* (Paris 1959).

8. The bulk of Leenhardt's papers are in the hands of M. R. H. Leenhardt, 59 Rue Claude Bernard, Paris 5ᵉ. All unpublished documents, usually cited by date unless otherwise specified, are from this collection. Some letters and journals (1917, 1922–1923) are held by Mme R.

Dousset-Leenhardt, 10 Rue de Tournon, Paris 6ᵉ. The Archives of the Former Société des Missions Evangéliques are housed in the Bibliothèque du Département Evangélique Français d'Action Apostolique (DEFAP), 102 Bd Arago, Paris 14ᵉ.

9. M. Leenhardt, *Le Mouvement éthiopien en Sud de l'Afrique, de 1896 à 1899* (Cahors 1902); repr. Académie des Sciences d'Outre-Mer (Paris 1976).

10. "Consecration de Maurice Leenhardt, Montpellier, 1902," TS, Leenhardt Papers (hereinafter LP).

11. This was recognized by his Marist competitors: see Father Provincial, "Rapport de Visite," 16 Oct. 1913, pp. 21–2, 25, Rome, Archives Pères Maristes, Océanie, Nouvelle-Calédonie, 208; however, development of a Melanesian priesthood has been slow and confined to the post-World War Two period. A full comparison of Protestant and Catholic evangelical practices is beyond the scope of this essay.

12. Maurice Leenhardt (hereinafter ML)—Parents, undated fragment, probably 1905, LP.

13. ML—Parents, 2 June 1903, LP.

14. ML—Jeanne Leenhardt, 13 Oct. 1919, LP. Leenhardt's thinking on conversion appears to anticipate recent "intellectualist" views of the process. See primarily Robin Horton, "African Conversion," *Africa,* XLI (1971), esp. 93–101. Horton distinguishes between (a) traditional religious systems which combine the experience of "communion" with "explanation-prediction-control" of the world's "space-time events" and (b) Christianity, which tends to abandon day-to-day control functions and concentrates on communion with a personal God. In Leenhardt's view, as in Horton's, full Christianization entails a general revolution in the ways a person communes with and manipulates his world. A consistently Christian ethic would thus result in what Burridge (op. cit., 17) calls a social situation of "generalized individuality." However, Leenhardt, as his thought developed in the conclusion of *Do Kamo* at least, strongly rejected any reduction of experience to an "individual" personal configuration.

15. ML—Parents, 10 Oct., 20 Nov. 1903, 22 Mar. 1905, LP.

16. ML—Parents, 31 Aug. 1911, LP.

17. ML—Parents, 6 Feb. 1904, LP.

18. ML—Boegner, 13 Feb. 1904, Paris, Archives of the Société des Missions Evangéliques (hereinafter SME).

19. ML—Parents, 13 Sept. 1904, LP.

20. ML, "Expériences sociales en terre canaque," *Revue du Christianisme Social,* n.s. (Oct.–Nov. 1921), 786–802, repr. in *Le Monde Non Chrétien,* LXVI (1963), 18.

See also ML, *Le catéchumène canaque,* Cahiers Missionaires, no. 1 (Paris 1922); *Do Kamo . . . ,* chs 11 and 12.

21. "Cahier d'Eleisha Nebay, 1911," trans. from the Houailou by R.-H. Leenhardt, LP.

22. ML—Parents, 1905, no month or day, LP.

23. Franz Leenhardt—Maurice, 24 Dec. 1902, LP.

24. ML—Parents, 1905, no month or day, LP.

25. *Journal des Missions Evangéliques,* II (1913), 309–13.

26. ML—Parents, 25 Oct. 1913, LP.

27. "La notion de dieu chez les mélanésiens," TS, n.d. (Lecture notes for a class at the SME school, Paris, probably late 1930s.) On the "dieu long" see ML, *Notes d'ethnologie Néo-Calédonnienne* (Paris 1930), 187, 233–4.

28. ML—Parents, 25 Oct. 1913, LP.

29. ML, *Gens . . . ,* 8.

30. ML, "Ethnologie," TS, n.d. (Lecture notes for a class at the SME school.)

31. ML—Parents, 19 Mar. 1915, LP; for details on Boesoou Erijisi, Leenhardt's remarkable ethnographic informant, see R.-H. Leenhardt, "Un Sociologue Canaque," *Cahiers d'Histoire du Pacifique,* IV (1976), 19–53.

32. ML, "Notes sur la traduction du Nouveau Testament en langue primitive," *Revue d'Histoire et de Philosophie Religieuse,* (May-June 1922), 216–17.

33. Ibid., 212; for a full discussion of "the Word" in Houailou usage, see ML, *Do Kamo . . . ,* chs 9 and 10.

34. ML—Parents, 4 June 1912, LP.

35. On Houailou duals and plurals see esp. ML, "La Personne mélanésienne," *Annuaire de l'Ecole Pratique des Hautes Etudes,* 5e Section, 1941–42 (Melun 1942), 5–17; idem, *Langues et dialectes de l'Austro Mélanésie* (Paris 1946), Intro., xxxiii–xxxix.

36. See, particularly, E. A. Nida and C. R. Taber, *The Theory and Practice of Translation* (Leiden 1969), 22–32, which sets out principles developed by Nida in a distinguished career as linguist and Bible translation theorist.

37. ML, "Notes sur la traduction du Nouveau Testament," 196.

38. ML, "La Bible en mission," *Evangile et Liberté,* XXI (Oct. 1934).

39. ML, "Notes sur la traduction . . . ," 218.

40. ML, *Notes d'ethnologie . . . ,* 234.

41. ML, "Modes d'expression en sociologie et en ethnologie," *Synthèse,* X, Proc. 6th International Significal Summer Conference (n.d., 1951?), 262. For an account of discovering that *bao* = cadaver, see *Do Kamo . . . ,* 80.

42. See ML, *Notes d'ethnologie . . . ,* 239.

43. See the very beautiful ritual discourses to and by the *kanya* in ML, *Documents néo-calédoniens* (Paris 1932), 341–51.

44. See ML, *Notes d'ethnologie . . . ,* 179–212; ML—Parents, 24 May 1914, LP.

45. ML, *Notes d'ethnologie . . . ,* 77–9, and 98 fn, where he traces the development of his thinking beyond evolutionism to the recognition of a reciprocal system. See also ML, "Observation de la pensée religieuse d'un peuple océanien et d'un peuple bantou," *Histoire générale des religions* (Paris 1948), I, 53; for the system of social exchanges see *Notes d'ethnologie,* ch. 5. (The kinship system, for ML, was not separate from myth.)

46. C. Lévi-Strauss, *La pensée sauvage* (Paris 1962), 285.

47. ML—Jeanne Leenhardt, 17 Aug. 1918, LP.

48. ML, "Notes sur la traduction . . . ," 210–11.

49. See the list of terms drawn from totemism provided by Pierre Métais in his valuable analysis of ML's translation: "Sociologue parce que linguiste," *Journal de la Société des Océanistes,* X (1954), 42, 44. On Christian appropriation of totemic terms see also ML's report in *Annuaire de l'Ecole Pratique des Hautes Etudes,* 5e Section, (1949–50), 31.

50. ML, *Gens . . . ,* ch. 1.

51. ML—Parents, 1904, no day or month, LP.

52. On the Christian God (Christ) as unity of male "power" and feminine "life," see ML, "Quelques éléments communs aux formes inférieures de la religion," M. Brillant and R. Aigran (eds), *Histoire des religions* (Paris 1953), 109; also ML—Parents, 25 Oct. 1919, LP.

53. Jeanne Leenhardt—children, 1 Feb. 1939, LP.

# 37

# Meaghan Morris
# 1950–

Meaghan Morris is a writer living in Sydney, Australia. Her work critiques, among other topics, culture, feminism, postmodernism, and film. A recent publication, *The Pirate's Fiancée: Feminism, Reading, Postmodernism* (1989), includes the essays "Room 101 or a Few Worst Things in the World," "Post-modernity and Lyotard's Sublime," and "Tooth and Claw: Tales of Survival and *Crocodile Dundee.*" She is the coeditor of *Michel Foucault: Toward a Radical Democratic Politics* (1985) and two anthologies, *Michel Foucault: Power, Truth, Strategy* (1980), and *Language, Sexuality, and Subversion* (1978). "Banality in Cultural Studies" first appeared in *Logics of Television* (1990), a collection of essays edited by Patricia Mellencamp.

As Mellencamp states in the "Prologue" to *Logics of Television,* Morris's essay presents a "general overview of the state of cultural studies and cultural critique." Rather than a "survey of the field," though, "Banality in Cultural Studies" examines Morris's "irritation about two developments in recent cultural studies" and offers a third possible strategy. Her first irritation is with Jean Baudrillard's use of the term "banality," a term valorized in Baudrillard because of its negative connotations; indeed, the term is used precisely for its negative connotations. In opposition to banality (or "mass cultural anarchy") is "fatality," a term privileged as "aesthetic order." While Baudrillard concludes that "a banal theory assumes . . . that the subject is more powerful than the object" and "a fatal theory knows . . . that the object is always *worse* than the subject," Morris demonstrates that Baudrillard's opposition between figuration and literalness is in fact simply a play between figurations, a return to metalanguage and exegesis.

Instead of the fatal-banal hierarchy that Baudrillard presents as an opposition is the more democratic view of recent cultural studies, apparent in the "British Cultural Studies" movement. However, and importantly, the work of this movement constitutes Morris's second irritation with developments in cultural studies. Part of her irritation stems from the tendency for the *criticism* itself to achieve banality. As Morris states, ethnography entails the analysis of a culture so that, at least while examining a culture, the analyst is ethnically located outside of it. Consequently, there exists a "gap between the cultural student and the culture studied." The analyst, in Morris's view, should analyze her or his own institutional position; instead, what occurs is "the people" becomes an "allegorical emblem of the critic's own activity." Banality is thus apparent in the repetitive, circular nature of such critiques.

Rather than remain lodged between the "fatal strategies" of Baudrillard and the, at times, false optimism of cultural studies, Morris looks to Michel de Certeau for an approach to the issues she raises in the essay. In *The Practice of Everyday Life,* de Certeau describes two "spaces" within the "science"—not the theory—of popular culture. One space he calls "polemological," or the analysis of "facts" produced "by *experience* of another place, and time spent on the other's terrain." The second is "utopian," or spaces that "deny the immutability and authority of facts." Importantly, together "both spaces refuse the fatality . . . of an established order." For Morris, de Certeau's two spaces preclude the analysis of culture as a "content"; instead, his definition of popular culture becomes a *"way of operating,"* and, in turn, a way of avoiding certain problems of recent cultural critiques. Still, de Certeau offers the possibility that "banality" is "the arrival at a *common* place . . . the outcome of a practice, something that 'comes into being' at the end of a trajectory."

# Banality in Cultural Studies

This paper takes a rather circuitous route to get to the point. I'm not sure that banality can have a point, any more than cultural studies can properly constitute its theoretical object. My argument *does* have a point, but one that takes the form of pursuing an aim rather than reaching a conclusion. Quite simply, I wanted to come to terms with my own irritation about two developments in recent cultural studies.

One was Jean Baudrillard's revival of the term "banality" to frame a theory of media. It is an interesting theory that establishes a tension between everyday life and catastrophic events, banality and "fatality"—using television as a metonym of the problems that result. Yet why should such a classically dismissive term as "banality" appear to establish, yet again, a frame of reference for discussing popular culture?

The other development has occurred in the quite different context that John Fiske calls "British Cultural Studies,"[1] and is much more difficult to specify. Judith Williamson, however, has bluntly described something that also bothers me: "left-wing academics . . . picking out strands of 'subversion' in every piece of pop culture from Street Style to Soap Opera."[2] In this kind of analysis of everyday life, it seems to be *criticism* that actively

strives to achieve "banality," rather than investing it negatively in the object of study.

These developments are not *a priori* related, let alone opposed (as, say, pessimistic and optimistic approaches to popular culture). They also involve different kinds of events. "Baudrillard" is an author, British Cultural Studies is a complex historical and political movement as well as a library of texts. But irritation may create relations where none need necessarily exist. To attempt to do so is the real point of this paper.

I want to begin with a couple of anecdotes about banality, fatality, and television. But since storytelling itself is a popular practice that varies from culture to culture, I shall again define my terms. My impression is that American culture easily encourages people to assume that a first-person anecdote is primarily oriented toward the emotive and conative functions, in Jakobson's terms, of communication: that is, toward speaker-expressive and addressee-connective activity, or an I/you axis in discourse. However, I take anecdotes, or yarns, to be primarily referential. They are oriented futuristically towards the construction of a precise, local, and *social* discursive context, of which the anecdote then functions as a *mise en abyme*. That is to say, anecdotes for me are not expressions of personal experience but allegorical expositions of a model of the way the world can be said to be working. So anecdotes need not be true stories, but they must be functional in a given exchange.

My first anecdote is a fable of origin.

TV came rather late to Australia: 1956 in the cities, later still in the country regions where the distance between towns was immense for the technology of that time. So it was in the early 1960s that in a remote mountain village—where few sounds disturbed the peace except for the mist rolling down to the valley, the murmur of the wireless, the laugh of the kookaburra, the call of the bellbird, the humming of chainsaws and lawnmowers, and the occasional rustle of a snake in the grass—the pervasive silence was shattered by the voice of Lucille Ball.

In the memory of many Australians, television came as Lucy, and Lucy *was* television. There's a joke in *Crocodile Dundee* where the last white frontiersman (Paul Hogan) is making first contact with modernity in his New York hotel, and he's introduced to the TV set. But he already knows TV: "I saw that twenty years ago at so-and-so's place." He sees the title, *"I Love Lucy,"* and says, "Yeah, that's what I saw." It's a throwaway line that at one level works as a formal definition of the "media-recycle" genre of the film itself. But in terms of the dense cultural punning that characterizes the film, it's also, for Australians, a very precise historical joke. Hogan was himself one of the first major Australian TV stars, finding instant stardom in the late 1960s by faking his way onto a talent-quest show, and then abusing the judges. Subsequently, he took on the Marlboro Man in a massive cigarette-advertising battle that lasted long enough to convert the slogan of Hogan's commercials ("Anyhow, have a Winfield") into a proverb inscrutable to foreigners. So Hogan's persona already incarnates a populist myth of indigenous Australian response to

Lucy as synecdoche of all American media culture.

But in the beginning was Lucy, and I think she is singled out in memory—since obviously it was not the only program available—because of the impact of her voice. The introduction of TV in Australia led not only to the usual debates about the restructuring of family life and domestic space, and to predictable fears that the Australian "accent" in language and culture might be abolished, but also to a specific local version of anxiety about the effects of TV on children. In "Situation Comedy, Feminism, and Freud: Discourses of Gracie and Lucy," Patricia Mellencamp discusses the spectacle of female comedians in the American 1950s "being out of control via language (Gracie) or body (Lucy)."[3] In my memory, Lucy herself combines both functions. Lucy was heard by many Australians as a screaming hysteric: as "voice," she was "seen" to be a woman out of control in both language *and* body. So there was concern that Lucy-television would, by some mimesis or contagion of the voice, metabolically transform Australian children from the cheeky little larrikins we were expected to be into ragingly hyperactive little psychopaths.

My own memory of this lived theoretical debate goes something like this. My mother and I loved Lucy, my father loathed "that noise." So once a week, there would be a small domestic catastrophe, which soon became routinized, repetitive, banal. I'd turn Lucy on, my father would start grumbling, Mum would be washing dishes in the next room, ask me to raise the volume, I'd do it, Dad would start yelling, Mum would yell back, I'd creep closer to the screen to hear, until finally Lucy couldn't make herself heard, and I'd retire in disgust to my bedroom, to the second-best of reading a novel. On one of the rare occasions when all this noise had led to a serious quarrel, I went up later as the timid little voice of reason, asking my father why, since it was only half an hour, did *he* make such a lot of noise. He said that the American voices (never then heard "live" in our small town) reminded him of the Pacific war. And that surely, after all these years, there were some things that, in the quiet of his own home, a man had a right to try to forget.

Looking back from the contradictions of the present, I can define from this story a contradiction which persists in different forms today. On the one hand, Lucy had a galvanizing and emancipating effect because of her loquacity and her relentless tonal insistence. Especially for Australian women and children, in a society where women were talkative with each other and laconic with men, men were laconic with each other and catatonic with women, and children were seen but not heard. Lucy was one of the first signs of a growing sense that women making a lot of noise did not need to be confined to the haremlike rituals of morning and afternoon tea or the washing up. On the other hand, my father's response appears, retrospectively, as prescient as well as understandable. The coming of Lucy, and of American TV, was among the first explicit announcements to a general public still vaguely imagining itself as having been "British" that Australia was now (as it had, in fact, been anyway since 1942) hooked into the media network of a different war machine.

My second anecdote follows logically from that, but is set in another world. Ten years later, after a whole cultural revolution in Australia and another war with the Americans in Asia, I saw a TV catastrophe one banal Christmas Eve. There we were in Sydney, couch-potatoing away, when the evening was shattered by that sentence which takes different forms in different cultures but is still perhaps the one sentence always capable of reminding people everywhere within reach of TV of a common and vulnerable humanity—"We interrupt this transmission for a special news flash."

Usually on hearing that, you get an adrenaline rush, you freeze, you wait to hear what's happened, then the mechanisms of bodily habituation to crisis take over to see you through the time ahead. This occasion was alarmingly different. The announcer actually stammered: "Er . . . um . . . something's happened to Darwin." Darwin is the capital of Australia's far north. Most Australians know nothing about it, and live thousands of miles away. It takes days to get into by land or sea, and in a well-entrenched national imaginary it is the "gateway" to Asia, and in its remoteness and "vulnerability," the likely port of a conventional invasion. This has usually been a racist nightmare about the "yellow peril" sweeping down, but it does also have a basis in flat-map logic. There's no one south of Australia but penguins.

So people panicked, and waited anxiously for details. But the catastrophe was that there was *no information*. Now, this was not catastrophe *on* TV—like the explosion of the space shuttle *Challenger*—but a catastrophe of and *for* TV. There were no pictures, no reports, just *silence*—which had long ceased to be coded as paradisal, as it was in my fable of origin, but was now the very definition of a state of total emergency. The announcer's stammer was devastating. He had lost control of all the mechanisms for assuring credibility;[4] his palpable personal distress had exposed us, unbelievably, to something like a *truth*. When those of us who could sleep woke up the next day to find everyday life going on as usual, we realized it couldn't have been World War III. But it took another twenty-four hours for "true" news to be reestablished, and to reassure us that Darwin had merely been wiped out by a cyclone. Whereupon we went into the "natural disaster" genre of TV living, and banality, except for the victims, resumed. But in the aftermath, a question surfaced. Why had such a cyclone-sensitive city not been forewarned? It was a very big cyclone—someone should have seen it coming.

Two rumors did the rounds. One was an oral rumor, or a folk legend. The cyclone took Darwin by surprise because it was a Russian weather warfare experiment that had either gone wrong or—in the more menacing variant—actually found its target. The other rumor made its way into writing in the odd newspaper. There had been foreknowledge: indeed, even after the cyclone there was a functioning radio tower and an airstrip which might have sent news out straight away. But these belonged to an American military installation near Darwin, which was not supposed to be there. And in the embarrassment of realizing the scale of the disaster to come, someone somewhere had made a decision to say nothing in the hope of averting discovery. If this was true, "they" needn't have worried. The story was never, to my knowledge, pursued further. We didn't really care. If there had been such an installation, it wasn't newsworthy; true or false, it wasn't catastrophic; true or false, it merged with the routine stories of conspiracy and paranoia in urban everyday life; and, true or false, it was—compared with the Darwin fatality count and the human interest stories to be had from cyclone survivors—just too banal to be of interest.

My anecdotes are also banal, in that they mark out a television contradiction which is overfamiliar as both a theoretical dilemma and an everyday experience. It is the contradiction between one's pleasure, fascination, thrill, and sense of "life," even birth, in popular culture and the deathly shadows of war, invasion, emergency, crisis, and terror that perpetually haunt the networks. Sometimes there seems to be nothing more to say about that "contradiction," in theory, yet as a phase of collective experience it does keep coming back around. So I want to use these two anecdotes now to frame a comparison between the late work of Baudrillard and some aspects

of "British" (or Anglo-Australian) cultural studies—two theoretical projects that have had something to say about the problem. I begin with Baudrillard, because "banality" is a working concept in his lexicon, whereas it is not a significant term for the cultural studies that today increasingly cite him.

In Baudrillard's terms, my anecdotes marked out a historical shift between a period of concern about TV's effects on the real—which is thereby assumed to be distinct from its representation (the *Lucy* moment)—and a time in which TV *generates* the real to the extent that any interruption in its processes of doing so is experienced as more catastrophic in the lounge room than a "real" catastrophe elsewhere. So I have simply defined a shift between a regime of production and a regime of simulation. This would also correspond to a shift between a more or less real Cold War ethos, where American military presence in your country could be construed as friendly or hostile, but you thought you should have a choice, and that the choice mattered; and a pure war (or, simulated chronic cold war) ethos, in which Russian cyclones or American missiles are completely interchangeable in a local imaginary of terror, and the choice between them is meaningless.

This analysis could be generated from Baudrillard's major thesis in *L'échange symbolique et la mort* (1976). The later Baudrillard would have little further interest in my story about Lucy's voice and domestic squabbles in an Australian country town, but might still be mildly amused by the story of a city disappearing for thirty-six hours because of a breakdown in communications. However, where I would want to say that this event was for participants a real, if mediated, experience of catastrophe, he could say that it was just a final flicker of real reality. With the subsequent installation of a global surveillance regime through the satellization of the world, the disappearance of Darwin could never occur again.

So Baudrillard would collapse the "contradiction" that I want to maintain: and he would make each polar term of my stories (the everyday and the catastrophic, the exhilarating and the frightful, the emancipatory and the terroristic) invade and contaminate its other in a process of mutual exacerbation. This is a viral, rather than an atomic, model of crisis in everyday life. If, for Andreas Huyssen, modernism as an adversary culture constitutes itself in an "anxiety of contamination" by its Other (mass culture),[5] the Baudrillardian text on (or of) mass culture is constituted by perpetually *intensifying* the contamination of one of any two terms by its other.

So like all pairs of terms in Baudrillard's work, the values "banality" and "fatality" chase each other around his pages following the rule of dyadic reversibility. Any one term can be hyperbolically intensified until it turns into its opposite. Superbanality, for example, becomes fatal, and a superfatality would be banal. It's a very simple but, when well done, dizzying logico-semantic game which makes Baudrillard's books very easy to understand, but any one term most difficult to define. A complication in this case is that "banality" and "fatality" chase each other around two books, *De la séduction* (1979) and *Les stratégies fatales* (1983).

One way to elucidate such a system is to imagine a distinction between two sets of two terms—for example, "fatal charm" and "banal seduction." Fatal charm can be seductive in the old sense of an irresistible force, exerted by someone who desires nothing except to play the game in order to capture and to immolate the desire of the other. That's what's fatal about it. Banal seduction on the other hand, does involve desire: desire for, perhaps, an immovable object to overcome. That's what's fatal for it. Baudrillard's next move is to claim that both of these strategies are finished. The only irresistible force today is that of the moving *object* as it flees and evades the subject. This

is the "force" of the sex-object, of the silent zombie-masses, and of femininity (not necessarily detached by Baudrillard from real women, but certainly detached from feminists).

This structure is, I think, a "fatal" travesty, or a "seduction" of the terms of Althusserian epistemology and *its* theory of moving objects. In *Les stratégies fatales,* the travesty is rewritten in terms of a theory of global catastrophe. The human species has passed the dead point of history: we are living out the ecstasy of permanent catastrophe, which slows down as it becomes more and more intense (*une catastrophe au ralenti,* slow-motion, or slowing-motion catastrophe), until the supereventfulness of the event approaches the uneventfulness of absolute inertia, and we begin to live everyday catastrophe as an endless dead point, or a perpetual freeze frame.

This is the kind of general scenario produced in Baudrillard's work by the logic of mutual contamination. However, an examination of the local occurrences of the terms "banal" and "fatal" in both books suggests that "banality" is associated, quite clearly and conventionally, with negative aspects of media—overrepresentation, excessive visibility, information overload, an obscene plenitude of images, a gross platitudinousness of the all-pervasive present.

On the other hand, and even though there is strictly no past and no future in Baudrillard's system, he uses "fatality" as both a nostalgic and a futuristic term for invoking a classical critical value, *discrimination* (redefined as a senseless but still rule-governed principle of selectiveness). "Fatality" is nostalgic in the sense that it invokes in the text, for the present, an "aristocratic" ideal of maintaining an elite, arbitrary, and avowedly artificial order. It is futuristic because Baudrillard suggests that in an age of overload, rampant banality, and catastrophe (which have become at this stage equivalents of each other), the last Pascalian wager may be to bet on the return, in the present, of what can only be a simulacrum of the past. When fatal charm can simulate seducing banal seduction, you have a fatal strategy. The animating myth of this return is to be, in opposition to critical philosophies of Difference (which have now become identical), a myth of *Fatum*—that is, Destiny.

So read in one sense, Baudrillard's theory merely calls for an aesthetic order (fatality) to deal with mass cultural anarchy (banality). What makes his appeal more charming than most other tirades about the decay of standards is that it can be read in the opposite sense. The "order" being called for is radically decadent, superbanal. However, there is a point at which the play stops.

In one of Baudrillard's anecdotes (an enunciative *mise en abyme* of his theory), set in some vague courtly context with the ambience of a mid—eighteenth-century French epistolary novel, a man is trying to seduce a woman. She asks, "Which part of me do you find most seductive?" He replies, "Your eyes." Next day, he receives an envelope. Inside, instead of the letter, he finds a bloody eye. Analyzing his own fable, Baudrillard points out that in the obviousness, the literalness of her gesture, the woman has purloined the place of her seducer.

The man is the banal seducer. She, the fatal seducer, sets him a trap with her question as he moves to entrap her. In the platitudinous logic of courtliness, he can only reply "Your eyes"—rather than naming some more vital organ which she might not have been able to post—since the eye is the window of the soul. Baudrillard concludes that the woman's literalness is fatal to the man's banal figuration: she loses an eye, but he loses *face*. He can never again "cast an eye" on another woman without thinking literally of the bloody eye that replaced the letter. So Baudrillard's final resolution of the play between banality and fatality is this: a banal theory assumes, like the platitudinous seducer, that

the subject is more powerful than the object. A fatal theory knows, like the woman, that the object is always *worse* than the subject (*"je ne suis pas belle, je suis pire . . ."*).

Nonetheless, in making the pun "she loses an eye, but he loses face," Baudrillard in fact enunciatively reoccupies the place of control of meaning by *de*-literalizing the woman's gesture, and returning it to figuration. Only the pun makes the story work as a fable of seduction, by draining the "blood" from the eye. Without it, we would merely be reading a horror story (or a feminist moral tale). So it follows that Baudrillard's figuration is, in fact, "fatal" to the woman's literality, and to a literal feminist reading of her story that might presumably ensue. In the process, the privilege of "knowing" the significance of the woman's fatal-banal gesture is securely restored to metalanguage, and to the subject of exegesis.

Recent cultural studies offers something completely different. It speaks not of restoring discrimination but of encouraging cultural democracy. It respects difference and sees mass culture not as a vast banality machine but as raw material made available for a variety of popular practices.

In saying "it," I am treating a range of quite different texts and arguments as a single entity. This is always imprecise, polemically "unifying," and unfair to any individual item. But sometimes, when distractedly reading magazines such as *New Socialist* or *Marxism Today* from the last couple of years, flipping through *Cultural Studies,* or scanning the pop-theory pile in the bookstore, I get the feeling that somewhere in some English publisher's vault there is a master disk from which thousands of versions of the same article about pleasure, resistance, and the politics of consumption are being run off under different names with minor variations. Americans and Australians are recycling this basic pop-theory article, too: with the perhaps major variation that English pop theory still derives at least nominally from a Left popul*ism* attempting to salvage a sense of life from the catastrophe of Thatcherism. Once cut free from that context, as commodities always are, and recycled in quite different political cultures, the vestigial *critical* force of that populism tends to disappear or mutate.

This imaginary pop-theory article might respond to my television anecdotes by bracketing the bits about war and death as a sign of paranoia about popular culture, by pointing out that it's a mistake to confuse conditions of production with the subsequent effects of images, and by noting that with TV one may always be "ambivalent." It would certainly stress, with the Lucy story, the subversive pleasure of the female spectators. (My father could perhaps represent an Enlightenment paternalism of reason trying to make everything cohere in a model of social totality.) With the Darwin story, it would insist on the creativity of the consumer/spectator, and maybe have us distractedly zapping from channel to channel during the catastrophe instead of being passively hooked into the screen, and then resisting the war machine with our local legends and readings. The article would then restate, using a mix of different materials as illustration, the enabling theses of contemporary cultural studies.

In order to move away now from reliance on imaginary bad objects, I'll refer to an excellent real article which gives a summary of these theses—Mica Nava's "Consumerism and Its Contradictions." Among the enabling theses—and they *have* been enabling—are these: consumers are not "cultural dopes" but active, critical users of mass culture; consumption practices cannot be derived from or reduced to a mirror of production; consumer practice is "far more than just economic activity: it is also about dreams and consolation, communication and confrontation, image and identity. Like sexuality, it consists of a multiplicity of fragmented and contradictory discourses."[6]

I'm not now concerned to contest these theses. For the moment, I'll buy the lot. What I'm interested in is first, the sheer proliferation of the restatements, and second, the emergence in some of them of a *restrictive definition* of the ideal knowing subject of cultural studies.

John Fiske's historical account in "British Cultural Studies and Television" produces one such restatement and restriction. The social terrain of the beginning of his article is occupied by a version of the awesomely complex Althusserian subject-in-ideology, and by a summary of Gramsci on hegemony. Blending these produces a notion of subjectivity as a dynamic field, in which all sorts of permutations are possible at different moments in an endless process of production, contestation, and reproduction of social identities. By the end of the article, the field has been vastly simplified: there are "the dominant classes" (exerting hegemonic force) and "the people" (making their own meanings and constructing their own culture "within, and sometimes against," the culture provided for them) (286).

Cultural studies for Fiske aims to understand and encourage cultural democracy. One way of understanding the *demos* is *"ethnography"*—finding out what the people say and think about their culture. But the methods cited are "voxpop" techniques common to journalism and empirical sociology—interviewing, collecting background, analyzing statements made spontaneously by, or solicited from, informants. So the choice of the term "ethnography" for these practices emphasizes a possible "ethnic" gap between the cultural student and the culture studied. The "understanding" and "encouraging" subject may share some aspects of that culture, but *in the process of interrogation and analysis* is momentarily located outside it. "The people" is a voice, or a *figure of* a voice, cited in a discourse of exegesis. For example, Fiske cites "Lucy," a fourteen year old fan of Madonna ("She's tarty and seductive . . . but it looks alright when she does it, you know, what I mean . . ."); and then goes on to translate, and diagnose, what she means: "Lucy's problems probably stem from her recognition that marriage is a patriarchal institution and, as such, is threatened by Madonna's sexuality" (273).

If this is again a process of embedding in metadiscourse a sample of raw female speech, it is also a perfectly honest approach for any academic analyst of culture to take. It differs from a discourse that simply appeals to "experience" to validate and universalize its own conclusions. However, such honesty should also require some analysis of the analyst's own institutional and "disciplinary" position—perhaps some recognition, too, of the double play of transference. (Lucy tells him her pleasure in Madonna: but what is his pleasure in Lucy's?) This kind of recognition is rarely made in populist polemics. What takes its place is first, a citing of popular voices (the informants), an act of translation and commentary, and then a play of *identification* between the knowing subject of cultural studies and a collective subject, "the people."

In Fiske's text, however, "the people" have no necessary defining characteristics—except an indomitable capacity to "negotiate" readings, generate new interpretations, and remake the materials of culture. This is also, of course, the function of cultural studies itself (and in Fiske's version, the study does include a "semiotic analysis of the text" to explore *how* meanings are made [272]). So against the hegemonic force of the dominant classes, "the people" in fact represent the most creative energies and functions of critical reading. In the end they are not simply the cultural student's object of study and his native informants. The people are also the textually delegated, allegorical emblem of the critic's own activity. Their *ethnos* may be constructed as other, but it is used as the ethnographer's mask.

Once "the people" are both a source of authority for a text and a figure of its own critical activity, the populist enterprise is not only circular but (like most empirical sociology) narcissistic in structure. Theorizing the problems that ensue is one way—in my view, an important way—to break out of the circuit of repetition. Another is to project elsewhere a misunderstanding or discouraging Other figure (often that feminist or Marxist Echo, the blast from the past) to necessitate and enable more repetition.

The opening chapter of Iain Chambers's *Popular Culture* provides an example of this, as well as a definition of what counts as "popular" knowledge that is considerably more restrictive than John Fiske's. Chambers argues that in looking at popular culture, we should not subject individual signs and single texts to the "contemplative state of official culture." Instead, it is a practice of "distracted reception" that really characterizes the subject of "popular epistemology." For Chambers, this distraction has consequences for the practice of writing. Writing can imitate popular culture (life) by, for example, "writing through quotations," and refusing to "explain . . . references fully." To explain would be to reimpose the contemplative stare and adopt the authority of the "academic mind."[7]

Chambers's argument emerges from an interpretation of the history of subcultural practices, especially in music. I've argued elsewhere my disagreement with his attempt to use that history to generalize about popular culture in The Present.[8] Here, I want to suggest that an image of the subject of pop epistemology as casual and "distracted" obliquely entails a revival of the figure that Andreas Huyssen, Tania Modleski, and Patrice Petro have described in various contexts as "mass culture as woman."[9] Petro, in particular, further points out that the contemplation/distraction opposition is historically implicated in the construction of the "female spectator" as site, and target, of a theorization of modernity by male intellectuals in Weimar.[10]

There are many versions of a "distraction" model available in cultural studies today: there are housewives phasing in and out of TV or flipping through magazines in laundromats as well as pop intellectuals playing with quotes. In Chambers's text, which is barely concerned with women at all, distraction is not presented as a female characteristic. Yet today's recycling of Weimar's distraction nonetheless has the "contours," in Petro's phrase, of a familiar female stereotype—distracted, absent-minded, insouciant, vague, flighty, skimming from image to image. The rush of associations runs irresistibly toward a figure of mass culture not as woman but, more specifically, as bimbo.

In the texts Petro analyzes, "contemplation" (of distraction in the cinema) is assumed to be the prerogative of male intellectual audiences. In pop epistemology, a complication is introduced via the procedures of projection and identification that Elaine Showalter describes in "Critical Cross-Dressing."[11] The knowing subject of popular epistemology no longer contemplates "mass culture" as bimbo, but takes on the assumed mass cultural characteristics in the writing of his own text. Since the object of projection and identification in post-subcultural theory tends to be black music and "style" rather than the European (and literary) feminine, we find an actantial hero of knowledge emerging in the form of the *white male theorist* as bimbo.

However, I think the problem with the notion of pop epistemology is not really, in this case, a vestigial antifeminism in the concept of distraction. The problem is that in antiacademic pop-theory writing (much of which, like Chambers's book, circulates as textbooks with exam and essay topics at the end of each chapter), a stylistic enactment of the "popular" as *essentially* distracted, scan-

ning the surface, and short on attention span, performs a retrieval, at the level of *enunciative* practice, of the thesis of "cultural dopes." In the critique of which—going right back to the early work of Stuart Hall, not to mention Raymond Williams—the project of cultural studies effectively and rightly began.

One could claim that this interpretation is possible only if one continues to assume that the academic traditions of "contemplation" really do define intelligence, and that to be "distracted" can therefore only mean being dopey. I would reply that as long as we accept to restate the alternatives in those terms, that is precisely the assumption we continue to recycle. No matter which of the terms we validate, the contemplation/distraction, academic/popular oppositions can serve only to limit and distort the possibilities of popular practice. Furthermore, I think that this return to the postulate of cultural dopism in the *practice* of writing may be one reason why pop theory is now generating over and over again the same article. If a cultural dopism is being enunciatively performed (and valorized) in a discourse that tries to contest it, then the argument in fact *cannot* move on, but can only retrieve its point of departure as "banality" (a word pop theorists don't normally use) in the negative sense.

For the thesis of cultural studies as Fiske and Chambers present it runs perilously close to this kind of formulation: people in modern mediatized societies are complex and contradictory, mass cultural texts are complex and contradictory, therefore people using them produce complex and contradictory culture. To add that this popular culture has critical and resistant elements is tautological—unless one (or a predicated someone, that Other who needs to be told) has a concept of culture so rudimentary that it excludes criticism and resistance from the practice of everyday life.

Given the different values ascribed to mass culture in Baudrillard's work and in pop theory, it is tempting to make a distracted contrast between them in terms of elitism and populism. However, they are not symmetrical opposites.

Cultural studies posits a "popular" subject "supposed to know" in a certain manner, which the subject of populist theory then claims to understand (Fiske) or mimic (Chambers). Baudrillard's elitism, however, is not an elitism of a knowing subject of theory but an elitism of the *object*—which is forever, and actively, evasive. There is a hint of "distraction" here, an echo between the problematics of woman and literalness and mass culture as bimbo which deserves further contemplation. A final twist is that for Baudrillard, the worst (that is, most effective) elitism of the object can be called, precisely, "theory." Theory is understood as an objectified and objectifying (never "objective") force strategically engaged in an ever more intense process of commodification. Like "distraction" it is distinguished by the rapidity of its *flight,* rather than by a concentrated pursuit.

However, it is remarkable, given the differences between them and the crisis-ridden society that each in its own way addresses, that neither of the projects I've discussed leaves much place for an unequivocally pained, unambivalently discontented, or momentarily *aggressive* subject. It isn't just negligence. There is an active process going on in both of discrediting—by direct dismissal (Baudrillard) or covert inscription as Other (cultural studies)—the voices of grumpy feminists and cranky leftists ("Frankfurt School" can do duty for both). To discredit such voices is, as I understand it, one of the immediate political functions of the current boom in cultural studies (as distinct from the intentionality of projects invested by it). To discredit a voice is something very different from displacing an analysis which has become outdated, or revising a strategy which no longer serves its purpose. It is to

character-ize a fictive position from which anything said can be dismissed as already heard.

Baudrillard's hostility to the discourses of political radicalism is perfectly clear and brilliantly played out. It is a little too aggressive to accuse cultural studies of playing much the same game. Cultural studies is a humane and optimistic discourse, trying to derive its values from materials and conditions already available to people. On the other hand, it can become an apologetic "yes, *but* . . ." discourse that most often proceeds *from* admitting class, racial, and sexual oppressions *to* finding the inevitable saving grace—when its theoretical presuppositions should require it at least to do both simultaneously, even "dialectically." And in practice the "but . . ."—that is to say, the argumentative rhetoric—has been increasingly addressing not the hegemonic force of the "dominant classes" but other critical theories (vulgar feminism, the Frankfurt School) inscribed as misunderstanding popular culture.[12]

Both discourses share a tendency toward reductionism—political as well as theoretical. To simplify matters myself, I'd say that where the fatal strategies of Baudrillard keep returning us to his famous Black Hole—a scenario that is so grim, obsessive, and, in its enunciative strategies, maniacally overcoherent that instead of speaking, a woman must *tear out her eye* to be heard—the voxpop style of cultural studies is on the contrary offering us the sanitized world of a deodorant commercial where there's always a way to redemption. There's something sad about that, because cultural studies emerged from a real attempt to give voice to much grittier experiences of class, race, and gender.

Yet the sense of frustration that some of us who would inscribe our own work as cultural studies feel with the terms of present debate can be disabling. If one is equally uneasy about fatalistic theory on the one hand and about cheerily "making the best of things" on the other, then it is a poor solution to consent to confine oneself to (and in) the dour position of rebuking both.

In *The Practice of Everyday Life,* Michel de Certeau provides a more positive approach to the politics of theorizing popular culture, and to the particular problems I have discussed.[13] One of the pleasures of this text for me is the range of moods that it admits to a field of study which—surprisingly, since "everyday life" is at issue—often seems to be occupied only by cheerleaders and prophets of doom. So from it I shall borrow—in a contemplative rather than a distracted spirit—two quotations to modify the sharp oppositions I've created, before discussing his work in more detail.

The first quotation is in fact from Jacques Sojcher's *La Démarche poétique.* De Certeau cites Sojcher after arguing for a double process of mobilizing the "weighty apparatus" of theories of ordinary language to analyze everyday practices, *and* seeking to restore to those practices their logical and cultural legitimacy. He then uses the Sojcher quotation to insist that in this kind of research, everyday practices will "alternately exacerbate *and disrupt* our logics. Its regrets are like those of the poet, and like him, it struggles against oblivion." So I will use his quotation in turn as a response to the terrifying and unrelenting coherence of Baudrillard's fatal strategies. Sojcher:

And I forgot the elements of chance introduced by circumstances, calm or haste, sun or cold, dawn or dusk, the taste of strawberries or abandonment, the half-understood message, the front page of newspapers, the voice on the telephone, the most anodyne conversation, the most anonymous man or woman, everything that speaks, makes noise, passes by, touches us lightly, meets us head on. (xvi)

The second quotation comes from a discussion of "Freud and the Ordinary Man," and the difficult problems that arise when "elitist writing uses the 'vulgar' [or, I would add, the 'feminine'] speaker as a disguise for a metalanguage about itself." For de Certeau, a recognition that the "ordinary" and the "popular" can act as a mask in analytical discourse does *not* imply that the study of popular culture is impossible except as recuperation. Instead, it demands that we show *how* the ordinary introduces itself into analytical techniques, and this requires a displacement in the institutional practice of knowledge:

Far from arbitrarily assuming the privilege of speaking in the name of the ordinary (it cannot *be* spoken), or claiming to be in that general place (that would be a false "mysticism"), or, worse, offering up a hagiographic everydayness for its edifying value, it is a matter of restoring historicity to the movement which leads analytical procedures back to their frontiers, to the point where they are changed, indeed disturbed, by the ironic and mad banality that speaks in "Everyman" in the sixteenth century, and that has returned in the final stages of Freud's knowledge. . . . (5)

In this way, he suggests, the ordinary "can reorganize the place from which discourse is produced." I think that this includes being very careful about our enunciative and "anecdotal" strategies—more careful than much cultural studies has been in its mimesis of a popular voice—and their relation to the institutional *places* we may occupy as we speak.

In spirit, de Certeau's work is much more in sympathy with the *bricoleur* impulse of cultural studies than with apocalyptic thinking. The motto of his book could be the sentence "People have to make do with what they have" (18). Its French title is *Arts de faire:* arts of making, arts of doing, arts of making do. Its project, however, is not a theory of popular culture but "a science of singularity": a science of the relationship that links "everyday pursuits to particular circumstances." So the study of how people use mass media, for example, is defined not in opposition *to* "high" or "elite" cultural analysis, but in connection *with* a general study of *activities*—cooking, walking, reading, talking, shopping. A basic operation in the "science" is an incessant movement between what de Certeau calls "polemological" and "utopian" spaces of making do (15−18): a movement which involves, as my quotations may suggest, both a poetics and a politics of practice.[14]

The basic assumption of a polemological space is summed up by a quotation from a Maghrebian syndicalist at Billancourt: "They always fuck us over." This is a sentence that seems inadmissible in contemporary cultural studies: it defines a space of struggle, and mendacity ("the strong always win, and words always deceive"). For the peasants of the Pernambuco region of Brazil, in de Certeau's main example, it is a socioeconomic space of innumerable conflicts in which the rich and the police are constantly victorious. But at the same time and in the same place, a utopian space is reproduced in the popular legends of *miracles* that circulate and intensify as repression becomes more absolute and apparently successful. De Certeau mentions the story of Frei Damiao, the charismatic hero of the region.

I would cite, as a parable of both kinds of space, a television anecdote about the Sydney Birthday Cake Scandal. In 1988, governments in Australia spent lavish sums of money on bicentenary celebrations. But it was really the bicentenary of Sydney as the original penal colony. In 1988 "Australia" was in fact only eighty-seven years old, and so the event was widely understood to be a costly effort at simulating, rather than celebrating, a unified national history. It promoted as our fable of

origin not the federation of the colonies and the beginnings of independence (1901) but the invasion of Aboriginal Australia by the British penal system—and the catastrophe that, for Aborigines, ensued.

A benevolent Sydney real-estate baron proposed to build a giant birthday cake above an expressway tunnel in the most famous social wastage-and-devastation zone of the city, so we could know we were having a party. The project was unveiled on a TV current affairs show, and there was an uproar—not only from exponents of good taste against kitsch. The network switchboards were jammed by people pointing out that, above the area that belongs to junkies, runaways, homeless people, and the child as well as adult prostitution trade, a giant cake would invoke a late eighteenth-century voice quite different from that of our first prison governor saying, "Here we are in Botany Bay." It would be Marie Antoinette saying, "let them eat cake." There was nothing casual or distracted about *that* voxpop observation.

The baron then proposed a public competition, again via TV, to find an alternative design. There were lots of proposals: a few of us wanted to build Kafka's writing machine from "In the Penal Colony." Others proposed an echidna, a water tower, a hypodermic, or a giant condom. The winner was a suburban rotary clothesline: Australia's major contribution to twentieth-century technology, and thus something of a symbol for the current decline in our economy. But in the end, the general verdict was that we'd rather make do with the cake. As one person said in a voxpop segment, "At least with the cake, the truth about the party is all now out in the open." So had the cake been built, it would have been, after all that polemological narrativity, a wildly utopian popular monument.

No monument materialized, and the story died down. However, it reappeared in a different form when an extravagant birthday party was duly held on January 26, 1988.

Two and a half million people converged on a few square kilometers of harbor foreshore on a glorious summer's day to watch the ships, to splash about, to eat and drink and fall asleep in the sun during speeches. The largest gathering of Aboriginal people since the original Invasion Day was also held, to protest the proceedings. The party ended with a fabulous display of fireworks, choreographed to music progressing "historically" from the eighteenth century to the present. The climax was "Power and the Passion," a famous song by Midnight Oil (Australia's favorite polemological rock band), which is utterly scathing about public as well as "popular" chauvinist culture in urban white Australia. Only those watching the celebrations on TV were able to hear it and to admire the fireworks dancing to its tune. The day after, a slogan surfaced in the streets and on the walls of the city and in press cartoons: "Let them eat fireworks."

For de Certeau, a polemological analysis is entailed by "the relation of procedures to the fields of force in which they act" (xvii). It maps the terrain and the strategies of what he loosely calls "established powers" (in opposition not to the "powerless" but to the nonestablished, to powers and possibilities not in stable possession of a singular *place* of their own). This analysis is an accompaniment, and not an alternative or a rival, to utopian tactics and stories. Polemological and utopian spaces are distinct, but in proximity: they are "alongside" each other, not in contradiction.

These terms need clarification, since it is not just a matter of opposing major to minor, strong to weak, and romantically validating the latter. A strategy is "the calculus of force-relationships which becomes possible when a subject of will and power (a proprietor, an enterprise, a city, a scientific institution) can be isolated from an 'environment' " (xix). Strategy presupposes a place of its own, one circumscribed as "proper," and so predicates

an exterior, an "outside," an excluded Other (and technologies to manage this relationship). Tactics, however, are localized ways of using what is made available—materials, opportunities, time and space for action—by the strategy of the other, and in "his" place. They depend on arts of *timing,* a seizing of propitious moments, rather than on arts of colonizing space.[15] They use "the place of the other," in a mode of *insinuation*—like the street slogans in my example, of course, but more exactly like the mysterious appearance of "Power and the Passion" in the festive choreography of State.

The "miracle" created by the appearance of this heretical song did not necessarily derive, unlike the graffiti, from a deliberate act of debunking—although it's nice to think it did. While Midnight Oil's public image in Australia is unambiguously political, it is just possible that for the ceremony planners, the reference may have been more like Ronald Reagan's "Born in the USA": a usage crucially inattentive to detail, but functional, and not inaccurate, in mobilizing parts of a resonant myth of how Sydney feels as a *place.* But the intention didn't matter: the flash of hilarity and encouragement the song gave viewers otherwise mortified by the Invasion festival would be, in de Certeau's terms, a product of *their* "tactical" use of the show, their insinuation of polemical significance into the place of programmed pleasure.

It is in this sense of popular practice as a fleeting appropriation, one which diverts the purposive rationality of an established power, that de Certeau's theory associates consumer "reading" with oral culture, and with the survival skills of colonized people: like dancers, travelers, poachers, and short-term tenants, or "voices" in written texts, "they move about . . . passing lightly through the field of the other" (131). In this movement, polemological space is created by an "analysis of facts": not facts as objectively validated by a regime of place, but facts produced by *experience* of another place, and time spent on the other's terrain. Polemological analysis in this sense accords no legitimacy to "facts." "They always fuck us over" may be a fact but not a law: utopian spaces deny the immutability and authority of facts, and together both spaces refuse the fatality (the *fatum,* "what has been spoken," destiny decreed) of an established order.

This general definition of popular culture as a *way of operating*—rather than as a set of contents, a marketing category, a reflected expression of social position, or even a "terrain" of struggle—is at once in affinity with the thematics of recent cultural studies and also, I think, inflected away from some of its problems.

Like most theories of popular culture today, it does not use "folk," "primitive" or "indigenous" cultures as a lost origin or ideal model for considering "mass" cultural experience. Unlike some of those theories, it does not thereby cease to think connections between them. Global structures of power and forces of occupation (rationalizing time and establishing place) do not drop out of the analytical field. On the contrary, imperialism and its knowledges—ethnology, travel writing, "communications"—*establish* a field in which analysis of popular culture becomes a tactical way of operating.

De Certeau shares with many others a taste for "reading" as privileged metaphor of a *modus operandi.* However, the reading he theorizes is not a figure of "writerly" freedom, subjective mastery, interpretive control, or caprice. To read is to "wander through an imposed system" (169)—a text, a city street, a supermarket, a State festivity. It is not a passive activity, but it is not independent of the system it uses. Nor does the figure of reading assert the primacy of a scriptural model for understanding popular culture. To read is not to write and rewrite but to travel: reading borrows, without establishing a "place" of its own. As a schooled activity, reading happens

at the point where "*social* stratification (class relationships) and *poetic* operations (the practitioner's construction of a text) intersect." So a reader's autonomy would depend on a transformation of the social relationships that overdetermine her relation to texts. But in order not to be another normative imposition, any "politics" of reading would also have to be articulated on an analysis of poetic practices already in operation.

In this framework, popular culture does not provide a space of exemption from socioeconomic constraints, although it may circulate stories of exemption denying the fatality of socioeconomic systems. At the same time, it is not idealized as a reservoir or counterplace for inversions of "propriety" (distraction vs. contemplation, for example). As a way of operating, the practice of everyday life has no place, no borders, no hierarchy of materials forbidden or privileged for use: "Barthes reads Proust in Stendhal's text: the viewer reads the landscape of his childhood in the evening news" (xxi).

De Certeau's insistence on the movement *between* polemological and utopian practices of making do makes it possible to say that if cultural studies is losing its polemological edge—its capacity to articulate loss, despair, disillusion, anger, and thus to learn from failure—Baudrillard's work has not lost its utopianism but has rather produced too much *convergence* between polemological and (nightmare) utopian spaces: his stories are negative miracles, working only to intensify the fatality of his "facts."

Yet de Certeau's formulations draw heavily on a distinction between having and not having a place (and on a "fleeting appropriation" of Derrida's critique of *le propre*) which can in turn pose difficulties for feminists, or indeed anyone today for whom "a room of one's own" is a utopian aspiration rather than a securely established premise, and for whom a stint of "short-term tenancy" in someone else's place seems less like denying fatality, and more like one's usual fate.

There are serious problems here (and not only for a feminist appropriation of de Certeau's work). Another is the way that any rhetoric of otherness may slide, by association or analogy between historically "othered" terms, toward assimilating its figures of displacement in an ever-expanding exoticism: peasants in Brazil, Maghrebian workers in Billancourt, Barthes in the library, and television viewers in Sydney can come into equivalence in a paradigm of *exempla* of desirably transient practice. And the political question of "positioning" in relation to "practice" in cultural studies is clearly not eliminated by a rhetorical shift from "having" words to "doing" words, from values of propriety to modes of operativity—or from territorializing to technicist frames of reference.

*The Practice of Everyday Life* doesn't eliminate or avoid these problems, although its solutions may not satisfy feminists. It deals with them through a historical critique of the "logics" of cultural analysis, the objects of study they constitute, and the limits they construct and confront. I need to refer briefly to this critique in order to consider the relation between place, storytelling, and a politics of "banality" in his theory.

There is an insistent "we" structuring de Certeau's discourse, which is not a humanist universal but an (otherwise undifferentiated) marker of a class position in knowledge. It locates the text's project (and the writer and reader of cultural analysis) in a "place"—the scholarly enterprise, the research institution. Whether or not de Certeau's reader is prepared to go along with his tenured (masculine) "we," its placing works to interrupt rather than facilitate any slide toward exoticism. It also creates intervals, or spaces, of polemological reflection on that utopia for analysis, the nonplace of the other. For as Wlad Godzich points out in a foreword to de Certeau's collection of essays *Heterologies,*

his "other" "is not a magical or a transcendental entity; it is the discourse's mode of relation to its own historicity in the moment of its utterance."[16]

In the quotations with which I began my discussion of *The Practice of Everyday Life,* the "regrets" of research involve a moment of remembering "the element of chance introduced by circumstances . . . everything that speaks, makes noises, passes by, touches us lightly, meets us head on." Since these fugitive encounters with the other are also the very object of analysis, remembering entails not only a poetics of regret but also a history of forgetting, a "struggle against oblivion." If the taste of strawberries or abandonment can "alternately exacerbate and disrupt our logics," it is not because of some essential inadequacy of "thought" (analysis) in relation to "feeling" (the popular), as Iain Chambers's mind/body dualism implies; nor is it because of a tantalizing gap in *being* founding the subject's pursuit of its objects (that famous "lack" still assumed, if parodied, by Baudrillard's theory of fatality). It is, rather, that what may transform analytical procedures at their frontiers is precisely a "banality" of which the repression has constituted *historically* an enabling, even empowering, condition for the study of popular culture.

This is a large thesis, which rests on several distinct arguments.[17] I can mention only two, in drastically simplified form. One is a historical account of how French scholarly interest in popular culture emerged during the nineteenth century from projects to destroy or "police" it, and how this primary "murder" inflects procedures still used today: for example, that play of identification which leads cultural historians into writing, in the name of the "popular," other-effacing forms of intellectual autobiography.[18] The second argument takes the form of an allegory of the relationship between European writing and "orality" since the seventeenth century.[19] It combines a history of a socioeconomic and technological space ("the scriptural economy") with an interpretation of the emergence of modern disciplines, and of the birth-in-death of "the other." The work of Charles Nisard (*Histoire des livres populaires,* 1954) is the focus for the first account, and Defoe's *Robinson Crusoe* (1719) is read as an inaugural text for the second.

They are linked by a claim that the scriptural economy entailed for intellectuals a "double isolation" from the "people" (in opposition to the "bourgeoisie") and from the *"voice"* (in opposition to the "written"): "Hence the conviction that far, too far away from economic and administrative powers, 'the People speaks' " (131–32). This new "voxpop" (my term, not his) becomes both an object of nostalgic longing and a source of disturbance. Thus Robinson Crusoe, master of the island, the white page, the blank space *(espace propre)* of production and progress, finds his scriptural empire haunted by the "crack" or the "smudge" of Man Friday's footprint on the sand—a "silent marking" of the text by what *will* intervene *as voice* ("a marking of language by the body") in the field of writing (154–55).[20] With the figure of Man Friday appears a new and long-lasting form of alterity defined *in relation to* writing: he is the other who must either cry out (a "wild" outbreak requiring treatment) or make his body the vehicle of the dominant language—becoming "his master's voice," his ventriloquist's dummy, his mask in enunciation.

If this is a large thesis, it is also today a familiar one, not least with respect to its form. Defining the "other" (with whatever value we invest in this term in different contexts) as the repressed-and-returning in discourse has become one of the moves most tried and trusted to (re)generate writing, remotivate scriptural enterprise, inscribe signs, maybe myths, of critical difference. De Certeau admits as much, describing the "problematics of repression" as a type of ideological criticism that doesn't change the workings of a system but endows the critic with an appearance of distance from it (41). However, his own emphasis is on "restoring historicity" in order to think the critic's *involvement* in the system, and thus the operations that may reorganize his place.

If the other figures mythically as "voice" in the scriptural economy, the voice in turn discursively figures in the primary form of quotation—a mark or trace of the other. Two ways of quoting have historically defined this voice: quotation as *pretext,* using oral "relics" to fabricate texts, and quotation-*reminiscence,* marking "the fragmented and unexpected return . . . of oral relationships that are structuring but repressed by the written" (156). De Certeau gives the first an eighteenth-century name, "the *science of fables*"; the second he calls "returns and turns of voices" *("retours et tours de voix"),* or "sounds of the body."

The science of fables involves all "learned" hermeneutics of speech—ethnology, psychiatry, pedagogy, and political or historiographical procedures which try to "introduce the 'voice of the people' into the authorized language." As "heterologies," or "sciences of the different," their common characteristic is to try to *write* the voice, transforming it into readable products. In the process, the position of the other (the primitive, the child, the mad, the popular, the feminine . . . ) is defined not only as a "fable," identical with "what speaks" *(fari),* but as a fable that "does not know" what it says. The technique enabling this positioning of the other (and thus the dominance of scriptural labor over the "fable" it cites) is *translation:* the oral is transcribed as writing, a model is constructed to read the fable as a system, and a meaning is produced. John Fiske's "ethnographic" fable of Lucy's response to Madonna provides a step-by-step example of this procedure.[21]

The "sounds of the body" marked in language by quotation-reminiscence are invoked by de Certeau in terms strongly reminiscent of a thematics of Woman—reso-nances, rhythms, wounds, pleasures, "soli-tary erections" (the *inaccessibility* of the voice, says de Certeau, makes "people" write), fragmentary cries and whispers, "aphasic enunciation"—"everything that speaks, makes noise, passes by, touches us lightly, meets us head on." Necessarily more difficult to describe than the science of fables, these returns and turns of voices are sug-gested, rather than represented, by examples: opera (a "space for voices" that emerged at the same time as the scriptural economy), *Nathalie Granger,* Marguerite Duras's "film of voices," but also the stammers, voice-gaps, vague rhythms, unexpectedly moving or memorable turns of phrase that mark our most mundane activities and haunt our every-day prose (162–63).

Perhaps these are the sounds that are ban-ished from Baudrillard's story of the eye—or rather by the "scriptural labor" of his subse-quent exegesis. Baudrillard finds a triumph of *literalness* in the woman's substitution of an eye for the letter. So, in the manner of the science of fables, he specifies a meaning for the fable that suits the antifemin*ist* discourse for which it acts as a pretext. However, he does this not by trying to "write" the woman's voice (body) but, on the contrary, by rephras-ing an extremist bodily gesture as an urbane triumph of writing.

But we could say instead that a rejection of *writing* is the primary reversal on which the story of the eye depends. The "translation" of the letter as body is precisely a refusal of "lit-eral-ness." The woman sends the eye as com-mentary (metadiscourse): as Baudrillard notes, her gesture cites and mocks the se-ducer's courtly platitude. But the "blood" in the envelope is also a reminder of the gap between the rhetorical promise of seduction and its material consequences, in this social code, for women.

In the epistolary novels to which Baudril-lard's fable refers (see, for example, *Les lettres de la Marquise de M\*\*\* au Comte de R\*\*\**, by Crébillon fils), the usual outcome is death, often by suicide, for the female co(r)respond-ent. So the eye sliding out of the envelope cheats death, as well as cheating the seducer of his pleasures. He loses face, but she merely gives him the eye. And it cheats on literary narrative; the eye in this fable is the mark of a high-speed, fast-forward reader who tears to the end of the story without submitting to the rituals of "writing." Something in this fable—perhaps a shudder—leaps from a woman to man in the circuit reserved for the letter, but it doesn't take the form of a pun. It has a historically resonant *eloquence* to which Baudrillard's discourse, even as it tells the story, remains resolutely deaf.

It is crucial to say, however, that in de Cer-teau's framework both of the major forms of quoting are understood positively as capable (when their history is not forgotten and the position of the "scribe" not denied) of leaving ways for the other to speak. It is precisely this capacity which makes possible a feminist reading of Fiske's and Baudrillard's stories, and which can enable feminist cultural criti-cism to resist, in turn, its own enclosure as a self-perpetuating, self-reiterating academic practice.

The science of fables uses voices to prolif-erate discourse: in the detour through differ-ence, quotation alters the voice that it desires and fails to reproduce, but is also altered by it. However, unlike an exoticism which multi-plies anecdotes of the same, a "heterological" science will try to admit the alteration pro-voked by difference. Its reflexivity is not rein-vested in a narcissistic economy of pleasure, but works to transform the conditions that make its practices possible, and the position-ing of the other these entail.

Quotation-reminiscence "lets voices out": rather than generating discourse, the sounds of the body interrupt it from an "other" scene. As "letting out," this kind of quotation seems to be involuntary: memories rush from that nonplace conveniently cast beyond the citing subject's "domain" of responsibility. However, it is in a *"labor"* of reminiscence that the body's sounds can interrupt discourse not only in the mode of event but as practice. De Certeau sees this "struggle against oblivion" in philosophies which (like Deleuze and Guattari's *Anti-Oedipus,* Lyotard's *Libidinal Economy*) strive to create "auditory space"; and in the "reversal" that has taken psychoanalysis from a "science of dreams" toward "the experience of what speaking voices *change* in the dark grotto of the bodies that hear them" (162, emphasis mine).

So while both of these "ways of quoting" belong to the strategy of the institution, and define the scholarly place, each therefore can be borrowed by tactical operations that— like the recognition of alterity, the labor of reminiscence—change analytical procedures by "returning" them to their limits, and insinuating the ordinary into "established scientific fields." The event of this change is what de Certeau calls "banality": the arrival at a *common* "place," which is not (as it may be for populism) an initial state of grace, and not (as it is in Baudrillard) an indiscriminate, inchoate condition, but on the contrary, the outcome of a practice, something that "comes into being" at the end of a trajectory. This is the banality that speaks in *Everyman,* and in the late work of Freud—where the ordinary is no longer the object of analysis but the *place* from which discourse is produced.

It is at this final point, however, that my reading can fellow-travel no further, and parts company with de Certeau's "we."

A feminist critique of *The Practice of Everyday Life* would find ample material to work with. De Certeau's Muse—the silent other to whom his writing would strive to give voice—is unmistakably The Ordinary Man.[22]

My problem here, however, is specifically with the characteristics of the *scholarly* "place" of enunciation from which the notion of banality is constructed, and for which it can work as a myth of transformation. For to invoke with de Certeau an "ironic and mad banality" that can insinuate itself into our techniques, and reorganize the place from which discourse is produced, is immediately to posit an awkward position for "scholarly" subjects for whom *Everyman* might not serve as well as *'I Love Lucy''* as a fable of origin, or indeed as a myth of "voice." For me as a feminist, as a distracted media baby, and also, to some extent, as an Australian, the reference to *Everyman* (and, for that matter, to Freud) is rather a reminder of the problems of disengaging my own thinking from patriarchal (and Eurocentric) cultural norms.

The analytical scene for de Certeau occurs in a highly specialized, professional place. Yet in contrast to most real academic institutions today, it is not already *occupied* (rather than nomadically "crossed") by the sexual, racial, ethnic, and popular differences that it constitutes as "other." Nor is it squarely *founded,* rather than "disrupted," by the ordinary experience encountered at its frontiers. It is a place of knowledge secured, in fact, by precisely those historic exclusions which have made it so difficult to imagine or *admit* the possibility of a scholarship "proper" to the other's "own" experience—except in the form of an error (essentialism), or apocalyptic fantasy (rupture, revolution). Construed from de Certeau's "here," the other as narrator, rather than object, of scholarly discourse remains, as a general rule, a promising myth of the future, a fable of changes to come.

In other words: in this place, the citing of alterity and the analytical labor of reminiscence promise something like the practice of a "writing cure" for the latter-day Robinson Crusoe.

This is a "fate" all the more awkward for me to assume in that for de Certeau, "place," "the proper," and even "closure" are not always necessarily *bad values,* but modes of spatial and narrative organization every-where at work in everyday social life. It is the primary function of any *story,* for example, to found a place, or create a field that authorizes practical actions (125). So there is no sugges-tion in his work that those who have been most intimately marked in history by Man Fri-day's Alternative (the cry, the impersonation) should not now, in writing their stories, thereby lay claim to a place. The utopian def-erral of an "other" narration in de Certeau's theory occurs, like the apotheosis of banality as the Ordinary *Man,* because the "place" of the other may never coincide with that of any subject of a discourse (nor, of course, the subject's with that of an actual speaker). To dream otherwise is a "false mysticism"—longing for Presence, denial of History, nos-talgia for God.

Unfortunately, since the other here is also "the discourse's mode of relation to *its own* historicity in the moment of its utterance" (emphasis mine), this argument encourages us to conclude that scholarly knowledge in the present must continue to be written, and transformed, from Crusoe's place. In practice, of course, de Certeau drew no such conclu-sion, writing that "the history of women, of blacks, of Jews, of cultural minorities, *etc.*" (my emphasis) puts into question "the sub-ject-producer" of history and *therefore* "the particularity of the place where discourse is produced."[23] But the *"etc."* points to a prob-lem with the rhetoric of otherness that lingers when the epistemology that sustained it is apparently revised. "Etc." is Man Friday's footprint: a unifying myth of a *common* oth-erness—Black, Primitive, Woman, Child, People, "Voice," Banality—deriving its value only from its function as negation (polemo-logical challenge, utopian hope) for that same singular writing subject of historical production.

I am skeptical that a theory grounded on (rather than tactically using) the category of otherness can even end up anywhere else.[24]

However, in the context of cultural studies, the immediate practical disadvantage of this construction of analysis is to reinscribe *alien-ation* from everyday life as a constitutive rather than contingent feature of the scholar's enunciative place. An old pathos of separa-tion creeps back in here, of which the polari-ties (elite/popular, special/general, singular/ "banal") mark not only the semantic organi-zation of de Certeau's discourse but the narrative thrust of his text. The main line of *The Practice of Everyday Life* moves from its beginnings in "A Common Place: Ordinary Language" to "The Unnamable," a meditation on that absolute other, ultimate frontier, and final banality, Death.

Rather than venturing any further on to that forbidding theoretical terrain, I shall shift the scene of my own analysis to a more congenial place.

One of the enduring lounge-room "institu-tions" of Australian TV is Bill Collins, host of an ancient show that was once *The Golden Years of Hollywood,* but is now just a time-slot for *Movies.* A former teacher, Collins has spent twenty years using his "place" to define what counts on television as knowledge of cinema history. He now has many competi-tors and probably not much power, but for years he had a monopoly—years when there were no old films in theaters, no video chains, and no systematic study of media in schools. So it is no exaggeration to say that Collins was one of the founders of Australian screen education.

His pedagogy has changed little with time. Collins is a trivia expert, respectful rather than mocking in his relentless pursuit of the detail. His address to the audience is avuncular, his construction of film auratic. Never raucous or unkind, rarely "critical," his scholarship is a perpetual effusion of an undemanding love. Usually placed in a "home study" decor with posters, magazines, and books, Collins repre-sents knowledge as a universally accessible domestic hobby. It is from his enthusiasms, rather than any formal training (which in this "place" is rather despised), that his authority derives. His "history" is a labyrinthine network of minuscule anecdotes: its grand theme is less the rise and fall of famous careers than the ebb and flow of fortune in the lives of the humbler figures near the bottom of the credits, or toward the edge of the frame. His own image expounds his theme: plump, owlish, chronically middle-aged, unpretentiously dressed, Collins has one eccentricity, a voice just a little bit pompous and prissy.

While I was working on this essay, he showed two films that seemed chosen to stimulate my thinking. Both were fables about "proper" places (malign in one case, benign in the other) and a principle of fatality at work in everyday life.

David Green's *The Guardian* (1984) could have been subtitled *Man Friday's Revenge.* Martin Sheen plays the white husband and father worried about the security of his apartment block, invaded by junkies from the street. After a murder and a rape inside, he persuades the other residents to hire a guardian (Louis Gossett, Jr.). Tough, streetwise, and black, the solitary "John" moves in and makes the place his own. A sinister conflict emerges. Sheen wants a flexible frontier: residents inside, desperados outside, ordinary peaceful neighbors moving in and out as before. Gossett demands strict closure, total control: he bashes visitors, kills intruders, and polices not only the building but the residents' everyday lives.

At last, the sleeping liberal awakens in the would-be white vigilante. Too late: charging off into the night to tackle Gossett *chez lui,* Sheen falls afoul of a ghetto gang. Pulverized by terror, he is saved at last by Gossett—to suffer the ignominy of his own abject gratitude for the guardian's greater violence. Back at the ranch, the two men lock gazes in the final scene of the film: black guardian stand-

ing triumphantly inside, undisputed master of the place; white resident creeping furtively outside, insecure and afraid between the zones of home and street—in each of which he will henceforth be but a tenant without authority.

The structural reversal is complete, the moral ambiguity of the moment absolute. Was Sheen's first mistake to accept violence by inviting Gossett in, or was it to deny the implications of this action and, by dithering, lose control? Either way, *The Guardian* dramatizes with white-and-black simplicity a problem besetting any thematics of place primarily articulated by binary oppositions between "haves" and "have-nots," self and other, propriety and mobility. In such a schema, the drifter's desire is colonized as the settler's worst nightmare.[25] The *other*'s desire for a place can be represented only in terms of a choice between the *status quo* (critique of property, romance of dispossession) or as a violent reversal of roles that intensifies the prevailing structuration of powers. Totalitarian violence is in the end the true successor to Sheen's liberal paranoia—and it is the only image that the film can admit of what "a room of one's own" for the (black) urban poor might mean.

If *The Practice of Everyday Life* provides a sophisticated attempt to undermine the fatality of this kind of system by introducing nonsymmetry to its terms—theorizing difference rather than contradiction between them, refusing to assign *a priori* a negative value to either side—it nevertheless leaves us stranded when it comes to developing, rather than arriving at, the critical practice of a feminism (for example) already situated *both* by knowledge and social experience of insecurity and dispossession, *and* by a politics of exercising established institutional powers. Similarly, this aspect of de Certeau's work may not be of much help with the problems of an emerging cultural criticism which is equally—though      not      indifferently—"at home" in a number of sometimes conflicting social sites (academy, media, community group as well as "home" and "street"), moving between them with an agility which may well owe more to imperatives derived from technological changes, and from shifts in employment patterns, than it does to transient desire.

Bill Collins introduced *The Guardian* with a promise that it would unsettle anybody who lived in an apartment. Screening Alfred Hitchcock's *The Trouble with Harry* (1955) for the first time on TV, he saved his lesson till last.

*The Trouble with Harry* provided the perfect counterpart to the pure polemological message ("they always fuck us over") of *The Guardian*. Subtle, elusive, hilariously amoral in its utopian treatment of death, it also promised a perfect ending for my essay. For in this film, one day in a quiet mountain village—where few sounds disturb the silence except for the drifting of autumn leaves, the bird song in the valley, the honking of an antique car horn, the popping of a shotgun, the call of an excited child, and the occasional rustle of a rabbit in the grass—the pervasive calm is shattered by the appearance of a corpse.

Harry is a strange body, in more ways than one. He is a foreigner to the valley: the curious insignificance of his death, the incongruity of his presence there, is established by repeated shots of his feet sticking up as he sprawls headfirst down the hillside. But as the locals begin to arrive, it seems that there may be more trouble in paradise than the mere apparition of Harry. One by one, the adults respond with astounding banality: they talk of blueberry muffins, coffee, elderberry wine, lemonade; a reader trips on the corpse and ignores it, going straight on with his book; a tramp steals Harry's shoes; an artist sketches the scene. The initial suspect, watching from the bushes, mutters: "Next thing you know they'll be televising the whole thing!"

As the mystery of these responses begins to be dispelled, another takes its place. The inhabitants of this tiny village barely know each other, and coexist in an anomic isolation far exceeding small-town discretion. This may be a not-quite-innocent paradise, but it isn't really a *place;* a utopia, but not a community. But when the truth of Harry's death starts to emerge from a casual chat about destiny, new relationships swiftly develop. During the ensuing narrative play between deception and detection, the corpse shifts repeatedly between temporary homes—in the ground, on the hillside, in the bathtub. Only when the full story has been told does Harry find his proper location (where he was in the beginning) and identity (as a banal victim of a fatal heart attack); couples are formed, first names exchanged, histories shared, community established; and, when the founding of a place is complete, "the trouble with Harry is over."

Grasping something like this in my first viewing, thrilling in an allegorical sensitivity to each phrase, every scene, that echoes *The Practice of Everyday Life,* I resolved to do a reading of the film—forgetting that to retrieve a given theory of popular culture from a text framed as an *exemplum* of both would be to produce, at the end of my trajectory, precisely the kind of "banality" I was setting out to question.

I did not long enjoy the contemplation of my intention. "Did you notice," asked Bill Collins in his meditative moment, "how everyone in this film seems to *want* to feel guilty?" *"That's not the point!"* I told the television, ready with my counterthesis. "Well," declared that irritating voice, "there's a Ph.D. in that!"

In a fascinating essay on the figure of the speaking voice in the work of Rousseau and Plato, Michèle Le Doeuff points out that this voice (indefinite, uncertain, irrational in its effects, *"celle dont on aurait pu penser qu'elle était la banalité meme"*) may function in philosophy not only as an emblem of the other but, therefore, as an instrument of demarcation whereby a theory can speak obliquely not of voices but of philosophy itself—its limits, its failures, and its problems of legitimacy.[26]

I suspect that in cultural studies, its function is rather the opposite. Parasitic on philosophy as cultural studies has been, it is perhaps today the discipline most at odds with the historic, self-legitimating dream of philosophical autonomy analyzed by Le Doeuff in *L'imaginaire philosophique*. Careless about its own epistemological grounding, its theoretical integrity, and its difference from "other" discourses, cultural studies has been more concerned (and, I think, rightly so) with analyzing and achieving political effects. It may be for this reason, then, and along with the historical determinations that de Certeau describes, that the "banality" of the speaking voice becomes in cultural studies a way of *suspending* the question of legitimation, and all the problems that question entails.

"Banality," after all, is one of the group of words—including "trivial" and "mundane"—whose modern history inscribes the disintegration of old European ideals about the common people, the common place, the common culture. In medieval French, the "banal" fields, mills, and ovens were those used communally. It is only in the late eighteenth century (and within the "scriptural economy") that these words begin to acquire their modern sense of the trite, the platitudinous, the unoriginal.

So if banality is an irritant that repeatedly returns to trouble cultural theory, it is because the very concept is part of the modern history of taste, value, and critique of judgment that constitutes the polemical field within which cultural studies now takes issue with classical aesthetics. "Banality" as mythic signifier is thus always a mask for questions of value, of value judgment, and "discrimination"—especially in the sense of how we distinguish

and evaluate *problems* (rather than cultural "products"), legitimate our priorities, and defend our choice of what matters.

This is a debate which has barely begun, and which is all the more complex in that the professional protocols inherited by cultural studies from established disciplines—sociology, literary criticism, philosophy—may well be either irrelevant or contentious. If I find myself, for example, in the contradictory position of wanting polemically to reject Baudrillard's use of "banality" as a framing *aesthetic* concept to discuss mass media, yet go on to complain myself of a syllogistic "banality" in British cultural studies, the dilemma can arise because the repertoire of critical strategies available to people wanting to theorize the discriminations that they make in relation to their experience of popular culture—without needing to defend the validity of that experience, still less that of culture *as a whole*—is still extraordinarily depleted.

And there is an extra twist to the history of banality. In the Oxford version of this history, it has a double heritage in, on the one hand, old English, *bannan*—to summon, or to curse—and a Germanic *bannan:* to proclaim *under penalty*. So banality is related to banishing, and also to wedding *bans*. In other words, it is a figure inscribing power in an act of *enunciation*. In medieval times it could mean two things besides "common place." It could mean to issue an edict or a summons (usually to war). That was the enunciative privilege of the feudal lord. Or it could mean to proclaim under orders: to line the streets, and cheer, in the manner required by the call *"un ban pour le vanqueur!"* To obediently voice a rhythmic applause is the "banal" enunciative duty of the common people, the popular chorus.

This two-sided historical function of banality—lordly pronouncement, mimetic popular performance—is not yet banished from the practice of theorizing the popular today. It's very hard, perhaps impossible, not to make the invoked "voice" of the popular perform itself obediently in just that medieval way in our writing. However, when the voice of that which academic discourses—including cultural studies—constitute *as* popular begins in turn to theorize its speech, then you have an interesting possibility. That theorization may well go round by way of the procedures that Homi Bhabha has theorized as "colonial mimicry," for example, but may also come around eventually in a different, and as yet utopian, mode of enunciative practice.[27] However, I think that this can happen only if the complexity of social experience investing our "place" as intellectuals today—including the proliferation of different places in and between which we may learn and teach and write—becomes a presupposition of, and not an anecdotal adjunct to, our practice.

For this reason, I think that feminists have to work quite hard in cultural studies *not* to become subjects of banality in that old double sense: not to formulate edicts and proclamations, yet to keep theorizing, not to become supermimics in the Baudrillardian sense of becoming, by reversal, the same as that which is mimicked, yet to refuse to subside either into silence or into a posture of reified difference. Through some such effort, pained and disgruntled subjects, who are also joyous and inventive practitioners, can begin to articulate our critique of everyday life.

## NOTES

1. John Fiske, "British Cultural Studies and Television," in *Channels of Discourse: Television and Contemporary Criticism,* ed. Robert C. Allen (Chapel Hill: University of North Carolina Press, 1987), pp. 254–89.

2. Judith Williamson, "The Problems of Being *Popular,*" *New Socialist* Sept. 1986:14–15.

3. Patricia Mellencamp, "Situation Comedy, Feminism, and Freud: Discourses of Gracie and Lucy," in *Studies in Entertainment: Critical Approaches to Mass Culture,* ed.

Tania Modleski (Bloomington: Indiana University Press, 1986), pp. 80–95.

4. Cf. Margaret Morse, "The Television News Personality and Credibility: Reflections on the News in Transition," in *Studies in Entertainment,* pp. 55–79.

5. Andreas Huyssen, *After the Great Divide: Modernism, Mass Culture, Postmodernism* (Bloomington: Indiana University Press, 1986), p. vii.

6. Mica Nava, "Consumerism and Its Contradictions," *Cultural Studies* 1.2 (May 1987):204–210. The phrase "cultural dopes" is from Stuart Hall, "Notes on Deconstructing 'the Popular,' " in *People's History and Socialist Theory,* ed. Raphael Samuel (London: Routledge & Kegan Paul, 1981), pp. 227–39.

7. Iain Chambers, *Popular Culture: The Metropolitan Experience* (New York: Methuen, 1986), pp. 12–13.

8. Meaghan Morris, "At *Henry Parkes* Motel," *Cultural Studies* 2:1 (1988):1–47.

9. Andreas Huyssen, "Mass Culture as Woman: Modernism's Other," in *After the Great Divide,* pp. 44–62; Tania Modleski, "Femininity as Mas(s)querade: A Feminist Approach to Mass Culture," in *High Theory/Low Culture,* ed. Colin MacCabe (Manchester: Manchester University Press, 1986), pp. 37–52; Patrice Petro, "Mass Culture and the Feminine: The 'Place' of Television in Film Studies," *Cinema Journal* 25.3 (Spring 1986):5–21.

10. Patrice Petro, "Modernity and Mass Culture in Weimar: Contours of a Discourse on Sexuality in Early Theories of Perception and Representation," *New German Critique* 40 (Winter 1987):115–46.

11. Elaine Showalter, "Critical Cross-Dressing: Male Feminists and the Woman of the Year," in *Men in Feminism,* ed. Alice Jardine and Paul Smith (New York: Methuen, 1987), pp. 116–32.

12. This sectarianism may be partly a result of the notions of "negotiated," "resistant," and "oppositional" *readings* that still play such a large part in our analyses. In the end, the aim of analysis becomes to generate one of these, thus repeatedly proving it possible to do so. Since there is little point in regenerating a "dominant" reading of a text (the features of which are usually presupposed by the social theory that frames the reading in the first place), the figure of a misguided but onside Other is necessary as a structural support to justify the exercise and guarantee the "difference" of the reading.

13. Michel de Certeau, *The Practice of Everyday Life,* trans. Steven F. Rendall (Berkeley: University of California Press, 1984), p. xvi.

14. A space for de Certeau is the product of, as well as

a potential arena for, a practice. Cf. *The Practice of Everyday Life,* Part III, "Spatial Practices."

15. I have tried to develop this notion of timing further in relation to the public use of live television in "Panorama: The Live, The Dead, and The Living," in *Island in the Stream: Myths of Place in Australian Cultural Criticism,* ed. Paul Foss (Sydney: Pluto, 1988).

16. Michel de Certeau, *Heterologies: Discourse on the Other,* trans. Brian Massumi (Manchester: Manchester University Press, 1986), p. xx.

17. It is unfortunate that de Certeau's theoretical essays remain better known in English than his work as a historian, and so are read in isolation from it. For background to the following discussion, cf. Michel de Certeau, *La possession de Loudun* (Paris: Julliard-Gallimard, 1970); *L'absent de l'histoire* (Paris: Mame, 1973); *La culture au pluriel* (Paris: 10–18, 1974); *L'écriture de l'histoire* (Paris: Gallimard, 1975); and with D. Julia and J. Revel, *Une politique de las langue, La Révolution française et les patois* (Paris: Gallimard, 1975).

18. Michel de Certeau, Dominique Julia, and Jacques Revel, "The Beauty of the Dead: Nisard," in *Heterologies,* pp. 119–36.

19. Michel de Certeau, *The Practice of Everyday Life,* Part IV, "Uses of Language."

20. De Certeau restricts the use of a writing/orality opposition in several important ways. First, there can be no *quest* for this voice "that has been simultaneously colonized and mythified" (132). There is no origin, authenticity, or spontaneity of presence to be found in a mythic voxpop, and no "pure" voice independent either of the scriptural systems that it inhabits or of the ways of "hearing"/receiving by which it is codified.

Second, "writing" and "orality" should not be construed as terms that *always* found a metaphysical opposition, the recurrence of which analysis can perpetually retrace. If "writing" and "orality" can function now as imaginary unities, they do so as a result of reciprocal distinctions made "within successive and interconnected historical configurations," from which they cannot be

isolated (133). (Cf. *L'écriture de l'histoire,* Part III, "Systèmes de sens: l'écrit et l'oral.")

Third, the orality in question is one *changed* by three or four centuries of Western fashioning. It cannot be "heard" except as insinuation in the text of the scriptural economy. In Defoe's "theoretical fiction," Man Friday's footprint is not another local trace of an eternal illusion of presence. It represents the emergence of something *novel* in Defoe's text, outlining "a *form* of alterity in relation to writing that will also impose its identity on the voice . . ." (155).

21. In this perspective, "pop epistemology" works in a slightly different way. It "writes the voice" by effacing scriptural labor, as well as the translation that makes "distraction" readable, thus producing a fable of the coincidence of its own writing with "what speaks" in popular culture. The problem here is not that the "materiality" of writing is effaced but that the relationship of this practice to the disciplinary history from which it emerges (and which it claims to contest) is simply ignored.

22. Certainly, he is a Man now marked as Woman, Child, or Savage (and the text is sensitive to the problem of assimilating any one of these terms to the bodies of people they have been used to represent). However, de Certeau's history of this marking presupposes the indifference of the primary figure.

23. *Heterologies,* pp. 217.

24. For a different view, cf. Elizabeth Grosz, "The 'People of the Book': Representation and Alterity in Emmanuel Levinas," *Art & Text* 26 (Sept.–Nov. 1987):32–40.

25. An extreme case is Jean Duvignaud, "Esquisse pour le nomade," in *Cause commune: Nomades et vagabonds* (Paris: 10–18, 1975), pp. 13–40.

26. Michèle Le Doeuff, "La philosophie dans le gosier," in *L'imaginaire philosophique* (Paris: Payot, 1980), pp. 171–79. Translation by Colin Gordon forthcoming (London: The Athlone Press).

27. Homi K. Bhabha, "Of Mimicry and Man: The Ambivalence of Colonial Discourse," *October* 28 (Spring 1984):125–33.

# 38

# Robert Con Davis
# 1948–

# Ronald Schleifer
# 1948–

Robert Con Davis and Ronald Schleifer are professors of English at the University of Oklahoma. They are also coeditors of the Oklahoma Project for Discourse and Theory, a book series whose publications address the concerns of cultural studies and contemporary discourse. Their own recent publications have cultural studies orientations, particularly Schleifer's *Rhetoric and Death: The Language of Modernism and Postmodern Discourse Theory* (1990) and Davis's *The Paternal Romance: Reading God-the-Father in Early Western Culture* (1993). They are coauthors of *Criticism and Culture* (1991), and with Nancy Mergler, *Culture and Cognition: The Boundaries of Literary and Scientific Inquiry* (1992).

Throughout *Criticism and Culture,* from which this essay is drawn, Davis and Schleifer test "critical modes against the tasks they set for themselves to perform." In "Notes Towards a Definition of Cultural Studies" (1991) they focus, as they say in the Preface to *Criticism and Culture,* on critics "who attempt to define culture and situate literary criticism within cultural studies." Consequently, the critics under scrutiny here "have turned generally from what they may *know* to what they may *do* in the context of the cultures they inhabit." Shoshana Felman's psychological critique of pedagogy, for instance, provides a means for viewing the function of language—of the utterance—rather than the "mere content of the statement." Such a study reorients literary studies and makes it "a kind of activism," one that necessitates "ethical and political choices." These choices and cultural activities are central to the discussion of feminist critiques, which have been instrumental in reorienting and thus transforming cultural understanding by critiquing both their own premises, as well as those of other critical practices. As Davis and Schleifer emphasize, feminist critiques are an "instance of cultural critique as a pedagogical mode—an exemplary instance of cultural studies." Such critiques constitute the critical viewpoint, the positioning of the "subject," within a specific historical and ideological context. It is just this interrelationship of the inner process (the individual) and the general process (a society of individuals) of culture that constitutes elements in both Geertz's analytic critique of the "institutions" of culture and Williams's more politically oriented "transformational" critique of culture. For both, as for the other critics this essay analyzes, cultural studies is essentially and necessarily "a participatory relation within the discourse of inquiry."

# Notes Towards a Definition of Cultural Studies

*The alternatives—either calling culture as a whole into question from outside under the general notion of ideology, or confronting it with the norms which it itself has crystallized—cannot be accepted by critical theory. To insist on the choice between immanence and transcendence is to revert to the traditional logic criticized in Hegel's polemic against Kant. . . . [I]f stubbornly immanent contemplation threatens to revert to idealism, to the illusion of the self-sufficent mind in command of both itself and of reality, transcendent contemplation threatens to forget the effort of conceptualization required. . . . The dialectical critic of culture must both participate in culture and not participate. Only then does he do justice to his object and to himself.*

Theodor Adorno
*Prisms*

The path of [*Criticism and Culture*] goes from eighteenth-century attempts to define the nature of critique through the institution of literary criticism in the twentieth century in the Anglo-American academy in response to a number of cultural texts and forces. We have explored the various ways in which critical practice in modern literary studies over the last thirty years has functioned fundamentally as the practice of critique within the contexts of Romantic and post-Romantic conceptions of subjectivity and language, and we have attempted to mark this exploration with commitments to particular culturally instituted values and social aims. Within historical and intellectual developments, we have examined the issue of ethical responsibility in criticism, which has moved to the centre of literary studies so that literary critics have turned generally from what they may *know* to what

they may *do* in the context of the cultures they inhabit. The study of literature has come to address this reconception or reorientation in many different guises—all of them, we believe, movements towards *critique*—as shown in the polemical debates Edward W. Said describes as the conflict between "the new subculture of theoretical opposition" and the "old traditions" now fighting against "theory" with "appeals to humanism, tact, good sense, and the like" (1983: 167). These are the very appeals Matthew Arnold used in response to the "terrible learning" of philology he opposed in 1862.

A hallmark of the "old tradition" is what Lillian Robinson has called its "apparently systematic neglect of women's experience in the literary canon," a silence about gender and an inability to reconsider "whether the great monuments are really so great, after all" (1983: 106, 108). For the Arnoldian tradition of humanism the rationale for inclusion in the canon—what makes a literary work "great"—is presented as self-evident and without need of discussion, the promotion of the self-evident drawing generally from the four basic assumptions about modes of inquiry in the "human sciences" that have governed our discussions in this book. These assumptions, and the "grounds" they form, make certain kinds of understanding possible by organizing the play of discourses in the human sciences, discourses that correspond to various focuses of cultural critique in psychology, linguistics, philosophy and history. Our point in [*Criticism and Culture*], like that of Said, Graff, Spivak and many others writing today about cultural studies and social institutions, is to test these critical modes against the tasks they set for themselves to perform. Most immediately, the test is of "literature" itself, as Miller says, against the "entire body of traditional inquiries in the human sciences" that the Arnoldians load on to literary study. To this end, we have challenged the "imperialism" of each of the grounds, their tendency to reduce and dismiss all other explanations and to make each ground, in turn, a kind of "base" for the superstructure and epiphenomena of other discursive formations. This tendency is at the heart of the blind and yet fierce resistance among contemporary versions of these grounds—Marxist, structuralist, psychoanalytic and deconstructive—to the institution of alternative modes of literary criticism and pedagogy. It is resistance to the rigours of unending critique.

Each of the grounds of criticism we explore tends to situate itself as a self-evident explanation for "everything" and then dismiss further inquiry. The study of literature reduced to the study of language, accordingly, becomes "scientific" in relation to other cultural formations, often refusing to traffic in the discussion of cultural values and constantly returning to the supposed objective nature of linguistic conditions. Limited to psychological study, criticism becomes a guide to the "inevitable" symptomatics of the text, diagnosing particular authors or even particular eras in terms of "health" or "disease," in a model of understanding based upon more or less autonomous subjects (or what Deleuze and Guattari describe in the broadest sense as the Western Oedipus). Based on religious and deconstructive concerns, literary criticism, in Stephen Greenblatt's words, often leads fairly directly "and predictably to the void," or at least to reifications of the "void" in various manifestations of the sublime (1985: 164). Finally, scaled to the study of history and society, criticism becomes a programme for social action—what Lentricchia calls "the production of knowledge to the ends of power" (1983: 11)—in which case the study of literature recognizes cultural values defined collectively and socially as power. This grounding gesture "marginalizes" (as "false consciousness," "ideology" or "self interest") what it cannot describe as belonging to the base of historical formation in the global historical explanation we discussed in the preceding chapter.

In each case, the tendency towards imperialism and resistance constitutes the slide of critique into "criticism" based on particular and often exclusive assumptions that often, as we mentioned earlier, appropriate all phenomena as *examples* of the "basic" mechanisms. These grounds account for particular discourses while claiming, in Raymond Williams's terms, "to exhaust the full range of human practice, human energy, human intention (. . . that extraordinary range of variations, both practiced and imagined, of which human beings are and have shown themselves to be capable)" (1977: 43). In each case there is a dimension, at least implicitly, of ethics which deals, in John Dewey's terms, "with conduct in its entirety, with reference . . . to what makes its conduct, its *ends,* its real meaning" (1891: 241). The definition of ethics as the ends of conduct even encompasses Julia Kristeva's description of contemporary social control in which the "coercive, customary manner of ensuring the cohesiveness of a particular group" is less evident. Instead, Kristeva argues in a definition compatible with Dewey's, that "ethics crops up wherever a code (mores, social contract) must be shattered in order to give way to the free play of negativity, need, desire, pleasure, and jouissance, before being put together again" (1980: 23). For Kristeva, ethics inhabits the work of negative critique, and for her, as for Dewey, the relationships between knowledge and power, the universal and the particular, are realized in the provisional descriptions of the ends of conduct made by institutional and transformational critique.

## CRITIQUE AND LEARNING

The potential of critique in literary studies has ethical implications for the understanding of "culture," and those implications are perhaps clearest in the institutional conduct of the study of literature. In "The Function of Criticism at the Present Time" Frye complains that the apparent arbitrary and unsystematic nature of the institutionalization of literary studies in Anglo-American higher education did "not . . . make any sense at all" (1949: 257). Earlier, Kenneth Burke had attempted to breach the interested complacency of "those persons who take the division of faculties in our universities to be an exact replica of the way in which God himself divided up the universe" (1937: 303) with a rhetorical and "sociological" understanding of literature. Recently, in *Professing Literature,* Gerald Graff traced the institutionalization of English studies in America and described how its structuring into chronological periods has served institutional, "departmental" interests rather than the ends of critique by avoiding the view of literary study and literature "as social products with a history that [readers] might have a personal and critical stake in" (1987: 258). The result is that professors have no need to critique their professional activity or their intellectual and social practice. "The notions of institution, genre, and language," as Robert Scholes has said, are examples of "powerful tools of thought . . . whose interrelatedness has only recently become apparent." "This new perception," he goes on, "is leading many scholars to reconsider the dimension of their academic disciplines, as they rediscover the very objects of their study" (1985: 3).

If critique calls into question the institutional structures that transmit knowledge (just as Nietzsche questioned the concept of "knowledge" itself), then it also questions the concepts of teaching and education. Shoshana Felman argues, for instance, that "teaching, like psychoanalysis, does not deal so much with *lack* of knowledge as with *resistances* to knowledge" (1987: 79); the critique of pedagogy, therefore, needs to situate pedagogy in relation to the relationships of power that discourse coordinates along with its "knowledge." She attempts to explore and analyse the relationships between knowledge and ignorance—between teacher and student—in a way suggestive of structuralism's reconsideration of language-effects as opposed to the unconscious structures which allow language to function. Parallel to both is post-structuralism's reconsideration of the "constative" and "performative" forces of discourse, and behind these—Foucault's caution about dialectical critique notwithstanding—is the Marxist relationship of base and superstructure, the relationship between supposedly transcendent, timeless ideas, beliefs and feelings about the world and the modes of cultural production—psychological, linguistic, philosophical and social modes—that give rise to those ideas.

Felman traces the relationship between knowledge and ignorance in teaching and psychoanalysis in ways that shed light on the rethinking of the profession and discipline of English studies more generally. Teaching, psychoanalysis teaches us, must learn to learn from ignorance, "ignorance" not simply as the absence of knowledge but as an orientation to knowledge as power and the situating of power that *"itself can teach us something"* (1987: 79), the aim of teaching being "not the transmission of ready-made knowledge; it is rather the creation of a new *condition* of knowledge" (1987: 80), or what could be called a new condition for the production of knowledge. The teacher's and the analyst's "competence, insists Lacan, lies in 'what I would call *textual knowledge,'*" which is, Felman says, "the very stuff the literature teacher is supposed to deal in . . . knowledge of the functioning of language, of symbolic structures, of the signifier, knowledge at once derived from—and directed towards—interpretation" (1987: 81).

Felman's description of the teacher using rather than "exchanging" knowledge also suggests a reorientation in English studies from a model of transmitting great works of art and the "tradition" which engenders or is constituted by these works, to the study of literature as a form of cultural critique that examines the conditions and realization of discourse in its various groundings. Teaching uncovers the conditions of knowledge, functioning through performative "utterances" as well as constative statements. "Misinterpretations of the psychoanalytical critique of pedagogy," Felman says, "refer exclusively to Lacan's or Freud's explicit *statements* about pedagogy, and thus fail to see the illocutionary force, the didactic function of the *utterance* as opposed to the mere content of the statement" (1987: 72–3). If it "is not a purely cognitive, informative experience," she says, but also an emotional, "transferential" one, then literary study must expand and re-structure itself to emphasize the functioning of language, of symbolic structures, of signification—knowledge at once derived from and directed towards the ongoing activity, the doing, of interpretation. This reorientation of literary studies, then, is an orientation towards cultural studies as a kind of activism in its various modes, as we have been suggesting throughout this book.

Such institutional "reorientation," of course, can be subject to its own critique. It's all well and good, one could object, to describe but not to make ethical choices, to define teaching as both cognitive and emotional, to say there are many ways to organize the discipline of English studies, but the fact is that such a "pluralism" simply demonstrates "complicity" with a repressive social order (Lentricchia 1983: 65), or an "inability to look into things all the way down to the bottom" (Miller 1985: 23). Such "pluralism"

could also be "mystified" apprehension of the effects that linguistic relationships occasion as substantialized "objects" in the world (Greimas 1966: 65). Pluralism may also embody the psychological resistance to the truth, as Freud often implies. The fact is, as each of these positions argues, sooner or later critique requires ethical and political choices.

In teaching, a "political" choice is made each time texts are ordered for a course. Lillian Robinson makes this point in describing the "turn from the construction of pantheons, which have no *prescribed* number of places, to the construction of course syllabi, [when] something does have to be eliminated each time something else is added, and here ideologies, aesthetic and extra-aesthetic, do necessarily come into play" (1983: 112). What does the teacher do? What is to be taught? What is the object of literary studies? Robinson argues that, in one way or another, the feminist critique answering these questions "humanizes" male critical theory and that such 'humanity' provides a basis for informed choice.

Underlying the self-evident opposition between "aesthetic" and "extra-aesthetic" considerations, as we have suggested, is the self-evident "truth" in need of further critique. The site of this opposition is where *literary* criticism becomes *cultural* criticism, where the four "grounds" we have been examining come together in constant competition. Sandra Gilbert stages such a competition between literary history and operative concepts from psychoanalysis in rewriting a feminist literary history in "Life's Empty Pack: Notes Toward a Literary Daughteronomy" (1985), and Henry Louis Gates Jr follows structuralist and post-structuralist "signifying" and "signification" in situating traditions in African-American literature in relation to itself and to a critical canon in "The Blackness of Blackness: A Critique of the Sign and the Signifying Monkey" (1984)—both critics arguing for restructuring and expansion of the literary canon. Gates situates himself and the object of literary study "in this space between two linguistic domains," standard American English and "American Negro usage" (1984: 293) and suggests that the use of *"signifying* as the slave's trope, the trope of tropes . . . a trope that subsumes other rhetorical tropes, including metaphor, metonymy, synecdoche and irony" (1984: 286) in contemporary black literature and criticism defines the themes and techniques of post-modern literary practice—much the way New Criticism used modernist texts to define and justify its critical formulations.

In this way, the practice of literary study itself is always forming canons, is always a *cultural* activity. Stanley Fish and others have argued that interpretive strategies condition and determine the so-called "facts" of discourse (1980: 165–66), the practices of criticism determining the objects of study. Criticism becomes critique, though, only when it becomes self-consciously framed in this activity. When it does so, *critique* itself necessarily becomes *cultural critique*—that is, the "signify'n" Gates describes, like the critical practice that allows him to see its significance, produces, as he says, "a critique of traditional notions of closure in interpretation" (1984: 304). The strongest of those notions for the *institution* of literary studies, like the "restrictive institution" we are hardly aware of "until we come into conflict with it," Robinson describes, is the very construction of objects of knowledge, the literary canon itself. Critique in the sense we have been discussing, therefore, is constitutive of literary and cultural study at the most basic level in the formation of the objects of study.

## FEMINIST CRITIQUES

Throughout *Criticism and Culture* we have consistently returned to various feminist critiques of gender formation for their produc-

tive engagement with the institutional and transformative concerns of cultural study. If critique entails a rethinking of the object of knowledge, it also means a rethinking of the subject of knowledge in ways that question the "grounds" of dominant critical activities. This challenge is foregrounded most dramatically in the cultural critique of gender, in which the diversity of approaches has developed with remarkable intensity, suggesting a development characteristic of a significant critical reorientation in the practices of criticism and in the potential for critique.

Evident in this reorientation is the urgency to understand literature *subjectively,* from the viewpoint of a *culturally* gendered subject, the project that has already led many to rethink their assumptions and practices. When Elaine Showalter cites Irving Howe's description of Michael Henchard's selling of his wife and daughter at the beginning of *The Mayor of Casterbridge* and Howe's assertion that to "shake loose from" and "discard" his wife "through the public sale of her body to a stranger" wrings a "second change out of life," she notes that "a woman . . . will have a different experience of this scene" (1979: 129) and that only the training in "androcentric" reading has obscured this difference. As Patrocinio Schweickart adds, "the feminist inquiry into the activity of reading begins with the realization that the literary canon is androcentric, and this has a profoundly damaging effect on women readers" (1986: 40). The reorientation effected by the inquiry into reading in relation to gender suggests that all readings are not the same and that "texts" are not endowed with transcendent ("constative") meanings but are historically and socially situated through gender markings—as well as, for example, class issues.

This situation is clear if we contrast the survey of feminist literary criticism Showalter presents in "Feminist Criticism in the Wilderness" with the "grounds" for literary study we have been exploring. Showalter isolates four approaches for feminist inquiry parallel to our four grounds. She, too, describes "theories of women's writing [which] presently make use of four models of difference: biological, linguistic, psychoanalytic, and cultural" (1981: 249). Three of the four categories coincide with ours, even though the order of their presentation is different. But the category in our discussion occupied by the philosophical approach to literature is Showalter's category of biology and gender difference, that is, the "natural" materiality of gendered existence. If, in part at least, philosophy is taken to be ontology, where we are most abstract, Showalter is at this point most concrete; where we explore post-structuralism as a language which can address the "situation" of humankind, as Hillis Miller says, as "something encountered in our relations to other people, especially relations involving love, betrayal, and the ultimate betrayal by the other of our love for him or her, the death of the other" (1985: 22), Showalter surveys literal and metaphorical articulations of the physical difference between men and women in "feminist criticism which itself tries to be biological, to write from the critic's body, . . . [criticism which is] intimate, confessional, often innovative in style and form" (1981: 251). She posits not abstract "grounds" but concrete models for difference, an approach that situates the act of reading and criticism in particular gendered contexts for culture.

Showalter's taxonomy for feminism, drawing from at least four areas of contemporary critical thought, indicates not just the interdisciplinary nature of feminist critiques but their explicitly critical orientation. An example is Hélène Cixous's drawing on both biology and psychoanalysis in her description of Little Red Riding Hood as "a little clitoris" in her psychoanalytically informed discussion in "Castration or Decapitation?" Cixous also relies on the opposition between nature and culture introduced by Lévi-Strauss (and critiqued, from the vantage of the gendered sub-

ject, by Kristeva) and examines the relations between female silence—the loss of speech—and female decapitation. Schweickart also examines the linguistic strategies of literature from a viewpoint that encompasses biological, psychological and cultural concerns with rhetoric, as do many other critics of gender and culture (1986).

Feminist critiques of culture *as critiques,* however, have proven ultimately not to be confinable to the grounding of biological, or "natural," gender differences, suggesting the resituated dimension of critique that has emerged strongly in feminist cultural criticism. Under pressure—that is, tested under the weight of numerous literary and social texts—the biological grounding of gender inquiry has given way, probably decisively, to other approaches to culture and ideology. The ideology of "natural" *men* and *women* with essential "sexual difference [merely] functions," Monique Wittig warns, "as censorship in our culture by masking, on the ground of nature, the social opposition between men and women." The ground of "masculine/feminine, male/female are the categories," she goes on, "which serve to conceal the fact that social differences always belong to an economic, political, ideological order" (1982: 64). In other words, the *idea* that there is a human nature structured irremediably within the categories of heterosexual opposition as situated and known within a particular culture "is only an *idea*" (1981: 47). In Wittig's and others' challenges to gender as a "natural" ground of cultural inquiry there is a reinstitution of Simone de Beauvoir's critique of "natural" gender in *The Second Sex* where she argued that "no biological, psychological, or economic fate determines the figure that the human female presents in society; it is civilization as a whole that produces this creature, intermediate between male and eunuch, which is described as feminine" (1952: 249).

Wittig's critique of the biological grounding of gender difference—and her consistent articulation of a lesbian critique in regard to the decidedly male underpinnings of the whole heterosexual order of Western culture—is a powerful formulation, at the very least, of the social construction of gender, a position that Wittig has advanced in other provocative critiques such as "On the Social Contract" (1989) and "Homo Sum" (1990). Her critique of gender breaks through the implicit biological "grounding" of many other feminist inquiries and mandates that no social practice or text can be naturalized, or removed from the contest with other social practices, based on the supposedly natural and unassailable categories of sexual difference. Henceforth, according to this critique, all social institutions must be understood as the management of power as marked by gender in the social construction of class and gender.

Wittig's position continues the critique of gender differences that we discussed in Freud, Lacan, and psychoanalysis generally in Chapter 3. There we also highlighted questions of sexual difference in relation to linguistic strategies and cultural understanding. Also in the critique of structuralism in Chapter 4 we followed Kristeva's weaving together of different discourses in "Stabat Mater"—a discourse of the maternal body and a discourse of cultural history—to articulate the multi-faceted relationship between an "experience" of womanhood that seemed, scandalously, impersonal and collective in relation to biology, language, psychology and cultural order. In Chapter 5 we examined Felman's Austinian critique of Derridean deconstruction and Derrida's and Spivak's genealogical critique of the concept of "woman." In the preceding chapter on social relations we examined Spivak's social critique of the historicization of Foucault from the vantage of the historical position of the (female) subaltern, and juxtaposed the claims of New Historicism with the particularities of feminist readings of

cultural artifacts. In other words, we have drawn out the elements of several feminist critiques in our own critical practice in this book to expose our own interests and simultaneously to facilitate the further shifting of grounds, even the grounds we necessarily assume in arguing our position. We have attempted to adopt the double gesture of critique in interrogating the suppositions of a narrative and its derivative modes of analysis, as suggested in Nietzsche's aphoristic style and Derrida's multiplication of analytic frames in philosophic critiques as well as Marx's attempt constantly to make contradiction both an object and a method of understanding.

In examining the ways in which contemporary literary and cultural criticism have become species of cultural critique by reorienting its inquiry in relation to a gendered subject of knowledge, we have followed feminist critiques that challenge literary theory to confront the difficult task of assimilating the findings of an expanding sphere of cultural inquiry. To the degree that this challenge has already been accepted in literary and cultural studies, we believe that a significant shifting of ground is already taking place, a decisive reorientation. It may well be that the future of literary studies is being decided as current feminist theory and cultural criticism are being formulated.

If this is so, it is because feminist critiques, more explicitly than other forms of cultural critique, call for social, linguistic and ideological interrogations of their own premises. In "Imperialism and Sexual Difference" Spivak tries to situate feminist criticism as it is practised within the context of middle-class academic life in the West, placing some modes of feminist practice within the context of New Critical formalism and structuralist and poststructuralist economies. She also enlarges that context to articulate feminism in relation to imperialism and the colonial tendency to universalize a particular situation into the human condition. She writes, 'even as we feminist critics discover the troping error of the masculist truth-claim to universality or academic objectivity, we perform the lie of constituting a truth of global sisterhood where the model remains male and female sparring partners of generalizable or universalizable sexuality who are the chief protagonists in that European context" (1986: 226). She notes, in particular, the "post-romantic concept of irony" which springs "from the imposition of her own historical and voluntarist" position with "U.S. academic feminism as a 'universal' model of the 'natural' reactions of the female psyche" (1986: 235). Such a practice, she argues, carries with it the *"structural* effect" specifically colonialist and imperialist in origin.

Like Wittig, Spivak articulates a critique of feminism informed by the advances that psychoanalysis, structuralism, post-structuralism and Marxism have brought to the examination of discourse in general. She reads literary texts in such a way that "discourses"—personal discourse, political discourse, and philosophic discourse—are seen to be *cultural* discursive practices. Together, in specific practices of literary and cultural critique, Spivak and also Wittig delineate the outlines of feminist practices in particular as part of a larger effort to demonstrate the reconception and reorientation of literary studies in the twentieth century as cultural critique.

Irigaray, Deleuze and Guattari, Spivak, and Wittig, among others, all redefine social behaviour that was previously unexamined or vaguely conceived as existing outside of an analytical frame in order to locate it in relation to cultural institutions and possibilities of transforming those institutions. They expose social behaviour in its cultural dimension as an instituted practice occurring at a particular historical moment. The force of this generalizing critique, consistent with the particularities of Annette Kuhn's and Tania Modleski's critiques of gender differences in popular cul-

ture within a larger ethics of cultural studies, has the potential to dislocate countless critical practices that have silently ignored the operations of power in supposedly neutral zones of gender (and genital) organization. It is for this transformative potential, and the opportunity not merely to understand but to change culture, that we have consistently highlighted feminist critiques of cultural understanding.

## THE INSTITUTED SUBJECT OF CULTURAL STUDIES

In the challenge of feminist critiques we see the instance of cultural critique as a pedagogical mode—an exemplary instance of cultural studies. Our strategy for cultural studies in the broadest sense is derived precisely from the critical reformulation of the four groundings of criticism in this book. Fundamental to that working model is the "instituted subjectivity" within cultural inquiry. Such instituted subjectivity is the complex interrelationship between the subject and object of cultural studies. As such, it is outside the opposition between subject and object of inquiry. By subjectivity we do not mean non-"objective" or non-rigorous and do not intend simply to denote the concept of culture implied in Raymond Williams" "structure of feeling," the common human "experience" as the absolute "ground" of all cultural elaboration and formations—an essentialist construction of "experience" as the irreducible "terrain of the lived" (quoted in Hall 1980: 66). From Williams' perspective, "culture" is the outgrowth of "experience" in the sense that "experience," as Stuart Hall says, is where "all the different practices [of culture] intersect" (Hall 1980: 63).

Rather, we have positioned the subjective nature of cultural studies according to what Hall calls the "structuralist" understanding of culture (1980: 64), which suggests that "experience," so called, is no ground of culture at all but, in its substantiated form, is the instituted "effect" of a specific cultural text and practice. That is, a particular culture at a particular moment produces "experience" in a specific configuration: in effect, first culture and then "experience." In this perspective, in which "experience" is not the natural foundation of culture, it becomes necessary to define and situate the critical viewpoint, or "subject," that constitutes any instance of experience being investigated. Analysis of the "subject" as a construction within a cultural frame then begins with the critic's own "subjective" historical placement, the investigator's own insertion into a historically and ideologically specific moment. The investigator then represents him- or herself in the activity of cultural discourse. Never simply personal, the subjective moment—the situating and constructing of a subject at a historical juncture—is a crucial reference for cultural studies in that it is the rigour of critique that this model has instead of "disinterestedness" or "objectivity." We have ended our discussion with feminism and a provisional definition of cultural studies precisely to mark our own "subjective" sense, our own placement in relation to intellectual and ethical practices.

Such placement, asserting some version of universality in conjunction with the particular, makes cultural inquiry an ethical activity. It is just this ethical activity that Derrida describes in "The Principle of Reason: The University in the Eyes of its Pupils" (1983). Derrida argues that institutional knowledge as produced in the Western university is a product of the eighteenth-century separation of pure knowledge from the practicality of ethics as it was expressed by Kant. In this scenario, aesthetics and art are the mediating terms between knowledge and ethics. Rigorously extending Kant's logic, Derrida projects social and cultural experience as texts with textual and aesthetic dimensions. He then situates the object of cultural studies in precisely that mediating position—constituted

simultaneously by knowledge and power. This organization of "disciplines" creates a sense of what it means to be *interested*. In this view, the cultural studies critic, for example, will not seek to perform a strictly "disinterested" inquiry but will always be enacting a participatory relation within the discourse of inquiry. The critic, in other words, cannot be an innocent observer passively recording an "other" world, as we discussed in relation to Foucault and Spivak, but is defined as a subject position in relation to knowledge and power. The resultant activity of a performative "knowing" grounds one's "interest" both as awareness but also as ethical responsibility for the discourse of inquiry itself. It follows that intellectual scrutiny must always be ethical engagement. Again, in that there is rigour but not disinterested objectivity from this viewpoint, it is important to acknowledge the roles the participant/observer may *and* may not occupy—that is, may *actually* occupy and be responsible for in ethical and ideological terms.

By "participants," further, we mean those subject to the particular constraints in a sphere of possibility in terms of what is thinkable and doable, what Foucault means by *pouvoir,* which not only describes the ideal of Power but also, as a verb, means "to be able," designating what is possible in the world as we know it—the limit of what can be done as it consistently constrains action posing a fair working definition of ideology. On this important point we think, for example, of Gulliver's situationally imposed limits in *Gulliver's Travels.* In Lilliput, or in any of the "other" worlds into which Gulliver is inserted, there is an outlandish asymmetry between his subjective intentions and the material conditions that constrain him. The tale's frequent and satiric reversals as Gulliver encounters enormously large and tiny people suggest the fundamental lack of any natural isomorphism between Gulliver as a culturally instituted subject and the social and material discourses in which he operates. That is, the narrative reversals mark Gulliver's own capability in every instance in relation to the possibilities of knowledge and power. His mediate distance between knowledge and power is, above all, textual in the psychological, linguistic, philosophical, and historical conceptions of text and marking we have explored throughout this book. Gulliver, gullibly situated like the rest of us, never quite understands this textuality; he never understands, *ideologically,* the mediated relationship between knowledge and power.

This misrecognition of ideology is the constitutional instability, the inevitable misrecognition, of ideology apprehended as a merely cognitive awareness of a text. Such cognition mistakes perception for unmediated apprehension, just as, at another extreme, Paulo Freire describes a kind of anti-Gulliver, an impossible ideal of a person who recognizes perfectly the implications of ideological and class struggle and who has the unerring ethical and critical "ability," as Freire says, "to perceive social, political, and economic contradictions" in society and culture (1968: 19). Such perfect recognition fails to take fully into account the instituted and limited subjectivity always necessary for the work of negativity—the work of critique—to continue within culture.

## THE TRANSFORMED OBJECT OF CULTURAL STUDIES

These notes towards a definition of cultural studies suggest something quite different from "disinterested" observation and indicate what we think of as a post-modern and post-structuralist *activism*—a cultural and political position wagered on an always to be enacted interpretation of a social text interwoven by social relations. The possibility of success for such a practice must continually be resituated within historical change as a virtual rather than an actual text—hence the need for ongoing contest and struggle to achieve cultural knowledge and change, and the necessity to reject the concept of the "last instance" of critique. The subjective and ideologically motivated "interest" of cultural studies derives from a commitment to a continual resituating within multiple contextual frames that include, and perhaps begin with, the local situation in institutions in which we can act as teachers and intellectuals and, in so doing, discover our mutual interests in a collectivity.

The critique of the subject is a key to cultural studies and formulates a critique of "culture" itself. In this critique, critics read the discourses and texts of contemporary culture to expose crucial oppositions and contradictions that govern the exercise of power, to expose what Homi K. Bhabha calls at one extreme "the political 'rationality' of the nation as a form of narrative—textual strategies, metaphoric displacements, subtexts and figurative stratagems" (1990: 2). Through such critiques Bhabha, Stuart Hall, Gayatri Spivak and other cultural critics work, in effect, continually to manoeuvre themselves into strategic conflicts with cultural practices in the interventionist style of one working from within an institution—as theorists and teachers in the academy—to change and transform culture. Such interventions must always be repeated in that they always succumb to the ideality of "reading" and the monumentality of "practice."

It is to underline the necessity of this repetition that Clifford Geertz describes cultural analysis as "intrinsically incomplete." He writes (1973) that the deeper cultural analysis "goes,"

the less complete it is. It is a strange science whose most telling assertions are its most tremulously based, in which to get somewhere with the matter at hand is to intensify the suspicion, both your own and that of others, that you are not quite getting it right. But that, along with plaguing subtle people with obtuse questions, is what being an ethnographer is like.

There are a number of ways to escape this—turning culture into folklore and collecting it, turning it into traits and counting it, turning it into institutions and classifying it, turning it into structures and toying with it. But they *are* escapes. The fact is that to commit oneself to a semiotic concept of culture and an interpretive approach to the study of it is to commit oneself to a view of ethnographic assertion as . . . "essentially contestable". (p. 29)

Such contestation defines culture as well as cultural studies. The four examples of "escape" that Geertz presents offer four different definitions of culture: the collection of folklore which, like the Arnoldian canonization of literature and art we examined in Chapter 2 [of *Criticism and Culture*], attempts to encompass a self-evident cultural tradition. The enumeration of cultural traits, as in scientifically modelled social sciences critiqued by structural linguistics and Marxism, attempts to define culture positivistically. The apprehension of intellectual structures, like the linguistically modelled analyses critiqued by post-structuralism and historicism, attempts to understand culture in terms of its hermetic and idealistic logic of signification. In this chapter we are foregrounding the last of these definitions of culture, the description of social institutions, in an attempt to see culture in terms of relationships of power. Two of these definitions—those of intellect and language—encompass what Raymond Williams calls the " 'inner' process" of culture. The others, scientific positivism and historical institutionalism, encompass what he calls the "general process" of culture.

As we saw in Chapter 1, Williams specifically describes the "complexity of the concept of 'culture' " we are trying to describe

here as both "a noun of 'inner' process, specialized to its presumed agencies in 'intellectual life' and 'the arts' " and "a noun of general process, specialized to its presumed configurations in 'whole ways of life' " (1977: 17). For Williams, "culture" encompasses an individual subject's "inner" world and a society of individuals conceived as a whole greater than the sum of its parts. For him, both definitions of culture are thoroughly historical. Throughout *Culture and Society,* for instance, he argues that the "idea" of culture in each of these senses responds to the growing industrialism of Britain, and more specifically to the fragmented individualism of laissez-faire capitalism. In his definition of culture, Williams above all wants to demonstrate that "culture," as both an inner process and a general process, can be subject to a transformational critique.

The historical and intellectual complexity of culture is subject to institutional critique. In his attempt to understand culture, Geertz develops what he calls the "essentially semiotic" conception of culture as textual (1973: 5), and he seeks to rescue social discourse "from its perishing occasions and fix it in perusable terms" (1973: 20). That is, this conception of culture attempts to avoid imprisonment "in the immediacy of its own detail" without falling into vacuously abstract generalizations (1973: 24). The collections of folklore or of the "facts" of positive science present the danger of detail. The abstractions of structuralism or of grand institutional histories present the danger of unsubstantial universals. Against these dangers, Geertz suggests that the "thick descriptions" of cultural institutions, seeking "a stratified hierarchy of meaningful structures" (1973: 7), can be achieved only by situating the events we call culture within the particularities of historical understanding. For Geertz within cultural analysis "the essential task of theory building . . . is not to codify abstract regularities but to make thick description possible, not to generalize across cases but to generalize within them" (1973: 26).

Williams pursues and achieves such an analysis in his tracing of the great nineteenth-century articulations of "culture" as a concept in *Culture and Society,* even if, unlike Geertz, his aim is the transformation rather than the understanding of culture. In this pursuit, however, Williams demonstrates the problem and danger of the strict separation between knowledge and power, institutional and transformational critique, and the object and subject of cultural studies. "A culture," Williams writes, "while it is being lived, is always in part unknown, in part unrealized. The making of a community is always an exploration, for consciousness cannot precede creation, and there is no formula for unknown experience" (1958: 334). This definition of culture substantiates Geertz's description of cultural studies as "essentially contestable" (1973: 29). It also substantiates the complex relationship between criticism and critique we have delineated in this book that describes the historicity of cultural studies as neither the prisoner of positive detail nor the working out of transhistorical destinies. Bakhtin's dialogical aesthetics attempts a similar complex historiography, as do Derrida's conceptual grammatologies. Lacanian psychoanalysis and the scientific semiotics of Jakobson attempt parallel synchronic critiques. In this definition Williams is attempting to *situate* historically what seems, in the Arnoldian tradition, to be a universal and transcendental idea. Both Williams and Geertz locate the contest in the word "culture" to define it not in terms of transcendent meaning nor in terms of local dialect, but within what Geertz calls "the flow of social discourse" (1973: 20).

Williams, as we have seen, pursues this contest historically, in the genealogy of "culture" which, as Foucault says, attempts to "record the singularity of events outside any monotonous finality; it must seek them in the most unpromising places, in what we tend to feel is without history—in sentiments, love, conscience, instinct [—in order] to isolate the different scenes where they engaged in different roles" (1971: 139–40). In this approach, culture itself, "what we tend to feel is without history," is realized within historical consciousness. This is the approach of critique—specifically the critiques of psychological, linguistic, conceptual and social formations we have traced in this book.

In creating the possibility of the realization and transformation of culture, Williams achieves what Geertz describes as the achievement of cultural studies at its best, the possibility of bringing "us in touch with the lives of strangers" (1973: 16). That those strangers are often ourselves—this, after all, is the discovery of contemporary feminism— is the promise of understanding and power of transformation that cultural studies offer. These are precisely the complex ends of making the familiar "odd," "peculiar," "unpleasant," "ignoble"—all that Arnold describes under the label of "terrible learning" (1862: 184–5). In such learning—the "terrible" learning of critique—the distinctions between inner and general processes, private responses and public responsibilities, break down. In it aesthetics and ethics, literary and cultural studies, are reoriented in relation to one another.

## REFERENCES

Adorno, Theodor, *Prisms,* trans. Samuel and Shierry Weber (Cambridge, MA: M.I.T. Press, 1981).

Arnold, Matthew, "On Translating Homer: Last Words," in *On the Classical Tradition,* ed. R. H. Super (Ann Arbor: University of Michigan Press, 1960), 168–216.

Bhabha, Homi K., ed., *Nation and Narration* (New York: Routledge, 1990).

Burke, Kenneth, "Literature as Equipment for Living," in *The Philosophy of Literary Form* (Berkeley and Los Angeles: University of California Press, 1973).

De Beauvoir, Simone, *The Second Sex,* trans. H.M. Parshley (New York: Bantam Books, 1952).

Dewey, John, "Outlines of a Critical Theory of Ethics," in *Early Works, Vol. 3, 1889–1892,* ed. Jo Ann Boydston (Carbondale: Southern Illinois University Press, 1969), 239–388.

Felman, Shoshana, *Jacques Lacan and the Adventure of Insight* (Cambridge, MA: Harvard University Press, 1987).

Foucault, Michel (1971), "Nietzsche, Genealogy, History," in *Language, Counter-Memory, Practice,* trans. Donald Bouchard and Sherry Simon (Ithaca, NY: Cornell University Press, 1977), 139–64.

Freire, Paulo, *Pedagogy of the Oppressed,* trans. Myra Berman Ramos (New York: Continuum, 1968).

Frye, Northrop (1949), "The Function of Criticism at the Present Time," in *Our Sense of Identity,* ed. Malcolm Ross (Toronto: University of Toronto Press, 1954), 247–265.

Gates, Henry Louis, "The 'Blackness of Blackness': A Critique of the Sign and the Signifying Monkey," in *Black Literature and Literary Theory* (New York: Oxford University Press, 1984), 285–321.

Geertz, Clifford, *The Interpretation of Cultures* (New York: Basic Books, 1973).

Gilbert, Sandra, "Life's Empty Pack: Notes Toward a Literary Daughteronomy," in *Critical Inquiry,* 11, (1985), 355–84.

Graff, Gerald, *Professing Literature: An Institutional History* (Chicago: University of Chicago Press, 1987).

Greenblatt, Stephen, "Shakespeare and the Exorcists," in *Shakespeare and the Question of Theory,* eds. Patricia Parker and Geoffrey Hartman (New York: Methuen, 1985), 163–187.

Greimas, A. J., *Structural Semantics,* trans. Daniele McDowell, Ronald Schleifer, and Alan Velie (Lincoln: University of Nebraska Press, 1983).

Hall, Stuart, "Cultural Studies: Two Paradigms," in *Media, Culture and Society,* 2 (1980), 57–72.

Kristeva, Julia, *Desire in Language,* trans. Thomas Gora, Alice Jardine, and Leon Roudiez (New York: Columbia University Press, 1980).

Lentricchia, Frank, *Criticism and Social Change* (Chicago: University of Chicago Press, 1983).

Miller, J. Hillis, "The Search for Grounds in Literary Study," in *Rhetoric and Form: Deconstruction at Yale,* ed. Robert Con Davis and Ronald Schleifer (Norman: University of Oklahoma Press, 1985), 19–36.

Robinson, Lillian, "Treason Our Text: Feminist Challenges to the Literary Canon," in *Feminist Criticism,* ed. Elaine Showalter (New York: Pantheon, 1985), 105–221.

Said, Edward W., *The World, the Text, and the Critic* (Cambridge, MA: Harvard University Press, 1983).

Schweickart, Patrocinio, "Reading Ourselves: Toward a Feminist Theory of Reading," in *Gender and Reading,* ed. Elizabeth Flynn and Patrocinio Schweickart (Baltimore: Johns Hopkins University Press, 1986), 31–62.

Scholes, Robert, *Textual Power* (New Haven: Yale University Press, 1985).

Showalter, Elaine, "Toward a Feminist Poetics," in *Feminist Criticism,* ed. Elaine Showalter (New York: Pantheon, 1985), 125–43.

———, "Feminist Criticism in the Wilderness," in *Feminist Criticism,* ed. Elaine Showalter (New York: Pantheon, 1985), 243–70.

Spivak, Gayatri Chakravorty, "Imperialism and Sexual Difference," in *Oxford Literary Review,* 8 (1986), 225–40.

Williams, Raymond, *Culture and Society: 1780–1950* (New York: Columbia University Press, 1958).

———, *Marxism and Literature* (New York: Oxford University Press, 1977).

Wittig, Monique, "One Is Not Born a Woman," in *Feminist Issues,* 1, No. 2 (Winter) (1981), 47–54.

———, "The Category of Sex, in *Feminist Issues,* 2, No. 1 (Fall) (1982), 63–68.

———, "On the Social Contract," in *Feminist Issues,* 9, No. 1 (Spring) (1989), 3–12.

———, "Homo Sum," in *Feminist Issues,* 10, No. 1 (Spring) (1990), 3–11.

# Index

Abel, Elizabeth, 63
Academic criticism/critique, 47, 82, 167, 172–173, 597
Academic world. *See also* Academic criticism/critique; Teaching
  and cultural studies, 20, 597, 602, 603
  Derrida's views of, 320–340, 676
  and feminism, 511, 674–675
  and humanism, 113
  and literary studies, 3–4, 72–82, 198–199, 670–671
  and theory, 113, 130
Acker, Kathy, 508
Adorno, Theodor, 668
Aesop's Fables, 172
Aesthetics, 8–9, 14, 24, 25, 37, 237, 300
  and cultural studies, 597, 603, 606, 671, 676, 679
  and ideology, 85–89
  and theory, 83–92, 93–108
Afanasyev, V., 270
African-American/Black Studies, 126, 130
African-Americans
  and cultural studies, 671–672
  and feminism, 52, 67, 224, 581–582, 587, 590
  and rhetoric and reader response, 193, 224
  and theory, 123–131, 148–149
Althusser, Louis, 97, 112, 303, 355–360, 378, 436, 467, 473, 617, 618, 619, 622
*Anatomy of Criticism* (Frye), 25, 87, 239, 373–374, 440
Apollinaire, Guillaume, 225
"Apostrophe, Animation, and Abortion" (Barbara Johnson), 162–163, 216–231
Archetypal criticism, 17, 371–374
Ardener, Shirley and Edwin, 65–66, 67, 68–69
Aristotle, 4, 8, 153, 157, 270, 321, 322, 323, 326, 329, 337, 434
Armstrong, Nancy, 441
Arnold, Matthew, 6, 18, 19, 20, 36–37, 45, 52, 74–82, 109, 110, 113, 114–117, 598–599, 600, 668, 678, 679

Art
  and criticism, 20, 34–45
  definitions of, 263, 598
  and historical critique, 38, 436
  and the public, 34–45
"Art as Technique" (Shklovsky), 13, 260, 261–272
Atwood, Margaret, 66
Auerbach, E., 97, 491
Auerbach, Nina, 53, 57
Austin, John L., 174, 297, 303, 307–319, 468, 674
Authorship, 299, 304, 342–353
Avenarius, Richard, 263

Babbitt, Irving, 22–23, 76
Bachelard, Gaston, 47, 158
Baker, Houston, 123
Bakhtin, Mikhail, 157, 436, 679
Baldick, Chris, 4–5
Baldwin, James, 128
Balibar, Etienne, 435, 436
Balzac, Honore, 362–363
"Banality in Cultural Studies" (Morris), 10, 91, 604–605, 642–666
Barthes, Roland, 12, 17–18, 20, 25, 46–50, 84, 85, 87–88, 97, 98, 99, 233, 238, 239, 241, 289, 304, 355, 361, 362–364
"Base and Superstructure in Marxist Cultural Theory" (Raymond Williams), 91, 435, 453–466
Bate, Walter Jackson, 76, 114, 117
Baudelaire, Charles, 215, 216–218, 219, 220, 225, 228–229
Baudrillard, Jean, 567, 604–605, 642, 643, 646–648, 651–652, 653, 656, 657, 659, 660, 664
Baym, Nina, 55, 67, 201
Beardsley, Monroe C., 24, 372
Behn, Aphra, 68
Belsey, Catherine, 3, 86, 234, 235–236, 299, 300–301, 302, 303, 354–370, 374, 378, 435–436, 441, 507, 508, 509
Bely, Andrey, 262, 263
Benhabib, Seyla, 85
Benjamin, Walter, 10–11, 21, 434, 437, 440, 445–452, 467, 468
Ben Michaels, Walter, 441

Bennett, Paula, 18, 164, 513–514, 535–548, 599
Bentham, Jeremy, 116
Benveniste, Emile, 225, 240–241, 356–357, 360
Bernikow, Louise, 537
*Beyond the Culture Wars: How Teaching the Conflicts Can Revitalize American Education* (Graff), 3–4, 163
*Beyond the Pleasure Principle* (Freud), 522–523
Bhabha, Homi K., 132, 134–136, 137, 138, 665, 677
Binswanger, Ludwig, 158, 159
Biography, 41–42, 433
Biological criticism, 51, 56–58, 129, 508, 566, 569–570, 579–570, 673–674
Birmingham Centre for the Study of Popular Culture, 601, 602
Black Arts Movement, 126, 128, 129, 130
Blackmur, R. P., 172
"The Blackness of Blackness: A Critique of the Sign and the Signifying Monkey" (Gates), 671–672
Blacks. *See* African-Americans
Blake, William, 38–39, 133
Blanchot, Maurice, 14, 110–112, 284
Bleich, David, 160, 161, 162, 195
Bloom, Allan, 72, 150
Bloom, Harold, 61, 63, 68–69, 196, 207
Blumberg, Rae Lessor, 582
Bobbitt, Philip, 484
Boccaccio, G., 269, 270
"The Body and Cinema: Some Problems for Feminism" (Kuhn), 511–513
Boegner, Alfred, 630
Boetticher, Budd, 426
Bogan, Louise, 51
Booth, A. Wayne, 191–192, 193, 194–195, 197
Borch-Jacobsen, Mikkel, 556
Brantlinger, Patrick, 601
Brecht, Bertolt, 437, 448, 467–471, 528